A+ In Depth

Jean Andrews, Ph.D.

THOMSON

COURSE TECHNOLOGY

Australia • Canada • Mexico • Singapore • Spain • United Kingdom • United States

A+ In Depth

is published by Premier Press, a division of Course Technology.

Senior Editor: Lisa Egan	**Associate Product Manager:** Tim Gleeson	**Production Editors:** Megan Belanger, Daphne Barbas
Senior Editor: William Pitkin III	**Associate Product Manager:** Nick Lombardi	**Quality Assurance:** Nicole Ashton
Developmental Editor: Deb Kaufmann	**Copy Editor:** Joan Fitzgerald	**Cover Design:** Mike Tamanachi
Senior Marketing Manager: Jason Sakos	**Senior Manufacturing Coordinator:** Laura Burns	**Compositor:** GEX Publishing Services

BRIEF CONTENTS

TABLE OF CONTENTS

Introduction

A+ In Depth was written to be the very best tool on the market today to prepare you to support personal computers. This book takes you from the just-a-user level to the I-can-fix-this level for common PC hardware and software concerns. This book achieves its goals with an unusually effective combination of tools that powerfully reinforce both concepts and hands-on real-world experience. It also provides thorough preparation for CompTIA's newly revised 2003 A+ Certification Exams.

This book includes:

- ◆ CoursePrep® A+ Test Preparation software. This software simulates the actual A+ exam environment so you are even more prepared for exam day.
- ◆ Comprehensive review and practice end-of-chapter material, including a chapter summary, key terms, and review questions.
- ◆ Step-by-step instructions on installation, maintenance, optimizing system performance, and troubleshooting.
- ◆ A wide array of photos and screen shots support the text, displaying in detail the exact hardware and software features you will need to understand to manage and maintain your PC.

In addition, the carefully structured, clearly written text is accompanied by graphics that provide the visual input essential to learning. Coverage is balanced—while focusing on new hardware and software, it also covers the real work of PC repair, where some older technology remains in widespread use and still needs support. For example, the book covers the latest ATX motherboard form factor, but also addresses the capabilities and maintenance of the AT motherboard form factor because many are still in use. Also included is thorough coverage of operating system and applications support. While Windows is the primary OS of choice for most PCs, DOS is given comprehensive coverage because it is still used in some troubleshooting situations when Windows will not load. Because Windows XP is currently the preferred Windows OS, two full chapters are devoted to supporting it. In addition, three chapters are dedicated to Windows 9x, Windows NT and Windows 2000, because these operating systems are still present in the workplace. Because occasionally a PC technician sees a Linux installation on the desktop, an appendix covers this OS.

This book provides thorough preparation for CompTIA's newly revised A+ 2003 Upgrade Certification examinations and maps completely to the revised exam objectives. This certification credential's popularity among employers is growing exponentially, and obtaining certification increases your ability to gain employment and improve your salary. To get more information on A+ Certification and its sponsoring organization, the Computing Technology Industry Association, see their Web site at *www.comptia.org*.

FEATURES

To ensure a successful learning experience, this book includes the following pedagogical features:

- ◆ **Learning Objectives:** Every chapter opens with a list of learning objectives that sets the stage for you to absorb the lessons of the text.
- ◆ **Comprehensive Step-by-Step Troubleshooting Guidance:** Troubleshooting guidelines are included in almost every chapter. In addition, Chapter 24 gives insights into general approaches to troubleshooting that help apply the specifics detailed in each chapter for different hardware and software problems.
- ◆ **Step-by-Step Procedures:** The book is chock-full of step-by-step procedures covering subjects from hardware installation and maintenance to optimizing system performance.
- ◆ **Art Program:** Numerous detailed photographs, three-dimensional art, and screenshots support the text, displaying hardware and software features exactly as you will see them in your work.

 Tips: Tip icons highlight additional helpful information related to the subject being discussed.

 A+ Icons: All of the content that relates to CompTIA's A+ 2003 Upgrade Certification exams, whether it's a page or a sentence, is highlighted with an A+ icon. The icon notes the exam name and the objective number. This unique feature highlights the relevant content at a glance, so you can pay extra attention to the material.

 **Caution Icon:** This icon highlights critical safety information. Follow these instructions carefully to protect the PC and its data and for your own safety.

♦ **End-of-Chapter Material:** Each chapter closes with the following features, which reinforce the material covered in the chapter.

  ♦ **Chapter Summary:** This bulleted list of concise statements summarizes all major points of the chapter.

  ♦ **Review Questions:** You can test your understanding of each chapter with a comprehensive set of review questions.

  ♦ **Key Terms:** The content of each chapter is further reinforced by an end-of-chapter key-term list. The definitions of all terms are included at the end of the book in a full-length glossary.

ACKNOWLEDGMENTS

Thank you to the wonderful people at Course Technology who continue to provide support, warm encouragement, patience, and guidance. Lisa Egan, Kristen Duerr, Daphne Barbas, and Nick Lombardi of CT. Thank you, Deb Kaufmann, the Developmental Editor, for your careful attention to detail and your genuine friendship, and to Joan Fitzgerald, our excellent copy editor. Thank you Tony Woodall of Omega Computer Systems for your above-and-beyond research efforts. Thank you, Nicole Ashton, John Bosco, John Freitas, Christian Kunciw, Vitaly Davidovich, Thomas Pedrick, and Marianne Snow for your careful attention to the technical accuracy of the book.

Thank you to all the people who took the time to voluntarily send encouragement and suggestions for improvements to the previous editions. Your input and help is very much appreciated. The reviewers all provided invaluable insights and showed a genuine interest in the book's success. Thank you to:

Tom Bledsaw, ITT Technical Institute

Bill Bruyn, Devry Phoenix

Tracy Dearinger, Sheridan College

Pauline Duewekey, Baker College at Mount Clemens

Mary Fastner, Brown Institute

Bryant Grigsby, Brown Institute

Garrett Krueger, Brown Institute

Don Locke, Center for Disease Control

Scott Maikkula, Brown Institute

David Mansheffer, Brown Institute

Mary Ellen O'Shields, Central Carolina Community College

Timothy Peterson, Brown Institute

Greg Stefanelli, Carroll Community College

Sheri Schultz, Brown Institute

Mike Sthultz, CLCX

Arthur Tamer, Brown Institute

Doug Waterman, Fox Valley Technical College

Tony Woodall, Omega Computers

Thank you to Sarah Sambol, Scott Johns, and Joy Dark who were here with me making this book happen. I'm very grateful.

This book is dedicated to the covenant of God with man on earth.

Some of the proceeds of this book go to Joy Land, a children's home in Hyderabad, A.P., India.

Jean Andrews, Ph.D.

PHOTO CREDITS

Figure 5-8	Courtesy of VIA Technologies, Inc.
Figure 5-9	Courtesy of Advanced Micro Devices (AMD), Inc.
Figure 19-15	Courtesy of D-Link Systems, Inc.
Figure 21-1	Courtesy of Brother International Corporation
Figure 21-6	Courtesy of Epson America, Inc.

Most other photos courtesy of Jennifer Dark

PROTECT YOURSELF, YOUR HARDWARE, AND YOUR SOFTWARE

When you work on a computer it is possible to harm both the computer and yourself. The most common accident that happens when attempting to fix a computer problem is erasing software or data. Experimenting without knowing what you are doing can cause damage. To prevent these sorts of accidents, as well as the physically dangerous ones, take a few safety precautions. The text below describes the potential sources of damage to computers and how to protect against them.

Power to the Computer

To protect both yourself and the equipment when working inside a computer, turn off the power, unplug the computer, and always use a grounding bracelet as described in Chapter 4. Consider the monitor and the power supply to be "black boxes." Never remove the cover or put your hands inside this equipment unless you know about the hazards of charged capacitors. Both the power supply and the monitor can hold a dangerous level of electricity even after they are turned off and disconnected from a power source.

Protect Against ESD

To protect the computer against electrostatic discharge (ESD), commonly known as static electricity, always ground yourself before touching electronic components, including the hard drive, motherboard, expansion cards, processors, and memory modules. Ground yourself and the computer parts, using one or more of the following static control devices or methods:

- ◆ **Ground bracelet or static strap:** A ground bracelet is a strap you wear around your wrist. The other end is attached to a grounded conductor such as the computer case or a ground mat, or it can plug into a wall outlet (only the ground prong makes a connection!). The bracelet also contains a current-limiting device called a resistor that prevents electricity from harming you.

- ◆ **Ground mats:** Ground mats can come equipped with a cord to plug into a wall outlet to provide a grounded surface on which to work. Remember, if you lift the component off the mat, it is no longer grounded and is susceptible to ESD.

- ◆ **Static shielding bags:** New components come shipped in static shielding bags. Save the bags to store other devices that are not currently installed in a PC.

The best solution to protect against ESD is to use a ground bracelet together with a ground mat. Consider a ground bracelet to be essential equipment when working on a computer. However, if you find yourself in a situation where you must work without one, touch the computer case before you touch a component. When passing a chip to another person, ground yourself. Leave components inside their protective bags until ready to use. Work on hard floors, not carpet, or use antistatic spray on the carpets. Generally, don't work on a computer if you or the computer have just come inside from the cold.

Besides using a grounding mat, you can also create a ground for the computer case by leaving the power cord to the case plugged into the wall outlet. This is safe enough because the power is turned off when you work inside the case. However, if you happen to touch an exposed area of the power switch inside the case, it is possible to get a shock. Because of this risk, in this book, you are directed to unplug the power cord to the PC before you work inside the case.

There is an exception to the ground-yourself rule. Inside a monitor case, there is substantial danger posed by the electricity stored in capacitors. When working inside a monitor, you *don't* want to be grounded, as you would provide a conduit for the voltage to discharge through your body. In this situation, be careful *not* to ground yourself.

When handling motherboards and expansion cards, don't touch the chips on the boards. Don't stack boards on top of each other, which could accidentally dislodge a chip. Hold cards by the edges, but don't touch the edge connections on the card.

Don't touch a chip with a magnetized screwdriver. When using a multimeter to measure electricity, be careful not to touch a chip with the probes. When changing DIP switches, don't use a graphite pencil, because graphite conducts electricity; a very small screwdriver works very well.

After you unpack a new device or software that has been wrapped in cellophane, remove the cellophane from the work area quickly. Don't allow anyone who is not properly grounded to touch components. Do not store expansion cards within one foot of a monitor, because the monitor can discharge as much as 29,000 volts of ESD onto the screen.

Hold an expansion card by the edges. Don't touch any of the soldered components on a card. If you need to put an electronic device down, place it on a grounded mat or on a static shielding bag. Keep components away from your hair and clothing.

Protect Hard Drives and Disks

Always turn off a computer before moving it, to protect the hard drive, which is always spinning when the computer is turned on (unless the drive has a sleep mode). Never jar a computer while the hard disk is running. Avoid placing a PC on the floor, where the user can accidentally kick it.

Follow the usual precautions to protect disks. Keep them away from magnetic fields, heat, and extreme cold. Don't open the floppy shuttle window or touch the surface of the disk inside the housing. Treat disks with care and they'll generally last for years.

COMPTIA AUTHORIZED CURRICULUM PROGRAM

The logo of the CompTIA Authorized Curriculum Program and the status of this or other training material as "Authorized" under the CompTIA Authorized Curriculum Program signifies that, in CompTIA's opinion, such training material covers the content of the CompTIA's related certification exam. CompTIA has not reviewed or approved the accuracy of the contents of this training material and specifically disclaims any warranties of merchantability or fitness for a particular purpose. CompTIA makes no guarantee concerning the success of persons using any such "Authorized" or other training material in order to prepare for any CompTIA certification exam.

The contents of this training material were created for the CompTIA A+ Certification exam covering CompTIA certification exam objectives that were current as of February, 2003.

HOW TO BECOME COMPTIA CERTIFIED:

This training material can help you prepare for and pass a related CompTIA certification exam or exams. In order to achieve CompTIA certification, you must register for and pass a CompTIA certification exam or exams.

In order to become CompTIA certified, you must:

1. Select a certification exam provider. For more information please visit *www.comptia.org/certification/general_information/test_locations.asp*.
2. Register for and schedule a time to take the CompTIA certification exam(s) at a convenient location.
3. Read and sign the Candidate Agreement, which will be presented at the time of the exam(s). The text of the Candidate Agreement can be found at *www.comptia.org/certification/general_information/candidate_agreement.asp*.
4. Take and pass the CompTIA certification exam(s).

For more information about CompTIA's certifications, such as their industry acceptance, benefits, or program news, please visit *www.comptia.org/certification/default.asp*.

CompTIA is a non-profit information technology (IT) trade association. CompTIA's certifications are designed by subject matter experts from across the IT industry. Each CompTIA certification is vendor-neutral, covers multiple technologies, and requires demonstration of skills and knowledge widely sought after by the IT industry.

To contact CompTIA with any questions or comments:

Please call + 1 630 268 1818

questions@comptia.org

1

INTRODUCING HARDWARE

In this chapter, you will learn:

♦ That a computer requires both hardware and software to work

♦ About the many different hardware components inside and connected to a computer

♦ How the CPU works and how it communicates with other devices

Like millions of other computer users, you have probably used your micro-computer to play games, explore the Internet, write papers, build spread-sheets, or create a professional-looking proposal or flyer. You can use all these applications without understanding exactly what goes on inside your computer case or monitor. But if you are curious to learn more about microcomputers, and if you want to graduate from simply being the end user of your computer to becoming the master of your machine, then this book is for you. This book focuses on all aspects of PC hardware and software. It is written for anyone who wants to understand what is happening inside the machine, in order to install new hardware and software, diagnose both hardware and software problems, and make decisions about purchasing new hardware and operating systems. In addition, this book prepares you to pass the A+ Core Hardware Service Technician exam and the A+ Operating System Technologies exam, the two exams required by CompTIA (*www.comptia.org*) for A+ Certification. The only assumption made here is that you are a computer user—that is, you can turn on your machine, load a software package, and use that software to accomplish a task. No experience in electronics is assumed.

This chapter introduces you to the inside of your computer, a world of elec-tronic and mechanical devices that has evolved over just a few years to become one of the most powerful technical tools of our society.

Hardware Needs Software to Work

In the world of computers, the term **hardware** refers to the computer's physical components, such as the monitor, keyboard, memory chips, and hard drive. The term **software** refers to the set of instructions that directs the hardware to accomplish a task. In Figure 1-1, a passenger directs a chauffeur who directs a car, just as a computer user directs software, which, in turn, controls hardware to perform a given task.

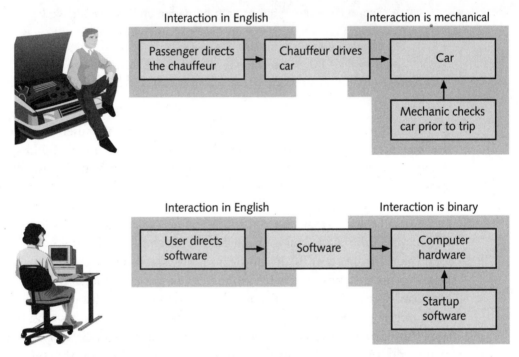

Figure 1-1   A user interacts with a computer much as a passenger interacts with a chauffeured car

In order to perform a computing task, software uses hardware for four basic functions: input, processing, output, and storage (see Figure 1-2). Also, hardware components must communicate both data and instructions among themselves, which requires an electrical system to provide power, since these components are electrical. In this chapter, we introduce the hardware components of a computer system and give you some initial insight into how they work. In Chapter 2, we address how hardware and software work together, focusing primarily on the sophisticated system of communication of data and instructions that includes both hardware and software.

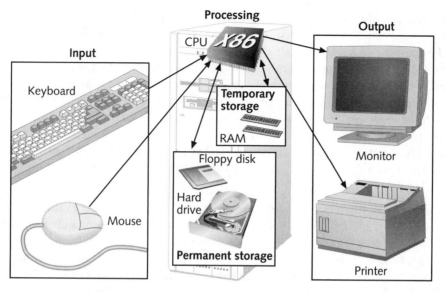

Figure 1-2 Computer activity consists of input, processing, storage, and output

Look again at Figure 1–1 and note that the interaction between the passenger and the chauffeur is in English, but that the chauffeur must translate these directions, such as "Go to the airport," into mechanical directions that the car can "understand," such as pressing the gas pedal, braking when necessary, and turning the wheel to control the car until it reaches the airport. In the same fashion, a computer user interacts with a computer in a language that the user and the software understand, but software must convert that instruction into a form that hardware can "understand."

As incredible as it might sound, every communication between hardware and software, or between software and other software, is reduced to a simple yes or no, which is represented inside the computer by two simple states: on and off (see Figure 1-3).

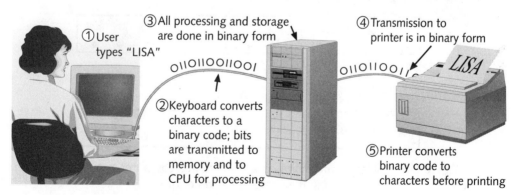

Figure 1-3 All communication, storage, and processing of data inside a computer are in binary until presented as output to the user

That was not always so. For almost half a century, people attempted to invent an electronic computational device that could store all 10 digits in our decimal number system and even some characters of our alphabet. Scientists attempted to store a charge in a vacuum tube, which is similar to a light bulb. The charge would later be "read" to determine what had been stored there. Each digit in our number system, one through nine, was stored with increasing degrees of charge, similar to a light bulb varying in power from dim to bright. However, the degree of "dimness" or "brightness" was difficult to measure, and it would change because the voltage in the equipment could not be accurately regulated. For example, an eight would be stored with a partially bright charge, but later it would be read as a seven or nine as the voltage on the vacuum tube fluctuated slightly.

Then, in the 1940s, John Atanasoff came up with the brilliant idea to store and read only two values, on and off. Either there was a charge or there was not a charge, and this was easy to write and read, just as it's easy to determine if a light bulb is on or off. This technology of storing and reading only two states is called binary, and the number system that uses only two digits, 0 and 1, is called the **binary number system**. A 1 or 0 in this system is called a **bit**, or binary digit. Because of the way the number system is organized, grouping is often done in groups of 8 bits, each of which is called a **byte**. (Guess what four bits are called? A nibble!)

In a computer, all counting and calculations use the binary number system. Counting in binary goes like this: 0, 1, 10, 11, 100, 101, and so forth. All letters and characters are converted to a binary code before being stored in a computer. The most popular coding scheme for letters and characters is **ASCII (American Standard Code for Information Interchange)**, which assigns an 8-bit code for letters, symbols, and other characters. For example, the uppercase letter A in binary ASCII code is 0100 0001, and the number 25 is 0001 1001 (see Figure 1-4). For more information about ASCII codes, see Appendix B.

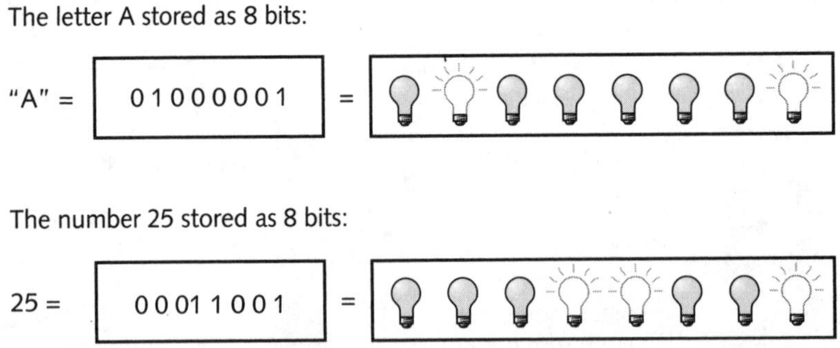

The letter A stored as 8 bits:

"A" =   01000001   = 🔆🔆🔆🔆🔆🔆🔆🔆

The number 25 stored as 8 bits:

25 =   00011001   = 🔆🔆🔆🔆🔆🔆🔆🔆

Figure 1-4   All letters and numbers are stored in a computer as a series of bits, each represented in the computer as on or off

Hexadecimal notation, or **hex**, is a shorthand way that the computer displays long binary numbers, making them easier for human beings to read and understand. The hex number system is built on multiples of two, just like the binary number system, which makes it simple for the computer to convert from binary to hex just before displaying a number on the screen. However, the hex number system has 16 numerals, which are 0, 1, 2, 3, 4, 5, 6, 7, 8, 9, A, B, C, D, E, and F. For more information about the hex number system, see Appendix C.

PC HARDWARE COMPONENTS

In this section, we cover the major hardware components of a microcomputer system used for input, output, processing, storage, electrical supply, and communication. Most input and output devices are outside the computer case. Most processing and storage components are inside the case, such as the **central processing unit (CPU)**, also called the **microprocessor** or **processor**. The CPU is the most important chip in the computer. As its name implies, this device is central to all processing the computer does. The CPU reads data received by input devices, and output from the CPU is written to output devices. The CPU writes data and instructions in storage devices and performs calculations and other data processing. Whether inside or outside the case, and regardless of the function the device performs, each hardware device requires these elements to operate:

- *A method for the CPU to communicate with the device.* The device must send data to and/or receive data from the CPU. The CPU might need to control the device by passing instructions to it, and/or the device might need to request service from the CPU.

- *Software to instruct and control the device.* A device is useless without software to control it. The software must know how to communicate with the device at the detailed level of that specific device, and the CPU must have access to this software in order to interact with the device. Each device responds to a specific set of instructions based on the device's functions. The software must have an instruction for each possible action you expect the device to accomplish.

- *Electricity to power the device.* Electronic devices require electricity to operate. Devices can receive power from the power supply inside the computer case, or they can have their own power supplied by a power cable connected to an electrical outlet.

In the next few pages, we take a sightseeing tour of computer hardware, looking first outside and then inside the case.

Hardware Used for Input and Output

$A+CORE$
  1.1
Most input/output devices reside outside the computer case. These devices communicate with components inside the computer case through a wireless connection or through cables attached to the case at a connection called a **port**, sending data and/or instructions to the computer and receiving them from the computer. Most computer ports are on the back of the case (Figure 1-5), but some models have ports on the front of the case for easy access. For wireless connections, a wireless device communicates with the system using a radiowave or infrared port. The most popular input devices are a keyboard and a mouse, and the most popular output devices are a monitor and a printer.

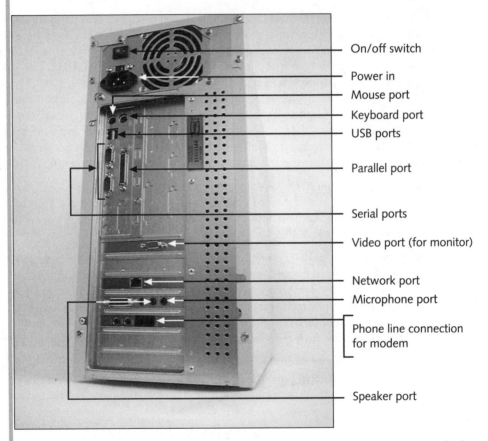

Figure 1-5   Input/output devices connect to the computer case by ports usually found on the back of the case

The **keyboard** is the primary input device of a computer (see Figure 1-6). Enhanced keyboards are the standard today and hold 102 keys. Ergonomic keyboards are curved to make them more comfortable for the hands and wrists. In addition, some keyboards come equipped with a mouse port—a plug used to attach a mouse (another input device) to the keyboard—although it is more common for the mouse port to be directly on the computer case. Electricity to run the keyboard comes from inside the computer case and is provided by wires in the keyboard cable.

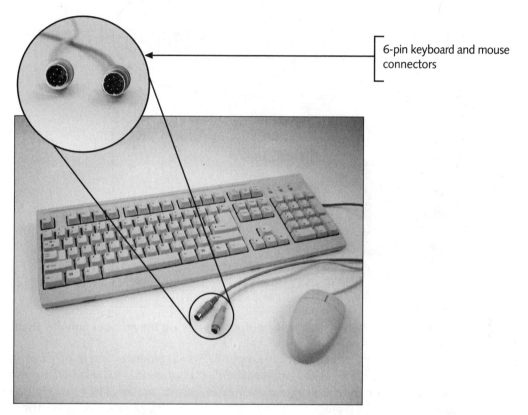

6-pin keyboard and mouse connectors

Figure 1-6   The keyboard and the mouse are the two most popular input devices

A **mouse** is a pointing device used to move a pointer on the screen and to make selections. The bottom of a mouse houses a rotating ball or an optical sensor that tracks movement and controls the location of the pointer. The one, two, or three buttons on the top of the mouse serve different purposes for different software. For example, Windows 2000 uses the left mouse button to execute a command and the right mouse button to display information about the command.

A+CORE 1.1 The monitor and the printer are the two most popular output devices (see Figure 1-7). The **monitor** is the visual device that displays the primary output of the computer. Hardware manufacturers typically rate a monitor according to the size of its screen (in inches) and by the monitor's resolution, which is the number of dots on the screen used for display.

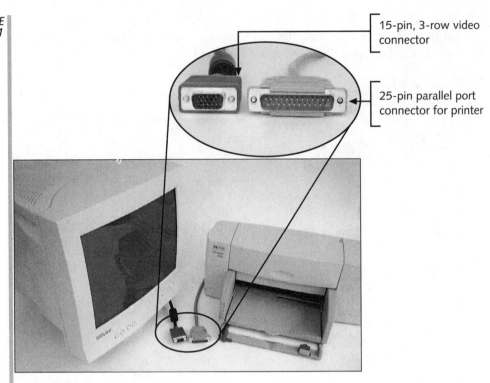

$A^{+}_{1.1}$

15-pin, 3-row video connector

25-pin parallel port connector for printer

Figure 1-7   The two most popular output devices are the monitor and the printer

A very important output device is the **printer**, which produces output on paper, often called **hard copy**. The most popular printers available today are ink-jet, laser, and dot matrix printers. The monitor and the printer need separate power supplies. Their electrical power cords connect to electrical outlets. Sometimes the computer case provides an electrical outlet for the monitor's power cord, eliminating the need for one more power outlet.

Hardware Inside the Computer Case

$A^{+}_{1.1}$ Most storage and all processing of data and instructions are done inside the computer case, so before we look at components used for storage and processing, let's look at what you see when you first open the computer case. Most computers contain these devices inside the case (see Figure 1-8):

- A motherboard containing the CPU, memory, and other components
- A floppy drive, hard drive, and CD-ROM drive used for permanent storage
- A power supply with power cords supplying electricity to all devices inside the case
- Circuit boards used by the CPU to communicate with devices inside and outside the case
- Cables connecting devices to circuit boards and the motherboard

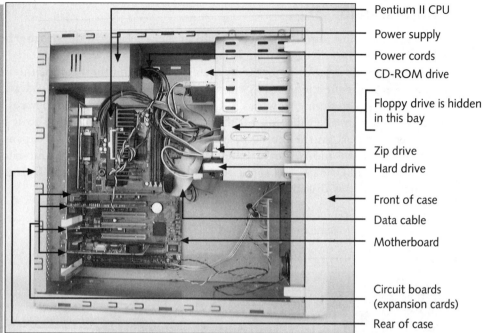

Pentium II CPU
Power supply
Power cords
CD-ROM drive
Floppy drive is hidden in this bay
Zip drive
Hard drive
Front of case
Data cable
Motherboard
Circuit boards (expansion cards)
Rear of case

Figure 1-8 Inside the computer case

Among the things you first notice when you look inside a computer case are boards that contain electronic components. A **circuit board** is a board that holds microchips, or integrated circuits (ICs), and the circuitry that connects these chips. All circuit boards contain microchips, which are most often manufactured using **CMOS (complementary metal–oxide semiconductor)** technology. CMOS chips require less electricity and produce less heat than chips manufactured using earlier technologies such as TTL (transistor-transistor logic). Some circuit boards, called **expansion cards**, are installed in long narrow **expansion slots** on the motherboard.

The other major components look like small boxes, including the power supply, hard drive, CD-ROM drive, and floppy drive. Devices that the CPU communicates with that are not directly on the motherboard are called **peripheral devices**; these are linked to the CPU by way of the motherboard. Peripheral devices can connect to the motherboard by way of ports and connectors directly on the motherboard or on expansion cards.

Two types of cables are inside the case: data cables, which connect devices to one another, and power cables or power cords, which supply power. Most often, you can distinguish between the two by their shapes. Data cables are flat and wide, and power cords are round and small. There are some exceptions to this rule, so the best way to identify a cable is to trace its source and destination.

The Motherboard

A+CORE 1.1

The largest and most important circuit board in the computer is the **motherboard**, also called the **main board** or **system board** (see Figure 1-9), which contains the CPU, the component where most processing takes place. The motherboard is the most complicated piece of equipment inside the case, and Chapter 5 covers it in detail. Because all devices must communicate with the CPU on the motherboard, all devices in a computer are either installed directly on the motherboard, directly linked to it by a cable connected to a port on the motherboard, or indirectly linked to it by expansion cards. Some ports on the motherboard extend outside the case to accommodate external devices such as a keyboard, and some ports provide a connection for a device inside the case, such as a floppy disk drive.

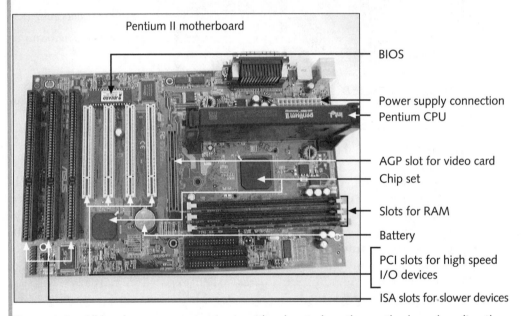

Figure 1-9   All hardware components are either located on the motherboard or directly or indirectly connected to it, because they must all communicate with the CPU

Figure 1-10 shows the ports provided to the outside of the case by a motherboard: a keyboard port, a mouse port, two serial ports, two USB ports, and a parallel port. A **serial port** is called a serial port because data is transferred serially (one bit follows the next); it is often used for an external modem or serial mouse (a mouse that uses a serial port). A **parallel port** transmits data in parallel and is most often used by a printer. A **USB (universal serial bus) port** is a newer port used by many different input/output devices such as keyboards, printers, scanners, and mice.

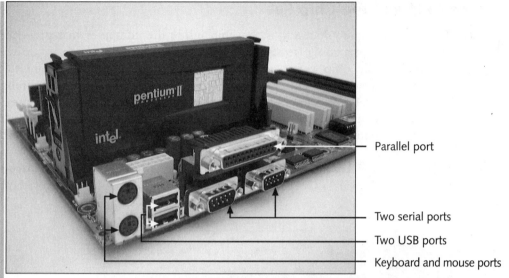

Parallel port

Two serial ports

Two USB ports

Keyboard and mouse ports

Figure 1-10   A motherboard provides ports for common I/O devices

Listed next are the major components found on all motherboards, some of which are labeled in Figure 1-9. The sections that follow discuss these components in detail.

Components used primarily for processing:

- Central processing unit (CPU), the computer's most important chip
- Chip set that supports the CPU by controlling many motherboard activities

Components used for temporary storage:

- Random access memory (RAM) used to hold data and instructions as they are processed

Components that allow the CPU to communicate with other devices:

- Traces, or wires, on the motherboard used for communication
- Expansion slots to connect expansion cards to the motherboard
- The system clock that keeps communication in sync

Electrical system:

- Power supply connections to provide electricity to the motherboard and expansion cards

Programming and setup data stored on the motherboard:

- Flash ROM, a memory chip used to permanently store instructions that control basic hardware functions (explained in more detail later in the chapter)
- CMOS setup chip that holds configuration data

The CPU and the Chip Set

A+CORE
1.1

The CPU, or microprocessor, is the chip inside the computer that performs most of the actual data processing (see Figure 1-11). The CPU could not do its job without the assistance of the **chip set**, a group of microchips on the motherboard that control the flow of data and instructions to and from the CPU, providing careful timing of activities (see Figure 1-12). While this book touches on different types of machines, it focuses on the most common personal computers (PCs), referred to as IBM-compatible. These are built around microprocessors and chip sets manufactured by Intel Corporation, AMD, VIA, SiS, Cyrix, and other manufacturers. The Macintosh family of computers, manufactured by Apple Computer, Inc., is built around a family of microprocessors manufactured by Motorola Corporation. You will learn more about the CPU and the chip set in Chapter 5.

Fan

CPU

CPU socket

Figure 1-11   Processing of data and instructions is done by the CPU (this Pentium with fan on top is made by Intel)

Storage Devices

A+CORE
1.1

In Figure 1-2, you saw two kinds of storage: temporary and permanent. The CPU uses temporary storage, called **primary storage** or **memory**, to hold both data and instructions temporarily while it is processing them. Primary storage is much faster to access than permanent storage. However, when they are not being used, the data and instructions must be kept in permanent storage, sometimes called **secondary storage**, such as a floppy disk, CD, or hard drive.

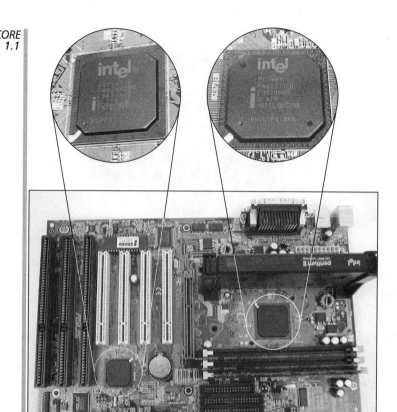

Figure 1-12 This motherboard uses two chips in its chip set (notice the lines coming from each chip used for communication)

Figure 1-13 shows an analogy to help you understand the concept of primary and secondary storage. Suppose you must do some research at the library. You go to the stacks, pull out several books, carry them to a study table, and sit down with your notepad and pencil to take notes and do some calculations. When you're done, you leave with your notepad full of information and calculations, but you don't take the books. In this example, the stacks are permanent storage, and the books (data and instructions) are permanently kept there. The table is temporary storage, a place for you to keep data and instructions as you work with them. The notepad is your output from all that work, and you are the CPU, doing the work of reading the books and writing down information. Reading a book that is lying on the table is much faster than running back and forth to the stacks every time you want to refer to it, which is what the CPU would have to do if it were not for primary storage, or memory. Also, you can see that the table (memory) gives fast but temporary access, while the stacks (secondary storage) give slow but permanent access.

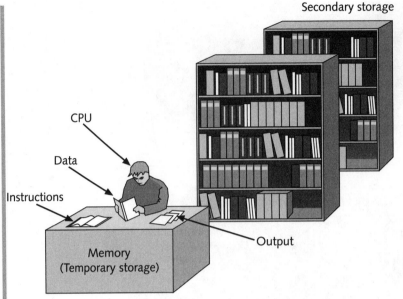

Figure 1-13   Memory is a temporary place to hold instructions and data while the CPU processes both

Primary Storage

Located on the motherboard and on other circuit boards, devices called memory or **RAM (random access memory)**, provide primary storage. RAM chips can be individually installed directly on the motherboard or in banks of several chips on a small board that plugs into the motherboard (see Figure 1-14). The most common types of boards that hold memory chips are called **SIMMs (single inline memory modules)**, **DIMMs (dual inline memory modules)**, and **RIMMs** (memory modules manufactured by Rambus, Inc.) See Figure 1-15. Most motherboards today use DIMMs. Any information stored in RAM is lost when the computer is turned off, because RAM chips need a continuous supply of electrical power to hold data or software stored in them. This kind of memory is called **volatile** because it is temporary in nature. By contrast, another kind of memory holds its data permanently, even when the power is turned off. This type of memory is **nonvolatile** and is called **ROM (read–only memory)**. You will see examples of ROM chips later in the chapter.

Figure 1-14 A SIMM, DIMM, or RIMM holds RAM and is mounted directly on a motherboard

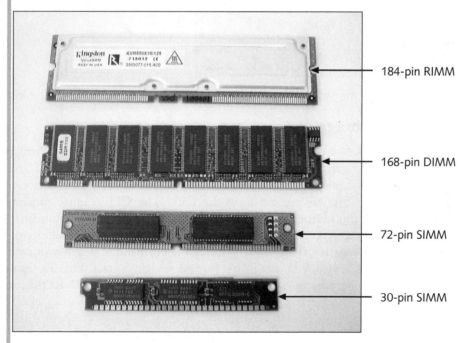

Figure 1-15 Types of RAM modules

Using Windows 9x or Windows 2000, you can see what type of CPU and how much memory you have installed. Right-click the My Computer icon on your desktop, select Properties from the shortcut menu, and click the General tab (see Figure 1-16). You can also see which version of Windows you are using. For Windows XP, click Start, right-click My Computer, and then select Properties from the shortcut menu. Then click the General tab.

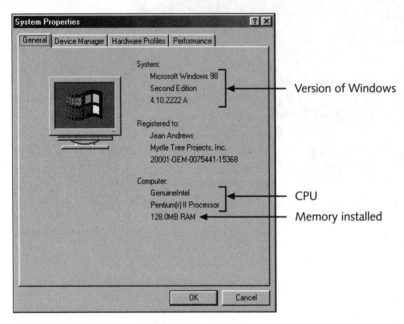

Figure 1-16   Use the System Properties window to see how much memory is installed

Secondary Storage

A+CORE
1.1

Recall that the RAM on the motherboard is called primary storage. Primary storage temporarily holds both data and instructions as the CPU processes them. These data and instructions are also permanently stored on devices such as CDs, hard drives, and floppy disks, in locations that are remote from the CPU. The CPU cannot process data and instructions from this remote storage (called secondary storage); they must first be copied into primary storage (RAM) for processing. The most important difference between these types of storage is that secondary storage is permanent. When you turn off your computer, the information in secondary storage remains intact. The five most popular secondary storage devices are hard disks, floppy disks, Zip drives, CD-ROMs, and DVDs.

A+CORE
1.1

> **TIP** Don't forget that primary storage, or RAM, is temporary; as soon as you turn off the computer, you lose any information there. That's why you should save your work frequently into secondary storage.

A **hard drive** is a sealed case containing platters or disks that rotate at high speed (see Figure 1-17). As the platters rotate, an arm with a sensitive read/write head reaches across the platters, both writing new data to them and reading existing data from them. Most hard drives today use a technology called EIDE (Enhanced Integrated Drive Electronics), which originated from IDE technology. IDE provides two connectors on a motherboard for two data cables (see Figure 1-18). Each IDE cable has a connection at the other end for an IDE device and a connection in the middle of the cable for a second IDE device. Therefore, a motherboard can accommodate up to four IDE devices in one system. Hard drives, Zip drives, CD-ROM drives, and tape drives, among other devices, can use these four IDE connections, which the chip set controls. A typical system has one hard drive connected to one IDE connector and a CD-ROM drive connected to the other (see Figure 1-19).

...rive with sealed cover removed

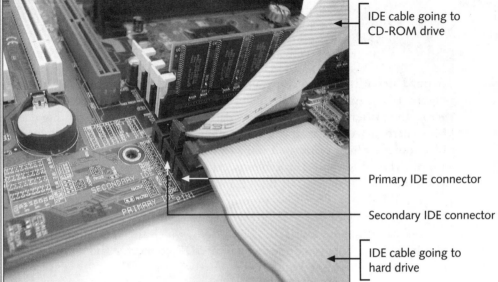

IDE cable going to
CD-ROM drive

Primary IDE connector

Secondary IDE connector

IDE cable going to
hard drive

Figure 1-18   A motherboard usually has two IDE connectors, each of which can
accommodate two devices; a hard drive usually connects to the
motherboard using the primary IDE connector

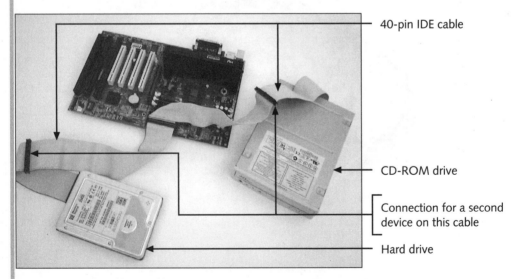

40-pin IDE cable

CD-ROM drive

Connection for a second
device on this cable

Hard drive

Figure 1-19   Two IDE devices connected to a motherboard using both IDE connections
and two cables

A+CORE 1.1   Figure 1-20 shows the inside of a computer case with three IDE devices. The CD-ROM drive and the Zip drive share an IDE cable, and the hard drive uses the other cable. Both cables connect to the motherboard at the two IDE connections. (You will learn more about IDE and EIDE in Chapter 8.)

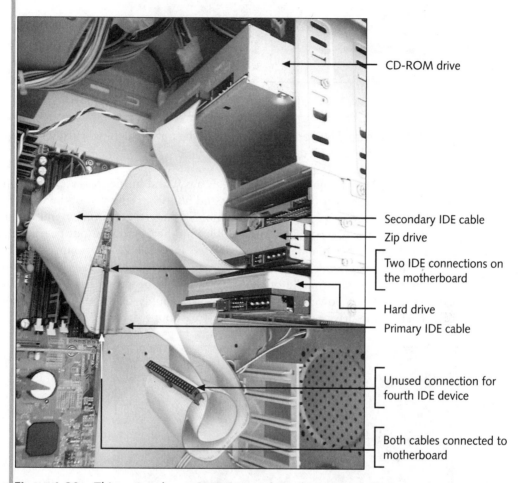

CD-ROM drive

Secondary IDE cable
Zip drive
Two IDE connections on the motherboard
Hard drive
Primary IDE cable

Unused connection for fourth IDE device

Both cables connected to motherboard

Figure 1-20   This system has a CD-ROM and Zip drive sharing the secondary IDE cable, and a hard drive using the primary IDE cable

A hard drive receives its power from the power supply through a power cord (see Figure 1-21). Look back at Figure 1-20 and you can see the power connections to the right of the cable connections on each drive. (The power cords in the figure are not connected, so you can see the cable configuration more easily.) How a hard drive works and how to install one are the subjects of Chapters 8 and 9.

$A^{+CORE}_{1.1}$

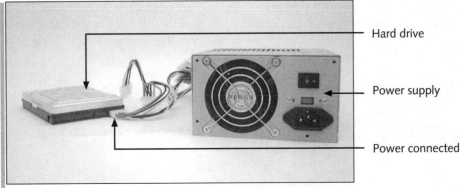

Figure 1-21   A hard drive receives power from the power supply by way of a power cord connected to the drive

Another secondary storage device almost always found inside the case is a floppy drive. Floppy drives come in two sizes: 3½ inches and 5¼ inches (the size of the disks the drives can hold). The newer 3½ inch disks use more advanced technology and actually hold more data than the older 5¼ inch disks. Older motherboards did not provide a connector for a floppy drive, but newer ones do (see Figure 1-22). A floppy drive cable can accommodate two drives. The drive at the end of the cable is drive A. If another drive were connected to the middle of the cable, it would be drive B in a computer system (see Figure 1-23). A power cord from the power supply that connects to a power port at the back of the drive provides electricity to a floppy drive.

Figure 1-22   A motherboard usually provides a connection for a floppy drive cable

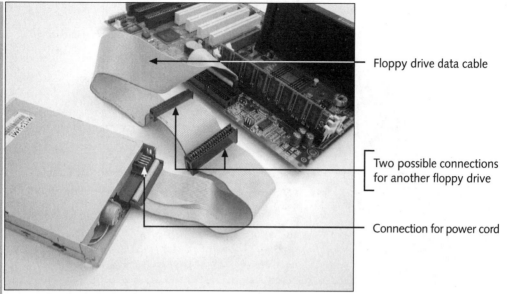

Floppy drive data cable

Two possible connections
for another floppy drive

Connection for power cord

Figure 1-23   One floppy drive connection on a motherboard can support one or two
floppy drives

Floppy drives are not as necessary as they once were, because the industry is moving toward storage media that can hold more data, such as CDs and Zip disks. For years, every PC and notebook computer had a floppy drive, but many newer notebook computers don't, and some manufacturers offer floppy drives on desktop systems as add-on options only.

A CD-ROM (compact disc read-only memory) drive is considered standard equipment on most computer systems today because most software is distributed on CDs. Figure 1-24 shows the rear of a CD-ROM drive with the IDE data cable and power cord connected. Don't let the name of the CD-ROM drive confuse you. It's really not memory, but secondary storage because, when you turn off the power, the data stored on a CD remains intact. Chapter 11 discusses different CD technologies and drives, some of which can both read and write data to the disc.

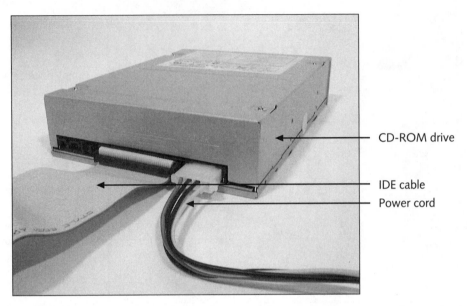

CD-ROM drive

IDE cable
Power cord

Figure 1-24   Most CD-ROM drives are EIDE devices and connect to the motherboard by way of an IDE data cable

Motherboard Components Used for Communication Among Devices

When you look carefully at the motherboard, you see many fine lines on both the top and the bottom of the board's surface (see Figure 1-25). These lines, sometimes called **traces**, are circuits, or paths, that enable data, instructions, and power to move from component to component on the board. This system of pathways used for communication and the protocol and methods used for transmission are collectively called the **bus**. (A **protocol** is a set of rules and standards that any two entities use for communication.) The paths, or lines, of the bus that are used to move data, called the **data bus**, are the part of the bus that we are most familiar with.

Binary data is put on a line of a bus by placing voltage on that line. We can visualize bits "traveling" down the bus in parallel, but in reality, the voltage placed on each line is not "traveling" but is all over the line. When one component at one end of the line wants to write data to another component, the two components get in sync for the write operation. Then the first component places voltage on several lines of the bus, and the other component immediately reads the voltage on those lines.

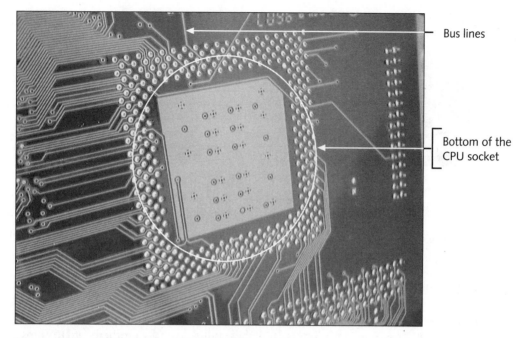

Bus lines

Bottom of the
CPU socket

Figure 1-25   On the bottom of the motherboard, you can see bus lines terminating at the
CPU socket

The CPU or other devices interpret the voltage, or lack of voltage, on each line on the
bus as binary digits (0s or 1s). Some buses have data paths that are 8, 16, 32, or 64 bits
wide. For example, a bus that has eight wires, or lines, to transmit data is called an 8-bit
bus. Figure 1-26 shows an 8-bit bus between the CPU and memory that is transmitting
the letter A (binary 01000001). All bits of a byte are placed on their lines of the bus at
the same time. Remember there are only two states inside a computer: on and off, which
represent zero and one. On a bus, these two states are no voltage for a zero and voltage
for a one. So the bus in Figure 1-26 has voltage on two lines and no voltage on the other
six lines, in order to pass the letter A on the bus. This bus is only 8 bits wide, but most
buses today are much wider: 16, 32, 64, or 128 bits wide. Also, most buses today use a
ninth bit for error checking. Adding a check bit to each byte allows the component reading the data to verify that it is the same data written to the bus.

The width of a data bus is called the **data path size**. A motherboard can have more than
one bus, each using a different protocol, speed, data path size, and so on. The main bus on
the motherboard that communicates with the CPU, memory, and the chip set goes by several names: **system bus**, memory bus, **host bus**, front side bus, or external bus. In our discussions, we use the term *system bus*. The data portion of most system buses on today's
motherboards is 64 bits wide with or without additional lines for error checking.

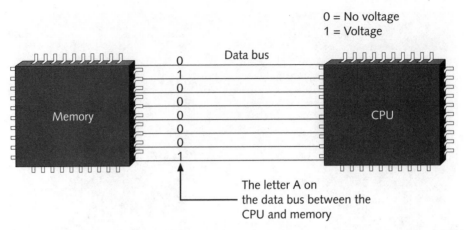

Figure 1-26 A data bus has traces, or lines, that contain voltage interpreted by the CPU and other devices as bits

One of the most interesting lines, or circuits, on a bus is the **system clock** or system timer, which is dedicated to timing the activities of the chips on the motherboard. A crystal on the motherboard (Figure 1-27), similar to that found in watches, generates continuous pulses to produce the system clock. Traces carry these pulses over the motherboard to chips and expansion slots to ensure that all activities are performed in a synchronized fashion. Remember that everything in a computer is binary, and this includes the activities themselves. Instead of continuously working to perform commands or move data, the CPU, bus, and other devices work in a binary fashion. Do something, stop, do something, stop, and so forth. Each device works on a clock cycle or beat of the clock. Some devices, such as the CPU, do two or more operations on one beat of the clock, and others do one operation per beat. Some devices might even do something on every other beat, but all work according to beats or cycles. You can think of this as similar to children jumping rope. The system clock (child turning the rope) provides the beats or cycles, while devices (children jumping) work in a binary fashion (jump, don't jump). In the analogy, some children jump two or more times per rope pass.

How fast does the clock beat? The beats, called the **clock speed**, are measured in **hertz (Hz)**, which is one cycle per second; **megahertz (MHz)**, which is one million cycles per second; and **gigahertz (GHz)**, which is one billion cycles per second. Most motherboard buses today operate at 100 MHz, 133 MHz, 200 MHz, or 400 MHz. In other words, data or instructions can be put on the system bus at the rate of 400 million every second. A CPU operates from 166 MHz to more than three GHz. In other words, the CPU can put data or instructions on its internal bus at this much higher rate. Although we often refer to the speed of the CPU and the motherboard bus, talking about the frequency of these devices is more accurate, because the term *speed* implies continuous flow, while the term *frequency* implies digital or binary flow: on and off, on and off.

Motherboard crystal
generates the system clock

Figure 1-27   The system clock is a pulsating electrical signal sent out by this component
that works much like a crystal in a wristwatch (one line, or circuit, on the
motherboard bus is dedicated to carrying this pulse)

The lines of a bus, including data, instruction, and power lines, often extend to the expansion slots (Figure 1-28). The size and shape of an expansion slot depend on the kind of bus it uses. Therefore, one way to determine the kind of bus you have is to examine the expansion slots on the motherboard. Figure 1-29 shows three types of expansion slots:

- PCI (Peripheral Component Interconnect) expansion slot used for high-speed input/output devices

- AGP (Accelerated Graphics Port) expansion slot used for a video card

- ISA (Industry Standard Architecture) expansion slot used by older and/or slower devices

With a little practice, you can identify these slots by their length, by the position of the breaks in the slots, and by the distance from the edge of the motherboard to a slot's position. Look for all three of these expansion slots in Figure 1-29.

In Chapter 5, you'll learn that each of these types of expansion slots communicates with the CPU by way of its own bus. There is a PCI bus, an AGP bus, and an ISA bus, each running at different speeds and providing different features to accommodate the expansion cards that use these different slots. But all these buses connect to the main bus or system bus, which connects to the CPU.

Pins on connector edge
of expansion card

PCI slot

Bus lines

Figure 1-28   The lines of a bus end at an expansion slot where they connect to pins that
connect to lines on the expansion card inserted in the slot

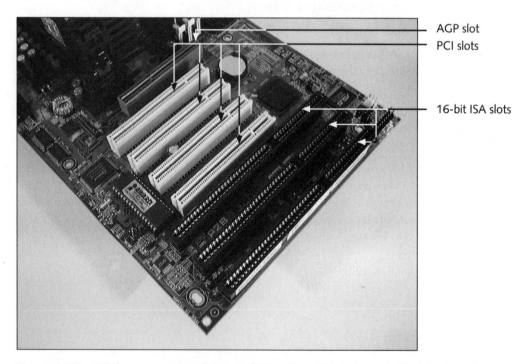

AGP slot
PCI slots

16-bit ISA slots

Figure 1-29   PCI bus expansion slots are shorter than ISA slots and offset farther; the one
AGP slot is set farther from the edge of the board

Interface (Expansion) Cards

A+CORE
    1.1

Circuit boards other than the motherboard inside the computer are sometimes called circuit cards, adapter boards, expansion cards, interface cards, or simply **cards**, and are mounted in expansion slots on the motherboard (see Figure 1-30). Figure 1-31 shows the motherboard and expansion cards installed in a computer case. By studying this figure carefully, you can see the video card installed in the one AGP slot, a sound card and network card installed in two PCI slots (the other two PCI slots are not used), and a modem card installed in an ISA slot (two ISA slots are not used). Figure 1-31 also shows the ports these cards provide at the rear of the PC case. You can see a full view of a video card in Figure 1-32. These cards all enable the CPU to connect to an external device or, in the case of the network card, to a network. The **video card** provides a port for the monitor. The sound card provides ports for speakers and microphones. The network card provides a port for a network cable to connect the PC to a network, and the modem card provides ports for phone lines. The technology to access these devices is embedded on the card itself, and the card also has the technology to communicate with the slot it is in, the motherboard, and the CPU.

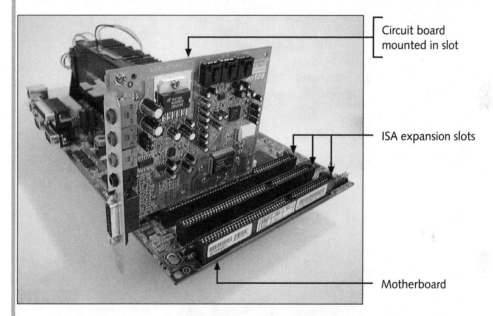

Circuit board
mounted in slot

ISA expansion slots

Motherboard

Figure 1-30   This circuit board is a sound card mounted in an ISA slot on
the motherboard

$A\!+\!{}^{CORE}_{1.1}$

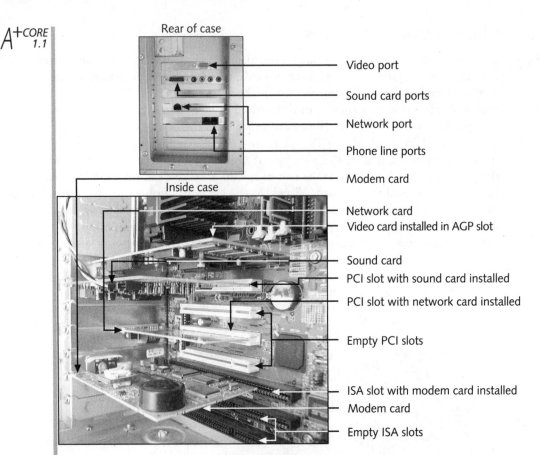

Rear of case

Video port

Sound card ports

Network port

Phone line ports

Modem card

Inside case

Network card
Video card installed in AGP slot

Sound card
PCI slot with sound card installed

PCI slot with network card installed

Empty PCI slots

ISA slot with modem card installed
Modem card

Empty ISA slots

Figure 1-31   Four cards installed on a motherboard providing ports for several devices

15-pin, 3-row
video port

Figure 1-32   The easiest way to identify this video card is to look at the port on the end
of the card

A+CORE
  1.1
The easiest way to determine the function of a particular expansion card (short of seeing its name written on the card, which doesn't happen very often) is to look at the end
of the card that fits against the back of the computer case. A network card, for example,
has a port designed to fit the network cable. An internal modem has one, or usually two,
telephone jacks as its ports. You'll get lots of practice in this book identifying ports on
expansion cards. However, as you examine the ports on the back of your PC, realize that
sometimes the motherboard provides ports of its own.

The Electrical System

A+CORE
  1.1
The most important component of the computer's electrical system is the power supply,
usually located near the rear of the case (see Figure 1-33). This **power supply** does not
actually generate electricity but converts and reduces it to a voltage that the computer
can handle. A power supply receives 110–120 volts of AC power from a wall outlet and
converts it to a much lower DC voltage. Older power supplies had power cables that provided either 5 or 12 volts DC. Newer power supplies provide 3.3, 5, and 12 volts DC. In
addition to providing power for the computer, the power supply runs a fan directly from
the electrical output voltage to help cool the inside of the computer case. Temperatures
over 185 degrees Fahrenheit (85 degrees Celsius) can cause components to fail. When a
computer is running, this fan and the spinning of the hard drive are the two primary
noisemakers.

Figure 1-33   Power supply with connections

Every motherboard has one or a pair of connections to provide electrical power from the
power supply to the motherboard and to other components that receive their power from
ports and expansion slots coming off the motherboard (see Figure 1-34). Each bus has wires,

A+CORE 1.1 or lines, designated to carry voltage to power expansion cards. Figure 1-35 shows the lines on the motherboard that are part of the bus ending at an expansion slot, some of which carry power. In Chapter 5, you will learn the specifics of which line carries what.

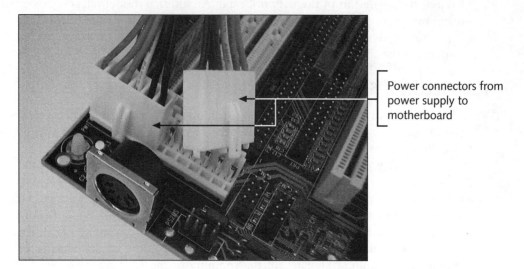

Power connectors from power supply to motherboard

Figure 1-34   The motherboard receives its power from the power supply by way of one or two connections located near the edge of the board

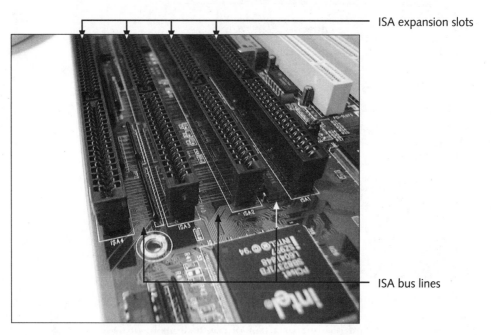

ISA expansion slots

ISA bus lines

Figure 1-35   Bus lines ending at expansion slots, some of which carry electrical power needed by cards

Instructions and Data Stored on the Motherboard

A+CORE
1.1

Some very basic instructions and data are stored on the motherboard—just enough to provide rudimentary information about the setup of the computer, to start the computer, and to search for an operating system stored on a secondary storage device such as a hard drive or floppy disk. These data and instructions are stored on special ROM (read-only memory) chips on the motherboard by setting physical switches on the board and through using CMOS configuration chips.

The distinction between hardware and software becomes vague in the case of ROM chips. Usually, it's easy to distinguish between hardware and software. For example, a floppy disk is hardware, but a file on the disk containing a set of instructions is software. This software file, sometimes called a **program**, might be stored on the disk today, but you can erase that file tomorrow and write a new one to the disk. In this case, a floppy disk is clearly a permanent physical entity, whereas the program is not. Sometimes, however, hardware and software are not so easy to distinguish. For instance, a ROM chip on a circuit board inside your computer has software instructions permanently etched into it during fabrication. This software is actually a part of the hardware and is not easily changed. In this case, hardware and software are closely tied together, and some people even give such hybrid components a new name: **firmware**.

These ROM chips hold programs or software that, among other things, tell the CPU how to perform many fundamental input/output tasks, and they are therefore sometimes called **BIOS (basic input/output system)** chips. See Figure 1-36 for an example of a **ROM BIOS** chip on a video card. The motherboard contains a vital ROM BIOS chip (Figure 1-37) that contains the programming necessary to start the computer and to perform other fundamental functions such as interacting with the floppy disk drive. As you add new hardware components to your system or new BIOS features become available, you might want to upgrade these utility programs. (You will learn how to do this in Chapter 5.) In the past, this meant buying new ROM chips and exchanging them on the motherboard. However, ROM chips on motherboards today can be reprogrammed. Called **flash ROM**, the software stored on these chips can be overwritten by new software that remains on the chip until it is overwritten.

Figure 1-36   A ROM BIOS chip on a video card holds programs that provide instructions to operate the card

Figure 1-37   The ROM BIOS chip on the motherboard contains the programming to start up the PC as well as perform many other fundamental tasks

Another chip on the motherboard contains a very small amount of memory, or RAM—enough to hold configuration or setup information about the computer. This is called the **CMOS configuration chip** or **CMOS setup chip**, or CMOS RAM. This chip, shown in Figure 1-38, is responsible for remembering system information such as how memory is allocated and which hard drives and floppy drives are present. A trickle of electricity from a small battery located on the motherboard or computer case, usually

A+CORE
1.1 close to the chip itself, powers the CMOS chip; thus, even though the CMOS chip is RAM (temporary memory), when the computer is turned off, the chip retains its data. When the computer is first turned on, it looks to this CMOS chip to learn what hardware it should expect to find.

Battery

CMOS setup chip

Figure 1-38   The CMOS setup chip, powered by a battery when the PC is turned off, contains data about the system configuration as well as the current time and date

> **TIP**   Even though a computer has many CMOS chips, the term CMOS chip has come to mean the one chip on the motherboard that holds the configuration or setup information. If you hear someone ask: "What does CMOS say?" or "Let's change CMOS," the person is talking about the configuration or setup information stored on this one CMOS chip. The program to change CMOS setup is stored in the ROM BIOS chip and can be accessed during the startup process.

A motherboard can also retain setup or installation information in different settings of jumpers or DIP switches on the board. **Jumpers** are considered open or closed based on whether a jumper cover is present on two small wires that extend from the motherboard (see Figure 1-39). A group of jumpers is sometimes used to tell the system the CPU's running speed, or to turn a power-saving feature on or off. A **DIP (dual inline package) switch** is similar to a light switch and is on or off depending on the direction in which the small switch is set. Many motherboards have at least one, often several, jumpers and perhaps a single bank of DIP switches (see Figure 1-40), although the trend is to include most setup information in CMOS rather than to have a jumper or switch on the board that has to be mechanically set.

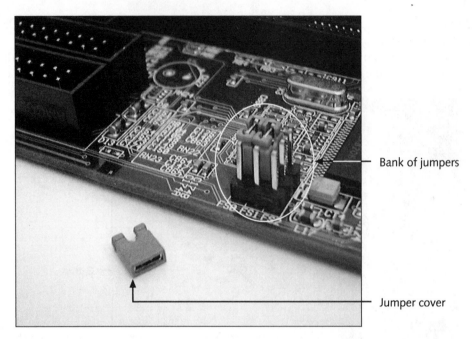

Bank of jumpers

Jumper cover

Figure 1-39   Setup information about the motherboard can be stored by setting a jumper
on (closed) or off (open). A jumper is closed if the cover is in place, connecting
the two wires that make up the jumper; a jumper is open if the cover is not
in place.

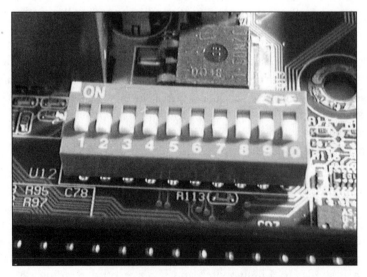

Figure 1-40   A motherboard can use a bank of DIP switches for configuration settings

CHAPTER SUMMARY

- ❏ A computer requires both hardware and software to work.

- ❏ The four basic functions of the microcomputer are input, output, processing, and storage of data.

- ❏ Data and instructions are stored in a computer in binary, which uses only two states for data—on and off, or 1 and 0—which are called bits. Eight bits equal one byte.

- ❏ Letters and other characters must be assigned a numeric value before they can be stored in a computer. The most popular coding scheme for letters and characters is ASCII (American Standard Code for Information Interchange), which assigns an 8-bit code for letters, symbols, and other characters.

- ❏ The four most popular input/output devices are the printer, monitor, mouse, and keyboard.

- ❏ The most important component inside the computer case is the motherboard, also called the main board or system board. It contains the most important microchip inside the case, the central processing unit (CPU), a microprocessor, as well as access to other circuit boards and peripheral devices. All communications between the CPU and other devices must pass through the motherboard.

- ❏ A ROM BIOS microchip is a hybrid of hardware and software with embedded programming. These chips are called firmware.

- ❏ Most microchips are manufactured using CMOS (complementary metal-oxide semiconductor) technology. Most CPUs are CMOS chips.

- ❏ Each hardware device needs a method to communicate with the CPU, software to control it, and electricity to power it.

- ❏ Devices outside the computer case connect to the motherboard through ports on the case. Common ports are serial, parallel, USB, game, keyboard, and mouse ports.

- ❏ A circuit board inserted in an expansion slot on the motherboard can provide an interface between the motherboard and a peripheral device or can itself be a peripheral. (An example is an internal modem.)

- ❏ The chip set on a motherboard controls most activities on the motherboard and includes several device controllers, including the USB controller, memory controller, IDE controller, and so forth.

- ❏ Primary storage, called memory or RAM, is temporary storage the CPU uses to hold data and instructions while it is processing both.

- ❏ RAM is stored on single chips, SIMMs, DIMMs, and RIMMs.

- ❏ Secondary storage is slower than primary storage, but it is permanent storage. The most common examples of secondary storage devices are floppy disk, hard drive, and CD-ROM drive.

❑ Most hard drives use EIDE (Enhanced Integrated Drive Electronics) technology, which can accommodate up to four EIDE devices on one system.

❑ The system clock is used to synchronize activity on the motherboard. To control the pace of activity, it sends continuous pulses over the bus that different components use.

❑ A motherboard has several buses, including the system bus, the PCI bus, the AGP bus, and the ISA bus.

❑ The frequency of activity on a motherboard is measured in megahertz (MHz), or 1 million cycles per second. The CPU operates at a much higher frequency than other components in the system, and its activity is measured in gigahertz (GHz), or 1 billion cycles per second.

❑ The power supply inside the computer case supplies electricity to components both inside and outside the case. Some components external to the case get power from their own electrical cable.

❑ ROM BIOS on a motherboard holds basic software needed to start a PC and begin the process of loading an operating system. Most ROM chips are flash ROM, meaning that these programs can be updated without exchanging the chip.

❑ The CMOS chip on a PC's motherboard stores setup, or configuration, information. This information can also be set by means of jumpers and DIP switches. When power to the PC is turned off, a battery on the motherboard supplies power to the CMOS chip.

KEY TERMS

ASCII (American
  Standard Code for
  Information
  Interchange)
binary number system
BIOS (basic input/out-
  put system)
bit
bus
byte
cards
central processing unit
  (CPU)
chip set
circuit board
clock speed

CMOS (complementary
  metal-oxide semi-
  conductor)
CMOS configuration
  chip
CMOS setup chip
data bus
data path size
DIMM (dual inline
  memory module)
DIP (dual inline
  package) switch
expansion card
expansion slot
firmware
flash ROM

gigahertz (GHz)
hard copy
hard drive
hardware
hertz (Hz)
hexadecimal notation
  (hex)
host bus
jumper
keyboard
main board
megahertz (MHz)
memory
microprocessor
monitor
motherboard

mouse
nonvolatile
parallel port
peripheral device
port
power supply
primary storage
printer
processor
program

protocol
RAM (random access
    memory)
RIMM
ROM (read-only
    memory)
ROM BIOS
secondary storage
serial port
SIMM (single inline

memory module)
software
system board
system bus
system clock
trace
USB (universal serial
    bus) port
video card
volatile

REVIEW QUESTIONS

1. The process that best characterizes all computer activity includes four specific, unique stages. They include _____, _____, _____, and _____.

2. The native language of the processor is based on the _____ number system.

    a. Decimal

    b. Hexadecimal

    c. Binary

    d. Octal

3. The binary representation of the number 18 in byte format is:

    a. 10010

    b. 00010010

    c. 100100

    d. 01000100

    e. None of the above

4. The hexadecimal number system is based on a collection of _____ unique values.

    a. 2

    b. 8

    c. 10

    d. 16

    e. None of the above

5. In order to communicate with the CPU, a device needs to post a "request for service" over the control bus. This "request for service" is referred to as:

   a. DMA

   b. I/O

   c. IRQ

   d. ROM address

   e. RAM address

6. The term that is associated with either a wireless or wired connection to the motherboard that allows communications with outside devices is called the:

   a. Keyboard

   b. Speaker

   c. Power supply

   d. Port

   e. Mouse

7. The device whose design is based on a rotating ball and sensors that track movement and controls the location of a pointer on screen is referred to as a:

   a. Keyboard

   b. Mouse

   c. Monitor

   d. CPU

   e. None of the above

8. The device that is best characterized as being associated with what is referred to as *resolution* or a collection of dots or pixels is referred to as a:

   a. Keyboard

   b. Mouse

   c. Monitor

   d. CPU

   e. None of the above

9. The type of microchip technology that was developed as a means of using less power and, consequently, producing less heat, is called _____ technology.

   a. CPU

   b. Peripheral device

   c. CMOS

   d. TTL

   e. Motherboard

10. The serial port transfers data _____ bit(s) at a time.

    a. 0

    b. 1

    c. 4

    d. 8

    e. 16

11. The parallel port transfers data _____ bit(s) at a time.

    a. 0

    b. 1

    c. 4

    d. 8

    e. 16

12. The _____ port allows multiple devices to be connected to a common bus, typically, in excess of 100 devices simultaneously.

    a. Serial

    b. Parallel

    c. Universal Serial Bus (USB)

    d. Integrated Device Electronics (IDE)

    e. Small Computer System Interface (SCSI)

13. Devices that are used as storage devices, but are considered to be volatile or temporary storage devices, are:

    a. RAM

    b. ROM

    c. Hard drive

    d. CD-ROM

    e. CPU

14. Devices that are used as storage devices, but are considered to be nonvolatile storage devices that are typically used to hold setup data are:

    a. RAM

    b. ROM

    c. Hard drive

    d. CD-ROM

    e. CPU

15. Which of the following are considered to be storage devices under the classifica-tion of *primary* storage?

    a. RAM

    b. ROM

    c. Hard drive

    d. CD-ROM

    e. Both c and d

16. Which of the following are considered to be storage devices under the classifica-tion of *secondary* storage?

    a. RAM

    b. ROM

    c. Hard drive

    d. CD-ROM

    e. Both c and d

17. Which term best describes a collection of related wires designed to carry data between devices on a motherboard?

    a. CPU

    b. Port

    c. Bus

    d. SIMM

    e. DIMM

18. Which of the following memory storage devices do *not* belong with the rest of the group?

    a. Hard drive

    b. Zip drive

    c. CD-ROM

    d. RAM

    e. DVD

19. A majority of hard drives today utilize the _____ interface connector to get data to and from the hard drive unit.

    a. Power

    b. RAM

    c. IDE

    d. CPU

    e. SCSI

20. The most popular hard drive data interface utilizes a collection of _____-wires in order to allow for the transfer of data between hard drive and hard drive interface connector on the motherboard.

    a. 8

    b. 16

    c. 34

    d. 40

    e. 50

21. A set of rules and/or standards that are imposed to ensure that two or more devices from different manufacturers can communicate without problem is referred to as:

    a. Trace

    b. Bus

    c. Interface

    d. Port

    e. Protocol

22. Which of the following do *not* represent expansion slots located on the system motherboard?

    a. PCI

    b. AGP

    c. ISA

    d. IDE

    e. None of the above

23. The power supply is tasked with the responsibility to convert:

    a. AC to DC power

    b. DC to AC power

    c. DC to DC power

    d. AC to AC power

    e. None of the above

24. Which of the following voltages are considered to be output voltages on newer power supplies used in microcomputer systems?

    a. 5V and 12V only

    b. 5V, 12V, and 3.3V

    c. 5V, 12V, and 120V

    d. 5V, 12V, 3.3V, and 120V

    e. None of the above

25. The term associated with software that is actually written into hardware and *not* changed often is:

    a. Program

    b. Software

    c. Firmware

    d. Hardware

    e. CPU

26. The name-assigned hardware that is tasked with the responsibility to hold instructions that are *not* changed often, but contains fundamental input/output instructions is referred to as:

    a. RAM

    b. Hard drive

    c. ROM BIOS

    d. CPU

    e. None of the above

27. Of the following pieces of solid-state memory, which would *not* be considered volatile memory?

    a. CMOS setup chip

    b. RAM

    c. CMOS RAM

    d. ROM

    e. None of the above

28. Jumpers are often used to program hardware to a particular configuration. If the manufacturer's literature states that a jumper pair on the system motherboard should be set to "closed," the jumper should be _____.

    a. In place

    b. Not in place

    c. Both a and b

    d. Neither a nor b

2

HOW HARDWARE AND SOFTWARE WORK TOGETHER

In this chapter, you will learn:

♦ How hardware and software interact

♦ How system resources help hardware and software communicate

♦ How an OS relates to BIOS, device drivers, and applications

♦ Different ways an OS can launch applications

Computer systems contain both hardware and software, and computer technicians must understand how they interact. Although the physical hardware is the visible part of a computer system, the software is the intelligence of the system that enables the hardware components to work. In this chapter, you'll see how operating system software controls several of the more significant hardware devices. You'll also see how an OS provides the interface that applications need to command and use hardware devices.

HARDWARE AND SOFTWARE INTERACTION: AN OVERVIEW

Let's begin with a review of the analogy used in Chapter 1, as shown in Figure 2-1, the comparison of a car to computer hardware. If a car is like a hardware system, then the people who service and drive the car are like software that manages and instructs the hardware. The mechanic and driver make the automobile a functioning tool that people can use to accomplish a task. Without their intelligence, skill, and direction, the car is nothing more than an interconnected assemblage of electronic and mechanical devices. Software provides a similar function for hardware. Software is the intelligence of the computer; it determines what hardware is present, decides how it is configured and used, and then uses that hardware to perform tasks.

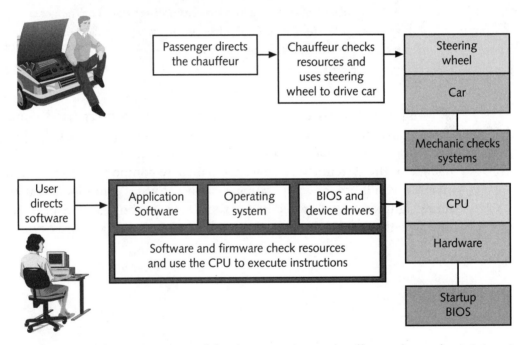

Figure 2-1   Software interacts with hardware much as a chauffeur and a mechanic interact with a car

Software consists of programs, written by programmers, that instruct computers to perform specific tasks. The first thing most people picture when they hear software mentioned is application software that users interact with, such as word-processing or database programs. However, this type of software does not control hardware directly; there are several layers between such applications and system hardware. An operating system acts as the middleman between applications and hardware. In general, an **operating system (OS)** is software that controls a computer. It manages hardware, runs applications, provides an interface for users, and stores, retrieves, and manipulates files.

A+ OS
  1.1
A computer might have several applications installed to meet users' various needs, but it only needs one operating system. Many operating systems are on the market, each designed to support different types of hardware systems and user needs:

- *DOS.* The first OS for IBM computers and IBM-compatible computers was DOS, the disk OS. Because DOS was written for early PCs, it has significant limitations today. DOS was the OS early versions of Windows used, including Windows 3.1 and Windows 3.11 (collectively called 3.x). Windows 3.x did not perform OS functions but simply served as a user-friendly intermediate program between DOS and applications and the user.

- *Windows 9x.* The more recent Windows 95, Windows 98, and Windows Me, collectively called Windows 9x, are true operating systems with a DOS core and a user-friendly interface. Windows 98 is a popular OS for desktop computers for home use, but Windows 2000 and Windows XP are quickly replacing it.

- *Windows NT, Windows 2000, and Windows XP.* Windows NT comes in two versions, Windows NT Workstation for workstations and Windows NT Server to control a network. Windows 2000 is an upgrade of Windows NT, and Windows XP is an upgrade of Windows 2000. Windows 2000 also comes in several versions, some designed for the desktop and others designed for high-end servers. Windows 2000 Professional is a popular OS for the corporate desktop. Windows 2000 Server, Advanced Server, and Datacenter Server are network server OSs. Windows XP currently comes in two main versions: Windows XP Home Edition and Windows XP Professional. Windows XP is expected to first replace Windows 9x and then replace Windows 2000. Windows.NET Server is soon to be released.

- *Unix.* Unix is a popular OS used to control and support networks and to serve Internet applications such as Web servers.

- *Linux.* A scaled-down version of Unix, Linux is provided free of charge in its basic form and allows open access to the programming code of the OS. It is often used for server applications.

- *OS/2.* Developed by IBM and Microsoft, OS/2 is used less commonly on home desktop PCs but is used in industrial settings and certain types of networks. Windows NT was developed using some core components of OS/2, and Microsoft intended it to replace OS/2.

- *Mac OS.* Available only for Apple Macintosh computers, Mac OS is often used for graphics applications and in educational settings.

Every OS is responsible for communicating with hardware, but the OS does not relate directly to the hardware. Rather, the OS uses the BIOS or device drivers to interface with hardware. Figure 2-2 shows these relationships. Therefore, most PC software falls into three categories:

- BIOS and device drivers
- Operating system (OS)
- Application software

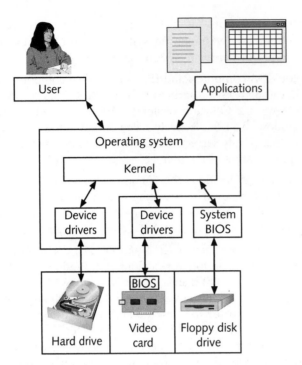

Figure 2-2   An OS relates to hardware by way of BIOS and device drivers

Device drivers are small programs stored on the hard drive that tell the computer how to communicate with a hardware device such as a printer, network card, or modem. These drivers are installed on the hard drive when the device is first installed.

Recall from Chapter 1 that the BIOS (basic input/output system) on the motherboard is hard-coded or permanently coded into a computer chip called the ROM BIOS chip. BIOS programs fall into three categories: programs to control I/O devices (called **system BIOS**), programs to control the startup of a computer (called **startup BIOS**), and a program to change the setup information stored in CMOS (called **CMOS setup**). Just as a mechanic is responsible for the condition of a car before turning it over to the driver, when a computer is turned on, first startup BIOS and then the OS are in control of preparing the computer for user interaction. Later sections in this chapter explain how this works, and Chapter 5 covers how CMOS setup changes CMOS RAM.

A PC technician must understand how BIOS or device drivers control hardware devices and how these devices and the CPU relate to each other. To understand how all this works, we begin with the system resources—the tools used for communication on the motherboard.

2

SYSTEM RESOURCES

A+CORE
1.4

Just as a chauffeur has resources or tools to control a car (such as controls on the console), and the car has resources to alert the chauffeur that it needs attention (such as the oil warning light), software has resources to control hardware, and hardware has resources to alert software that it needs attention. Think of a **system resource** as a tool used by either hardware or software to communicate with the other.

There are four types of system resources: memory addresses, I/O addresses, interrupt request numbers (IRQs), and direct memory access (DMA) channels. Table 2-1 lists these system resources used by software and hardware and defines each.

Table 2-1   System resources used by software and hardware

System Resource	Definition
IRQ	A line of a motherboard bus that a hardware device can use to signal the CPU that the device needs attention. Some lines have a higher priority for attention than others. Each IRQ line is assigned a number (0 to 15) to identify it.
I/O addresses	Numbers assigned to hardware devices that software uses to send a command to a device. Each device "listens" for these numbers and responds to the ones assigned to it.
Memory addresses	Numbers assigned to physical memory located either in RAM or ROM chips. Software can access this memory by using these addresses.
DMA channel	A number designating a channel on which the device can pass data to memory without involving the CPU. Think of a DMA channel as a shortcut for data moving to and from the device and memory.

As Table 2-1 explains, all four resources are used for communication between hardware and software. Hardware devices signal the CPU for attention using an IRQ. Software addresses a device by one of its I/O addresses. Software looks at memory as a hardware device and addresses it with memory addresses, and DMA channels pass data back and forth between a hardware device and memory.

All four system resources depend on certain lines on a bus on the motherboard. A bus such as the system bus has three components: the data bus carries data, the address bus communicates addresses (both memory addresses and I/O addresses), and the control bus controls communication (see Figure 2-3). It's impossible to truly understand system resources without relating them to physical lines on the bus. Therefore, we turn our attention next to a careful examination of one motherboard bus, before we look at each system resource in detail.

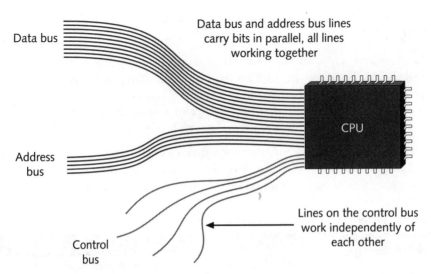

Figure 2-3   A bus consists of a data bus, an address bus, and a control bus

The 8-Bit and 16-Bit ISA Slots

A+CORE
4.3

In Chapter 1, you learned that all devices are directly or indirectly connected to the motherboard because they all depend on the CPU on the motherboard for processing their data. A device connects to the motherboard by a data cable, a slot, or a port coming directly off the motherboard. In any case, the device always connects to a single bus on the motherboard. Recall that there are several different buses on a motherboard. Our discussion here is limited to one of the first system buses used on the early PCs of the 1980s, because it is easy to understand. This bus was the only bus on the motherboard at the time and provided slots called **ISA (Industry Standard Architecture) slots**. Chapter 5 discusses in detail the current system bus and the other peripheral buses on today's motherboards. The first system bus had only eight lines for data, and, therefore, the first ISA slot had eight lines for data and was called the 8-bit ISA slot. Figure 2-4 shows an expansion slot for this bus with some of the pinouts labeled. A **pinout** is a description of how each pin on a bus, connection, plug, slot, or socket is used.

Some lines on the bus are used for data, addresses, and voltage; others are a variety of control lines. Looking at Figure 2-4, you can see that eight lines are used for data and 20 lines are used for addresses. These 20 lines can carry either memory addresses or I/O addresses. The CPU determines which type of address is using these lines by setting control lines B11 through B14, as shown in Figure 2-4 (memory read, memory write, I/O read, and I/O write). Since this bus has only 20 address lines, the largest address value that can travel on the bus is 1111 1111 1111 1111 1111, or 1,048,576 (1,024K or 1 MB). Managing a DMA channel requires two lines: DRQ (direct request) and DACK (direct acknowledge). Four DMA channels (0, 1, 2, and 3) on the first system bus connected to an 8-bit ISA slot.

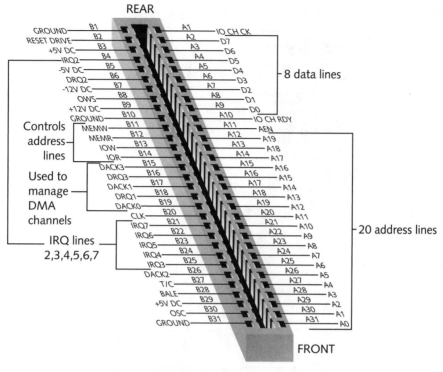

Figure 2-4 A 62-pin expansion slot for the 8-bit ISA bus

A+CORE 4.3 As computer technology improved, the 16-bit ISA slot was invented to provide more memory addresses, DMA channels, and IRQs. These were necessary to meet the demand for more memory, more devices operating at the same time, and faster data transfer. Figure 2-5 shows how the 16-bit ISA slot added an extension to the 8-bit slot, allowing eight additional data lines for a total of 16, five additional IRQ lines, four more DMA channels, and four additional address lines for a total of 24. Today, motherboards still use the 16-bit ISA slot, although they also use newer, faster buses. An 8-bit expansion card (an expansion card that processes only eight bits of data at one time) can use a 16-bit ISA expansion slot; it uses only the first part of the slot. Modem cards typically use an 8-bit ISA slot.

 Motherboards in the late 1980s had a variation of the ISA slot, the Extended ISA (EISA) slot, which was deeper than the ISA slot. The extra depth accommodated an additional group of pins set deep in the slot to yield a 32-bit data path. These 32-bit EISA slots are seldom seen today, and the 32-bit EISA expansion cards that used them are obsolete. It's difficult to distinguish an ISA slot from an EISA slot because, on the surface, they look the same. Check your motherboard documentation to determine which type of slot the board is using.

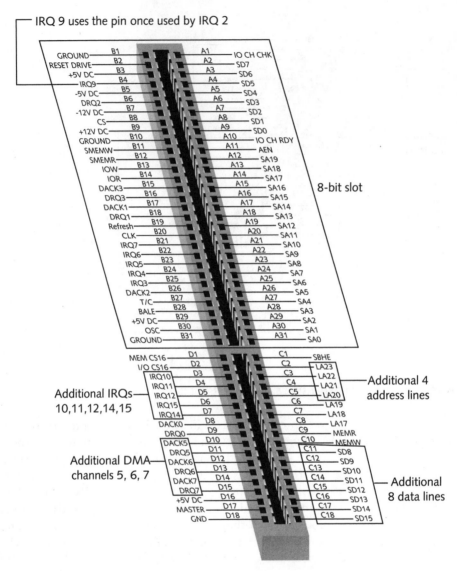

Figure 2-5 A 98-pin expansion slot for the 16-bit ISA bus

A+CORE 4.3 Although motherboards can contain buses that are faster and provide more options than the 16-bit system bus used with a 16-bit ISA slot, the basic functions haven't changed. You can still find lines on these buses for data, addresses, IRQs, and DMA channels, although it is common practice today for a line to perform several functions, called multiplexing, making it more difficult to pinpoint which lines are used for which resources on newer buses. A line can be used for more than one purpose because all devices, controllers, and the CPU using these lines are made aware of how a line is currently being used by reading voltage on a control line or by the different stages of the clock cycle.

$A+^{CORE}_{4.3}$ The first PCs only had one bus, the system bus, and everything on the motherboard ran at the speed of this one bus. This is not the case today. Because the ISA slots run at a much slower speed than the system buses of today, the ISA slots no longer connect directly to the system bus. ISA slots connect to a slow ISA interface, which connects to the medium-speed PCI bus, which connects to the faster system bus. This bus arrangement can be compared to road systems of the past and present. In the past, roads were all assigned the same speed limit, but today a slow street in a subdivision connects to a faster highway, which connects to an even faster freeway.

Now that you've been introduced to the way the system resources use the lines on a bus, let's turn our attention to a more detailed description of the four resources and how they work.

Interrupt Request Number (IRQ)

$A+^{CORE}_{1.4}$ When a hardware device needs the CPU to do something, for instance, when the keyboard needs the CPU to process a keystroke after a key has been pressed, the device needs a way to get the CPU's attention, and the CPU must know what to do once it turns its attention to the device. These interruptions to the CPU are called **hardware interrupts**, and the device initiates an interrupt by placing voltage on the designated **IRQ (interrupt request) line** assigned to it. This voltage on the line serves as a signal to the CPU that the device has a request that needs processing. Often, a hardware device that needs attention from the CPU is referred to as "needing servicing." Interrupts initiate many processes that the CPU carries out, and these processes are said to be "interrupt-driven."

Look back at Figure 2-4 for a moment, and find the IRQ lines (IRQ 2, 3, 4, 5, 6, and 7). Table 2-2 lists common uses for these IRQs. Eight IRQs are actually built into this bus, but IRQs 0 and 1 are not available for expansion cards (because they are used for the system clock and keyboard), so they are not given pins on the expansion slot. IRQ 2 was reserved in the early days of PCs because it was intended to be used as part of a link to mainframe computers. Thus, only five IRQs were available for devices, and each device had to have its own IRQ. This made it difficult for more than five devices to be connected to a PC at any one time.

Table 2-2   IRQ numbers for devices using the early 8-bit ISA bus

IRQ	Device
0	System timer (system clock)
1	Keyboard controller
2	Reserved (not used)
3	COM2
4	COM1
5	LPT2
6	Floppy drive controller
7	LPT1

A+CORE
1.4

In Table 2-2, notice the COM and LPT assignments. COM1 and COM2 are preconfig-ured assignments that can be assigned to serial devices such as modems, and LPT1 and LPT2 are preconfigured assignments that can be assigned to parallel devices such as printers. For example, rather than being assigned an IRQ and some I/O addresses, the modem uses the assignments previously made to COM2, which makes it easier to configure the modem and to avoid conflicts with other devices also needing an IRQ and some I/O addresses. You will learn more about COM and LPT assignments in Chapter 10.

On motherboards, the CPU actually doesn't know which IRQ is "up" because the inter-rupt controller manages that. If more than one IRQ is up at the same time, the inter-rupt controller selects the IRQ that has the lowest value to process first. For example, if a user presses a key on the keyboard at the exact time that she moves the mouse config-ured to use COM1, the keystroke is processed before the mouse action, since the keyboard is using IRQ 1 and the mouse on COM1 is using IRQ 4. Think of the interrupt controller as the "inside man" with the CPU. All devices wait outside the door for the controller to let the CPU know what they need. The controller chip on early motherboards was designed to handle only eight different IRQs.

When the 16-bit ISA bus appeared, more IRQs became available, so a second interrupt controller chip was added to the motherboard chip set. This second controller did not have access to the CPU, so it had to communicate with it through the first controller (see Figure 2-6). To signal the first controller, the second controller used one of the first controller's IRQ values (IRQ 2). But that was a problem because, even though IRQ 2 was supposed to be used only for mainframe computers hooked to the PC, some devices that used IRQ 2 had already been manufactured and were in use. Providing a way for these devices to work was accomplished by tying the new IRQ 9 to the old IRQ 2 pin on the 16-bit ISA bus. The result was that a device could still use the pin on the expan-sion slot for IRQ 2, but it was really IRQ 9, which you can see if you look carefully at Figure 2-4. Because of this, the IRQ priority level became: 0, 1, (8, 9, 10, 11, 12, 13, 14, 15), 3, 4, 5, 6, 7.

A+ OS
1.1
1.5
CORE
1.4

To see how the IRQs are assigned on your computer, use MSD for DOS and Device Manager for Windows 9x and Windows 2000/XP. (Windows NT does not have Device Manager.) For Windows 9x, click Start, point to Settings, click Control Panel, and double-click System. Click the Device Manager tab. Select Computer and click Properties. Figure 2-7 shows the Computer Properties dialog box. Notice in Figure 2-7 that IRQ 2 is assigned to the programmable interrupt controller and IRQ 9 is used by the video card.

2

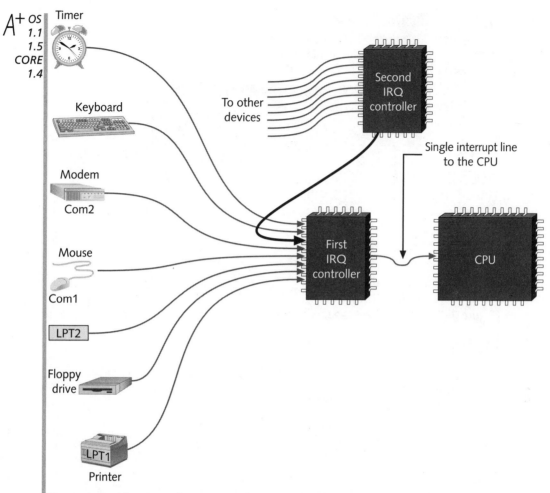

Figure 2-6 The second IRQ controller uses IRQ 2 to signal the first IRQ controller

For Windows 2000, a quick way to access Device Manager is to right-click My Computer on the desktop and select Properties from the shortcut menu. For Windows XP, click start, right-click My Computer, and select Properties from the shortcut menu. The System Properties window appears. Click the Hardware tab and then click the Device Manager button (see Figure 2-8). On the menu, click View, then if necessary click Resources by Type. Click the plus sign next to Interrupt request (IRQ) to open the list of assigned IRQs. Notice in the figure that several devices share IRQ 11.

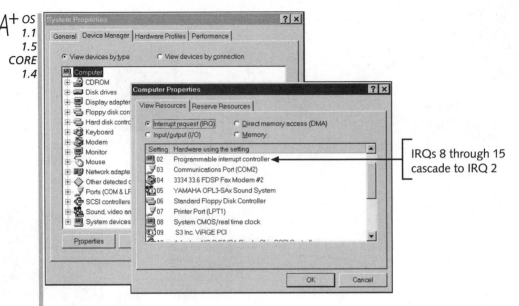

Figure 2-7 Use Device Manager to see how IRQs use your system

IRQs 8 through 15 cascade to IRQ 2

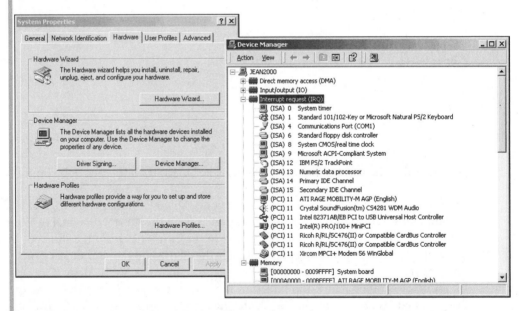

Figure 2-8 Windows 2000 Device Manager shows the current assignments for system resources

TIP Sharing IRQs is not possible with ISA devices on the ISA bus. However, newer buses are designed to allow more than one device to share an IRQ. In Chapter 5, you will see how the PCI and USB buses do this.

A+CORE
1.4

With interrupts, the hardware device or the software initiates communication by sending a signal to the CPU, but a device can be serviced in another way, called polling. With **polling**, software that is constantly running has the CPU periodically check the hardware device to see if it needs service. Not very many devices use polling as the method of communication; most hardware devices use interrupts. A joystick is one example of a device that does use polling. Software written to manage a joystick has the CPU check the joystick periodically to see if the device has data to communicate, which is why a joystick does not need an IRQ to work.

Memory Addresses

A+CORE
1.4

An operating system relates to memory as a long list of cells that it can use to hold data and instructions, somewhat like a one-dimensional spreadsheet. Each memory location or cell is assigned a number beginning with zero. These number assignments are made when the OS is first loaded and are called **memory addresses**. Think of a memory address as a seat number in a theatre (see Figure 2-9). Each seat is assigned a number regardless of whether someone sits in it. The person sitting in a seat can be data or instructions, and the OS refers to the person not by name but by seat number. For example, the OS might say, "I want to print the data in memory addresses 500 through 650." These addresses most often appear on the screen as hexadecimal (base 16 or hex) numbers in segment: offset form (for example, C800:5, which is 819,205 in decimal).

Figure 2-9 Memory addresses are assigned to each location in memory, and these locations can store data or instructions

 TIP See Appendix C for more information on the hexadecimal number system and how it applies to memory addresses.

The CPU uses the address bus to communicate the memory addresses it uses to access memory (see Figure 2-10). For example, if it wants to read the data in memory address

$A^{+CORE}_{1.4}$ 819,205, it puts the value 819,205 on the address bus. The memory controller, which is part of the chip set, reads the address and then puts the data stored in that memory address on the data bus, which the CPU reads. In this example, the CPU puts the binary value for 819,205, which is 11001000000000000101, on the address bus. Each line on the address bus must hold one of the bits for this number. In this case, 20 lines are required. Therefore, the number of lines on the motherboard devoted to the address bus limits the largest memory address the CPU can use.

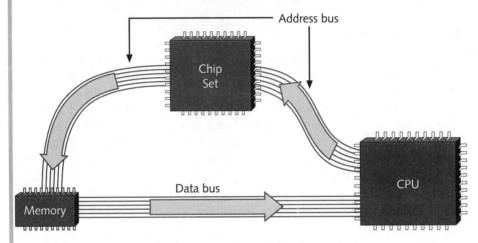

Figure 2-10   The CPU tells the memory controller from which memory address
              to fetch data

 TIP   Windows offers a calculator that can quickly convert binary, digital, and hexadecimal numbers. You can use it to follow along with the conversions used here. Enter a number in one number system, and then click another number system to make the conversion. To access the calculator in Windows 9x or Windows NT/2000/XP, click Start, Programs, Accessories, Calculator.

Remember that only 20 lines on the bus were available to early CPUs to handle addresses, so the largest memory address the CPU could use was 11111111111111111111, which is 1,048,575 or 1,024K or 1 MB of memory. DOS used this 1 MB of memory and divided it according to the scheme shown in Table 2-3.

Table 2-3   Division of memory under DOS

Range of Memory Addresses	Range Using Hex Terminology	Type of Memory
0 to 640K	0 to A0000	Conventional or base memory
640K to 1,024K	A0000 to FFFFF	Upper memory (A through F ranges)
Above 1,024K	100000 and up	Extended memory

2

A+CORE
1.4

DOS and applications used the first 640K of memory, and the BIOS and device drivers, discussed later in the chapter, used the addresses from 640K up to 1,024K. Then newer CPUs and motherboards were developed with 24 address lines and more, so memory addresses above 1,024K became available and were called **extended memory**. Windows 9x still uses these same divisions of memory, although it makes the most use of extended memory. Memory addresses are expressed using hexadecimal notation. Because the hex numbers in upper memory begin with A through F, the divisions of upper memory are often called the A range, B range, C range, and so on, up to the F range. Chapter 6 covers memory in more detail.

Table 2-3 applies to DOS and Windows 9x only. Windows NT/2000/XP uses an altogether different memory-mapping design, which has no conventional, upper, or extended memory; it's all just memory.

Using Windows 9x Device Manager, you can see how the first 1 MB of memory addresses are assigned (see Figure 2-11). To view the list, in the list of devices select Computer and click Properties, then click Memory. Notice in the figure that the system BIOS has been assigned memory addresses in the F range of upper memory. This F range is always reserved for motherboard BIOS, and other programs never request it. When the CPU is first turned on and needs a program to know how to boot up, it begins with the instructions stored on the ROM BIOS chip assigned to these memory addresses.

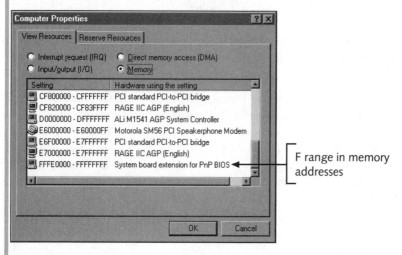

F range in memory addresses

Figure 2-11   Computer Properties window shows how the first megabyte of memory addresses are assigned

Shadowing ROM

Before finishing our discussion of memory, let's look at one other interesting use of ROM and RAM that helps clarify the use of memory addresses. Sometimes system BIOS programs are copied from the ROM BIOS memory into RAM because reading from RAM chips is generally faster than reading from ROM chips. The process of copying programs from ROM to RAM for execution is called **shadowing ROM**, or just

A+CORE
1.4

shadow RAM. If the ROM programs are executed directly from the ROM chips, the memory addresses are assigned to this ROM. If the programs are first copied to RAM and then executed, the same memory addresses are assigned to this area of RAM. The instructions work the same, either way.

>
> **TIP**   In the setup of your computer, you usually have the choice of whether to shadow system BIOS. For DOS and Windows 9x, accept the default setting for this option.

I/O Addresses

A+CORE
1.4

Another system resource made available to hardware devices is input/output addresses, or I/O addresses. **I/O addresses**, or **port addresses**, sometimes simply called ports, are numbers the CPU can use to access hardware devices, in much the same way it uses memory addresses to access physical memory. Recall that the address bus on the motherboard sometimes carries memory addresses and sometimes carries I/O addresses. If the address bus has been set to carry I/O addresses, then each device "listens" to this bus (see Figure 2-12). If the address belongs to it, then it responds; otherwise, it ignores the request for information. In short, the CPU "knows" a hardware device as a group of I/O addresses. If it wants to know the status of a printer or a floppy drive, for example, it places a particular I/O address on the address bus on the motherboard.

Table 2-4 lists a few common assignments for I/O addresses. Because these addresses are hex numbers, you sometimes see them written with 0x first, like this: 0x0040, or with the h last, like this: 0040h.

Because IBM made many address assignments when it manufactured the first PC in the late 1970s, common devices such as a hard drive, a floppy drive, or a keyboard use a range of predetermined I/O addresses that never change. Their BIOS is simply programmed to use these standard addresses and standard IRQs. Legacy devices (devices that use older technologies) were designed to use more than one group of addresses and IRQ, depending on how jumpers or DIP switches were set on the device. Newer devices, called Plug and Play devices, can use any I/O addresses or IRQ assigned to them during the boot process. You will learn more about this in Chapter 10.

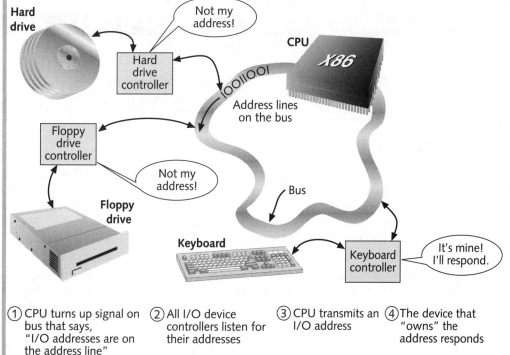

① CPU turns up signal on bus that says, "I/O addresses are on the address line"

② All I/O device controllers listen for their addresses

③ CPU transmits an I/O address

④ The device that "owns" the address responds

Figure 2-12   I/O address lines on a bus work much like an old telephone party line; all devices "hear" the addresses, but only one responds

Table 2-4   IRQs and I/O addresses for devices

IRQ	I/O Address	Device
0	0040-005F	System timer
1	0060-006F	Keyboard controller
2	00A0-00AF	Access to IRQs above 7
3	02F8-02FF	COM2 (covered in Chapter 10)
3	02E8-02EF	COM4 (covered in Chapter 10)
4	03F8-03FF	COM1 (covered in Chapter 10)
4	03E8-03EF	COM3 (covered in Chapter 10)
5	0278-027F	Sound card or parallel port LPT2 (covered in Chapter 10)
6	03F0-03F7	Floppy drive controller
7	0378-037F	Printer parallel port LPT1 (covered in Chapter 10)
8	0070-007F	Real-time clock
9-10		Available
11		SCSI or available

A+CORE
1.4

Table 2-4   IRQs and I/O addresses for devices (continued)

IRQ	I/O Address	Device
12	0238-023F	Motherboard mouse
13	00F8-00FF	Math coprocessor
14	01F0-01F7	IDE hard drive (covered in Chapters 8 and 9)
15	0170-0170	Secondary IDE hard drive or available (covered in Chapters 8 and 9)

DMA Channels

A+CORE
1.4

Another system resource used by hardware and software is a **DMA (direct memory access) channel**, a shortcut method that lets an I/O device send data directly to memory, bypassing the CPU. A chip on the motherboard contains the DMA logic and manages the process. Earlier computers had four channels numbered 0, 1, 2, and 3. Later, channels 5, 6, and 7 were added when the 16-bit ISA bus was introduced. You can see the lines on the bus needed to manage these channels in Figures 2-4 and 2-5. Each channel requires two lines to manage it, one for the DMA controller to request clearance from the CPU and the other used by the CPU to acknowledge that the DMA controller is free to send data over the data lines without interference from the CPU.

DMA channel 4 is used as IRQ 2 was used, to connect to the higher IRQs. In Figure 2-13, note that DMA channel 4 cascades into the lower DMA channels. DMA channels 0–3 use the 8-bit ISA bus, and DMA channels 5, 6, and 7 use the 16-bit ISA bus. This means that the lower four channels provide slower data transfer than the higher channels, because they don't have as many data paths available. Also, an 8-bit expansion card using only the 8-bit ISA bus cannot access DMA channels 5, 6, or 7, because it can't get to these pins on the extended expansion slot.

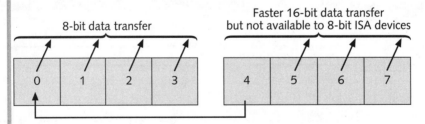

Figure 2-13   DMA channel 4 is not available for I/O use because it is used to cascade into the lower four DMA channels

Some devices, such as a hard drive, are designed to use DMA channels, and others, such as the mouse, are not. Those that use the channels might be able to use only a certain channel, say channel 3, and no other. Alternately, the BIOS might have the option of changing a DMA channel number to avoid conflicts with other devices. Conflicts occur when more than one device uses the same channel. DMA channels are not as popular as they once were, because their design makes them slower than newer methods. However, slower devices such as floppy drives, sound cards, and tape drives may still use DMA channels.

HOW AN OS RELATES TO OTHER SOFTWARE

Now that you have learned about system resources on the motherboard that enable interaction between hardware and software, we turn our attention to the OS and how it interfaces with hardware, BIOS, device drivers, and applications. All interaction between software and hardware is by way of the CPU. The CPU operates in two modes: 16-bit or 32-bit, which are sometimes called real mode and protected mode. There are several differences between these two modes, but fundamentally, in 16-bit mode or real mode the CPU processes 16 bits of data at one time and in 32-bit mode or protected mode, it processes 32 bits at a time.

TIP A newer CPU, the Intel Itanium operates in 64-bit mode. Windows XP 64-bit edition is designed to use this type of CPU.

An operating system must use the same mode the CPU is using. Therefore, we begin our discussion of software by looking more carefully at each of these modes.

Real (16-Bit) and Protected (32-Bit) Operating Modes

In **real mode**, illustrated in Figure 2-14, a CPU assumes that only one application or program is running at a time, which is called single tasking, so it gives that program direct access to all hardware devices including memory. It uses a 16-bit data path and 1 MB of memory addresses, unless a **memory extender** is used, which is an OS utility program that provides an OS with memory addresses above 1 MB (extended memory). The DOS and Windows 9x memory extender is Himem.sys, which you will learn to use in Chapter 6.

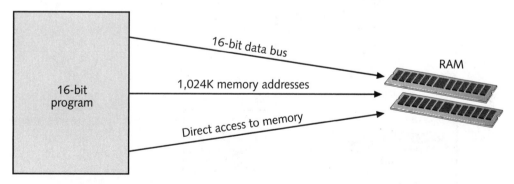

Figure 2-14   Real mode, or MS-DOS mode, provides single-tasking, 1,024K of memory addresses, direct access to RAM using a 16-bit data path

In **protected mode**, more than one program can run at the same time, which is a type of **multitasking**. In protected mode, each program can be safely contained within its own range of resources. Here lies the meaning behind the two terms, real and protected.

Real mode means that the software has "real" access to the hardware; protected mode means that more than one program can be running, and each one is "protected" from the other(s).

A+ OS
1.1

In protected mode, shown in Figure 2-15, more than one program can run, and the programs have access to memory addresses of 4096 MB (4 GB) or sometimes more, depending on the motherboard, CPU, and OS being used. In protected mode, the OS does not allow a program direct access to RAM but works as the mediator between memory and programs. This allows the OS some latitude in how it uses RAM. If the OS is low on RAM, it can store some data on the hard drive. This method of using the hard drive as though it were RAM is called **virtual memory**, and data stored in virtual memory is stored in a file on the hard drive called a **swap file** or **page file**. The OS manages the entire process, and the applications know nothing about this substitution of hardware resources for RAM. Programs running in protected mode just see memory addresses and have no idea where they are located.

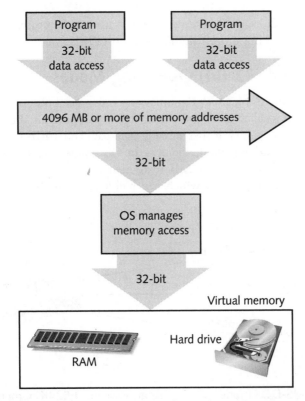

Figure 2-15 Protected mode is multitasking program access to more than 1,024K of memory addresses using 32-bit data segments where the OS manages direct memory access

Even after protected mode became available, hardware and software needed to be backward compatible (able to support older technology), so today's CPUs and operating systems still support real mode. In fact, the CPU starts in real mode and must be told to

2

switch to protected mode. For this reason, an OS starts in real mode and commands the CPU to switch to protected mode before allowing user interaction or loading an application. DOS and the MS-DOS mode of Windows 9x operate in real mode. Windows 9x and Windows NT/2000/XP start in real mode and then switch to protected mode. In protected mode, the OS allots CPU time to an application for a specified period and then preempts the processing to give the CPU to another application, in a process called **preemptive multitasking**. The end result is that the computer appears to be multitasking when it really is not. Windows 95 was the first version of Windows to provide preemptive multitasking. Table 2-5 summarizes the differences between real mode and protected mode.

Table 2-5   A CPU and an OS operate in either real mode or protected mode

Real Mode	Protected Mode
16-bit data path	32-bit data path
Using DOS, only one program runs at a time.	Using Windows 95 and later OSs, several programs can be loaded and running.
The CPU can access up to 1 MB of memory unless a memory extender is used.	The CPU can access 4 GB or more of memory.
Programs have direct access to hardware.	Programs access hardware by way of the operating system.

How an OS Uses Real and Protected Modes

The OS must be in sync with the CPU, using the same mode it is using. Not only must the OS be in sync with the CPU, but applications must be compiled to run in either real or protected mode. In addition, there is a mode that is a hybrid of real and protected mode that older software written for Windows 3.x used, where the mode is real but the intent is to run more than one program in a pseudo–protected environment. This unique Windows 3.x situation is important because it helps to make clear the different ways in which an OS can manage applications.

Windows 3.x was not really a full-fledged OS, but it did not act strictly like application software. It was installed by DOS and used DOS as its operating system, and, therefore, is considered a DOS application. Windows 3.x provided an operating *environment*, which refers to the overall support it provided to application software, and applications were installed under Windows 3.x. The two primary things that Windows 3.x provided that DOS did not were a graphical user interface (GUI) and a limited form of multitasking.

16-Bit and 32-Bit Software

Applications and device drivers written for Windows 3.x are called 16-bit Windows software. Data access is 16 bits at a time, and each program is written so that it should not infringe on the resources of other applications that might be running. Software programs written for Windows 95 and higher are called 32-bit drivers or 32-bit applications. In short, three general types of software run on PCs:

- 16-bit DOS software designed to run in real mode as the only program running and expecting direct access to hardware. Under DOS, an application might attempt to serve as its own device driver. These programs could use only the first 1 MB of memory.

- 16-bit Windows software designed for Windows 3.x to run where other programs might also be running. These applications might or might not attempt to access hardware resources directly and could most likely use extended memory.

- 32-bit Windows software designed to run in protected mode with other software and can be loaded in extended memory. These applications never attempt to access hardware directly.

Nearly all applications and device drivers written today are 32-bit, although 16-bit software still exists, and you must know how to support it in a Windows environment. You will learn more about supporting 16-bit applications and drivers in Chapter 12.

DOS, with or without Windows 3.x, is a real mode OS. Windows 9x is a hybrid operating system. Some of Windows 9x uses 16-bit data access (called 16-bit programs) and some uses 32-bit data access (called 32-bit programs). The Windows 9x 16-bit components exist primarily for backward compatibility with older hardware and software. Because the 32-bit programs access twice as much data at one time as 16-bit programs do, the 32-bit programs are faster. This fact largely explains why Windows 9x is faster than DOS. Windows NT/2000/XP are true 32-bit OSs; all OS programs are written using 32-bit coding methods.

A 32-bit OS allows a 16-bit program to run by providing it with an environment that appears to the program to be a 16-bit environment. This technique is called **virtual real mode**. Each Windows operating system has a method to provide a virtual real mode to a 16-bit application.

How an OS Uses BIOS and Device Drivers

Looking back at Figure 2-2, you can see that an operating system uses programs designed to interact with specific hardware devices. Two kinds of programs are used for this purpose, BIOS and device drivers. In Figure 2-2, you can see that some device drivers belong to the OS and others do not. You can also see that the total BIOS in a system can be located in several places in the system. The OS communicates with simple devices, such as floppy drives or keyboards, through BIOS, and with more complex devices, such as digital cameras or CD-ROM drives, through device drivers. We first look at the BIOS and then turn our attention to device drivers.

How an OS Uses System BIOS

System BIOS contains the programming instructions to run the simple hardware devices common to every system, specifically the keyboard and floppy disk drive. In addition,

2

system BIOS can be used to access the hard drive. In the case of the hard drive, an OS has a choice of using system BIOS or device drivers. Most often it uses device drivers because they are faster. One reason device drivers are faster than system BIOS is that device drivers are executed from RAM; BIOS is stored in ROM, and RAM access is faster than ROM access. However, sometimes the OS uses system BIOS to access the hard drive when older software requires it.

 TIP There is a good way to determine whether the BIOS or a device driver is controlling a device. If the device is configured using CMOS setup, most likely system BIOS controls it. If the device is configured using the OS, most likely a driver controls it.

For example, in Figure 2-16, the setup main menu for an Award BIOS system shows the ability to configure, or set, the system date and time, the Supervisor Password (power-on password), floppy drive diskettes, the hard drive, and the keyboard. Figure 2-17 shows another setup window for this same BIOS that can configure serial ports, an infrared port, and a parallel port. System BIOS can control all these devices. On the other hand, there is no setup window in this BIOS to control the DVD drive or Zip drive installed on this system. The BIOS is not aware of these devices; this means they are controlled by device drivers.

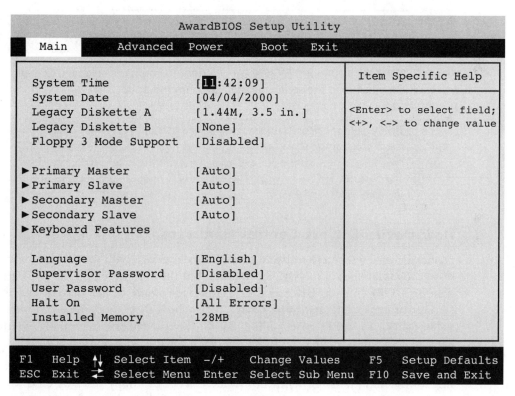

Figure 2-16   Use the BIOS setup main menu for Award BIOS to configure some of the devices controlled by system BIOS

```
                        Award BIOS Setup Utility
    Advanced

    ┌─────────────────────────────────────────────┬──────────────────────────┐
    │       I/O Device Configuration              │   Item Specific Help     │
    │                                             │                          │
    │   Onboard FDC Swap A & B      [No Swap]     │                          │
    │   Floppy Disk Access Control  [R/W]         │   <Enter> to select if   │
    │                                             │   switch drive letter    │
    │                                             │   assignments or not.    │
    │   Onboard Serial Port 1:      [3F8H/IRQ4]   │                          │
    │   Onboard Serial Port 2:      [2F8H/IRQ3]   │                          │
    │   UART2 Use Infrared          [Disabled]    │                          │
    │                                             │                          │
    │   Onboard Parallel Port:      [378H/IRQ7]   │                          │
    │   Parallel Port Mode:         [ECP + EPP]   │                          │
    │   ECP DMA Select:             [3]           │                          │
    │                                             │                          │
    └─────────────────────────────────────────────┴──────────────────────────┘

    F1   Help  ↕  Select Item  -/+   Change Values   F5   Setup Defaults
    ESC  Exit  ⇄  Select Menu  Enter Select Sub Menu  F10  Save and Exit
```

Figure 2-17   Use this Award BIOS setup window to configure several I/O devices,
including the serial, parallel, and infrared ports

 TIP   CMOS setup windows are accessed during startup. A system displays a message at the bottom of the screen saying something like, "Press Del to enter setup." Pressing the indicated key launches a program stored on the ROM BIOS microchip to change the contents of CMOS RAM. This BIOS setup program provides windows like those in Figures 2-16 and 2-17.

How Device Drivers Control Hardware

Device drivers, which are software designed to interface with specific hardware devices, serve the same functions as BIOS programs, but they are stored on the hard drive rather than on ROM chips, as BIOS is. The OS provides some device drivers, and the manufacturer of the specific hardware device with which they are designed to interface provides others. In either case, unlike BIOS, device drivers are usually written for a particular OS and might need to be rewritten for use with another.

When you purchase a printer, DVD drive, Zip drive, digital camera, scanner, or other hardware device, bundled with the device is a set of floppy disks or CDs that contain the device drivers (see Figure 2-18). You must install these device drivers under the operating system so it will have the necessary software to control the device. In most cases, you install the device and then install the device drivers. There are a few exceptions, such as a digital camera using a serial port to download pictures. In this case, you install the software to drive the digital camera before you plug in the camera. See the device documentation to learn what to do first. Later chapters cover device driver installations.

Figure 2-18   A device such as this CD-ROM drive comes packaged with its device drivers stored on a floppy disk or other media. Alternately, you can use device drivers built into the OS.

Device drivers come from a number of sources. Some come with and are part of the operating system, some come with hardware devices when they are purchased, and some are provided for downloading over the Internet from a device manufacturer's Web site.

There are two kinds of device drivers: 16-bit real-mode drivers and 32-bit protected-mode drivers. Windows 9x supports both, but Windows NT/2000/XP uses only 32-bit drivers.

Device Drivers Under Windows 9x   Windows 9x comes with 32-bit drivers for hundreds of hardware devices. Windows automatically loads these drivers into extended memory (memory above 1,024K) at startup, or when the device first needs them. However, Windows does not provide drivers for all older devices, so a system might sometimes need to use an older 16-bit real-mode device driver. These 16-bit drivers are loaded by entries in the **Config.sys**, **Autoexec.bat**, and **System.ini** files, text files used to configure DOS and Windows 3.x that Windows 9x supports for backward compatibility. These drivers use upper memory addresses. When the driver is installed, the driver installation program makes appropriate entries in these files.

 TIP   Under DOS, a program, such as a device driver that stays in memory until the CPU needs it, is called a **TSR (terminate-and-stay-resident)** program. The term is seldom used today, except when talking about real mode programs.

Windows uses Autoexec.bat and Config.sys to be backward compatible with DOS and uses System.ini to be backward compatible with Windows 3x. However, using 16-bit drivers can slow performance, so to get the most out of Windows 9x, you should use 32-bit protected-mode drivers designed for Windows 9x. When selecting a driver to install, be sure the driver claims to be Windows 9x compatible, which means it is a 32-bit driver and you can install the driver using the Add New Hardware Wizard. If the driver must be installed using a setup program that the driver manufacturer provides and cannot be installed using the Add New Hardware Wizard, then it is a 16-bit driver.

Windows 9x keeps information about 32-bit drivers in the Windows **registry**, a database of hardware and software settings, Windows configuration settings, user parameters, and application settings. Windows 32-bit drivers are sometimes called dynamic drivers because they can be loaded into memory when the device is accessed and then unloaded to conserve memory when the device is disconnected or turned off. Drivers that always remain in memory are called static drivers.

Sometimes, to address bugs, make improvements, or add features, manufacturers release device drivers that are more recent than those included with Windows or bundled with the device. Whenever possible, it is best to use the latest driver available for a device provided by the device manufacturer. You can usually download these updated drivers from the manufacturer's Web site. For example, suppose you have just borrowed a printer from a friend, but you forgot to borrow the CD with the printer drivers on it. You can go to the printer manufacturer's Web site, download the drivers to a folder on your PC, and install the driver under Windows. Figure 2-19 shows you a Web page from the Hewlett-Packard (HP) Web site showing a list of downloadable drivers for ink-jet printers. You will learn how to install, update, and troubleshoot drivers in later chapters.

Sixteen-bit drivers under Windows 9x can cause slow performance, so use 32-bit drivers whenever possible. Sometimes determining whether a device driver is 16-bit or 32-bit can be difficult. One way to identify whether Windows 9x is using a 16-bit driver is to go into Device Manager and look for an exclamation point beside the device, which indicates that the driver has a problem. This might indicate that the driver is a 16-bit driver. If a driver is loaded from Config.sys or Autoexec.bat, it is a 16-bit driver; if it is loaded from the registry, it is a 32-bit driver. System.ini can contain both types. Table 2-6 summarizes basic information about device drivers under Windows 9x.

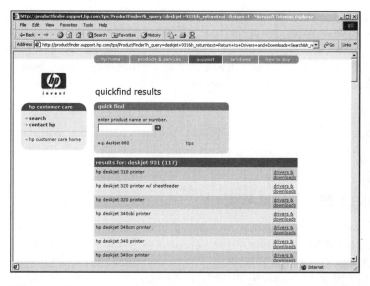

Figure 2-19   Download the latest device drivers from a manufacturer's Web site

Table 2-6   Two types of device drivers and how to use them under Windows 9x

Characteristic	16-Bit Device Drivers	32-Bit Device Drivers
Operating mode	Real mode	Protected mode
Use of memory	May use upper memory addresses	Stored in extended memory
How loaded	Loaded by a command line in Config.sys, Autoexec.bat, or System.ini	Automatically loaded from the registry by Windows 9x at startup or when the device is used
How changed	Edit the Config.sys or Autoexec.bat files	From Device Manager, select the device and use the Properties, Driver tab
How to identify the type	In Device Manager, look for an exclamation point beside the device name	Look to see how the driver is loaded, from the registry, System.ini, Autoexec.bat, or Config.sys. Also, look for no exclamation point beside the device name in Device Manager.
When to use this type	Use a 16-bit driver under Windows only when a 32-bit driver is not available. When operating under DOS, 16-bit drivers are required.	When you can, always use 32-bit drivers because they are faster and pose fewer configuration problems.

Device Drivers Under Windows 2000 Windows 2000/XP installs protected-mode drivers in the same way as Windows 9x, but Windows 2000/XP does not claim to support 16-bit device drivers. For Windows 2000/XP, always check the **HCL (hardware compatibility list)** to determine if a driver will work under Windows 2000/XP. Go to this Microsoft Web site and search for your device:

www.microsoft.com/windows2000/professional/howtobuy/upgrading/compat

If the device does not install properly or produces errors, check the manufacturer's Web site for a driver that the manufacturer says is compatible with Windows 2000/XP.

How an OS Launches Applications

Application software is designed to work on top of a particular OS. "On top of" here means that the application depends on the OS, such as Windows 98 or Windows XP, in order to run. An application depends on an OS to provide access to hardware resources, manage its data in memory and in secondary storage, and perform many other background tasks. For example, consider a situation in which Windows XP loads and executes an application. The application cannot run or even load itself without Windows XP, much as a document cannot be edited without a word-processing program. Windows XP stays available to the application for the entire time the application is running. The application passes certain functions to Windows XP, such as reading from a CD-ROM or printing.

An application written to work with one OS, such as Windows XP, does not necessarily work with another, such as a Macintosh system. There are, however, some exceptions. For instance, OS/2 is written so that any application designed to work with DOS also works with OS/2, an early selling point for OS/2. However, to take full advantage of an operating system's power and an application's power, buy application software written specifically for your OS.

Application software is downloaded from the Internet or comes written on floppy disks or on CD-ROMs; usually it must be installed on a hard drive in order to run. During the installation, the install program creates folders on the hard drive and copies files to them. For Windows, it also makes entries in the Windows registry, and it can place icons on the desktop and add entries to the Start menu. Because the install program does all the work for you, installing a software package usually is very easy and is covered in later chapters.

Loading Application Software Using the Windows Desktop

Once an application is installed, Windows 9x and Windows NT/2000/XP offer four ways to execute software:

- Place a shortcut icon directly on the desktop for the applications you use often and want to get to quickly. These shortcuts contain the command line used to execute the application. To view this command line, right-click an

2

application icon. A drop-down menu appears. From the menu, select Properties. The icon's Properties box appears (see Figure 2-20). From this box, you can view the complete command line that the icon represents. Chapter 12 explains how to create shortcuts for Windows.

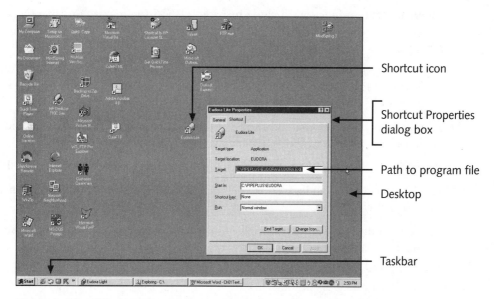

Shortcut icon

Shortcut Properties dialog box

Path to program file

Desktop

Taskbar

Figure 2-20 Windows has icons on the desktop that point to program files on the hard drive

- Click the Start button, select Programs (or All Programs in Windows XP), and select the program from the list of installed software.

- Use the Run command: Click the Start button on the Windows taskbar, and then click Run to display the Run dialog box (see Figure 2-21). In this box, enter a command line or click Browse to search for a program file to execute.

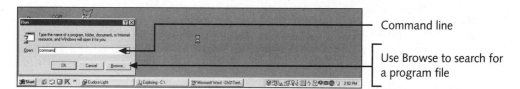

Command line

Use Browse to search for a program file

Figure 2-21 The Windows Run dialog box allows you to enter DOS-like commands

- Execute a program or launch an application file by double-clicking the file-name in Windows Explorer or My Computer.

CHAPTER SUMMARY

❏ An operating system controls the different hardware components that make up a computer and also provides an interface that a user or an application can use.

❏ Operating system functions include managing BIOS (programs permanently stored on hardware devices) and memory, interfacing between hardware and software, and performing tasks the user requests (such as formatting disks and copying or deleting files).

❏ Operating systems used for desktop computers include DOS, Windows 9x, Windows NT/2000/XP, Unix, a version of Unix called Linux, OS/2, and the Mac OS. Windows.NET Server will be released soon.

❏ Four system resources that aid in the communication between hardware and software are I/O addresses, IRQs, DMA channels, and memory addresses.

❏ An IRQ is a line on a bus that a device needing service uses to alert the CPU.

❏ A DMA channel provides a shortcut for a device to send data directly to memory, bypassing the CPU.

❏ Memory addresses are hexadecimal numbers, often written in segment: offset form, assigned to RAM and ROM so that the CPU can access both.

❏ The CPU places a device's I/O address on the address bus when it wants to initiate communication with the device.

❏ For DOS and Windows 9x, the three types of logical primary memory are conventional (or base) memory, upper memory, and extended memory. These assignments are rooted in how the 20-line memory address bus of early PCs limited memory to 1,024K. Windows 9x makes the most use of extended memory.

❏ Software manages memory by means of memory addresses that point to locations in RAM. The number of memory addresses is partly limited by the number of wires on the bus devoted to these addresses.

❏ RAM and ROM BIOS on the motherboard and other circuit boards need memory addresses assigned to them so the CPU can access them.

❏ The 8-bit ISA slot had a limited number of system resources available to it; the number increased with the invention of the 16-bit ISA slot.

❏ The number of wires on the bus assigned for the data path determines the size of the data segment that software can access at one time.

❏ COM and LPT are preconfigured assignments of system resources that a device can use. For example, COM1 is IRQ 4 and I/O addresses 03F8 through 03FF.

❏ Four types of software are BIOS or firmware, device drivers, operating systems (OSs), and application software. Sometimes device drivers are considered part of the OS.

❑ Operating systems use BIOS, manage secondary storage and primary storage, help diagnose problems with hardware and software, interface between hardware and software, and perform various housekeeping tasks.

❑ Application software relates to the OS, which relates to BIOS and device drivers to control hardware.

❑ A CPU can operate in real or protected mode. In real mode, it processes 16 bits at a time, and in protected mode, it processes 32 bits at a time.

❑ DOS uses real mode, which is limited to running a single program and using a 16-bit data path and 1,024K of memory addresses, unless a memory extender is used.

❑ Protected mode allows more than one program to run at a time, can use a 32-bit data path, and has more than 1,024K of memory addresses. In protected mode, the OS manages access to RAM and does not allow a program direct access to it.

❑ Virtual memory is "fake" memory: data is actually stored in a swap file on the hard drive. The OS makes applications think that they are using real memory.

❑ Device drivers are written using either 16-bit or 32-bit code. Most drivers today are 32-bit protected-mode drivers that Windows loads from the registry.

❑ Windows 9x loads older 16-bit device drivers from Autoexec.bat, Config.sys, or System.ini to be backward compatible with DOS and Windows 3.x.

❑ From the Windows desktop, programs can be launched from the Start menu, a shortcut icon on the desktop, the Run dialog box, Windows Explorer, or My Computer.

KEY TERMS

Autoexec.bat
CMOS setup
Config.sys
device driver
DMA (direct memory access) channel
extended memory
hardware interrupt
HCL (hardware compatibility list)
I/O address
IRQ (interrupt request) line

ISA (Industry Standard Architecture) slot
memory address
memory extender
multitasking
operating system (OS)
page file
pinout
polling
port address
preemptive multitasking
protected mode
real mode

registry
shadow RAM or shadowing ROM
startup BIOS
swap file
system BIOS
system resource
System.ini
TSR (terminate-and-stay-resident)
virtual memory
virtual real mode

REVIEW QUESTIONS

1. The small programs stored on hard drives, with the purpose of telling the computer how to communicate with a hardware device such as a network card, are referred to as:

   a. Operating systems

   b. Device drivers

   c. Application software

   d. Windows 9x

   e. None of the above

2. In the overall progression of operating systems and operating environments, Windows 3.x was the next product offered by Microsoft to provide operating system functionality to microcomputer systems it was installed on.

   a. True

   b. False

3. Windows 9x (including Windows 95, Windows 98, and Windows ME) are classified, according to Microsoft, as fully functional, stand-alone operating systems.

   a. True

   b. False

4. The operating system is responsible for communicating with system hardware. Which of the following is *not* one of the ways the operating system communicates with system hardware?

   a. Through the hardware directly

   b. Through instructions found in device drivers

   c. Through application software

   d. Through system BIOS

   e. None of the above

5. Of all the system resources available at the system level, which resource is responsible for assigning a physical memory address space to a set of BIOS instructions located on a device other than the motherboard?

   a. IRQ

   b. I/O address

   c. ROM address (memory address)

   d. DMA channel

   e. None of the above

6. Of all the system resources available at the system level, which resource is responsible for allowing *all* devices that need attention of the processor a session with the processor?

   a. IRQ

   b. I/O address

   c. ROM address (memory address)

   d. DMA channel

   e. None of the above

7. Of all the system resources available at the system level, which resource is responsible for allowing memory intensive devices access to memory without the intervention of the CPU?

   a. IRQ

   b. I/O address

   c. ROM address (memory address)

   d. DMA channel

   e. None of the above

8. Of all the system resources available at the system level, which resource is responsible for providing a portal to all devices that need to transfer data in and out of the operating system?

   a. IRQ

   b. I/O address

   c. ROM address (memory address)

   d. DMA

   e. None of the above

9. Communication between the operating system kernel and system hardware takes place through two methods; _____ _____, and _____ _____.

10. Of the three primary buses used by the CPU for data transfer, which bus is responsible for determining the maximum amount of physical memory that can be accessed by the processor?

    a. Data bus

    b. Address bus

    c. Control bus

    d. Power bus

    e. None of the above

11. Of the three primary buses used by the CPU for data transfer, which bus is responsible for getting data into the CPU's internal registers for data processing?

    a. Data bus

    b. Address bus

    c. Control bus

    d. Power bus

    e. None of the above

12. Of the three primary buses used by the CPU for data transfer, which bus is responsible for providing a path for devices to handshake with the CPU to provide device-specific status?

    a. Data bus

    b. Address bus

    c. Control bus

    d. Power bus

    e. None of the above

13. Assuming an 8-bit ISA bus, which of the following is not included in the interface?

    a. Address bus

    b. Control bus

    c. Data bus

    d. Power bus

    e. None of the above

14. The 16-bit ISA bus is characterized by a _____-pin expansion slot connector.

    a. 34

    b. 40

    c. 50

    d. 62

    e. 98

15. The 8-bit ISA bus is characterized by a _____-pin expansion slot connector.

    a. 34

    b. 40

    c. 50

    d. 62

    e. 98

2

16. Each Interrupt Controller is capable of handling eight interrupts. All AT-class microcomputers are based on a dual Interrupt Controller design. What is the accurate number of interrupts that are available to users for assignment to unique pieces of hardware?

 a. 7

 b. 8

 c. 15

 d. 16

 e. 32

17. Assuming a user has two serial devices that need to be connected to the PC, but one of the two devices is more critical in terms of priority of when the device is serviced by the processor. Which port should the service technician connect the device to in order to fulfill this requirement?

 a. COM1

 b. COM2

 c. LPT1

 d. LPT2

 e. Any of the above ports is acceptable.

18. In order for any user to view the assignment of Interrupts for a particular computer, assuming the Windows 2000 operating system, this can be accomplished by viewing:

 a. Add/Remove Hardware

 b. Add/Remove Programs

 c. Control Panel

 d. Device Manager

 e. None of the above

19. An address bus of 20 bits allows for a maximum physical memory space of:

 a. 1 MB

 b. 16 MB

 c. 32 MB

 d. 256 MB

 e. 4 GB

20. An address bus of 24 bits allows for a maximum physical memory space of:

 a. 1 MB

 b. 16 MB

 c. 32 MB

 d. 256 MB

 e. 4 GB

21. Memory address above the 1 MB limit is referred to as:

    a. Conventional or base memory

    b. Upper or reserved memory

    c. Expanded memory

    d. Extended memory

    e. Secondary memory

22. When an address is posted over the address bus, which statement can be said of how the devices hear and respond to the address?

    a. All devices hear and all devices respond to the devices' correct I/O address.

    b. All devices hear and only one device responds to the devices' correct I/O address.

    c. Only one device hears and all devices respond to the devices' correct I/O address.

    d. Only one device hears and only one device responds to the devices' correct I/O address.

    e. None of the above

23. Which of the following DMA channels are *not* available to 8-bit ISA devices?

    a. Channels 0-3

    b. Channels 4-7

    c. Channels 0-7

    d. Channels 0-15

    e. None of the above

24. In order for multitasking to occur, the CPU must be placed in one of two modes of operation, which is referred to as:

    a. Safe mode

    b. Normal mode

    c. Real mode

    d. Protected mode

    e. Ant mode

25. When a Pentium processor is running in 16-bit mode, the maximum amount of addressable memory is:

    a. 1 MB

    b. 16 MB

    c. 32 MB

    d. 4 GB

    e. None of the above

2

26. Running more than one program at a time can be accomplished if the micro-processor is running in:

    a. 16-bit mode

    b. 32-bit mode

    c. Both a and b

    d. Neither a nor b

27. Preemptive multitasking requires the CPU to be operating in:

    a. 16-bit mode

    b. 32-bit mode

    c. Both a and b

    d. Neither a nor b

28. Having an operating system running in 16-bit applications while running in 32-bit mode is referred to as:

    a. Real mode processing

    b. Protected mode processing

    c. Virtual real mode processing

    d. Hybrid mode processing

    e. None of the above

29. The term *legacy*, when used in the context of discussing hardware, refers to devices that are:

    a. Plug and play (PnP) compliant

    b. Non-plug and play (PnP) compliant

    c. Both a and b

    d. Neither a nor b

30. When loading device drives under the Windows 9x operating system, 16-bit drivers are loaded using:

    a. The System Registry

    b. The files CONFIG.SYS, AUTOEXEC.BAT, and SYSTEM.INI

    c. The specific application software

    d. All of the above

    e. None of the above

31. Windows 9x keeps information about 32-bit devices in the Windows System Registry.

    a. True

    b. False

32. Device drives listed as 16-bit device drivers reside in extended memory.

    a. True

    b. False

33. Upon reviewing the hardware contained in the Device Manager, a service technician sees a yellow exclamation point next to one of the devices. This symbol indicates to the service technician that that particular device is making use of a:

    a. 16-bit device driver

    b. 32-bit device driver

    c. Device that uses both a 16-bit and 32-bit device driver

    d. Device that uses neither a 16-bit nor a 32-bit device driver

34. Provide a list of four ways to execute application software under the Windows 9x operating system:

    a. _____

    b. _____

    c. _____

    d. _____

3

UNDERSTANDING THE BOOT PROCESS AND COMMAND LINE

> **In this chapter, you will learn:**
> ♦ To understand the process of booting to a command prompt
> ♦ To create and use Windows 9x rescue disks to troubleshoot and solve problems when booting Windows
> ♦ To use many commands at the command prompt

If you are working with an OS, you will see an interface on the monitor screen. This interface can be command driven, menu driven, or icon driven. For most OS tasks, you use a graphical user interface (GUI) such as the Windows desktop, which is both menu driven and icon driven. With a GUI, you can launch applications, use utilities such as Windows Explorer to copy a file or create a folder, and perform some limited troubleshooting tasks when problems arise. However, if the OS is not functioning to the extent that it can provide a desktop, a PC technician must troubleshoot the system using a command-driven interface. This chapter focuses on using the command line in real mode under Windows 9x, which is called MS-DOS mode. Real mode can be used to boot the computer and troubleshoot problems when Windows cannot boot to the Windows desktop. Learning to use the command line is important because it is the tried-and-true tool for the worst operating system problems. Also, Windows 9x uses DOS-like core components and, therefore, understanding and learning to use MS-DOS mode commands helps you understand this foundation of Windows. In addition, when troubleshooting problems with booting Windows 2000/XP, a command prompt provided by the Recovery Console is sometimes the only tool that is available in the worst-case situations. Many commands in this chapter also work at the Recovery Console command prompt. In short, knowing how to use the command prompt is essential to PC troubleshooting.

We begin the chapter by learning how a PC first boots up and loads the operating system. Then, you will learn how to create floppy disks that can be used to boot to a command prompt. Finally, we will look at some essential commands used when troubleshooting a failing system.

Booting Up Your Computer

Understanding what happens when you first turn on your PC and boot up to an operating system command prompt or desktop is essential to troubleshooting problems with the operating system. The term *booting* comes from the phrase "lifting yourself up by your bootstraps" and refers to the computer bringing itself up to an operable state without user intervention. Booting can refer to either a soft boot or hard boot. A **hard boot**, or **cold boot**, involves initially turning on the power with the on/off switch. A **soft boot**, or **warm boot**, involves using the operating system to reboot. For DOS, pressing the keys Ctrl, Alt, and Del at the same time performs a soft boot. For Windows 9x and Windows NT/2000/XP, one way to soft boot is to click Start, click Shut Down, select Restart from the Shut Down menu, and then click OK. You can also press Ctrl+Alt+Del and then select Shut Down from the Close Program dialog box that appears.

A hard boot is more stressful on your machine than a soft boot because of the initial power surge through the equipment. Also, a soft boot is faster. Always use the soft boot method to restart unless the soft boot method doesn't work. If you must power down, avoid turning off the power switch and immediately turning it back on without a pause, because this can damage the machine. Some PCs have a reset button on the front of the case. Pressing the reset button starts the boot process at an earlier point than does the operating-system soft boot and is, therefore, a little slower but might work when the OS soft boot fails. For newer motherboards, pressing the reset button restarts the system without actually powering off and thus eliminates the stress to the system caused by the initial surge when the power first comes on.

In this section, you will learn what happens when the PC is first turned on and the startup BIOS takes control and then loads the OS. You will then learn what happens when the essential components of the operating system are loaded from the hard drive or floppy disk. But first you should be familiar with the Plug and Play standard and understand what a file system is.

Plug and Play

$A+$CORE
4.4

Plug and Play (PnP) is a standard designed to make installation of hardware devices easier. PnP applies to the OS, the system BIOS, and the hardware devices themselves. If the BIOS is a Plug and Play BIOS, it begins the process of configuring hardware devices in the system. It gathers information about the devices and then passes that information to the operating system. If the operating system is also Plug and Play compliant, it uses that information to complete the hardware configuration process. For a system to be fully Plug and Play, the BIOS, the operating system, and all devices must support Plug and Play.

Windows 9x and Windows 2000/XP support Plug and Play, but Windows NT does not. However, Windows 2000/XP Plug and Play is more advanced than the Windows 9x version and does not use the startup BIOS to help with Plug and Play configurations.

3

A+CORE
4.4

Therefore, on a Windows 2000/XP system, it is not important that the motherboard BIOS be Plug and Play.

Legacy devices (older devices that are not Plug and Play) do not allow Windows or the motherboard BIOS to assign system resources (IRQs, I/O addresses, memory addresses, and DMA channels) to the device. For example, if a legacy sound card requires a certain group of upper memory addresses that are hard-coded into its on-board BIOS, there's nothing that Plug and Play can do about that. (Hard-coded is computer jargon for something being coded so that it cannot be changed.) If two non-Plug and Play hardware devices require the same resource and their BIOS does not provide for accepting a substitute, these two devices cannot coexist on the same PC.

> **TIP**   A Plug and Play hardware device will have something like Windows Ready or Windows Compliant written on the box.

ESCD (extended system configuration data) Plug and Play BIOS is an enhanced version of Plug and Play that creates a list of all the things you have done manually to the configuration that Plug and Play does not do on its own. This ESCD list is written to the BIOS chip so that the next time you boot, the startup BIOS can faithfully relay that information to Windows 9x. The BIOS chip for ESCD BIOS is a special RAM chip called Permanent RAM, or PRAM, that can hold data written to it without the benefit of a battery, which the CMOS setup chip requires.

What Is a File System?

A+ OS
1.1
1.4

An operating system is responsible for storing the files and folders on a secondary storage device such as a CD, floppy disk, or hard drive, using organizational methods called a **file system**. Windows uses several different file systems, all of which are discussed in later chapters. The most common file system for floppy disks and hard drives is the FAT file system.

FAT File System

The FAT file system is named after the **FAT (file allocation table)**, a table on a hard drive or floppy disk that tracks the locations of files on a disk. A disk is composed of **tracks**, which are concentric circles on the disk surface, shown in Figure 3-1. Each track is divided into several segments, each called a **sector**. A **cluster**, the smallest unit of space on a disk for storing data, is made up of one or more sectors. The FAT contains a list of clusters and which clusters are used for each file stored on the disk. The most recent version of FAT, FAT32, is a more efficient method of organization for large drives than FAT16 (the earlier version).

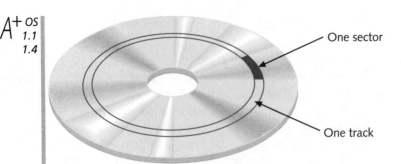

One sector

One track

Figure 3-1   A hard drive or floppy disk is divided into tracks and sectors. Several sectors make one cluster

Files and Directories

Regardless of the file system used, every OS manages a hard drive by using directories (Windows calls these folders), subdirectories, and files. A **directory table** is a list of files and subdirectories. When a hard drive is first installed and formatted, there is a single directory table on the drive called the **root directory**. For logical drive C, the root directory is written as C:\.

> A physical hard drive can be divided into logical drives, sometimes called volumes, such as drive C or drive D. You will learn more about logical drives and volumes in Chapter 8.

As shown in Figure 3-2, this root directory can hold files or other directories, which can have names such as C:\Tools. These directories, called **subdirectories**, **child directories**, or **folders**, can, in turn, have other directories listed in them. Any directory can have files and/or other directories listed in it, for example, C:\wp\data\myfile.txt in Figure 3-2. The C: identifies the logical drive. If the directory had been on a floppy disk, either A: or B: would have identified it. When you write the drive and directories pointing to the location of the file, as in this example, the drive and directories are called the **path** to the file. The first part of the file before the period is called the **filename** (myfile), and the part after the period is called the **file extension** (txt), which, for Windows and DOS, always has three characters or fewer. The file extension identifies the type file, such as .doc for Microsoft Word document files or .xls for Microsoft Excel spreadsheet files.

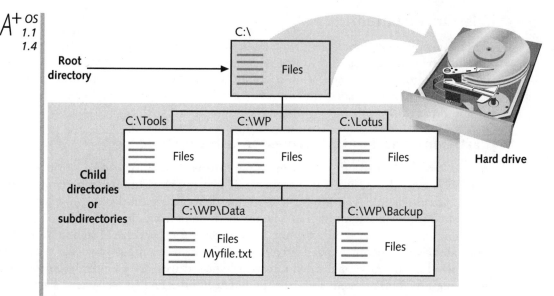

A+ OS
1.1
1.4

Figure 3-2   A hard drive is organized into groups of files stored in directories. The first directory is called the root directory. All directories can have child directories or subdirectories. Under Windows, a directory is called a folder.

File Naming Conventions

Because the OS assumes that filenames entered in a command issued at a command prompt follow the DOS naming convention, it is important to understand how to name files. Under DOS, a filename can contain up to eight characters, a separating period, and a file extension of up to three characters, like this: *filename.ext*. Characters can be the letters a through z, the numbers 0 through 9, and the following characters: _, ^, $, ~, !, #, %, &, -, {, }, (,), @, ', `. Be sure to not use a space, period, *, ?, or \ in a filename or file extension. Acceptable file extensions for program files are .com, .sys, .bat, and .exe. A **program file** contains a list of instructions for the OS to follow. For example, the DOS utility program to display information about the system is Msd.exe.

Under Windows 95 and later Windows OSs, filenames can be as long as 255 characters and can contain spaces. Before Windows 95, only the Macintosh OS used these long filenames. When using long filenames in Windows 9x, remember that the DOS portion of the system can only understand eight-character filenames with three-character extensions. When the DOS part of the system is operating, it truncates long filenames and assigns new eight-character names. Windows NT/2000/XP has no DOS core and therefore manages long filenames better. When using long filenames at the command prompt, put double quotation marks around the filename, like this: "My long file name.doc".

A+ OS
1.1

File Organization

By creating different directories on a hard drive, you can organize your program files and data files by placing programs in one directory and files created by those programs in a second directory. This organization is comparable to keeping paper records in separate folders. You can also organize files on other secondary storage media such as floppy disks or Zip drives.

Partitions and Logical Drives on a Hard Drive

A hard drive is divided into one or more **partitions**. A partition can be a primary partition or an extended partition (see Figure 3-3). A primary partition can have one logical drive and an extended partition can have one or more logical drives. Most hard drives have one primary partition with one logical drive in it called drive C: and one extended partition which can have one or more logical drives such as drive D: and drive E:. Each **logical drive**, sometimes called a **volume**, is formatted using its own file system. For example, if a hard drive is divided into two logical drives, drive C: might be formatted using the FAT32 file system and drive D: might use the FAT16 file system. Each logical drive has its own FAT, root directory, and subdirectories. In the discussion of the boot process that follows, you will see that during the boot, the system must know which logical drive to turn to on the hard drive to find and load the operating system.

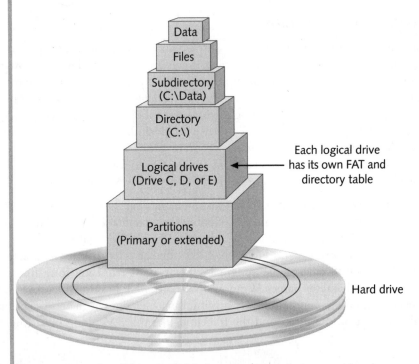

Figure 3-3   A hard drive is divided and organized at several levels

Startup BIOS Controls the Beginning of the Boot

A+CORE
2.1

A successful boot depends on the hardware, the BIOS, and the operating system all per-forming without errors. If errors occur, they might or might not stall or lock up the boot process. Errors are communicated as beeps or as messages on screen. See Appendix A, Error Messages and Their Meanings, for a listing of error messages and beep codes and what to do about them. The boot can be divided into four main steps: BIOS checking hardware, loading the OS, the OS initializing itself, and finally loading and executing an application. After a brief overview of all four, we will examine the first three steps in detail. (This chap-ter does not cover the fourth part, loading and executing an application.) Startup BIOS is in control for the first step; then it turns over control to the OS in the second step.

Step 1: POST. Startup BIOS tests essential hardware components. This test is called the **power-on self test (POST)**. The ROM BIOS startup program surveys hardware resources and needs, and assigns system resources to meet those needs (see Figure 3-4). The ROM BIOS startup program begins the startup process by reading configuration information stored in DIP switches, jumpers, and the CMOS chip, and then comparing that information to the hardware—the CPU, video card, floppy disk drive, hard drive, and so on. Some hardware devices have their own BIOSs that request resources from startup BIOS, which attempts to assign these system resources as needed.

Step 2: The ROM BIOS startup program searches for and loads an OS. Most often the OS loads from logical drive C on the hard drive. Configuration information on the CMOS chip tells startup BIOS where to look for the OS. Most newer BIOSs support loading the OS from the hard drive, a floppy disk, a CD, or a Zip drive. The BIOS turns to that device, reads the beginning files of the OS, copies them into memory, and then turns control over to the OS. This part of the loading process works the same for any operat-ing system; only the OS files being loaded change.

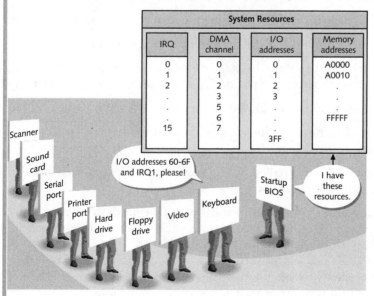

Figure 3-4   Boot Step 1: ROM BIOS startup program surveys hardware resources and needs and assigns system resources to satisfy those needs

Step 3: The OS configures the system and completes its own loading. The OS checks some of the same things that startup BIOS checked, such as available memory and whether that memory is reliable. Then the OS loads the software to control a mouse, CD-ROM, scanner, and other peripheral devices. These devices generally have device drivers stored on the hard drive.

Step 4: The user executes application software. When you tell the OS to execute an application, the OS must first find the application software on the hard drive, CD-ROM, or other secondary storage device, copy the software into memory, and then turn control over to it. Finally, you can command the application software, which makes requests to the OS, which, in turn, uses the system resources, system BIOS, and device drivers to interface with and control the hardware. At this point, the user is like the passenger in the back seat of the car with the chauffeur at the wheel. The trip has begun!

Now let's look at the first three steps in detail, beginning with the POST.

Power-on Self Test (POST) and Assignment of System Resources

When you turn on the power to a PC, the CPU begins the boot process by initializing itself and then turning to the ROM BIOS for instructions. The ROM BIOS then performs POST. Listed below are the key steps in this process.

- When the power is first turned on, the system clock begins to generate clock pulses.

- The CPU begins working and initializes itself (resetting its internal values).

- The CPU turns to memory address FFFF0h, which is the memory address always assigned to the first instruction in the ROM BIOS startup program.

- This instruction directs the CPU to run POST.

- POST first checks the BIOS program operating it and then tests CMOS RAM.

- A test determines that there has been no battery failure.

- Hardware interrupts are disabled. (This means that pressing a key on the keyboard or using another input device at this point does not affect anything.)

- Tests are run on the CPU, and it is initialized further.

- A check determines if this is a cold boot. If so, the first 16 KB of RAM is tested.

- Hardware devices installed on the computer are inventoried and compared to configuration information.

- The video card is tested and configured. During POST, before the CPU has checked the video system, beeps sometimes communicate errors. Short and long beeps indicate an error; the coding for the beeps depends on the BIOS. After POST checks and verifies the video controller card (note that POST does not check to see if a monitor is present or working), POST can use the monitor to display its progress.

A^{+CORE}
2.1

- POST checks RAM by writing and reading data. The monitor displays a running count of RAM during this phase.

- Next, the keyboard is checked, and if you press and hold any keys at this point, an error occurs with some BIOSs. Secondary storage—including floppy disk drives and hard drives—ports, and other hardware devices are tested and configured. The hardware that POST finds is checked against the data stored in the CMOS chip, jumpers, and/or DIP switches to determine if they agree. IRQ, I/O addresses, and DMA assignments are made; the OS completes this process later.

- Some devices are set up to go into "sleep mode" to conserve electricity.

- The DMA and interrupt controllers are checked.

- CMOS setup is run if requested.

- BIOS begins its search for an OS.

How the BIOS Finds and Loads the OS

After POST and the first pass at assignment of resources is complete, the next step is to load an OS. Most often the OS is loaded from logical drive C on the hard drive. A list of the minimum information required on the hard drive to load an OS follows. You can see some of these items labeled in Figure 3-5.

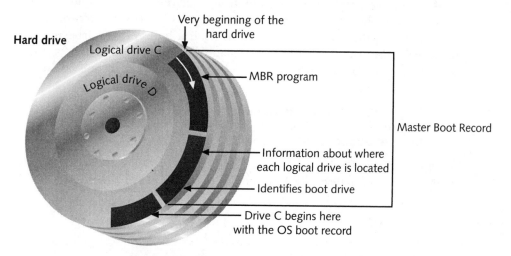

Figure 3-5 A hard drive might contain more than one logical drive; the partition table at the beginning of the drive contains information about the location of each logical drive, indicates which drive is the boot drive, and holds the Master Boot Record that begins the boot process for the operating system

- A small sector at the very beginning of the hard drive, called the **Master Boot Record (MBR)**, contains a program needed to locate the beginning of the OS on the drive.

- A **partition table** contains a map to the logical drives on the hard drive. Whether a hard drive has one or several logical drives, it always contains a single partition table, located at the very beginning of the drive, which tells BIOS these things: (1) how many partitions the drive has and how each partition is divided into one or more logical drives, (2) which partition contains the drive to be used for booting (called the **active partition**), and (3) where each logical drive begins and ends. Chapter 8 covers all this in more detail.

- At the beginning of the boot drive (usually drive C) is the OS **boot record**, which loads the first program file of the OS. For Windows 9x, that program is **Io.sys**, and for Windows NT/2000/XP, that program is **Ntldr**.

- The boot loader program for the OS (Io.sys or Ntldr) begins the process of loading the OS into memory. For Windows 9x, **Msdos.sys** is needed next, followed by Command.com. These two files, plus Io.sys, are the core components of the real-mode portion of Windows 9x. Windows NT/2000/XP has a different set of startup files.

The process by which the BIOS loads the OS begins with BIOS looking to CMOS setup to find out which secondary storage device should have the OS (see Figure 3-6). Setup might instruct the BIOS to look first on drive C, and, if it finds no OS there, then try drive A; or the order might be search A then C. If BIOS looks first to drive A and finds no disk in the drive, it turns to drive C. If it looks first to drive A and finds a disk in the drive, but the disk does not contain the OS (for Windows 9x, that means the OS boot record, Io.sys, Msdos.sys, and Command.com), then one of these or a similar error message appears:

```
Non-system disk or disk error, press any key
Bad or missing COMMAND.COM
No operating system found
```

You must replace the disk with one that contains the OS or simply remove the disk and press any key to force the BIOS to continue to drive C to find the OS.

3

Loading the MS-DOS Core of Windows 9x

A+ OS
1.2
1.3
2.5
3.2

This section describes what first happens during booting when only the MS-DOS core of Windows 9x is loaded, which brings the OS to a real-mode command prompt similar to a DOS command prompt. It's important for a PC technician to understand this real-mode DOS core because it is often used as a troubleshooting tool when the hard drive fails. You can boot to a command prompt in several ways, including booting from a Windows startup disk or using the Windows startup menu. You'll learn how to prepare a startup disk later in the chapter. Chapter 12 covers how to use the Windows startup menu.

In Step 2 of Figure 3-6, the BIOS locates the MBR on the hard drive, which looks to the partition table to determine where the logical boot drive is physically located on the drive. It then turns to the OS boot record of that logical drive.

The OS boot record is a very short program; it loads just one hidden file, which makes up the DOS core, into memory (see Figure 3-6, Step 3; and Figure 3-7). (A **hidden file** is a file that does not appear in the directory list.) The OS boot record program knows the filename, which is Io.sys. The Io.sys file contains the basic I/O software for real mode and requires that the Msdos.sys file be present. Msdos.sys is a text file that contains some parameters and switches that can be set to affect the way the OS boots. You will learn about the contents of Msdos.sys and how to change it to affect the boot process in Chapter 12.

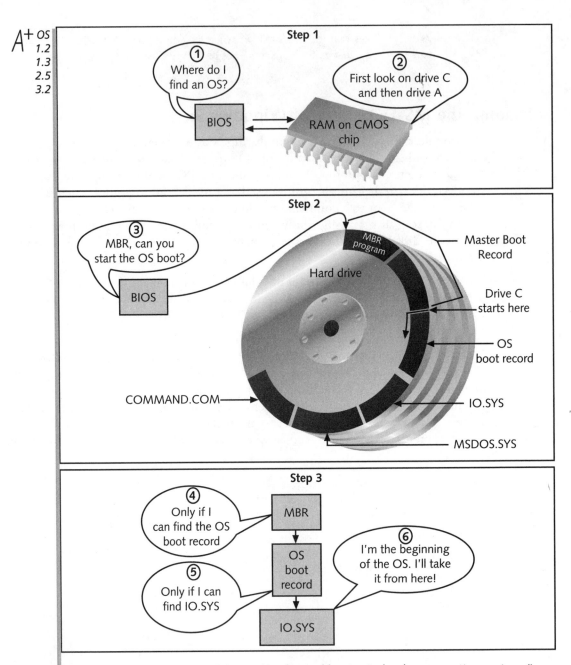

Figure 3-6 Boot Step 2: BIOS searches for and begins to load an operating system (in this example, Windows 9x is the OS)

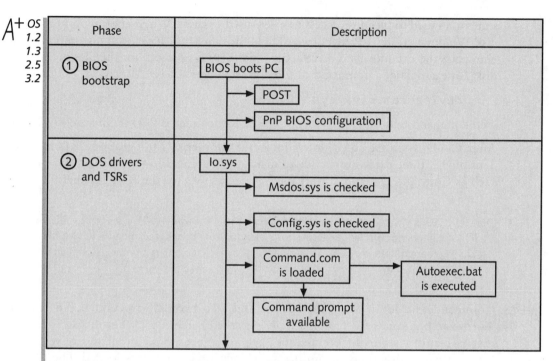

Phase	Description
① BIOS bootstrap	BIOS boots PC → POST → PnP BIOS configuration
② DOS drivers and TSRs	Io.sys → Msdos.sys is checked → Config.sys is checked → Command.com is loaded → Autoexec.bat is executed → Command prompt available

A+ OS 1.2 1.3 2.5 3.2

Figure 3-7   Boot Step 3: Operating system completes the boot process; MS-DOS core is loaded and command prompt presented to user

TIP The three OS files necessary to boot to a command prompt in Windows 9x are Io.sys, Msdos.sys, and Command.com. Config.sys and Autoexec.bat are not required but are used if they are present.

Once Io.sys is loaded into memory, the boot record program is no longer needed, and control is turned over to Io.sys. This program looks for Msdos.sys, reads it, and uses the settings in it. Io.sys then looks on the hard drive for a file named Config.sys. This configuration file contains commands that tell Io.sys how many files it can open at any one time (Files=) and how many file buffers to create (Buffers=). (A buffer is a temporary holding area for files.) Config.sys also includes the commands to load device drivers (Device=), as well as other information. An example of a typical command in Config.sys follows; it gives real-mode Io.sys access to memory above 1 MB, called extended memory:

```
Device=himem.sys
```

Several drivers can be loaded into memory from commands in Config.sys. Io.sys puts these programs in memory wherever it chooses. However, a program can request that it be put in a certain memory location.

Sometimes Config.sys is used to create a RAM drive. A **RAM drive** is an area of memory that looks and acts like a hard drive, but because it is memory, it is much faster. It is sometimes used to speed up access to often-used software. When booting from the startup disk, Windows creates a RAM drive to hold files after they have been uncompressed. This eliminates the need for hard drive access, and there is no room for the files on the floppy disk. An example of a command in Config.sys to create a RAM drive is:

```
device=ramdrive.sys 2048
```

The command tells the OS to create a RAM drive that is 2,048K in size.

After Config.sys is executed, Io.sys looks for another OS file, named Command.com. This file has three parts: more code to manage I/O, programs for internal OS commands such as Copy and Dir, and a short program that looks for the Autoexec.bat file.

> **TIP** Some OS commands are **internal commands**, meaning they are embedded in the Command.com file, and others are **external commands**, meaning they have their own program files. An example of an external command is Format, stored in the file Format.com.

 A+ OS
1.2
1.3

Command.com looks for Autoexec.bat and, if it's found, executes it. The filename **Autoexec.bat** stands for "automatically executed batch file." A **batch file** is a text file that contains a series of commands that are executed in order. Autoexec.bat lists OS commands that execute automatically each time the OS is loaded. The following commands are examples of commands that might be found in the Autoexec.bat file:

- The following Path command lists two paths, separated by semicolons. The OS uses the paths listed in the Path command to locate program files. You will learn more about the Path command later in the chapter.

```
PATH C:\;C:\Windows;
```

- The Set command is used to create and assign a value to an environmental variable that an application can later read. A software installation program might add a Set command to your Autoexec.bat file. Later, the software uses the environmental variable in the program. An example of a Set command assigning a path to the variable Mypath is:

```
Set Mypath=C:\VERT
```

- The Restart command causes the system to reboot.

```
Restart.com
```

- The Temp command lets applications know where to store temporary files. By default, DOS stores temporary files in C:\Temp, Windows 9x uses C:\Windows\Temp, Windows NT uses C:\Temp, and Windows 2000/XP uses C:\Winnt\Temp. Add the Temp command to Autoexec.bat if applications are putting temporary files in strange locations. An example of a Temp command is:

```
Temp=C:\Temp
```

A^{+CORE}
  1.1
  1.2
  1.3

3

- The Echo command turns on and off the displaying of commands and messages. Use it in a batch file to control output to screen.

   ```
   Echo off
   ```

A^{+} *OS*
  1.2
  1.3
The boot process into real mode with a command prompt is completed after Autoexec.bat has finished executing. At this point, Command.com is the program in charge, providing you with a command prompt and waiting for your command. On the other hand, if a program or menu was executed from Autoexec.bat, it might ask you for a command.

The command prompt indicates the drive that loaded the OS. If the OS files were loaded from a floppy disk, the command prompt is A:\>, (called the A prompt). If the OS was loaded from the hard drive, the command prompt is C:\> (the C prompt). The colon following the letter identifies the letter as the name of a drive, and the backslash identifies the directory on the drive as the root or main directory. The > symbol is the prompt symbol that the OS uses to say, "Enter your command here." This drive and root directory are now the default drive and default directory, sometimes called the current working drive or directory.

If you want to complete loading Windows, use the Win command. Enter this command at the C prompt:

   ```
   C:\> WIN
   ```

 Note that commands used at a command prompt are not case sensitive, that is, you can enter *WIN*, *Win*, or *win*.

EMERGENCY STARTUP DISKS

A^{+} *OS*
  3.2
Although you normally boot from a hard drive, problems with the hard drive sometimes make booting from a floppy disk necessary. A floppy disk with enough software to load an operating system is called a **bootable disk**, or **system disk**. A bootable disk with some utility programs to troubleshoot a failed hard drive is called a **rescue disk**, **emergency startup disk (ESD)**, or **startup disk**. Having a rescue disk available for an emergency is very important, and a PC technician should always have one or more on hand. For DOS, you have to create your own rescue disk, making sure it includes the necessary system files and any utilities that you might need in an emergency.

Beginning with Windows 95, the OS provided an automated method to create a rescue disk. This rescue disk is created under the Control Panel, Add/Remove Programs group. The files on the rescue disk vary with the version of Windows 9x. You can also create your own bootable disk or add your own utilities to the rescue disk that Windows creates. In some situations you need a startup disk, which you can use to boot up a PC for the first time after a new hard drive has been installed when the hard drive has nothing written on it. Windows NT/2000/XP each have a different set of startup disks.

A+ OS
3.2
In this section, you will learn several ways to create Windows 9x startup disks and then, in the remainder of the chapter, you will learn to use many of the utilities that Windows puts on these disks.

Windows 9x Startup Disks

A+ OS
3.2
Windows 9x can create a startup disk for you, complete with everything you need to troubleshoot a failed hard drive or prepare a new hard drive for use. The disk does not need to be created on the same computer that will use it, although in most cases you should use the same version of Windows as used by the computer that will be using the disk. Follow these directions to create a startup disk for Windows 9x.

1. Click **Start** on the Taskbar, point to **Settings**, and then click **Control Panel**.

2. In the Control Panel window, double-click the **Add/Remove Programs** icon.

3. Click the **Startup Disk** tab, and then click the **Create Disk** button (see Figure 3-8).

4. Windows might need the Windows CD to create the disk. Insert the CD if it is requested. Windows then creates the startup disk.

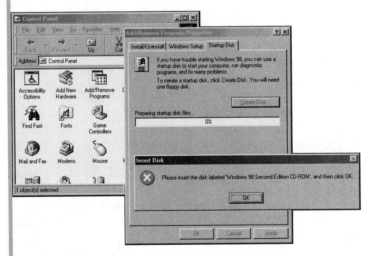

Figure 3-8   Windows might use the Windows CD to create a startup disk

Table 3-1 lists the files included on the startup disk for Windows 98, Second Edition (Windows 98 SE). Other versions of Windows 9x contain some, but not all, of these files.

A+ OS
3.2

Table 3-1   Files on the Windows 98 startup disk

File	Description
Aspi2dos.sys	Real-mode Adaptec CD-ROM driver
Aspi4dos.sys	Real-mode Adaptec CD-ROM driver
Aspi8dos.sys	Real-mode Adaptec CD-ROM driver
Aspi8u2.sys	Real-mode Adaptec CD-ROM driver
Aspicd.sys	Real-mode Adaptec CD-ROM driver
Autoexec.bat	Batch file that contains commands executed at startup
Btcdrom.sys	Mylex/BusLogic CD-ROM driver
Btdosm.sys	Mylex/BusLogic CD-ROM driver
Command.com	Command interpreter
Config.sys	Loads device drivers
Drvspace.bin	Accesses compressed hard drive
Ebd.cab	Cabinet file containing other utility program files
Ebd.sys	Identifies the startup disk
Extract.exe	Uncompresses the Ebd.cab file
Fdisk.exe	Partitions the hard drive
Findramd.exe	Locates the RAM drive during startup
Flashpt.sys	Mylex/BusLogic CD-ROM driver
Himem.sys	Extended memory manager
Io.sys	System boot file
Msdos.sys	Contains boot parameters
Oakcdrom.sys	Generic device driver for CD-ROM drives
Ramdrive.sys	Creates a RAM drive at startup
Readme.txt	Information about the startup disk
Setramd.bat	Searches for a drive letter to assign the RAM drive

The file Ebd.cab is a compressed file, called a **cabinet file**, that contains the several compressed files listed in Table 3-2. You will learn to use many of these commands later in
the chapter. During startup, the contents of the cabinet file are uncompressed and copied
to the RAM drive because there is not enough space for them on the floppy disk and
the startup disk assumes the hard drive might not be accessible. You can also use the
Extract command to extract specific files when the RAM drive is not active.

A+ OS
3.2

Table 3-2   Files contained in the cabinet file, Ebd.cab

File	Description
Attrib.exe	Changes file attributes
Chkdsk.exe	Determines the status of a disk and repairs it
Debug.exe	Debugging utility used to view contents of memory
Edit.com	Text editor used from a command prompt
Extract.exe	Extracts files from a cabinet file
Format.com	Formats a hard drive
Mscdex.exe	Microsoft utility to interface with a CD-ROM driver
Scandisk.exe	Checks and repairs hard drives
Scandisk.ini	Contains parameters for Scandisk.exe
Sys.com	Copies system files to a disk, making it bootable

Creating Your Own Bootable Rescue Disk for Windows 9x

Using Windows Explorer, you can create a system disk (Windows terminology for a bootable disk) and then copy program files to the disk that you might need in an emergency. The first step is to format the disk, which writes tracks on the disk and puts a file system on the disk. Chapter 7 covers more details of what happens during the format operation. To format a floppy disk in Windows 9x, follow these steps.

1. Click the **Start** button on the Taskbar, point to **Programs**, and then click **Windows Explorer**. Right-click either drive A or drive B. The shortcut menu in Figure 3-9 appears.

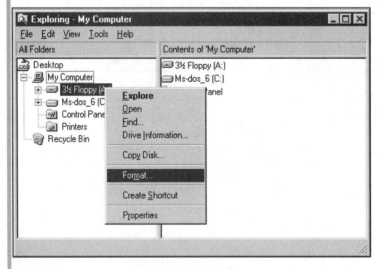

Figure 3-9   Menu for managing a floppy disk

2. Click **Format** on the menu. The dialog box shown in Figure 3-10 opens. Notice that you have three format options: Quick format (does not overwrite existing tracks), Full format (writes new tracks and sector markings), and an option to copy just the system files to the disk; these are the files needed to make the disk bootable. (Io.sys, Msdos.sys, and Command.com are copied to the disk.)

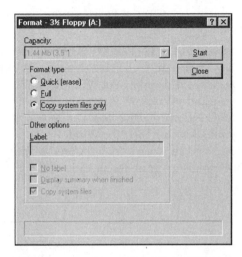

Figure 3-10 Format a disk in Windows 9x

3. If the disk has been preformatted at the factory, you can select the third option to copy system files only, but if the disk has never been formatted, select **Full**. Then click **Start**.

From a command prompt, you can create your own bootable rescue disk and manually copy OS utility files to it. To make a bootable rescue disk for Windows 9x, from the command prompt, type:

```
Format A:/S
```

The command erases any files currently on the disk in drive A, and the /S switch copies the two hidden files, Io.sys and Msdos.sys, and Command.com to the disk in drive A, making the disk bootable.

You might also want to put some utility programs on the disk to help in troubleshooting. In addition to the files listed in Tables 3-1 and 3-2, other files you might need are Xcopy.exe, MSD.exe, Mem.exe, and More.com. You will learn about these files later in the chapter.

 When Windows 9x (including Windows Me) creates a startup disk, it copies files to the disk from the \Windows\Command\EBD folder. You can also copy these files to a formatted disk to create a startup disk manually.

Using a Windows 9x Startup Disk with Another OS

In some situations, it is appropriate to use a startup disk created by one OS to boot a failed system that has a different OS installed. For example, suppose Windows NT/2000/XP refuses to boot. Using a different PC, you can create a startup disk under Windows 98 and then use it to boot the Windows NT/2000/XP PC. If you can successfully boot to an A prompt (A:\>), you have demonstrated that the hard drive or files stored on it are the source of the problem. However, it is best to use recovery procedures and disks native to the OS installed.

Suppose there is an important data file on the Windows NT/2000/XP computer and you don't have the proper recovery disks for the OS. You might be able to use the Windows 98 startup disk to recover the file. There are special considerations for Windows NT/2000/XP. These OSs support more than one file system, and a Windows 9x startup disk supports only FAT16 or FAT32. If a Windows NT/2000/XP hard drive has a different file system installed, such as NTFS (New Technology File System), then the Windows 9x startup disk cannot read that file system. In this situation, you can work from an A prompt, but you will not be able to access the hard drive. The solution is to create rescue disks under these operating systems that can read the file system.

USING THE COMMAND PROMPT

A+ OS
1.1
1.2
1.3
1.5

In this section, you will first learn how to access a command prompt and how to launch programs from the command prompt. Then you will learn to use several commands to manage files and folders and perform many utility tasks useful when troubleshooting a failing system.

Accessing a Command Prompt

A+ OS
1.1
1.2
1.3
1.5

There are several ways to get to a command prompt:

- From the Windows 9x desktop, you can access a command prompt by clicking Start, Programs, MS-DOS Prompt. A command prompt window, sometimes called a **DOS box**, appears, as shown in Figure 3-11. In it you can enter DOS-like commands discussed in this chapter. To exit the window, type Exit at the command prompt. For Windows 2000, to access a command prompt window, click Start, Programs, Accessories, Command Prompt. For Windows XP, click Start, All Programs, Accessories, Command Prompt.

- For all versions of Windows, you can also get a command prompt window using an alternate method: click Start, Run, and enter Command.com in the Run dialog box. For Windows NT/2000/XP, to get a 32-bit version of the 16-bit Command.com program, enter CMD.exe in the Run dialog box.

- When you boot from a bootable disk or rescue disk, you get a command prompt instead of the Windows desktop. Also, Windows 2000/XP has a Recovery Console that can be accessed using the Windows setup CD or setup disks. The Recovery Console provides a command prompt for DOS-like commands. This chapter does not cover how to access the Recovery Console.

A+ os
1.1
1.2
1.3
1.5

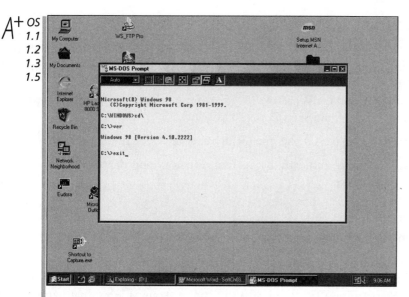

Figure 3-11   An MS-DOS Prompt window operates in the virtual real mode provided by
Windows 9x

If you want to get a true real-mode environment in Windows 9x, use one of these
methods:

- Click Start, click Shutdown, and select Restart in MS-DOS mode from
  the Shutdown dialog box. This method only works for Windows 95 and
  Windows 98. Windows Me, Windows NT, Windows 2000, and Windows XP do
  not support accessing real mode in this way. For Windows Me and Windows XP,
  create an MS-DOS startup disk, insert it in the floppy disk drive, and boot from
  that disk. Recall that the startup BIOS boot sequence must be drive A first and
  then drive C for you to be able to do this. Windows NT and Windows 2000 do
  not offer the option to create an MS-DOS startup disk, but, in a pinch, you can
  use one created on another PC to boot a Windows NT/2000 computer to a
  DOS prompt.

- You can also boot to a command prompt by holding down the Ctrl key or
  the F8 key while booting, which causes the OS to display a startup menu.
  From the menu, select Command prompt only.

To add a command prompt icon to your Windows 9x desktop for easy access, locate
the program file (Command.com or Cmd.exe) in Windows Explorer and, while holding
down the Ctrl key, drag the icon to your desktop. Another way to create the shortcut
is to click Start, point to Programs, Accessories, and Command Prompt. Right-click on
Command Prompt and select Create Shortcut from the shortcut menu.

Launching a Program Using the Command Prompt

In the last chapter, you learned how to launch a program from the Windows desktop. We now turn our attention to launching or running a program from a command prompt. We begin by looking at the command prompt the user sees and the information it provides. If you booted a Windows 98 PC from a bootable floppy disk into command prompt mode, you would see the A prompt (A:\>).

To make the hard drive (drive C) the default drive, enter C: at the A prompt.

The prompt now changes to indicate the current directory and drive in the root directory of drive C; it looks like this:

```
C:\>
```

A+ OS 3.3 Launching the Program File

At the command prompt, when you type a single group of letters with no spaces, the OS assumes that you typed the filename of a program file you want to execute, which is stored in the current directory. The OS attempts to find the program file by that name, copies the file into RAM, and then executes the program. Let's use, as our example, the program Mem.exe, a Windows 9x utility which displays how memory is currently allocated. The program file Mem.exe is stored on the hard drive in the C:\Windows\command folder. Note what happens in Figure 3-12 when you type *mem* at the A: prompt, like this:

```
A:\>mem
```

The OS says it cannot find the program to execute. It looked on the floppy disk (drive A) only for Mem.com, Mem.exe, or Mem.bat, the three file extensions that MS-DOS recognizes for programs. If the OS finds none of these files in the current directory, it stops looking and displays the error message:

```
Bad command or file name
```

To help the OS locate the program file, we must first change the default drive to the hard drive by giving the command:

```
A:\> C:
```

Notice in Figure 3-12 that the prompt changes to C:\>, indicating that the logical drive C on the hard drive is the default drive. Now we change the default directory on the hard drive to \Windows\Command using the **CD (change directory) command** like this:

```
C:\>CD\windows\command
```

(Remember that DOS and Windows commands are not case sensitive, so it makes no difference whether you type CD, Cd, or cd.) The prompt now looks like this:

```
C:\WINDOWS\COMMAND>
```

A+ OS
3.3

Figure 3-12 shows what happens when we enter the *mem* command again, and the OS locates and executes the program file.

```
A:\>mem
Bad command or file name

A:\>c:

C:\>cd\windows\command

C:\WINDOWS\COMMAND>mem

Memory Type            Total    Used       Free
- - - - - - - - - -    - - - - - - - -    - - - -    - - - - - -
Conventional            640K    160K       480K
Upper                     0K      0K         0K
Reserved                  0K      0K         0K
Extended (XMS)        130,036K  2,112K  127,924K

Total memory          130,676K  2,272K  128,404K

Total under 1 MB        640K    160K       480K

Largest executable program size        479K (490, 816 bytes)
Largest free upper memory block          0K       (0 bytes)
MS-DOS is resident in the high memory area.

C:\WINDOWS\COMMAND>
```

Figure 3-12 Finding a program file

There is another way to tell the OS where to look to find program files. As part of the boot procedure, you can use the Path command to give the OS a list of paths in which to look for executable program files beyond the default directory. Recall that by storing the Path command in the Autoexec.bat file, you can cause the command to execute automatically during the boot process. You can also execute the Path command any time after booting. The last Path command you execute overrides any previous ones. To see the list of presently active paths, type Path at the command prompt, and then press Enter. Figure 3-13 shows the results of this command. To enter a new list of paths, type Path followed by each path name, separating one path from the next with a semicolon, as shown in the second Path command in Figure 3-13.

```
C:\>path
PATH=F:\;A:\;G:\

C:\>path F:\;A:\G:\C:\;C:\Windows\Command

C:\>path
PATH=F:\;A:\G:\C:\;C\WINDOWS\COMMAND

C:\>
```

Figure 3-13   The Path command

In Figure 3-13, the first Path command displays the list of active paths, which are three logical drives, F, A, and G. The second Path command changes this list, giving the OS the same three logical drives as well as the drive C root directory and the C:\Windows\Command directory. The last Path command displays the new list of active paths.

When you tell the OS to execute a program, you can also include the path to that program file as part of the command line. For example, if the Mem.exe file is stored in the directory C:\Windows\Command, you can execute the program by typing:

A:\> C:\Windows\Command\Mem.exe

Here, you are telling the OS that the name of the program file is Mem.exe and that its location is the directory \Windows\Command on drive C. With this method, the directory and drive that contain the Mem program need not be the defaults, nor do you need to use the Path command.

In summary, using the MS-DOS mode of Windows 9x, the OS searches for executable program files using the following rules:

1. If no path is given before the filename, the OS looks in the current directory.

2. If a path is given before the filename in the command line, the OS looks in that path.

3. If no path is given and the file is not in the current directory, the OS looks in the paths given to it by the last Path command executed.

Although the Path command and Autoexec.bat are not necessary in Windows 9x, you can use them. If you have an Autoexec.bat file in your root directory when Windows 9x starts, it reads the Path command stored in that file. You can also store DOS commands in batch files and execute them from Windows 9x by double-clicking the filename of the batch file in Explorer.

If you don't have an Autoexec.bat file with a Path command, Windows 9x uses a default path of C:\Windows; C:\Windows\Command. Not all paths to program files must appear in the Path command, as they must in DOS.

3

Regardless of the method or OS used, when a program is launched from a command prompt or from the desktop, the following happens:

1. The OS receives the command to execute the application.

2. The OS locates the program file for the application.

3. The OS loads the program file into memory.

4. The OS gives control to the program.

5. The program requests memory addresses from the OS for its data.

6. The program initializes itself and possibly requests that data from secondary storage be loaded into memory.

7. The program turns to the user for its first instruction.

Using Commands to Manage a Floppy Disk or Hard Drive

A+ OS
1.4

You can use several OS commands to manage a floppy disk and hard drive. This section describes a number of commands with some of their more common options. For more information about these and other OS commands, type the command name at a command prompt, then type /? (slash and question mark).

You can use two **wildcards** with filenames to execute a command on a group of files or in an abbreviated filename if you do not know the entire name. The question mark (?) is a wildcard for one character, and the asterisk (*) is a wildcard for more than one character. For example, if you want to find all files in a directory that start with A and have a three-letter file extension, you would use the following command:

```
dir a*.???
```

Recall that DOS allows only eight characters for a filename and three for its extension; this is often called the 8.3 format. For filenames that do not meet this format, such as the filename Mydocument.doc, DOS displays the filename with the first few letters and a tilde (~) character:

```
Mydocum~.doc
```

If you have two documents that would have the same name if truncated in this manner, DOS also adds an identifying number. For example, if you have a document named Mydocument.doc and one named Mydocumentnew.doc, DOS truncates these:

```
Mydocu~1.doc
Mydocu~2.doc
```

When you boot using a DOS rescue disk, be aware of this file-naming convention. Also recall that when working from a command prompt window, you can use double quotation marks around long filenames and long folder names when using them in command lines.

$A^+_{\ 1.3}$ OS

Dir

Use this command to list files and directories. Some examples are:

DIR /P	List one screen at a time.
DIR /W	Use wide format, where details are omitted and files and folders are listed in columns on the screen.
DIR *.txt	Use wildcard character.
DIR Myfile.txt	Check that a single file is present.

Type

The Type command displays on screen the contents of text file. Some examples are:

Type Myfile.txt	Displays file contents.
Type Myfile.txt >PRN	Redirects output to printer.
Type Myfile.txt |More	Displays output one screen at a time.

Del or Erase

The Del or Erase command erases files or groups of files. If the command does not include drive and directory information, like the following examples, the OS uses the default drive and directory when executing the command.

For example, to erase all files in the A:\DOCS directory, use the following command:

        C:\> ERASE A:\DOCS*.*

To erase all files in the current default directory, use the following command:

        A:\DOCS> DEL *.*

To erase all files in the current directory that have no file extension, use the following command:

        A:\DOCS> DEL *.

To erase the file named Myfile.txt, use the following command:

        A:\> DEL MYFILE.TXT

Undelete

The Undelete command attempts to recover deleted files. Some variations of the Undelete command follow. Windows 9x has no Undelete command.

To list files that can be undeleted, without actually undeleting them, use the following command:

        A:\>UNDELETE /list

3

To recover deleted files without being prompted to confirm each file, use the following command:

```
A:\>UNDELETE /all
```

Recover

The Recover command attempts to recover a file from damaged sectors on a disk. Always specify the drive, path, and filename of the file you want to recover with the Recover command. If you want to recover several files, use the command on one file at a time. Windows 9x has no Recover command.

To recover the file named Myfile.txt on a floppy disk, use the following command:

```
RECOVER A:\DOCS\MYFILE.TXT
```

Whatever portion of the file that the Recover command can read is stored in the root directory and named A:FILE0000.REC (or the next available number). Copy this file to another disk before trying to recover the second file.

Because the Recover command might mark clusters as bad in the FAT, first use the Diskcopy or Copy command (described below) before using Recover. The Recover command can sometimes destroy data that might have been saved by other methods.

Diskcopy

The Diskcopy command makes an exact duplicate (sector by sector) of one floppy disk (called the source disk) to another disk of the same size and type (called the target disk).

To duplicate a floppy disk using only a single drive, use the following command:

```
C:\>DISKCOPY A: A:
```

The OS prompts you as many times as necessary to insert the source disk and then insert the target disk to make the exact copy. Diskcopy copies data from one disk to the other, byte by byte, including any hidden files, bad sectors, fragmented files, or other contents; it copies everything as is. For this reason, the copy can be faulty if the target disk has bad sectors. Diskcopy ignores the fact that a sector is marked as bad in the FAT and copies to it anyway. The Diskcopy command copies formatting information, so the target disk does not need to be formatted before copying.

A^+ OS 1.3 ## Copy

The Copy command copies a single file or group of files. The original files are not altered.

To copy a file from one drive to another, use the following command:

```
A:\>COPY drive:\path\filename.ext drive:\path\filename.ext
```

A+ OS
  1.3

The drive, path, and filename of the source file immediately follow the Copy command; the drive, path, and filename of the destination file follow the source filename. If you do not specify the filename of the copy, the OS assigns the file's original name. If you omit the drive or path of the source or the destination, then the OS uses the current default drive and path.

To copy the file Myfile.txt from the root directory of drive C to drive A, use the following command:

    C:\>COPY MYFILE.TXT A:

Because the command does not include a drive or path before the filename Myfile.txt, the OS assumes that the file is in the default drive and path.

To copy all files in the C:\DOCS directory to the floppy disk in drive A, use the following command:

    C:\>COPY C:\DOCS*.* A:

To make a backup file named System.bak of the System.ini file in the \Windows directory of the hard drive, use the following command:

    C:\WINDOWS> COPY SYSTEM.INI SYSTEM.BAK

If you use the Copy command to duplicate multiple files, the files are assigned the names of the original files. When duplicating multiple files, the destination portion of the command line cannot include a filename.

> **TIP** When trying to recover a corrupted file, you can sometimes use the Copy command to copy the file to a new media, such as from the hard drive to a floppy disk. During the copying process, if the Copy command reports a bad or missing sector, choose the option to ignore that sector. The copying process then continues to the next sector. The corrupted sector will be lost, but others can likely be recovered.

Xcopy /C /S /Y /D:

The Xcopy command is more powerful than the Copy command. It follows the same general command-source-destination format as the Copy command, but it offers several more options, outlined next, with a couple of useful examples.

Use the /S option with the Xcopy command to copy all files in the directory \DOCS, as well as all subdirectories under \DOCS and their files, to the disk in drive A.

    C:\>XCOPY C:\DOCS*.* A: /S

To copy all files from the directory C:\DOCS created or modified on March 14, 2003, use the /D switch, as in the following command:

    XCOPY C:\DOCS*.* A: /D:03/14/03

A^+ *OS*
1.3

Use the /Y option to overwrite existing files without prompting, and use the /C option to keep copying even when an error occurs.

Deltree

The Deltree command deletes the directory tree beginning with the subdirectory you specify, including all subdirectories and all files in all subdirectories in that tree. Use it with caution!

```
C:\>DELTREE [drive:]path
```

Mkdir [drive:]path or MD [drive:]path

The Mkdir (abbreviated MD, for make directory) command creates a subdirectory under a directory. To create a directory named \GAME on drive C, use this command:

```
MKDIR C:\GAME
```

The backslash indicates that the directory is under the root directory. To create a directory named CHESS under the \GAME directory, use this command:

```
MKDIR C:\GAME\CHESS
```

The OS requires that the parent directory GAME already exists before it creates the child directory CHESS.

Figure 3-14 shows the result of the Dir command on the directory \GAME. Note the two initial entries in the directory table, the . (dot) and the .. (dot, dot) entries. The Mkdir command creates two entries when the OS initially sets up the directory. You cannot edit these entries with normal OS commands, and they must remain in the directory for the directory's lifetime. The . entry points to the subdirectory itself, and the .. entry points to the parent directory, in this case, the root directory.

```
C:\>DIR \GAME /P

 Volume in drive C has no label
 Volume Serial Number is 0F52-09FC
 Directory of C:\GAME

.              <DIR>      02-18-93    4:50a
..             <DIR>      02-18-93    4:50a
CHESS          <DIR>      02-18-93    4:50a
NUKE           <DIR>      02-18-93    4:51a
PENTE          <DIR>      02-18-93    4:52a
NETRIS         <DIR>      02-18-93    4:54a
BEYOND         <DIR>      02-18-93    4:54a
        7 file(s)            0 bytes
                      9273344 bytes free

C:\>
```

Figure 3-14   Dir of the \GAME directory

$A^+_{1.3}$ os

Chdir [drive:]path or CD [drive:]path or CD..

The Chdir (abbreviated CD, for change directory) command changes the current default directory. Using its easiest form, you simply state the drive and the entire path that you want to be current:

```
CD C:\GAME\CHESS
```

The command prompt now looks like this:

```
C:\GAME\CHESS>
```

To move from a child directory to its parent directory, use the .. variation of the command:

```
C:\GAME\CHESS> CD..
C:\GAME>
```

Remember that .. always means the parent directory. You can move from a parent directory to one of its child directories simply by stating the name of the child directory:

```
C:\GAME> CD CHESS
C:\GAME\CHESS>
```

Do not put a backslash in front of the child directory name; doing so tells DOS to go to a directory named CHESS that is directly under the root directory.

Rmdir [drive:]path or RD [drive:]path

The Rmdir command (abbreviated RD, for remove directory) removes a subdirectory. Before you can use the Rmdir command, three things must be true:

- The directory must contain no files.

- The directory must contain no subdirectories.

- The directory must not be the current directory.

The . and .. entries are present when a directory is ready for removal. For example, to remove the \GAME directory in the above example, the CHESS directory must first be removed:

```
C:\> RMDIR C:\GAME\CHESS
```

Or, if the \GAME directory is the current directory, use this command:

```
C:\GAME> RD CHESS
```

Once you remove the CHESS directory, you can remove the \GAME directory. You must first leave the \GAME directory like this:

```
C:\GAME>CD..
C:\> RD \GAME
```

A^{+} *OS*
 1.3
 1.5
Attrib

The Attrib command displays or changes the read-only, archive, system, and hidden attributes assigned to files. To display the attributes of the file MYFILE.TXT, use this command:

```
ATTRIB MYFILE.TXT
```

To hide the file, use this command: `ATTRIB +H MYFILE.TXT`

To remove the hidden status of the file, use this command: `ATTRIB -H MYFILE.TXT`

To make the file a read-only file, use this command: `ATTRIB +R MYFILE.TXT`

To remove the read-only status of the file, use this command: `ATTRIB -R MYFILE.TXT`

To turn on the archive bit, use this command: `ATTRIB +A MYFILE.TXT`

To turn off the archive bit, use this command: `ATTRIB -A MYFILE.TXT`

The archive bit is used to determine if a file has changed since the last backup.

Unformat

The Unformat command might be able to reverse the effect of an accidental format. To unformat a disk, use this command:

```
UNFORMAT C:
```

Path

As discussed earlier in the chapter, the Path command lists where the OS should look to find executable program files. This command is discussed again to make the list of commands more complete. A sample Path command is:

```
PATH C:\;C:\DOS;C:\WINDOWS;C:\UTILITY
```

A semicolon separates each path from the next. You should put the most-used paths at the beginning of the line, because the OS searches the paths listed in the Path command line from left to right. The Path command goes in the Autoexec.bat file and can be executed from the OS prompt.

Sys Drive:

The Sys command copies the system files needed to boot to a disk or hard drive. Use the command if the system files on a drive are corrupt. You can access the drive, but you cannot boot from it. The command to copy system files to the hard drive is:

```
SYS C:
```

A^{+} *OS*
 1.5
 CORE
 3.1
Chkdsk [drive:] /F /V

The Chkdsk command reports information about a disk. Use the /F option to have Chkdsk fix errors it finds, including errors in the FAT caused by clusters marked as being used but not belonging to a particular file (called lost allocation units) and clusters

A+ OS
1.5
CORE
3.1

marked in the FAT as belonging to more than one file (called cross-linked clusters). To check the hard drive for errors and repair them, use this command:

```
CHKDSK C: /F
```

To redirect the output from the Chkdsk command to a file that you can later print, use this command:

```
CHKDSK C: >Myfile.txt
```

The /V option of the Chkdsk command displays all path and filename information for all files on a disk:

```
CHKDSK C: /V
```

Chkdsk is useful when using a startup disk; otherwise, use ScanDisk or disk error checking from the Windows desktop.

A+ OS
1.3
1.5

Scandisk Drive: /A /N /P

The Scandisk command scans a hard drive for errors and repairs them if possible. Scandisk checks the FAT, long filenames, lost and cross-linked clusters, directory tree structure, bad sectors, and compressed structure if the drive has been compressed using Windows DriveSpace or DoubleSpace. The /A parameter is used to scan all nonremovable local drives. Use this command only to display information without fixing the drive:

```
SCANDISK C: /P
```

Use this command to display information and fix errors:

```
SCANDISK C:
```

Use this command to start and stop Scandisk automatically:

```
Scandisk C: /N
```

If you use the above command, Scandisk still stops to report errors.

Scanreg /Restore /Fix /Backup

The Scanreg command restores or repairs the Windows 98 registry. It uses backups of the registry that Windows 98 Registry Checker automatically makes each day. To restore the registry from a previous backup, use this command:

```
SCANREG /RESTORE
```

A menu appears asking you which backup to use.

To repair a corrupted registry, use this command:

```
SCANREG /FIX
```

To create a new backup of the registry, use this command:

```
SCANREG /BACKUP
```

Don't use this last command if you are having problems with the registry.

$A^{+}_{}$ *OS*
1.3
1.5
2.5

Defrag Drive: /S

3

The Defrag command examines a hard drive or disk for **fragmented files** (files written to a disk in noncontiguous clusters) and rewrites these files to the disk or drive in contiguous clusters. Use this command to optimize a hard drive, that is, to improve its performance.

Use the /S:N option to sort the files on the disk in alphabetical order by filename.

```
DEFRAG C: /S:N
```

Use the /S:D option to sort the files on the disk by date and time.

```
DEFRAG C: /S:D
```

$A^{+}_{}$ *OS*
1.3

Ver

Use the Ver command to display the version of the operating system in use.

$A^{+}_{}$ *OS*
1.5

Extract filename.cab file1.ext /D

The Extract command extracts files from a cabinet file such as the Ebd.cab file on the Windows 98 startup disk. To list the files contained in the cabinet file, use this command:

```
EXTRACT EBD.CAB /D
```

To extract the file Debug.exe from the Ebd.cab file, use this command:

```
EXTRACT EBD.CAB DEBUG.EXE
```

To extract all files from the Ebd.cab cabinet file, use this command:

```
EXTRACT EBD.CAB *.*
```

Debug

The Debug program is an editor that can view and manipulate the components of a file system on floppy disks and hard drives, including the FAT, directories, and boot records. It can also be used to view the contents of memory and hexadecimal memory addresses. To access Debug, enter the command Debug at the command prompt.

$A^{+}_{}$ *OS*
1.3
1.5

Edit [path][filename]

The Edit program (Edit.com) is a handy, quick, and dirty way to edit text files while working at a command prompt. To edit the file Autoexec.bat on a floppy disk, use this command:

```
EDIT A:\AUTOEXEC.BAT
```

If the file does not already exist, Edit creates it. For the Autoexec.bat file on the Windows 98 startup disk, your screen should be similar to the one shown in Figure 3-15. After you have made your changes and want to exit from the editor, press the Alt key to activate the menus, and choose Exit from the File menu. When asked if you want to save your changes, respond Yes to exit the editor and save changes.

```
  File  Edit  Search  View  Options  Help
                      a:\AUTOEXEC.BAT
@ECHO OFF                                                                        ↑
set EXPAND=YES
SET DIRCMD=/O:N
set LglDrv=27 * 26 Z 25 Y 24 X 23 W 22 V 21 U 20 T 19 S 18 R 17 Q 16 P 15
set LglDrv=%LglDrv% O 14 N 13 M 12 L 11 K 10 J 9 I 8 H 7 G 6 F 5 E 4 D 3 C
cls
call setramd.bat %LglDrv%
set temp=c:\
set tmp=c:\
path=%RAMD%:\;a:\;%CDROM%:\
copy command.com %RAMD%:\ > NUL
set comspec=%RAMD%:\command.com
copy extract.exe %RAMD%:\ > NUL
copy readme.txt %RAMD%:\ > NUL

:ERROR
IF EXIST ebd.cab GOTO EXT
echo Please insert Windows 98 Startup Disk 2
echo.
pause
GOTO ERROR
                                                                                 ↓
F1=Help                                        Line:1      Col:1
```

Figure 3-15   Edit Autoexec.bat

> **TIP** In older versions of DOS, Qbasic.exe was required for Edit.com to work correctly.

Editing Autoexec.bat and Config.sys

If you make a mistake when editing Autoexec.bat or Config.sys, you can cause a boot problem. Before editing these files on your hard drive, always make a rescue disk. If you are editing one of these files on a rescue disk, you can make a backup copy of the file before you edit it or have a second rescue disk ready just in case.

Do not use word-processing software, such as Word or WordPerfect, to edit Autoexec.bat or Config.sys, unless you save the file as a text (ASCII) file. Word-processing applications place control characters in their document files that prevent the OS from interpreting the file correctly.

> **TIP** When working from a command prompt you can reboot your computer (Ctrl+Alt+Del) to execute the new Autoexec.bat file, or you can type Autoexec.bat at the command prompt. If the computer stalls during the boot, use another startup disk to reboot. You can also press the F5 key to bypass the startup files during the boot.

Fdisk /Status /MBR

The Fdisk command is used to prepare a hard drive for first use. It creates partitions and logical drives on the hard drive, displays partition information, and restores a damaged Master Boot Record. Table 3-3 shows options for this command. You will learn more about the Fdisk command in Chapters 8 and 9.

A+ OS
1.3

Table 3-3   Options for the Fdisk command

Fdisk Command Option	Description
/MBR	Repairs a damaged MBR program stored at the beginning of the partition table
/Status	Displays partition information for all hard drives in the system

> **TIP** Many real-mode commands, such as Fdisk/MBR, have equivalent commands in the Windows 2000/XP Recovery Console. The Recovery Console command similar to Fdisk/MBR is Fixmbr.

Format Drive: /S /V:Volumename /Q /U /Autotest

Recall that the Format command is used to format a disk or a hard drive. For a hard drive, first run Fdisk to partition the drive and create each logical drive. Then use Format to format each logical drive. Table 3-4 shows options for this command. Chapter 8 covers the details of what happens when you format a hard drive.

Table 3-4   Options for the Format command

Format Command Option	Description
V	Allows you to enter a volume label only once when formatting several disks. The same volume label is used for all disks. A volume label appears at the top of the directory list to help you identify the disk.
/S	Stores the system files on the disk after formatting. Writes the two hidden files and Command.com to the disk, making the disk bootable.
/Q	Re-creates the root directory and FATs if you want to quickly format a previously formatted disk that is in good condition. /Q does not read or write to any other part of the disk.
/F:size	Specifies the size of a floppy disk. If the size is not specified, the default for that drive is used. The common values for size are: /F:360 is 360K, double-density 5¼-inch disk /F:1.2 is 1.2 MB, high-density 5¼-inch disk /F:720 is 720K, double-density 3½-inch disk /F:1.44 is 1.44 MB, high-density 3½-inch disk

A+ OS
  1.3

Table 3-4   Options for the Format command (continued)

Format Command Option	Description
/U	Allows an unconditional format of the disk, which formats the disk more thoroughly by erasing all data. Use this option when you have been getting read/write errors on the disk.
/Autotest	Does not prompt the user before and during the format.

Using Batch Files

Suppose you have a list of OS commands that you want to execute several times. Perhaps you have some data files to distribute to several PCs in your office, and, having no LAN, you must walk from one PC to another, repeatedly doing the same job. A solution is to store the list of commands in a batch file on disk and then execute the batch file at each PC. Windows requires that the batch file have a .bat file extension. For example, store these five OS commands on a disk in a file named MYLOAD.BAT:

```
C:
MD\UTILITY
MD\UTILITY\TOOLS
CD\UTILITY\TOOLS
COPY A:\TOOLS\*.*
```

From the command prompt, you execute the batch file, just as you do other program files, by entering the filename, with or without the file extension:

```
A:\>MYLOAD
```

All commands listed in the file will execute, beginning at the top of the list. The batch file above creates a subdirectory under the C drive called Utility\Tools; changes that directory to the default directory, and copies all files from the \Tools directory in drive A into that new subdirectory. Look at any good book on DOS to find examples of the very useful ways you can implement batch files, including adding user menus.

CHAPTER SUMMARY

❑ When the OS loads from a hard drive, the BIOS first executes the Master Boot Record (MBR), which executes the OS boot record, which, for Windows 9x, attempts to find Io.sys on the hard drive.

❑ Io.sys, which uses Msdos.sys, and Command.com, form the core of real-mode Windows 9x. These three files are necessary to boot to a command prompt. Config.sys and Autoexec.bat are not required but are used if they are present. Other files are needed to load the GUI desktop and run GUI applications.

❑ Autoexec.bat and Config.sys are two files that contain commands used to customize the 16-bit portion of the Windows 9x load process.

3

❑ Windows NT/2000/XP uses a different set of startup files. The first file loaded and executed is Ntldr (NT loader).

❑ A floppy disk with enough software on it to load an operating system is called a bootable disk, or system disk. A bootable disk with some utility programs to troubleshoot a failed hard drive is called a rescue disk, emergency startup disk (ESD), or startup disk.

❑ Create a startup disk in Windows 9x using the Control Panel, Add/Remove Programs icon.

❑ The boot process can be divided into four parts: POST, loading the OS, the OS initializing itself, and loading and executing an application.

❑ Startup BIOS is in control when the boot process begins. Then the startup BIOS turns control over to the OS.

❑ The MBR is a small program at the very beginning of the hard drive that is needed to locate the beginning of the OS on the drive.

❑ A hard drive is divided into high-level divisions called partitions, and within the partitions, the drive is further divided into logical drives or volumes. Each logical drive has a file system such as FAT32 or FAT16.

❑ The hard drive partition table contains a map to the logical drives on the hard drive, including an indication of which drive is the boot drive.

❑ A hidden file is a file that does not appear in the directory list. One example is Io.sys, which contains the basic I/O software for real mode in Windows 9x.

❑ A RAM drive is an area of memory that looks and acts like a hard drive, only it performs much faster. The Windows 9x startup disk uses a RAM drive to hold program files assuming the hard drive is not accessible.

❑ The file Command.com has three parts: code to manage I/O, programs for internal OS commands such as Copy and Dir, and a short program that looks for the Autoexec.bat file.

❑ You can access a command prompt window, sometimes called a DOS box, in Windows 9x by clicking Start, Programs, and MS-DOS Prompt. You can also access it by clicking Start, Run, and typing Command.com in the Run dialog box.

❑ Windows NT/2000/XP uses CMD.exe, a 32–bit version of Command.com, to provide a command prompt window.

❑ The Fdisk command is used to partition a hard drive.

❑ The Format command is used to format floppy disks and logical drives. The /S option with the Format command makes a drive bootable. The Unformat command attempts to reverse the effect of an accidental format.

❑ The Del or Erase command deletes files or groups of files. The Undelete command attempts to recover erased files. The Recover command attempts to recover a file from damaged sectors on a disk.

❏ The Diskcopy command makes an exact duplicate of one floppy disk on another disk of the same size and type. The Copy command copies a single file or group of files. More powerful than the Copy command, the Xcopy command supports copying subdirectories.

❏ The Sys command copies the system files needed to boot to a disk or drive.

❏ Mkdir creates a subdirectory, Chdir changes the current directory, and Rmdir removes a subdirectory.

❏ The Attrib command displays or changes the read-only, archive, system, and hidden attributes assigned to files.

❏ The Path command specifies where the OS should look to find executable program files.

❏ Chkdsk and Scandisk both check drives for errors and repair them. Scandisk does a more thorough scan for Windows 9x and basically replaces Chkdsk.

❏ The Defrag command rewrites files on a hard drive in contiguous clusters in order to improve hard drive performance.

❏ The Scanreg command restores or repairs the Windows 98 registry.

❏ Batch files can be used to execute a group of commands using only a single command to execute the batch file.

KEY TERMS

active partition	FAT (file allocation table)	partition table
Autoexec.bat	file extension	path
batch file	file system	Plug and Play (PnP)
boot record	filename	POST (power-on self test)
bootable disk	folder	program file
cabinet file	fragmented file	RAM drive
CD (change directory) command	hard boot	rescue disk
child directory	hidden file	root directory
cluster	internal command	sector
cold boot	Io.sys	soft boot
Command.com	logical drive	startup disk
directory table	Master Boot Record (MBR)	subdirectory
DOS box	Msdos.sys	system disk
emergency startup disk (ESD)	Ntldr	track
external command	partition	volume
		warm boot
		wildcard

REVIEW QUESTIONS

The process of booting the computer refers to the system moving itself to an operable state without user intervention. Match the two types of boot processes with the descriptions provided:

3

1. Cold boot   a. Occurs when the user presses the key sequence Ctrl+Alt+Space bar

                      b. Occurs when the system is restarted using the Restart option on the Shut Down menu

2. Warm boot   c. Occurs when the system is powered up using the on/off switch

3. Which of the two forms of system boot offer(s) a less stressful way to get a system restarted should a problem with the operating system be encountered?

    a. Cold boot

    b. Warm boot

    c. Both offer the same low level of stress to the system.

    d. Neither a nor b

4. The philosophy of Plug and Play (PnP) was created to:

    a. Allow interface cards to be inserted or removed without powering down the system

    b. Ensure that gaming software could be played on all systems that conformed to the PnP standard

    c. Allow IBM-class and Macintosh-class systems to be compatible in terms of both hardware and software

    d. Make installation of hardware devices easier

5. Which of the following operating systems is *not* Plug and Play (PnP) compliant?

    a. Windows 9x

    b. Windows 2000

    c. Windows XP

    d. Windows NT

    e. None of the above

6. Which of the following operating systems does Plug and Play (PnP) technology *not* require startup BIOS to assist in PnP configurations?

    a. Windows 9x

    b. Windows 2000

    c. Windows XP

    d. Both b and c

    e. None of the above

7. Which of the following do *not* allow the assigning of system resources?

   a. PnP-compliant devices

   b. Legacy-based devices

   c. Both a and b

   d. Neither a nor b

8. The smallest unit of space on a disk for storing data is referred to as:

   a. Sector

   b. Cluster

   c. Track

   d. Cylinder

   e. None of the above

9. Whenever a form of secondary storage media is hi-level formatted, two core components are created; the _____ _____, and _____ _____.

10. All files are made up of two components. They include the:

    a. File name and file extension

    b. Directory and file name

    c. Directory and file extension

    d. Both b and c

    e. None of the above

11. The following file is to be saved on a computer that has DOS Version 6.22 installed on it:

    Mississippi.doc

    Will the file be saved as listed above?

    a. Yes

    b. No

12. Does the following represent a file that would be accepted for storage by Windows 98 SE?

    Maryland*98.doc

    a. Yes

    b. No

3

13. (For this particular question, assume that the system is being run under the Windows 2000 operating system.) If the user wanted to ensure the retention of the long file naming structure of the file:

Computer Technology is Changing.doc

It would require that the user save the file as:

a. Computer Technology is Changing.doc

b. "Computer Technology is Changing.doc"

c. *Computer Technology is Changing.doc*

d. All of the above would work

e. None of the above would work

14. The types of partitions that exist for data storage include:

a. Primary and Secondary partitions

b. Primary and Extended partitions

c. Physical and Logical partitions

d. Physical and Secondary partitions

e. Directory and Subdirectory partitions

The following list represents the four steps needed to complete the boot process:

a. Loading the operating system

b. BIOS checking hardware

c. Loading and executing an application

d. Operating system self-initialization

For questions 15–18, place the four steps above in sequential order, starting with the first step and finishing with the last step in the boot process.

15. First step of the boot process: _____

16. Next step of the boot process: _____

17. Next step of the boot process: _____

18. Last step of the boot process: _____

For questions 19–22, assign each of the four steps above definitions that best describe each step.

19. Begins the process of reading configuration information from switches, jumpers, and CMOS devices

20. Configuration information on the CMOS chip tells the startup BIOS where to look for critical system startup files

21. Critical system startup files are properly configured based on available memory and other hardware installed

22. Microsoft Internet Explorer is loaded

23. Information about where each logical drive is located on a single physical drive is found in the:

    a. Root directory

    b. First subdirectory off the root directory

    c. Partition table

    d. Master boot record

    e. Boot record

24. Which of the following provides a map of the logical drives on a physical hard drive?

    a. Root directory

    b. First subdirectory off the root directory

    c. Partition table

    d. Master boot record

    e. Boot record

25. Which of the following would be responsible for loading the first program file of the operating system?

    a. Root directory

    b. First subdirectory off the root directory

    c. Partition table

    d. Master boot record

    e. Boot record

26. What three critical operating system files are needed in order to start Windows 9x? (Be sure the files are in the proper order!)

    a. Ntldr, Msdos.sys, io.sys

    b. Io.sys, Msdos.sys, command.com

    c. Ntldr, io.sys, command.com

    d. Msdos.sys, io.sys, command.com

    e. Command.com, io.sys, msdos.sys

27. Explain the steps necessary to create a Windows 9x Startup Disk.

28. There are a number of ways in which to access what is referred to as a Command Prompt. If it is important to start a 16-bit version of the command.com in all versions of Windows, typing the _____ command in the "Run" field after activating the Start menu would accomplish this.

    a. Command.com

    b. Cmd.com

    c. Command prompt.exe

    d. Cmd16.com

    e. None of the above

29. Entering the command prompt while the system is booting up in Windows 98 requires the user to:

    a. Use a DOS boot disk

    b. Press the F8 key to enter Command Prompt mode

    c. Choose Command Prompt from the Start menu

    d. All of the above

    e. None of the above

30. In the following command sequence:

    xcopy c:\docs*.xls d:

    which statement best describes the function of the command sequence?

    a. Copy all files that have an .xls extension in the DOCS folder on the C: drive over to the root directory of D: drive

    b. Copy all DOCS files that have an .xls extension on the C: drive over to the D: drive

    c. Copy all files that have an .xls extension in the DOCS folder on the C: drive over to some location on the D: drive, location cannot be determined specifically

    d. Copy all files from the D: drive over to the C: drive in a folder called DOCS under the same name with an .xls extension

    e. None of the above

4

ELECTRICITY AND POWER SUPPLIES

In this chapter, you will learn:

♦ How electricity is measured

♦ How to protect your computer system against damaging changes in electrical power

♦ About different form factors and computer cases

♦ How to detect and correct power supply problems

♦ About Energy Star specifications

This chapter focuses on the power supply, which provides power to all other components inside the computer case. To troubleshoot problems with the power system of a PC, you need a basic understanding of electricity. This chapter begins by discussing how to measure electricity and the form in which it comes to you as house current. The chapter then addresses the power supply, backup power sources, how to measure power supply output, and how to change a defective power supply. Finally, it introduces you to form factors and explains how Energy Star devices save energy.

ELECTRICITY: A BASIC INTRODUCTION

To most people, volts, ohms, watts, and amps are vague words that simply have to do with electricity. If these terms are mysterious to you, they will become clear in this section which discusses electricity in nontechnical language and uses simple analogies.

Electricity is energy; water is matter. However, the two have enough in common to make some analogies. Consider Figure 4-1. The water system shown in the top part of the figure is closed—that is, the amount of water in the system remains the same because no water enters and no water leaves the system. The electrical system in the lower part of the figure is similar in several respects. Think of electricity as a stream of tiny charged particles (electrons) that flow like water along the path of least resistance.

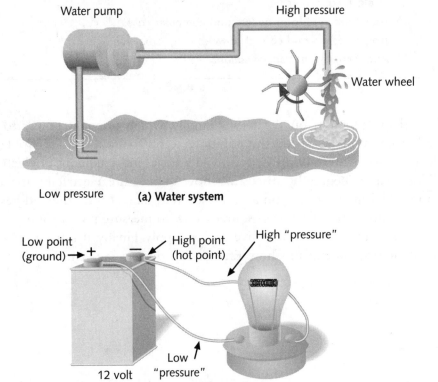

Figure 4-1   Two closed systems: (a) water system with pump, wheel, and pool;
(b) electrical system with battery and light bulb

Just as water flows down because of the force of gravity, electricity flows from negative to positive because of the force of like charges repelling one another. The water pump produces water pressure in the system by lifting the water, and a battery produces electrical pressure in the system by creating a buildup of negative charges (in the form of electrons) in one location, which are driven to move. This difference in charge, which is similar to water pressure in a water system, is called potential difference. Water seeks a place of rest, moving from a high to a low elevation, and electrons seek a place of rest by moving from a negatively charged location (sometimes called "hot") to a positively charged location (sometimes called "ground"). In the figure, water flows through the closed system, the water wheel harnesses some of its force and converts it to a form of energy, motion. Also in the figure, as the electrons flow in the closed electrical system called a circuit, the light bulb harnesses some of the force of the moving electrons and converts it to another form of energy, light. When the water returns to the pool, water pressure decreases and the water is at rest. When the electrons arrive at the positive side of the battery, electrical potential difference decreases, and the system is at rest.

 TIP Electron flow goes from the hot point, or negative terminal, to the ground or positive terminal. Because early theories of electricity assumed that electricity flowed from positive to negative, most electronics books show the current flowing from positive to negative. This theory is called conventional current flow; if it were used in Figure 4-1, the figure would show reversed positive and negative symbols.

Electrical energy has properties that we can measure in various ways. The preceding description (of an electrical system that includes a battery and a light bulb) illustrates some simple principles that apply to the most complex electrical systems. Next we use this simple electrical system to define four properties of electricity, all of which can be measured (see Table 4-1).

Table 4-1   Measures of electricity

Unit	Definition	An Example as Applied to a Computer
Volts (measures potential difference)	Abbreviated as V (for example, 110 V). Volts are measured by finding the potential difference between the electrical charges on either side of an electrical device in an electrical system.	An AT power supply supplies four separate voltages: +12 V, -12 V, +5 V, -5 V. An ATX power supply supplies these and also +3.3 V.
Amps or amperes (measures electrical current)	Abbreviated as A (for example, 1.5 A). Amps are measured by placing an ammeter in the flow of current and measuring that current.	A 17-inch monitor requires less than 2 A to operate. A small laser printer uses about 2 A. A CD-ROM drive uses about 1 A.

Table 4-1   Measures of electricity (continued)

Unit	Definition	An Example as Applied to a Computer
Ohms (measures resistance)	Abbreviated with the symbol Ω (for example, 20 Ω). Devices are rated according to how much resistance to electrical current they offer. The ohm rating of a resistor or other electrical device is often written somewhere on the device. The resistance of a device is measured when the device is not connected to an electrical system.	Current can flow in typical computer cables and wires with a resistance of near zero Ω.
Watts (measures power)	Abbreviated W (for example, 20 W). Watts are calculated by multiplying volts by amps.	A computer power supply is rated at 200 to 600 W.

Voltage

The first measure of electricity listed in Table 4-1 is potential difference. First, consider how to measure the water pressure. If you measure the pressure of the water directly above the water wheel and then measure the pressure just as the water lands in the pool, you find that the water pressure above the wheel is greater than the water pressure below it.

Now consider the electrical system. If you measure the electrical charge on one side of the light bulb and compare it to the electrical charge on the other side of the bulb, you see a difference in charge. The potential difference in charge creates an electrical force called **voltage**, which drives the electrons through the system between two points. Voltage is measured in units called **volts (V)**.

In Figure 4-2, the leads of a **voltmeter**, a device for measuring electrical voltage, are placed on either side of a light bulb that consumes some electrical power. The potential difference between the two points on either side of the device is the voltage in the closed system. Voltage is measured when the power is on.

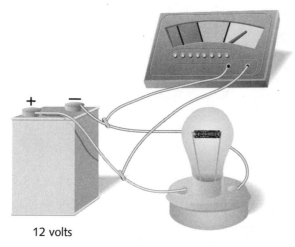

12 volts

Figure 4-2 A voltmeter measuring the voltage across a bulb and a battery

Amps

The volume of electrons (or electricity) flowing through an electrical system is called current. Look back at Figure 4-1. The volume or amount of water flowing through the water system does not change, although the water pressure changes at different points in the system. To measure that volume, you pick one point in the system and measure the volume of water passing through that point over a period of time. The electrical system is similar. If you measure the number of electrons, or electrical current, at any point in this system, you find the same value as at any other point, because the current is constant throughout the system. (This assumes that the entire closed water or electrical system has only a single pipe or a single wire.) Electrical current is measured in **amperes (A)**, abbreviated **amps**. Figure 4-3 shows an **ammeter**, a device that measures electrical current in amps. You place the ammeter in the path of the electrical flow so that the electrons must flow through the ammeter. The measurement, which you take with the power on, might not be completely accurate because the ammeter can influence the circuit.

 Because the current flows through an ammeter, check the rating of the ammeter before measuring amps to make sure it can handle the flow of electricity. More flow than the ammeter is designed to handle can blow the meter's fuse.

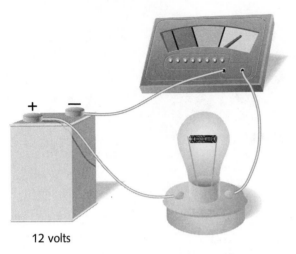

12 volts

Figure 4-3   Battery and bulb circuit with ammeter in line

Relationship Between Voltage and Current

Refer again to the water system in Figure 4-1. To increase the volume of water flowing through the system, you increase the difference in water pressure between the low and high points (which is called the pressure differential). As the pressure differential increases, the water flow (or current) increases, and as the water pressure differential decreases, the water flow (or current) decreases. Another way of saying this is: there is a direct relationship between pressure differential and current. An electrical system works the same way. As the electrical potential difference (or voltage) increases, the electrical current increases; as the voltage decreases, the current decreases. There is a direct relationship between voltage and current.

Ohms

Suppose you are working your water pump to full capacity. If you still want to increase the overall power of your water system—so the wheel turns faster to produce more mechanical energy—you could decrease the resistance to water flow, allowing more water to flow to push the wheel faster. You might use a larger pipe or a lighter water wheel, or, if the system has a partially open water valve, you could open the valve more; these alternatives all would lower resistance to water flow. As resistance decreases, current increases. As resistance increases (smaller pipes, heavier wheel, partially closed valve), current decreases.

Similarly, **resistance** in an electrical system is a property that opposes the flow of electricity. As electrical resistance increases, the flow of electrons decreases. As resistance decreases, the electricity increases. (A condition of low resistance that allows current to flow in a completed circuit is called **continuity**). When too much electricity flows through a wire, it creates heat energy (similar to friction) in the wire. This heat energy can cause the wire to melt or burn, which can result in an electrical fire, just as too much water current can cause a pipe to burst. Reducing the size of a wire reduces the amount of electricity that can safely flow through it. Electrical resistance is measured in **ohms (Ω)**.

Resistors are devices used in electrical circuits to resist the flow of electricity. These devices control the flow of electricity in a circuit, much as partially closed valves control the flow of water.

Relationships Among Voltage, Current, and Resistance

Voltage and current have a direct relationship. This means that when voltage increases, current increases. Resistance has an inverse relationship with voltage and current. This means that as resistance increases, either current or voltage decreases. As resistance decreases, either current or voltage increases. This last statement is known as Ohm's Law. A similar statement defines the relationship among the units of measure: volts, amps, and ohms. One volt drives a current of one amp through a resistance of one ohm.

Wattage

Wattage is the total amount of power needed to operate an electrical device. When thinking of the water system, you recognize that the amount of water power used to turn the water wheel is not just a measure of the water pressure that forces current through the system. The amount of power also depends on the amount of water available to flow. For a given water pressure, you have more power with more water flow and less power with less water flow. A lot of power results when you have a lot of pressure and a lot of current.

As with the water system, electrical power increases as both voltage and current increase. Wattage, measured in **watts (W)**, is calculated by multiplying volts by amps in a system (W = V × A). For example, 120 volts times 5 amps is 600 watts. Note that while volts and amps are measured to determine their value, watts are calculated from those values.

AC and DC

A+CORE
1.1
1.2

Electricity can be either AC, alternating current, or DC, direct current. **Alternating current (AC)** cycles or oscillates back and forth rather than traveling in only one direction. House current in the United States oscillates 60 times in one second (60 hertz), changing polarity from +110V to −110V and causing current to flow in different directions, depending on whether it's positive or negative in the cycle. AC is the most economical way to transmit electricity to our homes and workplaces. Decreasing current and increasing voltage (high pressure and low volume) can force alternating current to travel great distances. Decreasing voltage and increasing current (low pressure and high volume) when they reach their destination can make alternating current more suitable for driving our electrical devices.

A+CORE
  1.1
  1.2

Direct current (DC) travels in only one direction and is the type of current that most electronic devices require, including computers. A **rectifier** is a device that converts alternating current to direct current. A **transformer** is a device that changes the ratio of current to voltage. Large transformers reduce the high voltage on power lines coming to your neighborhood to a lower voltage before the current enters your home. The transformer does not change the amount of power in this closed system; if it decreases voltage, then it increases current. The overall power stays constant, but the ratio of voltage to current changes.

A computer power supply changes and conditions the house electrical current in several ways, functioning as both a transformer and a rectifier (see Figure 4-4). It steps down the voltage from the 110-volt house current to 3.3, 5, and 12 volts, or to 5 and 12 volts, and changes incoming alternating current to direct current, which the computer and its peripherals require. The monitor, however, receives the full 110 volts of AC voltage, converting that current to DC.

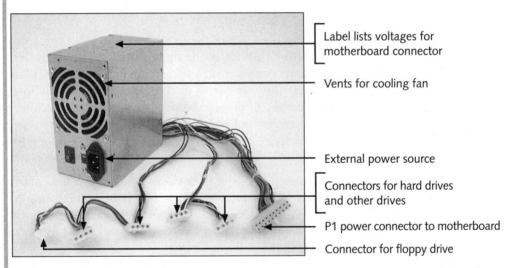

Label lists voltages for motherboard connector

Vents for cooling fan

External power source

Connectors for hard drives and other drives

P1 power connector to motherboard

Connector for floppy drive

Figure 4-4   Computer power supply with connections

Recall that direct current flows in only one direction, from hot to ground. For a PC, a line may be either +5 or −5 volts in one circuit, or +12 or −12 volts in another circuit, depending on whether the circuit is on the positive side or negative side of the power output. Several circuits coming from the power supply accommodate different devices with different power requirements.

Hot, Neutral, and Ground

When AC comes from the power source at the power station to your house, it travels on a hot line and completes the circuit from your house back to the power source on a neutral line, as seen in Figure 4-5.

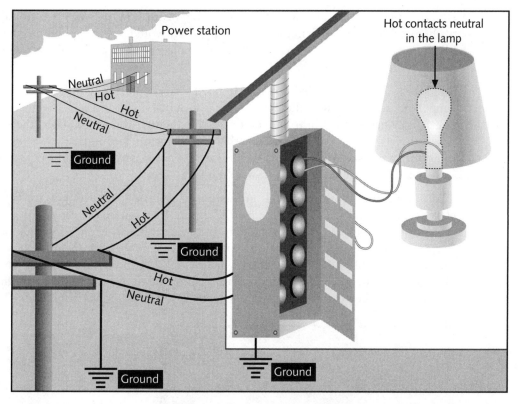

4

Figure 4-5   Normally hot contacts neutral to make a closed circuit in the controlled environment of an electrical device such as a lamp. An out-of-control contact is called a short, and the flow of electricity is then diverted to the ground.

When the two lines reach your house and enter an electrical device, such as a lamp or radio, electricity flows through the device to complete the circuit between the hot line and the neutral line. The device contains resistors and other electrical components that control the flow of electricity between the hot and neutral lines. The hot source seeks and finds ground by returning to the power station on the neutral line.

A short circuit, or a short, occurs when uncontrolled electricity flows from the hot line to the neutral line or from the hot line to ground. Electricity naturally finds the easiest route to ground. Normally that path is through some device that controls the current flow and then back through the neutral line. If an easier path (one with less resistance) is available, the electricity follows that path. This can cause a short, a sudden increase in flow that can create a sudden increase in temperature—enough to start a fire and injure both people and equipment. Never put yourself in a position where you are the path of least resistance between the hot line and ground!

A fuse is a component included in a circuit and designed to prevent too much current from flowing through the circuit. A fuse is commonly a wire inside a protective case, which is rated in amps. If too much current begins to flow, the wire gets hot and eventually melts, breaking the circuit, as an open switch would, and stopping the current flow. Many devices have fuses, which can be easily replaced when damaged. You will learn to test a fuse later in the chapter.

To prevent the uncontrolled flow of electricity from continuing indefinitely, which can happen because of a short, the neutral line is grounded. Grounding a line means that the line is connected directly to the earth, so that, in the event of a short, the electricity flows into the earth and not back to the power station. Grounding serves as an escape route for out-of-control electricity. The earth is at no particular state of charge and so is always capable of accepting a flow of current.

The neutral line to your house is grounded many times along its way (in fact, at each electrical pole) and is also grounded at the breaker box where the electricity enters your house. You can look at a three-prong plug and see the three lines: hot, neutral, and ground (see Figure 4-6). Generally, electricians use green or bare wire for the ground wire, white for neutral, and black for hot in home wiring for 110-volt circuits. In a 220-volt circuit, black and red are hot, white is neutral, and green or bare is ground. To verify that a wall outlet is wired correctly, use a simple receptacle tester, as shown in Figure 4-7.

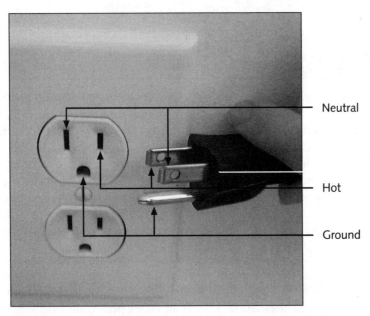

Neutral

Hot

Ground

Figure 4-6   A three-prong plug showing hot, neutral, and ground

Figure 4-7   Use a receptacle tester to verify that hot, neutral, and ground are wired correctly

CAUTION

Beware of the different uses of black wire. In PCs, black is used for ground, but in home wiring, black is used for hot!

Even though you might have a three-prong outlet in your home, the ground plug might not be properly grounded. To know for sure, test the outlet with a receptacle tester.

CAUTION

It's very important that PC components be properly grounded. Never connect a PC to an outlet or use an extension cord that doesn't have the third ground plug. The third line can prevent a short from causing extreme damage. In addition, the bond between the neutral and ground helps eliminate electrical noise (stray electrical signals) within the PC sometimes caused by other electrical equipment sitting very close to the computer.

Some Common Electronic Components

Understanding what basic electronic components make up a PC and how they work is important. Basic electronic components in a PC include transistors, capacitors, diodes, ground, and resistors. Figure 4-8 shows the symbols for these components.

Materials used to make these and other electronic components can be:

- *Conductors*. Material that easily conducts electricity, such as gold or copper
- *Insulators*. Material that resists the flow of electricity, such as glass or ceramic
- *Semiconductors*. Material such as silicon whose ability to conduct electricity, when a charge is applied, falls between that of a conductor and an insulator

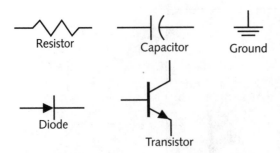

Figure 4-8   Symbols for some electronic components and ground

A **transistor** is an electronic device that can serve as a gate or switch for an electrical signal and can amplify the flow of electricity. Invented in 1947, the transistor is made of three layers of semiconductor material. A charge (either positive or negative, depending on the transistor's design) placed on the center layer can cause the two outer layers of the transistor to complete a circuit to create an "on" state. An opposite charge placed on the center layer can make the reverse happen, causing the transistor to create an "off" state. Manipulating these charges to the transistor allows it to hold a logic state, either on or off (translated to binary 0 or 1). When the transistor maintains this state, it requires almost no electrical power. Because the initial charge sent to the transistor is not as great as the resulting current that the transistor creates, sometimes a transistor is used as a small amplifier. The transistor is the basic building block of an integrated circuit (IC), which is used to build a microchip.

A **capacitor** is an electronic device that can hold an electrical charge for a period of time and can smooth the uneven flow of electricity through a circuit. Capacitors inside a PC power supply create the even flow of current the PC needs. Capacitors maintain their charge long after current is no longer present, which is why the inside of a power supply can be dangerous even when it is unplugged.

A **diode** is a semiconductor device that allows electricity to flow in only one direction. (A transistor contains two diodes.) One to four diodes used in various configurations can be used to convert AC to DC. Singularly or collectively, depending on the configuration, these diodes are called a rectifier.

As explained above, a resistor is an electronic device that limits the amount of current that can flow through it.

PROTECTING YOUR COMPUTER SYSTEM

Now that you have learned some basic information about how electricity works, understanding how power is supplied to a computer will be easier. But first, let's look at ways to protect your computer system. As you read the rest of the chapter, you will begin to look inside a computer and start taking it apart and putting it back together. Working on a computer, it is possible to harm both the computer and yourself. The most common accident when someone attempts to fix a computer problem is erasing software or data. Experimenting without knowing what you are doing can cause damage. You can take many safety precautions to prevent these sorts of accidents, as well as the ones that put you in physical danger. Here are a few general safety precautions to keep in mind:

A+CORE
3.2

4

- Make notes as you work so that you can backtrack later if necessary.

- When unpacking hardware or software, remove the packing tape and cellophane from the work area as soon as possible.

- Keep components away from your hair and clothing.

- Keep screws and spacers orderly and in one place, such as a cup or tray.

- Don't stack boards on top of each other: You could accidentally dislodge a chip this way.

- When handling motherboards and expansion cards, don't touch the chips on the boards. Hold expansion cards by the edges. Don't touch any soldered components on a card, and don't touch chips or edge connectors unless it's absolutely necessary.

- Don't touch a chip with a magnetized screwdriver.

- Don't use a graphite pencil to change DIP switch settings, because graphite is a conductor of electricity, and the graphite can lodge in the switch.

- In a classroom environment, after you have reassembled everything, have your instructor check your work before you put the cover back on and power up.

- Always turn off a computer before moving it. A computer's hard drive always spins while it is on, unless it has sleep mode. Therefore, it is important not to move, kick, or jar a computer while it is running.

- To protect disks, keep them away from magnetic fields, heat, and extreme cold. Don't open the shuttle window on a floppy disk or touch the disk's surface.

You will learn about additional safety precautions in the remainder of this section.

Protecting Against Electricity

To protect both yourself and the equipment when working inside a computer, turn off the power, unplug the computer, and always use a ground bracelet (which you will learn more about later). Never touch the inside of a computer that is turned on. In addition, consider the monitor and the power supply to be "black boxes." Never remove the cover or put your hands inside this equipment unless you know about the hazards of charged capacitors and have been trained to deal with them. Both the power supply and the monitor can hold a dangerous level of electricity even after you turn them off and disconnect them from a power source. The power supply and monitor contain enough power to kill you, even when they are unplugged.

Static Electricity

A+CORE
3.2

Electrostatic discharge (ESD), commonly known as **static electricity**, is an electrical charge at rest. A static charge can build up on the surface of an ungrounded conductor and on nonconductive surfaces such as clothing or plastic. When two objects with dissimilar electrical charges touch, static electricity passes between them until the dissimilar charges become equal. To see how this works, turn off the lights in a room, scuff your feet on the carpet, and touch another person. Occasionally you can see and feel the charge in your fingers. If you can feel the charge, then you discharged at least 3,000 volts of static electricity. If you hear the discharge, then you released at least 6,000 volts. If you see the discharge, then you released at least 8,000 volts of ESD. A charge of much less than 3,000 volts can damage electronic components. You can touch a chip on an expansion card or motherboard; damage the chip with ESD; and never feel, hear, or see the discharge.

ESD can cause two types of damage in an electronic component: catastrophic failure and upset failure. A catastrophic failure destroys the component beyond use. An upset failure damages the component so that it does not perform well, even though it may still function to some degree. Upset failures are more difficult to detect because they are not as easily observed.

CAUTION

A monitor can also damage components with ESD. Do not place or store expansion cards on top of or next to a monitor, which can discharge as much as 29,000 volts onto the screen.

To protect the computer against ESD, always ground yourself before touching electronic components, including the hard drive, motherboard, expansion cards, processors, and memory modules. Ground yourself and the computer parts, using one or more of the following static control devices or methods:

- *Ground bracelet or static strap.* A **ground bracelet** is a strap you wear around your wrist. One end attaches to a grounded conductor such as the computer case or a ground mat or plugs into a wall outlet. (Only the ground prong makes a connection!) The bracelet also contains a resistor that prevents electricity from harming you. Figure 4-9 shows a ground bracelet.

- *Ground mats.* Ground mats can come equipped with a cord to plug into a wall outlet to provide a grounded surface on which to work. If you lift the component off the mat, it is no longer grounded and is susceptible to ESD. Figure 4-10 shows a ground mat.

$A^{+CORE}_{3.2}$

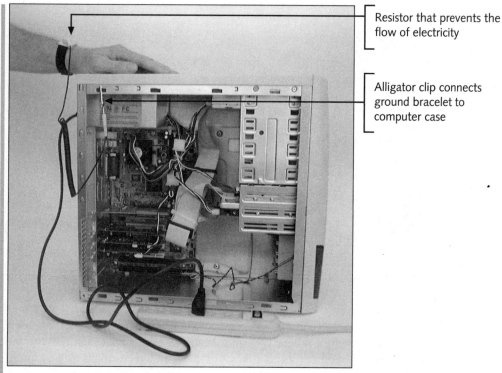

Resistor that prevents the flow of electricity

Alligator clip connects ground bracelet to computer case

4

Figure 4-9 A ground bracelet, which protects computer components from ESD, can clip to the side of the computer case and eliminates ESD between you and the case

- *Static shielding bags.* New components come shipped in static shielding bags. Save the bags to store other devices that are not currently installed in a PC. When working on a PC, you can also lay components on these bags (see Figure 4-11).

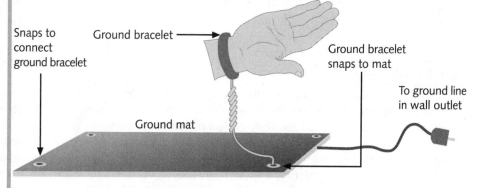

Snaps to connect ground bracelet

Ground bracelet

Ground bracelet snaps to mat

To ground line in wall outlet

Ground mat

Figure 4-10 A ground bracelet can be connected to a ground mat, which is grounded by the wall outlet

A+CORE
3.2

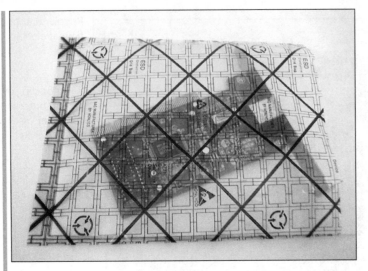

Figure 4-11   Static shielding bags help protect components from ESD

The best way to guard against ESD is to use a ground bracelet together with a ground mat. Consider a ground bracelet essential equipment when working on a computer. However, if you are in a situation where you must work without one, touch the computer case or the power supply before you touch a component. When passing a chip to another person, ground yourself and then touch the other person before you pass the chip. Leave components inside their protective bags until you are ready to use them. Work on hard floors, not carpet, or use antistatic spray on the carpets. Generally, don't work on a computer if you or the computer have just come from the cold, because the potential for ESD is higher.

TIP

Besides using a ground mat, you can also create a ground for the computer case by leaving the power cord to the case plugged into the wall outlet. This is safe enough because the power is turned off when you work inside the case. However, if you happen to touch an exposed area of the power switch inside the case, you may get a shock. Because of this risk, this book directs you to unplug the power cord to the PC before you work inside the case.

CAUTION

There are exceptions to the rule of always being grounded when you work with PCs. You *don't* want to be grounded when working inside a monitor or with a power supply or with high-voltage equipment such as a laser printer. These devices maintain high electrical charges, even when the power is turned off. Inside a monitor case, the electricity stored in capacitors poses substantial danger. When working inside a monitor, you don't want to be grounded, because you would provide a conduit for the voltage to discharge through your body. In this situation, be careful not to ground yourself. The situation is similar when working with a power supply. *Don't* wear a ground bracelet when working inside these devices, because you don't want to be the ground for these charges!

EMI (Electromagnetic Interference)

Another phenomenon that can cause electrical problems with computers is **electromagnetic interference (EMI)**. EMI is caused by the magnetic field produced as a side effect when electricity flows. EMI in the radio frequency range, which is called radio frequency interference (RFI), can cause problems with radio and TV reception. Data in data cables that cross an electromagnetic field can become corrupted, causing crosstalk. Using shielded data cables covered with a protective material can partially control crosstalk. Power supplies are also shielded to prevent them from emitting EMI.

> **TIP**
> PCs can emit EMI to other nearby PCs, which is one reason a computer needs to be inside a case. To help cut down on EMI between PCs, always install face plates in empty drive bays or slot covers over empty expansion slots.

If mysterious, intermittent errors persist on a PC, one thing to suspect is EMI. Try moving the PC to a new location. If the problem continues, try moving it to a location that uses an entirely different electric circuit. Using an inexpensive AM radio is one simple way to detect the presence of EMI. Turn the tuning dial away from a station into a low-frequency range. With the radio on, you can hear the static that EMI produces. Try putting the radio next to several electronic devices to detect the EMI they emit.

If EMI in the electrical circuits coming to the PC poses a significant problem, you can use a line conditioner to filter the electrical noise causing the EMI. Line conditioners are discussed later in the chapter.

Surge Protection and Battery Backup

In addition to protecting your PC against ESD and EMI, you need to consider how power coming into a computer is regulated. A wide range of devices on the market filter the AC input to computers and their peripherals (that is, condition the AC input to eliminate highs and lows) and provide backup power when the AC fails. These devices, installed between the house current and the computer, fall into three general categories: surge suppressors, power conditioners, and uninterruptible power supplies (UPSs). All these devices should have the UL (Underwriters Laboratory) logo, which ensures that the laboratory, a provider of product safety certification, has tested this device.

Surge suppressors protect equipment against sudden changes in power level, such as spikes from lightning strikes. Power conditioners and uninterruptible power supplies condition the power passing through them (that is, alter it to provide continuous voltages). Both provide a degree of protection against **spikes** (temporary voltage surges) and raise the voltage when it drops during **brownouts** (temporary voltage reductions). These devices are measured by the load they support in watts, volt-amperes (VA), or kilovolt-amperes (kVA).

A+CORE
1.8

To determine the VA required to support your system, multiply the amperage of each component by 120 volts and then add up the VA for all components. For example, a 17-inch monitor has 1.9 A written on the back of the monitor, which means 1.9 amps. Multiply that value times 120 volts, and you see that the monitor requires 228 VA. A Pentium PC with a 17-inch monitor and tape backup system requires about 500 VA of support.

Surge Suppressors

A **surge suppressor**, also called a **surge protector**, provides a row of power outlets and an on/off switch that protects equipment from overvoltages on AC power lines and telephone lines. A surge suppressor might be a shunt type that absorbs the surge, a series type that blocks the surge from flowing, or a combination of the two. The shunt-type suppressor is measured by **clamping voltage**, a term that describes the let-through voltage. Surge suppressors can come as power strips (note that not all power strips have surge protection), wall-mounted units that plug into AC outlets, or consoles designed to sit beneath the monitor on a desktop. Some provide RJ-11 telephone jacks to protect modems and fax machines from spikes.

Whenever a power outage occurs, unless you have a reliable power conditioner or UPS installed, unplug all power cords to the PC, printers, monitors, and the like. Sometimes when the power returns, sudden spikes are accompanied by another brief outage. You don't want to subject your equipment to these surges. When buying a surge suppressor, look for those that guarantee against damage from lightning and that reimburse for equipment destroyed while the surge suppressor is in use.

Surge suppressors are not always reliable, and once the fuse inside the suppressor blows, a surge suppressor no longer protects equipment from a power surge. It continues to provide power without warning that you have lost protection.

A **data line protector** serves the same function for your telephone line to your modem that a surge suppressor does for the electrical lines. Telephone lines carry a small current of electricity and need protection against spikes, just as electrical lines do. The let-through rating for a data line protector for a phone line should be no more than 260 volts.

Power Conditioners

In addition to providing protection against spikes, **power conditioners** also regulate, or condition, the power, providing continuous voltage during brownouts. These voltage regulators, sometimes called **line conditioners**, can come as small desktop units.

These electricity filters are a good investment if the AC in your community suffers excessive spikes and brownouts. However, a device rated under 1 kVA will probably only provide corrections for brownouts, not for spikes. Line conditioners, like surge suppressors, provide no protection against a total blackout (complete loss of power).

$A^{+CORE}_{1.8}$ | **Uninterruptible Power Supply**

Unlike a power conditioner, the **UPS (uninterruptible power supply)** provides backup power in the event that the AC fails completely. The UPS also offers some filtering of the AC. The power supplies in most computers can operate over a wide range of electrical voltage input, but operating the computer under these conditions for extended periods of time can shorten not only the power supply's life, but also the computer's. UPSs offer these benefits:

- Condition the line for both brownouts and spikes

- Provide backup power during a blackout

- Protect against very high spikes that could damage equipment

A UPS device suitably priced for personal computer systems is designed as either a standby device, an inline device, or a **line-interactive** device (which combines features of the first two). Several variations of these three types of UPS devices are on the market at widely varying prices.

A common UPS device is a rather heavy box that plugs into an AC outlet and provides one or more outlets for the computer and its peripherals (see Figure 4-12). It has an on/off switch, requires no maintenance, and is very simple to install.

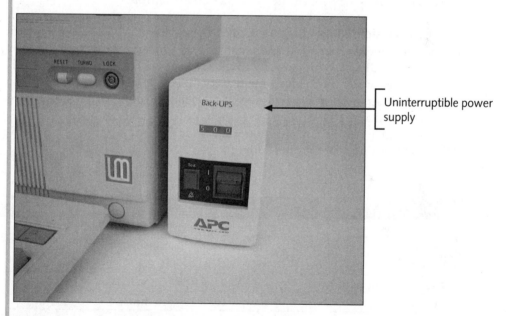

Figure 4-12   Uninterruptible power supply (UPS)

The Intelligent UPS Some UPSs can be controlled by software from a computer, to allow additional functionality. For example, from the front panel of some UPSs you can check for a weak battery. If the UPS is an **intelligent UPS**, you can perform the same function from utility software installed on your computer. To accommodate this feature, a UPS must have a serial port connection to the PC and a microprocessor on board. Some things this utility software and an intelligent UPS can do are:

- Diagnose the UPS

- Check for a weak battery

- Monitor the quality of electricity received

- Monitor the percentage of load the UPS is carrying during a blackout

- Automatically schedule the weak-battery test or UPS diagnostic test

- Send an alarm to workstations on a network to prepare for a shutdown

- Close down all servers protected by the UPS during a blackout

- Provide pager notification to a facilities manager if the power goes out

- After a shutdown, allow for startup from a remote location over phone lines

Windows NT, Windows 2000, and Windows XP offer support for intelligent UPSs. You can monitor and control the devices from the UPS dialog box accessible through Control Panel. Microsoft and American Power Conversion Corp. (APC), a leading manufacturer of UPSs, developed the Windows 2000 controls.

What to Consider When Buying a UPS   When you purchase a UPS, cost often drives the decision about how much and what kind of protection you buy. However, do not buy an inline UPS that runs at full capacity. A battery charger operating at full capacity produces heat, which can reduce the battery's life. The UPS rating should exceed your total VA or wattage output by at least 25 percent. Also be aware of the degree of line conditioning that the UPS provides. Consider the warranty and service policies as well as the guarantee the UPS manufacturer gives for the equipment that the UPS protects. Table 4-2 lists some UPS manufacturers.

Table 4-2   UPS manufacturers

Manufacturer	Web Site
MGE UPS Systems	www.mgeups.com
American Power Conversion Corp. (APC)	www.apcc.com
Tripp Lite	www.tripplite.com
Belkin Components	www.belkin.com
Invensys	www.bestpower.com
Liebert Corporation	www.liebert.com
Para Systems, Inc.	www.minuteman-ups.com
Toshiba International Corp.	www.tic.toshiba.com

THE COMPUTER CASE AND FORM FACTORS

A^{+}CORE
1.1
1.2
4.3

Power supplies and computer cases are often sold together and must be compatible with each other. Also, the power supply and case must fit the motherboard. For these reasons, we now turn our attention to the computer case. When you put together a new system, or replace components in an existing system, the form factors of the motherboard, power supply, and case must all match. The **form factor** describes the size, shape, and general makeup of a hardware component.

4

When you are deciding which form factor to use, the motherboard drives the decision because it determines what the system can do. After you've decided to use a certain form factor for the motherboard, then you must use the same form factor for the case and power supply. Using a matching form factor for the power supply and case assures you that:

- The motherboard fits in the case.

- The power supply cords to the motherboard provide the correct voltage, and the connectors match the connections on the board.

- The holes in the motherboard align with the holes in the case for anchoring the board to the case.

- Holes in the case align with ports coming off the motherboard.

- For some form factors, wires for switches and lights on the front of the case match up with connections on the motherboard.

Case, Power Supply, and Motherboard Form Factors

A^{+}CORE
1.1
1.2
4.3

Several form factors apply to power supplies, cases, and motherboards: the older and outdated XT, AT, ATX, LPX, NLX, and backplane systems. Each of these form factors has several variations. The four most common form factors used on personal computers today are the AT, Baby AT, ATX, and Mini-ATX. The most popular form factor is the ATX. This form factor and earlier, less common, and up-and-coming form factors are discussed next.

AT Form Factor

The **AT** form factor, sometimes called **full AT**, is used on older motherboards that measured 12" $\times$ 13.8". This form factor uses the full-size AT cases that the original IBM AT (Advanced Technology) personal computer used. A smaller, more convenient version of AT called the Baby AT came later. Full AT motherboards cannot be used with smaller AT cases or with newer ATX cases. Their dimensions and configuration make full AT systems difficult to install, service, and upgrade. Another problem with the AT form factor is that the CPU is placed on the motherboard in front of the expansion slots; long cards might not fit in these slots because they will bump into the CPU. You can visualize this problem by looking at the AT motherboard in Figure 4-13.

A+CORE
  1.1
  1.2
  4.3

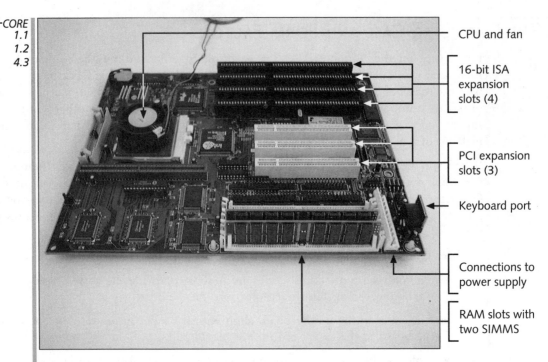

CPU and fan

16-bit ISA
expansion
slots (4)

PCI expansion
slots (3)

Keyboard port

Connections to
power supply

RAM slots with
two SIMMS

Figure 4-13   The CPU on the AT motherboard sits in front of the expansion slots

Recall that power supplies for AT systems supply +5, -5, +12, and -12 volts to the motherboard and other components. Most manufacturers no longer produce full AT boards.

Baby AT Form Factor

Improved flexibility over full AT made **Baby AT** the industry standard form factor from about 1993 to 1997. Power supplies designed for the Baby AT form factor blow air out of the computer case. At 13" × 8.7", Baby AT motherboards are smaller than full AT motherboards and fit in many types of cases, including newer ATX cases designed to provide backward compatibility. The design of Baby AT motherboards did not resolve the problem with the position of the CPU in relation to expansion slots. In addition, because of the motherboard's configuration and orientation within the case, drives and other devices are not positioned close to their connections on the motherboard. This means that cables might have to reach across the motherboard and not be long enough.

ATX Form Factor

ATX is the most commonly used form factor today. It is an open, nonproprietary industry specification originally developed by Intel in 1995. ATX improved upon AT by making adding and removing components easier, providing greater support for I/O devices and processor technology, and lowering costs. Components on the motherboard are arranged so as not to interfere with each other and for better position inside the case. Also, the position of the power supply and drives inside the case makes connecting them to the motherboard easier and makes it possible to reduce cable lengths, which can help reduce the potential for EMI and corrupted data. Connecting the switches and lights on the front of the case to components inside the case requires fewer wires, making installation simpler and reducing the potential for mistakes.

An ATX motherboard measures 12" × 9.6", so it's smaller than a full AT motherboard. On an ATX motherboard, the CPU and memory slots are rotated 90 degrees from the position on the AT motherboard. Instead of sitting in front of the expansion slots, the CPU and memory slots sit beside them, preventing interference with full-length expansion cards (see Figure 4-14).

The ATX power supply and motherboard use a single power connector called the P1 connector that includes, in addition to the voltages provided by AT, a +3.3-volt circuit for a low-voltage CPU. In addition to the P1 connector, one or more auxiliary connectors can be used to supply power to the CPU or CPU fan. Cases designed for Baby AT and LPX cannot accommodate ATX motherboards and power supplies, although many ATX cases can accommodate Baby AT motherboards.

An additional difference between AT and ATX systems is that the power supply fan blows air into rather than out of the case, cooling the processor directly. Using an ATX power supply can help lower noise and cooling cost, because the power supply has a side vent in just the right position to blow air on the processor and expansion cards. This can reduce the need to add additional fans and heat sinks.

Another feature of an ATX motherboard not found on AT boards is a **soft switch**, sometimes called the **soft power** feature. Using this feature, an OS, such as Windows 98 or Windows 2000/XP, can turn off the power to a system after the shutdown procedure is done. Also, CMOS can be configured to cause a keystroke or network activity to power up the system (wake on LAN). On older AT systems, when the PC is running and a user presses the power switch on the front of the case, the power turns off abruptly. The operating system has no opportunity to close down gracefully and, on the next power up, the system might have errors. With a soft switch controlling an ATX system and an operating system supporting the feature, if the user presses the power switch on the front of the case while the computer is on, the OS goes through a normal shutdown procedure before powering off.

4

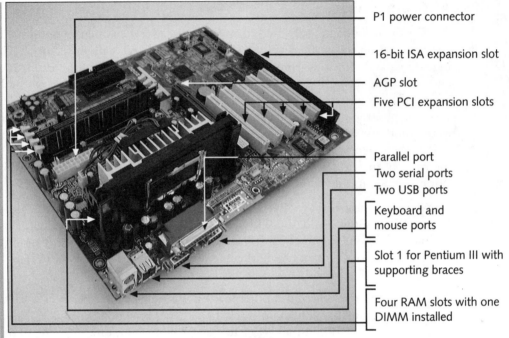
P1 power connector

16-bit ISA expansion slot

AGP slot
Five PCI expansion slots

Parallel port
Two serial ports
Two USB ports
Keyboard and
mouse ports

Slot 1 for Pentium III with
supporting braces

Four RAM slots with one
DIMM installed

Figure 4-14 The CPU on an ATX motherboard sits beside the expansion slots and does not block the room needed for long expansion cards

In addition to regular ATX, there are several other types of ATX boards. **Mini-ATX**, a smaller ATX board (11.2" × 8.2"), can be used with ATX cases and power supplies. **MicroATX** addresses some technologies that have come along since the original development of ATX. **FlexATX** allows for maximum flexibility in the design of system cases and boards and therefore can be a good choice for custom systems.

NLX Form Factor

NLX is a form factor for low-end personal computer motherboards and is used with low-profile cases. In NLX systems, the motherboard has only one expansion slot, in which a **riser card**, or **bus riser**, is mounted (see Figure 4-15). Expansion cards are mounted on the riser card, and the card also contains connectors for the floppy and hard drives. The motherboard itself includes a low-end video controller. The NLX form factor is designed to be flexible and to use space efficiently.

A+CORE
  1.1
  1.2

4

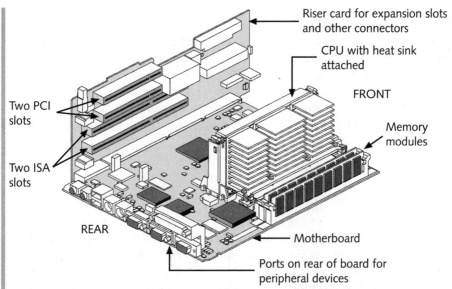

Riser card for expansion slots
and other connectors

CPU with heat sink
attached

FRONT

Two PCI
slots

Memory
modules

Two ISA
slots

REAR

Motherboard

Ports on rear of board for
peripheral devices

Figure 4-15 The NLX form factor uses a riser card that connects to the motherboard. The riser card provides expansion slots for expansion cards

LPX and Mini-LPX Form Factors

Western Digital originally developed **LPX** and **Mini-LPX**, which each have a riser card similar to NLX systems, and are often used in low-cost systems sold in large electronics stores. Difficult to upgrade, they cannot handle the size and operating temperature of today's faster processors. In addition, a manufacturer often makes proprietary changes to the standard LPX motherboard design, forcing you to use only the manufacturer's power supply. LPX and Mini-LPX use small cases called low profile cases and slimline cases, which the next section discusses.

Backplane Systems

Backplane systems do not use a true motherboard. The backplane is a board that normally sits against the back of a proprietary case with slots on it for other cards. **Active backplanes** contain no circuits other than bus connectors and some buffer and driver circuits. **Passive backplanes** contain no circuitry at all; the circuits are all on a mothercard, a circuit board that plugs into the backplane and contains a CPU. These systems are generally not used in personal computers. Passive backplanes are sometimes used for industrial rack-mounted systems and high-end file servers. A rack-mounted system is not designed for personal use, and often several of these systems are mounted in cases stacked on a rack for easy access by technicians.

Types of Cases

A+CORE
1.1

Several types and sizes of cases are on the market for each form factor. The computer case, sometimes called the chassis, houses the power supply, motherboard, expansion cards, and drives. The case has lights and switches on the front panel that can be used to control and monitor the PC. Generally, the larger the case, the larger the power supply and the more amps it carries. These large cases allow for the extra space and power needed for a larger number of devices, such as multiple hard drives needed in a server.

Cases for personal computers and notebooks fall into three major categories: desktop cases, tower cases, and laptop cases.

Desktop Cases

The classic case with four drive bays and around six expansion slots that sits on your desktop doing double duty as a monitor stand is called a desktop case. The motherboard sits on the bottom of a desktop case, and the power supply is near the back. Because of the space a desktop case takes, it has fallen out of favor in recent years and is being replaced by smaller and more space-efficient cases.

For low-end desktop systems, **compact cases**, sometimes called **low-profile** or **slim-line cases**, follow either the NLX, LPX, or Mini-LPX form factor. Likely to have fewer drive bays, they generally still provide for some expansion. You can see the rear of a compact case in Figure 4-16. An LPX motherboard that uses this case has a riser card for expansion cards, which is why the expansion card slots in the figure run parallel to the motherboard sitting on the bottom of the case.

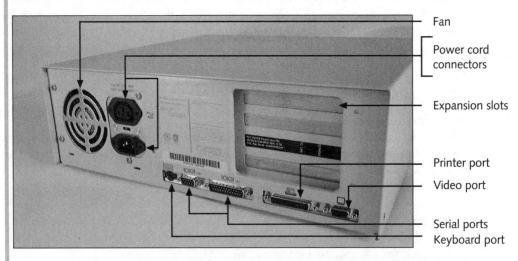

Fan

Power cord connectors

Expansion slots

Printer port

Video port

Serial ports
Keyboard port

Figure 4-16   Because the expansion slots are running parallel to the motherboard on the bottom of this desktop case, you know a riser card is used

$A^{+CORE}_{1.1}$ **Tower Cases**

A **tower case** can be as high as two feet and has room for several drives. Often used for servers, this type of case is also good for PC users who anticipate upgrading, because tower cases provide maximum space for working inside a computer and moving components around. Variations in tower cases include the minitower, midsize tower, and full-size tower.

Midsize towers, also called miditowers, are the most popular. They are midrange in size and generally have around six expansion slots and four drive bays, providing moderate potential for expansion. The minitower, also called a microtower, is the smallest type of tower case and does not provide room for expansion. Figure 4-17 shows a minitower that accommodates a Baby AT or a full ATX system. Full-size towers are used for high-end personal computers and servers. They are usually built to accommodate ATX, Mini-ATX, and Baby AT systems. Figure 4-18 shows examples of each of the three main tower sizes, as well as two desktop cases.

Figure 4-17   Minitower for a Baby AT or full ATX motherboard

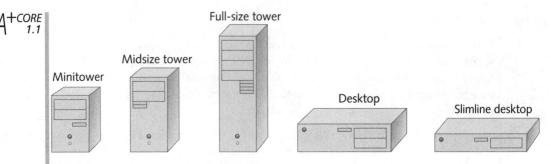

Figure 4-18   Tower and desktop cases

Notebook Cases

Notebook cases are used for portable computers that have all the components of a desktop computer. The cost and power of notebook systems varies widely. As with other small systems, notebooks can present difficulties in expansion. The smallest notebook cases are called subnotebooks. Notebook designs are often highly proprietary, but are generally designed to conserve space, allow portability, use less power, and produce less heat. The case fan in a notebook usually attaches to a thermometer and runs only when temperature needs to be lowered. Additionally, the transformer and rectifier functions of the power supply are often moved to an AC adapter on the power cable.

In summary, when selecting a computer case, remember that the case needs to fit its intended use. Many different manufacturers make cases and power supplies. Some specialize in high-end custom systems, while others make a variety of cases, from rack-mounted servers to low-profile desktops. Table 4-3 lists a few case and power supply vendors.

Table 4-3   Manufacturers of cases and power supplies for personal computers

Manufacturer	Web Site
Alien Media	www.alienmedia.com.au/cases
Axxion Group Corporation	www.axxion.com
Sunus Sunteck	www.suntekgroup.com
Enlight Corporation	www.enlightcorp.com
PC Power and Cooling	www.pcpowerandcooling.com
PCI Case Group	www.pcicase.co.uk/menu.htm
Casse Industry Corp.	www.kingspao.com
Colorcase	www.colorcase.com

DETECTING AND CORRECTING POWER SUPPLY PROBLEMS

If you assemble a PC from parts, most often you purchase a computer case with the power supply already installed. However, you might need to exchange the power supply of an existing PC because it is damaged or you need to upgrade to one with more power. In this section, you will learn how to troubleshoot the power system and power supply in your computer as well as how to upgrade and install power supplies. The first step in this process is to learn how to measure the voltage of a power supply.

Measuring the Voltage of a Power Supply

If you suspect a problem with a power supply, the simplest and preferred solution is to replace it with a new one. However, in some situations, you might want to measure the voltage output. When a power supply works properly, voltages all fall within an acceptable range (plus or minus 10 percent). However, be aware that even if measured voltage falls within the appropriate range, a power supply can still cause problems. This is because problems with power supplies are intermittent—in other words, they come and go. Therefore, if the voltages are correct, you should still suspect the power supply is the problem when certain symptoms are present. (You will learn about troubleshooting power supplies later in the chapter.) To learn for certain whether the power supply is the problem, replace it with a unit you know is good.

Using a Multimeter

A voltmeter measures the difference in electrical potential between two points, in volts, and an ammeter measures electrical current in amps. Figure 4-19 shows a **multimeter**, which can be used as either a voltmeter or an ammeter or can measure resistance or continuity (the presence of a complete circuit with no resistance to current), depending on a dial or function switch setting.

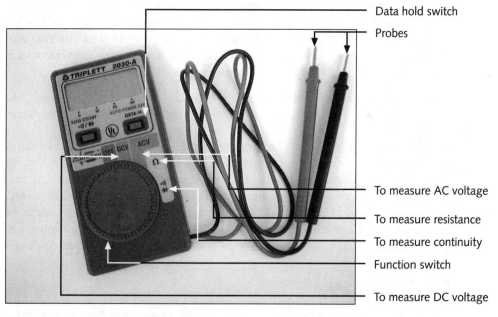

Figure 4-19   A digital multimeter

Less expensive multimeters commonly measure voltage, resistance, and continuity, but not amps. Measure voltage and amps while the electricity is on. Measure resistance and continuity while the electricity is off. For the specific details of how to use your multimeter, consult the manual, which explains what you can measure with the multimeter and how to use it.

Multimeters are sometimes small, portable, battery-powered units. Larger ones are designed to sit on a countertop and are powered by a wall outlet. A multimeter can provide either a digital or an analog display. A digital display shows the readings as digits on an LCD (liquid crystal display) panel. A digital multimeter is sometimes called a DMM (digital multimeter) or a DVM (digital voltage meter). An analog display shows the readings as a needle moving across a scale of values.

Before you begin to use a multimeter, you must tell it three things: (1) what you want it to measure (voltage, current, or resistance), (2) whether the current is AC or DC, and (3) what range of values it should expect. If you are measuring the voltage output from a wall outlet (110–120 V), the range should be much higher than when you are measuring the voltage output of a computer power supply (3–12 V). Setting the range high assures you that the meter can handle a large input without pegging the needle (exceeding the highest value the meter is designed to measure) or damaging the meter. However, if you set the range too high, you might not see the voltage register at all. Set the range low enough to ensure that the measure is as accurate as you need but not lower than the expected voltage. When you set the range too low on some digital multimeters, the meter reads OL on the display.

For example, to measure the voltage of house current, if you expect the voltage to be 115 volts, set the voltage range from 0 to somewhere between 120 and 130 volts. You want the high end of the range to be slightly higher than the expected voltage. To protect the meter, most meters do not allow a very large voltage or current into the meter when the range is set low. Some multimeters are **autorange meters**, which sense the quantity of input and set the range accordingly.

A meter comes with two test probes. One is usually red and the other black. Install the red probe at the positive (+) jack on the meter and the black probe at the negative (–) jack.

How to Measure Voltage   To measure voltage, place the other end of the black probe at the ground point and the other end of the red probe at the hot point, without disconnecting anything in the circuit and with the power on. For example, to measure voltage using the multimeter in Figure 4-19, turn the function switch dial to DCV for DC voltage measurement. This meter is autoranging, so that's all that needs to be set. With the power on, place the two probes in position and read the voltage from the LCD panel. The DATA-H (data hold) switch allows you to freeze the displayed reading.

CAUTION

When using a multimeter to measure voltage, current, or resistance, be careful not to touch a chip with the probes.

How to Measure Current   In most troubleshooting situations, you will measure voltage, not current. However, you should know how to measure current, which is discussed here. To measure current in amps, the multimeter itself must be part of the circuit. Disconnect the circuit at some point so that you can connect the multimeter in line to find a measure in amps. Not all multimeters can measure amps.

How to Measure Continuity   You can also use a multimeter to measure continuity. If there is little or no resistance (less than 20 ohms gives continuity in a PC) in a wire or a closed connection between two points, the path for electricity between the two points is unhindered or "continuous." This measurement is taken with no electricity present in the circuit.

For example, if you want to know that pin 2 on one end of a serial cable is connected to pin 3 on the other end of the cable, set the multimeter to measure continuity, and work without connecting the cable to anything. Put one probe on pin 2 at one end of the cable and the other probe on pin 3 at the other end. If the two pins connect, the multimeter shows a reading on the LCD panel, or a buzzer sounds (see the multimeter documentation). In this situation, you might find that the probe is too large to extend into the pinhole of the female connection of the cable. A straightened small paper clip works well here to extend the probe. However, be very careful not to use a paper clip that is too thick and might widen the size of the pinhole, because this can later prevent the pinhole from making a good connection.

One way to determine if a fuse is good is to measure continuity. Set a multimeter to measure continuity, and place its probes on each end of the fuse. If the fuse has continuity, then it is good. If the multimeter has no continuity setting, set it to measure resistance. If the reading in ohms is approximately zero, there is no resistance and the fuse is good. If the reading is infinity, resistance is infinite; the fuse is blown and should not be used.

How to Measure the Voltage of a Power Supply

To determine whether a power supply is working properly, measure the voltage of each circuit the power supply supports. First, open the computer case and identify all power cords coming from the power supply. Look for the cords from the power supply to the motherboard and other power cords to the drives (see Figure 4-20).

The computer must be turned on to test the power supply output. Be very careful not to touch any chips or disturb any circuit boards as you work. The voltage output from the power supply is no more than 14 volts, not enough to seriously hurt you if you accidentally touch a hot probe. However, you can damage the computer if you are not careful.

You can hurt yourself if you accidentally create a short circuit from the power supply to ground through the probe. If you touch the probe to the hot circuit and also to ground, you divert current from the computer circuit and through the probe to ground. This short might be enough to cause a spark or to melt the probe, which can happen if you allow the two probes to touch while one of them is attached to the hot circuit and the other is attached to ground. Make sure the probes only touch one metal object, preferably only a single power pin on a connector, or you could cause a short.

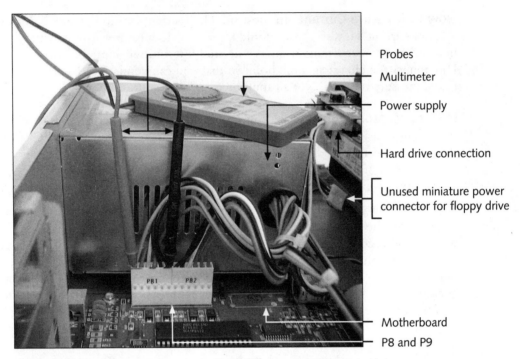

Figure 4-20   Multimeter measuring voltage on an AT motherboard

Because of the danger of touching a hot probe to a ground probe, you might prefer not to put the black probe into a ground lead too close to the hot probe. Instead, when the directions say to place the black probe on a lead very close to the hot probe, you can use a black wire lead on an unused power supply connection meant for a hard drive. The idea is that the black probe should always be placed on a ground or black lead.

All ground leads are considered at ground, no matter what number they are assigned. Therefore, you can consider all black leads to be equal. For an AT motherboard, the ground leads for P8 and P9 are the four black center leads 5, 6, 7, and 8. For an ATX motherboard, the ground leads are seven black leads in center positions on the ATX P1 power connector. The ground leads for a hard drive power connection are the two black center leads, 2 and 3.

We first discuss how to measure the power output for AT and ATX motherboards and then discuss the procedure for a secondary storage device.

Measuring Voltage Output to an AT Motherboard

1. Remove the cover of the computer. The voltage range for each connection is often written on the top of the power supply. The two power connections to the motherboard are often labeled P8 and P9. Figure 4-21 shows a closeup of the two connections, P8 and P9, coming from the power supply to the motherboard. Each connection has six leads, for a total of 12 leads. Of these 12, four

are ground connections and lead 1 is a "power good" pin, used to indicate that the motherboard is receiving power. Table 4-4 lists a common arrangement for these 12 leads .

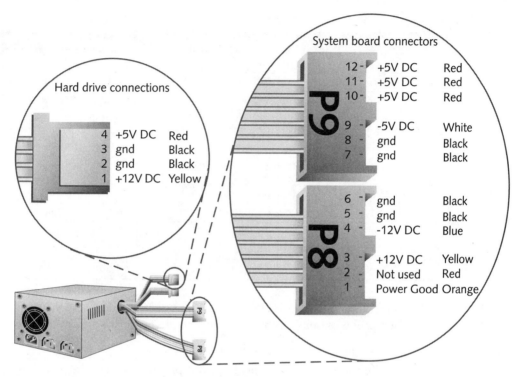

Figure 4-21 AT power supply connections

2. Set the multimeter to measure voltage in a range of 20 volts, and set the AC/DC switch to DC. Insert the black probe into the − jack and the red probe into the + jack of the meter.

3. Turn on the multimeter and turn on the computer.

4. To measure the +12-volt circuit and all four ground leads:

   a. Place the red probe on lead 3. The probe is shaped like a needle. (Alligator clips don't work too well here.) Insert the needle down into the lead housing as far as you can. Place the black probe on lead 5. The acceptable range is +10.8 to +13.2 volts.

   b. Place the red probe on lead 3, and place the black probe on lead 6. The acceptable range is +10.8 to +13.2 volts.

   c. Place the red probe on lead 3, and place the black probe on lead 7. The acceptable range is +10.8 to +13.2 volts.

   d. Place the red probe on lead 3, and place the black probe on lead 8. The acceptable range is +10.8 to +13.2 volts.

5. To measure the −12-volt circuit, place the red probe on lead 4, and place the black probe on any ground lead or on the computer case, which is also grounded. The acceptable range is −10.8 to 13.2 volts.

Table 4-4   Twelve leads to the AT motherboard from the AT power supply

Connection	Lead	Description	Acceptable Range
P8	1	"Power Good"	
	2	Not used or +5 volts	+4.4 to +5.2 volts
	3	+12 volts	+10.8 to +13.2 volts
	4	−12 volts	−10.8 to −13.2 volts
	5	Black ground	
	6	Black ground	
P9	7	Black ground	
	8	Black ground	
	9	−5 volts	−4.5 to −5.5 volts
	10	+5 volts	+4.5 to +5.5 volts
	11	+5 volts	+4.5 to +5.5 volts
	12	+5 volts	+4.5 to +5.5 volts

6. To measure the −5-volt circuit, place the red probe on lead 9, and place the black probe on any ground. The acceptable range is −4.5 to −5.5 volts.

7. To measure the three +5-volt circuits:

   a. Place the red probe on lead 10, and place the black probe on any ground. The acceptable range is +4.5 to +5.5 volts.

   b. Place the red probe on lead 11, and place the black probe on any ground. The acceptable range is +4.5 to +5.5 volts.

   c. Place the red probe on lead 12, and place the black probe on any ground. The acceptable range is +4.5 to +5.5 volts.

8. Turn off the PC and replace the cover.

Measuring Voltage Output to an ATX Motherboard   To measure the output to the ATX motherboard, follow the procedure just described for the AT motherboard. Recall that the ATX board uses 3.3, 5, and 12 volts coming from the power supply. Figure 4-22 shows the power output of each pin on the connector. Looking at Figure 4-22, you can see the distinguishing shape of each side of the connector. Notice the different hole shapes (square or rounded) on each side of the connector, ensuring that the plug from the power supply is oriented correctly in the connector. Also notice the notch on the connector and also on the pinout diagram on the right side of the figure. This notch helps orient you as you read the pinouts. Table 4-5 lists the leads to the motherboard and their acceptable voltage ranges.

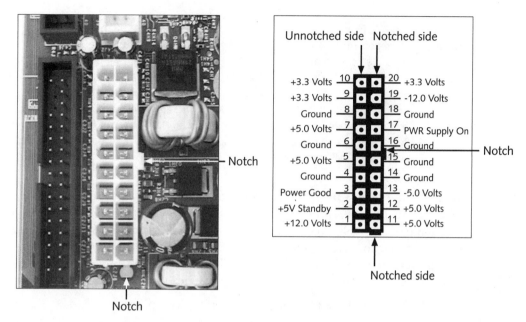

Figure 4-22   Power connection on an ATX motherboard

Table 4-5   Twenty leads to the ATX motherboard from the ATX power supply

Unnotched Side			Notched Side		
Lead	Description	Acceptable Range	Lead	Description	Acceptable Range (Volts)
1	+12 volts	+10.8 to +13.2V	11	+5 volts	+4.5 to +5.5V
2	+5 volts standby	+4.5 to +5.5V	12	+5 volts	+4.5 to +5.5V
3	Power Good		13	-5 volts	-4.5 to -5.5V
4	Black ground		14	Black ground	
5	+5 volts	+4.5 to +5.5V	15	Black ground	
6	Black ground		16	Black ground	
7	+5 volts	+4.5 to +5.5V	17	Pwr supply on	
8	Black ground		18	Black ground	
9	+3.3 volts	+3.1 to +3.5V	19	-12 volts	-10.8 to -13.2V
10	+3.3 volts	+3.1 to +3.5V	20	+3.3 volts	+3.1 to +3.5V

Dell ATX power supplies and motherboards made after 1998 might not use the standard P1 pinouts for ATX, although the power connectors look the same. For this reason, *never* use a Dell power supply with a non-Dell motherboard, or a Dell motherboard with a non-Dell power supply, without first verifying that the power connector pinouts match; otherwise, you might destroy the power supply, the motherboard, or both. Centrix International Corp. (*www.centrix-intl.com*) sells a pinout converter to convert the P1 connector of a Dell power supply or motherboard to standard ATX. Also, PC Power and Cooling (*www.pcpowerandcooling.com*) makes a power supply modified to work with a Dell motherboard.

Testing the Power Output to a Floppy or Hard Drive   The power cords to the floppy disk drive, hard drive, and CD-ROM drive all supply the same voltage: one +5-volt circuit and one +12-volt circuit. The power connection to any drive uses four leads; the two outside connections are hot, and the two inside connections are ground (see Figure 4-22). The power connection to a 3.5-inch floppy disk drive is usually a miniature connection, as shown in Figure 4-21. Follow these steps to measure the voltage to any drive:

1. With the drive plugged in, turn on the computer.

2. Set the multimeter to measure voltage as described earlier.

3. Place the red probe on lead 1, shown in the drive connection callout in Figure 4-22, and place the black probe on lead 2 or 3 (ground). The acceptable range is +10.8 to +13.2 volts.

4. Place the red probe on lead 4, and place the black probe on lead 2 or 3 (ground). The acceptable range is +4.5 to +5.5 volts.

You may choose to alter the method you use to ground the black probe. In Step 4 above, the red probe and black probe are very close to each other. You may choose to keep them farther apart by placing the black probe in a ground lead of an unused hard drive connection.

Upgrading Your Power Supply

A+CORE
1.10

Sometimes a power supply upgrade is necessary when you add new devices. If you are installing a hard drive or DVD drive and are concerned that the power supply is not adequate, test it after you finish the installation. Make as many as possible of the devices in your system work at the same time. For example, you can make both the new drive and the floppy drive work at the same time by copying files from one to the other. If the new drive and the floppy drive each work independently, but data errors occur when both work at the same time, suspect a shortage of electrical power.

If you prefer a more technical approach, you can estimate how much total wattage your system needs by calculating the watts for each circuit and adding them together, as discussed earlier in the section, "Surge Protection and Battery Backup." In most cases, the computer's power supply is more than adequate if you add only one or two new devices.

A+*CORE* *1.2* Most often you purchase a computer case with a power supply already installed, but you can purchase power supplies separately from cases. Power supplies for microcomputers range from 200 watts for a small desktop computer system to 600 watts for a tower floor model that uses many multimedia or other power-hungry devices. Most case vendors also make power supplies (see Table 4-3).

The easiest way to fix a power supply you suspect is faulty is to replace it. You can determine if the power supply really is the problem by turning off the PC, opening the computer case, and setting the new power supply on top of the old one. Disconnect the old power supply's cords and plug the PC devices into the new power supply. Turn on the PC and verify that the new power supply solves your problem before installing it.

Follow this procedure to install a power supply:

1. Turn off the power.

2. Remove all external power cables from the power supply connections.

3. Remove the case cover.

4. Disconnect all power cords from the power supply to other devices.

5. Determine which components must be removed before the power supply can be safely removed from the case. You might need to remove the hard drive, several cards, or the CD-ROM drive. In some cases, you may even need to remove the motherboard.

6. Remove all the components necessary to get to the power supply. Remember to protect the components from static electricity as you work.

7. Unscrew the screws on the back of the computer case that hold the power supply to the case.

8. Look on the bottom or back of the case for slots that hold the power supply in position. Often the power supply must be shifted in one direction to free it from the slots.

9. Remove the power supply.

10. Place the new power supply in position, sliding it into the slots the old power supply used.

11. Replace the power supply screws.

12. Replace all other components.

13. Before replacing the case cover, connect the power cords, turn on the PC, and verify that all is working.

14. Turn off the PC and replace the cover.

Introduction to Troubleshooting

A^{+CORE} 2.1 2.2 Troubleshooting a PC problem begins with isolating it into one of two categories: problems that prevent the PC from booting and problems that occur after a successful boot. Begin by asking the user questions like these to learn as much as you can:

- Please describe the problem. What error messages, unusual displays, or failures did you see?
- When did the problem start?
- What was the situation when the problem occurred?
- What programs or software were you using?
- Did you move your computer system recently?
- Has there been a recent thunderstorm or electrical problem?
- Have you made any hardware, software, or configuration changes?
- Has someone else used your computer recently?
- Can you show me how to reproduce the problem?

Next, ask yourself, "Does the PC boot properly?" Figure 4-23 shows you the direction to take, depending on the answer. If the screen is blank and the entire system is "dead"—no lights, no spinning drive or fan—then proceed to troubleshoot the power system.

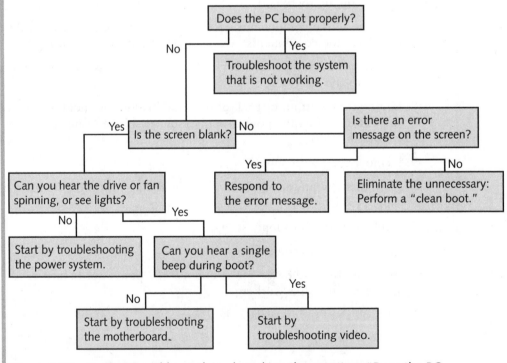

Figure 4-23   Begin PC problem solving by asking the question, "Does the PC boot properly?"

$A+$CORE
2.1
2.2

Recall from Chapter 3 that when POST completes successfully, it sounds a single beep indicating that all is well, regardless of whether the monitor is working or even present. If you hear the beep, then the problem is with the video, and the next step is to troubleshoot it. If you don't hear the beep or you hear more than one, then POST encountered an error. In that case, proceed to troubleshooting the motherboard, a subject Chapter 5 covers.

If an error message appears on the screen, then the obvious next step is to respond to the message. An example of such an error is "Keyboard not present." If the error message occurs as the OS loads, and you don't understand the message or know how to respond to it, begin by troubleshooting the OS.

If video works but the boot message is confusing or unreadable, then begin to eliminate the unnecessary. Perform a clean boot. For Windows 9x or Windows 2000/XP, the simplest way is to boot to safe mode. If that doesn't work, use your bootable rescue disk or disks.

If the PC boots properly, turn your attention to the system that is not working and begin troubleshooting there. In this chapter, since you are learning about electricity and power supplies, we will look more closely at how to troubleshoot the power system.

Troubleshooting the Power System

$A+$CORE
2.1

First, let's look at some general guidelines and some questions to ask when you have power problems:

- Are there any burnt parts or odors? (Definitely not a good sign!)
- Is everything connected and turned on? Are any cable connections loose? Is the computer plugged in?
- Are all the switches turned on? Computer? Monitor? Surge protector? Uninterruptible power supply? Separate circuit breaker? Is the wall outlet (or surge protector) good?
- If the fan is not running, turn off the computer, open the case, and check the connections to the power supply. Are they secure? Are all cards securely seated?

For most of the newer ATX power supplies, a wire runs from the power switch on the front of the ATX case to the motherboard. This wire must be connected to the pins on the motherboard and the switch turned on before power comes up. Check that the wire is connected correctly to the motherboard. Figure 4-24 shows the wire, which is labeled "REMOTE SW," connected to pins on the motherboard labeled "PWR.SW." If you are not sure of the correct connection on the motherboard, see the motherboard documentation. Next, check the voltage output from the power supply.

A+CORE
2.1

Remote SW

Figure 4-24   For an ATX power supply, the remote switch wire must be connected to the motherboard before power will come on

Then, remove all nonessential expansion cards (modem, sound card, mouse) one at a time. This verifies that they are not drawing too much power and pulling the system down. It is possible that the expansion cards are all good but that the power supply cannot provide enough current for all the add-on boards. Perhaps there are too many cards and the computer is overheating. The temperature inside the case should not exceed 113 degrees F (45 degrees C). You might need to add extra cooling fans, which the next chapter discusses.

Vacuum the entire unit, especially the power supply's fan vent, or use compressed air to blow out dust. Excessive dust insulates components and causes them to overheat. Use an ESD-safe service vac that you can purchase from electronic tools suppliers.

TIP

Remember from earlier in the chapter that strong magnetic or electrical interference can affect how a power system functions. Sometimes an old monitor emits too much static and EMF (electromagnetic force) and brings a whole system down. When you troubleshoot power problems, remember to check for sources of electrical or magnetic interference such as an old monitor or electric fan sitting near the computer case.

Troubleshooting the Power Supply Itself

Problems with the PC's power supply or the house current can express themselves in the following ways:

- The PC sometimes halts during booting. After several tries, it boots successfully.

- Error codes or beeps occur during booting, but they come and go.

- The computer stops or hangs for no reason. Sometimes it might even reboot itself.

- Memory errors appear intermittently.

- Data is written incorrectly to the hard drive.

- The keyboard stops working at odd times.

- The motherboard fails or is damaged.

- The power supply overheats and becomes hot to the touch.

An overheated system can cause intermittent problems. Use compressed air or an anti-static vacuum to remove dust from the power supply and the vents over the entire computer. Check that the power supply fan and the fan over the CPU both work.

A brownout (reduced current) of the house current or a faulty power supply might cause symptoms of electrical power problems. If you suspect the house current could be low, check other devices that are using the same circuit. A copy machine, laser printer, or other heavy equipment might be drawing too much power. Remove the other devices from the same house circuit.

A system with a standard power supply of about 250 watts that has multiple hard drives, multiple CD-ROM drives, and several expansion cards is most likely operating above the rated capacity of the power supply, which can cause the system to give unexpected reboots or intermittent, otherwise unexplained errors. Upgrade the power supply as needed to accommodate an overloaded power system.

If these suggestions don't correct the problem, check the power supply by measuring the voltage output or by exchanging it for one you know is good. For an AT motherboard, be certain to follow the black-to-black rule when attaching the power cords to the motherboard. Remember that the power supply might give correct voltages when you measure it but still be the source of problems.

An electrical conditioner might solve the problem of intermittent errors caused by noise in the power line to the PC. Try installing an electrical conditioner to monitor and condition voltage to the PC.

Troubleshooting the Power Supply Fan

An improperly working fan sometimes causes power supply problems. Usually just before a fan stops working, it hums or whines, especially when the PC is first turned on. If this has just happened, replace the fan if you are trained to service the power supply. If not, then replace the entire power supply, which is considered an **FRU (field replaceable unit)** for a PC support technician. If you replace the power supply or fan and the fan still does not work, the problem might not be the fan. A short somewhere else in the system drawing too much power might cause the problem. Don't operate the PC if the fan does not work. Computers without cooling fans can quickly overheat and

$A^{+CORE}_{2.1}$ damage chips. To troubleshoot a nonfunctional fan, which might be a symptom of another problem and not a problem of the fan itself, follow these steps:

1. Turn off the power and remove all power cord connections to all components, including the connections to the motherboard, and all power cords to drives. Turn the power back on. If the fan works, the problem is with one of the systems you disconnected, not with the power supply or its fan.

2. Turn off the power and reconnect the power cords to the drives. If the fan comes on, you can eliminate the drives as the problem. If the fan does not come on, try one drive after another until you identify the drive with the short.

3. If the drives are not the problem, suspect the motherboard subsystem. With the power off, reconnect all power cords to the drives.

4. Turn off the power and remove the power to the motherboard by disconnecting P8 and P9 or P1. Turn the power back on.

5. If the fan works, the problem is probably not the power supply but a short in one of the components powered by the power cords to the motherboard. The power to the motherboard also powers interface cards.

6. Remove all interface cards and reconnect plugs to the motherboard.

7. If the fan still works, the problem is one of the interface cards. If the fan does not work, the problem is the motherboard or something still connected to it.

Power Problems with the Motherboard

The motherboard, like all other components inside the computer case, should be grounded to the chassis. Look for a metal screw that grounds the board to the computer case. However, a short might be the problem with the electrical system if some component on the board makes improper contact with the chassis. This short can seriously damage the motherboard. Check for missing standoffs (small plastic or metal spacers that hold the motherboard a short distance away from the chassis), the problem that most often causes these improper connections.

Shorts in the circuits on the motherboard might also cause problems. Look for damage on the bottom of the motherboard. These circuits are coated with plastic, and quite often damage is difficult to spot.

Frayed wires on cable connections can also cause shorts. Disconnect hard drive cables connected directly to the motherboard. Power up with P8 and P9 or P1 connected but all cables disconnected from the motherboard. If the fan works, the problem is with one of the systems you disconnected.

CAUTION

Never replace a damaged motherboard with a good one without first testing or replacing the power supply. You don't want to subject another good board to possible damage.

A+CORE 1.2
1.9
2.1

Overheating

If your computer hangs after it has been running for a while, you may have an overheating problem. First, check whether there is airflow within the case. Open the case and make sure the CPU and power supply fans are turning and that cables will not fall into the fans and prevent them from turning when you close the case. While you have the case open, use an antistatic vacuum designed to be used around electronic equipment or a can of compressed air (both available at most computer supply stores) to blow dust off the motherboard and the CPU heat sink. Check the vents of the case, and clear any foreign material that may be blocking airflow.

After you close the case, leave your system off for a few hours. When you power up the computer again, let it run for 10 minutes, go into CMOS setup, check the temperature readings, and reboot. Next, let your system run until it shuts down. Power it up again and check the temperature in setup again. A significant difference in this reading and the first one you took after running the computer for 10 minutes indicates an overheating problem. Try adding an extra case fan or more powerful fans than those you already have. When adding extra fans, for every fan that blows air out of the case, use one that blows air into the case. Also, you can monitor the temperature inside the case using a temperature sensor that sounds an alarm when a high temperature is reached or uses software to alert you of a problem.

Be careful when trying to solve an overheating problem. Excessive heat itself may damage the CPU and the motherboard, and the hard reboots necessary when your system hangs may damage the hard drive. If you suspect damaged components, try substituting comparable components that you know are good.

ENERGY STAR SYSTEMS (THE GREEN STAR)

As you build or maintain a computer, one very important power consideration is energy efficiency and conservation. **Energy Star** systems and peripherals have the U.S. Green Star, indicating that they satisfy certain energy-conserving standards of the U.S. Environmental Protection Agency (EPA). Devices that can carry the Green Star are computers, monitors, printers, copiers, and fax machines. Qualifying devices are designed to decrease overall electricity consumption in the United States, to protect and preserve natural resources. These standards, sometimes called the **Green Standards**, generally mean that the computer or the device has a standby program that switches the device to sleep mode when it is not in use. During **sleep mode**, the device must use no more than 30 watts of power.

 TIP Office equipment is among the fastest growing source of electricity consumption in industrialized nations. Much of this electricity is wasted, because people often leave computers and other equipment on overnight. Because Energy Star devices go into sleep mode when they are unused, they create overall energy savings of about 50 percent.

Power Management Methods and Features

Computer systems use several different power management methods to conserve energy. Some are listed below:

- Advanced Power Management (APM), championed by Intel and Microsoft
- AT Attachment (ATA) for IDE drives
- Display Power Management Signaling (DPMS) standards for monitors and video cards
- Advanced Configuration and Power Interface (ACPI), used with Windows 98 and Windows 2000/XP and supported by system BIOS

These energy-saving methods are designed to work incrementally, depending on how long the PC is idle. The following sections discuss several specific features that can sometimes be enabled and adjusted using CMOS setup or using the OS. In CMOS setup, a feature might not be available, setup might include additional features, or a feature might be labeled differently from those described next. (How to change these settings is covered in the next chapter.)

- *Green timer on the motherboard.* This sets the number of minutes of inactivity that must pass before the CPU goes into sleep mode. You can enable or disable the setting and select the number of minutes.

- *Doze time.* **Doze time** is the time that elapses before the system reduces 80 percent of its power consumption. Different systems accomplish this in different ways. For example, when one system enters doze mode, the system BIOS slows down the bus clock speed.

- *Standby time.* **Standby time** is the time that elapses before the system reduces 92 percent of its power consumption. For example, a system might accomplish this by changing the system speed from turbo to slow and suspending the video signal.

- *Suspend time.* **Suspend time** is the time that elapses before the system reduces its power consumption by 99 percent. The way this reduction is accomplished varies. The CPU clock might be stopped and the video signal suspended. After entering suspend mode, the system needs warmup time so that the CPU, monitor, and other components can reach full activity.

- *Hard drive standby time.* **Hard drive standby time** is the amount of time before a hard drive shuts down.

Figure 4-25 shows the Power Management Setup screen of the CMOS setup for Award BIOS for an ATX Pentium II motherboard.

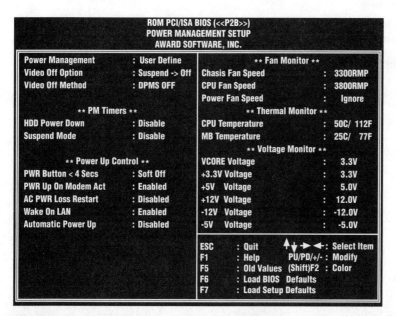

ROM PCI/ISA BIOS (<<P2B>>)
POWER MANAGEMENT SETUP
AWARD SOFTWARE, INC.

Power Management	: User Define	** Fan Monitor **	
Video Off Option	: Suspend -> Off	Chasis Fan Speed	: 3300RMP
Video Off Method	: DPMS OFF	CPU Fan Speed	: 3800RMP
		Power Fan Speed	: Ignore
** PM Timers **		** Thermal Monitor **	
HDD Power Down	: Disable	CPU Temperature	: 50C/ 112F
Suspend Mode	: Disable	MB Temperature	: 25C/ 77F
		** Voltage Monitor **	
** Power Up Control **		VCORE Voltage	: 3.3V
PWR Button < 4 Secs	: Soft Off	+3.3V Voltage	: 3.3V
PWR Up On Modem Act	: Enabled	+5V Voltage	: 5.0V
AC PWR Loss Restart	: Disabled	+12V Voltage	: 12.0V
Wake On LAN	: Enabled	-12V Voltage	: -12.0V
Automatic Power Up	: Disabled	-5V Voltage	: -5.0V

ESC : Quit	↑↓ → ← : Select Item
F1 : Help	PU/PD/+/- : Modify
F5 : Old Values	(Shift)F2 : Color
F6 : Load BIOS Defaults	
F7 : Load Setup Defaults	

Figure 4-25   A Power Management Setup screen showing power management features

Using the Video options on the left of the screen, you can enable or disable power management of the monitor. With power management enabled, you can control Energy Star features. The PM Timers feature controls doze, standby, and suspend modes for the hard drive. The Power Up Control determines the way the system can be controlled when it starts or when power to the computer is interrupted. The features on the right side of the screen monitor the power supply fan, CPU fan, optional chassis fan, temperatures of the CPU and the motherboard (MB), and voltage output to the CPU and motherboard.

Energy Star Monitors

Most computers and monitors sold today are Energy Star compliant, displaying the green Energy Star logo onscreen when the PC is booting. In order for a monitor's power-saving feature to function, the video card or computer must also support this function. Most monitors that follow the Energy Star standards adhere to the **Display Power Management Signaling (DPMS)** specifications developed by VESA (Video Electronics Standards Association), which allow for the video card and monitor to go into sleep mode simultaneously.

To view and change energy settings of an Energy Star monitor Using Windows 2000, right-click on the desktop and select Properties. The Desktop Properties window opens. Click the Screen Saver tab. If your monitor is Energy Star compliant, you will see the Energy Star logo at the bottom. When you click Power…, the Power Options Properties window opens, and you can change your power options (see Figure 4-26). Your power options might differ depending on the power management features your BIOS supports.

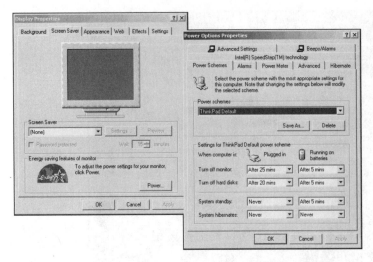

Figure 4-26   Changing power options in Windows 2000

 TIP   Problems might occur if system BIOS is turning off the monitor because of power management settings, and Windows 9x is also turning off the monitor. If the system hangs when you try to get the monitor going again, try disabling one or the other setting.

CHAPTER SUMMARY

❑ A combination of voltage, current, and resistance creates an electrical circuit.

❑ Electrical voltage is a measure of the potential difference in an electrical system.

❑ Electrical current is measured in amps, and electrical resistance is measured in ohms. One volt drives a current of one amp through a resistance of one ohm, which is one watt of power.

❑ Wattage is a measure of electrical power. Wattage is calculated by multiplying volts by amps in a system.

❑ Microcomputers require direct current (DC), which is converted from alternating current (AC) by the PC's power supply inside the computer case.

❑ A PC power supply is actually a transformer and rectifier, rather than a supplier, of power.

❑ Materials used to make electrical components include conductors, insulators, and semiconductors.

❑ A transistor is a gate or switch for an electrical signal, a capacitor holds an electrical charge, a diode allows electricity to flow in one direction, and a resistor limits electrical current.

4

❐ To protect a computer system against ESD, use a ground bracelet, ground mat, and static shielding bags.

❐ Protect a computer system against EMI by covering expansion slots (which also reduces dust inside the case), by not placing the system close to or on the same circuit as high-powered electrical equipment, and by using line conditioners.

❐ Devices that control the electricity to a computer include surge suppressors, line conditioners, and UPSs.

❐ A surge suppressor protects a computer against damaging spikes in electrical voltage.

❐ Line conditioners level the AC to reduce brownouts and spikes.

❐ A UPS provides enough power to perform an orderly shutdown during a blackout.

❐ There are two kinds of UPSs: the true UPS (called the inline UPS), and the standby UPS.

❐ The inline UPS is the more expensive, because it provides continuous power. The standby UPS must switch from one circuit to another when a blackout begins.

❐ Utility software at a remote computer or a computer connected to the UPS through a serial cable can control and manage an intelligent UPS.

❐ Data line protectors are small surge suppressors designed to protect modems from spikes on telephone lines.

❐ A form factor is a set of specifications for the size and configuration of hardware components such as cases, power supplies, and motherboards.

❐ The most common form factor today is ATX. There is an ATX variation called Mini-ATX. ATX superseded the earlier AT and Baby AT form factors.

❐ Other form factors include LPX and NLX, in which expansion cards are mounted on a riser card that plugs into the motherboard.

❐ Case types include desktop, low-profile or slimline desktops, minitower, midi-tower, full-size tower, and notebook. The most popular case type in use today is the miditower.

❐ A multimeter is a device that measures volts, amps, ohms, and continuity in an electrical system.

❐ Before replacing a damaged motherboard in a PC, first measure the output of the power supply to make sure that it did not cause the damage.

❐ A faulty power supply can cause memory errors, data errors, system hangs, or reboots; it can damage a motherboard or other components.

❐ To reduce energy consumption, the U.S. Environmental Protection Agency has established Energy Star standards for electronic devices,.

❐ Devices that are Energy Star compliant go into sleep mode in which they use less than 30 watts of power.

❐ PCs that are Energy Star compliant often have CMOS settings that affect the Energy Star options available on the PC.

KEY TERMS

active backplane

alternating current (AC)

ammeter

ampere or amp (A)

AT

ATX

autorange meter

Baby AT

backplane system

brownouts

bus riser

capacitor

clamping voltage

compact case

continuity

data line protector

diode

direct current (DC)

Display Power Management Signaling (DPMS)

doze time

electromagnetic interference (EMI)

Energy Star

electrostatic discharge (ESD)

field replaceable unit (FRU)

flexATX

form factor

full AT

Green Standards

ground bracelet

hard drive standby time

intelligent UPS

line conditioner

line-interactive UPS

low-profile case

LPX

microATX

Mini-ATX

Mini-LPX

multimeter

NLX

ohms (Ω)

passive backplane

power conditioner

rectifier

resistance

resistor

riser card

sleep mode

slimline case

soft power

soft switch

spikes

standby time

static electricity

surge suppressor or surge protector

suspend time

tower case

transformer

transistor

UPS (uninterruptible power supply)

volt (V)

voltage

voltmeter

wattage

watt (W)

REVIEW QUESTIONS

1. What are the two main types of power supplies used in PCs, and what power supply connectors do each use to power the motherboard?

2. What is the color code associated with power supply voltages used in a PC?

3. Explain the difference between the mini and Molex connectors, and describe the kinds of devices typically used with each connector.

4. Explain each of the two voltages that are supplied to each Molex connector, and explain what each voltage is responsible for controlling.

5. Explain the difference between spikes, surges, and sags, and what types of devices can be used to protect sensitive electronic equipment from the effects of these problems.

6. Besides offering power to a device in the event of a power failure, what else does the UPS provide the user?

7. Assuming an AT-class power supply, which of the answers below represents the complete set of DC voltages offered?

    a. +/– 5V, +/– 12V

    b. +/– 5V, +/– 12V, +3.3V

    c. +5V, +12V, +3.3V

    d. 120V

    e. None of the above; the AT-class power supply does not provide DC voltages.

8. Assuming a load of 6.75A, determine the amount of power required to be supplied by the power authority in the United States.

9. Which of the following electrical quantities best describes the flow of electrons through a device?

    a. Volts

    b. Amps

    c. Resistance

    d. Power

    e. None of the above

10. Which of the following can potentially render a computer inoperable due to its destructive properties?

    a. RAM

    b. ROM

    c. ESD

    d. EMI

    e. None of the above

11. At the very least, which type of device should be used to protect a computer from extreme power spikes?

    a. A new power supply

    b. A new computer

    c. A UPS

    d. A surge suppressor

    e. None of the above

4

12. Which of the following is the recommended place to physically connect the wire that extends out from the ground strap?

  a. The HOT lead of the AC outlet

  b. One of the +5V connections throughout the system

  c. The metal frame of the computer case

  d. The plastic enclosure of the keyboard

  e. None of the above; there is no need of such a cable.

Match the following components with their function or most significant attribute:

13. Transistor   a. device used to store energy and should be handled with care due to this characteristic

14. Diode   b. device that is used to allow the flow of current on a single direction only

15. Capacitor   c. device that is often referred to as an electronic switch, one that was used to replace vacuum tubes due to its high-speed switching capability

                   d. device that is used to supply four different voltages to a motherboard and peripheral devices

Match the following components with their function or most significant attribute:

16. Amp   a. unit given for the amount of electrical power consumed by a particular device

17. Watt   b. unit given to represent the amount of current passing through a particular circuit

18. Ohm   c. unit given to represent the amount of electrical resistance experienced in an electrical circuit

                   d. unit given to represent the potential difference between two points on a device

19. The primary function of the power supply is to:

  a. Convert AC voltage to DC voltage

  b. Convert DC voltage to AC voltage

  c. Convert DC voltage to DC voltage

  d. Convert AC voltage to AC voltage

20. A technician decides to use a volt-ohm meter (VOM) to check if a fuse is good or not. The VOM produces a reading of zero ohms. What does this indicate to the technician?

  a. That the VOM was not set on the proper scale

  b. That the fuse is good

  c. That the fuse is bad

  d. That the fuse is not powered

  e. None of the above

5

THE MOTHERBOARD

In this chapter, you will learn:

- ♦ About the types of motherboards
- ♦ About components on the motherboard
- ♦ A basic procedure for building a computer
- ♦ How to install a motherboard
- ♦ How to troubleshoot a motherboard

Chapter 1 introduced the basic hardware components of a computer. In this chapter, we begin to examine in detail how the components of a computer work in harmony and with accuracy. Our starting point is the motherboard, the central site of computer logic circuitry and the location of the most important microchip in the computer, the CPU.

 To understand the ideas in this chapter, you should (1) know the definitions of bit, byte, kilobyte, and hexadecimal (hex), and (2) be able to read memory addresses written in hex. (See Appendix C.)

TYPES OF MOTHERBOARDS

A+CORE
1.1
1.2
1.10
4.3

A motherboard's primary purpose is to house the CPU and allow all devices to communicate with it and with each other. As you learned in the last chapter, the two most popular motherboards are the older AT and the newer ATX. The AT motherboard has a power connection for 5- and 12-volt lines coming from the power supply. To accommodate newer CPUs that use less voltage, the ATX has lines for 5, 12, and 3.3 volts from the power supply. Figure 5-1 shows that the ATX motherboard uses a single 20-pin power connection called the **P1 connector**, but the AT board uses two power connections, the **P8 connector** and the **P9 connector**.

Each board is available in two sizes. ATX boards include more power-management features, support faster systems, and are easier to install. Table 5-1 summarizes AT and ATX boards and their form factors.

Table 5-1   Types of motherboards

Type of Motherboard	Description
AT	• Oldest type of motherboard still used in some systems • Uses P8 and P9 power connections (see Figure 5-1) • Measures 30.5 cm × 33 cm (12 inches × 13 inches)
Baby AT	• Smaller version of AT. Small size is possible because motherboard logic is stored on a smaller chip set. • Uses P8 and P9 power connections • Measures 33 cm × 22 cm (12 inches × 8.7 inches)
ATX	• Developed by Intel for Pentium systems • Has a more conveniently accessible layout than AT boards • Includes a power-on switch that can be software-enabled and extra power connections for extra fans • Uses a P1 connector (see Figure 5-1) • Measures 30.5 cm × 24.4 cm (12 inches × 9.6 inches)
Mini ATX	• An ATX board with a more compact design • Measures 28.4 cm × 20.8 cm (11.2 inches × 8.2 inches)

The main components on a motherboard follow:

■ CPU and its accompanying chip set (recall that the chip set is a group of chips on the motherboard that controls the timing and flow of data and instructions to and from the CPU)

■ System clock

$A^{+CORE}_{\ \ \ 1.1}$
1.10
4.3

5

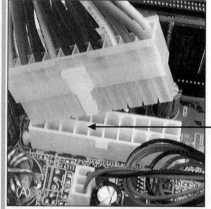

— P1 on an ATX motherboard

(A)

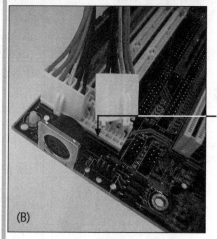

— P8 and P9 on an AT motherboard

(B)

Figure 5-1   ATX uses a single P1 power connection (A), but AT type motherboards use P8 and P9 power connections (B)

- ROM BIOS
- CMOS configuration chip and its battery
- RAM
- RAM cache (optional)
- System bus with expansion slots
- Jumpers and DIP switches
- Ports directly on the board
- Power supply connections

Of the components listed, you can replace or upgrade the following five: CPU, ROM BIOS chip, CMOS battery, RAM, and RAM cache. Because you can exchange these

A+CORE
1.1
1.10
4.3

items without returning the motherboard to the manufacturer, they are called field replaceable units (FRUs).

Before examining the most important motherboard components, let's look at the motherboard itself as a component (see Figures 5-2 and 5-3).

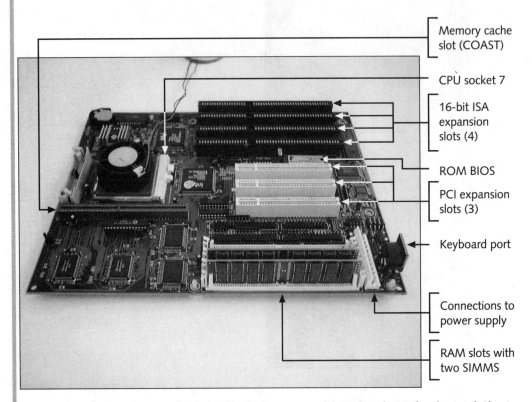

Memory cache slot (COAST)

CPU socket 7

16-bit ISA expansion slots (4)

ROM BIOS

PCI expansion slots (3)

Keyboard port

Connections to power supply

RAM slots with two SIMMS

Figure 5-2 A typical AT motherboard with memory cache and socket 7 for the Intel Classic Pentium CPU. The CPU with a fan on top is installed as well as two SIMM memory modules

When you buy a motherboard, your selection determines the following components:

- Types and speeds of CPU you can use

- Chip set on the board (already installed)

- Memory cache type and size

- Types and number of expansion slots: ISA, PCI, and AGP

- Type of memory, including what kind and how much of SRAM (on-board or inside CPU housing) and DRAM (SIMMs, DIMMs, or RIMMs)

- Maximum amount of memory you can install on the board and the incremental amounts by which you can upgrade memory

5

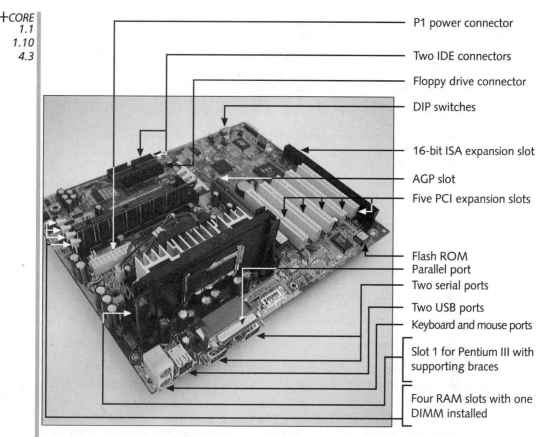

P1 power connector

Two IDE connectors

Floppy drive connector

DIP switches

16-bit ISA expansion slot

AGP slot

Five PCI expansion slots

Flash ROM
Parallel port

Two serial ports

Two USB ports

Keyboard and mouse ports

Slot 1 for Pentium III with
supporting braces

Four RAM slots with one
DIMM installed

Figure 5-3 An ATX motherboard with a Pentium III and one DIMM module installed

- Type of case you can use
- ROM BIOS (already installed)
- Type of keyboard connector
- Presence or absence of different types of proprietary video and/or proprietary local bus slots
- Presence or absence of IDE controllers and SCSI controller
- Presence or absence of COM ports, LPT ports, and mouse port

Because the motherboard determines so many of your computer's features, selecting the motherboard is a very important decision when you purchase a computer or assemble one from parts. Depending on which applications and peripheral devices you plan to use with the computer, you can take one of three approaches to selecting a motherboard. The first option is to select the board that provides the most room for expansion, so you can upgrade and exchange components and add devices easily. A second approach is to select the board that best suits the needs of the computer's current configuration, knowing that when you need to upgrade, you will likely switch to new technology and a new motherboard. The third approach is to select a motherboard that meets your present needs with moderate room for expansion.

Ask the following questions when selecting a motherboard:

- Does the motherboard support the CPU you plan to use?
- What type of BIOS does the motherboard use?
- What bus speeds and type of memory does the board support, and how much memory can the board hold?
- Does the board use many embedded devices?
- Does the board fit the case you plan to use?
- Does the board support your legacy cards?
- What is the warranty on the board?
- How extensive and user-friendly is the documentation?
- How much support does the manufacturer supply for the board?

Sometimes a motherboard contains a component more commonly offered as a separate device. A component on the board is called an embedded component or an on-board component. One example is support for video. The video port might be on the motherboard or might require a video card. The cost of a motherboard with an embedded component is usually less than the combined cost of a motherboard with no embedded component and an expansion card. If you plan to expand, be cautious about choosing a proprietary board that has many embedded components. Often such boards do not easily accept add-on devices from other manufacturers. For example, if you plan to add a more powerful video card, you might not want to choose a motherboard that contains an embedded video controller. Even though you can often set a switch on the motherboard to disable the proprietary video controller, there is little advantage to paying the extra money for it.

If you have an embedded component, make sure you can disable the component so you can use another external component if needed. You disable a component on the motherboard through jumpers on the board or through CMOS setup.

Table 5-2 lists some manufacturers of motherboards and their Web addresses.

Table 5-2   Major manufacturers of motherboards

Manufacturer	Web Address
Motherboards.com	www.motherboards.com
Abit	www.abit.com.tw
American Megatrends, Inc. (AMI)	www.megatrends.com or www.ami.com
ASUS	www.asus.com
Dell	www.dell.com
First International Computer of America, Inc.	www.fica.com
Gateway	www.gateway.com
Gigabyte Technology Co., Ltd.	us.giga-byte.com
IBM	www.ibm.com
Intel Corporation	www.intel.com
Iwill Corporation	www.iwill.net
Supermicro Computer, Inc.	www.supermicro.com
Tyan Computer Corporation	www.tyan.com

COMPONENTS ON THE MOTHERBOARD

Now that you have learned about types of motherboards, let's take a look at some components on the motherboard: the system clock, the CPU and chip set, ROM BIOS, RAM, buses and expansion slots, and components used to change hardware configuration settings (jumpers, DIP switches, and CMOS). You will learn where these components are on the motherboard and how they function.

The System Clock

Remember from Chapter 1 that the motherboard contains a system clock that keeps the beat for many motherboard activities. We use units called megahertz (MHz) to measure clock frequency. One megahertz (MHz) is equal to 1,000,000 beats, or cycles, of the clock per second. A single clock beat or cycle was once the smallest unit of processing the CPU or another device could execute, meaning that it could only do one thing for each beat of the clock. Today some CPUs can perform two activities per clock cycle.

Although the speed at which a CPU can operate is often called the CPU speed, it is more accurate—but less common—to speak of the CPU frequency. Speed implies continuous motion, and nothing is continuous about the way a CPU works. It works by doing something, waiting for the clock beat, doing something, waiting for the clock beat, and so forth. Activities are binary: doing and waiting, and are measured in frequency of activity. For example, you might say that a CPU can operate at a frequency of 550 MHz, but we inaccurately call this the speed of the CPU.

A **wait state** occurs when the CPU must wait for another component, for example, when slower dynamic RAM reads or writes data. To allow time for slow operation, CMOS setup information specifies that the CPU maintain a wait state. For example, if the CPU normally can do something in two clock beats, it is told to wait an extra clock beat, meaning that its cycle takes a total of three clock beats. It works for two beats and then waits one beat, which makes a 50 percent slowdown. Wait states might be incorporated to slow the CPU so that the rest of the motherboard activity can keep up. Wait states are set as part of the motherboard's default settings and are only changed in rare circumstances, for example, when the board becomes unstable.

The CPU and the Chip Set

IBM and IBM-compatible computers manufactured today use microprocessor chips made by Intel (*www.intel.com*) or AMD (*www.amd.com*), or to a lesser degree by Cyrix, which is currently owned by VIA Technologies (*www.via.com.tw*), or other manufacturers. Early CPUs by Intel were identified by model numbers: 8088, 8086, 80286, 386, and 486. After the 486 Intel introduced the Pentium CPU, and several Intel CPUs that followed include Pentium in their names. The model numbers can be written with or without the 80 prefix and are sometimes preceded with an i, as in 80486, 486, or i486.

How the CPU Works

The CPU contains three basic components: an input/output (I/O) unit, one or more arithmetic logic units (ALU), and a control unit (see Figure 5-4). The I/O unit manages data and instructions entering and leaving the CPU. The control unit manages all activities inside the CPU itself. The ALU unit does all comparisons and calculations. The CPU also needs places to store data and instructions as it works on them. Registers are small holding areas inside the CPU that work much as RAM does outside the CPU. Registers hold counters, data, instructions, and addresses that the ALU is currently processing. In addition to registers, the CPU has its own internal memory cache that holds data and instructions waiting to be processed by the ALU. Also notice in Figure 5-4 the external bus where data, instructions, addresses, and control signals are sent into and out of the CPU. The CPU has its own **internal bus** for communication to the internal cache. The CPU's internal bus operates at a much higher frequency than the external, or system, bus. The industry sometimes calls these internal and external buses the **back side bus** and the **front side bus**.

Older CPUs had only a single ALU, but beginning with the Pentium, CPUs contain at least two ALUs so the CPU can process two instructions at once. For the Pentiums, the front side data bus is 64 bits wide, but the back side data bus is only 32 bits wide, because of this dual-processing design. This is why the industry calls the Pentium a 32-bit processor; it processes 32 bits at a time internally, even though it uses a 64-bit bus externally. Intel recently released a 64-bit processor, called the Itanium, that has a 128-bit external data bus.

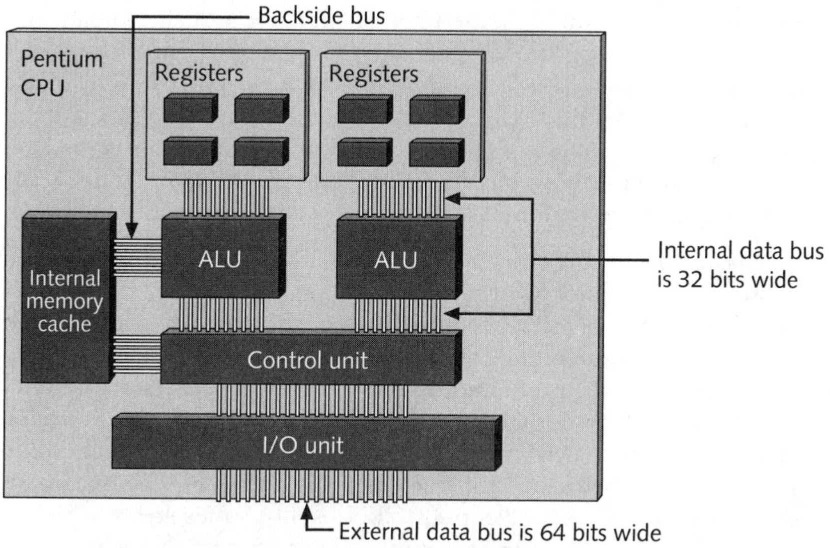

Figure 5-4 Beginning with the Pentium CPU, a CPU has two arithmetic logic units and can process two instructions at once

How to Rate CPUs

You need to know how to identify a CPU installed in a system and what performance to expect from that CPU. The following attributes are used to rate CPUs:

1. *CPU speed measured in gigahertz.* The first CPU used in an IBM PC was the 8088, which worked at about 4.77 MHz, or 4,770,000 clock beats per second. An average speed for a new CPU today is about 2 GHz, or 2,000,000,000 beats per second. In less than two seconds, this processor beats more times than your heart beats in a lifetime!
2. *Efficiency of programming code.* Permanently built into the CPU chip are programs that accomplish fundamental operations, such as comparing or adding two numbers. Less efficient CPUs require more steps to perform these simple operations than more efficient CPUs. These groups of instructions are collectively called the **instruction set**.
3. *Number of transistors.* The number of electronic switches, or transistors, in the processor circuitry is a measure of its overall computing power.
4. *Number of registers.* The more registers the CPU chip has, the less often the CPU has to access memory.
5. *Word size.* Word size, sometimes called the internal data path size, is the largest number of bits the CPU can process in one operation. Word size ranges from 16 bits (2 bytes) to 64 bits (8 bytes).

6. *Data path.* The data path, sometimes called the external data path size or the front side data bus, is the largest number of bits that can be transported into the CPU. The data path size is the same as the system bus size, or the number of bits that can be on the bus at one time. The data path in Figure 5-4 is 64 bits wide. The word size need not be as large as the data path size; some CPUs can receive more bits than they can process at one time, as in the case of the Pentium in Figure 5-4.

7. *Maximum number of memory addresses.* A computer case has room to physically house a lot of memory, but a CPU has only a fixed range of addresses that it can assign to this physical memory. How many memory addresses the CPU can assign limits the number of physical memory chips that the computer can use effectively. The minimum number of memory addresses a CPU can use is one megabyte (where each byte of memory is assigned a single address). Recall that one megabyte (MB) is equal to 1,024 kilobytes (K), which is equal to 1,024 × 1,024 bytes, or 1,048,576 memory addresses. The maximum number of memory addresses for Pentium CPUs is 4,096 megabytes, which is equal to 4 gigabytes (GB). The size of the address bus on a motherboard must match the number of pins the CPU uses for memory addresses; together these determine how many memory addresses the CPU can use.

8. *The amount of memory included with the CPU.* Most present-day CPUs have a memory cache on the processor chip and also inside the processor housing on a small circuit board. In documentation, the chip is sometimes called a die. Memory on the die is called internal cache, primary cache, level 1, or L1 cache. Memory not on the die is called secondary cache, level 2, or L2. In addition, some processors have L3 cache, which is further away from the CPU than L2 cache.

9. *Multiprocessing ability.* Some microchips are really two processors in one and can do more than one thing at a time. Others are designed to work in cooperation with other CPUs installed on the same motherboard.

10. *Special functionality.* There are also special-purpose CPUs such as the Pentium MMX, which is designed to manage multimedia devices efficiently.

Until Intel manufactured the Pentium series of chips, the three most popular ways of measuring CPU power were speed measured in megahertz, word size in bits, and data path size in bits. The criteria for measuring the power of a CPU have changed since the introduction of the Pentium. The word size and path size have remained the same for the last few years, so we have been more interested in clock speed, bus speed, internal cache, and especially, the intended functionality of the chip, such as its ability to handle graphics well (MMX technology). Now, with Intel's recent introduction of the Itanium CPU, word size and path size have increased and, once more, have become the attributes used to compare processors.

$A^{+CORE}_{1.10}$
4.3
4.4

The Pentium and Its Competitors

The most popular CPU microchips Intel manufactures for personal computers are the Pentium series of chips. A Pentium processor has two arithmetic logic units (ALUs), so it can perform two calculations at once; it is therefore a true multiprocessor. Pentiums have a 64-bit external path size and two 32-bit internal paths, one for each ALU. To compare the Pentium family of chips with its competitors, you need to understand bus speed, processor speed, the multiplier, and memory cache. Each is introduced here and discussed in more detail later in the chapter.

5

Recall that **bus speed** is the frequency or speed at which data moves on a bus. Remember also that a motherboard has several buses; later in the chapter you will learn the details of each. Each bus runs at a certain speed, some faster than others. Only the fastest bus connects directly to the CPU. This bus has many names. It's called the **motherboard bus**, or the **system bus**, because it's the main bus on the motherboard connecting directly to the CPU, or it's called the Pentium bus because it connects directly to the Pentium. It's called the **host bus** because other buses connect to it to get to the CPU, and it's also called the **memory bus** because it connects the CPU to RAM. It's called the external bus or the front side bus because it connects to the front side of the CPU that faces the outside world. Although the name memory bus is the most descriptive of the four, this book uses the more popular term, system bus. The common speeds for the system bus are 100 MHz, 133 MHz, 200 MHz, 400 MHz, and 533 MHz, although the bus can operate at several other speeds, depending on how the motherboard is configured.

> When you read that Intel supports a motherboard speed of 100 MHz or 133 MHz, the speed refers to the system bus speed. In documentation you sometimes see the system bus speed called the bus clock because the pulses generated on the clock line of the bus determine its speed. Other slower buses connect to the system bus, which serves as the go-between for other buses and the CPU.

Processor speed is the speed at which the CPU operates internally. If the CPU operates at 400 MHz internally but 100 MHz externally, the processor speed is 400 MHz, and the system bus speed is 100 MHz. In this case, the CPU operates at four times the speed of the bus. This factor is called the **multiplier**. If you multiply the system bus speed by the multiplier, you get the processor speed, or the speed of the CPU:

System bus speed × multiplier = processor speed

You can use jumpers on the motherboard or CMOS setup to set the system bus speed and multiplier, which then determine the CPU speed, or processor speed. Common multipliers are 1.5, 2, 2.5, 3, 3.5, and 4.

> Running a motherboard or CPU at a higher speed than that the manufacturer suggests is called overclocking and is not recommended, because the speed is not guaranteed to be stable. Also, the actual speed of the CPU might be slightly higher or lower than the advertised speed.

A+CORE
1.10
4.1
4.3

A **memory cache** is a small amount of RAM (referred to as static RAM, or SRAM) that is much faster than the rest of RAM, which is called dynamic RAM (DRAM). DRAM loses data rapidly and must be refreshed often. SRAM is faster than DRAM because SRAM does not need refreshing and can hold its data as long as power is available. The CPU processing of programming code and data can be speeded up by temporarily storing them in SRAM cache. The cache size a CPU can support is a measure of its performance, especially during memory-intensive calculations.

Recall that a memory cache can exist on the CPU die or inside the CPU housing on another die. A memory cache on the CPU die is called an **internal cache**, **primary cache**, or **Level 1 (L1) cache**. A cache outside the CPU microchip is called **external cache**, secondary cache, or **Level 2 (L2) cache**. L2 caches are usually 128K, 256K, 512K, or 1 MB in size. In the past, all L2 cache was contained on the motherboard, but beginning with the Pentium Pro, some L2 cache has been included, not on the CPU microchip like the L1 cache, but on a small circuit board with the CPU chip, within the same physical Pentium housing. If there is L2 cache in the processor housing and additional cache on the motherboard, then the cache on the motherboard is called **Level 3 (L3) cache**. Some advanced processors manufactured by AMD have L1, L2, and L3 cache inside the processor housing. In this case, the L3 cache is further removed from the CPU than the L2 cache, even though both are inside the CPU housing.

Also, remember that the bus between the processor and the L2 cache is called the back side bus, or cache bus, and is not visible, because it is completely contained inside the CPU housing (see Figure 5-5). This cache bus usually runs at half the speed of the processor.

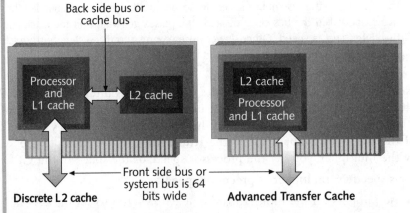

Figure 5-5   Some Pentiums contain L2 cache on separate dies (discrete L2 cache), and some contain L2 cache on the same die (Advanced Transfer Cache)

Some Pentium III CPUs contain L2 cache directly on the same die as the processor core, making it difficult to distinguish between L1 and L2 cache; this is called **Advanced Transfer Cache (ATC)**. ATC makes it possible for the Pentium III to fit on a smaller and

A^{+}CORE
_1.10_
_4.1_

less expensive form factor. The ATC bus is 256 bits wide and runs at the same speed as the processor. Pentium III L2 cache stored on a separate microchip within the CPU housing is called **discrete L2 cache** (see Figure 5-5). With discrete L2 cache, the Pentium III cache bus is 64 bits wide and runs at half the speed of the processor. All Pentium III processors have either 512K of discrete cache or 256K of ATC. The Pentium 4 uses 256K of ATC.

Some CPUs use a type of Level 1 cache called **Execution Trace Cache**. For example, the Pentium 4 has 8K of Level 1 cache used for data and an additional 12K of Execution Trace Cache containing a list of operations that have been decoded and are waiting to be executed. Many times a CPU decides to follow one branch of operations in a program of instructions rather than another branch. Only branches of operations that the CPU has determined will be executed are stored in the Execution Trace Cache, making the execution process faster.

Table 5-3 lists the six types of Pentium CPUs: Classic Pentium, Pentium MMX, Pentium Pro, Pentium II, Pentium III, and Pentium 4. Earlier variations of the Pentium II processor included the Celeron and Xeon. Recently, however, Intel stopped calling the Xeon the Pentium Xeon and simply refers to it as the Xeon, making it another group of CPUs different yet similar to the Pentiums. Several significant Intel CPUs are discussed below.

Table 5-3   The Intel Pentium and Xeon family of CPUs

Processor	Latest Processor Speeds (MHz or GHz)	Primary L1 Cache	Secondary L2 Cache	System Bus Speeds (MHz)
Classic Pentium	60 to 200 MHz	16K	None	66
Pentium MMX	133 to 266 MHz	32K	None	66
Pentium Pro	150 to 200 MHz	16K	256K, 512K, or 1 MB	60, 66
Pentium II	233 to 450 MHz	32K	256K, 512K	66, 100
Celeron	850 MHz to 1.8 GHz	32K or Execution Trace Cache	128K Advanced Transfer Cache or 256K Advanced Transfer Cache	Up to 400
Pentium II Xeon	400 or 500 MHz	32K	512K, 1 MB, or 2 MB	100
Pentium III	450 MHz to 1.33 GHz	32K	512K unified, non-blocking cache or 256K Advanced Transfer Cache	100, 133
Pentium III Xeon	600 MHz or 1 GHz	32K	256K, 1 MB, or 2 MB Advanced Transfer Cache	100 or 133

A+CORE
  1.10
   4.1

Table 5-3   The Intel Pentium and Xeon family of CPUs (continued)

Processor	Latest Processor Speeds (MHz or GHz)	Primary L1 Cache	Secondary L2 Cache	System Bus Speeds (MHz)
Xeon MP	1.4 GHz to 1.6 GHz	Execution Trace Cache	256K L2 Cache with 512K or 1 MB L3 Cache	400
Xeon DP	1.8 GHz to 2.4 GHz	Execution Trace Cache	256K or 512K Advanced Transfer Cache	400
Pentium 4	1.4 GHz to 2.8 GHz	Execution Trace Cache	256K or 512K Advanced Transfer Cache	400 or 533

Classic Pentium   Introduced in March 1993, the first Pentium chip has become affectionately known as the "Classic Pentium." Early problems with this first Pentium (which Intel later resolved) caused errors such as incorrect calculations on spreadsheets. The Classic Pentium is no longer manufactured.

Pentium MMX   The Pentium MMX (Multimedia Extension) targets the home market. It speeds graphical applications and performs well with games and multimedia software.

Pentium Pro   When the Pentium Pro was first released, Intel recommended it for 32-bit applications that rely heavily on fast access to large amounts of cache memory. It was the first Pentium to offer Level 2 cache inside the CPU housing, as well as other features not available on the Classic Pentium. The Pentium Pro was popular for computing-intensive workstations and servers, but, because it does not perform well in real mode, it does not perform well with older 16-bit application software written for DOS or Windows 3.x.

Pentium II   Designed for graphics-intensive workstations and servers, the Pentium II works well with 3-D graphic manipulation, CAD (computer-aided design), and multimedia presentations. The Pentium II is the first Pentium to use a slot (slot 1) instead of a socket to connect to the motherboard. (CPU sockets and slots are covered later in the chapter.) Intel patented slot 1, and, by doing so, tried to force its competitors to stay with the slower socket technology as they developed equivalent processors. The Pentium II can use the 100-MHz system bus with processor speeds up to 500 MHz.

The Celeron processor is a low-end Pentium II processor that targets the low-end multimedia PC market segment. It uses Level 2 cache within the processor housing and works well with Windows 9x and the most common applications.

The Pentium II Xeon processor is a fast, high-end Pentium II processor designed exclusively for servers and powerful workstations. It supports up to eight processors in one computer and is recommended for use with Windows NT, Windows 2000, and Unix operating systems.

A^+CORE
1.10
4.1

Pentium III   The Pentium III (see Figure 5-6) uses either a slot or a socket and runs with the 100-MHz or 133-MHz memory bus with a processor speed up to 1 GHz. The Pentium III introduced Intel's performance enhancement called SSE, for Streaming SIMD Extensions. (SIMD stands for single instruction, multiple data, and is a method MMX uses to speed up multimedia processing.) SSE is an instruction set designed to provide better multimedia processing than MMX.

Figure 5-6   This Pentium III is contained in a SECC cartridge that stands on its end in slot 1 on a motherboard

The Pentium III Xeon is a high-end Pentium III processor that runs on the 133 MHz system bus and is designed for mid-range servers and high-end workstations. It uses a 330-pin slot called the SC330 (slot connector 330), sometimes called slot 2, and is contained within a cartridge called a Single Edge Contact Cartridge (SECC).

Pentium 4   The Pentium 4 processor (see Figure 5-7) can currently run at up to 2.8 GHz. It provides increased performance for multimedia applications such as digital video, as well as for new Web technologies. It currently uses a 400- or 533-MHz system bus.

Some improvements that the Pentium 4 design provides are increased efficiency in creating digital files, faster ways to work with pictures, new ways for the user to interface with the computer (such as through natural speech), and greater responsiveness to Internet applications. Intel calls the processor architecture NetBurst which is supported by the Intel 845 and 850 chip sets.

A+CORE
1.10
4.1

CPU

Frame to hold cooler

Socket 478

Figure 5-7   The Pentium 4

Mobile Pentiums   There are mobile versions of several Intel Pentium processors. The Pentium II, Pentium III, Celeron, and Pentium 4 processors all have versions designed for use in notebook computers. The mobile Pentium 4 M (for Mobile) provides the highest performance for notebooks used for multimedia, video, and other data-intensive operations, and is designed to support many low power features that extend battery life. Currently available from 1.4 GHz to 2 GHz on a 400 MHz system bus, it uses the 845MP Intel chip set.

Competitors of the Advanced Pentiums   Table 5-4 shows the performance ratings of five competitors of the Pentium advanced processors. When VIA *(www.via.com.tw)* purchased Cyrix, it introduced a new processor, the VIA C3, which is similar to, but faster than, the Cyrix III processor (see Figure 5-8). The Cyrix and VIA processors use the same sockets as earlier Pentium processors.

Table 5-4   VIA and AMD competitors of the Intel processors

Processor	Latest Clock Speeds (MHz)	Compares to	System Bus Speed (MHz)	Socket of Slot
Cyrix M II	300, 333, 350	Pentium II, Celeron	66, 75, 83, 95, 100	Socket 7
Cyrix III	433 to 533	Celeron, Pentium III	66, 100, 133	Socket 370
VIA C3	Up to 1 GHz	Celeron	100 or 133	Socket 370

A+CORE
1.10
4.1

Table 5-4   VIA and AMD competitors of the Intel processors (continued)

Processor	Latest Clock Speeds (MHz)	Compares to	System Bus Speed (MHz)	Socket of Slot
AMD-K6-2	166 to 475	Pentium II, Celeron	66, 95, 100	Socket 7 or Super Socket 7
AMD-K6-III	350 to 450	Pentium II	100	Super Socket 7
AMD Athlon	Up to 1.9 GHz	Pentium III	200	Slot A or Socket A
AMD Duron	1 GHz to 1.3 GHz	Celeron	200	Socket A
AMD Athlon MP	1.4 GHz to 1.8 GHz	Pentium III	200 to 400+	OPGA

5

Figure 5-8   VIA C3 Processor

Earlier AMD *(www.amd.com)* processors used a special type of socket called Super Socket 7, which supports an AGP video slot and 100–MHz system bus. The AMD Athlon can use a proprietary 242-pin slot called Slot A, which looks like the Intel slot 1 and has 242 pins. Also, the AMD Athlon and the AMD Duron use a 462-pin socket called Socket A. The latest AMD processor is the Athlon MP, shown in Figure 5-9.

Intel Itaniums: The Next-Generation Processor

Intel's newest processor is the Itanium, Intel's first 64-bit processor for microcomputers. Recall from Chapter 2 that earlier processors always operated in real mode, using a 16-bit data path. Later, protected mode was introduced, which uses a 32-bit data path. Almost all applications written today use 32-bit protected mode, because all CPUs manufactured today for microcomputers use a 32-bit data path. Beginning with the Itanium, this will slowly change. Although the Itanium is designed for high-end enterprise servers, the industry fully expects 64-bit processors to reach the personal computer market eventually. To take full advantage of a 64-bit processor, such as the Itanium, software developers must recompile their applications to use 64-bit processing and write operating systems that use 64-bit data transfers. Microsoft provides a 64-bit version of Windows XP that works with the Itanium processor. Intel has promised that the Itanium will provide backward compatibility with older 32-bit applications, although the older applications will not be able to take full advantage of the Itanium's capabilities.

Figure 5-9   AMD Athlon MP Processor

Earlier CPUs use one of two types of instruction sets: **RISC (reduced instruction set computing)** or **CISC (complex instruction set computing)**. Generally slower than RISC CPUs, CISC CPUs have a larger number of instructions that programmers can take advantage of. The Itanium uses a new instruction set called the **EPIC (explicitly parallel instruction computing)** architecture. With EPIC, the CPU receives a bundle of instructions that contains programming instructions as well as instructions for how the CPU can execute two instructions at once in parallel, using the CPUs multiprocessing abilities.

Table 5-5 shows the specifications for the two Itanium processors. Note the inclusion of an L3 cache. The Itanium uses an L1 cache on the processor die and L2 and L3 caches on the processor board. The L2 cache is closer to the CPU than the L3 cache.

Table 5-5   The Intel Itanium processors

Processor	Current Processor Speeds	L1 Cache	L2 Cache	L3 Cache	System Bus Speed
Itanium	733 and 800 MHz	32K	96K	2 MB or 4 MB	266 MHz
Itanium 2	900 MHz to 1 GHz	32K	256K	1.5 MB or 3 MB	400 MHz

A^{+CORE}
1.2
2.1
1.9

CPU Heat Sinks and Cooling Fans

Because a CPU generates so much heat, computer systems use a cooling fan to keep temperatures below the Intel maximum limit of 185 degrees F/85 degrees C (see Figure 5-10). Good CPU cooling fans maintain a temperature of 90–110 degrees F (32–43 degrees C). At one time, CPU cooling fans were optional equipment used to prevent system errors and to prolong the life of the CPU. Today's power-intensive CPUs require one or more cooling fans to maintain a temperature that will not damage the CPU. High-end systems can have as many as seven or eight fans mounted inside the computer case. Ball-bearing cooling fans last longer than other kinds.

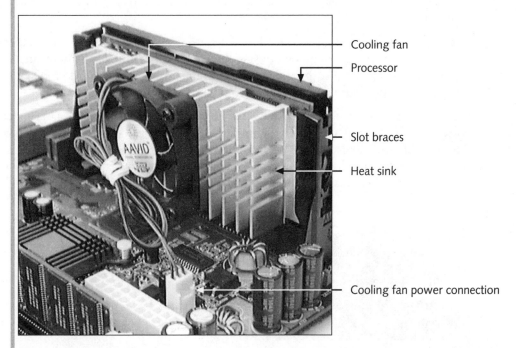

Figure 5-10   A CPU cooling fan mounts on the top or side of the CPU housing and is powered by an electrical connection to the motherboard

The cooling fan usually fits on top of the CPU with a wire or plastic clip. Sometimes a cream-like thermal compound is placed between the fan and the CPU. This compound draws heat from the CPU and passes it to the fan. The thermal compound transmits heat better than air and makes an airtight connection between the fan and the CPU. The fan is equipped with a power connector that connects to one of the power cables coming from the power supply or to a connector on the motherboard.

Older CPUs used a heat sink instead of a cooling fan. A **heat sink** is a clip-on device that mounts on top of the CPU; fingers or fins at its base pull the heat away from the CPU. Today most cooling fans designed to mount on the CPU housing also have a heat

A+CORE
1.2
1.9

sink attached, as shown in Figure 5-10. The combination heat sink and cooling fan is sometimes called a cooler. Heat sinks sometimes mount on top of other chips to keep them cool. For example, in Figure 5-7 you can see a heat sink mounted on top of a chip sitting behind the Pentium 4 CPU. Also notice in Figure 5-7 the frame to hold the cooler for the Pentium 4.

Some motherboards feature a power connection for the cooling fan that sounds an alarm if the fan stops working. Because the fan is a mechanical device, it is more likely to fail than the electronic devices inside the case. To protect the expensive CPU, you can purchase a temperature sensor for a few dollars. The sensor plugs into a power connection coming from the power supply and mounts on the side of the case. It sounds an alarm when the inside of the case becomes too hot.

Before installing a cooling fan, read the directions carefully. Clips that hold the fan and heat sink to the CPU frame or housing are sometimes difficult to install, and you must be very careful to use just the right amount of thermal compound. Too much compound can slide off the housing and damage circuits on the motherboard.

A good example of a CPU cooling fan is the Golden Orb fan by Thermaltake, Inc. (*www.thermaltake.com*) shown in Figure 5-11. Unlike some older fans, the Golden Orb can provide sufficient cooling for newer and hotter processors. A unique feature of the Golden Orb is that the heat sink is constructed around the fan, rather than beneath it. This helps the heat dissipate more quickly.

Figure 5-11   The Golden Orb cooling fan

Besides using fans and heat sinks to keep a CPU cool, there are some more exotic options such as refrigeration, peltiers, and water coolers. These solutions, for the most part, are used by hobbyists attempting to overclock a CPU to the max. A peltier is a heat sink carrying an electrical charge causing it to act as an electrical thermal transfer device. The peltier's top surface can be as hot as 500 degrees F while the bottom surface next to the CPU can be as cool as 45 degrees. The major disadvantage of a peltier is that this drastic difference in temperature can cause condensation inside the case when the PC is turned off. Refrigeration can also be used to cool a CPU. These units contain a small refrigerator compressor that sits inside the case and can reduce temperatures to below zero. The most popular method of cooling overclocked CPUs is a water cooler unit. A small water pump sits inside the computer case, and tubes move distilled water up and

A+CORE
1.2
1.9

over the CPU to keep it cool. Some manufacturers of these types of cooling systems are AquaStealth (*www.aquastealth.com*), asetek (*www.vapochill.com*), and FrozenCPU (*www.frozencpu.com*). Remember, overclocking is not a recommended best practice.

A+CORE
4.1

CPU Packages

Eight package types are used to house Intel processors in desktop PCs and high-end workstations:

- *SECC (Single Edge Contact Cartridge).* The processor is completely covered with a black plastic housing, and a heat sink and fan are attached to the housing. You can't see the circuit board or edge connector in an SECC package. The Pentium II and Pentium III use an SECC package in slot 1 with 242 contacts. The Pentium II Xeon and Pentium III Xeon use an SECC with 330 contacts. You can see the SECC in Figure 5-6.

- *SECC2 (Single Edge Contact Cartridge, version 2).* Similar to the SECC but without the heat sink thermal plate, and the edge connector on the processor circuit board is visible at the bottom of the housing. Pentium II and Pentium III use the SECC2 package with 242 contacts.

- *SEP (Single Edge Processor).* This package is similar to the SECC package, but the black plastic housing does not completely cover the processor making the processor the circuit board visible at the bottom of the housing. The first Celeron processors used the SEP package in slot 1. It has 242 contacts.

- *PPGA (Plastic Pin Grid Array).* The processor is housed in a square box designed to fit flat into Socket 370 (see Figure 5-12). Pins are on the underside of the flat housing, and heat sinks or fans can be attached to the top of the housing by using a thermal plate or heat spreader. The early Celeron processors used this package with 370 pins.

- *PGA (Pin Grid Array).* Pins on the bottom of this package are staggered and can be inserted only one way into the socket. The Xeon processors use this package with 603 pins.

- *OOI/OLGA (Organic Land Grid Array).* Used by some Pentium 4s, this 423-pin package is similar to the PGA package, but is designed to dissipate heat faster.

- *FC-PGA (Flip Chip Pin Grid Array).* This package looks like the PPGA package and uses Socket 370. Coolers can be attached directly to the top of the package. Some Pentium III and Celeron processors use this package.

- *FC-PGA2 (Flip Chip Pin Grid Array 2).* This package is similar to the FC-PGA package, but has a heat sink attached directly to the die of the processor. When used by a Pentium III or Celeron processor, it has 370 pins. When used by the Pentium 4, it has 478 pins.

- *PAC (Pin Array Cartridge).* The Itaniums use this flat cartridge, which is about the size of an index card. It uses either the PAC418 socket, which has 418 pins, or the PAC611 socket, which has 611 pins.

5

A+CORE
4.1
4.3

CPU Slots and Sockets

Recall from Chapter 2 that a slot or socket is the physical connection used to attach a device (the CPU) to the motherboard. The type of socket or slot supplied by the motherboard for the processor must match that required by the processor. Table 5-6 lists several types of sockets and slots that CPUs use. Slots 1 and 2 are proprietary Intel slots, and Socket A and Slot A are proprietary AMD connectors.

Figure 5-12 The Intel Celeron processor is housed in the PPGA form factor, which has pins on the underside that insert into Socket 370

Table 5-6 CPU sockets and slots

Connector Name	Used by CPU	Number of Pins	Voltage
Socket 4	Classic Pentium 60/66	273 pins 21 × 21 PGA grid	5 V
Socket 5	Classic Pentium 75/90/100/120/133	320 pins 37 × 37 SPGA grid	3.3 V
Socket 6	Not used	235 pins 19 × 19 PGA grid	3.3 V
Socket 7	Pentium MMX, Fast Classic Pentium, AMD KS, AMD KS, Cyrix M	321 pins 37 × 37 SPGA grid	2.5 V to 3.3 V
Super Socket 7	AMD KS-2, AMD KS-III	321 pins 37 × 37 SPGA grid	2.5 V to 3.3 V
Socket 8	Pentium Pro	387 pins 24 × 26 SPGA grid	3.3 V

$A+CORE$
4.1
4.3

Table 5-6   CPU sockets and slots (continued)

Connector Name	Used by CPU	Number of Pins	Voltage
Socket 370 or PGA370 Socket	Pentium III FC-PGA, Celeron PPGA, Cyrix III	370 pins in a 37 × 37 SPGA grid	1.5 V or 2 V
Slot 1 or SC242	Pentium II, Pentium III	242 pins in 2 rows, rectangular shape	2.8 V and 3.3 V
Slot A	AMD Athlon	242 pins in 2 rows, rectangular shape	1.3 V to 2.05 V
Socket A or Socket 462	AMD Athlon and Duron	462 pins, SPGA grid, rectangular shape	1.1 V to 1.85 V
Slot 2 or SC330	Pentium II Xeon, Pentium III Xeon	330 pins in 2 rows, rectangular shape	1.5 V to 3.5 V
Socket 423	Pentium 4	423 pins 39 × 39 SPGA grid	1.7 V and 1.75 V
Socket 478	Pentium 4	478 pins in a dense micro PGA (mPGA)	1.7 V and 1.75 V
Socket PAC418	Itanium	418 pins	3.3 V
PAC611	Itanium 2	611 pins	3.3 V
Socket 603	Xeon DP and MP	603 pins	1.5 and 1.7 V

Earlier Pentiums used a **pin grid array (PGA)** socket, with pins aligned in uniform rows around the socket. Later sockets use a **staggered pin grid array (SPGA)**, with pins staggered over the socket to squeeze more pins into a small space. PGA and SPGA sockets are all square or nearly square. Earlier CPU sockets, called dual inline pin package (DIPP) sockets, were rectangular with two rows of pins down each side. DIPP and some PGA sockets, called **low insertion force (LIF) sockets**, were somewhat troublesome to install because applying even force when inserting them was difficult. Current CPU sockets, called **zero insertion force (ZIF) sockets**, have a small lever on the side of the socket that lifts the CPU up and out of the socket. Push the lever down and the CPU moves into its pin connectors with equal force over the entire housing. The heat sink or fan clips to the top of the CPU. With this method, you can more easily remove and replace the CPU if necessary.

Most processors today come in more than one package, so it is important to match the processor package to the motherboard that has the right socket or slot. Slot 1, Slot A, and slot 2 are all designed to accommodate processors using SEP or SECC housings that stand on end much like an expansion card. Clips on each side of the slot secure the CPU in the slot. You can attach a heat sink or cooling fan to the side of the CPU case. Some motherboards with a slot 1 can accommodate processors that use flat packages, such as the Celeron housed in a PPGA package, by using a riser CPU card (see Figure 5-13). The riser card inserts into slot 1, and the Celeron processor inserts into Socket 370 on the riser card. This feature, sometimes called a slocket, allows you to upgrade an older Pentium II system to the faster Celeron. Always consult the motherboard documentation to learn which processors the board can support.

A+CORE
  4.1

Also, be aware of the processor's voltage requirements. For example, the Pentium 4 receives voltage from the +12-volt power line to the motherboard, rather than the lower-voltage lines that previous Pentiums used. For this reason, some motherboards include a new power connector, called the ATX12V. In some setups, a power cord designed to power a drive connects to this small connector. Another variation is the Celeron processor that uses 2.00 volts, and the Pentium III FC-PGA that uses either 1.60 or 1.65 volts. A motherboard built to support only the Celeron may not recognize the need to step down the voltage for a Pentium III FC-PGA processor. This overvoltage can damage the Pentium III. Again, it is always important to use only a processor and processor package that the motherboard documentation claims the board can support.

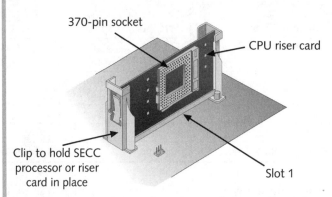

Figure 5-13   A riser card can be used to install a Celeron processor into a motherboard with slot 1

A+CORE
  4.3

CPU Voltage Regulator

As you can see from Table 5-6, different CPUs require different levels of voltage on the motherboard. Some CPUs require one voltage for external operations and another for internal operations. Those that require two different voltages are called **dual–voltage CPUs**. Others are called **single–voltage CPUs**. A CPU voltage regulator controls the amount of voltage to the CPU. Some CPUs require that you set the jumpers on the motherboard to control the voltage, and other CPUs automatically control the voltage without your involvement.

Figure 5-14 shows sample documentation of the jumper settings to use for various CPU voltage selections on a particular motherboard that requires jumpers to be set. Notice that the two jumpers called JP16, located near Socket 7 on the board, accomplish the voltage selection. For single voltage, for the Pentium, Cyrix 6x86, or AMD K5, both jumpers are open. Dual voltage, used by the Pentium MMX, Cyrix M2, and AMD K6, is selected by opening or closing the two jumpers according to the diagram. Follow the recommendations for your CPU when selecting the voltages from documentation.

A+CORE 4.3 | The Chip Set

Recall from Chapter 1 that a chip set is a set of chips on the motherboard that collectively controls the memory cache, external buses, and some peripherals. Intel makes the most popular chip sets, which are listed in Table 5-7. The Intel 440BX chip set is the first PC chip set to offer a system bus that runs at 100 MHz, allowing a Pentium II running at 350 MHz or 400 MHz to reach its full potential for performance in desktop PCs. Before this, the system bus slowed the CPU speed. The 440BX chip set is also the first chip set to use the mobile version of the Pentium II processor for notebooks. Often you see this chip set advertised with "AGP" in the name, as in the Intel 440BX AGP chip set. The 440GX chip set is an evolution of the 440BX.

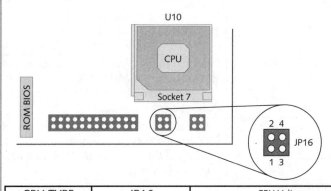

CPU TYPE	JP16	CPU Voltage	
		Core	I/O
Single Voltage Intel P54C/CQS/CT Cyrix 6x86 AMD K5	2 ⃝⃝ 4 1 ⃝⃝ 3 open	3.5 V	3.5 V
Dual Voltage Intel P55C/MMX Cyrix 6x86L/M2 AMD K6	2 ⃝⃝ 4 1 ⃝⃝ 3 open	2.8 V	3.4 V
	2 ●⃝ 4 1 ●⃝ 3 1-2 closed, 3-4 open	2.9 V	3.4 V
	2 ⃝● 4 1 ⃝● 3 1-2 open, 3-4 closed	3.2 V	3.4 V

Figure 5-14   CPU voltage regulator can be configured using jumpers on the motherboard to apply the correct voltage to the CPU

A+CORE
  4.3

Table 5-7   Intel chip sets

Common Name	Model Number	Comments
"E" chipset family	E8870	Supports up to four Itanium 2 processors using a 400-MHz system bus
	E7500	Supports dual Xeon processors using a 400-MHz system bus and up to 128 GB of memory
Intel i800 Series	860	Supports dual Xeon processors using a 400-MHz system bus and up to eight RIMMs
	850 and 850E	Designed for the Pentium 4 or Celeron and supports the 400-MHz or 533-MHz system bus using up to eight RIMMs. Supports ECC memory.
	845E	Designed for the Pentium 4 or Celeron supporting 400-MHz or 533 MHz system bus using two DIMM DDR modules. Supports ECC memory.
	845G or 845 GL	Designed for the Pentium 4 or Celeron and supports the 400-MHz or 533-MHz (845G only) system bus using two DIMM DDR or DIMM SDR modules
	845	Designed for the Pentium 4 or Celeron and supports the 400-MHz system bus using two DIMM DDR or three DIMM SDR modules. Supports ECC memory.
	840	Designed for dual processor systems using Pentium II Xeon or Pentium III Xeon processors
	820	Designed for Pentium II and Pentium III systems
	815, 815E, or 815EP	Designed for the Celeron or Pentium III and uses a 66/100/133 MHz system bus
	810	First Intel chip set to eliminate the PCI bus as the main device interconnection
Orion	460GX	Designed for up to four Itanium processors and four DIMMs
	450GX, KX	Supports Pentium Pro (includes support for multiprocessors)
	450NX	Designed for servers with multiple Pentium II or Pentium II Xeon processors
Natoma	440FX	Supports Pentium Pro and Pentium II (discontinued in January, 1999)
	440BX	Designed for servers and workstations (Pentium II and III)
	440GX	Designed for servers and workstations using the Pentium II Xeon and Pentium III Xeon
	440ZX	Designed for entry-level PCs using Pentium II
	440LX	Designed for Celeron processors

$\overset{+CORE}{A}\underset{4.3}{}$

Table 5-7   Intel chip sets (continued)

Common Name	Model Number	Comments
	440MX	Designed for notebook computers (M = mobile)
	440EX	Designed for smaller systems boards such as the Mini-ATX
Triton III	430VX	Value chip set, supports SDRAM
	430MX	Used for notebooks (M = mobile)
	430TX	Supports SDRAM, ultra DMA; replaced the VX and MX
Triton II	430HX	High performance, supports dual processors
Triton I	430FX	The oldest chip set, no longer produced

5

The 400 series of Intel chip sets uses the PCI bus as the interconnection between slower buses and the system bus. The Intel i800 series of chip sets introduced a new way for I/O buses to interface with the faster system bus and ultimately to the CPU. With the i800 series, the interconnection between buses is done using a hub interface architecture, in which all I/O buses connect to a hub, which connects to the system bus. This hub is called the hub interface, and the architecture is called Accelerated Hub Architecture (see Figure 5-15). The fast end of the hub, which contains the graphics and memory controller (GMCH), connects to the system bus and is called the hub's **North Bridge**. The slower end of the hub, called the **South Bridge**, contains the I/O Controller Hub (ICH). All I/O devices except display and memory connect to the hub by using the slower South Bridge. The 860 chipset hub can provide six channels of digital audio to support digital surround sound.

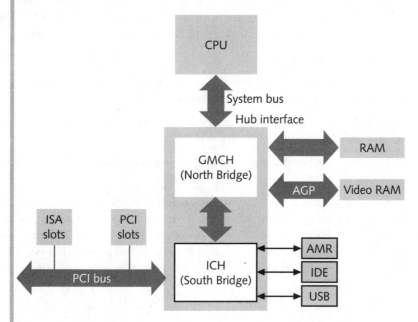

Figure 5-15   Using Intel 800 series Accelerated Hub Architecture, a hub interface is used to connect slower I/O buses to the system bus

A+CORE 4.3 Table 5-8 lists manufacturers of chip sets. Currently, Intel dominates the chip set market for several reasons. The major advantage that Intel has over other chip set manufacturers is that Intel knows more about its own Intel CPUs than other manufacturers do and produces the chip sets most compatible with the Pentium family of CPUs. Intel's investment in research and development also led to the development of the PCI bus, the universal serial bus, the AGP, and more recently, the Accelerated Hub Architecture.

Table 5-8 Chip set manufacturers

Company	URL
ALI, Inc.	www.aliusa.com
AMD	www.amd.com
Intel Corporation	www.intel.com
Philips Semiconductors	www.semiconductors.philips.com
Silicon Integrated Systems Corp. (known as SiS)	www.sis.com
Standard Microsystems Corp.	www.smsc.com
United Microelectronics Corp. (UMC)	www.umc.com
VIA Technologies, Inc. combined with AMD, Inc.	www.via.com.tw

ROM BIOS

A+CORE 1.10 A motherboard has ROM BIOS and RAM installed on it. The next chapter discusses RAM, and this section addresses ROM BIOS. Recall from earlier chapters that one ROM chip on the motherboard contains BIOS. BIOS manages the startup process (startup BIOS) and many basic I/O functions of the system (system BIOS). There are two methods to identify your motherboard and BIOS. First try the following:

1. Turn off the system power.

2. Turn on the power. While memory is counting on the screen, hold down the Pause/Break key to stop the startup process.

3. Look for the long string of numbers in the lower-left corner of your screen, which identifies the motherboard.

4. Look for the BIOS manufacturer and version number somewhere near the top of the screen.

If the above method does not work, try unplugging the keyboard and then turn on the PC. For older systems, the resulting keyboard error will stop the startup process. Many years ago, when a new device became available, such as the 3-1/2-inch floppy disk drive, your PC sometimes could not use the new device until you upgraded the BIOS. You did that by replacing the old BIOS chip with a new chip that supported the new device.

$A^{+}_{}\!\!\begin{smallmatrix}CORE\\1.10\end{smallmatrix}$ Now, however, it's much easier. Most of today's new devices are not supported by the system BIOS at all, but by device drivers, which are software programs installed on the hard drive as an add-on part of the OS. But, if some new feature does require a BIOS upgrade, you can do that with flash ROM. Installing a larger hard drive is an example of a hardware upgrade that might require a BIOS upgrade because the existing BIOS does not support large drives. Older BIOS supports hard drives with a capacity of up to only 504 MB. If you have this problem (large drive, old BIOS), you can solve it in one of two ways: either upgrade BIOS or use special software designed to get around the problem. Often the device manufacturer supplies such software. Table 5-9 lists BIOS manufacturers.

Table 5-9   BIOS manufacturers

Company	URL
American Megatrends, Inc. (AMI)	www.megatrends.com or www.ami.com
Phoenix Technologies (First BIOS, Phoenix, and Award)	www.phoenix.com
Compaq and Hewlett-Packard	thenew.hp.com
Dell	www.dell.com
IBM	www.ibm.com
Micro Firmware (BIOS upgrades)	www.firmware.com
Unicore (BIOS upgrades)	www.unicore.com

Technically speaking, flash ROM is called EEPROM (electrically erasable programmable read-only memory), because you can change the programming on the chip through software on your PC. The updated programming is retained until you change it again, even when you turn off your PC for long periods. Flash ROM allows you to upgrade system BIOS without replacing the ROM chip.

Makers of BIOS code are likely to change BIOS frequently, because providing the upgrade on the Internet is so easy for them. You can get upgraded BIOS code from manufacturers' Web sites or disks or from third-party BIOS resellers' Web sites or disks.

Figure 5-16 shows a sample Web site for flash ROM BIOS upgrades. See the Web site of the manufacturer of your BIOS or of the motherboard manufacturer for more information.

A+CORE
1.10

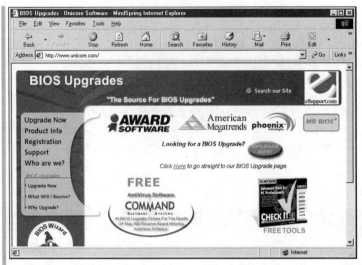

Figure 5-16   Flash ROM BIOS upgrades for most BIOS manufacturers can be downloaded from *www.unicore.com*

To upgrade flash ROM, follow the directions that came with your motherboard and the upgrade software itself. Generally, you perform these tasks:

1. Set a jumper on the motherboard, or change a setting in CMOS setup to tell the BIOS to expect an upgrade.

2. Copy the upgrade BIOS software to a bootable disk.

3. Boot from the disk and follow the menu options to upgrade the BIOS. If the menu gives you the option to save the old BIOS to disk, do so in case you need to revert to the old BIOS.

4. Set the jumper back to its original setting, reboot the system, and verify that all is working.

Be *very careful* that you upgrade the BIOS with the correct upgrade and that you follow the manufacturer's instructions correctly. Upgrading with the wrong file could make your system BIOS useless. If you're not sure that you're using the correct upgrade, *don't guess*. Check with the technical support for your BIOS before moving forward. Before you call technical support, have the information that identifies your BIOS available.

Buses and Expansion Slots

$A{+}CORE$
1.10

As cities grow, so do their transportation systems. Small villages have only simple, two-lane roads, but large cities have two-lane and four-lane roads, and major freeways, each with its own set of traffic laws, including minimum and maximum speeds, access methods, and protocols. As microcomputer systems evolved, so have their "transportation" systems. The earliest PC had only a single simple bus. Today's PCs have four or five buses, each with different speeds, access methods, and protocols. As you have seen, backward compatibility dictates that older buses be supported on a motherboard, even when faster, better buses exist. All this makes for a maze of buses on a motherboard.

5

Bus Evolution

Just as a city's road system improves to increase the speed and number of lanes of traffic, buses have evolved around these similar issues, data path and speed. Cars on a freeway travel at a continuous or constant speed, but traffic on a computer's CPU or bus is digital (on and off), rather than analog (a continuous) manner. The system clock keeps the beat for components. If a component on the motherboard works by the beat, or clock cycle, then it is synchronized, or in sync, with the CPU. For example, as explained earlier in the chapter, the back side bus of the Pentium II works at half the speed of the CPU. This means that the CPU does something on each clock cycle, but the back side bus is doing something on every other clock cycle.

Some components don't attempt to keep in sync with the CPU, even to work at a half or a third of clock cycles. These components work asynchronously with the CPU. They might work at a rate determined by the system clock or by another crystal on or off the motherboard. Either way, the frequency is much slower than the CPU's and not in sync with it. If the CPU requests something from one of these devices and the device is not ready, the device issues wait states to the CPU until it catches up.

Devices that use the 8-bit or 16-bit ISA bus are examples of these slower devices. The 16-bit ISA slot works at a rate of 8.33 MHz, compared to system bus speeds of 66 MHz to 400 MHz for faster buses. Buses that work in sync with the CPU and the system clock are called **local buses**. Buses that work asynchronously with the CPU at a much slower rate are called **expansion buses**. The system bus is a local bus, and the ISA bus is an expansion bus. Table 5-10 lists the various buses, in order of throughput speed from fastest to slowest.

A+CORE
  1.10

Table 5-10   Buses listed by throughput

Bus	Bus Type	Data Path in Bits	Address Lines	Bus Speed in MHz	Throughput in gigabytes/sec, megabytes/sec, or megabits/sec
System bus	Local	64	32	66, 75, 100 . . .	Up to 3.2 GB/sec
AGP	Local video	32	NA	66, 75, 100 . . .	Up to 528 MB/sec
PCI	Local I/O	32	32	33, 66	Up to 264 MB/sec
VESA or VL Bus	Local video or expansion	32	32	Up to 33	Up to 250 MB/sec
FireWire	Local I/O or expansion	1	Addresses are sent serially	NA	Up to 1.2 Gb/sec (gigabits)
MCA	Expansion	32	32	12	Up to 40 MB/sec
EISA	Expansion	32	32	12	Up to 32 MB/sec
16-bit ISA	Expansion	16	24	8.33	8 MB/sec
8-bit ISA	Expansion	8	20	4.77	1 MB/sec
USB	Expansion	1	Addresses are sent serially	3	Up to 480 Mbps

Some motherboard buses in Table 5-10 are outdated, and some are used today. Historically, the 8-bit ISA (Industry Standard Architecture) bus came first and was later revised to the 16-bit ISA bus to meet the demand for wider data path sizes. Then, in 1987, IBM introduced the first 32-bit bus, the MCA (Micro channel Architecture) bus, and competitors followed with the 32-bit EISA (Extended Industry Standard Architecture) bus. Because these buses are not synchronized with the CPU, they are all expansion buses. Of these buses, the only one still used today is the 16-bit ISA. A relatively new expansion bus is the universal serial bus (USB), which targets slow I/O devices such as the mouse, digital camera, and scanner. Its advantage is that USB devices are easily installed and configured.

A local bus is synchronized with the CPU. In the sense that a local bus is a bus that is close to, or "local to," the CPU, there is only one "true" local bus, the system bus, or memory bus, which connects directly to the CPU. All other buses must connect to the system bus to get to the CPU. A **local I/O bus** is a bus designed to support fast I/O devices such as video and hard drives; it runs synchronized with the system clock, which means that it is also synchronized with the CPU. One type of local I/O bus is the PCI bus, which is standard with Pentium systems. Local I/O buses did not always exist on a PC but were created as the need arose for a bus that was synchronized with the system clock, was not as fast as the system bus, and was faster than an expansion bus. The evolution of local I/O buses includes earlier proprietary designs, the VESA bus, the PCI bus, and the newer AGP bus. Of these, only the PCI and AGP buses are still sold. The FireWire, or IEEE 1394, bus is the latest local I/O bus and is becoming more popular.

A+CORE
1.10

Able to work either synchronously or asynchronously, it is classified as either a local or expansion bus. The older VESA bus could also be set to work either way.

5

Why So Many Buses?

When the first PCs were introduced in the early 1980s, the motherboard had only one bus, called the system bus, which ran at the same speed as the CPU (4.77 MHz). Everything on the motherboard working with the CPU or the bus kept the same beat, following the pulses of the one system clock. (This first bus is now called the 8-bit ISA bus.) Things today are not so simple. With speeds of different hardware components evolving at different rates, a single speed for all components is no longer practical. The CPU works at one speed, the bus connecting the CPU to memory works at a slower speed, and the bus communicating with I/O devices must work at an even slower speed. As manufacturers attempt to improve performance, they invent new buses to accommodate the characteristics of particular devices. In fact, the same motherboard might have as many as five or six different buses working at different speeds. Each bus has a set speed at which all components connected to it work. Some components convert data moving from bus to bus to the speed of the new bus.

What a Bus Does

Look on the bottom of the motherboard, and you see a maze of circuits that make up a bus. These embedded wires carry four kinds of cargo:

- *Electrical power.* Chips on the motherboard require power to function. These chips tap into a bus's power lines and draw what they need.

- *Control signals.* Some wires on a bus carry control signals that coordinate all the activity.

- *Memory addresses.* Components pass memory addresses to one another, telling each other where to access data or instructions. The number of wires that make up the memory address lines of the bus determines how many bits can be used for a memory address. The number of wires thus limits the amount of memory the bus can address.

- *Data.* Data passes over a bus in a group of wires, just as memory addresses do. The number of lines in the bus used to pass data determines how much data can be passed in parallel at one time. The number of lines depends on the type of CPU and determines the number of bits in the data path. (Remember that a data path is that part of the bus on which the data is placed; it can be 8, 16, 32, 64, or more bits wide.)

A+CORE
1.10

When comparing buses, users most often focus on the width of the data path and over-all bus speed. But you should also consider the type of expansion slot the bus allows. The bus that controls the expansion slot determines the number of fingers on the edge connector of the expansion card and the length of the edge connector. Figure 5-17 shows various bus connections.

On-Board Ports

Many motherboards contain **on-board ports** such as a keyboard port and a mouse port. In addition, a parallel printer port and one or two serial ports might be located directly on the motherboard. Few older motherboards contain more ports than these. Some systems also have a video or network port, and newer motherboards contain one or two USB ports.

> **TIP** You don't have to replace an entire motherboard if one port fails. Most ports on a motherboard can be disabled through CMOS setup. On older motherboards, look for jumpers or DIP switches to disable a port. Then use an expansion card for the port instead.

Relationship of CPU Speed to Bus Speed

Studies show that when the multiplier that determines CPU speed is large, the overall performance of the system is not as good as when the multiplier is small. This is a reasonable result because you are interested in the overall speed of the computer, which includes the CPU and the buses, not just the speed of the CPU. For example, a bus speed of 60 MHz and a multiplier of 5 yield a relatively fast CPU but a relatively slow system. It's better to have a bus speed of 80 MHz and a multiplier of 3 so that the bus runs fast enough to keep up with the CPU. See the motherboard documentation to learn how to set these speeds using jumpers, DIP switches, or CMOS setup. You will see an example later in this chapter.

You can change the speed of a computer in two ways:

1. Change the speed of the system bus. Whatever the system bus speed is, the PCI bus speed is one-half or one-third of that.

2. Change the multiplier that determines the speed of the CPU. The choices for the multiplier normally are 1.5, 2, 2.5, 3, 3.5, and so forth.

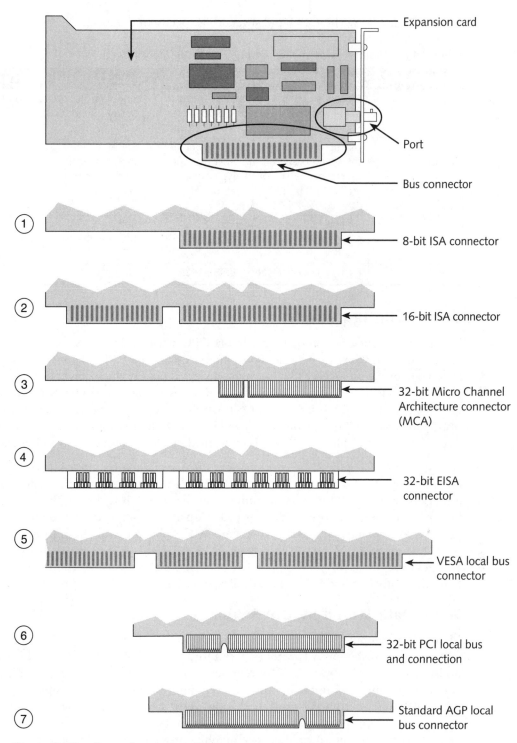

Figure 5-17   Seven bus connections on expansion cards

Table 5-11 lists how the CPU and several bus speeds are controlled.

Table 5-11 Motherboard speeds and how they are determined

Bus or Device	How Speed Is Determined	How Controlled
CPU	Processor speed = system bus speed × multiplier. Typical speeds are 500 MHz, 800 MHz, and 1 GHz.	Jumpers, DIP switches on the motherboard, CMOS setup set the multiplier.
Memory bus or system bus	Motherboard manufacturer recommends the speed based on the processor and processor's rated speed. Typical values are 100 MHz, 133 MHz, 200 MHz, 400 MHz, and 533 MHz.	Set by jumpers, DIP switches, or in CMOS setup. Most commonly set by jumpers.
PCI bus	System bus speed divided by 2 (divided by 3 for faster boards)	Setting the speed of the system bus sets the speed of the PCI bus.
ISA bus	Runs at only one speed: 8.33 MHz.	NA

Hardware Configuration

Hardware configuration information tells the CPU what hardware components are present in the system and how they are set up to interface with the CPU. Hardware configuration includes information such as how much memory is available, which power management features are present, and whether disk drives, hard drives, modems, serial ports, and the like are connected. Remember that during POST, BIOS looks to the system configuration information to determine the equipment it should expect to find and how that equipment interfaces with the CPU. The CPU uses this information later to process data and instructions.

As discussed in Chapter 2, the motherboard provides configuration information in three different ways: DIP switches, jumpers, and CMOS. Storing configuration information by physically setting DIP switches or jumpers on the motherboard or peripheral devices is inconvenient, because it often requires you to open the computer case to make a change. A more convenient method is to use the CMOS chip to hold the information in the small amount of RAM on the chip. A program in BIOS can then be used to easily make changes to setup. In this section, you will learn more about each method of storing configuration information. You will also see examples of CMOS setup screens.

Setup Data Stored by DIP Switches

Many older computers and a few newer ones store setup data using DIP switches on the motherboard, as shown in Figure 5-18. A DIP (dual inline package) switch has an ON position and an OFF position. ON represents binary 1 and OFF represents binary 0. If you add or remove equipment, you can communicate that to the computer by changing a DIP switch setting. When you change a DIP switch setting, use a pointed instrument, such as a ballpoint pen, to push the switch. Don't use a graphite pencil, because graphite conducts electricity. Pieces of graphite dropped into the switch can damage it.

Figure 5-18   DIP switches are sometimes used to store setup data on motherboards

Setup Data Stored by Jumpers

Most computers hold additional configuration information by using jumpers on the motherboard. A jumper consists of two pins sticking up side by side; a cover over the two pins makes a connection. The two pins and the connection together serve as electrical connectors on the motherboard. If the pins are not connected with a cover, the setting is considered OFF. If the cover is present, the setting is ON. If the cover is hanging on one pin, it is "parked" so you won't lose it. You can see all three situations in Figure 5-19.

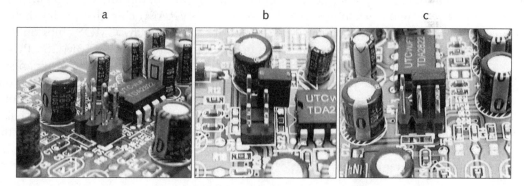

Figure 5-19   A 6-pin jumper group on a circuit board (a) has no pins covered, (b) has a cover parked on one pin, and (c) is configured with two jumpers capped or covered

For older motherboards, the presence of cache memory is a typical setting that was communicated to the computer by jumpers. Jumpers also are used to communicate the type and speed of the CPU to the system, or to disable a feature on the motherboard, such as keyboard power-up. (With this feature enabled, you can press a key to power up the system.) You change the jumper setting by removing the computer case, finding the correct jumper, and then either placing a metal cover over the jumper or removing the cover already there. Figure 5-20 shows a diagram of a motherboard with the keyboard power-up jumper shown.

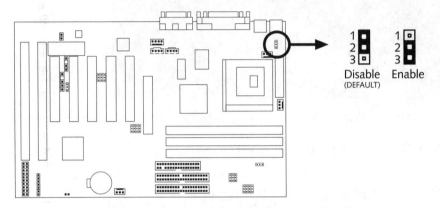

Figure 5-20   The keyboard power-up jumper allows you to use your keyboard to power up the computer

Setup Data Stored on a CMOS Chip

Computers today store most configuration information on one CMOS chip, also called the real-time clock/nonvolatile RAM (RTC/NVRAM) chip, that retains the data even when the computer is turned off. (There are actually many CMOS chips on a motherboard, used for various purposes.) On older computers (mostly IBM 286 PCs built in the 1980s), changes are made to the CMOS setup data using a setup program stored on a floppy disk. One major disadvantage of this method (besides the chance that you might lose or misplace the disk) is that the disk drive must be working before you can change the setup. An advantage of this method is that you cannot unintentionally change the setup. If you have an older computer and you do not have the floppy disk with the setup program, check the Web site of the motherboard manufacturer or the BIOS manufacturer for a replacement disk.

A+CORE 4.4 **Changing CMOS Using the Setup Program**   On newer computers, you usually change the data stored in the CMOS chip by accessing the setup program stored in ROM BIOS. You access the program by pressing a key or combination of keys during the boot process. The exact way to enter setup varies from one motherboard manufacturer to another. Table 5-12 lists the keystrokes needed to access CMOS setup for some common BIOS types.

A+CORE
4.4

Table 5-12 How to access CMOS setup

BIOS	Key to Press During POST to Access Setup
AMI BIOS	Del
Award BIOS	Del
Older Phoenix BIOS	Ctrl+Alt+Esc or Ctl+Alt+s
Newer Phoenix BIOS	F2 or F1
Dell computers using Phoenix BIOS	Ctrl+Alt+Enter
Older Compaq computer such as the Deskpro 286 or 386	Place the diagnostics disk in the disk drive, reboot your system, and choose Computer Setup from the menu.
Newer Compaq computers such as the ProLinea, Deskpro, Deskpro XL, Deskpro XE, or Presario	Press the F10 key while the cursor is in the upper-right corner of the screen, which happens just after the two beeps during booting.*
All other older computers	Use a setup program on the disk that came with the PC to access setup.

*For Compaq computers, the CMOS setup program is stored on the hard drive in a small, non-DOS partition of about 3 MB. If this partition becomes corrupted, you must run setup from a floppy disk. If you cannot run setup by pressing F10 at startup, suspect a damaged partition or a virus taking up space in conventional memory.

5

For the exact method you need to use to enter setup, see the documentation for your motherboard. A message such as the following usually appears on the screen:

        Press DEL to change Setup

or

        Press F8 for Setup

When you press the appropriate key or keys, a setup screen appears with menus and Help features that are often very user-friendly. Although the exact menus depend on the maker and version of components you are working with, the sample screens that follow will help you become familiar with the general contents of CMOS setup screens. Figure 5-21 shows a main menu for setup. On this menu, you can change the system date and time, the keyboard language, and other system features.

A+CORE
4.4

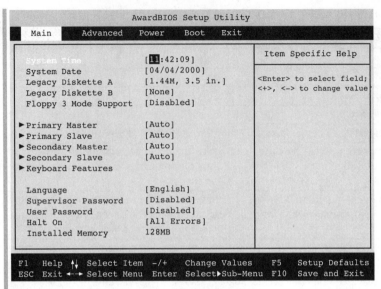

Figure 5-21   CMOS Setup Main menu

Recall the discussion of power management from Chapter 4. The power menu in CMOS setup allows you to configure automatic power-saving features for your system, such as suspend mode. Figure 5-22 shows a sample power menu.

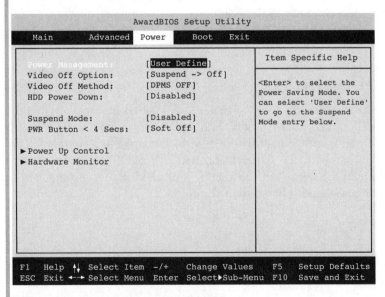

Figure 5-22   CMOS Setup Power menu

A+CORE 4.4 | Figure 5-23 shows a sample Boot menu in CMOS setup. Here, you can set the order in which the system tries to boot from certain devices. Most likely you will want to have the BIOS attempt to boot from the floppy drive first, and if no disk is present, turn to the hard drive. You will learn more about this in the installation procedures at the end of this chapter, as well as in later chapters.

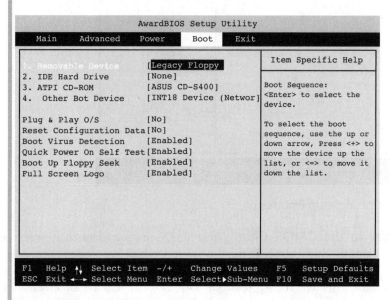

Figure 5-23   CMOS Setup Boot menu

Depending on which specific BIOS you are working with, an Advanced menu in the setup program or on other menus may contain other configuration options. When you exit the setup program, you can exit without saving your changes or exit and save your changes to the CMOS RAM chip. An exit screen such as the one shown in Figure 5-24 gives you various options, such as saving or discarding changes and exiting the program, restoring default settings, or saving changes and remaining in the program.

A+CORE
4.4

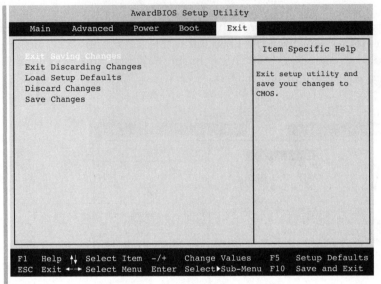

```
                    AwardBIOS Setup Utility
    Main      Advanced    Power     Boot      Exit

                                          ┌──────────────────────┐
    Exit Saving Changes                   │   Item Specific Help │
    Exit Discarding Changes               ├──────────────────────┤
    Load Setup Defaults                   │ Exit setup utility and│
    Discard Changes                       │ save your changes to  │
    Save Changes                          │ CMOS.                 │
                                          │                       │




    F1   Help ↑↓ Select Item  -/+   Change Values   F5   Setup Defaults
    ESC  Exit ←→ Select Menu   Enter Select▶Sub-Menu F10  Save and Exit
```

Figure 5-24   CMOS Setup Exit menu

Battery Power to the CMOS Chip   Most configuration data in newer computers is stored in a CMOS chip that is battery-powered when the system power is off (see Figure 5-25). The advantage of a CMOS chip over other types of chips is that a CMOS chip requires very little electricity to hold data. A small trickle of electricity from a nearby battery enables the CMOS chip to hold the data even while the main power to the computer is off. If the battery is disconnected or fails, setup information is lost. An indication that the battery is getting weak is that the system date and time are incorrect after the PC has been turned off.

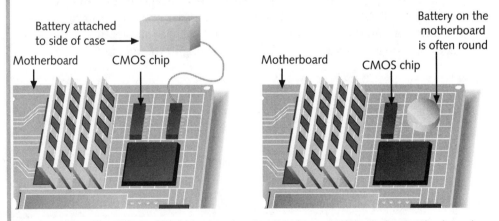

Figure 5-25   The battery that powers the CMOS chip may be on the motherboard or attached nearby

A+CORE
    4.4

There are several types of CMOS batteries:

- A 3.6 V lithium battery with a four-pin connector; connects with a Velcro strip
- A 4.5 V alkaline battery with a four-pin connector; connects with a Velcro strip
- A 3.6 V barrel-style battery with a two-pin connector; soldered on
- A 3 V lithium coin-cell battery

Figure 5-26 shows the coin cell, the most common type of CMOS battery.

5

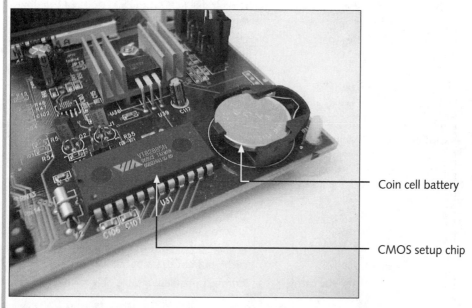

Coin cell battery

CMOS setup chip

Figure 5-26   The coin cell is the most common type of CMOS battery

Setting Startup Passwords in CMOS   Access to a computer can be controlled using a **startup password**, sometimes called a **power-on password**. During booting, or startup, the computer asks for a password. Entering an incorrect password terminates the boot process. The password is stored on the CMOS chip and is changed by accessing the setup screen. (This password is not the same as the OS password.) Many computers also provide a jumper near the CMOS chip that, when set to on, causes the computer to "forget" any changes made to default settings stored in CMOS. By jumping these pins, you can disable a password.

A+CORE
    2.1
    4.4

Lists of CMOS Settings   Motherboard manuals should contain a list of all CMOS settings, an explanation of their meanings, and their recommended values. When you purchase a motherboard or a computer, be sure the manual is included. If you don't have

A+CORE
  2.1
  4.4

the manual, you can sometimes go to the motherboard manufacturer's Web site and download the information you need to understand the specific CMOS settings of your computer. Table 5-13 lists some CMOS settings.

Table 5-13   CMOS settings and their purpose

Category	Setting	Description
Standard CMOS setup	Date and time	Used to set system date and time (called the real-time clock).
	Primary display	Used to tell POST and DOS (but not Windows) the type of video being used.
	Keyboard	Used to tell system if keyboard is installed or not installed. Useful if the computer is used as a print or file server and you don't want someone changing settings.
	Hard disk type	Used to record size and mapping of the drive.
	Floppy disk type	Choices are usually 3½ inch and 5¼ inch.
Advanced CMOS setup (a.k.a. BIOS Features setup)	Above 1 MB Memory test Memory parity Error check Numeric Processor test	Used to disable POST check of this memory to speed up booting. The OS checks this memory anyway. If you have a parity motherboard, used to enable parity checking to ensure that memory is correct. Enabled unless you have an old 386 or 486SX computer.
	System boot Sequence	Used to establish the drive the system turns to first to look for an OS. Normally drive A, then C.
	External cache Memory	Enable L2 cache. A frequent error in setup is to have cache but not use it because it's disabled here.
	Internal cache Memory	Normally enabled; disable only for old 386 computers.
	Password Checking option	Used to establish a startup password. Use this only if you need to prevent someone untrustworthy from using your PC.
	Video ROM Shadow C000, 16K	For DOS and Windows 9x, shadowing video ROM is recommended because ROM runs slower than RAM.
	System ROM Shadow F000, 64K	Enabling shadow system ROM is recommended.
	IDE multi-block mode	Enables a hard drive to read or write several sectors at a time. Depends on the kind of hard drive you have.
	Boot sector virus protection	Gives a warning when something is being written to the boot sector of the hard drive. Can be a nuisance if your software is designed to write to the boot sector regularly. When installing or upgrading an operating system, disable this protection so the OS install process can alter the boot sector without interruption.

A+CORE
2.1
4.4

Table 5-13   CMOS settings and their purpose (continued)

Category	Setting	Description
Advanced Chip Set Setup	AT bus clock selection	Gives the number by which the CPU speed is divided to get the ISA or EISA bus speed.
	ISA bus speed	Gives the number by which the PCI bus speed is divided to get the ISA bus speed.
	Bus mode	Can be set to synchronous or asynchronous modes. In synchronous mode, the bus uses the CPU clock. In asynchronous mode, it uses its own AT bus clock.
	AT cycle wait state	The number of wait states the CPU must endure while it interfaces with a device on the ISA or EISA bus. Increase this if an old and slow ISA card is not working well.
	Memory read wait state	Number of wait states the CPU must endure while reading from RAM.
	Memory write wait state	Number of wait states the CPU must endure while writing to RAM.
	Cache read option	Sometimes called "cache read hit burst." The number of clock beats needed to load four 32-bit words into the CPU's internal cache (4-1-1-1 is the usual choice).
	Fast cache read/write	Refers to external cache. Enable it if you have two banks of cache, 64K or 256K.
	Cache wait state	Refers to external cache. The number of wait states the CPU must use while accessing cache.
	AGP capability	Switches between AGP 1x, AGP 2x, and AGP 4x versions.
	AGP aperture size	Adjusts the amount of system memory AGP can address.
	VGA BIOS sequence	Determines order in which PCI/AGP is initialized; important mainly with dual monitors.
	Processor serial number	Allows processor ID# to be switched off for privacy (Pentium III only).
Power Menu (a.k.a. Power Management)	Power management	Disable or enable all power management features. These features are designed to conserve electricity.
	Video off method	Sets which way video to the monitor will be suspended.
	HDD power down	Disable or enable the feature to shut down the hard drive after a period of inactivity.
	Wake on LAN	Wake on LAN allows your PC to be booted from another computer on the same network. It requires an ATX power supply that supports the feature.

5

A+CORE
2.1
4.4

Table 5-13   CMOS settings and their purpose (continued)

Category	Setting	Description
	Wake on keyboard	Allows you to power up your PC by pressing a certain key combination.
IDE HDD Auto-detect	Automated query	Detects HDDs installed on either IDE channel; allows you to specify Normal, Large, or LBA mode.
Hardware Device Settings (only found on "jumper-less" motherboards)	CPU operating speed	Sets the appropriate speed for your CPU.
	External clock	Sets the system bus speed.
	I/O voltage	Sets the appropriate I/O voltage.
	Core voltage	Sets the appropriate core voltage.
Note: The titles, locations, and inclusion or exclusion of BIOS categories and settings depend on the manufacturer and/or BIOS version. For instance, Plug and Play may be a group of settings sharing a category with other settings in one version of BIOS, while Plug and Play may be its own category in another BIOS version.		

TIP   In documentation, a.k.a. stands for "also known as."

Protecting Documentation and Configuration Settings

A+CORE
2.1
4.4

If the battery goes bad or is disconnected, you can lose the settings saved in CMOS RAM. If you are using default settings, reboot with a good battery and instruct setup to restore the default settings. Setup has to autodetect the hard drive present, and you need to set the date and time, but you can easily recover from the problem. However, if you have customized some CMOS settings, you need to restore them. The most reliable way to do that is to keep a written record of all the changes you make to CMOS.

If you are permanently responsible for a computer, you should consider a written record of what you have done to this PC an essential tool for maintaining the PC. Use a small notebook or similar document, and keep CMOS settings, records of hardware and software installed, network settings, and similar information in the notebook. Suppose someone decides to tinker with a PC for which you are responsible, changes a jumper on the motherboard, and cannot remember which jumper he or she changed. The computer no longer works, and the documentation for the board is now invaluable. Lost or misplaced documentation makes the otherwise simple job of reading the settings for each jumper and checking them on the board a long and tedious research task. Keep the documentation well labeled in a safe place. If you have several computers to maintain, you might consider a filing system for each computer. Another method is to tape a cardboard folder to the inside top of the computer case and safely tuck the hardware documentation there. This works well if you are responsible for several computers spread over a wide area.

A+CORE
2.1
4.4

Regardless of the method you use, it's important that you keep your written record up to date and store it and the hardware documentation in a safe place. Leaving it in the care of users who might not realize its value is probably not a good idea. The notebook and documentation will be invaluable to you as you solve future problems with this PC.

5

Saving and Restoring CMOS Settings Using a Third-Party Utility Software

If you lose CMOS settings, another way to restore them is to use a backup of the settings that you have previously saved on a floppy disk. One third-party utility that allows you to save CMOS settings is Norton Utilities by Symantec (*www.symantec.com*).

You can also download a shareware utility to record CMOS settings. The files might change with new releases of the software.

1. Access the Internet and use a search engine to search for and go to a site offering Cmos.zip. Two current locations are *www.ibiblio.org/pub/micro/pc-stuff/ freedos/files/util/system/cmos.zip* and *www.computerhope.com/download/ hardware.htm*.

2. Select and download CMOS.ZIP. You can then exit the Internet.

3. Unzip the compressed file and print the contents of the documentation file.

4. Double-click the CMOS.EXE file you unzipped. The program shows the current content of CMOS memory in a DOS box.

5. Enter **S** (for Save) at the command line. Enter the drive letter of your floppy drive and a filename to save the current CMOS settings to floppy disk, such as **A:MYCMOS**.

6. Enter **Q** to quit the program.

When you want to retrieve the contents of the file from the floppy disk, run the CMOS.EXE program again, and enter **L** (for Load) at the command line, specifying the name of the file you saved on the floppy disk.

BUILDING A COMPUTER: AN INTRODUCTION

Now that you have learned about how motherboards work and what components they include, you can begin learning how to build your own computer. The final section of this chapter discusses in detail how a motherboard is installed. First, though, let's look at the overall process for building your own computer. In Chapter 4, you took your first look inside a computer and learned your way around by taking it apart. In this section, you will begin to learn how to put a new one together from separately purchased parts. You will need this information as you learn to install specific components in this chapter and the rest of the book. This is a general overview of the process and is not meant to include the details of all possible installation scenarios, which can vary according to the components and OS you are installing.

TIP Whenever you install or uninstall software or hardware, keep a notebook with details about the components you are working on, configuration settings, manufacturer's specifications, and other relevant information. This helps if you need to backtrack later and can also help you document and troubleshoot your computer system. Keep all hardware documentation for this system together with the notebook in an envelope in a safe place.

The general process for putting together a computer is as follows:

1. *Verify that you have all parts you plan to install.* Check device manufacturers' Web sites for updated BIOS and device drivers for your system.

2. *Prepare the computer case.* Installing the case fan, remove the plates that cover the drive bays, and install the spacers that keep the motherboard from touching the case. Because today's CPUs run at high temperatures, it is a good idea to have at least one case fan in addition to the power supply fan, to ensure good case ventilation. Also, preparing the case before actually installing components lessens the risk of damaging components as you install them.

3. *Install drives,* such as CD–ROM or DVD drive, hard drive, and floppy drive. Have a plan as to which drives to install in which locations, to avoid tangling cables or having them interfere with airflow or with access to other components. As you install drives, verify jumper settings for Master/Slave or SCSI ID.

4. *Determine proper configuration settings for the motherboard.* Especially important are any jumpers, DIP switches, or CMOS settings specifically for the CPU, and RAM speeds and timing. Gather as much information as possible from manufacturer documentation. Read the motherboard manual from cover to cover. You can also check manufacturer Web sites for suggestions for optimizing system settings.

5. *Set any jumpers or switches on the motherboard.* This is much easier to do before you put the board in the case.

6. *Install the CPU and CPU cooler.* The CPU comes already installed on some motherboards in which case you just need to install the cooler. You might need to add thermal grease.

7. *Install RAM* into the appropriate slots on the motherboard.

8. *Install the motherboard and attach cabling* that goes from the case switches to the motherboard and from the power supply to the drives. Pay attention to how cables are labeled and to any information in the documentation about where to attach them. (The next section covers details on how to install a motherboard.) Position and tie cables neatly together to make sure they don't obstruct the fans.

9. *Install the video card* (which can also be called the display adapter, video adapter, or graphics accelerator) on the motherboard. Usually this card goes into the AGP slot, as you learned in Chapter 1.

10. *Plug the computer into a power source, and attach the monitor and keyboard.* Note that you do not attach the mouse now. You do not need it for the initial setup. Although the mouse generally does not cause problems during setup, it is a good idea not to initially install anything you don't absolutely need.

11. *Boot the system and enter CMOS setup.* As you learned earlier in the chapter, there are several ways to do this, depending on what type of system you have.

12. *Make sure settings are set to the default.* If components come new from the manufacturer, they are probably already at default settings. If you are salvaging a component from another system, you may need to reset settings to the default. Generally a jumper or switch will set all CMOS settings to default settings. You will need to do the following while you are in CMOS:

    - Check the time and date.
    - Check the floppy drive type.
    - Make sure abbreviated POST is disabled. While you are setting up a system, you generally want the system to do as many tests as possible. Once you know the system is working, you can choose to abbreviate POST.
    - Set the boot order to drive A, then drive C, if you will be booting the OS from a floppy disk. Set the boot order to CD-ROM, then drive C, if you will be booting the OS from a CD. This determines which drive the system looks to for the OS. You may need to change the boot order later, as explained in Step 19.
    - Make sure autodetect hard disk is set so that the system automatically looks for drives.
    - Leave everything else as defaults unless you know that particular settings should be otherwise.
    - Save and exit.

13. *If you are booting from a floppy disk, insert a bootable setup disk* that contains the files that allow you to format the hard drive. (Refer to Chapter 3 for a list of files that should be on this disk.)

14. *Observe POST* and verify that no errors occur.

15. *Prepare the hard drive for the OS.* You will learn how to do this in Chapter 9.

16. *Reboot the system and run ScanDisk on drive C.* ScanDisk is an OS utility that checks the hard drive for errors and repairs them. Do this if the hard drive is not new. Chapter 9 covers this in detail.

17. *Connect the mouse.*

18. *Install the OS from CD or floppy.* Generally, it is best to install the OS before any expansion cards, such as a sound card or a modem card. Installing multiple cards at once can confuse Plug and Play, especially during OS installation. Unless you are very familiar with all components' resource requirements, it is almost always less trouble to install one device at a time on a new system. If

you are setting up multiple systems with the same configuration, build the first system one card at a time. If no major errors occur, then, on a second system, try installing all cards at once, after the OS has been loaded. If this approach is successful, then you can save a little time by installing all hardware devices before you install the OS. However, you should still reboot whenever you have the option, as the OS detects each device.

19. *Change the boot order in CMOS* so that it does not boot from a CD first. If you set the order as drive A, then drive C, you can boot from a floppy disk later as needed. This is the most common boot order.

20. *Check for conflicts with system resources.* For Windows, use Device Manager to verify that the OS recognizes all devices and that no conflicts are reported. If your motherboard comes with a CD that contains some motherboard drivers, install them now. Remember that the drivers that Windows installed for the devices it sensed might not be the latest drivers. Windows makes its best guess at what drivers to use, but if your version of Windows is older than some of your components, it might not have the correct or newest drivers for those devices. Using Device Manager, you can see what drivers are installed for a device. If Windows is not using the newest drivers, update the drivers using the latest drivers from the CD that comes with the device.

21. *Install any other expansion cards and/or drives,* and install appropriate drivers, one device at a time, rebooting and checking for conflicts after each installation.

22. *Verify that all is operating properly, and make any final OS and/or CMOS adjustments,* such as power management settings.

INSTALLING THE MOTHERBOARD

A+CORE
1.2
Now that you have learned about the general process of putting together a computer, you will learn how to install a motherboard. The following section provides you with information on how to install and configure a motherboard and how to test the installation.

CAUTION
As with any installation, remember the importance of using a ground strap to ground yourself when working inside a computer case, to protect components against ESD.

Preparing the Motherboard to Go into the Case

A+CORE
1.2
Before you begin preparing the motherboard, read the manual that comes with it from beginning to end. The steps in this procedure are general, and you will need to know information specific to your motherboard. Visually familiarize yourself with the configuration of the case and the motherboard.

Setting the Jumpers

The first step in preparing the motherboard to go in the case is to set the jumpers or DIP switches. When doing an installation, read the motherboard documentation carefully, looking for explanations of how jumpers and DIP switches on the board are used, which will differ from one motherboard to another. For example, a jumper group might control the system bus frequency and another group might control the CPU frequency multiple. Then set the jumpers and DIP switches according to the hardware you will be installing.

Adding the CPU, Fan, and Heat Sink

Now that you have set the jumpers on the motherboard, you are ready to add the CPU itself. The motherboard we are using in this example has a slot 1 for the Pentium II, which comes packaged either in a single edge contact cartridge (SECC) or a single edge processor package (SEPP) for the Celeron processor. For either processor, the motherboard uses a universal retention mechanism (URM), which is preinstalled on the board. Follow these steps to install the fan on the side of the processor first, and then install the processor on the motherboard:

1. Unfold the URM arms. Flip both arms up until they lock into position (see Figure 5-27).

2. Examine the fan and processor to see how the fan brace lines up with holes in the side of the SECC (see Figure 5-28).

URM supporting arms

Figure 5-27   Preparing URM arms to receive the CPU (the arms are in the upright position)

$A^{+CORE}_{1.2}_{1.9}$

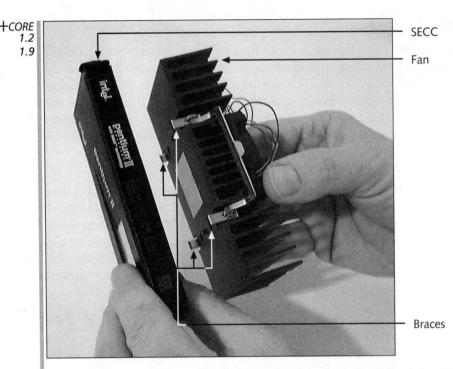

SECC

Fan

Braces

Figure 5-28 The braces on the fan align with holes in the side of the SECC

3. Place the fan directly on the side of the SECC. The two should fit tightly together, with absolutely no space between them.

4. After you fit the fan and SECC together, place the SECC on a table and push the clamp on the fan down and into place, to secure the fan to the SECC (see Figure 5-29).

Push clamp down

Figure 5-29 Push the clamp on the fan down until it locks in place, locking the fan to the SECC

A +CORE
 1.2
 1.9

5. Insert the fan and SECC into the supporting arms (see Figure 5-30). The SECC should fit snugly into slot 1, similar to the way an expansion card settles down into an expansion slot. The arms should snap into position when the SECC is fully seated. Be certain you have a good fit.

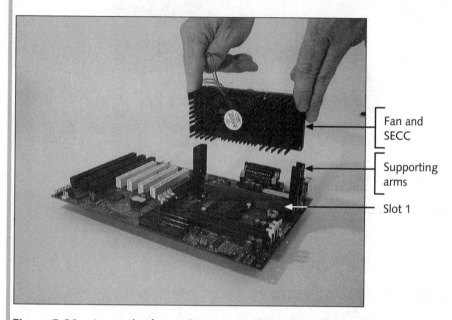

Figure 5-30   Insert the fan and SECC into the supporting arms and slot 1

6. Lock the SECC into position by pulling the SECC locks outward until they lock into the supporting arm lock holes.

7. Connect the power cord coming from the fan to the power connection on the motherboard (see Figure 5-31). Look for the power connection near slot 1. If you have trouble locating it, see the motherboard documentation.

A+*CORE*
   1.2

Power for CPU fan

Figure 5-31   Connect the fan power cord to the motherboard

The next step is to install RAM in the memory slots. Chapter 6 covers how to buy and install memory for a specific motherboard.

Installing the Motherboard in the Case

A+*CORE*
   1.2

Here are the steps for installing the motherboard in the case:

1. Install the faceplate. The **faceplate** or I/O shield is a metal plate that comes with the motherboard and fits over the ports to create a well-fitting enclosure around them. A case might have several faceplates designed for several brands of motherboards. Select the correct one and discard the others (see Figure 5-32). Insert the faceplate in the hole at the back of the case (see Figure 5-33).

2. Install the standoffs. **Standoffs**, also called **spacers**, are round plastic or metal pegs that separate the motherboard from the case, so that components on the back of the motherboard do not touch the case. Make sure the locations of the standoffs match the screw holes on the motherboard. If you need to remove a standoff to move it to a new slot, needle-nose pliers work well to unscrew the standoff. The case will have more holes than you need, in order to support several brands of motherboards.

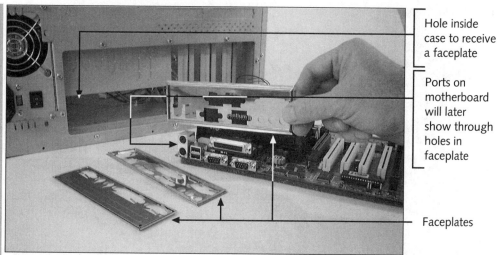

Hole inside
case to receive
a faceplate

Ports on
motherboard
will later
show through
holes in
faceplate

Faceplates

5

Figure 5-32 The computer case comes with several faceplates. Select the faceplate that fits over the ports that come off the motherboard. The other plates can be discarded.

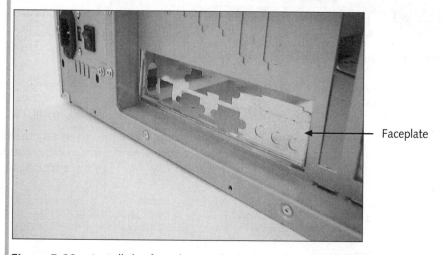

Faceplate

Figure 5-33 Install the faceplate in the hole at the rear of the computer case

3. Place the motherboard inside the case, and use screws to attach it to the case. Figure 5-34 shows how you must align the standoffs to the holes on the motherboard. The screws fit into the standoffs you installed earlier. There should be at least four standoff/screw sets, and there may be as many as six. Use as many as there are holes in the motherboard.

A⁺CORE 1.2

Holes for screws

Standoffs

Figure 5-34   Three standoffs and four screw holes are visible

4. Connect the power cord from the power supply to the P1 power connection on the motherboard. (If you are using an AT motherboard, you have two power connections, P8 and P9, which are connected using the black-to-black rule.)

5. Connect the wire leads from the front panel of the case to the motherboard. These are the wires for the switches and lights on the front of the computer. Because your case and your motherboard may not have been made by the same manufacturer, you need to pay close attention to the source of the wires to determine where they connect on the motherboard. For example, Figure 5-35 shows a computer case that has five wires from the front panel that connect to the motherboard.

The five connectors are:

- *Reset switch.* Used to reboot the computer
- *HDD LED.* Controls a light on the front panel that lights up when any IDE device is in use. (LED stands for light-emitting diode; an LED is a light on the front panel.)
- *Speaker.* Controls the speaker
- *Power LED.* Light indicating that power is on
- *Remote switch.* Controls power to the motherboard; must be connected for the PC to power up

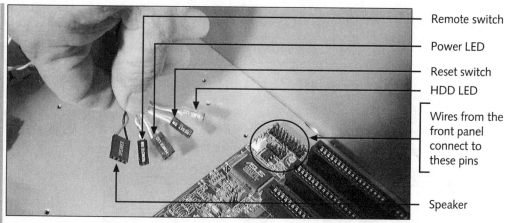

Remote switch

Power LED

Reset switch

HDD LED

Wires from the front panel connect to these pins

Speaker

Figure 5-35   Five wires from the front panel connect to the motherboard

To know which wire connects to which pins, see the motherboard documentation. Sometimes the documentation is not clear, but guessing is okay when connecting a wire to a connection. If it doesn't work, no harm is done.

TIP To help orient the connector on the motherboard pins, look for a small triangle embedded on the connector that marks one of the outside wires as pin 1 (see Figure 5-36). Look for pin 1 to be labeled on the motherboard as a small 1 embedded on the board to either the right or the left of the group of pins. Also, sometimes the documentation will mark pin 1 as a square pin in the diagram, rather than round like the other pins.

Figure 5-36   Look for the small triangle embedded on the wire lead connectors to orient the connector correctly to the motherboard connector pins

Completing the Installation

After you install the motherboard, you will install drives and other components. Later chapters cover how to do this. Finally, turn on the system and make sure everything is connected properly. You may need to change the hardware configuration settings discussed in the previous section. As you set configuration data, remember to create a rescue disk of these settings so that you can restore them if something goes wrong.

TROUBLESHOOTING THE MOTHERBOARD AND CPU

When troubleshooting the motherboard, use whatever clues POST can give you. Recall that, before video is checked out, POST reports any error messages as beep codes. When a PC boots, one beep indicates that all is well after POST. If you hear more than one beep, look up the beep code in Appendix A. Error messages on the screen indicate that video is working. If the beep code or error message is not in Appendix A, try the Web site of the ROM BIOS manufacturer for information. Figure 5-37 shows the Web site for AMI with explanations of beep codes produced by its startup BIOS.

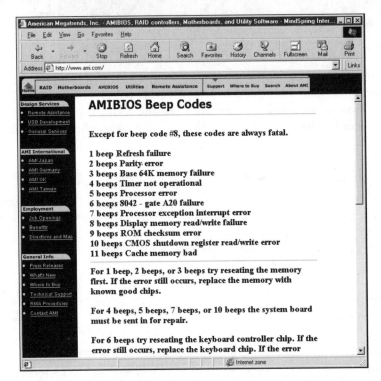

Figure 5-37   The ROM BIOS manufacturer's Web site is a good source of information about beep codes

Remember that you can try substituting good hardware components for those you suspect are bad. Be cautious here. A friend once had a computer that would not boot. He replaced the hard drive, with no change. He replaced the motherboard next. The computer booted up with no problem; he was delighted, until it failed again. Later he discovered that a faulty power supply had damaged his original motherboard. When he traded the bad one for a good one, the new motherboard also got zapped! Check the voltage coming from the power supply before putting in a new motherboard! (Instructions on troubleshooting the power supply are in Chapter 4.)

A+CORE
   2.1

A power-saving feature might be the source of the problem. Ask yourself, "Is the system in a doze or sleep Mode?" Many "green" systems can be programmed through CMOS to suspend the monitor or even the drive if the keyboard or CPU has been inactive for a few minutes. Pressing any key usually causes operations to resume exactly where the user left off. If you have just upgraded the CPU and the system will not boot, reinstall the old CPU, flash BIOS, and then try the new CPU again. Verify that you have installed thermal paste between the CPU and the heat sink.

If this doesn't resolve the problem, try these things:

- If the fan is running, reseat or replace the CPU, BIOS, or RAM. Try installing a DIMM in a different slot. A POST code diagnostic card is a great help at this point.

- Sometimes a dead computer can be fixed by simply disassembling it and reseating cables, adapter cards, socketed chips, and SIMMs, DIMMs, or RIMMs. Bad connections and corrosion are common problems.

- Check jumpers, DIP switches, and CMOS settings.

- Look for physical damage on the motherboard.

- Check CMOS for temperature reading that indicates overheating.

- Flash BIOS.

- A dead or dying battery may cause problems. Sometimes, after a long holiday, a weak battery causes the CMOS to forget its configuration.

- Reduce the system to essentials. Remove any unnecessary hardware, such as expansion cards, and then try to boot again.

- Exchange the CPU.

- Exchange the motherboard, but before you do, measure the voltage output of the power supply, in case it is producing too much power and has damaged the board.

CHAPTER SUMMARY

- ❑ The motherboard is the most complicated of all components inside the computer. It contains the CPU and accompanying chip set, the real-time clock, ROM BIOS, CMOS configuration chip, RAM, RAM cache, system bus, expansion slots, jumpers, ports, and power supply connections. The motherboard you select determines both the capabilities and limitations of your system.

- ❑ The most important component on the motherboard is the CPU, or central processing unit. The CPU is rated according to its speed, efficiency of programming code, word size, data path size, maximum number of memory addresses, size of internal cache, multiprocessing abilities, and special functions.

- ❑ Two kinds of static RAM cache for the slower DRAM are internal and external cache, sometimes called Level 1 and Level 2 or Level 3 cache, also called L1 and L2 or L3 cache.

❑ L1 cache is contained on the CPU microchip, and L2 and L3 cache are external to this microchip. L2 and L3 can be on the motherboard or in the CPU housing. If a processor has L2 cache, then cache on the motherboard is called L3 cache.

❑ The Itanium has L1, L2, and L3 cache.

❑ The Intel Pentium CPU family includes the Classic Pentium, Pentium MMX, Pentium Pro, Pentium II, Celeron, Pentium III, and Pentium 4. Intel's newest processor family is called the Itanium.

❑ AMD and VIA are Intel's chief competitors for the CPU market.

❑ Newer CPUs require extra cooling, which a CPU heat sink and cooling fan located on top of or near the CPU can accomplish.

❑ Common CPU sockets and slots are Socket 7, Socket 370, Socket 423, slot 1, Slot A, slot 2, and Socket 603. A slot looks like an expansion slot.

❑ Because some CPUs require one voltage for internal core operations and another voltage for external I/O operations, motherboards might have a voltage regulator on board.

❑ Some components can be built into the motherboard, in which case they are called on-board components, or they can be attached to the system in some other way, such as on an expansion card.

❑ ROM chips contain the programming code to manage POST and system BIOS and to change the CMOS settings. The setup or CMOS chip holds configuration information.

❑ A chip set is a group of chips on the motherboard that supports the CPU. Intel is the most popular manufacturer of chip sets.

❑ The total BIOS of a system includes the ROM BIOS on the motherboard as well as BIOS on expansion cards. Plug and Play BIOS is designed to work in harmony with Windows 9x to resolve resource conflicts from expansion cards and other devices. Flash ROM allows the ROM BIOS to be upgraded without changing the ROM chip.

❑ A bus is a path on the motherboard that carries electrical power, control signals, memory addresses, and data to different components on the board.

❑ A bus can be 16, 32, 64, or more bits wide. The first ISA bus had an 8-bit data path. The second ISA slot had a 16-bit data path.

❑ Some well-known buses are the 16-bit ISA, 32-bit MCA and EISA buses, and the two local buses, the VESA bus and the PCI bus. A local bus is designed to allow fast devices quicker and more direct access to the CPU than other buses do.

❑ Expansion slots can be located on the motherboard, but they are sometimes stacked vertically in the computer case on a second board devoted to that purpose.

❑ Jumpers on the motherboard can be used to set the motherboard speed and the CPU multiplier that determines the CPU speed.

❑ Sometimes the CPU must be slowed down to accommodate slower devices, by means of wait states that cause it to wait one clock beat. Wait states often reduce performance significantly.

❑ When building a new system, install the drives, motherboard, and expansion cards. Only install essential components before you install the OS. Then add other components one at a time, verifying that each component works before adding another.

❑ When installing the motherboard, install the CPU and memory, and set jumpers and DIP switches on the board before installing it in the case.

5

KEY TERMS

Advanced Transfer Cache (ATC)	instruction set	P9 connector
back side bus	internal bus	pin grid array (PGA)
bus speed	internal cache	power-on password
CISC (complex instruction set computing)	Level 1 (L1) cache	primary cache
	Level 2 (L2) cache	processor speed
	Level 3 (L3) cache	RISC (reduced instruction set computing)
discrete L2 cache	local bus	
dual-voltage CPU	local I/O bus	single-voltage CPU
EPIC (explicitly parallel instruction computing)	low insertion force (LIF) socket	South Bridge
		spacers
Execution Trace Cache	memory bus	staggered pin grid array (SPGA)
expansion bus	memory cache	standoffs
external cache	motherboard bus	startup password
faceplate	multiplier	system bus
front side bus	North Bridge	wait state
heat sink	on-board ports	zero insertion force (ZIF) socket
host bus	P1 connector	
	P8 connector	

REVIEW QUESTIONS

Questions 1–4 are based on the various designs of motherboards listed below. For each question, choose one of the choices below.

    a. AT

    b. Baby AT

    c. ATX

    d. Mini ATX

1. The original style motherboard design was referred to as a(n) _____ design.

2. Of the motherboard designs, which motherboard makes use of a P8/P9 power connector?

3. Which of the motherboard designs utilizes a more efficient, P1 power connector?

4. Which of the motherboard designs incorporates an additional 3.3V supply on the motherboard?

5. When the CPU is operating at a speed that is too fast for the device that it is communicating with, it imposes what is referred to as a _____ _____, which has the effect of slowing the processor down by adding additional clock ticks to each computing cycle.

Questions 6 and 7 are based on the three core CPU building blocks:

    a. I/O unit

    b. Arithmetic Logic Unit (ALU)

    c. Control Unit

6. Which of the above components manages all activities inside and out of the CPU?

7. Which of the above components manages data and instructions entering and leaving the CPU?

8. Which part of the CPU is used to hold counters, data, instructions, and addresses?

    a. Memory locations

    b. ALU

    c. Control unit

    d. Registers

    e. None of the above

9. The term given to the high-speed bus that is internal to the CPU and allows for communications between the ALU and internal memory cache is:

   a. Data bus

   b. Address bus

   c. Back side bus

   d. Control bus

   e. None of the above

10. The first processors used for the IBM-PC were rated at speeds of:

    a. 2 MHz

    b. 4.77 MHz

    c. 1 GHz

    d. 3.06 GHz

    e. None of the above

11. What is the definition of "word size"?

12. Another term associated with "data path" is:

    a. Address bus

    b. Back side data bus

    c. Front side data bus

    d. Control bus

    e. None of the above

13. The maximum number of physical addressable memory locations a CPU can address is determined by which bus structure?

    a. Address bus

    b. Back side data bus

    c. Front side data bus

    d. Control bus

    e. None of the above

14. The term "word size" is often used to describe the largest number of bits the CPU can process in one operation. It is also associated with which bus that the CPU utilizes?

    a. Internal address bus

    b. External address bus

    c. Internal data bus

    d. External data bus

    e. Control bus

15. A microprocessor with the following bus specifications:

    6-bit data bus

    8-bit address bus

    5-bit control bus

    can access how many physical memory locations?

    a. 32

    b. 64

    c. 128

    d. 256

    e. None of the above

16. Cache memory is often referred to as "look-ahead" memory for its ability to store previously decoded information for reference at a later time. Cache memory is available in different configurations. Which configuration of cache memory is found on the CPU die?

    a. L1

    b. L2

    c. L3

    d. All of the above

    e. None of the above

17. The Pentium microprocessor possesses what type of external data bus capacity?

    a. 16-bit

    b. 32-bit

    c. 64-bit

    d. 128-bit

    e. 256-bit

18. Assume that a Pentium microprocessor needs to run at a speed of 500 MHz, and the motherboard multiplier is set to 4. What is the speed of the system bus to allow this particular configuration?

    a. 4 MHz

    b. 100 MHz

    c. 125 MHz

    d. 500 MHz

    e. 2000 MHz

19. Cache memory is comprised of what specific type of memory?

    a. Static RAM

    b. Dynamic RAM

    c. ROM

    d. CD-ROM

    e. Hard disk

20. CPUs that employ Execution Trace Cache do so to optimize the way in which data is cached.

    a. True

    b. False

21. Intel's first true 64-bit processor is the:

    a. Pentium 4

    b. AMD Athlon MP

    c. Pentium 3

    d. Itanium

    e. Celeron

22. The heat sink, used with most current day processors, is used primarily to:

    a. Draw heat to the processor

    b. Draw heat away from the processor

    c. Depending on how they are configured, can do both

    d. Neither a nor b

23. In terms of CPU slots and sockets, which is used by Advanced Micro Devices (AMD) to interconnect the CPU to the motherboard?

    a. Slot 1 and slot 2

    b. Socket A and slot A

    c. Slot 1 and socket A

    d. Socket A and slot 2

    e. Socket A and socket B

5

24. Of the following socket configurations for Pentium processors, which was employed to squeeze more pins in the small amount of real estate reserved for the processor?

   a. PGA

   b. SPGA

   c. DIP

   d. SIMM

   e. DIMM

25. Upon executing system boot, what effect does holding down the Pause/Break key have on the boot sequence?

   a. It allows many of the POST procedures to be bypassed to allow for quicker system bootup.

   b. It restarts the boot process.

   c. It will stop the startup process.

   d. It will redirect the system to display error log information.

   e. None of the above

26. Buses that work in synchronization with the CPU and the system clock are referred to as:

   a. Local buses

   b. Expansion buses

   c. Synchronization buses

   d. Clock buses

   e. None of the above

27. Buses that work asynchronously with the CPU at a much slower rate are referred to as:

   a. Local buses

   b. Expansion buses

   c. Synchronization buses

   d. Clock buses

   e. None of the above

28. The PCI bus is an excellent example of a(n):

   a. Local bus

   b. Expansion bus

   c. Synchronization bus

   d. Clock bus

   e. None of the above

6

MANAGING MEMORY

In this chapter, you will learn:

- ♦ About the different kinds of physical memory and how they work
- ♦ How to upgrade and troubleshoot memory
- ♦ How DOS and Windows 9x view and manage memory

In earlier chapters, you learned how several important hardware components work and how to support them. This chapter looks at another component, memory, and examines how DOS and Windows 9x manage it.
Memory is required in order for a system to work. Memory is stored on
microchips, which are often stored on memory modules called SIMMs,
DIMMs, or RIMMs. Adding more memory to a system can sometimes
greatly improve performance.

PHYSICAL MEMORY

Recall that memory temporarily holds data and instructions as the CPU processes them and that computer memory is divided into two categories: ROM and RAM. ROM retains its data when the PC is turned off, but RAM loses all its data (except for data stored on the CMOS chip). ROM stores its data on chips socketed or soldered to the circuit boards. One or two ROM chips on a motherboard hold system BIOS and startup BIOS programs, and many devices and circuit boards such as video cards have ROM chips on them. In the 1980s, RAM chips were also socketed or soldered directly on motherboards, but today all RAM used as main memory is housed on SIMMs, DIMMs, or RIMMs. This section examines the different technologies of RAM and ROM, focusing on RAM technologies.

ROM on the Motherboard

A+CORE
1.1
1.10

Recall that ROM, or read-only memory, consists of memory chips that contain programs (called ROM BIOS) that are acid-etched into the chips at the factory (see Figure 6-1). The programs on a ROM chip (sometimes called firmware) are permanent; they cannot be changed. **EPROM (erasable programmable ROM)** chips can have their programs changed. They have a special window where an ultraviolet light erases the current memory contents, so that the chip can be reprogrammed. **EEPROM (electrically erasable programmable ROM)** chips (also known as flash ROM chips), also allow their programs to be changed. On EEPROM chips, a higher voltage is applied to a pin to erase its previous memory before a new instruction set or data is electronically written.

Newer ROM chips are usually soldered onto the motherboard and updated by flashing, as you learned in the last chapter. Older ROM chips were socketed onto the motherboard and replaced manually by removing the chip and inserting a new one in the socket.

RAM on the Motherboard

A+CORE
1.1
1.10

RAM, or random access memory, is divided into two categories: **static RAM (SRAM)** and **dynamic RAM (DRAM)**. DRAM, pronounced "DEE-RAM," is memory that needs to be refreshed every few milliseconds. To **refresh** RAM means that the computer must rewrite the data to the chip. Refreshing RAM is done by the memory controller, which is part of the chip set on the motherboard. Today most DRAM is stored on DIMMs and less commonly on RIMMs (see Figure 6-2).

A+CORE
1.1
1.10

6

Figure 6-1   The ROM BIOS on newer motherboards can be upgraded using software provided by the BIOS manufacturer

ROM BIOS chip

DIMM

Two extra slots for additional DIMMs

Figure 6-2   DRAM on most motherboards today is stored on DIMMs

Besides serving as main memory, RAM also provides a memory cache. These memory chips hold data as long as the power is on and are therefore called static RAM (SRAM), pronounced "ESS-RAM." A motherboard can have lots of main memory to hold data

A+CORE
1.1
1.10

and instructions as they are processed and a little memory cache to help speed up access time to main memory. Recall from Chapter 5 that cache memory is contained on the motherboard or inside the CPU housing. On the motherboard, it is either on individual chips or on a memory module called a **COAST (cache on a stick)**. Figure 6-3 shows a motherboard with 256K of SRAM installed on the board in two single chips. A COAST slot is available to hold an additional 256K. At first, the motherboard held all cache memory, then cache was stored inside the CPU housing, and more recently, some systems put the cache in both places.

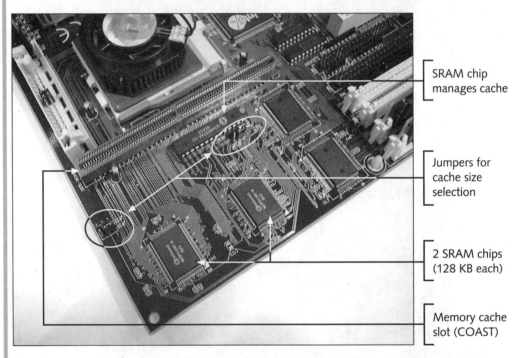

SRAM chip manages cache

Jumpers for cache size selection

2 SRAM chips (128 KB each)

Memory cache slot (COAST)

Figure 6-3　SRAM on this motherboard is stored in individual chips, and the board also has a COAST slot

DRAM and SRAM use several technologies summarized in Table 6-1. Of all the memory technologies listed, the two current DRAM technologies are Direct Rambus DRAM and Double Data Rate SDRAM (SDRAM II). Most SRAM is now inside the processor housing. Other technologies are considered obsolete, although you still need to be aware of them in case you see them on older motherboards you support. You will read more about these technologies in the following sections.

A+CORE
1.1
1.10
4.2

Table 6-1   Types of memory (SRAM and DRAM)

Main Memory (DRAM)	Cache Memory (SRAM)
DRAM, needs constant refreshing	SRAM, does not need refreshing
Slower than SRAM because of refreshing time	Faster but more expensive
Physically housed on DIMMs, SIMMs, and RIMMs	Physically housed on the motherboard on COAST modules or single chips or included inside the processor case
Technologies include: • FPM • EDO • BEDO • Synchronous DRAM (SDRAM) • SyncLink SDRAM (SLDRAM) • Double Data Rate SDRAM (DDR SDRAM or SDRAM II) • Direct Rambus DRAM	Technologies include: • Synchronous SRAM • Burst SRAM • Pipelined burst • Asynchronous SRAM • Housed within the processor case (new trend)
Memory addresses assigned	No memory addresses assigned

6

Static RAM Technologies

SRAM provides faster access than DRAM because data does not need to be constantly rewritten to SRAM, saving the CPU time used to refresh data in DRAM. Memory chips are made of transistors, which are switches. A SRAM transistor switch can stay in place as long as it has voltage available because each memory cell is comprised of several interlinked transistors, but DRAM transistor switches are charged by capacitors, which must be recharged. SRAM chips are more expensive than DRAM chips. Therefore, most computers have a little SRAM and a lot of DRAM. Table 6-2 summarizes how SRAM is used in different memory caches on and off the motherboard. Table 6-2 also summarizes the information about memory caches presented in Chapter 5.

Table 6-2   The location of memory caches in a system

Memory Cache	Where Located
L1 cache	On the CPU die. All CPUs today have L1 cache.
L2 cache	Inside the CPU housing. The first CPU to contain L2 was the Intel Pentium Pro.
L2 cache	On the motherboard of older systems.
L3 cache	Inside the CPU housing, further away from the CPU than the L2 cache. The Intel Itanium housing contains L3 cache.
L3 cache	On the motherboard when there is L2 cache in the CPU housing. Used with some newer AMD processors

How Memory Caching Works   Memory caching (see Figure 6-4) is a method used to store data or programs in SRAM for quick retrieval. Memory caching requires some

A+ *CORE*
1.1
1.10
4.2

SRAM chips and a cache controller. When memory caching is used, the cache controller anticipates what data or programming code the CPU will request next and copies that data or programming code to the SRAM chips. Then, if the cache guessed correctly, it can satisfy the CPU request from SRAM without accessing the slower DRAM. Under normal conditions, memory caching guesses right more than 90 percent of the time and is an effective way of speeding up memory access.

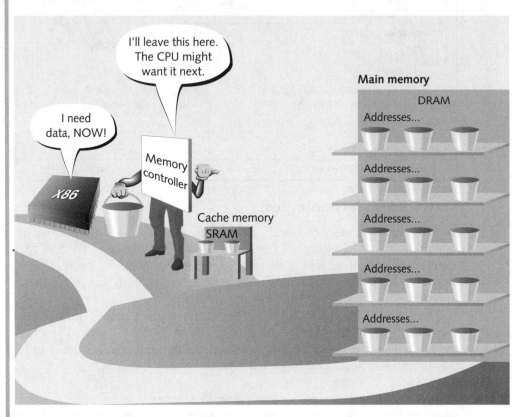

Figure 6-4   A memory cache (SRAM) temporarily holds data in expectation of what the CPU will request next

The memory controller sends data and control signals over the system bus. The methods used to coordinate how and when data and control signals are sent and read differ with various kinds of memory. SRAM uses a synchronous or asynchronous method (explained below). Synchronous SRAM is more expensive and about 30 percent faster than asynchronous SRAM. Here is a summary of the different types of SRAM:

- **Synchronous SRAM** requires a clock signal to manage or synchronize its control signals; the cache memory can then run in step with the CPU. Synchronous SRAM can be either burst or pipelined burst SRAM.

A+CORE
1.1
1.10
4.2

- With **burst SRAM**, data is sent in a two-step process: first the data address and then a series of data transmissions.

- **Pipelined burst SRAM** uses more clock cycles per transfer than does burst SRAM without pipelining but is less expensive.

- **Asynchronous SRAM** does not work in step with the CPU clock, so it cannot process as much data in one request and overall provides slower memory access.

To understand the difference between asynchronous and synchronous memory, consider this analogy. Children jump rope with a long rope, and one child on each end turns the rope. A child who cannot keep in step with the turning rope can only run through on a single pass and must come back around to make another pass. A child who can keep in step with the rope can run into the center and jump awhile, until he or she is tired and runs out. Which child performs the most rope-jumping cycles in a given amount of time? The one who keeps in step with the rope. Similarly, synchronous memory retrieves data faster than asynchronous memory, because it keeps time with the system clock.

SRAM on the Motherboard Systems today are generally built to include all the SRAM needed for optimum performance. If the cache memory is inside the CPU housing, you cannot control how much is present; it depends on the type of CPU you are using, so upgrading cache memory is not a concern. Older cache memory modules are expensive because they are seldom used anymore, so replacing the motherboard might be less expensive than upgrading the cache. Before you buy new SRAM, check the documentation for the motherboard to determine which kinds of SRAM the board supports, and then see what kind of SRAM the board already has. You might need to replace the existing SRAM on the board to upgrade to a larger or faster cache.

Dynamic RAM Technologies

In earlier PCs, main memory was stored on the motherboard as single, socketed chips, but today DRAM is always stored in either SIMMs, DIMMs, or RIMM modules, which plug directly into the motherboard. The major differences among these modules are the width of the data path that each type of module accommodates and the way data moves from the system bus to the module. Figure 6-5 shows some examples of memory modules.

6

A+CORE
1.1
1.10
4.2

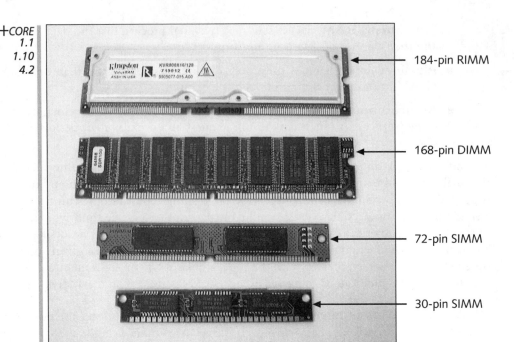

← 184-pin RIMM

← 168-pin DIMM

← 72-pin SIMM

← 30-pin SIMM

Figure 6-5   Types of RAM modules

Table 6-3 summarizes DRAM technologies. You will read more details about them in this section.

Table 6-3   DRAM memory technologies

Technology	Description	Used With
Conventional	Used with earlier PCs but currently not available.	• 30-pin SIMM
Fast page mode (FPM)	Improved access time over conventional memory. FPM may still be used today.	• 30-pin or 72-pin SIMM • 168-pin DIMM
Extended data out (EDO)	Refined version of FPM that speeds up access time. Still used on older motherboards.	• 72-pin SIMM • 168-pin DIMM
Burst EDO (BEDO)	Refined version of EDO that significantly improved access time over EDO. BEDO is seldom used today because Intel chose not to support it.	• 72-pin SIMM • 168-pin DIMM
Synchronous DRAM (SDRAM)	SDRAM runs in sync with the system clock and is rated by clock speed, whereas other types of memory run independently of (and slower than) the system clock.	• 66/100/133/150 MHz, 168-pin DIMM • 66/100/133 MHz, 144-pin SO-DIMM

Table 6-3   DRAM memory technologies (continued)

Technology	Description	Used With
DDR (Double Data Rate) SDRAM	A faster version of SDRAM that can run up to 400 MHz	• 200/266/300/333/370/400 MHz, 184-pin DIMM • 266 MHz, 200-pin SO-DIMM
Rambus DRAM (RDRAM)	RDRAM uses a faster system bus (800 MHz or 1066 MHz). Currently, a RIMM can use a 16- or 32-bit data path.	• 1066 MHz, 232-pin RIMM using a 32-bit data path • 800 MHz, 232-pin RIMM using a 32-bit data path • 1066 MHz, 184-pin RIMM using a 16-bit data path • 800 MHz, 184-pin RIMM using a 16-bit data path

6

A+CORE
1.1
4.2
4.3

The goal of each new technology is increasing overall throughput while retaining accuracy. **FPM (fast page mode)** was used on motherboards that ranged in speed from 16 to 66 MHz. **EDO (extended data out)** was used on motherboards rated at about 33 to 75 MHz, and SDRAM and Direct Rambus are used on motherboards rated 66 MHz and higher. The older the motherboard, the older the memory technology it can use, so, as a PC technician, you must be familiar with all these technologies even though the boards sold today only use the latest.

 Smaller versions of DIMMs and RIMMs, called SO-DIMMs and SO-RIMMs, are used in notebook computers. (SO stands for "small outline.")

SIMM Technologies   SIMMs first used FPM and then EDO technologies. FPM memory improved on the earlier memory types by sending the row address just once for many accesses to memory near that row. Earlier memory types required a complete row and column address for each memory access. SIMMs using FPM technology had 30 pins on the edge connector, and came in sizes of 256K to 4 MB. Later FPM SIMMs had 72 pins on the edge connector, came in sizes up to 16 MB, and were slightly longer. EDO memory improved on FPM memory. EDO memory is used on 72-pin SIMMs, some earlier DIMMs, and video memory, and often provides on-board RAM on various expansion boards.

SIMMs are rated by speed, measured in nanoseconds (ns). Common SIMM speeds are 60, 70, or 80 ns. This speed is a measure of access time, the time the CPU takes to receive a value in response to a request. Access time includes the time it takes to refresh the chips. An access time of 60 ns is faster than an access time of 70 ns. Therefore, the smaller the speed rating, the faster the chip.

DIMM Technologies   Next came DIMM technologies. DIMMs are also rated by speed and the amount of memory they hold. DIMMs have 168 or 184 pins on the edge

A+CORE
  1.1
  4.2
  4.3

connector of the board and hold from 8 MB to 2 GB of RAM. (There is also a 144-pin SDRAM DIMM that is not used with newer motherboards.) The first DIMMs used EDO or **burst EDO (BEDO)** and then **synchronous DRAM (SDRAM)** technology. A refined version of EDO, BEDO offers improved access time. BEDO is not widely used today because Intel chose to not support it. BEDO and EDO DIMMs have two notches on the edge connector.

Either 3.3 volts or 5.0 volts can power SDRAM modules. Purchase DIMMs that use the voltage supported by your motherboard. Your motherboard also determines if you can use buffered, unbuffered, or registered DIMMs. EDO DIMMs use buffers and SDRAM DIMMs use registers. Registers and buffers hold data and amplify a signal just before the data is written to the module. To determine which feature a DIMM has, check the position of the two notches on the DIMM module. In Figure 6-6, the position of the notch on the left identifies the module as registered (RFU), buffered, or unbuffered memory. The notch on the right identifies the voltage used by the module. The position of the notches not only helps identify the type of module but also prevents the wrong kind of module from being used on a motherboard.

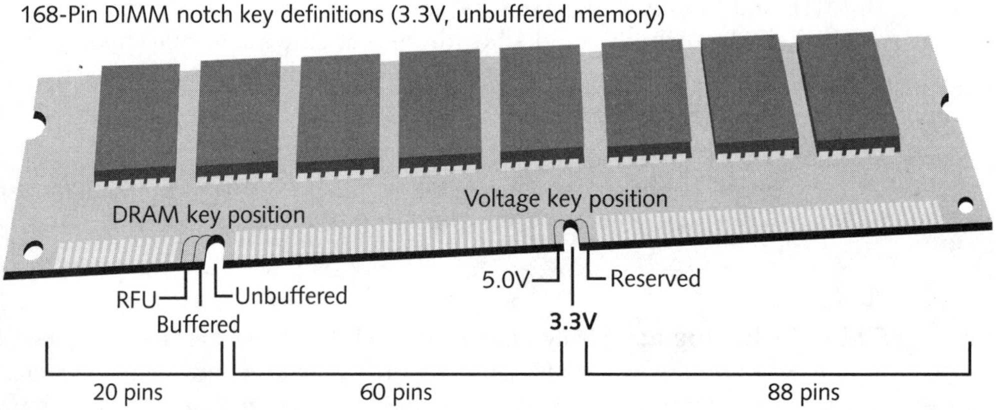

168-Pin DIMM notch key definitions (3.3V, unbuffered memory)

Figure 6-6   The positions of two notches on a DIMM identify the type of DIMM and the voltage requirement, and also prevent the wrong type from being installed on the motherboard

Synchronous DRAM is currently the most popular memory type. SDRAM is rated by the system bus speed and operates in sync with and at the same speed as does the system clock, whereas older types of memory (FPM, EDO, and BEDO) all run at constant speeds independent of the system bus speed. The SDRAM data path is 64 bits wide.

SDRAM currently comes in three variations: regular SDRAM, DDR SDRAM (SDRAM II), and SyncLink (SLDRAM). Of these technologies DDR SDRAM is the most popular.

A+CORE
1.1
4.2
4.3

Double Data Rate SDRAM (DDR SDRAM), sometimes called **SDRAM II**, runs twice as fast as regular SDRAM and can hold up to 2 GB of RAM. Instead of processing data for each beat of the system clock, as regular SDRAM does, it processes data when the beat rises and again when it falls, doubling the data rate of memory. If a motherboard runs at 100 MHz, then SDRAM II runs at 200 MHz with a data path of 64 bits. A consortium of 20 major computer manufacturers support DDR SDRAM. It is an open standard, meaning that its users pay no royalties. DDR SDRAM modules have only one notch on the edge connector, whereas regular SDRAM modules have two.

SyncLink DRAM (SLDRAM) was developed by a consortium of 12 DRAM manufacturers. It improved on regular SDRAM by increasing the number of memory banks that can be accessed simultaneously from four to sixteen. A **bank** is a location on the motherboard that contains slots for memory modules. Banks are discussed in more detail later in the chapter. SLDRAM did not have enough industry support and is now considered obsolete.

RIMM Technologies **Direct Rambus DRAM** (sometimes called **RDRAM** or **Direct RDRAM** or simply Rambus) is named after Rambus, Inc., the company that developed it. RDRAM data can travel on a 16- or 32-bit data path, and Rambus, Inc., is releasing a new RDRAM technology using a 64-bit data path soon. RDRAM works like a packeted network, not a traditional system bus, and can run at internal speeds of 800 MHz to 1066 MHz, using a 400- to 533-MHz system bus.

RDRAM uses RIMM memory modules. With RIMMs, each socket must be filled to maintain continuity throughout all sockets. If the socket does not hold a RIMM, then it must hold a placeholder module called a **C-RIMM (Continuity RIMM)** to ensure continuity throughout all slots. The C-RIMM contains no memory chips (see Figure 6-7). Concurrent RDRAM, an earlier version of Rambus memory, is not as fast as Direct RDRAM. Rambus designed the RDRAM technology but does not actually manufacture RIMMs: it licenses the technology to memory manufacturers. Because these manufacturers must pay licensing fees to use RDRAM, the industry might turn more to SDRAM memory advancements than to Rambus, even though Intel promotes RDRAM. Currently, the industry is on the fence. A good example is the Intel motherboard that supports the Pentium 4 processor, which can be bought to support either DIMMs or RIMMs.

6

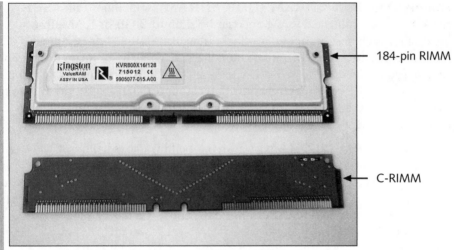

184-pin RIMM

C-RIMM

Figure 6-7   A C-RIMM or RIMM must be installed in every RIMM slot on a motherboard

Parity and Error Checking

In older machines, RAM existed as individual chips socketed to the motherboard in banks or rows of nine chips each. Each bank held one byte by storing one bit in each chip, with the ninth chip holding a parity bit (see Figure 6-8). On older PCs the parity chip was separated a little from the other eight chips. **Parity** refers to an error-checking procedure in which either every byte has an even number of ones or every byte has an odd number of ones. The use of a parity bit means that every byte occupies nine rather than eight bits.

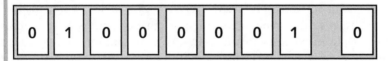

Figure 6-8   Eight chips and a parity chip represent the letter A in ASCII with even parity

Parity is a method of testing the integrity of the bits stored in RAM or some secondary medium, or testing the integrity of bits sent over a communications device. When data is written to RAM, the computer calculates how many ON bits (binary 1) are in the eight bits of a byte. If the computer uses odd parity, it makes the ninth or parity bit either a 1 or a 0, to make the number of ones in the nine bits odd. If it uses even parity, the computer makes the parity bit a 1 or 0 to make the number of ones in the nine bits even.

Later, when the byte is read back, the computer checks the odd or even state. If the number of bits is not an odd number for odd parity or an even number for even parity, a **parity error** occurs. A parity error always causes the system to halt. On the screen you see the error

A+CORE
  1.1
  4.2
message "Parity Error 1" or "Parity Error 2" or a similar error message about parity. Parity Error 1 is a parity error on the motherboard; Parity Error 2 is a parity error on an expansion board. RAM chips that have become undependable and cannot hold data reliably can cause parity errors. Sometimes this happens when chips overheat or power falters.

Older DRAM memory used parity checking, but today's memory uses an altogether new method of error checking called **ECC (error-correcting code)** that can not only detect but can also correct an error in a single bit. Memory modules today are either ECC or non-ECC, and there are some improvements in ECC that ECC memory might use. The first ECC method can detect and correct an error in one bit of the byte. Newer ECC methods can detect an error in two bits but cannot correct these double-bit errors.

6

Some older motherboards support **parity memory**, and some use only **nonparity memory**. If a SIMM has an odd number of chips, most likely it is parity memory; an even number of chips usually indicates nonparity memory. Most manufacturers use nonparity memory to save processing time and therefore money.

Some SDRAM memory modules support ECC. DIMMs that support ECC have a ninth chip on the module (the ECC chip), whereas it normally has only eight chips. The module is identified as a 71- or 72-bit DIMM instead of a 64-bit DIMM. ECC uses an extra 7 or 8 bits to verify the integrity of every 64 bits stored on the module and to correct any error, when possible. ECC memory costs more than regular memory but is more reliable.

When buying memory to add to a motherboard, know that in most cases, you must match the type of memory to the type the board supports. Older boards supported either parity or nonparity memory, and newer boards support either ECC or non-ECC memory. In some cases, you can install parity memory on a nonparity board or ECC memory on a non-ECC board, but error checking will not be enabled. To see if your motherboard supports parity or ECC memory, look for the ability to enable or disable the feature in CMOS setup, or check the motherboard documentation.

UPGRADING MEMORY

A+CORE
  1.2
To upgrade memory means to add more RAM to a computer. When first purchased, many computers have empty slots on the motherboard, allowing you to add SIMMs, DIMMs, or RIMMs to increase the amount of RAM. This section describes issues you should consider when purchasing and upgrading memory.

What to Look for When Buying Memory Chips and Modules

A+CORE
  1.2
Memory chips and memory modules come in different sizes, offer different speeds, and use different technologies and features. This section looks at several criteria you should use when buying memory.

Generally, use the fastest memory that your motherboard can support. The documentation for a motherboard states what memory speed to use on the board, usually written something like "Use 70 ns or faster." In this example, 60 ns works on this board, but 80-ns memory will cause problems. (Remember that the smaller the number, the faster the memory.) It is possible, but not recommended, to mix the speed of memory modules on a motherboard, but don't mix the speeds within a single memory bank.

When a computer first boots, the system must detect the type of memory installed. To do so, the system can use two methods: Parallel Presence Detect (PPD), which uses resistors to communicate the type of memory present, or Serial Presence Detect (SPD), which stores information about the memory type in EPROM. When purchasing memory for a system, you must match the method the module uses to what the motherboard expects. See the motherboard documentation to learn which type to buy. If the board does not specify the method used, assume PPD.

Another memory feature is **CAS Latency (CL)**, which reflects the number of clock cycles that pass while data is written to memory. Values are two or three clock cycles. CL2 (CAS Latency 2) is a little faster than CL3 (CAS Latency 3). Again, use the memory type that the motherboard manufacturer recommends.

Chips can be high-grade, low-grade, remanufactured, or used. Poor-quality memory chips can cause frequent **General Protection Fault (GPF)** errors in Windows, application errors, and errors that hang the system, so it pays to know the quality and type of memory you are buying. The next sections provide some guidelines to follow to ensure that you purchase high-quality memory chips.

Tin or Gold Leads

Memory modules and the banks that hold them can be either tin or gold. On a motherboard, the connectors inside the memory slots are made of tin or gold, as are the edge connectors on the memory modules. Once, all memory sockets were made of gold, but now most are made of tin to reduce cost. You should match tin leads to tin connectors and gold leads to gold connectors to prevent a chemical reaction between the two different metals, which can cause corrosion. Corrosion can create intermittent memory errors and even make the PC unable to boot.

Remanufactured and Used Modules

Stamped on each chip of a RAM module is a chip ID that identifies the date the chip was manufactured. Look for the date in the YYWW format, where YY is the year the chip was made, and WW is the week of that year. For example, 0210 indicates a chip made in the 10th week of 2002. Date stamps on a chip that are older than one year indicate that the chip is probably used memory. If some chips are old, but some are new, the module is probably remanufactured. When buying memory modules, look for ones with dates on all chips that are relatively close together and less than a year old.

A+*CORE*
 1.2
 1.9
 1.10
 4.2

Re-Marked Chips

New chips have a protective coating that gives them a polished, reflective surface. If the chip's surface is dull or matted, or you can scratch off the markings with a fingernail or knife, suspect that the chip has been re-marked. **Re-marked chips** have been used, returned to the factory, marked again, and then resold.

How Much and What Kind of Memory to Buy

A+*CORE*
 1.2
 1.9
 1.10
 4.2

When you add more memory to your computer, ask yourself these questions:

- How much memory do I have, and how much memory do I need?

- How many memory slots are on my motherboard, and what type and size of memory do these slots support?

- How much additional memory is cost-effective?

- What size and type modules should I buy to be compatible with the memory I already have installed?

This section discusses the answers to these questions in detail. To determine how much memory your system has, for Windows, right click on My Computer and select Properties from the drop-down menu. On the System Properties window, click the General tab. How much memory do you need? With the demands today's software places on memory, the answer is probably, "All you can get." Windows 95 and Windows 98 need 16 MB to 32 MB of memory. Windows 2000 and Windows XP require 64 MB of RAM. But for best performance, install 128 MB into a Windows 9x system and 256 MB into a Windows 2000/XP system.

To learn what type and size of memory modules your board supports, consult your motherboard documentation. Open the case and look at the memory sockets to determine how many sockets you have and what size and type of modules are already installed. If all slots are full, sometimes you can take out small-capacity modules and replace them with larger-capacity modules, but you can only use the size of modules that the board is designed to support.

Next decide how many and what size and type of modules to buy. To do that you need to understand how some modules are installed in banks and how a motherboard supports only a certain combination of modules.

How Much Memory Can Fit on the Motherboard?

To determine how much memory your computer can physically hold, read the documentation that comes with your computer. Not all sizes of memory modules fit on any one computer. Use the right number of SIMMs, DIMMs, or RIMMs with the right amount of memory on each module to fit the memory banks on your motherboard. Next let's look at several examples.

A+*CORE*
1.2
1.9
1.10
4.2

30-Pin SIMMs   On older motherboards, 30-pin SIMMs are installed in groups of four. SIMMs in each group or bank must be the same type and size. See the motherboard documentation for the exact combination of SIMMs in each bank that the board can support.

72-Pin SIMMs   To accommodate a 64-bit system bus data path, 72-pin SIMMs have a 32-bit data path and are installed in groups or banks of two. Most older motherboards that use these SIMMs have one to three banks that can be filled with two, four, or six SIMMs. The two SIMMs in each bank must match in size and speed. See the motherboard documentation for the sizes and type of SIMMs the board supports.

DIMMs   Most DIMMs have a 64-bit data path and can thus be installed as a single module rather than in pairs. There are DIMMs with a 128-bit data path that are not presently widely used. Pentium motherboards that use DIMM modules use only one socket to a bank, since a DIMM module accommodates a data path of 64 bits. DIMMs come as either single-sided modules (chips on only one side of the module) or double-sided modules (chips on both sides). Single-sided DIMMs come in 8, 16, 32, 64, and 128 MB sizes, and double-sided DIMMs come in 32, 64, 128, 256, and 512 MB, 1 GB, and 2 GB sizes.

For example, a Pentium motherboard might use 168-pin DIMM modules, and the documentation says to use unbuffered, 3.3V, PC100 DIMM SDRAM modules. The PC100 refers to the speed of the modules, meaning that the modules should be rated to work with a motherboard that runs at 100 MHz. You can choose to use ECC modules. If you choose not to, then CMOS setup should show the feature disabled. Three DIMM sockets are on the board, and each socket represents one bank. Figure 6-9 shows the possible combinations of DIMMs that can be installed in these sockets.

DIMM Location	168-pin DIMM		Total Memory
Socket 1 (Rows 0&1)	SDRAM 8, 16, 32, 64, 128, 256MB	x1	
Socket 2 (Rows 2&3)	SDRAM 8, 16, 32, 64, 128, 256MB	x1	
Socket 3 (Rows 4&5)	SDRAM 8, 16, 32, 64, 128, 256MB	x1	
	Total System Memory (Max 768MB)	=	

Figure 6-9   This table is part of the motherboard documentation and is used to show possible DIMM sizes and calculate total memory on the motherboard

RIMM Modules

When you purchase a system using RIMMs, all RIMM slots will be filled with either RIMMs or C-RIMMs. When you upgrade, you replace one or more C-RIMMs with RIMMs. Match the new RIMMs with those already on the motherboard following the recommendations of the motherboard documentation.

Table 6-4 gives one example of the RDRAM memory configuration for a motherboard. In the table, an RDRAM device is one chip on a RIMM module that has a 16- or 18-bit data path (with or without ECC). The board uses two RDRAM channels and has two

A+CORE
1.2
1.9
1.10
4.2

RIMM banks with two slots in each bank. Memory on a RIMM can be stored in one to four channels. Each bank serves one channel, which is why the motherboard is called a dual channel board. It uses PC600 or PC800 RDRAM, which refers to the speeds of 600 MHz or 800 MHz.

The board also supports two densities of RIMMs, either 128/144 Mb or 256/288 Mb, which refers to the amount of data each chip (device) on the RIMM can hold. A RIMM that has four chips, each of which holds 128 Mb or 16 MB of data, yields a RIMM that is 64 MB in size. A chip rated 144 Mb is the ECC version of a non-ECC 128-Mb chip. A 256-Mb RIMM has chips that each hold 32 MB of RAM. Multiply that by the number of devices on the RIMM for the RIMM size. The 288-Mb RIMM is the ECC version of the 256-Mb RIMM.

6

Table 6-4 One motherboard's memory configurations using RIMMs

Rambus Technology	4 RDRAM Devices per RIMM	6 RDRAM Devices per RIMM	8 RDRAM Devices per RIMM	12 RDRAM Devices per RIMM	16 RDRAM Devices per RIMM
128/144 Mb	64 MB	96 MB	128 MB	192 MB	256 MB
256/288 Mb	128 MB	192 MB	256 MB	384 MB	512 MB

The motherboard can hold up to four RIMMS. The first bank on this motherboard must contain two RIMMs, and the second bank can contain two RIMMs or two C-RIMMs. The RIMMs in each bank must have the same size and density, meaning that they must hold the same amount of memory and have the same number of DRAM devices or chips. The RIMMs in one bank must run at the same speed as RIMMs in the other bank, although the RIMMs in one bank can have a different size and density than the RIMMs in the other bank.

Match Memory Modules to the Motherboard

When you place memory on the motherboard, match the type of memory to the motherboard requirements. For example, if the motherboard supports RIMMs and the documentation says that you must use 600 or 800 speed RIMMs, then 700 speed RIMMs will not work. Also avoid mixing speeds on the same motherboard. For example, if you use a SIMM having one speed in one bank and a SIMM having another speed in the other bank, your computer works only as fast as the slower bank. Always put the slower SIMMs in the first bank. However, to ensure the most reliable results, use the same speed of SIMMs in all banks and also buy the same brand of SIMMs.

Reading Ads About Memory Modules

A+CORE
1.2
1.9
1.10
4.2

Figure 6-10 shows a typical memory module ad listing various types of SIMMs, DIMMs, and RIMMs. When you select memory, the number of pins, the speed, the size, and the type of module are all important. We will now examine the ad to see how it gives all this information to us.

A+CORE 1.2 4.2

MEMORY

72-PIN EDO

32MB	8X32 EDO	60NS		$14
64MB	16X32 EDO	60NS		$16
128MB	32X32 EDO	60NS		$99

168-PIN LONG DIMMS EDO

128MB	16X64	60NS 3.3VOLT	$37
128MB	16X72 (unbuffered)	60NS 3.3VOLT ECC	$47
126MB	16X72 (buffered)	60NS 3.3VOLT ECC	$57
256MB	32X72 (buffered)	60NS 3.3VOLT ECC	$127

168-PIN LONG DIMMS SDRAM (66MHz)

64MB	8X64	10NS	$15
128MB	16X64	10NS	$24

168-PIN SDRAM PC100/133/150

32MB	4X64	8NS	$12
64MB	8X64	8NS	$15
64MB PC133	8X64	7.5NS	$15
64MB	8X72	8NS	$24
128MB	16X64	8NS	$26
128MB PC133	16X64	7.5NS	$26
128MB	16X72	8NS	$28
128MB PC133	16X72	7.5NS	$29
256MB	32X64	8NS	$42
256MB PC133	32X64	7.5NS	$43
256MB	32X72	8NS	$49
256MB PC133	32X72	7.5NS	$46
512MB	64X72	8NS	$105
512MB PC133	64X64	7.5NS	$84
512MB PC133	64X72	7.5NS	$102
1024MB PC133	128X72	7.5NS	$269

DDR RAM PC1600/2100/2700

128MB	16X64	266MHZ	$26
128MB	16X72	266MHZ	$31
256MB	32X64	266MHZ	$52
256MB	32X72	200MHZ	$60
256MB	32X72	266MHZ	$60
256MB	32X64	333MHZ	$60
512MB	64X72	266MHZ	$117
512MB	64X64	333MHZ	$120
1024MB	128X72	266MHZ	$319

www.corsairmicro.com

CORSAIR   PC100/133/150

CM654S256-BX2	256MB	32X64	8NS	$69
CM654S256-133C2	256MB PC133	32X64 CAS2	7.5NS	$67
CM654S256-150C2	256MB PC150	32X64 CAS2	7NS	$69
CM724S256-133	256MB PC133	32X72	7.5NS	$73
CM724S256-BX2	256MB	32X72	8NS	$74
CM744S512-133	512MB PC133	64X72	7.5NS	$279
CM744S1024-133	1024MB PC133	128X72	7.5NS	$389

RAMBUS

CM616DR128A-800	128MB	RDRAM	800MHZ	$62
CM618DR128A-800	128MB	RDRAM	800MHZ	$64
CM616DR256A-800	256MB	RDRAM	800MHZ	$112
CM618DR128A-800	256MB	RDRAM	800MHZ	$132
CM616DR512-800	512MB	RDRAM	800MHZ	$304
CM618DR512-800	512MB	RDRAM	800MHZ	$322

*CHECK OUR WEBSITE FOR CURRENT PRICING AND SELECTION
ON PC 1066 RAMBUS MODULES FROM CORSAIR & KINGSTON*

VALUE SELECT MEMORY

VS128MB100	128MB	16X64 (SDRAM) 8NS	$28
VS128MB133	128MB PC133	16X64 (SDRAM) 7.5NS	$28
VS256MB100	256MB PC100	32X64 (SDRAM) 8NS	$47
VS256MB133	256MB PC133	32X64 (SDRAM) 7.5NS	$47
VS256REG133	256MB PC133	32X72 (SDRAM) 7.5NS	$53
VS512MB133	512MB PC133	64X64 (SDRAM) 7.5NS	$92
VS512MB133REG	512MB PC133	64X64 (SDRAM) 7.5NS	$119
VS128MB266	128MB PC2100	16X64 (DDR)	2.5CAS	$29
VS256MB266	256MB PC2100	32X64 (DDR)	2.5CAS	$62
VS512MB266	512MB PC2100	64X64 (DDR)	2.5CAS	$109
VS512MBECC266R	512MB PC2100	64X72 (DDR)	2.5CAS	$128
VS128MB800	128MB PC800	RDRAM	$57
VS128MBECC800	128MB PC800	ECCRDRAM	$59
VS256MB800	256MB PC800	RDRAM	$102
VS256MBECC800	256MB PC800	ECCRDRAM	$119

DDR RAM PC2100/2400/2700/3000/3200

CM64SD128-2400C2	128MB (CAS 2)	16X64 DDR	300MHZ	$43
CM64SD256-2400C2	256MB (CAS 2)	32X64 DDR	300MHZ	$79
CM64SD256-270CX2H	256MB (CAS 2)	32X64 DDR	333MHZ	$82
CM72SD256-2100	256MB	32X72 DDR	266MHZ	$87
CM72SD256R-2100	256MB (REG)	32X72 DDR	266MHZ	$90
CMX256A-3000C2	256MB (CAS 2)	32X64 DDR	370MHZ	$97
CM72SD512R-2100	512MB (REG)	64X72 DDR	266MHZ	$159
CM73SD512R-2100	512MB (REG)	64X72 DDR	266MHZ	$157
CMX512-2700C2	512MB (CAS 2)	64X64 DDR	333MHZ	$144
CMX512-3000C2	512MB (CAS 2)	64X64 DDR	370MHZ	$159
CMX512-3200	512MB (CAS 2.5)	64X64 DDR	400MHZ	$164

Figure 6-10   Typical memory ad

For each memory module, the ad lists the amount of memory, density, speed, and price. The ad lists SIMMs as 72-pin EDO memory, and the information includes the density of the module, which tells us (1) the width of the data bus, (2) if the module supports error checking, and (3) the size of the module. Here's how it works. The density is written as two numbers separated by an ×, such as 8 × 32, and is read "8 by 32." Let's start with the second number. If the second number is 32 or 64, then it's the width of the data bus in bits, grouped as eight bits to a byte. If the number is 36 or 72, then it's the width of the data bus plus an extra bit for each byte, used for either parity (for parity memory) or error checking and correction (for ECC memory). Look down the second column for SIMMs and note that this company offers only 32, which means the memory is not error checking and works on a 32-bit bus. When calculating the module's size, ignore the ninth bit and use only the values 32 or 64 to calculate size. Convert this number to bytes by dividing it by 8, and then multiply that value (number of bytes) by the number on the

A+CORE
1.2
4.2

left in the density listing, to determine the size of the module. For example, if the density is 8 × 32, then the size of the module is 8 × (32/8) = 8 × 4 = 32 MB.

There are several choices for DIMMs in the ad. For SDRAM, match the speed of the DIMM to the motherboard speed, and match other features to those specified for your motherboard. If the right-hand number in the density is 72, the DIMM is error-checking, and if the number is 64, the DIMM is not error-checking.

> **TIP** When reading memory ads for Rambus memory, 18 in the product code indicates error checking, and 16 does not.

6

Installing Memory

A+CORE
1.2

When installing RAM modules, remember to protect the chips against static electricity, as you learned in Chapter 4. Always use a ground bracelet as you work. Turn off the power and remove the cover to the case. Handle memory modules with care. Don't stack cards, because you can loosen a chip. Usually modules pop into place easily and are secured by spring catches on both ends. Look for the notches on one side or in the middle of the module that orient the module in the slot. For most SIMMs, the module slides into the slot at an angle, as shown in Figure 6-11. (Check your documentation for any instructions specific to your modules.) Place each module securely in its slot. Turn on the PC and watch POST count the amount of memory during the boot process. If the memory count is not what you expect, power off the system, then carefully remove and reseat each module. To remove a module, release the latches on both sides of the module and gently rotate the module out of the socket at a 45-degree angle.

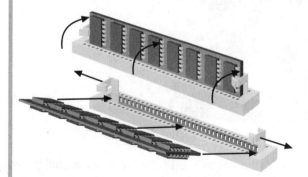

Figure 6-11   Installing a SIMM module

For DIMM modules, small latches on each side of the slot hold the module in place as shown in Figure 6-12. Pull the supporting arms on the sides of the slot outward. Look on the DIMM edge connector for the notches, which help you orient the DIMM correctly over the slot, and insert the DIMM straight down into the slot. When the DIMM is fully

A+CORE
1.2
1.10

inserted, the supporting arms should pop back into place. Figure 6-13 shows a DIMM being inserted into a slot on a motherboard.

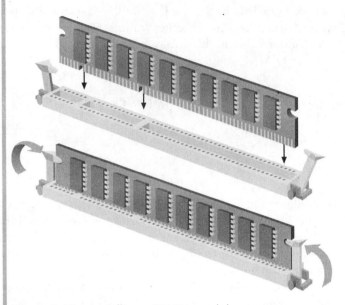

Figure 6-12   Installing a DIMM module

Figure 6-13   Insert the DIMM into the slot by pressing straight down until the supporting arms lock into position

For RIMM modules, if a C-RIMM is already in the slot, remove the C-RIMM and then insert the RIMM. Most often, placing memory on the motherboard is all that is necessary for installation. When the computer powers up, it counts the memory present without any further instruction and senses the features that the modules support, such

$A+$CORE
1.2

as parity or ECC. For some computers, you must tell the setup the amount of memory present. Read the motherboard documentation to determine what yours requires.

Troubleshooting Memory

$A+$CORE
2.1

When upgrading memory, if the computer does not recognize new SIMMs, DIMMs, or RIMMs, or if memory error messages appear, do the following:

- Check that you have the right memory modules supported by your motherboard.

- Check that you have installed the right size modules as stated in the motherboard documentation. Verify each module that was already installed or newly installed.

- Remove and reinstall the module. Make sure it sits in the socket at the same height as other modules.

- Remove the newly installed memory, and check whether the error message disappears. Try the memory in different sockets. Try installing the new memory without the old installed. If the new memory works without the old, then the problem is that the modules are not compatible.

- Clean the module edge connectors with a soft cloth or contact cleaner. Blow or vacuum dust from the memory sockets.

- Try flashing your BIOS. Perhaps BIOS has problems with the new memory that a BIOS upgrade can solve.

Recurring errors during normal operations can mean unreliable memory. If the system locks up or you regularly receive error messages about illegal operations and General Protection Faults occur during normal operation, and you have not just upgraded memory, do the following:

- Run a current version of antivirus software to check for viruses.

- Run diagnostic software such as PC-Technician to test memory.

- Are the memory modules properly seated? Remove and reinstall each one. For a DIMM module, try a different memory slot.

- Look for bent pins or chips installed the wrong way on cache memory.

- Replace memory modules one at a time. For example, if the system only recognizes six out of eight megabytes of RAM, swap the last two SIMM modules. Did the amount of recognized RAM change? You might be able to solve the problem just by reseating the modules.

- Sometimes a problem can result from a bad socket or a broken trace (a fine printed wire or circuit) on the motherboard. If so, you might have to replace the entire motherboard.

6

A+CORE
2.1

- The problem might be with the OS or applications. Download the latest patch for the software from the manufacturer's Web site.

- If you have just installed new hardware, the hardware device might be causing an error, which the OS interprets as a memory error. Try uninstalling the new hardware.

- A Windows error that occurs randomly and generates an error message with this or similar text, "exception fault 0E at >>0137:BFF9z5d0," is probably a memory error. Test, reseat, or replace RAM.

> **TIP** The utility Memtest86 is a good way to test for errors in your installed memory modules. Check the site *www.memtest86.com* to download this program.

HOW DOS ADDRESSES PHYSICAL MEMORY

Recall from Chapter 3 that Windows 9x has an underlying DOS core and when you boot from a Windows 9x rescue disk, you are loading and running the DOS core of Windows. Because this DOS rescue disk is a vital tool for a PC technician, it is important to understand how DOS manages physical memory using memory addresses. Also recall from Chapter 2 that a memory address is a number the CPU assigns to ROM or RAM to track the memory it can use. A CPU has a limited number of memory addresses that it can assign to physical memory, determined by the number of memory address lines available on the memory bus.

Both RAM and ROM must be assigned memory addresses so the CPU can access this memory. System BIOS stored on motherboard ROM chips must be assigned addresses by the CPU so that the CPU can access that programming. The assigning of addresses to both RAM and ROM occurs during booting, and is sometimes called memory mapping and is done by every OS. Figure 6-14 shows an example of how DOS and Windows 9x might map memory. The memory addresses available to the CPU are listed on the left, and the physical RAM and ROM that need these addresses are listed on the right. These RAM modules are on the motherboard, and ROM chips are on a sound card, network card, and video card in this example. RAM holds several device drivers, applications, and the OS.

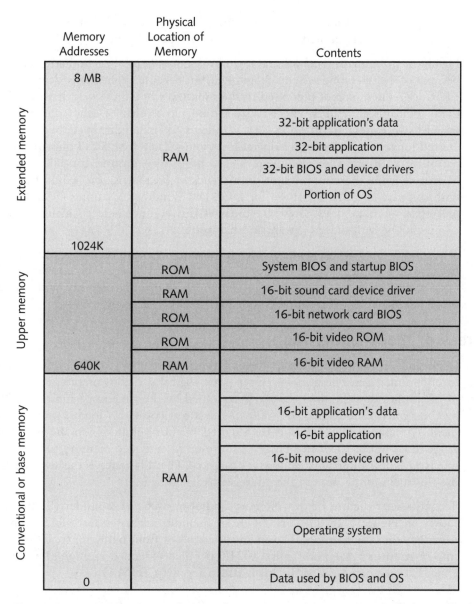

Figure 6-14   Memory map showing how ROM and RAM, on and off the motherboard, might be mapped to memory addresses

Programming stored on ROM chips is not usually copied into RAM, despite what many believe. It is simply assigned memory addresses by the CPU. These ROM programs become part of the total memory available to the CPU and do not use part of total RAM. The resources they use are memory addresses. RAM memory is still available to be assigned other addresses. The exception is shadowing ROM, in which programs stored on ROM are copied to RAM to improve performance.

Finally, memory management in DOS and Windows 9x presents limitations not so much because of the operating systems themselves, but because applications, device drivers, and BIOS used the standards presented to the industry when DOS was first introduced and these standards are still in effect today. Compared to that of other operating systems, memory management in DOS and Windows 9x is handicapped because DOS has existed longer than most other operating systems. Therefore, DOS must maintain compatibility with software and devices that have been around for a long time. Also, Microsoft made the commitment with Windows 9x that it, too, would be compatible with software and BIOS written for DOS and Windows 3.x using DOS. Probably the greatest limitation of Windows 9x today is this commitment to maintain backward-compatibility with older software and hardware.

Windows NT/2000/XP are not backward-compatible with older hardware and software because they do not manage memory in the same way. There is no conventional, upper, or extended memory; memory is just memory. Managing memory with these OSs is much simpler than managing memory with DOS or Windows 9x.

Areas of the Memory Map

DOS and Windows 9x manage several types of memory: conventional, upper, and extended memory. These memory types are logical divisions or categories rather than physical ones, and the divisions are determined by their memory addresses rather than by their physical location. The following sections cover this logical memory management. A segment of RAM can be assigned memory addresses in the upper memory range today but be assigned a range of addresses in extended memory tomorrow. It's still just RAM, no matter what address it's assigned. The difference is the way the CPU can use this memory because of the addresses assigned to it.

To get a clear picture of this memory-addressing schema, consider the memory map shown in Figure 6-15. The first 640K of memory addresses are called **conventional memory**, or base memory. The memory addresses from 640K up to 1024K are called **upper memory**. Memory above 1024K is called extended memory. The first 64K of extended memory is called the **high memory area (HMA)**.

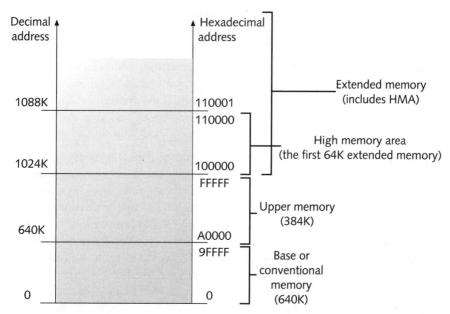

Decimal address — Hexadecimal address

Decimal address	Hexadecimal address	
1088K	110001	Extended memory (includes HMA)
	110000	
1024K	100000	High memory area (the first 64K extended memory)
	FFFFF	
640K	A0000	Upper memory (384K)
	9FFFF	Base or conventional memory (640K)
0	0	

Figure 6-15   Memory address map (not to scale) showing the starting and ending addresses of conventional, upper, and extended memory, including the high memory area

Conventional Memory

In the early 1980s, when IBM and Microsoft were designing the original PCs, they decided to make 640K of memory addresses available to the user, assuming this was plenty for anything the user would ever want to do. This 640K of addresses was intended to hold the OS, the applications software, and the data being processed. At that time, 640K of memory addresses was more than enough to handle all available applications. Today, 640K of memory addresses is inadequate, for the following reasons:

- Many applications are very large programs, requiring a considerable number of memory addresses to hold the programs as well as the data.

- Often more than one application runs at once, each requiring its own memory area for the program and data. Also, sometimes computers in a network serve more than one user at a time. In the early 1980s, a PC was expected to be used by a single user, operating one application at a time.

- Users expect software to provide a friendly graphical user interface, or GUI. Graphical user interfaces provide icons, graphics, and windows on a screen, all requiring large amounts of memory.

The problem caused by restricting the number of memory addresses available to the user to only 640K could have been easily solved by simply providing more addresses to the user in future versions of DOS. However, another original design decision ruled this out.

The next group of memory addresses, the 384K above conventional memory, called upper memory, was assigned to utility operations for the system. The system requires memory addresses to communicate with peripherals. The programs (such as BIOS on a video card or on the motherboard) and data are assigned memory addresses in this upper memory area. For example, the video BIOS and its data are placed in the very first part of upper memory, the area from 640K to 768K. All video ROM written for DOS-based computers assumes that these programs and data are stored in this area. Also, many DOS and Windows applications interact directly with video ROM and RAM in this address range.

Programs almost always expect data to be written into memory directly above the addresses for the program itself, an important fact for understanding memory management. Thus, if a program begins storing its data above its location in conventional memory, eventually it will "hit the ceiling," the beginning of upper memory assigned to video ROM. The major reason that applications have a 640K memory limit is that video ROM begins at 640K. If DOS and Windows 9x allowed applications into these upper memory addresses, all DOS-compatible video ROM would need to be rewritten, and many DOS applications that access these video addresses would not work. Know that 32-bit device drivers and applications under Windows 9x don't have this problem because they can run from extended memory and turn to the OS to access video.

Upper Memory

The memory map in Figure 6-15 shows that the memory addresses from 640K up to (but not including) 1024K are called upper memory. In the hexadecimal number system (see Appendix C), upper memory begins at A0000 and goes through FFFFF. Video ROM and RAM are stored in the first part of upper memory, hex A0000 through CFFFF (the A, B, and C areas of memory). Sixteen-bit BIOS programs for other legacy expansion boards are assigned memory addresses in the remaining portions of upper memory. BIOS on the motherboard (system BIOS) is assigned the top part of upper memory, from F0000 through FFFFF (the F area of upper memory). Upper memory often has unassigned addresses, depending on which boards are present in the system. Managing memory effectively involves gaining access to these unused addresses in upper memory and using them to store device drivers and TSR (terminate-and-stay-resident) programs.

Figure 6-16 shows that video memory addresses fall between A0000 and CFFFF. For VGA and Super VGA video, the A and B areas hold data sent to the video card, and the C area contains the video BIOS.

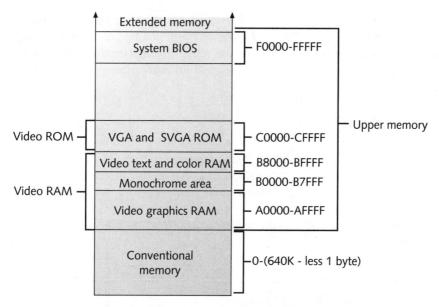

Figure 6-16   Memory map of upper memory showing starting and finishing addresses and video ROM and RAM assignments

Extended Memory and the High Memory Area

Memory above 1 MB is called extended memory. The first 64K of extended memory is called the high memory area, which exists because a bug in the programming for the older 286 CPU (the first CPU to use extended memory) produced this small pocket of unused memory addresses. Beginning with DOS 5, the OS capitalized on this bug by storing portions of itself in the high memory area, thus freeing some conventional memory where DOS had been stored. This method of storing part of DOS in the high memory area is called "loading DOS high." You will learn how to do this later in the chapter.

Extended memory is actually managed by the OS as a device (the device is memory) that is controlled by a device driver. To access extended memory, you need the device driver (called a memory manager) that controls it, and you must use applications that have been written to use the extended memory. The amount of extended memory you can have on your computer is limited by the amount of RAM that can be installed on your motherboard and the number of memory addresses the CPU and the memory bus can support.

DOS Utilities that Manage Memory

Windows 9x uses two utilities to manage memory above 640K: Himem.sys and Emm386.exe. **Himem.sys** is the device driver for all memory above 640K and allows DOS to access memory addresses above 1 MB. The program file **Emm386.exe** contains the software that loads device drivers and other programs into upper memory. Himem.sys is automatically loaded by Windows 9x during the boot process but can also be loaded by an entry in Config.sys when booting from a bootable floppy disk. Emm386.exe is not loaded automatically by Windows 9x, but you can load it by an entry in Config.sys.

A+ OS 1.2

Using Himem.sys

Himem.sys is considered a device driver because it manages memory as a device. It can be executed by the Device= command in Config.sys. Figure 6-17 shows an example of a very simple Config.sys file on a floppy disk that loads Himem.sys. The Config.sys file is being edited by the Edit.com text editor utility.

Figure 6-17   Config.sys set to use memory above 640K

To create the file on a floppy disk, you can use either of these two methods:

- Make drive A the default drive, and enter this command:

    `A:\> Edit Config.sys`

- Make drive C the default drive, and enter this command:

    `C:\> Edit A:Config.sys`

The second line in the Config.sys file, `device=A:\util\mouse.sys`, tells DOS to load into memory a device driver found on the floppy disk in the \Util directory, which allows you to use the mouse while in MS-DOS mode.

The third line in the Config.sys file, `device=A:\util\ansi.sys`, tells DOS to load the device driver Ansi.sys into memory. Ansi.sys helps control the keyboard and monitor, providing color on the monitor and an additional set of characters to the ASCII character set. For more information about ASCII and ANSI, see Appendix B.

Using Emm386.exe

In DOS and Windows 9x, Emm386.exe manages the memory addresses in upper memory. Before we see how to use it, let's examine memory when upper memory addresses are not available. To do that, we use the MEM command, which lets us view how memory is currently allocated. Use the /C option for a complete list and include the |MORE option to page the results on your screen. Figure 6-18 was produced using this command:

```
MEM /C |MORE
```

In Figure 6-18, the first column shows the programs currently loaded in memory. The second column shows the total amount of memory each program uses. The columns labeled Conventional and Upper Memory show the amount of memory being used by each program in each of these categories. This PC does not use upper memory for any of its programs. At the bottom of the screen is the total amount of free conventional memory (544,720 bytes) available to new programs to be loaded. Making this value as high as possible is the subject of the next section.

```
Modules using memory below 1 MB:

    Name        Total            Conventional        Upper Memory
    ----------  ---------------  ---------------     --------------
    MSDOS        18,672  (18K)    18,672  (18K)           0  (0K)
    HIMEM         1,168   (1K)     1,168   (1K)           0  (0K)
    DBLBUFF       2,976   (3K)     2,976   (3K)           0  (0K)
    IFSHLP        2,864   (3K)     2,864   (3K)           0  (0K)
    WIN           3,616   (4K)     3,616   (4K)           0  (0K)
    COMMAND       8,416   (8K)     8,416   (8K)           0  (0K)
    SAVE         72,768  (71K)    72,768  (71K)           0  (0K)
    Free        544,720 (532K)   544,720 (532K)          0  (0K)

Memory Summary:

    Type of Memory      Total         Used          Free
    ----------------  -----------   -----------   -----------
    Conventional         655,360       110,640       544,720
    Upper                      0             0             0
    Reserved                   0             0             0
    Extended (XMS)   133,156,864        69,632   133,087,232
                      -----------   -----------   -----------
-- More --
```

Figure 6-18   MEM report with /C option on a PC not using upper memory

Creating and Using Upper Memory Blocks

Figure 6-19 shows an example of a Config.sys file set to use upper memory addresses. The first line loads the Himem.sys driver. The second line loads the Emm386.exe file. Emm386.exe assigns addresses in upper memory to memory made available by the Himem.sys driver. The **noems** switch at the end of the command line says to Windows, "Do not create any simulated expanded memory." Expanded memory is an older type of memory above 1 MB that is no longer used by software. The command to load Emm386.exe must appear after the command to load Himem.sys in the Config.sys file.

A+ OS
1.2
1.3

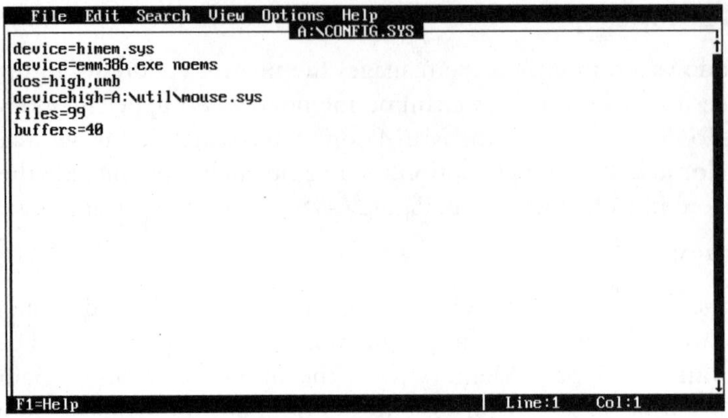

```
 File  Edit  Search  View  Options  Help
                      A:\CONFIG.SYS
device=himem.sys
device=emm386.exe noems
dos=high,umb
devicehigh=A:\util\mouse.sys
files=99
buffers=40




F1=Help                              Line:1    Col:1
```

Figure 6-19   Config.sys set to use upper memory

The command `DOS=HIGH,UMB` serves two purposes. This one command line can be broken into two commands like this:

```
DOS=HIGH
DOS=UMB
```

The `DOS=HIGH` portion tells the OS to load part of the DOS core into the high memory area ("loading DOS high"). Remember that the high memory area is the first 64K of extended memory. This memory is usually unused unless we choose to store part of DOS in it with this command line. Including this command in Config.sys frees some conventional memory that the OS would have used.

The second part of the command, `DOS=UMB`, creates upper memory blocks. An **upper memory block (UMB)** is a group of consecutive memory addresses in the upper memory area that has had physical memory assigned to it. The OS identifies blocks that system ROM or expansion boards are currently not using, and the memory manager makes these blocks available for use. This command `DOS=UMB` enables the OS to access these upper memory blocks. After the UMBs are created, they can be used in these ways:

- `Devicehigh=` command in Config.sys

- `Loadhigh` command in Autoexec.bat

- `Loadhigh` command at the command prompt (explained in the next section)

The next line in the Config.sys file in Figure 6-19 uses a UMB. The command `Devicehigh=A:\Util\Mouse.sys` tells the OS to load the mouse device driver into one of the upper memory blocks created and made available by the previous three lines. This process of loading a program into upper memory addresses is called loading high.

A^{+} OS
1.2
1.3

Loading Device Drivers High

Using the `Devicehigh=` command in Config.sys, rather than the `Device=` command, causes the driver to load high. With the `Devicehigh=` command, the OS stores these drivers in UMBs using the largest UMB first, then the next largest, and so on until all are loaded. Therefore, to make sure there is enough room to hold them all in upper memory, order the `Devicehigh=` command lines in Config.sys so that the largest drivers load first.

You can determine the amount of memory a device driver allocates for itself and its data by using the MEM command with the `/M filename` option:

```
MEM /M filename
```

The filename is the name of the device driver without the file extension.

You can also use a UMB from Autoexec.bat using the `Loadhigh` (`LH`) command. For example, to load high Mscdex.exe, a device driver to access a CD-ROM drive, use either command:

```
LH Mscdex.exe
Loadhigh Mscdex.exe
```

In either case, the program is loaded into the largest UMB available and does not use more precious conventional memory. Note that before the `Loadhigh` command can work, the program files Himem.sys and Emm386.exe must be available to the OS and these three lines must be added to Config.sys and executed by booting the computer:

```
Device=HIMEM.SYS
Device=EMM386.EXE NOEMS
DOS=UMB
```

If the Himem.sys and Emm386.exe files are not in the root directory of the boot device, you must include the path to the filename in the `Device=` line, like this:

```
Device=C:\DOS\HIMEM.SYS
```

> When a program is loaded high, two things can go wrong. Either the program might not work from upper memory, causing problems during execution, or there might not be enough room in the upper memory for the program and its data. If the program causes the computer to hang when you attempt to run it, or if it simply refuses to work correctly, remove it from upper memory.

6

CHAPTER SUMMARY

- SRAM is fast, static RAM and is used as a memory cache, which speeds overall computer performance by temporarily holding data and programming that the CPU may possibly use in the near future. SRAM does not require constant refreshing.

- DRAM (dynamic RAM) is slower than SRAM because it needs constant refreshing.

- DRAM is stored on three kinds of modules: SIMM, DIMM, and RIMM modules.

- SIMM memory modules can use either EDO or FPM technology. EDO is faster and only slightly more expensive than FPM, but the motherboard must support this type of memory to make use of its increased speed.

- DIMM memory modules can use either BEDO (burst EDO) or synchronous DRAM (SDRAM).

- Direct Rambus DRAM and Double Data Rate SDRAM (DDR SDRAM) are two technologies contending to be the next DRAM technology standard.

- Synchronous DRAM (which moves in sync with the system bus) is a faster kind of memory than the less expensive asynchronous DRAM (which does not move in sync with the system bus) found on SIMMs.

- When buying memory, use only gold edge connectors on memory modules that will be inserted in slots containing gold connections, and use only tin connectors in tin slots.

- When buying memory, beware of remanufactured and re-marked memory chips, because they have been either refurbished or re-marked before resale.

- RIMMs use a narrower data path than SIMMs or DIMMs in order to provide faster data transmission. Unlike with SIMMs and DIMMs, data moves from the system bus sequentially through each RIMM module.

- Older motherboards sometimes provided an extra COAST slot to upgrade SRAM, but most systems today come with an optimum amount of SRAM inside the CPU housing and/or on the motherboard.

- When upgrading memory, use the type, size, density, and speed of memory that the motherboard supports, and match the memory modules already installed.

- DOS added the Himem.sys memory manager extension to allow access to memory addresses above 1 MB. Windows 9x uses Himem.sys, along with Emm386.exe, to manage memory above 640K. Emm386.exe contains the software that loads 16-bit device drivers and other programs into upper memory.

- You can use a UMB (upper memory block) from Autoexec.bat with the **Loadhigh** (**LH**) command.

- The MEM command with the appropriate parameters shows exactly where in upper memory the UMBs are located and what software has been assigned addresses in upper memory.

KEY TERMS

asynchronous SRAM

bank

burst EDO (BEDO)

burst SRAM

CAS Latency (CL)

COAST (cache on a stick)

conventional memory

C-RIMM (Continuity RIMM)

Direct Rambus DRAM

Direct RDRAM

Double Data Rate SDRAM (DDR SDRAM)

dynamic RAM (DRAM)

ECC (error-correcting code)

EDO (extended data out)

EEPROM (electrically erasable programmable ROM)

Emm386.exe

EPROM (erasable programmable ROM)

FPM (fast page mode)

General Protection Fault (GPF)

high memory area (HMA)

Himem.sys

nonparity memory

parity

parity error

parity memory

pipelined burst SRAM

RDRAM

refresh

re-marked chips

SDRAM II

static RAM (SRAM)

synchronous DRAM (SDRAM)

synchronous SRAM

SyncLink DRAM (SLDRAM)

upper memory

upper memory block (UMB)

6

REVIEW QUESTIONS

1. Of the following types of solid-state memory, which type is written to *once* and read from *many* times?

   a. RAM

   b. SRAM

   c. DRAM

   d. ROM

   e. None of the above

2. Of the two types of volatile, power-dependent memory, which is considered to be faster?

   a. SRAM

   b. DRAM

   c. ROM

   d. CD-ROM

   e. None of the above

3. Of the various forms of solid-state memory, which requires that the data be "refreshed" in order for the data to be maintained?

   a. SRAM

   b. DRAM

   c. ROM

   d. CD-ROM

   e. None of the above

4. Of the various forms of solid-state memory, which is used in cache memory designs primarily due to its faster access times?

   a. SRAM

   b. DRAM

   c. ROM

   d. CD-ROM

   e. None of the above

5. Cache memory designs are classified according to their physical location with respect to the CPU. Which level cache memory system is located on the motherboard?

   a. L1 cache

   b. L2 cache

   c. L3 cache

   d. L4 cache

   e. None of the above

6. Of the various forms of DRAM technology, which design runs in conjunction with the system clock instead of independent of the system clock?

   a. Conventional

   b. FPM

   c. EDO

   d. Burst EDO

   e. SDRAM

7. Which of the following RAM module connectors is *not* considered to be standard?

   a. 30-pin SIMM

   b. 34-pin SIMM

   c. 72-pin SIMM

   d. 168-pin SIMM

   e. 184-pin SIMM

8. Typical data access times for SIMM modules are characterized as the time during which data is stable and available for use over the data bus. Common data access times for SIMMs used for system memory are:

   a. 60 nsec

   b. 60 msec

   c. 10 nsec

   d. 60 sec

   e. None of the above

9. Assuming a system that utilizes an even–parity error checking protocol, what would the parity bit be in order to protect the data byte 1 0 0 1 0 1 0 1?

   a. 0

   b. 1

   c. 1001

   d. 0101

   e. None of the above

10. Assuming a 486 microprocessor and a collection of 72-pin SIMMs, how many SIMMs are needed to make up a single bank of memory to interface with this processor?

   a. 1

   b. 2

   c. 3

   d. 4

   e. 5

11. An example of an address associated with conventional memory would be found in the range of addresses:

   a. 0 − 640kB

   b. 640kB − 1MB

   c. 1MB − 8MB

   d. 0 − 1MB

   e. 1024MB − 1088MB

12. The hexadecimal address "8567F" is associated with what range of memory?

   a. Base

   b. Upper

   c. High Memory

   d. Extended

   e. CD-ROM

13. Instructions from the Video BIOS are mapped to a region of memory called:

   a. Base

   b. Upper

   c. High Memory

   d. Extended

   e. CD-ROM

14. In order for operating systems such as Windows 98 to access all memory above the 1MB limit requires not only physical memory to be installed above 1MB, but memory managers. Which memory manager is required for the processor to access all installed memory above 1MB?

   a. Config.sys

   b. Autoexec.bat

   c. Himem.sys

   d. Emm386.exe

   e. None of the above

15. In order to manage memory in the upper memory area requires which memory manager to be installed?

   a. Config.sys

   b. Autoexec.bat

   c. Himem.sys

   d. Emm386.exe

   e. None of the above

16. Creating Upper Memory Blocks requires which memory manager(s)?

   a. Himem.sys

   b. Emm386.exe

   c. Both a and b

   d. Neither a or b

17. In an effort to optimize the region of space in Conventional Memory for programs and data, Microsoft developed a way of moving specific operating system components into what is referred to as Upper Memory Blocks (UMBs). The command *devicehigh=* is found in which user-configurable file?

   a. Config.sys

   b. Autoexec.bat

   c. Himem.sys

   d. Emm386.exe

   e. Both c and d

18. What is the address range, in hexadecimal, of the Upper Memory Space?
    a. 0 – 9FFFF
    b. A0000 – FFFFF
    c. 0 – A0000
    d. 0 – FFFFF
    e. None of the above

6

7

FLOPPY DRIVES

> ### In this chapter, you will learn:
>
> ♦ How floppy drives work
> ♦ How to manage floppy drives using Windows Explorer
> ♦ How to exchange and support floppy drives

In the last chapter, you learned about memory and how to support it. This chapter looks at another important component: floppy drives. Once considered essential devices for file storage and installing software on a computer, floppy drives are now mainly used for troubleshooting a failed boot and as a quick and easy way to transfer small files from one PC to another when a network is not available. In this chapter, you will learn how data is stored on a floppy disk, how to manage that data, and how to install a floppy disk drive on a PC. Much of what you learn about floppy drives in this chapter also applies to your study of hard drives in the next chapter.

HOW FLOPPY DRIVES WORK

Recall that memory is organized in two ways: physically (pertaining to hardware) and logically (pertaining to software). Similarly, data is stored physically and logically on a secondary storage device. Physical storage involves how data is written to and organized on the storage media, while logical storage involves how the OS and BIOS organize and view the stored data. This section explains first how data is physically stored on a floppy disk and then how the OS logically views the data.

How Data Is Physically Stored on a Floppy Disk

A+CORE 1.1

Years ago, floppy drives came in two sizes: 5¼ inches and 3½ inches. Today, new computers are equipped with only 3½-inch drives. However, because some older computers still have 5¼-inch floppy disk drives, this section covers 5¼-inch disks as well. Although physically larger, 5¼-inch disks do not hold as much data as 3½-inch disks, because they do not store data as densely. Table 7-1 summarizes the capacity of the four common types of floppy disks. The 5¼-inch double-density disks and the 3½-inch extra-high-density disks are hardly ever seen; most disks today are 3½-inch high-density and hold 1.44 MB of data.

Table 7-1   Floppy disk types

Type	Storage Capacity	Number of Tracks per Side	Number of Sectors per Track	Cluster Type
3½-inch extra-high-density	2.88 MB	80	36	2 sectors
3½-inch high-density	1.44 MB	80	18	1 sector
3½-inch double-density	720K	80	9	2 sectors
5¼-inch high-density	1.2 MB	80	15	1 sector
5¼-inch double-density	360K	40	9	2 sectors

Regardless of disk size and density, the physical hardware used to access a disk looks and works much the same way. Figure 7-1 shows the floppy drive subsystem, which consists of the floppy disk drive, its cable, and its connections. The data cable leaving the floppy drive leads to a controller for the drive on the motherboard. In older computers, the controller board plugged into an expansion slot. The board communicated with the CPU, passing data to and from the floppy disk. These controller boards were called I/O cards and often served multiple functions, having connections for a hard drive, floppy drive, and serial and parallel ports. Today, the controller is built into the motherboard so that the data cable goes directly from the drive to the motherboard.

A floppy drive is connected to either the controller card or motherboard by a 34-pin data cable. The cable has the controller connection at one end and a drive connection at the other. A second drive connection placed in the middle of the cable accommodates a second floppy drive. Having two drives share the same cable is a common practice for floppy drives as well as hard drives and other drives.

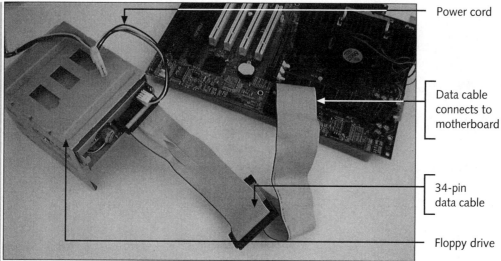

Power cord

Data cable
connects to
motherboard

34-pin
data cable

Floppy drive

Figure 7-1   Floppy drive subsystem: floppy drive, data cable, and power connection

Floppy drives receive power from the power supply by way of a power cord. The power cord plugs into the back of the drive and has a smaller connection than the power cord for other drives in the system.

Floppy disks, no matter what density or size, store data in much the same way. When first manufactured, disks have nothing on them; they are blank sheets of magnetically coated plastic. Recall from Chapter 3 that disks are organized in tracks and sectors. Before data can be written on the disk, it must first be mapped in concentric circles called tracks, which are divided into segments called sectors (see Figure 7-2).

The process of marking tracks and sectors to prepare the disk to receive data is called **formatting** the disk and is done using the Windows Explorer shortcut menu or using the Format command from a command prompt that you learned about in Chapter 3. Figure 7-2 shows a formatted 3½-inch double-density floppy disk. According to Table 7-1, there are 80 tracks, or circles, on the top side of the disk and 80 more tracks on the bottom. The tracks are numbered 0 through 79. Each side of the disk has nine sectors, numbered 1 through 9. Although the circles, or tracks, on the outside of the disk are larger than the circles closer to the center, all tracks store the same amount of data. Data is written to the tracks as bits, either 0s or 1s. Each bit is a magnetized, rectangular spot on the disk. Between the tracks and spots are spaces that are not magnetized. This spacing prevents one spot from affecting the magnetism of a nearby spot. The difference between a 0 spot and a 1 spot is the orientation of the magnetization of the spot on the disk surface.

A$+$$^{CORE}_{1.1}$

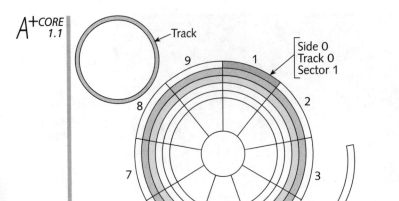

Figure 7-2 3½-inch double-density floppy disk showing tracks and sectors

Data is written to and read from the disk via a magnetic **read/write head** mechanism in the floppy drive (see Figure 7-3). Two heads are attached at the end of an actuator arm that freely moves over the surface of the disk. The arm has one read/write head above the disk and another below the disk. Moving in unison back and forth across the disk, the two heads lightly touch the surface of the disk, which spins at either 300 rpm (revolutions per minute) or 360 rpm, depending on the type of disk. (Note that the read/write heads of a hard drive never touch the surface. You will learn more about hard drives in the next chapter.) Data is written first to the bottom and then to the top of the disk, beginning at the outermost circle and moving in. Tunnel-erase heads on either side of the read/write head, as shown in Figure 7-4, ensure that the widths of the data tracks do not vary. As the data is written, the erase heads immediately behind and to the sides of the write head clean both sides of the magnetized spot, making a clean track of data with no "bleeding" from the track. The magnetized area does not spread far from the track. All tracks are then the same width, and the distance between tracks is uniform.

The disk is actually a piece of Mylar similar to that used for overhead transparencies. The surface of the Mylar is covered with a layer of either cobalt oxide or iron oxide (rust) that can hold a magnetic charge. Some floppy disks use another layer of Teflon to protect the oxide layer and to allow the read/write heads to move more smoothly over the surface. During formatting, the tracks are created by laying down a repeating character, the ÷ (division) symbol in ASCII code, which is hex F6 or binary 1111 0110. The tracks are divided into sectors, and a designated code marks the sector that starts a new track. For 3½-inch floppy disks, the sector address mark written on the disk during formatting marks the beginning sector. After formatting, actual data is written on the disk by overwriting the F6h patterns on the tracks.

A+CORE
1.1

Figure 7-3   Inside a floppy disk drive

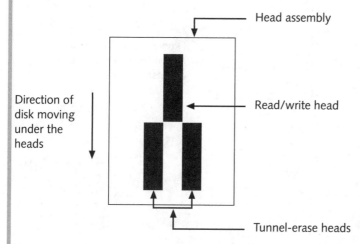

Figure 7-4   Uniform track widths are created by floppy drive read/write heads as the center head writes data while the two tunnel-erase heads clean up from behind

Different disk types use varying degrees of magnetic strength when data is written to a disk or when a disk is formatted. For example, a 3½-inch high–density disk can hold more data than a double-density disk because the data is written closer together. Data

A+CORE
1.1

on the high-density disk is recorded at about twice the magnetic strength as data on the double-density disk. The high-density disk surface is not as sensitive to a magnetic field as the double-density and therefore can handle data written to it with double the magnetic strength.

When data is read from the disk surface, the read/write head changes roles. It passes over a track, waiting for the right position on the disk to appear. When the correct sector arrives, the controller opens a gateway, and the magnetic charge on the disk passes voltage to the read/write head. The voltage is immediately amplified and passed to the controller, which in turn passes the data to the CPU.

How Data Is Logically Stored on a Floppy Disk

A+ OS
1.1
CORE
1.1

A **cluster**, sometimes called a **file allocation unit**, is a group of sectors that is the smallest unit on a disk used to hold a file or a portion of a file. "Sector" refers to the way data is physically stored on a disk, while "cluster" describes how data is logically organized. The BIOS manages the disk as physical sectors, but the OS considers the disk only a long list of clusters that can each hold a fixed amount of data (see Figure 7-5). The OS keeps that list of clusters in the file allocation table (FAT).

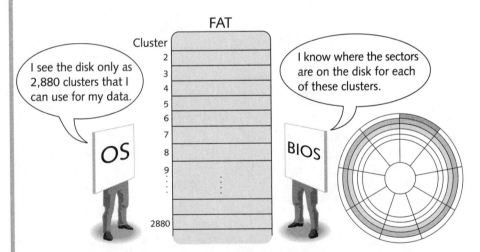

Figure 7-5 Clusters, or file allocation units, are managed by the OS in the file allocation table (FAT), but BIOS manages these clusters as one or two physical sectors on the disk

The 3½-inch high-density floppy disk has 80 tracks and 18 sectors per track on each side. Each side has 80 tracks × 18 sectors, or 1,440 sectors. This type of disk has only one sector per cluster, making 1,440 × 2 sides, or 2,880 clusters. Because each cluster holds 512 bytes (one sector) of data, a 3½-inch high-density floppy disk has 2,880 × 512 = 1,474,560 bytes of data. Divide this number by 1,024 to convert bytes to kilobytes. The storage capacity of

A+ OS
1.1
CORE
1.1
this disk is 1,440 kilobytes. Divide by 1,000 to convert kilobytes to megabytes, and the storage is 1.44 MB.

 There is a discrepancy in the way the computer industry defines a megabyte. Sometimes 1 megabyte = 1,000 kilobytes; at other times, we use the relationship 1 megabyte = 1,024 kilobytes.

The Formatting Process for a Floppy Disk

A+ OS
1.1
CORE
1.1
Formatting all floppy disks is similar, regardless of size or density. During formatting, the Format command without added options performs the following steps:

- Creates the tracks and sectors by writing tracks as a series of F6s in hex and, as necessary, writing the sector address mark to identify the beginning sector on a track

- Creates the boot record

- Creates two copies of the file allocation table (FAT)

- Creates the root directory

The next sections describe these basic steps in detail. Chapter 3 described options available with the Format command.

The Boot Record

The first sector of each floppy disk contains basic information about how the disk is organized. This information includes the number of sectors, the number of sectors per cluster, the number of bits in each FAT entry, and other basic information that an OS or BIOS needs to read the data on the disk. This information is stored in the first sector on the disk, called the **boot sector**, or **boot record**. At the end of the boot record is a small program, called the **bootstrap loader**, that can be used to boot from the disk. Table 7-2 shows the layout and contents of the boot record. The boot record indicates the version of DOS or Windows used to format the disk and is always located at the beginning of the disk at track 0, sector 1 (bottom of the disk, outermost track). This uniform layout and content allows any version of DOS or Windows to read any floppy disk. (You will learn about hard drive boot records in Chapter 8.)

The ninth item in Table 7-2 is the number of heads. A head refers to the read/write head, a part of the physical components of the drive. Because the disk always has only one top and one bottom with a read/write head assigned to each, the number of heads is always two. The last item in Table 7-2 is the program that searches for and loads Io.sys or Ntldr. If one of these files is on the disk, the file loads the rest of the OS files needed on the disk to boot; then the disk is said to be bootable.

7

Table 7-2   Contents of the floppy disk boot record

Bytes per sector
Sectors per cluster
Number of FATs
Size of the root directory
Number of sectors
Medium descriptor byte
Size of the FAT
Sectors per track
Number of heads (always two)
Number of hidden sectors
Program to load the OS

The File Allocation Table (FAT)

When formatting a floppy disk, after the boot record is created, the next step is to write two copies of the FAT to the disk. The FAT lists the location of files on the disk in a one-column table. Because the width of each entry in the column on a floppy disk is 12 bits, the FAT is called a 12-bit FAT, or **FAT12**. The FAT lists how each cluster (or file allocation unit) on the disk is currently used. A file is stored in one or more clusters that do not have to be contiguous on the disk. In the FAT, some clusters might be marked as bad (the 12 bits to mark a bad cluster are FF7h). These bits can be entered in the FAT during disk formatting or added later with the Recover command. An extra copy of the FAT immediately follows the first. If the first is damaged, sometimes you can recover your data and files by using the second copy.

The Root Directory Table

After creating the file allocation tables, the formatting process sets up the root directory table. Recall that the root directory, or main directory, is a table listing all files assigned to this table. The root directory contains a fixed number of rows to accommodate a predetermined number of files and subdirectories; the number of available rows depends on the disk type. A 3½-in high-density floppy disk has 224 entries in the root directory.

The root directory will later contain information about each file and subdirectory stored in it. Each directory entry is 32 bytes long, although only 22 bytes are used. Table 7-3 lists how the 22 bytes are used.

A+ OS
1.1
CORE
1.1

Table 7-3 Root directory information for each file

Root Directory Bytes	Usage
8	Name of file
3	File extension
1	Attribute byte (special meaning for each bit)
10	Not used
2	Time of creation or last update
2	Date of creation or last update
2	Starting cluster number in binary
4	Size of file in binary

7

Note that the root directory has no provision for the period (often referred to as "dot") that we normally see between the filename and the file extension in OS command lines. The period is not stored in directories but is only used in OS command lines to indicate where the filename ends and the file extension begins.

 TIP The long filenames in Windows 9x and Windows NT/2000/XP require more room in the directory. The directory provides for this extra room by using more than one entry for a single file, enough to accommodate the length of the filename. The directory stores both the long filename and the DOS version short filename.

Time and date of creation or last update are stored in a coded form that is converted to a recognizable form for display on the screen. The date and time come from the system date and time, which the OS gets from the real-time clock during the boot. At the command prompt, you can change these with the Date and Time commands. Using the Windows desktop, you can change the date and time in the Control Panel. The earliest date allowed is 1/1/1980.

File attributes are used for various purposes. One file attribute byte is broken into bits, and each bit has a specific meaning. The first two bits are not used. Tale 7-4 lists the meanings of the other six bits, beginning with the leftmost bit in the byte and moving to the right. Several of these bits can be changed using the Attrib command.

A+ OS
1.1
CORE
1.1

Table 7-4   Meaning of each bit in the directory attribute byte for each file (reading from left to right across the byte)

Bit	Description	Bit = 0	Bit = 1
1, 2	Not used		
3	Archive bit	Not to be archived	To be archived
4	Directory status	File	Subdirectory
5	Volume label	Not volume label	Is volume label
6	System file	Not system file	Is system file
7	Hidden file	Not hidden	Hidden
8	Read-only file	Read/write	Read-only

TIP   Bit 3, the archive bit, is a switch used to indicate whether the file has changed since the last backup and should be backed up next time a backup is made. You will learn more about backups in Chapter 9.

Notice that the root directory contains only the starting cluster number. To find out what other clusters store the file, look in the file allocation table. For example, suppose a file named Mydata.txt begins at cluster 5 and requires three clusters to hold the file. The OS takes the following steps to read the file. (The first three are numbered in Figure 7-6.)

1. The OS goes to the root directory and reads the name of the file (Mydata.txt) and the first cluster number (5).

2. The OS retrieves the contents of cluster 5 on the floppy disk, which is the first segment of the file.

3. The OS turns to the FAT, looks at the fifth position in the FAT, and reads 6, which says the next segment of the file is in cluster 6.

4. It retrieves the second segment of the file from cluster 6 on the floppy disk.

5. The OS turns to the sixth position in the FAT and reads 10, which says the next segment of the file is in cluster 10.

6. It retrieves the third segment of the file from cluster 10 on the floppy disk.

7. The OS turns to the tenth position in the FAT and reads all 1s in the FAT entry, which says this is the last cluster in the file. (If the FAT is FAT16, then an entry of 16 ones is written in the FAT. If it is FAT32, then an entry of 28 ones is written.)

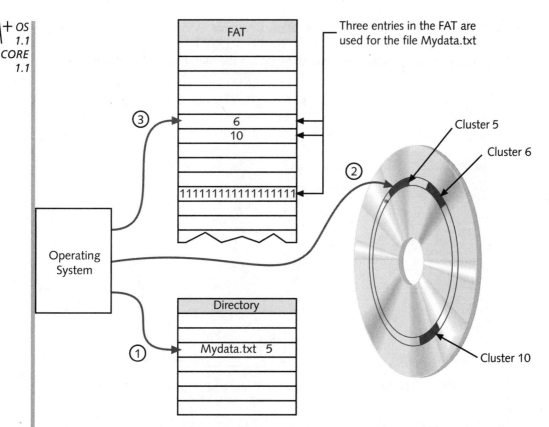

A+ OS
1.1
CORE
1.1

Figure 7-6 How an OS reads a file from the hard drive or a floppy disk

> By dividing the size of a file by the number of bytes per cluster and rounding up to the nearest whole number, you can determine how many clusters the file occupies.

The root directory and all subdirectories contain the same information about each file. Only the root directory has a limitation on the number of entries. Subdirectories can have as many entries as disk space allows. Because long filenames require more room in a directory than short filenames, assigning long filenames reduces the number of files that can be stored in the root directory.

Using Windows Explorer to Manage Floppy Disks and Hard Drives

A+ OS
1.1
1.5

In this section, you learn how to use Windows Explorer to manage floppy disks and hard drives. The section gives examples for Windows 98, but Windows Explorer in Windows NT/2000/XP works about the same way. You can open Windows Explorer

A+ OS
1.1
1.4
1.5

using several methods: (1) Click Start, Programs, Windows Explorer, (2) Right-click My Computer and select Explore from the menu, (3) Right-click Start and select Explore from the menu, or (4) open My Computer and, on the menu bar, click View, Explorer Bar, Folders.

Figure 7-7 shows computer resources in the My Computer folder as seen when using Windows Explorer. (You can also access My Computer by double-clicking the icon on the desktop in Windows 9x or Windows 2000. In Windows NT/2000/XP, start Windows Explorer by clicking Start, Programs (All programs in Windows XP), Accessories, Windows Explorer.)

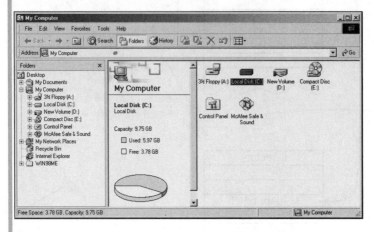

Figure 7-7 The My Computer view in Windows Explorer

Shortcut Menu Options

A+ OS
1.1
1.4
1.5

The easiest way to manage drives, disks, folders, and files in Windows Explorer is to use the shortcut menus. To access a shortcut menu, right-click the icon representing the item you want to work with. Figure 7-8 shows the shortcut menu for the floppy drive as an example.

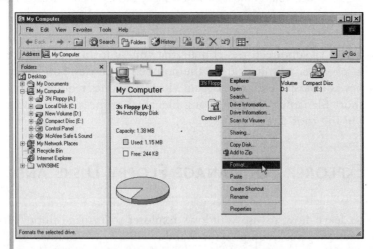

Figure 7-8 Use the shortcut menu to manage items in Explorer

A+ OS
1.1
1.4
1.5

Here are some tasks you can perform from a shortcut menu.

- If you select Explore, you can see the contents of the selected disk or folder in the floppy drive in the current Explorer window. If you select Open, the contents of the disk or folder appear in a separate window.

- The Create Shortcut option creates a shortcut icon for the selected item.

- Selecting the Properties option brings up a dialog box showing information about the selected item and allows you to change settings for the item.

- If you selected a disk or drive, the shortcut menu contains a Format option. Recall that you can use Explorer to format a floppy disk by selecting Format from the shortcut menu.

- The Backup option enables you to make a backup of a disk, and the Sharing option enables you to share a drive, folders, or files with other users on your network.

- For floppy drives, if you select Copy Disk, the dialog box shown in Figure 7-9 opens, where the disk listed under "Copy from" is the source disk and the disk listed under "Copy to" is the target disk. Click Start to copy the disk.

- The shortcut menu for files gives you additional options such as printing and e-mailing the file.

- The shortcut menu for a folder allows you to create a new file. The menu lists applications you can use to create the file.

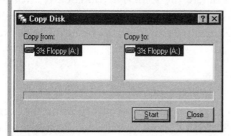

Figure 7-9   Copying a disk using Windows

As you can see, some options on shortcut menus are the same for files, folders, drives, and disks; others are specific to particular items. The additional shortcut menu options may differ, depending on what programs you have installed to work with a particular item.

Now let's look in more detail at ways to use Windows 9x Explorer to work with files and folders on your floppy disk or hard drive.

Create a New Folder

A+ OS
1.1
1.4
1.5

To create a folder (equivalent to using the MD command from the command line, which you learned in Chapter 3), do the following. Select the folder you want to be the parent folder by clicking the folder's name. For example, to create a folder named Games under the folder named Download, first click the Download folder. Then click the File menu.

7

A+ OS
1.1
1.4
1.5
Select New from the menu. Then select Folder from the submenu that appears. The new folder will be created under Download, but its name will be New Folder. The name New Folder is automatically selected and highlighted for the user to type a new name. Type Games to change the folder name to Games, as shown in Figure 7-10. The maximum depth of folders under folders depends on the length of the folder names.

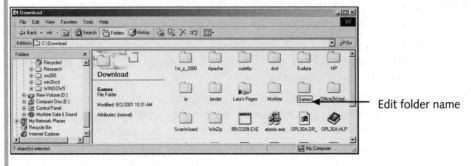

Edit folder name

Figure 7-10   Edit the new folder's name

Delete a Folder

A+ OS
1.1
1.4
1.5
To delete a folder (similar to using the RD command from the command line) from Explorer, right-click the folder and select Delete from the shortcut menu. A confirmation dialog box asks if you are sure you want to delete the folder. If you click Yes, you send the folder and all its contents, including subfolders, to the Recycle Bin. Empty the Recycle Bin to free your disk space. Files and folders sent to the Recycle Bin are not deleted until you empty it.

File Attributes

A+ OS
1.1
1.4
1.5
Using Explorer, you can view and change the file attributes (similar to using the command-line Attrib command). From Explorer, right-click a file and select Properties from the shortcut menu. The Properties window, shown in Figure 7-11 appears. From the Properties window, you can change the read-only, hidden, system, and archive attributes of the file.

Folder Properties

A+ OS
1.1
1.4
1.5
You can also view and change the properties assigned to folders. Select the folder and from the Explorer menu, click Tools, Folder Options, and then click the View tab. From this window you can change how and when files appear in the folder.

Windows identifies file type primarily by the file extension. In Windows Explorer, by default, Windows 9x hides the file extensions of those files for which it knows the application to use to open or execute the file. For example, just after installation, it hides .exe, .com, .sys, and .txt file extensions but does not hide .doc, .ppt, or .xls files until the software to open these files has been installed. To display all file extensions, on the View tab in the Folder Options window, uncheck Hide file extensions for known file types.

A+ OS
1.1
1.4
1.5

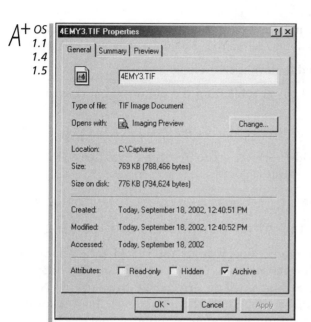

Figure 7-11   Properties of a file in Windows 2000

EXCHANGING AND SUPPORTING FLOPPY DRIVES

A+ CORE
1.2
When a floppy drive cannot read a disk or malfunctions in some other way, the problem can have many causes. This section describes problems that can occur with a floppy drive and its support system, how to replace the drive, and how to add an additional floppy drive to a computer system.

Many computers today come with one 3½-inch floppy drive, a hard drive, and a CD-ROM drive. The machine might have one or two empty bays for a second floppy drive or for a Zip drive. If you have no extra bay and want to add another drive, you can attach an external drive that comes in its own case and has its own power supply.

Floppy drives are now so inexpensive that repairing one is impractical. Once you've determined that the drive itself has a problem, open the case, remove the drive, and replace it with a new one. This procedure takes no more than 30 minutes, assuming that you don't damage or loosen something in the process and create a new troubleshooting opportunity.

Replacing a Floppy Drive

A+ CORE
1.2
Following is a five-step summary of how to replace a floppy drive. Each step is described in more detail in the next sections.

A+CORE
1.2
4.4

1. Check that the computer and other peripherals are working. Can you boot to the hard drive or another floppy drive? You should know your starting point.

2. Turn off the computer and remove the cover.

3. Unplug the data cable and power cable from the old drive. Unscrew and dismount the drive.

4. Slide the new drive into the bay. Reconnect the data cable and power cable.

5. Turn on the computer and check the setup. Test the drive. Turn off the computer and replace the cover.

Now let's look at each step in detail.

Check that the computer and other peripherals are working

Can you boot to the hard drive or another floppy drive? You should know your starting point. Imagine yourself in the following situation. You are asked to install a floppy disk drive in a computer. You remove the cover, install the drive, and turn on the PC. Nothing happens. No power, no lights, nothing. Or perhaps the PC does not boot successfully, giving errors during POST that appear to have nothing to do with your newly installed floppy drive. Now you don't know if you created the problem or if it existed before you started. That is why you check the computer before you begin and make sure you know what's working and what's not. The extra time is worthwhile and prevents a situation like this.

Before you start to work, you should do a quick system check of a PC:

- Turn on the computer and verify that it boots to the OS with no errors.

- Using Windows, open a program and perform a task from the program.

- Get a directory listing of files on a floppy disk and a CD-ROM.

- If the computer is connected to a printer, print a test page.

Turn off the computer and remove the cover

As you learned in Chapter 4, guard the computer against static electricity by using a ground bracelet, working on a hard floor (not on carpet), and grounding yourself before you touch any components inside the case. Never touch anything inside the case while the power is on. Remove the cover and put its screws in a safe place.

Next, prepare to remove the power cable. The power supply cable is a four-pronged cable that attaches to the back of the drive, as in Figure 7-12. The cable can be difficult to detach because the connection is very secure. Be careful not to apply so much pressure that you break the corner of the logic board. Steady the board with one hand while you dislodge the power cable with the other.

A+CORE
1.2

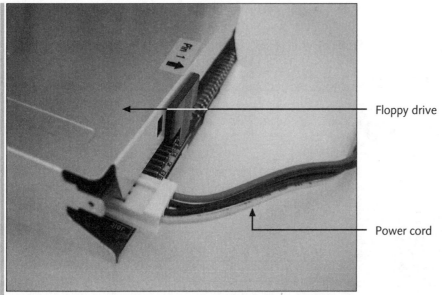

Floppy drive

Power cord

Figure 7-12 Power supply connection on the back of the drive (Note how well this drive manufacturer labeled pin 1 on the data connection.)

Unplug the data cable and power cable from the old drive, and unscrew and dismount the drive

Before removing the cables and the drive, note carefully how they are assembled, to help you reassemble them later. The data cable might go to an adapter card or directly to the motherboard. Before removing the cable, note that the cable has a color or stripe down one side. This edge color marks this side of the cable as pin 1. Look on the board to which the cable is attached. Verify that pin 1 or pin 2 is clearly marked, either by a number embossed on the board or by a square solder pad on the bottom of the circuit board, and that the colored edge aligns with pin 1 on both the board and the drive. Sometimes pin 1 on the floppy drive is marked, and sometimes the drive housing is constructed so that the cable built for the drive inserts in only one direction. Note the position of pin 1 on the drive.

Look at the cable connecting drive A to the floppy drive controller card or to the motherboard. There is a twist in the cable. This twist reverses these leads in the cable, causing the addresses for the first connection to be different from the addresses for the second connection that has no twist. The position of the twist on the cable determines which drive will be drive A (see Figure 7-13). This drive is always the one that the startup BIOS looks to first for a bootable disk, unless a change has been made in CMOS setup, instructing startup BIOS to look to a different drive. By switching the drive to before or after the twist, you exchange drives A and B. Some computers have two drives

A+CORE
A   1.2

attached to the same cable. In this case, the drive attached behind the twist is drive A, and the one attached before the twist is drive B. After you are familiar with the cable orientation and connection, remove the cable from the floppy drive.

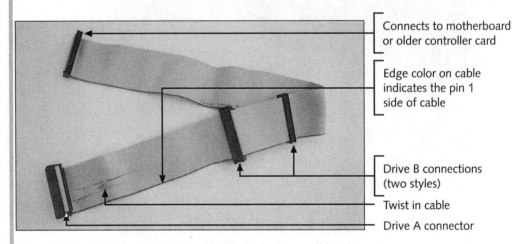

Connects to motherboard or older controller card

Edge color on cable indicates the pin 1 side of cable

Drive B connections (two styles)

Twist in cable

Drive A connector

Figure 7-13   Twist in cable determines which drive will be drive A

Now that the cable is detached, you can remove the floppy drive. Some drives have one or two screws on each side, attaching the drive to the drive bay. After you remove the screws, the drive usually slides to the front and out of the case. Sometimes you must lift a catch underneath the drive as you slide the drive forward. Be careful not to remove any screws that hold a circuit card on top of the drive to the drive housing; all this should stay intact.

Slide the new drive into the bay, reconnect the data cable and power cable

If the new drive is too narrow to fit snugly into the bay, you can buy an adapter kit with extensions for narrow drives that allow them to reach the sides of the bay. Screw the drive down with the same screws used on the old drive. Reaching the screw hole on the back of the drive might be difficult if it is against the side of the case. Make sure the drive is anchored so that it cannot slide forward or backward or up or down, even if a user turns the case on its side.

Next, you reconnect the data cable, making sure that the cable's colored edge is connected to the pin 1 side of the connection, as shown in Figure 7-14. Most connections on floppy drives are oriented the same way, so this one probably has the same orientation as the old drive. The power cable goes into the power connection in only one direction. Be careful not to offset the connection by one pin.

A^{+CORE}
  1.2
  4.4

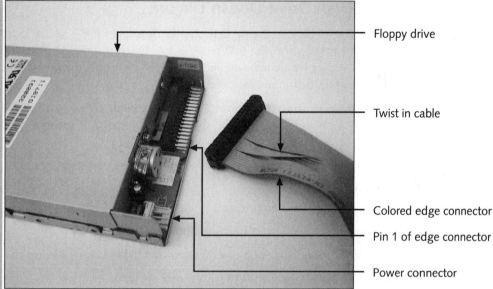

Floppy drive

Twist in cable

Colored edge connector
Pin 1 of edge connector

Power connector

7

Figure 7-14   Connect colored edge of cable to pin 1

Turn on the computer, check the setup, and test the drive

Double-check all connections and turn on the computer. If you changed disk types, you must inform CMOS setup by accessing setup and changing the drive type. Test the drive by formatting a disk or doing a Diskcopy. If you determine that all is well, replace the cover and you're done.

Note that you can run the computer with the cover off. If the drive doesn't work, having the cover off makes it easier to turn off the computer, check connections, and try again. Just make certain that you don't touch anything while the computer is on. Leaving the computer on while you disconnect and reconnect a cable is very dangerous for the PC and will probably damage something.

Adding a New Drive

A^{+CORE}
  1.2

Adding a new drive is no problem if you have an empty bay, an extra power cable, and an extra connection on the floppy drive data cable. Slide the drive into the bay, screw it down, connect the cable and power cable, change setup, and you're done. If you don't have an extra power cable, you can use a "Y" splitter on the power cable for the existing floppy drive, to provide the power connection.

You can test a floppy drive for accuracy and alignment using a digital diagnostic disk designed for that purpose and utility software such as TestDrive by MicroSystems Development Technologies, Inc. (*www.msd.com/diags*).

When a Floppy Disk Drive Doesn't Work

A+CORE
2.1

Sometimes a problem with the floppy drive arises during POST, and BIOS displays an error message. Error messages in the 600 range occur when the floppy drive did not pass the POST test. These problems can be caused by the power supply, the drive, the controller board (if one is present), or the motherboard.

Even if POST finds no errors, you might still have a problem. If you put a disk in a faulty drive and issue a command to access the disk, an error message such as the following might appear on the screen:

```
General failure reading drive A, Abort, Retry, Fail?
```

If nothing happens and the computer simply stops working, the problem might have several causes, including the following:

- The application you are running points to a different drive.
- Windows just encountered an unrelated error that has locked up the system.
- The system BIOS or CMOS setup is not correctly configured.
- The disk in the drive is not formatted.
- The floppy drive is bad.
- The shutter window on the floppy disk cannot open fully.
- The cable from the motherboard to the drive is damaged or poorly connected.
- The edge color on the cable is not aligned with pin 1.
- The power supply is bad.
- The power supply cable to the drive is loose or disconnected.
- The command just issued has a mistake or is the wrong command.
- The disk is inserted incorrectly.

You might discover more items to add to this list. I once helped someone with a drive error. We took the 3½-inch floppy disk out of the drive and opened the shuttle window (the spring-loaded metal cover that opens to reveal the disk inside the plastic housing) to find a blade of grass on the disk's surface. We removed the grass, and the disk worked perfectly. She then remembered that she had dropped the disk in the grass. When you have any computer trouble, check simple things first. Here are a few suggestions for solving drive problems:

- Remove the disk. Does the shuttle window move freely? Do you see any dirt, hair, or other foreign material on the disk's Mylar surface? Does the disk spin freely inside the housing cover? Some new disks simply need a little loosening up. Put the disk back in the drive, and try to access it again.
- Does the light on the correct drive go on? Maybe you are trying to access drive B, but the disk is in drive A.

- Does another disk work in the drive? If so, the problem is probably caused by the disk, not the drive. The exception is when the drive is out of alignment. When it is, the drive cannot read a disk that it did not format, although it might read a disk that it formatted with its own alignment. To test this possibility, try several disks and note whether the drive reads only those disks that it has recently formatted. If so, then you might have identified the problem, and you can replace the drive.

- Does the drive light come on? If not, the problem might be with the software or the hardware. Try to access the disk with other software. Can the OS access the drive with a simple Dir A: command? Can Windows Explorer access the disk? How about using the Chkdsk A: command? If the light doesn't come on even then, the problem might involve the power to the drive or the hardware connections inside the case. Does the other drive work? If neither light comes on, consider the power supply or the motherboard as the source of your problem.

- Does the light come on at boot and stay on? This is most likely caused by the cable not being attached correctly to pin 1. Check the edge color to see that it aligns with pin 1.

- Has this drive been used recently? Perhaps the system setup has lost CMOS data. The system might think it has a 720K drive when it really has a 1.44-MB drive. Access setup and check the drive specifications. Also check setup to see that Drive A and B have not been switched. Some CHOS have this option.

- Reboot the machine and try again. Many problems with computers disappear with a simple reboot. If a soft boot doesn't do it, try a hard boot.

- Try cleaning the drive's read/write heads. Use a head–cleaning kit that includes a paper disk and a cleaning solution. Follow the directions that come with the kit. You can purchase a kit at any store that sells computer supplies.

- If the drive still does not work with any disk and any software, then you must dig deeper. Inside the case, the hardware that can cause this problem is the drive itself, the data cable from the motherboard to the drive, the power supply, the power cable, or the motherboard. To find the culprit, replace each hardware component with a known good component, one component at a time, until the problem goes away. Having access to another working computer from which you can borrow parts is helpful.

> **TIP** When you try to discover which device is causing a problem during a troubleshooting session, you can trade a suspected device for one you know is good (called a known good device). You can also install the device you suspect is bad in a computer system you know is working. If the problem follows the device, then you know the device is bad.

- Turn off the computer and open the computer case. Check every connection from the motherboard to the drive. Check the power cable connection.

A+CORE
   2.1

- Take the power cable from the second working floppy drive, and put it on the nonworking one, to eliminate the power cable as the problem.

- Replace the data cable and try the drive again. Make sure to align the cable correctly with pin 1. If that does not work, exchange the drive itself and try again.

- If the drive still does not work, suspect the motherboard or the ROM BIOS on the motherboard. Try flashing ROM.

Some Common Error Messages and Their Meanings

A+CORE
   2.1

Here are some common error messages that might be caused by problems with a floppy drive, together with what they mean.

```
Non-system disk or disk error. Replace and strike any key
when ready.
No operating system found
```

These messages say that you are trying to boot from a disk that is not bootable. Remove the disk from the drive, and press any key. The computer bypasses the floppy drive and loads the OS from the hard drive. If you intended to boot from the floppy drive, the disk should have been formatted and made bootable as described in Chapter 3.

If you had no disk in the floppy drive, you can assume that some critical OS files are missing from the hard drive. In this case, boot from a bootable floppy disk or rescue disk, and check whether the files have been erased accidentally from your hard drive.

```
Bad or missing COMMAND.COM

Error in Config.sys line xx

Himem.sys not loaded

Missing or corrupt Himem.sys
```

These errors appear when the OS loads and the two hidden files are present, but system files such as Command.com, Config.sys, and Himem.sys, are not present, are corrupt, or, in the case of Config.sys, have an incorrect entry. Replace the missing or corrupt file. To test for errors in Autoexec.bat and Config.sys, you can hold down the F8 key while DOS loads. That causes lines in these files to execute one at a time as you watch the screen. Also, press F5 to bypass these two files during the boot.

```
Incorrect DOS version
```

This message appears when you try to use a DOS command such as Format or Backup. Remember that these are external commands in DOS because they require a program to execute that is not part of Command.com. DOS contains a number of programs that reside on the hard drive in a directory named \DOS or, in the case of Windows 9x, in a directory named \Windows\Command. When you enter the Format or Backup command, you execute these programs. DOS knows which version of DOS these programs belong to, and the error message indicates that the Format or Backup program you are

A+CORE
2.1

using does not belong to the same version of DOS that you have loaded. To determine the version of DOS currently loaded, use the VER command. If you get the error when trying to run a DOS application, try using the SETVER command in Config.sys.

Invalid Drive Specification

You are trying to access a drive that the OS does not know is available. For example, the error might appear in this situation: During booting, an error message indicates that BIOS cannot access the hard drive. You boot from a floppy disk in drive A and see an A prompt. You then try to access drive C from the A prompt, and you see the above message. DOS or Windows is telling you that it can't find drive C because it failed the test during POST. As far as the OS is concerned, the hard drive does not exist.

Not ready reading drive A:, Abort, Retry, Fail?

This message means the floppy disk in drive A is not readable. Perhaps the disk is missing or inserted incorrectly. The disk might have a bad boot record, errors in the FAT, or bad sectors.

General failure reading drive A:, Abort, Retry, Fail?

This message means the floppy disk is badly corrupted or not yet formatted. Sometimes this error means that the floppy drive is bad. Try another disk. If you determine that the problem is the disk and not the drive, the disk is probably unusable. A bad boot record sometimes gives this message.

Track 0 bad, disk not usable

This message typically occurs when you try to format a disk using the wrong disk type. Check your Format command. Most manufacturers write the disk type on the disk. If you have a 3½-inch floppy disk, you can tell if you are using a high-density or double-density disk by the see-through holes at the corners of the disk. The high-density disk has holes on two corners; the double-density has a hole on only one corner. Don't try to format a disk using the wrong density.

Write-protect error writing drive A:

The disk is write-protected and the application is trying to write to it. To write to a 3½-inch floppy disk, the write-protect window must be closed, that is, the switch must be toward the center of the disk so that you cannot see through the write-protect hole. To write to a 5¼-inch floppy disk, the write-protect notch must be uncovered.

CHAPTER SUMMARY

- ❑ Data is stored on floppy disks in concentric circles called tracks or cylinders. Each track is divided into sectors. Each sector holds 512 bytes of data.

- ❑ Different types of floppy disks vary according to the organization of tracks and sectors, the density at which data can be stored, and the intensity of the magnetic spots on the magnetized plastic surface of the disk.

- The smallest unit of space allocated to a file is called a cluster. On 3½-inch high-density floppy disks, 1 cluster is the same as 1 sector, which is 512 bytes.

- When a disk is formatted for use, the formatting process creates tracks and sectors and places a boot record, file allocation table (FAT), and root directory on the disk.

- The first sector of the disk, called the boot sector or the boot record stores basic information about how a floppy disk is organized. At the end of a boot record is a small program, called the bootstrap loader, that can be used to boot from the disk.

- The file allocation table (FAT) lists the location of files on a disk in a one-column table.

- Windows Explorer can be used to format a floppy disk and to manage files and folders on floppy disks and hard drives.

- Before beginning to install hardware such as a floppy drive, check the other peripherals so that, if you encounter any problems, you know whether they were preexisting or were caused during the installation.

- Error messages in the 600 range occur when a floppy drive does not pass the POST test.

- When troubleshooting a floppy drive, check the physical condition of the disk as well as error messages, CMOS settings, and cables connected to the drive.

KEY TERMS

boot record	cluster	formatting
boot sector	FAT12	read/write head
bootstrap loader	file allocation unit	

REVIEW QUESTIONS

1. The interrupt that has been reserved for use by the Floppy Drive Controller is:
   a. IRQ 7
   b. IRQ 5
   c. IRQ 6
   d. IRQ 13
   e. None of the above

2. Assuming a floppy drive interface cable with a twist, which connector is to be utilized such that the drive is recognized as Drive A: by the operating system?
   a. The connector immediately after the twist
   b. The connector immediately before the twist
   c. Either connector can be used.
   d. Neither connector can be used.

3. Typical protocol for connecting a floppy drive interface cable to a floppy drive unit is to orient the interface cable so that the wire with the red stripe coordinates with:

   a. The first pin of the floppy drive interface connector

   b. The last pin of the floppy drive interface connector

   c. The power connector of the floppy drive

   d. None of the above

4. The kind of data storage capability, number of tracks per side, and number of sectors per track that a user can expect from a 3 ½" high density floppy disk is:

   a. 1.44MB, 80, 36

   b. 1.44MB, 80, 18

   c. 1.44MB, 80, 9

   d. 1.44MB, 80, 15

   e. None of the above

5. The number of wires that can be expected in an interface cable for floppy drives is:

   a. 34

   b. 40

   c. 42

   d. 50

   e. None of the above

6. The smallest unit of storage that the operating system deals with, which is defined as a group of sectors is a:

   a. Sector

   b. Cluster

   c. Track

   d. Platter

   e. None of the above

7. Assuming a 3½" high density floppy disk, what are the maximum number bytes that are stored in a single cluster?

   a. 512

   b. 1,024

   c. 2,048

   d. 4,096

   e. None of the above

7

8. The kind of power connect that is most commonly used to power a 3½" floppy drive is a Molex connector.

   a. True

   b. False

9. The kind of error message a user would encounter if the disk in the floppy drive was *not* formatted would be:

   a. Bad command or file name

   b. General failure reading drive A:, Abort, Retry, Fail?

   c. Bad or missing COMMAND.COM

   d. Himem.sys not loaded

   e. None of the above

10. Kelly wants to install a second floppy drive into her computer. She finds the connector just *before* the twist available on the floppy drive interface cable. Which drive letter will be assigned to this particular drive once the system is started?

   a. A:

   b. B:

   c. C:

   d. D:

   e. None of the above

8

UNDERSTANDING AND INSTALLING HARD DRIVES

In this chapter, you will learn:

♦ About hard drive technologies

♦ How communication with hard drive BIOS is accomplished

♦ How a hard drive is logically organized to hold data

♦ How to install a hard drive

♦ How to solve hard drive installation problems

This chapter introduces hard drive technology and explains how a hard drive is logically organized. To understand how a hard drive works, it is important to know its physical characteristics as well as how the OS and BIOS communicate with the hard drive. You will also learn how to install a hard drive and what to do when you experience problems during or immediately after installation.

HARD DRIVE TECHNOLOGY

Two technologies are important to understanding how hard drives work: the technology used within the hard drive to read and write data to the drive, and the technology of how the hard drive interfaces with the system. You will first learn about different hard drive interfaces and then about the way the drive itself works.

Types of Hard Drive Interfaces

A+CORE
1.1
1.6
1.9
1.10
4.3

The majority of hard drives interface with the motherboard by means of **EIDE (Enhanced IDE)**, which is an interface standard that applies to other drives besides hard drives, including CD-ROM drives, Zip drives, tape drives, and so forth. EIDE is an extension of **IDE (Integrated Device Electronics**, formerly **Integrated Drive Electronics)** technology.

The EIDE Interface Standards

The EIDE standards define how hard drives and other drives such as CD-ROM drives, tape drives, and Zip drives relate to the system. The first standard that EIDE drives used was ATA-2. This standard allowed for up to four IDE devices on the same PC. These IDE devices could be hard drives, CD-ROM drives, or tape drives as well as other IDE devices. Drives other than hard drives can use the EIDE interface if they follow the **ATAPI (Advanced Technology Attachment Packet Interface)** standards. As standards developed, different drive manufacturers called them different names, which can be confusing. Standards today specify data transfer speed more than any other single factor. When selecting a drive standard, select the fastest standard you can, but keep in mind that the operating system, BIOS on the motherboard, and the drive must all support this standard. If one of these three does not, the other two will probably revert to a slower standard that all three can use.

Table 8-1 lists the different **ANSI (American National Standards Institute)** standards for IDE drives. The most popular standard today is Ultra ATA/100, which also supports older standards. If you install an ATA/100 hard drive on a single IDE cable with a slower drive, such as an ATA/66 CD-ROM drive, both drives will work but at the slower speed, 66 MB/sec. Also, ATA/66, ATA/100, and ATA/133 all use a special 40-pin IDE cable with 40 additional wires that reduce crosstalk on the cable. These 40 ground wires are in between the signal wires and all connect to ground. This special IDE cable is called an ATA/100 cable or an **80 conductor IDE cable**.

A+CORE
1.1
1.6
1.9
1.10
4.3

Table 8-1   Summary of ANSI interface standards for IDE drives

Standard (may have more than one name)	Speed	Description
IDE/ATA ATA	Speeds range from 2.1 MB/sec to 8.3 MB/sec	The first ANSI hard drive standard for IDE hard drives. Limited to no more than 528 MB. Supports PIO and DMA transfer modes.*
ATA-2 Fast ATA	Speeds up to 16.6 MB/sec	Breaks the 528-MB barrier. Allows up to four IDE devices. Supports PIO and DMA transfer modes.
ATA-3	Little speed increase	Improved version of ATA-2.
Ultra ATA Fast ATA-2 Ultra DMA DMA/33	Speeds up to 33.3 MB/sec	Defined a new DMA mode but only supports slower PIO modes.
Ultra ATA/66 Ultra DMA/66	Speeds up to 66.6 MB/sec	Uses a special 40-pin cable that provides additional ground lines on the cable to improve signal integrity.
Ultra ATA/100	Speeds up to 100 MB/sec	Uses the special 40-pin cable with additional grounding.
Ultra ATA/133	Speeds up to 133 MB/sec	Uses the special 40-pin cable with additional grounding and supports drives larger than 137 GB.

*   PIO (Programmed I/O) transfer mode uses the CPU to transfer data and is slower than DMA transfer mode that transfers data directly from the drive to memory without involving the CPU.

Using ATA/100 and earlier standards, BIOS and the OS address data on a hard drive using 28 bits for the address, making the largest addressable space on a hard drive 137 GB. A new ATA standard called ATA/ATAPI-6 was incorporated within the ATA/133 standard that allows 48 bits for the address, increasing the addressable space on a hard drive up to 144 petabytes (144,000,000,000,000,000 bytes). For your system to support drives larger than 137 GB, the OS, the system BIOS, the IDE controller, and the hard drive must all support the standard. Windows 98 and higher supports drives larger than 137 GB when a driver provided by the hard drive manufacturer is installed. Before investing in a drive larger than 137 GB, verify that your system BIOS and the IDE controller support it. If your motherboard does not support these drives, first check with the BIOS manufacturer for a possible update and flash BIOS. If an updated BIOS is not available, you can purchase an IDE controller that has compliant BIOS on the card.

There are two cabling methods used by drives larger than 137 GB: the drive can use an 80 conductor IDE cable used by ATA/100 and above (called parallel ATA or PATA), or the drive can use serial ATA (SATA). A serial IDE cable is much narrower and has fewer pins than a parallel IDE cable. The IDE controller must use the same type of connector and cabling method as the drive, although you can purchase an adapter to convert an 80 conductor IDE connection on a hard drive to a serial ATA connection. Also, if you want to install an IDE hard drive that uses a newer standard than your motherboard supports, you can install an IDE controller card to support the drive and disable the IDE controller on your motherboard.

8

A+CORE
1.1
1.6

> **TIP**   For more information on ATA/ATAPI-6, see the Technical Committee T13 Web site at *www.t13.org*. The T13 committee is responsible for the ATA standards.

> **TIP**   In most cases, a PC technician does not need to know which IDE standard a hard drive supports, because BIOS autodetection selects the best possible standard supported by both hard drive and BIOS. There are two exceptions. If two hard drives share the same IDE cable and the drives use different standards, both drives will run at the speed of the slower drive. For example, if you connect an ATA/66 drive and an ATA/100 drive on the same cable, both drives will run at 66 MB/sec. Another exception is when you install a new drive and BIOS does not recognize the drive or detects the drive and reports in CMOS setup that the drive has a smaller capacity than it actually does. In this situation, your older BIOS or IDE controller card does not support the newer IDE standard the drive is using. The solution is to flash BIOS, replace the controller card, or replace the motherboard.

A+CORE
1.10

Following the EIDE standard, a motherboard can support up to four EIDE devices. The motherboard offers two IDE connectors, or channels, a primary and secondary channel (see Figure 8-1). Each channel can accommodate an IDE data cable. The cable has two connectors on it: one connector in the middle of the cable and one at the far end for two EIDE devices. An EIDE device can be a hard drive, DVD drive, CD-ROM drive, Zip drive, or other type of drive. One device is configured to act as the master controlling the channel, and the other device on the channel is the slave. There are, therefore, four possible configurations for four IDE devices in a system:

- Primary IDE channel, master device
- Primary IDE channel, slave device
- Secondary IDE channel, master device
- Secondary IDE channel, slave device

These designations are made either by setting jumpers or DIP switches on the devices or by using a special cable-select data cable. You will see an example of an IDE installation later in the chapter.

> **TIP**   When installing a hard drive on the same channel with an ATAPI drive such as a CD-ROM drive, always make the hard drive the master and the ATAPI drive the slave.

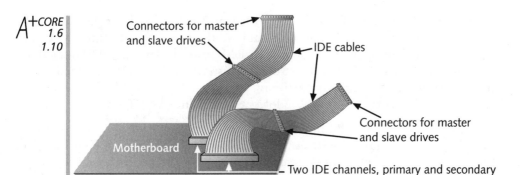

Connectors for master and slave drives

IDE cables

Connectors for master and slave drives

Motherboard

Two IDE channels, primary and secondary

Figure 8-1 A motherboard has two IDE channels; each can support a master and slave drive using a single IDE 40-pin cable

Other Interface Standards

Other than EIDE, the second most popular interface for hard drives as well as other drives is SCSI, which is not discussed in this chapter. Some other technologies used to interface between the hard drive and the system bus are IEEE 1394 and Fibre Channel. Chapter 10 discusses IEEE 1394, also known as FireWire and i.Link (named by Sony Corporation). IEEE 1394 uses serial transmission of data and is popular for multimedia and home entertainment applications. For example, Maxtor, Inc. (*www.maxtor.com*), a large hard drive manufacturer, makes a hard drive designed for home entertainment electronics that uses 1394 for the external hard drive interface (see Figure 8-2).

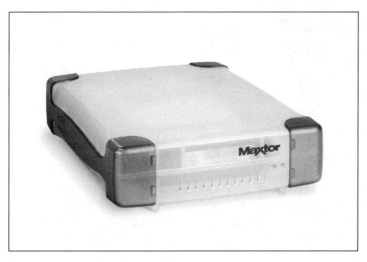

Figure 8-2 Maxtor 1394 external hard drive

A 1394 device connects to a PC through a 1394 port provided either directly on the motherboard or by way of a 1394 expansion card. Motherboard manufacturers have been slow to support 1394; most favoring support for USB instead. Generally, IDE is the slowest, SCSI is midrange, and 1394 is the fastest, with some overlaps in their speeds. For a system to use 1394, the operating system must support it. Windows 98, Windows 2000, and Windows XP support 1394, but Windows 95 and Windows NT do not.

Fibre Channel is another type of interface that can support hard drives. Fibre Channel is designed for use in high-end systems that have multiple hard drives. It competes with SCSI for these high-end solutions. As many as 126 devices can be connected to a single Fibre Channel bus, as compared to 16 SCSI devices, including the host adapter. Fibre Channel is faster than SCSI when more than five hard drives are strung together to provide massive secondary storage, but it is too expensive and has too much overhead to be a good solution for the desktop PC or workstation.

How Hard Drives Work

Hard drives have one, two, or more platters that stack together and spin in unison. Read/write heads are controlled by an actuator and move in unison across the disk surfaces as the disks rotate on a spindle (see Figure 8-3). PCs can use several types of hard drives, all having a magnetic medium on the platters.

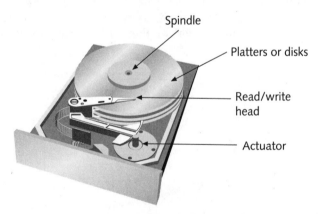

Figure 8-3   Inside a hard drive case

Figure 8-4 shows a hard drive with four platters. All eight sides of these four platters are used to store data, although on some hard drives the top side of the first platter just holds information used to track data and manage the disk. Each side, or surface, of one hard drive platter is called a **head**. (Don't confuse this with the read/write mechanism that moves across a platter, which is called a read/write head.) The drive in Figure 8-4 has eight heads. Each head is divided into tracks and sectors. The eight tracks shown in Figure 8-4, all of which are the same distance from the center of the platters, together make up one cylinder. If a disk has 300 tracks per head, it also has the same number of cylinders. As with floppy disks, data is written to a hard drive beginning at the outermost track. The entire first cylinder is filled before the read/write heads move inward and begin filling the second cylinder.

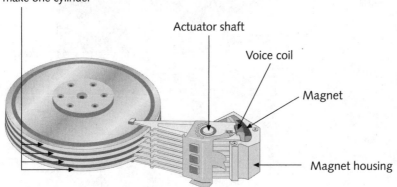

Eight tracks (one on each head) make one cylinder

Actuator shaft

Voice coil

Magnet

Magnet housing

Figure 8-4 A hard drive with four platters

The drive fits into a bay inside the computer case where it is securely attached with supports or braces and screws. This helps prevent the drive from being jarred while the disk is spinning and the heads are very close to the disk surface.

A hard drive requires a controller board filled with ROM programming to instruct the read/write heads how, where, and when to move across the platters and write and read data. For today's hard drives, the **hard drive controller** mounts on a circuit board on or inside the drive housing and is an integral part of it. The controller and drive are permanently attached to one another. Older drives such as MFM, RLL, ESDI, ST-506, and ST-412 had the controller board as a separate, large expansion card connected to the drive with two cables. Today, the controller of an IDE drive usually connects to the motherboard by way of a data cable from the drive to an IDE connection directly on the motherboard. Older motherboards had no IDE connection, so a small **adapter card** served as a simple pass-through from the drive to the motherboard. The data cable attached to the drive and the adapter card, which was inserted in an ISA slot on the motherboard. Sometimes an adapter card connects a hard drive to a motherboard to compensate for a motherboard BIOS that does not support a large-capacity drive. The adapter card contains the BIOS necessary to support the drive in the place of the system BIOS.

IDE Technology

Almost all hard drives on the market today use IDE standards, which use a varying number of sectors for each cylinder, depending on how close the cylinder is to the outer edge. Figure 8-5 shows a hardware subsystem including an IDE hard drive and its connection to a motherboard. In addition to the connection for the 40-pin data cable, the hard drive has a connection for the power cord from the power supply.

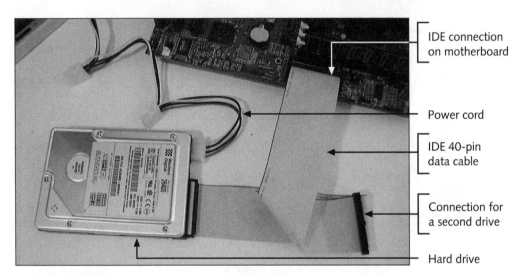

IDE connection
on motherboard

Power cord

IDE 40-pin
data cable

Connection for
a second drive

Hard drive

Figure 8-5   A PC's hard drive subsystem

Tracks and Sectors on an IDE Drive

Before learning how data is written to a hard drive, let's look at how track and sector markings are written to the drive. Older MFM and RLL technologies use a straightforward method of writing the tracks and sectors on the drive. They have either 17 or 26 sectors per track over the entire drive platter (see Figure 8-6). The larger tracks near the outside of the platter contain the same number of bytes as the smaller tracks near the center of the platter. This arrangement makes formatting a drive and later accessing data simpler but wastes drive space. The centermost track determines the number of bytes that a track can hold and forces all other tracks to follow this restriction.

Today's IDE drives eliminate this restriction. The number of sectors per track on an IDE drive is not the same throughout the platter. In this new formatting system, called **zone bit recording** (Figure 8-7), tracks near the center have the smallest number of sectors per track, and the number of sectors increases as the tracks grow larger. In other words, each track on an IDE drive is designed to have the optimum number of sectors appropriate to the size of the track. What makes this arrangement possible, however, is one fact that has not changed: every sector on the drive still has 512 bytes. Without this consistency, the OS would have a difficult time indeed communicating with the drive!

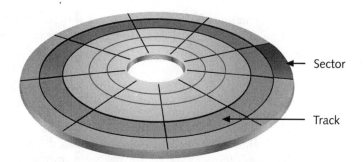

Figure 8-6   Floppy drives and older hard drives use a constant number of sectors per track

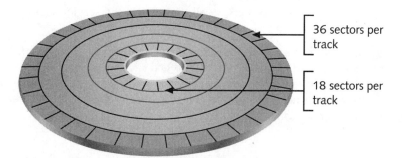

36 sectors per track

18 sectors per track

Figure 8-7   Zone bit recording can have more sectors per track as the tracks get larger

Because each track can have a different number of sectors, the OS cannot communicate with an IDE drive by contacting the hard drive controller BIOS and using sector and track coordinates, as it does with floppy disks and older hard drives. Newer, more sophisticated methods must be used that are discussed later in the chapter.

Low-Level Formatting

Recall from Chapter 7 that when the OS formats a floppy disk, it writes sector and track markings on the disk. With IDE drives, since the track and sector markings no longer follow a simple pattern, they are written on the hard drive at the factory. This process is called **low-level formatting**. The OS still executes the remainder of the format process (creating a boot sector, FAT, and root directory), which is called **high-level formatting** or **operating system formatting**.

With older RLL and MFM technology, the system BIOS, OS, or utility software such as Norton Utilities or SpinRite could perform the low-level format; even now a low-level format routine is still part of standard system BIOS. For an IDE drive, however, using system BIOS or standard utility software to low-level format would be a catastrophe. Formatting an IDE drive in this way could permanently destroy the drive, unless the drive controller BIOS were smart enough to ignore the command.

Because IDE drives are low-level formatted by the manufacturer, they cannot be low-level formatted as part of preventive maintenance, as older drives can. The track and sector markings on the drive created at the factory are normally expected to last for the life of the drive. For this reason IDE drives are often called disposable drives. When track and sector markings fade, as they eventually do, and the drive gives many "Bad Sector or Sector Not Found" errors or becomes unusable, you just throw the drive away and buy a new one!

However, options for formatting the IDE drive are becoming more commonplace. Some better-known IDE drive manufacturers offer a low-level format program specific to their drives. If an IDE drive continues to give errors or even totally fails, ask the manufacturer for a program to perform a low-level format of the drive. Sometimes the manufacturer only distributes these programs to dealers, resellers, or certified service centers.

 It's risky to low-level format an IDE drive using a format program other than one provided by the manufacturer, although some have tried and succeeded. Probably more drives have been permanently destroyed than saved by taking this risk, however. IDE drives last several years without a refresher low-level format. By that time, you're probably ready to upgrade to a larger drive anyway.

Table 8-2 lists hard drive manufacturers. The same manufacturers usually produce IDE drives and SCSI drives.

Table 8-2   Hard drive manufacturers

Company	URL
Conner Peripherals	www.seagate.com
Fujitsu America, Inc.	www.fujitsu.com
IBM PC Company	www.ibm.com
Maxell Corporation	www.maxell.com
Maxtor Corporation	www.maxtor.com
Seagate Technology LLC	www.seagate.com
Sony Corporation of America	www.sony.com
Western Digital Corporation	www.wdc.com

COMMUNICATING WITH THE HARD DRIVE BIOS

Now that you have learned about physical characteristics of a hard drive, let's look at how the OS and system BIOS communicate with the hard drive BIOS software, before moving to logical organization of hard drives. Recall from earlier in the chapter that, beginning with IDE hard drives, the number of sectors per track varies from one track to another. Therefore, with IDE drives, the OS and system BIOS could not count on using actual hard drive cylinder, head, and sector coordinates when requesting data through the hard drive BIOS (which is how requests were made with early hard drives; see Figure 8-8). Instead, sophisticated methods were developed so that system BIOS and the OS could communicate with the hard drive controller BIOS, but only the hard drive controller BIOS dealt with physically locating the data on the drive.

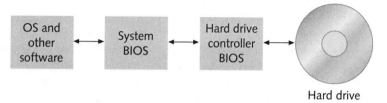

Hard drive

8

Figure 8-8   With older hard drives, cylinder, track, and sector information was communicated at each level

Calculating Drive Capacity on Older Drives

When hard drives were smaller and used a constant number of sectors per track, measuring drive capacity was straightforward. All sectors in a track held 512 bytes regardless of the track's radius. If you knew the number of tracks, heads, and sectors per track, you could calculate the storage capacity of a drive, because all tracks had the same number of sectors. Software and operating systems were written to interface with BIOS, which managed a hard drive by assuming that for each hard drive there was a fixed relationship among the number of sectors, tracks, heads, and cylinders.

If you know how many heads, cylinders (tracks), and sectors a drive has you can calculate the capacity of the drive. This information is usually written on the top of the drive housing. For example, the drive capacity for an older drive that has 855 cylinders, 7 heads, and 17 sectors/track is calculated as 855 cylinders × 7 heads × 17 sectors/track × 512 bytes/sector, which gives 52,093,440 bytes. Divide this value by 1,024 to convert to KB and then divide by 1,024 again to convert to MB, yielding a drive capacity of 49.68 MB.

> **TIP** When installing a hard drive, it was once necessary to tell CMOS setup the drive capacity by telling it how many heads, cylinders, and sectors the drive had. Today, most system BIOS offers **autodetection**, a method by which the BIOS detects the new drive and automatically selects the correct drive capacity and configuration.

Adjusting for More Complex Hard Drive Organization

As hard drive size and technology improved, the OS and other software required new methods to relate to hard drive BIOS because of two situations:

- Beginning with IDE technology, the number of sectors per track varied depending on the location of the track, which made it impossible for the OS and software to address the data on the hard drive using actual cylinder, head, and sector parameters.

- When hard drives were small, the maximum size of the parameters that the OS and software sent to hard drive BIOS was established. These maximum values placed limitations on the size hard drive that software can address using actual cylinder, head, and sector parameters. These parameters and values are discussed later in the chapter.

Although new technology was needed to address these issues, it was important for the industry to retain backward-compatibility so that legacy operating systems and other software could work with newer hard drives. As is common in the evolution of computers, clever methods were devised to "trick" older technology into working in newer environments. The older, legacy technology (in this case, software) still sees its world as unchanged because the newer technology (in this case, BIOS) shelters it from the new methodology. These "deceptions" happen at several stages of communication, in the following ways:

- *CHS mode or normal mode used for drives less than 528 MB.* The hard drive can use a complex cylinder, head, and sector organization that only the controller BIOS knows. However, the controller BIOS communicates to system BIOS in terms of the older methodology. When this method is used, the actual organization of the hard drive is called the **physical geometry** of the drive, and the organization communicated to system BIOS is called the **logical geometry** of the drive. This method is called **CHS (cylinder, head, sector) mode**, or **normal mode**. Using CHS mode, a drive can have no more than 1,024 cylinders, 16 heads, 63 sectors per track, and 512 bytes per sector. Therefore, the maximum amount of storage on a hard drive using CHS mode is 528 MB or 504 MB, depending on how the calculations are done (1K = 1,000 or 1K = 1,024).

- *Large mode or ECHS mode used for drives between 504 MB and 8.4 GB.* The hard drive controller BIOS sends the logical geometry to system BIOS, but system BIOS communicates a different set of parameters to the OS and other software. This method is called **translation**, and system BIOS is said to be in **large mode**, or **ECHS (extended CHS) mode**. Large mode is not as popular as LBA mode.

- *LBA mode used for drives larger than 504 MB.* The hard drive controller BIOS and system BIOS communicate using a method entirely different from cylinder, head, and sector information. System BIOS sends cylinder, head, and sector information to the software, which uses neither logical nor physical geometry. This method of translation is called **LBA (logical block addressing) mode**. System BIOS simply views the drive as a long list of sequential numbers (0, 1, 2, 3, …) called LBAs or addressable sectors. LBA mode is the most popular way of dealing with drives larger than 504 MB and is the only way of dealing with drives larger than 8.4 GB.

■ The OS and software can bypass the system BIOS altogether and communicate directly with the controller BIOS by using device drivers. Windows NT/2000/XP uses this method. True to its compromising nature, Windows 9x has its own 32-bit protected mode device drivers to access hard drives, bypassing system BIOS. However, to support DOS and other older software, Windows 9x also supports using system BIOS to access drives.

8

> **TIP** Don't confuse hard drive capacity with the capacity of a logical drive or volume. For example, when using large mode, a hard drive can be up to 8.4 GB, but each logical drive (for example, drive C) on the hard drive using the FAT16 file system can only be 2 GB or 4 GB, depending on the OS used. Therefore, if you are using FAT16 on a large-capacity hard drive, you are forced to use more than one logical drive (drives C, D, and E) on a single hard drive. However, if you use FAT32, your logical volume can be the size of the entire hard drive.

To use the operating system to report the capacity of a hard drive, at a command prompt, enter the command Chkdsk. For Windows 9x and Windows NT/2000/XP, using Windows Explorer, right-click the drive letter and select Properties from the shortcut menu. Report the capacity of each logical drive on the hard drive, and then add them together to get the entire hard drive capacity, assuming all space on the hard drive is partitioned and formatted. For Windows 9x, use Fdisk, and for Windows 2000/XP, use Disk Management to report the capacity of an entire hard drive regardless of whether or not the drive is fully partitioned and formatted.

Installations Using Legacy BIOS

A+CORE
1.2
1.10

Older (legacy) BIOS only supported drives less than 504 MB. Drives larger than 504 MB are called **large-capacity drives**, and the BIOS that support them is called **enhanced BIOS**. If you want to install a large-capacity drive on a PC whose BIOS does not support it, you have the following choices:

■ Let the BIOS see the drive as a smaller drive.

■ Upgrade the BIOS.

■ Upgrade the entire motherboard.

■ Use software that interfaces between the older BIOS and the large-capacity drive.

■ Use an adapter card that provides the BIOS to substitute for system BIOS.

A+CORE
1.2
1.10

This first option may or may not work, depending on your BIOS. Some BIOSs that do not support large-capacity drives do not recognize a large drive, but simply see the larger hard drive as a smaller drive they can support. In this case, the BIOS assigns a drive capacity smaller than the actual capacity. You can use this method, although it wastes drive space.

Most large-capacity drives come with software that performs the translation between an older BIOS and the large-capacity drive. Examples of such translation or disk overlay software are Disk Manager by Ontrack Data International, Inc. (*www.ontrack.com*), SpeedStor by Storage Dimensions, and EZ-Drive by StorageSoft (*www.storagesoft.com*). You can find the software on a floppy disk with the drive or download it from the drive manufacturer's Web site. Boot from a floppy disk with the software installed, and follow directions on the screen. A small partition or logical drive is created on the hard drive to manage the drive for the older BIOS. It's important to keep this disk in a safe place, in case you need it to access the hard drive because the software on the drive has become corrupted. A disadvantage of using this method is that if you boot from a regular bootable floppy disk, you might not be able to access the hard drive.

Some hard drives come with disk manager software already installed. For example, for some drives manufactured by Maxtor, the disk manager software is found in a directory called \MAX in a 112-MB partition that BIOS recognizes as drive C. The rest of the drive is assigned to other partitions or logical drives, such as drive D or drive E.

Adapter cards are available to provide the BIOS that substitutes for system BIOS. This is the recommended method if your motherboard does not have an upgrade for system BIOS. One manufacturer of these cards is Promise Technology, Inc.

The best solution is to upgrade BIOS. However, remember that the new BIOS must also relate correctly to the chip set on the motherboard. Follow the recommendations of the motherboard manufacturer when selecting a BIOS upgrade.

 TIP Some BIOSs support a method of data transfer that allows multiple data transfers each time software requests data. This method is called **block mode** and should be used if your hard drive and BIOS support it. However, if you are having problems with hard drive errors, you can try disabling block mode. Use CMOS setup to make the change.

HOW A HARD DRIVE IS LOGICALLY ORGANIZED TO HOLD DATA

A+ OS
1.1

This section covers how a file system works and how to install one on a hard drive. The goal of this section is to help you understand what must be written on a hard drive so that you can boot from it and get to a command prompt such as C:\> using the hard drive. For this to happen, the drive must have track and sector markings written on the drive, a file system must be installed, and files needed to boot the PC must be copied to the root directory of the drive.

A+ OS
1.1

Recall that today's hard drives come from the factory already low-level formatted (that is, with track and sector markings already in place). After one of these drives is physically installed and system BIOS has recognized the drive and determined the drive capacity, the next step is to install a file system on the drive. For current Windows operating systems, there are three choices of file systems, FAT16, FAT32, and NTFS. All Windows operating systems support FAT16. Windows 95 Second Edition, Windows 98, Windows 2000, and Windows XP support FAT32. Windows NT, Windows 2000, and Windows XP support NTFS. The NTFS file system is best installed during the Windows setup process or after Windows is installed, so this chapter does not cover it. You can install the FAT16 or FAT32 file system from a command prompt after booting from a startup disk.

Recall from Chapter 3 that for either file system, the high-level divisions are called partitions, and within the partitions, the drive is further divided into logical drives or volumes. Logical drives have letters assigned to them, such as drive C or drive D, and each logical drive has its own file system, such as FAT32 or NTFS, to manage files on the logical drive. This section discusses how partitions and logical drives are organized and used by the OS, and how to use OS commands to partition and format a hard drive for first use.

After physical installation, preparing a hard drive to hold files requires the following three steps:

1. *Low-level format.* This physically formats the hard drive and creates the tracks and sectors. For hard drives today, this has already been done by the time you buy the drive and does not involve an OS.

2. *Partitioning the hard drive.* Even if only one partition is used, this step is still required. The DOS and Windows Fdisk program sets up a partition table at the beginning of the hard drive. This table lists how many partitions are on the drive, their locations, and which partition is the boot partition. Within each partition, Fdisk also creates logical drives, assigning letters to these drives. Also, when using Windows 2000/XP, the Disk Management utility can be used to partition a drive and create logical drives. The Windows 2000/XP Recovery Console command Diskpart can also be used. In Windows XP, the Diskpart command is available at a command prompt as well.

3. *High-level format.* This process builds a file system for each logical drive. The OS must do this for each logical drive on the hard drive. As each logical drive is formatted, the OS creates an OS boot record, a root directory, and two copies of FAT for the logical drive, just as it does for a floppy disk. High-level formatting is done using the Format command or, in Windows 2000/XP, using Disk Management.

8

Hard Drive Partitions and Logical Drives

A+ OS
  1.4

Although you might have a 10-GB hard drive that is only a single physical drive, an OS can divide this single physical drive into more than one logical drive. (A logical drive is sometimes called a logical partition; don't let the two uses of the term *partition* confuse you; partitions and logical partitions are divisions at different levels.) Figure 8-9 shows a typical example with the hard drive divided into two partitions. The first partition contains one logical drive (drive C), and the second partition is divided into two logical drives (D and E). The partition table at the very beginning of the drive records all these divisions. The partition table is in the first sector of the hard drive on head 0, track 0, sector 1. This sector is called the master boot sector or the Master Boot Record (MBR). Table 8-3 lists the contents of a partition table. Don't confuse this first physical sector of the hard drive with sector 1 as Windows knows it. The OS's sector 1 comes after the physical sector 1 and is the first sector in the logical drive C.

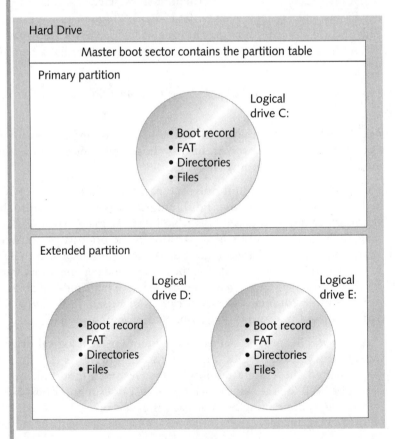

Figure 8-9   A hard drive is divided into one or more partitions that contain logical drives

Table 8-3   Hard drive partition table in the MBR

Item	Bytes Used	Description
1	446 bytes	Program that calls the boot program on the OS boot record
2	16-byte total 1 byte 3 bytes 1 byte 3 bytes 4 bytes 4 bytes	Description of the first partition Is this the bootable partition? (Yes = 90h, No = 00h) Beginning location of the partition System indicator; possible values are: 0 = Not a DOS partition 1 = DOS with a 12-bit FAT 4 = DOS with a 16-bit FAT 5 = Not the first partition 6 = Partition larger than 32 MB Ending location of partition First sector of the partition table relative to the beginning of the disk Number of sectors in the partition
3	16 bytes	Describes second partition, using same format as first partition
4	16 bytes	Describes third partition, using same format as first partition
5	16 bytes	Describes fourth partition, using same format as first partition
6	2 bytes	Signature of the partition table, always AA55

The partition table is exactly 512 bytes long, occupying one sector. During POST, the partition table program stored at the beginning of the Master Boot Record executes and checks the integrity of the partition table itself. If the partition table program finds any corruption, it refuses to continue execution, and the disk is unusable. If the table entries are valid, the partition table program looks in the table to determine which partition is the active partition, and it executes the bootstrap loader program in the boot record of that partition.

> **TIP** Sometimes the Master Boot Record is the target of a **boot sector virus**, which can cause problems with the boot process and data retrieval. The Windows 9x Fdisk /MBR command or the Windows 2000/XP Fixmbr command is used to repair damage to the program in the MBR.

The **active partition** is the partition on the hard drive used to boot the OS. It contains only a single logical drive (drive C) and is always the first partition on the drive. Windows 2000/XP calls the active partition the system partition.

$A^+_{\ \ 1.4}^{OS}$ Using DOS or Windows 9x, a hard drive can have one or two partitions. Using Windows NT/2000/XP, a drive can have up to four partitions. A partition can be a **primary partition** (having only one logical drive in the partition, such as drive C) or an **extended partition** (having more than one logical drive, such as drive D and drive E). There can be only one extended partition on a drive. Therefore, with DOS and Windows 9x, the drive can have one primary and one extended partition. Under Windows NT/2000/XP, the drive can have four partitions, but only one of them can be an extended partition. The active partition is always a primary partition.

$A^+_{\ \ 1.10}^{CORE}$ ## Choice of File Systems

After the hard drive is formatted and ready for use, you are not usually aware that the several logical drives on the hard drive all belong to the same hard drive. For example, Figure 8-10 shows three drives, C, D, and E, that are logical drives on one physical hard drive. If you right-click one drive, such as drive D in the figure, and select Properties from the shortcut menu, you can see the amount of space allotted to this logical drive and how much of it is currently used. Also note in the figure that drive D is formatted using the FAT32 file system. It is possible for one logical drive to be formatted with one file system and other logical drives on the same hard drive to be formatted with a different file system such as FAT16 or NTFS.

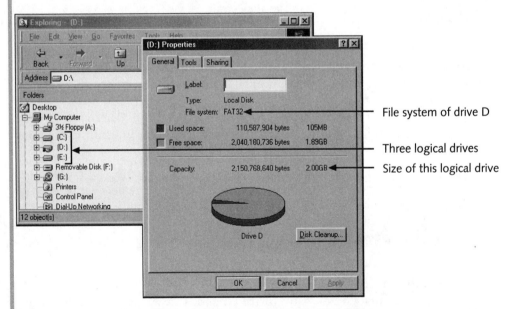

Figure 8-10   This hard drive contains three logical drives

  When partitioning a hard drive using the Windows 9x Fdisk utility, you have two choices for a file system, FAT16 or FAT32. Use FAT32 unless the same PC will also be running Windows NT, which does not support FAT32.

A+CORE
     1.10

FAT16

DOS and all versions of Windows support the FAT16 file system that uses 16 bits for each cluster entry in the FAT. Using FAT16, the smallest cluster size is four sectors. Since each sector is 512 bytes, a cluster that contains four sectors is 2,048 bytes. A one-character file takes up 2,048 bytes of space on a hard drive. For larger drives, the number of sectors in one cluster is even more. When the drive contains many small files, with cluster size so large, these files can create a lot of wasted space called **slack**.

Virtual File Allocation (VFAT)

Windows 95 and Windows for Workgroups offered an improved method of hard drive access, called **VFAT**, or **virtual file allocation table**. VFAT uses 32-bit protected-mode device drivers for hard drive access. In Windows for Workgroups, VFAT is called 32-bit file access. The Windows 95 version of VFAT supports long filenames of up to 255 characters. Using VFAT, the FAT still uses 16 bits per cluster entry. VFAT has been rendered outdated by FAT32.

FAT32

Beginning with Windows 95 OSR2, Microsoft offered a FAT that contains 32 bits per FAT entry instead of the older 12-bit or 16-bit FAT entries. Only 28 bits are used to hold a cluster number; the remaining four bits are not presently used.

FAT32 is efficient for logical drives up to 16 GB. In this range, the cluster size is 8K. After that, the cluster size increases to about 16K for drives in the 16-GB to 32-GB range. You are then reaching a drive size that warrants a more powerful file management system than FAT32, such as NTFS. Windows 2000/XP only supports FAT32 for drives up to 32 GB.

TIP If you are currently using FAT16 and are considering switching to FAT32, you can use a third-party utility such as PartitionMagic by PowerQuest Corporation (*www.powerquest.com*) to scan your hard drive and tell you how much of the drive is used for slack space. Knowing this can help you decide if the change will yield you more usable drive space.

NTFS

Windows NT/2000/XP supports **NTFS (New Technology file system)**. NTFS is designed to provide more security than does the FAT file system and uses a database called the **master file table (MFT)** to hold information about files and directories and their locations on the hard drive. Whereas the FAT file system writes the FAT and root directory at the beginning of a hard drive, NTFS writes the MFT at the end of a hard drive. Use NTFS under Windows NT/2000/XP when you have a large hard drive, you are not going to install Windows 98 on the drive as a second OS, and security is a concern.

8

A+CORE
1.10

It is best to install NTFS at the same time you install Windows NT/2000/XP from the setup CD, or you can convert a FAT file system to NTFS after Windows is installed. If you plan to install Windows NT/2000/XP using NTFS on a newly installed hard drive, you can still boot from a Windows 98 bootable disk and use Fdisk to partition the drive and install the FAT file system on the active partition. After you verify the hard drive is accessible and working using the FAT, you can then install Windows NT/2000/XP and NTFS.

How Many Logical Drives?

In addition to creating partitions on a hard drive and deciding which type of file system to use, Fdisk, Diskpart, or Disk Management is used to create logical drives within these partitions. The active or primary partition has only one logical drive, C. You specify how large this logical drive is when you set the size of the active partition. The extended partition can use all or some of the remaining free space on the drive (some space can go unused). You also decide how large the extended partition is, up to the amount of available free space on the drive. Within the extended partition, you can put several logical drives. You determine how many logical drives and what portion of the extended partition is allotted to each.

Some people prefer to use more than one logical drive to organize their hard drives, especially if they plan to have more than one OS on the same drive. However, the main reason you need multiple logical drives is to optimize space and access time to the drive. The larger the logical drive, the larger the cluster size, and the more slack or wasted space. When deciding how to allocate space to logical drives, the goal is to use as few logical drives as possible and still keep cluster size to a minimum.

Table 8-4 gives the information you need to decide how to slice your drive. Notice that the largest logical drive possible using DOS or Windows 9x FAT16 is 2 GB (this limitation is rooted in the largest cluster number that can be stored in a 16-bit FAT entry). For Windows NT/2000/XP, FAT16 logical drives can be no larger than 4 GB. However, you can see from the table that, to make a drive that big, the cluster size must be huge. Also, the largest hard drive that FAT16 can support is 8.4 GB; if the drive is larger than that, you must use FAT32. The sizes for logical drives using the NTFS file system are included to make the table complete.

When you use Fdisk, Diskpart, or Disk Managment to create a logical drive, a drive letter is assigned to each logical drive. For a primary partition, drive C is assigned to the one volume, and drives D and E and so forth are assigned to volumes in the extended partition. However, if a second hard drive is installed in a system, the program takes this into account when assigning drive letters. If the second hard drive has a primary partition, the program assigns it as drive D, leaving drive letters E, F, G, H, and so forth for the volumes in the extended partitions of both hard drives. For example, in a two-hard-drive system where each hard drive has a primary partition, an extended partition, and three logical drives, the drive letters for the first hard drive will be C, E, and F, and the drive letters for the second hard drive will be D, G, and H.

A+CORE
1.10

Table 8-4   Size of some logical drives compared to cluster size for FAT16, FAT32, and NTFS

File System	Size of Logical Drive	Size of Cluster
FAT16	Up to 128 MB	4 sectors per cluster
	128 to 256 MB	8 sectors per cluster
	256 to 512 MB	16 sectors per cluster
	512 MB to 1 GB	32 sectors per cluster
	1 GB to 4 GB*	64 sectors per cluster
FAT32	512 MB to 8 GB	8 sectors per cluster
	8 GB to 16 GB	16 sectors per cluster
	16 GB to 32 GB	32 sectors per cluster
	More than 32 GB**	64 sectors per cluster
NTFS	Up to 512 MB	1 sector per cluster
	512 MB to 1 GB	2 sectors per cluster
	More than 1 GB	4 sectors per cluster

* For DOS and Windows 9x, the largest FAT16 is 2 GB. For Windows NT/2000/XP, the largest FAT16 is 4 GB.

** Windows 2000/XP does not support FAT32 for drives larger than 32 GB.

If the second hard drive is not going to be the boot device, it does not have to have a primary partition. If you put only a single extended partition on that drive, then the program assigns the drive letters C, D, and E to the first drive and F, G, H, and so forth to the second drive.

When to Partition a Drive

There are several reasons to partition a drive:

- When you first install a new hard drive, you must partition it to prepare it for use.

- If an existing hard drive is giving errors, you can repartition the drive and reformat each logical drive to begin fresh. You will destroy all data on the drive, so back up important data first.

- If you suspect a virus has attacked the drive, you can back up critical data and repartition it to begin with a clean drive.

- If you want to wipe a hard drive clean and install a new OS, you can repartition a drive in preparation for formatting it with a new file system. If you do not want to change the size or number of partitions, you do not have to repartition the drive.

When installing Windows 9x, before you use the Windows 9x CD for Windows 9x upgrades, you can boot from a bootable disk that has the Fdisk.exe program file on it.

Then use Fdisk to partition the hard drive, and install enough of a previous version of Windows on it to boot from it. During a Windows 9x installation, if the drive is not partitioned, the install procedure automatically executes Fdisk to partition the drive.

You can use Fdisk to partition a drive or you can use third-party software such as PartitionMagic. Fdisk is simple and easy to use, but PartitionMagic has some advantages over Fdisk. A major one is that when Fdisk partitions a drive, it erases all data on the existing partitions that it changes or overwrites, but PartitionMagic protects data when it changes the partitions on the drive. Also, PartitionMagic has a more user-friendly GUI interface.

Sometimes you should not use Fdisk to partition a drive, such as when the drive has been partitioned by third-party software such as Disk Manager or SpeedStor. Recall that these products implement drive translation to enable a large hard drive to exist in a system whose system BIOS does not support large drives. To know if a large hard drive has been partitioned to do disk translation, look for entries in the Config.sys file that point to third-party software to manage the drive. Examples of these command lines are Dmdrvr.bin, Sstor.sys, Harddrive.sys, and Evdisk.sys. If you find lines with these filenames, use this third-party software to repartition the drive. Know that if you boot from a floppy disk, you cannot access a hard drive that is using drive translation, unless the floppy disk contains the right drivers provided by the drive translation software. Most drive translation software provides a way to create a floppy disk to be used in emergencies when the hard drive does not boot.

 TIP Fdisk under Windows 98 can incorrectly display the size of hard drives larger than 64 GB. The capacity will be reported as the true capacity minus 64 GB. For example, Fdisk will show a 120 GB drive to be 56 GB (120 GB - 64 GB). When using Windows 9x, for drives larger than 64 GB, check with the hard drive manufacturer for freeware that you can use to partition and format the drive. For instance, Western Digital has Data Lifeguard Tools and Maxtor has MaxBlast software.

What Happens During Formatting

After you partition a drive and create logical drives within each partition, you use the Format command to format each logical drive. (You will learn more about using these commands later in the chapter, when you learn how to install a drive.) The OS format for each logical drive creates these file system items at the beginning of each logical drive:

- OS boot record
- FAT
- Root directory

An OS boot record at the beginning of a logical drive is used during the boot process to inform the OS how the logical drive is organized. If the logical drive is the boot device, the boot program at the end of the boot record loads the first Windows hidden file, Io.sys, or Ntldr. Table 8-5 shows the complete record layout for the boot record. The medium descriptor byte tells the OS what type of disk this is. Table 8-6 gives the values of this descriptor byte.

Table 8-5   Layout of the boot record on each logical drive

Description	Number of Bytes
Machine code	11
Bytes per sector	2
Sectors per cluster	1
Reserved	2
Number of FATs	1
Number of root directory entries	2
Number of logical sectors	2
Medium descriptor byte	1
Sectors per FAT	2
Sectors per track	2
Heads	2
Number of hidden sectors	2
Total sectors in logical volume	4
Physical drive number	1
Reserved	1
Extended boot signature record	1
32-bit binary volume ID	4
Volume label	11
Type of file system (FAT12, FAT16, or FAT32)	8
Program to load operating system (bootstrap loader)	Remainder of the sector

8

Table 8-6   Disk type and descriptor byte

Disk Type	Descriptor Byte
3½-inch double-density floppy disk, 720K	F9
3½-inch high-density floppy disk, 1.44 MB	F0
Hard disk	F8

Recall from Chapter 7 that the total number of bytes for each file entry in a floppy drive directory is 32. The layout of the root directory is the same for hard drives as for floppy disks. Although earlier versions of Windows did limit the number of entries in the root directory, Windows 98 and later Windows OSs do not. Note, however, that Microsoft recommends that you keep only about 150 entries in any one directory. Having any more entries slows access to the directory.

INSTALLING A HARD DRIVE

A+CORE 1.2   Now that you know about hard drives, we turn our attention to the step-by-step process of installing an IDE hard drive. To install an IDE hard drive, do the following:

1. Set jumpers or DIP switches on the drive, physically install the drive inside the computer case, and attach the power cord and data cable.

2. Inform CMOS setup of the new drive, or verify that autodetect correctly detected the drive.

3. Use the Fdisk utility to create one or more partitions on the drive, and divide the extended partition (if there is one) into logical drives.

4. Use the Format command to high-level format each logical drive.

5. Install the OS and other software (covered in later chapters).

To install an IDE drive, you need the drive, a 40-pin data cable, and perhaps a kit to make the drive fit into a much larger bay. If the motherboard does not provide an IDE connection, you also need an adapter card.

Prepare for Installation

A+CORE 1.2   Remember from earlier chapters that keeping notes is a good idea whenever you install new hardware or software, or make any other changes to your PC system. As with installing any other devices, before you begin installing your hard drive, make sure you know where your starting point is, and take notes so that you can backtrack later if necessary. How is your system configured? Is everything working properly? Verify which of your system's devices are working before installing a new one. Later, if a resource conflict occurs and causes a device to malfunction, the information will help you isolate the problem.

> **TIP**
> When installing hardware and software, don't install too many things at once. If something goes wrong, you won't know what's causing the problem. Install one device, bring up the system, and confirm that the new device is working before installing another.

Make sure that you have a good bootable disk or Windows 9x rescue disk; test it to make sure it works. As always, just in case you lose setup information in the process, make sure you have a record of your CMOS setup on a disk or, at the least, write down any variations in setup from the default settings. Two good places to record CMOS settings are the notebook you keep about this computer and the manual for the motherboard.

Read Documentation

Before you take anything apart, carefully read all documentation for the drive and adapter card, and the part of your PC documentation that covers hard drive installation. Look for problems you have not considered, such as IRQ or DMA conflicts if this is a second hard drive for your system or if you have an older, limited version of system BIOS. Also check the setup of your computer to be sure it accommodates the size and type of hard drive you want to install. If you plan to choose a user-defined drive type in the setup (where you must enter the drive specifications), make sure your PC accepts the values you want. Check your motherboard documentation or CMOS setup screen.

Plan Drive Configuration

Remember, there can be up to two IDE controllers on a motherboard, the primary and secondary IDE controller. Each controller can support up to two drives, a master and a slave, for a total of up to four IDE drives in a system. When possible, leave the hard drive as the single drive on one controller, so that it does not compete with another drive for access to the controller and possibly slow down performance. Use the primary channel before you use the secondary channel. Put slow devices together on the same controller. For example, suppose you have a Zip drive, CD-ROM drive, and two hard drives. Since the two hard drives are faster than the Zip drive and CD-ROM drive, put the two hard drives on one controller and the Zip drive and CD-ROM drive on the other. Place the fastest devices on the primary channel and the slower devices on the secondary channel. If you have three or fewer devices, allow the fastest hard drive to be your boot device and the only device on the primary channel.

Make sure that you can visualize the entire installation. If you have any questions, find answers before you begin. Either keep reading until you locate the answer, call technical support, or ask a knowledgeable friend. You may discover that what you are installing will not work on your computer, but that is better than coping with hours of frustration and a disabled computer. You cannot always anticipate every problem, but at least you can know that you made your best effort to understand everything in advance. What you learn in thorough preparation pays off every time!

8

A+CORE
  1.2
Prepare Your Work Area and Take Precautions

The next step is to prepare a large, well-lit place to work. Set out your tools, documentation, new hardware, and notebook. Remember the basic rules concerning static electricity, which you learned in Chapter 4. Ground yourself and the computer; wear a ground bracelet during the installation. Avoid working on carpet in the winter, when there's a lot of static electricity.

Some added precautions for working with hard drives are:

- Handle the drive carefully.

- Do not touch any exposed circuitry or chips.

- Prevent other people from touching exposed microchips on the drive.

- When you first take the drive out of the static-protective package, touch the package containing the drive to a screw holding an expansion card or cover, or to a metal part of the computer case, for at least two seconds. This will drain the static electricity from the package and from your body.

- If you must set down the drive outside the static-protective package, place it component-side-up on top of the static-protective package on a flat surface.

- Do not place the drive on the computer case cover or on a metal table.

Turn off the computer and unplug it. Unplug the monitor and move it to one side. Remove the computer case cover. Check that you have an available power cord from the power supply.

> **TIP** If there are not enough power cords from a power supply, you can purchase a Y connector that can add an additional power cord.

Examine the locations of the drive bays and the length of the data cables. Decide which bay will hold which drive. Bays designed for hard drives will not have access to the outside of the case, unlike bays for Zip drives and other drives in which disks are inserted. Also, some bays are wider than others to accommodate wide drives such as CD-ROM drives and DVD drives (see Figure 8-11). Will the data cable reach the drives and the motherboard connector? If not, rearrange your plan for locating the drives in the bays, or purchase a custom-length data cable.

A⁺*CORE*
1.2
1.6

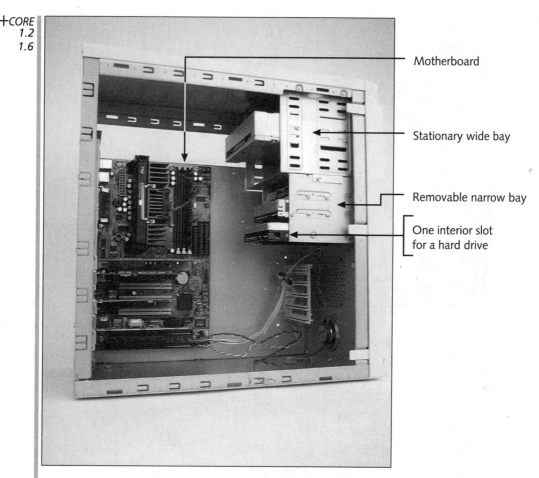

Motherboard

Stationary wide bay

Removable narrow bay

One interior slot
for a hard drive

8

Figure 8-11   Plan for the location of drives within bays

Set Jumpers and DIP Switches

A⁺*CORE*
1.2
1.6
Configuration is normally done by setting jumpers on the drive housing. Often, diagrams of the jumper settings are printed on the top of the hard drive housing (see
Figure 8-12). If they are not, see the documentation or visit the Web site of the drive
manufacturer. Figure 8-13 shows a typical jumper arrangement. Table 8-7 lists the
four choices for jumper settings for this drive. Note that your hard drive might not
have the first configuration as an option, but it should have a way of indicating if
the drive will be the master device. The factory default setting is usually correct for
the drive to be the single drive on a system. Before you change any settings, write
down the original ones. If things go wrong, you can revert to the original settings
and begin again. If a drive is the only drive on a controller, set it to single. For two
drives on a controller, set one to master and the other to slave.

A$^+$CORE
  1.2
  1.6

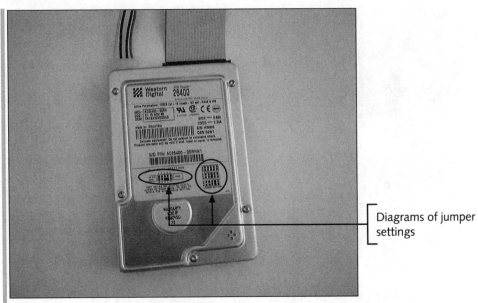

Diagrams of jumper settings

Figure 8-12   An IDE drive most likely will have diagrams of jumper settings for master and slave options printed on the drive housing

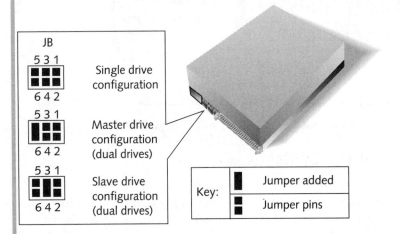

JB

5 3 1
6 4 2
Single drive configuration

5 3 1
6 4 2
Master drive configuration (dual drives)

5 3 1
6 4 2
Slave drive configuration (dual drives)

Key: ▮ Jumper added
        ▯ Jumper pins

Figure 8-13   Jumper settings on a hard drive and their meanings

Some hard drives have a cable-select configuration option. If you choose this configuration, you must use a cable-select data cable. When you use one of these cables, the drive nearest the motherboard is the master, and the drive farthest from the motherboard is the slave. You can recognize a cable-select cable by a small hole somewhere in the data cable.

A+*CORE*
1.2
1.6

Table 8-7 Jumper settings on an IDE hard drive

Configuration	Description
Single-drive configuration	This is the only hard drive on this IDE channel. (This is the standard setting.)
Master-drive configuration	This is the first of two drives; it most likely is the boot device.
Slave-drive configuration	This is the second drive using this channel or data cable.
Cable-select configuration	The cable-select data cable determines which of the two drives is the master and which is the slave.

Mount the Drive in the Bay

A+*CORE*
1.2
1.6

Next, look at the drive bay that you will use for the drive. The bay might be stationary, or it might be removable. With a removable bay, you first remove the bay from the computer case and mount the drive in the bay. Then you put the bay back into the computer case. In Figure 8-11, you can see a stationary bay for large drives and a removable bay for small drives, including the hard drive. In this example, you will see how the hard drive is installed in a computer case that has three other drives, a DVD drive, a Zip drive, and a floppy drive. Do the following to install the hard drive in the bay:

1. Remove the bay for the hard drive, and insert the hard drive in the bay. You can line up the drive in the bay with the front of the computer case (see Figure 8-14) to see how drives will line up in the bay. Put the hard drive in the bay flush with the front of the bay so it will butt up against the computer case once the bay is in position (see Figure 8-15). Line up other drives in the bay so they are flush with the front of the computer case. In our example, a floppy drive and Zip drive are already in the bay.

8

Stationary bay
for large drives

Floppy drive

Removable bay
for small drives

Figure 8-14 Line up the floppy drive in the removable bay so it's flush with the front of the case

A+CORE
1.2
1.6

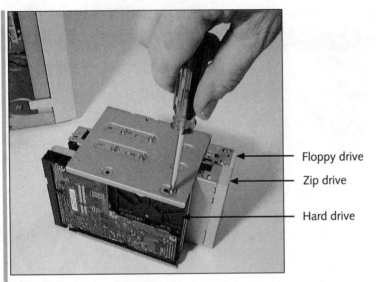

Floppy drive

Zip drive

Hard drive

Figure 8-15   Position the hard drive flush with the end of the bay

2. You must be able to securely mount the drive in the bay; the drive should not move when it is screwed down. Line up the drive and bay screw holes, and make sure everything will fit. After checking the position of the drive and determining how screws are placed, install four screws (two on each side) to mount the drive in the bay.

 **CAUTION**

Be sure the screws are not too long. If they are, you can screw too far into the drive housing and damage the drive itself.

Do not allow torque to stress the drive. For example, don't force a drive into a space that is too small for it. Also, placing two screws in diagonal positions across the drive can place pressure diagonally on the drive.

3. Decide whether to connect the data cable to the drive before or after you insert the bay inside the computer case, depending on how accessible the connections are. In this example, the data cables are connected to the drives first and then the bay is installed inside the computer case. In the photograph in Figure 8-16, the data cables for all the drives in the bay are connected to the drives.

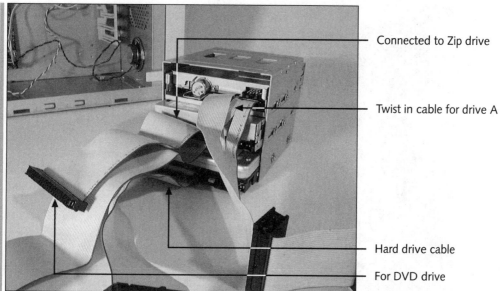

Connected to Zip drive

Twist in cable for drive A

Hard drive cable

For DVD drive

Figure 8-16   Connect the cables to all three drives

4. The next step is to place the bay back into position and secure the bay with the bay screw or screws (see Figure 8-17).

5. Install a power connection to each drive (Figure 8-18). In Figure 8-18, the floppy drive uses the small power connection, and the other drives use the large ones. It doesn't matter which of the power cords you use, because they all produce the same voltage. Also, the cord only goes into the connection one way.

6. Next, connect the data cable to the IDE connector on the motherboard. See Figure 8-19. Make certain pin 1 and the edge color on the cable align correctly at both ends of the cable. Normally, pin 1 is closest to the power connection.

A+CORE
1.2
1.6

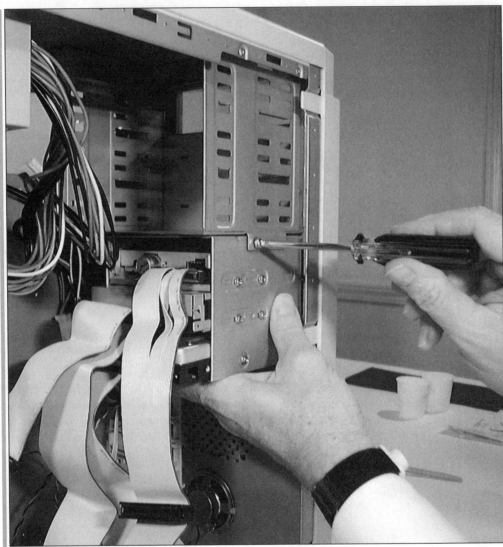

Figure 8-17 Secure the bay with the bay screw

A+CORE
1.2
1.6

Figure 8-18   Connect a power cord to each drive

8

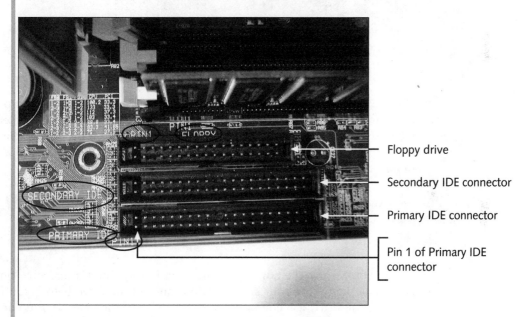

— Floppy drive

— Secondary IDE connector

— Primary IDE connector

⌐ Pin 1 of Primary IDE
└ connector

Figure 8-19   Floppy drive and two IDE connectors on the motherboard

A+CORE
1.2
1.6

7. If you are mounting a hard drive in an external bay, install a bay cover in the front of the case. Internal bays do not need this cover (see Figure 8-20).

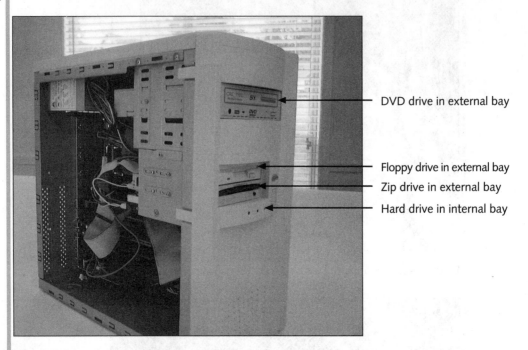

DVD drive in external bay

Floppy drive in external bay

Zip drive in external bay

Hard drive in internal bay

Figure 8-20   A tower case may have internal or external bays

8. When using a motherboard connection, if the wire connecting the motherboard to the hard drive light on the front of the case was not connected when the motherboard was installed, connect it now. If you reverse the polarity of the LED wire, the light will not work. Your motherboard manual should tell you the location of the LED wires on the motherboard.

 If the drive light does not work after you install a new drive, try reversing the LED wire on the motherboard pins.

9. Before you replace the computer case, plug in the monitor and turn on the computer. Verify that your system BIOS can find the drive before you replace the cover and that it recognizes the correct size of the drive. If you encounter problems, refer to the troubleshooting section at the end of this chapter.

If the Bay Is Too Large

If you are mounting a hard drive into a bay that is too large, a universal bay kit can help you securely fit the drive into the bay. These inexpensive kits should create a tailor-made

$A^{+}_{\ \ 1.2}^{CORE}$ fit. In Figure 8-21 you can see how the universal bay kit adapter works. The adapter spans the distance between the sides of the drive and the bay.

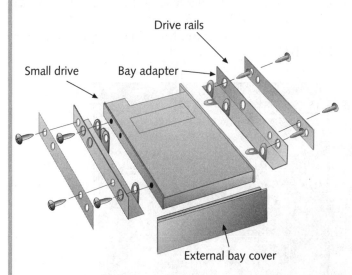

Drive rails

Small drive Bay adapter

External bay cover

Figure 8-21 Use a universal bay kit to make the drive fit the bay

Use CMOS Setup to Change Hard Drive Settings

$A^{+}_{\ \ 1.2}^{CORE}$
$_{4.4}$
When you first boot up after installing a hard drive, go to CMOS setup and verify that the drive has been recognized and that the settings are correct. Figures 8-22 through 8-25 show the four typical screens in setup programs, which allow you to change hard drive parameters. In Figure 8-22, you can see the choice for IDE HDD Auto Detection in the third item in the second column. For most hard drive installations, if Auto Detection is not enabled, enable it, save, and exit setup. Later, after you have rebooted with the new drive detected, you can return to setup, view the selections that it made, and make appropriate changes.

```
                    ROM PCI/ISA BIOS (<<P2B>>)
                       CMOS SETUP UTILITY
                      AWARD SOFTWARE, INC.

    STANDARD CMOS SETUP          SUPERVISOR PASSWORD
    BIOS FEATURES SETUP          USER PASSWORD
    CHIPSET FEATURES SETUP       IDE HDD AUTO DETECTION
    POWER MANAGEMENT SETUP       SAVE & EXIT SETUP
    PNP, AND PCI SETUP           EXIT WITHOUT SAVING
    LOAD BIOS DEFAULTS
    LOAD SETUP DEFAULTS

    Esc : Quit                   ↑↓→←: Select Item
    F10 : Save & Exit Setup      (Shift)F2 : Change Color
```

Figure 8-22 CMOS setup utility opening menu

Setup for Large-Capacity Hard Drives

A+CORE
1.2
4.4

Recall that the two ways BIOS relates to large-capacity drives are LBA and large mode. Notice in Figure 8-23 the column labeled *mode*, referring to how BIOS relates to the drive. Choices are normal, large, LBA, and auto. Most likely, when auto is the choice, setup automatically selects LBA.

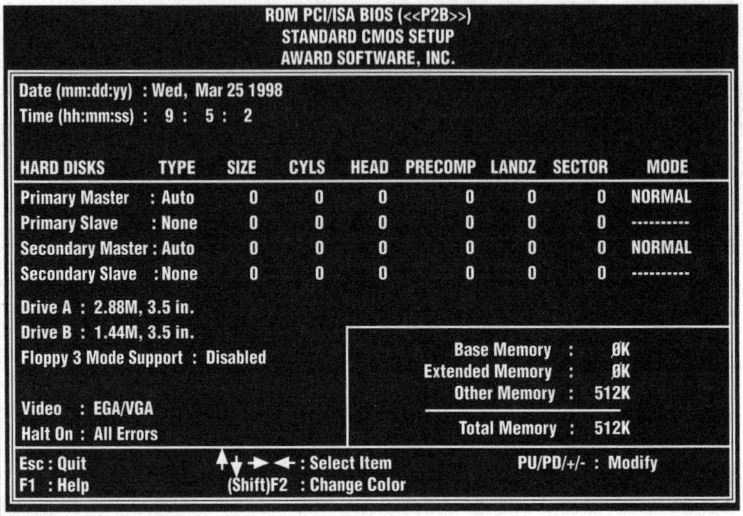

```
                    ROM PCI/ISA BIOS (<<P2B>>)
                      STANDARD CMOS SETUP
                      AWARD SOFTWARE, INC.

  Date (mm:dd:yy)  : Wed,  Mar 25 1998
  Time (hh:mm:ss) :  9 :  5 :  2

  HARD DISKS        TYPE    SIZE   CYLS   HEAD  PRECOMP  LANDZ  SECTOR    MODE

  Primary Master   : Auto     0      0      0       0      0       0    NORMAL
  Primary Slave    : None     0      0      0       0      0       0    ----------
  Secondary Master : Auto     0      0      0       0      0       0    NORMAL
  Secondary Slave  : None     0      0      0       0      0       0    ----------

  Drive A : 2.88M, 3.5 in.
  Drive B : 1.44M, 3.5 in.
  Floppy 3 Mode Support : Disabled          Base Memory    :     ØK
                                          Extended Memory  :     ØK
                                            Other Memory   :   512K
  Video   : EGA/VGA
  Halt On : All Errors                       Total Memory   :   512K

  Esc : Quit            ↑↓ → ← : Select Item        PU/PD/+/- : Modify
  F1  : Help          (Shift)F2  : Change Color
```

Figure 8-23   Standard CMOS setup

In Figure 8-24 (starting with the tenth item in the second column), you can see the hard drive features that the chip set on this motherboard supports. They are Ultra DMA, PIO, and DMA modes. Leave all these settings at Auto, and let BIOS make the choice according to its detection of the features your hard drive supports.

In Figure 8-25, the twelfth item of the first column indicates that BIOS on this motherboard supports block mode. From this screen you can also select the boot sequence (see ninth item in first column). Choices for this BIOS are A, C; A, CD Rom, C; CD Rom, C, A; D, A; F, A; C only; Zip, C; and C, A. Also notice on this screen (eighth item in the first column) that this BIOS supports booting from a SCSI drive even when an IDE drive is present. Booting from the IDE drive is the default setting.

$A^{+}_{\substack{CORE \\ 1.2 \\ 4.4}}$

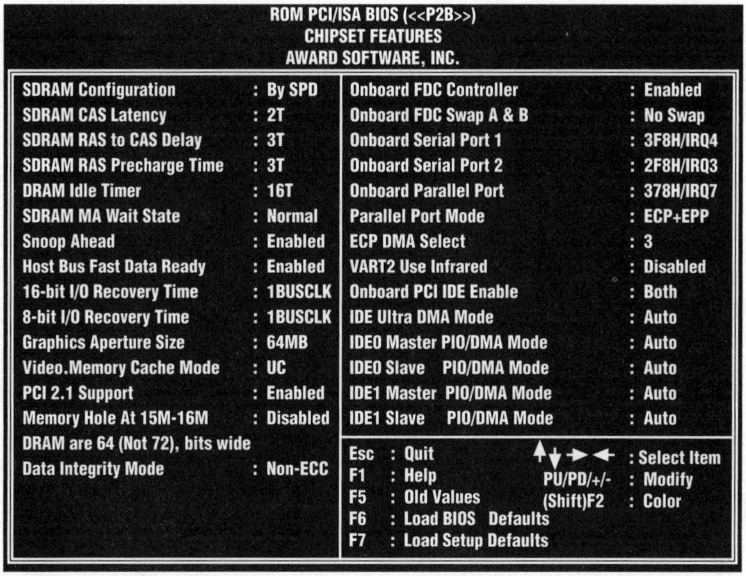

```
                    ROM PCI/ISA BIOS (<<P2B>>)
                       CHIPSET FEATURES
                      AWARD SOFTWARE, INC.

 SDRAM Configuration        : By SPD   Onboard FDC Controller     : Enabled
 SDRAM CAS Latency          : 2T       Onboard FDC Swap A & B      : No Swap
 SDRAM RAS to CAS Delay     : 3T       Onboard Serial Port 1       : 3F8H/IRQ4
 SDRAM RAS Precharge Time   : 3T       Onboard Serial Port 2       : 2F8H/IRQ3
 DRAM Idle Timer            : 16T      Onboard Parallel Port       : 378H/IRQ7
 SDRAM MA Wait State        : Normal   Parallel Port Mode          : ECP+EPP
 Snoop Ahead                : Enabled  ECP DMA Select              : 3
 Host Bus Fast Data Ready   : Enabled  VART2 Use Infrared          : Disabled
 16-bit I/O Recovery Time   : 1BUSCLK  Onboard PCI IDE Enable      : Both
 8-bit I/O Recovery Time    : 1BUSCLK  IDE Ultra DMA Mode          : Auto
 Graphics Aperture Size     : 64MB     IDE0 Master PIO/DMA Mode    : Auto
 Video.Memory Cache Mode    : UC       IDE0 Slave  PIO/DMA Mode    : Auto
 PCI 2.1 Support            : Enabled  IDE1 Master PIO/DMA Mode    : Auto
 Memory Hole At 15M-16M     : Disabled IDE1 Slave  PIO/DMA Mode    : Auto
 DRAM are 64 (Not 72), bits wide
 Data Integrity Mode        : Non-ECC  Esc  : Quit          ↑↓→← : Select Item
                                       F1   : Help     PU/PD/+/-  : Modify
                                       F5   : Old Values  (Shift)F2 : Color
                                       F6   : Load BIOS  Defaults
                                       F7   : Load Setup Defaults
```

Figure 8-24   CMOS setup for chip set features

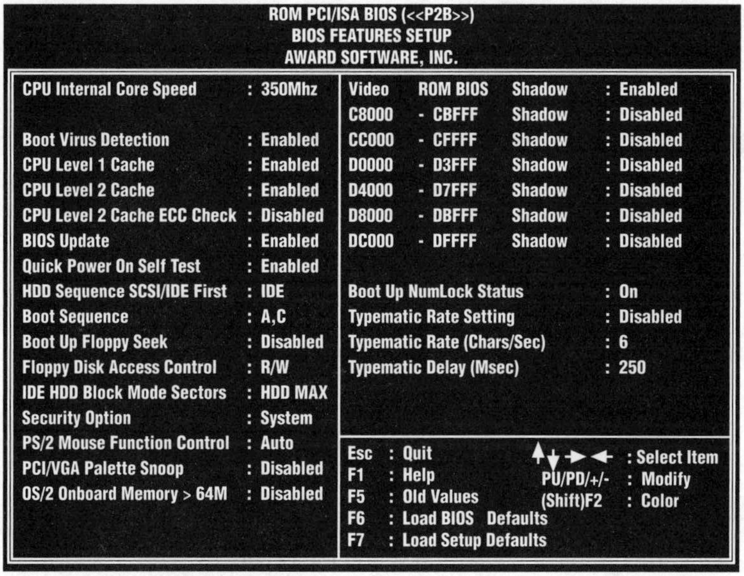

```
                    ROM PCI/ISA BIOS (<<P2B>>)
                       BIOS FEATURES SETUP
                      AWARD SOFTWARE, INC.

 CPU Internal Core Speed    : 350Mhz   Video   ROM BIOS  Shadow    : Enabled
                                       C8000  - CBFFF    Shadow    : Disabled
 Boot Virus Detection       : Enabled  CC000  - CFFFF    Shadow    : Disabled
 CPU Level 1 Cache          : Enabled  D0000  - D3FFF    Shadow    : Disabled
 CPU Level 2 Cache          : Enabled  D4000  - D7FFF    Shadow    : Disabled
 CPU Level 2 Cache ECC Check: Disabled D8000  - DBFFF    Shadow    : Disabled
 BIOS Update                : Enabled  DC000  - DFFFF    Shadow    : Disabled
 Quick Power On Self Test   : Enabled
 HDD Sequence SCSI/IDE First: IDE      Boot Up NumLock Status       : On
 Boot Sequence              : A,C      Typematic Rate Setting       : Disabled
 Boot Up Floppy Seek        : Disabled Typematic Rate (Chars/Sec)   : 6
 Floppy Disk Access Control : R/W      Typematic Delay (Msec)       : 250
 IDE HDD Block Mode Sectors : HDD MAX
 Security Option            : System
 PS/2 Mouse Function Control: Auto
 PCI/VGA Palette Snoop      : Disabled Esc  : Quit          ↑↓→← : Select Item
 OS/2 Onboard Memory > 64M  : Disabled F1   : Help     PU/PD/+/-  : Modify
                                       F5   : Old Values  (Shift)F2 : Color
                                       F6   : Load BIOS  Defaults
                                       F7   : Load Setup Defaults
```

Figure 8-25   CMOS setup for BIOS features

After you confirm that your drive is recognized and that all its settings are correct, you use the Fdisk and Format commands to set the logical organization of the drive.

Use Fdisk to Partition a Drive

A+ OS
1.5

To use Fdisk, boot from a startup disk that has the Fdisk.exe utility on it and enter Fdisk at the command prompt. The Fdisk opening menu shown in Figure 8-26 appears. Select option 1 to create the first partition. The menu in Figure 8-27 appears. Use option 1 to create the primary DOS partition. If you plan to install Windows 9x later, be sure this partition is at least 150 MB, preferably more. Make this first partition the active partition, which is the partition used to boot the OS. Fdisk automatically makes this partition drive C.

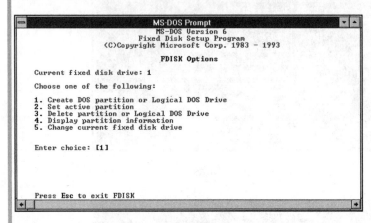

Figure 8-26   Fixed disk setup program (FDISK) menu

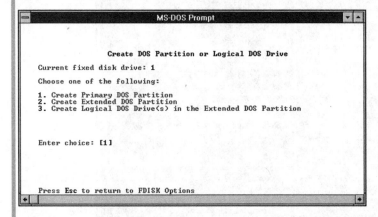

Figure 8-27   FDISK menu to create partitions and logical drives

Next, use option 2, shown in Figure 8-27, to create an extended DOS partition using the remainder of the hard drive. Then use option 3 to create logical drives in the extended partition.

A+ OS
1.5

When you create logical drives using Fdisk, you decide how large you want each drive to be. If you have at least 512 MB available for the drive, a message appears asking, "Do you wish to enable large disk support (Y/N)?" If you respond Y, then Fdisk assigns the FAT32 file system to the drive. Otherwise, it uses FAT16.

When Fdisk is completed, the hard drive has a partition table, an active and extended partition, and logical drives within these partitions. As seen in Figure 8-26, you can choose option 4 to display partition information (see Figure 8-28). After you exit the FDISK window, reboot the PC before you format the logical drives.

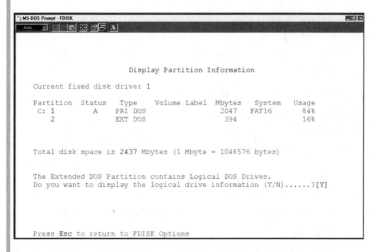

Figure 8-28   Fdisk displays partition information

Format Each Logical Drive

Now that the hard drive is partitioned and logical drives are created and assigned drive letters, the next step is to format each logical drive. The three commands used to format logical drives C, D, and E are:

```
Format C:/S
Format D:
Format E:
```

In the Format command line, the /S option makes the drive bootable, and the drive letter tells the OS which drive to format.

Using Windows to Partition and Format a New Drive

If you are installing a new hard drive in a system that is to be used for a new Windows installation, it is not necessary to boot from a bootable startup disk. After you have physically installed the drive, boot from the Windows setup CD and follow the directions on the screen to install Windows on the new drive. The setup process partitions and formats the new drive before it begins the Windows installation. If you are installing a second hard drive in a system that already has Windows 2000/XP installed on the first hard drive, use Windows to partition and format the second drive. After physically installing the second hard drive, boot into Windows as usual. Then use Disk Management to partition and format the new drive. This chapter does not cover the details of using Disk Management.

TROUBLESHOOTING HARD DRIVE INSTALLATIONS

A+CORE
2.1

Sometimes trouble crops up during the installation process. Keeping a cool head, thinking things through carefully a second, third, and fourth time, and using all available resources will most likely get you out of any mess. Installing a hard drive is not difficult unless you have an unusually complex situation.

For example, your first hard drive installation should not involve installing a second SCSI drive in a system that has two SCSI host adapters. Nor should you install a second drive in a system that uses an IDE connection for one drive on the motherboard and an adapter card in an expansion slot for the other drive. If a complicated installation is necessary and you have never installed a hard drive, consider asking for expert help. Know your limitations. Start with the simple and build your way up. Using what you have learned in this chapter, you should be able to install a single IDE drive in a PC or install a second slave IDE drive. After mastering that, tackle something more complicated.

Here are some errors that might occur during a hard drive installation, their causes, and what to do about them. (The next chapter covers troubleshooting hard drives after installation.) This list has been compiled from experience. Everyone makes mistakes when learning something new, and you probably will, too. You can then add your own experiences to this list.

- We physically installed an IDE hard drive. We turned on the machine and accessed CMOS setup. The hard drive was not listed as an installed device. We checked and discovered that autodetection was not enabled. We enabled it and rebooted. Setup recognized the drive.

- When first turning on a previously working PC, we received the following error message: "Hard drive not found." We turned off the machine, checked all cables, and discovered that the data cable from the motherboard to the drive was loose. We reseated the cable and rebooted. POST found the drive.

- We had physically installed a new hard drive, replaced the cover on the computer case, and booted the PC with a bootable floppy disk in the drive. POST beeped three times and stopped. Recall that diagnostics during POST are often communicated by beeps if the tests take place before POST has checked video and made it available to display the messages. Three beeps on most computers signal a memory error. We turned off the computer and checked the memory SIMMs on the motherboard. A SIMM positioned at

A+CORE
2.1

the edge of the motherboard next to the cover had been bumped as we replaced the cover. We reseated the SIMM and booted from a floppy disk again, this time with the cover still off. The error disappeared.

- We physically installed a new hard drive and turned on the computer. We received the following error: "No boot device available." We forgot to insert a bootable disk. We put the disk in the drive and rebooted the machine successfully.

- We physically installed the hard drive, inserted a floppy disk in the disk drive, and rebooted. We received the following error message: "Configuration/CMOS error. Run setup." This error message is normal for an older BIOS that does not support autodetection. POST found a hard drive it was not expecting. The next step is to run setup.

- We physically installed the card and drive and tried to reboot from a floppy disk. Error message 601 appeared on the screen. Any error message in the 600 range refers to the floppy disk. Because the case cover was still off, we looked at the connections and discovered that the power cord to the floppy disk drive was not connected. (It had been disconnected earlier to expose the hard drive bay underneath.) We turned off the machine and plugged in the cable. The error disappeared.

- The hard drive did not physically fit into the bay. The screw holes did not line up. We got a bay kit, but it just didn't seem to work. We took a break, went to lunch, and came back to make a fresh start. We asked others to help view the brackets, holes, and screws from a fresh perspective. It didn't take long to discover the correct position for the brackets in the bay.

- We set the jumpers on a hard drive and physically installed the drive. We booted and received the following error message: "Hard drive not present." We rechecked all physical connections and found everything okay. After checking the jumper settings, we realized that we had set them as if this were the second drive of a two-drive system, when it was the only drive. We restored the jumpers to their original state. In this case, as in most cases, the jumpers were set at the factory to be correct when the drive is the only drive.

If the computer will not recognize a newly installed hard drive, check the following:

- Does your system BIOS recognize large drives? Check CMOS setup.

- Does the manual state that you must first do a "low-level" format or run a Disk Manager? IDE drives are already low-level formatted. Older drives require the user to perform this routine.

- Has the Fdisk utility been successfully run? Choose "Display Partition Information" from the Fdisk menu to verify the status.

- Format C:/S is the last required "format" step. Has this been done?

- Has the CMOS setup been correctly configured?

8

- Are there any DIP switches or jumpers that must be set?

- Have the power cord and data cable been properly connected? Verify that the data cable stripes are connected to pin 1 on the edge connectors of both the motherboard and the drive.

- Check the Web site of the drive manufacturer for suggestions, if the above steps are not productive.

CAUTION

One last warning. When things are not going well, you can tense up and make mistakes more easily. *Be certain to turn off the machine before doing anything inside!* Not doing so can be a costly error. For example, a friend had been trying and retrying to boot for some time, and got frustrated and careless. He plugged the power cord into the drive without turning the PC off. Smoke went up and everything went dead. The next thing he learned was how to replace a power supply!

CHAPTER SUMMARY

- Most hard drives today use IDE technology, which has a complex method of organizing tracks and sectors on the disks.

- Several ANSI standards pertain to hard drives, including IDE, ATA, Fast ATA, Ultra ATA, Ultra ATA/66, Ultra ATA/100, and Ultra ATA/133.

- An IDE device such as a hard drive can be installed as a master drive, slave drive, or single drive on a system.

- The EIDE standards support two IDE connections, a primary and a secondary. Each connection can support up to two IDE devices for a total of four devices on a system.

- IDE devices under the EIDE standard can be hard drives, CD-ROM drives, tape drives, Zip drives, and others.

- Hard drive capacity for drives less than 8.4 GB is determined by the number of heads, tracks, and sectors on the disk, each sector holding 512 bytes of data.

- Large-capacity hard drives must have either LBA mode or large mode set in CMOS in order for system BIOS to support the drive. Without this support, other options can be used, including device driver software or a special EIDE adapter card specific to the drive.

- For the FAT file system, the DOS or Windows operating system views a hard drive through a FAT (file allocation table), which lists clusters, and a directory, which lists files.

❏ A hard drive is divided into partitions, which might also be divided into logical drives, or volumes. A Master Boot Record (MBR) at the beginning of the hard drive contains a table of partition information. Each logical drive contains a boot record, FAT, and root directory for the FAT file system.

❏ Physical geometry is the actual organization of heads, tracks, and sectors on the drive, whereas logical geometry is head, track, and sector information that the hard drive controller BIOS presents to system BIOS and the OS. The logical geometry may not be the same as the physical geometry, but, for drives less than 8.4 GB, should yield the same capacity when calculations are made.

❏ Drives larger than 8.4 GB use LBA mode, whereas the BIOS and OS view the drive as addressable sectors. The capacity of the drive is calculated as the number of addressable sectors multiplied by the number of bytes in one sector, which is almost always 512 bytes.

❏ System BIOS and software can use CHS, large mode, or LBA mode to manage a hard drive. The size of the drive and the drive manufacturer determine the mode used.

❏ The FAT, or file allocation table, lists all clusters on the hard drive and describes how each is allocated. FAT16 uses 16-bit entries, VFAT enabled Windows to use 32-bit protected-mode device drivers for hard drive access, and FAT32 uses 32-bit entries to hold the cluster numbers.

❏ DOS and the first release of Windows 95 support the FAT16 file system for hard drives. Windows 95 Release 2 and Windows 98 support FAT16 and FAT32 file systems. Windows NT supports FAT16 and the NTFS file systems. Windows 2000 and XP support FAT16, FAT32, and NTFS file systems.

❏ The FAT16 file system can be used for hard drives less than 8.4 GB. DOS and Windows 9x FAT16 logical drives cannot exceed 2 GB. Windows NT/2000/XP FAT16 logical drives cannot exceed 4 GB.

❏ Installing a hard drive includes setting jumpers or DIP switches on the drive; physically installing the adapter card, cable, and drive; changing CMOS setup; and partitioning, formatting, and installing software on the drive.

❏ Protect the drive and the PC against static electricity during installation.

❏ Most BIOSs today can autodetect the presence of a hard drive if the drive is designed to give this information to BIOS.

❏ For DOS or Windows 9x, a drive must have one primary partition and can have one extended partition. The drive boots from the primary partition. The extended partition can be subdivided into several logical drive partitions. Windows NT/2000/XP supports four partitions, one of which can be an extended partition.

❏ Use more than one partition to optimize cluster size, to handle drives greater than 2 GB when using FAT16, or to improve the organization of software and data on the drive.

❑ The OS, or high-level, format for the FAT file system creates the FATs, root directory, and boot record on the drive and marks any bad clusters in the FAT that the low-level format previously identified.

KEY TERMS

80 conductor IDE cable	ECHS (extended CHS) mode	logical geometry
active partition	EIDE (Enhanced IDE)	low-level formatting
adapter card	enhanced BIOS	master file table (MFT)
ANSI (American National Standards Institute)	extended partition	normal mode
	hard drive controller	NTFS (New Technology file system)
ATAPI (Advanced Technology Attachment Packet Interface)	head	operating system formatting
	high-level formatting	
	IDE (Integrated Device Electronics or Integrated Drive Electronics)	physical geometry
autodetection		primary partition
block mode		slack
boot sector virus	large-capacity drive	translation
CHS (cylinder, head, sector) mode	large mode	VFAT (virtual file allocation table)
	LBA (logical block addressing) mode	zone bit recording

REVIEW QUESTIONS

1. Devices that are considered to be non-hard drive-related may make use of the EIDE standard as long as they follow the _____ standards.

   a. SCSI

   b. HIMEM.SYS

   c. EMM386.EXE

   d. ATAPI

   e. ANSI

2. The most common interface cable used for the interconnection between EIDE-based controlling and controlled devices uses _____ wires.

   a. 34

   b. 40

   c. 50

   d. 62

   e. 80

3. The ANSI standard that allowed the interface of IDE-based devices that were larger than 528 MB was:

a. ATA

b. ATA-2 (Fast ATA)

c. Ultra ATA

d. Ultra ATA/100

e. Ultra ATA/133

4. Of the various cabling methods for drive devices, which is used for devices that are larger than 137 GB in size?

a. 34-wire cable

b. 40-wire cable

c. 50-wire cable

d. 62-wire cable

e. 80-wire cable (ATA/100)

5. The two EIDE connectors found on a motherboard allow devices to be configured as:

a. Primary/secondary master/slave

b. Primary/extended master/slave

c. Both a and b

d. Neither a nor b

6. Assuming a standard IDE cable, which connector is to be used to allow master/slave operation?

a. First connector for master, second connector for slave

b. First connector for slave, second connector for master

c. IDE devices use choice A, and EIDE devices use choice B.

d. EIDE devices use choice A, and IDE devices use choice B.

e. It does not matter which connector an IDE-/EIDE-compliant device uses.

7. In older hard drive designs like ST-506/412, the hard drive controller was integrated mounts on a circuit board inside the drive housing as an integral part of the drive assembly.

a. True

b. False

8. The number of data interface cable(s) used to connect the actual physical drive to its controlling electronics (based on the ESDI protocol) is two.

a. True

b. False

9. In order to address the issue of fixed or static sectors per track used in MFM- or RLL-based technology, newer drives use a more dynamic design where the sector density on the outside tracks is greater than that of the inside tracks. This dynamic design is referred to as:

   a. Hi-level formatting

   b. Low-level formatting

   c. Zone-bit recording

   d. Operating-system recording

   e. None of the above

10. The process that allows a more dynamic design of sector density where the sector density on the outside tracks is greater than that of the inside tracks is accomplished by which formatting method?

    a. Hi-level formatting

    b. Low-level formatting

    c. Zone-bit recording

    d. Operating-system recording

    e. None of the above

11. For IDE-/EIDE-based devices, the system BIOS contains the instructions necessary to accomplish the task of ensuring that the sector density on the outside tracks is greater than that of the inside tracks.

    a. True

    b. False

12. Assuming the following EIDE hard drive geometry/configuration:

    Cylinders: 768

    Heads: 8

    Sectors/Track: 62

    Determine the drive capacity in MB

    a. 380928 MB

    b. 0.36328125 MB

    c. 195035136 MB

    d. 186 MB

    e. None of the above

13. Assuming an IDE hard drive that has a capacity of 12.5 GB, which mode is used by the drive controller to communicate with the system BIOS about the size and geometry of the hard drive?

    a. CHS mode

    b. ECHS mode

    c. LBA mode

    d. FAT16

    e. FAT32

14. The maximum capacity hard drive supported by legacy BIOS was:

    a. 256 MB

    b. 504 MB

    c. 512 MB

    d. 1 GB

    e. None of the above

15. Which of the following files system(s) are supported by all versions of Windows?

    a. FAT16

    b. FAT32

    c. NTFS

    d. Both a and b

    e. All of the above

16. The following list represents the steps necessary to prepare a hard drive for use after physical installation:

    ❑ Partitioning the hard drive

    ❑ High-level format

    a. True

    b. False

17. The partition table contains the Master Boot Record (MBR).

    a. True

    b. False

18. Each logical drive of a partitioned hard drive contains the following:

    a. MBR, FAT, directories, files

    b. FAT, directories, subdirectories, files

    c. MBR, boot record, FAT, directories, files

    d. Boot record, FAT, directories, files

    e. Partition table, boot record, FAT, directories, files

8

19. When a physical hard drive is partitioned into four parts, a series of four
    _____ drives is created.

    a. Physical

    b. Logical

    c. Primary

    d. Formatted

    e. None of the above

20. When a drive is partitioned into three parts, the partition table looks as follows:

    a. One primary partition, one extended

    b. One primary partition, two extended

    c. One primary partition, one secondary

    d. One primary partition, two secondary

    e. One primary partition, two logical

21. In order for the operating system to boot from a particular partition, it must be
    setup as _____.

    a. Primary

    b. Secondary

    c. Extended

    d. Active

    e. On

22. A service technician is about to install Windows 98 on a hard drive, with the
    intention of also installing Windows NT on the same PC. Which file system
    should the technician choose?

    a. FAT16

    b. FAT32

    c. NTFS

    d. HPFS

    e. Any of the above would be acceptable.

23. Of the file systems offered for use with PCs, which provides a great level of
    security?

    a. FAT16

    b. FAT32

    c. NTFS

    d. All of the above offer equal file security.

    e. None of the above

24. Assuming the Windows 2000 operating system, what is the largest logical drive size, assuming a FAT16 file system?

    a. 1 GB

    b. 2 GB

    c. 4 GB

    d. 16 GB

    e. 32 GB

25. High-level formatting creates the following on each logical drive:

    a. Boot record, FAT, root directory

    b. MBR, boot record, FAT root directory

    c. Partition table, MBR, boot record, FAT root directory

    d. MBR, boot record, FAT root directory, files

    e. Boot record, FAT, root directory, files

8

9

OPTIMIZING AND PROTECTING HARD DRIVES

In this chapter, you will learn:

♦ About supporting hard drives and making backups

♦ About viruses and other computer infestations, and how to protect against them

♦ How to troubleshoot hard drives

In the previous chapter you learned about hard drive technology and installation. In this chapter, you will learn about supporting hard drives. You will learn how to optimize hard drive performance through disk compression and caching for hard drives. This chapter also discusses different types of viruses that can infect your hard drive as well as how to remove and prevent them. You will also learn what to do when a hard drive fails or produces errors and how important it is to keep good backups of the file system and data. No amount of experience replacing defective hard drives can substitute for good backups. The data itself is often the most valuable thing in your computer case.

MANAGING HARD DRIVES

The hard drive is the most important secondary storage device in your computer. In this section, you learn about Windows utilities to protect, optimize, and maintain hard drives. Some of these utilities can be accessed from a command prompt and some from the Windows desktop.

Defrag and Windows Disk Defragmenter

A+CORE
1.5
1.9
3.1

The Defrag command detects and repairs fragmentation. **Fragmentation** occurs when a single file is placed in several cluster locations that are not right next to each other. The clusters that make up a file are together called a **chain**. When a hard drive is new and freshly formatted, the OS writes files to the drive beginning with cluster 2, placing the data in consecutive clusters. Each new file begins with the next available cluster. Later, after a file has been deleted, the OS writes a new file to the drive, beginning with the first available cluster in the FAT. If the OS encounters used clusters as it writes the file, it simply skips these clusters and uses the next available one. In this way, after many files have been deleted and added to the drive, files become fragmented. On a well-used hard drive, it is possible to have a file stored in clusters at 40 or more locations. Fragmentation is undesirable because (1) when the OS has to access many different locations on the drive to read a file, access time slows down, and (2) if the file becomes corrupted, recovering a fragmented file is more complicated than recovering a file in one continuous chain.

For these reasons, one routine maintenance task is to **defragment** the hard drive periodically. To do this, you can run the Defrag command from a command prompt or use a graphical Disk Defragmenter utility available from the Windows desktop. With Windows NT, you must use third-party software, as Windows NT does not include a defragmenter command. Regardless of the method used, you should defragment your hard drive every six months or so as part of a good maintenance plan.

To use Windows 9x or Windows 2000 Disk Defragmenter, first close all open applications. Then choose Start, Programs, Accessories, and then System Tools. (For Windows XP, choose Start, All Programs, Accessories, and System Tools.) For Windows XP, the menu in Figure 9-1 appears. Click Disk Defragmenter. From the Disk Defragmenter window you can select a drive and defragment it.

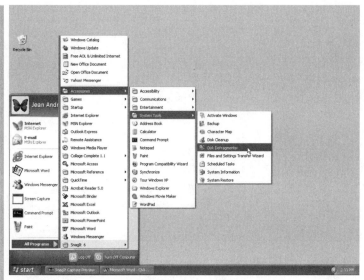

A+CORE
1.5
1.9
3.1

Figure 9-1 Windows XP System Tools contains Disk Defragmenter

TIP Defragmenting a large hard drive may take a long time, so plan for this before you begin. For Windows 9x, if you want to watch the progress as it moves through the FAT, click Show Details on the Disk Defragmenter dialog box.

Use ScanDisk to Correct Cross-Linked and Lost Clusters

A+CORE
1.5
1.9
3.1

As you learned in Chapters 7 and 8, a directory on a floppy disk or hard drive is a table holding information about files in that directory or folder. The directory contains the number of the first cluster in the file. The FAT holds the map to all the other clusters in the file. Occasionally, the mapping in the FAT becomes corrupted, resulting either in lost clusters or cross-linked clusters, as shown in Figure 9-2. Here, File 3 has lost direction and points to a cluster chain that belongs to File 4. Clusters 29 through 31 are called **cross-linked clusters** because more than one file points to them, and clusters 15 through 17 and 28 are called **lost clusters** or **lost allocation units** because no file in the FAT points to them.

In Chapter 3, you learned about the Chkdsk and ScanDisk commands. Chkdsk /F can be used to repair cross-linked and lost clusters. The Windows 9x ScanDisk utility is an improvement over Chkdsk and was designed to replace it. ScanDisk can repair cross-linked and lost clusters, check the FAT for other problems with long filenames and the directory tree, scan the disk for bad sectors, and repair problems with the structure of a hard drive that has been compressed using Windows DriveSpace or DoubleSpace. The Chkdsk command is supported by all versions of Windows. ScanDisk can be used from a command prompt or from the Windows desktop using Windows 9x. For Windows 2000/XP, using Windows Explorer, right-click on the drive and select Properties from the shortcut menu. Click the Tools tab and then click Check Now.

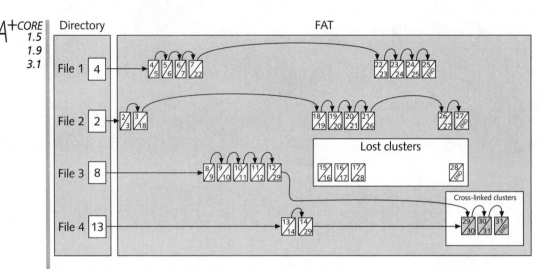

Figure 9-2 Lost and cross-linked clusters

From the Windows 9x desktop, click Start, Programs, Accessories, System Tools, and then ScanDisk. The ScanDisk utility first asks which drive you want to scan and gives you the choice of a Standard or Thorough scan (see Figure 9-3). The Standard scan checks files and folders for errors. The Thorough scan does all that the standard scan does and also checks the disk surface for bad sectors. Click Start to begin the scan.

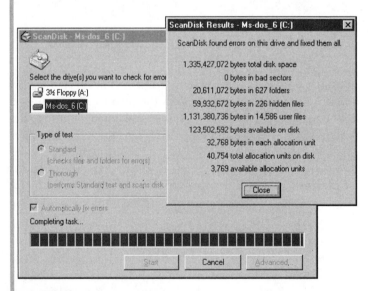

Figure 9-3 ScanDisk results

Use ScanDisk from a Windows 9x startup disk or from the desktop for both troubleshooting and maintenance. Like Defrag, ScanDisk is a good tool to run occasionally to check the health of the drive and possibly avert future problems.

Disk Compression

Disk compression software can help meet the ever-increasing demand for more space on hard drives to hold improved software. Software packages requiring 200 to 250 MB of hard drive space were unheard of three or four years ago but are now common. Hard drive sizes have increased proportionately. Even so, we often seek ways to cram more onto nearly full hard drives.

Software to manage disk compression works by (1) storing data on your hard drive in one big file and managing the writing of data and programs to that file and (2) rewriting data in files in a mathematically coded format that uses less space. Most disk compression programs combine these two methods. This section covers disk compression methods in several versions of Windows.

Disk compression does save hard drive space, but you need to carefully consider the risks involved as well as performance issues such as longer disk access time. If you do choose to use disk compression, keep good backups of both the data and the software. If the data and software on your drive are especially valuable, you may want to invest in a larger hard drive instead of using compression.

9

Disk Compression in Windows 9x

A **compressed drive** under Windows 9x is not a drive at all; it's a file. Figure 9-4 shows the two parts of a compressed drive. The **host drive**, in this case drive H, is not compressed and is usually a very small partition on the drive, generally under 2 MB. The host drive contains a special file called a **CVF (compressed volume file)**. The CVF holds everything on drive C, compressed into just one file.

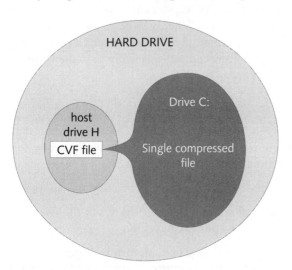

Figure 9-4   A compressed drive

Although several disk compression utilities are on the market, Windows 9x offers its own, called **DriveSpace**. DriveSpace does the following to compress a drive:

- Assigns a different drive letter to the hard drive, such as H

- Compresses the entire contents of the hard drive into a single file on drive H

- Sets up the drive so that Windows 9x and other applications view this compressed file as drive C

- Configures Windows 9x so that each time it boots, the DriveSpace driver loads and manages the compressed drive

 DriveSpace does not work with FAT32 under Windows 98.

To compress a drive in Windows 98 using DriveSpace, first make backups of important data. Then click Start, Programs, Accessories, then System Tools. Select DriveSpace and follow the steps to select and compress the drive.

 If a Windows 9x utility such as DriveSpace is missing from a menu list, the component might not have been installed when Windows was installed. To install a Windows component after Windows is installed, go to Control Panel, select Add/Remove Programs, and click the Windows Setup tab.

Disk Compression in Windows 2000 and Windows XP

Using the NTFS file system in Windows 2000/XP, you can compress a single file or folder or you can compress the entire NTFS volume. When you place a file or folder on a compressed volume, it will be compressed automatically. When you read a compressed file from a compressed volume, it will be decompressed automatically and then will be recompressed when you save it back to the compressed volume.

To compress an NTFS volume:

1. Open Windows Explorer.

2. Locate and right-click the root folder for the volume you want to compress. You will find it in the left pane of Windows Explorer.

3. Select **Properties** from the shortcut menu. The Properties box appears.

4. If necessary, click the **General** tab (see Figure 9-5). Click the check box labeled **Compress drive to save disk space**. Click **OK**.

5. The Confirm Attribute Changes dialog box appears. Indicate whether you want to compress only the root folder or the entire volume, and then click **OK** to begin compression.

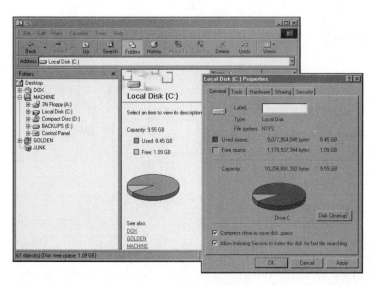

Figure 9-5   Compressing an NTFS volume

Disk Caching

A+ OS
2.5

A **disk cache** is a temporary storage area in RAM for data being read from or written to a hard drive, and is used to speed up access time to the drive. The process of disk caching works like this:

1. The CPU asks for data from a hard drive.

2. The hard drive controller sends instructions to the drive to read the data and then sends the data to the CPU.

3. The CPU requests more data, quite often data that immediately follows the previously read data on the hard drive.

4. The controller reads the requested data from the drive and sends it to the CPU. Without a cache, each CPU request requires that data be read from the hard drive, as indicated in the top part of Figure 9-6.

With a hard drive cache, the cache software handles the requests for data, as shown in the lower part of Figure 9-6. The cache program reads ahead of the CPU requests by guessing what data the CPU will request next. Since most data that the CPU requests is in consecutive areas on the drive, the cache program guesses correctly most of the time. The program stores the read-ahead data in memory (RAM). When the CPU requests the next set of data, if the cache program guessed right, the program can send that data to the CPU from memory without having to go back to the hard drive. Some cache software caches entire tracks at a time; other software caches groups of sectors.

9

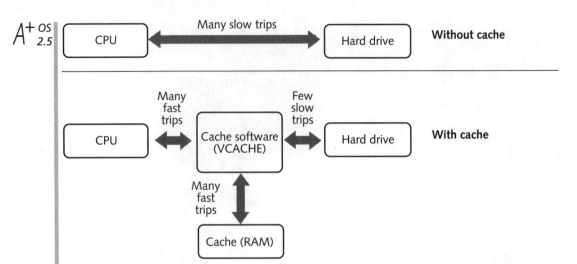

Figure 9-6 A CPU asking a hard drive for data without cache (upper part) and with cache (lower part)

Hardware Cache or Software Cache

There are two kinds of hard drive caches: hardware and software. Some hard drive controllers have a **hardware cache** built right into the controller circuit board. The BIOS on the controller contains the cache program, and RAM chips on the controller hold the cache.

A **software cache** is a cache program stored on the hard drive like other software and is usually loaded into memory when a computer is booted. The software cache program uses system RAM to hold the cache.

There are advantages and disadvantages to both kinds of hard drive cache. A hardware cache does not use RAM on the system board, but a software cache uses RAM for both the cache program itself and the data being cached. Therefore, a disadvantage of a software cache is that it uses RAM that might otherwise be used for applications software and its data.

On the other hand, a software cache is faster because of where the data is stored. Since data is stored in RAM, when the CPU is ready for the data, the data only needs to travel from RAM to the CPU on the system bus, the fastest bus on the motherboard. Since the hardware cache is on the controller board, when the CPU is ready for data stored in this cache, the data must travel from the controller board over one or more buses to the CPU.

Another disadvantage of a hardware cache is that it is a permanent part of the hard drive controller, and today's hard drives have the controller built into the drive housing. Exchanging hard drives to upgrade to a faster hardware cache is impractical, whereas upgrading to a faster software cache is a viable option.

A^+ os
2.5

> **TIP** When buying a new hard drive, check whether it includes hardware caches as an option. A controller with its own hardware cache is slightly more expensive than one without a cache.

How Disk Caching Methods Have Changed

As operating system technologies have changed, so have software disk caching methods. Here is a summary of how different OSs have accomplished disk caching.

- *DOS.* Before disk caching came along, DOS used buffers to speed disk access. A **buffer** is an area in memory where data waiting to be read or written is temporarily stored. Disk caches do a better job of speeding disk access than buffers, so the only reason to use buffers today is to satisfy the requirements of older software that uses them. Buffers are implemented by putting the Buffers=[*number*] command in Config.sys. This command specifies how many buffers DOS is to make available for use while data is being read.

- *DOS with Windows 3.x.* DOS with Windows 3.x used **SMARTDrive**, a 16-bit real mode software cache utility that came with DOS and Windows 3.x. SMARTDrive caches data both being read from and written to the hard drive, and caches data being read from floppy disks.

- *Windows 9x.* Windows 9x has a built-in 32-bit, protected-mode software cache called **VCACHE**, which is automatically loaded by Windows 9x without entries in Config.sys or Autoexec.bat. VCACHE doesn't take conventional memory or upper memory space the way SMARTDrive does, and it does a much better job of caching.

- *Windows NT/2000/XP.* Versions of Windows after Windows 9x use automated disk caching as an inherited Windows component. When working with caching under these versions of Windows, you can monitor physical disk performance using counters.

9

Making Backups

A **backup** is an extra copy of a data or software file that can be used if the original file becomes damaged or destroyed. Losing data due to system failure, a virus, file corruption, or some other problem really makes you appreciate the importance of having backups. This section covers the hardware and software needed to make backups of data and software from a hard drive. Windows 9x and Windows NT/2000/XP offer backup tools, which are also covered in this section.

> **TIP** With data and software, here's a good rule of thumb: if you can't get along without it, back it up.

You can use sophisticated methods to create backups in which the backup process is selective, only backing up what's changed, what has not been recently backed up, and so forth. Traditionally, these methods all involve backing up to tapes, because a tape is most likely to be large enough to contain an entire backup of a hard drive. In the discussions below of specific backup methods, tape is our medium. These backup methods are designed to reuse tapes and to make the backup process more efficient. On a network, often the backup medium is a device such as another hard drive or a tape drive on a computer somewhere on the network. Full, incremental, and differential backup methods speed up the backup process, and scheduled backups minimize the inconvenience to users. Selective backups only back up data that changes often on the hard drive. By selecting only certain critical folders on the drive to back up, the backup routine goes much faster, and recovery of lost data is much easier.

The Child, Parent, Grandparent Method

Before you perform routine hard drive backups, devise a backup plan or procedure. One common plan, called the **child, parent, grandparent backup method**, makes it easy to reuse tapes. This method is explained in Table 9-1. Put the plan in writing, and keep a log of backups performed.

Table 9-1   The child, parent, grandparent backup method

Name of Backup	How Often Performed	Storage Location	Description
Child backup	Daily	On-site	Keep four daily backup tapes, and rotate them each week. Label the four tapes Monday, Tuesday, Wednesday, and Thursday. A Friday daily (child) backup is not made, because on Friday you make the parent backup.
Parent backup	Weekly	Off-site	Perform the weekly backup on Friday. Keep five weekly backup tapes, one for each Friday of the month, and rotate them each month. Label the tapes Friday 1, Friday 2, Friday 3, Friday 4, and Friday 5.
Grandparent backup	Monthly	Off-site, in a fireproof vault	Perform the monthly backup on the last Friday of the month. Keep 12 tapes, one for each month. Rotate them each year. Label the tapes January, February, and so on.

Full, Incremental, and Differential Backups

Some backup methods are more efficient because they do not always create a complete backup of all data. A **full backup** backs up all data from the hard drive or an area of the hard drive. An **incremental backup** backs up only files that have changed or been created since the last backup, whether that backup is itself an incremental or full backup. **Differential backups** back up files that have changed or been created since the last full backup.

Begin by performing a full backup. The next time you back up, choose the incremental method to back up only files that have changed or been created since the full backup. The second time you perform an incremental backup, you back up only the files that have changed or been created since the last incremental backup.

For example, using the child, parent, grandparent method, you can perform a full backup each Friday. Monday through Thursday, you perform incremental backups. The advantage of this method is that incremental backups are faster and require less storage space than full backups. The disadvantage is that, to recover data, you must begin with the last full backup and work your way forward through each incremental backup until the time that the data was lost. This process can be time consuming. Plan to make a full backup after at least every sixth or seventh incremental backup. The Windows 9x and Windows NT/2000/XP backup utilities support incremental backups.

If you create differential backups with the child, parent, grandparent method, create a full backup on Fridays. On Monday, do a differential backup to back up all files that have changed since Friday. On Tuesday, a differential backup also backs up all files that have changed since Friday (the full backup). Differential backups don't consider whether other differential backups have been performed. Instead, they compare data only to the last full backup, which is how differential backups and incremental backups differ. Another difference is that incremental backups mark files as having been backed up, but differential backups do not. The advantage of differential backups over incremental ones is that if you need to recover data, you only need to recover from the last full backup and the last differential backup. Differential backups are not supported by Windows 95 but are supported by Windows 98 and Windows NT/2000/XP.

Scheduling Backups

Backups can be performed manually by a user sitting at the computer or can be scheduled to run automatically without user interaction. A scheduled backup is performed automatically by software when the computer is commonly not in use, such as during the middle of the night. Windows 98 and Windows NT/2000/XP support scheduling any program (including backup tasks) to execute at designated dates and times without user intervention.

Using Windows 98, do the following to create a program called Batch.bat to run a backup and schedule it to run at 11:59 p.m. every Monday night:

1. Using Notepad or WordPad, type this command line, where the tape drive is E and the /S parameter tells the OS to include subdirectories when copying (hidden files are not copied, but data is not usually hidden):

   ```
   Xcopy C:\Data\*.* E: /S
   ```

2. Save the file as **\Data\Batch.bat**, and exit the text editor.

3. Double-click **My Computer** on the desktop, and then double-click **Scheduled Tasks** to open the Scheduled Tasks window (see Figure 9-7).

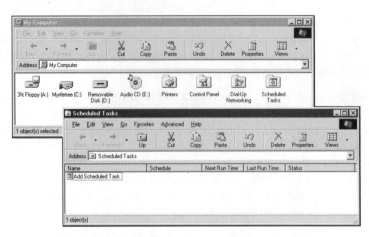

Figure 9-7   Add a scheduled task under Windows 98

4. Double-click **Add Scheduled Task**. The Scheduled Task Wizard appears. Select the program to schedule; click **Browse**, find and click the **Batch.bat** file in the \Data folder, and then click **Open**.

5. Enter a name for the scheduled task, select how often to perform the task, and then click **Next** (see Figure 9-8).

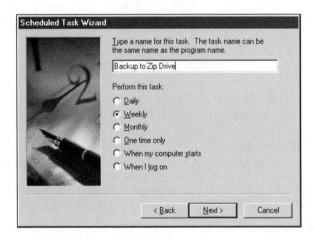

Figure 9-8   Name the scheduled task and select how often it runs

6. Enter the start time and select the day of the week for the task to execute. For example, enter **11:59 PM every Monday**. Click **Next**.

7. The wizard reports the scheduled task parameters. Click **Finish**.

8. To change settings for a scheduled task, double-click **My Computer**, double-click **Scheduled Tasks**, and then right-click the task in the Scheduled Tasks window. Select **Properties** from the shortcut menu. The task Properties dialog box opens (see Figure 9-9).

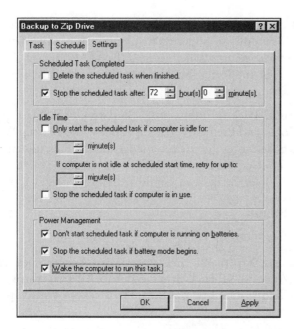

Figure 9-9   With some computers, the task scheduler can power up the computer to run the task

9. Click the **Settings** tab to change the task settings. Notice at the bottom of the Settings sheet that you can direct the scheduler to wake the computer to perform the task. This feature requires a motherboard that supports the option for software to power up the PC. To learn if your motherboard supports the feature, see CMOS setup or the motherboard documentation. If not, then the PC must be turned on for the scheduler to work.

You have just learned how to use a batch file to execute a scheduled backup. Windows offers a more powerful and sophisticated utility called Windows Scripting Host (WSH), which uses Windows commands to execute scripts written in a scripting language such as VBScript or JScript. This utility is also good for making backups. The script is stored in a file that can be placed as an icon on the desktop. To run the script, type *wscript.exe filename* in the Run dialog box, substituting the name of the script file for *filename*, or double-click the desktop icon. You can also make a script file run as a scheduled task.

A^{+} *OS* **Backup Software**
 1.5

Most tape drives come with some backup software. You can also purchase third-party backup software or use Windows 9x, or Windows NT/2000/XP for backing up your hard drive. Because the software only backs up files that are not currently in use, close all files before performing a backup.

$A+$ os
1.5

Windows 9x Backup Utility Windows 9x offers a backup utility that can back up to removable disks and tape drives. Windows 98 supports many popular backup devices that Windows 95 did not, including those using parallel ports, IDE/ATAPI devices, and SCSI devices. To use drives and tapes not supported by Windows 9x, use third-party backup software.

To use the Windows 98 Microsoft Backup utility (msbackup.exe), click Start, point to Programs, Accessories, System Tools, and then click Backup. Follow the Backup Wizard as it steps you through the process of selecting the backup media and the files, folders, or logical drives you want to back up. To select what to back up, the wizard takes you to a backup window similar to the Windows 2000/XP Backup window discussed next.

Windows 2000/XP Backup Utility

To perform a backup for Windows 2000/XP (using NEbackup.exe), follow these steps:

1. For Windows 2000, on the Start menu, click **Programs**, **Accessories**, **System Tools**, **Backup**. For Windows XP, click **Start**, point to **All Programs**, **Accessories**, **System Tools**, and click **Backup**. The Backup Wizard appears. Click **Advanced Mode**.

2. The Backup utility opens. Click the **Backup** tab (see Figure 9-10). If you want to perform a backup immediately, check the drive and subfolders to back up. Note the box labeled **Backup media or file name** in the lower-left corner, which says where to back up to. Click the **Start Backup** button in the lower-right corner to perform the backup.

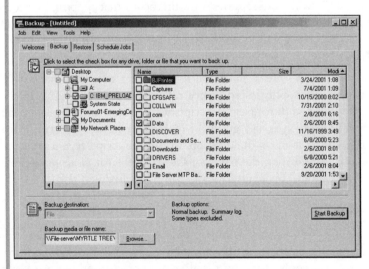

Figure 9-10 You can perform an immediate backup from the Backup tab

3. To perform a scheduled backup, begin by clicking the **Schedule Jobs** tab. Select a date on which you want to schedule a backup, and then click the **Add Job** button.

A+ OS
1.5

4. The Backup Wizard opens. On the first screen, click **Next**. Select **Backup selected files, drives, or network data** and click **Next**.

5. On the next screen, the Backup Wizard allows you to select what you want to back up. Select what you want to back up, and then click **Next**.

6. Follow the steps through the wizard to select the type of backup (Normal, Copy, Incremental, Differential, or Daily) and specify how to verify the data after backup, control access to the backed-up data, and label the backed-up data. When asked if you want to perform the backup now or later, select **Later** and click **Next**.

7. The When to Back Up window appears (see Figure 9-11) for you to specify when to perform the backup and give it a name. Note that you can perform an immediate backup from the wizard instead of using the method you learned in Step 1. After specifying a name and date for the job, click the **Set Schedule** button.

9

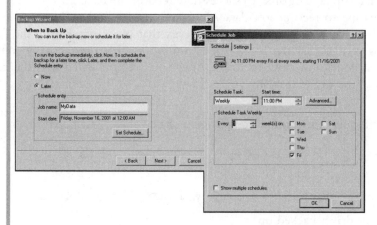

Figure 9-11   Select a name and date for the backup job

8. The Schedule Job window appears, also shown in Figure 9-11. Schedule how often the backup is to occur, and then click **OK**.

9. Click **Next** in the wizard, and follow the remaining instructions to complete the backup. At the end of the process, the wizard gives you an on-screen report summarizing information about the backup.

To recover files, folders, or the entire drive from backup using the Windows 2000 Backup utility, click the Restore tab on the Backup window (see Figure 9-10). Select the backup job to use for the restore process. The Backup utility displays the folders and files that were backed up with this job. You can select the ones that you want to restore.

A+ OS
2.1

Disk Cloning Software

For Windows 9x, you can back up a hard drive so that you can replicate the drive to a different computer or to another drive on the same computer, such as when you deploy a new operating system with application software on multiple computers in a corporate or educational lab. This process, called **disk cloning** or **disk imaging,** is best done with

$A^+_{2.1}$ OS software designed for that purpose. Examples of disk imaging software are Drive Image by PowerQuest (*www.powerquest.com*), ImageCast by Innovative Software (*www.imagecast.com*), and Norton Ghost by Symantec Corp (*www.symantec.com*).

Planning for Disaster Recovery

The time to prepare for disaster is before it occurs. If you have not prepared, the damage from a disaster will most likely be greater than if you had made and followed disaster plans. Suppose the hard drive on your PC stopped working and you lost all its data. What would be the impact? Are you prepared for this event? Backups are important, but you should also know how to use them to recover lost data. Also know when the backup was made and what to do to recover information entered since the last backup. Here's where careful recordkeeping pays off.

When you perform a backup for the first time or set up a scheduled backup, verify that you can use the backup tape or disks to successfully recover the data. This is a very important step in preparing to recover lost data. After you create a backup, erase a file on the hard drive, and use the recovery procedures to verify that you can re-create the file from the backup. This verifies that the backup medium works, that the recovery software is effective, and that you know how to use it. After you are convinced that the recovery works, document how to perform it.

 TIP Verify that your recovery plan works by practicing it before disaster occurs.

Always record your regular backups in a table with the following information:

- Folders or drives backed up
- Date of the backup
- Type of backup
- Label identifying the tape, disk, or other media

Refer to this table to recover data lost days or weeks before you discovered that it should be recovered. Keep the records in a notebook. You can also store the records in a log file (a file where events are logged or recorded) each time you back up.

Disk and Volume Types and Fault Tolerance

Some methods of hard drive partitioning are more fault tolerant than others. **Fault tolerance** is a computer's ability to respond to a fault or catastrophe, such as a hardware failure or power outage, so that data is not lost.

Windows 9x does not support fault tolerance. Windows NT uses a slightly different terminology to describe fault-tolerant volumes than does Windows 2000/XP. Windows 2000/XP implements fault tolerance by using a type of hard drive configuration first introduced by

Windows 2000 called dynamic disks. We first explain what a dynamic disk is and then look at different ways to implement fault tolerance under each OS.

Basic Disks and Dynamic Disks

Windows 2000/XP offers two ways to configure a hard drive: as a basic disk or a dynamic disk. A **basic disk** is the same as the configuration used with DOS, Windows 9x, and Windows NT. By default, Windows 2000/XP uses basic disk configuration. With basic disk configuration, you generally create partitions of a set size and then do not change them. If you want to change the size of a partition, you either have to reinstall Windows (if Windows is installed on that partition) or use special third-party software that allows you to change the size of a partition without losing your data. Within partitions, you create logical drives (sometimes called basic volumes) of set size.

Dynamic disks don't use partitions or logical drives; instead, they use **dynamic volumes**, which are called dynamic because you can change their size. Data to configure the disk is stored in a disk management database that resides in the last 1 MB of storage space at the end of a hard drive. DOS, Windows 9x, and Windows NT cannot read dynamic disks. Dynamic disks are compatible only with Windows 2000 and Windows XP.

 TIP Because a dynamic disk requires 1 MB of storage for the disk management database, if you are partitioning a basic disk and expect that one day you might want to convert it to a dynamic disk, leave 1 MB of space on the drive unpartitioned, to be used later for the disk management database.

A dynamic volume is contained within a dynamic disk and is a logical volume similar to a logical drive in a basic disk. There are three types of dynamic volumes:

- A **simple volume** corresponds to a primary partition on a basic disk and consists of disk space on a single physical disk.

- A **spanned volume** appears as a simple volume but can use space from two or more physical disks. It fills the space allotted on one physical disk before moving on to the next. This increases the amount of disk space available for a volume. However, if one physical disk on which data that is part of a spanned volume fails, all data in the volume is lost.

- A **striped volume** also can use space from two or more physical disks and increases the disk space available for a simple volume. The difference between a spanned volume and a striped volume is that a striped volume writes to the physical disks evenly rather than filling allotted space on one and then moving on to the next. This increases disk performance as compared to access time with a spanned volume.

Figure 9-12 illustrates the difference between basic disk and dynamic disk organization. A basic disk or a dynamic disk can use any file system supported by Windows 2000/XP (FAT16, FAT32, and NTFS). Once Windows 2000/XP is installed, you can use the Windows 2000/XP Disk Management utility to switch from basic to dynamic or dynamic to basic and change the file system on either type disk. Dynamic drives offer little advantage for a system with only a single hard drive, especially considering that only Windows 2000 and Windows XP can read dynamic drives.

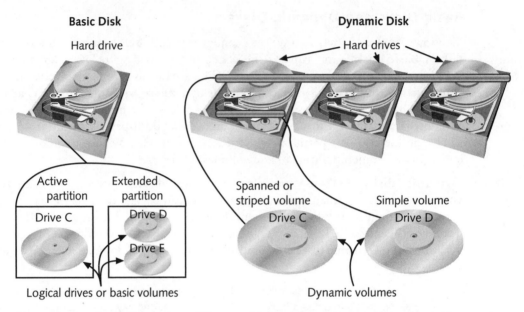

Figure 9-12   Basic disks use partitions and logical drives to organize a hard drive, and dynamic disks use dynamic volumes to organize multiple hard drives

A+CORE 1.6 1.7 Implementing Fault Tolerance

In order to provide fault tolerance, data is duplicated as it is written to a drive. One data duplication method is **RAID (redundant array of inexpensive disks** or **redundant array of independent disks)**, which involves writing data to multiple hard drives to provide better performance and data recovery. The different types of volumes and types of RAID are listed and described in Table 9-2. Your hard drive controller or motherboard and the OS must support RAID. If your PC or server motherboard does not support RAID drives, you can install a RAID-compliant IDE controller card and disable the IDE controller on your motherboard.

A+CORE
1.6
1.7
1.9

Table 9-2   Types of volumes and RAID levels

Volume Type or RAID Level	Intended Purpose	Description
Simple	Uses only a single hard drive	Simple volumes on dynamic disks are equivalent to the basic drive.
Spanned	Increases system performance and volume capacity	Data fills up one drive before moving on to the next. The set of drives is treated as a single volume (a single virtual drive). Reading from more than one disk can improve performance.
RAID 0: Disk striping without parity	Increases system performance and volume capacity	With disk striping, data is alternately written to two or more hard drives, creating a single logical drive on one or more physical drives. Because more than one drive is doing the work, performance improves.
RAID 1: Disk mirroring or disk duplexing	Provides fault tolerance	Data is written twice, once to each of two drives. Disk mirroring uses only a single HDD controller. Disk duplexing uses two controllers, one for each drive.
RAID 5: Disk striping with parity	Increases performance and volume capacity and provides fault tolerance	Data is written to three or more drives, and parity information is distributed across these drives, so that if one drive fails, the other drives can recreate the data stored on the failed drive.

Table 9-3 summarizes which methods are used by the various OSs. The table uses the prevalent terms in the documentation for each OS to describe the methods supported.

Table 9-3   Types of volumes and RAID used in different versions of Windows

Windows Version	Volume Types Supported
Windows 9x	---
Windows NT	RAID-0 (striped), RAID-1 (mirrored), RAID-5
Windows 2000	Simple, spanned, striped (RAID-0), mirrored (RAID-1), RAID-5
Windows XP	Simple, spanned, striped (RAID-0), mirrored (RAID-1), RAID-5

Windows 2000 Professional and Windows XP support RAID 0 and call it a striped volume. In addition to spanned volumes and striped volumes, Windows 2000 Server and Windows XP support RAID 1, which they call a mirrored volume, and RAID 5, which they call a RAID-5 volume.

To create any type of RAID volume under Windows 2000 or Windows XP, you must use dynamic drives. However, if you are upgrading from Windows NT and already have a RAID system set up, Windows 2000 and Windows XP support the setup using basic drives. The primary advantage of using dynamic drives over basic drives is that the 1-MB database not only contains information about the volumes on its hard drive, but also contains information about all volumes on all hard drives in the system. This database is automatically replicated on all drives. If one database fails, it is quickly and automatically restored using a copy of the database on another drive.

A+CORE
1.6
1.7
1.9

TIP   For file servers using RAID 5 that must work continuously and hold important data, it might be practical to use hardware that allows for hard drive hot-swapping, which means you can remove one hard drive and insert another without powering down the computer. However, hard drives that can be hot-swapped cost significantly more than regular hard drives.

VIRUSES AND OTHER COMPUTER INFESTATIONS

A+ OS
3.3

Statistics show that in 2001, one in 10 corporate desktop computers were infected with a computer infestation, and the rate of infestation is increasing 15 percent each year. A computer support person needs to know how to protect computers against computer infestations (including viruses), how to recognize them, and how to get rid of them. Understanding what infestations are, how they work, and where they hide helps technicians deal with them successfully. A computer **infestation** is any unwanted program transmitted to a computer without the knowledge of the user or owner and is designed to do varying degrees of damage to data and software. Computer infestations do not damage PC hardware. However, when boot sector information is destroyed on a hard drive, the hard drive can appear to be physically damaged. What most people call viruses really fall into four categories of computer infestations: viruses, Trojan horses, worms, and logic bombs. The four types of infestations differ in the way they spread, the damage they do, and the way they hide.

Because viruses are by far the most common kind of computer infestation, one of the most important defenses against them is **antivirus (AV) software** designed to discover and remove a virus. This section looks at several AV programs and how to use them effectively.

Understanding Computer Infestations

A+ OS
3.3

A **virus** is a program that replicates by attaching itself to other programs. The infected program must be executed for a virus to run. The virus might then simply replicate or also do damage by immediately performing some harmful action. A virus might be programmed to perform a negative action in the future, such as on a particular date (for instance, Friday the 13th), or when some logic within the host program is activated.

A virus differs from a **worm**, a program that spreads copies of itself throughout a network without a host program. A worm is seldom seen outside a network, where it creates problems by overloading the network as it replicates. Worms do damage by their presence rather than by performing a specific damaging act, as a virus does. A worm overloads memory or hard drive space by replicating repeatedly.

A **Trojan horse** is a third type of computer infestation that, like a worm, does not need a host program to work; rather it substitutes itself for a legitimate program. Trojan horses cannot replicate themselves. (This last statement has some exceptions. One Trojan horse program was disguised as an automatic backup utility downloadable from the Internet. When used, it created backups and replicated itself to the backups. It was programmed to damage several systems on Friday the 13th. In this case, the Trojan horse program is also

A+ OS
3.3

considered a virus because of its ability to replicate.) Because Trojan horse infestations generally cannot replicate and require human intervention to move from one location to another, they are not as common as viruses.

A **logic bomb** is dormant code added to software and triggered at a predetermined time or by a predetermined event. For example, an employee might put code in a program to destroy important files if his or her name is ever removed from the payroll file. Also, viruses, Trojan horses, logic bombs, and worms can occur in combination such as when a virus gains access to a network by way of a Trojan horse. The virus plants a logic bomb within application software on the network that sets off a worm when the application executes.

Where Viruses Hide

A program is called a virus because (1) it has an incubation period (does not do damage immediately), (2) it is contagious (can replicate itself), and (3) it is destructive. There are several types of viruses and methods that viruses use to avoid detection by antivirus software.

9

Boot Sector Virus   A **boot sector virus** hides in a boot sector program. It can hide on a hard drive either in the program code of the Master Boot Record or in the boot record program that loads the OS on the active partition of the hard drive. On a floppy disk, a boot sector virus hides in the boot program of the boot sector. One of the most common ways a virus spreads is from a floppy disk used to boot a PC. When the boot program is loaded into memory, so is the virus, which can then spread to other programs.

Many CMOS setups have an option that can protect against some boot sector viruses. It prevents writing to the boot sector of the hard drive. This feature must be turned off before installing Windows 9x or Windows NT/2000/XP, which must write to the boot sector during installation. Windows 9x does not tell you that you must turn the feature off and start the installation over until about halfway through the installation.

File Viruses   A **file virus** hides in an executable (.exe or .com) program or in a word-processing document that contains a macro. A **macro** is a small program contained in a document and can be automatically executed when the document is first loaded or later by pressing a key combination. For example, a word-processing macro might automatically read the system date and copy it into a document when you open the document. Viruses that hide in macros of document files are called macro viruses. **Macro viruses** are the most common viruses spread by e-mail, hiding in macros of attached document files.

A+ OS
3.3

One well-known example of a macro virus is Melissa, first introduced in 1999 in a Word 97 macro. The virus spread around the world within one working day. The e-mail that initially spread Melissa looked like this:

> From: (name of infected user)
>
> Subject: Important Message From (name of infected user)
>
> To: (50 names from alias list)
>
> Here is that document you asked for ... don't show anyone else ;-)
>
> Attachment: LIST.DOC

When the recipient opened the document, a macro executed and immediately e-mailed the List.doc to 50 e-mail addresses listed in the user's address book. The virus infected other Word documents, which, when e-mailed, also spread the virus.

One type of file virus searches a hard drive for files with .exe file extensions and then creates another file with the same filename with a .com file extension, and stores itself there. When the user launches a program, the OS first looks for the program name with the .com file extension. It then finds and executes the virus. The virus is loaded into memory and loads the program with the .exe extension. The user appears to have launched the desired program. The virus is then free to do damage or spread itself to other programs.

Multipartite Viruses A **multipartite virus** is a combination of a boot sector virus and a file virus. It can hide in either type of program.

Cloaking Techniques

A virus is programmed to attempt to hide from antivirus (AV) software. AV software can only detect viruses identical or similar to those it has been programmed to search for and recognize. AV software detects a known virus by looking for distinguishing characteristics called **virus signatures**, which is why it is important to update your AV software.

 TIP Antivirus software cannot detect a virus it does not know to look for. Therefore, upgrade your AV software regularly to keep your protection current as new viruses are discovered.

A virus attempts to hide from AV software in two ways: by changing its distinguishing characteristics (its signature) and by attempting to mask its presence. Three types of viruses categorized according to their cloaking techniques are polymorphic, encrypting, and stealth viruses.

Polymorphic Viruses A **polymorphic virus** changes its distinguishing characteristics as it replicates. Mutating in this way makes it more difficult for AV software to recognize the presence of the virus.

A^+ OS
3.3

Encrypting Viruses   One key symptom AV software looks for is a program that can replicate itself. An **encrypting virus** can transform itself into a nonreplicating program to
avoid detection. However, it must revert to a replicating program to spread or replicate and
can then be detected by AV software.

Stealth Viruses   A **stealth virus** actively conceals itself, using one or more of the following techniques:

- Because AV software can detect a virus by noting the difference between a program's file size before the virus infects it and after the virus is present, the virus
  alters OS information to mask the size of the file it hides in.

- The virus monitors when files are opened or closed. When it sees that the file it
  is hiding in is about to be opened, it temporarily removes itself or substitutes a
  copy of the file that does not include the virus. The virus keeps a copy of this
  uninfected file on the hard drive just for this purpose.

The Damage an Infestation Can Cause

Viruses, worms, and Trojan horses have not been known to physically damage a hard drive
or other hardware device. The damage they do ranges from minor, such as displaying bugs
crawling around on a screen, to major, such as erasing everything written on a hard drive.
Infestation damage is called the payload and can be accomplished in a variety of ways. A
virus can be programmed to drop its payload only in response to a triggering event such
as a date, opening a certain file, or pressing a certain key. Figure 9-13 shows the results of
a harmless virus that simply displays garbage on the screen.

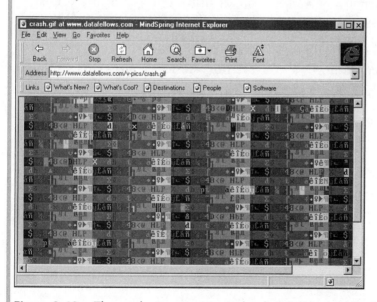

Figure 9-13   The crash virus appears to be destructive, making the screen show only
garbage, but does no damage to hard drive data

$A^+_{\ 3.3}\ ^{OS}$ ## How Infestations Spread

Understanding how infestations spread is essential to understanding how to protect your computer against them. Some computers are more vulnerable than others, depending on user habits. Here is a list of user activities that make a computer susceptible to infestations.

- Trading floppy disks containing program files

- Connecting the computer to an unprotected network

- Buying software from unreliable sources

- Downloading programs from the Internet

- Using floppy disks from unknown sources

- Using shared network programs

- Using used, preformatted floppy disks

- Reading e-mail that automatically executes a word processor to read attached files

- Executing attachments to e-mail messages without first scanning them for viruses

- Not write-protecting original program disks

How a Virus Replicates   Once a program containing a virus is copied to your PC, the virus can spread only when the infected program executes. The process is shown in Figure 9-14. Recall from earlier chapters that the first step in executing a program, whether it is stored in a program file or in a boot sector, is to load the program into memory. Viruses hidden in a program can then be executed from memory. A virus can either be a **memory-resident virus** and stay in memory, still working, even after the host program terminates, or a **non-memory-resident virus** that is terminated when the host program is closed.

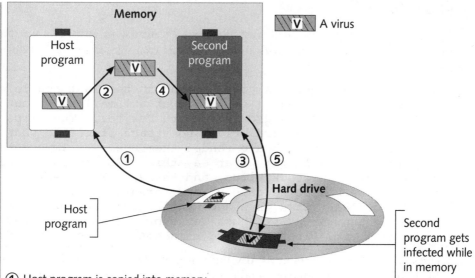

A^+ OS 3.3

(1) Host program is copied into memory.
(2) The virus may or may not move itself to a new location in memory.
(3) A second program is opened and copied into memory.
(4) The virus copies itself to the second program in memory.
(5) The newly infected second program is written back to the hard drive.

Figure 9-14   How a virus replicates

After a virus is loaded into memory, it looks for other programs loaded into memory. When it finds one, it copies itself there and into that same program file on disk. In Figure 9-14, you can see that a virus becomes more dangerous the longer it stays loaded into memory and the more programs that are opened while it is there. For this reason, if you want to use a computer that has been used by other people, such as in a computer lab, always reboot before you begin work to clear memory of programs. Use a hard boot, not just a soft boot, to erase all memory-resident programs (including a memory-resident virus) from memory.

How a Trojan Horse Gets into Your Computer   A Trojan horse is an infestation masquerading as a legitimate program. One interesting example of a Trojan horse is the AOL4FREE program. Originally this illegal program could provide unauthorized access to America Online. After AOL blocked the program's usefulness, a new program emerged, also called AOL4FREE. It was not an online access program but a destructive Trojan horse. People passed the program around, thinking that it would provide illegal access to AOL; however, if executed, it actually erased files on their hard drives.

A+ OS
  3.3

Virus Hoaxes

A virus hoax is a letter or e-mail warning about a nonexistent virus. The warning is itself a pest because it overloads network traffic. Here's an example of a virus hoax e-mail message I received:

> There is a new virus going around in the last couple of
> days!! DO NOT open or even look at any mail that you get
> that says: "Returned or Unable to Deliver." The virus will
> erase your whole hard drive and attach itself to your
> computer components and render them useless. Immediately
> delete any mail items that say this. AOL has indicated this
> is a very dangerous virus, and there is NO remedy for it at
> this time.Please be careful and forward to all your online
> friends ASAP. This is a new email virus and not a lot of
> people know about it; just let everyone know, so they won't
> be a victim. Please forward this email to your friends!!!

Viruses grow more powerful every day, but it is unlikely that this message is accurate. It is unlikely that a virus can render computer components useless. No virus has been known to do actual physical damage to hardware, although viruses can make a PC useless by destroying programs or data, and a few viruses have been able to attack system BIOS code on the motherboard. However, some can hide in macros in word-processing documents attached to e-mail messages, and a few viruses are able to hide in Web pages transmitted as e-mail messages and interpreted by e-mail software when you first open the messages. But what's most important, don't be gullible and take the bait by forwarding the message to someone else. The potential damage a hoax like this can do is to overload an e-mail system with useless traffic, the real intent of the hoax. When I received this e-mail, over a hundred names were on the distribution list.

Before forwarding a virus warning, you can check the Web sites of virus software manufacturers such as the ones listed later in this section. In addition, here are some Web sites that specialize in debunking virus hoaxes:

- *hoaxbusters.ciac.org* by Computer Incident Advisory Capability
- *www.hoaxinfo.com* by Jeff Richards
- *www.hoaxkill.com* by Oxcart Software
- *www.viruslist.com* by Kaspersky Lab
- *www.vmyths.com* by Rhode Island Soft Systems, Inc.

There are many sources for checking for virus hoaxes. Using a search engine, type "virus hoax," a similar phrase, or the name of the virus or virus warning, and you'll find a wealth of information. Always check before sending!

Protecting Against Computer Infestations

A+ OS 3.3 You can do a lot to protect your computer against viruses and other infestations. Your first line of defense is to make backups and use antivirus software regularly. After that, use wisdom when managing programs. Here are some general guidelines:

- Buy antivirus software and set your computer to run the AV program automatically at startup.

- Keep your AV software current by periodically downloading upgrades from the Internet. Many antivirus programs now offer an automatic update feature.

- Set a virus scan program to automatically scan word-processing documents and other e-mail attachments when they are opened. Some Web-based e-mail clients, such as Yahoo! Mail, offer the option to scan attachments before downloading them.

- Establish and faithfully execute a plan to make scheduled backups of your hard drive to protect against potential infestation damage.

- Only buy software from reputable vendors.

- Don't trade program files on floppy disks.

- Don't use floppy disks from unknown sources, and always scan floppy disks for viruses, no matter where they came from.

- Download software from the Internet sparingly, and then always scan program files for viruses before executing them.

- Never use pirated software.

- Format floppy disks before first use.

- Write-protect original program floppy disks, or use CDs to install programs.

- In a business environment, adopt strict company policies against using unauthorized software.

- Before using a running computer that others have used, hard-boot the computer.

- Set your computer CMOS settings to boot from drive C, then drive A.

- Turn on antivirus protection for your MBR in the CMOS settings, if available.

Virus Symptoms

Here are some warnings that suggest a virus is at work:

- A message appears that a downloaded document contains macros, or an application asks whether it should run macros in a document. (It is best to disable macros if you cannot verify that they are from a trusted source and that they are free of viruses or worms.)

9

A^+ *OS*
3.3

- A program takes longer than normal to load.

- The number and length of disk accesses seem excessive for simple tasks.

- Unusual error messages occur regularly.

- Less memory than usual is available.

- Files mysteriously disappear or appear.

- Strange graphics appear on your computer monitor, or the computer makes strange noises.

- There is a noticeable reduction in disk space.

- The system cannot recognize the hard drive when you boot from a floppy disk.

- The system cannot recognize the CD-ROM drive, although it worked earlier.

- Executable files have changed size.

- Executable files that once worked no longer work and give unexpected error messages.

- The access lights on the hard drive and floppy drive turn on when there should be no activity on that device. (However, sometimes an OS performs routine maintenance on the drive when the system has been inactive for a while.)

- Files constantly become corrupted.

- Strange or bizarre error messages appear.

- DOS or Windows error messages about the FAT or partition table appear.

- The hard drive boots but hangs before getting a DOS prompt or Windows desktop.

- File extensions or file attributes change without reason.

- The virus scanner software displays a message.

- The number of bad sectors on the hard drive continues to increase.

- The MEM command reveals unfamiliar TSRs loaded into memory.

What to Do When You Suspect a Virus Infestation

If you suspect a virus, run a virus scan program to detect and delete the virus. If the antivirus software is not already installed, you can still use it. Consult the documentation for instructions on how to proceed. In many cases, the installation process detects the virus and eliminates it before continuing the installation. However, if the AV software does not recognize the virus or if the virus successfully hides, the AV program cannot detect the virus. If the AV software found nothing, but you still suspect a virus, get the latest upgrade of your AV software and try it or another AV program. Also download recent virus definitions; these are usually part of automatic AV software updates. If you know the name of the virus, check the Web site of the antivirus software for information about the virus and how to remove it.

A+ OS
3.3

Table 9-4 lists popular antivirus software and Web sites that provide information about viruses.

Table 9-4   Antivirus software and information

Antivirus Software	Web Site
Norton AntiVirus by Symantec, Inc.	www.symantec.com
Dr. Solomon's Software	www.drsolomon.com
McAfee VirusScan by McAfee Associates, Inc.	www.mcafee.com
ESafe by Aladdin Knowledge Systems, Ltd.	www.esafe.com
F-Prot by Frisk Software International	www.f-prot.com
Command AntiVirus by Command Software	www.commandcom.com
PC-cillin by Trend Micro (for home use)	www.antivirus.com
NeaTSuite by Trend Micro (for networks)	www.antivirus.com

9

When selecting antivirus software, look for the following capabilities:

- Download new software upgrades and virus definitions from the Internet so that your software knows about new viruses

- Automatically execute at startup

- Detect macros in a word-processing document as it is loaded by the word processor

- Automatically monitor files being downloaded from the Internet including e-mail attachments and attachments sent during a chat session such as when using AOL Instant Messenger

- Virus alerts sent to your e-mail address to inform you of a dangerous virus and the need to update your antivirus software

- The ability to scan both automatically and manually for viruses

Using Antivirus Software

Antivirus software can work at different times to scan your hard drive or a floppy disk for viruses. Most AV software can be configured to scan memory and the boot sector of your hard drive for viruses each time your PC boots. Often it's not practical to have AV software scan the entire hard drive each time you boot, because that takes too much time. Consider scheduling the AV software to run at the same time every day, such as during lunch hour.

Some AV software can run continuously in the background and scan all programs that execute. However, the software can cause problems with other software, especially during installations. If you have a problem installing a new application, try terminating your AV software.

Set your AV software to scan files as they are downloaded from the Internet or a network and to scan documents for macro viruses each time a document is opened by a word processor.

TROUBLESHOOTING HARD DRIVES

This section contains information you can use to troubleshoot your hard drive. You will learn about error messages, tools that you can use to troubleshoot and maintain your hard drive, how to solve common hard drive problems, and some general troubleshooting guidelines.

An Ounce of Prevention

Taking good care of your hard drive is not difficult, but it does require a little time. Before we begin a discussion of hard drive troubleshooting and data recovery, here are some precautions you can take to protect your data and software as well as the drive itself.

- *Make backups and keep them current.* It's so important that it's worth saying again: keep backups to use if the original data get damaged or deleted. Never trust a computer; it'll let you down. Keep data files in directories separate from the software, to make backing up data easier. Back up the data as often as every four hours of data entry. Rotate the backup disks or tapes by keeping the last two or three most recent backups.

- *Run antivirus software regularly.* If you lose software or data on your hard drive, there's a good chance the source of the problem is a virus. Your best defense against data and software corruption is to install and run antivirus software. Keep the software current because new viruses are constantly turned loose.

- *Defragment files and scan the hard drive occasionally.* A fragmented hard drive increases access time, and reading and writing files wears out the drive. If you are trying to salvage a damaged file, it is much more difficult to recover a fragmented file than one stored in contiguous clusters. Regularly scan your hard drive for lost or cross-linked clusters.

- *Don't smoke around your hard drive.* To a read/write head, a particle of smoke on a hard drive platter is like a 10-foot boulder on the highway. Hard drives are not airtight. One study showed that smoking near a computer reduced the average life span of a hard drive by 25 percent.

- *Don't leave the PC turned off for weeks or months at a time.* Once my daughter left her PC turned off for an entire summer. At the beginning of the new school term, the PC would not boot. We discovered that the Master Boot Record had become corrupted. PCs are like cars in this respect: long spans of inactivity can cause problems.

- *High humidity can be dangerous for hard drives.* High humidity is not good for hard drives. I once worked in a basement with PCs, and hard drives failed much too often. After we installed dehumidifiers, the hard drives became more reliable.

- *Be gentle with a hard drive.* Don't bump the PC or move it when the drive is spinning.

■ *Take precautions when moving a hard drive or changing CMOS setup.* If you move a hard drive with important data on it from one computer to another, make backups first and verify that both computers use the same translation method (LBA or large mode). Don't change CMOS setup options for the hard drive unless you know what you're doing because changing modes in setup can destroy data, causing the drive to need repartitioning and reformatting.

Resolving Common Hard Drive Problems

Although the hard drive itself is a hardware component, problems with hard drives can be caused by software as well. Problems can also be categorized as those that prevent the hard drive from booting and those that prevent data from being accessed. In this section, you will learn about hardware and software problems with hard drives.

When a user brings a problem to you, begin troubleshooting by interviewing the user, being sure to include these questions:

■ Can you describe the problem and show me how to reproduce it?

■ Was the computer recently moved?

■ Was any new hardware or software recently installed?

■ Was any software recently reconfigured or upgraded?

■ Did someone else use your computer recently?

■ Does the computer have a history of similar problems?

Once you gather this basic information, you can begin diagnosing and addressing the hard drive problems.

If a hard drive is not functioning and data is not accessible, setting priorities helps focus your work. For most users, data is the first priority unless they have a recent backup. Software can also be a priority if it is not backed up. Reloading software from the original installation disks or CD-ROM can be time consuming, especially if the configuration is complex or you have written software macros or scripts but did not back them up.

If you have good backups of both data and software, hardware might be your priority. It could be expensive to replace, but downtime can be costly, too. The point is, when trouble arises, determine your main priority and start by focusing on that.

Be aware of the resources available to help you resolve a problem:

■ Documentation often lists error messages and their meanings.

■ The Internet can also help you diagnose hardware and software problems. Go to the Web site of the manufacturer of the product, and search for the FAQs (frequently asked questions) list or bulletin board. It's likely that others have encountered the same problem and posted the question and answer. If you search and cannot find your answer, then you can post a new question.

■ Technical support from the ROM BIOS, hardware, and software manufacturers can help you interpret an error message, or it can provide general support in diagnosing a problem. Most technical support is available during working hours by telephone. Check your documentation for telephone numbers. An experienced computer troubleshooter once said, "The people who solve computer problems do it by trying something and making phone calls, trying something else and making more phone calls, and so on, until the problem is solved."

 TIP Remember one last thing. After making a reasonable and diligent effort to resolve a problem, getting the problem fixed could become more important than resolving it yourself. There comes a time when you might need to turn the problem over to a more experienced technician.

Troubleshooting Hard Drives with Third-Party Software

To troubleshoot hard drive problems, you might need to use third-party utility software. Three popular utility software programs are Norton Utilities, SpinRite, and PartitionMagic. The following descriptions tell you what to expect from the software when a hard drive fails. Note that these are *not* complete listings of the utility software functions, nor of all available software. See specific software documentation for more detail.

■ *Norton Utilities* (*www.symantec.com*) offers several easy-to-use tools to prevent damage to a hard drive, recover data from a damaged hard drive, and improve system performance. Many functions of these tools have been taken over and improved by utilities included with recent versions of Windows. The most commonly used Norton Utilities tools now are the recovery tools. Two examples are Norton Disk Doctor, which automatically repairs many hard drive and floppy disk problems without your intervention, and UnErase Wizard, which allows you to retrieve accidentally deleted files. When using Norton Utilities, be certain you use the version of the software for the operating system you have installed. Using Norton with the wrong OS can do damage.

■ *PartitionMagic* by PowerQuest Corporation (*www.powerquest.com*) lets you manage partitions on a hard drive more quickly and easily than with Fdisk for Windows 9x or Disk Management for Windows NT/2000/XP. You can create new partitions, change the size of partitions, and move partitions without losing data or moving the data to another hard drive while you work. You can switch between FAT16 and FAT32 without disturbing your data, and you can hide and show partitions to secure your data.

■ *SpinRite* by Gibson Research (*www.grc.com*) is hard drive utility software that has been around for years. Still a DOS application without a sophisticated GUI interface, SpinRite has been updated to adjust to new drive technologies. It supports FAT32, SCSI, Zip drives, and Jaz drives. You can boot your PC from a floppy disk and run SpinRite from a floppy, which means that it doesn't require much system overhead. Because it is written in a language closer to the binary code that the computer understands, it is more likely to detect underlying hard drive problems than software that uses Windows, which can stand as a masking layer between the software and the hard drive. SpinRite analyzes the entire hard drive surface, performing data recovery of corrupted files and file system information. Sometimes, SpinRite can recover data from a failing hard drive when other software fails.

> **TIP** Always check compatibility between utility software and the operating system with which you plan to use it. One place you can check is the service and support section of the software manufacturer's Web site.

Hardware Problems

Hardware problems usually show up at POST, unless there is physical damage to an area of the hard drive that is not accessed during POST. Hardware problems often make the hard drive totally inaccessible.

Sometimes older drives refuse to spin at POST. Drives that have trouble spinning often whine at startup for several months before they finally refuse to spin altogether. If your drive whines loudly when you first turn on the computer, never turn off the computer. One of the worst things you can do for a drive that is having difficulty starting up is to leave the computer turned off for an extended period of time. Some drives, like old cars, refuse to start if they are unused for a long time. Also, data on a hard drive sometimes "fades" off the hard drive over time.

Do not trust valuable data to a drive that has this kind of trouble. Plan to replace the drive soon. In the meantime, make frequent backups and leave the power on.

The read/write heads at the ends of the read/write arms on a hard drive get extremely close to the platters but do not actually touch them. This minute clearance between the heads and platters makes hard drives susceptible to destruction. Should a computer be bumped or moved while the hard drive is operating, a head can easily bump against the platter and scratch the surface. Such an accident causes a "hard drive crash," often making the hard drive unusable.

If the head mechanism is damaged, the drive and its data are probably total losses. If the first tracks that contain the partition table, boot record, FAT, or root directory are damaged, the drive could be inaccessible, although the data might be unharmed.

Here's a trick that might work for a hard drive whose head mechanism is intact but whose first few tracks are damaged. Find a working hard drive that has the same partition table information as the bad drive. Take the computer case off, place the good drive on top of the bad drive housing, and connect a spare power cord and the IDE data cable to the good drive. Leave a power cord connected to the bad drive. Boot from a disk. No error message should show at POST. Access the good drive by entering C: at the A prompt. The C prompt should show on the monitor screen.

9

Without turning off the power, gently remove the data cable from the good drive and place it on the bad drive. Do not disturb the power cords on either drive or touch chips on the drive logic boards. Immediately copy the data you need from the bad drive to floppy disks, using the Copy command. If the area of the drive where the data is stored, the FAT, and the directory are not damaged, this method should work.

Here's another trick for an older hard drive having trouble spinning when first turned on. Remove the drive from the case, hold it firmly in both hands, and give the drive a quick and sudden twist that forces the platters to turn inside the drive housing. Reinstall the drive. It might take several tries to get the drive spinning. Once the drive is working, immediately make a backup and plan to replace the drive soon.

Hard Drive Not Found If your system BIOS cannot find your drive, giving an error message such as "Hard drive not found," the reason is most likely a loose cable or adapter card. Here are some things to do and check:

- Confirm that both the monitor and computer switches are turned on.

- Sometimes startup BIOS displays numeric error codes during POST. Errors in the 1700s or 10400s generally mean fixed disk problems. Check the Web site of the BIOS manufacturer for explanations of these numeric codes.

- Check CMOS setup for errors in the hard drive configuration.

- Turn off the computer and monitor before you do anything inside the case.

- Remove and reattach all drive cables. Check for correct pin 1 orientation.

- If you're using a controller card, remove and reseat it or place it in a different slot.

- Check the jumper or DIP switch settings on the drive.

- Inspect the drive for damage such as bent pins on the connection for the cable.

- Determine if the hard drive is spinning by listening to the hard drive or lightly touching the metal drive (with power on).

- Check the cable for frayed edges or other damage.

- Check the installation manual for things you might have overlooked. Look for a section about system setup, and carefully follow all directions that apply.

- Be sure the power cable and disk data cable connections are good.

- If the drive still does not boot, exchange the three field-replaceable units—the data cable, the adapter card (optional), and the hard drive itself—for a hard drive subsystem. Perform the following procedures in order:
    - Reconnect or swap the drive data cable.
    - Reseat or exchange the drive adapter card, if one is present.
    - Exchange the hard drive for a known good unit.

- If the hard drive refuses to work but its light stays on even after the system has fully booted, the problem might be a faulty controller on the hard drive or motherboard. Try replacing the hard drive and then the motherboard.

A bad power supply or a bad motherboard also might cause a disk boot failure. If the problem is solved by exchanging one of the field-replaceable units listed, you still must reinstall the old unit to verify that the problem was not caused by a bad connection.

Invalid Drive or Drive Specification   If you get the error message "Invalid drive or drive specification," the system BIOS cannot read the partition table information. Boot from a floppy disk, and use the Fdisk command to examine the table. If it is corrupt, which might be the result of a boot sector virus, try the Fdisk /MBR command to restore the master boot program. If this does not work, you can repartition the drive, but you will lose all data on the drive. If the data is important and is not backed up, try third-party data recovery software to recover the drive and its data before repartitioning.

There is a danger in using the Fdisk/MBR command. Some viruses detect when the MBR is altered or when an attempt is made to alter it, and do further damage at that time. Also, some third-party drive encryption software alters the MBR. If Fdisk/MBR overwrites the data encryption program in the MBR, encrypted data on the hard drive might not be readable. If you have important data on the drive that is not backed up, try to recover the data before using Fdisk/MBR.

Restoring the partition table is impossible if the track is physically damaged. The partition table is written on the very first sector of the hard drive, and this sector must be accessible. If it is accessible, you can create a primary partition that covers the damaged area, which you will never use. Create an extended partition for the remainder of the drive. You will not be able to use this hard drive as your boot device, but it can be used as a secondary hard drive. Another thing you can do is to use third-party partition software that allows you to decide where on a hard drive you want to put a partition.

Don't perform a low-level format on an IDE drive unless the drive is otherwise unusable. Use the low-level format program recommended by the manufacturer, and follow its instructions. Call the drive manufacturer's technical support to find out how to get this program, or check the manufacturer's Web site for details.

Damaged Boot Record   If the boot record on a hard drive is damaged, you might get an error message such as "Invalid media type," "Non-DOS disk," or "Unable to read from Drive C." Try third-party data recovery software such as GetDataBack by Runtime Software (*www.runtime.org*) to repair the boot record. If that doesn't work, reformat the volume.

Damaged FAT or Root Directory or Bad Sectors   Error messages that indicate a damaged FAT or root directory or bad sectors somewhere on the hard drive are "Sector not found reading drive C, Abort, Retry, Ignore, Fail?", "Bad Sector," and "Sector Not Found." Try using ScanDisk to repair the damage. If that doesn't work, try third-party recovery software, which might be able to recover the FAT or root directory. If these don't work, reformat the drive. If there is important data on the drive that is not backed up, before you format, try using the Copy command from a command prompt to copy these files to another medium.

Cannot Boot from the Hard Drive Error messages that indicate the hard drive is not bootable are "Non-system disk or disk error...," "Invalid system disk...," and "Command file not found." First verify that the drive can be accessed from a floppy disk. Boot from a rescue disk, and enter C: at the command prompt. If you can access the drive, the problem is missing or corrupted system files on drive C. Do these things:

- For Windows 9x, try the Sys C: command to copy Io.sys, Msdos.sys, and Command.com from the rescue disk to the hard drive.

- Use ScanDisk to scan the drive for errors.

- Run a current version of an antivirus program.

Drive Retrieves and Saves Data Slowly If the drive retrieves and saves data slowly, run Defrag to rewrite fragmented files to contiguous sectors. Slow data retrieval might be caused by fragmented files that have been updated, modified, and spread over different portions of the disk.

Software Problems with Hard Drives

Here are some general software causes of hard drive problems. The root cause of many of these problems is a virus:

- Corrupted OS files

- Corrupted partition table, boot record, or root directory, making all data on the hard drive inaccessible

- Corrupted area of the FAT that points to the data, the data's directory table, or the sector markings where the data is located

- Corrupted data

Resolving Hard Drive and Data Access Problems The software problems listed earlier can prevent data or programs on the hard drive from being accessible. For a hard drive and its data to be accessible by DOS or Windows, these items, listed in the order they are accessed, must be intact for a FAT file system: the partition table, the boot record, the FAT, the root directory, the system files, and data and program files.

- *Partition table.* When the partition table is damaged, BIOS tries to load the OS, first reading the master boot program at the beginning of the partition table information on the hard drive. If the partition table is damaged, this error message appears:

  ```
  Invalid drive or drive specification
  ```

In this case, you should still be able to boot from a floppy disk. When you get to the A prompt and try to access the hard drive by entering C:, you get the same error. To restore the boot program which is at the very beginning of the partition table (MBR, or Master Boot Record) information, for Windows 9x or Windows NT, use this command:

```
A> Fdisk /Mbr
```

For Windows 2000/XP, use this command from the Recovery Console:

```
Fixmbr
```

Often, these commands solve the problem of a damaged partition table.

■ *Boot record.* If the OS boot record on a hard drive is damaged, you cannot boot from the hard drive. After you boot from a floppy disk and try to access the hard drive, you might get one of these error messages:

```
Invalid media type
```

```
Non-DOS disk
```

```
Unable to read from Drive C
```

If the OS boot record is damaged, the best solution is to recover it from the backup copy you made when you first became responsible for the PC. (You can use Norton Utilities to make the backup.) If you don't have a backup, try to repair the boot record using Norton Disk Doctor or SpinRite.

■ *FAT and root directory.* The partition table and boot record are easily backed up to disk; they do not change unless the drive is repartitioned or reformatted. Always back them up as soon as you can after you buy a new computer or become responsible for a working one. Unlike the partition table and the boot record, the FAT and the root directory change often and are more difficult to back up. The success of Windows or third-party utilities in repairing a damaged FAT or root directory depends on the degree of damage to the tables. If these tables are damaged, you may receive this error message:

```
Sector not found reading drive C, Abort, Retry, Ignore, Fail?
```

Try copying important files on the drive to another medium. If you encounter the error, type I to ignore the bad sector and continue copying. Norton Disk Doctor might be able to repair the FAT or root directory.

■ *System files.* If the two OS hidden files (Io.sys and Msdos.sys) are missing or corrupted, you should see one of these error messages:

```
Non system disk or disk error...
```

```
Invalid system disk...
```

Use the following command to copy the two hidden files and the Command.com file from a rescue disk to the hard drive:

```
A:\> Sys C:
```

9

■ *Data and program files.* Data and program files can become corrupted for many reasons, ranging from power spikes to user error. If the corrupted file is a program file, the simplest solution might be to reinstall the software or recover the file from a previous backup. How to restore a data file that is not backed up is covered in the next section, along with problems that can cause data and program file corruption.

Data and Program File Corruption   To restore a data file that is not backed up, you have three options:

■ Use operating system tools and commands to recover the file.

■ Use third-party software such as Norton Utilities or SpinRite to recover the file.

■ If neither of these approaches works, you can turn to a professional data recovery service. These services can be expensive, but, depending on how valuable the data is, the cost might be justified.

When a data file or program file is damaged, portions of the file may still be intact. The basic approach to recovering data in this situation is to create a new file on another disk or on the hard drive, containing all the sectors from the original file that can be read from the damaged disk or hard drive. Use the Copy command and when you get an error message, try to move on to the next sector. Some of the file might be copied to the new medium. Then edit the newly created file to replace the missing data.

How successfully an OS recovers data depends on how badly damaged the file is. A few examples of how data commonly becomes damaged and what can be done to recover it are discussed below. If a file has been accidentally erased, or the disk or hard drive is otherwise damaged, remember these two things:

■ Don't write anything to the disk or hard drive, because you might overwrite data that you could otherwise recover.

■ If you are recovering data from a floppy disk, use Diskcopy in DOS or, for Windows, use Copy Disk in Explorer to make a copy of the disk before you do anything else. If Copy Disk or Diskcopy doesn't work, try copying the disk with a third-party program such as Norton Utilities.

Here are some problems you may experience with files and the file system:

■ *Corrupted file header.* If an application cannot open or read one of its data files, the file header might be corrupted. Many applications place header information (called the file header) at the beginning of the file. This data follows a different format from the rest of the file. The application uses it to identify the file and its contents. If the file header is lost or corrupted and an application needs that header to read the file, you can sometimes recover the contents by treating the file as an ASCII text file.

- *Lost clusters.* A disk can develop lost clusters (lost allocation units) if a program cannot properly close a file it has opened. For example, if you boot your computer while an application is running (not a good thing to do for this very reason), the application does not have the opportunity to close a file and may lose clusters. Another way clusters can be lost is if you remove a floppy disk from a drive while the drive light is still on (also not a good thing to do). Some older applications, such as early versions of MS Access, might not complete writing a file to a floppy disk until the application is closed or another data file is opened. In this case, you must close the application or open a new file before it is safe to remove the floppy disk.

  Lost clusters are clusters that are not incorporated into a file. The Chkdsk and Scandisk commands turn the clusters into a file with the name File0000.chk or a similar filename with a higher number and store the file in the root directory. To use this utility at a command prompt to access lost clusters, use the command with the /F option, like this:

  ```
  C:\> Chkdsk A:/F
  ```

  Often the file created can be used by the application that it belongs to, although you might have to change the file extension so the application will recognize the file. You can also use Windows 9x ScanDisk to accomplish the same results.

  If the drive is compressed, try booting to a command prompt and using ScanDisk to recover the compressed data. Include the name of the compressed volume file on the host drive, like this:

  ```
  Scandisk drvspace.nnn
  ```

  or

  ```
  Scandisk dblspace.nnn
  ```

  Substitute the file extension for the compressed volume file on the host drive (for example, Drvspace.001 or Dblspace.001).

- *Erased file.* A deleted file can sometimes be recovered. First look for the file in the Recycle Bin. If it's not there, at a command prompt try the Unerase or Undelete command, which recovers some erased files.

Getting Technical Support

Sometimes you may not be able to solve a hard drive problem on your own. The first step toward getting more help is to check the Web site of the hard drive manufacturer. Search for the hard drive, and look for problems with solutions. If you still need more help, you might need to call technical support. To make calls to technical support more effective, have as much of the following information as you can available before you call:

- Drive model and description
- Manufacturer and model of your computer
- Exact wording of error message, if any
- Description of the problem
- Hardware and software configuration for your system

CHAPTER SUMMARY

- ☐ To improve hard drive performance, use Disk Defragmenter regularly.

- ☐ Disk compression works by storing data on a drive in one big file, either managing how data and programs are written to that file or rewriting data files in a mathematically coded format that uses less space. Most compression software combines these two methods.

- ☐ Volumes can be compressed under Windows 2000/XP as long as they are using NTFS.

- ☐ Disk caching uses temporary storage to speed up access to hard drive data and can be controlled either by hardware or software.

- ☐ DOS uses buffers rather than disk caching. Windows 3.x and 9x use built-in caching programs. Windows NT/2000/XP use automated caching.

- ☐ Three third-party utility software programs used to work with hard drives are Norton Utilities, SpinRite, and PartitionMagic.

- ☐ The child, parent, grandparent backup method involves reusing tapes by making daily, weekly, and monthly backups.

- ☐ A full backup backs up all data from a hard drive. A differential backup backs up files that have changed or been created since the last full backup. An incremental backup backs up only files that have changed or been created since the last backup, whether or not it was a full backup.

- ☐ You can create backups using utilities included with tape drives or with Windows, or you can purchase third-party software.

- ☐ Disk cloning replicates a hard drive to a new computer.

- ☐ For disaster recovery, it is important to create and test a plan that includes keeping records of backups and recovery procedures.

❏ To create a RAID volume using Windows 2000 or Windows XP, you must use a dynamic drive.

❏ Viruses, which replicate by attaching themselves to other programs, are the most common type of computer infestation. Other types include Trojan horses, worms, and logic bombs.

❏ Viruses can hide in the boot sector, files, macros within files, or in both the boot sector and a file.

❏ Types of viruses that attempt to hide from antivirus software are polymorphic viruses, encrypting viruses, and stealth viruses.

❏ Damage from viruses ranges from an altered monitor display to the erasure of files or even an entire hard drive.

❏ Use antivirus software regularly both to clean out known viruses and to scan for undetected and unmanifested ones.

❏ Hard drive problems can be caused by hardware or software problems, and tend to fall into two categories: those that prevent the hard drive from booting and those that prevent data from being accessed.

❏ Common hard drive problems are corruption in OS files, the partition table, the boot record, the root directory, the FAT, sector markings, or data itself.

❏ For DOS or Windows to access a hard drive using the FAT file system, the following items must be intact, listed in the order in which they are accessed: the partition table, the boot record, the FAT, the root directory, the system files, and data and program files.

❏ High humidity, smoking near the PC, and leaving the PC turned off for long periods can damage a hard drive.

❏ ScanDisk and Chkdsk can be used to recover lost allocation units caused when files are not properly closed by the application creating them.

❏ When data is lost on a hard drive, don't write anything to the drive if you intend to try to recover the data.

❏ Low-level formats should be used as a last resort to restore an unreliable IDE hard drive. Use only the low-level format program recommended by the drive manufacturer.

9

KEY TERMS

antivirus (AV) software
backup
basic disk
boot sector virus
buffer
chain
child, parent, grandparent backup method
compressed drive
cross-linked clusters
CVF (compressed volume file)
defragment
differential backup
disk cache
disk cloning
disk compression
disk imaging

DriveSpace
dynamic disk
dynamic volume
encrypting virus
fault tolerance
file virus
fragmentation
full backup
hardware cache
host drive
incremental backup
infestation
logic bomb
lost allocation units
lost clusters
macro
macro virus
memory-resident virus

multipartite virus
non-memory-resident virus
polymorphic virus
RAID (redundant array of inexpensive disks *or* redundant array of independent disks)
simple volume
SMARTDrive
software cache
spanned volume
stealth virus
striped volume
Trojan horse
VCACHE
virus
virus signature
worm

REVIEW QUESTIONS

1. In terms of the way that files are stored on stored media, a collection of related clusters that deal with the same file is referred to as a _____.

   a. Defragmented file

   b. Fragmented file

   c. Lost cluster

   d. Chain

   e. Allocation unit

2. The concept associated with a single file that is placed in several cluster locations that are located one after another is _____.

   a. Defragmented file

   b. Fragmented file

   c. Lost cluster

   d. Chain

   e. Allocation unit

3. The FAT contains the number of the first cluster in a file.

   a. True

   b. False

4. Assuming that three unique files point to the same group of clusters on a disk is an example of:

   a. Normal cluster allocation

   b. Cross-linked clusters

   c. Lost allocation units

   d. Disk fragmentation

   e. Disk defragmentation

5. Assuming that *no* unique files point to a group of clusters on a disk that do hold data is an example of:

   a. Normal cluster allocation

   b. Cross-linked clusters

   c. Lost allocation units

   d. Disk fragmentation

   e. Disk defragmentation

6. Another term associated with the concept of "lost clusters" is:

   a. Normal cluster allocation

   b. Cross-linked clusters

   c. Lost allocation units

   d. Disk fragmentation

   e. Disk defragmentation

7. The improved system utility that comes with Windows 9x that is capable of repairing cross-linked and lost clusters is:

   a. Format

   b. ScanDisk

   c. ChkDsk

   d. Fdisk

   e. Defrag

8. A compressed drive under Windows 9x is *not* a drive, rather, it is a file.

   a. True

   b. False

9. With respect to disk compression under Windows 9x, the host drive contains a special file called a _____.

    a. ZIP file

    b. Compressed volume file

    c. JPG file

    d. CHK file

    e. None of the above; disk compression under Windows 9x is a drive, not a file.

10. The system utility that allows disk compression to occur in Windows 9x is:

    a. Defrag

    b. ScanDisk

    c. PKZIP

    d. DriveSpace

    e. None of the above

11. Of the two types of system cache—hardware cache and software cache—which type makes use of RAM in conjunction with controller BIOS to coordinate a more efficient use of data transfer?

    a. Hardware cache

    b. Software cache

    c. Both a and b

    d. Neither a nor b

12. Which of the following system utilities is the Windows 2000 operating system tool for disk caching?

    a. Buffer

    b. SMARTDrive

    c. VCACHE

    d. DriveSpace

    e. None of the above

A service technician configured backup software on a company server to conduct a full system backup on Sunday evening, where 2,000 files were backed up. Assume that two new files were created on Monday, and three new files were created on Tuesday.

13. If an incremental backup was performed at the close of business on both Monday and Tuesday on separate backup tapes, how many files were backed up on Tuesday's backup tape?

    a. 2

    b. 3

    c. 5

    d. 2,003

    e. 2,005

14. Instead of an incremental backup being performed, if a differential backup was performed at the close of business on both Monday and Tuesday on separate backup tapes, how many files were backed up on Tuesday's backup tape?

    a. 2

    b. 3

    c. 5

    d. 2,003

    e. 2,005

15. Instead of an incremental *or* differential backup being performed, if a full backup was performed at the close of business on both Monday and Tuesday on separate backup tapes, how many files were backed up on Tuesday's backup tape?

    a. 2

    b. 3

    c. 5

    d. 2,003

    e. 2,005

16. When creating a dynamic disk, which of the following configurations allows two or more physical disks to be written evenly to the physical disks in the dynamic disk instead of filling one disk then moving to the next disk in the dynamic disk cluster?

    a. Simple volume

    b. Spanned volume

    c. Striped volume

    d. All of the above

    e. None of the above

17. When considering RAID for the implementation of fault tolerance, which level RAID allows data to be alternatively written to two or more hard drives, thus creating a single "logical" drive on one or more physical drives?

    a. RAID 0

    b. RAID 1

    c. RAID 5

    d. All of the above

    e. None of the above

18. Which levels of RAID are supported within the core of Windows 9x?

    a. RAID 0

    b. RAID 1

    c. RAID 5

    d. All of the above

    e. None of the above

19. In dealing with computer infestations, which form of infestation does *not* need a host program to work, but substitutes itself for a legitimate program?

    a. Worm

    b. Trojan horse

    c. Logic bomb

    d. Polymorphic virus

    e. All of the above

20. Which of the following works hard to avoid detection by changing its distinguishing characteristics as it replicates?

    a. Worm

    b. Trojan horse

    c. Logic bomb

    d. Polymorphic virus

    e. All of the above

10

SUPPORTING I/O DEVICES

In this chapter, you will learn:

♦ How to install peripheral I/O devices

♦ How to use ports and expansion slots for add-on devices

♦ About keyboards and how to troubleshoot them

♦ About different types of pointing devices

♦ How monitors and video cards relate to the system, and how to troubleshoot them

---

This chapter focuses on how to install and support I/O devices. You will first learn about the procedures and guidelines common to most installations, including how to use serial, parallel, USB, and IEEE 1394 ports, as well as expansion slots. Then you will learn about the essential I/O devices for a PC: keyboard, mouse, and video. This chapter builds the foundation for Chapter 11, in which you will learn about multimedia devices.

BASIC PRINCIPLES OF PERIPHERAL INSTALLATIONS

When you add a new peripheral to a computer, the device needs a device driver or BIOS, system resources (which might include an IRQ, DMA channel, I/O addresses, and upper memory addresses), and application software. Consider these fundamental principles:

- The peripheral is a hardware device controlled by software. You must install both the hardware and the software.

- Software might be of different types. For example, a device could require driver software that interfaces directly with the hardware device and an application software package that interfaces with the driver. You must install all levels of software.

- Remember from Chapter 2 that more than one peripheral device might attempt to use the same computer resources. This conflict could disable one or both devices. Possible conflicts arise when more than one device attempts to use the same IRQ, DMA channel, I/O addresses, or (for 16-bit drivers) upper memory addresses.

Installation Overview

A+CORE
1.4
1.5
1.10

You follow three basic steps to install an add-on device:

1. Install the device.

2. Install the device driver.

3. Install the application software.

The device can be either internal (installed inside the computer case) or external (installed outside the case). Devices installed inside the case are drives (hard drives, floppy drives, CD-ROM drives, DVD drives, Zip drives, etc.) or devices inserted in expansion slots on the motherboard (a modem card, video capture card, and so forth). You can install an external device using an existing port (serial, parallel, USB, IEEE 1394 port, and so forth), or a port provided by an interface card installed in an expansion slot. Figure 10-1 shows the back of a PC case with several ports labeled. Only one of these ports, the video port, does not come directly off the motherboard.

An example of an external device that might use an expansion card is a scanner. When you buy a scanner, the package might include an expansion card that provides a port for the scanner. You are buying:

- Scanner

- Expansion card that interfaces with the computer (for example, a SCSI host adapter to provide a SCSI port for the scanner)

- Cable to connect the scanner to its expansion card

- Device driver on disk

- Application software for using the scanner

- Documentation

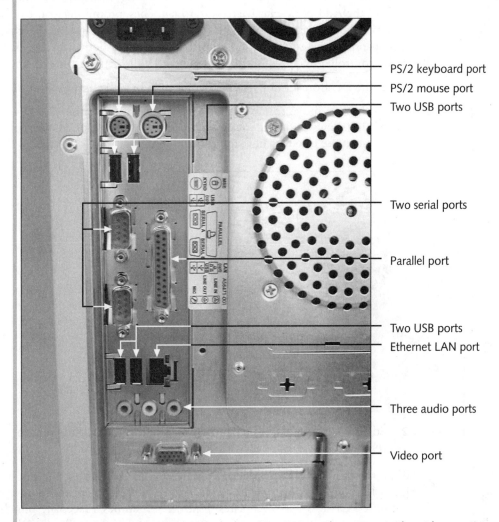

PS/2 keyboard port
PS/2 mouse port
Two USB ports

Two serial ports

Parallel port

Two USB ports
Ethernet LAN port

Three audio ports

Video port

Figure 10-1   Rear of computer case showing ports; only one port (the video port) is not coming directly off the motherboard

Installing the hardware includes installing the expansion card in an expansion slot on the motherboard and then plugging in the scanner itself. After physically installing the device, you need to install the device driver. The driver and scanner expansion card are specific for each brand and model of scanner; however, the application software might work with most scanners. In fact, you might have several applications that use the same hardware device.

The rest of this section discusses hardware devices and application software in detail, and reviews some of what you have learned about device drivers, before turning to standard ports for installing devices on a computer system.

Installing a Hardware Device

A+CORE
1.2
1.4
1.9
1.10

When installing an external device, turn off the PC and plug in the device and reboot. If the device is PnP, the Add New Hardware Wizard launches, prompting you to install the device drivers. You'll see examples of installing external devices later in the chapter. To install a PnP expansion card such as a video card, modem card network card, IEEE 1394 controller, USB controller, wireless NIC, or sound card, follow these general directions:

- Protect the PC from ESD by using an antistatic bracelet and ground mat.

- Unplug the PC, move things out of the way, and remove the case cover. Figure 10-2 shows a computer case with panels on the side. Remove the screws on the rear of the case that hold the panel in place, and slide the panel to the rear.

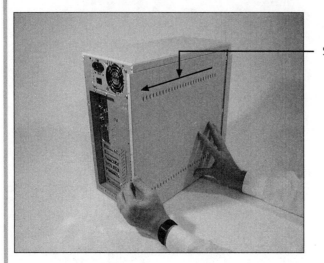

Slide to rear

Figure 10-2   Some cases have panels on each side; slide the panel to the rear to remove it

- Locate the slot you plan to use, and remove the faceplate from the slot. In Figure 10-3, you can see two PCI slots that have their faceplates removed, and two more PCI slots with faceplates in place. Sometimes a faceplate punches out, and sometimes you remove a faceplate screw to remove the faceplate.

- Insert the expansion card in the expansion slot. Be careful to push the card directly into the slot, without rocking it from side to side. Rocking it from side to side can widen the expansion slot, making it more difficult to keep a good contact. If you have a problem getting the card into the slot, you can put the end away from the side of the case in the slot first and gently rock the card from front to rear into the slot. The card should feel snug in the slot. You can almost feel it drop into place. Later, if the card does not work, most likely it is not seated securely in the slot. Check that first and then, if possible, try a different slot.

- Insert the screw that connects the card to the case (see Figure 10-3). Be sure to use this screw; if it's not present, the card can creep out of the slot over time.

10

Figure 10-3   Secure an expansion card in the slot with a screw

- Replace the case cover, power cord, and other peripherals. (If you like, you can leave the case cover off until you've tested the device, in case it doesn't work and you need to reseat it.)

- Plug in whatever device is intended to use the port on the rear of the card. For example, for a video card, plug in the monitor; for a sound card, plug in the speakers; or for a modem card, plug in the phone line.

- Reboot the PC. The Add New Hardware Wizard launches, prompting you to install the device drivers. Install the drivers and finish the wizard.

- Test the device.

It is not likely that you will purchase devices today that are not Plug and Play, but many legacy devices are still around, and you, as a PC support technician, must know how to support them. Special concerns when dealing with legacy devices are covered in various sections throughout the chapter.

$A^{+}\!\frac{CORE}{}$ *1.2*
1.4
1.9
1.10
When installing specialized devices such as CAD/CAM devices, security card readers, or temperature sensors, always read the documentation carefully before you begin. Installation goes much like other more common devices and generally follows the same procedures outlined above.

USING PORTS AND EXPANSION SLOTS FOR ADD-ON DEVICES

$A^{+}\!\frac{CORE}{}$ *1.1*
1.4
1.5
2.1
4.3
6.2
Devices can be plugged directly into a port (serial, parallel, USB, or IEEE 1394), or they can use an expansion card plugged into an expansion slot. This section provides details of both kinds of installations.

All computers come with one or two serial ports, one parallel port, and, on newer computers, one or more USB ports or an IEEE 1394 port. Newer motherboards have several on-board ports, but, on older motherboards, an **I/O controller card** in an expansion slot supplies the serial and parallel ports. Table 10-1 shows the speeds of various ports, from fastest to slowest.

Table 10-1   Data transmission speeds for various port types

Port Type	Maximum Speed
IEEE 1394/FireWire	1.2 Gbps (gigabits per second)
Hi-Speed USB	480 Mbps (megabits per second)
Original USB	12 Mbps
Parallel	1.5 Mbps
Serial	115.2 Kbps (kilobits per second)

Using Serial Ports

$A^{+}\!\frac{CORE}{}$ *1.1*
1.4
1.5
2.1
4.3
6.2
Chapter 1 introduced you to serial ports, which transmit data in single bits, or serially. You can identify these ports on the back of a PC case by (1) counting the pins and (2) determining whether the port is male or female. Figure 10-4 shows serial ports, a parallel port, and a game port, for comparison. On the top is one 25-pin female parallel port and one 9-pin male serial port. On the bottom is one 25-pin male serial port and a 15-pin game port. Serial ports are sometimes called DB-9 and DB-25 connectors. DB stands for data bus and refers to the number of pins on the connector. Serial ports are almost always male ports, and parallel ports are almost always female ports.

To simplify the allocation of system resources, two configurations for serial ports were designated COM1 and COM2, and later two more configurations were designated COM3 and COM4. These COM assignments each represent a designated IRQ and I/O address range, as seen in Table 10-2. Think of the serial ports as physical ports, and think of COM1 and COM2 as logical assignments to these physical ports, much as a phone number is a logical assignment to a physical telephone. In reality, COM1 is just a convenient way of saying IRQ 4 and I/O address 03F8h. Also notice in Table 10-2 that the two parallel port configurations are named LPT1 and LPT2 and each is assigned an IRQ and I/O address range.

A+CORE
1.1
1.4
1.5
2.1
4.3
4.4
5.1
6.2

DOS, all the Windows operating systems, and most applications that use serial devices know about and comply with these assignments. For example, you can tell your communications software to use COM1 to communicate with a modem, and it then knows that the modem is using IRQ 4 to signal the CPU and is "listening" for instructions by way of I/O addresses 03F8h through 03FFh.

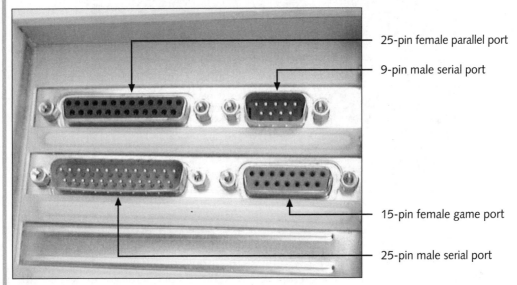

25-pin female parallel port

9-pin male serial port

15-pin female game port

25-pin male serial port

Figure 10-4   Serial, parallel, and game ports

Table 10-2   Default port assignments on many computers

Port	IRQ	I/O Address (in Hex)	Type
COM1	IRQ 4	03F8 – 03FF	Serial
COM2	IRQ 3	02F8 – 02FF	Serial
COM3	IRQ 4	03E8 – 03EF	Serial
COM4	IRQ 3	02E8 – 02EF	Serial
LPT1	IRQ 7	0378 – 037F	Parallel
LPT2	IRQ 5	0278 – 027F	Parallel

Serial ports were originally intended for input and output devices, and parallel ports were intended for printers. Serial ports can be configured for COM1, COM2, COM3, or COM4.

Most serial and parallel ports today connect directly to the motherboard, and the COM and LPT assignments are made in CMOS setup. The ports can also be enabled and disabled in setup. Sometimes the setup screen shows the COM assignments, and sometimes you see the actual IRQ and I/O address assignments (see Figure 10-5). Older I/O controller cards used jumpers and DIP switches to configure the serial and parallel ports on the card.

10

A+CORE
  1.4
  1.5
  2.1
  4.3
  4.4
  5.1
  6.2

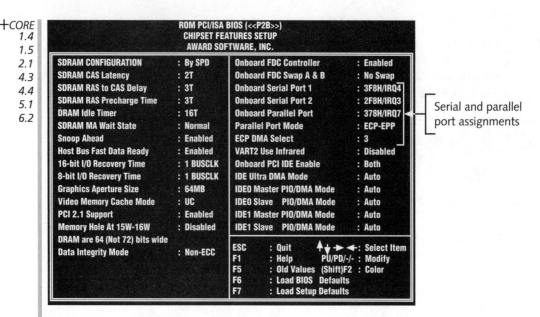

Figure 10-5 CMOS setup screen for chipset features

To verify that the port is configured correctly for any Windows OS, use Device Manager. Click the + sign beside Ports to reveal the list of ports. Click a communications port, such as COM1, and then click Properties. Click the Port Settings tab. You see the Properties dialog box in Figure 10-6, for Windows 9x, but other Windows OSs look the same. Note that the drop-down list shows the bits per second, or baud rate, of the port, which is currently set at 115,200 bps.

A serial port conforms to the standard interface called RS-232c (Reference Standard 232 revision c) and is sometimes called the RS-232 port. This interface standard originally called for 25 pins, but since microcomputers only use nine of those pins, manufacturers often installed a modified 9-pin port. Today some computers have a 9-pin serial port, some have a 25-pin serial port, and some have both. Both ports work the same way. The 25-pin port uses only nine pins; the other pins are unused. Serial 25-pin ports are often found on modems. You can buy adapters that convert 9-pin ports to 25-pin ports, and vice versa, to accommodate a cable you already have.

One of the nine pins on a serial port transmits data in a sequence of bits, and a second pin receives data sequentially. The other seven pins are used to establish the communications protocol. Recall from Chapter 1 that a protocol is a set of agreed-upon communication rules established before data actually passes from one device to another. Table 10-3 describes the functions of the pins of a serial port connection to a modem connected to another remote modem and computer. External modems sometimes use lights on the front panel to indicate the state of these pins. The labels on these modem lights are listed in the last column of the table.

A+CORE
1.4
1.5
2.1
4.3
4.4
5.1
6.2

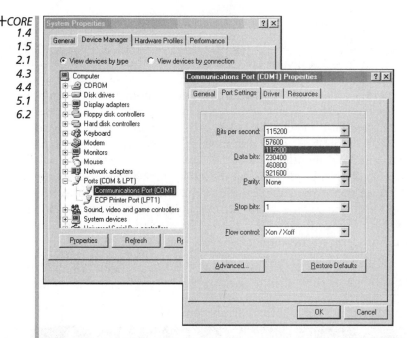

Figure 10-6 Properties of the COM1 serial port in Windows 9x

Table 10–3 is included not so much to explain the use of each pin as to show that more than just data is included in a serial communication session. Also, when the system is using serial ports, one of the devices is called the **DTE (Data Terminal Equipment)** and the other device is called the **DCE (Data Communications Equipment)**. For example, a modem is called the DCE, and the computer on which it is installed is called the DTE.

Table 10-3 9-pin and 25-pin serial port specifications

Pin Number for 9-Pin	Pin Number for 25-Pin	Pin Use	Description	LED Light
1	8	Carrier detect	Connection with remote is made.	CD or DCD
2	3	Receive data	Receiving data	RD or TXD
3	2	Transmit data	Sending data	SD or TXD
4	20	Data terminal ready	Modem hears its computer.	TR or DTR
5	7	Signal ground	Not used with PCs	
6	6	Data set ready	Modem is able to talk.	MR or DSR
7	4	Request to send	Computer wants to talk.	RTS
8	5	Clear to send	Modem is ready to talk.	CTS
9	22	Ring indicator	Someone is calling.	RI

10

$A{+}^{CORE}_{\substack{1.4 \\ 1.5}}$ ## Null Modem Connection

When two DTE devices, such as two computers, are connected, software can transmit data between the devices over a special cable called a **null modem cable**, or a **modem eliminator**, without the need for modems. The cable is not a standard serial cable but has several wires cross-connected in order to simulate modem communication. For example, two computers can be connected by a null modem cable using their serial ports. Based on the 9-pin specifications in Table 10-3, each computer expects to send data on pin 2 and receive data on pin 3. A 9-pin null modem cable would connect pin 2 on one end of the cable to pin 3 on the other end of the cable with a single wire. Similarly, pin 3 would connect to pin 2 on the other end of the cable, so that the received data on one end is the sent data on the other end. Crossing pins 2 and 3 allows data to be sent from one computer and received by the other on the serial port pins that each computer expects to use. Standard modem software can often be used to transmit data, but because there are no actual modems in the connection, very fast, accurate transfer is possible.

Table 10-4 describes the pins connected and crossed for a 25-pin null modem cable. Figure 10-7 shows the same information as a graphic.

Table 10-4 Pin connections for a 25-pin null modem cable

Pin on one end is	Connected to the pin on the other end	So that
2	3	Data sent by one computer is received by the other.
3	2	Data received by one computer is sent by the other.
6	20	One end says to the other end, "I'm able to talk."
20	6	One end hears the other end say, "I'm able to talk."
4	5	One end says to the other, "I'm ready to talk."
5	4	One end hears the other say, "I'm ready to talk."
7	7	Both ends are grounded.

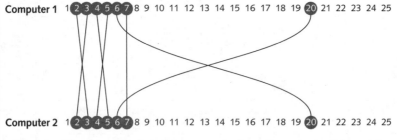

Figure 10-7 Wire connections on a 25-pin null modem cable used to transmit data

Infrared Transceivers

A+CORE
1.4
1.5
1.8
2.1
4.3
5.1
6.2

An infrared transceiver that supports infrared devices, such as wireless keyboards, mice, and printers, often connects to a serial port. In addition, a PC might use an infrared device to connect to a network. If the transceiver is Plug and Play, connect the device and turn on the PC. Windows automatically detects and installs the infrared driver, using the Add New Hardware Wizard. For legacy transceivers, install the transceiver using the Add New Hardware icon in Control Panel, or run the device driver setup program. The transceiver uses the resources of the serial port for communication and also creates a virtual infrared serial port and virtual infrared parallel port for infrared devices. During the installation, you are told what these virtual ports are and given the opportunity to change them. For example, if you physically connect the transceiver to COM2, the virtual ports will be COM4 for infrared serial devices and LPT3 for an infrared printer. The IRQ and I/O addresses for the infrared system are those assigned to COM2. To activate the transceiver, double-click the Infrared icon in Control Panel. If the icon is not visible, press F5 to refresh Control Panel.

In addition, sometimes a motherboard provides a 5-pin connection for its own proprietary IrDA-compliant infrared transceiver. In this case, the transceiver mounts on the outside of the case, and a wire goes through a small hole in the case to connect to the 5-pin connection. The motherboard manual instructs you to use CMOS setup to enable "UART2 Use Infrared." **UART (universal asynchronous receiver-transmitter)** refers to the logic on the motherboard that controls the serial ports on the board.

When you enable COM2 to use infrared, the COM2 serial port is disabled because the infrared transceiver is using the resources for that port. The transceiver drivers are then installed and used the same way as described earlier.

A common problem with infrared devices is the line-of-sight issue: there must be an unobstructed "view" between the infrared device and the receiver. This is the main reason the industry is moving away from infrared and toward other wireless technologies. Radio technology such as Bluetooth or 802.11b is becoming the most popular way to connect a wireless I/O device because with radio waves there is no line-of-sight issue.

10

Using Parallel Ports

A+CORE
1.5
2.1
4.3

Parallel ports, commonly used by printers, transmit data in parallel, eight bits at a time. If the data is transmitted in parallel over a very long cable, the data integrity is sometimes lost because bits may separate from the byte they belong to. Most parallel cables are only six feet (1.8 meters) long, though no established standard sets maximum cable length. However, avoid using a parallel cable longer than 15 feet (4.5 meters) to ensure data integrity. Hewlett-Packard recommends that cables be no longer than 10 feet (3 meters).

Parallel ports were originally intended to be used only for printers. However, some parallel ports are now used for input devices. These bidirectional parallel ports are often used for fast transmission of data over short distances. One common use is to download and upload data from a PC to a laptop. Some external CD-ROM drives use a bidirectional parallel

A+CORE
1.5
2.1
4.3
4.4
5.1

port to transmit and receive data. If you use an existing parallel port to install a peripheral device, installation is very simple. Just plug the device into the port and load the software. To accommodate a second parallel port, configure the port as LPT2. An example of this is described in the next section.

The uses of the pin connections for a 25-pin parallel port are listed in Table 10-5.

Table 10-5   25-pin parallel port pin connections

Pin	Input or Output from PC	Description
1	Output	Strobe
2	Output	Data bit 0
3	Output	Data bit 1
4	Output	Data bit 2
5	Output	Data bit 3
6	Output	Data bit 4
7	Output	Data bit 5
8	Output	Data bit 6
9	Output	Data bit 7
10	Input	Acknowledge
11	Input	Busy
12	Input	Out of paper
13	Input	Select
14	Output	Auto feed
15	Input	Printer error
16	Output	Initialize paper
17	Output	Select input
18	Input	Ground for bit 0
19	Input	Ground for bit 1
20	Input	Ground for bit 2
21	Input	Ground for bit 3
22	Input	Ground for bit 4
23	Input	Ground for bit 5
24	Input	Ground for bit 6
25	Input	Ground for bit 7

Types of Parallel Ports

Parallel ports fall into three categories: standard parallel port (SPP), **Enhanced Parallel Port (EPP)**, and **Extended Capabilities Port (ECP)**. The standard parallel port is sometimes called a normal parallel port or a Centronics port, named after the 36-pin Centronics connection used by printers (see Figure 10-8). A standard port allows data to flow in only one direction and is the slowest of the three types of parallel ports. EPP and

A+CORE
1.5
2.1
4.3

ECP are both bidirectional. ECP was designed to increase speed over EPP by using a DMA channel; therefore, when using ECP mode you are using a DMA channel. Over the years hardware and software manufacturers both have implemented several parallel port designs, all attempting to increase speed and performance. To help establish industry standards, a committee supported by the Institute of Electrical and Electronics Engineers (IEEE) was formed in the early 1990s and created the **IEEE 1284** standards for parallel ports. These standards require backward compatibility with previous parallel port technology. Both EPP and ECP are covered under the IEEE 1284 specifications.

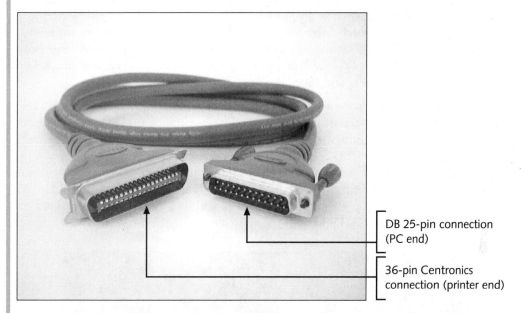

DB 25-pin connection (PC end)

36-pin Centronics connection (printer end)

Figure 10-8   A parallel cable has a DB-25 connection at the PC end of the cable and a 36-pin Centronics connection at the printer end of the cable. Printers can use this 36-pin Centronics connection or the smaller and less common mini-Centronics connector that also has 36 pins.

TIP   When using EPP or ECP printers and parallel ports, be sure to use a printer cable that is IEEE 1284 compliant. Look for the label somewhere on the cable. Older, noncompliant cables will not work properly with these printers.

Configuring Parallel Ports

When configuring a parallel port, if the port is on an I/O card, look to the documentation for the card to learn how to assign system resources to the port. If the parallel port is coming directly off the motherboard, then look to CMOS setup to configure the port (look back at Figure 10-5). Setup can have up to three different settings for parallel ports. For the BIOS in this figure, choices for parallel port mode are Normal, EPP, ECP, and EPP + ECP. If you select ECP or EPP + ECP, you must also make an ECP DMA selection. Choices are DMA Channel 1 or 3.

A^{+} *CORE*
1.4
1.5
4.3

> **TIP** If you have trouble using a serial or parallel port, check CMOS setup to make sure the port is enabled. If you have problems with resource conflicts, try disabling ECP mode for the parallel port. EPP mode gives good results and does not tie up a DMA channel.

Using USB Ports

A^{+} *CORE*
1.4
1.5
2.1
4.3
5.1

A relatively new I/O bus is the USB, originally created by a seven-member consortium including Compaq, Digital Equipment, IBM, Intel, Microsoft, NEC, and Northern Telecom. It is designed to make the installation of slow peripheral devices as effortless as possible. USB is much faster than regular serial ports and uses higher-quality cabling. USB is also much easier to manage, since it eliminates the need to resolve resource conflicts manually. USB is expected to ultimately replace both serial and parallel ports as the technology matures and more devices are built to use USB.

USB allows for **hot-swapping** and is **hot–pluggable**, meaning that a device can be plugged into a USB port while the computer is running, and the host controller will sense the device and configure it without your having to reboot the computer. Some I/O devices that use a USB connection are mice, joysticks, keyboards, printers, scanners, monitors, modems, digital cameras, fax machines, and digital telephones. One to four USB ports are found on most new motherboards (see Figure 10-9), and older motherboards that have no USB ports can be upgraded by adding a PCI-to-USB controller card in a PCI slot to provide a USB port.

Figure 10-9   A motherboard with two USB ports and a USB cable; note the rectangular shape of the connection as compared to the nearby serial and parallel D-shaped ports

A⁺CORE
1.4
1.5
4.3
2.1
5.1

USB Version 1 (sometimes called Basic Speed USB or Original USB) allows for two speeds, 1.5 Mb (megabits) per second and 12 Mb per second, and works well for slow I/O devices. USB Version 2 (sometimes called Hi-Speed USB) allows for up to 480 Mb per second, which is 40 times faster than Original USB. Hi-Speed USB is backward compatible with slower USB devices. The USB Implementers Forum, Inc. (*www.usb.org*), the organization responsible for developing USB, has adopted the symbols shown in Figure 10-10 to indicate if the product is certified by the organization as compliant with Original USB or Hi-Speed USB.

Figure 10-10   Hi-Speed and Original USB logos appear on products certified by the USB Forum

A **USB host controller**, which for most motherboards is included in the chip set, manages the USB bus. Sometimes a motherboard has two USB controllers; each is enabled and disabled in CMOS setup. As many as 127 USB devices can be daisy chained together using USB cables, so one device provides a USB port for the next device. Figure 10-11 shows a keyboard and a mouse daisy chained together and connecting to a single USB port on an iMac computer. There can also be a standalone **hub** into which several devices can be plugged.

10

Figure 10-11   A keyboard and a mouse using a USB port daisy-chained together

A+CORE
1.4
1.5
2.1
4.3
5.1

For full-speed devices, use Hi-Speed USB cables, which can be up to 16.4 feet (5 meters) long, to connect devices or a device and a hub. The USB cable has four wires, two for power and two for communication. The two power wires (one carries voltage and the other is ground) allow the host controller to provide power to a device. The connector on the host computer or hub end is called the A-Male connector, and the connector on the device end of the cable is called the B-Male connector. The A-Male connector is flat and wide, and the B-Male connector is square.

In USB technology, the host controller polls each device, asking if data is ready to be sent or requesting to send data to the device. The host controller manages communication to the CPU for all devices, using only a single IRQ, I/O address range, and DMA channel. The OS and the USB host controller automatically assign system resources at startup.

Windows 95 OSR 2.1 was the first Microsoft OS to support USB, although Windows 98 offers much improved USB support. Windows 95 with the USB update, Windows 98, Windows 2000, and Windows XP support Original USB, but Windows NT does not. Using Windows XP, you can download a patch for the OS that supports Hi-Speed USB.

A+CORE
1.2
2.1
4.3
5.1

Preparing to Install a USB Device

To install a USB device, you need:

- A motherboard or expansion card that provides a USB port
- An OS that supports USB
- A USB device
- A USB device driver

Windows 98 provides many USB device drivers. If you are installing a USB device, don't use a device driver from the manufacturer that claims to work only for Windows 95. Windows 98 and later OSs made several improvements in USB support that you should take advantage of.

Installing a USB Device

Follow these steps to install a USB device:

1. Using Device Manager, verify that the USB host controller driver is installed under Windows. See Figure 10-12 for an example of Device Manager under Windows 98. Note in the figure the symbol for USB. If the controller is not installed, install it from the Control Panel by double-clicking the **Add New Hardware** icon. If you have a problem installing the controller, verify that support for USB is enabled in setup.

2. Turn off the PC and plug in the USB device. When you reboot, Windows should launch the Add New Hardware Wizard to install the device drivers. If the wizard does not launch, go to the Control Panel and use the Add New Hardware icon. If that fails to install the drivers, look for and run the setup program on the CD or floppy disk that came with the device. After the drivers are installed, you should see the device listed in Device Manager. Verify that Windows sees the device with no conflicts and no errors.

A⁺CORE
1.2
2.1
4.3
5.1

3. Install the application software to use the device. For example, most scanners come with some software to scan and edit images. After you install the software, use it to scan an image.

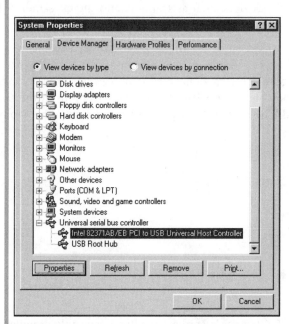

Figure 10-12   Using Device Manager, verify that the USB host controller is installed

10

> **TIP** If USB devices do not work, use CMOS setup to make sure USB support is enabled on the motherboard.

Using IEEE 1394 Ports

A⁺CORE
1.2
1.4
1.5
2.1
4.3
5.1

FireWire and **i.Link** are common names for another peripheral bus officially named **IEEE 1394** (or sometimes simply called 1394) after the group that designed the bus. The Institute of Electrical and Electronics Engineers was primarily led by Apple Computer and Texas Instruments in the initial design. FireWire is similar in design to USB, using serial transmission of data, but faster. FireWire supports data speeds as high as 1.2 Gbps (gigabits per second), much faster than USB. Whereas USB is targeted to replace slow serial and parallel ports, FireWire is likely to replace SCSI as a solution for high-volume, multimedia external devices such as digital camcorders, DVDs, and hard drives. SCSI is a very fast, but difficult to configure, peripheral bus.

FireWire devices can be daisy chained together and managed by a host controller using a single set of system resources (an IRQ, an I/O address range, and a DMA channel). One host controller can support up to 63 FireWire devices. Just as with USB, FireWire must

A+CORE
1.2
1.4
1.5
2.1
4.3
5.1

be supported by the operating system. Windows XP, Windows 2000, and Windows 98 all support FireWire. (Windows 95 and Windows NT do not.) The 1394 Trade Association has developed a new standard, **IEEE 1394.3**, designed for peer-to-peer data transmission. Using this new standard, imaging devices such as scanners and digital cameras can send images and photos directly to printers without involving a computer.

IEEE 1394 ports are sometimes found on newer high-end motherboards and are expected to become standard ports on all new motherboards, as commonplace as USB ports are now. These ports have two types of connectors: a 4-pin port that does not provide voltage to a device and a 6-pin port that does. See Figure 10-13. The two extra pins in the 6-pin port are used for voltage and ground. The cable for a 6-pin port is fatter than the 4-pin cable.

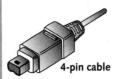

(Device requires AC adapter.)

4-pin cable

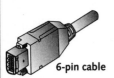

(Two pins are used for voltage and ground.)

6-pin cable

Figure 10-13   Two types of IEEE 1394 cable connectors; the 6-pin cable provides voltage to the device from the PC

The four wires used for data in a 1394 cable are two pairs of shielded twisted-pair cable wrapped in a common cord. Shielding refers to enclosing wires in a protective covering to reduce interference, and twisted-pair refers to the fact that two wires are twisted to reduce interference. Some network cabling is also shielded and uses twisted-pair wires. In fact, IEEE 1394 uses a design similar to Ethernet, the most popular network design. Just as with Ethernet, data is broken into small packets before it is sent over 1394 cable. Each device on the IEEE 1394 network can communicate with any other device on the network without involving the computer's CPU.

IEEE 1394 uses **isochronous data transfer**, meaning that data is transferred continuously without breaks. This works well when transferring real-time data such as that received by television transmission. Because of the real-time data transfer and the fact that data can be transferred from one device to another without involving the CPU, IEEE 1394 is an ideal medium for data transfers between consumer electronics products such as camcorders, VCRs, TVs, and digital cameras.

Figure 10-14 shows an example of how this might work. A person can record a home movie using a digital camcorder and download the data through a digital VCR to a 1394-compliant external hard drive. The 1394-compliant digital VCR can connect to and send data to the hard drive without involving the PC. The PC can later read the data off the hard drive and use it as input to video-editing application software. A user can edit the data and design a

A+CORE
1.2
1.4
1.5
2.1
4.3
5.1

professional video presentation complete with captioning and special effects. Furthermore, if the digital camcorder is also 1394-compliant, it can download the data directly to the PC by way of a 1394 port on the PC. The PC can then save the data to a regular internal hard drive.

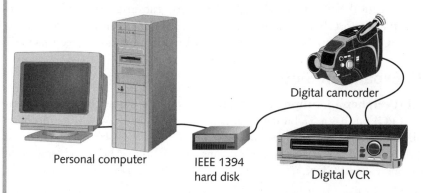

Digital camcorder

Personal computer   IEEE 1394
hard disk   Digital VCR

Figure 10-14   IEEE 1394 can be used as the interface technology to connect consumer audio/visual equipment to a PC

10

The current standard for IEEE 1394 is IEEE 1394.A, which supports speeds of 100, 200, or 400 Mbps, and allows for cable lengths up to 4.5 meters (15 feet). Just as with USB, devices using this standard are hot-pluggable. A new standard under development, IEEE 1394B, will support speeds up to 3.2 Gbps (gigabits per second) and extend the maximum cable length to 100 meters (328 feet).

Windows 98, Windows 2000, and Windows XP support IEEE 1394. Windows 98 Second Edition supports IEEE 1394 storage devices but not IEEE 1394 printers and scanners. Windows 2000/XP supports all these devices. For Windows 98 Second Edition, you can download an update from the Microsoft Web site (*windowsupdate.microsoft.com*). The update solves previous problems that occurred when devices were removed while the PC was still running.

To use a 1394 port with Windows, follow these steps:

1. Verify that Windows recognizes that an IEEE 1394 controller is present on the motherboard. Using Device Manager, look for the 1394 Bus Controller listed as an installed device. Click the + sign beside the controller in Device Manager to see the specific brand of 1394 controller that the board contains. If the controller is not installed or is not working, reinstall the driver. In Control Panel, double-click the **Add New Hardware icon**. If you have problems installing the driver, verify that 1394 support is enabled in setup.

2. Plug the device into the 1394 port. Install the device drivers for the 1394-compliant device. Without rebooting, you should be able to use the Add New Hardware icon in Control Panel. For example, after you have installed the drivers for a camcorder, you should see the device listed in Device Manager under Sound, video, and game controllers. If you don't see the device listed, turn the device off and then on.

A+CORE
1.2
1.4
1.5
2.1
4.3
5.1

3. Install the application software to use the device. A 1394–compliant camcorder is likely to come bundled with video-editing software, for example. Run the software to use the device.

For motherboards that don't support IEEE 1394, you can install an IEEE 1394 host adapter to provide the support. For example, FireBoard Red is an expansion card by Unibrain, Inc. that uses a PCI expansion slot and follows the IEEE 1394A standard. See *www.unibrain.com*.

Using PCI Expansion Slots

A+CORE
4.3

The **PCI (Peripheral Component Interconnect) bus** is now the standard local I/O bus. A standard PCI bus has a 32-bit data path and runs at 33 MHz when the motherboard runs at 66 MHz. However, the PCI specifications can also use a 64-bit data path and can run at a speed of 66 MHz when the system bus runs at 133 MHz. Also, an addendum to the PCI specifications, called PCI-X, released in September 1999, enables PCI to run at 133 MHz.

One advantage of the PCI local bus is that devices connected to it can run at one speed while the CPU runs at a different speed. The PCI bus expansion slots are shorter than ISA slots (see Figure 10-15) and set a little farther away from the edge of the motherboard. Also, PCI slots are usually white. Figure 10-16 shows the pinouts (position and meaning of each pin) for the standard PCI slot.

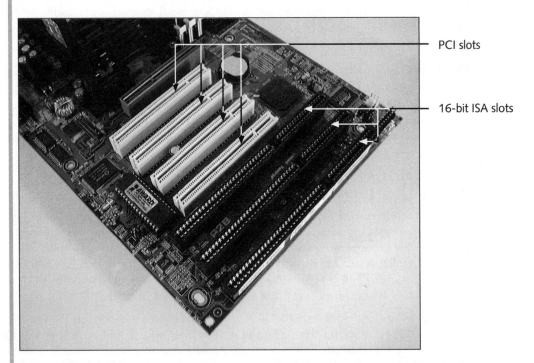

PCI slots

16-bit ISA slots

Figure 10-15 PCI bus expansion slots are shorter than ISA slots and offset farther

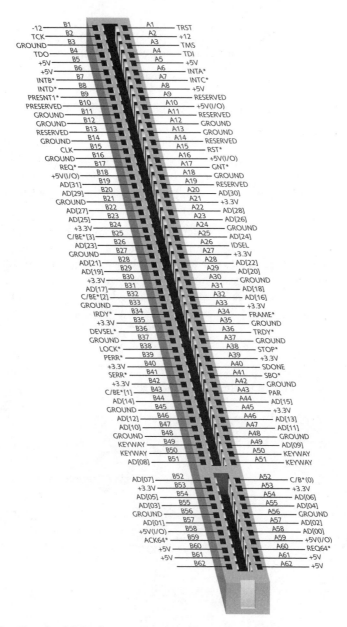

Figure 10-16   Standard PCI slot pinouts

Recall that the PCI bus is a local bus, meaning that it runs in sync with the system clock and the CPU. Because the PCI bus is faster than the ISA bus, PCI slots are often used for fast I/O devices such as network cards or SCSI host adapters. The PCI bus master, which is part of the motherboard chip set, manages the PCI bus and the expansion slots. The PCI bus master assigns IRQ and I/O addresses to PCI expansion cards, which is why you don't see jumpers or DIP switches on these cards. To be more accurate, the PCI bus assigns resources to a PCI slot; move the card to a different slot to assign a new set of resources to it.

> **TIP** When installing a PCI card, most likely you do not need to configure the IRQ or I/O address for the card, because the startup BIOS and PCI bus controller do this for you.

The PCI bus uses an interim interrupt between the PCI card and the IRQ line to the CPU. PCI documentation calls these interrupts A, B, C, and D, and so forth. One interrupt is assigned to each PCI expansion slot. The PCI bus master then maps each of these internal PCI bus interrupts to IRQs, using the IRQs available after legacy ISA bus devices claim their IRQs. The startup BIOS records which IRQs have been used by ISA devices and then assigns the unused ones to the PCI bus master during the boot process.

> **TIP** Newer motherboards sometimes have a communication and networking riser (CNR) slot that can accommodate a small network card, sound card, or modem card, or they can have an audio modem riser (AMR) slot that can accommodate a small modem or sound card. These small riser cards are inexpensive, since most of the logic to support the card is contained within the motherboard chip set. The CNR or AMR slots make it possible to add the card at a low cost, without using a PCI or ISA slot.

Use Device Manager to see which IRQ has been assigned to a PCI device. For example, Figure 10-17 displays the resources assigned to a PCI network card for Windows 2000. Notice that the IRQ assigned to the card is IRQ 9.

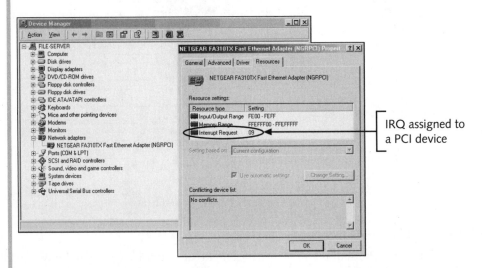

Figure 10-17   Use Device Manager to determine which IRQ has been assigned to a PCI device

Sometimes BIOS gives the PCI bus master an IRQ that a legacy ISA device needs, which can prevent either device from working. In CMOS setup, you can specify which IRQ to assign to a PCI slot, or you can tell setup that a particular IRQ is reserved for a legacy device, and thereby prevent the PCI bus from using it. See Figure 10-18.

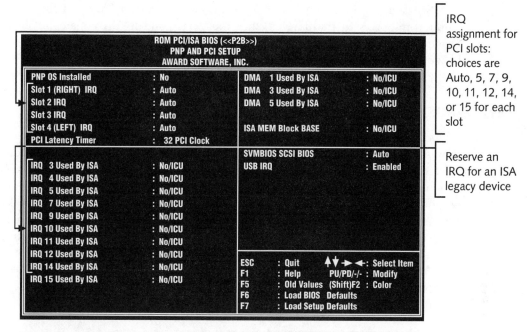

IRQ assignment for PCI slots: choices are Auto, 5, 7, 9, 10, 11, 12, 14, or 15 for each slot

Reserve an IRQ for an ISA legacy device

Figure 10-18   CMOS setup screen for Plug and Play and PCI options

If two heavy-demand PCI devices end up sharing an IRQ, they might not work properly. If you suspect this is the case, try moving one of the devices to a different PCI slot, so that a device with a heavy demand (such as a 1394 adapter) is matched with a low-demand device (such as a modem).

Using ISA Expansion Slots

A+CORE
1.4
1.10
4.3

Used on the first IBM 8088 PCs in the early 1980s, the ISA bus had an 8-bit data path. Later, IBM revised the ISA bus to have a 16-bit path. The IBM AT personal computer used this bus, which is why the 16-bit bus is sometimes called the AT bus. IBM wanted this bus to be backward-compatible with the older 8-bit ISA bus, so that the older 8-bit circuit boards would fit into the newer AT computers. To maintain compatibility, IBM kept the old 62-line slot connector and added another slot connector beside it to provide the extra 8 bits. Slots with both connectors are called 16-bit slots. Many new motherboards have at least one 16-bit slot, which can be used by either an 8-bit or 16-bit ISA card. The trend for newer motherboards is not to have any ISA slots, as few new ISA devices are being manufactured. You saw the pinout descriptions of the 8-bit and 16-bit ISA slots in Chapter 2.

A+*CORE*
1.4
1.10
4.3

Using legacy ISA bus devices is a little more difficult than using either USB or PCI, because the configuration is not as automated. The ISA bus itself does not manage system resources, as do USB and PCI bus masters. It is up to the ISA device to request system resources at startup. If the ISA device does not support Plug and Play, then you select the I/O address, DMA channel, and IRQ by setting jumpers or DIP switches on the card. If the ISA device is Plug and Play compliant, then at startup Plug and Play allocates the required resources to the device. Once the device and its drivers are installed, look at Device Manager to find out what resources it is using. To discover if a device is Plug and Play compliant, look for "Ready for Windows" on the box or read the documentation.

KEYBOARDS

A+*CORE*
1.2

Keyboards have either a traditional straight design or a newer ergonomic design, as shown in Figure 10-19. The word ergonomic means "designed for safe and comfortable interaction between human beings and machines." The ergonomically safer keyboard is designed to keep your wrists high and straight. Some users find it comfortable, and others do not. Figure 10-20 demonstrates the correct position of hands and arms at the keyboard. Keyboards also differ in the feel of the keys as you type. Some people prefer more resistance than others, and some like more sound as the keys make contact. A keyboard might have a raised bar or circle on the F and J keys to help your fingers find the home keys as you type. Another feature is the depth of the ledge at the top of the keyboard that holds pencils, etc. Some keyboards have a mouse port on the back of the keyboard, and specialized keyboards have trackballs or magnetic scanners for scanning credit cards in retail stores.

Figure 10-19   An ergonomic keyboard

Computer keyboards have been criticized by users who work with them for hours at a time because they can cause a type of repetitive stress injury (RSI) known as carpal tunnel syndrome (CTS). CTS is caused by keeping the wrists in an unnatural position and having to execute the same motions (such as pressing keys on a keyboard) over prolonged periods.

A+CORE
1.2
1.5

Figure 10-20   Keep wrists level, straight, and supported while at the keyboard

10

You can help prevent carpal tunnel syndrome by keeping your elbows at the same level as the keyboard and keeping your wrists straight and higher than your fingers. I've found that a keyboard drawer that slides out from under a desk surface is much more comfortable, because the keyboard is low enough for me to keep the correct position. If I'm working at a desk with no keyboard drawer, I sometimes type with the keyboard in my lap to relieve the pressure on my arms and shoulders.

Keyboards use one of two common technologies in the way the keys make contact: foil contact or metal contact. When you press a key on a foil-contact keyboard, two layers of foil make contact and close a circuit. A small spring just under the keycap raises the key again after it is released.

The more expensive and heavier metal-contact keyboards generally provide a different touch to the fingers than foil-contact keyboards. Made by IBM and AT&T, as well as other companies, the metal-contact keyboards add an extra feel of solid construction that is noticeable to most users, giving the keystroke a clear, definitive contact. When a key is pressed, two metal plates make contact, and again a spring raises the key when it is released.

Keyboard Connectors

A+CORE
1.2
1.5

Keyboards connect to a PC by one of four methods: a PS/2 connector (sometimes called a mini-DIN), a DIN connector, a USB port, or the more recently available wireless connection. The DIN connector (DIN is an acronym of the German words meaning "German industry standard") is round and has five pins. The smaller round PS/2 connector has six pins. See Figure 10-21. Table 10-6 shows the pinouts for both connector types. If the keyboard you use has a different connector from the keyboard port of your computer, use a keyboard connector adapter, like the one shown in Figure 10-22, to convert DIN to

A+CORE
1.2
1.5

PS/2 or PS/2 to DIN. Also, some keyboards are cordless, using radio transmission (or, for older cordless devices, infrared) to communicate with a sensor connected to the keyboard port. For example, a cordless keyboard made by Logitech (*www.logitech.com*) uses a receiver that plugs into a normal keyboard port.

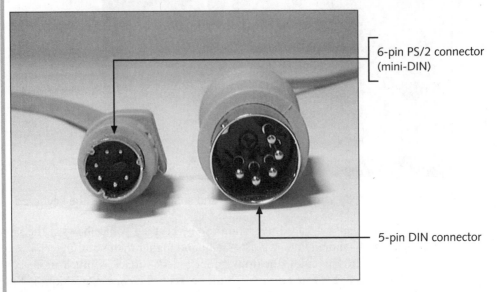

Figure 10-21   Two common keyboard connectors are a PS/2 connector and a DIN connector

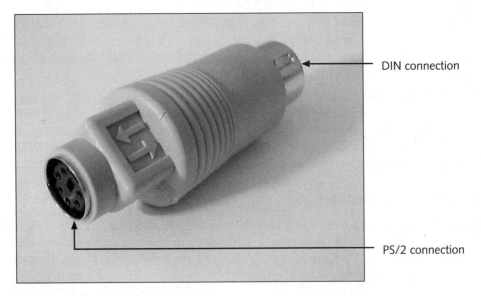

Figure 10-22   A keyboard adapter

Table 10-6   Pinouts for keyboard connectors

Description	6-pin Connector (PS/2)	5-Pin Connector (DIN)
Keyboard data	1	2
Not used	2	3
Ground	3	4
Current (+5 volts)	4	5
Keyboard clock	5	1
Not used	6	-

Installing Keyboards

A+CORE 1.2   Most often, installing a keyboard simply means plugging it in and turning on the PC. Because the system BIOS manages the keyboard, no keyboard drivers are necessary. The exception to this is a wireless keyboard that needs a driver to work. In this case, you must use a regular keyboard to install the software to use the wireless keyboard. Plug in the receiver, insert the CD or floppy drive, and run the setup program on the disk. You can then use the wireless keyboard.

Troubleshooting Keyboards

A+CORE 2.1   Often dirt, food, or drink in the keyboard causes one or more keys to stick or not work properly. Because of its low cost, the solution for a keyboard that doesn't work is most often to replace it. However, you can try a few simple things to repair one.

A Few Keys Don't Work

If a few keys don't work, remove the caps on the bad keys with a chip extractor. Spray contact cleaner into the key well. Repeatedly depress the contact in order to clear it. Don't use rubbing alcohol to clean the key well, because it can leave a residue on the contact. If this method of cleaning solves the problem, then clean the adjacent keys as well.

Turning the keyboard upside down and lightly bumping multiple keys with your flat palm will help loosen and remove debris.

The Keyboard Does not Work at all

If the keyboard does not work at all, first determine that the cable is plugged in. PC keyboard cables may become loose or disconnected. If the cable connection is good and the keyboard still does not work, swap it with another keyboard of the same type that you know is in good condition, to verify that the problem is in the keyboard, not the computer.

If the problem is in the keyboard, check the cable. If possible, swap the cable with a known good one, perhaps from an old discarded keyboard. Sometimes a wire in a PC keyboard cable becomes pinched or broken. Most cables can be easily detached from the keyboard by removing the few screws that hold the keyboard case together, then simply unplugging

A+CORE
2.1

the cable. Be careful as you work; don't allow the keycaps to fall out! In Chapter 4 you learned how to use a multimeter to test a cable for continuity. You can use this method to verify that the cable is good.

On the motherboard, the chip set and the ROM BIOS chip both affect keyboard functions. You might choose to flash BIOS to verify that system BIOS is not the source of the problem. Otherwise, the entire motherboard might have to be replaced, or you can try substituting a USB keyboard for the PS/2 keyboard.

Key Continues to Repeat After Being Released

This problem can be caused by a dirty contact. Some debris may have conductive properties, short the gap between the contacts, and cause the key to repeat. Try cleaning the key switch with contact cleaner.

Very high humidity and excess moisture sometimes short key switch contacts and cause keys to repeat, because water is an electrical conductor. The problem usually resolves itself after the humidity level returns to normal. You can hasten the drying process by using a fan (not a hot hair dryer) to blow air at the keyboard.

Keys Produce the Wrong Characters

This problem is usually caused by a bad chip. PC keyboards actually have a processor mounted on the logic board inside the keyboard. Try swapping the keyboard for one you know is good. If the problem goes away, replace the keyboard.

Major Spills on the Keyboard

When coffee or drinks with sugar in them spill on the keyboard, they create a sticky mess. The best solution to stay up and running is to simply replace the keyboard. You can try to save the keyboard by thoroughly rinsing it in running water, perhaps from a bathroom shower. Make sure the keyboard dries thoroughly before you use it. Let it dry for two days on its own, or less if you set it out in the sun or in front of a fan.

For a list of keyboard manufacturers, see Table 10-7 at the end of the next section, "Pointing Devices."

POINTING DEVICES

A pointing device allows you to move a pointer on the screen and perform tasks such as executing (clicking) a command button. Common pointing devices are the mouse, the trackball, and touch pads (see Figure 10-23).

Figure 10-23   The most common pointing devices: a mouse, a trackball, and a touchpad

Mouse technologies include the wheel mouse and the optical mouse. Inside a wheel mouse is a ball that moves freely as you drag the mouse on a surface. As shown in Figure 10-24, two or more rollers on the sides of the ball housing turn as the ball rolls against them. Each roller turns a wheel. The turning of the wheel is sensed by a small light beam as the wheel "chops" the light beam when it turns. The chops in the light beams are interpreted as mouse movement and sent to the CPU. One of two rollers tracks the x-axis (horizontal) movement of the mouse, and a second roller tracks the y-axis (vertical) movement.

10

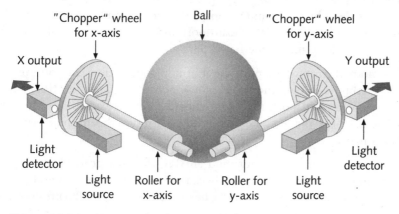

Figure 10-24   How a wheel mouse works

A+CORE
1.2

An optical mouse replaces the ball in a standard mouse with a microchip, miniature red light, and camera. The light illuminates the work surface, the camera takes 1,500 snapshots every second, and the microchip reports the tiniest changes to the PC. An optical mouse works on most surfaces and doesn't require a mouse pad. The bottom of an optical mouse has a tiny hole for the camera rather than a ball, and the light glows as you work.

A mouse can have two or three buttons. Software must be programmed to use these buttons. Almost all applications use the left button. Windows uses the right button to display shortcut menus. The center button has recently been converted into a scroll wheel that you can use to move through large documents on screen. Many applications allow you to customize mouse button functions.

A+CORE
1.2

A mouse can connect to the computer by several methods:

- By using the serial port (the mouse is then called a **serial mouse**)
- By using a dedicated round mouse port coming directly from the motherboard (**motherboard mouse** or **PS/2-compatible mouse**)
- By using a mouse bus card that provides the same round mouse port (**bus mouse**) as discussed above
- By using a USB port
- By using a Y-connection with the keyboard so that both the keyboard and the mouse can share the same port
- By using a cordless technology whereby the mouse sends signals to a sensor on the PC or to an access point connected to the PC

Except for the cordless mouse, all of the above produce the same results (that is, the mouse port type is transparent to the user). Therefore, the advantages and disadvantages of each connection type are based mainly on the resources they require. The motherboard mouse is most users' first choice because the port on the motherboard does not take any resources that other devices might need. If you are buying a new mouse that you plan to plug into the motherboard port, don't buy a bus mouse unless the motherboard documentation states that you can use a bus mouse. The motherboard port and the bus port are identical, but a bus mouse might not work on the motherboard port.

If you have a motherboard mouse port, use it. If it becomes damaged, you can switch to a serial port or USB port. The motherboard mouse port most likely uses IRQ 12. If you are not using a mouse on this port, the motherboard might release IRQ 12 so that other devices can use it. Check the documentation for your motherboard to determine how the unused IRQ is managed.

The serial mouse requires a serial port and an IRQ for that port. Most people prefer a USB or bus mouse to a serial port mouse because they can assign the serial ports to other peripheral devices. A bus mouse can use a bus card if the motherboard does not have a mouse port.

Cleaning the Mouse

A+CORE
1.2
1.3

The rollers inside the wheel mouse housing collect dirt and dust and occasionally need cleaning. Remove the cover of the mouse ball from the bottom of the mouse. The cover usually comes off with a simple press and shift or turn motion. Clean the rollers with a cotton swab dipped in a very small amount of liquid soap.

Other Pointing Devices

Other pointing devices are trackballs, touch pads and touch screens. A trackball is really an upside-down wheel mouse. You move the ball on top to turn rollers that turn a wheel sensed by a light beam. A touch pad allows you to duplicate the mouse function, moving the pointer by applying light pressure with one finger somewhere on a pad that senses the x, y movement. Some touch pads let you double-click by tapping their surfaces. Buttons on the touch pad serve the same function as mouse buttons. Use touch pads or trackballs where surface space is limited, because they remain stationary when you use them. Touch pads are popular on notebook computers.

A+CORE
1.2
1.3
2.1

A touch screen is an input device that can be embedded inside a monitor for a desktop system or a LCD panel in a notebook or the touch screen can be installed on top of the monitor screen or LCD panel as an add-on device. As an add-on device, the touch screen has its own AC adapter to power it. The touch screen is a grid that senses clicks and drags similar to those created by a mouse and sends these events to the computer by way of a serial or USB connection. When installing a touch screen add-on device, follow the manufacturer's directions to attach the touch screen to the monitor or LCD panel, connect the USB or serial cable and the power cable, and then install the touch screen device drivers and management software. Reboot the PC. The touch screen must then be calibrated to account for the monitor's resolution using the management software. If the resolution is later changed, the touch screen must be recalibrated. The screen can be cleaned with a damp cloth using a solution of alcohol and water.

Table 10-7 gives sources for more information about keyboards and pointing devices.

10

Table 10-7   Manufacturers of keyboards and pointing devices

Manufacturer	Web Site
Mitsumi	www.mitsumi.com
Logitech	www.logitech.com
Microsoft	www.microsoft.com
Intel	www.intel.com
Belkin	www.belkin.com
Keytec, Inc	www.magictouch.com

Troubleshooting a Mouse

A+CORE
1.2
2.1

If the mouse does not work or the pointer moves like crazy over the screen, do the following to troubleshoot the mouse:

- Check the mouse port connection. Check for dust or dirt inside the mouse. Reboot the PC.

- Try a new mouse.

- Using Device Manager and the Add New Hardware icon in Control Panel, first uninstall and then reinstall the mouse driver. Reboot the PC.

- Reboot the PC and select the logged option from the startup menu to create the Bootlog.txt file. Continue to boot and check the log for errors.

COMPUTER VIDEO

The primary output device of a computer is the monitor. The two necessary components for video output are the video controller and the monitor itself.

Monitors

A+CORE 1.1 The common types of monitors today are rated by screen size, resolution, refresh rate, and interlace features. Many older VGA (Video Graphics Adapter) monitors are still in use, but most sold today meet the standards for Super VGA. Monitors use either the older CRT (cathode-ray tube) technology used in television sets or the newer LCD (liquid crystal display) technology used in notebook PCs and also available for desktops. LCD monitors for desktops are called **flat panel monitors** or flat panel displays.

How a CRT Monitor Works

Most monitors use CRT technology, in which the filaments at the back of the cathode tube shoot a beam of electrons to the screen at the front of the tube, as illustrated in Figure 10-25. Plates on the top, bottom, and sides of the tube control the direction of the beam. The beam is directed by these plates to start at the top of the screen, move from left to right to make one line, and then move down to the next line, again moving from left to right. As the beam moves vertically down the screen, it builds the image. By turning the beam on and off and selecting the correct color combination, the grid in front of the filaments controls what goes on the screen when the beam hits that portion of the line or a single dot on the screen. When hit, special phosphors on the back of the monitor screen light up and produce colors. The grid controls which one of three electron guns fires, each gun targeting a different color (red, green, or blue) positioned on the back of the screen.

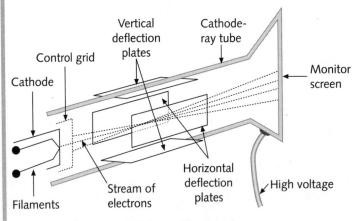

Figure 10-25   How a CRT monitor works

A+CORE 1.1 **Choosing the Right Monitor** How a monitor works and the features available on monitors are summarized in Table 10-8 and discussed next.

Table 10-8 Some features of a monitor

Monitor Characteristic	Description
Screen size	Diagonal length of the screen surface
Refresh rate	The number of times an electronic beam fills a video screen with lines from top to bottom in one second
Interlaced	The electronic beam draws every other line with each pass, which lessens the overall effect of a lower refresh rate.
Dot pitch	The distance between adjacent dots on the screen
Resolution	The number of spots, or pixels, on a screen that can be addressed by software
Multiscan	Monitors that offer a variety of refresh rates so they can support several video cards
Green monitors	Monitors that save electricity and support the EPA Energy Star program

10

Screen Size The screen size of a monitor is the one feature that most affects price. The larger the screen size, the more expensive the monitor. Common screen sizes are 14 inches, 15 inches, 17 inches, and 21 inches. Macintosh computers can use special monitors designed for page layouts on legal-sized paper. The 15-inch monitor is most popular, and the small 14-inch monitor is losing popularity.

When you match a monitor to a video card, a good rule of thumb is to match a low-end video card to a small, 14-inch monitor, a midrange video card to a 15-inch monitor, and a high-end video card to a 17-inch or larger monitor, to get the best performance from both devices. However, you can compare the different features of the video card to those of the monitor, such as the resolutions supported, the refresh rate, and the bandwidth. **Bandwidth** as it applies to analog communication is the difference between the highest and lowest frequencies that an analog communications device such as a video cable can carry.

Monitor sizes are measured on the diagonal. The monitor I'm now using is advertised as having a 17-inch screen. The actual dimensions of the lighted screen are 9½ inches by 11½ inches. The diagonal measurement of the lighted area is 15 inches, and the diagonal measurement of the screen surface is 17 inches.

Refresh Rate The **refresh rate**, or vertical scan rate, is the number of times in one second an electronic beam can fill the screen with lines from top to bottom. Refresh rates differ among monitors. The Video Electronics Standards Association (VESA) set a minimum refresh rate standard of 70 Hz, or 70 complete vertical refreshes per second, as one requirement of Super VGA monitors. Slower refresh rates make the image appear to flicker, while faster refresh rates make the image appear solid and stable. The refresh rate is set by using the Display icon in the Control Panel.

$A\genfrac{}{}{0pt}{}{\text{+CORE}}{\text{1.1}}$ **Interlaced or Noninterlaced** **Interlaced** monitors draw a screen by making two passes. On the first pass, the electronic beam strikes only the even lines, and on the second pass, the beam strikes only the odd lines. The result is that a monitor can have a slow refresh rate with a less noticeable overall effect than there would be if the beam hit all lines for each pass. Interlaced monitors generally have slightly less flicker than **noninterlaced** monitors, which always draw the entire screen on each pass. Buy an interlaced monitor if you plan to spend long hours staring at the monitor. Your eyes will benefit.

Dot Pitch **Dot pitch** is the distance between the spots, or dots, on the screen that the electronic beam hits. Remember that three beams build the screen, one for each of three colors (red, green, and blue). Each composite location on the screen is really made up of three dots and is called a triad. The distance between a color dot in one triad and the same color dot in the next triad is the dot pitch. The smaller the pitch, the sharper the image. Dot pitches of .28 mm or .25 mm give the best results and cost more. Although less expensive monitors can have a dot pitch of .35 mm or .38 mm, that can still create a fuzzy image, even with the best video cards.

Resolution **Resolution** is a measure of how many spots on the screen are addressable by software. Each addressable location is called a **pixel** (for picture element), which is composed of several triads. Because resolution depends on software, the video controller card must support the resolution, and the software you are using must make use of the monitor's resolution capabilities. The standard for most software packages is 800 × 600 pixels, although many monitors offer a resolution of 1,024 × 768 pixels or higher. The resolution is set in Windows from the Display icon in Control Panel and requires a driver specific for that resolution. Higher resolution usually requires more video RAM.

Multiscan Monitors **Multiscan monitors** offer a variety of vertical and horizontal refresh rates so they can support a variety of video cards. They cost more but are much more versatile than other monitors.

Green Monitors A Green monitor saves electricity, making a contribution to conserving natural resources. A Green monitor meets the requirements of the EPA Energy Star program and uses 100 to 150 watts of electricity. When the screen saver is on, the monitor should use no more than 30 watts of electricity.

Monitors and ELF Emissions

There is some debate about the danger of monitors giving off ELF (extremely low frequency) emissions of electromagnetic fields. Standards to control ELF emissions are Sweden's MPR II standard and the TCO '95 standards. The TCO '95 standards also include guidelines for energy consumption, screen flicker, and luminance. Most monitors manufactured today comply with the MPR II standard, but very few comply with the more stringent TCO '95 standards.

A+CORE
1.1
1.3

Flat Panel Monitors

Flat panel monitors are increasing in popularity, although they still cost much more than comparable CRT monitors. Flat panel monitors take up much less desk space than CRT monitors, are lighter, and require less electricity to operate. An LCD panel produces an image using a liquid crystal material made of large, easily polarized molecules. Figure 10-26 shows the layers of the LCD panel that together create the image. At the center of the layers is the liquid crystal material. Next to it is the layer responsible for providing color to the image. These two layers are sandwiched between two grids of electrodes. One grid of electrodes is aligned in columns, and the other electrodes are aligned in rows. The two layers of electrodes make up the electrode matrix. Each intersection of a row electrode and a column electrode forms one pixel on the LCD panel. Software can manipulate each pixel by activating the electrodes that form it. The image is formed by scanning the column and row electrodes, much as the electronic beam scans a CRT monitor screen.

The polarizer layers outside the glass layers in Figure 10-26 are responsible for preventing light from passing through the pixels when the electrodes are not activated. When the electrodes are activated, light on the back side of the LCD panel can pass through one pixel on the screen, picking up color from the color layer as it passes through.

10

Two kinds of LCD panels are on the market today: **active-matrix** and **dual-scan passive matrix** displays. A dual-scan display is less expensive than an active-matrix display and provides a lower quality image. With dual-scan display, two columns of electrodes are activated at the same time. With active-matrix display, a transistor that amplifies the signal is placed at every intersection in the grid, which further enhances the pixel quality.

Flat panel monitors are built to receive either an analog signal or a digital signal from the video card and have two ports to accommodate either signal. If the signal is analog, it must be converted to digital before the monitor can process it. Flat panel monitors are designed to receive an analog signal so that you can use a regular video card that works with a CRT monitor, thus reducing the price of upgrading from a CRT to an LCD monitor. As you will see in the upcoming discussion of video cards, video cards convert digital data from the CPU to analog before sending it to the monitor. Therefore, with analog flat panel monitors, the data is converted from digital to analog and back to digital before being used by the flat panel monitor. These conversions reduce the quality of the resulting image. For the best output, use a digital flat panel monitor along with a digital video card designed to support the monitor.

A+CORE
1.2

Installing Dual Monitors

To increase the size of your Windows desktop, you can install more than one monitor for a single computer. The following dual-monitor installation procedure assumes that you use Windows 9x and that you already have a monitor installed. Setting up dual monitors gives you more space for your Windows desktop as well as some redundancy if one goes down. To install a second monitor and a dual-monitor setup:

1. Verify that the original video card works properly, determine whether it is PCI or AGP, and decide whether it is to be the primary monitor.

A+CORE
1.2
1.3

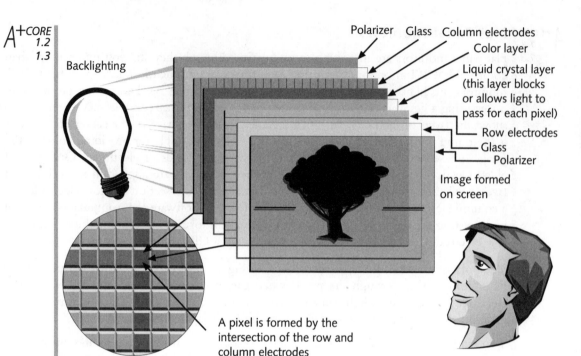

Figure 10-26   Layers of an LCD panel

2. Install a second adapter card in the PCI slot nearest to the AGP slot if the original monitor has an AGP adapter, or in the PCI slot immediately next to the original PCI adapter if the original monitor has a PCI adapter, and attach the second monitor.

3. If CMOS has the setting, adjust CMOS to initialize the primary adapter first, if necessary.

4. Boot the system. Windows recognizes the new hardware and may prompt you for the location of the drivers. At this time, a message appears saying that if you can see the message, the installation was successful, and telling you to adjust the display properties.

5. Open **Display Properties** from Control Panel. The Display Properties window shown in Figure 10-27 appears. Select the **Settings** tab.

6. Notice that the two monitors in the figure are labeled 1 and 2. (If the two monitors are not present, try rebooting your PC.) Click the image of the new monitor (number 2), or select the correct adapter from the drop-down menu under Display. Click **Yes** to enable the monitor.

7. Adjust the settings to your preferences, and check the **Extend my Windows desktop onto this monitor** box. To save the settings, click **Apply**.

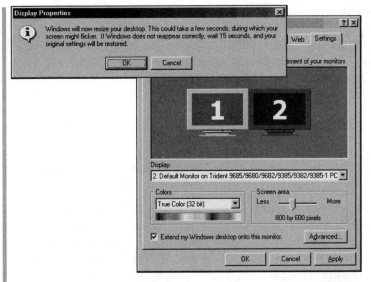

Figure 10-27 You must choose to activate a second monitor before it will be used by Windows

> **TIP** Settings for each video adapter that you add to your system must be saved/applied individually. Up to nine separate adapters can be added to a single system.

8. The dialog box also shown in Figure 10-27 appears. Click **OK** to apply the settings.

Once you add a second monitor to your system, you can move from one monitor to another simply by moving your mouse. Switching from one monitor to the other does not require any special keystroke or menu option.

Video Cards

Recall that the video controller card is the interface between the monitor and the computer. These cards are sometimes called graphic adapters, video boards, graphics cards, or display cards. Sometimes the video controller is integrated into the motherboard. If you are buying a motherboard with an integrated video controller, make sure that you can disable the controller on the motherboard if it needs replacement or gives you trouble. You can then install a video card and bypass the controller on the motherboard.

The quality of a video subsystem is rated according to how it affects overall system performance, video quality (including resolution and color), power-saving features, and ease of use and installation. Because the video controller on the video card is separate from the core system functions, manufacturers can use a variety of techniques to improve performance without being overly concerned about compatibility with functions on the motherboard. An example of this flexibility is the many ways memory is managed on a video controller. This section discusses the buses video cards use, how a video card works, and the features available on video cards, especially video memory. Two main features to look for in a video card are the bus it uses and the amount of video RAM it has or can support. Also know that a motherboard might have its own on-board video controller and video port, but that this video subsystem is probably very basic and lacks many of the features you'll read about in this section.

The Buses Used by Video Cards

Three buses have been used for video cards in the last 10 years or so, the VESA bus, the PCI bus, and the AGP bus. The VESA and AGP buses were developed specifically for video cards, and the PCI bus is used for many types of cards, including a video card.

Several years ago, in an attempt to create a standard for local 32-bit buses, many manufacturers endorsed the **VESA (Video Electronics Standards Association) VL bus**. Many motherboards offered the VESA local bus for video and memory circuit boards. The expansion slot for a VESA local bus included the 16 bits for the ISA slot plus an added extension with another 116 pins (see Figure 10-28). About 1995, the faster PCI bus replaced the VESA bus. Nowadays you seldom see a PC that uses a VESA video card.

A+CORE
   4.3

More recently, an even faster bus, the AGP bus, has replaced the PCI bus for video cards, although a PCI bus is used for a second video card if a system has two monitors (dual monitors). The AGP is designed to provide fast access to video. Motherboards have a single AGP slot to support one AGP video card (see Figure 10-29). AGP is more like a port than a bus, because it does not allow for expandability and supports only a single card. The faster AGP bus has a direct connection to the CPU without having to use the slower PCI bus.

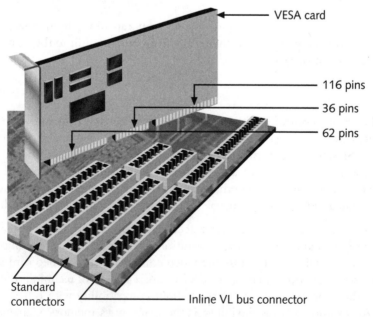

VESA card

116 pins

36 pins

62 pins

Standard
connectors

Inline VL bus connector

Figure 10-28   VESA local bus expansion slot

A+ CORE 4.3

AGP slot

Figure 10-29   A motherboard has only one AGP slot, which is used to support a video/graphics card

10

The AGP bus runs at the same speed as the system bus, connects directly to it, and has a 32-bit-wide data path. AGP runs faster than PCI, which runs at half the system bus speed. AGP also offers additional features that give it an overall better performance for video than PCI. It offers an improved rendering of 3-D images when software is designed to use it.

AGP can share system memory with the CPU to do its calculations and, therefore, it does not always have to first copy data from system memory to video memory on the graphics card. This feature, known as direct memory execute (DIME), is probably the most powerful feature of AGP. The first AGP specification defined AGP 2X, which allowed AGP to transfer two cycles of data during a single AGP clock beat. The AGP 2.0 specification defined AGP 4X, which can transfer four cycles of data during a single AGP clock beat, yielding an overall data throughput of more than 1 GB/sec (gigabytes per second). Compare that to the throughput of the PCI bus, which is either 132 or 264 MB/sec.

Figure 5-36 shows a 132-pin AGP slot on a motherboard. Another AGP standard, called the AGP Pro, has provision for a longer slot. This 180-pin slot has extensions on both ends that contain an additional 20 pins on one end and 28 pins on the other end that are used to provide extra voltage to the AGP video card in the slot. AGP Pro is used for high-end video cards that consume more than 25 watts of power. The first AGP Pro standard ran at the same speed as AGP 4X. The latest AGP standard is AGP 8X that runs at eight cycles of data per clock cycle (2.1 Gbps).

When matching video cards to AGP slots, be aware of the several variations in AGP slots. All AGP speeds support a 3.3 V slot identified by a notch or key near the right end of the slot and a 1.5 V slot identified by a notch or key near the left end of the slot. In addition, there is an AGP universal slot that has no notch and can accommodate either 1.5 V or 3.3 V cards. The AGP Pro slot might be a 1.5 V, 3.3 V, or universal slot. AGP slots on a motherboard are backward compatible with older AGP standards, but you should not use a faster AGP video card in a slower AGP slot. Also, when using an AGP Pro video card, leave the PCI slot next to it empty in order to improve ventilation and prevent overheating.

A+CORE
4.3

In order for AGP to work at its full potential, the motherboard must run at a minimum of 100 MHz, and the operating system must support AGP. Windows 98, Windows 2000, and Windows XP support AGP. See *www.agpforum.org* and *developer.intel.com/technology/agp/* for more information.

A+CORE
1.9
4.2

Graphics Accelerators

One of the more important advances made in video cards in recent years is the introduction of graphics accelerators. A **graphics accelerator** is a type of video card that has its own processor to boost performance. With the demands that graphics applications make in the multimedia environment, graphics accelerators have become not just enhancements, but common necessities.

The processor on a graphics accelerator card is similar to a CPU but specifically designed to manage video and graphics. Some features included on a graphics accelerator are MPEG decoding, 3-D graphics, dual porting, color space conversion, interpolated scaling, EPA Green PC support, digital output to flat panel display monitors, and application support for popular high-intensity graphics software such as AutoCAD and Quark. All these features are designed to reduce the burden on the motherboard CPU and perform the video and graphics functions much faster than the motherboard CPU.

Video Memory

Older video cards had no memory, but today they need memory to handle the large volume of data generated by increased resolution and color. Video memory is stored on video cards as memory chips. The first video cards to have memory all used DRAM chips, but now video memory chips can use several technologies.

The amount of data a video card receives from the CPU for each frame (or screen) of data is determined by the screen resolution (measured in pixels), the number of colors, (called color depth and measured in bits), and enhancements to color information (called alpha blending). The more data required to generate a single screen of data, the more memory is required to hold that data. Memory on the video card that holds one frame of data before it is sent to the monitor is called a frame buffer.

Several factors affect the amount of memory required for the frame buffer, which can be as much as 8 MB. However, in addition to needing memory to hold each frame buffer, a graphics accelerator card might also need memory for other purposes. Software that builds 3-D graphics on screen often uses textures, and sometimes a graphics card holds these textures in memory to build future screens. Large amounts of video RAM keep the card from having to retrieve these textures from the hard drive or system RAM multiple times. In addition, to improve performance, the graphics card might use double or triple buffering, in which the card holds not just the frame being built, but the next one or two frames. Because of texturing and triple buffering, a card might need as much as 32 MB of RAM. See the graphics card documentation for information about memory recommendations for maximum performance.

There are several types of video memory and, when upgrading the memory on a video card, you must match the memory to the card. One type of memory, called **video RAM**, or **VRAM**, is designed so that video memory can be accessed by both the input and output processes at the same time, and is, therefore, a type of dual-ported memory. Three other types of memory chips designed to improve performance of video cards are WRAM, SGRAM, and 3-D RAM.

A+ CORE
1.9
4.2

SGRAM (synchronous graphics RAM) is similar to SDRAM, discussed in Chapter 6, but designed specifically for video card processing. SGRAM, like SDRAM, can synchronize itself with the CPU bus clock, which makes the memory faster. SGRAM also uses other methods to increase overall performance for graphics–intensive processing but is not dual-ported memory. It is used on moderate to high-end cards when the very highest resolutions are not required.

WRAM (window RAM) is a type of dual-ported RAM but faster and less expensive than VRAM. WRAM was named more for its ability to manage full-motion video than for its ability to speed up Microsoft Windows video processing. WRAM's increased speed is primarily due to its own internal bus on the chip, which has a data path that is 256 bits wide. WRAM is used on high-end graphics cards with very high resolutions and true color.

Some video processing involves simulating 3-D graphics; **3-D RAM** was designed specifically to improve this performance. Much of the logic of 3-D processing is embedded on the chip itself. A graphics card chip set normally calculates which pixel of a 3-D graphic to display, depending on whether or not the pixel is behind other pixels and, therefore, out of sight in a 3-D graphic. After the pixel is drawn, a calculation is made as to whether or not the pixel is seen. If the pixel is not to be visible, the chip set writes it back to memory for use later. With 3-D RAM, the chip set simply passes the data to the 3-D RAM chip that draws the pixel and decides whether or not to display it without involving the chip set.

For more information about video cards, including graphics accelerators, see the Web sites of the manufacturers listed in Table 10-9.

10

Table 10-9   Video card manufacturers

Manufacturer	Web Site
ASUSTeK Computer, Inc.	www.asus.com
ATI Technologies, Inc.	www.ati.com
Creative Technology, Ltd.	www.creative.com
Gainward Co., Ltd.	www.gainward.com
Hercules Computer Technology	www.hercules.com
Matrox Graphics, Inc.	www.matrox.com
MSI Computer Corporation	www.msicomputer.com
nVidia	www.nvidia.com
VisionTek	www.visiontek.com

Troubleshooting Video Problems

A+ CORE
2.1
OS
3.3

For monitors as well as other devices, do the easy things first. Make simple hardware and software adjustments. Also, remember the "trade good for suspected bad" method. Many monitor problems are caused by poor cable connections or bad contrast/brightness adjustments. Also check if the monitor is still under warranty. Remember that many warranties are voided when an unauthorized individual works inside the monitor. When servicing a monitor, take the time to clean the screen with a soft dry cloth.

A+CORE
2.1
OS
3.3

> **TIP** When you turn on your PC, the first thing you see on the screen is the firmware on the video card identifying itself. You can use this information to search the Web, especially the manufacturer's Web site, for troubleshooting information about the card.

Typical monitor problems and how to troubleshoot them are described next.

Power Light (LED) Does Not Go on; No Picture

- Is the monitor plugged in? Verify that the wall outlet works by plugging in a lamp, radio, etc.

- If the monitor power cord is plugged into a power strip or surge protector, verify that the power strip is turned on and working and that the monitor is also turned on. Look for an on/off switch on the front and back of the monitor. Some monitors have both.

- If the monitor power cord is plugged into the back of the computer, verify that the connection is tight and the computer is turned on.

- A blown fuse could be the problem. Some monitors have a fuse that is visible from the back of the monitor. It looks like a black knob that you can remove (no need to go inside the monitor cover). Remove the fuse and look for the broken wire indicating a bad fuse.

- The monitor may have a switch on the back for choosing between 110 volts and 220 volts. Check that the switch is in the right position.

If none of these solutions solves the problem, the next step is to take the monitor to a service center.

Power LED Light Is on, No Picture on Power-up

- Check the contrast adjustment. If there's no change, then leave it at a middle setting.

- Check the brightness adjustment. If there's no change, then leave it at a middle setting.

- Make sure the cable is connected securely to the computer.

- If the monitor-to-computer cable detaches from the monitor, exchange it for a cable you know is good, or check the cable for continuity.

- If this solves the problem, reattach the old cable to verify that the problem was not simply a bad connection.

- Confirm that the proper system configuration has been set up. Some older motherboards have a jumper or DIP switch you can use to select the monitor type.

- Test a monitor you know is good on the computer you suspect to be bad. Do this and the previous step to identify the problem. If you think the monitor is bad, make sure that it also fails to work on a good computer.

A+CORE
2.1
3.1
OS
3.3

■ Check the CMOS settings or software configuration on the computer. When using Windows 9x or Windows 2000/XP, boot into safe mode (for Windows 9x press F5 during the boot, and for Windows 2000/XP, press F8 and then choose safe mode from the menu) to allow the OS to select a generic display driver and low resolution. If this works, change the driver and resolution.

■ Reseat the video card. For a PCI card, move the card to a different expansion slot. Clean the card's edge connectors, using a contact cleaner or a white eraser. Do not let crumbs from the eraser fall into the expansion slot.

■ If there are socketed chips on the video card, remove the card from the expansion slot and, using a screwdriver, press down firmly on each corner of each socketed chip on the card. Chips sometimes loosen because of thermal changes; this condition is called **chip creep**.

■ Trade a good video card for the video card you suspect is bad. Test the video card you think is bad on a computer that works. Test a video card you know is good on the computer that you suspect may be bad. Whenever possible, do both.

■ If the video card has socketed chips that appear dirty or corroded, consider removing them and trying to clean the pins. You can use a clean pencil eraser to do this. Normally, however, if the problem is a bad video card, the most cost-effective measure is to replace the card.

■ Go into CMOS setup and disable the shadowing of video ROM.

■ Test the RAM on the motherboard with diagnostic software.

■ For an older motherboard that supports both VESA and PCI, if you are using a VESA video card, try using a PCI card. For a motherboard that is using an AGP video card, try using a PCI video card in a PCI slot.

■ Trade the motherboard for one you know is good. Sometimes, though rarely, a peripheral chip on the motherboard of the computer can cause the problem.

Power on, but Monitor Displays the Wrong Characters

■ Wrong characters are usually not the result of a bad monitor but of a problem with the video card. Trade the video card for one you know is good.

■ Exchange the motherboard. Sometimes a bad ROM or RAM chip on the motherboard displays the wrong characters on the monitor.

Monitor Flickers and/or Has Wavy Lines

■ Monitor flicker can be caused by poor cable connections. Check that the cable connections are snug.

■ Does the monitor have a degauss button to eliminate accumulated or stray magnetic fields? If so, press it.

A+CORE
2.1
OS
3.3

- Check if something in the office is causing a high amount of electrical noise. For example, you might be able to stop a flicker by moving the office fan to a different outlet. Bad fluorescent lights or large speakers can also produce interference. Two monitors placed very close together can also cause problems.

- If the vertical scan frequency (the refresh rate at which the screen is drawn) is below 60 Hz, a screen flicker may appear. Use Control Panel, Display icon to make the adjustment. Use the highest refresh rate offered.

- For older monitors that do not support a high enough refresh rate, your only cure may be to purchase a new monitor.

- Before making a purchase, verify that the new monitor will solve the problem.

- Check Control Panel, Display, Settings to see if a high resolution (greater than 800 × 600 with more than 256 colors) is selected. Consider these issues:

  1. The video card might not support this resolution/color setting.

  2. There might not be enough video RAM; 2 MB or more may be required.

  3. The added (socketed) video RAM might be a different speed than the soldered memory.

No Graphics Display or the Screen Goes Blank when Loading Certain Programs

This problem may be caused by the following:

- A special graphics or video accelerator card is not present or is defective.

- Software is not configured to do graphics, or the software does not recognize the installed graphics card.

- The video card does not support the resolution and/or color setting.

- There might not be enough video RAM; 2 MB or more might be required.

- The added (socketed) video RAM might be a different speed than the soldered memory.

- The wrong adapter/display type is selected. Start Windows from safe mode to reset the display.

Screen Goes Blank 30 Seconds or One Minute After the Keyboard Is Left Untouched

A Green motherboard (one that follows energy-saving standards) used with an Energy Saver monitor can be configured to go into standby or doze mode after a period of inactivity. This might be the case if the monitor resumes after you press a key or move the mouse. Doze times can be set for periods from as short as 20 seconds to as long as one hour. The power LED light normally changes from green to orange to indicate Doze Mode. Monitors and video cards using these energy-saving features are addressed in Chapter 4.

A+*CORE*
 2.1
 OS
 3.3

You might be able to change the doze features by entering the CMOS menu and looking for an option such as Power Management, or in Windows by opening Control Panel and selecting Display, Screen Saver.

Some monitors have a Power Save switch on the back. Make sure this is set as you want.

> **TIP** Problems might occur if the motherboard power-saving features are turning off the monitor, and Windows screen saver is also turning off the monitor. If the system hangs when you try to get the monitor going again, try disabling one or the other. If this doesn't work, then disable both.

Poor Quality Color Display

For this problem, try the following:

- Read the documentation for the monitor to learn how to use the color-adjusting buttons to fine-tune the color.

- Exchange video cards.

- Add more video RAM; 2 MB or 4 MB might be required for higher resolutions.

- Check if a fan or large speaker (speakers have large magnets) or a nearby monitor could be causing interference.

Picture out of Focus or out of Adjustment

For this problem, try the following:

- Check the adjustment knobs on the control panel on the outside of the monitor.

- Change the refresh rate. Sometimes this can make the picture appear more focused.

- You can also make adjustments inside the monitor that might solve the problem. If you have not been trained to work inside the monitor, take the monitor to a service center.

Crackling Sound

Dirt or dust inside the unit might be the cause. Someone trained to work on the inside of the monitor can vacuum inside it.

To Configure or Change Monitor Settings and Drivers in Windows

If the video card is supported by Windows, you can change the driver and settings by double-clicking the Display icon in Control Panel. For drivers not supported by Windows, you can reinstall the drivers by using the CD or floppy disks that come with the video card. The settings for this type of driver can most likely be changed through Control Panel's Display icon.

10

A +CORE
1.2
1.8
2.1
OS
3.3
To Change the Video Driver Configuration

Double-click the Display icon in Control Panel or right-click on the Desktop and select Properties from the shortcut menu. Select the Settings tab to change the color palette, the resolution (for example, from 800 × 600 to 1600 × 1200), or the driver for the video card or monitor type. Click Advanced on the Settings tab to show the Change Display Type window. From this window, you can change the video card or the monitor type. For Windows XP, click Advanced, Adapter tab, Properties, and the Driver tab. (See Figure 10-30.)

If you increase the resolution, the Windows icons and desktop text become smaller. Select Large Fonts on the Appearance tab.

A +CORE
1.2
OS
3.3
Returning to Standard VGA Settings

When the display settings don't work, return to standard VGA settings as follows:

- For Windows 9x or Windows 2000/XP, reboot the system and press the F8 key after the first beep.

- When the Microsoft Windows 9x Startup menu or the Windows 2000/XP Advanced Options menu appears, select safe mode to boot up with minimal configurations and standard VGA display mode. For Windows 2000/XP you can also try Enable VGA Mode from the Advanced Options menu.

- Double-click the Display icon in Control Panel, and reset to the correct video configuration.

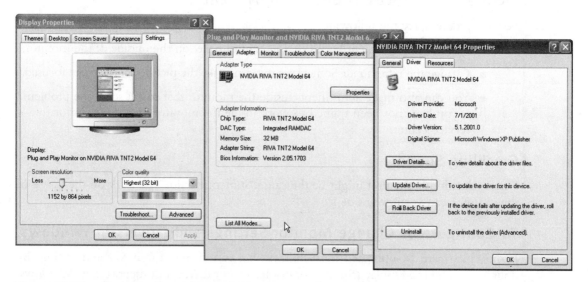

Figure 10-30 Updating the video card drivers in Windows XP

CHAPTER SUMMARY

- Adding new devices to a computer requires installing hardware and software and resolving possible resource conflicts.

- All hardware devices require some resources from a computer, which might include an IRQ, DMA channel, I/O addresses, and, for legacy devices, some upper memory addresses to contain their device drivers.

- Use Device Manager under Windows to determine what resources currently installed devices use.

- Most computers provide two serial ports and one parallel port to be used for a variety of devices. Newer motherboards also provide one or more USB ports and an IEEE 1394 port.

- The PCI bus is presently the most popular local bus. The VESA local bus is a standard designed by the Video Electronics Standards Association for video cards. For video cards, the VESA bus was replaced by PCI, which was then replaced by the AGP bus.

- Generally, expansion cards use PCI slots or older and slower ISA slots.

- A null modem connection is used to connect two computers using their serial ports and a cable, but no modems.

- The UART chip controls serial ports.

- Because data might get corrupted, parallel cables should not exceed 15 feet (4.5 meters) in length. HP recommends that the cables not exceed 10 feet (3 meters).

- Three types of parallel ports are standard, EPP, and ECP. The ECP type uses a DMA channel.

- Serial ports are sometimes configured as COM1, COM2, COM3, or COM4, and parallel ports can be configured as LPT1, LPT2, or LPT3.

- The USB bus only uses one set of system resources for all USB devices connected to it, and USB devices are hot-pluggable.

- The IEEE 1394 bus provides either a 4-pin or 6-pin connector, uses only one set of system resources, and is hot-pluggable.

- The PCI bus runs in sync with the CPU, and the PCI controller manages system resources for all PCI cards. Resources are assigned to PCI slots during startup.

- A keyboard can use a DIN, PS/2, USB, or wireless connection.

- Two types of monitors are CRT and LCD. CRT costs less but LCD takes less desktop space.

- Features to consider when purchasing a monitor are screen size, refresh rate, interlacing, dot pitch, resolution, multiscan ability, and Green Standards used by the monitor.

- A video card is rated by the bus that it uses and the amount of video RAM on the card. Both features affect the overall speed and performance of the card.

- Some types of video memory are SGRAM, WRAM, and 3-D RAM.

10

KEY TERMS

3-D RAM

active matrix

bandwidth

bus mouse

chip creep

DCE (Data Communications Equipment)

dot pitch

DTE (Data Terminal Equipment)

dual-scan passive matrix

ECP (Extended Capabilities Port)

EPP (Enhanced Parallel Port)

FireWire

flat panel monitor

graphics accelerator

hot-pluggable

hot-swappable

hub

IEEE 1284

IEEE 1394

IEEE 1394.3

i.Link

interlaced

I/O controller card

isochronous data transfer

modem eliminator

motherboard mouse

multiscan monitor

noninterlaced

null modem cable

PCI (Peripheral Component Interconnect) bus

pixel

PS/2-compatible mouse

refresh rate

resolution

serial mouse

SGRAM (synchronous graphics RAM)

UART (universal asynchronous receiver-transmitter)

USB host controller

VESA (Video Electronics Standards Association)

VL bus

VRAM (video RAM)

WRAM (window RAM)

REVIEW QUESTIONS

1. The three steps to install an add-on device include:

   a. _____

   b. _____

   c. _____

2. The serial port on the back of the microcomputer is recognized by:

   a. A 9-pin female connector (DB-9F)

   b. A 9-pin male connector (DB-9M)

   c. A 15-pin female connector (DB-15F)

   d. A 25-pin female connector (DB-25F)

   e. All of the above qualify for serial port connectors.

3. The parallel port on the back of the microcomputer is recognized by:

   a. A 9-pin female connector (DB-9F)

   b. A 9-pin male connector (DB-9M)

   c. A 15-pin female connector (DB-15F)

   d. A 25-pin female connector (DB-25F)

   e. All of the above qualify for serial port connectors.

4. When installing new hardware devices into an existing microcomputer, the two tasks that should be accomplished before actually installing the new hardware include:

   a. _____

   b. _____

5. The kind of data transmission speed a user can expect using a FireWire port is:

   a. 115.2 kbps

   b. 1.5 Mbps

   c. 12 Mbps

   d. 480 Mbps

   e. 1.2 Gbps

6. The protocol for interrupt requests is such that IRQ values that are closer to zero have a higher priority. A service technician needs to install two devices through a serial port, where one of the devices requires a higher priority in terms of device servicing by the CPU. Which port should the service technician place the serial device on to ensure a higher priority of one serial device over the other?

   a. LPT1

   b. LPT2

   c. COM1

   d. COM2

   e. None of the above

7. Complete the following table with default port assignments:

Port	IRQ	I/O Address	Port Type
		03F8-03FF	
		03E8-03EF	
		0378-037F	

8. When two pieces of Data Terminal Equipment, such as two microcomputers, want to communicate with each other over a conventional telephone line using modems, it is customary to connect the microcomputer to the external modem using a cable referred to as a "null modem cable."

   a. True

   b. False

9. The logic component that is used to control serial ports is:

    a. RAM

    b. ROM-BIOS

    c. UART

    d. CPU

    e. Hard drive

10. In order to ensure data integrity over a parallel port, it is recommended that cable lengths be restricted to:

    a. 10 feet

    b. 50 feet

    c. 100 feet

    d. 250 feet

    e. No restriction

11. Parallel port configurations fall into three categories; they include:

    a. _____

    b. _____

    c. _____

12. Of the three parallel port configurations that are available, which two provide for bidirectional communications between the port and device?

    a. _____

    b. _____

13. Of the two bidirectional parallel port configurations, which utilizes a DMA channel to increase data transfer rates?

14. Of the following ports, which allows hot-swapping of devices in and out of the port?

    a. Serial

    b. Parallel

    c. Game

    d. USB

    e. PS/2 ports

15. Which of the following do *not* support IEEE 1394 bus?

    a. Windows 98

    b. Windows 2000

    c. Windows XP

    d. Windows NT

    e. All of the above support IEEE 1394.

16. Standard PCI bus offers a data path of:

    a. 8 bits

    b. 16 bits

    c. 32 bits

    d. 64 bits

    e. 128 bits

17. Which of the following is *not* commonly used when interfacing a keyboard to a microcomputer?

    a. PS/2

    b. DIN

    c. USB

    d. COM

    e. All of the above connectors are used for keyboard interface.

18. The number of pixels that can be addressed on a screen by software is referred to as:

    a. Screen size

    b. Refresh rate

    c. Dot pitch

    d. Resolution

    e. None of the above

10

19. The number of times a screen is completely written over the course of a second's worth of time is referred to as:

    a. Screen size

    b. Refresh rate

    c. Dot pitch

    d. Resolution

    e. None of the above

20. The term "interlacing," with respect to monitors, refers to:

    a. The drawing of an entire screen's worth of information in a single pass

    b. The drawing of an entire screen's worth of information in two passes

    c. The drawing of an entire screen's worth of information in three passes

    d. None of the above

21. In terms of image quality, which type of image display used with laptop computers offers the best picture?

11

MULTIMEDIA DEVICES AND MASS STORAGE

In this chapter, you will learn:

♦ About multimedia devices such as sound cards, digital cameras, and MP3 players

♦ About optical storage technologies such as CD and DVD

♦ About tape drives and removable drives

♦ How certain hardware devices are used for backups and fault tolerance

♦ How to troubleshoot multimedia and mass storage devices

The ability to create output in a vast array of media—audio, video, and animation, as well as text and graphics—has turned PCs into multimedia machines. The multimedia computer has much to offer, from video conferencing for executives to tools for teaching the alphabet to four-year-olds. This chapter examines multimedia devices, what they can do, how they work, and how to support them. You will also learn about storage devices such as CD, DVD, removable drives, and tape drives, including installation and troubleshooting. These mass storage devices are used to hold multimedia data and, in some cases, to hold backups.

MULTIMEDIA ON A PC

The goal of multimedia technology is to create or reproduce lifelike representations for audio, video, and animation. Remember that computers store data digitally and ultimately as a stream of only two numbers: 0 and 1. In contrast, sights and sounds have an infinite number of variations and are analog in nature. The challenge for multimedia technology is to bridge these two worlds.

CPU Technologies for Multimedia

Two enhancements by Intel to CPU technology designed with multimedia applications in mind are **MMX (Multimedia Extensions)**, used by the Pentium MMX, Pentium Pro, and Pentium II, and **SSE (Streaming SIMD Extension)**, used by the Pentium III. (**SIMD**, which stands for **single instruction, multiple data**, is a process that allows the CPU to receive a single instruction and then execute it on multiple pieces of data rather than receiving the same instruction each time the data is received.) The Pentium 4 uses both MMX and SSE. Multimedia software tends to use input/output operations more than it performs complex computations. Both MMX and SSE were designed to speed up the repetitive looping of multimedia software and manage the high-volume input/output of graphics, motion video, animation, and sound. MMX technology added new instructions designed for repetitive processing, more efficient ways to pass those instructions to the CPU, and increased CPU cache. SSE added improvements to 3-D graphics and speech recognition. To compete with SSE, AMD introduced 3DNow!, a CPU instruction set that helps AMD processors perform better in 3D graphics and other multimedia data processing.

 To know if software or hardware is taking advantage of a CPU enhancement for multimedia, look on the product package for the Intel MMX, Intel SSE, or AMD 3DNow! symbols.

Multimedia Devices

Now let's look at some specific devices used for multimedia support. Many multimedia capabilities are added to a system using sound cards and other adapter cards. There are also externally attached devices such as digital cameras or MP3 players. In this section, you will learn about these and other devices.

Sound Cards

A sound card is an expansion card that records sound, saves it in a file on your hard drive, and plays it back. Some cards give you the ability to mix and edit sound, and even to edit the sound using standard music score notation. Sound cards have ports for external stereo speakers and microphone input. Also, sound cards may be Sound Blaster compatible, which means that they understand the commands sent to them that have been written for a Sound Blaster card, which is generally considered the standard for PC sound cards. Some play CD audio by way of a cable connecting the CD to the sound card. For good quality sound you definitely need external speakers and perhaps an amplifier.

Sound passes through three stages when it is computerized: (1) digitize or input the sound, that is, convert it from analog to digital, (2) store the digital data in a compressed data file, and later (3) reproduce or synthesize the sound (digital to analog). Each of these stages is discussed next, followed by a discussion of sound card installation. Table 11-1 lists some sound card manufacturers.

Table 11-1   Sound card manufacturers

Abit	www.abit.com.tw
Aopen	www.aopen.com
Elements	www.elements-pc.com
Guillemot Corporation	us.guillemot.com
SIIG	www.siig.com
Syba	www.syba.com
Turtle Beach	www.tbeach.com

11

TIP A good source for information about hardware devices (and software) is a site that compares product prices, features, and technical specifications, such as *www.cnet.com* or *www.pricewatch.com*. On the CNET Networks and Price Watch sites, you can also find company information and product reviews.

Sampling and Digitizing the Sound

Converting sound from analog to digital storage is done by first sampling the sound and then digitizing it. When you record sound, the analog sound is converted to analog voltage by a microphone and passed to the sound card, where it is digitized. The critical factor in the performance of a sound card is the accuracy of the samples (determined by the sample size, which can be either 8 or 16 bits). The **sampling rate** of a sound card (the number of samples taken of the analog signal over a period of time) is usually expressed as samples (cycles) per second, or **hertz (Hz)**. One thousand hertz (one kilohertz) is written as kHz. A low sampling rate provides a less accurate representation of the sound than does a high sampling rate. Our ears detect up to about 22,000 samples per second, or hertz. The sampling rate of music CDs is 44,100 Hz, or 44.1 kHz. When you record sound on a PC, the sampling rate is controlled by the recording software.

The larger the sample size, the more accurate the sampling. If 8 bits are used to hold one number, then the sample range can be from –128 to +127. This is because 1111 1111 in binary equals 255 in decimal, which, together with zero, equals 256 values. Sound samples are considered to be both positive and negative numbers, so the range is –128 to +127 rather than 0 to 255. However, if 16 bits are used to hold the range of numbers, then the sample range increases dramatically, because 1111 1111 1111 1111 in binary is 65,535 in decimal, meaning that the sample size can be –32,768 to +32,767, or a total of 65,536 values. Music CDs use this 16-bit sample size.

Thus, an 8-bit sound card has a sample size of 256. A 16-bit sound card has a sample size of 65,536. Sound cards typically use 8- or 16-bit sample sizes, with a sampling rate from 4,000 to 44,000 samples per second. For high-quality sound, use a 16-bit sound card. Samples may also be recorded on a single channel (mono) or on two channels (stereo).

> **TIP** Don't confuse the sample size of 8 bits or 16 bits with the ISA bus size that the sound card might use to attach to the motherboard. A sound card may use an 8-bit sample size but a 16-bit ISA bus. When you hear people talk about an 8-bit sound card, they are speaking of the sample size, not the bus size.

 A+CORE 1.2

Installing a Sound Card

Most sound cards come with a device driver as well as all the software needed for normal use, such as application software to play music CDs. The installation of a sample sound card is described following. The card used is a PnP Creative Labs Sound Blaster card that uses a PCI slot and supports a 128-voice wave table (a table of stored sample sounds that is used to reconstruct and reproduce recorded sound). It works under DOS 6+, Windows 9x, and Windows NT/2000/XP. The card comes with drivers and software on a CD-ROM and a user's guide.

The three main steps in this example of a sound card installation are to install the card itself in an empty PCI slot on the motherboard, install the driver, and then install the applications stored on the CD that comes with the sound card.

The Sound Blaster card shown in Figure 11-1 has three internal connections (connections to something inside the case) and one jumper group that enables or disables a speaker amplifier. If you are using a speaker system with an external amplifier, disable the amplifier on the card by setting the jumper on the sound card to "disable amplifier."

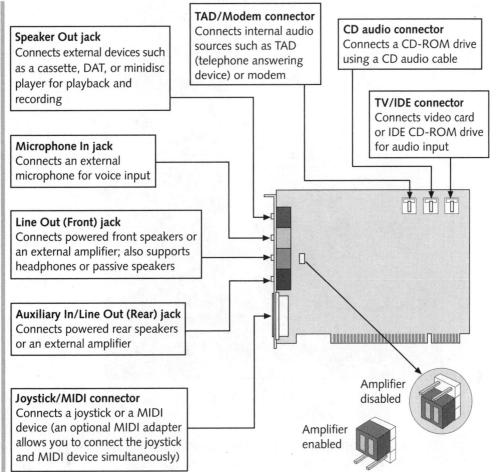

Speaker Out jack
Connects external devices such as a cassette, DAT, or minidisc player for playback and recording

TAD/Modem connector
Connects internal audio sources such as TAD (telephone answering device) or modem

CD audio connector
Connects a CD-ROM drive using a CD audio cable

TV/IDE connector
Connects video card or IDE CD-ROM drive for audio input

Microphone In jack
Connects an external microphone for voice input

Line Out (Front) jack
Connects powered front speakers or an external amplifier; also supports headphones or passive speakers

Auxiliary In/Line Out (Rear) jack
Connects powered rear speakers or an external amplifier

Joystick/MIDI connector
Connects a joystick or a MIDI device (an optional MIDI adapter allows you to connect the joystick and MIDI device simultaneously)

Amplifier disabled

Amplifier enabled

Figure 11-1   The Sound Blaster sound card has three internal connections and one jumper group that controls amplifier support

Follow these steps to install a sound card:

1. Make sure that you are properly grounded. Wear a grounding bracelet and follow other procedures to guard against ESD, as described in Chapter 4.

2. Turn off the PC, remove the cover, and locate an empty expansion slot for the card. Since this installation uses the connecting wire from the sound card to the CD-ROM drive (the wire comes with the sound card), place the sound card near enough to the CD-ROM drive so that the wire can reach between them.

3. Attach the wire to the sound card (see Figure 11-2) and to the CD-ROM drive.

A+CORE
1.2

Figure 11-2 Connect the wire to the sound card that will make the direct audio connection from the CD

4. Remove the cover from the slot opening at the rear of the PC case, and place the card into the PCI slot, making sure that the card is seated firmly. Use the screw taken from the slot cover to secure the card to the back of the PC case.

5. Check again that both ends of the wire are still securely connected and that the wire is not hampering the CPU fan, then replace the case cover.

6. Plug in the speakers to the ports at the back of the sound card, and turn on the PC. The speakers may or may not require their own power source. Check the product documentation or manufacturer's Web site for more information.

 There can be several ports on a sound card. Most likely the speaker ports are the green center ports on the card.

Notice that the installation in the example was in a system using a CD-ROM drive. Later in the chapter, you'll see an example of a sound card installed in a system with a DVD drive. If you are using a speaker system with an amplifier, disable the amplifier on the card. To do so, set the jumper on the sound card to disable amplifier support (see Figure 11-1).

A+CORE 1.2 Installing the Sound Card Driver

After the card is installed, the device drivers must be installed. The next example uses a driver installation under Windows 98 as an example. When Windows 98 starts, it detects that new hardware is present. The New Hardware Found dialog box opens, indicating that it discovered the Sound Blaster PCI128. Follow these steps to install the sound card driver:

1. The New Hardware Wizard gives you this option: **Search for the Best Driver for Your Device (Recommended)**. Select this option and click the **Next** button.

2. Clear all check boxes and check only the **Specify a Location** check box.

3. Click the **Browse** button and point to the driver path, such as **D:\Audio\English\Win98drv**.

   In this example, the CD-ROM drive is drive D, and the sound card's user guide listed the location of the driver on the CD. Substitute your CD-ROM drive letter and, for other sound card installations, see the documentation for the location of the driver on the CD-ROM.

4. Click **Next** to continue the driver installation.

5. Click **Finish** when the installation is complete, and reboot your PC.

With most sound cards, on the CD containing the sound card driver, you can find some application software for the special features offered by the card. Sometimes, as is the case with this Sound Blaster card, this software is installed at the same time as the drivers, so you can use the software at this point in the installation. For other sound cards, you can install the additional software after driver installation is complete and the sound card is working. See the documentation that comes with the sound card to learn if application software is present, and how and when to install it.

After you have installed the driver, rebooted, and entered Windows, verify that the card and the driver are correctly installed in Windows 98 by using Device Manager.

1. Click **Start**, point to **Settings**, click **Control Panel**, and then double-click **System**.

2. Select the **Device Manager** tab. Figure 11-3 shows the sound card installed.

3. To see the resources used by the card, select the card and click **Properties**. The Properties box appears. Click the **Resources** tab.

Troubleshooting problems with sound cards is covered later in the chapter.

11

Digital Cameras

A+CORE 1.8

Digital cameras are becoming more popular as quality improves and prices decrease. Digital camera technology works much like scanner technology, except it is much faster. It essentially scans the field of image set by the picture taker and translates the light signals

A+CORE
1.8

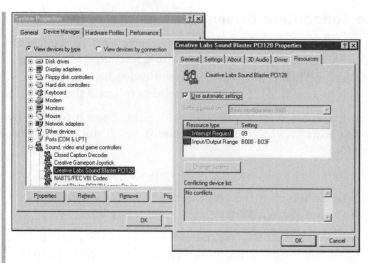

Figure 11-3   Device Manager shows the sound card installed and the resources it is using

into digital values, which can be stored as a file and viewed, manipulated, and printed with software that interprets the stored values appropriately.

TWAIN is a standard format used by digital cameras and scanners for transferring images. To transfer images to your PC, first install the software bundled with your camera or other device that contains the images. You can transfer images from the camera to your computer's hard drive using a cable supplied with the camera. The cable might attach directly to the camera or connect to a cradle the camera sits in to recharge or upload images. The cable can use a serial, parallel, USB, or FireWire (IEEE 1394) connection. The camera can also use a wireless or infrared connection, or it can use an external storage medium such as a flash RAM card to upload images. CompactFlash, SmartMedia, SanDisk, and Sony Memory Sticks are different types of flash RAM cards. Figure 11-4 shows a SmartMedia card from a digital camera inserted into a FlashPath card that can then be inserted into a floppy disk drive to upload images to the PC. Some printers are also capable of uploading images directly from flash RAM cards. You can use a site such as www.cdnet.com or www.compusa.com to find and compare other digital cameras and flash card readers.

After the images are on the PC, use the camera's image-editing software, or another program such as Adobe PhotoShop, to view, touch up, and print the picture. The picture file, which is usually in **JPEG (Joint Photographic Experts Group)** format, can then be imported into documents. JPEG is a common compression standard for storing photos. Most JPEG files have a .jpg file extension.

Most digital cameras also have a video-out port that allows you to attach the camera to any TV, using a cable provided with the camera. You can then display pictures on TV or copy them to videotape. Table 11-2 lists manufacturers of digital cameras.

FlashPath

SmartMedia

Figure 11-4 The small SmartMedia card holds the digital images from a digital camera, and FlashPath allows a PC to read SmartMedia by way of a floppy disk drive

11

Table 11-2 Digital camera manufacturers

Canon	www.usa.canon.com
Casio	www.casio.com
Epson	www.epson.com
Fujifilm	www.fujifilm.com
Hewlett-Packard	www.photosmart.com
Kodak	www.kodak.com
Minolta	www.minolta.com
Nikon	www.nikonusa.com
Olympus	www.olympusamerica.com
Sony	www.sony.com/di
Toshiba	www.toshiba.com

MP3 Players

A popular audio compression method is **MP3**, a method that can reduce the size of a sound file as much as 1:24 without much loss of quality. An MP3 player is a device or software that plays MP3 files. MP3 players are small but can store a lot of information. Figure 11–5 shows a typical MP3 player.

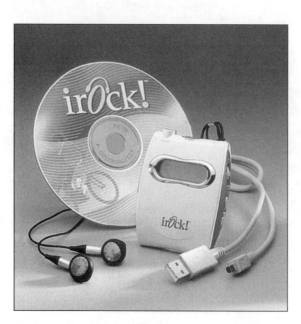

Figure 11-5   An MP3 player with player software, headphones, and cable used to download MP3 files from a PC

Compression Methods Used with MP3 Players

One of the better-known multimedia data compression standards is MPEG, an international standard for data compression for motion pictures, video, and audio. Developed by the **Moving Pictures Experts Group (MPEG),** it tracks movement from one frame to the next and stores only what changes, rather than compressing individual frames. MPEG compression can yield a compression ratio of 100:1 for full-motion video (30 frames per second, or 30 fps).

There are currently several MPEG standards: MPEG-1, MPEG-2, MPEG-3, and MPEG-4. MPEG-1 is used in business and home applications to compress images. MPEG-2 is used to compress video films on DVD-ROM. MPEG-3 is used for audio compression, and MP3 is a type of MPEG-3 compression. MPEG-4 is used for video transmissions over the Internet.

MPEG compression is possible because it cuts out or drastically reduces sound that is not normally heard by the human ear. In the regular audio CD format (uncompressed), one minute of music takes up about 10 MB of storage. The same minute of music in MP3 format takes only about 1 MB of memory. This makes it possible to download music in minutes rather than hours. Sound files downloaded from the Internet are most often MP3 files. MP3 files have an .mp3 file extension. For more information about MPEG and MP3, see *www.mpeg.org*.

How MP3 Players Work

Most portable MP3 players today store MP3 files in onboard memory or hard drives, which can be expanded using an add-on flash RAM card such as SmartMedia, CompactFlash, or Memory Stick. MP3 files are downloaded from the PC to the MP3 player, in contrast to using a digital camera, which transfers or uploads data to the PC.

You can download and purchase MP3 music files from Web sites such as EMusic (*www.emusic.com*) and MP3.com (*www.mp3.com*). Once the files are downloaded to your PC, you can play them on your PC using MP3 player software such as Windows Media Player or MusicMatch Jukebox (see *www.musicmatch.com*), transfer them to a portable MP3 player, or convert them into an audio CD if your computer has a rewritable CD drive. There are also CD/MP3 players that can play CDs in either standard audio format or MP3 format. A CD can store 10 hours or more of music in MP3 format. You can also play the MP3 files directly from the Internet without first downloading them, which is called **streaming audio**. MP3 files are generally transferred to portable devices using a USB or serial cable.

Also, you can convert files from your regular music CDs into MP3 files (a process called ripping), and play them on your computer or download them to an MP3 player. "Ripper" software copies the music file from the CD, and encoder software compresses the file into MP3 format. CD rippers, MP3 encoders, and MP3 player software can be downloaded from the Internet. For example, see the MusicMatch site at *www.musicmatch.com*.

Table 11-3 lists some manufacturers of MP3 players.

Table 11-3   MP3 player manufacturers

Creative Labs	*www.creative.com*
I-Jam	*www.ijamworld.com*
Imation	*www.imation.com*
Intel	*www.intel.com*
Panasonic	*www.panasonic.com*
Pine Technology	*www.xfxforce.com*
Samsung	*www.samsungusa.com*
Sensory Science (owned by SONICblue)	*www.sensoryscience.com*
SONICblue	*www.sonicblue.com*
Sony	*www.sel.sony.com*

Video Capture Card

An NTSC (National Television Standards Committee) video capture card is another multimedia option. With this card, you can capture input from a camcorder or directly from TV. Video can be saved as motion clips or stills, edited, and, with the right card, copied back to video tape for viewing with a VCR and television. Look for these features on a video capture card:

- An IEEE 1394 (FireWire) port to interface with a digital camcorder
- Data transfer rates, which affect price
- Capture resolution and color-depth capabilities
- Ability to transfer data back to the digital camcorder or VCR
- Stereo audio jacks
- Video-editing software bundled with the card

Other options include a TV tuner that makes it possible to turn your PC into a television, complete with instant replay and program scheduling. Ports on a video capture card might include an antenna or cable TV port for input and a TV or VCR port for output. Other ports are a PC monitor video port and possibly an IEEE 1394 port for a camcorder. Expect the card to fit into an AGP slot and take the place of your regular video card. For an excellent example of a video capture card, see the All-in-Wonder RADEON card from ATI Technologies at *www.ati.com*.

Table 11-4 lists some manufacturers of video capture cards.

Table 11-4   Video capture card manufacturers

ASUS	www.asus.com
ATI	www.ati.com
Creative Labs	www.creative.com
Matrox	www.matrox.com
Pinnacle Systems	www.pinnaclesys.com
SONICblue	www.sonicblue.com

OPTICAL STORAGE TECHNOLOGY

CDs and DVDs are popular storage media for multimedia data, and CDs are the most popular way of distributing software. Both DVD and CD-ROM technologies use patterns of tiny pits on the surface of a disc to represent bits, which a laser beam can then read. This is why they are called optical storage technologies. CD-ROM drives use the **CDFS (Compact Disc File System)** or the **UDF (Universal Disk Format) file system**, and DVD-drives only use the newer UDF. Windows supports both file systems, which include several standards used for audio, photographs, video, and other data. Most CD-ROM drives support several CDFS formats, and most DVD drives support CDFS and several UDF formats. In this section, you will learn about the major optical storage technologies, including their similarities and differences, their storage capacities, and variations within each type.

CD-ROM

A+CORE
1.1

Of the multimedia components discussed in this chapter, the most popular is the CD-ROM drive. CD-ROMs are used to distribute software and sound files. CD-ROM drives are read-only devices. Read/writable CDs and drives are discussed later in the chapter.

During the manufacturing process, data can be written to a CD-ROM disc only once, because the data is actually embedded in the surface of the disc. Figure 11-6 shows a CD-ROM surface laid out as one continuous spiral of sectors of equal length that hold equal amounts of data. If laid out in a straight line, this spiral would be 3.5 miles long. The surface of a CD-ROM stores data as pits and lands. **Lands** are raised areas and **pits** are recessed areas on the surface; each represents either a 1 or a 0, respectively. The bits are read by the drive with a laser beam that distinguishes between a pit and a land by the amount of deflection or scattering that occurs when the light beam hits the surface.

Figure 11-6 The spiral layout of sectors on a CD-ROM surface

11

A small motor with an actuator arm moves the laser beam to the sector on the track it needs to read. If the disc were spinning at a constant speed, the speed near the center of the disc would be greater than the speed at the outer edge. To create the effect of **constant linear velocity (CLV)**, the CD-ROM drive uses a mechanism that speeds up the disc when the laser beam is near the center of the disc, and slows down the disc when the laser beam is near the outer edge. Thus, the beam is over a sector for the same amount of time, no matter where the sector is. (Since the outer edge has more sectors than the inner edge, the light beam needs more time to read near the outer edge than it does near the inner edge.) The transfer rate of the first CD-ROM drives was about 150K per second of data (150 KBps), with the rpm (revolutions per minute) set to 200 when the laser was near the center of the disc. This transfer rate was about right for audio CDs. To show video and motion without a choppy effect, the speed of the drives was increased to double speed (150K per sec × 2), quad speed (150K per sec × 4), and so on. CD-ROM drives with speeds at 72 times the audio speed are not uncommon now. Audio CDs must still drop to the original speed of 200 rpm and a transfer rate of 150 KBps.

Because of the problems of changing speeds using CLV, newer, faster CD-ROM drives use a combination of CLV and **constant angular velocity (CAV)**, the same technology used by hard drives, whereby the disc rotates at a constant speed.

When you choose a CD-ROM drive, look for the multisession feature, which means that the drive can read a disc that has been created in multiple sessions. To say a disc was created in **multisessions** means that data was written to the disc at different times rather than in a single long, continuous session.

Some CD-ROM drives have power-saving features controlled by the device driver. For example, when the drive waits for a command for more than five minutes, it enters Power Save Mode, causing the spindle motor to stop. The restart is automatic when the drive receives a command.

Table 11-5 lists manufacturers of CD-ROM drives.

Table 11-5   CD-ROM drive manufacturers

Acer Peripherals	*global.acer.com*
Addonics Technologies	*www.addonics.com*
ASUS	*www.asus.com*
Axonix	*www.axonix.com*
Benq	*www.benq.com*
Circo Technology	*www.circotech.com*
Creative Labs	*www.creativelabs.com* or *www.creative.com*
Hewlett-Packard	*www.hpcdwriter.com*
Panasonic	*www.panasonic.com*
Samsung	*www.samsung.com*
Sanyo	*www.sanyo.com*
Sony	*www.sony.com*
TDK	*www.tdk.com/multimedia*

A+CORE
2.1
3.1

Caring for CD-ROM Drives and Discs

Most problems with CD-ROMs are caused by dust, fingerprints, scratches, surface defects, or random electrical noise. Don't use a CD-ROM drive if it is standing vertically, such as when someone turns a desktop PC case on its side to save desk space. Use these precautions when handling CDs or DVDs:

- Hold the CD by the edge; do not touch the bright side of the disc where data is stored.

- To remove dust or fingerprints, use a clean, soft, dry cloth.

- Do not write or paste paper on the surface of the CD. Don't paste any labels on the top of the CD, because this can imbalance the CD and cause the drive to vibrate.

- Do not subject the CD to heat or leave it in direct sunlight.

- Do not use cleaners, alcohol, and the like on the CD.

- Do not make the center hole larger.

- Do not bend the CD.

- Do not drop the CD or subject it to shock.

- If a CD gets stuck in the drive, use the emergency eject hole to remove it. Turn off the power to the PC first. Then insert an instrument such as a straightened paper clip into the hole to eject the tray manually.

- When closing a CD tray, don't push on the tray. Press the close button on the front of the drive.

How a CD-ROM Drive Can Interface with the Motherboard

CD-ROM drives can interface with the motherboard in several ways:

- Use an IDE interface; it can share an IDE connection and/or cable with a hard drive. IDE is the most popular interface method for CD-ROM drives. These drives follow the **ATAPI (Advanced Technology Attachment Packet Interface)** standard, an extension of the IDE/ATA standard that allows tape drives, CD-ROM drives, and other drives to be treated just like another hard drive on the system.

- Use a SCSI interface with a SCSI host adapter.

- Use a proprietary expansion card that works only with CD-ROMs from a particular manufacturer.

- Use a proprietary connection on a sound card.

- Be a portable drive and plug into an external port on your PC, such as a USB port or SCSI port.

Most CD-ROM drives are Plug and Play compliant. These drives allow a system to avoid resource conflicts. Boxes marked "Designed for Windows" indicate Plug and Play CD-ROM drives.

Installing a CD-ROM Drive

Once installed, the CD-ROM or CD-RW drive becomes another drive on your system, such as drive D or E. After it is installed, you access it just like any other drive by typing D: or E: at the command prompt, or by accessing the drive through Windows Explorer. The major differences are (1) the CD-ROM drive is read-only (you cannot write to it) and (2) a CD-ROM drive is slower to access than a hard drive.

The most popular interface for a CD-ROM drive is IDE, although you will occasionally see a SCSI CD-ROM drive. Figure 11-7 shows the rear of an IDE CD-ROM drive. Note the jumper bank that can be set to cable select, slave, or master. Recall from Chapter 8 that, for Enhanced IDE (EIDE), there are four choices for drive installations: primary master, primary slave, secondary master, and secondary slave. If the drive will be the second drive installed on the cable, then set the drive to slave. If the drive is the only drive on the

11

A+CORE
1.2

cable, choose master, because single is not a choice. The cable select setting is used if a special IDE cable-select cable determines which drive is master or slave. If the CD-ROM
drive shares an IDE channel with a hard drive, make the hard drive the master and the
CD-ROM drive the slave.

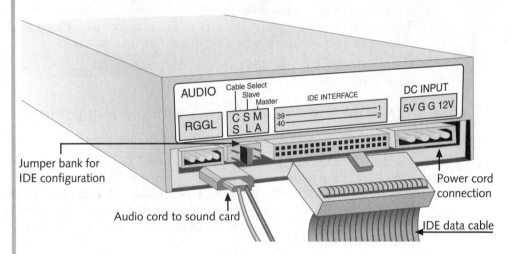

Figure 11-7   Rear view of an IDE CD-ROM drive

When given the choice of putting the CD-ROM drive on the same cable with a hard
drive or on its own cable, choose to use its own cable. A CD-ROM drive that shares a
cable with a hard drive can slow down the hard drive's performance. Most systems today
have two IDE connections on the motherboard, so most likely you will be able to use
IDE2 for the CD-ROM drive.

Follow these general steps to install a CD-ROM drive, using safety precautions to protect
the system against ESD:

1. Open the case and slide the drive into an empty bay. If the bay uses rails, screw
   the rails in place. If you have no rails, then put two screws on each side of the
   drive, tightening the screws so the drive can't shift, but avoiding overtightening
   them. Use the screws that come with the drive; screws that are too long can
   damage the drive. If necessary, buy a mounting kit to extend the sides of the
   drive so that it fits into the bay and attaches securely.

2. Connect a power cord to the drive.

3. For IDE drives, connect the 40-pin cable to the IDE adapter and the drive,
   being careful to follow the pin 1 rule: match the edge color on the cable to
   pin 1 on both the adapter card and the drive. Generally, the colored edge is closest
   to the power connector.

4. Attach the audio cord if you have a sound card. Don't make the mistake of attaching a miniature power cord designed for a 3 ½-inch disk drive coming from the power supply to the audio input connector on the sound card. The connections appear to fit, but you'll probably destroy the drive by doing so.

5. Some drives have a ground connection, with one end of the ground cable attaching to the computer case. Follow the directions included with the drive.

6. Check all connections and turn on the power. Press the eject button on the front of the drive. If it works, then you know power is getting to the drive. Put the case cover back on.

7. Turn on the PC. If the drive is Plug and Play, Windows automatically launches the Found New Hardware Wizard. Windows supports IDE CD-ROM drives using its own internal 32-bit drivers without add-on drivers, so the installation of drivers requires little intervention on your part. If the Found New Hardware Wizard does not launch, click **Start**, **Settings**, **Control Panel**, and double-click **Add New Hardware**. Click **Next** when you are prompted to begin installing the software for the new device. Complete the installation by following the directions of the Add New Hardware Wizard.

8. Windows assigns the next available drive letter to the drive. To dictate what the drive letter should be, use Device Manager. Access Device Manager, select the CD-ROM drive, and click **Properties**, then click the **Settings** tab (see Figure 11-8), where the drive is designated E:. Select a range of letters to be used by the drive, and click **OK**.

When you update or install additional features on applications software, some software expects the same drive letter to be used as when the CD-ROM drive was first installed. Permanently setting the CD-ROM drive letter satisfies the requirements of this software.

9. The drive is now ready to use. Press the eject button to open the drive shelf, and place a CD in the drive. Data on CDs is written only on the bottom, so be careful to protect it. Now access the CD using Explorer (use the assigned drive letter).

If you have a problem reading the CD, verify that you placed the CD in the tray label-side-up and that the format is compatible with your drive. If one CD doesn't work, try another—the first CD may be defective or scratched.

A CD-ROM drive can be set so that when you insert a CD, software on the CD automatically executes, a feature called Autorun or Autoplay. To turn the feature on, from Device Manager, right-click the CD-ROM drive and select Properties. From the Properties window, select the Settings tab and select Auto insert notification. To prevent a CD from automatically playing when the feature is enabled, hold down the Shift key when inserting the CD.

11

A+CORE
1.2
OS
2.4

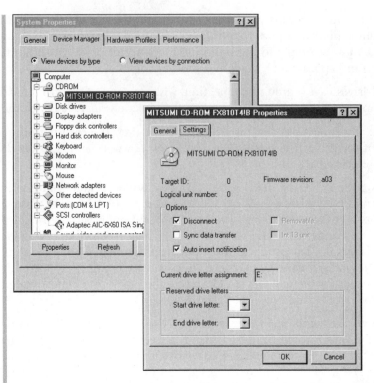

Figure 11-8 You can specify the drive letter assigned to the CD-ROM drive from the Properties box for the drive

Accessing the CD-ROM Drive when Booting from a Floppy Disk

In Chapter 3 you created a Windows emergency startup disk to start a system in the event of a hard drive failure. This rescue disk needs to include tools to access the CD-ROM drive, because Windows is normally loaded from a CD-ROM. When you are recovering from a failed hard drive, you will not have access to the 32-bit Windows CD-ROM drivers on the hard drive. Windows 98 and later versions of Windows automatically add the real-mode CD-ROM device drivers to their rescue disks, but Windows 95 does not. This section explains how to add this functionality to a Windows 95 rescue disk.

Two files are required to access a CD-ROM drive while in real mode: the 16-bit device driver provided by the manufacturer of the CD-ROM drive (or a generic real-mode driver that works with the drive), and the 16-bit real-mode OS interface to the driver, Mscdex.exe. The device driver is loaded from Config.sys, and Mscdex.exe is loaded from Autoexec.bat.

For example, let's say your CD-ROM drive comes with a floppy disk that includes the following files:

- *Install.exe*. CD-ROM installation program
- *Cdtech.sys*. CD-ROM device driver
- Instruction files and documentation

To make your Windows 95 rescue disk capable of accessing the CD-ROM drive when you boot from this disk, first you need to copy two files to the root directory of your Windows 95 rescue disk: Mscdex.exe from the C:\Windows\Command folder and Cdtech.sys from the floppy disk bundled with your CD-ROM drive. Then add this or a similar command to the Config.sys file (the parameters in the command lines are explained below):

```
DEVICE = A:\CDTECH.SYS /D:MSCD001
```

Put this or a similar command in your Autoexec.bat file on the floppy disk:

```
MSCDEX.EXE /D:MSCD001 /L:E /M:10
```

The explanations of these command lines are as follows:

- When the program Mscdex.exe executes, it uses the MSCD001 entry as a tag back to the Config.sys file to learn which device driver is being used to interface with the drive. In this case it is Cdtech.sys.

- To Mscdex.exe, the drive is named MSCD001 and is being managed by the driver Cdtech.sys.

- Mscdex.exe will use Cdtech.sys as its "go-between" to access the drive.

- Mscdex.exe also assigns a drive letter to the drive. If you want to specify a certain drive letter, use the /L: option in the command line. In our example, the CD-ROM drive will be drive E. If you don't use the /L: option, then the next available drive letter is used.

- The /M: option controls the number of memory buffers.

- If the files referenced in these two commands are stored on the floppy disk in a different directory from the root directory, then include the path to the file in front of the filename.

If your hard drive fails and you start up from your rescue disk, once the CD-ROM drivers are loaded and the CD-ROM drive is recognized, you can copy files needed to troubleshoot the system from the Windows 9x CD, which, in this case, is in drive E. If you decide to reinstall Windows, you can type E:\Setup at the command prompt.

CD-R and CD-RW

A CD-ROM is a read-only medium, meaning that CD-ROM drives can only read, not write. In the past, writing to a CD required expensive equipment and was not practical for personal computer use. Now, **CD-R (CD-recordable)** drives and disks are much more affordable, making burning your own CDs a viable option. These CD-R discs can be read by regular CD-ROM drives and are excellent ways to distribute software or large amounts of data. Besides allowing for a lot of data storage space on a relatively inexpensive medium, another advantage of distributing software and/or data on a CD-R disc is that you can be assured no one will edit or overwrite what's written on the disc.

You can tell the difference between a CD and a CD-R disc by the color of the bottom of the disk. CD-R discs have blue, black, or some other color tint, and CDs are silver. When you purchase and install a CD-R drive, good software to manage the writing process is an important part of the purchase, because some less robust software can make burning a disc a difficult process. Also, some CD-R drives are multisession drives, and some are not.

Also available, at a higher cost, is a **CD-RW (CD-rewritable)** drive, which allows you to overwrite old data with new data. The process of creating a CD-RW disc is similar to that used for CD-R discs. The chemicals on the surface of the CD-RW disc are different, allowing the process of writing a less reflective spot to the surface of the disc to be reversed so that data can be erased. One drawback to CD-RW discs is that the medium cannot always be read successfully by older CD-ROM drives or by some audio CD players.

CD-RW discs are useful in the process of developing CDs for distribution. A developer can create a disc, test for errors, and rewrite to the disc without wasting many discs during the development process. After the disc is fully tested, CD-R discs can be burned for distribution. The advantages of distributing on CD-R discs rather than CD-RW discs are that CD-R discs are less expensive and can be read by all CD-ROM drives.

> **TIP**   A CD-R or CD-RW is expected to hold its data for many years; however, you can prolong the life of a CD-R or CD-RW by protecting it from exposure to light.

DVD

A+CORE
1.1

With multimedia, the ability to store massive amounts of data is paramount to the technology's success. The goal of storing a full-length movie on a single unit of a computerized, inexpensive storage medium has been met by more than one technology, but the technology that has clearly taken the lead in popularity is **DVD (digital video disc** or **digital versatile disc)** technology (see Figure 11-9). It takes up to seven CDs to store a full-length movie, and only one DVD. A DVD can hold 8.5 GB of data, and, if both the top and bottom surfaces are used, it can hold 17 GB of data, which is enough for more than eight hours of video storage. DVD uses the Universal Disk Format (UDF) file system.

When you look at the surface of a CD and a DVD, it is difficult to distinguish between the two. They both have the same 5-inch diameter and 1.2-mm thickness, and the same shiny surface. However, a DVD can use both the top and bottom surface for data. If the top of the disc has no label, data is probably written on it, and it is most likely a DVD. Because DVD uses a shorter wavelength laser, it can read smaller, more densely packed pits, which increases the disc's capacity. In addition, a second layer is added to DVD, an opaque layer that also holds data and almost doubles the capacity of the disc.

Figure 11-9   A DVD device

DVD uses MPEG-2 video compression and requires an MPEG-2 controller to decode the compressed data. This decoder can be firmware on a controller card that comes bundled with the DVD drive, software that comes bundled with the DVD drive and is installed at the time the DVD drive is installed, or the decoder is contained on a video capture card. Audio is stored on DVD in Dolby AC-3 compression. This audio compression method is also the standard used by HDTV (high-definition TV). Dolby AC-3 compression is also known as Dolby Digital Surround or Dolby Surround Sound. It supports six separate sound channels of sound information for six different speakers, each producing a different sound. These speakers are known as Front Left and Right, Front Center, Rear Left and Right, and Subwoofer. Because each channel is digital, there is no background noise on the channel, and a sound engineer can place sound on any one of these speakers. The sound effects can be awesome!

Besides DVD-ROM, new DVD devices have recently come on the market that are read-writable. Table 11-6 describes these devices.

Table 11-6   DVD devices

DVD Device	Description
DVD-ROM	Read-only device. A DVD-ROM drive can also read CD-ROMs.
DVD-R	DVD recordable. Uses a similar technology to that used by CD-R drives. Holds about 4.7 GB of data. Can read DVD-ROM discs.
DVD-RAM	Recordable and erasable. Multifunctional DVD device that can read DVD-RAM, DVD-R, DVD-ROM, and CD-R discs.
DVD-R/RW or DVD-ER	Rewritable DVD device, also known as erasable, recordable device. Media can be read by most DVD-ROM drives.
DVD+R/RW	A technology similar to and currently competing with DVD-RW. Can read DVD-ROM and CD-ROM discs but is not compatible with DVD-RAM discs.

The last three items in Table 11-6 compete with one another. All have similar, but not identical, features, so compatibility and standards are issues. It's yet to be seen which of these three media will prevail in the marketplace, although DVD-RAM appears to be moving ahead. When purchasing one, pay close attention to compatibility with other media, such as CD-ROM, and to the availability and price of discs.

Table 11-7 lists manufacturers of DVD drives.

Table 11-7   DVD drive manufacturers

Acer Communications and Multimedia	www.acercm.com
Addonics	www.addonics.com
Creative Labs	www.creative.com
Hewlett-Packard	www.hp.com
IBM	www.ibm.com
Intel	www.intel.com
Pioneer	www.pioneerelectronics.com
Sony Electronics	www.sel.sony.com
Toshiba	www.toshiba.com

A+CORE 1.2

Installing a DVD Drive

For our example of installing a DVD drive we are using the Creative PC-DVD Encore by Creative Labs, Inc. (*www.americas.creative.com*) because it uses a hardware decoder. That makes its installation more complicated than the installation of a software decoder. Except for the documentation and a sample DVD game disc, the parts included in the DVD drive kit are shown in Figure 11-10. The data coming from the DVD drive is split into video data and sound data. Recall that video data must be decoded before being sent to the monitor, and sound data must be decoded before being sent to a regular sound card (one that does not process Dolby sound). In both cases, this is accomplished by the DVD decoder card. Figure 11-11 shows the flow of data in the completed system.

A good example of a DVD drive that uses a software decoder is the Creative Lab's Ovation 16x. This IDE drive comes with an audio cable, IDE cable, and CD that contains the drivers and decoder software. Installation is much simpler than the example here because there is no decoder card to install.

Decoder card-to-sound card cable

DVD drive-to-decoder card cable (audio)

IDE data cable

DVD drive

TV out cable

DVD application software

VGA loopback cable

Driver files
DVD decoder card

Figure 11-10   Parts included in the DVD drive kit

11

To help make the final installation of parts easier to visualize, we set up the installation outside the case and took the photo shown in Figure 11-12. This photo was taken simply to help you understand the final installation. No power was on while the components were in this position!

The DVD decoder card (Figure 11-13) has connections for audio in, audio out, video in, and video out. In addition, there are two other external ports, one for TV out and one for Dolby digital sound out. Use the TV out port to play DVD movies from your PC, and use the Dolby port if you have a Dolby speaker system.

The rear of the DVD drive is shown in Figure 11-14, and a diagram of the rear panel is shown in Figure 11-15. Looking closely at Figure 11-14, note that the jumper is set so that the drive will be a slave on the IDE connection.

Looking at the location of the bay for the DVD drive, we decide to connect the audio cable first, slide the drive into the bay, and then connect the remaining cable and cord. Survey your own situation for the best approach. Follow these steps to install the DVD components:

1. Turn off the PC and remove the case cover. Confirm that the jumper on the DVD drive is set to slave (the default setting).

2. Connect the DVD drive audio cord to the analog audio connection on the rear of the drive.

3. Remove the faceplate covering the bay opening on the front of the computer case.

A+CORE
1.2

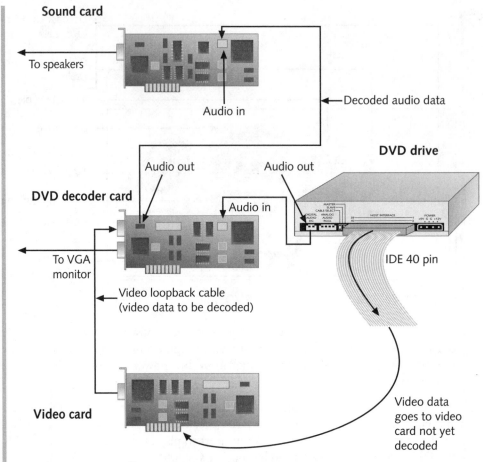

Figure 11-11   Data flow in the DVD subsystem

4. Slide the drive into the bay from the front of the bay.

5. Secure the drive in the bay with two screws on each side of the drive.

6. Attach the IDE data cable to the drive, carefully aligning the edge color of the cable with pin 1 on the drive.

7. Connect a power cord to the power connection on the drive.

8. Connect the audio cord coming from the DVD drive to the audio in connection on the DVD decoder card.

9. Connect the second audio cord first to the audio out connection on the DVD decoder card and then to the audio in connection on the sound card (refer back to Figure 11-12). The cord has two plugs at the sound-card end. Select the plug that fits the sound-card connection.

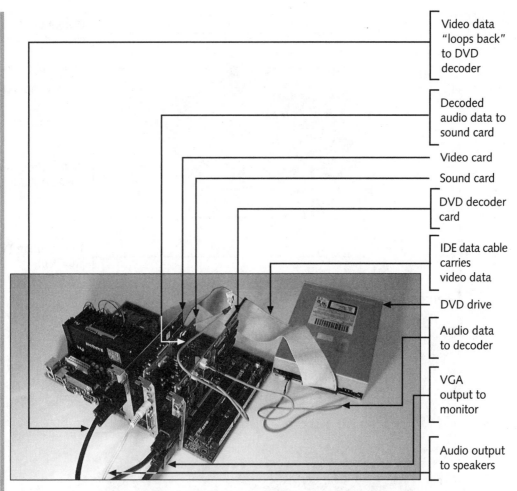

A+CORE
1.2

Video data
"loops back"
to DVD
decoder

Decoded
audio data to
sound card

Video card

Sound card

DVD decoder
card

IDE data cable
carries
video data

DVD drive

Audio data
to decoder

VGA
output to
monitor

Audio output
to speakers

11

Figure 11-12   The complete DVD subsystem, including the drive (right) and various
components installed on the motherboard (left)

10. Insert the DVD decoder card in a PCI expansion slot, and secure it with a screw.

11. Replace the case cover. Install the video loopback cable (see Figure 11-16),
which presents video data to the DVD decoder for decoding before the
decoder sends the video data on to the monitor.

12. Turn on the PC. Windows recognizes and uses the drive as a CD-ROM drive
without additional device drivers. To use the drive as a DVD drive, you must
install the device drivers that come bundled with the drive. Insert the installation disk in the floppy disk drive, and enter **A:Setup** in the Run dialog box to
start the installation.

A+CORE
   1.2

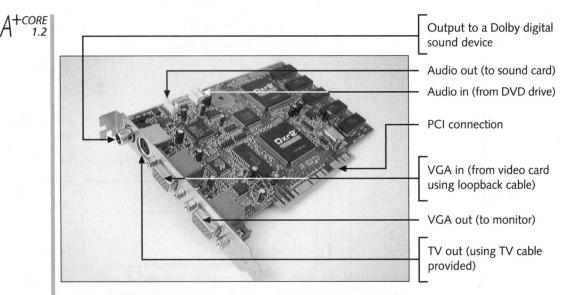

Output to a Dolby digital
sound device

Audio out (to sound card)

Audio in (from DVD drive)

PCI connection

VGA in (from video card
using loopback cable)

VGA out (to monitor)

TV out (using TV cable
provided)

Figure 11-13   DVD decoder card

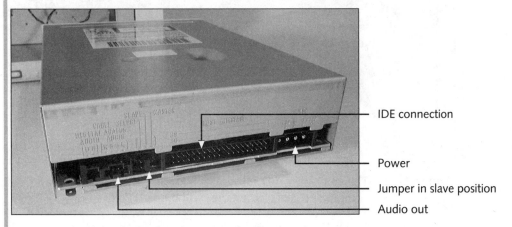

IDE connection

Power

Jumper in slave position

Audio out

Figure 11-14   Rear of DVD drive (see Figure 11-15 for an explanation of each
connection)

In the next two sections, we look at two more types of drives used for storage and backups:
tape drives and removable drives.

TAPE DRIVES

A+CORE
   1.2

Tape drives (Figure 11-17) are inexpensive mass storage devices. They are the tried-and-true
way of backing up an entire hard drive or portions of it. Tape drives are more convenient

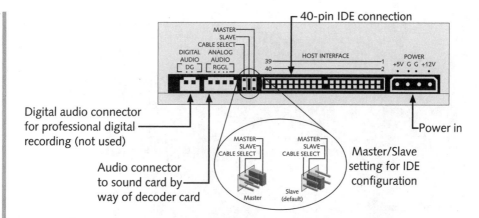

Figure 11-15   Rear panel of the DVD drive

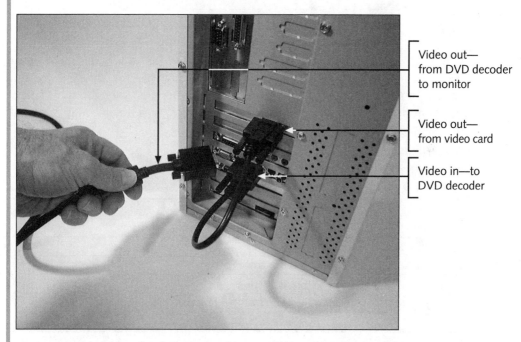

Figure 11-16   The video loopback cable installed in the DVD subsystem

for backups than floppy disks or other types of removable disks. Tapes have capacities of anywhere from several hundred kilobytes to several gigabytes and come in several types and formats. Although tape drives don't require that you use special backup software to manage them, you might want to invest in specialized software to make backups as efficient and effortless as possible. Many tape drives come with bundled software, and Windows offers a Backup utility that can use tape drives. Several of the more common standards and types of tape drives and tapes are described in this section.

$A^{+CORE}_{1.2}$

Figure 11-17   An external tape drive

The biggest disadvantage of using tape drives is that data is stored on tape by **sequential access**, meaning that, in order to read data from anywhere on the tape, you must start at the beginning of the tape and read until you come to the sought-after data. Sequential access makes recovering files slow and inconvenient, which is why tapes are not used for general-purpose data storage.

Table 11-8 lists some manufacturers of tape drives.

Table 11-8   Tape drive manufacturers

DLT	www.dlttape.com
Exabyte	www.exabyte.com
Hewlett-Packard	www.hp.com
Iomega	www.iomega.com
Quantum Corporation	www.quantum.com
Seagate	www.seagate.com
Sony	www.sony.com

How a Tape Drive Interfaces with a Computer

A tape drive can be external or internal. An external tape drive costs more but can be used by more than one computer. A tape drive can interface with a computer in these ways:

- An external tape drive can use the parallel port (see Figure 11-18) with an optional pass-through to the printer (so that the drive and the printer can use the same parallel port).

$A^{+CORE}_{1.2}$

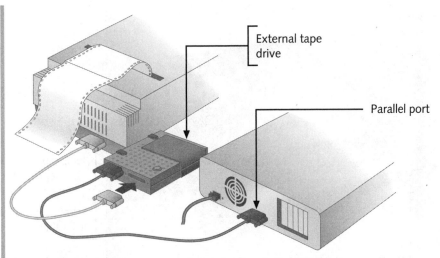

Figure 11-18 An external tape drive can use the parallel port for input/output, with an optional pass-through to the printer

11

- An external or internal drive can use a SCSI bus. This method works well if the tape drive and the hard drive are on the same SCSI bus, which contains a data pass–through just to the SCSI system.

- An external or internal drive can use its own proprietary controller card or the floppy drive interface.

- An internal drive can use the IDE ATAPI interface.

Currently, the most popular tape drive interfaces are IDE ATAPI and SCSI. Figure 11–19 shows the rear of an ATAPI tape drive. You can see the connections for a power supply and a 40-pin IDE cable as well as jumpers to set the drive to master, slave, or cable select. This setup is similar to any IDE device. When installing an ATAPI tape drive, avoid putting the drive on the same IDE data cable as the hard drive, because it might hinder the hard drive's performance. A typical configuration is to install the hard drive as the sole device on the primary IDE channel and let a CD-ROM drive and tape drive share the second channel. Set the CD-ROM drive to master and the tape drive to slave on that channel.

A+CORE
1.2

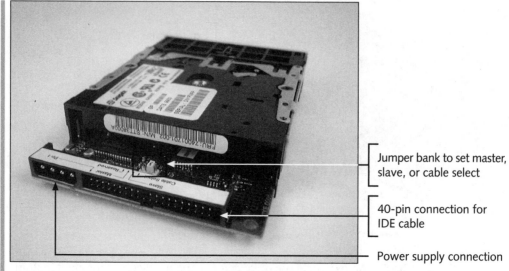

Jumper bank to set master,
slave, or cable select

40-pin connection for
IDE cable

Power supply connection

Figure 11-19   The rear of an ATAPI IDE tape drive

The Tapes Used by a Tape Drive

Tape drives accommodate one of two kinds of tapes: full-sized **data cartridges** are
4 × 6 × ⅝ inches, and the smaller **minicartridges**, like the one in Figure 11-20, are
3¼ × 2½ × ⅝ inches. Minicartridges are more popular because their drives can fit into a
standard 5½-inch drive bay of a PC case.

Write-protect switch

Figure 11-20   Minicartridge for a tape drive has a write-protect switch

Standards for writing data to tapes have not developed as well as consumers would like, making it necessary to match tapes to tape drives carefully when purchasing and using them. Several standards have been promoted by different organizations as well as by individual manufacturers. One group of standards is **QIC (Quarter-Inch Committee** or **quarter-inch cartridge)** which is not used much today. A popular and improved group of standards based on QIC is the **Travan standards** developed by 3M.

REMOVABLE DRIVES

A removable drive can be either an external or internal drive. Using a removable drive provides several advantages:

- Increases overall storage capacity of a system

- Makes it easy to move large files from one computer to another

- Serves as a convenient medium for making backups of hard drive data

- Makes it easy to secure important files (To keep important files secure, keep the removable drive in a safe when it is not in use.)

When purchasing a removable drive, consider how susceptible the drive is when dropped. The **drop height** is the height from which the manufacturer says you can drop the drive without making it unusable. Also consider how long the data will last on the drive. The **half life** (sometimes called life expectancy or shelf life) of the disk is the time it takes for the magnetic strength of the medium to weaken by half. Magnetic media, including traditional hard drives and floppy disks, have a half life of five to seven years, but writable optical media such as CD-Rs have a half life of 30 years.

An internal removable drive should also be Plug and Play compliant, meaning that the drive can interface with Plug and Play BIOS and with Windows 9x and Windows 2000/XP installations without manually setting switches and jumpers.

Types of Removable Drives

One type of removable drive is the Iomega 3½-inch Zip drive, which stores 100 MB or 250 MB of data on each of its disks and has a drop height of 8 feet (see Figure 11-21). An internal 100-MB Zip drive costs less than $100 and uses an IDE interface. The external Zip drive plugs into the parallel port, a USB port, or a SCSI port. The drive and disk look like a traditional 3½-inch floppy disk drive and disk, but the disk is slightly larger. If you include a Zip drive on a new PC, consider it an add-on, not a replacement for the standard 3½-inch floppy disk drive. Zip drives cannot read standard 3½-inch floppy disks.

Two other removable drive technologies are SuperDisk, developed by Imation, which stores 120 MB of data and SuperDisk, manufactured by Maxell that stores 240 MB of data. SuperDisk 120 MB drives are backward-compatible with double-density (720K) and high-density (1.44 MB) floppy disks, and SuperDisk 240 MB drives are back-compatible with SuperDisk 120 MB drives and both sizes of floppy disks. The SuperDisk is really two disk

Figure 11-21   An internal Zip drive kit includes the IDE Zip drive, documentation, drivers on floppy disk, and one Zip disk

drives in one. It can use the old technology to read from and write to regular floppy disks, and it can use laser technology to read/write to 120 MB or 240 MB disks. SuperDisk is up to 27 times faster than regular floppy drives. One advantage SuperDisk has over Zip drives is its backward compatibility with regular floppy disks. A disadvantage of SuperDisk is that the medium is not as popular as Zip drives, so if you plan to exchange disks with other users, most likely you will want to use a Zip drive. SuperDisk drives can be purchased as external (parallel port and USB) or internal drives.

The Iomega Jaz drive is one example of a removable hard drive that stores 1 GB or 2 GB of data on each removable disk. Both the internal and external models use a SCSI connection, although you can purchase an adapter to enable the external SCSI Jaz drive to use a USB port. Iomega advertises that you can back up 1 GB of data from your fixed hard drive to the Jaz drive in five minutes. The drop height is 3 feet.

A+CORE 1.2 Installing a Removable Drive

1.8
2.1

Installing an internal removable drive is similar to installing a hard drive. For an IDE drive, set the drive to master or slave on an IDE channel. If the external or internal drive is a SCSI drive, the SCSI host adapter must already be installed and configured. Do the following to install an external drive:

1. Identify the connectors. Many removable drives use either the parallel port, a USB port, or a SCSI port for connection. A parallel drive has a 25-pin connector for the cable to the 25-pin parallel port on the back of the PC, and another 25-pin connector for the printer cable. A SCSI drive has a 25-pin, 50-pin, or 68-pin connector on the drive for the cable to the PC, and another connector for the next SCSI device on the external SCSI bus. For USB, there might be a second USB connection on the device for pass-through to another USB device.

$A+$*CORE*
1.2
1.8
2.1

2. For a parallel device, turn off your PC and connect the parallel cable from the drive to the parallel port on the PC. If you have a printer, connect the printer cable to the printer port on the drive. Go to Step 6.

3. For a USB device, connect the USB cable to the USB port. Go to Step 6.

4. For a SCSI device, with the SCSI host adapter installed, connect the SCSI cable to the drive and to the SCSI port on the host adapter.

5. For a SCSI drive, set the drive's SCSI ID. You might also need to set the host adapter to recognize an external device. See the documentation for the host adapter.

6. Check all your connections and plug the AC power cord for the drive into a wall socket.

7. Turn on your PC and install the software. See the installation procedures in the documentation that came with the removable drive. Most often, the software is on an accompanying disk.

8. If you have problems, turn off everything and check all connections. Power up and try again.

11

TROUBLESHOOTING GUIDELINES

$A+$*CORE*
2.1
OS
3.3

This section covers some troubleshooting guidelines for CD-ROM, CD-RW, DVD, DVD-RW, and tape drives as well as sound cards. Remember, with these components, as with others you have learned about, not to touch chips on circuit boards or disk surfaces where data is stored, stack components on top of one another, or subject them to magnetic fields or ESD.

Problems with CD-ROM, CD-RW, DVD, or DVD-RW Installation

$A+$*CORE*
2.1
OS
3.3

The following are general guidelines to use when a CD-ROM, CD-RW, DVD, or DVD-RW drive installation causes problems:

Computer Does Not Recognize the Drive (No Drive D Listed in Windows Explorer)

- Check the data cable and power cord connections to the drive. Is the stripe on the data cable correctly aligned to pin 1? (Look for an arrow or small 1 printed on the drive. For a best guess, pin 1 is usually next to the power connector.)

- For an IDE drive, is the correct master/slave jumper set? For example, if both the hard drive and the CD-ROM or DVD drive are hooked to the same ribbon cable, one must be set to master and the other to slave. If the CD-ROM or DVD drive is the only drive connected to the cable, then it should be set to single or master.

- For an IDE drive, is the IDE connection on the motherboard disabled in CMOS setup?

A+CORE
2.1
OS
3.3

- If you are using a SCSI drive, are the proper IDs set? Is the device terminated if it is the last item in the SCSI chain? Are the correct SCSI drivers installed?

- If you are booting from a Windows 9x startup disk, check drivers, including entries in Config.sys and Autoexec.bat, and verify that Mscdex.exe is in the correct directory.

- Is another device using the same port settings? Check system resources listed in Device Manager. Is there an IRQ conflict with the IDE primary or secondary channel or the SCSI host the drive is using?

- Suspect a boot virus. This is a common problem. Run a virus scan program.

Troubleshooting Sound Problems

A+CORE
2.1
OS
3.3

Problems with sound can be caused by a problem with the sound card itself, but they can also be a result of system settings, bad connections, or a number of other factors. Here are some questions you can try to answer to diagnose the problem.

- Is the sound cable attached between the drive and the analog audio connector on the sound card?

- Are the speakers turned on?

- Is the speaker volume turned down?

- Are the speakers plugged into the line "Out" or the "Spkr" port of the sound card (the middle port)?

- Is the transformer for the speaker plugged into an electrical outlet on one end and into the speakers on the other end?

- Is the volume control for Windows turned down? (To check for Windows 98, click Start, Programs, Accessories, Multimedia, Volume Control.)

- Does the sound card have a "diagnose" file on the install disk?

- Does Device Manager report a problem with the card? Is another device using the same I/O addresses or IRQ number?

- Using Device Manager, uninstall the sound card and then reinstall it using the Add New Hardware applet in Control Panel.

- To check for a bad connection, turn off the computer and remove and reinstall the sound card.

- Replace the sound card with one you know is good.

Troubleshooting Tape Drives

A +CORE
 2.1
 OS
 3.3

The following is a list of tape drive problems you might encounter and suggestions for dealing with them.

A Minicartridge Does Not Work

- If you are trying to write data, verify that the minicartridge is write-enabled.

- Are you inserting the minicartridge correctly? Check the user guide.

- Check that you are using the correct type of minicartridge. See the user guide.

- Is the minicartridge formatted? The software performs the format and can take an hour or more.

- Retension the tape. Use the backup software to do this. Some tape drives require this, and others do not. Retensioning fast-forwards and rewinds the tape to eliminate loose spots.

- Take the minicartridge out and reboot. Try the minicartridge again.

- Try using a new minicartridge. The old one may have worn out.

- As with floppy disks, if the tape was removed from the drive while the drive light was on, the data being written at that time may not be readable.

Data Transfer Is Slow

- Does the tape software have an option for optimizing speed and/or data compression? Try turning one, and then the other, off and on.

- Some tape drives can use an optional accelerator card to speed up data transfer. See the tape drive user guide.

- Try a new minicartridge.

- If the tape drive can do so, completely erase the tape and reformat it. Be sure that the tape drive can perform this procedure before you tell the software to do it.

- If you have installed an accelerator card, verify that the card is connected to the tape drive.

- Check that there is enough memory for the software to run.

The Drive Does Not Work After the Installation

- Check that pin 1 is oriented correctly to the data cable at both ends.

- Check for a resource conflict. The tape drive normally requires an IRQ, DMA channel, and I/O address.

The Drive Fails Intermittently or Gives Errors

- The tape might be worn out. Try a new tape.

11

$A+^{CORE}_{\substack{2.1 \\ OS \\ 3.3}}$

- Clean the read/write head of the tape drive. See the tape drive user guide for directions.

- For an external tape drive, move the drive as far as you can from the monitor and computer case.

- Reformat the tape.

- Retension the tape.

- Verify that you are using the correct tape type and tape format.

CHAPTER SUMMARY

❏ Multimedia PCs and devices are designed to create and reproduce lifelike presentations of sight and sound.

❏ All computer communication is digital. To be converted to digital from analog, sound and images are sampled, which means their data is measured at a series of representative points. More accurate sampling requires more space for data storage.

❏ MMX and SSE by Intel and 3DNow! by AMD improve the speed of processing graphics, video, and sound, using improved methods of handling high-volume repetition during I/O operations.

❏ To take full advantage of MMX, SSE, or 3DNow! technology, software must be written to use its specific capabilities.

❏ Installing a sound card includes physically installing the card, then installing the sound card driver and sound application software.

❏ The middle plug on the sound card is used for the speaker out, or sound out, function.

❏ Digital cameras use light sensors to detect light and convert it to a digital signal stored in an image file using JPEG format.

❏ MP3 is a version of MPEG compression used for audio files. Portable MP3 players store and play MP3 files downloaded from a PC, using internal memory and flash storage devices.

❏ A video capture card allows you to capture input from a camcorder or directly from TV.

❏ CD-ROMs are optical read-only devices with data physically embedded into the surface of the disc.

❏ The speed of some CD-ROM drives slows down as the laser beam moves from the inside to the outside of the disc.

❏ CD-ROM drives can have an IDE or SCSI interface, or they can connect to the system bus through a proprietary expansion card or through a connection on a sound card.

❑ The most common interface for CD-ROM drives is IDE, which uses the ATAPI standard, an extension of the IDE/ATA standard developed so that tape drives, CD-ROM drives, and other drives can be treated just like another drive on the system.

❑ Data is only written to the shiny underside of a CD-ROM, which should be protected from damage.

❑ A DVD can store a full-length movie and uses an accompanying decoder card to decode the MPEG-compressed video data and Dolby AC-3 compressed audio.

❑ Tape drives are an inexpensive way to back up an entire hard drive or portions of it. Tape drives are more convenient for backups than floppy disks or other types of removable disks.

❑ The three most popular removable drives are Zip, SuperDisk, and Jaz drives.

KEY TERMS

ATAPI (Advanced Technology Attachment Packet Interface)

CD-R (CD-recordable)

CD-RW (CD-rewritable)

CDFS (Compact Disc File System)

constant angular velocity (CAV)

constant linear velocity (CLV)

data cartridge

drop height

DVD (digital video disc or digital versatile disc)

half life

hertz (Hz)

JPEG (Joint Photographic Experts Group)

lands

minicartridge

MMX (Multimedia Extensions)

MP3

MPEG (Moving Pictures Experts Group)

multisession

pits

QIC (Quarter-Inch Committee or quarter-inch cartridge) standards

sampling rate

sequential access

SIMD (single instruction, multiple data)

SSE (Streaming SIMD Extension)

streaming audio

Travan standards

Universal Disk Format (UDF) file system

11

REVIEW QUESTIONS

1. A variety of enhancements to CPU technology were designed specifically with multimedia applications in mind. Which of these enhancements offered improvements to 3-D graphics and speech recognition specific to Intel microprocessors?

   a. MMX

   b. SSE

   c. 3DNow!

   d. All of the above

   e. None of the above

2. The process of digitizing sound is done by sampling the digital wave to create an analog wave or representation.

   a. True

   b. False

3. When digitizing sound, as more samples are taken, what can be said about the accuracy and memory requirements of the procedure?

   a. The greater the samples, the more accurate the sound wave sampling, and requires a lower memory requirement

   b. The greater the samples, the more accurate the sound wave sampling, and requires a higher memory requirement

   c. The lower the samples, the more accurate the sound wave sampling, and requires a lower memory requirement

   d. The lower the samples, the more accurate the sound wave sampling, and requires a higher memory requirement

4. The minimum sampling rate for CDs that contain music is:

   a. 1,000 samples per second

   b. 9,600 samples per second

   c. 22,000 samples per second

   d. 44,100 samples per second

   e. 88,200 samples per second

5. Assuming an 8-bit per sample sample size, what is the sample range that can be expected?

   a. 8 samples

   b. 255 samples

   c. 44,100 samples

   d. 88,200 samples

   e. None of the above

6. The ability to scan an image directly into an application, without having to first exit that application and scan the image via a different application, is the advantage of using the _____ format, used by digital cameras and scanners.

   a. JPG

   b. TWAIN

   c. Serial

   d. Parallel

   e. FireWire

7. List three types of Flash RAM cards that are used with digital cameras.

   a. _____

   b. _____

   c. _____

8. The most common picture image files used by digital cameras is the _____ file format.

   a. Zip

   b. LZW

   c. GIF

   d. JPG

   e. MP3

9. A file compression algorithm that is specifically designed as an audio compression routine is the _____ algorithm.

   a. Zip

   b. LZW

   c. GIF

   d. JPG

   e. MP3

10. The algorithm that offers compression ratios of 100:1 for full-motion video signals is better known as the _____ standard.

    a. Zip

    b. JPG

    c. GIF

    d. MP3

    e. MPEG

11

11. The ability to play MP3 files directly from the Internet, without downloading them first, is referred to as:

    a. Compression

    b. Decompression

    c. Downloading

    d. Uploading

    e. Streaming

12. Of the two file systems that are available for optical media, which of these are used with DVD drives only?

    a. FAT

    b. MP3

    c. CDFS

    d. UDF

    e. NTFS

13. When information is embedded onto the surface of a CD-ROM, logic 1 is represented by _____, and logic 0 is represented by _____.

    a. Hills, valleys

    b. Valleys, hills

    c. Lands, pits

    d. Pits, lands

    e. Ridge, valley

14. The Data Transfer Rate (DTR) for a CD-ROM drive that is classified as a 10x rating is:

    a. 150 kBps

    b. 300 kBps

    c. 1.5 MBps

    d. 3.0 MBps

    e. None of the above

15. CD-ROM drives can be interfaced to a motherboard using the IDE interface, thanks to which standard?

    a. Primary IDE

    b. Secondary IDE

    c. Extended IDE

    d. ATAPI

    e. FAT16

16. Assume that a user requests a writable CD-ROM drive that will not need to rewrite data to a CD-ROM after it has been written one time. Fulfilling this request requires the installation of which type of CD-ROM drive?

    a. CD-ROM drive

    b. CD-R drive

    c. CD-RW drive

    d. DVD drive

    e. Any of the above

17. Which of the following removable drives has a maximum data storage capacity of 250MB on a single removable platter?

    a. Floppy drive

    b. CD-ROM

    c. Zip drive

    d. Jaz drive

    e. Tape drive

11

12

SUPPORTING WINDOWS 9x

> **In this chapter, you will learn:**
> - About the Windows 9x architecture
> - How to install Windows 9x and how to install hardware and applications using Windows 9x
> - About tools for using and managing Windows 9x
> - About the Windows 9x boot process
> - How to troubleshoot Windows 9x

As a PC support technician, you need to know how to install, use, and troubleshoot the Windows OSs commonly used today. You need a general knowledge of how hardware works and a detailed knowledge of how Windows and other types of software work. In Chapter 2, you learned how hardware and software work together, and in Chapter 3, you were introduced to the DOS portion of Windows 9x. This chapter covers how Windows 9x is structured, how it is used, how it works with various software programs and hardware devices, and how to troubleshoot it. Although Windows 9x is gradually being replaced by newer Windows OSs like Windows 2000 and Windows XP, it is still in use, and you need to know how to work with it.

Windows 9x has had several releases, including Windows 95, Windows 95 Service Release 2 (SR2), Windows 98, Windows 98 Second Edition (SE), and Windows Me (Millennium Edition). Each of these OSs uses the same basic architecture, and each release improves on previous versions and adds new features.

> **TIP** To learn which version of Windows is installed, right-click the My Computer icon and select Properties from the shortcut menu. The System Properties window opens. Click the General tab.

WINDOWS 9X ARCHITECTURE

Like other OSs, Windows 9x has a shell and a kernel. A **shell** is that portion of the OS that relates to the user and to applications. The shell provides a command, menu, or icon interface to the user using various interface tools such as Windows Explorer, the Control Panel, or My Computer.

The core, or **kernel**, of the OS is responsible for interacting with hardware. It has more power to communicate with hardware devices than the shell so that applications operating under the OS cannot get to hardware devices without the shell passing those requests to the kernel. This structure provides a more stable system.

The two most important parts of the shell are the user component and the GDI. The **user component** manages input from the keyboard and other user devices, output from the user interface, and the **GDI (Graphics Device Interface)**. The GDI is a component of the OS responsible for presenting the graphical interface to the user and providing graphics support to output devices. The purposes of each component are listed in Table 12-1.

Table 12-1   Core components of Windows 9x

Component Name	Main Files Holding the Component	Functions
Kernel	Kernel32.dll, Krnl386.exe	Handles the basic OS functions such as managing memory, file I/O, and loading and executing programs
User	User32.dll, User.exe	Controls the mouse, keyboard, ports, and desktop, including the position of windows, icons, and dialog boxes
GDI	GDI32.dll, GDI.exe	Draws screens, graphics, and lines, and manages printing

The Windows 9x core relates to users, software, and hardware by way of several modules, as seen in Figure 12-1. Configuration data is primarily stored in the Windows 9x registry, a database that also contains the initialization information for applications, a database of hardware and software settings, Windows configuration settings, user parameters, and application settings. In addition, some data is kept in text files called initialization files, which often have an .ini or .inf file extension.

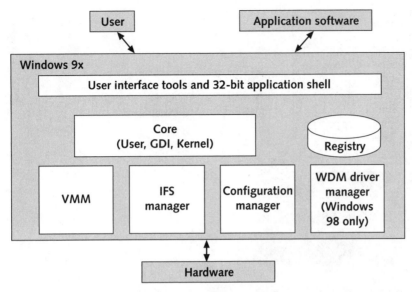

Figure 12-1   The Windows 9x architecture as it relates to the user, application software, and hardware

Virtual Machines

Before we look at the different components in Figure 12-1, you need to understand how these components relate to applications and hardware. Applications call on the OS to access hardware or other software by using an **application programming interface (API) call**. When applications are first loaded by Windows 9x, the methods to access hardware and software are made available to the software through an interface called a **virtual machine**. An application sees a virtual machine as a set of resources made available to it through these predefined APIs. An OS can provide a virtual machine to a single application that commands all the resources of that virtual machine, or the OS can assign a virtual machine to be shared by two or more applications. Think of virtual machines as multiple logical machines within one physical machine, similar in concept to several logical drives within one physical drive.

Figure 12-2 shows several virtual machines that Windows 9x can provide. In the figure, the system virtual machine (system VM) is the most important VM under Windows 9x and is where all OS processes run. It can also support 32-bit and 16-bit Windows application programs, but DOS programs run in their own virtual machines.

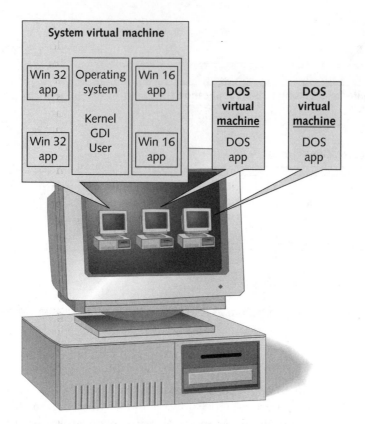

Figure 12-2   Windows 9x uses the virtual machine concept

A DOS program expects to directly control the hardware of the entire PC, memory included. If a DOS program begins to use memory addresses not assigned to it, errors occur in a multitasking environment. Windows 9x solves this problem by providing the DOS program with its own virtual machine. In effect, the application program says, "I want all of memory and all of this and all of that." Windows 9x says, "OK, here they are," and gives the program its own PC, including all the virtual memory addresses it wants from 0 to 4 GB as well as its own virtual hardware! As far as the DOS program is concerned, it can go anywhere and do anything within its own PC. The DOS application program does not try to communicate with any other application program or to access the data of another program, because it thinks there are no other programs; it controls its entire world, and it's the only program in it. That's a virtual machine.

 One important result of running DOS programs in individual virtual machines is that when a DOS program makes an error, the virtual machine it is using hangs, but other programs and the OS are isolated from the problem and thus are not affected.

Windows 16-bit application programs offer a slightly different challenge to Windows 9x. These programs make some of the same mistakes that DOS programs do and can cause the system to hang. However, they also sometimes expect to access other programs and their data. The 16-bit Windows programs don't expect to control the hardware directly and are content to route their requests to Windows. Windows 9x places these programs within the system virtual machine because they communicate with hardware through the OS, but Windows 9x puts these programs together in their own memory space so they can share memory addresses.

A+ OS
3.1
3.3

The result of this arrangement is that when a 16-bit Windows program causes an error called a Windows Protection Error or a General Protection Fault, it can disturb other 16-bit programs, causing them to fail. However, it does not disturb DOS programs in their own virtual machines or 32-bit programs that don't share their virtual memory addresses.

Components of Windows 9x

We now turn our attention to the OS components that create, configure, and manage the virtual machines used by software and the OS. Figure 12-1 serves as a simple but complete reference point for all components of Windows 9x, illustrating how they relate to the user, hardware, software, and to each other. As you can see, Windows 9x architecture uses a modular approach that divides functions into separate program groups, making each component easier to update and implement. The major components are shown in Figure 12-1 and listed here:

12

- The **VMM (Virtual Machine Manager)** is the component responsible for managing virtual machines and all the resources needed by each application running in them. The VMM also manages memory and virtual memory for applications. Virtual memory is discussed later in the chapter.

- The **IFS (Installable File System) manager** is responsible for all disk access.

- The **Configuration Manager** is responsible for the Plug and Play features of Windows 9x and other hardware configuration tasks such as providing system resources to hardware devices.

- The **WDM (Win32 Driver Model)** driver manager, introduced with Windows 98, is the component responsible for managing device drivers. The WDM makes it possible for device drivers written for Windows 98 to also work with Windows NT/2000/XP.

INSTALLING WINDOWS 9X, HARDWARE, AND SOFTWARE

In Chapter 3, you learned how to boot a computer to a C prompt on a working hard drive. In this chapter, you learn how to install Windows 9x from that point. You will also learn how to install hardware and applications with Windows 9x.

Installing Windows 9x

Remember as you proceed with Windows 9x installation that there are separate installation CDs for installing Windows 9x on a PC without Windows (Microsoft labels the OS as Windows 9x for a New PC) and for installing Windows 9x on a PC with an earlier version of Windows (Microsoft labels the OS as Windows 9x Upgrade). The CDs for installing Windows on a new PC are significantly more expensive than the upgrade CDs. To use the upgrade CDs, a previous version of Windows must be installed on your hard drive.

A problem arises if you have just replaced a failed hard drive with a new hard drive and you want to do a fresh installation using a Windows 9x Upgrade CD. During the OS installation, the upgrade CD asks you to provide a Microsoft floppy disk or CD from an earlier version of Windows. If you cannot provide the CD or floppy, the upgrade installation terminates and you must use the more expensive version, Windows 9x for a New PC.

First, let's look at what's on the Windows 9x installation CD and how to prepare your hard drive for installation.

What's on the Windows 9x CD

The Windows 9x installation CD contains all the files you need to complete installation of the OS, as well as some system administration tools, instructions and tutorials, and other utilities. The CD includes a setup Wizard that guides you through the process of installation and does not require you to work with the OS files themselves.

The Windows 9x installation CD includes files you can use for the following tasks:

- Installing the OS
- Customizing configuration of the operating system
- Configuring and optimizing your desktop
- Network administration
- Diagnosing and troubleshooting system errors
- File management

Figure 12-3 shows the opening screen of the Windows 98 CD. It provides links to find information on software available with Windows 98, play video clips showing the multimedia features of Windows 98, browse the CD for a particular file or program, and add or remove software.

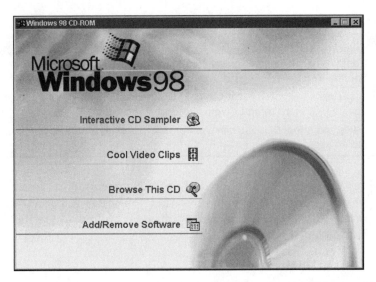

Figure 12-3   The opening screen of the Windows 98 CD provides links you can use to navigate the CD

Important folders on the CD and their contents include:

- *CD sample* contains subfolders that provide a catalog of and demos of Microsoft products.

- *Drivers* lists hardware drivers by category.

- *Oldmsdos* contains old DOS tools that can be useful in setup and troubleshooting.

- *Sysrec* contains system recovery tools.

Table 12-2 lists some important files on the Windows 9x CD.

Table 12-2   Important files on the Windows 9x CD

File	Function
Autorun.inf	Launches the interactive interface for the CD (This is the interface shown in Figure 12-3)
Readme.txt	Explains the layout of the CD and gives the locations of other readme files
Setup.exe	Begins installation of the OS
Batch.exe	Creates files that can be used for automated Windows 9x installations
Checklinks.exe	Contains the Link Check Wizard, which can help you find and fix broken links and program shortcuts
Netmon.386	Contains the Network Monitor, which enables you to monitor network performance remotely for Windows 9x computers

12

Table 12-2   Important files on the Windows 9x CD (continued)

File	Function
Regserv.exe	Contains the Microsoft Remote Registry, which provides a means to view and edit the Windows 9x registry remotely
Textview.exe	Launches a text viewer that can quickly display text files without opening and operating a more complex word-processing application
Where.exe	Gives you a tool that you can use from the command line to locate a specific file on your hard drive

This list does not give a comprehensive inventory of the contents of the installation CD but is an overview of what you will find there. After you install Windows 9x, you can refer to the CD at any time to access utilities and tutorials on how to use the operating system and the tools included with it.

A+ OS 2.1 ## Preparing for Installation

Before installing Windows 9x, verify that the hardware requirements are met. Table 12-3 shows the minimum and recommended hardware requirements for Windows 9x. In order for Windows 9x to perform satisfactorily, the PC should meet the recommended requirements.

Table 12-3   Minimum and recommended hardware requirements for Windows 9x

Description	Windows 95	Windows 98	Windows Me
Processor	486 or higher	486DX (Pentium is recommended)	Pentium 150 MHz
RAM	4 MB (8 MB is recommended)	16 MB (24 MB is recommended)	32 MB
Free hard drive space	50 MB	195 MB (315 MB is recommended)	320 MB

Windows 9x is most likely to be installed as an upgrade from DOS with Windows 3.x, as an upgrade from Windows 95 to Windows 98, or on a clean hard drive. If you are having problems with your current operating system and applications, consider doing a clean install rather than an upgrade. A **clean install** ignores any settings in the currently installed OS, including information about installed hardware or software. Therefore, after the clean install, you must reinstall all hardware and applications. Before deciding to do a clean install, verify that you have all the application software installation CDs or floppy disks and then back up all data on the drive. Also take time to verify that the backup of data is good and that you have all device driver software.

You do not need to format the hard drive, although you should delete all folders on the hard drive used for the OS or applications, including the \Windows folder, files, and sub-folders before you begin the installation. This forces Setup to perform a clean install and

A+ OS 2.1

make certain no corrupted system files or applications remain. If you like, you can also format the hard drive. Do this if you suspect a virus is present. If you suspect a boot sector virus is present, use the Fdisk/MBR command (discussed in Chapter 9) to rewrite the master boot sector program. Then do the clean install.

After Windows 9x is installed, reinstall all the application software and then, if you formatted the hard drive, restore the data from backups. This method takes longer than an upgrade, but gives you the advantage of a fresh start. Any problems with corrupted applications or system settings will not cause you problems in the new installation.

An **upgrade install** carries forward as much information as it can about what the current OS knows concerning installed hardware and software, user preferences, and other settings. An upgrade is faster than a clean install because you don't need to reinstall software and hardware. However, problems with an old installation sometimes carry forward into the upgrade.

You can perform an upgrade or a clean install with either the Windows 9x for a New PC or the Windows 9x Upgrade CD. If you are doing an upgrade, the old operating system must be in good enough shape to boot up because you must begin an upgrade from within the currently installed OS.

Installing Windows 9x as a Clean Installation

You can change CMOS settings to specify the order in which system BIOS looks for an OS on the drives on your PC. You might need to change the boot order in CMOS, depending on how you plan to load the OS. Older PCs could boot only from a hard drive or floppy disk. This meant that to use a CD-ROM drive, you first had to boot these PCs from floppy disks and then install the CD-ROM drivers. There are more choices with newer PCs, some of which can boot from a hard drive, floppy drive, Zip drive, CD-ROM drive, or other type of drive. These newer PCs have drivers for drive types other than hard drives and floppy drives written into their BIOS, allowing you to boot from a different medium.

TIP

If the PC is on a network, it is possible to install the OS from another computer on the network. However, if you want to do an upgrade, you must begin the upgrade from within the current OS. Therefore, if you are performing an installation across a network, you are forced to do a clean install.

Windows 9x comes on a set of floppy disks or on a CD. If you are installing the OS from floppy disks, you can boot from the hard drive or floppy disk. To boot from the floppy disk, insert the Windows 9x Disk 1, which is bootable, and boot the PC. At the A prompt, enter the command *Setup.exe*. You can also boot from a hard drive, go to a C prompt, and insert the Windows 9x Disk 1 in the floppy disk drive. Enter the command *A:\Setup* to execute the Setup program on the floppy disk. Either way, the Windows 9x setup screen appears. Follow the directions on the screen.

> **TIP** Your CD-ROM drive might be configured to run a CD automatically when it is first inserted. This Autoplay feature causes the Setup opening menu to appear without your entering the Setup command. To disable the feature, hold down the Shift key while inserting the CD.

If you are installing the OS from a CD (if your PC can boot from a CD-ROM drive) insert the CD in the drive and reboot. If your PC cannot boot from a CD, boot from a floppy disk or hard drive, then insert the CD in the CD-ROM drive, and enter the command *D:\Setup.exe*, substituting the drive letter of your CD-ROM drive for *D* if necessary.

> **TIP** To speed up the installation, you can copy the files and folders on the Windows 98 CD to a folder on your hard drive and run the Setup program from that folder. Also, having the Windows 98 CD files on your hard drive makes it easier to access the files later when adding Windows components or updating drivers.

Installing Windows 9x as an Upgrade

If you are doing an upgrade, before you begin the installation, prepare your hard drive by doing these things:

- Verify that you have enough space on the hard drive. Delete files in the Recycle Bin and temporary directories.

- Run ScanDisk to check and repair errors on the hard drive. From Windows 95, click Start, Programs, Accessories, System Tools, ScanDisk, and scan each logical drive in the system. From a Windows startup disk or from DOS, enter the command *Scandisk* at the command prompt.

- Run a current version of antivirus software to check for viruses.

- Check Config.sys and Autoexec.bat for potential problems. Verify that any hardware devices using device drivers loaded from these files work under the old OS so you know your starting point if problems occur under the new OS.

- The Windows 9x upgrade process moves commands in Autoexec.bat used to load TSRs required for 16-bit Windows programs to Winstart.bat. Look for the Winstart.bat file in the root directory after the installation is done. If setup does not find any TSRs to put in the file, it will not be created.

- If TSRs such as QEMM386 (a memory manager by Quarterdeck) are loaded from Config.sys or Autoexec.bat, and problems arise because they run during the installation, disable them by converting these lines to remarks or comments by typing *REM* at the beginning of the command lines. Later, after the installation, you can activate them again by removing the REMs at the beginning of lines.

A+ OS
2.1

- If you are connected to a network, verify that the connection works. If it does, Windows setup should be able to reestablish the connection correctly at the end of the installation.

- If you are upgrading from Windows 95 to Windows 98, create a Windows 95 rescue disk for use in the event that the installation fails.

- Decide if you want to use FAT16 or FAT32 for your file system. If you choose FAT16, you can later convert to FAT32 using the Windows Drive Converter. After Windows 98 is installed, to access the Converter, click Start, Programs, Accessories, System Tools, Drive Converter (FAT32). As an alternative, you can use the Run dialog box. For the 16-bit version, enter *cvt.exe*, and for the 32-bit version, enter *cvt1.exe*, and then click OK. The Drive Converter Wizard steps you through the process.

- If you are installing Windows on a compressed drive, be aware that the registry can reside on any compressed drive, but the swap file can reside on a compressed drive only if the drive is compressed using protected-mode software such as DriveSpace. (Recall that compressed drives, discussed in Chapter 9, are hard drives that have a portion of their data compressed in order to save space on the drive.) DriveSpace marks the area for the swap file as uncompressible. If your drive is compressed with real-mode compression software, such as DoubleSpace, then know that you cannot put the swap file on this compressed drive. Best practice is to back up the data and then uncompress the drive. You can later compress it using Windows 98 DriveSpace.

> **TIP** If you used DOS DoubleSpace (available with DOS 6 and 6.2) to compress the drive, type DBLSPACE at the DOS prompt. If you used DriveSpace (available with DOS 6.22), type DRVSPACE. These utilities give you statistics about the compressed drive and also allow you to change the size of the uncompressed part of the drive, called the host drive.

After you prepare your hard drive for an upgrade installation, do the following to get to the setup screen:

1. Start the PC, loading the current operating system.

2. Close all open applications, including any antivirus software that is running.

3. Insert the CD in the CD-ROM drive or the floppy disk in the floppy drive. When upgrading from Windows 95 to Windows 98, open the Run dialog box and enter the command **D:\Setup.exe**, substituting the drive letter for the CD-ROM drive or floppy drive for D. Click **OK**.

4. Follow the instructions on the setup screen. When you have the opportunity to select the folder to install Windows, select the folder that the current OS is installed in; most likely that is \Windows. If you use the same folder, Setup uses whatever settings it finds there.

12

A+ OS
2.1
2.2

Installation Process from the Setup Screen

After you get to the setup screen, the installation process is the same, no matter whether you are doing an upgrade or a clean install. When installing Windows 9x, you have the option of creating the Startup disk as discussed earlier. Be sure to do that to help prepare for emergencies. During the installation, you are also asked to choose from four setup options:

- *Typical.* This option installs all components that are usually installed with Windows 9x. Most often, this is the option to choose.

- *Portable.* Use this option when installing Windows 9x on a notebook computer.

- *Compact.* Use this option if you are short on hard drive space and want the smallest possible installation. No optional components are installed during the installation. After the installation, if you need a component, you can install it by double-clicking the Add/Remove Programs applet in the Control Panel.

- *Custom.* Use this option if you know you need components not normally installed under the Typical installation. You have the opportunity to select any group of components to include in the installation.

During the installation, Setup records information in log files. The primary log file is Setuplog.txt, a text file that Windows uses when it is recovering from a crash to determine how far it got in the installation. Figure 12-4 shows a portion of Setuplog.txt in which the system ran a virus check on CMOS and began checking drives. The Detection Log (Detlog.txt) keeps a record of hardware detected, as shown in Figure 12-5.

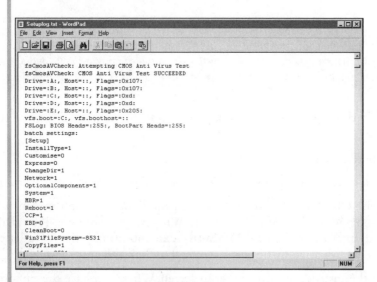

Figure 12-4   Windows records information about the setup process in Setuplog.txt

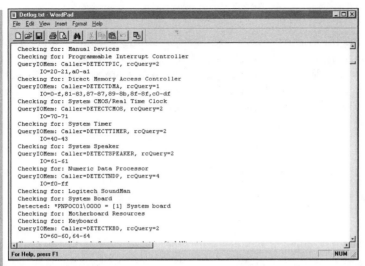

Figure 12-5   The Detlog.txt file shows what hardware has been detected

If the system fails to respond during the hardware detection phase, an entry is recorded in Detcrash.log, a binary file Windows uses to help recover from a crash caused by a hardware problem. Windows does not use the contents of Detlog.txt; it is created only for the benefit of the user.

For example, if Setup suspects that a network card is present, because it sees a network driver installed in Config.sys, it records in Setuplog.txt and Detlog.txt that it is about to look for the card. If it finds the card, it records the success in Detlog.txt. However, if an error occurs while Setup searches for the card, an entry is made in the Detcrash.log file.

If the system crashes while trying to detect the network card and Setup is then restarted, it looks at Detcrash.log and Setuplog.txt to determine what it was trying to do at the time of the crash. It skips that step and goes to the next step, so it doesn't make the same mistake twice.

Although Setup might crash several times during the installation process, progress is still being made. By reading the content of the log files, Setup is able to skip steps that cause a problem and move forward.

> **TIP**   Be careful not to delete the log files during the installation process, especially if you've just experienced a crash. Also, restart by using the power on/power off method so that the ISA bus is fully initialized, which does not always happen during a warm boot.

In certain situations you might want to force Setup to begin installation at the beginning instead of looking to Setuplog.txt for the entry point, for example, when you think you might have resolved a problem with hardware and want Setup to attempt to find the hardware again. To do that, delete Setuplog.txt to force a full restart.

12

$A^+_{2.1}$ OS **Configuring the Windows 9x Startup with Msdos.sys**

In Windows 9x, the file Msdos.sys is a text file containing several parameters that affect how the OS boots. You can change some entries in this file to customize the boot process. The file is a hidden, read-only, system file, so before you can edit it, you must first use the Attrib command at the command prompt or menus from Explorer to make the file available for editing. Also, make a backup copy of the file in case you want to revert to the form it was in before changes were made.

From a command prompt, follow these steps to change the options in Msdos.sys:

1. Go to an OS command prompt.

2. Go to the root directory of your hard drive by entering:

   CD\

3. Make the file available for editing by entering:

   ATTRIB -R -H -S MSDOS.SYS

4. Make a backup copy of the file by entering:

   COPY MSDOS.SYS MSDOS.BK

5. Use Edit.com to edit the file by entering:

   EDIT MSDOS.SYS

6. Save the file and return it to a hidden, read-only, system file by entering:

   ATTRIB +R +H +S MSDOS.SYS

Table 12-4 lists each entry in the Msdos.sys file and its purpose. You can refer to this table as you read about the different options available when installing and configuring Windows 9x.

Table 12-4   Contents of the Msdos.sys file options section

Command Line Variable Name	Purpose of the Values Assigned to the Variable
AutoScan	0 = computer does not scan hard drive. 1 = default. Prompts the user before running ScanDisk on the hard drive when booting up after the computer was not shut down properly. 2 = automatically scans without prompting the user.
BootMulti	0 = default. Boot only to Windows 9x. 1= allows for a dual boot.
BootWin	1 = default. Boot to Windows 9x. 0 = boot to previous version of DOS.
BootGUI	1 = default. Boot to Windows 9x with the graphic user interface. 0 = boot only to the command prompt for DOS 7.0 (the DOS core of Windows 95) or 7.1 (the DOS core of Windows 98). Autoexec.bat and Config.sys will be executed, and you will be in real-mode DOS.

Table 12-4   Contents of the Msdos.sys file options section (continued)

Command Line Variable Name	Purpose of the Values Assigned to the Variable
BootMenu	0 = default. Don't display the Startup Menu. 1= display the Startup Menu.
BootMenuDefault	1 through 8 = the value selected from the Startup Menu by Default. (Normally this value should be 1.)
BootMenuDelay	n = number of seconds delay before the default value in the Startup Menu is automatically selected.
BootKeys	1= default. The function keys work during the boot process (F4, F5, F6, F8, Shift+F5, Ctrl+F5, Shift+F8). 0 = disable the function keys during the boot process. (This option can be used to help secure a workstation.)
BootDelay	n = number of seconds the boot process waits (when it displays the message "Starting Windows 95" or "Starting Windows 98") for the user to press F8 to get the Startup Menu (default is 2 seconds).
Logo	1= default. Display the Windows 9x logo screen. 0 = leave the screen in text mode.
Drvspace	1= default. Load Drvspace.bin, used for disk compression, if it is present. 0 = don't load Drvspace.bin.
DoubleBuffer	1= default. When you have a SCSI drive, enables double buffering for the drive (See the drive documentation.) 0 = don't use double buffering for the SCSI drive.
Network	1= if network components are installed, include the option "Safe mode with network support" in the Startup Menu. 0 = don't include the option on the Startup Menu. (This is normally set to 0 if the PC has no network components installed. The Startup Menu is renumbered from this point forward in the menu.)
BootFailSafe	1= (default). Include Safe mode in the Startup Menu. 0 = don't include Safe mode in the Startup Menu.
BootWarn	1= (default). Display the warning message when Windows 9x boots into Safe mode. 0 = don't display the warning message.
LoadTop	1= default. Load Command.com at the top of conventional memory. 0 = don't load Command.com at the top of conventional memory. (Use this option when there is a memory conflict with this area of memory.)

12

Figure 12-6 shows a sample Msdos.sys file. The lines containing **x**s at the bottom of the file are used to ensure that the file size is compatible with other programs.

```
[Paths]
WinDir=C:\WIN95
WinBootDir=C:\WIN95
HostWinBootDrv=C

[Options]
BootMulti=1
BootGUI=1
BootMenu=1
Network=0
;
;The following lines are required for compatibility with other programs.
;Do not remove them (MSDOS.SYS needs to be >1024 bytes).
;xxxxxxxxxxxxxxxxxxxxxxxxxxxxxxxxxxxxxxxxxxxxxxxxxxxxxxxxxxxxxxa
;xxxxxxxxxxxxxxxxxxxxxxxxxxxxxxxxxxxxxxxxxxxxxxxxxxxxxxxxxxxxxxb
;xxxxxxxxxxxxxxxxxxxxxxxxxxxxxxxxxxxxxxxxxxxxxxxxxxxxxxxxxxxxxxc
;xxxxxxxxxxxxxxxxxxxxxxxxxxxxxxxxxxxxxxxxxxxxxxxxxxxxxxxxxxxxxxd
;xxxxxxxxxxxxxxxxxxxxxxxxxxxxxxxxxxxxxxxxxxxxxxxxxxxxxxxxxxxxxxe
;xxxxxxxxxxxxxxxxxxxxxxxxxxxxxxxxxxxxxxxxxxxxxxxxxxxxxxxxxxxxxxf
;xxxxxxxxxxxxxxxxxxxxxxxxxxxxxxxxxxxxxxxxxxxxxxxxxxxxxxxxxxxxxxg
;xxxxxxxxxxxxxxxxxxxxxxxxxxxxxxxxxxxxxxxxxxxxxxxxxxxxxxxxxxxxxxh
;xxxxxxxxxxxxxxxxxxxxxxxxxxxxxxxxxxxxxxxxxxxxxxxxxxxxxxxxxxxxxxi
;xxxxxxxxxxxxxxxxxxxxxxxxxxxxxxxxxxxxxxxxxxxxxxxxxxxxxxxxxxxxxxj
;xxxxxxxxxxxxxxxxxxxxxxxxxxxxxxxxxxxxxxxxxxxxxxxxxxxxxxxxxxxxxxk
;xxxxxxxxxxxxxxxxxxxxxxxxxxxxxxxxxxxxxxxxxxxxxxxxxxxxxxxxxxxxxxl
;xxxxxxxxxxxxxxxxxxxxxxxxxxxxxxxxxxxxxxxxxxxxxxxxxxxxxxxxxxxxxxm
;xxxxxxxxxxxxxxxxxxxxxxxxxxxxxxxxxxxxxxxxxxxxxxxxxxxxxxxxxxxxxxn
;xxxxxxxxxxxxxxxxxxxxxxxxxxxxxxxxxxxxxxxxxxxxxxxxxxxxxxxxxxxxxxo
;xxxxxxxxxxxxxxxxxxxxxxxxxxxxxxxxxxxxxxxxxxxxxxxxxxxxxxxxxxxxxxp
;xxxxxxxxxxxxxxxxxxxxxxxxxxxxxxxxxxxxxxxxxxxxxxxxxxxxxxxxxxxxxxq
;xxxxxxxxxxxxxxxxxxxxxxxxxxxxxxxxxxxxxxxxxxxxxxxxxxxxxxxxxxxxxxr
;xxxxxxxxxxxxxxxxxxxxxxxxxxxxxxxxxxxxxxxxxxxxxxxxxxxxxxxxxxxxxxs
```

Figure 12-6   A sample Msdos.sys file

A+ OS 2.2 Upgrading from Windows 95 to Windows 98

You have just learned the basic installation process for Windows 9x. This section discusses things to consider when upgrading to Windows 98 from Windows 95. Upgrading is relatively easy, because the two OSs are similar. Follow these guidelines when upgrading from Windows 95 to Windows 98:

- As with any OS installation, you need to check whether your hardware is compatible with the OS you are planning to install. In this case, most hardware that works with Windows 95 works with Windows 98.

- Use up-to-date virus software and virus definitions to scan for viruses on your hard drive.

- You also need to check software packages and programs for compatibility. You can do this by checking the documentation or the manufacturer's Web site for each program. If you plan an OS upgrade, a software manufacturer can often provide a downloadable **patch**, also called a **service pack**, to make the software compatible with the new OS. The search utility at *www.microsoft.com/windows/compatible/* provides a quick way to determine whether a particular product has been tested for compatibility with Windows.

■ Make sure you have at least one full backup of your system as it was under Windows 95. If the upgrade to Windows 98 fails for any reason, you can use your Windows 95 backup to restore the system to the point where you were before you attempted to upgrade. How to perform a backup is covered in Chapter 9.

After you back up your system and make sure its hardware and software are compatible with Windows 98, use the following procedure to perform the upgrade:

1. If your system BIOS runs a program to protect the boot sector of your hard drive from viruses, enter CMOS setup and disable the program because it might interfere with the installation. After the installation you can turn the program back on.

2. Start Windows 95 and close any open applications. If you have antivirus software running in the background, close the software. Close any icons open in the System Tray.

3. Insert the upgrade CD in the CD-ROM drive. Click **Start**, **Run**, and enter **D:\Setup** in the Run dialog box (where D is the drive letter of the CD-ROM drive), then click **OK**.

4. When the Setup program opens, it provides a series of windows to guide you through the setup process. All you have to do is follow the prompts and provide any requested information. Always create the emergency startup disk when you are prompted to do so.

5. After Setup is complete, open and test some applications you already had installed under Windows 95. Any problem you have with a particular application may be solved by uninstalling and then reinstalling it, or installing any patches necessary to make it work with Windows 98.

6. After the upgrade from Windows 95 to Windows 98 is complete and you have verified that your system works, it is a good idea to back up your system again.

Downloading and Installing Updates for Windows 9x

Between releases of OS versions, manufacturers often produce OS updates in the form of patches or service packs that add features, fix bugs, or address security issues. The Microsoft Web site, *windowsupdate.microsoft.com*, provides you with a list of updates available for your OS. In Windows 98 and Windows Me, you can access this page by clicking Windows Update on the Start menu. The update process examines your system and recommends available updates for you to select, download, and install following directions on the screen.

12

Installing Hardware with Windows 9x

A+ OS
1.1
2.4

After a hardware device is physically installed in a system, the next step is to install the software necessary to interface with it. This software, called a device driver, is written to interface with the specific device and the specific operating system. Knowing how to install and troubleshoot device drivers is an essential skill of a PC support technician.

For Windows 9x or Windows 2000/XP, when a new device is installed and you power up the PC, Windows recognizes it and immediately launches the Found New Hardware Wizard. If the wizard does not launch automatically, you can start it manually. Go to Control Panel and double-click the Add New Hardware icon, which launches the wizard.

> **TIP** The Control Panel contains several applets, or small programs, that are used to manage Windows. You can view these applets in a list or as icons. Use the View menu in Control Panel to change their appearance.

One step in the wizard is to select the hardware device from a list of devices. If you click OK, Windows uses a Windows driver for the device, or you can click Have Disk to use your own drivers (see Figure 12-7). If you have a driver on a floppy disk or CD or you downloaded a driver from the Internet to a folder on your hard drive, click Have Disk and point the wizard to the disk, CD, or folder on the hard drive that contains the driver. Sometimes you must select a folder on the disk or CD for the operating system to use, such as \Win98 to locate the drivers to install under Windows 98 (or \Win2k for Windows 2000).

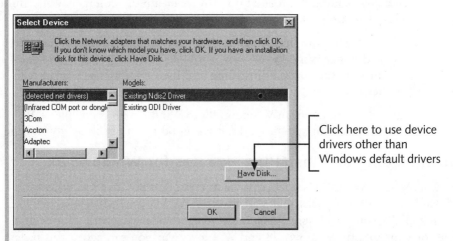

Figure 12-7   To use device drivers supplied by the device manufacturer, click Have Disk

A+ OS 1.1 2.4 Viewing and Changing Current Device Drivers

You can view and change current device drivers from the Control Panel. For example, in Windows 98, to view the current video driver, click Start, Settings, Control Panel, and then double-click Display. Click the Settings tab to view the currently installed display driver, as shown in Figure 12-8.

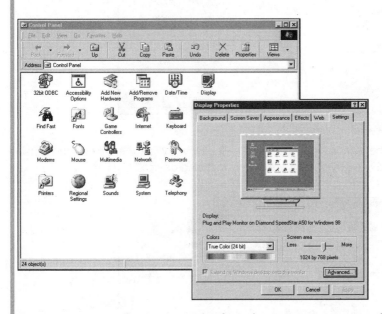

Figure 12-8   Use the Settings tab of Display Properties to view the currently installed display driver

To change the video card driver, click Advanced, click the Adapter tab, and then click the Change button. You see the Windows 98 Update Device Driver Wizard. Click Next to see the dialog box in Figure 12-9, which includes options to let Windows 98 search for a new driver from its list of Windows drivers or to display a list of all the drivers in a specific location, so you can select the driver you want. To provide your own driver, click the second option and then click Next. Then click Have Disk to provide the new driver from a floppy disk, a CD, or a file downloaded from the Internet.

If the new driver fails, try uninstalling and then reinstalling the device. To uninstall a device, access Device Manager (click Start, Settings, Control Panel, double-click System, then click Device Manager), select the device, and then click Remove (see Figure 12-10). Then reboot the PC and allow the Found New Hardware Wizard to launch.

12

A+ OS
1.1
2.4

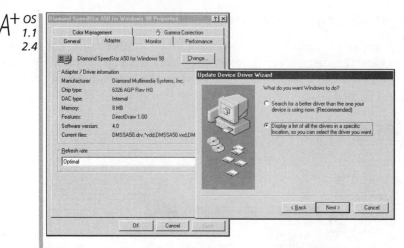

Figure 12-9 The Windows 98 Update Device Driver Wizard enables you to install a new device driver for a previously installed device

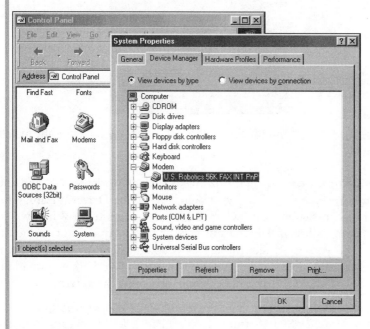

Figure 12-10 Use Device Manager to uninstall a device

A+ OS
2.4

Plug and Play and Hardware Installations

Plug and Play (PnP) is a set of design specifications for both hardware and software that works to make hardware installations effortless. For a system to be truly Plug and Play, it must meet these criteria:

- The system BIOS must be PnP. (To know if your BIOS is PnP, you can use MSD, a 16-bit command-line diagnostic utility.)

- All hardware devices and expansion cards must be PnP-compliant.

- The OS must be Windows 9x or another OS that supports PnP.

- A 32-bit device driver must be available (from the device manufacturer or ˙ Windows).

If all these things are true, hardware installation should be just a matter of installing the new hardware device, turning on the PC, and perhaps providing the 32-bit driver, if it is not included with Windows 9x. During the boot process, Windows 9x surveys the devices and their needs for resources and allocates resources to each device. Windows 9x is free to assign these resources to the devices and avoids assigning the same resource to two devices. For PnP to work, each device in the system must be able to use whatever resources the OS assigns to it.

 Keep in mind that Windows 9x is a compromise OS, attempting to bridge the 16-bit world and the 32-bit world. It makes many compromises between these two worlds.

Although it supports 16-bit device drivers and applications, Windows 9x works better using 32-bit drivers and 32-bit applications for four main reasons:

- 32-bit drivers and applications are generally much faster than 16-bit software.

- 32-bit drivers and applications can be stored in extended memory, releasing more of the first megabyte of memory.

- 32-bit drivers can be loaded dynamically, meaning that they are loaded into memory when needed and removed when not needed, thus conserving memory. In contrast, 16-bit drivers must be stored in conventional or upper memory and remain there as long as the OS is running.

- 32-bit applications can share data with other 32-bit applications, are generally better designed, and make better use of OS resources.

If you are using older 16-bit drivers under Windows 9x, search for 32-bit drivers to replace them. Look on the device manufacturer's Web site or the Microsoft Web site.

12

A^+ OS
2.4

> **TIP** To learn whether a driver is 16-bit or 32-bit, look at how Windows loads it. If the driver is a 32-bit driver written for Windows 9x, it is loaded from the registry. System.ini can contain both 16-bit and 32-bit drivers. If the driver is loaded from Autoexec.bat or Config.sys, it is a 16-bit driver written for DOS.

During the Windows 9x installation, Windows 9x setup tries to substitute 32-bit drivers for all 16-bit drivers it finds in use, and, if it can, eliminates the Autoexec.bat and Config.sys files altogether. However, if it can't substitute a 32-bit driver for an older 16-bit driver, it puts (or keeps) the proper lines in the Config.sys file and sets itself up to use the older driver.

Installing Applications in Windows 9x

As the bridge between earlier and later versions of Windows, Windows 9x can use both 16-bit and 32-bit software. This section shows you how to install both.

Preparing for Software Installation

As with installing hardware, you can do several things to prepare your system and to increase the likelihood that installing software on Windows 9x will be successful:

- *Check available resources*. Check your computer resources to make sure you have (1) enough space on your hard drive, (2) the minimum requirements for memory, and (3) the proper CPU and video monitor. Read the documentation for the software you are installing, and make sure you can fulfill any other requirements of the particular software program. The minimum requirements for the software should be listed in the installation manual. Remember that you should not completely fill your hard drive with software and data, because the operating system needs extra space for temporary files and for the swap file, which changes size depending on how much space is needed.

> **TIP** For best performance with Windows 9x, allow a minimum of 100 MB of unused hard drive space for working temporary files used by applications.

- *Protect the original software*. After the installation is complete, put the original floppy disks or CDs from which you installed the software in a safe place. If you have the original software handy, reinstalling it will be easier should something go wrong with the installed software.

- *Back up the registry and system configuration files*. Many older software packages edit Config.sys, Autoexec.bat, Win.ini, and/or System.ini files during the installation. Newer software might add its own entries to the Windows registry. Before you begin the installation, make backup copies of all these files so that you can backtrack if you want to. (You will learn more about backing up the registry later in the chapter.)

Performing Software Installation

To install software designed for Windows 9x, access the Control Panel and double-click the Add/Remove Programs icon. Insert the software CD in the CD-ROM drive or the floppy disk in the floppy disk drive, and then click the Install button. Follow directions on the setup screen. If the CD-ROM drive is set to Autorun, a setup screen might appear automatically as soon as you insert the software installation CD in the drive. For older software, click Start and Run to display the Run dialog box. Enter the drive and name of the installation program, for example, *A:Install* or *D:Setup*. Either way, the installation program loads and begins executing. If the installation program asks you a question you cannot answer, you can always abandon the installation and try again later.

Most software asks you for a serial number unique to your copy of the software. The number is probably written on the CD-ROM or on the first floppy disk, or it might be stamped on the documentation. Write the serial number on the floppy disk or on the CD case, so that you have it if you lose the documentation later. Copyright agreements often allow you to install the software on only one computer at a time. This serial number identifies the copy of the software that you have installed on this machine.

After the installation is complete and the software is working, update your backup copies of Autoexec.bat, Config.sys, System.ini, Win.ini, and the registry so that they, too, reflect the changes that the application software made to these configuration files.

Troubleshooting Software Installations

If you have difficulty installing software in Windows 9x, try the following:

- If an application locks up when you first open it, try deleting all files and folders under \Windows\Temp. A software installation sometimes leaves files and folders in the Windows temporary directories. To conserve space on the hard drive, delete all files and folders under \Windows\Temp.

- Look at the Readme.htm hypertext file in the \Windows directory, which will point you to the Programs.txt file, also in the \Windows directory. If there is a software problem that was known when Windows shipped, information about the problem and what to do about it might be in these text files. You can also check the Web site of the software manufacturer or the Microsoft Web site for additional insight.

12

TIP A **hypertext** file is a text file that contains hypertext tags to format the file and create hyperlinks to different points in the file or to other files. Hypertext files are used on the World Wide Web and are read and displayed using a Web browser such as Microsoft Internet Explorer or Netscape Navigator. To read a hypertext file using Windows Explorer, double-click the filename and your default browser will open the file.

Supporting DOS Applications Under Windows 9x

Windows 3.x used **PIF (program information file)** files to manage the virtual machine environment for DOS applications and provided a PIF editor to alter these files. Each application had its own PIF file that was used to specify the DOS environment that Windows 3.x created for it. If an application had no PIF file, Windows 3.x used the settings in the _Default.pif file in the \Windows\System folder.

Windows 9x manages the environment for DOS applications in a similar, but slightly different, fashion. The Apps.inf file contains a section named [PIF95] that contains a master list of settings to be used for all DOS applications listed in the file.

If you want to customize the settings for a DOS application, use the Properties feature of the DOS program file, which creates an individual PIF for the program file and serves as the PIF editor. Right-click the program filename, and select Properties from the menu that appears. Windows searches for the program's PIF file and, if none is found, creates one using default values. If Windows 9x was installed over Windows 3.x, then _Default.pif still exists in the \Windows\System directory and default values are read from it. Regardless of where the default values come from, any changes made are stored in the PIF for the application. To make the changes, using Explorer, right-click the program filename and select Properties from the shortcut menu. Click the Program tab. (*Note*: the Program tab will not be present for Windows applications.) See Figure 12-11.

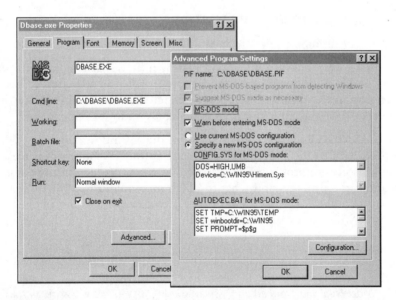

Figure 12-11   Properties sheets for a DOS application affect the way Windows 9x provides an environment for the application

If you select Use current MS-DOS configuration, Windows executes the contents of Dosstart.bat, stored in the Windows folder. **Dosstart.bat** is a type of Autoexec.bat file that executes in two situations: when you select Restart the computer in MS-DOS mode from the shutdown menu, or when you run a program in MS-DOS mode. This file can be used to load real-mode device drivers, but Set commands are not executed.

If you select Specify a new MS-DOS configuration, you can change the Autoexec.bat and Config.sys files used for this MS-DOS mode only. For example, if the application runs slowly in DOS mode and does a lot of disk accessing, you can add entries to run real-mode SmartDrive here. SmartDrive is a 16-bit driver used to manage disk caching. It is not normally run under Windows 9x, having been replaced by the faster 32-bit Vcache, which is built into Windows 9x. In this situation, since Windows 9x does not manage disk access in MS-DOS mode, loading SmartDrive from this window is appropriate, since Vcache will not be running.

Real Mode vs. Virtual Real Mode

An OS that supports protected mode can allow a 16-bit program written to work in real mode to run in virtual real mode (sometimes referred to as virtual DOS mode). Figure 12-12 shows the difference between real mode and virtual real mode. In virtual real mode, the program "thinks" it is really working in a real-mode environment. It "thinks" that:

- It is the only program running.
- It has all memory available to it, all 1,024K of memory addresses that directly point to RAM.
- It accesses data using a 16-bit data path.

Underneath this environment, the OS is managing memory for the application. It receives the data in a 16-bit path but is free to use a 32-bit data path to access memory and is also free to use virtual memory for the data.

Recall the two types of 16-bit applications: those written for DOS and those written for Windows 3.x. DOS 16-bit applications expect to run in real mode with no other applications running with them. A Windows 3.x 16-bit application expects to allow Windows to manage memory for it and expects that other applications might also be running in a cooperative multitasking environment.

12

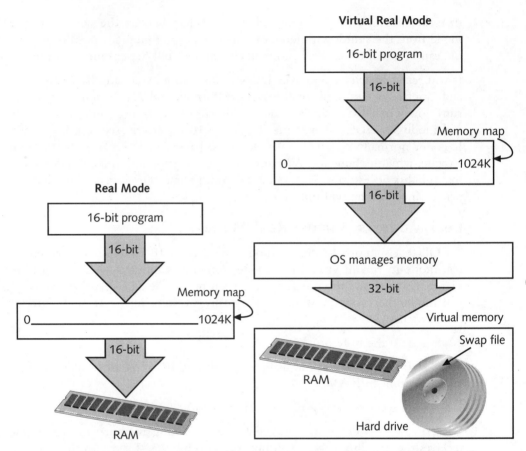

Figure 12-12   Virtual real mode provides "DOS in a box" to a 16-bit application that was written to run in real mode

When Windows 9x runs a 16-bit DOS application, the application ordinarily runs in virtual DOS mode in a virtual DOS machine (VDM), sometimes called a **DOS box**, rather than in real mode. In a VDM, the application "thinks" it is running in real mode, but the OS is managing hardware resources using 32-bit drivers and providing virtual memory to the application. If you want a DOS application to have a "real" real mode rather than a virtual real mode, access the Properties box for the application. For example, once again using Edit.com as our example of a 16-bit application, right-click the program filename in Explorer (or right-click the shortcut icon to the program), and select Properties. Click the Program tab and click Advanced. The Advanced Program Settings box appears (refer back to Figure 12-11). Click MS-DOS mode to run the application in real mode. You can then choose to give the program its own private set of Config.sys and Autoexec.bat settings to be executed before the program runs. This information is stored in the PIF created for the shortcut. When you execute the shortcut or program, Windows 9x shuts down and reboots in real mode before executing the program.

> **TIP** To access real mode in Windows 9x, select Start and Shutdown. When the Shut Down Windows dialog box appears, select Restart in MS-DOS mode.

TOOLS TO MANAGE AND TROUBLESHOOT WINDOWS 9X

A+ OS
1.5
3.2

Now that you know how to install and upgrade Windows 9x and how to install hardware and software, let's look at some tools used with it. As a PC technician, you need to be familiar with a wide variety of ways to manage and troubleshoot Windows 9x, from simple keyboard shortcuts and desktop tasks to tools such as Device Manager and Dr. Watson. Table 12-5 lists several tools to monitor and improve system performance, control the OS, and help with troubleshooting. Several major tools are covered in this section.

Table 12-5   Windows 9x system performance and troubleshooting tools

Tool	Win 95	Win 98/ME	Description
Automatic Skip Driver Agent Filename: Asd.exe Location: \Windows		X	Automatically skips drivers that prevent Windows from loading and records problems encountered in the log file Asd.log. To run, select Automatic Skip Driver Agent from the Tools menu of the System Information window.
Microsoft System Information Filename: MSInfo32.exe Location: \Program Files\ Common files\Microsoft shared\Msinfo	X	X	Displays system information, including installed hardware and device drivers. To run, click Start, Programs, Accessories, System Tools, System Information or type Msinfo32.exe in the Run dialog box.
Hardware Diagnostic tool (Hwinfo.exe)		X	Displays the same information as System Information, but in text form. Enter hwinfo /ui ub the Run dialog box.
Registry Checker Filename: Scanreg.exe Location: \Windows\Command		X	Backs up, verifies, and recovers the Registry. To run, select Registry Checker from the Tools menu of the System Information window.
Windows Update Filename: Iexplore.exe Location: *www.microsoft.com/windowsupdate*	X	X	Download service packs (fixes) for Windows from the Microsoft Web site.
System options in Control Panel	X	X	Several applets in Control Panel can be used in monitoring and tweaking system performance.
System Configuration Utility Filename: MsConfig Location: \Windows\System		X	Allows you to temporarily modify the system configuration to help with troubleshooting. To run, select System Configuration Utility from the menu Tools of the System Information window or type Msconfig in the Run dialog box.

12

A+ OS
1.5
3.1
3.2

Table 12-5 Windows 9x system performance and troubleshooting tools (continued)

Tool	Win 95	Win 98/ME	Description
System File Checker Filename: Sfc.exe Location: \Windows\System		X	Verifies system files. This tool scans for changed, deleted, or corrupted system files and restores them from the originals on the Windows CD-ROM. To run, select System File Checker from the Tools menu of the System Information window.
System Monitor Filename: Sysmon.exe Location: \Windows		X	System Monitor tracks the performance of some important system components. To run, click Start, Programs, Accessories, System Tools, System Monitor.
Microsoft Backup (\Program Files\Accessories\ Backup\Msbackup.exe)	X	X	Backs up files and folders to prevent loss when your hard drive fails. To run, click Start, Programs, Accessories, System Tools, Backup.
System Recovery Filename: pcrestor.bat Location: On the Windows 98/Me CD in \Tools\Sysrec		X	Uses a full system backup created by Microsoft Backup to reinstall Windows and restore the system to its state as of the last backup.
Dr. Watson Filename: Drwatson.exe Location: \Windows		X	Traps errors in log files created by applications and takes a snapshot of the system to use for troubleshooting.
Scheduled Task Wizard Filename: Mstask.exe Location: \Windows\System	X	X	Schedule tasks such as MS Backup to run at predetermined times.
Version Conflict Manager Filename: Vcmui.exe Location: \Windows		X	Installs Windows files over a newer file that might be in the \Windows folder and subfolders.
System Configuration Editor Filename: Sysedit.exe Location: \Windows\System	X	X	Text editor to edit files that configure how Windows loads. To run it, enter Sysedit.exe in the Run dialog box. Sysedit automatically opens Protocol.ini, System.ini, Win.ini, Config.sys, and Autoexec.bat for editing.
Task Manager Filename: Taskman.exe Location: \Windows	X	X	Run, switch and end applications, and access the Shutdown menu. To run it, type Taskman in the Run dialog box.
Signature Verification Tool Filename: sigverif.exe Location: \Windows		X	Checks system drivers for digital signatures given them by Microsoft, which ensures they have been tested by Microsoft. To run it, use the System Information window.
Digital Signature Check		X	Identifies drivers that have been digitally signed by Microsoft to verify their integrity. To use it, enable this key in the registry: HKEY_LOCAL_MACHINE\Software\Microsoft\Driver Signing.

Keystroke Shortcuts in Windows

Table 12-6 lists a few handy keystrokes to use when working with Windows, including the function keys you can use during startup. You can also use the mouse to accomplish some of these tasks, but keystrokes are faster for experienced typists. Also, in some troubleshooting situations, the mouse is not usable. At those times, knowing these keystrokes is very valuable.

Table 12-6   Keystrokes that make working with Windows easier

General Action	Keystrokes	Description
While loading Windows	F4	Load previous version of DOS.
	F5	Start in safe mode.
	F8 or Ctrl	Display Startup menu.
	Shift + F8	Step-by-step confirmation.
Working with text anywhere in Windows	Ctrl + C Ctrl + Ins	Shortcut for Copy.
	Ctrl + A	Shortcut for selecting all text.
	Ctrl + X	Shortcut for Cut.
	Ctrl + V Shift + Ins	Shortcut for Paste.
	Shift + arrow keys	Hold down the Shift key, and use the arrow keys to select text, character by character.
Managing programs	Alt + Tab	Hold down the Alt key and press Tab to move from one loaded application to another.
	Ctrl + Esc	Display Start menu.
	Alt + F4	Close a program window, or, if no window is open, shut down Windows.
	Double-click	Double-click an icon or program name to execute the program.
	Ctrl + Alt + Del	Display the Task List, which you can use to switch to another application, end a task, or shut down Windows.
Managing files, folders, icons, and shortcuts	Ctrl + Shift while dragging a file	Create a shortcut.
	Ctrl while dragging a file	Copy a file.
	Shift + Delete	Delete a file without placing it in the Recycle Bin.
	F2	Rename an item.
	Alt + Enter	Display an item's Properties window.

12

Table 12-6   Keystrokes that make working with Windows easier (continued)

General Action	Keystrokes	Description
Selecting items	Shift + click	To select multiple entries in a list (such as filenames in Explorer), click the first item, hold down the Shift key, and click the last item you want to select in the list. All items between the first and last are selected.
	Ctrl + click	To select several nonsequential items in a list, click the first item to select it. Hold down the Ctrl key and click other items anywhere in the list. All items you have clicked are selected.
Using menus	Alt	Press the Alt key to activate the menu bar.
	Alt, letter	After the menu bar is activated, press a letter to select a menu option. The letter must be underlined in the menu.
	Alt, arrow keys	After the menu bar is activated, use the arrow keys to move over the menu tree.
	Alt, arrow keys, Enter	After the menu bar is activated and the correct option is highlighted, press Enter to select the option.
	Esc	Press Escape to exit a menu without making a selection.
Managing the desktop	Print Screen	Copy the desktop into the Clipboard.
	Ctrl + Esc	Display the Start menu and move the focus to the menu. (Use the arrow keys to move over the menu.)
	Alt + M	After the focus is on the Start menu, minimize all windows and moves the focus to the desktop.
Working with windows	Ctrl + Tab and Ctrl + Shift + Tab	Move through tabbed pages in a dialog box.
	Shift + Close (X) button on a window	Close current folder and its parent folders.
	F5	Refresh the contents of a window.
Using the Windows key (key labeled with the Windows flag icon)	Win	Display the Start menu.
	Win + E	Start Windows Explorer.
	Win + M	Minimize all windows.
	Win + Tab	Move through items on task bar.
	Win + R	Display the Run dialog box.
	Win + Break	Display the System Properties window.
Using the Applications key (key labeled with a box and arrow icon)	Application key	When an item is selected, display its shortcut menu.

Managing the Windows 9x Desktop

From the Windows 9x desktop you can make applications automatically load at startup, create shortcuts to files and applications, and make the environment more user-friendly. In this section, you will learn some ways to manage the Windows 9x desktop.

To control display settings, right-click anywhere on the desktop and select Properties from the shortcut menu. The Display Properties window appears as shown in Figure 12-13.

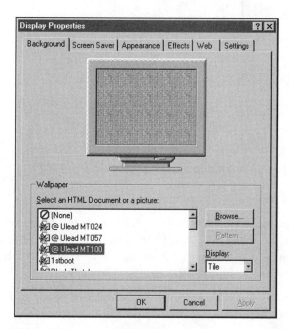

Figure 12-13   The Display Properties window lets you change settings for your desktop

Some of the more common things you can do from each tab on the window are:

- *Background*. Select desktop wallpaper or pattern.

- *Screensaver*. Select screensaver and change its settings; change power settings for monitor.

- *Appearance*. Pick and customize a color scheme for the desktop.

- *Effects*. Specify icon settings.

- *Web*. Set Active Desktop properties.

- *Settings*. Change color range and display size.

A+ OS
1.1
You can also hide and unhide the taskbar at the bottom of the desktop. To do that, click Start, Settings, Taskbar, and Start Menu. The Taskbar Properties window appears. (You can also reach this window by right-clicking the Taskbar and selecting Properties from the shortcut menu.) Then click the Taskbar Options tab and select Auto hide (see Figure 12-14).

A+ OS
1.1

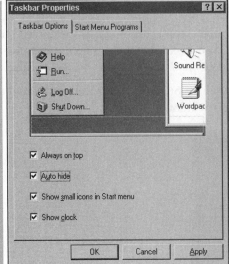

Figure 12-14   Use the Taskbar Properties window to change taskbar settings

Working with Shortcuts

A **shortcut** on the desktop is an icon that points to a program that can be executed or to a file or folder. The user double-clicks the icon to load the software. A shortcut can be created in several ways. One way is through the Start Menu Programs tab on the Taskbar Properties window you saw in Figure 12-14.

From here, click the Add button. The Create Shortcut Wizard appears, as shown in Figure 12-15. Enter the name of the program you want to create a shortcut to, or browse for the file on your computer. In this example, we are creating a desktop shortcut to the Notepad application.

Once you enter or select the name of the program for which you want to create a shortcut, click Next. You then have the option to select where to place the shortcut. Select Desktop at the top of the folder list to create a desktop shortcut, and then click Next. Follow the directions in the wizard to complete the process. Remember that you can create a shortcut for a program or a data file, name it, and select where to place it (either on the desktop or on the Start menu). If you want a program to load whenever Windows 9x starts, create a shortcut and put the shortcut in the Startup folder of the Start menu. All items in the Startup folder execute automatically when Windows 9x starts.

Here are some other ways to create a shortcut:

- Select (single-click) the file, folder, or program in Explorer or in a My Computer window. From the File menu, select Create Shortcut.

- In Explorer, on the File menu, click New and then click Create Shortcut.

- Right-click the file, folder, or program to which you want to create a shortcut, and select Create Shortcut from the menu.

- Drag the file, folder, or program to the desktop.

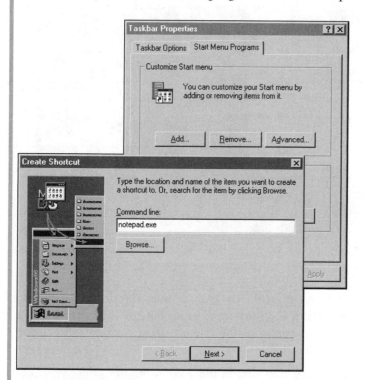

Figure 12-15   Select the item you want to point the shortcut to

> To edit a shortcut, right-click the shortcut and select Properties from the menu. To delete a shortcut, select Delete from this same menu.

Managing Icons

An icon on the desktop can be a shortcut to an application, or it can represent a file that belongs to an application. The telltale sign of the difference is the small bent-arrow shortcut symbol on the icon, as seen in Figure 12-16. The icon on the right represents the document file MyLetter1.doc stored in the \Windows\Desktop folder, and the icon on the left is a shortcut to the file MyLetter2.doc, which can be stored anywhere on the drive. Also shown in Figure 12-16 are the contents of the \Windows\Desktop folder as seen by Explorer. You can add an icon to the desktop by putting a file in this folder. One way to delete an icon on the desktop is to delete the corresponding file in this folder; however, as you will see, this method can cause problems.

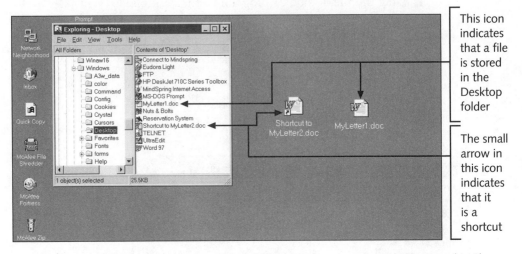

This icon indicates that a file is stored in the Desktop folder

The small arrow in this icon indicates that it is a shortcut

Figure 12-16 One icon is a shortcut, and the other icon represents a file stored in the Desktop folder

If you delete a shortcut icon from the desktop or the \Windows\Desktop folder, such as Shortcut to MyLetter2.doc, the shortcut is gone, but the actual file that the shortcut points to is not deleted. If you delete a document icon, such as MyLetter1.doc, the document itself is deleted.

An error can occur if the actual document file, MyLetter2.doc, is deleted, but the shortcut to the deleted document remains on the desktop. Figure 12-17 shows a sample error message that occurs when this shortcut is used.

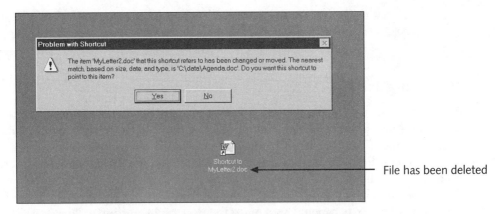

File has been deleted

Figure 12-17 The file that the shortcut points to has been deleted, which causes an error when the shortcut is used

Device Manager

$A+$ *OS*
1.5
3.2

Device Manager gives a graphical view of hardware devices configured under Windows and the resources and drivers they use. Using Device Manager, you can make changes, update drivers, and uninstall device drivers. You can also use Device Manager to print a report of system configuration. When a device driver is being installed, Windows 9x might inform you of a resource conflict, or the device simply might not work. Use Device Manager as a useful fact-finding tool for resolving the problem.

Device Manager is one tab on the System Properties window. To access System Properties, right-click the My Computer icon on the desktop and select Properties from the shortcut menu, or double-click the System icon in Control Panel. From the System Properties window, click the Device Manager tab. The list of devices appears, as seen in Figure 12-18.

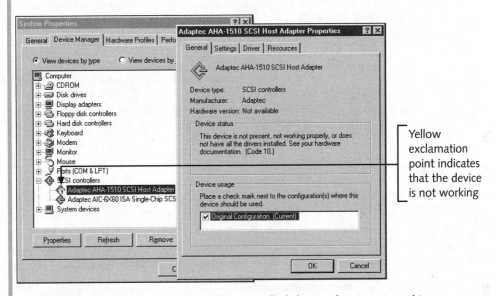

12

Figure 12-18   The Properties box of an installed device that is not working

A + sign next to the device name indicates that you can click the plus sign for a list of manufacturers and models installed. The open diamond symbol indicates a SCSI device, and the three-forked symbol is used for USB. Symbols that indicate a device's status are:

- A red X through the device name indicates a disabled device.

- An exclamation point on a yellow background indicates a problem with the device. (The device might still be functioning.)

A+ OS
1.5
3.2

- A blue I on a white field indicates that automatic settings were not used and resources have been manually assigned. It does not indicate a problem with the device.

- For Windows Me, a green question mark indicates a compatible driver is installed (not the driver designed for the device), which means the device might not be fully functional.

To see a better explanation of a problem, click the device and select Properties. The Device Properties dialog box that opens can give you helpful information about solving problems including I/O addresses, DMA channels, and IRQs used by the device, as well as the names of devices that are also attempting to use the same resources.

In fact, before you start hardware installation, you might want to use Device Manager to print a summary of all hardware installed on the PC and resources being used. This printout can be a record of your starting point before the installation as well as a tool to help resolve conflicts during the installation. To print this summary, access Device Manager and click Print. From the Print dialog box, select All Devices and System Summary for a complete listing.

> **TIP** If you have a problem with an installed device, use Device Manager to uninstall the device. Select the device and click the Uninstall button. Then reboot and reinstall the device, looking for problems during the installation that point to the source of the problem. Sometimes reinstalling a device is all that is needed to solve the problem.

Dr. Watson

A+ OS
3.1
3.2

A troubleshooting tool you can use when you have problems running an application is Dr. Watson. **Dr. Watson** is a Windows utility that can record detailed information about the system, errors that occur, and the programs that caused them in a log file named \Windows\Drwatson\WatsonXX.wlg, where XX is an incrementing number. Start Dr. Watson (see Figure 12-19), and then reproduce the application error.

Next, look at the events logged in the Dr. Watson window under the Diagnosis tab. Use this information to check the Microsoft Web site, *support.microsoft.com*, for the problem and solution. For errors that you cannot reproduce at will, you can load Dr. Watson each time Windows starts by creating a shortcut to Drwatson.exe in the Startup folder.

A+ OS
3.1
3.2

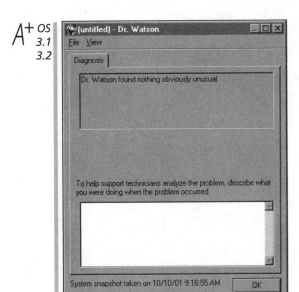

Figure 12-19   The Dr. Watson opening window

12

The Windows 9x Registry

In supporting and troubleshooting Windows 9x, you need to understand the role of the registry and .ini files. The registry is a database of configuration information and settings for users, hardware, applications, and the OS. Starting with Windows 9x, the registry takes over the essential functions of .ini files. However, Windows 9x still supports .ini files for compatibility with Windows 3.x and legacy software and hardware devices. Entries that 16-bit Windows applications make in Win.ini and System.ini are not added to the registry because these applications cannot access the registry. Entries made in .ini files by applications that can access the registry are copied into the registry. In this section, you will examine how the registry is organized, what kinds of information are in the registry, how and why you might edit the registry, and how to recover from a corrupted registry.

A+ OS
1.1
1.2

How the Registry Is Organized

The registry organizes information in a hierarchical database with a treelike, top-to-bottom design. The Windows 9x System.ini file contains setup parameters. Figure 12-20 shows a portion of the System.ini file. Notice that section names appear in square brackets, key names to the left of the equal signs, and values assigned to these key names to the right of the equal signs. The Windows 9x registry takes on a similar but enhanced design that allows for keys to cascade to several levels on the tree. Figure 12-21 shows a portion of a Windows 9x registry. Consider names on the left of the window as similar to section names in System.ini; these names are called **keys** by Windows 9x. On the right of the window are value names, such as ScreenSaveTime, and to the right of each name is the **value data** assigned to that name, such as "60." The value names, called values by

A+ OS
1.1
1.2

Windows 9x, are similar to the key names in System.ini, and the value data are similar to the values assigned to key names in System.ini.

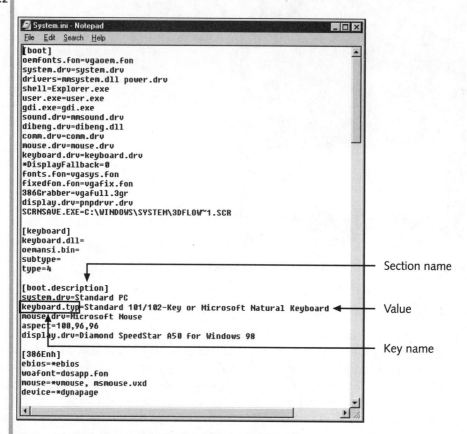

Figure 12-20 A sample Windows 98 System.ini file

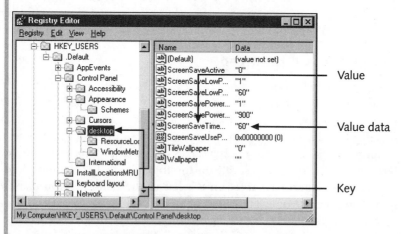

Figure 12-21 Structure of the Windows 9x registry

A+ OS
1.1
1.2

The registry is organized into the six major keys, or branches, listed in Table 12-7. The registry is contained in two files, System.dat and User.dat, located in the Windows directory as hidden, read-only, system files, although the information forms only a single database.

Table 12-7   Six major branches, or keys, of the Windows 9x registry

Key	Description
HKEY_CLASSES_ROOT	Contains information about file associations and OLE data (This branch of the tree is a mirror of HKEY_LOCAL_MACHINE\ Software\Classes.)
HKEY_USERS	Includes user preferences, including desktop configuration and network connections
HKEY_CURRENT_USER	If there is only one user of the system, this is a duplicate of HKEY_USERS. For a multiuser system, this key contains information about the current user preferences.
HKEY_LOCAL_MACHINE	Contains information about hardware and installed software
HKEY_CURRENT_CONFIG	Contains the same information in HKEY_LOCAL_MACHINE\ Config and has information about printers and display fonts
HKEY_DYN_DATA	Keeps information about Windows performance and Plug-and-Play information

12

A+ OS
3.1

Recovering from a Corrupted Registry

Windows 95 has a way to recover from a corrupted registry that is different from the method used by Windows 98/Me. These methods are discussed next.

Windows 95 Backup of the Registry   Windows 95 maintains a backup copy of the two registry files and names the backup files System.da0 and User.da0. Each time Windows 95 boots successfully, it makes a new backup of the two registry files. If Windows 95 has trouble loading and must start in safe mode, it does not back up the registry.

If Windows 95 does not find a System.dat file when it starts, it automatically replaces it with the backup System.da0. If both System.dat and User.dat are missing, or if the WinDir= command is missing in Msdos.sys, Windows 9x tells you that the registry files are missing and starts in safe mode. It then displays the Registry Problem dialog box. Click the Restore From Backup and Restart buttons to restore the registry files from System.da0 and User.da0. If these files are also missing, the registry cannot easily be restored. You can either restore the files from your own backups or run Windows 9x Setup. There is another option. Look for the file System.1st in the root directory of the hard drive. This is the System.dat file created when Windows 9x was first installed. In an emergency, you can revert to this file.

A+ OS
1.5
3.1

Windows 98/Me Registry Checker   Windows 98/Me offer a utility called the Registry Checker, which is not available with Windows 95. It automatically backs up the registry each day, and by default, it keeps the last five days of backups. In an emergency,

A+ OS
1.5
3.1

you can recover the registry from one of these backups. You can also tell Registry Checker to make an additional backup on demand, for example, when you make changes to the registry and want to back them up before you make new changes.

To access Registry Checker, select Start, point to Programs, Accessories, System Tools, and then click System Information. The Microsoft System Information window opens (see Figure 12-22). From the menu bar, select Tools and then Registry Checker. Registry Checker tells you if the registry is corrupted and fixes it, if allowed. You can also create a new backup at this time.

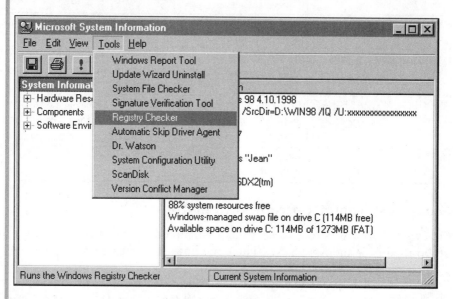

Figure 12-22   The Registry Checker is available under Programs, Accessories, System Tools, System Information Tool; it is used to back up, restore, and repair the Windows 98 registry

Backups are kept in cabinet files in the \Windows\Sysbckup folder as rb001.cab, rb002.cab, and so on. To revert to one of these backups, you must first be in MS-DOS mode. For Windows Me, boot from a bootable disk. For Windows 98, boot from a bootable disk or boot to an MS-DOS prompt from the Windows 98 startup menu. (Windows Me does not have this option on the startup menu.) From the MS-DOS prompt (not a DOS box within a Windows session), use the commands in Table 12-8 to repair or recover the registry.

A+ OS
1.5
3.1

Table 12-8 Commands used to repair or recover the Windows 98 or Windows Me registry

Command	Purpose
Scanreg /Restore	Restores the registry from a previous backup. A screen appears asking you which backup to use.
Scanreg /Fix	Repairs the corrupted registry. If the problem is inherent to the registry itself, this might work. If you want to undo a successful change to the registry, then use the Restore option instead.
Scanreg /Backup	Creates a new backup of the registry at the DOS prompt. Don't do this if the registry is giving you problems.
Scanreg /Opt	Optimizes the registry. ScanReg looks for and deletes information in the registry that is no longer used. This reduces the size of the registry, which might speed up booting.
Scanreg /?	Help feature of ScanReg.

Modifying the Registry

On rare occasions you might need to edit the registry manually. For example, if a virus infected your registry, an antivirus technical staff person might direct you to edit the registry and delete any entries added by the virus. The first step in editing the registry is to back up the two registry files System.dat and User.dat. The next step is to use Regedit.exe, located in the Windows folder. You can use Explorer to locate the file, then double-click it, or you can click Start, then Run, and type Regedit in the Run dialog box. When you do, the window in Figure 12-23 opens. Open one branch of the tree by clicking the + sign to the left of the key, and close the branch by clicking the – sign. To search for an entry in the registry, click Edit and then click Find.

12

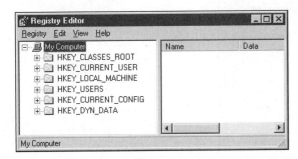

Figure 12-23 The six major keys, or branches, of the registry seen in the Registry Editor

Managing Memory with Windows 9x

Memory management did not change fundamentally from DOS to Windows 9x; with Windows 9x memory is still organized as conventional, upper, and extended as it is under DOS. However, Windows 9x made some improvements in the allocation of this memory and in automating the process that makes managing memory easier. In effect,

Windows 9x, which is mostly a 32-bit OS, "lives" in extended memory together with its device drivers and applications and uses only base and upper memory for 16-bit components. If you are using all 32-bit drivers and applications in a Windows 9x environment, memory management requires no work on your part. Just let Windows 9x automate the process for you. This section covers some other ways memory is managed in Windows 9x.

$A+$ OS
1.1
2.5

Windows 9x Swap File

Virtual memory uses hard drive space so that it acts like memory. Windows stores virtual memory in a file called a **swap file**. The purpose of virtual memory is to increase the amount of memory available. Of course, because a hard drive is much slower than RAM, virtual memory works considerably slower than real memory. For example, a hard drive may have a data access time of 10 milliseconds (ten millionths of a second, abbreviated 10 ms), whereas RAM speed may be 60 nanoseconds (60 billionths of a second or 60 ns).

Windows 9x automates virtual memory management, and Microsoft recommends you allow that. To see what virtual memory options Windows 9x offers, click Start, point to Settings, click Control Panel, select System, and then select the Performance tab. Click Virtual Memory and the dialog box in Figure 12-24 appears. These settings are used to tell Windows how to manage the swap file. Unless you have good reason to do otherwise, check Let Windows manage my virtual memory settings.

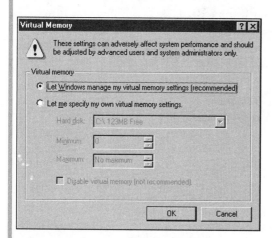

Figure 12-24   Options for managing virtual memory in Windows 9x

One reason you might want to manage virtual memory yourself is to make the file size permanent in order to prevent Windows from resizing the file, which can slow down performance. To improve performance, first defragment the hard drive so there is plenty of unfragmented space for the file. Then set the maximum and minimum file sizes to the same value, which forces the size to not change. If you have the available hard drive space, set the size to about 2.5 times the amount of RAM.

A+ OS
1.1
2.5

Notice in Figure 12-24 that you can specify the location of the swap file. The name of the swap file in Windows 9x is **Win386.swp**, and its default location is C:\Windows. You can choose to put the swap file on a compressed drive, but Windows does not compress the swap file itself, in order to better ensure the file's safety.

Virtual Machine Manager

How does Windows 9x provide virtual memory addresses to DOS and 16-bit Windows application programs? By **memory paging**, which involves swapping blocks of memory stored in RAM to the hard drive. Memory paging is managed by the Virtual Machine Manager (VMM).

As you can see in Figure 12-26, Windows 9x stores virtual memory in a swap file and provides virtual memory addresses to application programs. In Figure 12-25, you see three sets of virtual memory addresses. Each set can contain up to 4 GB of addresses, depending on the amount of virtual memory available. The top set is being used by two 16-bit applications. The second set of virtual addresses is being used by a single DOS application, and a third set of addresses is being used by a 32-bit application. Each virtual machine for DOS has a set of virtual memory addresses. The 16-bit Windows programs share a single set of virtual memory addresses, and each 32-bit program has its own individual set of addresses.

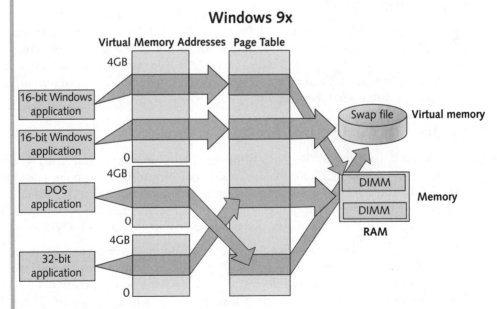

Figure 12-25   How Windows 9x manages memory

In Figure 12-25, all these virtual addresses map onto the page table, which in turn maps onto either physical memory (RAM) or virtual memory on the hard drive (the swap file). Not all virtual memory addresses in Windows 9x have physical or virtual memory assigned to them. These virtual addresses remain unassigned until an application program uses them.

A+ OS
 1.1
 2.5

In Windows 9x, the VMM controls the page table, moving 4K pages in and out of physical RAM. If a program requests memory that the memory manager knows is stored in the swap file, the manager generates a **page fault**, which causes the manager to go to the drive to return the data from the swap file to RAM. This action is called a **page-in**. If RAM is full, the manager takes a page and moves it to the swap file, which is called a **page-out**.

If RAM is full much of the time, the VMM might spend excessive time moving pages in and out of RAM. That can cause excessive hard drive use, decrease overall system performance, and even cause the system to lock up or applications to fail. This situation, sometimes called **disk thrashing**, can cause premature hard drive failure. Symptoms of excessive memory paging are:

- Very high CPU use

- Very slow system response

- Constant hard drive use

To avoid excessive memory paging, leave fewer application programs open at the same time or install more RAM.

BOOTING WINDOWS 9x

In Chapter 3, you learned how to boot to a command prompt. In this section, you will learn about the startup process in Windows 9x, including the differences between booting Windows 95 and booting Windows 98/Me. Finally, you will learn how to cause an application to load at startup. First, though, you'll learn more about important files that Windows 9x uses when booting up.

Files Used to Customize the Startup Process

A+ OS
 1.2
 1.5

Windows 9x uses several files to control the startup process. Recall that DOS requires Io.sys, Msdos.sys, and Command.com in the root directory of the boot device in order to load. In addition, Autoexec.bat and Config.sys are text files that can contain settings for environmental variables and commands to load drivers and TSRs. Windows 9x supports Autoexec.bat and Config.sys for backward compatibility with DOS.

If Autoexec.bat or Config.sys files are present in the root directory, the command lines in them are executed during the boot. They are used to customize the loading process. Just as DOS uses text files to hold information about what is loaded, Windows 3.x also uses text files to hold custom settings that help control the loading process. These files are called initialization files, and some entries in these files are read and used by Windows 9x. However, most Windows 9x settings are stored in the Windows registry rather than in text files.

A+ OS
1.2
1.5

These text files can be edited with the Edit.com program from the command prompt or any text editor from within Windows. The Windows System Configuration Editor **(Sysedit)** is a handy Windows text editor designed to be used with these files. To use Sysedit, type *sysedit* in the Run dialog box. These files automatically appear for editing: Autoexec.bat, Config.sys, **Win.ini**, **System.ini**, and **Protocol.ini** (see Figure 12-26).

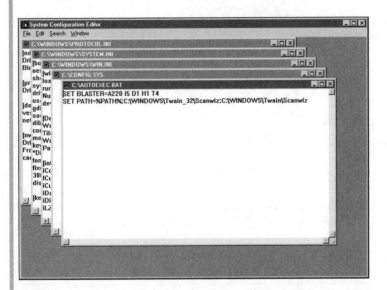

Figure 12-26   Sysedit can be used to edit Windows system files

12

Recall that an **initialization file**, which has an .ini file extension, is used by Windows or application software to store configuration information needed when Windows or an application is first loaded. An application can have its own .ini files and registry and can also store its information in the Windows .ini files and the Windows registry. Table 12-9 shows Windows .ini files, which Windows 9x supports for backward compatibility with Windows 3.x.

System.ini and Win.ini are used by both Windows 3.x and Windows 9x. A sample Windows 9x System.ini file is shown in Figure 12-20. The two sections required for the boot process are [boot] and [386Enh]. Windows 3.x kept many more entries in these sections than does Windows 9x, which really only uses these files for backward compatibility with older applications.

A+ OS
1.2
1.5

Table 12-9   Windows .ini files

Windows Initialization File	General Purpose of the File
System.ini	Contains hardware settings and multitasking options for Windows. The [386Enh] section loads protected mode (32-bit) drivers for older applications, which may cause problems in more recent operating systems.
Progman.ini	Contains information about Program Manager groups
Win.ini	Contains information about user settings, including printer, fonts, file associations, and settings made by applications
Control.ini	Contains information about the user's desktop, including color selections, wallpaper, and screen saver options
Mouse.ini	Contains settings for the mouse
Protocol.ini	Contains information about the configuration of the network

Initialization files are only read when Windows or an application using .ini files starts up. If you change the .ini file for an application, you must restart the software for the change to take effect. If you want the application to ignore a line in the .ini file, you can turn the line into a **comment** line by putting a semicolon or the letters REM at the beginning of the line.

CAUTION

Sometimes it is necessary to manually edit an .ini file that belongs to an application, but you should normally not edit System.ini or other Windows 9x initialization files. Incorrect changes to these files might result in Windows not running correctly, and Windows sometimes overwrites these files when changes are made to Windows through the Control Panel.

We now turn our attention to the Windows 9x startup process, in which these and other files are used.

The Windows 9x Startup Process

A+ OS
2.3

Windows 9x first loads in real mode and then switches to protected mode. With DOS, the two core real-mode system files responsible for starting up the OS, Io.sys and Msdos.sys, remain in memory, running even after the OS is loaded. With Windows 9x, Io.sys is responsible for only the initial startup process performed in real mode. Then control is turned over to Vmm32.vxd, which works in protected mode, and Io.sys is terminated. Recall that Windows 9x includes a file named Msdos.sys, but it is only a text file that contains some parameters and switches that can be set to affect the way the OS boots.

Startup in Windows 9x is a five-phase process, as shown in Figure 12-27. We will look at each phase.

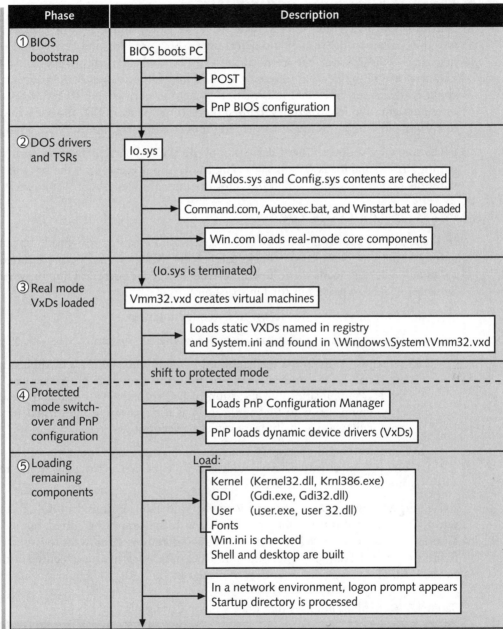

Phase	Description
① BIOS bootstrap	BIOS boots PC → POST → PnP BIOS configuration
② DOS drivers and TSRs	Io.sys → Msdos.sys and Config.sys contents are checked → Command.com, Autoexec.bat, and Winstart.bat are loaded → Win.com loads real-mode core components
③ Real mode VxDs loaded	(Io.sys is terminated) Vmm32.vxd creates virtual machines → Loads static VXDs named in registry and System.ini and found in \Windows\System\Vmm32.vxd
④ Protected mode switch-over and PnP configuration	shift to protected mode → Loads PnP Configuration Manager → PnP loads dynamic device drivers (VxDs)
⑤ Loading remaining components	Load: Kernel (Kernel32.dll, Krnl386.exe) GDI (Gdi.exe, Gdi32.dll) User (user.exe, user 32.dll) Fonts Win.ini is checked Shell and desktop are built In a network environment, logon prompt appears Startup directory is processed

Figure 12-27   Windows 9x core components and the loading process

A^{+} OS
2.3
2.5

Phase 1: BIOS POST and Bootstrap

Startup BIOS begins the process. If the BIOS is a Plug and Play (PnP) BIOS, it examines the devices on the system and determines which are Plug and Play compliant. BIOS first enables the devices that are not Plug and Play and then tries to make the Plug and Play devices use the leftover resources. It also looks to permanent RAM for information about hardware and uses that information to help in configuring PnP devices that have their configuration information recorded there. It performs POST and saves information that Windows Configuration Manager later uses to complete the hardware configuration.

BIOS looks for a device (hard drive, floppy disk, CD-ROM drive, and so forth) containing the OS and loads Windows 9x. The Master Boot Record on the boot device executes the bootstrap loader, which looks for the initial hidden file of Windows 9x (Io.sys).

Phase 2: The OS Is Loaded

In Phase 2, BIOS turns control over to Io.sys, which creates a real-mode operating system environment. Next, Io.sys checks the text file Msdos.sys for boot parameters. Then Io.sys automatically loads the following drivers if they are present: Himem.sys, Ifshlp.sys, Setver.exe, and Drvspace.bin (or Dblspace.bin).

- Himem.sys provides access to extended memory.

- 16-bit programs use Ifshlp.sys to access the file system.

- Setver.exe is included for backward compatibility with DOS applications that expect all DOS components to be from the same version. Setver.exe "asks" the DOS application what version of DOS it expects to use and presents DOS components to that application as if they were all from that version, even if they are actually from different versions.

- Drvspace.bin and Dblspace.bin provide disk compression. One of these two files is loaded only if Io.sys finds Dlbspace.ini or Drvspace.ini in the root directory of the boot drive.

Io.sys also sets several environmental variables to default settings. In DOS, these default settings were loaded from Config.sys. Entries in Io.sys cannot be edited, but an entry in Config.sys overrides the default entry in Io.sys. Therefore, if you want to use settings different from the default, put the command in Config.sys, which is executed at this point in the load. The default Io.sys entries are listed in Table 12-10.

Table 12-10   Entries in Io.sys that once were in Config.sys

Entry	Description
Buffers=30	The number of file buffers to create
DOS=HIGH	The DOS core of Windows 9x is loaded into the high memory area (HMA).
Files=60	The number of files that can be open at one time under 16-bit applications

Table 12-10   Entries in Io.sys that once were in Config.sys (continued)

Entry	Description
Himem.sys	Himem.sys is loaded to manage extended memory in Windows 9x.
Lastdrive=Z	The last letter that can be assigned to a logical drive
Setver.exe	A program that tells DOS applications that the version of DOS they are looking for is the version they are using. The program allows some older DOS applications to run that might otherwise hang.
Shell=Command.com /P	Loads Command.com and executes Autoexec.bat
Stacks=9,256	The number of frames of instructions that can be held in memory in a queue at one time. Used for backward compatibility with older applications

Next, Io.sys loads Command.com and follows instructions stored in Autoexec.bat and Winstart.bat. The default assignments made to environmental variables that were stored in Autoexec.bat in DOS are listed below:

- Tmp=c:\windows\temp
- Temp=c:\windows\temp
- Prompt=pg
- Path=c:\windows;c:\windows\command

The Tmp and Temp variables are used by some software to locate where to put their temporary files. You can change any of these by making an entry in Autoexec.bat. Next, Io.sys loads Win.com. Then Win.com loads other real-mode core components.

Phase 3: Static VxDs

In Phase 3, Io.sys relinquishes control to the virtual machine manager (VMM) component housed in Vmm32.vxd along with some virtual device drivers. A **virtual device driver (VxD)** is a driver that works with a virtual machine to provide access to hardware for software running in the VM. Under Windows 3.x, these VxDs were loaded from System.ini and had a .386 file extension. Under Windows 9x, if stored in individual files, they have a .vxd file extension. They are called **static VxDs** because once they are loaded into memory, they remain there. (Conversely, **dynamic VxDs** are loaded into and unloaded from memory as needed.)

Vmm32.vxd is built specifically for a particular computer when Windows 9x is installed and contains some VxDs critical for a successful boot; each installation of Windows will have a different build of this file. (The VxD drivers now included in Vmm32.vxd were listed in the [386enh] section of System.ini under Windows 3.x.) Vmm32.vxd terminates Io.sys and, while still in real mode, loads static VxD device drivers as identified in

12

A+ OS
2.3
1.1

four different locations. They can be embedded in Vmm32.vxd, named in the registry or System.ini, or stored in the .vxd files in the \Windows\System\Vmm32 directory.

If you suspect a problem with a VxD that is part of the Vmm32.vxd file, then store a new version of the .vxd file in the \Windows\System\Vmm32 directory. If Windows finds a VxD driver there, it uses that driver instead of the one embedded in Vmm32.vxd. Also, VxD drivers are listed in the registry and in System.ini. Normally, the entries are the same, and entries are only listed in System.ini for backward compatibility. However, if an entry in System.ini differs from an entry in the registry, the value in System.ini is used.

Phase 4: Protected-Mode Switchover and PnP Configuration

At the beginning of Phase 4, Vmm32.vxd switches to protected mode and loads Configuration Manager. Configuration Manager is responsible for configuring legacy and PnP devices. It uses any information that PnP BIOS might have left for it and loads the 32-bit VxDs for the PnP devices.

Phase 5: Loading the Remaining Components

In Phase 5, with Vmm32.vxd still in control, the three core components are loaded, then fonts and other associated resources are loaded. Win.ini is checked and commands stored there are executed to allow backward compatibility. The shell and user desktop are loaded. If the computer is working in a networked environment, a logon dialog box is displayed, and the user can log on to Windows 9x and the network. Finally, any processes stored in the Startup directory are performed.

Differences Between the Windows 95 and Windows 98/Me Boot Process

Windows 98 made some minor changes in what happens during startup to speed up the boot process. For instance, Windows 95 waits two seconds, displaying "Starting Windows 95" so that you can press a key to alter the boot process. Windows 98 eliminated this two-second wait and, in its place, allows you to press and hold the Ctrl key as it loads. If you do that, you see the startup menu that is also available with Windows 95.

Loading an Application at Startup

A+ OS
2.3
1.1

If you want an application to load automatically at startup, you can:

- Place a shortcut in the C:\Windows\All Users\Startup Menu\ Programs\Startup folder

- Put the name of the program file in the Load= or Run= line in Win.ini

- Manually edit the registry key HKEY_LOCAL_MACHINE\SOFTWARE\ Microsoft\Windows\CurrentVersion\Run

TROUBLESHOOTING WINDOWS 9x

This section covers Windows 9x troubleshooting. It is important for you to know how to troubleshoot problems that occur during a Windows installation, problems that occur during the boot process, and problems that occur during normal Windows operations.

Troubleshooting Windows 9x Installations

Table 12-11 lists some problems that might occur while installing Windows 9x and what to do about them.

Table 12-11 Some problems and solutions when installing Windows 9x

Symptom	Description and Solution
An error message about BIOS appears during installation.	This is most likely caused by BIOS not allowing changes to the boot sector to protect it from viruses. Disable the feature in CMOS setup.
Windows 9x stalls during the first restart after installation.	This is probably caused by legacy hardware not configured correctly. Try the following: ■ Remark (REM) out all entries in Config.sys and Autoexec.bat. ■ Disable the ISA enumerator by commenting out this line in System.ini: Device=ISAPNP.386.
During the first restart after installation, an error message appears with information about a bad or missing file.	This is probably caused by an error in Config.sys or Autoexec.bat. Try renaming both files so they are not executed. If this solves the problem, then comment out each line in the file, one at a time, until you know which line caused the problem.
During the first restart after the installation, you get an error message about a missing or damaged VxD file.	Run Windows setup again and select the option Verify or replace the missing VxD (virtual device driver).
After upgrading from Windows 95 to Windows 98, the startup screen still says Windows 95.	This can be caused by one of two problems. The Io.sys file might not have been updated. Use the Sys C: command to replace it. The file Logo.sys is in the root directory, which overrides the logo screen embedded in Io.sys. Delete or rename the file.
"Invalid system disk" error appears during setup.	■ Suspect a boot sector virus. Run a current version of antivirus software. ■ If this error occurs while installing Windows when disk management software such as DiskPro is running, Windows might have damaged the hard drive MBR. To recover from this problem, see the documentation for the disk management software.

12

>
> **TIP** For specific error messages that occur during installation and what to do about them, go to the Microsoft Web site *support.microsoft.com* and search for the error message.

Troubleshooting the Windows 9x Boot Process

A+ OS
2.3
3.1

When the boot process does not complete correctly, you can go through these basic steps to troubleshoot it:

1. Check and address any error messages that occur during a normal boot.

2. If you cannot boot to a normal desktop, boot in safe mode and begin troubleshooting there.

3. If you cannot boot using safe mode, the GUI portion of the OS is not functioning. Boot to the command prompt using the startup menu. Use commands at the C prompt for troubleshooting.

4. If the startup menu is not accessible, the MS-DOS core of the OS is not functioning. Boot from an emergency startup disk and try to access drive C.

5. If you cannot access drive C, then the hard drive is not accessible.

Error Messages Received While Loading Windows 9x

Error messages are your first indications that something is going wrong with the Windows 9x boot process. You can use these messages to figure out how to solve some Windows 9x boot problems. Table 12-12 shows error messages that Windows 9x might produce and gives advice about what to do when you see them. Specific errors are covered later in this section.

Table 12-12   Error messages received while loading Windows 9x

Error Message or Problem	What to Do
MS-DOS compatibility mode	■ Windows is using real-mode drivers to access the hard drive rather than the preferred 32-bit drivers. After backing up the Config.sys and System.ini files, remove any references to real-mode drivers for the hard drive in these files. ■ The problem might be due to an outdated motherboard BIOS. Consider updating the BIOS.
Bad or missing file Real mode driver missing or damaged Error in config.sys line xx	■ Verify that Config.sys, Autoexec.bat (root directory of the hard drive) and System.ini (Windows folder) are present and in the right location. ■ Check Config.sys and Autoexec.bat for errors using the step-by-step confirmation option from the Windows 9x startup menu. To check System.ini, rename the file so that it will not be used and boot with a bare bones version of the file. ■ Look in the Win.ini file for applications that are attempting to load at startup but have been deleted or uninstalled. Check the Load= or Run= lines.

A+ OS
2.3
3.1

Table 12-12   Error messages received while loading Windows 9x (continued)

Error Message or Problem	What to Do
Cannot open file *.inf	■ This error is caused by insufficient memory. Disable any TSRs running in Autoexec.bat. ■ Close any applications that are running or remove them from the Start folder.
Insufficient disk space	■ Run ScanDisk and Defragmenter. Check free space on the hard drive.
Invalid system disk Bad or missing command.com	■ Suspect a boot sector virus. Run a current version of antivirus software. ■ Io.sys could be missing or corrupted. Restore the file from a backup or an emergency startup disk. To restore all real-mode files needed to begin loading Windows 9x, do the following: (1) boot from a Windows 9x emergency startup disk, (2) restore Io.sys, Msdos.sys, Drvspace.bin, and Command.com by executing the command SYS C:, (3) remove the floppy disk and reboot.
Invalid VxD dynamic link call from IFSMGR	This error is caused by a missing or corrupted Msdos.sys file. Restore the file from a backup or from an emergency startup disk.
Missing system files	Run the SYS C: command.
System Registry file missing	Either System.dat or User.dat is corrupted or missing. For Windows 95, restore them by using either System.da0 or User.da0. For Windows 98/Me, run ScanReg.
VxD error returns to command prompt	A VxD file is missing or corrupted. Run Windows Setup from the Windows 9x CD and choose Verify installed components.
Error containing the text "Kernel32.dll"	An error that contains this text probably indicates a corrupted kernel. Try restoring system files. If that doesn't work, reinstall Windows. *Note*: this error may appear at other times, not just during the boot process.

12

Windows has several tools you can use to help troubleshoot problems with booting.

- Use System Configuration Utility (Msconfig) to limit what loads during the boot in order to attain the cleanest possible boot.

- Use Device Manager to disable a device that you think is causing a problem.

- Use Automatic Skip Driver Agent (ASDA) to keep Windows from installing a driver that might be corrupted, including built-in Windows drivers.

- The Windows 9x startup menu includes safe mode, the command prompt, and other troubleshooting options.

Microsoft Windows 9x Startup Menu

Normally, when you load Windows, the message "Starting Windows" appears and then the OS loads. However, you can force the menu to appear rather than the "Starting Windows" message by tapping the F8 key or holding down the Ctrl key during the boot.

Startup Menu Options

A+ OS
2.3
3.1

The Microsoft Windows 9x startup menu options are:

1. Normal

2. Logged (\BOOTLOG.TXT)

3. Safe Mode

4. Safe Mode with network support

5. Step-by-step confirmation

6. Command prompt only

7. Safe Mode command prompt only

8. Previous version of MS-DOS

What to expect when you select each option on the menu is described next. Option 4 appears if the OS is configured for a network, and Option 8 appears if a previous version of DOS was retained during the Windows 9x installation.

Normal   In Msdos.sys, if BootGUI=1, then this option starts Windows 9x. If BootGUI=0, then this option boots to the DOS 7.0 or DOS 7.1 prompt (the DOS core of Windows 9x). Either way, the commands in Autoexec.bat and Config.sys are executed.

If a problem appears when you boot in normal mode but does not appear when you boot in safe mode, then suspect that Config.sys, Autoexec.bat, System.ini, and Win.ini are the sources of your problem. To eliminate Config.sys or Autoexec.bat as the source of the problem, boot using the step-by-step confirmation option on the startup menu. To eliminate Win.ini or System.ini as the source of the problem, use the following procedure:

1. Change the name of the System.ini file in the Windows folder to System.sav.

2. Find the System.cb file in the Windows folder and make a copy of it. Rename the copy System.ini. Do not rename the original System.cb file because you may need it at another time.

3. In the [boot] section of the System.ini file, add this line and then save the file:

   ```
   drivers=mmsystem.dll
   ```

4. Change the name of the Win.ini file in the Windows folder to Win.sav.

5. Restart your computer.

If this works, the problem was in the Win.ini or System.ini files, and you can reexamine these files in detail to determine the exact source of the problem.

A+ OS
2.3
3.1
3.2

> **TIP** If your mouse stops working when you copy the System.cb file and rename it System.ini, add the following lines in the specified sections of the new System.ini file:
> ```
> [boot]
> mouse.drv=mouse.drv
> [386Enh]
> mouse=*vmouse,imsmouse.vxd
> ```

Logged (\BOOTLOG.TXT)   This option is the same as Normal, except that Windows 9x tracks the load and startup activities and logs them to the Bootlog.txt file. A portion of a sample Bootlog.txt file is shown in Figure 12-28. Notice that this file contains information about which components loaded successfully and which did not. This file can be a helpful tool when troubleshooting.

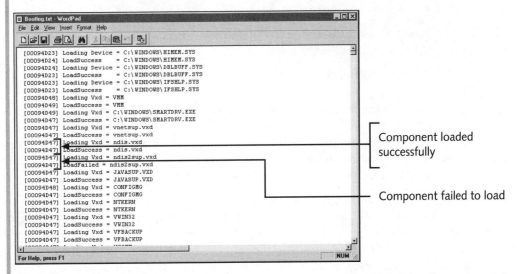

Figure 12-28   The Bootlog.txt file contains information about successful and unsuccessful boot activities

Safe Mode   When you have problems with the Windows 9x boot process but no error message appears during the boot, you can use safe mode to troubleshoot the problems. You can reach safe mode either from the startup menu or by pressing F5 while Windows is loading. Figure 12-29 shows Windows 98 booted into safe mode. Safe mode does not execute entries in the registry, Config.sys, Autoexec.bat, and the [Boot] and [386Enh] sections of System.ini. Also, when you enter safe mode, Windows 98/Me include support for networks, but Windows 95 does not.

A+ OS
2.3
3.1
3.2

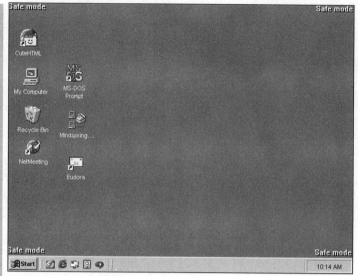

Figure 12-29   Windows 98 safe mode

Safe mode starts Windows 9x with a minimum default configuration to give you an opportunity to correct an error in the configuration. For example, if you selected a video driver that is incompatible with your system, when Windows 9x starts, it detects the problem and enters safe mode with a standard VGA driver selected. You can then go to Device Manager, select the correct driver, and restart Windows.

From the startup menu, you can choose to enter safe mode yourself if you know of a problem you want to correct. For example, if you selected a group of background and foreground colors that makes reading the screens impossible, you can reboot and choose safe mode. Safe mode gives you the standard color scheme along with the VGA mode. Go to Display Properties, make the necessary corrections, and reboot.

Sometimes you will use safe mode for troubleshooting when you don't know exactly what the problem is. In that situation, once you are in safe mode, use the following checklist:

- Use a current version of antivirus software to scan for a virus.

- Sometimes loading in safe mode is all that is needed. Try to reboot the PC in normal mode.

- If the Safe Recovery dialog box appears, select the option of Use Safe Recovery. Windows 9x then attempts to recover from previous boot problems. Try to boot again.

- If you had problems with a device installation before the Windows failure, disable or remove the device in Device Manager. Reboot after disabling each device that you suspect to be a problem.

A+ OS
2.3
3.1
3.2

- If you have just made configuration changes, undo the changes and reboot.

- Look for real-mode drivers or TSRs (programs loaded in Config.sys, Autoexec.bat, or System.ini) that might be causing a problem and disable them by inserting a semicolon or a REM at the beginning of the command line.

- Try to boot again. If the problem is still not solved, restore the registry. For Windows 95, make backups of System.dat and User.dat. Then overwrite them with System.da0 and User.da0. For Windows 98/Me, use ScanReg to restore the registry from backups. (How to do this was covered earlier in the chapter.)

A+ OS
1.5
2.3
3.1
3.2

- Run ScanDisk to repair errors on and optimize the hard drive. While in safe mode, select Start, Programs, Accessories, System Tools, ScanDisk. Under Type of Test, select Thorough. (See Figure 12-30.)

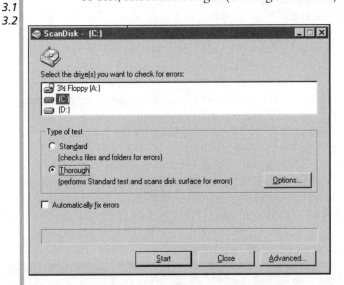

Figure 12-30 Use ScanDisk to check the hard drive for errors

A+ OS
2.3
3.1
3.2

- Run the Defragmenter utility to optimize the drive. (You will learn more about this later in the chapter.)

- For Windows 98/Me, run System File Checker to verify system files.

- For Windows 98/Me, run Automatic Skip Driver Agent (covered later in the chapter) to skip loading any driver that causes a problem. Reboot and examine the Asd.log file for recorded errors.

- For Windows 98/Me, use the System Configuration Utility to reduce the system to essentials and reboot. If the problem goes away, restore one item at a time until the problem returns. In this manner, you can identify the item that is the source of the problem.

12

A^+ *OS*
2.3
3.1
3.2

- Using Explorer, search for files in system folders that have changed recently. To sort file and folder names by date last modified using Explorer, click Modified. To reverse the sort order, hold down the Ctrl key while clicking Modified. If software or drivers have been installed recently, suspect that they might be the source of the problem.

Safe Mode with Network Support   This option allows you access to the network when booting into safe mode. It is useful if Windows 95 is stored on a network server and you need to download changes to your PC in safe mode. This option is not available on the startup menus in Windows 98/Me, which automatically include network support.

To eliminate the network connection as a source of a boot problem you are troubleshooting, first boot in safe mode without network support and then boot in safe mode with network support. If the boot without network support succeeds but the boot with network support gives errors, then suspect that the network drivers might be the source of the problem. For Windows 98/Me, disable the network card in Device Manager to eliminate the network drivers as the source of the problem.

Step-by-Step Confirmation   This option asks for confirmation before executing each command in Io.sys, Config.sys, and Autoexec.bat. You can accomplish the same thing by pressing Shift+F8 when the message "Starting Windows 95/98" appears.

A^+ *OS*
1.2
2.3
3.1
3.2

Command Prompt Only   This option executes the contents of Autoexec.bat and Config.sys but doesn't start Windows 9x. You get a DOS prompt. Type WIN to load Windows 9x. This command executes the file Win.com. You can use several switches with the WIN command when troubleshooting the OS. Table 12-13 lists these switches.

Table 12-13   Switches Used with the WIN command

Command/Switch	Purpose
WIN /D:M	Starts Windows in safe mode
WIN /D:F	Turns off 32-bit disk access; use this option if there appears to be a problem with hard drive access
WIN /D:S	Instructs Windows not to use memory address F000:0, which is used by BIOS
WIN /D:V	Instructs Windows that the system BIOS should be used to access the hard drive rather than the OS
WIN /D:X	Excludes all upper memory addresses from real mode drivers

In a troubleshooting situation, try each switch until you find one that works. You can then identify the source of the problem and can sometimes put entries in the System.ini file to make the switch a permanent part of the load.

A+ OS
2.3
3.1
3.2

Safe Mode Command Prompt Only   This option does not execute the commands in Autoexec.bat or Config.sys. You get a DOS prompt.

Previous Version of MS-DOS   This option loads a previous version of DOS if one is present. You can get the same results by pressing F4 when the message "Starting Windows 95/98" appears. This option is not available in Windows 98 SE or Windows Me.

Troubleshooting with the Startup Menu

If you tried using the tools recommended in the previous sections, but have not yet identified the source of the problem, use the following checklist to troubleshoot using the startup menu:

- Try a hard boot. A soft boot might not do the trick, because TSRs are not always "kicked out" of RAM with a soft boot.

- If you have not already done so, try safe mode next.

- Try the option Step-by-step confirmation next. Look for error messages caused by a missing or corrupted driver file. Try not allowing real-mode drivers to load. After the problem command within Autoexec.bat or Config.sys is identified, you can eliminate the command or troubleshoot it. Specific commands in these files and their purposes were covered in Chapter 3.

- Use the Logged option next, and examine the Bootlog.txt file that is created to see if it identifies the problem.

- Try booting using the Command prompt only option. From the command prompt, run the real-mode version of ScanDisk, which you can find in the \Windows\Command folder, to scan the hard drive for errors. From a command prompt, enter this command: C:\Windows\Command\Scandisk. If the Scandisk.exe program on the hard drive is corrupted, use the one on the emergency startup disk.

- For Windows 98/Me, from the command prompt, type Scanreg/Fix and try to reboot.

- For Windows 98/Me, from the command prompt, next type Scanreg/Restore and select the latest known good backup of the Windows 9x registry. Try to reboot.

- From the command prompt, you can use the WIN command with the switches listed in Table 12-13. If one of these commands solves the problem, look for real-mode drivers that might be in conflict, eliminating those that you can. Examine Bootlog.txt for errors and try booting from safe mode again.

- Try booting with the Safe Mode command prompt only. Remember that when you are in safe mode, the registry is not executed. If you suspect a corrupted registry, restore it to its last saved version as you learned to do earlier. Then try the WIN command with or without the switches, as necessary.

12

$A+$ *OS*
2.3
3.1
3.2

Using the Startup Disk for Troubleshooting

If you cannot solve the boot problems you are experiencing by using the troubleshooting utilities within Windows or on the startup menu, use an emergency startup disk to recover from the failed boot. If you do not have an emergency startup disk, create one on another computer and use it to work with the computer that has the problem. Before using the startup disk, it is a good idea to check it for viruses on a working computer by scanning it with antivirus software. If you find a virus on the emergency startup disk, destroy the disk and use a working computer to create a new one.

To use the emergency startup disk, place it in the floppy disk drive and turn on the PC. It will boot to a startup menu or to an A prompt, depending on the version of Windows 9x you are using. Figure 12-31 shows the Startup Menu.

```
Microsoft Windows 98 Startup Menu
_____


1. Start Computer With CD-ROM Support.
2. Start Computer Without CD-ROM Support.
3. View the Help File.

   Enter A Choice:              Time Remaining: 30




F5=Safe Mode Shift+F5=Command Prompt Shift+F8=Step Configuration[N]
```

Figure 12-31 Windows 98 rescue disk startup menu

If you are using a version for which the startup disk boots to a menu, select the first option, which is to start the PC with CD-ROM support. The OS then examines the system for problems and provides an A prompt where you can enter commands.

If the system failed to boot from the hard drive, the first step in troubleshooting at this point is to see if you can access the hard drive. To do that, enter DIR C: at the A prompt. If this step works, then the problem lies in the software used on the hard drive to boot, including the OS boot record, OS hidden files, and command interface files. If you cannot access the hard drive, the problem is with the partition table, the Master Boot Record, hard drive, its cabling, or its power source. In this case, you need to examine the hard drive for errors.

A+ OS
2.3
3.1
3.2

Use Fdisk to examine the partition table. If the table is corrupted, most likely you have lost everything on your hard drive. Try using the Fdisk /MBR command to restore the Master Boot Record on the drive. If this does not work, try creating new partitions on the drive and formatting the drive. All data and software on the drive will be lost. If you cannot use Fdisk on the drive, treat the problem as a hardware problem.

After you complete troubleshooting the hard drive, eliminating physical problems with the hard drive subsystem, CMOS, and the partition table, the next step is to run the Windows 9x Setup program. When given the opportunity, select Verify installed components. Setup then restores damaged or missing system files.

Troubleshooting Windows 9x Hardware and Software

A+ OS
3.2

Here are some general tips for troubleshooting hardware and software:

- Begin by asking the user questions like the ones listed in Chapter 4 to learn as much as you can about the problem and how to reproduce it.

- Try rebooting the computer. The problem with the device may disappear when Windows redetects it.

- Frequent system lockups might indicate corrupted memory modules. Try using memory testing software to check for intermittent memory errors, which indicate the module needs replacing. An example of memory testing software is DocMemory by CST, Inc. (*www.docmemory.com*).

- For external devices such as monitors, printers, and scanners, try turning on the device before turning on the computer. If your computer is on and you are rebooting, leave the device on and online.

- If a device doesn't work with one application, try it with another. If the problem only occurs with one application, the problem is probably not with the hardware device but with that application.

- Check Device Manager for errors it reports about the device. If it reports errors, use the Hardware Troubleshooter in Device Manager to help resolve the problem or go to the Microsoft Web site and search for the error message.

- The driver might be corrupted or need updating. Look on the Web for updated device drivers. Search the device manufacturer's Web site or the Microsoft Web site for information about problems with the device and solutions.

- Use Device Manager to uninstall the device and then reinstall it. If you uninstall the device and then reboot, Windows should recognize an uninstalled device and automatically launch the Found New Hardware Wizard. If it doesn't launch, then chances are the device is not working or is not PnP.

12

A+ OS
3.2

- For PnP devices on expansion cards such as sound cards, modems, and network cards, if you uninstall the device in Device Manager and Windows does not recognize the device when you reboot, the device might not be working. The expansion card needs to be reseated or moved to a different expansion slot. If that doesn't work, the card needs replacing.

- If none of these things work, ask yourself what changed since the device last worked. For example, maybe you added another hardware device that conflicts with the one you are using, or maybe you have added software that conflicts with the software that the problem device is using. Try disabling other devices or try uninstalling software that you suspect is causing the problem. Use Automatic Skip Driver Agent to eliminate other devices that might prevent this one from working.

- The problem might be caused by lack of resources. If your system is running low on memory or has too many applications open, it might not be able to support a device. A corrupted Windows system file or registry can also cause problems with hardware devices. Try verifying system files or restoring the registry from backup.

- Check the registry key HKEY_LOCAL_MACHINE\SOFTWARE\ Microsoft\Windows\CurrentVersion\Run.

- Check the hard drive. Run ScanDisk and Defrag. Delete unneeded files and empty the Recycle Bin. Generally clean up the hard drive, making plenty of room for the swap file and temporary files used by applications.

- Suspect a virus. Run a current version of antivirus software. Clean or delete all files that contain viruses. Restore system files.

- Check for applications loaded at startup that use system resources. Close applications not currently in use.

- Look for icons in the **System Tray**, the small area on the right side of the taskbar at the bottom of the screen. These icons represent small applets that are loaded at startup and take system resources. Keep these icons to a minimum.

- Clean up the registry using the Scanreg /opt command.

- Remove extraneous software such as fancy screen savers and desktop wallpaper and photos.

- For software problems, try uninstalling and reinstalling the application. Search the Web site of the software manufacturer for fixes, upgrades, and suggestions to solve the problem.

Windows Help and the Microsoft Web Site

Windows Help might provide useful information when you try to resolve a problem. To access the Troubleshooting tool of Windows Help, click Start, click Help, and then click Troubleshooting. The Help information includes suggestions that can lead you to a solution. For example, in Figure 12-32, the Hardware Troubleshooter suggests that you check to see that the device is not listed twice in Device Manager. If this is the case, you should remove the second occurrence of the device.

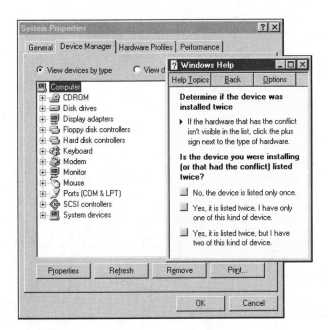

Figure 12-32   Troubleshooter making a suggestion to resolve a hardware conflict

Also, the Microsoft Web site, *support.microsoft.com* (see Figure 12-33), has lots of information on troubleshooting. Search for the device, an error message, a Windows utility, a symptom, a software application, an update version number, or key words that lead you to articles about problem and solutions. You can also go to *www.microsoft.com* to browse for links on hardware and software compatibility.

 For those serious about learning to provide professional support for Windows 95 or Windows 98, two good books are *Microsoft Windows 95 Resource Kit* and *Microsoft Windows 98 Resource Kit*, both by Microsoft Press.

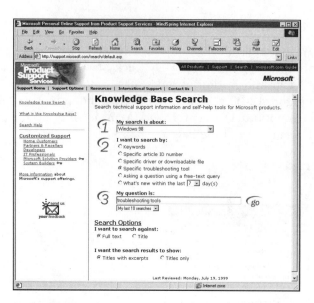

Figure 12-33   Microsoft Technical Support Web site

CHAPTER SUMMARY

❑ The Windows 9x core consists of the kernel, the user, and the GDI, and relates to users, software, and hardware by way of the following modules: the VMM, the IFS manager, the Configuration Manager, and the WDM driver manager.

❑ Virtual memory uses hard drive space as memory in order to increase the total amount of memory available. In Windows, virtual memory is stored in the swap file.

❑ Although Windows 9x supports 16-bit drivers, using 32-bit drivers whenever possible is best because they are faster, can be stored in extended memory, and can be dynamically loaded.

❑ Virtual machines are multiple logical machines within one physical machine. If an application crashes or produces another type of error within a virtual machine, only that virtual machine is affected, instead of the entire system.

❑ Before installing 9x as an upgrade, verify that you have enough hard drive space, run ScanDisk or Chkdsk, run antivirus software, back up critical system files, disable TSRs that might cause problems if they run during installation, verify that any network connections work, make sure that the swap file is on a drive compressed with protected-mode software, and decide whether you want to use FAT16 or FAT32.

❏ If Windows is already installed and you want to do a clean install, when you reach the setup screen install the new OS in a different folder than the one used by the currently installed OS, which is probably \Windows.

❏ Upgrading from Windows 95 to Windows 98 is relatively easy because the two OSs are similar. Before performing the upgrade, check hardware and software compatibility, run antivirus software, and back up your system. The Setup Wizard on the Windows 98 CD will guide you through the setup process. After setup is complete, test installed applications and back up your system again.

❏ When adding new hardware to Windows 9x, use the Add New Hardware Wizard. Select the hardware from a list of devices to use a Windows driver, or click Have Disk to use your own drivers (from a manufacturer's disk or downloaded from the Internet to a folder on your hard drive).

❏ For a Windows 9x system to be truly Plug and Play, the system BIOS must be PnP, all hardware devices and expansion cards must be PnP compliant, and a 32-bit device driver must be available for any installed hardware device.

❏ Dosstart.bat is a type of Autoexec.bat file that executes when you select Restart the computer in MS-DOS mode or when you run a program in MS-DOS mode.

❏ An OS that supports protected mode can create a virtual real mode for a 16-bit application so that the application thinks it is the only program running, has all memory available to it, and accesses data using a 16-bit data path. Windows 9x ordinarily runs a 16-bit DOS application in a virtual DOS machine.

12

❏ Windows keystroke shortcuts are useful for experienced typists who may find them faster than the mouse; they are also useful in troubleshooting situations when the mouse does not work.

❏ In the Display Properties window, you can change the background, screensaver, appearance, icon effects, Active Desktop settings, color range, and display size for the desktop.

❏ Starting with Windows 9x, the Windows registry takes over the essential functions of .ini files. However, Windows 9x still supports System.ini and Win.ini for backward compatibility with legacy hardware devices and legacy software applications.

❏ The registry is contained in two files, System.dat and User.dat. Windows 95 maintains backups of these files, called System.da0 and User.da0, that you can use when troubleshooting. Windows 98/Me keep compressed backup files of the registry and system files in cabinet files named Ra000.cab, Ra001.cab, and so forth.

❏ Changes in Control Panel, Device Manager, and other locations in Windows 9x can change the registry automatically. The Regedit utility is used to edit the registry manually.

❏ The Registry Checker (Scanreg.exe) backs up, verifies, and recovers the registry. It automatically backs up the registry every day and keeps the last five days of backups.

❏ The System Configuration Utility (Msconfig) allows you to modify the system configuration temporarily to help with troubleshooting. It reduces the startup process to essentials.

❏ The Dr. Watson utility (Drwatson.exe) helps you troubleshoot applications by trapping errors in log files and taking a snapshot of the system.

❏ The System Configuration Editor (Sysedit.exe) is a text editor used to edit system files. When you run Sysedit, it automatically opens Protocol.ini, System.ini, Win.ini, Config.sys, and Autoexec.bat.

❏ Device Manager lists hardware devices installed on a system. For more information about a specific device in Device Manager, click the device and select Properties.

❏ Initialization files, which have the .ini file extension, are used by Windows or application software to store configuration information needed when Windows or an application first loads.

❏ The five phases of the Windows 9x boot process are BIOS POST and bootstrap, loading the OS, the loading of real mode VxDs, protected-mode switchover and PnP configuration, and loading remaining components.

❏ Applications are loaded at startup by a shortcut in the Startup folder, the name of the program file in the Load= or Run= line in Win.ini, or an entry in the registry.

❏ When troubleshooting Windows 9x boot problems, first check error messages, then boot in safe mode, then boot to the command prompt using the startup menu, and finally try booting from an emergency startup disk.

❏ To force the Windows 9x startup menu to appear, hold down either the Ctrl key or the F8 key during the boot.

❏ In Logged mode, Windows tracks startup activities and logs them to the Bootlog.txt file.

❏ You can reach safe mode either from the Windows startup menu or by pressing F5 while Windows is loading.

❏ Safe mode starts Windows 9x with a minimum default configuration to give you an opportunity to correct an error in the configuration.

❏ Choosing Command Prompt Only from the startup menu executes the contents of Autoexec.bat and Config.sys but does not start Windows. Instead it brings you to a DOS prompt. Use the WIN command to load Windows 9x.

❏ Use the startup disk to recover from a failed boot when you cannot solve the problem using the startup menu or cannot boot from the hard drive. If you do not have a startup disk or if the one you have has a virus, use a working computer to create a new one.

KEY TERMS

application program interface (API) call

clean install

comment

Configuration Manager

disk thrashing

DOS box

Dosstart.bat

Dr. Watson

dynamic VxD

GDI (Graphics Device Interface)

hypertext

IFS (Installable File System) manager

initialization files

kernel

keys

memory paging

page fault

page-in

page-out

patch

PIF (program information file)

Plug and Play (PnP)

Protocol.ini

service pack

shell

shortcut

static VxD

swap file

Sysedit

System.ini

System Tray

upgrade install

user component

value data

virtual device driver

virtual machine

VMM (Virtual Machine Manager)

WDM (Win32 Driver Model)

Win.ini

Win386.swp

REVIEW QUESTIONS

1. Which of the following operating systems was *not* included in the Windows 9x suite of products?

   a. Windows 95 OSR2

   b. Windows 98

   c. Windows 98 SE

   d. Windows ME

   e. None of the above

2. Which of the following files is used to control the mouse, keyboard, ports, and desktop?

   a. Kernel32.dll

   b. User32.dll

   c. GDI32.dll

   d. Msdos.sys

   e. Io.sys

3. Which of the following serves to manage memory, file I/O, and loading and executing programs?

   a. Kernel32.dll

   b. User32.dll

   c. GDI32.dll

   d. Msdos.sys

   e. Io.sys

4. Applications call on the operating system to access hardware and other software by using a(n) _____.

   a. Interrupt Vector Table

   b. Virtual Memory Manager

   c. System registry

   d. Application Programming Interface

   e. Configuration Manager

5. Which component of Windows 9x is responsible for all disk access?

   a. The Virtual Memory Manager (VMM)

   b. The Installable File System (IFS)

   c. The Configuration Manager

   d. The Win32 Driver Model (WDM)

   e. None of the above

6. Which component of Windows 9x is responsible for the Plug and Play features of Windows 9x and other hardware configuration tasks, such as providing system resources to hardware devices?

   a. The Virtual Memory Manager (VMM)

   b. The Installable File System (IFS)

   c. The Configuration Manager

   d. The Win32 Driver Model (WDM)

   e. None of the above

7. Which of the following files launches the interactive interface for the Windows 9x CD?

   a. Autorun.inf

   b. Autoexec.bat

   c. Setup.exe

   d. Checklinks.exe

   e. Config.sys

8. Which minimum microprocessor is required in order to install and run Windows 98?

   a. 386SX

   b. 386DX

   c. 486SX

   d. 486DX

   e. Pentium

9. What is the minimum secondary storage requirement in order to install and run Windows 98?

   a. 4 MB

   b. 16 MB

   c. 32 MB

   d. 50 MB

   e. 195 MB

10. A service technician would like to install Windows 98 onto an older system. The technician will be installing this operating system for the first time, but realizes that there are utilities in some of the core folders that normally do *not* come with the Windows 98 installation. Which choice should the technician make during the operating system installation?

    a. Typical

    b. Portable

    c. Compact

    d. Custom

    e. Special

11. If the system fails to respond during the hardware detection phase, an entry is recorded in the _____ file; a binary file Windows uses to help recover from a crash caused by a hardware problem.

    a. Detcrash.log

    b. Detlog.txt

    c. Autoexec.bat

    d. Config.sys

    e. Setup.ext

12

12. In Windows 98, each function in the startup core has a very significant purpose. In Windows 9x, the _____ file is a text file containing several parameters that affect how the OS boots.

    a. Autoexec.bat

    b. Config.sys

    c. MSDOS.sys

    d. IO.sys

    e. Command.com

13. Some core operating systems have their specific file attributes set to "read-only" in an effort to protect them from ever getting deleted and/or modified. How is the "read-only" attribute set such that the operating system *can* modify these files if need be?

14. Which of the Command Line Variable Names will allow for a dual boot between Windows 9x and another operating system, such as DOS?

    a. AutoScan

    b. BootMulti

    c. BootWin

    d. BootGUI

    e. Boot Menu

15. In order to uninstall a device in Windows 9x, it can be accomplished by using the _____.

    a. Control Panel

    b. Start Menu

    c. The Update Device Driver Wizard

    d. Device Manager

    e. Fdisk

16. In order for a system to be *truly* Plug and Play (PnP) compliant, it must meet the following criteria:

    a. _____

    b. _____

    c. _____

    d. _____

17. During software installation, it is a good idea to back up specific system core and system configuration files. These include:

    a. _____

    b. _____

    c. _____

    d. _____

    e. _____

18. Assuming a 32-bit operating system, if a 16-bit application needs to be executed, it is run in what mode?

    a. Real mode

    b. Virtual real mode

    c. Protected mode

    d. Virtual protected mode

    e. Safe mode

19. Which key sequence allows the user to move from one loaded application to another?

    a. Ctrl+Alt+Delete

    b. Alt+Tab

    c. Ctrl+X

    d. Ctrl+Shift+Tab

    e. Ctrl+Esc

20. Using the Device Manager, which symbol represents a problem with a device, but shows that the device might still be functioning?

    a. A red X through the device

    b. A yellow exclamation point

    c. A blue I on a white field

    d. A green question mark

21. Which of the major keys in the Windows 9x registry is responsible for keeping information about Windows performance and PnP information?

    a. HKEY_USERS

    b. HKEY_CURRENT_USER

    c. HKEY_LOCAL_MACHINE

    d. HKEY_CURRENT_CONFIG

    e. HKEY_DYN_DATA

12

22. Which of the following files represent backup copies of the system registry files?

    a. System.da0, User.da0

    b. System.dat, User.dat

    c. Kernel32.exe, User.exe

    d. User32.exe, GDI.exe

    e. Autoexec.bat, Config.sys

23 Virtual memory uses hard drive space so that it acts like memory. Windows stores virtual memory in a special file. What is the name of this file?

    a. Autoexec.bat

    b. Config.sys

    c. Himem.sys

    d. EMM386.exe

    e. None of the above

24. The Windows System Configuration Editor is called:

    a. Notepad

    b. Word

    c. Sysedit

    d. Edit

    e. System Registry

25. The startup of Windows 9x is a five-phase process. Name the five phases:

    a. _____

    b. _____

    c. _____

    d. _____

    e. _____

13

UNDERSTANDING AND INSTALLING WINDOWS 2000 AND WINDOWS NT

In this chapter, you will learn:

♦ About Windows NT/2000/XP architecture
♦ How to install Windows 2000 Professional
♦ How to install hardware and applications with Windows 2000
♦ How to install and support Windows NT Professional

Windows NT, Windows 2000, and Windows XP share the same basic Windows architecture and have similar characteristics. Windows NT introduced a new file system, NTFS, that represents a break with past Windows operating systems; Windows 2000 and Windows XP use it as well. Windows 2000 is the culmination of the evolution of Microsoft operating systems from the 16-bit DOS operating system to a true 32-bit, module-oriented operating system, complete with desktop functionality, user-friendly Plug and Play installations, and other easy-to-use features. Windows XP includes additional multimedia support, making the final step for Microsoft to announce the merging of Windows 9x operating systems and Windows NT operating systems into a single OS. (There will be no future updates to Windows 9x, as Microsoft considers this OS a legacy technology.) This chapter lays the foundation for understanding the architecture of Windows NT/2000/XP and then shows you how to install Windows 2000 Professional. You will also learn how to install hardware and software under Windows 2000. Because a PC support technician occasionally sees Windows NT still used, the last part of the chapter covers Windows NT installation and support.

WINDOWS NT/2000/XP ARCHITECTURE

For the corporate desktop or home PC, in most cases you would choose Windows XP rather than Windows 2000. However, if you must select between Windows 98 and Windows 2000, Windows 2000 is the better choice for the corporate desktop. Because of its improved power management, Windows 2000 is also a better choice for notebook computers. For the business environment, Windows 2000 is more secure and reliable and offers better support for very large hard drives. Windows 98 is the better choice for the home PC. Windows 98 works better than Windows 2000 with games, music, and video, and supports the widest variety of hardware and software products.

Windows 2000 includes four operating systems:

- *Windows 2000 Professional* was designed to replace both Windows 9x and Windows NT Workstation as a personal computer desktop or notebook OS. It is an improved version of Windows NT Workstation, using the same new technological approach to hardware and software, and has all the popular features of Windows 9x, including Plug and Play.

- *Windows 2000 Server* is the improved version of Windows NT Server and is designed as a network operating system for low-end servers.

- *Windows 2000 Advanced Server* is a network operating system that has the same features as Windows 2000 Server but is designed to run on more powerful servers.

- *Windows 2000 Datacenter Server* is a network operating system that is a step up from Windows 2000 Advanced Server. It is intended for use in large enterprise operations centers.

Now let's look at the architecture of Windows NT/2000/XP in more detail, including how the OS relates to applications, networking features, and the management of hard drives and memory.

Windows NT/2000/XP Modes

Windows NT/2000/XP operates in two modes, user mode and kernel mode, which each take advantage of different CPU functions and abilities (see Figure 13-1). This section explains both modes.

User Mode

User mode is a processor mode in which programs have only limited access to system information and can access hardware only through other OS services. The OS has several **subsystems**, or OS modules, that use this mode and interface with the user and with applications. The Windows tools you use, such as Windows Explorer, run primarily in user mode. In Figure 13-1, note the Win32 subsystem, which is probably the most important user mode subsystem because it manages and provides an environment for all 32-bit programs, including the user interface (such as the one for Explorer). The Win32 security subsystem provides logon to the system and other security functions, including privileges for file access.

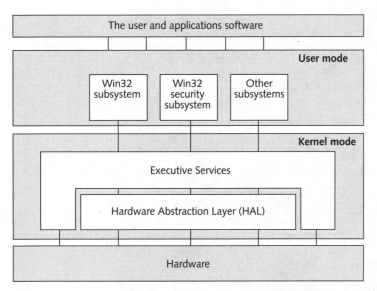

Figure 13-1   User mode and kernel mode in Windows NT/2000/XP and how they relate to users, application software, and hardware

All applications relate to Windows NT/2000/XP by way of the Win32 subsystem, either directly or indirectly. Figure 13-2 shows how various programs that run under Windows NT/2000/XP interact with subsystems. For instance, each legacy DOS application resides in its own NTVDM. An **NTVDM (NT virtual DOS machine)** is a carefully controlled environment that Windows NT/2000/XP provides. In it a DOS application can interface with only one subsystem and cannot relate to anything outside the system, so it is similar to the Windows 9x virtual DOS machine introduced in Chapter 12. All 16-bit Windows 3.x applications reside in a **Win16 on Win32 (WOW)** environment. Within the WOW, these 16-bit applications can communicate with one another and the WOW, but that's as far as their world goes. Figure 13-2 shows three 16-bit Windows 3.x applications residing in a WOW that resides in one NTVDM. Because each DOS application expects to run as the only application on a PC, each has its own NTVDM.

You can see in Figure 13-2 that 32-bit applications do not require an NTVDM and can relate to the Win32 subsystem directly, because they are written to run in protected mode. They can also use a single line of communication (called single-threading) with the Win32 subsystem or multiple lines for interfacing (called **multithreading**) with the Win32 subsystem, depending upon what the process requests. A **thread** is a single task that the process requests from the kernel, such as the task of printing a file. A **process** is a program or group of programs that is running, together with the system resources assigned to it, such as memory addresses, environmental variables, and other resources. Sometimes a process is called an instance, such as when you say, "Open two instances of Internet Explorer." Technically, you are saying to open two Internet Explorer processes. An example of multithreading is Microsoft Word requesting that the subsystem read a large file from the hard drive and print a job at the same time. Single-threading happens when the application does not expect both processes to be performed at the same time but simply passes one request followed by another.

13

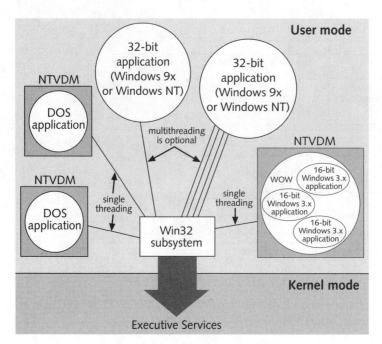

Figure 13-2 Environment subsystems in Windows NT/2000/XP user mode include NTVDMs for DOS and Windows 3.x applications and optional multithreading for 32-bit applications

Kernel Mode

Kernel mode is a processor mode in which programs have extensive access to system information and hardware. Kernel mode is used by two main components: the HAL (hardware abstraction layer) and a group of components collectively called executive services. The **HAL (hardware abstraction layer)** is the layer between the OS and the hardware. The HAL is available in different versions, each designed to address the specifics of a particular CPU technology. **Executive services** interface between the subsystems in user mode and the HAL. Executive services components manage hardware resources by way of the HAL and device drivers. Windows NT/2000/XP was designed to port easily to different hardware platforms. Because only the components operating in kernel mode actually interact with hardware, they are the only parts that need to be changed when Windows NT/2000/XP moves from one hardware platform to another.

Applications in user mode have no access to hardware resources. In kernel mode, executive services have limited access to hardware resources, but the HAL primarily interacts with hardware. Limiting access to hardware mainly to the HAL increases OS integrity because more control is possible. With this isolation, an application cannot cause a system to hang by making illegal demands on hardware. Overall performance is increased because the HAL and executive services can operate independently of the slower, less efficient applications using them.

Networking Features

A+CORE
6.2
OS
4.1

A workstation running Windows NT/2000/XP can be configured to work as one node in a workgroup or one node on a domain. A **workgroup** is a logical group of computers and users that share resources (Figure 13-3), where the control of administration, resources, and security on a workstation is controlled by that workstation. Each computer maintains a list of users and their rights on that particular PC. A Windows **domain** is a group of networked computers that share a centralized directory database of user account information and security for the entire set of computers (Figure 13-4). A workgroup uses a **peer-to-peer** networking model, and a domain uses a **client/server** networking model. Using the client/server model, the directory database is controlled by a Network Operating System (NOS). Popular NOSs are Windows NT/2000, Windows .NET, Novell Netware, Unix, Linux, and Mac OS. Windows for the desktop has network client software built in for Windows (Microsoft Client), Mac (AppleTalk), and Novell Netware (NWLink). Alternately, for Novell Netware, you can install Novell client software.

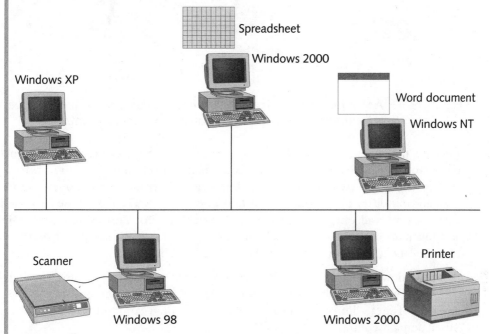

Figure 13-3   On a peer-to-peer network, no single computer controls the network and each computer controls its own resources

In a Windows NT/2000 or Windows .NET domain, a network administrator manages access to the network through a centralized database. In Figure 13-4, you see the possible different components of a Windows domain. Every domain has a **domain controller**, which stores and controls a database of (1) user accounts, (2) group accounts, and (3) computer accounts. This database is called the directory database or the **security accounts manager (SAM)** database.

A+ OS
   4.1

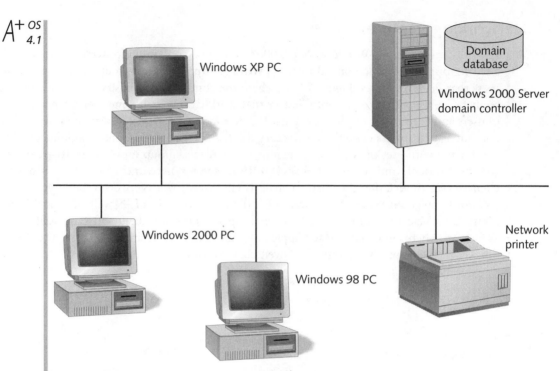

Figure 13-4   A Windows domain is a network where security on each PC or other device
is controlled by a centralized database on a domain controller

Because the domain controller database is so important, Windows allows for backup copies of the database to exist on more than one computer in the domain. Under Windows NT, a network can have a primary domain controller and one or more backup domain controllers. The **primary domain controller (PDC)** holds the original directory database, and read-only copies are stored on **backup domain controllers (BDCs)**. An administrator can update the database on the PDC from any computer on the network, and the BDCs later get a copy of the updated database.

With Windows 2000, a network can have any number of domain controllers, each keeping a copy of the directory that can be edited. An administrator can update the directory on any one of these domain controllers, which will then communicate the change to the other domain controllers.

When Windows NT and Windows 2000 domain controllers are on the same network, conflicts can result because of the differences in the way the domain controllers work in each OS. For this reason, Windows 2000 runs in two modes: native mode and mixed mode. **Native mode** is used when no Windows NT domain controllers are present, and **mixed mode** is used when there is at least one Windows NT domain controller on the network. Mixed mode is necessary in a situation where a large network is being upgraded from Windows NT to Windows 2000 and some servers have been upgraded

A+ OS
   4.1

but others have not. When installing Windows 2000 Server, the installer can choose mixed mode during the installation process and later migrate to native mode by using the Computer Management console, which you will learn about in the next chapter. Once you change a domain to native mode, you cannot change it back to mixed mode.

In addition to native mode and mixed mode, another networking feature new to Windows 2000 is **Active Directory**, a directory database service that allows for a single administration point for all shared resources on a network. In Windows 2000, the security accounts manager (SAM) database is part of Active Directory. Active Directory can track file locations; peripheral devices, including printers, scanners, and other hardware; databases; Web sites; users; services; and so forth. It uses a locating method similar to that used by the Internet. Windows 2000 Server versions provide Active Directory, and Windows 2000 Professional acts as an Active Directory client, or user, of the directory.

Windows NT/2000/XP Logon

Regardless of whether Windows NT/2000/XP computers are networked or not, every Windows NT/2000/XP workstation has an **administrator account** by default. An administrator has rights and permissions to all computer software and hardware resources and is responsible for setting up other user accounts and assigning them privileges. During the Windows NT/2000/XP installation, you enter a password to the default administrator account. When the workstation is part of a Windows workgroup, after the OS is installed, you can log on as an administrator and create local user accounts. If the workstation is part of a domain, a network administrator sets up global user accounts that apply to the entire domain, including giving access to the local workstations. Local user accounts, as well as other ways to secure a workstation, are covered in Chapter 16.

When Windows NT/2000/XP starts up, you must log on before you can use the OS. For Windows NT/2000, you see the logon screen when you press Ctrl+Alt+Del. Windows XP displays a logon screen by default. To log on, enter a username and password, and click OK. Windows NT/2000/XP tracks which user is logged on to the system and grants rights and permissions according to the user's group or to specific permissions granted this user by the administrator. If you do not enter a valid account name and password, Windows NT/2000/XP does not allow you access to the system.

How Windows NT/2000/XP Manages Hard Drives

A+ OS
   1.4
   2.1

Windows NT incorporated new ways of managing hard drives that are also used in Windows 2000 and Windows XP. Windows NT/2000/XP assigns two different functions to hard drive partitions holding the OS (see Figure 13-5). The **system partition**, normally drive C, is the active partition of the hard drive. This is the partition that contains the OS boot record. Remember that the MBR looks to this OS boot record for the boot program as the first step in turning the PC over to an OS. The other partition, called the **boot partition**, is the partition where the Windows NT/2000/XP operating system is stored.

13

A+ OS
  1.4
  2.1

> **TIP** Don't be confused by the terminology here. It is really true that, according to Windows NT/2000/XP terminology, the Windows OS is on the boot partition, and the boot record is on the system partition, although that might seem backward. The PC boots from the system partition and loads the Windows NT/2000/XP operating system from the boot partition.

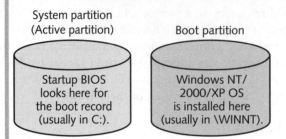

Figure 13-5   Two types of Windows NT/2000/XP hard drive partitions

The system partition and the boot partition can be the same partition or separate partitions. Windows NT/2000/XP is designed to use two partitions in this way so that the Windows system files do not have to be stored on the same partition used to boot the OS. For Windows NT, both partitions can be formatted with either FAT16 or NTFS. Windows 2000/XP use NTFS, FAT16, or FAT32, although NTFS under Windows NT is not compatible with an NTFS volume under Windows 2000/XP. Know that Windows 9x and DOS cannot read files stored on an NTFS volume. If you want these OSs to access the volume, you must use the FAT16 or FAT32 file system.

Recall that Windows 9x, using Fdisk, can create two partitions: a primary partition and an extended partition. The primary partition contains drive C, and the extended partition can contain several volumes or logical drives. Also recall that each FAT16 volume can be no larger than 2 GB. Using Windows NT/2000/XP, you can have up to four partitions. The first partition must be a primary partition and, if it is the boot device, can have only a single drive C. There can be up to four primary partitions on the drive, each containing a single logical drive. However, one of the four partitions can be an extended partition, which means it can have several volumes or logical drives. Because of the way Windows NT/2000/XP uses the FAT, each FAT16 volume can be up to 4 GB. However, to make the volume compatible with Windows 9x, limit the size to 2 GB.

Now that you've seen how partitions work in Windows NT/2000/XP, let's look at how file systems work.

A Choice of File Systems

Table 13-1 summarizes which file systems are supported by which operating systems. You need this information to plan your Windows NT/2000/XP installation. Windows versions not discussed in this chapter are included for comparison. Windows NT/2000/XP does not support the High Performance File System (HPFS) used by OS/2. If a hard drive

A+ OS
1.4
2.1

is using HPFS, use the Windows NT/2000/XP Convert.exe utility to convert an HPFS partition to an NTFS partition. This program can also convert a FAT16 partition to NTFS.

Table 13-1   Operating system support for file systems

	DOS	Windows 95	Windows 98	Windows NT	Windows 2000	Windows XP
FAT16	X	X	X	X	X	X
FAT32		X (for OSR2)	X		X	X
NTFS				X	X	X

> **TIP** Although Windows NT 4.0 does not support FAT32, you can use third-party utility software packages, such as FAT32 for Windows NT 4.0 by Winternals (*www.winternals.com*) to manage the interface, making it possible for Windows NT to read from and write to FAT32.

When a hard drive is formatted for NTFS, each cluster can range from 512 bytes on smaller disks to 4K on larger disks. Clusters are numbered sequentially by logical cluster numbers (LCN) from the beginning to the end of the disk. Each cluster number is stored in a 64-bit entry, compared to either 16 bits for FAT16 or 32 bits for FAT32.

The FAT file system uses three components to manage data on a logical drive: the FAT, directories, and data files. In contrast, the NTFS file system uses a database called the **master file table (MFT)** as its core component. The MFT tracks the contents of a logical drive using one or more rows in the table for each file or directory on the drive. As shown in Figure 13-6, the MFT contains in one record, or row, information about each file, including header information (abbreviated H in Microsoft documentation), standard information (SI) about the file (including date and time); filename (FN); security information about the file, called the security descriptor (SD); and data about the location of the file. Entries in the MFT are ordered alphabetically by filename to speed up a search for a file listed in the table.

13

Referring again to Figure 13-6, note the data area in the MFT record is 2K for small hard drives but can be larger for larger hard drives. For small files, if the data can fit into the 2K area, the file, including its data, is fully contained within the MFT.

If the file is moderately large and the data does not fit into the MFT, the data area in the MFT becomes an extended attribute (EA) of the file, which points to the location of the data. The data itself is moved outside the table to clusters called runs. The record in the MFT for this moderately large file contains pointers to these runs. Each data run, or cluster, assigned to the file is given a 64-bit virtual cluster number (VCN). The MFT maps the VCNs for the file onto the LCNs for the drive. This mapping is stored in the area of the MFT record that would have contained the data if the file had been small enough. If the file is so large that the pointers to all the VCNs cannot be contained in one MFT record, then additional MFT records are used. The first MFT record is called the base file record and holds the location of the other MFT records for this file.

A+ OS
1.4
2.1

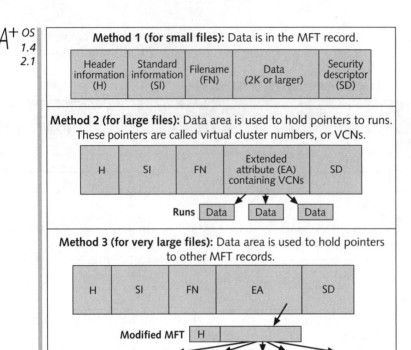

Figure 13-6 The Windows NT/2000/XP file system Master File Table uses three methods to store files, depending on the file size

Advantages of NTFS and FAT

When choosing between the NTFS file system and the FAT16 or FAT32 file system, consider the advantages that NTFS offers over FAT:

- NTFS is a recoverable file system. NTFS retains copies of its critical file system data and automatically recovers a failed file system, using this information the first time the disk is accessed after a file system failure.

- NTFS under Windows 2000/XP supports encryption (encoding files so they can't be deciphered by others) and disk quotas (limiting the hard drive space available to a user). Windows NT NTFS does not support these features.

- NTFS supports compression (reducing the size of files and folders). (Windows 9x supports compression of an entire logical drive but not compression of individual files or folders.)

- NTFS provides added security in the event you boot from floppy disks:
  - If the file system for the active partition of a PC is FAT, you can boot from a DOS or Windows 9x boot disk and bypass the Windows NT/2000/XP security logon. When you use NTFS, you can boot from a DOS or Windows 9x boot disk to an A:\> prompt, but you cannot access the hard drive. Under Windows 2000/XP, you can use the Recovery Console to

A+ OS
1.4
2.1

access files on an NTFS partition, but the Windows logon is required. Using Windows NT, you can boot from the three Windows NT startup disks, logon, and access an NTFS partition.

- If you boot a PC using a DOS or Windows 9x boot disk, you can access the hard drive of a Windows NT/2000/XP system that uses the FAT file system, but you cannot access an NTFS file system.

- If you boot a PC using the Windows 2000/XP Recovery Console or the three Windows NT startup disks, you can only access the NTFS file system if you provide an administrator account and password. In fact, if the administrator forgets his or her password to the OS, the hard drive is not accessible and the only recourse is to reload the OS.

- NTFS supports mirroring drives, meaning that two copies of data can be kept on two different drives to protect against permanent data loss in case of a hard drive crash. This feature makes the NTFS an important alternative for file servers.

- NTFS uses smaller cluster sizes than does FAT16 or FAT32, making more efficient use of hard drive space when small files are stored.

- NTFS supports large-volume drives. NTFS uses 64-bit cluster numbers, whereas FAT16 uses 16-bit cluster numbers and FAT32 uses 32-bit cluster numbers. Because the number of bits assigned to hold each cluster number is so large, the cluster number itself can be large, and the table can accommodate very large drives with many clusters. Overall, NTFS is a more effective file system for drives over 1 GB and offers more robust drive compression, allowing compression of individual folders and files.

13

The advantages of the FAT file system over NTFS include:

- The FAT file system has less overhead than the NTFS file system and, therefore, works best for hard drives that are less than 500 MB.

- The FAT file system is compatible with Windows 9x and DOS operating systems. If you plan to use either DOS or Windows 9x on the same hard drive as Windows NT/2000/XP, use the FAT file system so that DOS and Windows 9x can access files used by Windows NT/2000/XP.

- In the event of a serious problem with Windows NT/2000/XP, if you are using FAT on the active partition of the drive, you can boot the PC from a DOS or Windows 9x startup disk and access the drive.

You can choose to have Windows NT/2000/XP use NTFS by directing it to convert the hard drive from FAT to NTFS or by having Windows NT/2000/XP partition a drive so that one partition of the drive uses the FAT format and the other uses the NTFS format. Windows NT/2000/XP allows you to format logical drives with either FAT or NTFS on the same extended partition.

Memory in Windows NT/2000/XP

A+ OS
1.1
2.5

As you learned in earlier chapters, managing memory under DOS and Windows 9x can be complicated because of having to deal with conventional, upper, and extended memory

A+ OS
1.1
2.5

for backward compatibility. Windows NT/2000/XP eliminates that complexity, because memory is simply memory; in other words, all memory addresses are used the same way. It also loses some backward compatibility.

The Windows NT/2000/XP memory management model is illustrated in Figure 13-7, which shows the object-oriented approach to memory management. The application or device driver only says, "I want memory." It cannot tell Windows which physical memory or which memory addresses it wants or even the range of addresses it wants to fall within. Windows uses its virtual memory manager to interface between the application or driver and the physical and virtual memory that it controls. Memory is allocated in 4K segments called **pages**. Applications and devices written for Windows NT/2000/XP only know how many pages they have. The virtual memory manager takes care of the rest. It is free to store these pages in RAM or on the hard drive in the swap file named **Pagefile.sys** (see Figure 13-7).

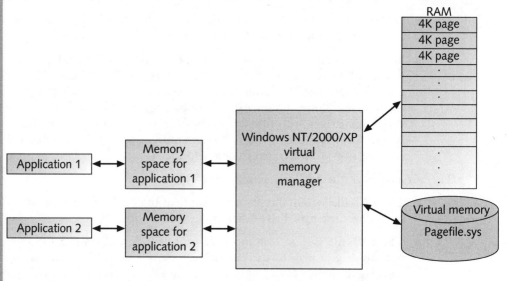

Figure 13-7   Windows NT/2000/XP memory management

INSTALLING WINDOWS 2000 PROFESSIONAL

A+ OS
2.1

This section looks at installing Windows 2000 on a system with a newly installed hard drive, called a clean install, and also installing Windows 2000 as an upgrade from Windows 9x or Windows NT, called an upgrade installation. Just as with Windows NT and Windows XP, Windows 2000 can be installed to be dual-booted with another OS. Before any type of installation, verify that your system meets the minimum requirements for Windows 2000. You must have at least 650 MB of free space on your hard drive, at least 64 MB of RAM, and a 133 MHz Pentium-compatible CPU or higher.

Plan the Installation

A+ OS
2.1

Before you install Windows 2000, you need to select a file system (NTFS, FAT16, or FAT32) and verify that your computer, your peripheral hardware devices, and your software qualify for Windows 2000. The best way to verify compatibility in these three areas is to visit the Microsoft Web site at *www.microsoft.com/windows2000/professional/howtobuy/ upgrading/compat* (see Figure 13-8). Here is a brief explanation of why you must verify all three components:

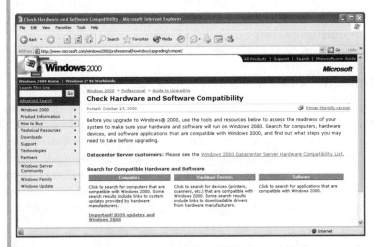

Figure 13-8 Use the Microsoft Web site to verify that your computer, peripheral devices, and applications all qualify for Windows 2000

13

- Windows NT/2000/XP does not use system BIOS to interface with hardware devices. For that reason, a hardware device must be specifically designed to interact with Windows NT/2000/XP. Don't assume that because a device is compatible with Windows NT, it works with Windows 2000. In some instances this is not the case, so check the HCL for Windows 2000 to be sure.

- Software applications must also qualify for Windows 2000. If an application is not listed on the Microsoft Web site, it might still work with Windows 2000. You can verify compatibility by checking with the application manufacturer's Web site or technical support, or you can just install the application under Windows 2000 and test it yourself.

- Your motherboard BIOS must meet the **Advanced Configuration and Power Interface (ACPI)** standards developed by Intel, Microsoft, and Toshiba, which apply to system BIOS, the OS, and certain hardware devices and software to control when a device goes into an inactive state in order to conserve power. To take full advantage of Windows 2000 power management abilities, your system BIOS must be ACPI-compliant. If your BIOS is not ACPI-compliant and you install Windows, Windows does not install ACPI support but installs an older HAL that does not support ACPI. If you later flash your BIOS to make it ACPI-compliant, you have to reinstall Windows to include ACPI support.

A^+ _OS_
_2.1_

>
> **TIP** If you have problems with Windows 2000 or NT detecting your hard drive, the problem might be out-of-date system BIOS. Try flashing BIOS and then try the Windows installation again.

Microsoft calls a BIOS that is ACPI-compliant a "good BIOS" and puts it on the Good BIOS list. The Microsoft site allows you to search for ACPI-compatible computers by model and manufacturer. The Microsoft Web site tells you if the system is compatible with Windows 2000 and sometimes provides a link to the BIOS Web site where you can download an upgrade to the BIOS. If you are upgrading BIOS, do that before you begin the Windows 2000 installation. You can install Windows 2000 on a system that is not ACPI-compliant, but you cannot use some of its power management features.

Installing Windows 2000 on Networked Computers

If you are installing Windows 2000 on a networked PC, consider where the Windows 2000 installation files are stored. You can install the OS from a CD in the computer's CD-ROM drive, or you can store the files on a file server on the network and perform the installation from the file server. If you will be doing multiple installations on the network, consider using a file server. Copy all the files from the \i386 folder on the Windows 2000 CD to a folder on the file server and then share that folder on the network. Later, during the installation, when you are ready for the CD, point the setup program to the file server folder instead.

Windows 2000 offers a number of options for installation that can be automated so you don't need to sit at the computer responding to the questions that setup asks during the installation process. One method, called an **unattended installation**, is performed by storing the answers to installation questions in a text file or script that Windows 2000 calls an **answer file**. A sample answer file is stored on the Windows 2000 CD. If you must perform many installations on computers that have the same Windows 2000 setup, it might be worth your time to develop an answer file to perform unattended installations. How to set up unattended installations is beyond the scope of this chapter. Another option is drive imaging. After the installation, use the sysprep.exe utility to remove configuration settings such as the computer name that uniquely indentifies this PC. Then clone the entire hard drive to a new PC using third-party drive-imaging software.

>
> **TIP** To learn how to create an unattended installation of Windows 2000, go to the Microsoft Support Web site (_support.microsoft.com_) and search for the Microsoft Knowledge Base article Q216258. You can also search the Web site for other articles on this subject.

When installing Windows 2000 on a network, just as with other operating systems, you need to know how to configure the computer to access the network. You should know these things before you begin the installation:

- The computer name and workgroup name for a peer-to-peer network

A+ OS
  2.1

- The username, user password, computer name, and domain name for a domain network

- For TCP/IP networks, how the IP address is assigned, either dynamically (gets its IP address from a DHCP server when it first connects to the network) or statically (IP address is permanently assigned to the workstation). If the IP address is statically assigned, you need the IP address for the workstation. (DHCP servers, which are used to assign IP addresses when a computer connects to a network, are covered in Chapter 18.)

Upgrade or Clean Install?

If you are installing Windows 2000 on a new hard drive, then you are doing a clean install. If Windows 9x or Windows NT is already installed on the hard drive, then you have three choices:

- You can perform a clean install, overwriting the existing operating system and applications.

- You can perform an upgrade installation.

- You can install Windows 2000 in a second partition on the hard drive and create a dual-boot situation.

Each of these options has advantages and disadvantages.

Clean Install, Erasing Existing Installations   If the hard drive does not have a lot of important data on it or has data that can be backed up, a clean install that overwrites the existing installation has some advantages. One advantage is that you get a fresh start. With an upgrade, problems with applications or the OS might follow you into the Windows 2000 load. If you erase everything (format the hard drive), then you are assured that the registry as well as all applications are as clean as possible. The disadvantage is that, after Windows 2000 is installed, you must reinstall application software on the hard drive and restore the data from backups. If you do a clean install, you can choose to format the hard drive first, or simply do a clean install on top of the existing installation. If you don't format the drive, the data will still be on the drive, but the previous operating system settings and applications will be lost.

If you decide to do a clean install, verify that you have all the application software CDs or floppy disks and software documentation. Back up all the data, and verify that the backups are good. Then, and only then, format the hard drive or begin the clean install without formatting the drive. If you don't format the hard drive, be sure to run a current version of antivirus software before you begin the installation.

Upgrade the Existing Operating System   All versions of Windows 9x and Windows NT Workstation 3.51 and higher can be upgraded to Windows 2000. The advantages of upgrading are that all applications and data and most OS settings are carried forward into the new Windows 2000 environment, and the installation is faster. If you perform an

13

upgrade, you must begin the installation while you are in the current OS. If you are working from a remote location on the network, you cannot do an upgrade.

> **TIP** You cannot upgrade a compressed Windows 9x drive. You must uncompress it before you can upgrade to Windows 2000 Professional.

Create a Dual Boot   The ability to boot from both Windows 2000 and another OS, such as DOS or Windows 9x, is called a **dual boot**. Don't create a dual boot unless you need two operating systems, such as when you need to verify that applications and hardware work under Windows 2000 before you delete the old OS. Windows 2000 does not support a second operating system on the same partition, so you must have at least two partitions on the hard drive. All applications must be installed on each partition to be used by each OS.

> **TIP** Recall that Windows NT/2000/XP can support up to four partitions on a hard drive. All four can be primary partitions (which can have only one logical drive), or one of the partitions can be an extended partition (which can have several logical drives). For the first primary partition, the active partition, that drive is drive C. For a dual boot with Windows 2000, one OS is installed in the active partition on drive C, and the other OS is installed on another partition's logical drive.

You must decide what file system to use for the Windows 2000 partition: FAT16, FAT32, or NTFS. If you choose to use a dual boot with DOS, use FAT16 for the Windows 2000 partition so that DOS can read the partition. For Windows 9x, use either the FAT16 or FAT32 file system, not NTFS, so that Windows 9x can read the Windows 2000 partition.

Windows 2000 uses the latest version of NTFS, the one introduced by Windows NT Server 4.0, NTFS Version 5.0 (NTFS5). NTFS4 is used by Windows NT Workstation 4.0. The NTFS5 version includes numerous enhancements over previous versions but cannot be read by Windows NT Workstation 4.0 unless Windows NT 4.0 Service Pack 4 is applied. For this reason, if you create a dual boot between Windows 2000 and Windows NT using NTFS for both operating systems, you can encounter the following problems:

- The file system data structures might not be the same.

- Disk utilities, such as Chkdsk under Windows NT, might not work on the drive.

- Windows NT cannot read encrypted files and folders.

- You cannot use Windows 2000 to repair a damaged Windows NT 4.0 NTFS partition. Windows NT 4.0 only allows access to an NTFS drive from within Windows NT 4.0 and not from any other OS.

For these reasons, using a dual boot between Windows 2000 and Windows NT is not recommended.

A^+ *OS*
  2.1
  2.2

Planning an Upgrade from Windows 9x to Windows 2000

Because the Windows 9x registry and the Windows 2000 registry are not compatible, transfer of information from one to the other will not be as complete as with an upgrade from Windows NT to Windows 2000 where information in the registry is easily ported into the new OS. Until you perform the upgrade, you cannot know exactly what Windows 2000 was able to import from Windows 9x, although Setup might inform you or ask for additional help in some cases.

To test your system and be alerted to potential problems, running the Check Upgrade Only mode of Windows 2000 Setup is a good idea. This does not actually install Windows 2000 but instead just checks for compatibility and reports any upgrade issues with hardware or software. Run the utility to produce the report, Upgrade.txt, which is stored in the C:\Windows directory.

Hardware Compatibility   One issue to consider in upgrading from Windows 9x to Windows 2000 is that Windows 2000 does not import drivers from Windows 9x, because they are generally not compatible. As you learned earlier, a hardware device must be designed to be compatible with Windows 2000. If you want to install a device but its driver is not included in Windows 2000, you might have to download a driver from either the Microsoft site or the manufacturer's Web site. Check for compatibility and make sure you have all the required device drivers before you begin your Windows 9x-to-Windows 2000 upgrade. Windows 2000 attempts to carry over installed hardware devices that are compatible with Windows 2000, asking for new drivers where necessary; it ignores and does not install incompatible devices. If Setup cannot find a critical driver such as the driver to control a hard drive, it cancels the upgrade.

Another thing you need to know is that Windows 2000 deletes all the Windows 9x system files and replaces them with Windows 2000 system files in the same directory.

13

Software Compatibility   Basically, the main advantage of performing an upgrade from Windows 9x to Windows 2000 rather than doing a clean install of Windows 2000 is that you do not have to reinstall software that is compatible with Windows 2000. If an application was written for Windows 9x, it might or might not be compatible with Windows 2000. Windows 9x applications store registry data differently from Windows 2000 applications and may rely on APIs specific to Windows 9x. If an application doesn't work after you upgrade to Windows 2000, try reinstalling it. If that doesn't work, check the software manufacturer's Web site for a patch or upgrade.

Planning an Upgrade from Windows NT to Windows 2000

Upgrading to Windows 2000 from Windows NT is much easier than upgrading from Windows 9x. However, you need to be aware of some considerations before performing the upgrade:

- You must install networking on Windows NT 3.51 machines before upgrading, or you cannot log on to Windows 2000.

A^+ OS
2.1
2.2

- If you are upgrading from Windows NT using NTFS, Setup automatically upgrades to the Windows 2000 version of NTFS.

- ·If you are upgrading from Windows NT using FAT16 or Windows NT with third-party software installed that allows it to use FAT32, Setup asks you whether you want to upgrade to NTFS.

Hardware Compatibility   Generally, most hardware devices and their corresponding drivers that worked under Windows NT work under Windows 2000 as well, although some third-party drivers might need to be updated for Windows 2000. As always, it is a good idea to check the HCL on the Microsoft Web site or run the Check Upgrade Only mode of Windows 2000 Setup.

Software Compatibility   Nearly all applications that run with Windows NT Workstation 3.51 and later will run with Windows 2000 without modification. Here are some exceptions:

- Antivirus software and third-party network software, both of which must be removed before upgrading to Windows 2000

- Some disk management tools

- Custom tools for power management, which are replaced in Windows 2000 by ACPI. Windows 2000 also provides minimal support for APM (Advanced Power Management), which must be removed before the upgrade. Windows 2000 considers APM a legacy tool, uses it only on notebook computers, and uses only enough APM features to support a notebook computer's battery. With ACPI-compliant BIOS, the BIOS senses information about the system and turns that information over to the OS to make decisions and manage the power management functions of the system.

- Custom solutions that are workarounds for Windows NT not supporting Plug and Play, which are unnecessary in Windows 2000 because it provides complete support for Plug and Play

- Software to monitor and control a UPS (uninterruptible power supply)

Now that you know about advantages and disadvantages of installing Windows 2000 as a clean install and as an upgrade, including issues to consider with specific upgrades, let's look at step-by-step procedures for how to do both.

> **TIP**   When installing Windows from across the network to a remote PC, you can only do a clean install. In this situation, run the Winnt.exe setup program. When working at the local computer, to perform a clean install, you can boot from the Windows CD or run Winnt32.exe from a command prompt. If you want to perform an upgrade, you must execute the Winnt32.exe program from within Windows. In any case, the program executed is called Setup in Windows documentation.

Clean Installation

A^+ OS
2.1
2.2

The Windows 2000 package comes with documentation and a CD. For United States distributions, the package includes a floppy disk to provide 128-bit data encryption.

(This disk is not included in distributions to other countries because of laws that prohibit 128-bit data encryption software from leaving the United States.)

If your PC is capable of booting from a CD, then insert the CD and turn on the PC. The Welcome to the Windows 2000 Setup Wizard screen appears (see Figure 13-9). Select Install a new copy of Windows 2000, click Next, and proceed to Step 6 below. However, if your PC does not boot from a CD and you have a clean, empty hard drive, first create a set of Windows 2000 setup disks to boot the PC and to begin the installation process. The remaining installation is done from the CD.

Figure 13-9   Using the Setup Wizard, you can do an upgrade, do a clean install, or create a dual boot

To make the four setup disks, follow these directions:

1. Using a working PC, format four floppy disks.

2. Place the Windows 2000 CD in the CD-ROM drive and a formatted floppy disk in the floppy disk drive. For Windows 9x, click **Start**, **Run**, and enter this command in the Run dialog box: **D:\bootdisk\makeboot.exe A:**, substituting the drive letter of the CD-ROM drive for D: and the letter of the floppy drive for A:.

3. Insert new disks in the drive as requested. Label the disks Windows 2000 Setup Disks 1, 2, 3, and 4.

4. Now begin the Windows 2000 installation. Boot the PC from the first setup disk created above. You will be asked to insert each of the four disks in turn and then asked to insert the Windows 2000 CD.

5. The Windows 2000 license agreement appears. Accept the agreement and the Welcome screen appears, as shown in Figure 13-9. The setup process is now identical to that of booting directly from the CD. Save the four setup floppy disks in case you have future problems with Windows 2000.

13

A+ OS
2.1

6. Windows 2000 searches the hard drive for partitions and asks which partition to use. If the partitions are not created, it creates them for you. You are asked to decide which file system to use. If the hard drive has already been formatted with the FAT16 or FAT32 file system, you are asked if you want to upgrade to the NTFS file system. Be aware that if you convert the file system to NTFS, you cannot revert to FAT16 or FAT32. You can also convert from FAT16 or FAT32 to NTFS after the installation is complete. If the hard drive is already partitioned and contains a partition larger than 2 GB and if you select the FAT file system, then Windows 2000 automatically formats the drive using the FAT32 file system. It puts the entire partition in one logical FAT32 drive.

7. During installation, you are given the opportunity to change your keyboard settings for different languages, enter your name and company name, and enter the product key found on the CD case. You are also given the opportunity to enter date and time settings and an administrator password. Be sure to remember the password. It is required when you log on to the system later to set up new users and perform other administrative tasks. If you forget it and no one else has administrator privileges, you might have to reinstall Windows 2000.

8. If Setup recognizes that you are connected to a network, it provides the Networking Settings window to configure the computer to access the network. If you select Typical settings, then Setup automatically configures the OS for your network. After the installation, if the configuration is not correct, you can make changes.

9. At this point in the installation, you are asked to remove the Windows 2000 CD and click **Finish**. The computer then restarts. After Windows 2000 loads, it completes the process of connecting to the network. You are asked questions about the type of network. (For example, does the network use a domain or workgroup?) When the configuration is complete, verify that you have access to the network if there is one.

Clean Install When the Hard Drive Has an Operating System Installed

A+ OS
2.1

Using Windows 9x, if your PC automatically detects a CD in the CD-ROM drive, follow these directions to do a clean install when another OS is already installed:

1. Using antivirus software, scan memory and your hard drive for viruses.

2. Insert the Windows 2000 CD in the CD-ROM drive. If your PC detects the CD, a window opens with the message "This CD-ROM contains a newer version of Windows than the one you are presently using. Would you like to upgrade to Windows 2000?" Answer **No**. The Install Windows 2000 window appears (see Figure 13-10).

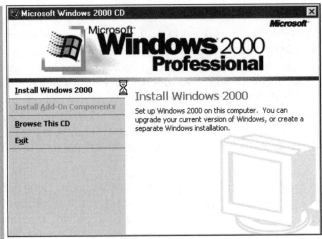

A+ OS
2.1

Figure 13-10   Windows 2000 Setup window

3. Click **Install Windows 2000**. The Windows Setup Wizard opens, as in Figure 13-9. Select **Install a new copy of Windows 2000 (Clean Install)**. Windows displays the license agreement and asks you to accept it. Enter the product key from the back of the CD case, and you will be given the opportunity to select special options.

4. After a reboot, the installation process continues as described above.

If your PC does not automatically recognize a CD, then insert the CD in the CD-ROM drive and do the following:

1. Click **Start**, **Run**. In the Run dialog box, enter the command: **D:\i386\ winnt32.exe**. Substitute the drive letter of the CD-ROM drive for D:.

2. The Windows 2000 Setup Wizard appears, as in Figure 13-9. Select **Install a new copy of Windows 2000 (Clean Install)**. The installation process continues as described above.

Upgrade Installation

A+ OS
2.1

To upgrade your operating system from Windows 9x or Windows NT using the Windows 2000 CD, first prepare for the installation:

1. Verify that all devices and applications are Windows 2000–compatible. Download and install any patches or upgrades from hardware or software manufacturers.

2. Using antivirus software, scan memory and your hard drive for viruses.

3. Back up all critical system files and data files. Back up the registry in case you need to backtrack to the current installation. If you have important data on your hard drive, back up the data.

4. Close all applications and disable any virus-scanning software. If the hard drive is compressed, decompress the drive.

13

A+ OS
2.1
2.4

You are now ready to perform the upgrade. Do the following:

1. Insert the Windows 2000 CD in the CD-ROM drive. If your system is set to detect the CD automatically, it runs the setup program and shows a message asking if you want to upgrade your computer to Windows 2000. Answer **Yes** and the installation process begins. If Windows does not detect the CD, click **Start**, **Run**, enter **D:\i386\winnt32.exe** in the Run dialog box, and then click **OK**. Substitute the drive letter of the CD-ROM drive for D:. On the Welcome to Windows 2000 Setup Wizard Screen, select **Upgrade to Windows 2000 (Recommended)**. Follow the directions on the screen.

2. Windows 2000 Setup performs the upgrade in two major stages: the Report phase and the Setup phase. During the Report phase, Windows 2000 Setup scans the hardware, device drivers, current operating system, and applications for compatibility. In this phase, you are given the opportunity to provide third-party DLL files that make a device driver or application Windows 2000-compatible, if Setup recognizes that the device driver or application will not work without the fix. Next, Setup generates a report of its findings. If its findings indicate that an unsuccessful installation is likely, you can abandon the installation and perhaps check with hardware and software manufacturers for fixes. In the Report phase, Setup also creates an answer file that it uses during the Setup phase, installs the Windows 2000 boot loader, and copies Windows 2000 installation files to the hard drive.

3. The PC reboots and the Setup phase begins, which has two parts: the Text mode and the GUI mode. In the Text mode, Setup installs a Windows 2000 base in the same folder that the old OS is in, usually C:\Windows for Windows 9x and C:\WINNT for Windows NT. The target folder cannot be changed at this point. Setup then moves the Windows registry and profile information to %windir%\setup\temp, where %windir% is the path to the Windows folder, most likely C:\Windows\setup\temp.

4. The PC reboots again and the GUI mode of Setup begins. Setup reads information that it saved about the old Windows system and makes appropriate changes to the Windows 2000 registry. It then migrates application DLLs to Windows 2000 and reboots for the last time. The upgrade is done.

TIP During installation, Windows 2000 records information about the installation to a file called Setuplog.txt. This file is useful when troubleshooting any problems that occur during installation.

After the Installation: Backing Up the System State

A+ OS
2.1
2.4

After you have completed installing Windows 2000, do the following:

1. Access the Internet and download and install all OS service packs, updates, and patches.

2. Verify that all hardware works and install additional devices, such as printers, as needed.

3. Create user accounts for Windows 2000. (Chapter 16 covers creating user accounts.) You can also install additional Windows components at this time.

A^+ *OS*
2.1
2.4

4. Verify that the system functions properly, and back up the system state. This backup of the system can later be used to help you recover the OS in the event of system failure. (You will learn more about recovering from system failure in the next chapter.)

A^+ *OS*
1.1
1.5

Windows 2000 calls the files critical to a successful operating system load the **system state data**. This includes all files necessary to boot the OS, the Windows 2000 registry, and all system files in the %SystemRoot% folder, the folder in which Windows 2000 is installed. For an upgrade, the folder will most likely be C:\Windows, the original Windows folder before the upgrade. For a clean install, the default folder is C:\WINNT. When you back up the system state data, you cannot select which of these files you want to back up because Windows 2000 always backs up all of them. Here is the process:

1. Click **Start**, point to **Programs**, **Accessories**, **System Tools**, and then click **Backup**. The Backup dialog box opens. Click the **Backup** tab (see Figure 13-11).

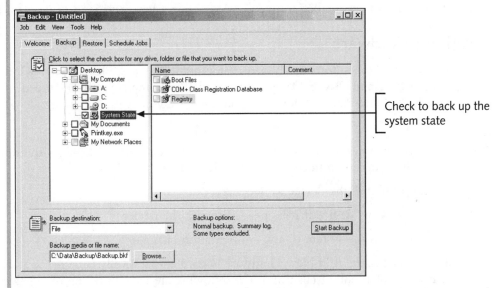

Figure 13-11   Back up the Windows 2000 registry and all critical system files

2. Check the **System State** box in the list of items you can back up. Notice in Figure 13-11 that the system state includes the boot files and the registry. It also includes the COM+ (Component Object Model) Registration Database, which contains information about applications and includes files in the Windows folders.

3. Select the destination for the backup. You can back up to any media, including a folder on the hard drive, Zip drive, tape drive, or network drive. Click **Start Backup** to begin the process.

Later, if you have problems with a corrupted Windows 2000 installation, you can click the Restore tab in the Backup window illustrated in Figure 13-11 to restore the system to its state at the last backup.

> **TIP** When you back up the system state, the registry is also backed up to the folder %SystemRoot%\repair\RegBack. If you later have a corrupted registry, you can copy files from this folder to the registry folder, which is %SystemRoot%\System32\Config.

INSTALLING HARDWARE AND APPLICATIONS UNDER WINDOWS 2000

A+ OS 2.4 This section discusses how to install hardware and software with Windows 2000 and includes special considerations for legacy hardware. As with Windows 98, Windows 2000 has an Add New Hardware Wizard that automatically launches when new hardware is detected, and software is best installed from the Add/Remove Programs icon of Control Panel.

Installing Hardware

A+ OS 2.4 Windows 2000 can automatically detect and install Plug and Play devices, as long as you also have Plug and Play BIOS and Plug and Play-compliant drivers and devices. If a device is Plug and Play, Windows 2000 automatically does the following:

- Identifies the device you are installing

- Determines what system resources the device needs and assigns them so that there are no conflicts with other devices

- Configures the device as necessary

- Loads any device drivers needed to run the device

- Informs the system of any configuration changes

For PnP devices, the Add New Hardware Wizard automatically launches at startup. Any user can complete the installation if the following are true: installing the device drivers can be done without user input, all files necessary for a complete installation are present, the drivers have been digitally signed (**digital signatures** are digital codes used to authenticate the source of files), and there are no errors during installation. If one of these conditions is false, the installation is abandoned until someone with administrator privileges logs on.

Most devices designed to work with Windows 2000 are Plug and Play compatible. If a device is not Plug and Play, you can use the Add/Remove Hardware applet in Control Panel to install the device if you are logged on with administrator privileges.

A+ OS
2.4

If you are using the Add/Remove Hardware Wizard, you have to provide such information as where the driver for the device is located. Some devices that don't work with Windows 2000 may be completely incompatible and will not work at all. If you install a device and have a problem with it, you can attempt to update the device driver as follows:

1. In the Control Panel, double-click the **System** icon.

2. The System Properties window opens. Select the **Hardware** tab (see Figure 13-12).

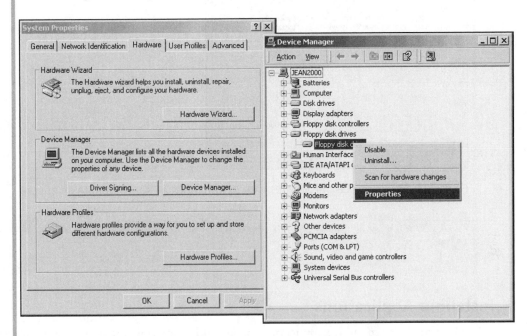

Figure 13-12   Use Device Manager to access a device's properties

3. Click the **Device Manager** button. The Device Manager opens, as shown in Figure 13-12. Expand the device class tree by clicking the plus sign, and locate the device for which you want to update a driver. For this example, we are using the floppy disk drive.

4. Right-click the floppy drive and select **Properties** from the shortcut menu (see Figure 13-12).

5. The Floppy disk drive Properties window opens (see Figure 13-13). On the **Driver** tab, click **Update Driver**. The Update Device Driver Wizard appears. If an update exists, follow directions onscreen to update the driver.

A^{+} OS
2.4

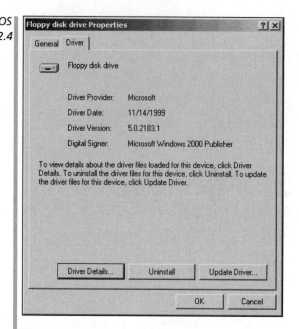

Figure 13-13   A device's Properties window provides a way to update its drivers

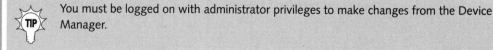

You must be logged on with administrator privileges to make changes from the Device Manager.

Installing Applications

The process of installing applications in Windows 2000 is not much different than that of earlier versions of Windows. If you are familiar with the installation wizards and setup programs used with Windows 9x, you should recognize all but a few minor details of these same components in Windows 2000.

The Windows 2000 Add/Remove Programs utility looks significantly different than in Windows 9x, and it provides more options. From the Windows 2000 Add/Remove Programs window, you can change or remove presently installed programs (Figure 13-14); add new programs from a CD-ROM, a floppy disk, or from Microsoft over the Internet; and add or remove Windows components. In Figure 13-14, note the expanded drop-down menu in the upper-right corner showing how you can sort the view of presently installed programs.

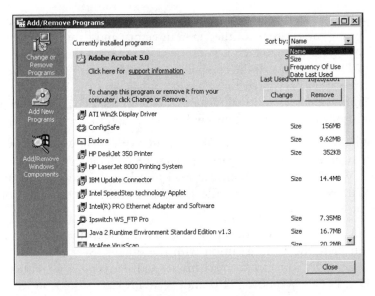

Figure 13-14   Making changes to currently installed programs

SUPPORTING WINDOWS NT

Though Windows 2000 and Windows XP are gradually replacing Windows NT, Windows NT is still around; therefore, knowing how to support it is important. Much of what you learn in this section carries over to later Windows OSs. First we will look at different ways to install Windows NT, and then we'll look at how to troubleshoot the Windows NT boot process.

Installing Windows NT as the Only OS

Windows NT comes with three disks that contain a simplified version of Windows NT, enough to boot a PC. If the hard drive does not contain an OS, the installation begins by booting from these three disks. After Windows NT is loaded from these three disks, it can access the CD-ROM drive, and installation continues from the CD. The program on the CD executed at that point is Winnt.exe, a 16-bit program. A faster version of Winnt.exe on the CD-ROM named Winnt32.exe, a 32-bit program, can, in certain situations, be used instead of Winnt.exe. Winnt32.exe can be run only after Windows NT has already been installed for the first time; it is used to upgrade from an older NT version to a newer version or to reinstall a corrupted version. It must be executed from within Windows.

The three startup disks can later be used to boot the PC if files on the hard drive become corrupted. You can also create a new set of bootable disks.

Installing Windows NT as the Second OS on the Hard Drive

A+ OS
2.1
2.3

Installing Windows NT on a hard drive to create a dual boot begins differently, but is otherwise the same as installing Windows NT as the only OS. The Windows NT installation

A+ OS
2.1
2.3

files are stored in the \i386 directory on the CD-ROM drive. If hard drive space is plentiful, you can copy the contents of the \i386 directory and its subdirectories to the hard drive and install from there, which is faster because access to the hard drive is faster than access to the CD-ROM drive. If the computer is connected to a network, the contents of the \i386 directory can be copied to a network server, and the Winnt.exe program can be executed from the server to install Windows NT on the PC, if certain conditions exist. (Installations from servers are not covered in this chapter.)

Remember that Windows NT can coexist on the same PC with either Windows 9x or DOS. In a dual boot arrangement, the system partition must be FAT rather than NTFS, so that the non-NT OS (Windows 9x or DOS) can read it. When Windows 9x is used for a dual boot, the Windows 9x Msdos.sys file has the multiboot configuration entry, BootMulti=1.

Windows NT resides on the boot partition, which can also be formatted for the FAT16 file system and can share the same partition with the other OS or reside on a second partition, such as drive D. You can format this second partition with either FAT or NTFS. If drive D is NTFS, Windows 9x cannot read any data stored on that drive. If drive D is a FAT16 partition, either OS can read data from either drive.

After both operating systems are installed, a **boot loader menu** appears, asking which OS to boot. The disadvantages of a dual boot are that application software cannot be shared between the two OSs; you must install applications in each OS. Also, you must reboot the PC to move from one OS to the other.

To install Windows NT with Windows 9x loaded, insert the Windows NT installation CD in the drive. If the PC autodetects the CD, you see the Windows NT opening screen. Click Windows NT Setup. If the PC does not autodetect the CD, click Start, Run and enter this command in the Run dialog box D:\i386\Winnt.exe. (Substitute the drive letter of your CD-ROM drive for D.) If you want a dual boot, do not choose to store Windows NT in the C:\Windows folder because it will overwrite Windows 9x.

After the installation is complete, when the PC reboots, it detects two OSs and shows a boot loader menu that gives you the choice between Windows NT Workstation Version 4.0 and Microsoft Windows (Windows 95 or 98). Select Windows NT Workstation version 4.0, which then loads.

Troubleshooting the Windows NT Boot Process

In this section, you will learn how to troubleshoot the Windows NT boot process and about some diagnostic tools that you can use for maintenance and troubleshooting. Many general troubleshooting tips you learned in earlier chapters apply to Windows NT as well. Troubleshooting the Windows 2000 boot process is covered in Chapter 14.

Listed below are the things you can do and the order in which you should do them to troubleshoot a failed Windows NT boot. You will learn more about these tools and processes in this section. Windows NT does not have a safe mode as does Windows 9x, nor does it have several of the useful troubleshooting utilities of Windows 9x that you learned about in the last chapter.

To recover from a failed Windows NT boot:

- If the Windows NT startup menu appears (it will if it thinks there is a problem you need to know about), use the Last Known Good configuration to return to the last registry values that allowed for a successful boot. Any configuration changes since the last good boot will be lost.

- If you cannot boot from the hard drive, boot using the three boot disks that came with the OS. If you don't have these three disks, you can create them on a working PC. Check for corrupted boot and system files that you can replace. (How to create the three boot disks is covered later in this section.)

- Boot from the three disks, and select the option "To repair a damaged Windows NT version 4.0 installation."

- Try reinstalling Windows NT in the same folder it currently uses. Tell the Setup program this is an upgrade.

- As a last resort, if you are using the NTFS file system and you must recover data on the hard drive, move the hard drive to another system that runs Windows NT and install the drive as a secondary drive. You might then be able to recover the data.

A+ OS
2.3
Last Known Good Configuration

Each time Windows NT boots and the first logon is made with no errors, the OS saves a copy of the hardware configuration from the registry, which is called the **Last Known Good configuration**. (All hardware configuration sets stored in the registry, including the Last Known Good, are called control sets.) The next time the PC boots, if an error occurs, it can use the Last Known Good configuration.

13

The key in the registry that contains the Last Known Good configuration is HKEY_LOCAL_MACHINE\HARDWARE.

If Windows NT detects the possibility of a problem, it adds the Last Known Good option to the Windows NT startup menu. You can select this Last Known Good option to revert to the control set used for the last good boot. For example, if you install a new device driver, restart Windows NT, and find that the system hangs, you can use the Last Known Good option to revert to the previous configuration.

Because the configuration information is not saved to the Last Known Good control set until after the logon, if you have trouble with the boot, don't attempt to log on. Doing so causes the Last Known Good to be replaced by the current control set, which might have errors.

For example, if you install a new video driver, restart Windows, and find the screen very difficult to read, don't log on. Instead, press the reset button to reboot the PC. When given the choice, select Last Known Good from the startup menu.

To prevent hard drive corruption, if you have problems booting Windows NT, wait for all disk activity to stop before pressing the reset button or turning off the PC, especially if you are using the FAT file system.

A+ OS
2.1
2.3
3.1
3.2

If you accidentally disable a critical device, Windows NT decides to revert to the Last Known Good for you. You are not provided with a menu choice.

Reverting to the Last Known Good causes the loss of any changes made to the hardware configuration since the Last Known Good was saved. Therefore, it is wise to make one hardware configuration change at a time and reboot after each change. That way, if problems during booting are encountered, only the most recent change is lost. When installing several hardware devices, install them one at a time, rebooting each time.

> **TIP** If you have problems booting in Windows NT, don't log on. If you do, you will over-write your previous Last Known Good.

Windows NT Boot Disks

With Windows 9x and DOS, any single floppy disk could be formatted as a boot disk or system disk. Windows NT is different. It requires three disks to hold enough of Windows NT to boot. However, just as with Windows 9x, formatting a single disk just to hold data or software can be done using Explorer, but you cannot make the disk a startup disk as is the case with Windows 9x.

If you try to boot from a disk that has been formatted by Windows NT, this error message appears:

```
BOOT: Couldn't find NTLDR
Please insert another disk
```

If the original three disks to boot Windows NT become corrupted or are lost, you can make extra copies using Winnt32.exe if you are running Windows NT, or using Winnt.exe if you are running another OS, such as DOS or Windows 9x. You do not have to be working on the PC where you intend to use the disks in order to make them, since the disks don't contain unique information for a specific PC.

Creating Windows NT Boot Disks   Do the following to create boot disks using Windows NT:

1. Click **Start**, **Run**, and then enter the path and name of the program with the /OX parameters. These parameters say to create only the set of three disks, without performing a complete installation. Note the E:\i386\winnt32.exe/ox entry in the Run dialog box of Figure 13-15. This is the command line from within Windows NT used to create the disks when drive E contains the Windows NT installation CD.

A+ OS
  2.3
  3.1
  3.2

Figure 13-15   Using Winnt32.exe to create a set of boot disks

2. The program asks for the location of the installation files. In this example, you would enter E:\i386. You are then prompted to insert three disks. The program creates the disks beginning with disk 3, then 2, then 1.

Windows NT does not have a safe mode as does Windows 9x, so if the PC later cannot boot Windows NT from the hard drive, these three disks can be used to load Windows NT, which loads using a generic VGA mode. After Windows NT is loaded, use the Emergency Repair Disk to restore critical system files to their state at the time the last update was made to the Emergency Repair Disk.

The Windows NT Emergency Repair Disk

A fourth important disk is the **Emergency Repair Disk (ERD)**, which does contain information unique to your OS and hard drive. You are given the opportunity to create the disk during installation. Always create this disk, because it is your record of critical information about your system that can be used to fix a problem with the OS.

The ERD enables restoration on your hard drive of the Windows registry, which contains all the configuration information for Windows. In addition, the disk includes information used to build a command window to run DOS-like commands. The files on the ERD are listed in Table 13-2. Files stored on the ERD are also written to the hard drive during the installation process. Using Explorer, you can see the files listed in the \winnt_root\repair folder.

13

Table 13-2   Files on the Windows NT Emergency Repair Disk

File	Description
Setup.log	A read-only, hidden system file used to verify the files installed on a system
System._	A compressed file containing part of the registry
Sam._	A compressed file containing some of the security part of the registry
Security._	A compressed file containing some of the security part of the registry
Software._	A compressed file containing software information in the registry
Default._	A compressed file containing part of the registry
Config.nt	The Windows NT version of Config.sys used in creating a command window
Autoexec.nt	The Windows NT version of Autoexec.bat
Ntuser.da_	A compressed file containing information about authorized users of the system

A+ OS
2.3
3.1
3.2

After the installation, you can create a new ERD or update the current one by using the Rdisk.exe utility in the \winnt_root\system32 folder. You should update the disk any time you make any major changes to the system, for example, when you install hardware or software. To use the Rdisk.exe utility, click Start, Run, and then either click Browse or enter the path to the utility. Add the /S option so that the utility also updates the registry.

If Windows NT is stored on drive D, the command line is:

D:\WINNT\System32\rdisk.exe /s

First, files are updated in the *\winnt_root*\repair directory; then you are given the opportunity to create a new ERD.

Using the Boot Disks and the ERD to Recover from a Failed Boot

In case of problems with the OS, you can do several things to attempt to load Windows NT from the hard drive, which are beyond the scope of this book. However, in the case of a hard drive failure, you can boot from the three boot disks that come with the Windows NT CD or that you made using either Winnt.exe or Winnt32.exe. The Windows NT programs on these disks may also request that you provide the ERD. Insert the first boot disk, and reboot. You will be prompted to insert disk 2, followed by disk 3. The Setup menu in Figure 13-16 then appears. Select the option to repair a damaged installation by pressing R, and follow directions on screen.

```
Windows NT Workstation Setup

Welcome to Setup.
The Setup program for the Microsoft(R) Windows NT(TM) OS version 4.0
prepares Windows NT to run on your computer.

        *To learn more about Windows NT Setup before continuing, press F1
        *To set up Windows NT now, press ENTER
        *To repair a damaged Windows NT version 4.0 installation, press R
        *To quit Setup without installing Windows NT, press F3
```

Figure 13-16   Windows NT Workstation Setup Menu

> **TIP** Windows NT does not have a Device Manager. When installing and troubleshooting hardware, look for individual icons in the Control Panel to manage hardware devices. For a detailed report of the system configuration, use the WinMSD command. At a command prompt enter Winmsd /a /f. The command creates the report in the current directory.

CHAPTER SUMMARY

❑ Windows 2000 is actually a suite of operating systems: Windows 2000 Professional, Windows 2000 Server, Windows 2000 Advanced Server, and Windows 2000 Datacenter Server.

❑ The two architectural modes of Windows NT/2000/XP are user mode and kernel mode. Kernel mode is further divided into two components: executive services and the hardware abstraction layer (HAL).

❑ A process is a unique instance of a program running together with the program resources and other programs it may use. A thread is one task that the process requests from the kernel, such as the task of printing a file.

❑ An NTVDM provides a DOS-like environment for DOS and Windows 3.x applications.

❑ Windows 3.x 16-bit applications run in a WOW.

❑ A workgroup is a group of computers and users sharing resources. Each computer maintains a list of users and their rights on that particular PC. A domain is a group of networked computers that share a centralized directory database of user account information and security.

❑ Of all Windows NT/2000/XP accounts, the administrator account has the most privileges and rights and can create new user accounts and assign them rights.

❑ Windows 2000 can run in native mode and mixed mode. Native mode is used when all domain servers are Windows 2000 servers. Mixed mode is used when a domain has both Windows 2000 and Windows NT servers controlling the domain.

❑ Windows NT can operate using two different file systems: FAT16 and NTFS. NTFS offers more security and power than does FAT16, but FAT16 is backward-compatible with older OSs. Windows 2000/XP supports FAT16, FAT32, and NTFS. NTFS under Windows 2000/XP is not compatible with NTFS under Windows NT.

❑ Windows NT/2000/XP offers a clean install and an upgrade installation. A clean install overwrites all information from previous operating system installations on the hard drive.

❑ System BIOS, hardware, and software must be compatible with Windows 2000. Check the HCL and the Compatible Software Applications list on the Microsoft Web site before beginning an installation. If you need to flash BIOS, do it before you begin the installation.

❑ A PC can be configured to dual boot between Windows NT or 2000 and another OS, such as Windows 9x or DOS.

❑ Windows 2000 supports a dual boot, but each operating system must be installed in its own partition, and an application must be installed twice, once for each OS.

❑ A Windows 2000 upgrade installation is done in two phases, the Report phase and the Setup phase.

❑ Windows 2000 supports Plug and Play and automatically launches the Add New Hardware Wizard when it senses a new device has been installed on the system.

❑ Windows 2000 has a Device Manager to view, uninstall, and update devices.

❑ Applications can be installed in Windows 2000 using the Add/Remove Programs applet in Control Panel.

❑ Four disks are important in recovering from a failed Windows NT boot. Three disks are required to boot Windows NT, and an Emergency Repair Disk (ERD) can be prepared to recover critical system files on the hard drive.

13

KEY TERMS

ACPI (Advanced Configuration and Power Interface)

Active Directory

administrator account

answer file

backup domain controller (BDC)

boot loader menu

boot partition

client/server

digital signature

domain

domain controller

dual boot

Emergency Repair Disk (ERD)

executive services

(HAL) hardware abstraction layer

kernel mode

Last Known Good configuration

master file table (MFT)

mixed mode

multithreading

native mode

NTVDM (NT virtual DOS machine)

Pagefile.sys

pages

peer-to-peer

primary domain controller (PDC)

process

security accounts manager (SAM)

subsystems

system partition

system state data

thread

unattended installation

user mode

Win16 on Win32 (WOW)

workgroup

REVIEW QUESTIONS

1. Windows 2000 includes four operating systems. These are:

   a. _____

   b. _____

   c. _____

   d. _____

2. The operating systems found under the name Windows NT, Windows 2000, and Windows XP operate in two modes. They include _____ mode and _____ mode.

3. With the operating system running in _____ mode, programs have only limited access to system information and can access hardware only through other operating system services.

4. With the operating system running in _____ mode, programs have extensive access to system information and hardware.

5. Which of the following subsystems provides logon to the system and other security features, including privileges for file access?

   a. Win32

   b. Win16

   c. DOS

   d. Executive Services

   e. Hardware Abstraction Layer

6. Whether directly or indirectly, all applications relate to Windows NT, Windows 2000, and Windows XP by way of the _____ subsystem.

   a. Win32

   b. Win16

   c. DOS

   d. Executive Services

   e. Hardware Abstraction Layer

7. Windows 3.x was based on DOS as the operating system foundation. With that in mind, which type of environment do all 16-bit Windows 3.x applications reside in Windows NT/2000/XP?

   a. Win16

   b. Win32

   c. NT Virtual DOS machine (NTVDM)

   d. Win16 on Win32 (WOW)

   e. Executive Services

8. All 32-bit applications do not require an NTVDM and can relate to the Win32 subsystem directly.

   a. True

   b. False

9. The term _____ refers to a single task that the process requests from the kernel, such as printing a file.

   a. NTVDM

   b. Program

   c. Thread

   d. Process

   e. Hardware Abstraction Layer

10. The term _____ refers to a program or group of programs that is running, together with the system resources assigned to it, such as memory addresses, environmental variables, and other resources.

   a. NTVDM

   b. Program

   c. Thread

   d. Process

   e. Hardware Abstraction Layer

11. Kernel mode is used by two main components: _____ and _____.

13

12. The _____ components manage hardware resources by way of the Hardware Abstraction Layer (HAL) and device drivers.

13. A _____ is a logical group of computers and users that share resources.

    a. Peer-to-peer network

    b. Client/server network

    c. Workgroup

    d. Domain

    e. Domain controller

14. A _____ is a group of networked computers that share a centralized directory database of user account information and security for the entire set of computers.

    a. Peer-to-peer network

    b. Client/server network

    c. Workgroup

    d. Domain

    e. Domain controller

15. Under Windows NT, there can be two primary domain controllers (PDC) in a single domain.

    a. True

    b. False

16. In Windows 2000, the _____ is a directory database service that allows for a single administration point for all shared resources on a network.

    a. PDC

    b. BDC

    c. Kernel

    d. Active Directory

    e. System Partition

17. In Windows NT/2000/XP, the _____ partition is the active partition on the hard drive; it contains the operating system boot record.

    a. System

    b. Boot

    c. Primary

    d. Extended

    e. Secondary

18. With Windows NT, which file systems are *not* allowed for formatted partitions?

    a. FAT16

    b. FAT32

    c. NTFS

    d. All are allowed

    e. None of the above

19. With Windows 2000 and Windows XP, which file systems are *not* allowed for formatted partitions?

    a. FAT16

    b. FAT32

    c. NTFS

    d. All are allowed

    e. None of the above

20. Which file system is compatible with Windows 98?

    a. FAT

    b. NTFS

    c. Both a and b

21. Which file system uses smaller cluster sizes?

    a. FAT

    b. NTFS

    c. Both a and b

22. Which file system has less overhead?

    a. FAT

    b. NTFS

    c. Both a and b

23. Which file system supports compression of individual files or folders?

    a. FAT

    b. NTFS

    c. Both a and b

24. The virtual memory manager allows the exchange of memory in _____ segments called "pages."

    a. 4 KB

    b. 8 KB

    c. 256 KB

    d. 512 KB

    e. 1 MB

13

25. A service technician would like to configure a new system to allow a dual boot with Windows 98 and Windows 2000. The technician should *not* set up the file system as:

a. FAT16

b. FAT32

c. NTFS

d. Any of the above are valid.

e. None of the above

14

MANAGING AND TROUBLESHOOTING WINDOWS 2000

In this chapter, you will learn:

- ◆ About the Windows NT/2000/XP boot process
- ◆ How to troubleshoot the Windows 2000 boot process
- ◆ How to use maintenance and troubleshooting tools to support Windows 2000

I n the last chapter, you learned about the Windows NT/2000/XP architecture and how to install Windows 2000 and Windows NT. You also learned how to troubleshoot the Windows NT boot process. As you learned in the last chapter, Windows NT does not provide many support tools to aid in troubleshooting when the OS does not boot correctly. Windows 2000 and Windows XP have more troubleshooting tools and options. Some of these tools and options work with both Windows 2000 and Windows XP, and some work with only one OS or the other. In this chapter, you learn about the details of the Windows NT/2000/XP boot process and specifically how to troubleshoot the Windows 2000 boot process. In addition, this chapter covers supporting and troubleshooting Windows 2000 after it boots, including problems you might have with system errors and performance. In the next two chapters, you will learn about Windows XP.

UNDERSTANDING THE WINDOWS NT/2000/XP BOOT PROCESS

A+ OS
1.2
2.3

Understanding the boot process and making changes to it are critical when supporting Windows NT/2000/XP. In this section you learn what happens during the boot process as well as how to solve boot problems. The following is a look behind the scenes with a description of each step in the boot process. As you read, refer to Table 14-1 for an outline of the boot sequence for Intel-based computers.

1. *BIOS executes POST.* First, startup BIOS performs POST, which executes regardless of which OS is present. After POST, BIOS turns to the hard drive to load an OS. Remember from earlier chapters that BIOS looks for the partition information at the beginning of the hard drive.

2. *BIOS executes the MBR program.* The first thing in the partition information that BIOS needs is the MBR (Master Boot Record) containing the master boot program. Remember that the master boot program is the very first thing written in the first sector of a hard drive. The master boot program is followed by the partition table itself, and both are stored in the master boot record. BIOS executes this master boot program, which examines the partition table, looking for the location of the active partition on the drive, and then turns to the first sector of the active partition to find and load the program in the boot sector of that active partition. So far in the boot process, nothing is different between Windows NT/2000/XP and other OSs.

Table 14-1   Steps in the Intel-based CPU boot process

Description	Step
POST (power-on self test) is executed.	1. Performed by startup BIOS
MBR (Master Boot Record) is loaded, and the master boot program within the MBR is run. (The master boot program is at the very beginning of the hard drive, as part of the partition table information. The program searches for and loads the OS boot record of the active partition.)	2. Performed by startup BIOS
The boot sector from active partition is loaded, and the program in this boot sector is run.	3. Performed by MBR program
Ntldr (NT Loader) file is loaded and run.	4. Performed by boot sector program
The processor is changed from real mode to flat memory mode, in which 32-bit code can be executed.	5. Performed by Windows NT/2000/XP loader
Minifile system drivers (described below) are started so files can be read.	6. Performed by Windows NT/2000/XP loader
Read Boot.ini file and build the boot loader menu described in the file. (This menu is discussed in Chapter 13.)	7. Performed by Windows NT/2000/XP loader

A+ OS
1.2
2.3

Table 14-1   Steps in the Intel-based CPU boot process (continued)

Description	Step
If the user chooses Windows NT/2000/XP, then run Ntdetect.com to detect hardware present; otherwise, run Bootsect.dos.	8. Performed by Windows NT/2000/XP loader
Ntldr reads information from the Registry about device drivers and loads them. Also loads the Hal.dll and Ntoskrml.exe.	9. Performed by Windows NT/2000/XP loader
Ntldr passes control to Ntoskrml.exe; load is complete.	10. Last step performed by the loader

3. *The MBR program executes the OS boot program.* Remember that when DOS or Windows 9x boots, the OS boot sector contains the name of the initial OS load program, Io.sys. When Windows NT/2000/XP is installed, it edits this boot sector of the active partition, instructing it to load the Windows NT/2000/XP program Ntldr at startup, instead of Io.sys. (It does this even when the PC is configured for a dual boot.)

4. *The boot program executes Ntldr.* With the execution of Ntldr, Windows NT/2000/XP then starts its boot sequence. This program is responsible for loading Windows NT/2000/XP and performing several chores to complete the loading process. It then passes control to the OS.

5. *Ntldr changes the processor mode and loads a file system.* Up to this point, the CPU has been processing in real mode. Windows NT/2000/XP does not process in real mode. Ntldr is a 32-bit program that begins by changing the CPU mode from real mode to a 32-bit mode called **32-bit flat memory mode** in order to run its 32-bit code. Next a temporary, simplified file system called the **minifile system** is started so that Ntldr can read files from either a FAT or an NTFS file system.

6. *Ntldr reads and loads the boot loader menu.* Ntldr then is able to read the **Boot.ini** file, a hidden text file that contains information needed to build the boot loader menu. The menu appears and the user can make a selection or, after the preset time expires, the default selection is used.

7. *Ntldr uses Ntdetect.com.* If Ntldr is to load Windows NT/2000/XP as the OS, Ntldr runs the program Ntdetect.com, which checks the hardware devices present and passes the information back to Ntldr. This information is used later to update the Windows NT/2000/XP registry concerning the Last Known Good hardware profile used.

8. *Ntldr loads the OS and device drivers.* Ntldr then loads Ntoskrnl.exe, Hal.dll, and the System hive. The System hive is a portion of the Windows NT/2000/XP registry that includes hardware information that is now used to load the proper device drivers for the hardware present. You will learn more about the System hive in Chapter 16.

14

A+ OS
1.2
2.3

9. *Ntldr passes control to Ntoskrnl.exe.* Ntldr then passes control to Ntoskrnl.exe, and the boot sequence is complete.

10. *An operating system other than Windows NT/2000/XP is chosen.* If a selection was made from the boot loader menu to load an OS other than Windows NT/2000/XP, such as DOS or Windows 9x, Ntldr does not load Ntdetect.com nor complete the remaining chores to load Windows NT/2000/XP. Instead, Ntldr loads and passes control to the program Bootsect.dos, which is responsible for loading the other OS.

> **TIP** When repairing a corrupted hard drive, a support person often copies files from one PC to another. However, the Bootsect.dos file contains information from the partition table for a particular hard drive and cannot be copied from another PC.

The files needed to boot Windows NT/2000/XP successfully are listed in Table 14-2. (In the table, references to *winnt_root* follow Microsoft documentation conventions and mean the name of the directory where Windows NT/2000/XP is stored, which is \\Winnt by default. Also, sometimes Microsoft refers to this root folder as %SystemRoot%.)

Table 14-2 Files needed to boot Windows NT/2000/XP successfully

File	Location
Ntldr	Root folder of the system partition (usually C:\\)
Boot.ini	Root folder of the system partition (usually C:\\)
Bootsect.dos	Root folder of the system partition (usually C:\\)
Ntdetect.com	Root folder of the system partition (usually C:\\)
Ntbootdd.sys*	Root folder of the system partition (usually C:\\)
Ntoskrnl.exe	*winnt_root*\\system32 folder of the boot partition
Hal.dll	*winnt_root*\\system32 folder of the boot partition
System	*winnt_root*\\system32\\config folder of the boot partition
Device drivers	*winnt_root*\\system32\\drivers folder of the boot partition

*Ntbootdd.sys is used only with a SCSI boot device.

Customizing the Windows NT/2000/XP Boot Process

A+ OS
2.3

The Boot.ini file contains information about how the Windows NT/2000/XP boot is configured and can be used to customize the boot process. As you learned earlier in this chapter, Ntldr reads this file and uses it to see what operating systems are available and how to set up the boot. Figure 14-1 shows an example of a Boot.ini file for Windows 2000.

There are two main sections in Boot.ini: the [boot loader] section and the [operating systems] section. The [boot loader] section contains the number of seconds the system gives the user to select an operating system before it loads the default operating system; this is called a timeout. In Figure 14-1, the timeout is set to 30 seconds. If the system is set for a dual boot, the path to the default operating system is also listed in the [boot loader] section.

A+ OS
2.3

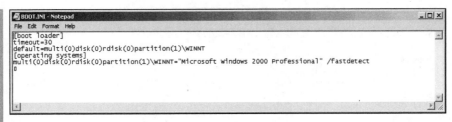

Figure 14-1   A sample Boot.ini file

The [operating systems] section of the Boot.ini file provides a list of operating systems that can be loaded, including the path to the boot partition of each operating system. Here is the meaning of each entry in Figure 14-1 that points to the location of the OS:

- *Multi(0).* Use the first hard drive controller.

- *Disk(0).* Used only when booting from a SCSI hard drive.

- *Rdisk(0).* Use the first hard drive.

- *Partition(1).* Use the first partition on the drive.

You can add switches to the [operating systems] section of the Boot.ini file, either by editing the file manually or through the System Properties window. In Figure 14-1, the only switch used in this Boot.ini file is /fastdetect, which causes the OS not to attempt to inspect any peripherals connected to a COM port at startup.

The recommended way to change Boot.ini settings, which is also easier and safer than editing the file manually, is through the System Properties window. For Windows 2000, do the following:

1. On the Start menu, point to **Settings** and then click **Control Panel**.

2. Double-click the **System** icon.

3. The System Properties window opens. Click the **Advanced** tab (see Figure 14-2).

4. Click the **Startup and Recovery** button.

5. The Startup and Recovery window opens (see Figure 14-3). Change settings as desired and then click **OK** to save them (or Cancel if you do not want to save them).

14

A^+ OS
2.3

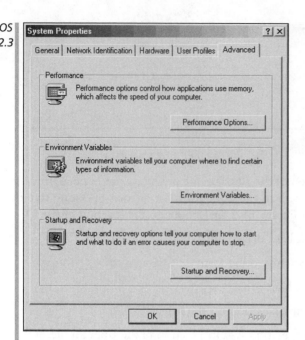

Figure 14-2   You can access startup and recovery options from the System Properties window

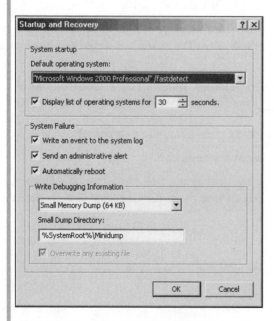

Figure 14-3   Changing the default operating system and timeout value in the Startup and Recovery window changes the Boot.ini settings

A+ OS
2.3

> In order to view or edit the Boot.ini file using a text editor such as Notepad, you must first change the folder options to view hidden system files. To do that, in Windows Explorer, select the root directory, click Tools, Folder Options, and then select the View tab. Uncheck the option to *Hide protected operating system files.*

TROUBLESHOOTING THE WINDOWS 2000 BOOT PROCESS

A+ OS
2.3
3.2

When problems arise with booting, as with all PC problems, try the simple things first. Turn off the power and restart the system. Check for loose cables, switches that are not on, stuck keys on the keyboard, a wall outlet switch that has been turned off, and similar easy-to-solve problems. The next step is to determine at what point in the boot process the system fails. Ask what has happened since the last successful boot. Has new hardware or software been installed? Has there been a power surge or electrical storm? Has a user tinkered with the system? If you cannot pinpoint the source of the problem, then several tools can help you troubleshoot the boot process. Windows 2000 offers an Advanced Options menu, which includes starting the computer in safe mode. Use this option to prevent many device drivers and system services that normally load during the boot process from loading. You can then fix or disable these devices or services once the OS loads. The second utility, called the Recovery Console, is new in Windows 2000. Its command-line interface lets you perform maintenance and repairs to the hard drive. Another tool is the emergency startup disk, which is used to recover from problems with corrupted or missing operating system files or a corrupted hard drive boot sector. These three tools are discussed next.

Advanced Options Menu

A+ OS
2.3
3.2

As a PC boots, when the message *Starting Windows* appears at the bottom of the screen, press the F8 key to display the Windows 2000 **Advanced Options menu**, shown in Figure 14-4. As with the Windows 9x startup menu, this menu can be used to diagnose and fix problems when booting Windows 2000. The purpose of each menu option is outlined in the following sections.

14

Safe Mode

Safe mode boots the OS with a minimum configuration and can be used to solve problems with a new hardware installation or problems caused by user settings. Safe mode boots with the mouse, monitor with basic video, keyboard, and mass storage drivers loaded. It uses the default system services (it does not load any extra services) and does not provide network access. When you boot in safe mode, you see "Safe Mode" in all four corners of your screen. You have a GUI interface in safe mode. Once the OS loads in safe mode, you can disable the problem device, scan for viruses, run diagnostic software, or take other appropriate action to diagnose and solve problems. When you load Windows 2000 in safe mode, all files used for the load are recorded in the Ntbtlog.txt file.

A+ OS
2.3
3.2

Windows 2000 Advanced Options Menu
Please select an option:

       Safe Mode
       Safe Mode with Networking
       Safe Mode with Command Prompt

       Enable Boot Logging
       Enable VGA Mode
       Last Known Good Configuration
       Directory Services Restore Mode (Windows 2000 domain controllers only)
       Debugging Mode

       Boot Normally

Use ↑ and ↓ to move the highlight to your choice.
Press Enter to choose.

Figure 14-4   Press the F8 key at startup to display the Windows 2000 Advanced
                 Options menu

Safe Mode with Networking

Use this option when you are solving a problem with booting and need access to the network to solve the problem. For example, if you have just attempted to install a printer, which causes the OS to hang when it boots, and the printer drivers are downloaded from the network, boot into safe mode with networking. Uninstall the printer and then install it again from the network. Also use this mode when the Windows 2000 installation files are available on the network, rather than the Windows 2000 installation CD, and you need to access these files.

Safe Mode with Command Prompt

This safe mode option does not load a GUI desktop automatically. Use it to get a command prompt. If the first safe mode option does not load the OS, then try this option.

Enable Boot Logging

When you boot with this option, Windows 2000 loads normally and you access the regular desktop. However, all files used during the load process are recorded in a file, Ntbtlog.txt. Use this option to see what did and did not load during the boot process. If you have a problem getting a device to work, check Ntbtlog.txt to see what driver files loaded. Boot logging is much more effective if you have a copy of Ntbtlog.txt that was made when everything worked as it should. Then you can compare the good load to the bad load, looking for differences.

Enable VGA Mode

Use this option when the video setting is such that you can't see the screen well enough to fix a bad setting. This can happen because of a corrupted video driver or when a user creates a desktop with black fonts on a black background, or something similar. Booting in this mode gives you a very plain VGA video. Go to the Display settings, correct the problem, and reboot normally.

Last Known Good Configuration

Just as with Windows NT, Windows 2000 keeps the Last Known Good configuration in the registry. Use this option if you suspect the system was configured incorrectly. It restores Windows 2000 to the settings of the last successful boot, and all system setting changes made after this last successful boot are lost.

> **TIP** Each time the system boots completely and the user logs on, the Last Known Good is saved. If you have booted several times since a problem started, the Last Known Good will not help you recover from the problem, since all saved versions of the Last Known Good reflect the problem.

Directory Services Restore Mode (Windows 2000 Domain Controllers Only)

This option applies only to domain controllers and is used as one step in the process of recovering from a corrupted Active Directory. Recall that Active Directory is the domain database managed by a domain controller that tracks users and resources on the domain. The details of how all this works are beyond the scope of this chapter.

Debugging Mode

This mode gives you the opportunity to move system boot logs from the failing computer to another computer for evaluation. Connect another computer to the failing computer by way of the serial port. In this mode, Windows 2000 sends all the boot information to the serial port. The details of how to do this can be found in the *Windows 2000 Professional Resource Kit* (Microsoft Press).

14

Recovery Console

The Advanced Options menu can help if the problem is a faulty device driver or system service. However, if the problem goes deeper than that, the next tool to use is the **Recovery Console**. Use it when the operating system does not start properly or hangs during the load. The Recovery Console does not use a GUI, and with it you can access the FAT16, FAT32, and NTFS file systems.

The purpose of the Recovery Console is to allow you to repair a damaged registry, system files, or file system on the hard drive. You must enter the Administrator password in order to use the Console and access an NTFS volume. You are not allowed into all folders, and you cannot copy files from the hard drive to a floppy disk without setting certain parameters. If the registry is so corrupted that the Recovery Console cannot read the password in order to validate it, you are not asked for the password, but you are limited in what you can do at the Console.

A+ OS
2.3
3.1

The Recovery Console software is located on the Windows 2000 CD and also on the four Windows 2000 setup disks. If you have not already created the setup disks, you can go to a working Windows 2000 PC and create the disks by following the directions given in Chapter 13. Follow these steps to load Windows 2000 from the disks and access the Recovery Console:

1. Insert the first of the four setup disks, and restart the PC. You are directed to insert each of the four disks in turn, and then the Setup screen appears as shown in Figure 14-5.

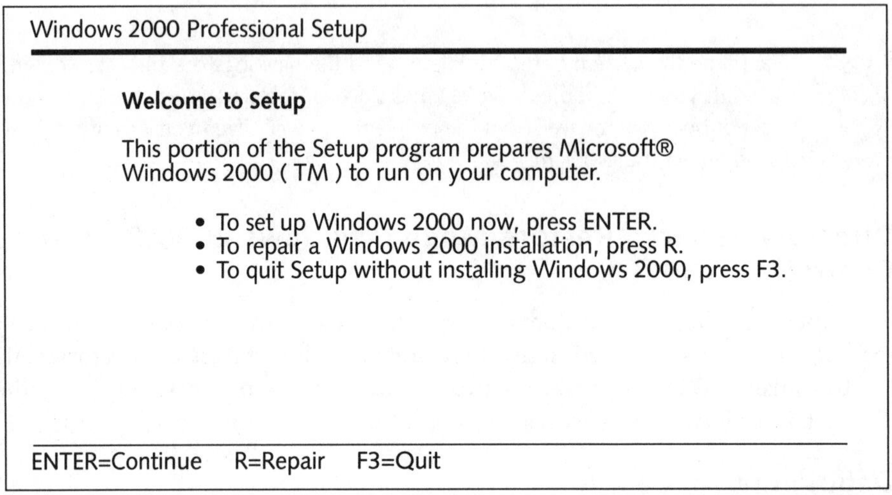

Windows 2000 Professional Setup

───

Welcome to Setup

This portion of the Setup program prepares Microsoft®
Windows 2000 (TM) to run on your computer.

   • To set up Windows 2000 now, press ENTER.
   • To repair a Windows 2000 installation, press R.
   • To quit Setup without installing Windows 2000, press F3.

───

ENTER=Continue   R=Repair   F3=Quit

Figure 14-5   Use this Windows Setup screen to access the Recovery Console

2. Type **R** to select the To repair a Windows 2000 installation option. The Windows 2000 Repair Options window opens. See Figure 14-6. Type **C** to select the Recovery Console.

3. The Windows 2000 Recovery Console window opens. See Figure 14-7. The Recovery Console looked at the hard drive and determined that only a single Windows 2000 installation was on the drive installed in the C:\Winnt folder. (The Winnt folder might be on a different drive on your machine.) Press **1** and then press **Enter** to select that installation.

4. Enter the Administrator password, and press **Enter**. If you don't know the password, you cannot use the console.

A+ OS
2.3
3.1

Windows 2000 Professional Setup

Windows 2000 Repair Options:

- To repair a Windows 2000 installation by using the recovery console, press C.

- To repair a Windows 2000 installation by using the emergency repair process, press R.

If the repair options do not successfully repair your system, run Windows 2000 Setup again.

C=Console   R=Repair   F3=Quit

Figure 14-6 Windows 2000 offers two repair options

Microsoft Windows 2000 (TM) Recovery Console.

The Recovery Console provides system repair and recovery functionality.

Type EXIT to quit the Recovery Console and restart the computer.

1: C:\WINNT

Which Windows 2000 installation would you like to log onto
(To cancel, press ENTER)? 1
Type the Administrator password:
C:\WINNT>

Figure 14-7 The Windows 2000 Recovery Console command prompt

14

5. You now have a command prompt. You can use a limited group of DOS-like commands at this point to recover a failed system. These commands are listed and described in Table 14–3. To leave the Recovery Console and start Windows 2000, type **Exit** at the command prompt.

 At the command prompt, to retrieve the last command, press F3. To retrieve the command one character at a time, press the F1 key.

A+ OS
2.3
3.1

Table 14-3   Commands available from the Recovery Console

Command	Description
Attrib	Changes the attributes of a file or folder, works the same as the DOS version, as in the following example: `Attrib -r -h -s filename` This command removes the read, hidden, and system attributes from the file.
Batch	Carries out commands stored in a batch file: `Batch file1 file2`. The commands stored in file1 are executed, and the results written to file2. If no file2 is specified, results are written to the screen.
Cd	Displays or changes the current directory.
Chkdsk	Checks a disk and repairs or recovers the data.
Cls	Clears the screen.
Copy	Copies a single uncompressed file, for example, `Copy A:\File1 C:\Winnt\File2` copies the file on the floppy disk named File1 to the hard drive, Winnt folder, naming the file File2. Use the command to replace corrupted files.
Del	Deletes a file: `Del File1`.
Dir	Lists files and folders.
Disable	Used when a service or driver starts and prevents the system from booting properly: `Disable servicename` This command disables a Windows 2000 system service or driver, restarts the computer without it, and helps you determine the problem.
Diskpart	Creates and deletes partitions on the hard drive. Enter the command with no arguments to display a user interface.
Enable	Enables a Windows 2000 system service or driver: `Enable servicename`.
Exit	Quits the Recovery Console and restarts the computer.
Expand	Expands a compressed file and copies it from a floppy disk or a CD to the destination folder, for example: `Expand A:\File1 C:\Winnt` expands the file on the floppy disk, copying it to the hard drive.
Fixboot	Rewrites the OS boot sector on the hard drive. If a drive letter is not specified, the system drive is assumed. `Fixboot C:` Use this command when the boot sector is damaged.
Fixmbr	Rewrites the Master Boot Record boot program. This command is the same as `Fdisk/MBR`. Use this command when the Master Boot Record is damaged.
Format	Formats a logical drive. If no file system is specified, NTFS is assumed: `Format C:/fs:FAT32` Uses FAT32 file system `Format C:/fs:FAT` Uses FAT16 file system
Help	Help utility appears for the given command: `Help Fixboot`.
Listsvc	Lists all available services.
Logon	Allows you to log on to an installation with the Administrator password.
Map	Lists all drive letters and file system types.
Md or Mkdir	Creates a directory: `MD C:\TEMP`.

A+ OS
2.3
3.1

Table 14-3   Commands available from the Recovery Console (continued)

Command	Description
More or Type	Displays a text file on screen: `TYPE filename.ext`.
Rd or Rmdir	Deletes a directory: `RD C:\TEMP`.
Rename or Ren	Renames a file: `Rename File1.txt File2.txt`.
Set	Displays or sets Recovery Console environmental variables.
Systemroot	Sets the current directory to the directory where Windows 2000 is installed.
Type	Displays contents of a text file: `Type File1.txt`.

Using the Recovery Console to Restore the Registry

If you suspect that the Windows 2000 registry is damaged, you can use the Recovery Console commands to restore the registry from the last backup that you created. (This process also works for the Windows XP registry.) The registry consists of five files, Default, Sam, Security, Software, and System, which are stored in the %SystemRoot%\System32\Config folder. A backup of the registry is stored in the %SystemRoot%\Repair\RegBack folder every time you back up the system state (see Figure 14-8).

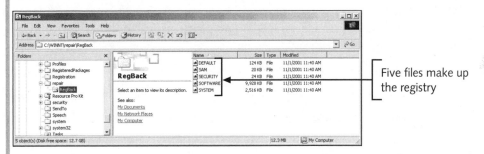

Five files make up the registry

Figure 14-8   Windows puts a backup of the registry in the C:\WINNT\repair\RegBack folder

To restore the registry from this backup using the Recovery Console, first rename the registry files so that you can backtrack if necessary. From the Recovery Console command prompt, perform the steps outlined in Table 14-4. These actions restore the registry to its state at the time of the last backup.

Table 14-4   Steps to restore the Windows 2000/XP registry

Command	Description
1. `Systemroot`	Makes the Windows folder the current folder.
2. `CD System32\Config`	Makes the Windows registry folder the current folder.

14

$A+$ _OS_
2.3
3.1
3.2

Table 14-4   Steps to restore the Windows 2000/XP registry (continued)

Command	Description

3. `Ren Default Default.save`
   `Ren Sam Sam.save`
   `Ren Security Security.save`
   `Ren Software Software.save`
   `Ren System System.save`
	Renames the five registry files.

4. `Systemroot`	Returns to the Windows folder.
5. `CD repair\RegBack`	Makes the registry backup folder the current folder.

6. `Copy default C:\Winnt\system32\config`
   `Copy Sam C:\Winnt\system32\config`
   `Copy Security C:\Winnt\system32\config`
   `Copy Software C:\Winnt\system32\config`
   `Copy System C:\Winnt\system32\config`
	Copies the five registry files from the backup folder to the registry folder.

Installing the Recovery Console

Although the Recovery Console is often launched from the Windows CD to recover from system failure, you can also install it on your working system so it appears on the OS startup menu. Use it to address less drastic problems that occur when you can access the menu. To install the Recovery Console:

1. Open a command window in Windows 2000.

2. Change from the current directory to the \i386 folder on the Windows 2000 CD.

3. Enter the command **winnt32 /cmdcons**. The Recovery Console is installed.

4. Restart your computer. Recovery Console should now be shown with the list of available operating systems on the OS startup menu.

Emergency Repair Process

$A+$ _OS_
2.3
3.1
3.2

If options on the Advanced Options menu fail to recover the system and the Recovery Console fails to do so, your next option is the **Emergency Repair Process**. Use this option only as a last resort because it restores the system to the state it was in immediately after the Windows 2000 installation. All changes since the installation are lost. The process uses an Emergency Repair Disk (ERD), but the disk does not contain the same information as does the Windows NT ERD (Windows NT Emergency Repair Disk).

Recall that the Windows NT ERD contains a copy of the registry and that you should update the disk any time you make significant changes to the registry. You can then use the disk to repair a corrupted registry, restoring it to its state when you last updated the ERD.

The Windows 2000 ERD contains information about your current installation but does not contain a copy of the registry because it is too large to fit on a single floppy disk. The Windows 2000 ERD points to a folder on the hard drive where the registry was backed

A+ OS
2.3
3.1
3.2

up when Windows 2000 was installed. This folder is %SystemRoot%\repair, which most likely is C:\Winnt\repair.

Using the Windows 2000 ERD to recover from a corrupted registry returns you to the installation version of the registry, and you lose all changes to the registry since that time. Because of the way the ERD works, you do not need to update the disk once you've created it. Before a problem occurs, follow these directions to create the disk:

1. Click **Start**, point to **Programs**, **Accessories**, and **System Tools**, and then click **Backup**. The Backup window appears with the Welcome tab selected. See Figure 14-9. Select **Emergency Repair Disk**.

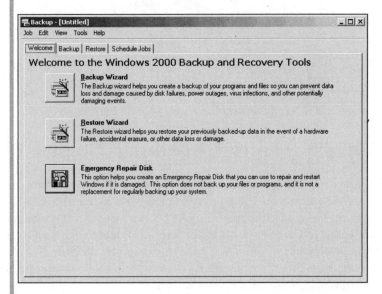

Figure 14-9   Use the Backup window to back up the registry and create an emergency repair disk

2. The Backup tab and the Emergency Repair Diskette dialog box open. If you check the box shown in Figure 14-10, the system backs up your registry to a folder under the Repair folder, %SystemRoot%\repair\RegBack.

3. Click **OK** to create the disk. Label the disk Windows 2000 Emergency Repair Disk, and keep it in a safe place.

If your hard drive fails, you can use the ERD to restore the system, including system files, boot files, and the registry, to its state at the end of the Windows 2000 installation. To do that, follow these steps:

1. Boot the PC from the four Windows 2000 setup disks. The Setup menu appears (refer back to Figure 14-5). Select option **R**.

2. When the Windows 2000 Repair Options window opens (refer back to Figure 14-6), select option **R**.

14

A+ OS
2.3
3.1
3.2

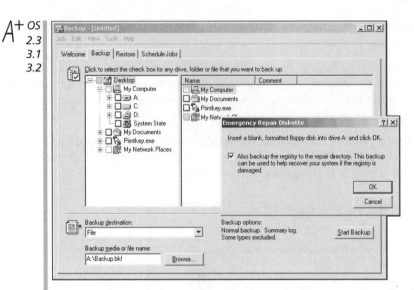

Figure 14-10   Create an ERD and back up the registry to the hard drive

3. You are instructed to insert the Emergency Repair Disk. Follow the instructions on the screen to repair the installation.

If this process does not work, then your next option is to reinstall Windows 2000. It is a good idea to use Windows 98 ScanDisk on a Windows 98 startup disk to scan the hard disk surface for errors before you do the installation. If you suspect that a virus damaged the file system, also use the Fixmbr command or the Fdisk /MBR command discussed in earlier chapters to replace the master boot program in case it has been corrupted by the virus. Windows 2000 also offers a utility called InoculateIT Antivirus AVBoot, which is a command-line tool that can scan memory, the MBR sector, and OS boot sectors for viruses.

TOOLS FOR MAINTENANCE AND TROUBLESHOOTING

A+ OS
1.5

In this section, you will learn about many tools you can use for maintenance and troubleshooting in Windows 2000. You learned about some tools earlier in this chapter, as well as in previous chapters on other versions of Windows. All tools discussed in this section work under Windows XP, although in some cases, the menus have changed slightly. Of the tools discussed in this section, all except Windows File Protection, Microsoft Management Console, and automated Windows Update are available under Windows NT. In this section, you will learn how to use tools to manage hard disks, applications, system processes, and other Windows components.

Using the Backup Tool to Restore the System State

A+ OS
1.5

In Chapter 13, you learned how to back up the system state after installing Windows 2000 and verifying that the system is working. To use the backup (Ntbackup.exe) to restore the system state after the system fails or the registry becomes corrupted, begin the same way

A+ OS
 1.5

you did to make the backup by clicking Start, pointing to Programs, Accessories, and System Tools, and then clicking Backup. The dialog box opens showing the Backup tab. Click the Restore tab, which is shown in Figure 14-11.

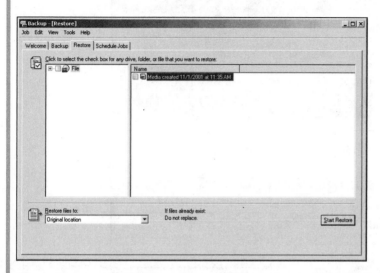

Figure 14-11   Restore the system state from the Restore tab of the Backup window

From the Restore tab, you select the backup you want to restore and, in the drop-down menu in the lower-left corner, the location to which it is to be restored. Click the Start Restore button in the lower-right corner to start the process. Remember that you can restore the system state as a way of restoring the registry.

Windows 2000 Support Tools

A+ OS
 3.3

Windows 2000 offers several support tools that you can install. They are located in the \Support\Tools folder on the Windows 2000 CD. To install them, run the Setup program located in that folder. Enter this command in the Run dialog box: D:\Support\Tools\Setup.exe. Substitute the drive letter of your CD-ROM drive for D in the command line if necessary. The list of tools installed is shown in Figure 14-12.

One of these utilities is Dependency Walker, which lists all the files used by an application. It can be useful when troubleshooting a failed application installation if you have a report of files used by the application on a computer where the installation is good or to help resolve General Protection Faults. Compare the reports, looking for DLL files that are missing on the bad installation, are not the correct size, or are incorrectly date stamped. Software applications often use DLL files for added functionality and to relate to the operating system. To use the utility, click Start, point to Programs, Windows 2000 Support Tools, and Tools, and then click Dependency Walker. Figure 14-13 shows a Dependency Walker window. Click File, Open, and select the main executable file for an application. In the figure, Apache.exe is selected. Apache is a popular Web server application. The window lists all supporting files that Apache.exe uses and how they depend on one another.

14

A+ OS
3.3

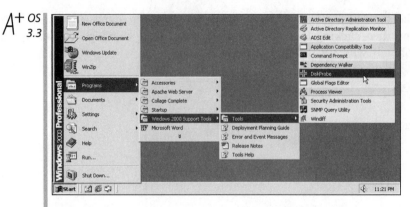

Figure 14-12   Windows 2000 support tools

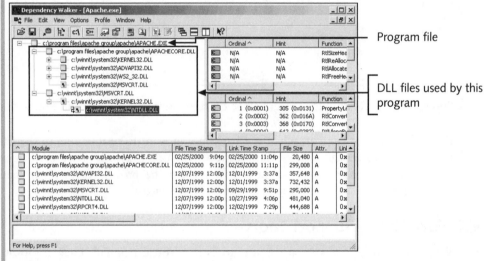

Figure 14-13   You can use Dependency Walker to solve problems with applications

Windows File Protection

Windows 2000 provides a feature called **WFP (Windows File Protection)** to protect system files such as .sys, .dll, or .exe files from modification. Earlier versions of Windows sometimes allowed these files to be overwritten by unsigned, non-Microsoft versions during program installations. Changes to shared system files can cause errors within a program, incompatibility between two or more programs, mismatches between file versions, or even system instability.

WFP prevents these problems and protects files from modification through two tools. One is a background process that notifies WFP when a protected file is modified. WFP then checks the file signature to see whether it is the correct Microsoft version of the file. If the file version is not correct, WFP looks in the Dllcache folder, which contains cached copies of system files or asks that the Windows 2000 CD be inserted so that WFP can find the file and restore it from the CD. Replacing incorrect system files with correct ones from the Windows 2000 CD requires administrative permissions. If a non-administrator user is logged on when WFP activates, WFP does not prompt that user to insert the Windows 2000 CD but waits until an administrator logs on to request the CD and replace the file.

 TIP   If a file has been modified, is correctly signed as a Microsoft-approved version, and is not present in the Dllcache folder, WFP adds it to that folder to be used as the correct version on future scans.

When WFP restores a file, it shows the following message by default, replacing *file_name* with the name of the system file it restored:

```
A file replacement was attempted on the protected system
file file_name. To maintain system stability, the file has
been restored to the correct Microsoft version. If
problems occur with your application, please contact the
application vendor for support.
```

If you see this message, carefully note what application was working at the time and what happened just before the message. In addition to software installations, viruses, and software applications, errors can cause attempted modifications to system files. It is important to have as much information as possible in order to figure out which applications might need to be scanned for viruses or replaced altogether.

The other tool that WFP provides is the **SFC (System File Checker)**. The system or an administrator might use this tool in several situations. If the administrator set the system to perform an unattended installation, after Setup is completed, the SFC checks all protected system files to see whether they were modified by programs added during the installation, as well as the catalog files that contain the file signatures. If any incorrect modifications have been made or if any important system files are unsigned, WFP retrieves a copy of the file from the Dllcache folder or requests it from the Windows 2000 CD.

14

An administrator can also activate the SFC manually from a command prompt and use it to verify that the system is using correct versions of all protected system files, either as a preventative maintenance measure or when it is suspected that system files have become corrupted or deleted. To use System File Checker, from the command prompt, the administrator types *Sfc.exe* with one of the switches listed in Table 14-5. You can also access the Run dialog box from the Start menu and type C:\Winnt\system32\sfc.exe /scannow (or another switch).

Table 14-5   Switches for the Sfc.exe utility

Switch	Function
/cachesize=x	Sets, in megabytes, the size of the file cache.
/cancel	Discontinues scans of protected system files.
/enable	Enables normal operation of WFP.

Table 14-5   Switches for the Sfc.exe utility (continued)

Switch	Function
/purgecache	Empties the file cache and immediately scans all protected system files, populating the Dllcache folder with confirmed correct versions of system files (may require insertion of the Windows 2000 CD as source for correct versions).
/quiet	Replaces incorrect versions of system files with correct ones without prompting the user.
/scanboot	Performs a scan of protected system files every time the system boots.
/scannow	Performs an immediate scan of protected system files.
/scanonce	Performs a scan of protected system files the next time the system boots.
/?	Displays a list of available switches for the sfc command.

Disk Properties Window

A+ OS
1.4
1.5
2.5

The Disk Properties window provides a way for you to perform routine maintenance on a drive. To access the window, using Windows Explorer, right-click the icon for the drive that you want to work with, and select Properties from the shortcut menu. The Properties window for the selected drive opens, as shown in Figure 14-14. The General tab, which appears in front when you first open the window, provides information about the name, type, and file system of the selected drive, as well as the amount of free and used space.

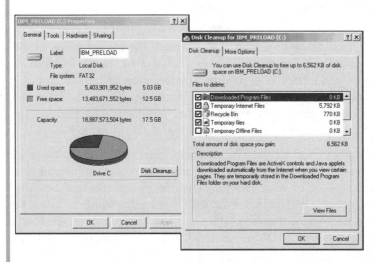

Figure 14-14   The Disk Properties window provides a shortcut to disk management tools

Notice that the drive in Figure 14-14 is using the FAT32 file system. Compare this window for a FAT32 disk to the window shown in Figure 14-15 for an NTFS disk. One difference in the two windows is the Disk Properties window for an NTFS disk includes the option for drive compression at the bottom of the window. For an NTFS disk, check Compress drive to save disk space, and then click Apply to compress the volume. Later, if you decide to not use compression, clear the check box.

A+ OS
1.4
1.5
2.5

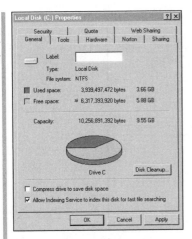

Figure 14-15 Disk Properties window for an NTFS disk

> **TIP** If you are using NTFS, you can also compress a single folder or file from the General tab of its Properties window.

If you click the Disk Cleanup... button to the right of the drive space graphic, the Disk Cleanup window opens with the Disk Cleanup tab showing, as shown in Figure 14-14. From this view, you can select nonessential files to delete in order to save drive space. Disk Cleanup tells you how much total space you can save and how much space each type of removable file is taking; it also describes each type of file. Included in the list are temporary files created by applications that the application no longer needs.

Going back to the Properties window for the drive, if you click the Tools tab, you can access three drive management tools that you are already familiar with: ScanDisk (listed as Error checking), Backup, and Defrag.

Computer Management

A+ OS
1.4
1.5
2.5

Computer Management is a window that consolidates several Windows 2000 administrative tools that you can use to manage the local PC or other computers on the network. To use most of these tools, you must be logged on as an administrator, although you can view certain settings and configurations in Computer Management if you are logged in with lesser privileges. To access Computer Management, from the Control Panel open the Administrative Tools window and then double-click the Computer Management icon. The Computer Management window appears. See Figure 14-16. Some tasks you can perform from this window include monitoring problems with hardware, software, and security. You can share folders, view device configurations, add new device drivers, start and stop services, and manage server applications.

14

A+ OS
1.4
1.5
2.5

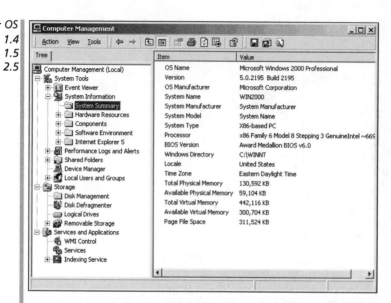

Figure 14-16   Windows 2000 Computer Management combines several administrative tools into a single easy-to-access window

> By default, the Administrative Tools group is located in the Control Panel. In addition, you can add the Administrative Tools group to the Start menu under Start, Programs, Administrative Tools. To do that, right-click the taskbar and select Properties. On the Taskbar and Start Menu Properties window, select the Advanced tab. Check Display Administrative Tools, and click OK.

A+ OS
1.5

Disk Management

The Computer Management console contains a tool called **Disk Management** that you can use to create partitions on basic disks or volumes on dynamic disks and to convert a basic disk to a dynamic disk. This graphical, user-friendly utility replaces the Fdisk utility of earlier Windows OSs. To access the utility, in the Computer Management console select Disk Management or enter Diskmgmt.msc in the Run dialog box.

When Disk Management first loads, it examines the drive configuration for the system and displays all drives laid out in a graphical format so you can see how each drive is allocated.

The Disk Management window shown in Figure 14–17 displays three drives. Disk 0 is a basic hard drive using the NTFS file system. Disk 1 is a dynamic hard drive that has not yet been allocated into volumes. The third drive is a CD-ROM drive shown with a CD in the drive.

A+ OS
1.5

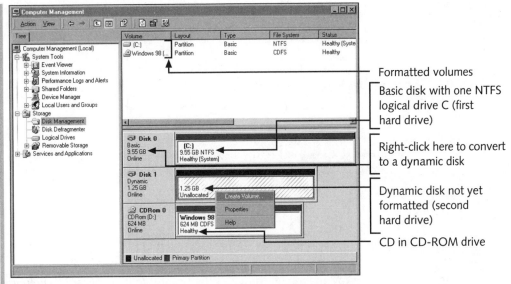

Figure 14-17   Create a volume on an unallocated dynamic disk

After you install a new second hard drive in the system, when you first access Disk Management, it asks if you want to create a basic disk or dynamic disk using the new drive. Then Disk Management displays the new disk with unallocated space, as shown in Figure 14-17. This second hard drive has been designated as a dynamic disk.

To create a volume on this dynamic disk, do the following:

1. Right-click an unallocated area of the drive, and select **Create Volume** from the shortcut menu (see Figure 14-17).

2. The Create Volume Wizard launches. Click **Next** to continue.

3. On the next screen (see Figure 14-18), select a volume type, either Simple volume, Spanned volume, or Striped volume. In our example, only Simple volume is available, because we are working with only one dynamic drive. You need to have more than one dynamic drive to specify a volume as striped or spanned. Click **Next** to continue.

4. Follow the wizard through the process of specifying the volume size, a drive letter, file system (NTFS, FAT, or FAT32), and allocation unit size (default is 512 bytes). The wizard then creates the dynamic volume.

The process for creating a partition on a basic disk is similar; the main difference is that the wizard is called the Create Partition Wizard. Access it by right-clicking the unallocated portion of the basic disk, selecting Create Partition, and following the directions in the wizard.

14

A+ OS
1.5

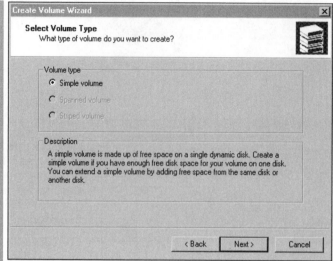

Figure 14-18   Disk Management provides the Create Volume Wizard to help you create volumes

Microsoft Management Console

A+ OS
1.1

When Windows combines several administrative tools in a single window, the window is called a **console**. Individual tools within the console are called **snap-ins**. An example of a console is Computer Management. Event Viewer and System Information are two snap-ins in that console. Another example of a console is Recovery Console, introduced earlier in the chapter. Windows 2000/XP offers a way for you to create your own customized consoles using the console-building utility **Microsoft Management Console (MMC)**. Table 14-6 lists some available snap-ins for MMC.

Table 14-6   Some MMC snap-ins

Snap-in	Description
Active X Control	Enables you to add Active X controls to your system.
Certificates	Provides certificate management at the user, service, or computer level.
Component Services	Links to the Component Services management tool, which is located on the Control Panel.
Computer Management	Links to the Computer Management tools on the Control Panel.
Device Manager	Lets you see what hardware devices you have on your system and configure device properties.
Disk Defragmenter	Links to the Disk Defragmenter utility.
Disk Management	Links to the Disk Management tool.
Event Viewer	Links to the Event Viewer tool, which displays event logs for the system.

A+ OS
1.1

Table 14-6   Some MMC snap-ins (continued)

Snap-in	Description
Fax Service Management	Enables you to manage fax settings and devices.
Folder	Enables you to add a folder to manage from MMC.
Group Policy	Provides a tool to manage group policy settings.
Indexing Service	Searches files and folders using specified parameters.
IP Security Policy Management	Manages Internet communication security.
Link to Web Address	Enables you to link to a specified Web site.
Local Users and Groups	Provides a tool to manage settings for local users and groups.
Performance Logs and Alerts	Gives you an interface from which to set up and manage logs of performance information and alerts about system performance.
Removable Storage Management	Enables you to manage settings and configuration information for removable storage devices such as Zip drives and tape backup drives.
Security Configuration and Analysis	Enables you to manage configuration of security settings for computers that use security template files.
Services	Provides a centralized interface for starting, stopping, and configuring system services.
Shared Folders	Provides information about shared folders, open files, and current sessions.
System Information	Contains information about the system that you can use when troubleshooting.

Creating a Customized Console

As with the Computer Management console, you must have administrative privileges to perform most tasks from the MMC. You can use MMC to create your own customized consoles. You can also save a console in a file, which is assigned an .msc file extension. Store the file in the C:\Documents and Settings*user*\Start Menu\Programs\Administrative Tools folder to make it appear as a program when you click Start, and point to Programs, Administrative Tools. In the path, substitute the name of the user. For example, for the Administrator, the path to the .msc file is C:\Documents and Settings\Administrator\Start Menu\Programs\Administrative Tools.

14

 TIP   After you create a console, you can copy the .msc file to any computer or place a shortcut to it on the desktop.

A+ OS
1.1

Follow these directions to open MMC and create a console that contains some popular utility tools:

1. Click **Start**, **Run**, enter **MMC** in the Run dialog box, and then click **OK**. An empty console window appears, as shown in Figure 14-19.

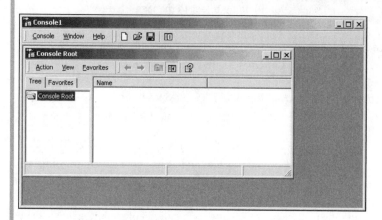

Figure 14-19   An empty console

2. Click **Console** on the menu bar, and then click **Add/Remove Snap-in**. The Add/Remove Snap-in window opens. The window illustrated in Figure 14-20 is empty because no snap-ins have been added to the console.

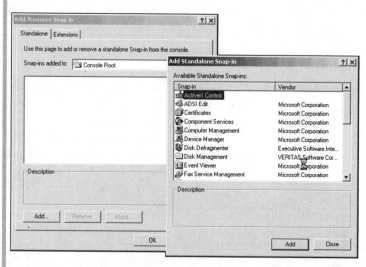

Figure 14-20   List of snap-ins available to be added to a console

3. Click **Add**. You see a list of snap-ins that can be added to a console, as shown in Figure 14-20. Select a snap-in and then click **Add**.

4. A dialog box opens that allows you to set the parameters for the snap-in. The dialog box offers different selections, depending on the snap-in being added.

A+ OS
1.1
When you have made your selections, click **Finish**. The new snap-in appears in the Add/Remove Snap-in window.

5. Repeat Steps 3 and 4 to add all the snap-ins that you want to the console. When you finish, from the Add Standalone Snap-in window illustrated in Figure 14-21, click **Close**, then click **OK**.

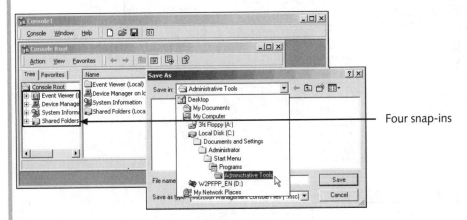

Figure 14-21   Saving a console with four snap-ins

6. Figure 14-21 shows a console with four snap-ins added. To save the console, click **Console** on the menu bar, and then click **Save As**. The Save As dialog box opens.

7. The default location for the console file is shown in Figure 14-21. This is the location that ensures the console appears as an option under Administrative Tools on the Start menu. Select this location for the file, name the file, and click **Save**.

8. Close the console window by clicking **Console**, **Exit**.

To use the console, click Start, Programs, Administrative Tools, and select the console.

14

A+ OS
1.5
3.1
3.2
3.3

Event Viewer

The Event Viewer MMC snap-in connects to the Event Viewer tool, which displays logs about significant system events that occur in Windows NT/2000/XP or in applications running under these OSs such as a hardware or network failure, OS error messages, a device or service that has failed to start, or General Protection Faults. Three different logs are shown in Event Viewer, and are displayed in Windows 2000, as shown in Figure 14-22:

- *The application log* records application events that the developer of the program sets to trigger a log entry. One type of event recorded in this log is an error recorded by the Dr. Watson utility, which you will learn about later in the chapter.

- *The security log* records events based on audit policies, which an administrator sets to monitor user activity such as successful or unsuccessful attempts to access a file or log on to the system. Only an administrator can view this log.

A^+ *OS*
1.5
3.1
3.2
3.3

- *The system log* records events triggered by Windows components, such as a device driver failing to load during the boot process. Windows NT/2000/XP sets which events are recorded in this log. All users can access this log file.

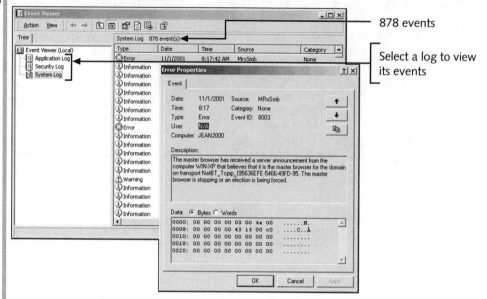

878 events

Select a log to view
its events

Figure 14-22   Use Event Viewer to see information about security audits in the security log and error, warning, or information events for the system and application logs

Three types of events are recorded in the system and application logs:

- *Information* events are recorded when a driver, service, or application functions successfully.

- *Warning* events are recorded when something happens that may indicate a future problem but does not necessarily indicate that something is presently wrong with the system. For example, low disk space might trigger a warning event.

- *Error* events are recorded when something goes wrong with the system, such as a necessary component failing to load, data getting lost or becoming corrupted, or a system or application function ceasing to operate.

A+ OS
 1.5
 3.1
 3.2
 3.3

You can open Event Viewer from the Computer Management Console, or you can locate it by double-clicking the Administrative Tools icon in the Control Panel. To view a log within Event Viewer, in the left pane click the log that you want to view. This generates a summary of events that appears in the right pane. Double-click a specific event to see details about it (see Figure 14-22).

Notice in the figure that 878 events are listed in the system log. You may only want to view certain events and not the entire list to find what you're looking for. To filter events, right-click on a log in the left pane, and select Filter from the shortcut menu. To filter events, you can use several criteria which are listed in Table 14-7.

Table 14-7   Log properties that can be used to filter events

Property	Description
Category	The category that the event falls under, such as an attempt to log on to the system or access a program.
Computer	The name of a computer on the system.
Event ID	A number that identifies the event and makes tracking events easier for support personnel.
Event source	The application, driver, or service that triggered the event.
Event type	The type of event, such as information, error, or warning.
From: To:	The range of events that you want to view. You can view the events from first to last event, or you can view all events that occurred on a specific date and in a specific time range.
User	The logon name for a user.

Another way you can avoid a ballooning log file is to set a size limit and specify what happens when the log reaches this limit. If you right-click a log, select Properties from the shortcut menu, and click the General tab, you can set the maximum size of the log in megabytes (as well as view general information about the log). You can set it so that the log overwrites events as needed, overwrites events that are more than a specified number of days old, or does not overwrite events at all. Select this last option when system security is high and you do not want to lose any event information. If you select this option, the system simply stops recording events when the log file reaches the maximum size (see Figure 14-23).

To allow the system to record events in the log after a log reaches maximum size, you have to review the events and clear the log manually by clicking the Clear Log button from the Properties window or selecting Clear All Events from the Action menu. Before clearing the log, Event Viewer gives you a chance to save it.

14

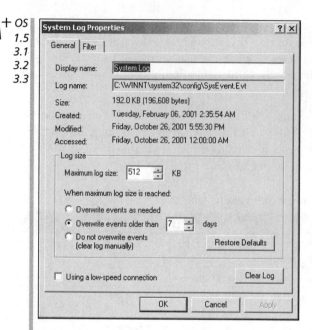

$A^+_{\text{1.5}}$ OS
3.1
3.2
3.3

Figure 14-23   View information about a log, including maximum size of the log file, in the Log Properties window

Performance Monitoring and Optimization

Maintaining optimal performance, or addressing performance problems when they develop, involves a three-part process in which you analyze data provided by monitoring tools such as Task Manager and System Monitor, determine areas in which performance is below the baseline, and identify and take the steps necessary to correct the problem.

Principles for Optimizing Performance

Here are some principles to remember when trying to optimize performance on your Windows NT/2000/XP system:

- One of the most important things you can do is establish a **baseline** of acceptable performance for your system, defining what you consider normal performance under a typical workload. Baselines can be created when the OS is first installed, when major changes are made, and on a periodic basis such as once a month. Figure out what resources the system uses when you are running all required programs and services. That will help you decide whether you need to add more resources (such as more RAM) to the system. Heavily used Windows 2000 computers may benefit from having as much as 512 MB of RAM, whereas machines used more moderately may only need 128 MB of RAM.

- If you add RAM, remember that you also need to increase the size of the paging file. You might also increase paging file size if the peak usage of the paging file is too close to the limit.

- Replacing one component may not help much if other components have not been upgraded. For example, if you install a faster CPU, you need to look at the amount of RAM and the size of the hard drive as well.

- Each application is assigned a priority level, which determines its position in the queue for CPU resources. This priority level can be changed for applications that are already loaded by using Task Manager. If an application performs slowly, increase its priority. You should only do this with very important applications, because giving an application higher priority than certain background system processes can sometimes interfere with the operating system.

- In general, upgrading an existing PC is recommended as long as the cost of the upgrade stays below half the cost of buying a new machine. Even if you just keep the case, power supply, and an expansion card or two, buying a new motherboard and hard drive can be almost like having a whole new system at a lower cost.

The rest of this section discusses two tools that you can use to monitor system performance: Task Manager and System Monitor.

Task Manager

A+ OS
1.5
3.2

Task Manager (Taskman.exe) allows you to view the applications and processes running on your computer as well as performance information for the processor and the memory. There are three ways that you can access Task Manager:

- Press Ctrl+Alt+Delete. The Windows Security window opens. Click the Task Manager button.

- Right-click a blank area on the taskbar, and select Task Manager from the shortcut menu.

- Press Ctrl+Shift+Esc.

Task Manager has three tabs: Applications, Processes, and Performance. Under the Applications tab (see Figure 14-24), each application loaded can have one of two states: Running or Not Responding. If an application is listed as Not Responding, you can end it by selecting it and clicking the End Task button at the bottom of the window. You will lose any unsaved information in the application.

The Processes tab lists system services and other processes associated with applications, together with how much CPU time and memory the process uses. This information can help you determine which applications are slowing down your system. The Performance tab, seen in Figure 14-25, shows more detail about how a program uses system resources. You can use these views to identify which applications and processes use the most CPU time.

14

A+ OS
1.5
3.2

Figure 14-24   The Applications tab in Task Manager shows the status of active applications

On the Performance tab in Figure 14-25, note the four frames at the bottom of the window. These frames give the following information:

- The *Totals* frame indicates how much the system is currently being used by counting handles (indicates a device or file is being accessed), threads (unit of activity within a process), and processes (programs running). Use these entries to know how heavily the system is used.

- The *Physical Memory* frame lists Total (amount of RAM), Available (RAM not used), and System Cache (RAM in use). Use these entries to know if you must upgrade RAM.

- The *Commit Charge* frame lists Total (current size of virtual memory, also called the page file or swap file), Limit (how much of the paging file can be allocated to applications before the size of the paging file must be increased), and Peak (maximum amount of virtual memory used in this session). Use these entries to learn if you must increase the size of the paging file.

A+ OS
  1.5
  3.2

- The *Kernel Memory* frame indicates how much RAM and virtual memory the OS uses. This frame lists Total (sum of RAM and virtual memory), Paged (how much of the paging file the OS uses), and Nonpaged (how much RAM the OS uses). Use this frame to learn how much memory the OS is using. If usage is high, look for OS processes you can eliminate.

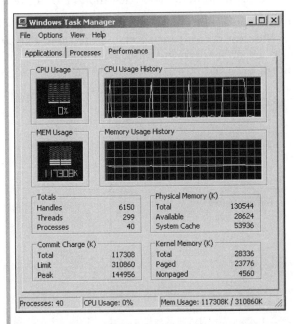

Figure 14-25   The Performance tab shows more detail about how system resources are being used

By reading the information in the frames in Figure 14-25, you can see that the OS is using about 28 MB of memory. The system contains about 130 MB of RAM, and the maximum paging file size is set to about 311 MB. How to change the maximum and initial size of the paging file is covered in the section, "Managing Virtual Memory," later in the chapter.

14

A+ OS
  1.5
System Monitor

In most cases, you can get what information you need from Task Manager to determine if the system needs performance tuning or upgrading. If this information is not detailed enough, use System Monitor, which provides more detail than Task Manager on system performance. There are three components of System Monitor: objects, instances, and counters. Objects are hardware or software system components, and instances are multiples of objects. For example, Microsoft Word is an object, but if you have Word open in two separate windows on the desktop, then two instances of this one object are running. Counters show information on specific characteristics of an object and constantly gather data and update the counter display. You can specify which counters to show for an object.

A+ OS
1.5

Important objects to monitor using System Monitor include Memory, Paging File, Processor, and Physical Disk (the hard drive). In the following example, we will access System Monitor and then add and view counters for the Memory object.

1. In the Control Panel, double-click the **Administrative Tools** icon.

2. From the Administrative Tools window, double-click the **Performance** icon.

3. The Performance window opens. See Figure 14-26. System Monitor is highlighted and the System Monitor details pane shows on the right. The pane is blank because no objects are presently being monitored. Right-click that pane and select **Add Counters** from the shortcut menu (see Figure 14-26).

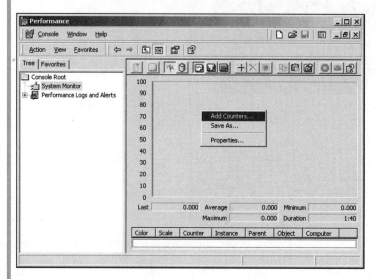

Figure 14-26   Access System Monitor through the Performance window

4. The Add Counters window opens (Figure 14-27). From the Performance object drop-down list, select the **Memory** object.

5. You have the option to view all counters, but that makes a messy, hard-to-read display. By default, the radio button is selected beside the option Select counters from list. Locate and click the **Available Bytes** counter, which tells you how much physical memory remains. Click **Add**.

6. Scroll down the list until you see the **Page Faults/sec** counter. This tells you how many pages were requested but not immediately available in memory. Click **Add**.

7. Click **Close** to close the Add Counters window.

A^{+} OS
1.5

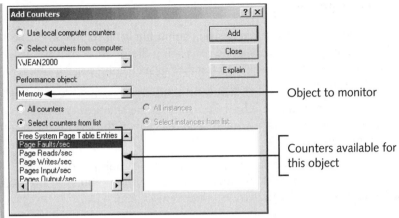

Figure 14-27   In the Add Counters window, select a performance object and counters
to monitor

Figure 14-28 shows System Monitor in the process of monitoring the two counters you
selected. The lines tracking the counters are color-coded to match the counters listed at the
bottom of the graph. Look at the left side of the graph. The line representing Page Faults/sec
begins at 0 and spikes when an application is opened. The line representing Available Bytes
begins at 30 and dips lower, showing fewer bytes are available when applications are active.
The vertical line on the right moves to the right as monitoring continues.

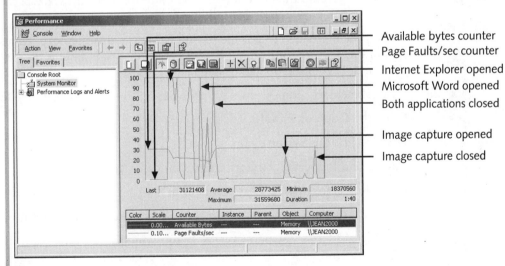

14

Figure 14-28   System Monitor shows how changes in system activity affect the selected
object and counters

Managing Virtual Memory

A+CORE
1.9
OS
2.5

Under Windows 2000, the default size of the paging file is set to 1.5 times the amount of RAM installed. You might need to change the paging file in order to improve system performance. Here are some guidelines to remember in managing paging files:

- Set the initial and maximum sizes of the file to the same value. This prevents disk fragmentation that might result from setting them to two different values. Windows 2000 does not normally need to change the size of the paging file during processing.

- To calculate the appropriate size of a paging file, multiply the counter Paging File object, % Usage Peak counter, which shows how much of the paging file the system is using, by the size of Pagefile.sys.

- Two situations in which you might want to change the size of the paging file are when 70% of the paging file is being used or when the Memory object, % Committed Bytes In Use counter, reaches 85%.

- When changing the size of a paging file, remember that you need to balance the file size with disk space usage and that Windows 2000 requires at least 5 MB of free space on a disk. In other words, don't make the file too large, especially when the disk it is stored on is active or has limited space. Test performance as you change paging file size, and make changes gradually.

- Moving the paging file to a volume other than the boot volume can help conserve disk space on the boot volume and optimize performance, especially when a system has multiple hard disks.

- When deciding where to put the paging file, know that memory dumps (covered in the next section) cannot be captured if the paging file is on a different physical disk from the operating system.

To change virtual memory settings and paging file size in Windows 2000, do the following:

1. Open the **Control Panel**.

2. Double-click the **System** icon.

3. The System Properties window opens. Click the **Advanced** tab.

4. Click the **Performance Options** button.

5. The Performance Options window opens. Click the **Change...** button.

6. The Virtual Memory window opens. In this window, you can change the paging file size and view information about the paging file and the registry. Figure 14-29 shows all three windows.

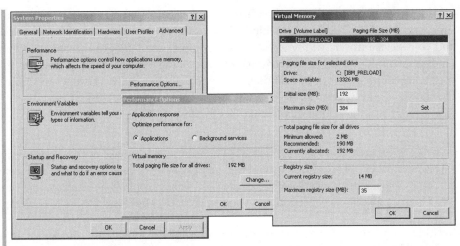

Figure 14-29   Use the System Properties window to change paging file settings

Dr. Watson and Memory Dumps

A+ OS
3.1
3.2
3.3

Two tools that can produce text output useful in diagnosing problems with the OS and applications are Dr. Watson and memory dumps. Recall from Chapter 12 that Dr. Watson is used to debug errors in applications by recording error events to a log file. It can help solve problems such as when an application fails to install or load, when the system locks, or when error messages appear. In Windows 2000, these events are recorded in the Drwtsn32.log file. Dr. Watson automatically launches when an application error occurs, or you can launch it manually by entering Drwtsn32.exe in the Run dialog box or at a command prompt. The log file is written to the\Documents and Settings*user*\Documents\DrWatson folder.

Another tool that helps you understand what happened when an error occurs is a **memory dump**. It saves the contents of memory at the time a stop error halts the system in a file called a **dump file**. A **stop error** is an error so severe that the operating system stops all processes. How to capture and interpret memory dumps is beyond the scope of this book.

Windows Update

A+ OS
2.2
3.2

In the process of maintaining and troubleshooting Windows 2000, remember that the Microsoft site offers patches, fixes, and updates for known problems and has an extensive knowledge base documenting problems and their solutions. You learned how to download a Windows update in Chapter 12; the process is basically the same for Windows 2000 as it is for Windows 9x. You can access Windows Update by going to the Microsoft site *windowsupdate.microsoft.com*, or you can click Windows Update on your Start Menu, which takes you directly to the site.

If you think you might later want to uninstall a critical update or service pack, select the option to Save uninstall information. Later, to uninstall the fix, again execute the downloaded file. When given the option, select Uninstall a previously installed service pack.

14

In addition to critical updates and service packs that Microsoft creates to address known problems with Windows, the Windows Update tool also uses ActiveX controls to scan your system, find your device drivers and system files, and compare these files to the ones on the Windows Update server. If you do not already have Active Setup and the ActiveX controls installed on your computer, a prompt to install them will pop up when you access the site. After Windows Update scans your system and locates update packages and new versions of drivers and system files, it offers you the option of selecting files for download.

> **TIP** Because ActiveX controls have open access to the Windows operating system, there is some risk of an ActiveX control causing damage to data or software on your computer. Some system administrators require that ActiveX controls be disabled when they are not specifically needed for tasks such as Windows Update downloads.

In addition to the information in this chapter, other important sources of information about Windows 2000 are the Microsoft Web site at *support.microsoft.com* and the *Windows 2000 Professional Resource Kit* by Microsoft Press. The *Resource Kit* includes a CD that contains additional Windows 2000 utilities. These resources can further help you understand Windows 2000 and solve problems with the OS. Also remember that user manuals are an excellent source of information as well as the Web, training manuals and product installation documentation.

> **TIP** In addition to the support tools described here, third-party diagnostic software can be of help. For example, ConfigSafe by imagineLAN, Inc. (*www.imaginelan.com*) is a utility that tracks configuration changes to Windows 9x or Windows NT/2000/XP and can restore the system to a previously saved configuration.

CHAPTER SUMMARY

- The boot process for Windows NT, Windows 2000, and Windows XP works the same under each OS, although the tools to troubleshoot a failed boot are slightly different for each OS.

- The boot process can be customized with entries in Boot.ini. The Boot.ini file can be edited with a text editor, but it is best to change the file using the System Properties window.

- Tools to use to troubleshoot problems with loading Windows 2000 are the Advanced Options menu, the Recovery Console, and the Emergency Repair Process.

- To access the Advanced Options menu, press F8 when starting Windows 2000.

- The Advanced Options menu includes safe mode, safe mode with networking, safe mode with command prompt, enable boot logging, enable VGA mode, Last Known Good configuration, directory services restore mode, and debugging mode.

- The Recovery Console is a command interface with a limited number of commands available to troubleshoot a failing Windows 2000 load. The console requires that you enter the Administrator password.

❏ Access the Recovery Console by first booting from the Windows 2000 CD or from the four setup disks, or the console can be installed under the startup menu and accessed from there.

❏ Using the Recovery Console, you can restore the registry to the state it was in at the time of the last backup of the registry.

❏ The Emergency Repair Process lets you restore the system to its state at the end of the Windows 2000 installation. Don't use it unless all other methods fail because you will lose all changes made to the system since the installation. It requires the emergency startup disk.

❏ Back up the Windows 2000 system state on a regular basis using the Backup utility. This backup includes system files, files to load the OS, and the registry. Back up the system state before editing the registry.

❏ Windows 2000 Support Tools can be installed from the Windows 2000 CD and include several utilities to support hardware and applications.

❏ Windows File Protection (WFP) protects the system files against an application, a virus, or a user changing or deleting them. System File Checker is part of the WFP system.

❏ The Disk Properties window gives information about a disk and can be used to clean up a disk, defragment a disk, and check and repair errors on a disk using ScanDisk.

❏ Disk Management is a tool found in the Computer Management console. Disk Management replaces Fdisk in older Windows OSs and is used to partition and format a hard drive and to convert a basic disk to a dynamic disk.

❏ Microsoft Management Console (MMC) can be used to create customized consoles to manage the OS.

❏ Event Viewer is used to view system, application, and security events.

❏ When monitoring performance, begin by establishing a baseline that helps determine what performance should be expected of a system.

❏ Task Manager is used to measure performance, giving information about the processor, memory, the hard drive, and virtual memory.

❏ System Monitor gives more detail than Task Manager and can be used to monitor object and instance performance over time by using counters that you select for monitoring.

❏ Virtual memory is managed in Windows 2000 from the System applet of Control Panel, Advanced tab.

❏ Information about application errors and stop errors can be recorded by Dr. Watson and memory dumps.

❏ Windows Update uses the Microsoft Web site to download patches and fixes to Microsoft OSs and applications.

❏ Additional sources of support for Windows 2000 include the Microsoft support Web site at *support.microsoft.com* and the *Windows 2000 Professional Resource Kit* by Microsoft.

14

KEY TERMS

32-bit flat memory mode	dump file	SFC (System File Checker)
Advanced Options menu	Emergency Repair Process	snap-ins
baseline	memory dump	stop error
Boot.ini	Microsoft Management Console (MMC)	WFP (Windows File Protection)
console	minifile system	
Disk Management	Recovery Console	

REVIEW QUESTIONS

1. The NT Loader file, NTLDR, is loaded and executed during the boot process. This file is expected to be in which file location in order to execute properly?

   a. The root directory of the system partition

   b. The \winnt_root\system 32 folder of the boot partition

   c. The \winnt_root\system 32\config folder of the boot partition

   d. The \winnt_root\system 32\drivers folder of the boot partition

   e. None of the above

2. The program that is responsible for loading Windows NT/2000/XP and performing several chores to complete the loading process before passing control to the operating system is:

   a. NTLDR

   b. MBR

   c. NTDETECT

   d. MSDOS

   e. SETUP

3. Statements such as:

   ```
   Default=multi(0)disk(0)rdisk(0)partition(1)
   ```

   are found in which file?

   a. Autoexec.bat

   b. Config.sys

   c. System.ini

   d. Boot.ini

   e. Win.ini

4. The term *disk(0)* refers to:

   a. Using the first hard disk, drive 0

   b. Using the first partition on the drive

   c. Using the first hard drive controller

   d. Using a SCSI hard drive

   e. Using a hard drive *remotely*; not physically installed in the system

5. The term *multi(0)* refers to:

   a. Using the first hard disk, drive 0

   b. Using the first partition on the drive

   c. Using the first hard drive controller

   d. Using a SCSI hard drive

   e. Using a hard drive *remotely*; not physically installed in the system

6. Pressing the F8 key upon system boot results in the following direct action:

   a. Entry into Safe Mode with Networking

   b. Entry into Safe Mode with Command Prompt

   c. Enable Boot Logging

   d. Recovery Console

   e. None of the above

7. Which of the following are *only* available on Windows 2000 Domain Controllers?

   a. Entry into Safe Mode with Networking

   b. Entry into Safe Mode with Command Prompt

   c. Enable Boot Logging

   d. Recovery Console

   e. None of the above

8. In Windows 2000, the number of files that make up the System Registry are:

   a. One

   b. Two

   c. Four

   d. Five

   e. Unable to determine, as the number changes regularly

14

9. Windows 2000 provides a feature called Windows File Protection (WFP) to protect specific system files. Which of the following are *not* protected from modification with WFP?

   a. .sys

   b. .com

   c. .exe

   d. .dll

   e. All of the above are protected using WFP.

10. Enabling the Disk Properties window provides the user a way to perform routine maintenance on a particular drive unit. Upon careful comparison of the Disk Properties window between a system running Windows 2000 and Windows NT, one shows an option "Compress drive to save disk space." This option is found on which system?

    a. Windows 2000

    b. Windows NT

    c. Both a and b

    d. Neither a nor b

11. What are the three types of events that are recorded in the system and application logs?

    a. _____

    b. _____

    c. _____

12. Pressing the key sequence Ctrl+Alt+Delete results in the following direct action:

    a. Cold boot

    b. Warm boot

    c. Task Manager window

    d. Windows Security window

    e. None of the above

13. The Task Manager reports on system performance characteristics of all but the following by way of "tabs"?

    a. Applications

    b. Processes

    c. Performance

    d. Memory usage

    e. All are reported by the Task Manager

15

INSTALLING AND USING WINDOWS XP PROFESSIONAL

In this chapter, you will learn:

♦ About the features and architecture of Windows XP

♦ How to install Windows XP

♦ How to use Windows XP

♦ How to install hardware and applications with Windows XP

A+ OS
1.1

Windows XP is the latest generation of Microsoft operating systems. Windows XP currently comes as Windows XP Home Edition, Windows XP Professional, and Windows XP 64-bit Edition, although an edition for the advanced server market, named Windows .NET, is likely to be available by the time this book is published. This chapter focuses on Windows XP Professional, which is the upgrade from Windows 2000 Professional. Features of Windows XP that you already learned about in chapters on earlier versions of Windows are not covered in detail, where they have not changed in Windows XP; more discussion is given to new features or changes to existing ones. This chapter builds the foundation you will need to manage and provide technical support for Windows XP, the focus of the next chapter.

FEATURES AND ARCHITECTURE OF WINDOWS XP

Windows XP integrates features of Windows 9x and 2000, while providing added support for multimedia and networking technologies. The look and feel of Windows XP differs slightly from its predecessors, and utilities and functions are organized differently under menus and windows. You'll learn about many of these differences in this chapter.

> **TIP** Windows XP is replacing all previous versions of Windows in the home market and for the corporate desktop. If your hardware and applications qualify, select Windows XP Home Edition for a home PC over Windows 98/Me. For a corporate environment, choose Windows XP Professional over Windows NT/2000. The only exception is compatibility issues with older hardware and software.

Windows XP Features

Windows XP Home and Windows XP Professional have these features, among others:

- A new user interface, shown in Figure 15-1. Notice how different it looks from the desktops of earlier Windows versions such as Windows 98 and Windows 2000.

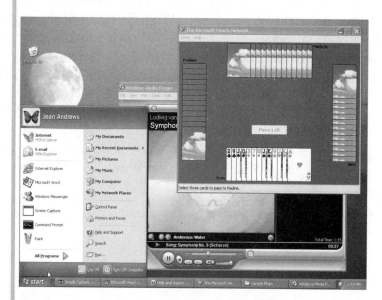

Figure 15-1 The Windows XP desktop and Start menu

- The ability for two users to be logged on simultaneously. Each user has a separate profile, and Windows XP can switch between users, keeping a separate set of applications open for each user.

- Windows Media Player for Windows XP, a centralized application for working with digital media

- Windows Messenger for instant messaging, conferencing, and application sharing
- An expanded Help feature
- Advanced security features

In addition to these features of Windows XP Home edition, Windows XP Professional offers:

- A way for someone to remotely control your computer called Remote Desktop
- A way for an administrator to manage user profiles from a server (roaming profiles)
- Additional security features
- Multilingual capabilities
- Support for new higher-performance processors

There is also Windows XP 64-bit Edition, designed to be used with a high-end 64-bit CPU such as the Intel Itanium. This Windows XP version is designed mostly for servers or heavily technical workstations that run scientific and engineering applications and need greater amounts of memory and higher performance than standard desktop PCs. For example, an aircraft designer who uses software to simulate how various conditions affect aircraft materials might use Windows XP 64-bit Edition on a system that supports resource-intensive simulation and animation applications.

Windows Internet Explorer, Windows Media Player, a firewall, and other Microsoft products are tightly integrated with the Windows XP operating system. Some users see this as a disadvantage, and others see it as an advantage. Tight integration allows applications to interact easily with other applications and the OS, but, on the other hand, makes it more difficult for third-party software to compete with Microsoft applications.

Windows XP provides several enhancements over Windows 2000 and other earlier versions. Table 15-1 summarizes the advantages and disadvantages of Windows XP.

15

Table 15-1   Advantages and disadvantages of Windows XP

Advantages	Disadvantages
Provides better integration of Windows 9x and NT than did Windows 2000	Requires nearly a gigabyte of hard drive space for the operating system itself, and at least a 233 MHz processor with 64 MB of RAM
Offers significant GUI enhancements over earlier versions of Windows	Programs used with Windows XP may need more than the minimum system requirements for the operating system
Adds features but uses only slightly more total memory for the OS than does Windows 2000	Nearly eliminates support for device drivers not approved by Microsoft
Adds advanced file sorting options, such as sorting pictures by resolution or sound files by artist	Security concerns with centralized storage of online information in Microsoft Passport, a repository of the user IDs and passwords you use on the Internet

A^+ *OS*
  1.1

Table 15-1   Advantages and disadvantages of Windows XP (continued)

Advantages	Disadvantages
Includes built-in support for compressed files	
Has improved troubleshooting tools and is generally more stable than previous Windows OSs	

Windows XP Architecture

A^+ *OS*
  1.1

Windows XP uses the same kernel architecture as Windows NT and Windows 2000, with components operating in either user mode or kernel mode. Figure 15-2 shows how the different OS components relate. Notice in the figure that some low-level device drivers such as those that access the hard drive have direct access to hardware, just as they do with Windows NT and Windows 2000. All 16-bit and 32-bit applications relate to the kernel by way of the Win32 subsystem operating in user mode. As you will learn in the next chapter, the boot process is also the same, and the files needed for a successful boot are the same as those for Windows NT/2000.

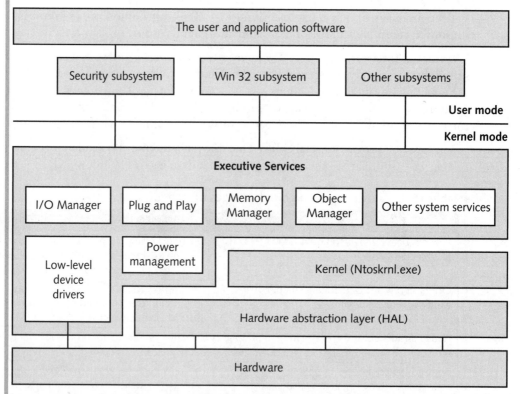

Figure 15-2   The Windows XP architecture uses the same basic structure and components as Windows NT and Windows 2000

A+ OS
1.1

Windows XP is generally more stable than Windows NT and Windows 2000. It was designed to avoid situations that occurred with Windows NT/2000, which caused drivers and applications to bring these systems down. Installing Windows XP should also be easier than installing Windows NT or Windows 2000. In addition, Windows XP has increased security, including a built-in Internet firewall designed to protect a home PC connected directly to the Internet by way of an always-on connection such as cable modem or DSL. Firewalls, cable modem, and DSL are covered in Chapters 18 and 19.

INSTALLING WINDOWS XP

A+ OS
2.1

Installing Windows XP involves many of the same considerations and decisions that you learned about when installing Windows 2000. In this section, you learn how to install Windows XP as a clean install and as an upgrade, including how to set up a dual boot.

Planning the Installation

A+ OS
2.1

Before installing Windows XP, do the following:

- Verify that the system meets the minimum and recommended requirements shown in Table 15-2.

- Check the hardware compatibility list (HCL) to verify that all installed hardware components are compatible with Windows XP.

- Decide how you will partition your hard drive and what file system you will use.

- For a PC on a network, decide whether the PC will be configured as a workstation in a workgroup or as part of a domain. (Workgroups and domains were covered in Chapter 13.)

- Make a final checklist to verify that you have done all of the above and are ready to begin the installation.

15

Table 15-2   Minimum and recommended requirements for Windows XP Professional

Component or Device	Minimum Requirement	Recommended Requirement
One or two CPUs	Pentium II 233 MHz or better	Pentium II 300 MHz or better
RAM	64 MB	128 MB up to 4 GB
Hard drive partition	2 GB	2 GB or more
Free space on the hard drive partition	640 MB (bare bones)	2 GB or more
CD-ROM drive	12x	12x or faster
Accessories	Keyboard and mouse or other pointing device	Keyboard and mouse or other pointing device

> 💡 **TIP** Remember that the requirements of an OS vary depending on which version you have installed and what applications and hardware you have installed with it.

Minimum Requirements and Hardware Compatibility

Recall from earlier chapters that you can use the My Computer icon on the Windows desktop to determine the current CPU and available RAM. To see how much hard drive space is available, using Windows Explorer, right-click the drive letter and select Properties from the shortcut menu. Part of the installation process for an upgrade is to clean up the hard drive, which might free some hard drive space. Even though Windows XP requires only 640 MB to install, you cannot achieve acceptable results unless you have at least 1.5 GB of free hard drive space on the volume that holds Windows XP.

There are several ways you can verify that software and hardware qualify for Windows XP. One way is to run the Readiness Analyzer. Use this command from the Windows XP CD, substituting the drive letter for your CD-ROM drive for D in the command line:

```
D:\I386\Winnt32 /checkupgradeonly
```

Depending on the release of Windows XP, your path might be different. The process takes about 10 minutes to run and displays a report you that can save and later print. The default name and path of the report is C:\Windows\compat.txt. The report is important if you have software you are not sure will work under Windows XP. If the analyzer reports that your software will not work under Windows XP, you might choose to upgrade the software or set up a dual boot with your old OS and Windows XP (dual-boot setup is covered later in the chapter).

Readiness Analyzer also checks hardware compatibility. Another way to verify your hardware is to go to the Microsoft Web site at *www.microsoft.com/hwdq/hcl*. Search on each hardware device by type (see Figure 15-3). There might be a copy of the Windows XP Professional HCL in the hcl.txt file on the Windows XP CD in the support folder. But for the most up-to-date information, use the Microsoft Web site.

If your hardware does not qualify for Windows XP, check the hardware manufacturer's Web site for an upgrade and download the upgrade drivers before you begin the installation. If you plan to erase the hard drive as part of the installation, store these drivers on floppy disks or on a network drive until you're ready to install them under Windows XP. If you cannot find an upgrade, sometimes a device will work if you substitute a Windows driver written for a similar device. Check the documentation for your device, looking for information about other devices it can emulate. It is especially important to know that your network card or modem card qualifies for Windows XP before you install the OS because you need the card to access the Internet to get upgrades. If you are not sure an important hardware component qualifies, then install Windows XP as a dual boot with your current OS. Later, when you get the component working under Windows XP, you can uninstall the other OS.

A+ OS
2.1

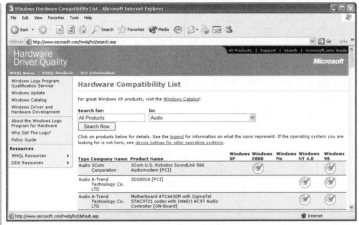

Figure 15-3   Search for each hardware component by type to determine if it qualifies for Windows XP

Hard Drive Partitions and File Systems

Windows XP needs at least a 2-GB partition for the installation and should have about 1.5 GB of free space on that partition. You can install Windows XP on the same partition as another OS, but Windows XP overwrites the existing OS on that partition. If you do not have a free 2-GB partition for the installation, you must delete smaller partitions and repartition the drive. Deleting a partition erases all data on it, so be sure to create backups first. Follow these general directions to ensure that partitions on the hard drive are adequate to install Windows XP:

- For Windows 9x, use Fdisk at the command prompt, and, for Windows 2000, use Disk Management to determine what partitions are on the drive, how large they are, what logical drives are assigned to them, and how much free space on the drive is not yet partitioned.

- If existing partitions are too small, look at the free space on the drive. If there is enough free space that is not yet partitioned, use that free space to create a new partition that is at least 2 GB.

- If you cannot create a 2-GB or larger partition, back up your data, delete the smaller partitions, and create a 2-GB active partition on the drive.

- If you have free space on the drive for other partitions, don't partition them at this time. First install Windows XP and then use Disk Management under Windows XP to partition the remaining free space on the drive.

The same concerns about selecting a file system for Windows 2000 apply to Windows XP. The file systems supported by Windows XP are the same as those supported by Windows 2000: FAT16, FAT32, and NTFS. Recall that the NTFS file system used by Windows 2000 is incompatible with the Windows NT NTFS file system, causing a

15

A+ OS
2.1
2.2

potential problem when installing Windows 2000 and Windows NT on the same PC as a dual boot. Because the Windows XP NTFS file system is the same as that of the Windows 2000 NTFS file system, a dual boot between these two OSs should be no problem. Here are the general directions for selecting a file system:

- Use the NTFS file system if you are interested in file and folder security, file compression, control over how much disk space a user is allowed, or file encryption.

- Use the FAT16 or FAT32 file system if you are setting up a dual boot with Windows 9x and each OS must access all partitions. When using FAT16, so that the partition will be compatible with Windows 9x, make it no larger than 2 GB.

- Use the FAT16 file system if you are setting up a dual boot with MS-DOS or Windows NT and each OS must access all partitions.

Joining a Workgroup or a Domain

If you are installing Windows XP on a network, you must decide how you will access the network. If you have less than 10 computers networked together, Microsoft recommends that you join these computers in a workgroup in which each computer controls its own resources. In this case, each user account is set up on the local computer, independently from user accounts on other PCs. There is no centralized control of resources. For more than 10 computers, Microsoft recommends that you use a domain controller running a network operating system such as Windows 2000 Server to control network resources. (Windows XP Professional installed on a workstation can then be a client on this Windows network. Also, it is expected that Microsoft will soon release Windows .NET, a server OS.) You will also want to use a domain controller if you want to administer and secure the network from a centralized location or if several centralized resources on the network are shared by many users. How to manage workgroups is covered in Chapter 18, but managing a domain controller is beyond the scope of this book.

Upgrade or Clean Install?

If you plan to set up a dual boot, then you will perform a clean install for Windows XP. If you already have an OS installed and you do not plan a dual boot, then you have a choice between an upgrade and a clean install. Things to consider when making this decision are:

- You can use the less expensive upgrade version of Windows XP Professional to upgrade from Windows 98, Windows Me, Windows NT 4.0, and Windows 2000 to Windows XP Professional.

- You can use the less expensive upgrade version of Windows XP Home Edition to upgrade from Windows 98 or Windows Me to Windows XP Home Edition.

- If you currently have Windows 95 installed, you must do a clean install using the more expensive For a New PC version of Windows XP Professional or Windows XP Home Edition.

A+ OS
  2.1
  2.2

■ Regardless of whether you have an OS currently installed, you can still choose to do a clean install if you want a fresh start. Unless you erase your hard drive, reformat it, or delete partitions before the upgrade, data on the hard drive is not erased even if you convert to a new file system during the installation. However, OS settings and installed software do not carry forward into the new installation.

Final Checklist

Before you begin the installation, complete the final checklist shown in Table 15-3 to verify that you are ready.

Table 15-3   Checklist to complete before installing Windows XP

Things to Do	Further Information
Does the PC meet the minimum or recommended hardware requirement?	CPU: RAM: Hard drive size: Free space on the hard drive:
Have you run the Readiness Analyzer or checked the Microsoft Web site to verify that all your hardware and software qualify?	List hardware and software that need to be upgraded:
Do you have the product key available?	Product key:
Have you decided how you will join a network?	Workgroup name: Domain name: Computer name:
Will you do an upgrade or clean install?	Current operating system: Does the old OS qualify for an upgrade?
Is your hard drive ready?	Size of the hard drive partition: Free space on the partition: File system you plan to use:

For a clean install, will you set up a dual boot?	List reasons for a dual boot:
	For a dual boot
	    Size of the second partition:
	    Free space on the second partition:
	    File system you plan to use:

Have you backed up important data on your hard drive?	Location of backup:

15

Installation Process

A+ OS
  2.1
  2.2

Follow these general directions to perform a clean install of Windows XP on a PC that does not already have an OS installed:

1. Boot from the Windows XP CD, which displays the menu in Figure 15-4. This menu might change slightly from one Windows XP build to another. Select the first option and press Enter. If your PC does not boot from a CD,

$\overset{+}{A}\ \underset{2.1}{\overset{OS}{}}$

go to a command prompt and enter the command D:\i386\Winnt.exe, substituting the drive letter for your CD-ROM drive for D. (The path might vary depending on the release of Windows XP.) The End-User License agreement appears. Accept the agreement.

```
Windows XP Professional Setup
====================== =

    Welcome to Setup.

    This portion of the Setup program prepares Microsoft ( R )
    Windows ( R ) XP to run on your computer.

        •   To set up Windows XP now, press ENTER.

        •   To repair a Windows XP installation using Recovery Console,
            press R.

        •   To quit Setup without installing Windows XP, press F3.


ENTER=Continue  R=Repair  F3=Quit
```

Figure 15-4 Windows XP Professional Setup opening menu

2. Setup lists all partitions that it finds on the hard drive, the file system of each partition, and the size of the partition. It also lists any unpartitioned free space on the drive. From this screen, you can create and delete partitions and select the partition on which you want to install Windows XP. If you plan to have more than one partition on the drive, only create one partition at this time. The partition must be at least 2 GB in size and have 1.5 GB free. After the installation is done, you can use Disk Management to create the other partitions. Figure 15-5 shows an example of the list provided by Setup when the entire hard drive has not yet been partitioned.

3. If you created a new partition in Step 2, Setup asks you which file system you want to use to format the partition, NTFS or FAT. If the partition is at least 2 GB in size, the FAT file system will be FAT32. Select a file system for the partition. The Setup program formats the drive, completes the text-based portion of setup and loads the graphical interface for the rest of the installation. The PC then restarts.

4. Select your geographical location from the list provided. Windows XP will use it to decide how to display dates, times, numbers, and currency. Select your keyboard layout. Different keyboards can be used to accommodate special characters for other languages.

A+ OS
2.1

```
Windows XP Professional Setup
======================= =

    The following list shows the existing partitions and
    unpartitioned space on this computer.

    Use the UP and DOWN ARROW keys to select an item in the list.

        •   To set up Windows XP on the selected item, press ENTER.

        •   To create a partition in the unpartitioned space, press C.

        •   To delete the selected partition, press D.


    ┌─────────────────────────────────────────────────┐
    │  28663 MB Disk 0 at Id 0 on bus 0 on atapi [MBR] │
    │                                                  │
    │  Unpartitioned space                  28663 MB   │
    │                                                  │
    │                                                  │
    │                                                  │
    └─────────────────────────────────────────────────┘


    ENTER=Install     C=Create Partition     F3=Quit
```

15

Figure 15-5   During setup, you can create and delete partitions and select a partition on which to install Windows XP

5. Enter your name, the name of your organization, and your product key.

6. Enter the computer name and the password for the Administrator account. This password is stored in the security database on this PC. If you are joining a domain, the computer name is the name assigned to this computer by the network administrator managing the domain controller.

 It is *very* important that you not forget the Administrator password. You cannot log onto the system without it.

7. Select the date, time, and time zone. The PC might reboot.

A+ OS
2.1

8. If you are connected to a network, you will be asked to choose how to configure your network settings, Typical or Custom. The Typical setting installs Client for Microsoft Networks, File and Printer Sharing, and TCP/IP using dynamically assigned IP addresses. The Custom setting allows you to configure the network differently. If you are not sure which to use, choose the Typical settings. You can change them later. How networks are configured is covered in Chapter 18.

9. Enter a workgroup or domain name. If you are joining a domain, the network administrator will have given you specific directions on how to configure user accounts on the domain.

For a clean install on a PC that already has an OS installed, follow these general directions:

1. Close any open applications. Close any boot management software or antivirus software that might be running in the background.

2. Insert the Windows XP CD in the CD-ROM drive. Autorun launches the opening window shown in Figure 15-6.

3. Select the option to **Install Windows XP**. On the next screen, under Installation Type, select **New Installation**. Read and accept the licensing agreement. The installation process works the same as described above, picking up with Step 3.

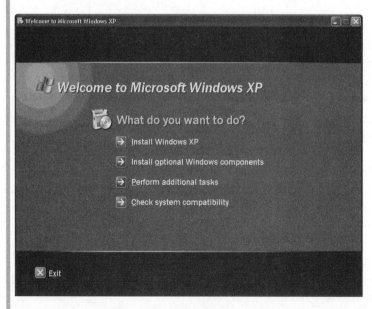

Figure 15-6 Windows XP Setup menu

A+ os
  2.1

When performing an upgrade to Windows XP, follow these general directions:

1. Before you begin the installation, do the following to prepare the system:

   - Clean up the hard drive: erase unneeded or temporary files, empty the Recycle Bin, run Disk Defragmenter, and do a ScanDisk of the drive.

   - If you have determined that you must upgrade hardware or software and that these upgrades are compatible with your old OS, perform the upgrades and verify that the hardware or software is working.

   - If you do not have the latest BIOS for your motherboard, flash your BIOS.

   - Back up important files.

   - Scan the hard drive for viruses using a current version of antivirus software.

   - If you have a compressed hard drive, uncompress the drive. The only exception to this is that if you are using Windows NT file compression on an NTFS drive, you do not need to uncompress it.

   - Uninstall any hardware or software that you know is not compatible with Windows XP and for which you have no available upgrade.

2. Insert the Windows XP Upgrade CD in the CD-ROM drive. The Autorun feature should launch the Setup program, with the menu shown in Figure 15-6.

3. If the Setup menu does not appear, you can enter the Setup command in the Run dialog box. Select the option to **Install Windows XP**.

4. On the next screen, under Installation Type, select **Upgrade**. The menu gives you two options:

   - *Express Upgrade.* This upgrade uses existing Windows folders and all the existing settings it can.

   - *Custom Upgrade.* This upgrade allows you to change the installation folder and the language options. Using this option, you can also change the file system to NTFS.

5. Select the type of upgrade, and accept the licensing agreement.

6. Select the partition on which to install Windows XP. If the drive is configured as FAT and you want to convert to NTFS, specify that now. Note that Windows XP has an uninstall utility that allows you to revert to Windows 98 if necessary. This uninstall tool does not work if you convert FAT to NTFS.

7. Setup performs an analysis of the system and reports any compatibility problems. Stop the installation if the problems indicate that you will not be able to operate the system after the installation.

8. For an upgrade from Windows 98 or Windows Me to Windows XP, the Setup program converts whatever information in the registry it can to Windows XP. At the end of the installation process, you are given the opportunity to join a

15

domain. For Windows NT and Windows 2000 upgrades, almost all registry entries are carried forward into the new OS, and the information about a domain is not requested because it is copied from the old OS into Windows XP.

Upgrading from Windows NT or Windows 2000 to Windows XP is the easiest type of upgrade because these operating systems all have similar registries and support applications and devices in the same way. Nearly all applications that run on Windows NT or Windows 2000 will run on Windows XP. When upgrading from Windows NT to Windows XP, the NTFS file system is automatically converted to the Windows XP version.

> **TIP**
> Antivirus software designed to be used with the Windows NT NTFS file system might not run under the Windows XP NTFS file system because of the way some antivirus programs filter software as it accesses the file system. You might have to upgrade your antivirus software after Windows XP is installed.

Setting Up a Dual Boot

You can configure Windows XP to set up a dual boot with another operating system. Start the installation as you would for a clean install on a PC with another operating system already installed. When given the opportunity, choose to install Windows XP on a different partition than the other OS. Windows XP recognizes that another OS is installed and sets up the Startup menu to offer it as an option for booting. After the installation, when you boot with a dual boot, the Startup menu automatically appears, asking you to select an operating system, as shown in Figure 15-7.

Please select the operating system to start:

    Microsoft Windows XP Professional
    Microsoft Windows 98

Use the up and down arrow keys to move the highlight to your choice.
Seconds until highlighted choice will be started automatically: xx
Press ENTER to choose.

For troubleshooting and advanced startup options for Windows, press F8.

Figure 15-7   Menu that appears for a dual boot

A+ OS
  2.1

The first active partition (drive C) must be set up with a file system that both operating systems understand. For example, for a dual boot with Windows 98, use the FAT32 or FAT16 file system. For a dual boot with Windows 2000, use either the FAT or the NTFS file system. You should install the other operating system first, and then you can install Windows XP in a different partition. When you install Windows XP on another active partition or an extended partition, it places only the files necessary to boot in the first active partition, which it calls the system partition. This causes Windows XP to initiate the boot rather than the other OS. The rest of Windows XP is installed on a second partition, which Windows XP calls the boot partition. This is the same way that Windows NT and Windows 2000 manage a dual boot with an older OS.

> **TIP** When setting up a dual boot, always install the older operating system first.

Earlier Windows operating systems were not aware of applications installed under the other OS in a dual boot, but Windows XP is. For example, if you set up a dual boot with Windows XP and Windows 98, an application installed under Windows 98 can be executed from Windows XP. This application might be listed under the Start menu of Windows XP. If it is not, you can use Windows XP Explorer to locate the program file. Double-click the application to run it from Windows XP. This makes implementing a dual boot easier because you don't have to install an application under both OSs.

After the Installation

A+ OS
  2.1

Immediately after you have installed Windows XP, there are several things to do to activate the OS, prepare it for use, and back up the hard drive in preparation for a disaster. These steps are discussed in this section.

15

Product Activation

Product activation is a method used by Microsoft to prevent unlicensed use of its software so that you must purchase a Windows XP license for each installation of Windows XP. The license was introduced with Microsoft Office XP, and Microsoft says it will continue using product activation in all future Microsoft products. The first time you log on to the system after the installation is complete, the Activate Windows dialog box appears giving these three options (see Figure 15-8):

- Yes, let's activate Windows over the Internet now.

- Yes, I want to telephone a customer service representative to activate Windows.

- No, remind me to activate Windows every few days.

A+ OS
2.1

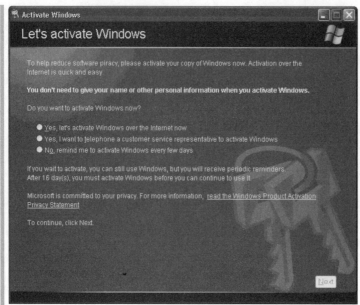

Figure 15-8 Product activation is a strategy used by Microsoft to prevent software piracy

If you choose to activate Windows over the Internet and are connected to the Internet at the time, the process is almost instant. Windows XP sends a numeric identifier to a Microsoft server, which sends a certificate activating the product on your PC. You have up to 60 days after installation to activate Windows XP; after that the system will not boot. If you install Windows XP from the same CD on a different computer and you attempt to activate Windows from the new PC, a dialog box appears telling you of the suspected violation of the license agreement. You can call a Microsoft operator and explain what caused the discrepancy. If your explanation is reasonable (for example, you uninstalled Windows XP from one PC and installed it on another), the operator can issue you a valid certificate. You can then type the certificate value into a dialog box to complete the boot process.

Now access the Internet and download any service packs, updates, or patches for the OS from the Microsoft Web site. You can also install any additional Windows components at this time.

Transferring User Files and Preferences to a New PC

Windows XP offers a utility that helps you transfer user files and preferences from one computer to another that has just had Windows XP installed. The **User State Migration Tool (USMT)** transfers user files and folders and displays properties, taskbar options, and browser and e-mail settings from a Windows 9x or Windows NT/2000/XP computer. This utility can help make a smooth transition because a user who is moving from one PC to another does not have to copy files and reconfigure OS settings. The process involves three steps:

1. Use a Windows XP computer to create a disk that contains the Files and Settings Transfer Wizard. This PC does not need to be the same PC that will later receive the transfer.

A+ OS
2.1

2. Use the disk on the source computer (the user's old computer) to run the Wizard and copy the user state to a server hard drive or removable media such as a Zip drive.

3. On the destination computer (the user's new computer), use the Wizard to transfer the user state to this computer.

To begin the process, use the Files and Settings Transfer Wizard to create the disk. To access the Wizard, click Start, All Programs, Accessories, System Tools, Files and Settings Transfer Wizard. The Wizard launches and the Welcome to the Files and Settings Transfer Wizard window opens. Click Next and the Wizard asks if this is the New computer or Old computer. Select New computer and then click Next. Figure 15-9 shows the next screen, on which you can choose to create the disk or declare that you are ready to put the information on the new computer. On the screen, note that you can also use the Windows XP CD to launch the Wizard on the old computer rather than creating the disk.

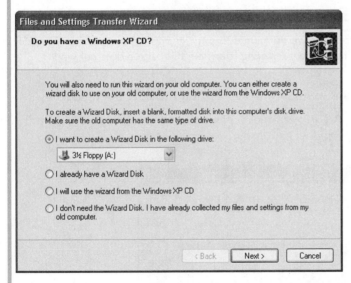

Figure 15-9   The first step in using the Files and Settings Transfer Wizard is to create the Wizard disk

After you have created the disk or chosen to use the Windows XP CD, go to the old computer, launch the Wizard, and retrieve the files and settings. Then return to this screen on the new computer, and choose to put the information on the new computer.

Instead of using the Wizard, you can also use two commands at the command prompt. Scanstate copies the information to a server or removable media, and Loadstate copies the information to the destination computer. These utilities can be included in batch files and executed automatically when implementing Windows XP over a large number of computers in an enterprise. For details on how to use the command lines in a batch file, see the *Windows XP Resource Kit* by Microsoft Press.

15

 **Preparing for Later Problems with the OS**

After the installation is complete, hardware and software are installed, and user preferences are set, it is a good idea to guard against later problems with the OS by creating a backup of the hard drive. Windows XP offers a utility called the **Automated System Recovery (ASR)** process that allows you to restore an entire hard drive volume or logical drive to its state at the time the backup of the volume was made. This process creates the backup and also creates an ASR floppy disk that allows you to use the backup to recover the system later. You will learn how to recover a failed system using a backup in the next chapter. In this section, you learn how to create the backup.

The backup file created will be just as large as the contents of the hard drive volume, so you will need a massive backup medium such as another partition on this or another local hard drive or file server, a tape drive, or a writeable CD-R or CD-RW drive.

CAUTION

Do not back up the logical drive or volume to a folder on the same volume. The ASR backup process allows you to do this, but restoring later from this backup does not work.

Follow these directions to create the backup and the ASR floppy disk:

1. Click **Start**, **All Programs**, **Accessories**, **System Tools**, **Backup**. The Backup and Restore window appears (see Figure 15-10).

Figure 15-10 Use the Backup or Restore Wizard to back up the hard drive partition after the Windows XP installation is complete

2. Click the **Advanced Mode** link. The Backup Utility window appears. Click **Automated System Recovery Wizard**. On the following screen, click **Next**.

3. The Backup Destination window appears. Select the location of the medium to receive the backup and insert a disk into the floppy disk drive. This disk will become the ASR disk. Click **Next**.

4. Click **Finish**. The backup process shows its progress as seen in Figure 15-11.

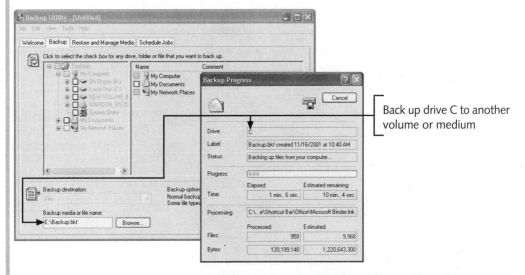

Back up drive C to another volume or medium

Figure 15-11   The Backup utility can create a backup of drive C and an ASR disk to be used later for the Automated System Recover utility

5. When the backup is finished, label the ASR disk with the name of the disk, the date it was created, and the computer's name, and put it in a safe place.

> **TIP** Just as with Windows 2000, you can back up the system state as discussed in Chapter 13. If you back up the system state when you complete an installation and a failure occurs in the future, you can restore the system state without overwriting user data on the hard drive. This is less drastic than the Automated System Recovery process that restores the entire volume.

USING WINDOWS XP

Now that you have learned how to install Windows XP successfully and guard the system against potential failure, let's take a closer look at how it works and what it can do. One difference you will note immediately on using Windows XP for the first time is the desktop shown in Figure 15-12. When the OS is first installed, the Recycle Bin is the only shortcut on the desktop. Also note that the Start menu is organized with a more graphical look. Notice in Figure 15-12 that the user name for the person currently logged on shows at the top of the Start menu. Applications at the top of the Start menu are said to be "pinned" to the Start menu and are permanently listed there until you change them in a Start menu setting. Applications that are used often are listed below the pinned applications and can change from time to time. The programs in the white column of the Start menu on the left side are user oriented, and the programs in the dark column on the right side of the menu are OS oriented.

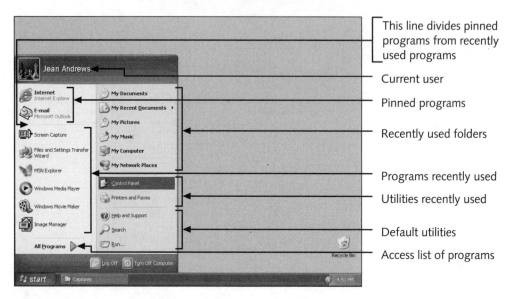

Figure 15-12 The Windows XP desktop and Start menu

When you click All Programs, the list of currently installed software appears. Figure 15-13 shows the default entries under Accessories, System Tools. You have already seen two of these, Backup, and Files and Settings Transfer Wizard. Also, after Windows is installed, you can use the Activate Windows option on this menu to activate Windows XP. You will learn about some other options on this menu later in this chapter and in the next chapter.

When you drill down to windows and menus on these windows, you will notice you have more control over how and where things appear. Overall, if you are familiar with earlier versions of Windows, learning to use Windows XP is easy and intuitive. One example of how you can change the way a window appears is through the Control Panel. To access the Control Panel, click Start and Control Panel. Figure 15-14 shows the Control Panel in Category View. Select a category in order to see the applets in that category, or click Switch to Classic View to see the applets when you first open the Control Panel as you did with earlier versions of Windows.

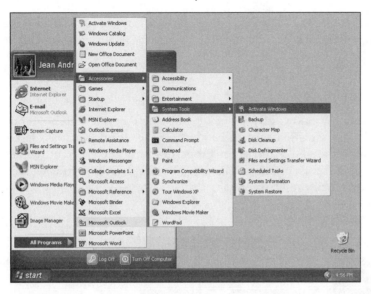

Figure 15-13   Click Start, All Programs to view the list of currently installed software

View items rather than categories

Figure 15-14   The Control Panel is organized by category, although you can easily switch to Classic View

Customizing the Windows XP Desktop

You can do several things to customize the Windows XP desktop. For example, you can change the background on the desktop (called the wallpaper), create shortcuts, and control what goes in the system tray. This section looks at each of these ways to make the desktop look and work the way you want it to.

15

TIP Each user account has a different desktop configuration, so if you want to create a customized desktop for a user, you must first log on to the system under that user account.

Managing Shortcuts

When you first install Windows XP, by default, only the Recycle Bin shows on the desktop. To add other shortcuts that normally were on the Windows 2000 desktop, right-click anywhere on the desktop and select Properties from the shortcut menu. (You can also select the Display icon in Control Panel.) The Display Properties window appears (see Figure 15-15). Click the Desktop tab.

Figure 15-15   Managing the Windows XP desktop

Click Customize Desktop to display the Desktop Items window, also shown in Figure 15-15. You can check My Documents, My Computer, My Network Places, and Internet Explorer to add these icons to the desktop. Also notice on this window the option to have Windows clean up your desktop by moving any shortcuts that you have not used in the last 60 days to a separate folder.

You can add a program shortcut to the desktop by right-clicking a program name in the Start, All Programs list and then selecting Copy from the shortcut menu. Then right-click anywhere on the desktop, and select Paste from the shortcut menu. A shortcut is created and placed on the desktop. You can also use Windows Explorer to create a shortcut. From Explorer, right-click a program filename or the filename of a document or data file, and then select Create Shortcut from the shortcut menu (see Figure 15-16). Then, drag the shortcut created to the desktop.

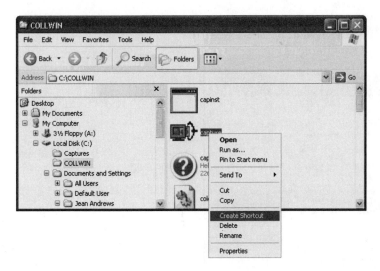

Figure 15-16   Create a shortcut to a file using the file's shortcut menu in Explorer

A+ OS 1.1 Windows XP Taskbar and System Tray

The taskbar can be controlled from the Taskbar and Start Menu windows. Access these windows by using the Taskbar and Start menu icon in Control Panel or by right-clicking the taskbar and selecting Properties. Either way, the window in Figure 15-17 appears. From it you can add items to and remove items from the Start Menu, control how the taskbar manages items in the system tray, and specify how the taskbar is displayed.

You might want to display frequently used programs as icons in the taskbar. To do that, right-click the taskbar, select Toolbars, and then click Quick Launch. Also, the system tray can sometimes become cluttered with several icons for running services such as the volume control and network connectivity. Windows XP automatically hides these icons. To unhide them, click the left arrow on the right side of the taskbar. In addition, by using the options available on the taskbar shortcut menu, you can add programs to the Quick Launch toolbar, customize taskbar properties, and add new toolbars to the taskbar.

Windows Messenger

By default, when Windows XP first starts, it loads Windows Messenger, which takes up system resources even if you are not using it. To stop Windows Messenger from loading at startup, on the Windows Messenger menu, click Tools and then click Options. The Options window opens as shown in Figure 15-18. Click the Preferences tab and uncheck Run this program when Windows starts. Click OK.

15

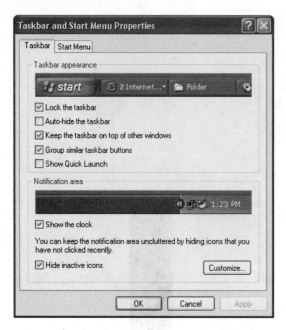

Figure 15-17 Use the Taskbar and Start Menu Properties window to control what appears in the Start Menu and Taskbar

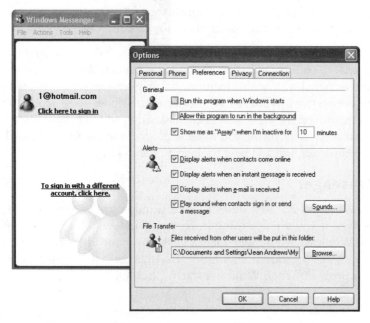

Figure 15-18 Disable Windows Messenger at startup

Managing Audio and Video

Windows XP has several built-in features to manage audio and video, including support for inputting images from digital cameras and scanners, a Windows Movie Maker for editing video, and Windows Media Player, Version 8. (Windows Me has Media Player, Version 7.) With Media Player you can play DVDs, CDs, and Internet radio. There's a jukebox for organizing audio files, including MP3 files used on music CDs. You can also burn your own music CDs using Media Player with a CD-R or CD-RW drive. To access the Media Player, click Start, All Programs, Windows Media Player. Figure 15-19 shows the Media Player window.

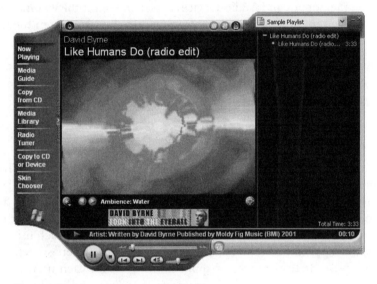

Figure 15-19   Windows Media Player

As with older versions of Windows, you can record and manage sound from the Entertainment group of Windows and manage sounds for Windows events from the Sounds applet in Control Panel. To record sound, if you have a microphone connected to a sound card, click Start, All Programs, Accessories, Entertainment, and Sound Recorder. The Sound Recorder appears, as shown in Figure 15-20. Click the Record button (red dot in lower-right corner) to record and save a sound, such as your own voice, in a sound file. There are several types of sound files, including MP3 files (with the .mp3 file extension), which can be used on audio CDs, and Wave files (with the .wav file extension). Windows uses .wav files to record sound. Later, you can substitute this .wav file for one of the Windows sounds that plays when you open or close applications, shut down Windows, or perform many other Windows activities that can be accompanied by sound. To change the sounds for various Windows events, from Control Panel, open the Sounds and Audio Devices applet, and select the Sounds tab.

15

Figure 15-20   Record sounds using Windows Sound Recorder

Media Player has its own volume control, but there is another way to adjust sound. From the Control Panel, open the Sounds and Audio Devices applet and select the Volume tab. If you check Place volume icon in the taskbar, you can easily adjust the sound from the taskbar.

> **TIP** Two ways to control sound volume are to use the Windows controls or use the manual controls on an amplifier or speaker.

Multiple Logins and Remote Assistance

Windows XP allows more than one user to be logged in at the same time. To switch from one account to another, click Start, Log Off. The Log Off Windows dialog box opens, giving you two choices: Switch User and Log Off. Click Switch User and then select a new account from the list of user accounts. After you enter a password, the screen goes blank and then the desktop configured for the new user appears. Each user can have his or her own set of applications open at the same time. When users switch back and forth, Windows keeps separate instances of applications open for each user.

Windows XP also offers a new feature called **Remote Assistance**. Using this utility, a user sitting at the PC can give a support technician at a remote location full access to the desktop. The technician can use the desktop just as she would if sitting in front of the PC. This is useful when an inexperienced user has trouble following the technician's directions as the technician investigates and troubleshoots problems with Windows XP.

INSTALLING HARDWARE AND APPLICATIONS

In this section, you will learn how to install hardware and applications under Windows XP, and you will also learn several ways to solve problems with both. Later in this chapter and the next chapter, you will learn about more tools and procedures you can use to troubleshoot a failed system, program, or hardware device. We will first look at how to install hardware.

Installing Hardware

A+ OS
2.4
3.2

Since Windows XP is relatively new to the market, a device might not come with a Windows XP-compatible driver. To see if a hardware device has a driver known to be compatible with Windows XP, visit the Microsoft Web site *www.microsoft.com/technet,* and search on the driver or device. Download the latest driver from the Microsoft Web site or the Web site of the device manufacturer. Windows XP offers three processes that help solve problems with devices:

- Verifying that the driver is certified by Microsoft

- Providing a way to automatically find an update for a driver

- Rolling back a driver in case an updated driver fails

As with earlier Windows operating systems, when Windows XP first starts, if it senses a new device, it automatically launches the Found New Hardware Wizard, which gives you two options:

- Install the software automatically (Recommended)

- Install from a list or specific location (Advanced)

Select the option to Install the software automatically, and then click Next. During the installation process, you have the opportunity to click Have Disk to provide a driver supplied by the manufacturer, rather than selecting the device from a list, which results in using a Windows driver. First attempt to use the Windows XP driver. If it causes problems, search both the Microsoft Web site and the manufacturer's Web site for the latest updated driver. If the Wizard does not automatically launch when you start Windows, you can start it using the Add Hardware icon in Control Panel.

Using Device Manager

After a device is installed, you can use Device Manager to verify that Windows XP sees no problems with the device. There is more than one way to access Device Manager. One is to click Start, right-click My Computer, and then select Manage from the shortcut menu. The Computer Management window appears (see Figure 15-21). This powerful tool offers several important utilities to support Windows XP, some of which you learned about in earlier chapters, that function as they did with Windows 2000 (such as Event Viewer), and some of which you will learn about in this chapter. Under System Tools, click Device Manager to view it. With Device Manager selected, use the View menu to control how you view devices and resources in Device Manager, similarly to previous versions of Windows. Another way to access Device Manager is to open the System applet in the Control Panel, select the Hardware tab, and click Device Manager.

15

A+ OS
2.4
3.2

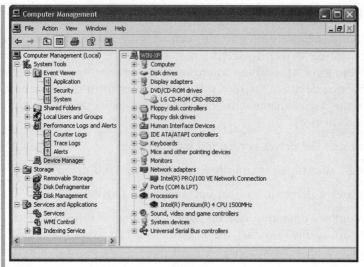

Figure 15-21   Device Manager is one tool available in the Computer Management window

Using Device Manager, you can verify that there are no resource conflicts with the device and that it works properly as viewed by Windows XP. From Device Manager, Windows XP offers a way to update a driver using the Update Device Driver Wizard. Right-click a device and select Properties from the shortcut menu. The Properties window for that device appears (see Figure 15-22). Select the Driver tab and click Update Driver to launch the Wizard, and follow directions on the screen. The Wizard goes to the Microsoft Web site, searches for updates to the driver, informs you if there is an update, and asks permission to install the update. Windows XP only suggests an update if the hardware ID of the device exactly matches the hardware ID of the update. A hardware ID is a number assigned to a device by the manufacturer that uniquely identifies the product.

 TIP   If you do not have an always-on connection to the Internet, connect to the Internet before you launch the Update Device Driver Wizard.

If you update a driver and the new driver does not perform as expected, you can revert to the old driver by using the Driver Rollback feature. To revert to a previous driver, from the Properties window for the device (see Figure 15-22), click Roll Back Driver. If a previous driver is available, it will be installed. In many cases, when a driver is updated, Windows saves the old driver in case you want to revert to it. Note that Windows does not save printer drivers when they are updated and also does not save any drivers that are not functioning properly at the time of an update.

A+ OS
2.4
3.2

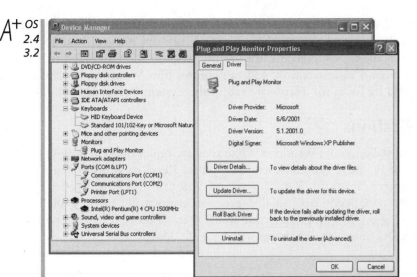

Figure 15-22   Use the Properties window for a device to obtain an updated driver from the Microsoft Web site

You can also copy an older driver from another PC or a backup medium to this PC for a rollback. Two files are needed: a .sys file and an .inf file. The .sys file is the actual driver, and the .inf file contains information about the driver. Put these files in the %systemroot%\ system32\reinstallbackups\ folder, and then perform the rollback.

 By default, Device Manager does not show legacy devices that are not Plug and Play. To view installed legacy devices, on the View menu of Device Manager, check Show hidden devices (see Figure 15-23).

15

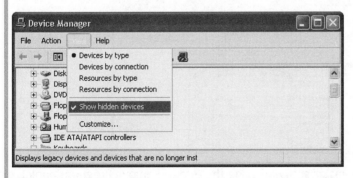

Figure 15-23   By default, Windows XP does not display legacy devices in Device Manager. Show these hidden devices by using the View menu

A+ OS
2.4
3.2

Windows 2000 and Windows XP support the verification of digital signatures assigned to device drivers. If you suspect a problem with a driver, run **Sigverif.exe** to scan for drivers that are not digitally signed. To use the utility, enter the command in the Run dialog box. Also, during an installation, you can control how Windows handles a driver not digitally signed by using the Hardware tab of the System Properties window.

Installing Applications

Applications are installed under Windows XP as they are under other Windows OSs. You can use the Add or Remove Programs icon in Control Panel, or you can run the application's setup program from the Run dialog box. You can only install software if you have Administrator privileges. An installed program is normally made available to all users when they log on. If a program is not available to all users, try installing the program files in the Documents and Settings\All Users folder.

> **TIP** You can cause a program to launch automatically each time you start Windows by putting a shortcut to the program in the Startup menu folder for the user. For each user, this folder is Documents and Settings*Username*\\Start Menu\\Programs\\Startup. If you want the software to start up automatically for all users, put the shortcut in this folder: Documents and Settings\\All Users\\Start Menu\\Programs\\Startup.

Software is uninstalled using the Add and Remove Programs applet in Control Panel. Open the applet and select the software to uninstall (see Figure 15-24). Then click the Change/Remove icon. If other users are logged on to the system, the Warning message in Figure 15-24 appears. Log everyone off and then uninstall the software.

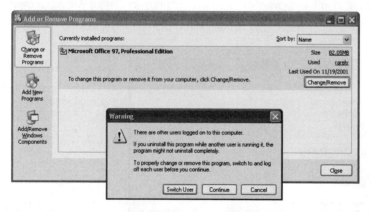

Figure 15-24   To uninstall software using the Add or Remove Programs applet, only one user, an administrator, should be logged on to the system

Installing Legacy Software

DOS and Windows 9x applications that would not work under Windows NT and Windows 2000 are more likely to work under Windows XP. Some legacy applications that you should not attempt to run under Windows XP are older versions of antivirus software, and maintenance and cleanup utilities. In these cases, it is best to upgrade your software to versions designed to work under Windows XP.

If a legacy application does not start up and run successfully after you have installed it, try the following:

- Check the Microsoft Web site for updates to Windows XP or the Microsoft application (*windowsupdate.microsoft.com*). How to perform Windows XP updates is covered in the next chapter.

- Check the software manufacturer's Web site for updates or suggestions on how to run the software under Windows XP.

- Consider upgrading the software to a later version.

- Use the Windows XP Compatibility Mode utility.

The **Compatibility Mode utility** provides an application with the environment it expects from the operating system it was designed for, including Windows 95, Windows 98, Windows Me, Windows NT, and Windows 2000. (Compatibility mode does not apply to DOS applications.) There is more than one way to use the utility, but the easiest way is to create a shortcut on the desktop to an installed application and then set the properties of the shortcut to use compatibility mode. After you create the shortcut to the application, right-click it and select Properties from the shortcut menu. The Properties window displays (see Figure 15-25). Select the Compatibility tab. Check *Run this program in compatibility mode for,* and then select the operating system that you want Windows XP to emulate. Click Apply to apply the change. Run the software to find out whether the problem is solved.

15

If it is not solved, if you like, you can provide Microsoft with information that might help it fix the problem in some future Windows XP update. To provide the information, run the Program Compatibility Wizard. Click Start, All Programs, Accessories, Program Compatibility Wizard. Follow directions on the Wizard screen to locate the program file. After you locate the program file, you are asked to test the application and then respond to the questions shown in Figure 15-26.

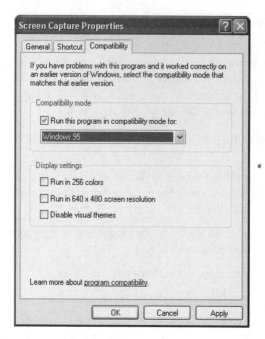

Figure 15-25   Setting Windows XP to run a legacy program in compatibility mode

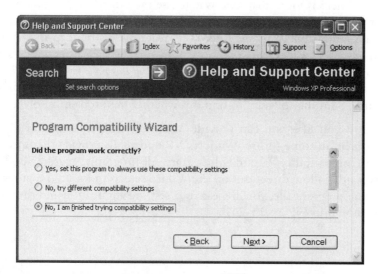

Figure 15-26   Using the Program Compatibility Wizard

If you answer, "No, I am finished trying compatibility settings," then the screen in Figure 15-27 appears. If you respond Yes to the question, "Would you like to send this information to Microsoft?", then the information needed to help Microsoft solve problems with the application is transmitted to the Microsoft Web site over the Internet.

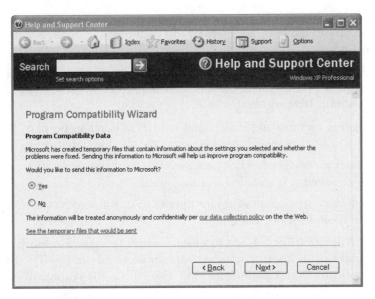

Figure 15-27   If running a legacy program in compatibility mode does not solve the problem, you can send helpful information to Microsoft

---

CHAPTER SUMMARY

❑ There are presently three versions of Windows XP: Windows XP Home Edition, Windows XP Professional, and Windows XP 64-bit Edition. Windows .NET is expected to be released soon.

❑ Windows XP integrates features of Windows 9x and 2000, while providing added support for multimedia and networking technologies.

❑ Although the Windows XP interface looks different from that of earlier versions of Windows and the OS organizes some utilities and functions differently, Windows XP is built on the same basic architecture as Windows NT and Windows 2000 and has the same basic kernel structure.

❑ Windows XP requires only 640 MB of free hard drive space for installation; however, acceptable performance cannot be achieved without 1.5 GB of free space on the Windows XP partition.

❑ Windows XP supports the same file systems as Windows 2000: FAT16, FAT32, and NTFS.

❑ You can install Windows XP as a dual boot with Windows 2000, because they both use the same version of NTFS. To dual boot Windows XP with Windows 9x or Windows NT, you must use FAT32. Always install the other OS first, and install Windows XP on a different partition than another OS.

15

❑ A clean install is required if you plan to dual boot Windows XP with another OS. Perform an upgrade if you have another version of Windows installed and you do not plan to dual boot.

❑ Before upgrading to Windows XP, clean up the hard drive by deleting unnecessary files and running Disk Defragmenter and ScanDisk, uncompress the drive, and delete known incompatible software.

❑ An Express Upgrade uses existing folders and settings as much as possible. A Custom Upgrade allows you to changes folders, language, and the file system.

❑ Unlike earlier versions of Windows, Windows XP is aware of applications installed under another OS when it is installed as a dual boot.

❑ Microsoft uses product activation to prevent the use of its software products, including Windows XP, on more than one computer.

❑ The User State Migration Tool (USMT) enables a user to make a smooth transition from one computer to another by transferring user files and settings. The Scanstate and Loadstate commands accomplish the same thing from the command prompt.

❑ Differences in the Windows XP desktop from earlier versions include the absence (by default) of any shortcuts other than the Recycle Bin and the more graphical organization of the Start menu.

❑ In the Windows XP Control Panel, you can view applications in Category View or Classic View to see them as they looked in earlier versions of Windows.

❑ Windows XP allows more than one user to be logged on at the same time, each with their own instances of open applications.

❑ Windows XP offers processes to help find updates for a driver, roll back a driver if an update fails, and verify that a driver is certified by Microsoft.

❑ The Computer Management, Disk Management, and Device Manager tools work much the same way in Windows XP as they did in Windows 2000.

❑ Windows XP Device Manager hides legacy devices (non–Plug and Play devices) by default.

❑ You can only install software in Windows XP if you have administrator privileges.

❑ DOS applications and older Windows applications that did not work under earlier versions of Windows are more likely to work under Windows XP.

❑ Compatibility mode in Windows XP provides an application written for Windows 9x or later with the environment for which it was designed.

KEY TERMS

Automated System Recovery (ASR)	product activation	Sigverif.exe
	Remote Assistance	User State Migration Tool (USMT)
Compatibility Mode utility		

REVIEW QUESTIONS

1. Windows XP uses the same kernel architecture as Windows NT and Windows 2000.

   a. True

   b. False

2. The minimum processor requirement for the installation of Microsoft Windows XP Professional is:

   a. Pentium 233

   b. Pentium 300

   c. Pentium II 233

   d. Pentium II 300

   e. Pentium IV

3. The minimum hard drive partition needed to install Microsoft Windows XP Professional is:

   a. 640 KB

   b. 100 MB

   c. 640 MB

   d. 1 GB

   e. 2 GB

4. The recommended hard drive partition needed to install Microsoft Windows XP Professional is:

   a. 640 KB

   b. 100 MB

   c. 640 MB

   d. 1 GB

   e. 2 GB

5. Running the Readiness Analyzer to verify software and hardware qualification prior to operating system installation requires the following command string:

   a. d:\I386\Winnt32\checkupgradeonly

   b. d:\I386\Winnt32/checkupgradeonly

   c. d:\I386\Winnt32/readanalyzer

   d. d:\I386\Winnt32/system

   e. None of the above

6. Use FAT16 and FAT32 file system if you are setting up a dual boot with Windows 9x, and each operating system must access all partitions.

   a. True

   b. False

7. To repair a Windows XP Installation:

    a. Start the Recovery Console

    b. Start the Performance Monitor

    c. Start the My Computer routine

    d. Start the Network Neighborhood routine

    e. None of the above

8. Of the two types of upgrades for Windows XP, Express and Custom Upgrades, which upgrade uses existing Windows folders and all the existing settings it can?

    a. Express

    b. Custom

    c. Both a and b

    d. Neither a nor b

9. Of the tools available in Windows XP, which tool transfers user files and folders and displays properties, taskbar options, and browser and e-mail settings from a Windows 9x or Windows NT/2000/XP computer?

    a. My Computer

    b. The Settings folder in the Control Panel

    c. The User State Migration Tool (USMT) Utility

    d. The Automated System Recovery (ASR) Utility

    e. The Compatibility Mode Utility

10. Windows XP offers a utility called the _____ process that allows the user to restore an entire hard drive volume or logical drive to its state at the time the backup of the volume was made.

    a. My Computer

    b. Settings folder in the Control Panel

    c. User State Migration Tool (USMT) Utility

    d. Automated System Recovery (ASR) Utility

    e. Compatibility Mode Utility

11. The _____ provides an application with the environment it expects from the operating system it was designed for, including Windows 95, Windows 98, Windows ME, Windows NT, and Windows 2000.

    a. My Computer icon

    b. Settings folder in the Control Panel

    c. User State Migration Tool (USMT) Utility

    d. Automated System Recovery (ASR) Utility

    e. Compatibility Mode Utility

16

MANAGING AND SUPPORTING WINDOWS XP

In this chapter, you will learn:

- ♦ How to use Windows XP features to secure the PC and protect users and their data
- ♦ About the Windows NT/2000/XP registry
- ♦ About tools for troubleshooting and maintaining Windows XP
- ♦ How to troubleshoot the Windows XP boot process

You were introduced to Windows XP in the last chapter and learned how to install and use it. This chapter takes you further in learning to support this OS. You will learn about security features that protect the Windows XP system, its users, and their data. You'll also learn how the Windows NT/2000/XP registry is organized and how to edit it, and about many troubleshooting tools available under Windows XP. Finally, you will learn how to troubleshoot the Windows XP boot process. In later chapters, you will learn more about how Windows XP is used on networks and about additional security features it has when networked.

SECURITY USING WINDOWS NT/2000/XP

A+ OS
1.4

Security under Windows NT/2000/XP has two goals: to secure the system resources including hardware and software from improper use, and to secure users' data from improper access. In this section you will learn about some features of Windows NT/2000/XP that support these goals. At the heart of Windows NT/2000/XP security is the concept of user accounts.

User Accounts and Profiles

A+ OS
1.4

A **user account** defines a user to Windows and records information about the user including the user name, password used to access the account, groups that the account belongs to, and the rights and permissions assigned to the account. There are three types of user accounts in Windows NT/2000/XP:

- **Global user accounts**, sometimes called domain user accounts, are used at the domain level, created by an administrator, and stored in the SAM (security accounts manager) database on a domain controller. A user can log on to any computer on the networked domain using a global user account, and the information about a global user account's rights and permissions apply to each workstation in the domain. The centralized SAM database is part of Active Directory, a repository of information used to manage a Windows network that is itself managed by Windows 2000 Server or soon-to-come Windows .NET.

- A **local user account** is created on a local computer and allows a user access to only that one computer. An administrator creates a local user account, assigns a user name and password to the account, and gives the account rights and permissions. As a general rule, a user account should have no more rights than a user needs to do his or her job. For example, an administrator responsible for setting up and maintaining user accounts in an office workgroup can set the permissions on a user account to deny the user the right to install a printer, install software, or do any other chores that change the PC software or hardware environment.

- **Built-in user accounts**. Every Windows XP workstation has two built-in user accounts that are set up when the OS is first installed: an administrator account and a guest account. An administrator has rights and permissions to all computer software, data, and hardware resources. Under Windows NT/2000/XP, the administrator can create other user accounts and assign corresponding rights and permissions to individual accounts, to groups of selected accounts, or to all accounts that use the computer. A guest account has very limited privileges and gives someone who does not have a user account access to a computer. The guest account is useful in a business environment where many people use a single computer for limited purposes and it is not practical for all of them to have unique user accounts.

A+ OS
1.4

How user accounts are set up depends on whether the computer is a standalone workstation (not networked), belongs to a workgroup, or belongs to a domain. Recall from Chapter 13 that in a workgroup, each computer manages the security for its own resources. Each local user account is set up on the local computer independent of other accounts on other PCs, and there is no centralized control of resources. If a user on one computer needs access to resources on another computer in the workgroup, the other computer must have the same user account and password that the first computer does. This chapter focuses on setting up security for standalone workstations and for workstations in a workgroup. It does not cover managing user accounts at the domain level.

After an administrator creates a local user account and the user logs on for the first time, the system creates a **user profile** for that user. When the user changes settings to customize his or her computer and then logs off, the user profile is updated so that settings can be restored the next time the user logs on.

If the computer is networked to other computers in a Windows workgroup, the administrator must create a user account on each computer in the workgroup that this user needs to access. When the user logs on to each computer in the workgroup, he or she would have to reestablish the user profile at each computer, re-creating desktop settings and application settings for each computer unless the administrator implements a feature called roaming user profiles. With **roaming user profiles**, settings established by a user at one computer are stored in a file on a file server on the network and shared with all computers in the workgroup. When a user moves from one computer to another computer in the workgroup, the roaming profile follows the user so that he or she does not have to redo settings at each computer.

Another type of profile used with workgroups is a **mandatory user profile**. This profile is a roaming user profile that applies to all users in a user group, and individual users cannot change that profile. It is used in situations where users only perform specific job-related tasks. A profile that applies to a group of users is called a **group profile**. An administrator creates roaming and mandatory profiles using the Computer Management console under the Administrative Tools applet in the Control Panel.

You can view all profiles stored on a Windows XP computer by using the System Properties window. Click Start and right-click My Computer. Select Properties and then click the Advanced tab. Under User Profiles, click the Settings button (see Figure 16-1). Next, we turn our attention to how to create and manage local user accounts.

16

A+ OS
  1.4

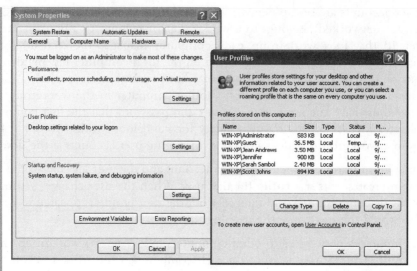

Figure 16-1   View all user profiles stored on this PC using the System Properties window

Administering Local User Accounts

When setting up accounts for users where security is a concern, you should follow a few guidelines about passwords for both users and administrators:

- Usernames for Windows NT/2000/XP logon can consist of up to 15 characters.

- Passwords can be up to 127 characters.

- Do not use a password that is easy to guess, such as one consisting of real words, your telephone number, or the name of your pet.

- The most secure type of password is a combination of letters, numbers, and even non-alphanumeric characters.

- User accounts can be set up with or without passwords. Passwords provide greater security. Where security is a concern, always set a password for the Administrator account.

- Passwords can be controlled by the administrator, but generally, users should be allowed to change their own passwords.

An administrator can create a user account using the Computer Management console or the User Accounts applet in Control Panel. If the account is created in Computer Management it will have Limited privileges. If it is created using the Control Panel, it will have Administrator privileges. To create a local user account using Computer Management, follow these steps:

1. Log on to the computer as the administrator.

2. Click **Start** and right-click **My Computer**. Select **Manage** from the short-cut menu. The Computer Management console window opens. (Note that

A+ OS
1.4

you can also access Computer Management by way of the Control Panel, Administrative Tools applet.)

3. Expand **Local Users and Groups** by clicking the plus sign to its left. Right-click **Users** and select **New User** from the shortcut menu. The New User window opens (see Figure 16-2).

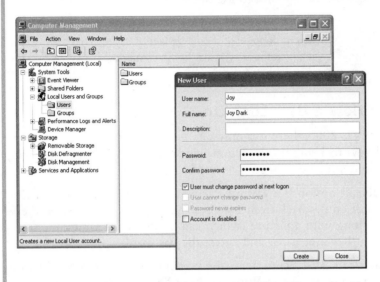

Figure 16-2 Create a user account using either Computer Management or the User Accounts applet in Control Panel

4. The account is created with the default type Limited, which means the account cannot create, delete, or change other accounts; make system-wide changes; or install software. If you want to give the account Administrator privileges, then open the **Control Panel** and double-click the **User Accounts** applet.

5. The User Accounts window opens listing all accounts. To make changes to an account, select the account.

6. In the next window, you can choose to change the name of the account, change the password, change the picture icon associated with the account, change the account type, or delete the account. Click **Change the account type**.

7. In the next window, select **Computer administrator** and click **Change Account Type**. Click **Back** twice on the menu bar to return to the opening window.

Sometimes a user forgets his or her password or the password is compromised. If this happens and you have Administrator privileges, you can access the account through the Control Panel or the Computer Management Console to provide the user with a new password. This action is called resetting the password. However, resetting a password under Windows XP causes the OS to lock the user out from using encrypted e-mail or files or using Internet passwords stored on the computer.

16

A+ OS
1.4

For this reason, each new user should create a **forgotten password floppy disk** for use in the event the user forgets the password. To create the disk, open the User Accounts applet in Control Panel, click your account, and select Prevent a forgotten password under Related Tasks in the left pane of this window. Follow the wizard to create the disk. If a user enters a wrong password at logon, he or she has the opportunity to use the forgotten password floppy disk to log on.

> **TIP** The forgotten password floppy disk should be kept in a protected place so that others cannot use it to gain unauthorized access to the computer.

A+ OS
2.4

Controlling How a User Logs On

With Windows NT/2000, there was only one way to log on to the system: pressing the Ctrl+Alt+Del keys to bring up the logon window. In a Windows XP workgroup, you have some options as to how logging on works:

- The default option is a Welcome screen that appears when the PC is first booted or comes back from a sleep state. All users are listed on the Welcome screen along with a picture (which can be the user's photograph); a user clicks on his or her user name and enters the password.

- Instead of the Welcome screen, the user must press Ctrl+Alt+Del to get to a logon window similar to Windows NT/2000.

- Fast User Switching enables more than one user to be logged on to the system. If this option is disabled, only one user can log on at a time. If the option is enabled, when a user clicks Start, Log Off, then the Log Off Windows dialog box offers three options, Switch User, Log Off, and Cancel. When Fast User Switching is disabled, the Switch User option does not display. Disable Fast User Switching when you want to conserve resources because performance is poor when several users leave applications open.

To change the way a user logs on, from Control Panel, open the User Accounts applet. Click Change the way users log on or off (see Figure 16-3). Make your selections and click Apply Options to close the dialog box.

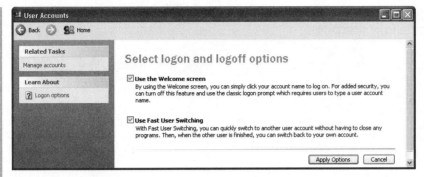

Figure 16-3 Options to change the way users log on or off

User Groups

User groups are an efficient way for an administrator to manage multiple user accounts that require the same privileges and similar profiles. When installed, Windows XP sets up several user groups including:

- Administrators, who have access to all parts of the system, can install or uninstall devices and applications, and can perform all administrative tasks.

- **Backup Operators** can back up and restore any files on the system regardless of their having access to these files.

- **Power Users** can read from and write to parts of the system other than their own local drive, install applications, and perform limited administrative tasks.

- **Limited Users** (known as Users in Windows NT/2000) have read-write access only on their own folders, read-only access to most system folders, and no access to other users' data. They cannot install applications or carry out any administrative responsibilities.

- **Guests** use a workstation once or occasionally and have limited access to files and resources. A guest account has permission to shut down a computer.

Creating a New User Group

You can also create your own user group and customize the permissions and profiles for this group of users. To create a new group:

1. Click **Start**, right-click **My Computer**, and select **Manage** from the menu.

2. The Computer Management console opens. Expand **Local Users and Groups** by clicking the plus sign.

3. To create a new group, right-click the **Groups** folder and select **New Group**... from the shortcut menu.

4. The New Group window opens, as shown in Figure 16-4. In this window, enter a name and description of the new group and click the **Add** button to find and select users to add to this group. When finished, click **Create** to finish creating the group.

16

A+ OS
2.4

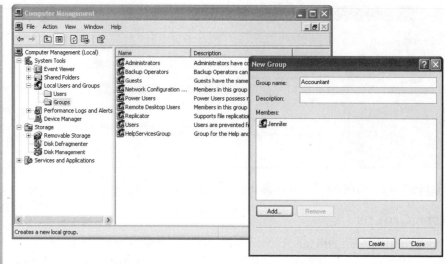

Figure 16-4   Create a new user group

You can also change the profile settings assigned to users in a group. For example, to control what a user or a user group can do, including the ability to change the system date and time, go to the Control Panel and access the Administrative Tools applet. Double-click the Local Security Policy icon. The Local Security Settings window appears (see Figure 16-5). Under Local Policies, the User Rights Assignment group lists several activities, which can be managed by changing the user groups that have the right to do these activities. Right-click Change the system time, and then select Properties from the shortcut menu. The Change the system time Properties window appears, as shown in Figure 16-5. From this window you can add and remove the user groups that have the right to change the system time.

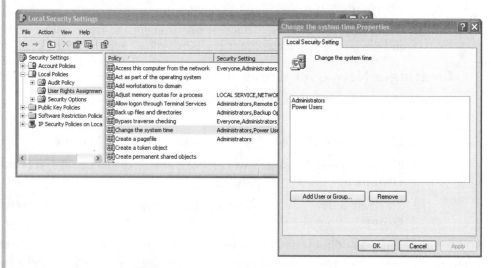

Figure 16-5   Local policies can be assigned to a user group, affecting all users in the group

A^{+} *OS*
     2.4

Group Policy

Another way to control how the system can be used is by applying settings called a **Group Policy** to your computer. Group Policy is normally intended to be used on a domain, although you can use it on a standalone computer or a computer in a workgroup. Group Policy can be applied to your computer, regardless of the currently logged-on user (called Computer Configuration) or can be applied to each user who logs on (called User Configuration). The Group Policy console is a Microsoft Management Console (MMC) snap-in that can be accessed by typing gpedit.msc in the Run dialog box. From the console you can control such things as how Media Player, Internet Explorer, and NetMeeting work, as well as many Windows settings and components. For a standalone computer or a computer in a workgroup, use Computer Configuration instead of User Configuration to implement Group Policy settings.

Disk Quotas

An administrator can set **disk quotas**, which limit how much disk space a user can access. This is important when two or more users are using a single computer and need to share its storage capacity. A disk quota does not specify where a user's files must be located; it just specifies how much total space the user can take up on a volume. The disk quota set applies to all users. You can only set disk quotas if you are using NTFS.

To set disk quotas:

1. Log on as an administrator, and open **My Computer**.

2. Find the partition that you want to set a disk quota on. Right-click it and select **Properties** from the shortcut menu.

3. Click the **Quota** tab and the **Enable quota management** check box. See Figure 16-6.

4. In this view, you can specify that users have unlimited access to disk space, you can specify the amount of space for users, and you can set a level of disk space used that will trigger a warning message to a user. For this example, all users are restricted to 500 MB of storage space and warned when they have used 400 MB.

5. Click the **Limit disk space to** radio button, enter **500** in the box next to it, and select **MB** from the drop-down menu to the right of the box.

6. In the box next to **Set warning level to**, enter **400**, then select **MB** from the drop-down menu. This warns users when they have used 400 MB of their allotted 500 MB of storage space.

7. Click **Deny disk space to users exceeding quota limit** so that no user can use more than the specified amount of disk space.

16

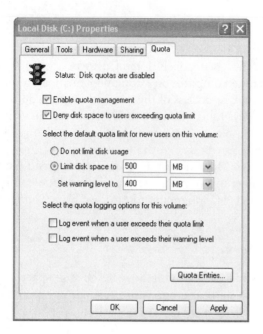

Figure 16-6   Setting disk quotas

8. Click **OK**. You are prompted to enable disk quotas. Click **OK** to respond to the prompt (see Figure 16-7).

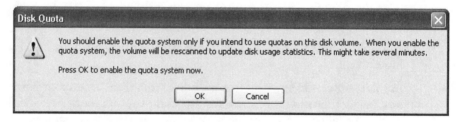

Figure 16-7   The prompt at the end of the quota-setting process gives you information about enabling quotas

EFS (Encrypted File System)

A+ OS
1.4
Another Windows 2000/XP security feature is the **Encrypted File System (EFS)**. EFS applies only to the Windows 2000/XP NTFS file system. In the past, it was possible to bypass an existing operating system's security measures by installing a new operating system or booting from a startup disk. In Windows 98, a password could be put on a file using a FAT file system, but you could boot from a startup disk, get to the file at the command prompt, copy it to a floppy disk, and access the file without using the password. That method does not work with EFS, which protects encrypted data even when someone who is not authorized to view those files or folders has full access to a computer's

A+ OS
1.4

data storage. When an unauthorized user attempts to access a file encrypted using EFS, he receives the error "Access Denied."

Encryption is the process of putting readable data into code that must be translated before it can be accessed, usually by using a **key** that encrypts the data and also provides a way to "unlock" the code and translate it back into readable data.

> **TIP** Do not confuse the term *key* as it is used in encryption with the term *registry key* which applies to information placed in the registry.

To ensure that a file can be accessed if a user is not available or forgets the password to log on to the system, an administrator for the OS can decrypt a file. In this case, the administrator is called a data recovery agent (DRA).

How to Use Encryption

A user does not have to go through a complex process of encryption to use EFS; from a user's perspective, it's just a matter of placing a file in a folder marked for encryption. Encryption can be implemented at either the folder or file level. If a folder is marked for encryption, every file created in the folder or copied to the folder will be encrypted. At the file level, each file must be encrypted individually. Encrypting with EFS at the folder level is encouraged and considered a best practice strategy because it provides greater security: any file placed in an encrypted folder is automatically encrypted so the user doesn't have to remember to encrypt it. An encrypted file remains encrypted if you move it from an encrypted folder to an unencrypted folder on the same logical drive.

In the following example, you encrypt the My Documents folder for an existing user named User2, create a file in that folder that automatically becomes encrypted because the folder is encrypted, and decrypt the folder so that others can access it.

1. In Windows Explorer, locate the My Documents folder for User2. In this example, the correct path is C:\Documents and Settings\User2\My Documents.

2. Right-click the **My Documents** folder, and choose **Properties** from the shortcut menu. The My Documents Properties window appears (see Figure 16-8).

3. On the **General** tab, click the **Advanced** button. The Advanced Attributes window appears.

16

A+ OS
1.4

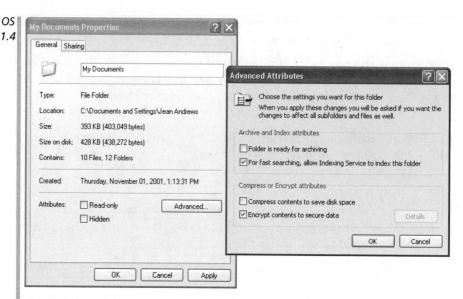

Figure 16-8   Encrypt folder contents

4. Check the box labeled **Encrypt contents to secure data**, and click **OK** (see Figure 16-8).

5. Click **Apply**. This causes the Confirm Attribute Changes window to open if any files or folders exist in the selected folder (see Figure 16-9).

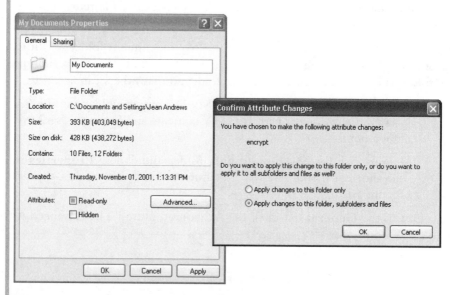

Figure 16-9   Apply changes to all folder contents

A+ OS
1.4

6. In this example, the subfolder My Pictures exists within the My Documents folder. If necessary, click the radio button next to the option **Apply changes to this folder, subfolders, and files** to encrypt any objects in this folder and its subfolders. (If you do not want to apply the changes to all subfolders and files, you select Apply changes to this folder only.) Click **OK**.

7. Open Microsoft Word, type some text in a file, and save the file in User2's My Documents folder. This file is automatically encrypted, because the My Documents folder is encrypted. If an unauthorized user attempts to access the encrypted document, the user receives an error message.

To allow others on the network to view this file, you would move or copy it to a folder that is not encrypted. Encryption is removed automatically when a file is sent over the network or moved off a logical drive where the folder is encrypted. If you move the file to another folder on the same logical drive or volume, you have to decrypt it manually. In this next example, you allow other users to view the file stored on your local hard drive by moving the file to a folder that is not encrypted, sharing the folder, and decrypting the file.

To decrypt a file, from the file's Properties window, click the Advanced button. On the Advanced Attributes window, uncheck Encrypt contents to secure data.

The Cipher Command

If you are encrypting a large number of files or folders from a command prompt or using a batch file, you can use the Cipher command:

```
CIPHER [/E, /D] [/S:dir] [pathname[…]]
```

- /E encrypts the specified files or folders.

- /D decrypts the specified files or folders.

- /S:dir applies the action to the specified folder (directory) and all its subfolders.

- Pathname is the path to and the name of the file or folder that is to be encrypted or decrypted.

For example, at the command prompt, to decrypt all files in the C:\Public folder, use this command:

```
Cipher /D C:\Public\*.*
```

Internet Connection Firewall

A+ OS
4.2

Windows 2000/XP offers several security features that protect the system from unauthorized access over a network or over the Internet, which you will learn about in later chapters. One feature new to Windows XP is Internet Connection Firewall. A **firewall** is hardware or software that protects a computer or network from unauthorized access. **Internet Connection Firewall (ICF)** is Windows XP software designed to protect a PC from unauthorized access from the Internet when the PC is connected directly to the Internet.

16

> **TIP** You should not use ICF on a PC that has Internet access from a LAN (local area network) because it can prevent others on the LAN from accessing resources on the PC.

ICF works by examining every communication that comes to the PC to determine if the communication has been initiated by the PC or is being initiated by an outside device or computer. If the communication is initiated by some source other than the PC, it is refused. With ICF, you can browse the Web, but those on the Web cannot initiate a communication with your PC in order to gain unauthorized access to data stored there.

To enable ICF, open the Network Connections applet in Control Panel and right-click on the network connection icon that you use to connect to the Internet. This might be a connection to the Internet by way of a dial-up modem, a cable modem, or a DSL connection. (All these connection types are covered in later chapters.) The connection Properties box opens as shown in Figure 16-10 for a modem connection. Click the Advanced tab and select Protect my computer and network by limiting or preventing access to this computer from the Internet. If you would like the firewall to record dropped packets in a log file, click Log Dropped Packets. Click OK. Remember, don't do this for a regular network connection if you want others on the network to have access to resources on your PC.

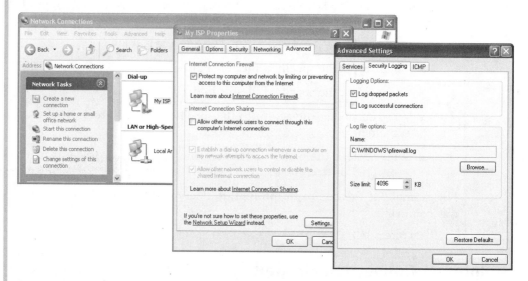

Figure 16-10   Enable Internet Connection Firewall and log dropped packets

We now turn our attention to several utilities that allow you to customize and troubleshoot Windows XP. We begin by looking at the Windows NT/2000/XP registry and learning how to edit it.

THE WINDOWS NT/2000/XP REGISTRY

A+ OS
1.1
1.2

The Windows NT/2000/XP registry is a hierarchical database containing information about all the hardware, software, device drivers, network protocols, and user configuration needed by the OS and applications. Many components depend on this information, and the registry provides a secure and stable location for it. Table 16-1 lists ways in which some components use the registry.

The next section looks at how the registry is organized, how to view the contents of the registry, how to back up and recover the registry, and how Windows makes changes to the registry.

Table 16-1   Components that use the Windows NT/2000/XP registry

Component	Description
Setup programs for devices and applications	Setup programs can record configuration information in the registry and query the registry for information needed to install drivers and applications.
User profiles maintained and used by the OS	Windows maintains a profile for each user that determines the user's environment. User profiles are kept in files, but, when a user logs on, the profile information is written to the registry, where changes are recorded, and then later written back to the user profile file. The OS uses this profile to control user settings and other configuration information specific to this user.
Files active when Ntldr is loading the OS	During the boot process, NTDetect.com surveys present hardware devices and records that information in the registry. Ntldr loads and initializes device drivers using information from the registry, including the order in which to load them.
Device drivers	Device drivers read and write configuration information from and to the registry each time they load. The drivers write hardware configuration information to the registry and read it to determine the proper way to load.
Hardware profiles	Windows can maintain more than one set of hardware configuration information (called a **hardware profile**) for one PC. The data is kept in the registry. An example of a computer that has more than one hardware profile is a notebook that has a docking station. Two hardware profiles describe the notebook, one docked and the other undocked. This information is kept in the registry.
Application programs	Many application programs read the registry for information about the location of files the program uses and various other parameters that were stored in .ini files under Windows 9x.

16

How the Registry Is Organized

A+ OS
1.1
1.2

When studying how the registry is organized, keep in mind that there are two ways to look at this organization: physical and logical.

Logical Organization of the Registry

Logically, the organization of the registry looks like an upside-down tree with five branches, called keys or subtrees (see Figure 16-11), which are categories of information stored in the registry. Each key is made up of several subkeys that may also have subkeys, and subkeys hold, or contain, values. Each value has a name and data assigned to it. Data in the registry is always stored in values, the lowest level of the tree.

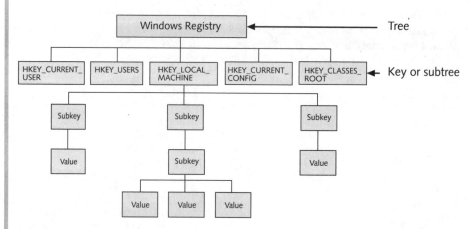

Figure 16-11 The Windows NT/2000/XP registry is logically organized in an upside-down tree structure of keys, subkeys, and values

Figure 16-12 shows the Windows Registry Editor, the window you see when you first open the editor: there are five high levels, one for each key or subtree. Notice in the figure that the HKEY_CURRENT_USER subtree has been opened to show subkeys under it; several subkeys have their own subkeys. If you click on a subkey that has a value assigned to it, that value appears on the right side of the window. Later in this section, you will see how to edit values in the registry.

The five subtrees of the registry, shown in Figure 16-12, are listed in Table 16-2 together with their primary functions. As you can notice in the table, the HKEY_LOCAL_MACHINE subtree is the mainstay key of the registry.

A^+ OS
1.1
1.2

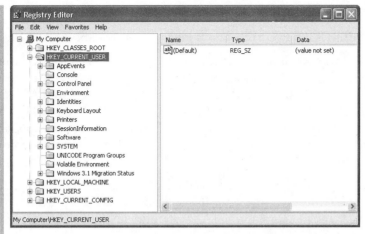

Figure 16-12   Windows Registry Editor shows the five high-level subtrees in the Windows NT/2000/XP registry

Table 16-2   The five subtrees of the Windows NT/2000/XP registry

Subtree (Main Keys)	Primary Function
HKEY_CURRENT_USER	Contains information about the currently logged-on user
HKEY_CLASSES_ROOT	Contains information about software and the way software is configured. This key points to data stored in HKEY_LOCAL_MACHINE.
HKEY_CURRENT_CONFIG	Contains information about the active hardware configuration, which is extracted from the data stored in the HKEY_LOCAL_ MACHINE subkeys called SOFTWARE and SYSTEM
HKEY_USERS	Contains information used to build the logon screen and the ID of the currently logged-on user
HKEY_LOCAL_MACHINE	Contains all configuration data about the computer, including information about device drivers and devices used at startup. The information in this key does not change when different users log on.

16

Physical Organization of the Registry

The physical organization of the registry is quite different from the logical organization. Physically, the registry is stored in five files called **hives**. There is no one-to-one relationship between the subtrees and these five files, even though there are five of each. Figure 16-13 shows the way the subtrees are stored in hives, as follows:

- HKEY_LOCAL_MACHINE consists of four hives, the SAM hive, the Security hive, the Software hive, and the System hive.

- HKEY_CURRENT_CONFIG data is kept in portions of two hives: the Software hive and the System hive.

- HKEY_CLASSES_ROOT data is kept in a portion of the Software hive.

A+ OS
1.1
1.2

- HKEY_USERS data is kept in the Default hive.

- HKEY_CURRENT_USER data is kept in a portion of the Default hive.

From Figure 16-13, you can also see that some subtrees use data contained in other sub-trees. For instance, the HKEY_CURRENT_USER data is a subset of the data in the HKEY_USERS subtree. HKEY_CURRENT_CONFIG and HKEY_CLASSES_ROOT subtrees use data contained in the HKEY_LOCAL_MACHINE subtree. However, don't let this physical relationship cloud your view of the logical relationship among these sub-trees. Although data is shared among the different subtrees, logically speaking, none of the five subtrees is subordinate to any other.

The registry hives are stored in the \%SystemRoot%\system32\config folder as a group of files. In a physical sense, each hive is a file. Each hive is backed up with a log file and a backup file, which are also stored in the \%SystemRoot%\system32\config folder.

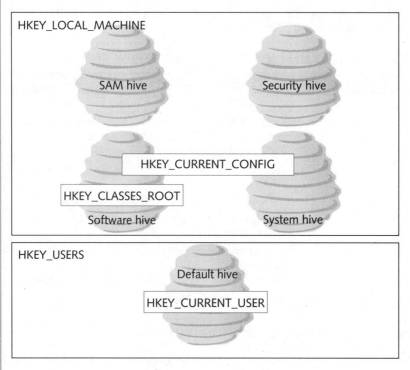

Figure 16-13   The relationship between registry subtrees (keys) and hives

Editing the Registry

A+ OS
1.5

When you make a change in Control Panel, Device Manager, or many other places in Windows NT/2000/XP, the registry is modified automatically. This is the only way most users will ever change the registry. However, on rare occasions you might need to edit the registry manually, for example, when you are following the directions of Microsoft

A+ OS
  1.5

technical support staff to delete references in the registry to viruses or worms. Changes to the registry take effect immediately and are permanent.

Before you edit the registry, you should back it up so that you can restore it if something goes wrong. Backing up the system state, which you learned to do in Chapter 13, is one way to back up the registry. In Chapter 13, you backed up the system state after a Windows 2000 installation, but you can also back up the system state at any time. When the system state is backed up, the Backup utility also puts a copy of the registry files in the %SystemRoot%\repair folder.

Windows NT/2000 offers two registry editors, each with a slightly different look and feel, although they both accomplish the same thing:

- Regedt32.exe located in the \%SystemRoot%\system32 folder, which shows each key in a separate window. Use it to edit the registry.

- Regedit.exe located in the \%SystemRoot% folder, which shows all keys in the same window and has a look and feel similar to Explorer. Use it to search and view the registry.

To access a registry editor, type the program name in the Run dialog box. With Windows XP, typing either Regedt32 or Regedit in the Run dialog box launches the Regedit.exe program.

The example below uses Regedit.exe under Windows XP to view the registry and look at registry values. To access Regedit.exe, double-click the filename in Explorer or enter the filename in the Run dialog box. Figure 16-14 shows a detailed view of the registry.

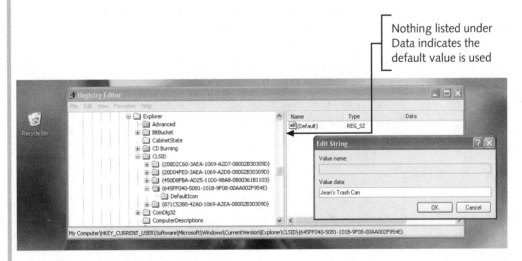

Figure 16-14   Editing a registry subkey value

Let's look at one example of editing the registry. Follow these directions to first back up the system state before editing the registry:

1. Click **Start**, **All Programs**, **Accessories**, **System Tools**, **Backup**. The Backup or Restore Wizard appears.

A^+ *OS*
1.5

2. Click **Advanced Mode**. The Backup Utility window appears. Click the **Backup** tab.

3. Check the **System State** box, and under **Backup media or file name:**, select the location to store the backup.

4. Click **Start Backup**. In the dialog box that appears, click **Start Backup** again to confirm the action. After the backup is done, click **Close** to close the Backup utility.

To change the name of the Recycle Bin on the Windows XP desktop for the currently logged on user, do the following:

1. To open Registry Editor, click **Start**, **Run** and type **Regedit** in the Run dialog box. Click **OK**. The Registry Editor window appears.

2. Locate the following subkey, which is the name of the Recycle Bin on the Windows desktop, by double-clicking the yellow folder icon of each subkey, moving down through the tree to the lowest subkey value. As you move down the tree, if the currently selected subkey has a value, that value appears in the right pane of the window.

   HKEY_CURRENT_USER\Software\Microsoft\Windows\CurrentVersion\Explorer\CLSID\645FF040-5081-101B-9F08-00AA002F954E

3. Figure 16-14 shows the subkey. The right pane shows nothing listed under Data, so the default value is used, which is the value for Recycle Bin. Position the window on the screen so that you can see the Recycle Bin icon.

4. Double-click the name of the value in the right pane. The Edit String dialog box appears. The Value data should be empty in the dialog box. If a value is present, you selected the wrong value. Check your work and try again.

5. Enter a new name for the Recycle Bin. For example, in Figure 16-14, the new name is "Jean's Trash Can." Click **OK**.

6. To see your change, right-click somewhere on the desktop and select **Refresh** from the shortcut menu. The name of the Recycle Bin changes.

7. To restore the name to the default value, on the Registry Editor window, again double-click the name of the value. The Edit String dialog box appears. Delete your entry and click **OK**.

8. To verify the change is made, right-click on the screen and select **Refresh** from the shortcut menu. The Recycle Bin name should return to its default value.

A+ OS
1.5

From these directions, you can see that changes made to the registry take effect immediately. Therefore, take extra care when editing the registry. If you make a mistake and don't know how to correct a problem you create, then you can restore the system state to recover.

OTHER MAINTENANCE AND TROUBLESHOOTING TOOLS

A+ OS
3.1
3.2

This section discusses other commonly used tools that Windows XP provides for maintenance and troubleshooting. Some tools are new or changed in Windows XP, and some operate just as they do in Windows 2000. Table 16-3 lists several tools and their functions. Some tools are executed from a command line (have an .exe file extension), others are Microsoft Management Console snap-ins (have an .msc file extension), and others are graphical tools built into Windows XP (such as Device Manager). MMC was discussed in Chapter 14. MMC snap-ins are executed from the Run dialog box or can sometimes be accessed using Windows menus. Some command-line programs can be executed from the Run dialog box, and all can be executed from a command prompt window.

Several tools listed in the table are discussed later in the chapter. For more extensive information about any of these tools, search Help and Support on your Windows XP computer, search the Microsoft Knowledge Base at *support.microsoft.com*, or see the book, *Microsoft Windows XP Professional Resource Kit Documentation* by Microsoft Press. In addition, to get help about a command-line tool, from a command prompt, enter the tool name followed by /?. For example, to get help about Defrag, enter Defrag /?.

Table 16-3   Windows XP maintenance and troubleshooting tools

Tool	Description
Add or Remove Programs in Control Panel	Uninstall software that is causing a problem
Automated System Recovery (ASR)	Drastically recovers a failed system. Only use as a last resort, because the logical drive on which Windows is installed is formatted and restored from the most recent backup. All data and applications written to the drive since the last backup are lost.
Backup (Ntbackup.exe)	Backs up and restores data and software
Boot logging	An option on the Advanced Options startup menu to log events to the Ntbtlog.txt file
Bootcfg (Bootcfg.exe)	Views and edits the contents of the Boot.ini file used to hold startup settings
Cacls.exe	Changes access control lists (ACL) assigned to a file or group of files to control what users have access to a file and the type of access they have (read, write, change, or full). For more information on CACLS, type Help Cacls at a command prompt.
Chkdsk (Chkdsk.exe)	Checks and repairs errors on a logical drive
Cipher.exe	Displays and changes the encryptions applied to files and folders using the NTFS file system

16

A+ OS
3.1
3.2

Table 16-3   Windows XP maintenance and troubleshooting tools (continued)

Tool	Description
Compact.exe	Displays and changes the compressions applied to files and folders using the NTFS file system
Computer Management (Compmgmt.msc)	Console provides access to several snap-ins used to manage and troubleshoot a system
Convert.exe	Converts a FAT16 or a FAT32 logical drive to NTFS
Defrag.exe	A command-line tool to defragment a logical drive or floppy disk, it is similar to the graphic tool, Disk Defragmenter.
Dependency Walker (Depends.exe)	Provides a list of files needed for an application to load
Device Driver Roll Back	Replaces a driver with the one that worked before the current driver was installed
Device Manager	Displays and changes device drivers and other hardware settings
DirectX Diagnostic Tool (Dxdiag.exe)	Used to troubleshoot problems with the DirectX application programming interface (API) used by Microsoft
Disk Cleanup (Cleanmgr.exe)	Deletes unused files to make more disk space available
Disk Defragmenter (Dfrg.msc)	Defragments a logical drive or floppy disk
Disk Management (Diskmgmt.msc)	Displays and changes partitions on hard drives and formats drives
DiskPart (Diskpart.exe)	A command-line tool to manage partitions and volumes of a hard drive similar to the graphic tool, Disk Management. Use DiskPart to write scripts to automate disk management tasks.
Dr. Watson (Drwtsn32.exe)	Records errors and information about those errors when applications fail. Errors are recorded in a log file named **Drwatson.log**. Note this is a different name than the log filename in Windows 2000, which is Drwtsn32.log.
Driver Signing and Digital Signatures (Sigverif.exe)	Verifies that drivers, system files, and software have been approved by Microsoft
Error Reporting	Produces an error report and sends it to Microsoft when the error occurs and the PC is connected to the Internet
Event Viewer (Eventvwr.msc)	Records and displays system problems
Expand.exe	Extracts a file from a cabinet file or compressed file
Fsutil (Fsutil.exe)	Displays information about drives and file systems and does advanced management tasks on those drives
Group Policy (Gpedit.msc)	Displays and changes policies controlling users and the computer
Help and Support	Provides helpful information, connects to Windows newsgroups, enables Remote Assistance, and steps you though many other troubleshooting tasks

A+ OS
  3.1
  3.2

Table 16-3 Windows XP maintenance and troubleshooting tools (continued)

Tool	Description
Last Known Good Configuration	A startup option used when normal or safe mode do not work. Using this tool, you can revert the system back to before a driver or application that is causing problems was installed.
Performance Monitor (Perfmon.msc)	Reports information about performance problems
Program Compatibility Wizard	Looks at legacy software and attempts to resolve issues that prevent the software from working in Windows XP
Recovery Console	Provides a command line to perform troubleshooting tasks when the desktop will not load
Registry Editor (Regedit.exe)	Displays and changes entries in the registry
Remote Assistance	Allows a user to share his computer with a support technician at a remote location so that the technician can control the computer
Remote Desktop	Allows a support technician to control a Windows XP computer remotely
Runas.exe	Runs a program using different permissions than those assigned to the currently logged-on user
Safe Mode	Loads the Windows desktop with a minimum configuration and then used to troubleshoot problems with device drivers, display settings, and other startup options that are causing problems
SC (Sc.exe)	Communicates commands to the Service Controller, which starts, stops, and manages programs that run in the background such as device drivers or Internet Connection Firewall
Services (Services.msc)	Graphical version of SC
System Configuration Utility (Msconfig.exe)	Controls settings used to troubleshoot a failing system
System File Checker (Sfc.exe)	Verifies the version of all system files when Windows loads
System Information (Msinfo32.exe)	Displays information about hardware, applications, and Windows that is useful when troubleshooting. Figure 16-15 shows a view of the System Information window.
System Information (Systeminfo.exe)	A version of System Information to be used from a command-prompt window. Information is listed on screen as text only. To direct that information to a file, use the command Systeminfo.exe >Myfile.txt. Later the file can be printed and used to document information about the system.
System Restore	Used to restore the system to a previously working condition, it restores the registry, some system files, and some application files.
Task Killing Utility (Tskill.exe)	Stops a process or program currently running. Useful when managing background services such as an e-mail server or Web server.
Task Lister (Tasklist.exe)	Lists currently running processes similar to the list provided by Task Manager

16

A+ OS
3.1
3.2

Table 16-3   Windows XP maintenance and troubleshooting tools (continued)

Tool	Description
Task Manager (Taskman.exe)	Lists and stops currently running processes. Use Task Manager to stop a locked-up application
Uninstall Windows XP Professional	Used to uninstall Windows XP and revert back to a previously installed OS
Windows File Protection	Protects system files and restores overwritten system files as needed
Windows Update (Wupdmgr.exe)	Updates Windows by examining the system, comparing it to available updates on the Microsoft Web site, and recommending appropriate updates

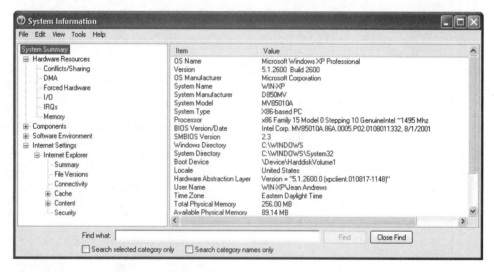

Figure 16-15   The System Information window displays important information about the system's hardware, software, and environment

Help on the Web

Microsoft offers help and updates on the Web. In earlier chapters, you learned to use the Microsoft Knowledge Base at *support.microsoft.com*. This section shows you how to access the Windows Update feature and Windows XP newsgroups.

A+ OS
2.2

Windows Update

Windows XP has an automated way to update the OS, applications, and device drivers made available on the Microsoft Web site. If no user interaction is required, anyone can perform the update, but if decisions must be made during the update, only someone with administrator privileges can perform the update. To do an update including updating the OS,

A+ OS
2.2

software and drivers, click Start, All Programs, and Windows Update. The Update Wizard takes you to the Microsoft Windows Update Web site (see Figure 16-16). Click Scan for updates and follow the directions on screen. This update process includes updating drivers, a process that can also be started from Device Manager, as you learned in the last chapter.

If an update is available for your computer, a screen similar to that shown in Figure 16-17 appears. Note in the figure that the update process found one critical update, nine updates to Windows XP that it does not consider critical, and no updates for drivers. To view information about these updates, click them. In this example, the critical update was designed to solve a problem with security, and the nine noncritical updates were about running Java applets, connecting to a UPS (uninterruptible power supply) service, using a CD burner, running legacy applications using compatibility mode, problems with the Files and Settings Transfer Wizard, problems using Remote Assistance across a firewall, and problems with Windows Messenger and Movie Maker. By default, only the critical update is selected for installing. To install noncritical updates, select the updates you want and then click Add. After you have selected what to update, click *Review and install updates* and follow directions on the screen.

> Windows XP does not ship with support for USB 2.0 (USB Hi-Speed). If you have a USB 2.0 port on your PC, the Update Wizard will recommend that you update the USB driver to support USB 2.0 unless you have already installed a third-party USB 2.0 driver. If you want to download the Microsoft USB 2.0 driver, first uninstall the third-party driver and then perform Windows Update.

Windows Newsgroups

If you have exhausted your sources of information and still have not resolved a problem, sometimes you can get help from a Windows newsgroup. To access a newsgroup, click Start, Help and Support. On the Help and Support window, click Get support, or find information in Windows XP newsgroups. Then click Go to a Windows Web site forum. Click Go to Windows Newsgroups. In the forum, you can post a question or read questions and answers posted by other users. Microsoft does not support this forum, so be careful about following the advice of users posting answers to questions on the forum.

In addition to newsgroups and the Microsoft Web site, many good Windows support Web sites exist. To get a very long list of these sites, go to a search engine on the Web such as *www.google.com* and enter Windows Help in the search box.

16

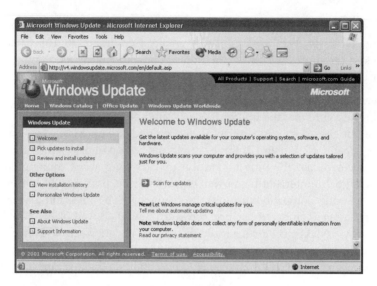

Figure 16-16   The Windows Update utility manages the process of downloading updates from the Microsoft Web site

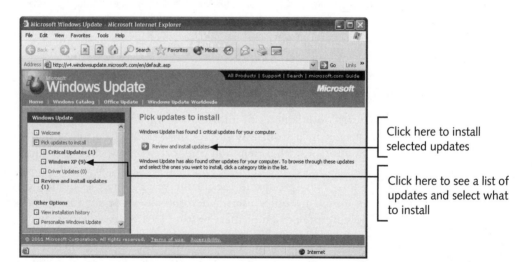

Click here to install selected updates

Click here to see a list of updates and select what to install

Figure 16-17   Windows Update process found updates appropriate to this computer

TROUBLESHOOTING THE BOOT PROCESS

$A+$ *OS*
2.3
3.1
3.2

The Windows XP boot process works the same way as the Windows NT and Windows 2000 boot process. Refer to Chapter 14 for a review of the process and the files required for a successful boot. Many tools you learned about in Chapter 14 to recover from a failed Windows 2000 boot also work under Windows XP. They are briefly mentioned in this section to make the troubleshooting process complete. In addition, Windows XP has added two tools for solving problems with the boot process: System Restore and Automated System Recovery. The tools to use when troubleshooting a failed boot are listed below in the order you should use them. Each tool discussed is more drastic than the one before it, affecting more of the system, installed hardware and software, and user data.

- Last Known Good Configuration and, in certain situations, Driver Rollback
- Safe mode from the Advanced Options menu
- System Restore
- Recovery Console
- Automated System Recovery
- Reinstall Windows XP using the Windows XP CD

You learned how to use the Last Known Good Configuration in Chapter 14, under Windows NT and Windows 2000. In addition, you can use Driver Rollback discussed in Chapter 15 if you suspect that a single device driver is the source of the problem. The Windows XP Advanced Options menu, shown in Figure 16-18, is also similar to that of Windows 2000. Refer to Chapter 14 for a discussion of each of the options on the menu and how to use them. Try Safe Mode with Networking first. If that doesn't work, try Safe Mode.

 To access the Advanced Options menu, press F8 while Windows is loading.

The next tool to use if these don't work is System Restore, a tool new to Windows XP, which is discussed next. If that doesn't work, then try the Recovery Console. Commands for the Recovery Console for Windows XP are the same as for Windows 2000 and were covered in Chapter 14. If the Recovery Console fails, then use the Automated System Recovery process to restore the hard drive to its state as of the last ASR backup. If you don't have an ASR backup, then your only recourse is to reinstall Windows XP following directions given earlier in the chapter. Be sure to scan for viruses before you reinstall.

16

A+ OS
2.3
3.1
3.2

```
Windows Advanced Options Menu
Please select an option:

        Safe Mode
        Safe Mode with Networking
        Safe Mode with Command Prompt

        Enable Boot Logging
        Enable VGA Mode
        Last Known Good Configuration (your most recent settings that worked)
        Directory Services Restore Mode (Windows domain controllers only)
        Debugging Mode

        Start Windows Normally
        Reboot
        Return to OS Choices Menu

Use the up and down arrow keys to move the highlight to your choice.
```

Figure 16-18   Windows XP Advanced Options menu

System Restore

A+ OS
2.3
3.1

The **System Restore** utility is new to Windows XP. It is similar to ScanReg used on previous versions of Windows; however, System Restore cannot be executed from a command prompt. ScanReg is not included in Windows XP. If you can load Windows XP, then you can use System Restore to restore the system state to its condition at the time a snapshot was taken of the system settings and configuration. The restore process does not affect user data on the hard drive but can affect installed software and hardware, user settings, and OS configuration settings. The restoration is taken from a snapshot of the system state, called a **restore point**, that was created earlier. The system automatically creates a restore point before you install new software or hardware or make other changes to the system. You can also manually create a restore point at any time. To create a restore point, do the following:

1. Click **Start**, **All Programs**, **Accessories**, **System Tools**, and **System Restore**. The System Restore window appears.

2. The System Restore window gives you two choices: Restore my computer to an earlier time and Create a restore point. Select **Create a restore point**, and then click **Next**.

3. Type a description of the restore point such as "Just before I updated the video driver." The system automatically assigns the current date and time to the restore point.

4. Click **Create** and then **Close**. The restore point is saved.

A+ OS
2.3
3.1

Before using System Restore to undo a change, if the change was made to a hardware device, first try Driver Rollback so that as few changes as possible to the system are lost. If Driver Rollback does not work or is not appropriate, do the following to revert the system back to the restore point:

1. Click **Start**, **All Programs**, **Accessories**, **System Tools**, and **System Restore**.

2. If necessary, click **Restore my computer to an earlier time**, and then click **Next**. A window appears as shown in Figure 16-19. Notice the two restore points in the figure, one created by the system and one created manually.

3. Select the date and time and the specific restore point. Click **Next** twice.

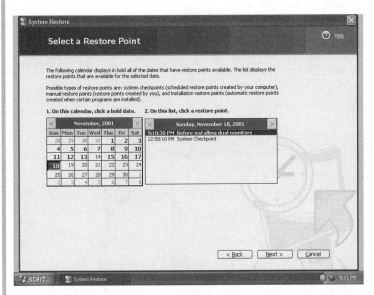

Figure 16-19   Restore points are automatically created daily and every time software or hardware is installed

16

Windows XP reboots and restores the system state to the settings saved in the restore point. Changes to user data are not affected but any installation or configuration changes made after the restore point are lost.

When selecting a restore point, select a point as close to the present as you can so that as few changes to the system as possible are lost. If System Restore does not work, try booting into safe mode and using it there. When you select Safe Mode from the Advanced Options menu, Windows XP asks if you want to go directly to System Restore rather than to safe mode. If safe mode does not work, then try going directly to System Restore.

A+ OS
2.3
3.1

> **TIP** The main difference between System Restore and Automated System Recovery is that System Restore does not affect user data on the hard drive, but Automated System Recovery does. In order to make it possible to recover a failed system without destroying data, make it a habit to always create a restore point every time you make a change to the system.

Windows XP Startup Disk

A+ OS
2.3
3.1
3.2

Using Windows Explorer, you can create an MS-DOS startup disk that can be used to boot into MS-DOS mode giving you an A prompt. If the hard drive is not using the NTFS file system, then you can access the drive and recover data files. You cannot launch Windows XP using the startup disk or use it to recover from a failed installation. To create a startup disk, using Windows Explorer, right-click drive A and select Format from the shortcut menu. The Format window opens, as shown in Figure 16-20. Check Create an MS-DOS startup disk, and then click Start. The unhidden files put on the startup disk are shown in the Explorer window in Figure 16-21. In addition to these files, Autoexec.bat, Config.sys, and the Windows 98 versions of Io.sys and Msdos.sys are also placed on the disk as hidden files.

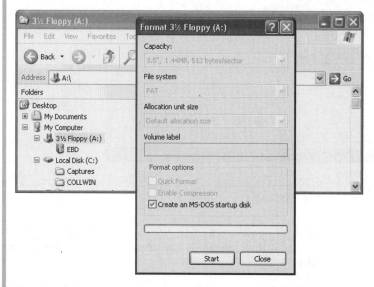

Figure 16-20   Windows XP gives you the ability to create an MS-DOS startup disk

A+ OS
2.3
3.1
3.2

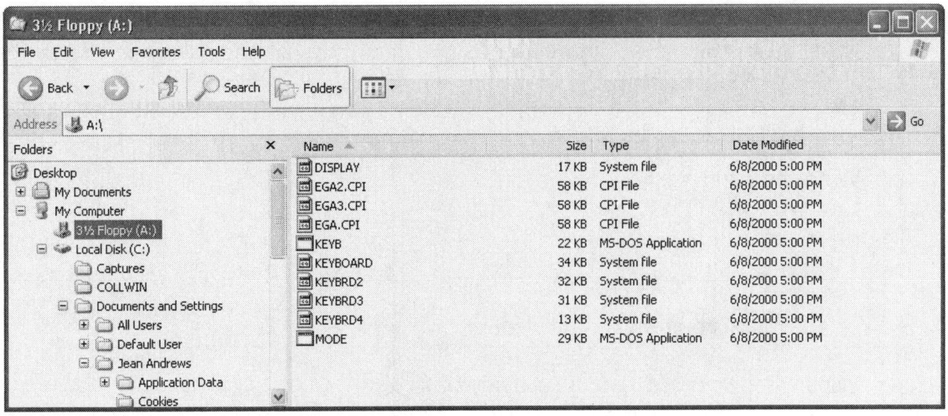

Figure 16-21   Files on the MS-DOS startup disk created by Windows XP

Automated System Recovery

A+ OS
2.3
3.1
3.2

After you finished the Windows XP installation, if you created the Automated System Recovery disk set, you can use this or a later set of the recovery disks to restore the system partition to its state when the backup was made. You will lose any changes made to the volume or logical drive holding Windows XP since the backup. Everything on the volume since the ASR backup and disk were made is lost, including software and device drivers installed, user data, and any changes to the system configuration. For this reason, it's a good idea to make fresh copies of the ASR disk set periodically. You learned how to make this backup and disk in the previous chapter.

If you use the Automated System Recovery process, know that you will lose all data stored on the Windows XP volume since the last backup was made.

To restore the hard drive to its state when the last ASR disk set was made, do the following:

1. Insert the Windows XP CD in the CD-ROM drive, and hard boot the PC.

2. A message says "Press any key to boot from CD." Press any key.

3. A blue screen appears with the message, "Press F6 to load RAID or SCSI drivers." If your system uses RAID or SCSI, press **F6**.

4. At the bottom of the blue screen, a message says, "Press F2 to run the Automated System Recovery process." Press **F2**.

5. The screen shown in Figure 16-22 appears, instructing you to insert the ASR floppy disk. Insert the disk and then press **Enter**.

6. Windows XP Setup does the following:
   - Loads files it needs to run
   - Repartitions and reformats the drive
   - Installs Windows from the Windows XP CD

16

A+ OS
2.3
3.1

- Launches the Automatic System Recovery Wizard to restore the Windows system state, applications, and data to what they were at the time of the last ASR backup.

```
Windows Setup
============




Please insert the disk labeled:

Windows Automated System Recovery Disk

Into the floppy drive.



Press any key when ready.
```

Figure 16-22   Automatic System Recovery process must have the ASR floppy disk

The ASR recovery process erases everything on the volume being restored. Figure 16–23 shows one of the above steps in the recovery process, in which you reformat the logical drive just before the Windows XP installation process begins.

```
Windows XP Professional Setup
=============================



Please wait while Setup formats the partition

\Device\Harddisk0\Partition1

on 28663 MB Disk 0 at Id 0 on bus 0 on atapi [MBR].


┌──────────────────────────────────────────────┐
│ Setup is formatting...          45%          │
│ ┌──────────────────────────────────────────┐ │
│ │▒▒▒▒▒▒▒▒▒▒▒▒▒▒▒▒▒▒                         │ │
│ └──────────────────────────────────────────┘ │
└──────────────────────────────────────────────┘
```

Figure 16-23   As part of the Automatic System Recovery process, Windows XP Setup repartitions and reformats the volume holding Windows XP

Error Messages and Their Meanings

A+ OS
2.3
3.1
3.3

Table 16-4 lists some Windows XP error messages and what they mean. Most of these errors occur when booting.

Table 16-4   Windows XP error messages and their meanings

Error Message	What It Means and What to Do About It
Invalid partition table Error loading operating system Missing operating system	The program in the MBR displays these messages when it cannot find the active partition on the hard drive or the boot sector on that partition. Use Fdisk or Diskpart from a command prompt to check the hard drive partition table for errors. Sometimes Fdisk/mbr might solve the problem. Third-party recovery software such as PartitionMagic might help. If a setup program came bundled with the hard drive (such as Data Lifeguard from Western Digital or MaxBlast from Maxtor), use it to examine the drive. Check the hard drive manufacturer's Web site for other diagnostic software.
A disk read error occurred NTLDR is missing NTLDR is compressed	A disk is probably in the floppy disk drive. Remove the disk and reboot. When booting from the hard drive, these errors occur if Ntldr has been moved, renamed, or deleted, or is corrupted, if the boot sector on the active partition is corrupted, or you have just tried to install an older version of Windows such as Windows 98 on the hard drive. First try replacing Ntldr. Then check Boot.ini settings.
An error displays in text against a blue screen and then the system halts. These Windows NT/2000/XP errors are called **stop errors** or **blue screens (BSOD)**. Some stop errors follow.	Stop errors are usually caused by viruses, errors in the file system, a corrupted hard drive, or a hardware problem.
Stop 0x00000024 or NTFS_File_System	The NTFS file system is corrupt. Immediately boot into the Recovery Console, and copy important data files that have not been backed up to another media before attempting to recover the system.
Stop 0x00000050 or Page_Fault_in_Nonpaged_Area	Most likely RAM is defective.
Stop 0x00000077 or Kernel_Stack_Inpage_Error	Bad sectors are on the hard drive, there is a hard drive hardware problem, or RAM is defective. Try running Chkdsk or, for the FAT file system, run Scandisk using a Windows 98 startup disk.
Stop 0x0000007A or Kernel_Data_Inpage_Error	There is a bad sector on the hard drive where the paging file is stored; there is a virus or defective RAM. Try running Chkdsk or Scandisk.
Stop 0x0000007B or Inaccessible_Boot_Device	There is a boot sector virus or failing hardware. Try Fdisk/mbr or fixmbr.

16

CHAPTER SUMMARY

- Windows NT/2000/XP requires a valid user account before you can use Windows. The user account identifies the user to Windows. Permissions assigned to a user account control what the user can and cannot do and access in Windows.

- Local user accounts apply to a single standalone computer or a single computer in a workgroup, and global user accounts are managed from a domain controller and apply to every computer in the domain.

- When using Windows in a domain, global user account information is stored in the SAM, which is part of Active Directory in Windows 2000 Server and Windows .NET.

- When a user makes changes to the system, the changes are often recorded in the user profile so the next time the user logs on, these changes automatically take effect.

- Methods that administrators can use to manage and secure multiple computers and users include roaming user profiles, mandatory user profiles, and group profiles.

- Passwords on user accounts are needed to secure computers and their resources. Passwords should not be easy to guess and should be a combination of letters, numbers, and non-alphanumeric characters.

- An administrator can create a user account using the Computer Management console or the User Accounts applet in Control Panel.

- Resetting a password under Windows XP causes the OS to lock out the user from using encrypted e-mail or files or using Internet passwords stored on the computer. For that reason, it is a good idea for a user to create a Windows XP forgotten password floppy disk.

- Windows XP user groups include Administrators, Backup Operators, Power Users, Limited Users, and Guests. In this list, each group has fewer permissions and rights than the previous group.

- Using disk quotas, an administrator can limit the amount of hard drive space a user can use.

- File and folder encryption in Windows 2000/XP requires using the NTFS file system.

- Internet Connection Firewall (ICF) prevents communication from the Internet from accessing the system if the communication has not been initiated by the local computer.

- The Windows NT/2000/XP registry is organized logically into five subtrees or keys and organized physically into five files called hives. There is no one-to-one correspondence between the subtrees and the hives.

- The registry is edited using a registry editor, which is accessed by entering Regedit in the Run dialog box. Changes to the registry are immediate, so always make a backup of the system state before editing the registry.

❑ Windows XP offers many troubleshooting and maintenance tools. Some are available from the command line. Others are Microsoft Management Console (MMC) snap-ins, and still others are built into Windows XP.

❑ You can get help on the Web for Windows XP. Microsoft offers Windows Update and Microsoft Knowledge Base. There are also Windows newsgroups and other Web sites where you can get help.

❑ Two recovery tools new to Windows XP are Automated System Recovery and System Restore.

❑ The Automated System Recovery (ASR) process creates a backup and an ASR floppy disk that can be used to restore the backup of the volume or logical drive holding Windows XP.

❑ The Windows XP System Restore utility is similar to ScanReg in earlier versions of Windows but cannot be executed at a command prompt. System Restore restores the system state using restore points, which are snapshots of the system state.

KEY TERMS

Backup Operator	global user account	mandatory user profile
blue screen (BSOD)	Group Policy	Power User
built-in user account	group profile	restore point
disk quota	Guest	roaming user profile
Drwatson.log	hardware profile	stop error
Encrypted File System (EFS)	hive	System Restore
encryption	Internet Connection Firewall (ICF)	user account
firewall	key	user profile
forgotten password floppy disk	Limited user	
	local user account	

16

REVIEW QUESTIONS

1. A user account defines a user to Windows and records information about the user including the username, password used to access the account, groups that the account belongs to, and the rights and permissions of the account. Which of the following accounts is used at the domain level and stored in the SAM database on a domain controller?

   a. Global User Account

   b. Local User Account

   c. Built-In User Accounts

   d. Security Accounts

   e. Roaming Account

2. After an administrator creates a local user account and the user logs on for the first time, the system creates a _____ for the user.

   a. Group profile

   b. User profile

   c. Roaming user profile

   d. Mandatory user profile

   e. None of the above

3. The maximum number of characters allowed for usernames in Windows NT/2000/XP logons is _____.

   a. 8

   b. 15

   c. 6

   d. 127

   e. 255

4. Passwords in Windows NT/2000/XP can be up to _____ characters.

   a. 8

   b. 15

   c. 6

   d. 127

   e. 255

5. User groups are an efficient way for administrators to manage multiple user accounts that require the same privileges and similar profiles. Which user group can read from and write to parts of the system other than their own local drive, install applications, and perform limited administrative tasks?

   a. Administrator

   b. Backup operator

   c. Power users

   d. Limited users

   e. Guests

6. Another way to control how the system can be used is by applying settings called a _____ to your computer.

   a. User System Setting Policy

   b. User Policy

   c. Group Policy

   d. Management Console Policy

   e. None of the above

7. The concept _____ refers to the idea that limits how much disk space a user can access.

   a. Group Policy

   b. Disk Quota

   c. Quota tab

   d. Roaming User Profile

   e. None of the above

8. The term(s) _____ refers to the process of putting readable data into code that must be translated before it can be accessed.

   a. Group Policy

   b. Disk Quota

   c. Quota tab

   d. Encryption

   e. Decryption

9. A _____ is hardware or software that protects a computer or network from unauthorized access.

   a. Security Policy

   b. Cipher Command

   c. Firewall

   d. Security Control Panel

   e. Network Connection applet

10. The subkey _____ contains all current configuration data about the computer, including information about device drivers and devices used at startup.

   a. HKEY_CURRENT USER

   b. HKEY_CURRENT_CONFIGURATION

   c. HKEY_CLASSES_ROOT

   d. HKEY_USERS

   e. HKEY_LOCAL_MACHINE

11. In order to edit the System Registry, which of the following utilities is the only one that can be used in Windows XP?

   a. Regedt32.exe

   b. Regedit.exe

   c. Fdisk.exe

   d. Registry_editor.exe

   e. None of the above

16

17

SUPPORTING MODEMS

In this chapter, you will learn:

♦ How modems work and how to install them

♦ About software that modems use to communicate with the OS

♦ Guidelines for troubleshooting modems

Almost all home computers and many corporate desktop computers have modems. This chapter focuses on how modems work as well as how to install and troubleshoot them. In Chapters 18 and 19, you will learn how to connect a PC to a network and how to connect a PC to the Internet using a modem, cable modem, DSL, or other hardware for the connection.

ALL ABOUT MODEMS

A **modem** is a device used by a PC to communicate over a phone line. A modem can be an external device (see Figure 17-1) connected to a USB or serial port, or it can be a modem card (see Figure 17-2) using either an ISA or PCI slot.

Figure 17-1   SupraSonic external modem

Figure 17-2   3Com U.S. Robotics 56K Winmodem modem card

Table 17-1 lists some modem manufacturers.

Table 17-1   Modem manufacturers

Manufacturer	Web Site
3Com U.S. Robotics	www.usr.com
Creative Labs	www.americas.creative.com
Zoom	www.zoom.com

A+CORE
1.1
4.3 To reduce the total cost of a computer system, some motherboards have a small expansion slot, less than half the length of a PCI slot, called an **audio/modem riser (AMR)** slot (see Figure 17-3) or a **communication and networking riser (CNR)** slot. The small slot accommodates a small, inexpensive type of modem card called a **modem riser card**. In addition, the AMR slot can support an audio riser card, and the CNR slot can support an audio riser card or a networking riser card. Part of a riser card's audio, modem, or networking logic is on the card and part is on a controller on the motherboard.

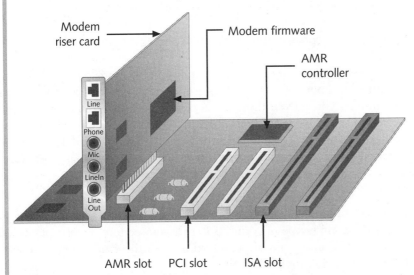

Figure 17-3   An audio/modem riser slot can accommodate an inexpensive modem riser card

Regardless of the type of modem card or external device, a modem is both hardware and firmware. Firmware on ROM chips on the device contains the protocol and instructions needed to format and convert data so that it can be transported over phone lines to a receiving modem on the other end. In general, modems are considered hardware, but it is fundamental to understanding communications that you also consider them to be firmware.

Computers are digital; regular phone lines are analog. Earlier chapters discussed the difference between digital data and analog data, and Figure 17-4 shows how this concept applies to phone lines. Data stored inside a PC is communicated to a modem as binary, or digital, data (0s and 1s). A modem converts this data into an analog signal (in a process called **modulation**) that can travel over a phone line, and then the modem at the receiving end converts the signal back to digital data (in a process called **demodulation**) before passing it on to the receiving PC. The two processes of MOdulation/DEModulation lead to the name of the device: modem.

17

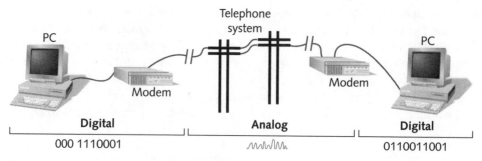

Figure 17-4   Modems convert a digital signal to analog and then back to digital

Sound traveling over regular phone lines is transmitted as analog signals, meaning that there are an infinite number of sound values, just as there are an infinite number of sound values in the human voice. Even though the data from a PC is inherently digital, it too must be converted to an analog signal in order to be transmitted over phone lines. PC data must be converted from two simple states or measurements (0 and 1, or off and on) to waves (like sound waves) that have a potentially infinite number of states or measurements. Modems use different characteristics of waves to correspond to the 0s and 1s of digital communication.

A+CORE 1.5   On a PC, the modem provides a connection for a regular phone line called an **RJ-11** connection, which is the same type of connection that you see for a regular phone wall outlet (Figure 17-5). In addition to a line-in connection from the wall outlet, a modem also has an extra RJ-11 connection for a telephone.

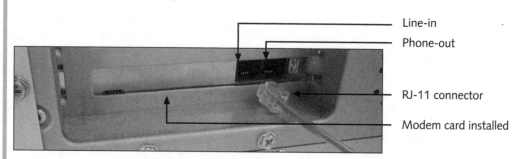

Figure 17-5   An RJ-11 connection on a modem is the same as that used for a regular phone connection

A+CORE 6.2   A modem must be able to both receive and transmit data. Communication in which transmission can be in only one direction at a time is called **half-duplex**; an example of this type of communication is a CB radio. A modem that can only communicate in one direction at a time is called a half-duplex modem. Communication that allows transmission in both directions at the same time is called **full-duplex**; a regular voice phone conversation is an example of full-duplex communication. If a modem can communicate in both directions at the same time, it is a full-duplex modem; most modems today are full-duplex.

How Modems Are Rated

Using Windows, you can view the properties of an installed modem on a PC. Many people install their modems by simply choosing settings supplied by others, or by allowing the installation program to use default options. This section explains what each modem property means and how it affects the modem's performance and compatibility with other modems.

Getting Started

When you first use a modem to make a dial-up call to another PC, you hear the modem making noises as the dial-up is completed. What you hear are the sounds of the two modems establishing the rules of communication between them. The process is called **handshaking**, or **training**. In this handshaking phase, the calling modem and the receiving modem communicate the protocols and determine speeds they can support, decide how to handle data compression and error checking, and agree on what methods of data transfer to use. The protocols agreed on must be supported by both modems, and they attempt to use the faster and more reliable protocols first.

Modem Speeds

The speed at which a modem passes data over phone lines is partly determined by the transmission standard the modem is using. Modem speed is usually measured in **bits per second (bps)**. On older, slower modems, you might find the speed expressed as **baud rate**, which is the number of times a signal changes in one second. On older modems, the baud rate is equal to the bps rate, because one signal represents one bit. On more modern modems, one signal can represent more than one bit, so faster modems are measured in bps (and baud rates may differ from bps rates). When modem speed is measured using baud rate, the number of bps is always equal to or a multiple of the baud rate. The most commonly rated modem speed in use today is 56.6 Kbps, although there are still a few modems around that are rated at 28.8 Kbps or 33.6 Kbps.

The maximum speed of a modem is often written into the manufacturer's name for the modem. To see what your modem's rating is when using Windows 9x, click Start, point to Settings, click Control Panel, and double-click Modems. You see the Modems Properties dialog box in Figure 17-6. In this figure, the installed modem is labeled as a U.S. Robotics 56K Fax Internal PnP modem. The 56K portion of the name indicates the maximum speed of the modem: 56 Kbps. To see similar information in Windows 2000/XP, from Control Panel, double-click Phone and Modem Options, and then click the Modem tab.

17

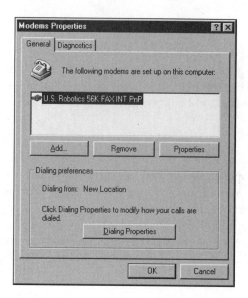

Figure 17-6   The maximum modem speed is often included in the modem name (in this case, 56 Kbps)

The Ceiling on Modem Speeds

Many factors limit modem speeds. Analog phone lines were designed to provide only sufficient audio signal quality to support the transmission of the human voice, affecting the ability to attain high transmission speeds for data. Newer digital phone lines have limitations as well. Older phone lines (installed before 1940) were analog from beginning to end, with no digital components. This is not true today. Regular (analog) telephone lines are always analog as they leave a house or office building; however, the analog signals are almost always converted to digital signals at some point in the transmission. These digital signals are then transmitted and converted back to analog signals at some point before they travel the last step between the local central telephone company office and the phone of the person receiving the call.

TIP   Because of the sampling rate (8,000 samples every second) used by phone companies when converting an analog signal to digital, taking into account the overhead of data transmission (bits and bytes sent with the data that are used to control and define transmissions), the maximum transmission rate that a modem can attain over a regular phone line is about 56,000 bps or 56 Kbps.

Other factors further limit modem speed. The line often has some disturbance, called **noise**, which can be caused by lines bumping against one another in the wind, bad wiring, lightning, or interference from nearby fluorescent lighting, radios, or TVs. This reduction in line quality is called a dirty or noisy line. A line that consistently produces high-quality results is called a clean line.

Modem Standards

The telecommunications industry sets standards to determine modem speed and protocols. The industry-approved standards for international communication were written by the **CCITT (Comité Consultatif International Télégraphique et Téléphonique)**. In 1992, the CCITT was incorporated into the **ITU (International Telecommunication Union)**, an intergovernmental organization approved by the United Nations to be responsible for adopting standards governing telecommunications. You might see the standards used by modems referred to as the CCITT standards (more commonly) or as the ITU standards. The CCITT standards are listed in Table 17-2. Look for a modem that supports the most standards including the latest standard, **V.92**. The more standards a modem supports, the better it can communicate with a variety of other modems.

 Avoid purchasing a modem using only a proprietary standard, because it may be able to communicate only with another modem produced by the same manufacturer.

Table 17-2   Modem transmission standards

Standard	Applies Mainly to	Description
Bell 212A	Speed (up to 1,200 bps)	This older standard supports 1,200 bps.
CCITT V.32	Speed (up to 9,600 bps)	This standard runs at 9,600 bps, includes error checking, and can negotiate standards with other modems. This standard was used for quite some time.
HST	Speed (up to 14.4 Kbps)	This older proprietary standard, created by U.S. Robotics, supports 9,600 or 14,400 bps. (U.S. Robotics also supports the CCITT standards.)
CCITT V.32bis	Speed (up to 14.4 Kbps)	This standard is an improvement over V.32 (up to 14.4 Kbps); bis means *second* in Latin and has a speed of 14,400 bps.
CCITT V.34	Speed (up to 33.6 Kbps)	This standard transmits at 28,800 bps, or 28.8 Kbps. Optional higher speeds are 31.2 Kbps and 33.6 Kbps.
MNP Class 4	Error correction	Developed by Microcom, Inc. and called the Microcom Networking Protocol (MNP), this standard provides error detection and correction and also automatically adjusts the speed of transmission according to the quality of the phone line. Earlier classes of MNP standards for error correction are Class 2 and Class 3.
CCITT V.42	Error correction	This error-correcting standard adopted the methods used by MNP Class 4. Data corrupted during transmission is automatically retransmitted using this standard. A modem can use this standard for error correction and one of the standards listed above for speed.

17

Table 17-2   Modem transmission standards (continued)

Standard	Applies Mainly to	Description
MNP Class 5	Data compression	The MNP Class 5 standard provides data compression, which can double normal transmission speeds between modems. It is common to see both MNP Class 4 and MNP Class 5 supported by a modem. They are sometimes called MNP-4 and MNP-5.
CCITT V.42bis	Data compression	An improved version of V.42 that also uses data compression. Many modems use the V.42bis standard for data compression and error checking and, at the same time, use the V.34 standard for data transmission protocols.
V.44	Data compression	An improved version of V.42bis.
K56flex	Speed (up to 56 Kbps)	One of two earlier standards used to attain a speed of up to 56 Kbps. This standard was backed by Lucent Technologies and Rockwell International Corp.
x2	Speed (up to 56 Kbps)	One of two earlier standards that supports a speed of 56 Kbps. This standard was supported by U.S. Robotics.
V.90	Speed (up to 56 Kbps)	The current standard used to attain speeds of 56 Kbps. It replaces both K56flex and x2.
V.92	Speed (up to 56 Kbps)	Improves on V.90 adding three new features: quick connect (reduces handshake time), modem on hold (allows call waiting without breaking the connection to the ISP), and improved upload speeds for large files.

TIP Although most modems today are rated and advertised to transmit at 56 Kbps, they seldom accomplish this speed. When one PC communicates with another, even if both PCs are equipped with 56K modems and using clean phones lines, the actual speed attained will most likely not exceed 34 Kbps. When you connect to your ISP (Internet service provider) using a 56 Kbps modem, if the ISP uses a digital connection to the phone company, you can achieve higher transmission speeds.

Data Compression

A modem includes firmware housed on the modem that can perform error correction and data compression. These and other functions of data communication can be performed by either hardware (firmware on the modem) or software (programs on the PC).

When data compression is performed by a modem, it applies to all data transmitted by the modem. If data compression is performed by the software on the PC, it applies to single-file transfer operations. Data compression done by the modem follows either the MNP-5, CCITT V.42, or V.42bis protocol. All three protocols also perform error correction.

Error Correction

As seen in Table 17-2, several standards include error correction; one modem often supports more than one standard. During the handshaking process, the answering modem tries to establish an error-correction protocol with the other modem by first suggesting the fastest, best standard. If the calling modem responds by accepting that standard, then both use it. If the calling modem does not support the suggested protocol, then the two modems negotiate to find the best protocol they both can use or simply decide not to use error correction.

Error correction works by breaking up data into small packets called **frames**. The sending modem performs some calculations on a frame of data and sums these calculations into a checksum. A **checksum** is a summary calculation of data and is used later to check or verify the accuracy of the data when received. A checksum works somewhat like a parity bit, except it is a little more complicated and applies to more data. The checksum is attached to the data frame, and they are transmitted together. The receiving modem performs the same calculations and compares its answer to the checksum value received. If the values do not agree, then the receiving modem requests a new transmission of the packet. This process does slow down data transmission, especially on dirty or noisy phone lines, but accuracy is almost 100 percent guaranteed.

More About Handshaking

Now that you understand several different protocols that must be established between two modems before they can communicate data, you can better understand what happens when two modems perform a handshake. Here are some key points about the process:

- When a modem answers an incoming call, this answering modem sends a modem tone, sometimes called a **guard tone**, which the calling modem recognizes as another modem and not a human voice, and so it does not break the connection.

- The answering modem sends a signal called the **carrier**. This is an unmodulated (unchanging) or continuous tone at a set frequency (also called pitch), that depends on the speed of communication the answering modem attempts to establish with the calling modem. This process, called "establishing carrier," sounds like static, which you hear during handshaking.

- After carrier is established, the two modems enter the equalization stage, which sounds like hissing or buzzing on the line. Both modems are testing the line quality and compensating for poor quality by changing the way they transmit. When this process completes, the speed of transmission, called the **modem speed** or the **line speed**, is set between them.

- The speakers on the modems are now turned off. Next the modems begin to talk about how they will transmit data. The answering modem asks if the other modem can support MNP-4, MNP-5, V.42, V.42bis, and so on. After some interchange, the methods of data transmission are agreed upon, and handshaking is complete. The two modems can now communicate.

17

External modems show you what is happening by turning lights on and off on the front of the modem and displaying messages on an LCD panel (called a display readout). Internal modems, of course, don't have these lights available for you to see, so communications software sometimes displays a pseudo-modem panel on your computer screen.

When a modem is first activated (turned on), it initializes itself and then raises (turns on) its Clear to Send (CTS) signal and, for an external modem, the CTS light also goes on. When the PC receives the CTS signal from its modem, it raises its Request to Send (RTS) signal in order to begin a call. For external modems, the RTS or RS light goes on.

 TIP Communications technicians use the terms *raising* and *dropping* signals to mean that the signal has either started or stopped, respectively.

Serial Port (UART) Settings

Recall from Chapter 10 that the chip responsible for any communication over a serial port is called the UART (universal asynchronous receiver-transmitter). An external modem is likely to use a serial port, and an internal modem has serial port (UART) logic on the modem card. Therefore, in addition to modem-to-modem communication, we must consider UART-to-UART (serial port to serial port) communication. The settings that control serial-port communication are called **port settings**. These port settings are described in Table 17-3. The speed of the transmission between the serial port and a device it is connected to, such as a modem, is measured in bits per second (bps) and called the **port speed**.

 TIP Don't confuse modem settings with port settings. Modem settings control modem-to-modem communication, and port settings control UART-to-modem communication.

Table 17-3   Port settings control how a serial port communicates

Port Setting	Description	Common Values
Bits per second	What will be the speed of the transmission in bps? The port speed should usually be about four times the modem speed.	2400; 4800; 9600; 19,200; 38,400; 57,600; 115,200; 230,400; 460,800; 921,600 bps
Data bits	How many bits are to be used to send a single character of data? Only 7 bits are required for standard ASCII characters, but in most cases, you should use 8 bits.	7 or 8 bits
Parity	Will there be error checking, and if so, what will be its format? In most cases, let the modem do error checking and use no parity checking on the serial port.	Odd, even, or none

Table 17-3   Port settings control how a serial port communicates (continued)

Port Setting	Description	Common Values
Stop bits	What will be the code to indicate that a character (its string of bits) is starting or ending? In most cases, use 1 bit.	1, 1.5, or 2 bits
Flow control	How will the flow of data be controlled? **Flow control** stops the flow of data if the receiving port is being overloaded. Flow control is controlled by software (Xon/Xoff) or hardware (RTS/CTS). Always use RTS/CTS.	Software (Xon/Xoff) or hardware (RTS/CTS)

To understand how port settings and modem settings affect communication, look at Figure 17-7. Communication between the DTE and the DCE (computer and modem) is controlled by the port settings (RS-232, digital, port speed), and communication between two DCE devices (two modems) is controlled by the modem settings (phone line, analog, line speed).

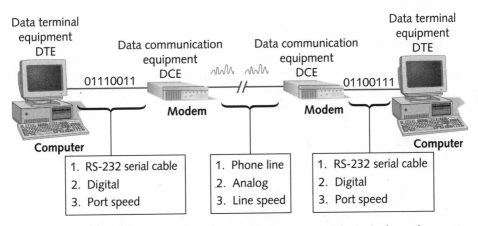

Figure 17-7   A computer communicates with a modem differently from the way a modem communicates with another modem

17

To see the modem and port settings using Windows 98, open Device Manager and select the modem. Then click Properties. The modem Properties dialog box opens. Click the Connection tab (see Figure 17-8). In this window, click the Advanced button and the Advanced Connection Settings window opens, also shown in Figure 17-8. From these two windows you can see all the port settings listed in Table 17-3, except the port speed, which is on the Modem tab of the modem's Properties dialog box.

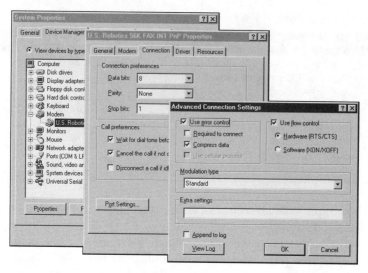

Figure 17-8   Port and modem settings under Windows 98

Under Windows 2000/XP, open Device Manager and right–click the modem. Select Properties from the shortcut menu. The modem's Properties dialog box opens. Click the Modem tab to view the port speed. If the modem is an internal modem, you cannot view or change the other port settings. To view the port setting for an external modem using a serial port, in Device Manager, right-click the serial port and select Properties. The serial port's Properties dialog box opens as shown in Figure 17-9.

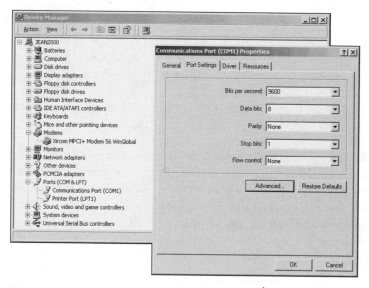

Figure 17-9   Port settings for a Windows 2000 serial port

Regardless of the expansion slot an internal modem uses, it has its own UART on the modem card and provides its own serial port logic to the computer system. This is why an internal modem must be configured to have its own COM port assigned to it for its UART to control. A typical configuration for a PC is to have COM1 assigned to the serial mouse and COM2 assigned to the internal modem. (An external modem does not need a COM port assigned to it, because it uses the port assignments already configured on the system.) The UART on the motherboard is not used by the internal modem, because the modem is not using the COM ports on the motherboard.

> **TIP** Sometimes a COM port on a motherboard can compete for resources with the COM port on an internal modem, causing a conflict. In this case, use CMOS setup to disable the conflicting COM port on the motherboard.

Modem Features

In addition to the UART logic, speed, protocols, data compression, and error correction used to rate a modem, there are other features. Some additional abilities you might want to look for in a modem are:

- *Caller ID* (provided that you subscribe to that service from the phone company) is supported.

- *Display readout* on external modems provides information about the status of the modem. (See Chapter 10, Table 10-3, for a list of modem lights and their meanings. The modem can also have an LCD panel for messages such as Training or Idle.)

- *Flash ROM* allows you to upgrade your modem to support future standards.

- *Plug and Play for Windows* makes modem installation more automatic.

- *Voice/data capability* allows the modem to also serve as a telephone, complete with a built-in speaker and microphone.

- *Auto-answer* makes it possible for the modem to receive incoming calls while you are away from the PC.

- The type of expansion slot (ISA or PCI) an internal modem uses or the port (serial port or USB port) an external modem uses affects ease of installation and the performance of the modem.

Installing and Configuring a Modem

A+CORE
1.2
1.4
1.8

Follow these general steps to install an internal modem:

1. Read the modem documentation.

2. Determine which serial port is available on your system.

A+*CORE*
1.2
1.4
1.8

3. Set any jumpers or DIP switches on the modem card. (See your documentation for details about your card. An example is shown in Figure 17-10. Common jumper and DIP switch settings are for COM ports, IRQ, and I/O addresses, and to indicate whether the card will use Plug and Play.)

Jumper bank for
IRQ setting

Jumper bank for COM
port selection

Figure 17-10   A modem might have jumpers to set IRQ and COM values; the default jumper settings should be set to use Plug and Play rather than dictate these values

4. Turn off your computer and remove the case. Find an empty slot, remove the faceplate, and save the screw. Mount the card firmly in the slot, and replace the screw to anchor the card.

5. Replace the cover. (You can test the modem before replacing the cover.)

6. Plug the telephone line from the house into the line jack on the modem. The second RJ-11 jack on the modem is for an optional telephone. It connects a phone so that you can more easily use this same phone jack for voice communication.

For an external modem, follow these general steps:

1. If the modem does not come with a cable, buy a high-quality cable. Don't skimp on price. Connect the cable to the modem and to the serial or USB port.

2. Plug the electrical cord from the modem into an 110V AC outlet.

3. Plug the telephone line from the house into the line jack on the modem. The second jack on the modem is for an optional telephone.

Turn on your computer and follow these steps to configure the modem using Windows 98:

1. When you turn on the PC. Windows 9x Plug and Play detects a new hardware device. Allow the OS to identify the modem and install the drivers, or provide your own disk. You might have to boot twice: once to allow Plug and Play to detect the UART and again to detect the modem. Also, if your modem has add-on features such as a Fax service, you might have to reboot again as this feature is installed. Follow onscreen directions until you reach the Windows 98 desktop.

TIP Sometimes an installation disk has several directories, one for each operating system it supports. For example, for Windows 98, look for a directory named \WIN98.

2. After the modem drivers are installed, configure the modem. Click **Start**, point to **Settings**, click **Control Panel**, and then double-click **Modem**. The Modem Properties box opens. Click the installed modem and then click **Properties**.

3. Use the properties listed below unless you have a specific reason to do otherwise (such as to compensate for a noisy phone line).

   - Set the modem speed at the highest value in the drop-down list, which is the highest value supported by this modem.

   - Set the port protocol at "8, No, and 1," which is computer jargon for 8 bits, no parity, and 1 stop bit.

   - Use hardware flow control.

4. If you want to use Windows 98 to make calls without using other software, create a Dial-Up Networking connection. Double-click the **My Computer** icon, and then double-click **Dial-Up Networking**. The Dial-Up Networking window opens. The Make New Connection wizard opens, as in Figure 17-11.

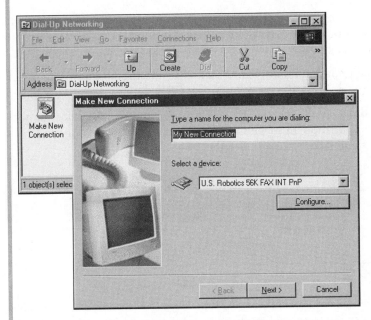

Figure 17-11   Create a Dial-Up Networking connection

5. Follow the connection wizard to specify the name of the connection and the phone number to call. When the wizard is done, the connection icon appears in the Dial-Up Networking window. Double-click the icon to make the call.

17

A+*CORE*
1.2
1.4
1.8
For Windows 2000/XP, installation is performed as it is for Windows 9x. However, some options in the modem Properties dialog box are slightly different. To configure the modem, from Control Panel, double-click the Phone and Modem Options icon. When the Phone and Modem Options dialog box opens, click the Modems tab. Select the modem and click Properties. The modem Properties dialog box opens. Configure the modem using this dialog box.

Problems during modem installation and ways to detect and resolve conflicts are covered in the Troubleshooting section later in this chapter. The last step after the modem installation is complete is to test the modem using communications software.

An excellent utility you can use to test a modem is HyperTerminal, a quick and easy way to make a phone call from a Windows PC. Later in the chapter, you will learn how to use commands in HyperTerminal to troubleshoot a modem. The following procedure is designed to verify that your modem works. Follow these steps to test your modem:

1. For Windows 2000/XP and Windows 98, click **Start**, point to **Programs** (for Windows XP, point to **All Programs**), **Accessories**, **Communications**, and click **HyperTerminal**. For Windows 95, click **Start**, point to **Programs**, **Accessories**, and click **HyperTerminal**.

2. For Windows 98, double-click the **Hypertrm.exe** icon in the HyperTerminal window.

3. When you see the Connection Description dialog box, enter a descriptive name for your connection (such as **test modem**), and select an icon for the shortcut. Click **OK**.

4. Enter the phone number to dial, and select the modem from the list of dial-up devices (most likely it's the only entry). Click **OK**.

5. Click **Dial** to make the call. Even if you dial an out-of-service number, you can still hear your modem make the call. This confirms that your modem is installed and configured to make an outgoing call.

 TIP If you don't see HyperTerminal under the Accessories group of Windows, it might not be installed. To install a Windows utility, use the Add/Remove Programs icon in Control Panel.

THE AT COMMAND SET

One of the pioneers of modem communications, Hayes Microcomputer Products, developed a language for PCs to use to control modems. Hayes did not patent or copyright the language, so most modems today are built to understand this language. Any modem that contains the logic to understand this language is said to be Hayes-compatible, and the language has become a de facto standard. (A de facto standard is a standard that has no official backing but is considered a standard because of widespread use and industry acceptance.)

The Hayes language for modem control is called the **AT command set** because, when the modem receives commands, each command line is prefaced with AT for ATtention. A modem that uses this language stays in command mode any time it is not connected to another modem. When a modem is in command mode and bits and bytes are sent to it from a PC, the modem interprets the bytes as commands to be followed, rather than as data to be sent over a phone line. It leaves command mode when it either receives an incoming call or dials out, and returns to command mode when a call is completed or a special escape sequence is sent to it by its computer.

Other manufacturers of modems have added to the Hayes AT command set; Table 17-4 lists a few of the core AT commands that most modems understand. Commands that begin with the ampersand character (&) are part of the extended command set; the others are part of the basic command set. When a modem is in command mode, it responds to each command with OK or gives the results after performing the command. You can type a command from a communications software window to be executed immediately or enter a command from a dialog box for the modem configuration to be executed later when the modem makes a call.

All communication between software and a modem, including AT commands, uses the **TAPI (Telephony Application Programming Interface)**, a standard jointly developed by Intel and Microsoft, to connect a PC to telephone services. **Telephony** is the technology of telephones, and TAPI is a type of API (application programming interface) that Windows can use when it needs to command the modem.

Table 17-4   AT commands for Hayes-compatible modems

Command	Description	Some Values and Their Meanings
AT	Gets the modem's attention	AT (Modem should respond with OK.)
*70	Disable call waiting	ATDT*70,4045551212
+++	Escape sequence: tells the modem to return to command mode. You should pause at least 1 second before you sequence. After you end it, wait another second before you send another command. Don't begin this command with AT.	+++ (Follow each + with a short pause; use this when trying to unlock a hung modem; don't begin the command begin with AT.)
On	Go Online: tells the modem to return to online data mode. This is the reverse command for the escape sequence above.	ATO0 Return online ATO1 Return online and retrain (perform training or handshaking again with the remote system)
A/	Repeat last command: repeat last command performed by the modem. Don't begin the command with AT, but do follow it with Enter. Useful when redialing a busy number.	

17

Table 17-4   AT commands for Hayes-compatible modems (continued)

Command	Description	Some Values and Their Meanings
I*n*	Identification: instructs the modem to return to product identification information	ATI0 Return the product code ATI3 Return the modem ROM version
Z*n*	Reset: instructs the modem to reset and restore the configuration to that defined at power on	ATZ0 Reset and return to user profile 0 ATZ1 Reset and return to user profile 1
&F	Factory default: instructs the modem to reload the factory default profile. In most cases, use this command to reset the modem rather than using the Z command	AT&F (This method is preferred to ATZ when trying to solve a modem problem)
A	Answer the phone: instructs the modem to answer the phone, transmit the answer tone, and wait for a carrier from the remote modem	
D*n*	Dial: tells the modem to dial a number. Several parameters can be added to this command. A few are listed on the right.	ATD5551212 Dial the given number ATDD Causes the dialing to pause ATDP Use pulse dialing ATDT Use tone dialing ATDW Wait for dial tone ATD& Wait for the credit card dialing tone before continuing with the remaining dial string
H*n*	Hang up: tells the modem to hang up	ATH0 Hang up ATH1 Hang up and enter command mode
M*n*	Speaker control: instructs the modem as to how it is to use the speaker	ATM0 Speaker always off ATM1 Speaker on until carrier detect ATM2 Speaker always on
L*n*	Loudness: sets the loudness of the modem's speaker	ATL1 Low ATL2 Medium ATL3 High
X*n*	Response: tells the modem how it is to respond to a dial tone and busy signal	ATX0 Blind dialing; the modem does not need to hear the dial tone and will not hear a busy signal ATX4 Modem must first hear the dial tone and responds to a busy signal (This is the default value.)

The commands in Table 17-4, which you can use to control a modem from HyperTerminal, are the same commands that software uses to communicate with modems. Knowing these commands can be useful when you troubleshoot a problem connecting a modem with an ISP. To use HyperTerminal to control a modem using the AT command set, follow these steps:

1. For Windows 2000/XP and Windows 98, click **Start**, point to **Programs** (for Windows XP, click **All Programs**), **Accessories**, **Communications**, and click **HyperTerminal**. For Windows 95, click **Start**, point to **Programs**, **Accessories**, and click **HyperTerminal**.

2. For Windows 9x, double-click the **Hypertrm.exe** icon in the HyperTerminal window.

3. When the Connection Description dialog box opens, click **Cancel**. You see an empty HyperTerminal window. Type **AT** and press **Enter**. The modem responds with OK to acknowledge the command session. See Figure 17-12.

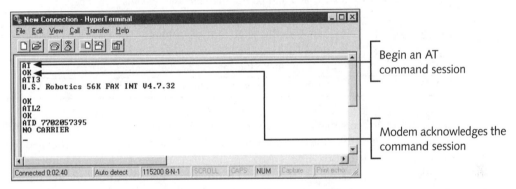

Figure 17-12   HyperTerminal can be used to control a modem using the AT command set

4. Enter any AT command; spaces are allowed. For example, in Figure 17-12, the ATI3 command causes the modem to report its ROM version, the ATL2 command sets the loudness to medium, and the ATD command followed by a phone number causes the modem to dial a number. Notice in the figure that the modem responds that no modem was connected on the other end (NO CARRIER).

Table 17-5 shows an example of an interchange between a modem and a user. Other examples of AT commands and their meanings are listed in Table 17-6.

Table 17-5   An example of a dialog between a user and a modem

Source	Command or Response	Description
From user	ATD 5551221 [Enter]	Dial the specified phone number.
From modem	CONNECT 19200	Modem responds with the agreed-on bps. At this point, you can transfer data using a utility provided by the communications software. Then wait at least 1 second before issuing the next command.
From user	+++	Escape sequence telling the modem to return to command mode (then pause 1 second)

Table 17-5 An example of a dialog between a user and a modem (continued)

Source	Command or Response	Description
From modem	OK	Modem responds by giving you the OK response.
From user	ATH0 [Enter]	Disconnect the line.
From modem	OK	Modem responds by giving you the OK response.

Table 17-6 Some examples of AT commands

Command	Description
ATDT 5552115	Dial the given number using tone dialing.
ATDP 5552115	Dial the given number using pulse dialing.
ATD 9,5552115	Dial 9 and pause, then dial the remaining numbers. (Use this method to get an outside line from a business phone.)
AT&F1DT9,5552115	Restore the default factory settings. Dial using tone dialing. Pause after dialing the 9. Dial the remaining numbers.
ATM2L2	Always have the speaker on. Set loudness of speaker at medium.
ATI3	Report the modem ROM version.

You can use AT commands to help diagnose problems with modems. To have Windows 98 perform a diagnostic test of a modem, in the Control Panel, click the Modems icon. A Modems Properties box opens (see Figure 17-13). Select the COM port the modem is installed on and click More Info. Wait a moment as the OS communicates with the modem and then displays a list of AT commands and their responses in the More Info dialog box also shown in Figure 17-13.

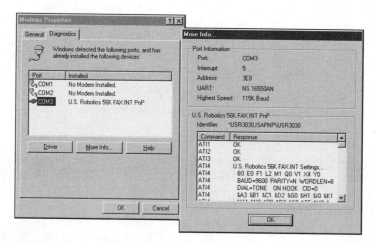

Figure 17-13 Windows 98 uses AT commands to perform a diagnostic test of a modem

For Windows 2000/XP, you can make a similar diagnostic test. Open Device Manager, right-click on the modem, and select Properties from the shortcut menu. The modem's Properties box opens. Click the Diagnostics tab and then click the Query Modem button.

TROUBLESHOOTING GUIDELINES FOR MODEMS

A+CORE
2.1

This section provides a guide to solving problems with modems and communicating over phone lines. Some keys to troubleshooting are to determine what works and what doesn't work, find out what worked in the past but doesn't work now, and discover what has changed since things last worked. Much of this can be determined by asking the user and yourself questions and by trying the simple things first. Below is a list of problems you may encounter with your modem and suggestions on how you can proceed.

The modem does not respond

- Make sure the modem is plugged into the phone jack.

- If you are using an external modem, make sure it is plugged into the computer and that the connection is solid.

- There are two RJ-11 ports on a modem. Check that the phone line from the wall outlet is connected to the line-in port.

- Plug a phone directly into the wall jack you are using, and make sure that there is a dial tone.

- If necessary, make sure to instruct the modem to dial an extra character to get an outside line, such as 9 or 8.

If this is a new installation that has never been used, check these things:

- Make sure the modem and the software are set to the same COM port and IRQ.

- Make sure no other device is configured to the same COM port or IRQ as the modem.

- For an internal modem, check that the DIP switches and jumpers agree with the modem properties in the OS.

- For an internal modem, using CMOS setup, disable the COM port the modem is set to use, so there will be no conflicts. For an external modem, verify that the COM port the modem is using is enabled. Check Device Manager for reported errors on the modem and the port the modem is using.

- If you are using an internal modem, try installing it in a different expansion slot. If you are using an external modem with a serial port card, move the card to a different slot and try to install the modem. If you are using an external modem, substitute a known-good serial cable. For a USB modem, verify that USB is enabled in CMOS setup.

- Check that the software correctly initialized the modem. If you did not give the correct modem type to the software, it may be trying to send the wrong initialization command. Try AT&F. (Under Windows 9x, click Start, point to Settings, and click Control Panel. Double-click Modems. Select the modem and click

17

$A^{+CORE}_{\ \ 2.1}$

Modem Properties, Connection, Advanced. The dialog box in Figure 17-14 opens. Enter the AT&F command under Extra settings.) Retry the modem. (For Windows 2000/XP, from Control Panel, double-click Phone and Modem Options. Click the Modems tab and then click Properties. On the modem properties dialog box, click the Advanced tab and enter the command under Extra initialization commands.)

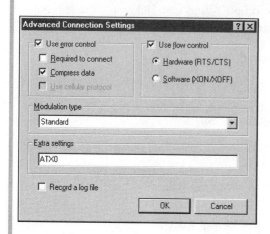

Figure 17-14   The Extra settings box allows you to send extra AT commands to the modem on any call

- Make sure you have enough RAM and hard drive space. Then close all other applications currently running, reboot the PC, and try the modem again.

The modem says there is no dial tone, even though you can hear it

- Make sure the phone cord from the wall outlet is plugged into the line jack on the modem.

- The modem might not be able to detect the dial tone, even if you can hear it. Try unplugging any other equipment plugged into this same phone line, such as a fax machine.

- Try giving the ATX0 command before you dial. Enter the command under Extra Settings, as in Figure 17-14. If that doesn't help, then remove the ATX0 command.

- Straighten your phone lines! Don't let them get all twisted and crossed with other heavy electrical lines.

- If there has been a recent lightning storm, the modem may be damaged. Replace the modem with one you know works.

$A^{+CORE}_{2.1}$ **The modem dials and then says that the other end is busy, even when you know that it is not**

- This can happen with international calls if the modem does not recognize the signal as a ring. Try giving the ATX0 command first.
- Straighten the phone lines and remove extra equipment, as described above.

The sending modem and the receiving modem take a very long time to negotiate the connection

- This is probably because of a noisy phone line. Try calling again or use a different number.
- Remove other equipment from your line. A likely suspect is a credit card machine.
- Turn off data compression and try again.
- Turn off error correction and try again.
- Try forcing your modem to use a slower speed.

During a connection, it sounds as if the handshaking starts all over again

Modems normally do this if the phone line is noisy and would cause a lot of data to become corrupted; it's called retraining and can sometimes solve the problem as the modems renegotiate, compensating for the noisy line. Do the things listed above to clear your line of equipment and twisted phone lines.

File transfers are too slow

Make sure your modem is configured to use data compression, if possible.

The modem loses connection at odd times or is slow

- Check the communications software for the speed assigned to it. People often set the communications software speed to the modem speed instead of the port speed, which is what the software asks for and which should be about four times the modem speed.
- You may have a noisy phone line. Try the connection using the same brand and model of modem on both lines. If performance is better, the problem is most likely the phone line.
- Is the phone line from the modem to the jack too long? About four feet is the limit; otherwise, electromagnetic interference may be the problem.
- Straighten the phone lines and clear the line of any extra equipment.
- Reinstall the modem. Allow Windows to detect the modem for you and install its own drivers.

17

$A^{+CORE}_{2.1}$ ## The modem drops the connection and gives the NO CARRIER message

- Most likely the connection was first dropped by the remote modem. Is someone trying to use a phone extension on this line?

- Disable call waiting. To do this, put *70 before the dialing number. Some communications software has a setting to disable call waiting. If not, you can put these three characters in the Extra settings box of Advanced Connections Settings (see Figure 17-14).

- Remove extra equipment from the line, and straighten the phone lines.

- Check the modem settings and make sure "Error control required to connect" is not checked.

- Try using a different modulation type under Advanced Connection Settings of your modem properties.

- The remote modem may not support the high speeds used. Try reducing the port speed to 9600 or lower.

When the weather is bad, the connection disconnects often

This is caused by a dirty phone line. Remove any extra equipment and straighten the lines. (This can help your connection regardless of weather conditions.)

When large files are downloaded, some data is lost

Make sure that hardware flow control is on and that software flow control is off for the software, the COM port, and the modem. (Use software settings options, the COM port Properties box, and the modem Properties box.)

The connection fails when large files are uploaded or downloaded

There may be a buffer overflow. Try these things to gain better control of data flow:

- Make sure that hardware flow control is on and that software flow control is off for the software, the COM port, and the modem.

- Is the serial port speed set too high for your UART chip? Lower the port speed.

- For an external modem, try a different cable.

You get nothing but garbage across the connection

- Check the port settings. Try 8 data bits, no parity, and one stop bit (8, No, and 1).
- Slow down the port speed.
- Slow down the modem speed.
- Try a different modulation type.

CHAPTER SUMMARY

- Modem cards use either an ISA slot or a PCI slot, although the motherboard on some systems has a shortened CNR or AMR slot that supports a modem riser card.

- External modems use a serial or USB port.

- Modems are both hardware and firmware.

- Modems convert digital computer signals to analog signals (through modulation) for transmission over phone lines, then back into digital signals on the receiving end (through demodulation).

- A modem can be either half-duplex (like a CB radio, with which communication can travel in only one direction at a time) or full duplex (like a regular voice phone conversation, in which communication can travel in two directions at once).

- Modems are classified according to how they set communication rules (handshaking), and how fast they pass data over phone lines (measured in bits per second).

- The most commonly used modem speed rating today is 56.6 Kbps. The current standard for 56 Kbps transmission is the V.92 standard.

- Modem standards were written by the CCITT, now called the ITU. The more standards a modem supports, the more easily it can communicate with other modems.

- The firmware housed on a modem can perform error correction and data compression. These data communication functions can also be performed by software on the PC.

- Features to look for in a modem include caller ID, display readout, Flash ROM, Plug and Play, the ability to serve as a telephone, and auto-answer.

- Computers are classified as DTE, and modems are classified as DCE. Communication between DTEs through DCEs is affected by the port speed on either end and by the communication speed between the two DCEs.

- Port settings include the port speed, data bits required to send a single character, parity for error checking, stop bits to communicate when a character ends, and flow control to stop data flow when necessary.

- HyperTerminal is a Windows utility used to test modem connection and troubleshoot a modem. From HyperTerminal, you can control the modem using the AT command set, which contains the same commands used in communication between the modem and the PC.

- As with other devices, when troubleshooting a modem, determine what does and does not work, what worked in the past but doesn't work now, and what has changed since things last worked.

- Common causes of modem problems include line noise, bad connections, interference from other devices, and speed mismatches.

17

KEY TERMS

AT command set

audio/modem riser (AMR)

baud rate

bits per second (bps)

carrier

CCITT (Comité Consultatif International Télégraphique et Téléphonique)

checksum

communication and networking riser (CNR)

demodulation

error correction

flow control

frame

full-duplex

guard tone

half-duplex

handshaking

ITU (International Telecommunications Union)

line speed

modem

modem riser card

modem speed

modulation

noise

port settings

port speed

RJ-11

TAPI (Telephony Application Programming Interface)

telephony

training

V.92

REVIEW QUESTIONS

1. In order to reduce the total cost of a computer system, some motherboards have a small expansion slot that is half the length of typical expansion slots, called a(n) _____ slot.

   a. PCI

   b. AMR

   c. EISA

   d. SCSI

   e. IDE

2. The process of converting data into an analog signal is referred to as _____.

   a. Modulation

   b. Demodulation

   c. Full-duplex

   d. Half-duplex

   e. Baud rate

3. The process of converting a signal into digital data is referred to as _____.

 a. Modulation

 b. Demodulation

 c. Full-duplex

 d. Half-duplex

 e. Baud rate

4. The bi-directional transmission of data or signals one direction at a time is referred to as _____ information transfer.

 a. Modulation

 b. Demodulation

 c. Full-duplex

 d. Half-duplex

 e. Baud rate

5. The bi-directional transmission of data or signals at the same time is referred to as _____ information transfer.

 a. Modulation

 b. Demodulation

 c. Full-duplex

 d. Half-duplex

 e. Baud rate

6. Data can be represented either as a stream of 1s and 0s, or as a waveform that continuously changes over time. Data that is represented by a series of 1s and 0s is referred to as:

 a. Analog data

 b. Digital data

 c. Full-duplex

 d. Half-duplex

 e. Modulation

7. Data that is represented by a waveform that continuously changes over time is referred to as:

 a. Analog data

 b. Digital data

 c. Full-duplex

 d. Half-duplex

 e. Modulation

17

8. The connector a user would expect to connect a typical telephone line to on the modem is referred to as a(n):

   a. Serial port

   b. Parallel port

   c. RJ-45

   d. RJ-11

   e. PCI

9. The term _____ refers to the process by which devices communicate with each other with the purpose of establishing rules and protocols, as well as sharing state information from each device.

   a. Baud rate

   b. Modulation

   c. Bits per second

   d. Handshaking

   e. Noise

10. In the most recent modem designs, the terms "baud rate" and "bits per second" have the same meaning.

    a. True

    b. False

11. When using conventional telephone networks, which of the following represents the highest data transfer rate in bps a user can expect from recent modem designs?

    a. 300

    b. 1,200

    c. 28,800

    d. 33,600

    e. 56,000

12. Which of the following will cause a modem to "scale back" or reduce the speed at which the modem transfers data?

    a. A high performance microprocessor

    b. Increased system memory

    c. The presence of lightning in the local vicinity

    d. All of the above

    e. None of the above

13. Which of the following modem transmission standards are classified as data compression standards?

    a. V.34

    b. V.42

    c. MNP Class 5

    d. V.92

    e. All of the above

14. Formatting data into frames for the purpose of ensuring that data can be sent with integrity is referred to as _____.

    a. Data compression

    b. Data protocols

    c. Data error correction

    d. Handshaking

    e. Port speed

15. When a modem answers an incoming call, the tone that is sent is referred to as a _____ tone.

    a. Guard

    b. Carrier

    c. Initiating

    d. Terminating

    e. Acknowledgment

16. The following port setting is used to deal with errors in data transmission.

    a. Bits per second

    b. Data bits

    c. Parity

    d. Stop bits

    e. Flow control

17. The modem is considered to be the _____ in the path of data flow between origination and destination points.

    a. DTE

    b. DCE

    c. Phone line

    d. Port

    e. Computer

17

18. The AT-command string required for Hayes-compatible modems to allow the modem to dial phone numbers using tone dialing is _____.

    a. ATZ0

    b. ATDP

    c. ATDT

    d. ATH0

    e. AT

19. The software tool used in Windows 98/2000/NT that allows for control of a modem through modem-based language strings is _____.

    a. My Computer

    b. Internet Explorer

    c. Device Manager

    d. HyperTerminal

    e. Add/Remove Hardware

CHAPTER

18

PCs ON A NETWORK

In this chapter, you will learn:

♦ About different types of physical network architectures

♦ How networking works with Windows

♦ How to install a network card and a network protocol using Windows

♦ About sharing resources on a network

♦ Troubleshooting tools and tips for network connections

♦ How to connect networks to each other

This chapter discusses how to connect PCs in networks and how to connect those networks to each other. You'll learn how local networks are built, how bridges and switches can segment large local networks, and how routers connect networks. You'll also learn about the different technologies used to connect PCs and networks to the Internet, the largest network of all; and how to support PCs connected to a network. You will also learn how computers are identified on a network, how to share computer resources over a network, and how to troubleshoot a network connection. In the next chapter, you'll learn how to connect to the Internet and how to use the resources on it.

PHYSICAL NETWORK ARCHITECTURES

A+CORE
6.3

Connecting devices on a **LAN (local area network)** provides a way for workstations, servers, printers, and other devices to communicate and share resources. There are several LAN architectures, or ways of structuring a network. The architecture of a network describes its overall design, including its physical components, network technologies, interfacing software, and the protocols needed to establish reliable communication among nodes on the network. (A **node**, or **host**, is one device on the network such as a workstation, server, or printer.) The four most popular physical network architectures (sometimes called hardware protocols) for local networks are Ethernet, wireless LAN, token ring, and FDDI. An older type of network technology is Attached Resource Computer network (ARCnet), which is seldom seen today. This section discusses the most popular architectures, including the network problems they were designed to solve as well as their advantages and disadvantages.

> **TIP**   The **Institute of Electrical and Electronics Engineers (IEEE)** creates standards for computer and electronics industries. The networking standard IEEE 802 consists of a series of specifications for networking. For example, IEEE 802.2 describes the standard for Logical Link Control, which defines how networks that use different protocols communicate with each other. For more information on the IEEE 802 standards, see the IEEE Web site, *www.ieee.org*.

A+CORE
6.3
OS
4.1

Before we get into the details of network architecture, you need to know a few terms and what they mean:

- A PC makes a direct connection to a network by way of a **network adapter**, which is most often an expansion card called a **network interface card (NIC)**, using a PCI slot. However, the adapter can also be an external device providing a network port. The device can connect to the PC using a USB port, SCSI external port, or serial port. In addition, the adapter can be embedded on the motherboard, which provides the network port. In any case, the adapter must match the type and speed of the physical network being used, and the network port must match the type of connectors used on the network. Laptops can make connections to a network through a PC Card NIC, a built-in network port, or an external device that connects to the laptop by way of a USB port. (You will learn about PC Cards in Chapter 20.)

- Communication on a network follows rules of communication called network protocols. Communication over a network happens in layers. The OS on one PC communicates with the OS on another PC using one set of protocols, and the NIC communicates with other hardware devices on the network using another set of networking protocols. Examples of OS protocols are NetBEUI and TCP/IP, and examples of hardware protocols are Ethernet and token ring. You'll learn more about these protocols later in the chapter.

- Data is transmitted on a network in pieces called **packets**, **datagrams**, or **frames**. Information about the packet that identifies the type of data, where it came from, and where it's going is placed at the beginning and end of the data. Information at the beginning of the data is called a header, and information at the end of the data is called a trailer.

A+CORE
6.3
OS
4.1

- Packets have a maximum size depending on the type of network. The networking protocols are responsible for breaking the data into segments small enough for the network and for adding identifying information to each packet.

- The NIC uses checksum values to verify data integrity. A checksum is a calculated value that can be compared to the value calculated by the receiving NIC. If the two values are not the same, the packet is assumed to be corrupted. This technique of calculating and comparing values is called a **CRC (cyclical redundancy check)**.

Ethernet

A+CORE
1.5
6.1
6.2

Ethernet is the most popular network architecture used today. The three variations of Ethernet are primarily distinguished from one another by speed: 10-Mbps Ethernet, 100-Mbps or Fast Ethernet, and Gigabit Ethernet. These three types are described below. Figure 18-1 shows several types of cables used with Ethernet, and Table 18-1 compares cable types and Ethernet versions.

- *10-Mbps Ethernet.* The first Ethernet specification was invented by Xerox Corporation in the 1970s, and in 1980 it was enhanced and became known as Ethernet IEEE 802.3. This type of Ethernet operates at 10 Mbps (megabits per second) and uses either **shielded twisted-pair (STP) cable**, **unshielded twisted-pair (UTP) cable**, or **coaxial cable**. STP uses a covering around the pairs of wires inside the cable that protects it from electromagnetic interference caused by electrical motors, transmitters, or high-tension lines. It costs more than unshielded cable, so it's only used when the situation demands it. Twisted-pair cable uses a connector that looks like a large phone jack called an **RJ-45 connector**, and thin coaxial cable uses a **BNC connector**. There are several variations of this speed of Ethernet. **10BaseT** Ethernet uses UTP cable that is rated by category. CAT-3 (category 3) is less expensive than the more popular CAT-5 cable. **10Base5** Ethernet (sometimes called **ThickNet**) uses thick coaxial cable such as RG8. **10Base2** Ethernet (sometimes called **ThinNet**) uses a less expensive, smaller coaxial cable such as RG58.

- *100-Mbps Ethernet or Fast Ethernet.* This improved and most popular version of Ethernet (sometimes called **100BaseT** or **Fast Ethernet**) operates at 100 Mbps and uses UTP or STP cable. 100BaseT networks can support slower speeds of 10 Mbps so that devices that run at either 10 Mbps or 100 Mbps can coexist on the same LAN. Two variations of 100BaseT are 100BaseTX and 100BaseFX. The most popular variation is 100BaseTX, CAT-5 twisted-pair cable enhanced CAT-5 (CAT-5e), or CAT-6 that has less crosstalk than CAT-5 or CAT-5e. 100BaseFX uses fiber-optic cable, shown in Figure 18-1. Fiber cable comes in three types: single-mode (thin, difficult to connect, expensive, and best performing), multi-mode (most popular), and plastic fiber (thick, easy to connect, short cable lengths required).

18

A+CORE
6.1
6.2

- *1000-Mbps Ethernet or Gigabit Ethernet.* The latest version of Ethernet operates at 1,000 Mbps and uses twisted-pair cable and fiber-optic cable. Not yet widely used, **Gigabit Ethernet** is expected to be used for high-speed LAN backbones and for server-to-server connections.

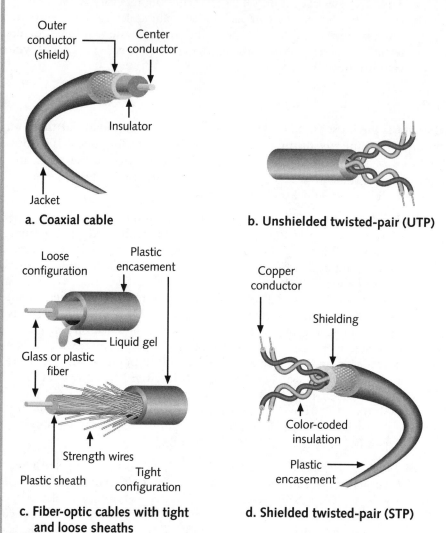

a. Coaxial cable

b. Unshielded twisted-pair (UTP)

c. Fiber-optic cables with tight and loose sheaths

d. Shielded twisted-pair (STP)

Figure 18-1   Networking cables

Important coaxial cables you should be aware of are RG59 used for cable TV and VCR transmission, RG6 which has greater shielding than RG59 and is used for Satellite Dish signals and video applications requiring greater shielding, RG8 used by ThickNet Ethernet and RG58 used by ThinNet Ethernet. Also, the outside jacket of coaxial cable is normally made of extruded PVC (poly vinyl chloride) which is not safe when used inside plenums (areas between the floors of buildings). More expensive plenum cable covered with Teflon is used in these situations.

A+*CORE*
6.1
6.2

Table 18-1   Variations of Ethernet and Ethernet cabling

Cable System	Speed	Cables and Connectors	Maximum Cable Length
10Base2 (ThinNet)	10 Mbps	Coaxial uses a BNC connector	185 meters or 607 feet
10Base5 (ThickNet)	10 Mbps	Coaxial uses an AUI 15-pin D-shaped connector	500 meters or 1,640 feet
10BaseT and 100BaseT (twisted-pair)	10 or 100 Mbps	UTP or STP uses an RJ-45 connector	100 meters or 328 feet
10BaseF, 10BaseFL, 100BaseFL, 100BaseFX, or 1000BaseFX (fiber-optic)	10 Mbps, 100Mbps, or 1 Gbps	Fiber-optic cable uses an ST or SC fiber-optic connector	500 meters up to 2 kilometers (6,562 feet)

Ethernet Topology

Ethernet networks can be configured as either a bus topology or a star topology. Topology is the arrangement or shape used to physically connect devices on a network to one another. Figure 18-2 shows examples of bus and star topologies. A **bus topology** connects each node in a line and has no central connection point. Cables just go from one computer to the next, and then the next. A **star topology** connects all nodes to a centralized hub. PCs on the LAN are like points of a star around the hub in the middle, which connects the nodes on the LAN.

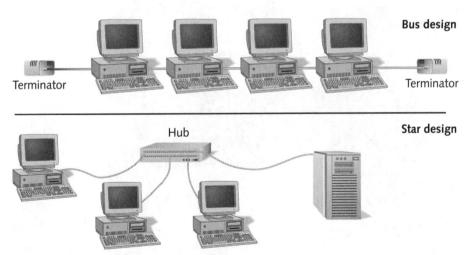

Bus design

Terminator   Terminator

Hub   **Star design**

Figure 18-2   Ethernet is a simple and popular network technology

18

The star arrangement is more popular because it is easier to maintain than the bus arrangement. In a star topology, a hub passes all data that flows to it to every device connected to it. An Ethernet hub **broadcasts** the data packet to every device, as shown in Figure 18-3. Think of a **hub** as just a pass-through and distribution point for every device connected to it, without regard for what kind of data is passing through and where the data might be going. See Figure 18-4.

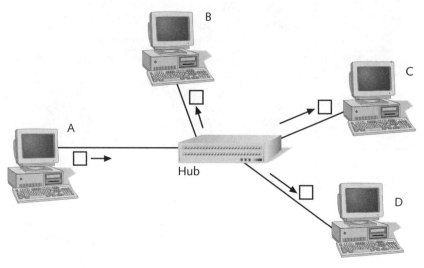

A+*CORE*
6.1

Figure 18-3   Any data received by a hub is replicated and passed on to every device connected to it

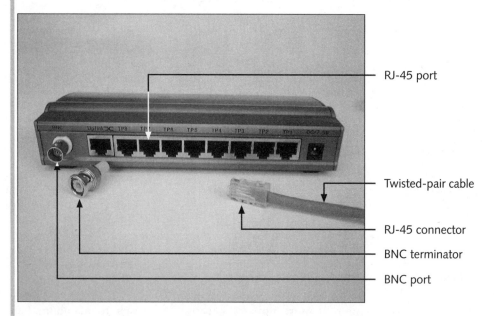

Figure 18-4   A hub is a pass-through device to connect nodes on a network

In Figure 18-3, when computer A sends data to the hub, the hub replicates the data and sends it to every device connected to it. Computers B, C, and D each get a copy of the data. It's up to these computers to decide if the data is intended for them. For this reason, a hub can generate a lot of unnecessary traffic on a LAN, which can result in slow performance when several nodes are connected to the hub.

As networks grow, more hubs can be added. Figure 18-5 shows an example of a network that uses three hubs in sequence. The hubs themselves form a bus network, but the computers connected to each hub form a star. This combination network configuration, which uses a logical bus for data delivery but is wired as a physical star, is an example of a **star bus topology**.

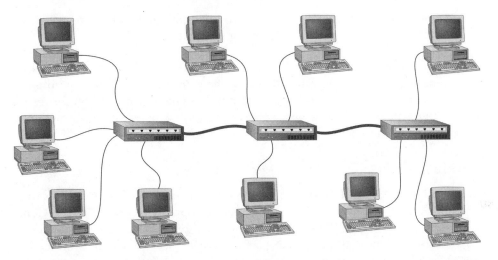

Figure 18-5   A star bus network uses more than one hub

Repeaters

Because signals transmitted over long distances on a network can weaken (in a process called **attenuation**), devices are added to amplify signals in large LANs (see Figure 18-6). For example, if a 10Base2 (ThinNet) Ethernet cable exceeds 185 meters (607 feet), amplification is required. A **repeater** is a device that amplifies signals on a network. There are two kinds of repeaters. An **amplifier repeater** simply amplifies the incoming signal, noise and all. A **signal-regenerating repeater** reads the signal and then creates an exact duplicate of the original signal before sending it on. Ethernet uses a signal-regenerating repeater.

18

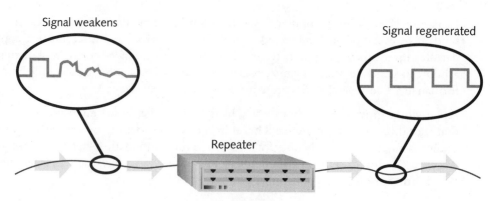

Figure 18-6 A repeater on a network restores the clarity of the signal, which degrades over a distance because of attenuation

Repeaters help overcome limitations on the length of cables that can be used, because with a repeater, signals can travel further. But there are still limitations, because Ethernet networks limit the maximum amount of time a signal can take to reach the network, and because repeaters can slow down travel time, too many repeaters can cause problems on a network. A hub acts as a signal-regenerating repeater.

Wireless LANs

A+CORE
1.3
1.8
5.1
6.2
6.3

Wireless LAN (WLAN) technology, as the name implies, uses radio waves or infrared light instead of cables or wires to connect computers or other devices. Connections are made using a wireless NIC (network interface card), which includes an antenna to send and receive signals. Wireless LANs are popular in places where networking cables are difficult to install, such as outdoors or in a historic building with wiring restrictions, or where there are many mobile users, such as on a college campus. Wireless devices can communicate directly (such as a handheld device communicating with a PC via an infrared connection), or they can connect to a LAN by way of a wireless **access point (AP)** as shown in Figure 18-7. Access points are placed so that nodes can access at least one access point from anywhere in the covered area. When devices use an access point, they communicate through the access point instead of communicating directly.

A LAN using a bus formation is often depicted in a logic diagram as a straight line with devices connecting to it, and a LAN using a ring formation is sometimes depicted as a circle. This method merely shows that devices are connected and is a nondescriptive way of drawing a LAN that might use a bus, ring, or star topology. Since most LANs are Ethernet, the most common way of drawing a LAN is to use a straight line.

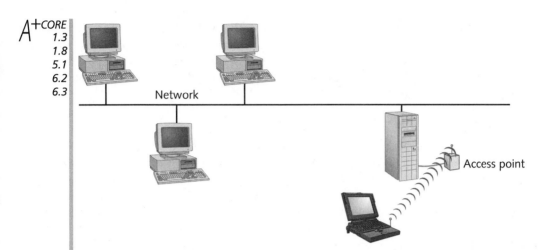

A+CORE
1.3
1.8
5.1
6.2
6.3

Figure 18-7   Nodes on a wireless LAN connect to a cabled network by way of an access point

The first IEEE standard that outlined wireless LAN specifications was IEEE 802.11, published in 1990. Most current wireless LAN devices operate under the 1999 IEEE **802.11b** standard also called **Wi-Fi**, and called **AirPort** by Apple Computers, although there are other wireless technologies available, such as Bluetooth. 802.11b uses a frequency range of 2.4 GHz and has a distance range of about 100 meters. **Bluetooth** is a standard for short-range wireless communication and data synchronization between devices. This standard was developed by a group of electronics manufacturers, including Ericsson, IBM, Intel, Nokia, and Toshiba, and it is overseen by the Bluetooth Special Interest Group. Bluetooth, which has a range of only 10 meters, also works in the 2.4 GHz frequency range, is easy to configure, and is considered a viable option for short-range connections such as connecting a PDA to a cell phone so that the PDA can connect to a remote network.

 For more information on Wi-Fi, see *www.wi-fi.org*, and for more information on AirPort, see *www.apple.com*. For information on Bluetooth, see *www.bluetooth.com*.

18

IEEE has two more up-and-coming wireless standards, 802.11a and 802.11g. 802.11a works in the 5.0 GHz frequency range and is, therefore, not compatible with 802.11b. It has a shorter range from wireless device to an access point (50 meters compared to 100 meters for 802.11b), but is much faster than 802.11b and does not have to deal with interference from cordless phones, microwave ovens, and Bluetooth devices, as does 802.11b. It is expected that 802.11b and 802.11a devices will coexist for some time. 802.11g is another IEEE wireless standard that is not yet widely available; it will be compatible with 802.11b, but faster.

Although wireless LANs have some obvious advantages in places where running cables would be difficult or overly expensive, wireless LANs tend to be slower than wired networks,

A+CORE
1.3
1.8
5.1
6.2
6.3

especially when they are busy. Another problem with wireless LANs is security. Companies are reluctant to use them when it is possible for an unauthorized person with a receiving device to intercept wireless LAN transmissions. Security on a wireless LAN is accomplished by filtering the MAC addresses of wireless NICs allowed to use the access point and by encrypting data sent over the wireless LAN.

Token Ring and FDDI

A+CORE
6.1
OS
4.1

Token ring is an older LAN technology developed by IBM that transmits data at 4 Mbps or 16 Mbps. Physically, a token ring network is arranged in a star topology, because each node connects to a centralized device and not to other nodes in the network. However, a token actually travels in a ring on the network. The token is either free or busy, and a node must have the token to communicate. Because it is physically a star and logically a ring, it is sometimes called a **star ring topology**. The centralized device to which the network nodes connect is called a **Controlled-Access Unit (CAU)**, a **Multistation Access Unit (MSAU** or sometimes just **MAU)**, or a **Smart Multistation Access Unit (SMAU)**. STP cables for token ring use either an IDC (IBM Data Connector) or UDC (Universal Data Connector) connector. Token ring technology is less popular today than Ethernet technology.

Fiber Distributed Data Interface (**FDDI**, pronounced fiddy) uses a token that travels in a ring like token ring. But with FDDI, data frames travel on the ring without the token, and multiple nodes can have data on the ring at the same time. Nodes on a FDDI network can be connected in a ring using a **ring topology**, meaning that each node is connected to two other nodes, although most FDDI networks use hubs in a physical star topology. FDDI provides data transfer at 100 Mbps, which is much faster than token ring or regular Ethernet and a little faster than Fast Ethernet, which also runs at about 100 Mbps. It is often used as the network technology for a large LAN in a large company. FDDI can also be used as a backbone network to connect several LANs in a large building.

How NICs Work

An internal NIC plugs into a motherboard expansion slot, provides a port or ports (or antenna in the case of a wireless NIC) for connection to a network, and manages the communication and hardware network protocol for the PC. An external NIC provides the same functions and can use a PC Card slot or USB port. An individual NIC can be designed to support Ethernet, token ring, FDDI, or wireless architectures, but only one architecture. However, it might be designed to handle more than one cabling system. See Figure 18-8 for some examples of network cards. The network card and the device drivers controlling the network card are the only components in the PC that are aware of the type of physical network being used. In other words, the type of network in use is transparent to the applications software using it.

A network card sends and receives data to and from the system bus in parallel, and sends and receives data to and from the network in series. In addition, the network card is responsible for converting the data it is transmitting into a signal that is in a form appropriate to the network. For example, a fiber-optic FDDI card contains a laser diode that converts data to light pulses before transmission, and a twisted-pair Ethernet card converts data from the 5-volt signal used on the motherboard to the voltage used by twisted-pair cables. The component on the card responsible for this signal conversion is called the **transceiver** (transmitter-receiver). It is common for an Ethernet card to contain more than one transceiver, each with a different port on the back of the card, in order to accommodate different cabling media. This type of Ethernet card is called a **combo card** (see Figure 18-9).

A^+ *OS*
    4.1

a. FDDI

b. Token ring

c. Ethernet

d. Wireless

18

Figure 18-8   Four different types of network cards: a. FDDI, b. token ring, c. Ethernet, and d. wireless

A+CORE
    1.5

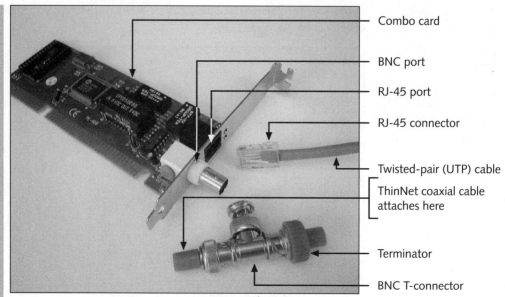

Combo card

BNC port

RJ-45 port

RJ-45 connector

Twisted-pair (UTP) cable

ThinNet coaxial cable
attaches here

Terminator

BNC T-connector

Figure 18-9   This Ethernet combo card can use either a BNC or RJ-45 connection,
depending on the cabling system used

Different networks have different ways of identifying network nodes. Ethernet, WLAN, and token ring cards have MAC addresses hard-coded on the card by their manufacturers. Called **MAC (Media Access Control) addresses**, **hardware addresses**, **physical addresses**, **adapter addresses**, or, in the case of Ethernet, Ethernet addresses, these addresses are 6-byte (48-bit) hex addresses unique to each card. Part of the MAC address refers to the manufacturer; therefore, no two adapters should have the same MAC address.

Network cards require an IRQ, an I/O address, and, for DOS and Windows 9x real mode, upper memory addresses. If the network card is on the PCI bus, then the PCI bus controller manages the IRQ and I/O address requirements. Network cards may be Plug and Play, or they can use jumpers or DIP switches on the card to determine which resources to request. When selecting a network card, three things are important:

- The speed and type of network to which you are attaching (for example, 100BaseT Ethernet, token ring, FDDI, type of WLAN, or a proprietary network standard)

- Except for wireless connections, the type of cable you are using (for example, shielded twisted-pair, coaxial, or fiber-optic cable)

- The type of slot you are using (PCI or ISA). PCI is faster than ISA and is the preferred choice.

Segmenting a Network

As you have learned, when two or more computers are connected, they form a network and are sometimes connected by hubs. For small networks, hubs are sufficient, but in larger networks, more intelligent devices are needed that can help reduce the traffic on the network. Bridges and switches are used to divide networks into segments, which decreases the amount of traffic on the overall network. This section describes how bridges and switches work and explains how they differ from each other.

Before we discuss these devices, you need to understand the following terms and concepts:

- All communication on a local network uses the MAC address of the NIC to identify the destination computer. Other computers on the network receive the packet, but, because it is not addressed to them, they discard it.

- Bridges and switches are more intelligent than hubs and make decisions about whether or not to allow traffic to pass or where to forward that traffic, reducing traffic on each segment and improving network performance.

A network engineer will add a bridge or switch at a strategic place on the network, such as between two floors or between two buildings, to contain heavy traffic within each of two segments created by the bridge. Bridges and switches use MAC addresses, which they store in routing tables, to determine where to send packets.

To help you understand how bridges work, suppose your town has a river running through it, as shown in Figure 18-10. Traffic on the West Side must pass over the bridge to reach the East Side. At the bridge stands a bridge attendant who looks at the source and destination addresses of each traveler (packet). Suppose that a traveler from the West Side approaches the bridge attendant. The attendant looks at the address where the traveler wants to go (the destination address). The attendant then searches for the destination address in his routing table. If he finds the address in the table, the table tells which side the address is on. He then grants or refuses the traveler permission to pass, based on that knowledge. If the attendant does not find the destination address in the routing table, he allows the traveler to cross. Also, the attendant updates his routing table by adding information he has just learned. By knowing that the traveler came from the West Side and knowing the source address of the traveler, he can enter this source address into his routing table as one address on the West Side. At first, the attendant doesn't know much about addresses on each side, but as many travelers come from both sides of the bridge, his table becomes more complete, and he becomes more efficient at his job.

18

Figure 18-10 A bridge is an intelligent device making decisions concerning network traffic

A **bridge** on a network works in a similar way to our hypothetical bridge separating two sides of town with an attendant. A network bridge keeps a routing table for each network segment it connects to. The tables start out empty, and all data packets that reach the bridge from one segment are passed on to the other segment connected to the bridge. As packets appear at the bridge, the bridge records the source MAC address in its routing table for that segment. The next time a packet appears at the bridge, the bridge looks at the packet's destination and routes it across the bridge only if the destination is on a different network segment or it does not recognize the destination. Figure 18-11 shows a bridge device.

To understand the difference between a bridge and a switch, we must look at a more complicated situation that involves three or more network segments, as shown in Figure 18-12. When a packet arrives at a bridge, the bridge searches the routing table of only that segment. The bridge makes only a single decision: "Is this packet destined for a node on its own network segment?" If the answer is "Yes," then the packet is refused. It will reach its destination without using the bridge. If the answer is "No," then the bridge simply broadcasts the packet to all other network segments connected to it, except the network segment that the packet came from. In Figure 18-12, if a packet arrives from network segment A, the bridge searches its routing table for network segment A. If it doesn't find the MAC address of the packet in that table, it broadcasts the packet to network segments B and C.

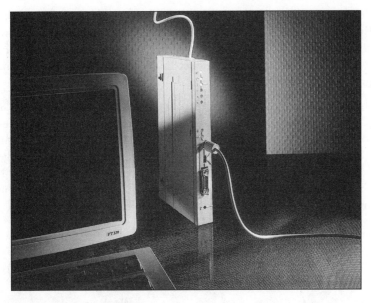

Figure 18-11   A bridge

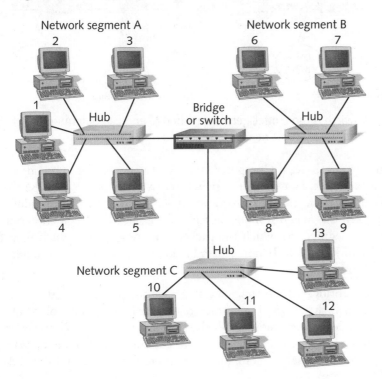

Figure 18-12   A bridge or switch connects two or more segments and decides whether or not to allow the packet to pass through, depending on its destination MAC address

18

You can now clearly see why bridging does not work well with large networks (such as the Internet). Broadcasting messages over several large networks would produce much unnecessary traffic on those networks. Bridging is effective at separating high-volume areas on a LAN and works best when used to connect LANs that usually do not communicate outside their immediate network.

A **switch**, on the other hand, does not work by sending broadcast messages. Just like a bridge, a switch keeps a table of the MAC addresses of all the devices connected to it. It uses this table to determine which path to use when sending packets. Recall the discussion of Figure 18-10 for a moment. Like a bridge, a switch does not let a packet pass to other networks if it is addressed to a location on its own network segment. However, unlike a bridge, a switch passes a packet only to its destination network segment, instead of to all segments other than the one it came from (the source). Figure 18-13 compares how a bridge works with how a switch works.

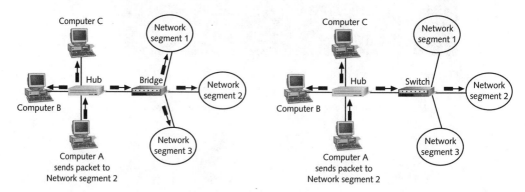

Figure 18-13   A switch is more intelligent than a bridge and can determine which network segment a packet needs to be sent to

For example, in Figure 18-12, if Computer 10 on Network segment C sends a packet to Computer 7 on Network segment B, the switch receives the packet because the hub on Computer 10's network segment is broadcasting. Using the destination address in the header of the packet, the switch searches all tables for all network segments connected to it to determine the segment to which the packet is addressed. The switch then forwards the packet to Network segment B, rather than broadcasting the packet to all network segments connected to it.

Network cards, hubs, bridges, and switches are all part of the physical infrastructure of a network. As you've learned, that physical infrastructure uses a hardware protocol to control communication between devices. For most LANs, that protocol is Ethernet. However, in addition to the hardware protocol, there is a layer of network communication at the operating system level. The OS can use one of several communication protocols such as TCP/IP or AppleTalk.

For example, a Windows network might use TCP/IP to communicate at the OS level, and the devices on the LAN (hubs, NICs, and bridges) might use Ethernet. The next section looks at the different OS networking protocols, how they work, and how to configure a computer to use them.

WINDOWS ON A NETWORK

A+CORE
6.2
OS
4.1

At the physical network level, Windows supports Ethernet, ATM, token ring, and other networking protocols. At the operating system level, Windows supports the three suites of protocols shown in Figure 18-14 and listed below. AppleTalk, which is shown in the figure but not listed here, is the default networking protocol for Macintosh computers. The figure also shows the different ways a computer or other device on the network can be addressed. Use this figure as a reference point throughout this section in order to understand the way the protocols and addresses relate on the network.

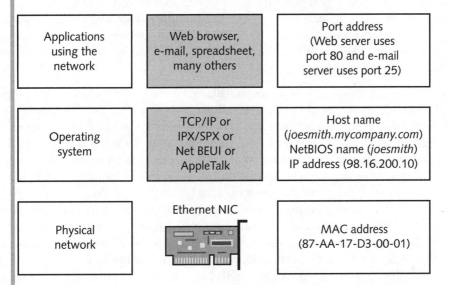

Figure 18-14   An operating system can use more than one method to address a computer on the network, but at the network level, a MAC address is always used to address a device on the network

- **TCP/IP (Transmission Control Protocol/Internet Protocol)** is the protocol suite used on the Internet and so should be your choice if you want to connect your network to the Internet, with each workstation having Internet access. Novell NetWare, Linux, Unix, and Mac OS also support TCP/IP.

18

$A+$*CORE*
  6.2
  OS
  4.1

- **IPX/SPX (Internetwork Packet Exchange/Sequenced Packet Exchange)** is a NWLink protocol suite designed for use with Novell NetWare operating system. Novell Netware is an OS designed to control access to resources on a network, similar to Windows 2000 Server. An OS designed to manage a network is called a **network operating system (NOS).** IPX/SPX is somewhat similar to TCP/IP but is not supported on the Internet.

- **NetBEUI (NetBIOS Extended User Interface)** is a proprietary Windows protocol suite used only by Windows computers and is a good choice if your network is isolated from the Internet. NetBEUI is faster than TCP/IP but does not support routing to other networks and therefore is not supported on the Internet.

To use one of these protocols on a network, the first step is to physically connect the computer to the network by installing the NIC in the computer and connecting the network cable to the hub or other network device. (For wireless LANs, after installing the NIC, you put the computer within range of an access point.) The next step is to install the protocol in the operating system. Once the protocol is installed, it automatically associates itself with any NICs it finds, in a process called binding. **Binding** occurs when an operating system-level protocol such as TCP/IP associates itself with a lower-level hardware protocol such as Ethernet. When the two protocols are bound, communication continues between them until they are unbound, or released.

You can determine which protocols are installed in Windows by looking at the properties of a network connection. For example, for Windows 2000, from Control Panel, double-click the Network and Dial-up Connections icon. Then right-click the Local Area Connection icon (see Figure 18-15). The Local Area Connection Properties dialog box opens, as shown in the figure. In this figure, you can see that two of the three protocols provided with Windows 2000 are installed because they are checked. In this situation, this PC is using a TCP/IP network, but one network printer on the network uses IPX/SPX and does not support TCP/IP. Because this PC uses that printer, it must have IPX/SPX installed. (A **network printer** is a printer that any user on the network can access, through its own network card and connection to the network, through a connection to a standalone print server, or through a connection to a computer as a local printer, which is shared on the network.) There is no problem with more than one operating system protocol operating on the network at the same time.

Addressing on a Network

$A+$*CORE*
  6.2
  OS
  4.2

Every device on a network has a unique address. Part of learning about a network is learning how a device (such as a computer or a printer) or a program (such as a Web server) is identified on the network. On a network, four methods are used to identify devices and programs:

- *Using a MAC address.* As you learned earlier, a MAC address is a unique address permanently embedded in a NIC and identifying a device on a LAN. A MAC address is a value expressed as six pairs of hexadecimal numbers and letters, often separated by hyphens. The MAC address is used only by devices inside the local network and is not used outside the LAN.

A+CORE
6.2
OS
4.2

- *Using an IP address.* An **IP address** is a 32-bit address consisting of a series of four 8-bit numbers separated by periods that identifies a computer, printer, or other device on a TCP/IP network such as the Internet or an intranet. (An **intranet** is a company network that uses TCP/IP.) Each of the four numbers can be no larger than 255. An example of an IP address is 109.168.0.104. Consider a MAC address a local address and an IP address a long-distance address.

- *Using character-based names.* Character-based names include domain names, **host names**, and **NetBIOS (Network Basic Input/Output System)** names used to identify a PC on a network with easy-to-remember letters rather than numbers. (Host names and NetBIOS names are often just called **computer names**.)

- *Using a port address.* A port address is a number between 0 and 65,535 that identifies a program running on a computer. These port addresses are not the same as the port addresses, also called I/O addresses, discussed in previous chapters. Port addresses will be covered in the next chapter.

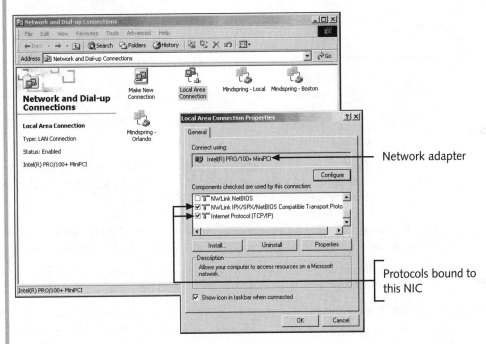

Figure 18-15 Two of three Windows 2000 network protocols are installed and bound to this network adapter

Figure 18-14 shows examples of each of these addresses and at what layer of the network they are used. The sections that follow explain the different address types in more detail.

18

MAC Addresses

MAC addresses are used at the lowest (physical) networking level for NICs and other networking devices on the same network to communicate. If a host does not know the MAC address of another host on the same network, it uses the operating system to discover the MAC address. Because the hardware protocol (for example, Ethernet) controls traffic only on its own network, computers on different networks cannot use their MAC addresses for communication. In order for the host to communicate with a host on another LAN across the corporate intranet or Internet, it must know the address of the host used by the TCP/IP protocols. These addresses are IP addresses (see Figure 18-16).

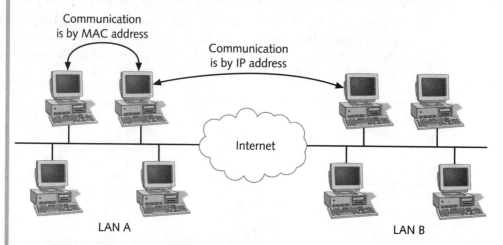

Figure 18-16   Computers on the same LAN use MAC addresses to communicate, but computers on different LANs use IP addresses to communicate over the Internet

If your PC is connected to the Internet or any other TCP/IP network, follow these directions to display the IP address and the NIC's MAC address in Windows 9x:

1. Click **Start**, **Run**. In the Run dialog box, type **winipcfg** and then press **Enter**. The IP Configuration window opens (see Figure 18-17).

2. Click the NIC on the drop-down list of network devices. The Adapter Address that appears is the MAC address; in this case, it is 00-20-78-EF-0C-5A.

3. Click the **OK** button.

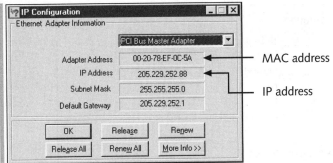

MAC address

IP address

Figure 18-17   Use the Windows 9x Winipcfg utility to display a PC's IP address and
MAC address

Windows NT/2000/XP uses Ipconfig instead of Winipcfg. If you are using
Windows 2000/XP, follow these instructions to see your MAC address and IP address:

1. Click **Start**, **Programs** (for Windows XP, **All Programs)**, **Accessories**, and
   then **Command Prompt**. A command prompt window appears.

2. At the command prompt, type **ipconfig/all | more**. The screen shown in
   Figure 18-18 appears.

3. The | more option causes the results to appear one screen at a time instead of
   scrolling by so fast you cannot read them. Press **Enter** to see each screen.

4. To exit the command prompt window, type **Exit** at the command prompt.

IP Addresses

All protocols of the TCP/IP suite identify a device on the Internet or an intranet by its IP
address. An IP address is 32 bits long, made up of 4 bytes separated by periods, as in this
address: 190.180.40.120. The largest possible 8-bit number is 11111111, which is equal to
255 in decimal, so the largest possible IP address in decimal is 255.255.255.255, which in
binary is 11111111.11111111.11111111.11111111. Each of the four numbers separated
by periods is called an **octet** (for 8 bits) and can be any number from 0 to 255, making a
total of 4.3 billion potential IP addresses (256 × 256 × 256 × 256). Because of the allocation scheme used to assign these addresses, not all of them are available for use.

The first part of an IP address identifies the network, and the last part identifies the host.
It's important to understand how the bits of an IP address are used in order to understand
how routing happens over interconnected networks such as the Internet and how
TCP/IP can locate an IP address anywhere on the globe. When data is routed over interconnected networks, the network portion of the IP address is used to locate the right network. Once the data arrives at the local network, the host portion of the IP address is used
to identify the one computer on the network that is to receive the data. Finally, the IP
address of the host must be used to identify its MAC address so the data can travel on the
host's LAN to that host. The next section explains this in detail.

18

A+CORE
6.2

Windows 2000 IP Configuration

Host Name ....: JEAN2000
Primary DNS Suffix ....:
Node Type................................: Hybrid
IP Routing Enabled ....: No
WINS Proxy Enabled.................: No
DNS Suffix Search List ....: prestige.net

Ethernet adapter Local Area Connection:

Connection-specific DNS Suffix .: prestige.net
Description ....: Intel(R) PRO/100+ MiniPCI
Physical Address ....: 00-10-A4-90-1B-AA
DHCP Enabled...........................: Yes
Autoconfiguration Enabled ....: Yes
IP Address ....: 192.168.1.101
Subnet Mask ....: 255.255.255.0
Default Gateway ....: 192.168.1.1
DHCP Server ....: 192.168.1.1
DNS Servers..............................: 208.220.88.13
                                            64.8.16.13
Lease Obtained ....: Wednesday, August 01, 2001 2:14:06 AM
Lease Expires ....: Tuesday, August 07, 2001 2:14:06 AM

Figure 18-18   Results of Windows 2000 Ipconfig/all | more command shows the current
                    IP configuration for this network

Classes of IP Addresses

When a business, college, or some other organization applies for IP addresses, a range of addresses appropriate to the number of hosts on the organization's networks is assigned. IP addresses that can be used by companies and individuals are divided into three classes: Class A, Class B, and Class C, based on the number of possible IP addresses in each network within each class. IP addresses are assigned to these classes according to the scheme outlined in Table 18-2.

You can determine the class of an IP address and the size or type of company to which an address is licensed by looking at the address. What is more important, you also can determine what portion of an IP address is dedicated to identifying the network and what portion is used to identify the host on that network.

Table 18-2 Classes of IP addresses

Class	Network Octets (Blanks in the IP address stand for octets used to identify hosts.)	Total Number of Possible Networks or Licenses	Host Octets (Blanks in the IP address stand for octets used to identify networks.)	Total Number of Possible IP Addresses in Each Network
A	0.__.__.__ to 126.__.__.__	127	__.0.0.1 to __.255.255.254	16 million
B	128.0.__.__ to 191.155.__.__	16,000	__.__.0.1 to __.__.255.254	65,000
C	192.0.0.__ to 223.255.255.__	2,000,000	__.__.__.1 to __.__.__.254	254

Figure 18-19 shows how each class of IP address is divided into the network and host portions. A Class A address uses the first octet (leftmost) for the network address and the remaining octets for host addresses. A Class A license assigns a single number that is used in the first octet of the address, which is the network address. The remaining three octets of the IP address can be used for host addresses that uniquely identify each host on this network. The first octet of a Class A license is a number between 0 and 126. For example, if a company is assigned 87 as its Class A network address, then 87 is used as the first octet for every host on this one network. Examples of IP addresses for hosts on this network are 87.0.0.1, 87.0.0.2, and 87.0.0.3. (The last octet does not use 0 or 255 as a value, so 87.0.0.0 would not be valid.) In the example's address 87.0.0.1, the 87 is the network portion of the IP address, and 0.0.1 is the host portion of the address. Because three octets can be used for Class A host addresses, one Class A license can have approximately $256 \times 256 \times 254$ host addresses, or about 16 million IP addresses. Only very large corporations with heavy communication needs can get Class A licenses.

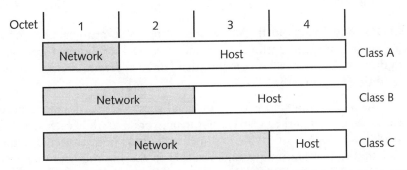

Figure 18-19 The network portion and host portion for each class of IP addresses

A Class B address uses the first two octets for the network portion and the last two for the host portion. A Class B license assigns a number for each of the first two leftmost octets, leaving the third and fourth octets for host addresses. How many host addresses are there in one Class B license? The number of possible values for two octets is about 256×254 or about 65,000 host addresses in a single Class B license. (Some IP addresses are reserved, so these numbers are approximations.) The first octet of a Class B license is a number between 128 and 191, which gives about 63 different values for a Class B first octet. The second number can be between 0 and 255, so there are approximately 63 × 256, or about 16,000, Class B networks. For example, suppose a company is assigned 135.18 as the network address for its Class B license. The first two octets for all hosts on this network are 135.18, and the company uses the last two octets for host addresses. Examples of IP addresses on this company's Class B network are 135.18.0.1, 135.18.0.2, and 135.18.0.3. In the first example listed, 135.18 is the network portion of the IP address, and 0.1 is the host portion.

A Class C license assigns three octets as the network address. With only one octet used for the host addresses, there can be only 254 host addresses on a Class C network. The first number of a Class C license is between 192 and 223. For example, if a company is assigned a Class C license for its network with a network address of 200.80.15, some IP addresses on the network would be 200.80.15.1, 200.80.15.2, and 200.80.15.3.

Class D and Class E IP addresses are not available for general use. Class D addresses begin with octets 224 through 239 and are used for **multicasting**, in which one host sends messages to multiple hosts, such as when the host transmits a video conference over the Internet. Class E addresses begin with 240 through 254 and are reserved for research.

A^+ OS 4.1 | Different Ways of Assigning IP Addresses

When a small company is assigned a Class C license, it obtains 254 IP addresses for its use. If it has only a few hosts (say, less than 25 on a network), many IP addresses go unused, which is one reason that there is a shortage of IP addresses. But suppose that the company grew, now has 300 workstations on the network, and is running out of IP addresses. There are two approaches to solving this problem: (1) use private IP addresses and (2) use dynamic IP addressing. Many companies combine both methods. An explanation of each of these solutions follows.

Public, Private, and Reserved IP Addresses

When a company applies for a Class A, B, or C license, it is assigned a group of IP addresses that are different from all other IP addresses and are available for use on the Internet. The IP addresses available to the Internet are called **public IP addresses**.

One thing to consider, however, is that not all of these 300 workstations need to have Internet access, even though they may be on the network. So, while each workstation may need an IP address to be part of the TCP/IP network, those not connected to the Internet don't need addresses that are unique and available to the Internet and therefore can use private IP addresses. **Private IP addresses** are IP addresses used on private intranets isolated from the Internet. Because the hosts are isolated from the Internet, no conflicts arise.

$A+$ OS
   4.1

In fact, a small company most likely will not apply for a license of public IP addresses at all but instead rely solely on private IP addresses for its internal network. A company using TCP/IP can make up its own private IP addresses to use on its intranet. IEEE recommends that the following IP addresses be used for private networks:

- 10.0.0.0 through 10.255.255.255

- 172.16.0.0 through 172.31.255.255

- 192.168.0.0 through 192.168.255.255

> IEEE, a nonprofit organization, is responsible for many Internet standards. Standards are proposed to the networking community in the form of an RFC (Request for Comment). RFC 1918 outlines recommendations for private IP addresses. To view an RFC, visit the Web site *www.rfc-editor.org*.

When assigning isolated IP addresses, also keep in mind that a few IP addresses are reserved for special use by TCP/IP and should not be used. They are listed in Table 18-3.

Table 18-3   Reserved IP addresses

IP address	How it is used
255.255.255.255	Broadcast messages
0.0.0.0	Currently unassigned IP address
127.0.0.1	Indicates your own workstation

All IP addresses on a network must be unique for that network. A network administrator may assign an IP address to a standalone computer (for example, if someone is testing networking software on a PC that is not connected to the network). As long as the network is a private network, the administrator can assign any IP address he or she desires, although a good administrator avoids using the reserved addresses.

$A+$ OS
   4.1
   4.2

Dynamically Assigned IP Addresses   If an administrator must configure each host on a network manually, assigning it a unique IP address, the task of going from PC to PC to make these assignments and keeping up with which address is assigned to which PC can be an administrative nightmare. The solution is to have a server automatically assign an IP address to a workstation each time it comes onto the network. Instead of permanently assigning IP addresses (called **static IP addresses**) to workstations, an IP address (called a **dynamic IP address**) is assigned for the current session only. When the session terminates, the IP address is returned to the list of available addresses. Because not all

18

A+ os
4.1
4.2

workstations are online at all times, fewer IP addresses than the total number of workstations can satisfy the needs of the network. Also, you can use private IP addresses for the range of IP addresses that can be assigned to workstations. When a workstation has an IP address assigned to it, it is said that the workstation is leasing the IP address. **Internet service providers (ISPs)**, organizations through which individuals and businesses connect to the Internet, use dynamic IP addressing for their subscribers.

The server that manages these dynamically assigned IP addresses is called a **DHCP (Dynamic Host Configuration Protocol)** server. In this arrangement, workstations are called DHCP clients. DHCP software resides on both the client and the server to manage the dynamic assignments of IP addresses. DHCP client software is built into Windows 9x and Windows NT/2000/XP.

When you configure a DHCP server, you specify the range of IP addresses that can be assigned to clients on the network. Figure 18-20 shows the configuration window for a DHCP server embedded as firmware on a router. (Routers are used to connect networks and are discussed later in the chapter.) The configuration window is accessed using a Web browser on the network and entering the IP address of the router in the Web browser address box. In the figure, you can see that the router's IP address is 192.168.1.1, and the starting IP address to be assigned to clients is 192.168.1.100. Because the administrator specified that the server can have up to 50 clients, the range of IP addresses is therefore 192.168.1.100 to 192.158.1.149. Also shown in the figure is a list of currently assigned IP addresses and the MAC address of the computer that currently leases that IP address.

When a PC first connects to the network, it attempts to lease an address from the DHCP server. If the attempt fails, it uses an Automatic Private IP Address (APIPA) in the address range 169.254.x.x.

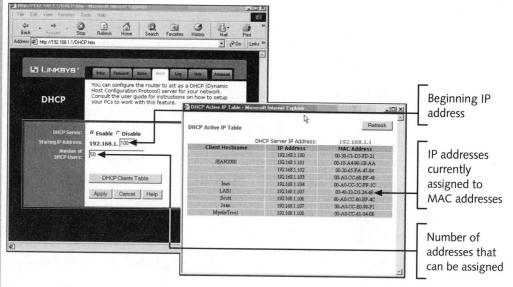

Figure 18-20   A DHCP server has a range of IP addresses it can assign to clients on the network

A+ OS
4.1
4.2

Network Address Translation If hosts on a network using private IP addresses need to access the Internet, a problem arises because the private IP addresses are not allowed on the Internet. The solution is to use **NAT (Network Address Translation)**, which uses a single public IP address to access the Internet on behalf of all hosts on the network using other IP addresses. Using NAT, when a computer on the network tries to access the Internet, it must go through a server, router, or other device that substitutes its own IP address for that of the computer requesting the information. Because the device is standing in proxy for other hosts that want Internet access, it is called a **proxy server**. Figure 18-21 shows how a proxy server stands between the network and the Internet. This proxy server has two network cards installed. One card connects to the LAN, and the other connects to a cable modem and on to the ISP and the Internet.

> **TIP** Windows 98 SE, Windows Me, Windows 2000, and Windows XP offer a NAT service called Microsoft Internet Connection Sharing (ICS). With it, two or more PCs on a home network can share the same IP address when accessing the Internet. Under ICS, one PC acts as the proxy server for other PCs on the home network.

Because a proxy server stands between a LAN and the Internet, it often does double duty as a firewall. Recall from Chapter 16 that a firewall is software or hardware that protects a network from illegal entry. Because networks are so often attacked by worms and hackers from the Internet, even a small LAN often has a router or other device between the LAN and the Internet that serves as a proxy server, DHCP server, and firewall. As a firewall, it filters out any unsolicited traffic coming from the Internet.

Host Names and NetBIOS Names

Each computer on a TCP/IP network is assigned an IP address, but these numbers are hard to remember. Host names and NetBIOS names use characters rather than numbers to identify computers on a network and are easier to remember and use than IP addresses. In addition, a company might have a **domain name** that can be used to identify the network. An example of a domain name is *amazon.com*. Domain names are covered in the next chapter.

Recall that NetBEUI is a proprietary Windows network protocol used for Windows LANs not connected to the Internet. NetBEUI supports NetBIOS, a protocol that applications use to communicate with each other. Before TCP/IP became such a popular protocol, Windows assumed that the protocol of choice would be NetBEUI and that all computers on a network would be assigned a NetBIOS name such as *joesmith* or *Workstation12*. These names usually are assigned when the operating system is installed. In contrast, TCP/IP identifies computers by IP addresses, but TCP/IP also allows a computer to be assigned a character-based host name such as *joesmith*. The host name can also have a domain name attached that identifies the network: *joesmith.mycompany.com*. On a TCP/IP network, the NetBIOS name or host name must be associated with an IP address before one computer can find another on the network. This process of associating a character-based name with an IP address is called **name resolution**.

18

A^+ *OS*
  4.1
  4.2

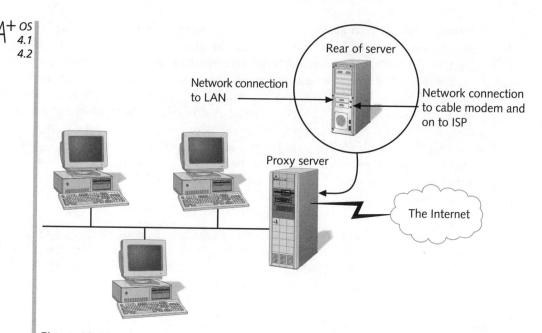

Figure 18-21   A proxy server stands between a private network and the Internet

Two name resolution services track relationships between character-based names and IP addresses: **DNS (Domain Name System**, also called **Domain Name Service)** and Microsoft **WINS (Windows Internet Naming Service)**. DNS tracks host names and WINS tracks NetBIOS names. Windows networks sometimes use a combination of DNS and WINS.

Windows 98 assumes that a computer name is a NetBIOS name, which can have only 15 characters, but Windows 2000 and Windows XP assume that the computer name is a host name that uses the TCP/IP convention for host names. If the name is 15 characters or fewer, it works as a NetBIOS name or a TCP/IP name on either a NetBEUI network or a TCP/IP network. If a host name is used, it can be up to 63 characters including letters, numbers, and hyphens, as long as the computer is not part of a workgroup. If the computer is part of a workgroup, the host name should not exceed 15 characters. Microsoft is slowly abandoning NetBIOS as the default naming convention in favor of TCP/IP host names.

Remember that applications that use NetBEUI use NetBIOS API calls to communicate with other applications on the network. Applications that use TCP/IP to communicate over the network use a type of API call known as **WinSock (Windows Sockets)**. WinSock is a part of the utility software installed with TCP/IP.

$A+$ OS
4.1

An application can make a NetBIOS API call to another computer on a network and identify the remote computer by its NetBIOS name even though the network uses TCP/IP. When dealing with these hybrid networks, you should know that the NetBIOS name of the remote computer must be related to an IP address before TCP/IP can make the connection.

Now that you know about the operating system protocols used on a network and how various types of addresses identify computers and devices on the network, let's turn our attention to how to install and configure a NIC and how to configure the OS to access and use resources on a network.

How Computers Find Each Other on a LAN

When an application using NetBIOS or WinSock wants to communicate with another computer on the same TCP/IP LAN, the requesting computer knows the name of the remote computer. Before TCP/IP communication can happen between the two computers, the first computer must discover the IP address of the remote PC. For Windows 98 using NetBIOS names, the computer runs through the following checklist in the order shown to discover the IP address. (A Windows 2000/XP computer using just TCP/IP and not NetBEUI uses DNS to resolve the name, not WINS, and begins at Step 5. If NetBEUI is running on this Windows 2000/XP computer, it tries DNS first, beginning at Step 5, and then turns to NetBEUI Steps 1 through 4 to resolve the name.)

1. The computer checks the NetBIOS name cache. This cache is information retained in memory from name resolutions made since the last reboot.

2. If the computer has the IP address of a WINS server, it queries the server. A WINS server is a Windows NT/2000 server on the network that maintains a database of NetBIOS names and IP addresses.

3. The computer sends a broadcast message to all computers on the LAN asking for the IP address of the computer with the broadcasted NetBIOS name.

4. The computer checks a file named **LMHosts**, which is stored in the \Windows folder on the local computer. This file, called a host table, contains the NetBIOS names and associated IP addresses of computers on the LAN if someone has taken the time to manually make the entries in the file.

5. If the IP address is still not discovered, the computer assumes that the network is using DNS instead of WINS, so it checks the file named **Hosts** in the \Windows folder. The Hosts file is another host table that contains host names and associated IP addresses and is similar to the information kept by DNS servers.

6. If the computer has the IP address of a DNS server, it queries the DNS server.

Both the LMHosts and Hosts host tables are in the \Windows folder. LMHosts serves as a local table of information similar to that maintained by a WINS server for NetBIOS names, and Hosts serves as a local table of information similar to that kept by a DNS server.

18

If you look in the \Windows folder of a Windows 9x computer or the \Winnt\System32\ drivers\etc folder of a Windows 2000/XP computer, you will see a sample of each file named LMHosts.SAM and Hosts.SAM, where the SAM stands for sample. Open each file with Notepad to examine it. Entries in a host table file beginning with the # symbol are comments and are not read by the name resolution process. The sample files contain many commented lines. You can add your entries to the bottom of the file without the # symbol. An example of a Hosts file is shown in Figure 18-22. It tells this computer what the IP address of the domain name *apache.test.com* is. Recall that a domain name is a name of a network. In the example, apache is the host name, and the domain name is test.com. The **fully qualified domain name (FQDN)** is *apache.test.com*, which is often loosely called the domain name.

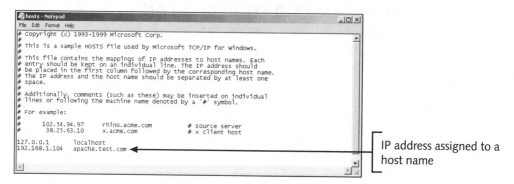

IP address assigned to a
host name

Figure 18-22   An entry in your client Hosts file will tell the client the IP address of an
intranet Web site when no DNS service is running in Windows 98

In this example, the computer named *apache.test.com* is used as a Web server for a private network. In order for those on the network to use this domain name, the Hosts file on each PC must have the entry shown in Figure 18-22, and the Web server must have the same IP address at all times. One way to accomplish this is to assign a static IP address to the server. Alternately, if your DHCP server supports this feature, you can configure it to assign the same IP address to your Web server each time if you tell the DHCP server your Web server's MAC address.

INSTALLING A NETWORK CARD AND CONNECTING TO A NETWORK

A+CORE
6.2
Connecting a PC to a network requires a NIC, network cable (called a **patch cable** or a straight-through cable), and a device for the PC to connect to, such as a hub. (Wireless PCs require a wireless NIC and require the PC to be within range of an access point.)

The simplest network of all does not use hubs, bridges, or switches, and consists of two PCs connected by a **crossover cable**, which is a network cable in which the read wire and the write wire on one PC exchange functions when they are connected to the second PC.

A+*CORE*
6.2

Installing a network card and connecting the PC to a network involves three general steps: (1) put the NIC in the PC, and install the NIC's drivers, (2) configure the NIC using Windows, so that it has the appropriate addresses on the network and the correct network protocols, and (3) test the NIC to verify that the PC can access resources on the network. This section discusses these steps using Windows 9x and Windows 2000/XP. In the following sections you will learn how to manage resources on the network and how to troubleshoot a failed network connection.

Installing a NIC Using Windows 9x

A+*CORE*
1.2
1.9
6.2

To install a NIC using Windows 9x, do the following:

1. Set DIP switches or jumpers if necessary, and physically install the network card in the PC. (If the card is Plug and Play, it most likely has no jumpers or DIP switches to set.)

2. Turn on the PC. The Found New Hardware wizard launches to begin the process of loading the necessary drivers to use the new device. It is better to use the manufacturer's drivers, not the Windows drivers. When given the opportunity, click **Have Disk** and insert the floppy disk or CD that came bundled with the NIC.

3. After the Windows desktop loads, to verify that the drivers installed successfully, open **Device Manager**. Select the card from the list of devices, and click **Properties**. The card's Properties window appears (see Figure 18-23). Look for any conflicts or other errors reported by Device Manager. If errors are reported, try downloading updated drivers from the Web site of the network card's manufacturer. You'll find other troubleshooting tips for installing NICs later in this chapter.

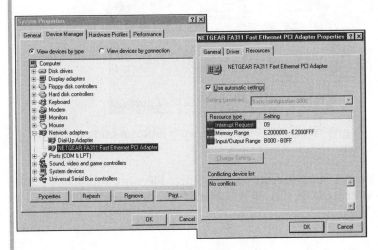

18

Figure 18-23   A network adapter's resources show in the Properties option of the Device Manager window

4. Connect a network patch cable to the NIC port and to the network hub or a wall jack connected to a hub. You are now ready to configure the NIC to access the network.

Connecting to a NetBEUI Network

Networks isolated from the Internet are likely to use the NetBEUI protocol, and networks that have Internet access are likely to use TCP/IP. This section shows you how to configure a NetBEUI network. TCP/IP is covered in the next section.

To use NetBEUI to connect to a network using Windows 98, do the following:

1. First verify that NetBEUI is installed, and install it as follows if necessary. Access the **Control Panel** and double-click the **Network** applet. The Network window opens.

2. Click **Add** to display the Select Network Component Type window, as shown in Figure 18-24.

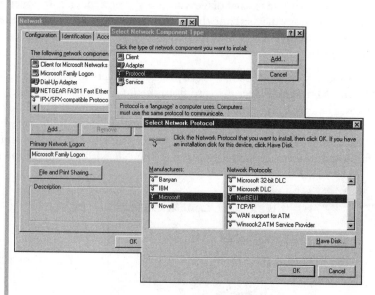

Figure 18-24 Using Windows 98, install a network protocol using the Network applet in Control Panel

3. Select **Protocol**, click **Add**, and the Select Network Protocol window opens. Select **Microsoft** on the left and **NetBEUI** on the right. See Figure 18-24. Click **OK**.

A+CORE
1.2
1.9
6.2

When you return to the Network window, notice that NetBEUI is automatically bound to any network cards it finds. In the list of network components, look for NetBEUI followed by an arrow and the name of the network card. In binding, a protocol is associated with a network card or a modem card. Also, if the Network Neighborhood icon was not on your desktop, it should be there now that a network protocol is installed.

Assigning NetBIOS Names The only configuration that NetBEUI requires is that the computer be given a NetBIOS name. NetBIOS is a protocol that applications use to communicate, and a NetBIOS name for a computer can consist of up to 15 characters. Windows 9x assumes that a computer name is a NetBIOS name. To assign a NetBIOS name to a Windows 9x computer, follow these directions:

1. Access the **Control Panel** and double-click the **Network** icon.

2. Click the **Identification** tab. See Figure 18-25.

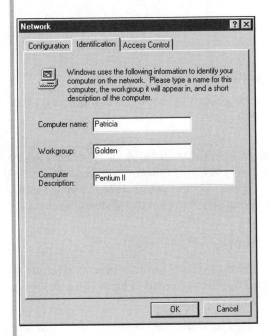

Figure 18-25   Each computer in a workgroup in Windows 98 must be assigned a name that other users on the network will see in their Network Neighborhood window

18

3. Enter the name of the workgroup (Golden in this example). Recall that a workgroup is a group of computers on a network that share files, folders, and printers. All users in the workgroup must have the same workgroup name entered on this window.

A^{+CORE}
1.2
1.9
6.2
OS
1.1

4. Enter the NetBIOS name of the computer (Patricia in this example). Each computer name must be unique within the workgroup.

5. Click **OK** to exit the window.

On the desktop, open Network Neighborhood. You should be able to see this and other computers on the network. Figure 18-26 shows an example of Network Neighborhood.

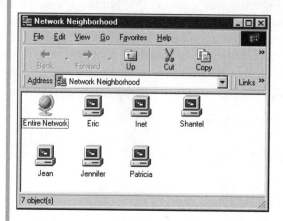

Figure 18-26   Windows 98 Network Neighborhood shows all computers on the LAN in a common workgroup

TIP   Network Neighborhood for Windows 9x and My Network Places for Windows 2000/XP can be viewed on the desktop and in Windows Explorer. By default, Windows 98 puts Network Neighborhood in both places, Windows 2000 puts My Network Places in both places, and Windows XP puts My Network Places only in Windows Explorer.

A^{+CORE}
1.2
1.9
6.2
OS
4.1
4.2

Connecting to a TCP/IP Network

NetBEUI works as long as you don't need to connect to the Internet or route requests to other networks. For these situations, TCP/IP is needed. This section describes how to install and configure TCP/IP using Windows 98.

To install and configure TCP/IP, you need to know the answers to these questions, which are supplied by your network administrator:

1. Will the PC use dynamic or static IP addressing?

2. If static IP addressing is used, what are the IP address, subnet mask, and gateway for this computer?

3. How is DNS to work? Do you enable or disable it? If enabled, what are the IP addresses of your DNS servers?

4. Is a proxy server used to connect to other networks (including the Internet)? If so, what is the IP address of the proxy server?

A+CORE
  1.2
  1.9
  6.2
  OS
  4.1
  4.2

Here is a quick explanation of what all these questions mean. You will learn more about them in the next chapter. In dynamic addressing the computer asks a DHCP server for its IP address each time it connects to the network. The server also gives the PC its subnet mask and gateway so that the computer knows how to communicate with other hosts that are not on its own network. A **gateway** is a computer or other device that allows a computer on one network to communicate with a computer on another network. A **default gateway** is the gateway a computer uses to access another network if it does not have a better option. A **subnet mask** is a group of four dotted decimal numbers that tells TCP/IP if a remote computer's IP address is on the same or a different network. A **DNS server** is a computer that can find an IP address for another computer when only the host name and domain name are known.

Installing and Configuring TCP/IP Using Windows 98   If TCP/IP is not already installed, you must install it. For Windows 98, do the following:

1. Access the Control Panel and double-click the **Network** icon. The Network window opens.

2. Click **Add** to display the Select Network Component Type window, as shown in Figure 18-27.

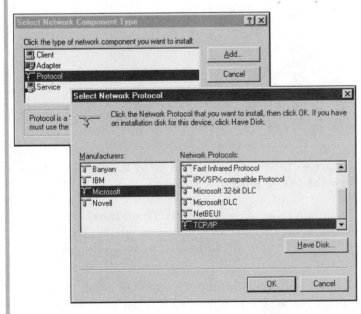

Figure 18-27   To install TCP/IP in Windows 98, use the Select Network Protocol dialog box

3. Select **Protocol**, click **Add**, and the Select Network Protocol window opens. Select **Microsoft** on the left and **TCP/IP** on the right. See Figure 18-27. Click **OK**. The system asks for the Microsoft Windows 98 CD and requests that you reboot the system.

18

A+CORE
1.2
1.9
6.2
OS
4.1
4.2

4. When you return to the Network window, notice that TCP/IP is automatically bound to any network cards or modems that it finds installed.

The next step is to configure TCP/IP for each of the bindings listed that you will use. Most likely, you will be using dynamic IP addressing, and the DNS service is initially disabled (later the DHCP server will tell the PC to enable it). The DHCP server might also act as the proxy server so that computers inside the network can make connections to computers outside the network using the proxy server's public IP address. In Windows 98, to configure TCP/IP bound to a NIC to communicate over a local network, do the following:

1. In the Network window, select the item where TCP/IP is bound to the NIC. (In Figure 18-28, that item is TCP/IP->NETGEAR FA311 Fast Ethernet PCI Adapter.) Then, click **Properties**. The TCP/IP Properties window appears.

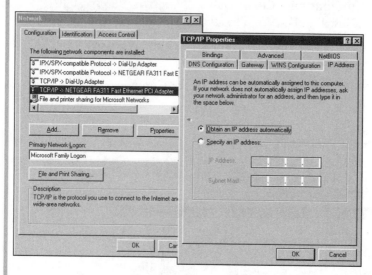

Figure 18-28   To configure TCP/IP in Windows 98, select the binding and click Properties to view the TCP/IP Properties window

2. If static IP addressing is used, click **Specify IP address**, and then enter the IP address and subnet mask supplied by your administrator. If dynamic IP addressing is used, click **Obtain an IP address automatically**. Most likely this will be your selection.

3. Click the **DNS Configuration** tab, and choose to enable or disable DNS (see Figure 18-29). If you enable DNS, enter the IP addresses of your DNS servers. If your network administrator gave you other specific values for the TCP/IP configuration, you will find the tabs for these settings on this window. But, in most cases, this is all that is needed to configure TCP/IP.

4. When finished, click **OK** to exit the Properties window, and then **OK** to exit the Network window.

A⁺CORE
1.2
1.9
6.2
OS
4.1
4.2

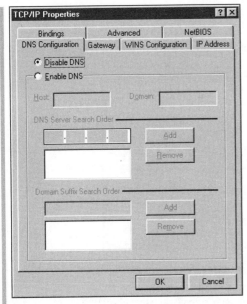

Figure 18-29   Configure DNS service under TCP/IP for Windows 98

5. On the desktop, verify that you can see your computer and others on the network in Network Neighborhood on the desktop. If you don't see others on the network, reboot the PC.

Installing a NIC Using Windows 2000/XP

A⁺CORE
1.2
1.9
6.2
OS
4.1
4.2

After a NIC is physically installed and the PC is turned on, Windows 2000/XP automatically detects the card and guides you through the process of installing drivers. After the installation, verify that the card is installed with no errors by using Device Manager. In Device Manager, the network card should be listed under Network adapters. Right-click the card and select Properties to view the card's properties.

Another way to access the NIC Properties window in Windows 2000/XP is to use the Network and Dial-up Connections applet in the Control Panel:

1. For Windows 2000, open the **Control Panel** and double-click the **Network and Dial-up Connections** icon. For Windows XP, in **Control Panel**, double-click **Network Connections**.

2. When the dialog box opens, right-click the **Local Area Connection** icon.

3. From the shortcut menu, select **Properties** to view the Local Area Connection Properties window (see Figure 18-30). Click **Configure**. The Properties window for the card appears. (Another way to access the Network and Dial-up Connections applet is to right-click My Network Places on the desktop and select Properties from the shortcut menu.)

18

A+CORE
1.2
1.9
6.2
OS
4.1
4.2

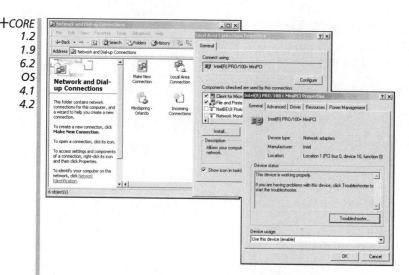

Figure 18-30   NIC Properties window under Windows 2000

To connect a Windows 2000 computer to a network using NetBEUI, using the Properties window of the local area connection, if necessary, install the NetBEUI Protocol, which automatically binds itself to the NIC providing this local network connection. Then assign a name to the computer. Remember to limit the name to 15 characters.

For Windows 2000/XP, follow these directions to give a computer name to a computer:

1. Right-click **My Computer** and select **Properties** from the shortcut menu. The System Properties window appears.

2. For Windows 2000, click the **Network Identification** tab, and then click the **Properties** button. The Identification Changes window appears (see Figure 18-31). For Windows XP, click the **Computer Name** tab, then click the **Change** button.

3. Enter the Computer name (JEAN2000 in the example shown in Figure 18-31).

4. For a workgroup, select Workgroup and enter the workgroup name (GOLDEN in this example). If the PC is to join a domain (a network where logging on is controlled by a server), enter the name of the domain here, such as *mycompany.com*. When configuring a PC on a network, always follow the specific directions of the network administrator responsible for the network.

5. Click **OK** to exit the Windows 2000 Identification Changes window or the Windows XP Computer Name Changes window, and click **OK** to exit the System Properties window.

6. On the Windows 2000 desktop, open the **My Network Places** icon, and double-click **Computers Near Me** to view this and other computers on the network. For Windows XP, click **Start**, **My Network Places**, and then click **View workgroup computers**.

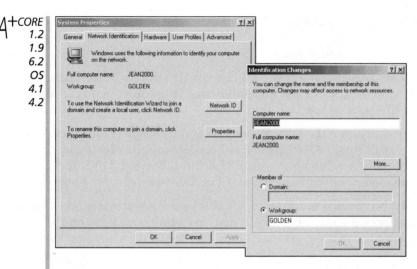

A+CORE
1.2
1.9
6.2
OS
4.1
4.2

Figure 18-31   Windows 2000 uses the Identification Changes dialog box to assign a host name to a computer on a network

Installing and Configuring TCP/IP Using Windows 2000/XP

For Windows 2000/XP, when a network card is installed, TCP/IP is installed by default. However, if TCP/IP has been uninstalled or gives you problems, you can install it again. Use the same procedure given earlier to install NetBEUI under Windows 2000/XP, this time selecting TCP/IP as the network protocol to install.

To set the TCP/IP properties for the connection, follow the steps below.

1. Using Control Panel, for Windows 2000 open the **Network and Dial-up Connection** applet, and for Windows XP, open the **Network Connections** applet. Right-click the **Local Area Connection** icon, and then select **Properties** from the shortcut menu. See Figure 18-32.

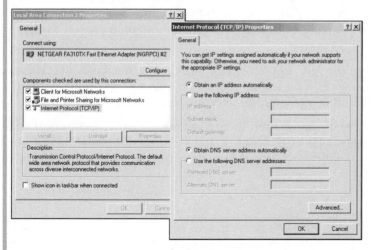

18

Figure 18-32   Configure a TCP/IP connection using Windows 2000

A+*CORE*
1.2
1.9
6.2
OS
4.1
4.2

2. Select **(Internet Protocol) TCP/IP** from the list of installed components, and then click the **Properties** button. The TCP/IP Properties dialog box opens, which is also shown in Figure 18-32.

3. For dynamic IP addressing, select **Obtain an IP address automatically**. For static IP addressing, select **Use the following IP address**, and enter the IP address, Subnet mask, and Default gateway.

4. To disable DNS until the DHCP server gives the computer the DNS server address, select **Obtain DNS server address automatically**. If you have the IP addresses of the DNS servers, click **Use the following DNS server addresses**, and enter the IP addresses. Click **OK** twice to close both windows.

5. Open **My Network Places** and verify that your computer and other computers on the network are visible. If you don't see other computers on the network, reboot the PC.

Installing a Wireless NIC

A+*CORE*
1.2
1.3
1.8
6.2
6.3

Installing a wireless NIC works the same way as installing a regular NIC except you must use the NIC's configuration software to specify wireless network parameters. A wireless connection requires the computer to be within an acceptable range of an access point or another wireless device that it will communicate with directly. This distance is determined by the type of wireless technology used, which most likely will be 802.11b. This wireless standard supports ranges from 100 meters to more than 500 meters depending on the speed at which the access point or other computer is configured to run. Generally, the higher the speed, the shorter the range between devices.

Do the following to install and configure a wireless NIC in a PC or notebook:

1. Install the wireless NIC and turn on the computer. A wireless NIC uses an internal or external antennae. If it has an external antennae, raise it. The computer immediately detects the device and launches the Found New Hardware Wizard. Follow the wizard to load the device drivers using the CD that came bundled with the NIC. If Windows prompts you to restart the computer, do so.

2. Configure the NIC to use the same wireless parameters as the access point or other computer. Run a setup program on the CD that came with the NIC to install the NIC configuration software, and then launch the software.

3. Consult the documentation to find out how to use the software. Figure 18-33 shows an example of the configuration window for a wireless NIC, but yours might look different. Using the configuration software, you can view the status

A+CORE
1.2
1.3
1.8
6.2
6.3

of the wireless connection and change the wireless parameters. Figure 18-33 shows an example of wireless configuration software reporting the following information about the connection:

- *State.* The state is the status of the current connection and reports the BSS ID (basic service set identifier), which is the MAC address of the access point device that the NIC is currently using.

- *Current Channel.* 802.11b uses 14 different channels. The United States can use channels 1 through 11. The access point device is configured to use one of these eleven channels, which is reported by the NIC software.

- *Current Tx Rate.* Current transmission rate, which is 11 Mbits/sec in the figure.

- *Throughput, Link Quality, and Signal Strength.* These values indicate throughput rate and how strong the signal is.

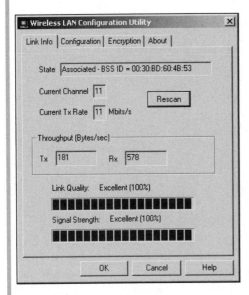

Figure 18-33 Wireless NIC configuration software reports the status of the current connection

18

Figure 18-33 also shows a Rescan button. You can click this button to tell the NIC to scan for a new access point.

4. Click the **Configuration tab** to change how the NIC functions (see Figure 18-34). Most likely, you will not need to change any defaults. Changes you can make on this screen include:

- *Mode.* The mode indicates if the computer is to communicate through an access point (Infrastructure mode) or if the computer is to communicate directly with another wireless device (Ad Hoc mode).

A+*CORE*
1.2
1.3
1.8
6.2
6.3

- *SSID.* The SSID (service set identifier) is currently set to ANY, which says the NIC is free to connect to any access point it finds. You can enter the name of an access point in order to specify this NIC should connect only to a specific access point. If you don't know the name assigned to a particular access point, ask the network administrator responsible for managing the wireless network.

- *Tx Rate.* You can specify the transmission rate or leave it at fully automatic so that the NIC is free to use the best transmission rate possible.

- *PS Mode.* When disabled, the PC is not allowed to enter sleep mode; network communication continues uninterrupted. Enable PS Mode to allow the PC to go into sleep mode.

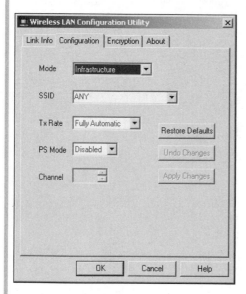

Figure 18-34   Configure how a wireless NIC will connect to a wireless LAN

5. This NIC supports encrypted wireless transmission. To enable encryption, click the **Encryption tab** (see Figure 18-35). Select 64-bit or 128-bit encryption, and enter a secret passphrase. This passphrase is a word, such as ourpassphrase, which generates a digital key used for encryption. Every computer user on this wireless network must enter the same passphrase, which can be changed at any time. Click **OK** to close the configuration software.

6. The next step is to configure the NIC to use TCP/IP or NetBEUI. How to configure TCP/IP and NetBEUI is covered earlier in the chapter and works the same way for wireless NICs as it does for regular NICs.

A+CORE
1.2
1.3
1.8
6.2
6.3

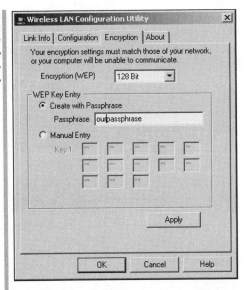

Figure 18-35   Enter a passphrase that generates a key to be used for 128-bit encryption to secure a wireless LAN

After the NIC is configured to use the OS network protocol, you should immediately see network resources in My Network Places or Network Neighborhood. If you don't, then try rebooting the PC.

Also, it is possible that the access point has been configured for MAC address filtering in order to control which wireless NICs can use the access point. Check with the network administrator to determine if this is the case, and, if necessary, give the administrator the NIC's MAC address to be entered into a table of acceptable MAC addresses.

USING RESOURCES ON THE NETWORK

Now you have learned how networks are structured, how to install NICs, and how to set up Windows networking. Let's look at how to use resources on a network once it's been set up. This section covers how to share folders, files, applications, and even entire hard drives. In Chapter 21 you will learn how to share printers on a network.

Sharing Files, Folders, and Applications

A+ OS
1.1
4.1

If users on a LAN working on a common project need to share applications and files or need to share printers, then all these users must be assigned to the same workgroup or domain on the LAN. Recall that Windows 9x makes shared resources available by way of Network Neighborhood, and Windows 2000/XP uses My Network Places. Open either icon to see

18

A^+ *OS*
1.1
4.1

the names of all computers on the network. Figure 18-36 shows My Network Places. Drill down to see shared files, folders, and printers in your workgroup. Using Network Neighborhood or My Network Places, you can copy files from one computer to another, use shared applications installed on one computer from another computer, and share printers.

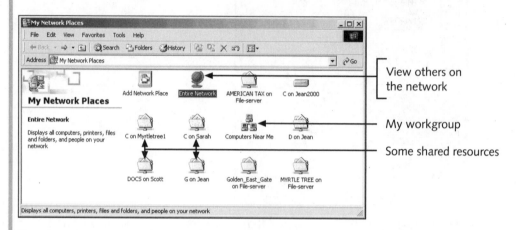

Figure 18-36   View and access shared resources on the network using My Network Places in Windows 2000

Workgroups can be effective when several people work on a common project. For example, if a group of people is building a Web site, sharing resources on the LAN is an effective method of passing Web pages around as they are built. Or one computer on the LAN can be designated as the file server. The user of this computer makes a portion of hard drive space available for the Web site files. All users have access to this one resource, and the Web site files are kept neatly in a single location. When using workgroups, it is the responsibility of each user to protect the resources being shared by using password protection for read and write privileges to files and folders.

To share resources over a peer-to-peer network, you must first install Client for Microsoft Networks and File and Printer Sharing. Client for Microsoft Networks is the Windows component that allows you to use resources on the network made available by other computers, and File and Printer Sharing allows you to share resources on your computer with others in your workgroup. After these components are installed, the last thing to do is to share the folders, files, or printers that you want others to be able to access. All these steps are covered in this section.

A^+ *OS*
4.1

Installing Windows 98 Components Needed to Share Resources

For Windows 98, to install Client for Microsoft Networks and File and Printer Sharing:

1. Use the **Control Panel** to access the **Network** applet. In the Network window, click **Add**. The Select Network Component Type dialog box opens.

2. Select **Client** and click then **Add**. The Select Network Client window opens. See Figure 18-37.

A+ OS
  4.1

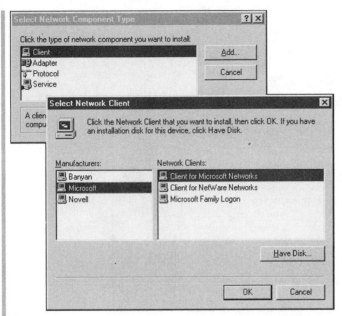

Figure 18-37   In Windows 98, install Client for Microsoft Networks so users on the LAN can connect to other PCs to share files, folders, and printers

3. Select **Microsoft** on the left and **Client for Microsoft Networks** on the right. Click **OK** and, if needed, insert the Windows 98 CD.

4. Install the service for sharing files and printers with others on the Microsoft network. In the Network window, click **Add**. The Select Network Component Type dialog box opens.

5. Click **Service** and then click **Add**. The Select Network Service window opens. See Figure 18-38.

6. Select **File and printer sharing for Microsoft Networks**, and then click **OK**. Insert the Windows 98 CD.

7. Turn on file and printer sharing. Click **File and Print Sharing**. The File and Print Sharing window opens. See Figure 18-39. Check both options to share both files and printers, and then click **OK**.

18

A^{+} *OS*
4.1

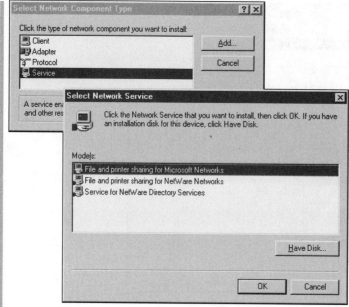

Figure 18-38   Install Windows 98 file and printer sharing for Microsoft Networks to be used to share files and printers on a LAN

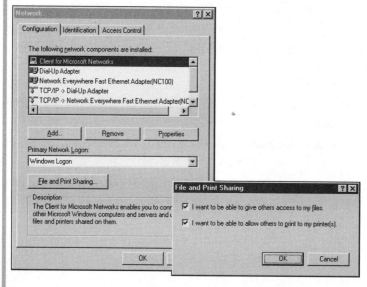

Figure 18-39   Turn on Windows 98 file and printer sharing so others on the LAN can access resources on this PC

A+ OS
4.1

When they are installed, Client for Microsoft Networks and File and Printer Sharing should automatically bind themselves to the TCP/IP protocol. You can verify this by accessing the TCP/IP Properties window and clicking the Bindings tab. Verify that Client for Microsoft Networks and File and Printer Sharing are checked.

Windows 2000/XP Components Needed to Share Resources

Client for Microsoft Networks and File and Printer Sharing are installed by default during a Windows 2000/XP installation. However, if you have a problem sharing resources on a LAN, you can try to uninstall and reinstall them. Both these actions are performed using the Local Area Connection Properties window accessed earlier by way of the Control Panel (see Figure 18-40). Click Install on the General tab. The Select Network Component Type window appears, which is also shown in Figure 18-40. Select Client and then click Add. You will need the Windows 2000 or Windows XP CD or other access to the installation files.

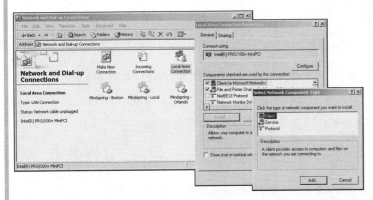

Figure 18-40   Use the Network and the Dial-up Connections applet in Control Panel to install a network protocol using Windows 2000

Sharing Files and Folders with the Workgroup

After the computer is configured for file and printer sharing, using Windows 98 or Windows 2000/XP, follow these example directions to make a folder on drive C named \data available to others on the LAN:

18

1. Using Windows Explorer, select the folder. In this example, we are using **C:\data**. Right-click the folder name. If the system is configured for file and printer sharing, the shortcut menu lists Sharing. For Windows 98 or Windows 2000, select **Sharing**. See Figure 18-41. For Windows XP, select **Sharing and Security**. The data Properties dialog box opens, as shown in Figure 18-42.

2. For Windows 2000 or Windows 98, click the **Shared As** option button, and for Windows XP, check **Share this folder on the network**. Enter a name for the shared folder. In the figure, the name is JEAN'S DATA. This action makes the folder available to others on the network. They can see the folder when they open My Network Places or Network Neighborhood on their desktop.

A+ OS
4.1

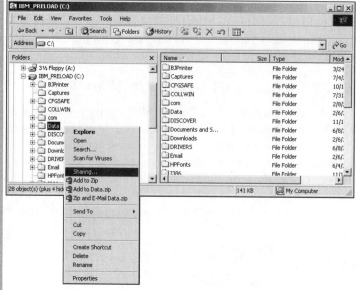

Figure 18-41   In Windows 98, use Windows Explorer to password protect a file or folder shared on a network

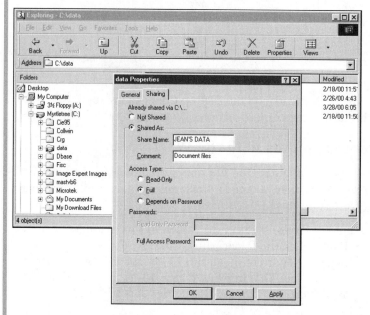

Figure 18-42   Using Windows 98, a user on a network can share a folder with others on the network

A+ OS
4.1

3. For Windows 98 or Windows 2000, in the section labeled Access Type, click the **Depends on Password** option button.

4. To allow others the right to make changes to the folder, enter a password under **Full Access Password**. For read-only access, enter a different password. Click **OK** to exit the window.

5. For added security when using Windows 2000/XP, set up a user account and password for each user who will have access to shared resources. This added security requires that a user give a valid password before accessing shared files, folders, or printers on the Windows 2000/XP PC.

6. For Windows XP, to allow others the right to change your files, check **Allow network users to change my files**.

When using the option Depends on Password, be sure to enter a password in both fields. With this option, if a password field is empty, then no password is required to have that type of access to the folder. Distribute the two passwords to those people who need to access the folder. You control the access rights (permissions) by selecting which password(s) you give.

> **TIP** Applications can also be shared with others in the workgroup. If you share a folder that has a program file in it, a user on another PC can double-click the program file in My Network Places or Network Neighborhood and execute it remotely on their desktop. This is a handy way for several users to share an application that is installed on a single PC.

Network Drive Maps

A **network drive map** is one of the most powerful and versatile methods of communicating over a network. By using network file service (NFS) client/server software, the network drive map makes one PC (the client) appear to have a new hard drive, such as drive E, that is really hard drive space on another host computer (the server). Even if the host computer uses a different OS, such as Unix, the drive map still functions. Using a network drive map, files and folders on a host computer are available even to network-unaware DOS applications. The path to a file simply uses the remote drive letter instead of a local drive such as drive A or drive C. To set up a network drive under Windows 98 or Windows 2000/XP, follow these steps:

1. On the host computer, using directions given earlier in the chapter, share the drive or folder on a drive that you want to allow others to have access to.

2. On the remote computer that will use the network drive, while connected to the network, access **Windows Explorer**. Click the **Tools** menu shown in Figure 18-43. Select **Map Network Drive**.

18

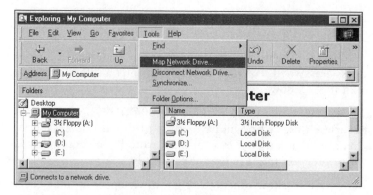

Figure 18-43   Mapping a network drive to a host computer in Windows 98, using Windows Explorer

3. The Map Network Drive dialog box appears, as in Figure 18-44. Select a drive letter from the drop-down list.

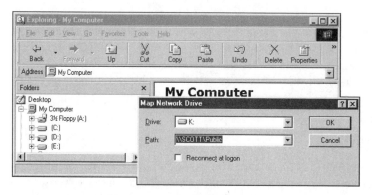

Figure 18-44   To map a network drive in Windows 98, enter a drive letter to use on your PC and the path to the host computer

4. Enter a path to the host computer. Use two backslashes, followed by the name of the host computer, followed by a backslash and the drive or folder to access on the host computer. For example, to access the folder Public on the computer named Scott, enter **\\Scott\Public** and then click **OK**.

5. Figure 18-45 shows the results of the drive mapping. Windows Explorer displays a new drive K. Folders listed on the right side of the figure are on the host PC.

 If a network drive does not work, go to Network Neighborhood or My Network Places, and verify that the network connection is good.

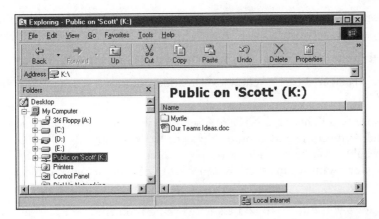

Figure 18-45   Content on the right side of Windows Explorer belongs to the host computer. This computer sees it as belonging to its drive K

Direct Cable Connection

Windows 9x and Windows NT/2000/XP offer a direct cable connection service that allows you to connect two PCs, using either a null modem cable (a cable that connects two PCs using their serial ports) or a parallel cable. Each end of the parallel cable must have a PC connector, not a printer connector. Buy a parallel cable with two DB-25 male/male connections, or buy an adapter for a printer cable. Direct Cable Connection is a handy utility when all you need to do is have two PCs share files or printers and a cable can reach between them, or when you want to allow a guest computer to access shared network resources that a host computer can access.

To set up a direct cable connection, set up both computers to share their resources. In Windows 9x/NT/2000, install the Direct Cable Connection component under Windows (from Control Panel, use the Add/Remove Programs applet). Then run Direct Cable Connection on both computers (click Start, Programs, Accessories, Communications, and Direct Cable Connection). A Direct Cable Connection dialog box appears asking if you want to be the host or guest PC. Make one PC the host and the other the guest. Next, select a port for the connection, either a serial or parallel port. The host computer then waits for the guest computer to initiate communication. Use Windows Explorer on the guest computer to view the shared folders on the host computer. In Windows XP the process is similar, but you use the New Connection Wizard to set up the connection. Click Start, All Programs, Accessories, Communications, and New Connection Wizard. Follow the prompts to Set up an advanced connection, and Connect directly to another computer.

18

TROUBLESHOOTING A NETWORK CONNECTION

A+CORE
2.1
6.2
OS
3.3
4.1

If you have problems connecting to the network, follow the guidelines below. First, here are some symptoms of NIC problems:

- You cannot make a connection to the network.

A+CORE
2.1
6.2
OS
3.3
4.1

- Network Neighborhood or My Network Places does not show any other computers on the network.

- You receive an error message while you are installing the NIC drivers.

- Device Manager shows a yellow exclamation point or a red X beside the name of the NIC.

- There are two lights on a NIC: one stays on steadily to let you know there is a physical connection, and another blinks to let you know there is activity. If you see no lights, you know there is no physical connection between the NIC and the network. This means there is a problem with the network cable, the card, or the hub.

Here are some ways you can try to address networking problems:

- Determine whether other computers on the network are having trouble with their connections. If the entire network is down, the problem is not isolated to the PC and the NIC you are working on.

- Try rebooting the PC to reset the network connections. For a network controlled by a domain server, be sure you log off the current session before you turn off the PC, so that the server will not think you are still logged on and be unable to log you back on until it times out. When you power the PC back up, configure the network protocols.

- Make sure the NIC and its drivers are installed by checking for the NIC in Device Manager. Try uninstalling and reinstalling the NIC drivers.

- For a legacy network card that cannot successfully connect to the network, the problem might be an IRQ conflict. Check Device Manager for conflicts.

- Check the network cable to make sure it is not damaged and that it does not exceed the recommended length for the type of network you are using.

- Connect the network cable to a different port on the hub. If that doesn't help, you may have a problem with the cable or the NIC itself. Uninstall the NIC drivers, replace the NIC, and then install new drivers.

- Check to see whether you have the most current version of your motherboard BIOS. The motherboard manufacturer should have information on whether an upgrade is available.

- When a network drive map is not working, first check Network Neighborhood or My Network Places, and verify that you can access other resources on the remote computer. You might need to log onto the remote computer with a valid user ID and password.

A+CORE
2.1
OS
3.3
4.1

Sometimes you might have trouble with a network connection due to a TCP/IP problem. Windows TCP/IP includes several diagnostic tools useful in troubleshooting problems with TCP/IP. You will learn about several of these in the next chapter. The most useful is **Ping (Packet Internet Groper)**, which tests connectivity and is discussed here. Ping sends a signal to a remote computer. If the remote computer is online and hears the signal, it responds. Ipconfig under Windows NT/2000/XP and Winipcfg under Windows 9x test the TCP/IP configuration. Try these things to test TCP/IP configuration and connectivity:

- For Windows NT/2000/XP, at the command prompt, enter *Ipconfig /all*, or, for Windows 9x, click Start, Run, enter *Winipcfg* in the Run dialog box, and then click OK. If the TCP/IP configuration is correct and an IP address is assigned, the IP address, subnet mask, and default gateway appear along with the adapter address. For dynamic IP addressing, if the PC cannot reach the DHCP server, then it assigns itself an IP address. This is called IP autoconfiguration. The Winipcfg window and the results of the Ipconfig command both show the IP address as the IP Autoconfiguration Address, and the address begins with 169. In this case, suspect that the PC is not able to reach the network or the DHCP server is down. Try to release the current IP address and lease a new address. To do this with Winipcfg, with the network card selected, click the Release button and then click the Renew button. For Ipconfig, first use the *Ipconfig /release* command, and then use the *Ipconfig /renew* command.

- Next, try the loopback address test. At a command prompt, enter the command *Ping 127.0.0.1* (with no period after the final 1). This IP address always refers to your local computer. It should respond with a reply message from your computer. If this works, TCP/IP is likely to be configured correctly. If you get any errors up to this point, then assume that the problem is on your PC. Check the installation and configuration of each component such as the network card and the TCP/IP protocol suite. Remove and reinstall each component, and watch for error messages, writing them down so that you can recognize or research them later as necessary. Compare the configuration to that of a working PC on the same network.

- Next, Ping the IP address of your default gateway. If it does not respond, then the problem may be with the gateway or with the network to the gateway.

- Now try to Ping the host computer you are trying to reach. If it does not respond, then the problem may be with the host computer or with the network to the computer.

- If you have Internet access and substitute a domain name for the IP address in the Ping command, and Ping works, then you can conclude that DNS works. If an IP address works, but the domain name does not work, the problem lies with DNS. Try this command: *ping www.course.com*.

18

CONNECTING NETWORKS

So far you have learned how LANs can be structured and how to set them up, including how to divide large ones into segments using bridges and switches. Other devices and technologies are used to connect networks, allowing them to communicate with each other within a building or over a large geographical area as a **WAN (wide area network)**. This section discusses routers, which are used to connect networks, as well as bandwidth technologies that networks use to communicate with each other.

Routers

Routers (see Figure 18-46) are responsible for data traveling across interconnected networks. A router can route data to the correct network in a way that is similar to a switch's method. However, a router can also forward a message to its correct destination over the most efficient available route, to destinations far removed from the LANs it is connected to. Switches and bridges use MAC addresses to make decisions, but, for TCP/IP, routers use IP addresses to determine the path by which to send a packet.

Figure 18-46 A typical router for a large network

Figure 18-47 shows a simplified view of the way networks work together to send data over the maze of many networks called the Internet. A user in California must pass through many networks to gain access to a server in New York. Each network operates independently of all other networks but can receive a packet from another network and send it on to a third network—while it also manages its own internal traffic. A router is a **stateless** device, meaning that it is unconcerned about the data that it is routing but is concerned about the destination address of that data.

Routers that connect networks belong to more than one network. In Figure 18-47, Network B contains four routers: Routers 1, 2, 3, and 4. But Routers 3 and 4 also belong to Network C. Network C contains Router 8, which also belongs to the same network as the server in New York that the user wants to access.

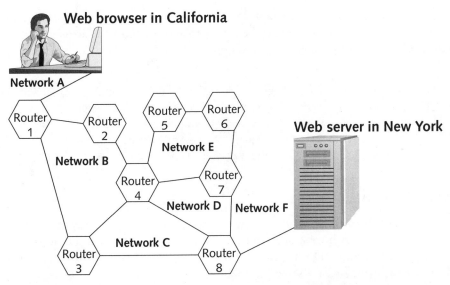

Figure 18-47 The Internet is a web of interconnecting, yet independent, networks

How many paths are there on the Internet by which the user in California can access the server in New York? One path is through Router 1, then 3, then 8, and finally to the server. Data going from the server to the user may travel a different path than data traveling from the user to the server. In fact, if a lot of data is divided into several packets, each packet may take a different route. The packets may not arrive at the user's PC in the same order in which they were sent and may have to be reassembled before they are presented to the application that will use them.

In Figure 18-47, a router that belongs to a network has an IP address for that network. However, if a router belongs to more than one network, it has a unique IP address for each network. Physically, this is accomplished by having one NIC for each network a router belongs to, with each NIC having a unique IP address. Router 4 in the diagram belongs to four networks (B, C, D, and E) and would, therefore, have four network cards and four IP addresses, one for each network.

A router can transmit a data packet to a remote network (a network it is not directly connected to) only if the protocol used to produce the data packet is a **routable protocol**. Recall that Windows supports several networking protocols: TCP/IP, NWLink, IPX/SPX, NetBEUI, and AppleTalk. TCP/IP is routable, as is IPX/SPX. AppleTalk is by the MAC OS. NetBEUI is not routable.

A **brouter** functions as both a bridge and a router. The device can route routable protocols including TCP/IP and IPX/SPX packets, and, in these cases, works as a router. It forwards packets that are not routable, such as NetBEUI packets, to other local networks in the manner that a bridge forwards packets.

Like switches, routers use tables to determine the best route by which to send the data to its destination. When the router receives a packet, it first looks at the packet's destination IP address. When it has the address, the router can use the tables and current network conditions to decide which path would be best for the packet. If there is no good route directly to the destination, the router may forward the packet to another router. When a packet is sent across a network, it may go through several routers.

> A router "learns" about new routes and best routes as it attempts to send packets. You can see the effects of what routers learn when you first attempt to access a new Web site with your browser. If the browser is slow to respond, click Stop and Refresh to cause the browser to resend the request. The new attempt often receives a quicker response because the routers along the way learned about routes that did or did not work.

Bandwidth Technologies

A+CORE
6.2
6.3

When you study the infrastructure of networks and how they connect to each other, much attention is given to how much data can travel over a given communication system in a given amount of time. This measure of data capacity is called **bandwidth** and also called **data throughput** or **line speed**. The greater the bandwidth, the faster the communication. In analog systems, bandwidth is the difference between the highest and lowest frequency that a device can transmit. Frequencies are measured in cycles per second, or hertz (Hz). In digital systems such as computers and computer networks, bandwidth is a measure of data transmission in bits per second (bps), thousands of bits per second (Kbps), or millions of bits per second (Mbps). The Internet depends on technologies that provide varying degrees of bandwidth, each serving a different purpose and following a different set of standards. A list of bandwidth technologies, their speeds, and their uses is shown in Table 18-4. Different bandwidth technologies are used for LANs and larger networks, since the larger the network, the more bandwidth it requires. In this section, you will learn about some common bandwidth technologies.

Table 18-4   Bandwidth technologies

Technology	Maximum Throughput Speeds	Common Uses
GSM mobile telephone service	9.6 to 14.4 Kbps	Wireless technology used for personal and business mobile telephones
Regular telephone (POTS, for Plain Old Telephone Service)	Up to 56 Kbps	Home and small business access to an ISP using a modem
X.25	56 Kbps	Provides communication between mainframes and terminals
ISDN	64 Kbps to 128 Kbps	Small to medium size business access to an ISP
IDSL	128 Kbps	(ISDN Digital Subscriber Line) Home and small business access to an ISP
DSL Lite or G.Lite	Up to 384 Kbps upstream and up to 6 Mbps downstream	Less expensive version of DSL

A+CORE
6.2
6.3

Table 18-4   Bandwidth technologies (continued)

Technology	Maximum Throughput Speeds	Common Uses
ADSL (Asymmetric Digital Subscriber Line)	640 Kbps upstream and up to 6.1 Mbps downstream	Most bandwidth is from ISP to user
SDSL (Symmetric DSL)	1.544 Mbps	Equal bandwidths in both directions
HDSL (High-bit-rate DSL)	Up to 3 Mbps	Equal bandwidths in both directions
Cable modem	512 Kbps to 5 Mbps	Home or small business to ISP
VDSL (Very-high-rate DSL)	Up to 55 Mbps over short distances	Future technology of DSL under development
802.11b wireless	5.5 Mbps or 11 Mbps	Most popular wireless
802.11a wireless	Up to 54 Mbps	Not readily available
Frame Relay	56 Kbps to 45 Mbps	Businesses that need to communicate internationally or across the country
Fractional T1	n times 64 Kbps (where n = number of channels or portions of a T1 leased)	Companies expecting to grow into a T1 line, but not yet ready for a T1
T1	1.544 Mbps	To connect large companies to branch offices or an ISP
Token Ring	4 or 16 Mbps	Used for local network
Ethernet	10 or 100 Mbps	Most popular technology for a local network
T3	45 Mbps	Large companies that require a lot of bandwidth and transmit extensive amounts of data
OC-1	52 Mbps	ISP to regional ISP
FDDI	100 Mbps	Supports network backbones from the1980s and early 1990s; also used to connect LANs across multiple buildings
ATM	25, 45, 155, or 622 Mbps	Large business networks and LAN backbones
OC-3	155 Mbps	Internet or large corporation backbone
Gigabit Ethernet	1 Gbps	Not readily available
OC-24	1.23 Gbps	Internet backbone, uses optical fiber
OC-256	13 Gbps	Major Internet backbone, uses optical fiber
SONET (Synchronous Optical Network)	51, 155 , 622, 1244, or 2480 Mbps	Major backbones

18

A+CORE
6.2
6.3

Here is a summary of some of the more common bandwidth technologies:

- *Regular telephone lines.* Regular telephone lines, the most common way to connect to an ISP, require an internal or external modem. As you learned in Chapter 17, a modem converts a PC's digital data (data made up of zeros and ones) to analog data (continuous variations of frequencies) that can be communicated over telephone lines.

- *Cable modem.* **Cable modem** communication uses cable lines that already exist in millions of households. Just as with cable TV, cable modems are always connected (always up). Cable modem is an example of broadband media. **Broadband** refers to any type of networking medium that carries more than one type of transmission. With a cable modem, the TV signal to your television and the data signals to your PC share the same cable. Just like a regular modem, a cable modem converts a PC's digital signals to analog when sending them and converts incoming analog data to digital.

- *ISDN.* **ISDN (Integrated Services Digital Network)** is a technology developed in the 1980s that uses regular phone lines, and is accessed by a dial-up connection. ISDN is actually an early implementation of DSL. For home use, an ISDN line is fully digital and consists of two channels, or phone circuits, on a single pair of wires, called B channels, and a slower channel used for control signals, called a D channel. Each B channel can support speeds up to 64,000 bps. The two lines can be combined so that, effectively, data travels at 128,000 bps, about three to five times the speed of regular phone lines.

- *DSL.* **DSL (Digital Subscriber Line)** is a broadband technology that uses ordinary copper phone lines and uses a range of frequencies on the copper wire that are not used by voice, thus making it possible for you to use the same phone line for voice and DSL at the same time. The voice portion of the phone line requires a dial-up as normal, but the DSL part of the line is always connected.

- *Satellite access.* People who live in remote areas and want high-speed Internet connections often are limited in their choices. DSL and cable modems may not work where they live, but satellite access is available from pretty much anywhere. Technology is even being developed to use satellites to offer Internet access on commercial airlines. Customers can use their own laptops to connect to the Internet through a connection at their seats to a satellite dish in the airplane. A satellite dish mounted on top of your house or office building communicates with a satellite used for communication by an ISP offering the satellite service.

- *Wireless access.* Wireless refers to several technologies and systems that don't use cables for communication, including public radio, cellular phones, one-way paging, satellite, infrared, and private, proprietary radio. Because of its expense and the concern that increasing use of wireless might affect our health, as well as airplane control systems, pacemakers, and other sensitive electronic devices, wireless is not as popular as wired data transmission. Wireless is an important technology for mobile devices and for Internet access in remote locations where other methods are not an option.

CHAPTER SUMMARY

❑ The most popular physical network architectures for LANs are Ethernet, token ring, FDDI, and wireless LAN.

❑ Ethernet uses a logical bus and can be configured as a star topology, in which all nodes connect to a centralized hub, or a bus topology, which connects nodes in a line and has no central connection point. An Ethernet hub broadcasts all data that flows through it on to every node connected to it. It does not make decisions about where to send packets.

❑ Token ring networks are physically configured in a star topology but are logically rings because of how data packets travel on them. A data packet is preceded by a token, which travels in one direction around the ring, up and down the connection from the PC to the hub.

❑ A FDDI network uses tokens and is structured as a ring but does not require a centralized hub as a token ring network does. It is faster than token ring.

❑ Wireless LANs make connections using radio or infrared technology. A wireless LAN can be used in combination with a wired LAN.

❑ A PC connects to a network using a NIC (network interface card), which communicates with NICs on other PCs using a set of hardware protocols (such as Ethernet or token ring). The OSs on the two computers use a different set of protocols (such as NetBEUI or TCP/IP) to communicate.

❑ NICs and the device drivers that control them are designed to work with a particular network architecture and are the only PC components that are aware of the type of physical network being used. A NIC can be designed to use more than one type of cabling.

❑ A NIC is identified by a MAC address, a physical address unique to the device that is assigned at the factory and generally does not change.

❑ Bridges and switches are used to segment large networks, decreasing the overall amount of traffic on the network and making it easier to manage.

❑ A bridge that connects several network segments only decides whether a packet is destined for a computer on its own segment and, if it is not, sends the packet to all other network segments. A switch sends a packet only to the network segment for which it is destined. Both keep source and destination MAC addresses in routing tables and learn new addresses as packets are sent.

❑ Network protocols break data into packets small enough for the network on which they will be traveling. Before they are transmitted on the network, headers and trailers that tell where data came from and where it is going are added to the packets.

❑ The three protocols that Windows supports for network communication are TCP/IP (the protocol suite for the Internet), IPX/SPX (designed for use with Novell NetWare), and NetBEUI (a proprietary Windows protocol for use on networks isolated from the Internet). Only TCP/IP is supported on the Internet.

18

❑ When a protocol is installed on a computer, it automatically binds itself to any NICs it finds. More than one protocol can be associated with a single NIC.

❑ The four types of addresses on a Windows network are MAC addresses, IP addresses, character-based names (such as NetBIOS names, host names, domain names), and port addresses.

❑ MAC addresses are used only for communication within a network.

❑ IP addresses identify devices on the Internet and other TCP/IP networks. They consist of four numbers separated by periods. The first part of an IP address identifies the network, and the last identifies the host. The class of an IP address determines how much of the address is used as the network identifier and how much is used for the host identifier.

❑ IP addresses can either be public or private. For private IP addresses to be able to access the Internet, they must go through NAT (network address translation) so that their requests all appear to be coming from a single public IP address for that network.

❑ Character-based names, such as fully qualified domain names, are used as an easy way to remember IP addresses.

❑ The IP address associated with a host name can change. DNS (Domain Name Service) and WINS (Windows Internet Naming Service) track the relationship between host names and IP addresses. DNS is more popular because it works on all platforms.

❑ Windows 98 assumes that a computer name is a NetBIOS name, which can have up to 15 characters. Windows 2000 and Windows XP assume that a computer name is a host name, which follows the TCP/IP convention and can have up to 63 characters.

❑ Applications that use TCP/IP for network communication use WinSock to make API calls to the OS.

❑ When installing a NIC, physically install the card, install the device drivers, install the networking protocol you intend to use, configure the protocol, and give the computer a name.

❑ NetBEUI is a fast network protocol that can be used on an isolated network. For Internet access, use TCP/IP. TCP/IP requires that the PC be assigned an IP address.

❑ When configuring TCP/IP, you must know if IP addresses are statically or dynamically assigned.

❑ Two files on a PC track IP addresses and related NetBIOS or host names. LMHosts tracks NetBIOS names on a NetBEUI network, and Hosts tracks host names on a TCP/IP network.

❑ Before users on a network can view or access resources on a PC, Client for Microsoft Networks and File and Printer Sharing for Microsoft Networks must be installed, and the resources must be shared.

❑ Network drive mapping makes one PC appear to have a new hard drive when that hard drive space is actually on another host computer. Use Windows Explorer to map a network drive.

◻ Direct cable connection between two PCs using either a null modem cable or a parallel cable allows two PCs to share files or printers.

◻ When troubleshooting a NIC on a PC, check connections in the rest of the network, cabling and ports for the PC, the NIC itself (substituting one known to be working), BIOS, and device drivers.

◻ Ping is a useful TCP/IP utility to check network connectivity.

◻ Two other useful troubleshooting tools are Ipconfig (Windows NT, Windows 2000, and Windows XP) and Winipcfg (Windows 9x), which test TCP/IP configuration.

◻ Routers are used to connect networks. If a router belongs to more than one TCP/IP network, it has a unique IP address for each network and routes packets according to IP addresses.

◻ Routers are more efficient than switches in choosing routes for packets over long distances.

◻ TCP/IP and IPX/SPX are routable networking protocols. NetBEUI, a Microsoft proprietary protocol, is not.

◻ Bandwidth measures how much data can travel over a given communication system in a given amount of time. Common bandwidth technologies include regular telephone lines, cable modem, ISDN, DSL, satellite access, and wireless access.

KEY TERMS

10Base2
10Base5
10BaseT
100BaseT
802.11b
access point (AP)
adapter address
AirPort
amplifier repeater
attenuation
bandwidth
binding
Bluetooth
BNC connector
bridge
broadband
broadcast
brouter

bus topology
cable modem
coaxial cable
combo card
computer name
Controlled-Access Unit (CAU)
CRC (cyclical redundancy check)
crossover cable
data throughput
datagram
default gateway
DHCP (Dynamic Host Configuration Protocol)
DNS (Domain Name System, also called Domain Name Service)

DNS server
domain name
DSL (Digital Subscriber Line)
dynamic IP address
Ethernet
Fast Ethernet
Fiber Distributed Data Interface (FDDI)
frame
fully qualified domain name (FQDN)
gateway
Gigabit Ethernet
hardware address
host
host name
Hosts

18

hub
Institute of Electrical and Electronics Engineers (IEEE)
Internet Service Provider (ISP)
intranet
IP address
IPX/SPX (Internetwork Packet Exchange/ Sequenced Packet Exchange)
ISDN (Integrated Services Digital Network)
LAN (local area network)
line speed
LMHosts
MAC (Media Access Control) address
multicasting
Multistation Access Unit (MSAU or MAU)
name resolution
NAT (Network Address Translation)
NetBEUI (NetBIOS Extended User Interface)

NetBIOS (Network Basic Input/Output System)
network adapter
network drive map
network interface card (NIC)
network operating system (NOS)
network printer
node
octet
packet
patch cable
physical address
Ping (Packet Internet Groper)
private IP address
proxy server
public IP address
repeater
ring topology
RJ-45 connector
routable protocol
router
shielded twisted-pair (STP) cable
signal-regenerating repeater

Smart Multistation Access Unit (SMAU)
star bus topology
star ring topology
star topology
stateless
static IP address
subnet mask
switch
TCP/IP (Transmission Control Protocol/ Internet Protocol)
ThickNet
ThinNet
token ring
transceiver
unshielded twisted-pair (UTP) cable
WAN (wide area network)
Wi-Fi
WINS (Windows Internet Naming Service)
WinSock (Windows Sockets)
wireless LAN (WLAN)

Review Questions

1. The connecting of devices to provide a way for workstations, servers, printers, and other devices to communicate and share resources is the definition of a:

   a. Packet

   b. LAN

   c. Topology

   d. Hub

   e. Repeater

2. A PC makes a direct connection to a network by way of a(n) _____.

   a. NIC

   b. Repeater

   c. Hub

   d. Switch

   e. Gateway

3. Which of the following represents the media to allow devices to interconnect on a network that is characterized by two wires covered by a metallic mesh to protect the wires from interference?

   a. Coaxial cable

   b. UTP

   c. STP

   d. Fiber-optic cable

   e. All of the above

4. The maximum cable length for the cable system ThinNet is:

   a. 100 meters

   b. 200 meters

   c. 500 meters

   d. 2,000 meters

   e. 607 feet

5. The maximum cable length for the cable system ThickNet is:

   a. 100 meters

   b. 200 meters

   c. 500 meters

   d. 2,000 meters

   e. 607 feet

6. The maximum cable length for the cable system 10BaseT is:

   a. 100 meters

   b. 200 meters

   c. 500 meters

   d. 2,000 meters

   e. 607 feet

18

7. The maximum cable length for the cable system 100BaseFX is:

   a. 100 meters

   b. 200 meters

   c. 500 meters

   d. 2,000 meters

   e. 607 feet

8. Which of the following bus topologies is characterized by systems connecting to a line with no central connection point?

   a. Bus topology

   b. Star bus topology

   c. Star topology

   d. Token ring

   e. None of the above

9. Which of the following bus topologies is characterized by using a logical bus for data delivery with a centralized connection point?

   a. Bus topology

   b. Star bus topology

   c. Star topology

   d. Token ring

   e. None of the above

10. Which of the following bus topologies is characterized by systems connecting to a line with no central connection point for data delivery but also utilizes a configuration that has one or more centralized connection points?

    a. Bus topology

    b. Star bus topology

    c. Star topology

    d. Token ring

    e. None of the above

11. Which of the following bus topologies is characterized by the use of controlled access units, multistation access units, and smart multistation access units?

    a. Bus topology

    b. Star bus topology

    c. Star topology

    d. Token ring

    e. None of the above

12. Which of the following broadcast network devices allows signals to pass through and acts as a distribution point for every device connected to it?

   a. Hub

   b. Switch

   c. Repeater

   d. Bridge

   e. Wireless access point

13. Which of the following broadcast network devices restores the clarity of the signal that is passed through it as a result of signal attenuation?

   a. Hub

   b. Switch

   c. Repeater

   d. Bridge

   e. Wireless access point

14. Which of the following broadcast network devices allows the network to be segmented through use of a routing table and uses network broadcast?

   a. Hub

   b. Switch

   c. Repeater

   d. Bridge

   e. Wireless access point

15. Which of the following broadcast network devices allows the network to be segmented through use of a routing table and does *not* use network broadcast?

   a. Hub

   b. Switch

   c. Repeater

   d. Bridge

   e. Wireless access point

16. Wireless networks make use of a(n) _____ in order for wireless devices to communicate directly with an existing LAN.

   a. Hub

   b. Switch

   c. Repeater

   d. Bridge

   e. Wireless access point

18

17. All of IEEE Communications Standards for wireless communications (802.x) are compatible.

   a. True

   b. False

18. IEEE 802.11b is based on the frequency spectrum of _____ with a distance range of 100 meters.

   a. 49 MHz

   b. 900 MHz

   c. 2400 MHz

   d. 5000 MHz

   e. None of the above

19. IEEE 802.11a is based on the frequency spectrum of _____ with a distance range of 100 meters.

   a. 49 MHz

   b. 900 MHz

   c. 2400 MHz

   d. 5000 MHz

   e. None of the above

20. A technical consultant meets with a new client who expresses a need to have a wireless network installed. The consultant concludes that high data throughput over the wireless network is crucial. Which IEEE standard should the consultant implement as part of the solution for this customer?

   a. IEEE 802.11a

   b. IEEE 802.11b

   c. IEEE 802.11s

   d. IEEE 1394

   e. None of the above

21. The MAC address refers to:

   a. The identification of the system computer at the source of communications

   b. The identification of the system computer at the destination of communications

   c. The identification of the network interface card used on a particular system computer

   d. The identification of the Microcomputer Advanced Computer value used to determine maximum data throughput

   e. None of the above

22. In the case of Ethernet, the MAC address is _____ in size.

   a. 2 bytes

   b. 4 bytes

   c. 6 bytes

   d. 8 bytes

   e. None of the above

23. Which of the following use MAC addresses in order to determine where to send packages of data?

   a. Bridges

   b. Switches

   c. Both a and b

   d. Neither a nor b

24. Of the following protocols, which is considered the protocol used on the Internet?

   a. TCP/IP

   b. IPX/SPX

   c. NetBEUI

   d. MAC address

   e. None of the above

25. Of the following protocols, which is considered to be the protocol of choice if the network is isolated from the Internet?

   a. TCP/IP

   b. IPX/SPX

   c. NetBEUI

   d. MAC address

   e. None of the above

26. The term "binding" refers to an association between a particular protocol, such as IPX/SPX, and NIC hardware.

   a. True

   b. False

27. The IP portion of a TCP/IP address is _____ bytes in length.

   a. 2

   b. 4

   c. 6

   d. 8

   e. 256

18

28. A single octet refers to _____ bit(s).

    a. 1

    b. 8

    c. 16

    d. 24

    e. 32

29. The number of octets that make up the host portion of a Class B IP address is:

    a. 1

    b. 2

    c. 3

    d. 4

    e. 8

30. _____ IP addresses refer to those addresses used on special intranets that are isolated from the Internet.

    a. Public IP addresses

    b. Private IP addresses

    c. Reserved IP addresses

    d. All of the above

    e. None of the above

31. Dynamic IP addresses are assigned for the current connect session only; when the session is over, the address is returned to the list of available addresses.

    a. True

    b. False

32. The type of IP addressing scheme that is employed by ISPs is _____ IP addressing.

    a. Static

    b. Dynamic

    c. Both a and b

    d. Neither a nor b

33. The type of server configuration that manages dynamically assigned IP addresses is called a _____ server.

    a. IP

    b. TCP/IP

    c. DHCP

    d. Proxy

    e. Print

34. When installing and configuring a wireless network, the installer must choose between two specific configurations: infrastructure and ad hoc mode. If the installer decides that computers on the network need to communicate with each other by way of an access point, the network should be configured as:

    a. Infrastructure mode

    b. Ad hoc mode

    c. Either a or b

    d. Neither a nor b

35. If the installer decides that one wireless device must communicate directly with another wireless device, the network should be configured as:

    a. Infrastructure mode

    b. Ad hoc mode

    c. Either a or b

    d. Neither a nor b

36. What type of network devices would be used in an environment that consists of several network segments with differing protocols and architectures and also determines the best path for sending data and filtering broadcast traffic to the local segment?

    a. NIC

    b. Bridge

    c. Switch

    d. Router

    e. Gateway

37. Of the various channel technologies that exist, what kind of bandwidth can be expected from a T1 channel?

    a. 56,000 bps

    b. 1.544 Mbps

    c. 45 Mbps

    d. 155 Mbps

    e. None of the above

18

PCs ON THE INTERNET

In this chapter, you will learn:

♦ About the TCP/IP suite of protocols

♦ How to connect to the Internet using dial-up, DSL, and cable modem connections

♦ About supporting common Internet clients such as Web browsers, e-mail clients, and file transfer software

In earlier chapters, you learned how different versions of Windows work on a single PC. In Chapter 18, you learned about connecting PCs to a network. This chapter takes the next logical step in effectively using PCs by discussing connections to the Internet using Windows. You will learn how the TCP/IP suite of protocols is used, how to create and troubleshoot dial-up and broadband connections to the Internet, and how to support popular applications that use the Internet, such as Web browsers, e-mail clients, and FTP software.

THE TCP/IP SUITE OF PROTOCOLS

In Chapter 18, you learned how the operating system uses TCP/IP to make resources on a network available to the user and how to install and configure the hardware and software necessary to do this. This chapter focuses on the applications on a desktop computer that use TCP/IP to access resources on a local network and on the Internet.

Most applications that use the Internet are **client/server applications**, which means the application has two components. The application (client) software makes a request for data from server software running on another computer. The DHCP software introduced in Chapter 18 is an example of client/server software. A DHCP client on one PC requests an IP address from a DHCP server on another computer. The World Wide Web itself is probably the most popular client/server application: the client is a Web browser, and the server is a Web host. The requested data is called a Web page, which can have graphics, sound, and video embedded as part of the requested data (see Figure 19-1).

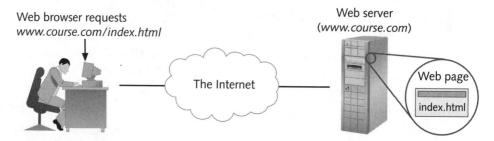

Web browser requests
www.course.com/index.html

Web server
(www.course.com)

The Internet

Web page

index.html

Figure 19-1   A Web browser (client software) requests a Web page from a Web server (server software); the Web server returns the requested file or files to the client

A PC support technician must know how to connect PCs to the Internet and support common client/server applications used on the Internet. Before we turn our attention to these applications, in this section, you learn more about how the protocols in the TCP/IP suite are used on intranets and the Internet to support these applications. First we look at how a client addresses a server application on another computer.

Using IP and Port Addresses to Identify Services

A server on the Internet or an intranet might be running a Web server application, an e-mail server application, and an FTP server application, all at the same time. (**FTP**, the **File Transfer Protocol**, is a quick and easy way to move files over a TCP/IP network.) Each service is an executable program running under the OS on that server. For example, one Web server is Apache HTTP Server by the Apache Software Foundation *(www.apache.org)*, and an e-mail server is Ntmail by Gordano LTD *(www.ntmail.co.uk)*. The Apache and Ntmail programs can both be running as background servers on a computer. How does a Web browser on a client PC say, "I want to speak with the Web server" and

A+ OS
4.2

an e-mail program say, "I want to speak with the e-mail server," if both programs are running on the same computer using the same IP address? The answer is by using an identifying number, called a **port**, **port address**, or **port number**, that has been assigned to each service when it is started. (Don't confuse these port addresses with I/O addresses assigned to hardware devices, which were discussed in previous chapters.)

Each service "listens" at its assigned port. A network administrator can assign any port number to a server, but there are established port numbers for common services and protocols. A Web server is normally assigned port 80, and an e-mail server receiving mail is normally assigned port 25, as shown in Figure 19-2. Port assignments are shown at the end of an IP address, following a colon. Using these default port assignments, the Web server would communicate at 138.60.30.5:80, and the e-mail server would communicate at 138.60.30.5:25. Another example of a port number assigned to a common service is the use of port 119 for **NNTP (Network News Transfer Protocol)**, the protocol used for newsgroups.

Figure 19-2   Each server running on a computer is addressed by a unique port number

19

Unless the administrator has a good reason to do otherwise, he or she uses the common port assignments listed in Table 19-1. (One reason not to use the default port assignments is concern about security. Some malicious software targets systems using default port assignments.) If a Web server is assigned a different port number, it can be accessed by entering the IP address of the server in the address box of the Web browser, followed by a colon and the port number of the Web server, like this: 138.60.30.5:8080.

A+ OS
  4.2

Table 19-1   Common TCP/IP port assignments for well-known services

Port	Protocol	Service	Description
20	FTP	FTP	File transfer data
21	FTP	FTP	File transfer control information
23	Telnet	Telnet	Telnet, an application used by Unix computers to control a computer remotely
25	SMTP	E-mail	Simple Mail Transfer Protocol; used by client to send e-mail
80	HTTP or HTTPS	Web browser	World Wide Web protocol
109	POP2	E-mail	Post Office Protocol, version 2; used by client to receive e-mail
110	POP3	E-mail	Post Office Protocol, version 3; used by client to receive e-mail
119	NNTP	News server	News servers
143	IMAP	E-mail	Internet Message Access Protocol, a newer protocol used by clients to receive e-mail

The Web browser initiates a request using an IP address and port number but is unaware of all that happens in order for the request to reach the Web server. Also notice in Table 19-1 that each service has one or more designated protocols. These protocols are the rules of communication between the client and server components of the applications. We now have yet another layer of communication protocols used in networking. Recall from the last chapter that at the lowest networking level, the network or hardware protocol controls communication among physical networking devices such as Ethernet NICs and hubs. The next layer up is the OS protocol used on the network, such as TCP/IP, AppleTalk, or NetBEUI. Now, on top of the hardware and OS protocols, we add a third level of protocols that control how applications such as those listed in Table 19-1 communicate using the network. These applications protocols are all supported by TCP/IP and are discussed in the next section, together with other protocols that are part of the TCP/IP suite. Figure 19-3 shows all these different layers of protocols and how they relate to one another. Note in the figure that each protocol can be classified as a TCP/IP protocol including the OS and applications protocols, or it is classified as a network (hardware) protocol used by networking hardware such as a phone line, NIC, or hub. As you read this section, this figure can serve as your roadmap to the different protocols.

TCP/IP Protocol Layers

A+ OS
  4.2

Within the TCP/IP suite, several protocols operate and the more significant ones are introduced in this section, from the top layer down. However, you should know that the TCP/IP protocol suite includes more protocols than just these.

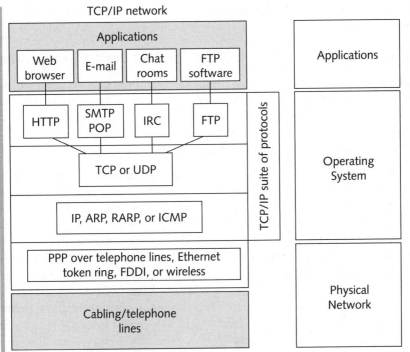

Figure 19-3 How software, protocols, and technology on a TCP/IP network relate to each other

Applications Protocols

Four of the most common applications that use the Internet are Web browsers, e-mail, chat rooms, and FTP. When one of these applications wants to send data to a counterpart application on another host, it makes an API call to the operating system, which handles the request. (An API call is a common way for an application to ask an operating system to do something.) The API call causes the OS to generate a request. For Web browsers, the request will be an HTTP request. **HTTP (Hypertext Transfer Protocol)** is the protocol used for the World Wide Web and used by Web browsers and Web servers to communicate. In other words, HTTP formats the request, and encrypts and compresses it as necessary. It adds an HTTP header to the beginning of the data that includes the HTTP version being used and how the data is compressed and encrypted, if that was done. Later, when the response is received from the server, it decrypts and decompresses it as necessary before passing it on to the browser.

Once the response is passed to the browser, a session is established. **Sessions** (established communication links between two software programs), sometimes called **sockets**, are managed by the browser and Web server using HTTP. However, TCP/IP at the OS level can also create a limited type of session.

19

$A+$ OS
4.2

Later in the chapter, you will learn more about Web and e-mail protocols and how they work.

TCP/IP Protocols Used by the OS for Network Communication

Looking back at Figure 19-3, you can see three layers of protocols between the applications protocols and the physical network protocols. These three layers make up the heart of TCP/IP communication. In the figure, TCP or UDP manages communication with the applications protocols above them as well as the protocols shown underneath TCP and UDP, which control communication on the network.

Remember from the last chapter that all communication on a network happens by way of packets delivered from one location on the network to another. When a Web browser makes a request for data from a Web server, a packet is created and an attempt is made to deliver that packet to the server. In TCP/IP, the protocol that guarantees packet delivery is **TCP (Transmission Control Protocol)**. TCP makes a connection, checks whether the data is received, and resends it if it is not. TCP is therefore called a **connection-oriented protocol**. TCP is used by applications such as Web browsers and e-mail. **UDP (User Datagram Protocol)** does not guarantee delivery (does not first connect and check whether data is received), thus UDP is called a **connectionless protocol** or a **best-effort protocol**. Guaranteed delivery takes longer and is used when it is important that data reach its destination accurately. UDP is primarily used for broadcasting and other types of transmissions, such as streaming video or sound over the Web, where guaranteed delivery is not as important as fast transmission.

Moving down the protocol layers, TCP and UDP pass a request to **IP (Internet Protocol)**, which is responsible for breaking up and reassembling data into packets and routing them to their destination (see Figure 19-4).

Up to this point, the data with its header information is one long stream of bytes, sometimes too much data for transmission over a network. IP looks at the size of the data and breaks it into individual packets, which can be up to 4K in size. IP adds its own IP header, which includes the IP address of its host (source IP address) and that of the server (destination IP address), and then passes the packet off to the hardware.

If TCP is used to guarantee delivery, TCP uses IP to establish a session between client and server in order to verify communication has taken place. When a TCP packet reaches its destination, an acknowledgment is sent back to the source (see Figure 19-5). If the source TCP does not receive the acknowledgment, it resends the data or passes an error message back to the higher-level application protocol.

Figure 19-4 TCP turns to IP to prepare the data for networking

Figure 19-5   TCP guarantees delivery by requesting an acknowledgment

19

Other protocols that operate in this part of the transmission process include the following:

- **ARP (Address Resolution Protocol)** is responsible for locating a host on a local network.

- **RARP (Reverse Address Resolution Protocol)** is responsible for discovering the Internet address of a host on a local network.

$A^+_{4.2}$ *OS*

- **ICMP (Internet Control Message Protocol)** is responsible for communicating problems with transmission. For example, if a packet exceeds the number of routers it can pass through on its way to its destination (called a **time to live (TTL)** or a **hop count**), a router kills the packet and returns an ICMP message to the source, saying that the packet has been killed.

Network Protocols Used by Hardware

As you learned in earlier chapters, network protocols used by PC hardware to communicate on a network are included in the firmware and drivers on a single NIC or, for phone-line connections, by a modem and its drivers. The protocol used depends on the type of physical network that the data is traveling on. For example, for a regular phone line, the most popular protocol today is **PPP (Point-to-Point Protocol)** and the device managing that protocol is a modem. PPP is sometimes called a **line protocol** or, less commonly, a **bridging protocol**. You will learn more about PPP later in the chapter. An earlier version of a line protocol is **Serial Line Internet Protocol (SLIP)**, which does not support encrypted passwords and is seldom used today. As you learned in the last chapter, Ethernet is the most popular network technology used for LANs, and its network or hardware protocol is Ethernet.

TCP/IP Utilities

$A^+_{4.1}$ *OS*

When TCP/IP is installed as a Windows 9x or Windows NT/2000/XP component, a group of utility tools are also installed that can be used to troubleshoot problems with TCP/IP. The most commonly used TCP/IP utilities are Ping, Winipcfg, and Ipconfig, which you learned about in the last chapter. Table 19-2 lists these and other TCP/IP utilities and gives a purpose for each. The program files are found in the \Windows or \Winnt folder.

Table 19-2 Utilities installed with TCP/IP on Windows

Command	Description
ARP (Arp.exe)	Manages the IP-to-Ethernet address translation tables used to find the MAC address of a host on the network when the IP address is known
Getmac (Getmac.exe)	Windows utility (new in Windows XP) that displays the NIC's MAC address
Ipconfig (Ipconfig.exe)	Displays the IP address of the host and other configuration information (A command similar to Ipconfig used by Unix is config.) Some parameters are: Ipconfig /all Displays all information about the connection Ipconfig /release Releases the current IP address Ipconfig /renew Requests a new IP address Ipconfig /? Displays information about Ipconfig
FTP (Ftp.exe)	Transfers files over a network

A+ OS
4.1

Table 19-2 Utilities installed with TCP/IP on Windows (continued)

Command	Description
Nbtstat (Nbtstat.exe)	Displays current information about TCP/IP and NetBEUI when both are being used on the same network
Netstat (Netstat.exe)	Displays information about current TCP/IP connections
Ping (Ping.exe)	Verifies that there is a connection on a network between two hosts
Route (Route.exe)	Allows you to manually control network routing tables
Telnet (Telnet.exe)	Allows you to communicate with another computer on the network remotely, entering commands to control the remote computer
Tracert (Tracert.exe)	Traces and displays the route taken from the host to a remote destination; Tracert is one example of a trace routing utility
Winipcfg (Winipcfg.exe)	Displays IP address and other configuration information in a user-friendly window (not available under Windows NT/2000/XP) On the Winipcfg window, use Release and Renew to cause the system to release the current IP address and request a new one, which can sometimes solve TCP/IP connectivity problems when using a DHCP server

Microsoft SNMP Agent

In addition to the utilities that are automatically installed with TCP/IP, another useful utility is Microsoft SNMP Agent. This utility can be installed after you install TCP/IP, and you can find it on the Windows setup CD. **SNMP (Simple Network Management Protocol)** provides system management tools for networks. A system administrator can monitor remote connections to computers running Windows clients with SNMP Agent. The administrator will most likely use the utility sparingly because it can be a security risk. For more information about SNMP, see RFC 1156 (*www.rfc-editor.org*).

Using NSLookup

An interesting tool that lets you read information from the Internet name space is NSLookup, which requests information about domain name resolutions from the DNS server's zone data. Zone data is information about domain names and their corresponding IP addresses kept by a DNS server. The NSLookup utility program is included in Windows 2000/XP. For example, using Windows 2000, to retrieve what the DNS server knows about the domain name *www.microsoft.com*, follow these directions:

1. Open a command window: Click **Start**, **Programs**, **Accessories**, **Command Prompt**. A command window appears.

2. Enter the command: **Nslookup www.microsoft.com**. Figure 19-6 shows the results. Notice in the figure that the DNS server knows about three IP addresses assigned to *www.microsoft.com*. It also reports that this information is nonauthoritative, meaning that it is not the authoritative, or final, name server for the *www.microsoft.com* computer name.

19

A+ OS
4.1

```
Command Prompt                                                          _ | □ | X
Microsoft Windows 2000 [Version 5.00.2195]
(C) Copyright 1985-1999 Microsoft Corp.

C:\>nslookup www.microsoft.com
Server:  linux4.prestige.net
Address:  208.220.88.13

Non-authoritative answer:
Name:     www.microsoft.akadns.net
Addresses:  207.46.197.102, 207.46.197.100, 207.46.230.218
Aliases:  www.microsoft.com


C:\>
```

Figure 19-6   The NSlookup command reports information about the Internet name space

CONNECTING TO THE INTERNET

A+CORE
1.8
6.3
OS
4.2

This section covers three ways to connect to the Internet: via a standard dial-up connection, DSL, and cable modem. You will learn how each type of connection is made as well as some advantages and disadvantages of each.

Dial-up Networking

A+CORE
1.8
6.3
OS
4.2

To connect to the Internet over a phone line using a dial-up connection, you need to have a modem installed on your PC, as well as drivers to control the modem. In Chapter 17 you learned how to install and use a modem. In the last chapter, you learned how to install TCP/IP and bind it to your NIC; the same procedure is used for binding TCP/IP to a modem. This section assumes that TCP/IP is installed and bound to the modem. It covers how to connect to the Internet, beginning with how to install and configure the Dial-up Networking feature in Windows and continuing with how to create and test the connection to your Internet service provider (ISP).

When a Windows PC connects to a network using a modem and regular phone line, the process is called **dial-up networking**. In effect, the modem on the PC acts like a network card, providing the physical connection to the network and the firmware at the lowest level of communication. After the dial-up connection is made, the PC's application software relates to the network as though it were directly connected to the network using a network card, but a network card is not needed. The modems and phone lines in between are transparent to the user, although transmission speeds with direct network connections are much faster than those of dial-up connections.

This section covers how to use dial-up networking utilities in Windows 9x and Windows 2000/XP. Note that in Windows 9x, Dial-up Networking and Network Connections are two different applets located under My Computer. In Windows 2000,

A^+CORE
1.8
6.3
OS
4.2

a single applet in the Control Panel called Network and Dial-up Connections combines both functions, and in Windows XP, this single Control Panel applet is called Network Connections.

How Dial-up Networking Works

Dial-up networking works by using PPP to send packets of data over phone lines. The network protocol (TCP/IP, NetBEUI, or IPX/SPX) packages the data, making it ready for network traffic, and then PPP adds its own header and trailer to these packets. Figure 19-7a shows how this works. The data is presented to the network protocol, which adds its header information. Then the packet is presented to the line protocol, PPP, which adds its own header and trailer to the packet and presents it to the modem for delivery over phone lines to a modem on the receiving end.

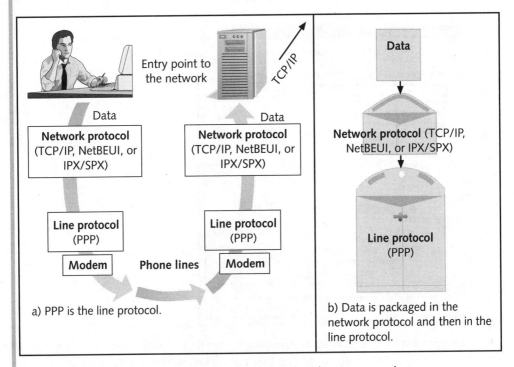

a) PPP is the line protocol.

b) Data is packaged in the network protocol and then in the line protocol.

Figure 19-7   PPP allows a PC to connect to a network using a modem

19

The modem on the receiving end is connected to a PC or server. The receiving computer strips off the PPP header and trailer information and sends the packet on to the network still packaged in the TCP/IP protocols, or whatever protocols the network is using. In Figure 19-7b, you can see how these two protocols act like envelopes. Data is put in a TCP/IP envelope for travel over the network. This envelope is put in a PPP envelope for travel over phone lines. When the phone line segment of the trip is completed, the PPP envelope is discarded.

A+CORE
1.8
6.3
OS
4.2

Creating a Dial-up Connection in Windows 98

To use Windows 98 or Windows NT to communicate with a network over phone lines, Dial-up Networking must be installed as an OS component on your PC using the Add/Remove Programs applet in Control Panel. (Network and Dial-up Connections in Windows 2000 and Network Connections in Windows XP are installed by default.)

When Windows 98 installs Dial-up Networking, it also "installs" a dial-up adapter. In terms of function, think of this dial-up adapter as a virtual network card. Remember that in the last chapter, you learned how TCP/IP is bound to a network interface card. A dial-up adapter is a modem playing the role of a network card for dial-up networking. After Dial-up Networking is installed, open the Device Manager to see your "new" dial-up adapter listed under Network adapters, as in Figure 19-8. You can also see it listed as an installed network component in the Network window of the Control Panel.

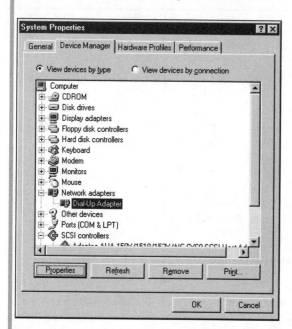

Figure 19-8   After Dial-up Networking is installed, a new virtual network device, a dial-up adapter, is listed as an installed hardware device

After installing Dial-up Networking, you create an icon in the Dial-up Networking group and then use the icon to make a connection. After you make the connection, you can use any Internet application, such as a Web browser or e-mail client, for which you have the software installed on your PC.

A+CORE
1.8
6.3
OS
4.2

Making a New Connection in Windows 98

To create a new dial-up networking connection in Windows 98:

1. After Dial-up Networking is installed, click **Start**, point to **Programs**, **Accessories**, **Communications**, and then click **Dial-up Networking**. The Dial-Up Networking dialog box appears, as in Figure 19-9.

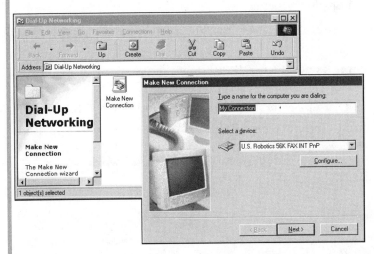

Figure 19-9   Creating a Windows 98 Dial-up Networking Connection icon

2. Double-click **Make New Connection**. The Make New Connection Wizard appears, also shown in Figure 19-9. Click **Next** to move past the first screen.

3. Enter a name for the connection. When you are connecting to the Internet, you can use the name of your ISP and the city in which the server is located. An example would be Earthlink Boston. If your modem is already installed, it appears in the modem list.

4. In the next dialog box, type the phone number to dial, and then click **Next** to continue.

5. Click **Finish** to build the icon. The icon appears in the Dial-Up Networking window.

Setting up a Connection to Your ISP

In order for your PC to connect to your ISP and use the Internet, you need answers to the following questions:

- What is the phone number of the ISP?

- What is your user ID and password for the ISP?

19

A+*CORE*
1.8
6.3
OS
4.2

- Will DNS servers be assigned at connection? If not, what is the IP address of one or two DNS servers?

- How will your IP address be assigned (most likely dynamic)?

To set up an ISP connection in Windows 98, do the following:

1. Right-click the icon you created for the connection, and select **Properties** from the drop-down menu.

2. Click the **General** tab. Verify that the correct phone number for your ISP is entered.

3. Click **Server Types**. Figure 19-10 shows the resulting dialog box. Verify that these selections are made:

    - Type of Dial-up Server: **PPP Internet, Windows NT Server, Windows 98**

    - Advanced Options: Select **Enable software compression** (software compression is most likely to be enabled, but this option really depends on what the ISP is doing) and **Log on to network**.

    - Allowed Network Protocols: **TCP/IP**

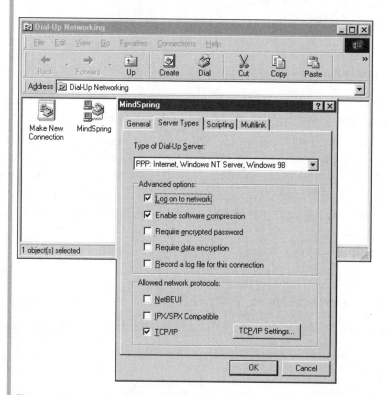

Figure 19-10   Configuring the server type for a connection to the Internet in Windows 9x

A+CORE
1.8
6.3
OS
4.2

4. Click **TCP/IP Settings** to open the TCP/IP Settings dialog box, as shown in Figure 19-11. Verify that these settings (or other settings as specified by your ISP) are chosen:

- **Server assigned IP address**
- **Specify name server addresses**
- **Use IP header compression**
- **Use default gateway on remote network**

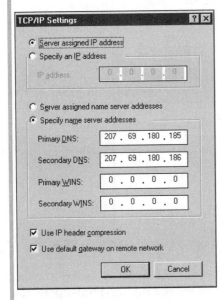

Figure 19-11 TCP/IP settings for a connection to the Internet in Windows 9x

5. Enter the IP addresses of the primary and secondary DNS servers. (This information is provided by your ISP. If it is not provided, then select Server assigned name server addresses.)

6. Click **OK** twice to complete building the Dial-up Networking connection.

7. To connect to your ISP, double-click the icon you created for it, which is now correctly configured. The first time you use the icon, you enter the user ID and password to connect to your ISP. Check the option to remember the user name and password if you don't want to have to enter it every time, but remember that this might not be wise if others who cannot be trusted have access to your PC.

8. Click **Connect**. You should now hear the modem making the connection.

19

A+CORE
1.8
6.3
OS
4.2

Creating a Dial-up Connection in Windows 2000

Windows 2000 adds more wizards to make the configuration process easier than it was with Windows 98. To create a new dial-up connection to the Internet in Windows 2000:

1. From the Start menu, click **Programs**, **Accessories**, **Communications**, and **Network and Dial-up Connections.**

2. The Network and Dial-up Connections window opens, as shown in Figure 19-12. Double-click the **Make New Connection** icon. If the Location Information screen opens, click **Next** to continue to the Network Connection Wizard.

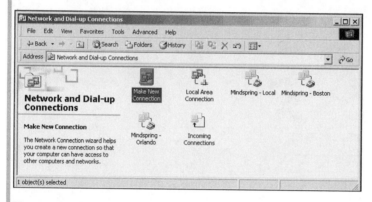

Figure 19-12   Network and Dial-up Connections applet in Windows 2000

3. The Network Connection Wizard opens. Click **Next** to skip the welcome screen. On the next screen, select the second option, **Dial-up to the Internet**, and then click **Next**.

4. The Internet Connection Wizard opens. Select the option to configure an Internet connection manually, and then click **Next**.

5. Choose how you connect to the Internet. For this example, select the option **I connect through a phone line and a modem**, and then click **Next** (see Figure 19-13). Notice in Figure 19-13 that you can also choose to connect through a LAN at this point. (This option was not available through a wizard in Windows 9x.)

6. Follow the directions in the remainder of the wizard to enter the phone number to dial to connect to your ISP, your username and password, a name for the connection, and whether to set up a new e-mail account. (For this example, assume that you already have an e-mail account, and choose not to set up a new one.)

7. On the final screen of the wizard, which informs you that you have created the connection successfully and can access it through your browser, click

Finish to close the wizard. Your new connection is shown in the Network and Dial-up Connections window.

8. If you want to create a shortcut to the dial-up connection on the desktop, right-click the icon in the Network and Dial-up Connections window, and select **Create Shortcut** on the shortcut menu.

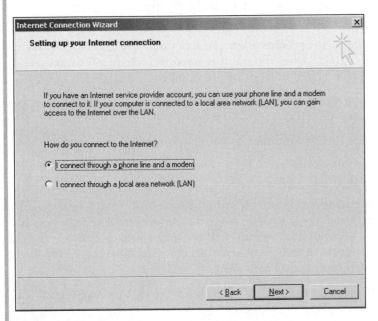

Figure 19-13 Using the Windows 2000 Internet Connection Wizard

9. A message appears saying, "Windows cannot create a shortcut here. Do you want the shortcut to be placed on the desktop instead?" Click **Yes** to create a shortcut on the desktop.

The procedure for creating a dial-up networking connection from Windows XP is similar to the procedure in Windows 2000. Double-click the Network Connections icon from the Windows XP Control Panel, and in the window that appears, click the option to create a new dial-up connection, then follow the wizard's instructions.

19

Dial-up Networking Problems

In this section, you learn about some of the most common problems and errors that you may encounter with dial-up networking and what to do about them. As always, check the simple things first before trying more difficult solutions.

A+CORE
1.8
6.3
OS
4.2

You cannot make a connection   If you have a problem connecting to the Internet using a dial-up connection, first find out what works and what doesn't work. Try the following:

- Find out the answers to these questions: At what point does the connecting process fail? Do you hear the modem hissing? If so, the problem is probably with the user ID and password. If not, then the problem might be the phone number, phone line, or modem. Is the phone line plugged in? Does the phone line work? Can you hear a dial tone?

- Check the Dial-up Networking connection icon for errors. Is the phone number correct? Does the number need to include a 9 to get an outside line? Has a 1 been added in front of the number by mistake?

- Try dialing the number manually from a phone. Do you hear beeps on the other end?

- Try another phone number.

- Does the modem work? Check Device Manager for reported errors about the modem.

- Print the Modemlog.txt file from a successful connection on another computer and the same file from the unsuccessful connection on the problem computer. Compare the two printouts to identify the point in the connection at which an error occurs. (See Chapter 17 for directions to log modem events to a text file.)

- Are all components installed? Check for the dial-up adapter and TCP/IP, and check the configuration of each.

- Reboot your PC and try again.

- Try removing and reinstalling each network component. Begin with TCP/IP.

- For Windows 9x, sometimes older copies of the Windows socket DLL may be interfering with the current Windows 9x socket DLL. (Windows 9x may be finding and executing the older DLL before it finds the newer one.) Search for and rename any files named Winsock.dll except the one in the \Windows\System directory.

You can connect, but you get the message "Unable to resolve hostname..."   This error message means that TCP/IP is not able to determine how to route a request to a host. Right-click the Dial-up Networking connection icon, select Properties, and check for these things:

- Under Server Type, try making TCP/IP the only network protocol allowed.

- Under TCP/IP settings, check the IP addresses of the DNS servers.

A+CORE
  1.8
  6.3
  OS
  4.2

- Make sure *Using the default gateway* is selected.
- Try *not* selecting IP header compression.

After connecting, you get the error message "Unable to establish a compatible set of network protocols" This error is most likely to be caused by a problem with the installation and configuration of Dial-up Networking or TCP/IP. Try these things:

- Verify that the dial-up adapter and TCP/IP are installed and configured correctly.
- Remove and reinstall TCP/IP. Be sure to reboot after the installation.
- For Windows 9x, try putting the PC in a different workgroup.
- Compare the modem log file to one created during a successful connection.

When you double-click the Web browser, the modem does not dial automatically
When this occurs, right-click the browser icon and select Properties from the drop-down menu. Under the Connection tab, check Connect to the Internet as needed.

DSL and Cable Modem Connections

A+CORE
  1.8
  6.3
  OS
  4.2

Recall that DSL and cable modem are called broadband technologies because they support the transmission of more than one kind of data at once. These connections can carry voice, data, sound, and video simultaneously. When using cable modem or DSL (as well as ISDN or satellite), if you are connecting a single PC to the Internet using an ISP, then the TCP/IP settings are no different from those used by a modem-to-phone line connection. In most cases, cable modem and DSL, like LANs, use a network card in the PC for the physical connection to the network, which in this case is the Internet. The network card provides a network port for a network cable. (Some newer cable modems use USB to connect to a PC.) For cable modem service to the Internet, the network or USB cable connects to a cable modem. For DSL, the phone line connects to a DSL box, which might also be a small router. The connection between the NIC and the broadband device most likely uses **PPPoE (Point-to-Point Protocol over Ethernet)**, a protocol specifically designed to support broadband connections. PPPoE is included in Windows XP.

For cable modem and DSL Internet connections, generally the installation goes like this:

1. Install the network card and the drivers to control the card.
2. Use a network cable to connect the PC to a cable modem or DSL box.
3. Install TCP/IP and bind TCP/IP to the card.
4. Configure TCP/IP to connect to the Internet or LAN.
5. Install the applications software (for example, a browser) to use the connection.

19

A+CORE
1.8
6.3
OS
4.2

In the following section, you'll learn about the different ways to connect to the Internet using these faster-than-phone line connections and the details of installing these services.

Cable Modem

A cable modem uses a regular TV cable to connect to a TV cable wall outlet. Figure 19-14 illustrates what the arrangement looks like. The cable modem also has an electrical connection to provide power to the box. A cable modem connects to a network card or USB port in your PC. Your cable modem company will provide you with the TCP/IP settings to use to configure TCP/IP. For a home installation, some cable modem companies will do the entire installation for you. You might need to purchase the cable modem and NIC, or they might be included in the installation fee. A service technician comes to your home, installs the network card if necessary, and configures your PC to use the service.

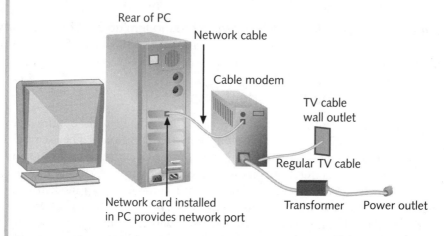

Figure 19-14   Cable modem connecting to a PC through a network card installed on the PC

If you don't have on-site service from the cable modem company, follow these instructions to install cable modem:

1. Install the network card and drivers. For most cable modem companies, the MAC address of the network card in the PC or the MAC address of the NIC in the cable modem must be entered in an online list of valid addresses that identify your PC or cable modem as a subscriber to the cable modem service. When the PC first connects to the service, the system recognizes the PC and assigns it a valid IP address, subnet mask, IP address of the default gateway, and IP address of a domain name server. If the cable company help desk technician needs the MAC address of the PC, use Winipcfg or Ipconfig to display it. If the technician needs the MAC address of the cable modem, look for it printed somewhere on the back of the cable modem.

2. Configure TCP/IP to use the network card, using the TCP/IP configuration information provided by the cable modem company.

A^{+CORE}
1.8
6.3
OS
4.2

3. Shut down the PC and connect one end of the network or USB cable to the network or USB port on the back of the PC. Connect the other end of the cable to the cable modem. Be sure the cable modem is plugged in and turned on. There is usually a switch on the back of the box. Connect the TV cable from the TV cable outlet to the cable modem. (Refer back to Figure 19-14.) Turn on the PC.

4. When the PC starts, you should immediately be connected to the Internet. Test the connection using your Web browser or e-mail client. If you are not connected, try the following:

   ■ For Windows 9x, use Winipcfg to access the IP Configuration window. Select the network card. Click **Release All**. Wait a moment and click **Renew**. Check for Internet connectivity again. For Windows 2000/XP, use Ipconfig /release and Ipconfig /renew to lease a new IP address, and then check for connectivity again.

   ■ If the above did not work, turn off the PC and the cable modem. Wait a full five minutes until all connections have timed out at the cable modem company. Turn on the cable modem, and then turn on the PC. After the PC boots up, again check for connectivity.

   ■ If this doesn't work, call the cable modem help desk. The technician there can release and restore the connection at that end, which should restore service.

DSL and ISDN

DSL/ISDN service is provided by the local telephone company. The telephone company's responsibility for the phone system ends at your house. Inside your house, you are responsible for your home phone network. A DSL/ISDN connection uses a DSL/ISDN converter box that is sometimes combined with a router as a single device so that more than one PC can use the DSL/ISDN line. The device connects to the PC by way of a network cable and card.

As with cable modem, a technician from the phone company most likely will do a DSL/ISDN installation for you. The installation process on the PC works the same as that of cable modem.

Sharing Internet Connections

A^{+CORE}
1.8
6.3
OS
4.2

There are several ways that computers on a LAN or WLAN can share an Internet connection. Here are a few options:

   ■ If one computer on the LAN has a direct connection to the Internet by way of a phone line, cable modem, or DSL, it can serve as a host computer for others on the LAN. Windows 98 and Windows XP **Internet Connection Sharing (ICS)** is designed to manage this type of connection. Using ICS, the host computer uses NAT and acts as the proxy server for the LAN. Windows XP ICS also includes a firewall.

19

A^+ OS
4.2

- For broadband connections (cable modem and DSL), the broadband converter box can connect to a network device such as a router that manages the connection for the entire network. The router has a network connection to the converter box and one or more network ports for devices on the network. In this situation, the router is likely to also have firewall software embedded in it and is controlled by way of a Web browser. A user on any computer on the network can enter the IP address of the router in a Web browser window and bring up the software on the router to configure the router. The router can serve as a DHCP server, a NAT proxy server, and a firewall.

- The router can also serve as a wireless access point for computers to connect wirelessly to the Internet. An example of a router that is also a wireless access point is the AirPlus D1-714P+ by D-Link (*www.dlink.com*) shown in Figure 19-15. It has one port for the converter box, four ports for computers on the network, and a parallel printer port designed to manage a network printer. The router can also support several computers with wireless adapters.

Figure 19-15   This D-Link router allows computers on a LAN to share a broadband Internet connection and also is an access point for computers with wireless adapters

Windows Internet Connection Sharing

To use Internet Connection Sharing in Windows 98 or Windows XP, the computer that has a direct connection to the Internet by way of a phone line, cable modem, or DSL is the host computer. Follow these general directions to configure the LAN for Internet Connection Sharing using Windows XP:

1. Following directions earlier in the chapter, install and configure the hardware (modem, cable modem, or DSL) to connect to the Internet, and verify the connection is working.

2. Open the Network Connections window in the Windows XP Control Panel, and click on the link to **Set up a home or small office network**. The Network Setup Wizard opens. Click **Next** on this window and the next.

A+ OS
4.2

3. Select the connection method for your host computer, which is **This computer connects directly to the Internet. The other computers on my network connect to the Internet through this computer**. Click **Next**.

4. The wizard looks at your hardware connections (NIC or modem) and selects the one that it sees as a "live" connection. Verify it is selected correctly and then follow the wizard to enter a description for your computer, your computer name, and your workgroup name.

5. The next screen of the wizard offers you the option of creating a Network Setup Disk that you can use to quickly configure every other computer on the LAN that is to use the Internet connection (see Figure 19-16). Select the option to **Create a Network Setup Disk**, insert a blank floppy disk in the drive, and click **Next**.

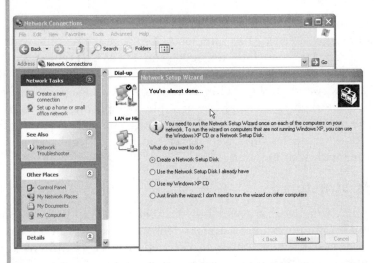

Figure 19-16   Create a Network Setup Disk to configure other computers on the LAN

6. The next screen gives you the option to format the disk. If it needs formatting, click **Format Disk**. Otherwise, click **Next**.

7. The wizard tells you that to use the disk, insert it into the next computer on the network, and run the program on the disk named Netsetup.exe. Click **Next** and then click **Finish**.

8. Recall from Chapter 16 that you can enable Internet Connection Firewall to protect the connection to your ISP against unsolicited activity from the Internet. On the host computer only, to enable Internet Connection Firewall, in the Network Connections windows, right click on the network connection, and select **Properties** from the shortcut menu. On the Properties box, click

19

$A^+_{}$ *OS*
  4.2

the **Advanced** tab and select **Protect my computer and network by limiting or preventing access to this computer from the Internet**.

9. Use the Network Setup Disk on each computer on the LAN that is to use the shared connection.

Supporting Internet Clients

Now that you've learned how to connect to the Internet, let's look at some ways of using it. Earlier in the chapter in Table 19-1, you saw a list of application services that use the Internet. In this section, you will learn how to support some of the most common Internet clients: Web browsers, e-mail, and FTP.

Supporting Web Browsers

$A^+_{}$ *OS*
  4.1
  4.2

A Web browser is a software application on a user's PC that is used to request Web pages from a Web server on the Internet or an intranet. A Web page is a text file with an .htm or .html file extension. It can include text coded in **HTML (Hypertext Markup Language)** that can be interpreted by a Web browser to display formatted text and graphics, as well as play sounds. If the HTML code on the Web page points to other files used to build the page such as a sound file or a photograph file, these files are also downloaded to the browser. In this section, you will learn about the addresses that Web browsers use to locate resources on a Web server and how to troubleshoot common problems that occur with Web browsers.

How a URL Is Structured

Earlier in the chapter you saw that a Web browser requests a Web page by sending an IP address followed by an optional port number. This works well on an intranet, but on the Internet, a more user-friendly address is preferred. A **URL (Uniform Resource Locator)** is an address for a Web page or other resource on the Internet. Figure 19-17 shows the structure of a URL.

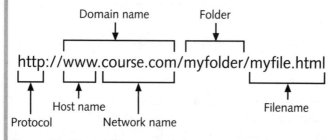

Figure 19-17 A URL contains the protocol used, the host name of the Web server, the network name, and the path and filename of the requested file

The first part of the URL shown in Figure 19-17 indicates the protocol, which in this case is HTTP. If secure HTTP were used to encrypt the data being transmitted, the protocol shown would be **HTTPS (HTTP secure)** and the secure protocol being used is SSL (secure socket layer). The protocol part of the URL specifies the rules, or protocol, the Web server should use when transmitting the page to the browser. A Web server is sometimes called an HTTP server.

Recall from Chapter 18 that a host name identifies a server or another computer within a network. In this example, the host name is *www* (a Web server), and *course.com* is the name of the Course Technology network, sometimes called the domain name. A name that contains not only the network name (in this case, *course.com*) but also the host on that network is, as you learned in Chapter 18, called a fully qualified domain name (FQDN) (in this case, *www.course.com*). The Web page requested is located in the folder *myfolder* on the *www* server, and the file within that folder is named *myfile.html*. The FQDN must be resolved to an IP address before the request can happen.

The last segment, or suffix, of a domain name is called the **top-level domain** (*.com* in our example) and tells you something about the organization or individual that owns the name. Some domain names in the United States end in the suffixes listed in Table 19-3. There are other endings as well, including codes for countries, such as .uk for the United Kingdom. With the growth of the Internet, there has been a shortage of available domain names; because of this shortage, additional suffixes are being created.

Table 19-3   Suffixes used to identify top-level domain names

Domain Suffix	Description
.air	Aviation industry
.biz	Businesses
.com	Commercial institutions
.coop	Business cooperatives
.edu	Educational institutions
.gov	Government institutions
.info	General use
.int	Organizations established by international treaties between governments
.mil	U.S. military
.museum	Museums
.name	Individuals
.net	Internet providers or networks
.org	Nonprofit organizations
.pro	Professionals

19

Domain names stand for IP addresses and provide an easy way to remember them, but domain names and IP addresses are not necessarily permanently related. A host computer can have a certain domain name, can be connected to one network and assigned a certain

A+ OS
4.1
4.2

IP address, and then can be moved to another network and assigned a different IP address. The domain name can stay with the host while it connects to either network. It is up to a name resolution service, such as DNS or WINS, to track the relationship between a domain name and the current IP address of the host computer.

Using Internet Explorer, you can control support options such as how scripts are handled by clicking Tools, Internet Options. The Internet Options window opens. Click the Advanced tab.

Solving Browser Performance Problems

If you notice poor browser performance, use the tools you have seen in earlier chapters, such as Defrag, ScanDisk, and System Information, to make sure that you have enough free hard drive space, that the hard drive is clean, and that the virtual memory settings are optimized. If you perform these tasks and the browser is still slow, try the procedures given below using the most popular browser, Internet Explorer, as an example.

Internet Explorer If Internet Explorer (IE) is slow even after you have taken steps to optimize your system, do the following:

1. Right-click the **Internet Explorer** icon on the desktop, and then click **Properties** on the shortcut menu. The Internet Properties window opens, as shown in Figure 19-18 for Windows 2000. (If the icon is not on the desktop, double-click the **Internet** or **Internet Options** applet in Control Panel.)

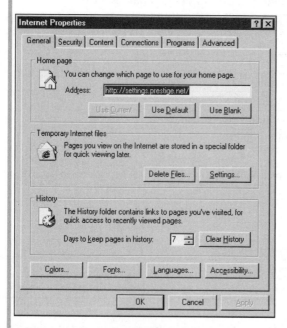

Figure 19-18   Use the Internet Properties dialog box to control the Internet Explorer environment

A+ OS
4.1
4.2

2. Click **Delete Files** under the Temporary Internet files heading to clean out the IE cache. The Delete Files dialog box appears asking you to confirm the deletion. Click **OK**. IE must search the entire cache each time it accesses a Web page. If the cache is too big, performance is affected.

3. Click **Clear History** under the History heading to clean out the shortcuts cache. The Internet Options dialog box appears, asking you to confirm the deletions. Click **OK**. If this cache gets too big, performance slows down. Also, if you reduce the number of days that Internet Explorer keeps pages in the history folder, performance might improve because there will be less material for Internet Explorer to search. For example, change the number of days to keep pages in history from the default value of 20 to 7.

4. Click **OK** to close the window.

Suppress Image Downloading   Slow browser performance can be caused by a slow Internet connection. In this case, one thing you can do is to suppress the downloading of images. Image files can be large and account for most of the downloaded data from Web sites. For Internet Explorer 5.x, you can download and install Web Accessories for Internet Explorer 5.x, which can be used to suppress the downloading of images from Web sites. (IE version 6 includes the ability to suppress downloading images without added software.) If the Microsoft site has been updated since the writing of this book, you may need to search for the Web Accessories for Internet Explorer. Follow these directions:

1. Go to this Microsoft Web site: *www.microsoft.com/windows/ie/downloads/archive/default.asp*.

2. Scroll down and click the heading **Web Accessories**, and then scroll down and click the **Download it now** link.

3. Another page opens, with more information about the Internet Explorer 5.x Web Accessories. On the right side of the page, in a box labeled Download, click the link to the file **ie5wa.exe.**

4. Click **OK** to save the file on disk. When the download window opens, choose to download it to a location on your hard drive, and then click **Save**. Remember where you saved the file.

5. After you download the file ie5wa.exe, double-click it, then click **Yes** to install accessories.

6. Close the IE browser window, and reopen it.

7. To use the IE Web Accessories to suppress downloading images, right-click the IE menu bar. If Favorites is already checked and on your menu bar, you can move on to Step 8. If it is not, click **Links** on the shortcut menu. This action adds the Links menu to the menu bar items.

19

8. Click **Favorites** on the menu bar, click **Links**, and then click **Toggle Images**. Web pages should now download without their images. You may have to click the **Refresh** button on your toolbar for the changes to take effect on an open page.

9. To reset the browser to download images, click **Favorites**, click **Links**, and then click **Toggle Images** again.

IE version 6 includes the option to suppress images, sound, animation, and video. Use the following procedure:

1. Open the **Tools** menu and then click **Internet Options**.

2. The Internet Options window opens. Click the **Advanced** tab.

3. Scroll down to the multimedia section of the check box list, and clear the check box or boxes for the feature or features that you do not wish to display (**Show pictures**, **Play animations**, **Play videos**, or **Play sounds**).

To display an individual video or picture when you have cleared the related check boxes, right-click the icon with which it has been replaced on the Web page.

Browser Updates and Patches

Browser manufacturers are continually improving their products, and generally speaking, you should use the most current version of the browser to take advantage of the latest features and fixes to known problems. However, if you have an older computer or operating system, you might not want to update a browser that requires a lot of system resources, because your older PC might not be able to support it. In this case, it's better to keep an older version on your PC unless you are having problems with your version.

If you are using Internet Explorer, check the Windows support Web site at *support.microsoft.com* to find information about specific problems with Internet Explorer. Search for the product and the error message for articles that describe the problem and possible solutions. Also check the Windows update Web site at *windowsupdate.microsoft.com* for updates or patches for known Internet Explorer problems. Download the patch and install it following the same general instructions you have seen in earlier chapters.

If you are not using the latest version of your Web browser, try downloading the latest version. If you use your browser for banking on the Internet, be sure to download a version that supports 128-bit encryption for better security features. If the new version creates problems on your system, you can revert to your original version by uninstalling the new version.

Supporting E-mail

A+ OS
4.2 E-mail is a client/server application used to send text messages to individuals and groups of individuals. When you send an e-mail message, it travels from your computer to your e-mail server. Your e-mail server sends the message to the recipient's e-mail server. The recipient's e-mail server sends it to the recipient's PC, but not until the recipient asks that it be sent by logging in and downloading e-mail. Different parts of the process are controlled by different protocols.

Figure 19-19 shows the journey made by an e-mail message as well as the protocols that control the different parts of the journey. The sender's PC and e-mail server both use **SMTP (Simple Mail Transfer Protocol)** to send an e-mail message to its destination. Once the message arrives at the destination e-mail server, it remains there until the recipient requests delivery. The recipient's e-mail server uses one of two protocols to deliver the message: either **POP (Post Office Protocol)** or **IMAP4 (Internet Message Access Protocol, version 4)**, a newer e-mail protocol. The current version of POP is version 3, often abbreviated as POP3. IMAP is slowly replacing POP for receiving e-mail.

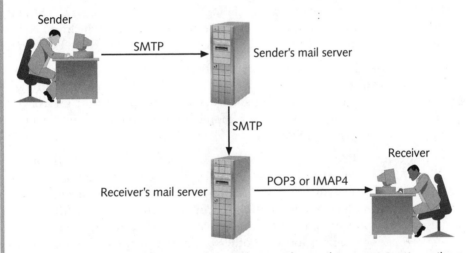

Figure 19-19   The SMTP protocol is used to send e-mail to a recipient's mail server, and POP3 or IMAP4 protocol is used to download e-mail to the client

19

TIP   SMTP is defined in RFC821 and RFC822 (see *www.rfc-editor.org*). When e-mail experts speak of error messages created during e-mail transactions, they sometimes call these messages 822 messages.

E-mail client software communicates with an e-mail server when it sends and receives e-mail. Two common e-mail clients are Eudora and Microsoft Outlook Express. Figure 19-19 shows a user with one e-mail server. In fact, it's possible to have two e-mail servers, one for sending e-mail and the other for receiving e-mail. Figure 19-20 shows this arrangement.

A+ OS
  4.2

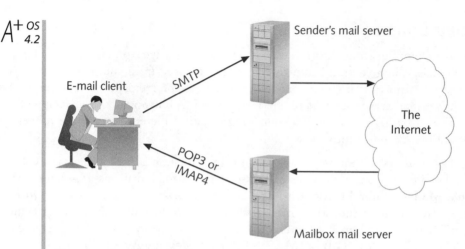

Figure 19-20   An e-mail client can use one server to send e-mail and another to receive e-mail

The e-mail server that takes care of sending e-mail messages (using the SMTP protocol) is often referred to as the SMTP server. The e-mail server from which you collect messages sent to you is often referred to as the POP server, because it uses the POP protocol.

When you configure your e-mail client software for the first time, you need to enter the addresses of your e-mail servers. If you are connecting to e-mail via an Internet service provider, the ISP can tell you these addresses. For example, if your ISP is *MyISP.net*, you might have an outgoing mail server address of *smtp.myISP.net* and an incoming mail server address of *pop3.myISP.net*.

In most e-mail client software, you enter the addresses of your POP or IMAP server and your SMTP server in a dialog box when setting up the program, along with your e-mail address you will use when sending e-mail. Look for menus or icons labeled Options, Preferences, Configuration, Setup, or similar names. After you enter the addresses, the software saves this and other configuration information in an initialization file, the Windows registry, or some other location. When you first log on to the e-mail server, you will be asked for your user ID and password, which are used to validate your right to access the account.

Supporting FTP

A+ OS
  4.2

A common task of communications software is file transfer, the passing of files from one computer to another. For file transfer to work, the software on both ends must use the same protocol. The most popular way to transfer files over the Internet is with FTP, which can transfer files between two computers using the same or different operating systems. For example, when upgrades for software become available, software vendors often provide files for customers to download to their PCs via FTP. This service is commonly provided by Windows NT, 2000, or Unix servers that offer access to files using FTP and

A+ OS
1.4
4.2
are called FTP servers or FTP sites. These commercial FTP sites only provide the ability to download a file to your PC. However, the FTP utility itself offers remote users the ability to copy, delete, and rename files, make directories, remove directories, and view details about files and directories, provided the user has the appropriate permissions on the FTP site.

Most communications applications provide an FTP utility that has a unique look and feel, but the basics of file transfer are the same from one utility to another. If you don't have graphical FTP software installed on your PC, you can use FTP commands from a command prompt.

FTP from a Command Prompt

FTP can be initiated at a DOS, Windows 9x, or Windows NT/2000/XP command prompt, if a connection to a network or the Internet is established. A sample set of FTP commands entered at the command prompt is shown in Table 19-4.

Table 19-4   A sample FTP session from a command prompt

Command Entered at the Command Prompt	Description
FTP	Execute the FTP program, ftp.exe.
OPEN 110.87.170.34	Open a session with a remote computer having the given IP address.
LOGIN: XXXXXX	The host computer provides a prompt to enter a user ID for the computer being accessed.
PASSWORD: XXXXXX	The host computer requests the password for that ID. Logon is then completed by the host computer.
CD /DATA	Change directory to the /DATA directory.
GET YOURFILE.DAT	Copy the file YOURFILE.DAT (or whatever file you want) from the remote computer to my computer.
PUT MYFILE.DAT	Copy the file MYFILE.DAT (or whatever file you want) from your computer to the remote computer.
BYE	Disconnect the FTP session.

File Transfer Using FTP Software

FTP client software can be downloaded from the Internet or directly from your ISP. This example looks at how to execute FTP using such software:

1. Start the FTP utility software. In this example we are using WS_FTP Pro by Ipswitch (*www.ipswitch.com*). The FTP utility screen appears similar to the one in Figure 19-21. Note that more recent versions of WS_FTP Pro might look and work slightly differently.

2. Click **Connect** to log on to an FTP site. A Session Profile dialog box appears, similar to the one in Figure 19-21.

19

A^{+} OS
1.4
4.2

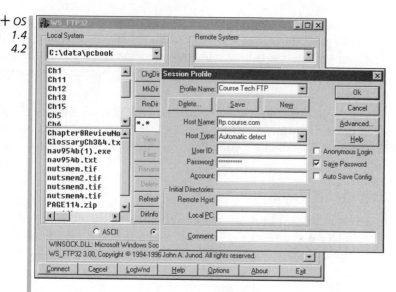

Figure 19-21   A typical FTP utility provided by an Internet service provider

3. Enter the Host Name, for example *ftp.course.com*. Enter the User ID and Password for this host computer, and then click **OK**.

4. The connection is made and your ID and password are passed to the host. After you have been authenticated by the host computer, a screen similar to that in Figure 19-22 appears.

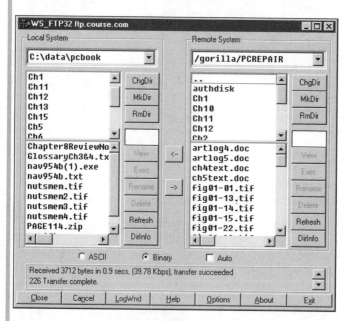

Figure 19-22   An FTP utility screen showing local and remote files

A+ OS
1.4
4.2

5. The files on the left belong to you, and the files on the right belong to the remote host computer. You can drag and drop files either to or from the other computer, or you can use the commands at the bottom of the window. Notice in Figure 19-22 the choices toward the bottom of the window: ASCII, Binary, or Auto. These choices refer to the format to be used to transfer the files. Use ASCII only for text files, and use Binary for all others. If you are not sure which to use, choose **Auto**.

6. When the transfer of files is complete, click **Exit** to leave the utility.

Many Web pages provide a link on the page offering you the ability to download a file. Click the link to download the file. It is likely that this file is not being downloaded from the Web server but rather from an FTP server. When you click the filename on the Web page, the program controlling the page executes FTP commands to the FTP server to download the file to you. If you receive an error, you can sometimes solve the problem by going directly to the company's FTP server and using an FTP utility (such as the one used above) to download the file or even see a list of other files that you might also like to download.

> **TIP** A Web browser can also serve as an FTP client. Enter the URL of the FTP server in the address box (for example, *ftp.course.com*). The browser changes menu options to become an FTP client. For Internet Explorer, to log onto the FTP server, on the menu bar, click File, and then click Login As. The Log On As dialog box appears for you to enter a user ID and password. Files and folders on the FTP server then display in the browser window.

CHAPTER SUMMARY

- Ports are used to address particular software or services running on a computer. Common port assignments are port 80 for HTTP (Web browser requests), port 25 for SMTP (sending e-mail), port 110 for POP3 (receiving e-mail), and port 20 for FTP.

- Generally, an API call is a way for an application to ask an operating system to do something. A browser uses an API call to access a Web server and make its request for information.

- TCP guarantees that a packet reaches its destination and so is called a connection-oriented protocol. UDP does not guarantee delivery and so is called a connectionless or best-effort protocol.

- IP is responsible for breaking data into packets and passing them from TCP or UDP to the hardware.

- PPP is used in dial-up networking to send packets of data over phone lines. It manages network transmission from one modem to another.

19

❑ Winipcfg and Ipconfig report configuration information about the current TCP/IP connection for a device and can release and restore the IP address. Winipcfg is supported in Windows 9x, and Windows NT/2000/XP support Ipconfig.

❑ Other TCP/IP utilities useful in solving networking problems are Tracert, Ping, and Nbtstat.

❑ Before you can create a dial-up connection to the Internet, you need to have a modem installed along with the drivers to run it, as well as TCP/IP installed and bound to the modem.

❑ The Windows Dial-Up Networking utility is used to connect to a network using a modem and a phone line. When a dial-up connection is made, a PC's application software relates to the network as though the computer were directly connected to the network using a network card.

❑ You can create a new dial-up networking connection in Windows 9x and Windows NT through the Dial-Up Networking applet in My Computer, through the Network and Dial-Up Connections applet in the Control Panel of Windows 2000, and through the Network Connections applet in the Control Panel of Windows XP.

❑ When experiencing problems with dial-up networking, make sure the modem is working, all necessary components are installed, and the phone number to dial and other settings are configured correctly.

❑ DSL and cable modem are broadband Internet connections that use a converter box connected to a NIC in a PC by way of a network cable. The connection can use the PPPoE protocol.

❑ Computers can share an Internet connection. Windows 98 and Windows XP use Internet Connection Sharing (ICS) to manage the connection on the host computer, or you can use a router that stands between the converter box and the network.

❑ Use a firewall on the host computer or router to protect the network from unsolicited activity from the Internet.

❑ A URL consists of a protocol, a host name, a network or domain name, and a top-level domain extension. Common top-level domains include .com for commercial institutions, .gov for divisions of government, and .org for nonprofit organizations.

❑ When you experience poor browser performance, try cleaning up your hard drive and making sure your system settings are optimized. If that doesn't work, try clearing your browser cache, clearing the Web page history, suppressing image downloads, or downloading updates.

❑ E-mail uses SMTP to send messages and POP3 to receive messages. POP3 is being replaced by IMAP. Your ISP will provide you with information on the server types and addresses that it uses to send and receive e-mail.

❑ FTP is used to transfer files from one computer to another, whether or not the computers are using the same operating system. Both computers must have an FTP utility installed. It can be executed from user-friendly GUI software or from a command prompt.

KEY TERMS

ARP (Address Resolution Protocol)

best-effort protocol

bridging protocol

client/server application

connectionless protocol

connection-oriented protocol

dial-up networking

FTP (File Transfer Protocol)

hop count

HTML (HyperText Markup Language)

HTTP (HyperText Transfer Protocol)

HTTPS (HTTP secure)

ICMP (Internet Control Message Protocol)

IMAP4 (Internet Message Access Protocol, version 4)

Internet Connection Sharing (ICS)

IP (Internet Protocol)

line protocol

NNTP (Network News Transfer Protocol)

POP (Post Office Protocol)

port

port address

port number

PPP (Point-to-Point Protocol)

PPPoE (Point-to-Point Protocol over Ethernet)

RARP (Reverse Address Resolution Protocol)

session

SLIP (Serial Line Internet Protocol)

SMTP (Simple Mail Transfer Protocol)

SNMP (Simple Network Management Protocol)

socket

TCP (Transmission Control Protocol)

time to live (TTL)

top-level domain

UDP (User Datagram Protocol)

URL (Uniform Resource Locator)

REVIEW QUESTIONS

19

1. Most applications on the Internet are _____ applications.

   a. Peer-to-peer

   b. Client/server

   c. Multitasking

   d. Monotasking

   e. None of the above

2. DHCP software is an example of:

   a. Peer-to-peer

   b. Client/server

   c. Multitasking

   d. Monotasking

   e. None of the above

3. An efficient method of transferring information, typically in the form of files, over a TCP/IP network is:

   a. SMTP

   b. HTTP

   c. FTP

   d. POPx

   e. Telnet

4. The service that is used by UNIX computers to control a computer remotely is referred to as:

   a. SMTP

   b. HTTP

   c. FTP

   d. POPx

   e. Telnet

5. Which service is used by the client to receive e-mail?

   a. SMTP

   b. HTTP

   c. FTP

   d. POPx

   e. Telnet

6. Which of the following is used to format requests, encrypt and compress data, and is recognized as the protocol most used for the World Wide Web to communicate?

   a. SMTP

   b. HTTP

   c. FTP

   d. POPx

   e. Telnet

7. The term(s) reserved for communications links between two different software programs once a response is passed to the Web browser is:

   a. Sessions

   b. Sockets

   c. Both a and b

   d. Neither a nor b

8. Which of the following protocols guarantees packet delivery to a particular server?

   a. TCP/IP

   b. TCP

   c. UDP

   d. ARP

   e. None of the above

9. Which of the following protocols are considered to be a connectionless protocol?

   a. TCP/IP

   b. TCP

   c. UDP

   d. ARP

   e. None of the above

10. Which of the follow protocols is responsible for breaking up and reassembling data into packets and routing them to their destination?

    a. TCP/IP

    b. TCP

    c. UDP

    d. ARP

    e. None of the above

11. Of the following protocols used by hardware, which does *not* support encrypted passwords and is seldom used today?

    a. PPP

    b. SLIP

    c. ICMP

    d. ARP

    e. RARP

19

12. Which of the following network utilities displays information about current TCP/IP connections?

    a. Nbtstat

    b. Netstat

    c. Ping

    d. Telnet

    e. Tracert

13. Which of the following network utilities allows communication with another computer on the network remotely, entering commands to control the remote computer?

    a. Nbtstat

    b. Netstat

    c. Ping

    d. Telnet

    e. Tracert

14. Which of the following network utilities verifies that there is a connection on a network between two hosts?

    a. Nbtstat

    b. Netstat

    c. Ping

    d. Telnet

    e. Tracert

15. Which of the following network utilities displays current information about TCP/IP and NetBEUI when both are being used on the same network?

    a. Nbtstat

    b. Netstat

    c. Ping

    d. Telnet

    e. Tracert

16. When a Windows-based PC connects to a network using a modem and regular phone line, the process is referred to as _____ networking.

    a. Peer-to-peer

    b. Client/server

    c. PDC/BDC

    d. Dial-up

    e. PPP

17. In the following URL, identify the *domain name* portion of the URL:

    http://www.course.com/A+Project/hardware.html

    a. course.com

    b. www.course.com

    c. A+Project

    d. hardware.html

    e. www

18. In the following URL, identify the *host name* portion of the URL:

    http://www.course.com/A+Project/hardware.html

    a. course.com

    b. www.course.com

    c. A+Project

    d. hardware.html

    e. www

19. In the following URL, identify the *network name* portion of the URL:

    http://www.course.com/A+Project/hardware.html

    a. course.com

    b. www.course.com

    c. A+Project

    d. hardware.html

    e. www

20. In the following URL, identify the *filename* portion of the URL:

    http://www.course.com/A+Project/hardware.html

    a. course.com

    b. www.course.com

    c. A+Project

    d. hardware.html

    e. www

19

NOTEBOOKS AND PDAs

In this chapter, you will learn:

♦ How to support, upgrade, and add peripheral devices to notebooks
♦ About technologies relating to personal digital assistants (PDAs)

So far in this book, you've learned how computers work, about some of the devices used to work with them, about operating systems, and how to connect a PC to a network. Most devices and software you've learned about have related to desktop computers, which are stationary and cannot be moved easily. This chapter covers two types of devices that are more portable: notebook computers and personal digital assistants (PDAs). As a PC technician, you must be familiar with these devices and aware of specific concerns when supporting them.

NOTEBOOK COMPUTERS

A+CORE
1.2
1.3
1.10

A **notebook** or **laptop computer** is a computer designed to be portable (see Figure 20-1). Notebooks use the same technology as PCs but with modifications to use less power, take less space, and operate on the move. This section discusses the special needs of supporting notebooks and shows how to add memory to a notebook, add peripheral devices, and find online resources for notebook support.

Figure 20-1   A notebook is a computer designed for portability

Notebooks and their replacement parts cost more than desktop PCs with similar features, because their components are designed to be more compact and to endure movement when in use. They use thin LCD panels instead of CRT monitors for display, compact hard drives that can withstand movement even during operation, and small memory modules and CPUs that require less power than regular components. Recall that LCD monitors, including notebook LCD panels, use several different technologies and that active matrix (sometimes called thin film transistor or TFT) technology generally gives better quality than does passive matrix (sometimes called dual-scan twisted nematic or DSTN) technology.

 TIP LCD panels on notebooks are fragile and can be damaged fairly easily. Take precautions against damaging a notebook's LCD panel.

The types and features of notebooks vary widely, as they do for PCs. However, notebooks are generally purchased as a whole unit that includes both hardware and software, and you are not as likely to upgrade the hardware and OS on a notebook as you might be for a desktop PC. In fact, some notebook manufacturers refuse to support a notebook that has had the OS upgraded or new hardware components added. When supporting any notebook, pay careful attention to the stipulations on the warranty that accompanies it. Some warranties are voided if you open the notebook case or install memory, batteries, or a hard drive that was not made by, or at least authorized by, the notebook's manufacturer.

In contrast, most desktop PCs are designed to be highly modular, letting you easily interchange, upgrade, and enhance components. In fact, PCs are often assembled from components purchased from various vendors and manufacturers. Notebook computers' design, on the other hand, can be very proprietary, which means that many of the skills needed to support them are brand-specific. In this section, we'll look at a few universal support issues, but remember that procedures can vary from one notebook brand to another.

Windows 98 Notebook Features

The Windows 98 features designed to support notebooks include:

- *Multilink Channel Aggregation*, a feature that allows you to use two modem connections at the same time to speed up data throughput when connected over phone lines. It works on both regular analog phone lines and ISDN. To use the feature, you must have two phone lines and two modem cards that are physically designed to connect two phone lines at the same time.

- *ACPI (Advanced Configuration and Power Interface)*, developed by Intel, Microsoft, and Toshiba to control power on notebooks and other devices. ACPI allows a device to turn on a notebook or allows a notebook to turn on a device. For example, if you connect an external CD-ROM drive to the notebook, it can turn on the notebook, or the notebook can cycle up and turn on an external CD-ROM drive. The BIOS of the notebook and the device must support ACPI for it to work.

- *Improved power management*, including automatically powering down a PC Card when it is not in use, support for multiple battery packs, and individual power profiles. Power profiles are described in the next section.

- *Improved support for PC Cards*, adding several new drivers.

- *Microsoft Exchange* lets a user select what e-mail to download when traveling with a notebook. Downloading large e-mail messages with attachments takes a long time over a modem. You might prefer to have this e-mail downloaded later when you are connected directly to the network.

 When returning from a trip with a notebook, you might want to update your desktop PC with all e-mail documents and other files created or updated during the trip. To do this, use Windows 9x **Briefcase**, a system folder used to synchronize files between two computers. Briefcase automatically updates files on the original computer to the most recent version. You can use a null modem cable, disk, or network for the file transfer.

20

Windows 2000 Notebook Features

Windows 2000 Professional has several features designed to support notebooks. Windows 2000 has stronger power management and security features than does Windows 98 for notebook computers. New Windows 2000 features include:

- *Offline Files*, which replaces Windows 9x Briefcase, stores shared network files and folders in a cache on the notebook hard drive so you can use them offline. When you reconnect to the network, Offline Files synchronizes the files in the cache with those on the network.

- *Hibernate mode* and support for ACPI and APM (Advanced Power Management) have been improved.

- *Improved battery support* includes the ability to use two batteries and to monitor battery performance with greater control.

- *Hot-swapping* of IDE devices and floppy disk external drives.

- **Folder redirection** lets you point to an alternate location on a network for a folder. This feature can make the location of a folder transparent to the user.

Windows XP Notebook Features

Windows XP includes several features to make mobile computing easier, including power management features that build on similar capabilities in earlier versions of Windows. It also includes the ability to create **hardware profiles**, which specify which devices are to be loaded on startup for a particular user or set of circumstances. For example, you might set two different hardware profiles for a notebook computer, one for when it is on the road and one for when it is at home connected to a home network.

To create a hardware profile in Windows XP for a mobile user, follow these steps:

1. From the **Start** menu, open the **Control Panel**.

2. Double-click the **System** icon.

3. The System Properties dialog box opens. Click the **Hardware** tab.

4. Click the **Hardware Profiles** button at the bottom of the Hardware tab. The Hardware Profiles dialog box opens (Figure 20-2).

5. Click **Profile1 (Current)** and then click the **Copy** button.

6. Type a new name for the profile, and then click **OK**.

7. Under When Windows starts, select either the option for Windows XP to wait for you to select a hardware profile or the option for Windows XP to start with the first profile listed if you don't select one in the specified number of seconds.

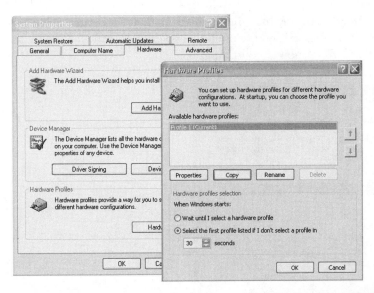

Figure 20-2 Windows XP allows you to set a hardware profile for each user

8. Restart the computer and, when prompted, select the new hardware profile.

9. Open the **System Properties** window. Click the **Hardware** tab, click **Device Manager**, and then double-click the icon for a device that you want enabled or disabled in the new profile.

10. Click the **General** tab in the Properties window for the device and in the area for device usage, select the option to enable the device, and disable it for the current profile or for all hardware profiles.

Power Management

A+CORE 1.2 — A notebook can be powered in several ways including an AC adapter (to use regular house current to power the notebook), a DC adapter (to use DC power such as that provided by automobile cigarette lighters), and a battery pack. Types of batteries are the older and mostly outdated Ni-Cad (nickel-cadmium) battery, the longer-life NiMH (nickel-metal-hydride) battery, and the current Lithium Ion battery that is more efficient than earlier batteries. A future battery solution is the fuel cell battery that is supposed to provide a continuous operating time of up to 10 hours. A notebook user might need one or more batteries and a DC adapter for travel and an AC adapter at home and for recharging the batteries. Always power down the notebook before switching power sources.

Windows 98 and Windows 2000/XP have features to help manage power consumption. The goal is to minimize power consumption to increase the time before a battery pack needs recharging. Using Windows 98, to access the power management window, click Start, point to Settings, click Control Panel, and double-click the Power Management icon. Figure 20-3 shows the Power Management Properties dialog box for one notebook.

20

(Other brands of notebooks may have different tabs in their Properties dialog box.) Use this dialog box to create, delete, and modify multiple power management schemes to customize how Windows 98 manages power consumption.

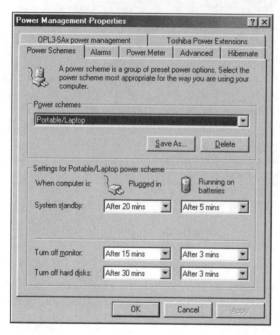

Figure 20-3   The Power Management Properties box of Windows 98 allows you to create and manage multiple power schemes

For example, one power-saving feature of Windows 98 puts a notebook into hibernation. When a computer hibernates, it stores whatever is currently in memory and then shuts down. When it returns from hibernating, it restores everything to the way it was before the shutdown. When hibernating, the notebook uses a very small amount of power. When you step away from the notebook for a few minutes, direct the notebook to hibernate in order to save power. Before you direct a notebook to hibernate, make sure you know the keystrokes or buttons required to restore the system to an active state without turning off the computer.

If the notebook supports hibernating, to configure Windows 98 to cause the notebook to hibernate when you close the lid of the notebook, do the following:

1. In the Power Management Properties dialog box, click the **Hibernate** tab (see Figure 20-4), and verify that hibernate support is enabled. If there is no Hibernate tab, your notebook does not support hibernating.

2. Click the **Advanced** tab. Figure 20-5 shows the Advanced page, which you use to control what happens when you press the shutdown button or close the lid of the notebook.

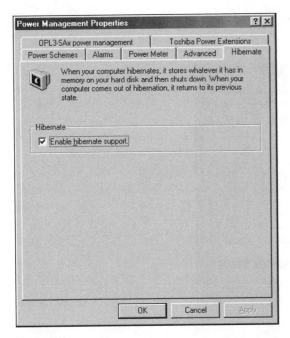

Figure 20-4   Verify that hibernate support is enabled

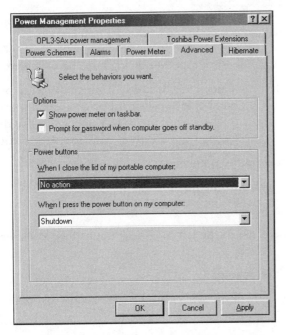

Figure 20-5   The Advanced tab of Power Management allows you to control the behavior of the power button and what happens when you close the lid of your notebook

20

3. Click the list arrow for "When I close the lid of my portable computer," and select **Hibernate** (see Figure 20-6).

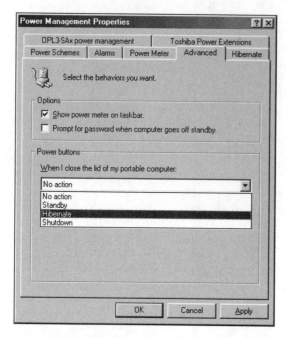

Figure 20-6   Choices of action when you close the lid of your notebook

4. Click **Apply** and **OK** to close the Properties dialog box and save your changes.

If you need to use the notebook for extended periods away from an electrical outlet, you can use extra battery packs. When the notebook signals that power is low, remove the old battery and replace it with a charged one. See the notebook's user guide for directions. Here is an example of directions for exchanging the battery pack for one notebook:

1. Save your work and turn off the notebook.

2. Remove all cables connected to the notebook.

3. Set the notebook on its back.

4. Slide the battery release panel to the left to expose the battery, as shown in Figure 20-7.

5. Lift the battery out of the computer.

6. Before placing a new battery in the slot, clean the edge connectors of the battery with a clean cloth.

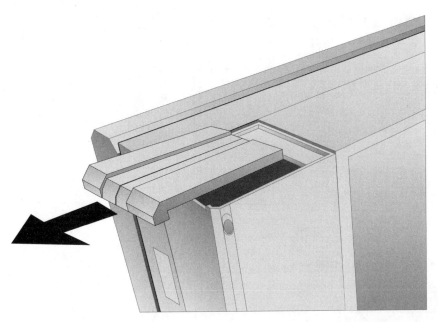

Figure 20-7 Slide the battery release panel to the left to expose the battery pack

To extend the life of your battery, don't leave it in while the notebook is turned on and connected to an electrical outlet. When using the notebook while it is connected to an electrical outlet, remove the battery from the case. To recharge the battery, leave the notebook turned off while it is connected to an electrical outlet with the battery inserted. To keep some older battery types operating at optimum performance, you have to let the battery almost completely discharge then recharge it completely before using it again. Some newer battery types do not require this. Check the documentation for your particular notebook and battery, and never use a battery charger on a battery type other than the one for which it was designed.

Windows 2000 improves the power management features of Windows 98, adding ACPI and APM. In Windows 2000, you can monitor and manage batteries on notebooks that are ACPI- and APM-enabled. You can access the battery meter directly by adding the battery status icon to the taskbar (see Figure 20-8). Follow these steps:

1. On the **Start** menu, click **Settings**, **Control Panel**.

2. Double-click **Power Options** to open the Power Options Properties dialog box.

3. Click the **Advanced** tab.

4. Click the check box labeled **Always show icon on the taskbar**, then click **OK**.

Note that the Power Options box also offers tabs on which you can create power profiles and set alarms to alert you when battery power is low or critical.

20

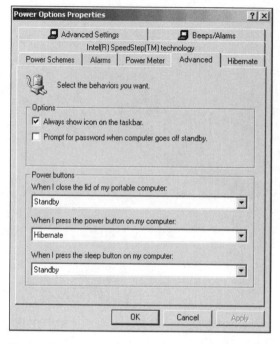

Figure 20-8   Use the Power Options Properties window to specify what to do when you close the lid, press the power button, or press the sleep button

Windows XP also includes power management features for notebooks, including support for ACPI and ACM. You can access these features from the Power Options icon in Control Panel in Classic view, or from Performance and Maintenance, then Power Options in Category view. In the Power Options window, click the Power Schemes tab to select a **power scheme**, a collection of settings for a particular set of circumstances, such as for home/office desk use or portable/laptop use.

Upgrading Memory

A+CORE
1.3
4.2
4.3

Notebooks use four types of memory (see Figure 20-9) that are all smaller than regular SIMMs, DIMMs, or RIMMs. **SO-DIMMs** (**small outline DIMMs**, pronounced "sew-dims") come in two types. 72-pin SO-DIMMs, which support 32-bit data transfers, use FPM or EDO (which you learned about in Chapter 6) and could be used as single modules in 386 or 486 machines but must be used in pairs in Pentium machines. 144-pin SO-DIMMs, which support 64-bit data transfers, use EDO and SDRAM and can be used as single modules in Pentium machines. Another type of memory for notebooks is the 160-pin **SO-RIMM (small outline RIMM)**, which uses a 64-bit data path and the Rambus technology discussed in Chapter 6. Also, before notebooks used memory modules, some notebooks provided memory slots to accommodate memory stored on a small card the size of a credit card. This **credit card memory** was installed by inserting it in this special memory slot, which looks like the PC Card slots for different add-on devices discussed later in the chapter, but can only be used for memory. Sub-notebooks sometimes use 144-pin MicroDIMMs that are smaller than 50-DIMMs and have a 64-bit data path.

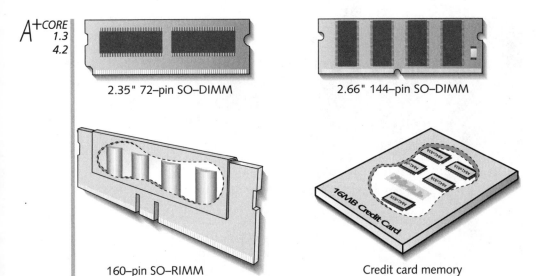

2.35" 72–pin SO–DIMM   2.66" 144–pin SO–DIMM

160–pin SO–RIMM   Credit card memory

Figure 20-9   Four types of memory used on notebook computers

CAUTION

Before upgrading memory, make sure you are not voiding your warranty. Search for the best buy, but make sure you use memory modules made by or authorized by your notebook's manufacturer and designed for the exact model of your notebook. Installing generic memory might save money but might also void the notebook's warranty.

A+CORE 1.3

To install memory, see the notebook user guide for directions. The following is an example of how to install memory on one notebook. Directions vary from one notebook computer to another.

1. Turn off the notebook and remove all cables.

2. Lift the keyboard brace, as shown in Figure 20-10. (Your notebook might have a different way to enter the system—for example, from the bottom of the case.)

3. Turn the keyboard over and toward the front of the notebook (see Figure 20-11). The keyboard is still connected to the notebook by the ribbon cable.

4. Lift the plastic sheet covering the memory module socket.

20

$A^{+CORE}_{\ \ 1.3}$

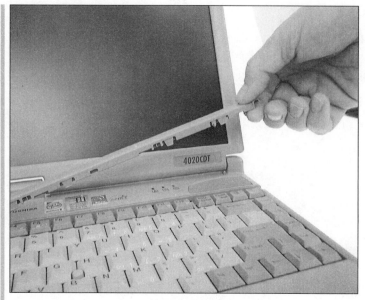

Figure 20-10   Lift the keyboard brace

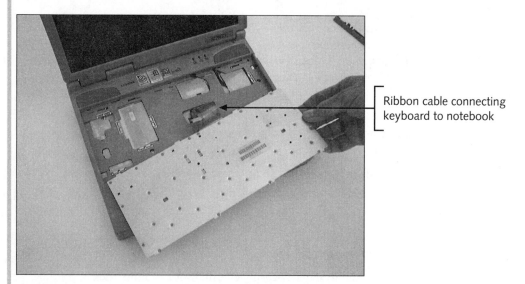

Ribbon cable connecting keyboard to notebook

Figure 20-11   Turn the keyboard over toward the front of the notebook to expose memory module sockets

5. Insert the SO-DIMM module into the socket. See Figure 20–12. The socket braces should snap into place on each side of the module when the module is in position.

6. Replace the keyboard and keyboard brace. (If you entered from the bottom, you might be replacing a cover on the bottom of the case in this step.)

7. Power up the notebook so that it can detect the new memory.

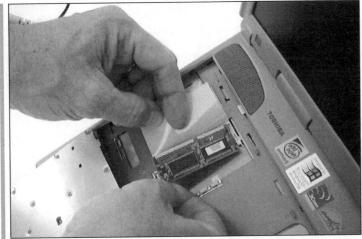

Figure 20-12 Install the SO-DIMM into the memory socket

Other Field Replaceable Units for Notebooks

Besides memory, other field replaceable units (FRUs) for notebooks might be the hard drive, the LCD panel, the motherboard, the CPU, the keyboard, the PC Card socket assembly, the CD-ROM drive, the floppy drive, a sound card, a pointing device, the AC adapter, the battery pack, and the DC controller. Parts either made or approved by the notebook manufacturer must be used to replace all these parts. The **DC controller** is a card inside the notebook that converts voltage to CPU core voltage. The DC controller can support battery mode, AC adapter mode, and various sleep modes, and must be specifically rated for the notebook's processor.

A hard drive for a notebook computer can be an external or internal drive. External devices, including hard drives, connect to ports on the notebook or to a port provided by a PC Card. Internal notebook drives are much smaller than desktop drives; for a comparison, see Figure 20-13. When installing an internal hard drive floppy drive, CD/CD-RW drive, DVD/DVD-RW drive or removable drive, follow specific directions given by the notebook's manufacturer. For example, to replace the hard drive for the notebook shown in Figure 20-14, first remove the floppy disk drive to reveal the hard drive under it. Remove the screws holding the hard drive in place, remove the drive, and replace it with a drive designed to fit this particular cavity.

A notebook does not contain the normal PCI and ISA expansion slots found in desktop systems. Most internal cards such as modems, SCSI host adapters, IEEE 1394 controllers, USB controllers, and network adapters use proprietary slots designed and supported by the notebook manufacturer. It is expected that the notebook industry will soon embrace a more generic method of connecting an internal card to a notebook using the Mini PCI Card specifications. The standards include three types of cards, Type I, II and III, that specify how the internal card provides a port on the notebook. Type I and II cards connect to the motherboard using a 100-pin stacking connector, and Type III cards use a 124-pin stacking connector and are smaller than the Type I and II cards and are expected to be the most popular.

20

$A^{+CORE}_{1.3}$

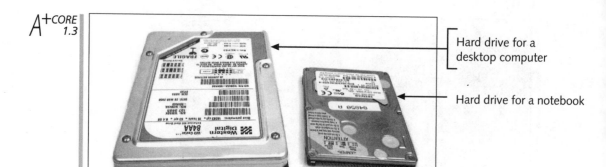

Hard drive for a
desktop computer

Hard drive for a notebook

Figure 20-13   Hard drives for notebooks are smaller than hard drives for desktop computers

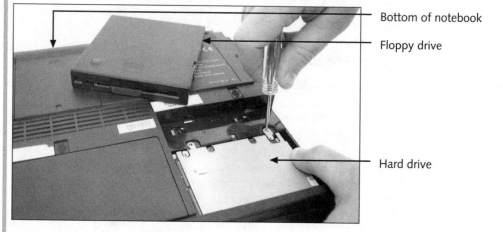

Bottom of notebook

Floppy drive

Hard drive

Figure 20-14   First remove the floppy drive to reveal the hard drive cavity

Connecting Peripheral Devices to Notebooks

$A^{+CORE}_{\substack{1.3 \\ 5.1}}$ A notebook provides ports on its back or sides (see Figure 20-15), which are used for
connecting peripherals. Some notebooks have fewer ports than the one in Figure 20-15
and are designed to be used with a port replicator, such as the one shown in Figure 20-16,
or a docking station, shown in Figure 20-17. A **port replicator** provides a means to connect
a notebook to a power outlet and provides additional ports to allow a notebook to easily
connect to a full-sized monitor, keyboard, and other peripheral devices. A **docking station**
provides the same functions as a port replicator, but also adds secondary storage, such as a
Zip drive or floppy disk drive.

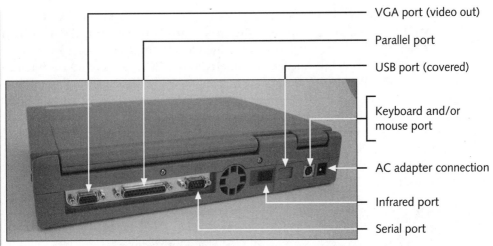

VGA port (video out)

Parallel port

USB port (covered)

Keyboard and/or mouse port

AC adapter connection

Infrared port

Serial port

Figure 20-15   Ports on the back of a notebook

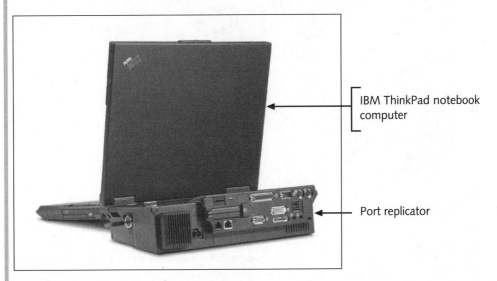

IBM ThinkPad notebook computer

Port replicator

Figure 20-16   A port replicator makes it convenient to connect a notebook computer to resources and peripherals at your office

20

Figure 20-17   An IBM ThinkPad dock, an example of a docking station

A+CORE
1.3
1.10
5.1

A popular way to add peripheral devices to a notebook is to use **PC Cards**, also called **PCMCIA (Personal Computer Memory Card International Association) Cards** in **PC Card slots** (see Figure 20-18), formally called **PCMCIA slots**. A PC Card is about the size of a credit card, but thicker, and inserts into a PC Card slot. Once intended only for memory cards, PC Card slots can now be used by many devices, including modems, network cards for wired or wireless networks, CD-ROMs, sound cards, SCSI host adapters, IEEE 1394 controllers, USB controllers, and hard disks. Unlike PCs, notebooks don't have the traditional expansion slots that connect to an I/O bus to add peripheral devices to a system. In notebooks, PC Card slots connect to the 16-bit PCMCIA I/O bus on the notebook motherboard. Some docking station PCs also have a PC Card slot, so that the device you use with your notebook can also be attached to the docking station.

Figure 20-18   Many peripheral devices are added to a notebook using a PC Card slot; here, a modem PC Card is inserted in a PC Card slot

The PCMCIA organization has developed four standards for these slots. The latest PCMCIA specification, **CardBus**, improves I/O speed, increases the bus width to 32 bits, and supports lower-voltage PC Cards while maintaining backward compatibility with earlier standards. Three standards for PCMCIA slots pertain to size and are named Type I, Type II, and Type III. Generally, the thicker the PC Card, the higher the standard. A thick hard drive card might need a Type III slot, but a thin modem card might only need a Type II slot. Type I cards can be up to 3.3-mm thick and are primarily used for adding RAM to a notebook PC. Type II cards can be up to 5.5-mm thick and are often used as modem cards. Type III cards can be up to 10.5-mm thick, large enough to accommodate a portable disk drive. When buying a notebook PC, look for both Type II and Type III PC Card slots. Often, one of each is included. For improved performance, look for 32-bit CardBus slots.

The operating system must provide two services for the PC Card, a socket service and a card service. The socket service establishes communication between the PC Card and the notebook when the card is first inserted and then disconnects communication when the card is

A+CORE
1.3
1.10
5.1

removed. The card service provides the device driver to interface with the card once the socket is created.

The PC Card might contain a data cable to an external device, or it might be self-contained. For example, in Figure 20-19, the PC Card on the left is the interface between the notebook PC and an external CD-ROM drive. The card is inserted in the PC Card slot, and the data cable from the PC Card connects to the external CD-ROM drive, which requires its own power supply connected to a wall outlet. The PC Card on the right in Figure 20-19 is a modem card; when inserted in the PC Card slot, it provides a direct connection for the telephone line to the modem (see Figure 20-20).

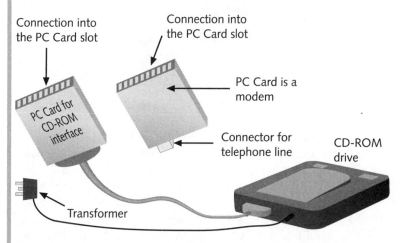

Figure 20-19   Two examples of PC Cards, one self-contained (the modem), the other connected to an external device (the CD-ROM drive)

Figure 20-20   Connect the phone line to the modem PC Card

Another popular use of a PC Card is to interface with a network. Figure 20-21 shows a PC Card that serves as the NIC to an Ethernet 100BaseT network. The RJ-45 connection is at

20

A^{+CORE}
1.3
1.10
5.1

the end of a small cord connected to the PC Card. This small cord is called a dongle or pigtail and is used so that the thick RJ-45 connection does not have to fit flat against the PC Card.

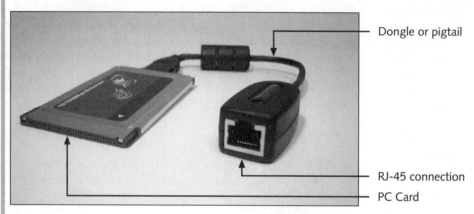

Dongle or pigtail

RJ-45 connection

PC Card

Figure 20-21 This PC Card serves as a NIC for an Ethernet 100BaseT network

PC Cards can be hot-swapped, but you must stop one card before inserting another. Hot-swapping allows you to remove one card and insert another without powering down the PC. For example, if you currently use a wireless network card in the PC Card slot of a Windows 2000 notebook and want to switch to a CD-ROM card, first turn off the network card, then remove the network card and insert the CD-ROM card with the attached external CD-ROM drive. For Windows 2000, to stop the card, use the Add/Remove Hardware icon in Control Panel. The Add/Remove Hardware Wizard starts; click Next and on the next screen select Uninstall/Unplug a device, and click Next again. On the next screen, select Unplug/Eject a device. A list of devices appears (see Figure 20-22). Select the device and click Next. The final screen tells you that you can safely unplug the device and gives you the option to display an Unplug/Eject icon in the taskbar when the device is used again. In Windows 9x, to stop a card, use the PC Card icon in the Control Panel; for Windows XP, use the Safely Remove Hardware icon in the system tray.

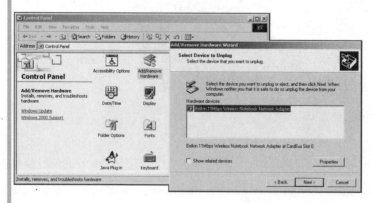

Figure 20-22 Before removing a PC Card from the notebook, stop the card (open the socket)

TIP A bug in Windows XP causes the system to hang if you remove a PC Card while the system is in sleep mode or is hibernating. To solve the problem, download the latest service pack for Windows XP.

The first time you insert a PC Card in a notebook, the Found New Hardware Wizard launches and steps you through the installation process in which you can use the drivers provided by the hardware manufacturer or use Windows drivers. The next time you insert the card in the notebook, the card is detected and starts up without help.

Other smaller slots used on notebooks include a slot for a Secure Digital (SD) Card and a slot for a CompactFlash Card. Both cards are about the size of a postage stamp. These slots are used primarily for flash memory but can also be used for other devices. For example, IBM uses a CompactFlash Type II slot for its Microdrive, a miniature 1 GB hard drive that is useful for storing multimedia files.

There are several flash memory products on the market including CompactFlash Type I and II, SmartMedia (introduced in Chapter 11), Microdrive, Secure Digital (SD), Memory Stick, and MagicGate. These flash cards can be used in sockets designed specifically for them or you can purchase adapter sleeves that enable the cards to use a PC Card slot. The card must be PCMCIA compliant.

Flash cards and PC Cards can also be read by desktop computers when the card is inserted in a card reader that can handle the specific format. For example, one card reader is the SwapBox PC Card Reader by SCM Microsystems (*www.scmmicro.com*). The card reader interfaces with a desktop computer by way of an ISA or PCI slot. PC Cards, such as a modem card or Ethernet card, can be inserted in the reader which can handle Type I, II, and III PC Cards. In addition, when used with adapter sleeves, the SwapBox can accept other PCMCIA-compliant cards such as SmartMedia and CompactFlash cards.

USB ports have become a popular way of adding devices to notebooks. For example, if the notebook does not have an RJ-45 port for an Ethernet connection, you can buy a device to plug into the USB port that provides the Ethernet port. Another example shown in Figure 20-23 is a wireless keyboard and mouse that use a receiver connected to a USB or PS/2 port. Installing this keyboard and mouse on a Windows 2000/XP notebook is very simple. You simply plug the receiver into the port. Windows displays a message that it has located the device and the mouse and keyboard are ready to use. This ease of installation is fast making USB the preferred method of connecting peripheral devices.

Online Resources for Troubleshooting Notebooks

Except for the differences discussed in this section, notebooks work identically to desktop PCs, and the troubleshooting guidelines in previous chapters also apply to notebooks. When troubleshooting notebooks, be especially conscious of warranty issues; know what you can do within the guidelines of the warranty. The documentation that comes with a notebook is much more comprehensive than what comes with a PC and most often contains troubleshooting guidelines for the notebook. Remember that the loaded OS and the hardware configuration are specific to the notebook, so you can rely on the notebook's manufacturer

20

A+CORE
1.3

for support more than you can for a desktop PC. Sometimes a notebook is designed so that the hard drive can be replaced or upgraded without violating warranties. See the notebook documentation for details. For questions about supporting a notebook that are not answered in the documentation, see the notebook manufacturer's Web site. Some popular manufacturers of notebooks and their Web sites are listed in Table 20-1.

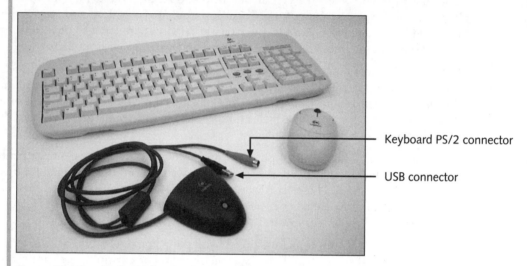

Keyboard PS/2 connector

USB connector

Figure 20-23   This wireless keyboard and mouse by Logitech use a receiver that connects to either a USB or keyboard port

Table 20-1   Notebook manufacturers

Manufacturer	Web site
Acer America	global.acer.com
ARM Computer	www.armcomputer.com
Compaq Computer	www.hp.com
Dell Computer	www.dell.com
Gateway	www.gateway.com
Hewlett-Packard	www.hp.com
IBM	www.ibm.com
Micron PC	www.micronpc.com
PC Notebook	www.pcnotebook.com
Sony	www.sonystyle.com
Toshiba America	www.csd.toshiba.com
WinBook	www.winbook.com

PDAs

Notebooks provide portability or flexibility, but even the smallest have to be carried in a case the size of a briefcase and can be cumbersome in some situations, especially for simple tasks such as checking addresses, viewing stock prices, or recording and receiving short messages. **PDAs (personal digital assistants)**, sometimes called personal PCs or hand-held PCs, provide greater ease of use for such situations. A PDA, such as a Palm Pilot or a Pocket PC, is a small, handheld computer with its own operating system and applications. Figure 20-24 shows the Compaq iPAQ H3800 PDA with its universal cradle and cable, which are used to connect to a PC.

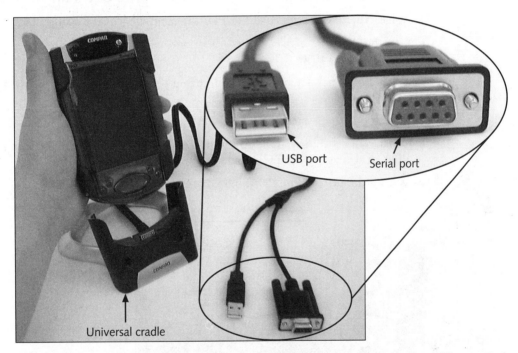

Figure 20-24   The Compaq iPAQ H3800 PDA comes with a cradle and a cable to attach to a USB or serial port on another computer

Like a notebook, a PDA is battery-powered, uses either a grayscale or color active matrix or dual-scan passive matrix display, and can sometimes benefit from additional memory. Other PDA hardware includes a stylus used to operate the PDA by touching the screen. You tap the screen with the stylus to open applications or make menu selections. You can also hold down the stylus to scroll through menu options. For quick access to commonly used applications such as a calendar or an address book, most PDAs provide application buttons below the screen that you can press to bring up the application. A PDA might use an AC/DC adapter that can plug into the PDA itself or into the universal cradle. Some PDAs have optional accessories such as the fold-out keyboard shown in Figure 20-25.

20

When purchasing a PDA, first decide how you will use it, and then match the features of the PDA to its intended purpose. Here are the main things to consider when purchasing a PDA. The next sections cover several of these items.

- What applications come with the PDA, and what applications can be added later?

- How easy is the PDA to use, and how thorough is its documentation?

- How easy is it to keep the PDA synchronized with your desktop computer or notebook, and will your organization approve the type of PDA synchronization?

- What support is available on the manufacturer's Web site? What software for the PDA can be downloaded from this site? What is the cost of that software?

- What type of batteries does the PDA use, and what is the battery life?

- Can the PDA use e-mail and the Web, and what extra hardware and software is required to do that?

- What additional devices can be purchased to make the PDA more versatile and easier to use?

- What operating system does the PDA use? How easy is the OS to use?

- What is the warranty? Does the warranty cover such things as dropping the PDA or damaging the LCD panel by pressing too hard on it?

- What is the price of the PDA, and what is the price of additional years of warranty?

PDA snaps in here

Figure 20-25   This fold-out keyboard attaches to a PDA

Battery Life on a PDA

Battery life on a PDA varies by model, and short battery life is one of the largest complaints against PDAs. Some PDAs use rechargeable batteries, and others do not. If your PDA's battery runs down all the way and discharges, you lose all the data and applications on it! Many manufacturers suggest that you get in the habit of setting your PDA in its cradle whenever you are not carrying it, and that you never trust it with data or downloaded software for more than a few hours. It is a good idea to have a cradle and adapter wherever you use your PDA; you may want to keep one at your home, another at your office, and another in your briefcase.

Applications on a PDA

You can use a PDA to store addresses and phone numbers, manage a calendar, run word processing, send and receive e-mail, access Web sites, play music, and exchange information with a desktop computer. Some PDAs come with all application software preinstalled, and others require the user to download applications at additional cost. Other PDAs support only the preinstalled applications and cannot download others. Some PDAs allow you to download e-mail or Web site content from a desktop computer or a notebook, and others can access the Internet directly by way of a modem or wireless connection. Not all Web sites are designed to be accessed by a PDA, and the Web content a PDA can read is more limited than the content a desktop or notebook computer can read.

Connecting a PDA to a PC

A+CORE
1.8

Typically, a PDA comes with a universal cradle that has an attached cable to connect to a desktop computer or notebook by way of a serial or USB port, or a PDA might use an infrared connection. The process by which the PDA and the PC "talk" to each other through the universal cradle, cable, and USB or serial connection is called **synchronization**. This process enables you to back up information on your PDA to the PC, work with PDA files on the PC, and download applications to the PDA that you downloaded from the Web using the PC. Special software, such as ActiveSync by Microsoft, might be needed to perform synchronization between the PDA and the other computer attached via the cable. You need to install this software before connecting the PDA to the PC. Follow the instructions in the PDA documentation and on the CD included with it to install the software.

Some PDAs can also synchronize with a desktop or notebook computer through wireless technology. The Compaq PDA shown in Figure 12-24 supports the Bluetooth standard introduced in Chapter 18. For wireless synchronization to occur, both the PDA and the PC must be set up to use the same wireless standard (for example, Bluetooth, Wi-Fi, or 802.11a). The PC and the PDA must each have a wireless transmitter/receiver (transceiver) and software installed to use it. Some PDAs have an embedded transceiver, and others require an add-on device. Again, study the PDA documentation to learn if a PDA supports wireless technology.

To set up a PDA and a PC to communicate, do the following:

- Read the PDA documentation about how to synchronize it with the PC and install on the PC the synchronization software that came bundled with the PDA. If the synchronization software must first be launched, launch it.

- Connect the PDA to the PC by way of a USB cable or serial cable that most likely also came bundled with the PDA.

- The PDA and PC should immediately synchronize. Data entered on one device should be reflected on the other.

20

$A+CORE$
1.8

If you have problems, check these things:

- Is the USB or serial cable plugged in at both ends?
- For a USB connection, verify the USB controller is working in Device Manager with no conflicts.
- Is the USB or serial port enabled in CMOS setup?
- Is the PDA turned on?
- Check the PDA documentation for other things to do and try.
- Uninstall and reinstall the PDA software on the PC.
- Check the Web site of the PDA manufacturer for problems and solutions.

PDA Manufacturers and Operating Systems

There are two main OSs for PDAs: Pocket PC and Palm OS. You may also see Pocket PC referred to as Windows CE 3.0; Windows CE was an earlier Microsoft handheld OS. Given the prominence of Microsoft Windows in most markets it has entered, it is interesting to note that Palm OS and Pocket PC have basically equal shares of the market for PDA OSs. The principal difference between the two OSs is in the applications they support. Pocket PC is considered a more versatile OS that can better be used to download and run applications similar to those supported by Windows, such as Microsoft Word or Excel. Palm OS is less complex, easier to use, and considered the better choice if the PDA is to be used only for simple tasks such as using e-mail, an address book, or a calendar. Table 20-2 lists some manufacturers of PDAs running Palm OS, and Table 20-3 lists some manufacturers of PDAs running Pocket PC.

Table 20-2   Manufacturers of Palm OS PDAs

Manufacturer	Web Site
HandEra	www.handera.com
Handspring	www.handspring.com
IBM	www.ibm.com
Palm	www.palm.com
Samsung	www.samsungelectronics.com/pda

Table 20-3   Manufacturers of Pocket PC PDAs

Manufacturer	Web Site
Casio	www.casio.com/personalpcs
Compaq	www.hp.com
Hewlett-Packard	www.hp.com
Toshiba	www.toshiba.com

> **TIP** Hewlett-Packard sponsors a forum to promote open source software (programming code is made public and no royalties are paid) to use the Linux operating system on handheld computers. For more information, see *www.handhelds.org*.

CHAPTER SUMMARY

- Notebook computers are designed for travel. They use the same technology as PCs, with modifications for space, portability, and power conservation. A notebook generally costs more than a PC with the same specifications.

- When supporting notebooks, pay careful attention to what the warranty allows you to change on the computer.

- Windows 98 notebook computer features include Multilink Channel Aggregation, ACPI and APM, improved support for and management of PC cards, and the Briefcase.

- Windows 2000 notebook features support high–end notebooks better than Windows 9x and include offline files, improved battery support, hot-swapping, and folder redirection.

- Windows XP notebook support includes the ability to create hardware profiles and power schemes that manage the computer's attached devices and power settings differently, depending on whether the computer is connected to a port replicator or not.

- A notebook can be powered by its battery pack or by an AC adapter connected to a power source.

- Notebooks use credit card memory, SO-DIMMs, and SO-RIMMs for upgrading memory.

- Upgrading memory on a notebook varies from one notebook to another; see the notebook's user guide for specific instructions.

- When upgrading components on a notebook, including memory, use components that are the same brand as the notebook, or use only components recommended by the notebook's manufacturer.

- PC Cards are a popular way to add peripheral devices to notebooks. The latest PC Card specification is CardBus. There are three types of PC Cards, which vary in thickness: Types I, II, and III.

- Notebook settings and procedures vary more widely from model to model than those of desktop computers. Check the manufacturer's documentation and Web site for information specific to your notebook model.

- A PDA provides even more portability than a notebook computer for applications such as address books and calendars. PDAs are designed to provide handheld computing power and can interface with a desktop or notebook computer to transfer files and applications.

- PDAs synchronize with PCs through a USB, serial, or wireless port. For wireless, check that the PC and PDA support the same wireless standard.

20

KEY TERMS

Briefcase	PC Card	port replicator
CardBus	PC Card slot	power scheme
credit card memory	PCMCIA (Personal	SO-DIMM (small outline
DC controller	Computer Memory	DIMM)
docking station	Card International	SO-RIMM (small outline
folder redirection	Association) Card	RIMM)
hardware profiles	PCMCIA slot	synchronization
laptop computer	PDA (Personal Digital	
notebook	Assistant)	

REVIEW QUESTIONS

1. Of the following types of displays used for laptops, which offers the best overall image quality?

    a. CRT monitor

    b. Active matrix

    c. Passive matrix

    d. Both b and c

    e. None of the above

2. The feature that allows a notebook running the Windows 98 operating system to turn devices on, as well as have devices turn on a notebook, is referred to as:

    a. Multilink Channel Aggregation

    b. ACPI

    c. Power Management

    d. Microsoft Exchange

    e. None of the above

3. In terms of upgrading memory for a notebook, which of the smaller memory used allows for at least 32-bit data transfers?

    a. SIMM

    b. DIMM

    c. RIMM

    d. SO-DIMM

    e. All of the above

4. Another term/acronym given to peripheral devices that are user-changeable in notebook or laptop computers is:

   a. CPU

   b. AC

   c. DC

   d. IDE

   e. FRU

5. To address the issue of limited connection points from the notebook to peripheral devices, notebook manufacturers have developed the _____ to provide additional connection points, as well as secondary storage capability.

   a. Port replicator

   b. Docking station

   c. Hub

   d. Switch

   e. Network

6. Many peripherals are added to notebook computers by way of a _____ bus, which has been designed around a card-type interface of various types.

   a. Serial

   b. Parallel

   c. SCSI

   d. PCMCIA

   e. IDE

7. Which of the following is *not* representative of flash memory products that are used in notebook computers?

   a. CompactFlash Type I

   b. CompactFlash Type II

   c. CompactFlash Type III

   d. SmartMedia

   e. Microdrive

8. Of the operating systems most used with notebook computers, which is most likely to "recognize" the newer USB-type devices once they are inserted into the notebook without the need for additional device drivers to be installed into the computer by way of manufacturer's disk?

   a. Windows 95

   b. Windows 98

   c. Windows 2000

   d. All of the above

   e. None of the above

20

9. The term associated with the coordinating of data on a notebook with that on a PDA is _____.

   a. Connecting

   b. Synchronizing

   c. Transferring

   d. Purging

   e. None of the above

10. Which of the following operating systems are most likely to be found on a current PDA?

    a. Windows 98

    b. Windows ME

    c. Windows CE

    d. Windows XP

    e. None of the above

21

SUPPORTING PRINTERS

In this chapter, you will learn:

♦ How printers work
♦ How to install printers and share them over a local area network
♦ How to troubleshoot printer problems

This chapter discusses the three main types of printers, how they work, and how to support them. Printers connect to a PC by way of a parallel port, serial port, USB port, or wireless (radio or infrared) connection. You'll also learn how to install a printer, how to share a printer with others on a network, and how to troubleshoot printer problems.

HOW PRINTERS WORK

A+CORE 5.1 This section discusses how printers work, what types of printers there are, and how to support them. Local printers connect directly to a computer by way of a parallel port, serial port, USB port, infrared connection, wireless connection, IEEE 1394 port, SCSI port, or PC Card connection, or a computer can access a network printer by way of the network. Printers can have a variety of options including extra paper trays to hold different sizes of paper, special paper feeders, staplers, collators, and sorters. Printers can also be combined with fax machines, copiers and scanners in the same machine. Most often, printers are powered by AC power, but some printers use batteries. Let's begin by looking at several types of printers for desktop computing.

Laser Printers

A+CORE 5.1 Laser printers are a type of electrophotographic printer and range from small, personal desktop models to large network printers capable of handling and printing large volumes continuously. Figure 21-1 shows an example of a typical laser printer for a desktop computer system.

Figure 21-1   A desktop laser printer

Laser printers require the interaction of mechanical, electrical, and optical technologies to work. Understanding how they work will help you support and service them. This section also explains why the safety precautions stated in laser printer user manuals are necessary.

How a Laser Printer Works

Laser printers work by placing toner on an electrically charged rotating drum and then depositing the toner on paper as the paper moves through the system at the same speed the drum is turning. Figure 21-2 shows the six steps of laser printing. The first four use the printer components that undergo the most wear. They are contained within the removable cartridge to increase the printer's life. The last two steps are performed outside the cartridge. Follow the steps of laser printing below while you refer to Figure 21-2.

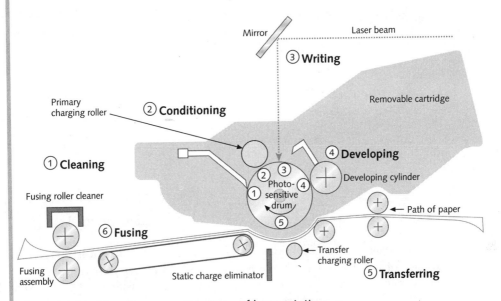

Figure 21-2   The six progressive steps of laser printing

1. *Cleaning.* The drum is cleaned of any residual toner and electrical charge.

2. *Conditioning.* The drum is conditioned to contain a high electrical charge.

3. *Writing.* A laser beam discharges a lower charge to only those places where toner is to go.

4. *Developing.* Toner is placed on the drum where the charge has been reduced.

5. *Transferring.* A strong electrical charge draws the toner off the drum onto the paper. This is the first step that takes place outside the cartridge.

6. *Fusing.* Heat and pressure fuse the toner to the paper.

Note that Figure 21-2 shows only a cross-section of the drum, mechanisms, and paper. Remember that the drum is as wide as a sheet of paper. The mirror, blades, and rollers in the drawing are also as wide as paper. Also know that toner responds to a charge and moves from one surface to another if the second surface has a more positive charge than the first. As you visualize the process, first note the location of the removable cartridge in the drawing, the photosensitive drum inside the cartridge turning in a clockwise direction, and the path of the paper, which moves from right to left.

21

A+CORE
5.1

Step 1: Cleaning. Figure 21-3 shows a clear view of the cleaning step. First a sweeper strip cleans the drum of any residual toner, which is swept away from the drum by a sweeping blade. A cleaning blade completes the physical cleaning of the drum. Next the drum is cleaned of any electrical charge by erase lamps (located in the hinged top cover of the printer), which light the surface of the drum to neutralize any electrical charge left on the drum.

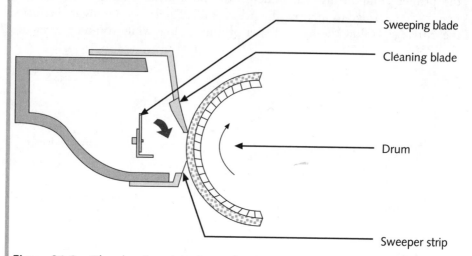

Figure 21-3   The cleaning step cleans the drum of toner and electrical charge

Step 2: Conditioning. The conditioning step puts a uniform electrical charge of −600V on the surface of the drum. The charge is put there by a primary charging roller or primary corona, which is charged by a high-voltage power supply assembly. The primary charging roller in Figure 21-2 is inside the toner cartridge and regulates the charge on the drum, ensuring that it is a uniform −600 V.

Step 3: Writing. In the writing step, the uniform charge applied in Step 2 is discharged only where you want the printer to print. This is done by controlling mirrors to reflect laser beams onto the drum in a pattern that re-creates the image desired. This is the first step in which data from the computer must be transmitted to the printer. Figure 21-4 shows the process. Data from the PC is received by the formatter (1) and passed on to the DC controller (2), which controls the laser unit (3). The laser beam is initiated and directed toward the octagonal mirror called the **scanning mirror**. The scanning mirror (4) is turned by the scanning motor in a clockwise direction. There are eight mirrors on the eight sides of the scanning mirror. As the mirror turns, the laser beam is directed in a sweeping motion that can cover the entire length of the drum. The laser beam is reflected off the scanning mirror, focused by the focusing lens (5), and sent on to the mirror (6), which is also shown in Figure 21-2. The mirror deflects the laser beam to a slit in the removable cartridge and on to the drum (7).

$A^{+}{}^{CORE}_{5.1}$

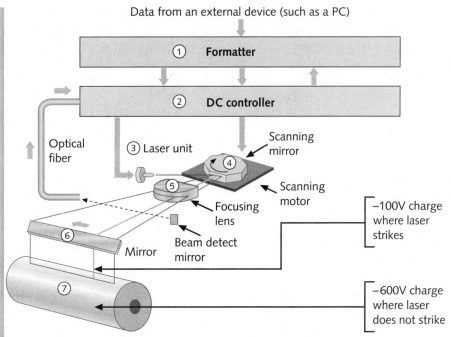

Data from an external device (such as a PC)

Figure 21-4   The writing step, done by an invisible laser beam, mirrors, and motors, causes a discharge on the drum where the image will be

The speed of the motor turning the drum and the speed of the scanning motor turning the scanning mirror are synchronized so that the laser beam completes one pass, or scanline, across the drum and returns to the beginning of the drum (right side of the drum in Figure 21-4) to begin a new pass, until it completes the correct number of passes for each inch of the drum circumference. For example, for a 1200 dots per inch (dpi) printer, the beam makes 1200 passes for every one inch of the drum circumference. The laser beam is turned on and off continually as it makes a single pass down the length of the drum, so that dots are written along the drum on every pass. For a 1200-dpi printer, 1200 dots are written along the drum for every inch of linear pass. The 1200 dots per inch down this single pass, along with 1200 passes per inch of drum circumference, together accomplish the resolution of 1200 × 1200 dots per square inch of many desktop laser printers.

TIP   A laser printer can produce better quality printouts than a dot-matrix printer, even when printing at the same dpi, because it can vary the size of the dots it prints, creating a sharp, clear image. HP calls this technology of varying the size of dots **REt (Resolution Enhancement technology)**.

21

In a laser printer, where the laser beam strikes the surface of the drum, the drum discharges from its conditioned charge of −600V down to −100V where toner will be placed on the drum. Toner does not stick to the highly charged areas of the drum.

A+CORE 5.1

Just as the scanning laser beam is synchronized to the rotating drum, the data output is synchronized to the scanning beam. Before the beam begins moving across the scanline of the drum, the **beam detect mirror** detects the laser beam by reflecting it to an optical fiber. The light travels along the optical fiber to the DC controller, where it is converted to an electrical signal that synchronizes the data output. The signal is also used to diagnose problems with the laser or scanning motor.

The laser beam has written an image to the drum surface as a −100 V charge. The −100 V charge on this image area will be used in the developing stage to transmit toner to the drum surface.

Step 4: Developing. Figure 21-5 shows the developing step, in which toner is applied by the developing cylinder to the discharged (−100 V) areas of the drum. Toner transfers from the cylinder to the drum as the two rotate very close together. The cylinder is coated with a layer of toner, made of black resin bonded to iron, which is similar to the toner used in photocopy machines. The toner is held on the cylinder surface by its attraction to a magnet inside the cylinder. (A toner cavity keeps the cylinder supplied with toner.) A **control blade** prevents too much toner from sticking to the cylinder surface. The toner on the cylinder surface takes on a negative charge (between −200 V and −500 V) because the surface is connected to a DC power supply called the DC bias.

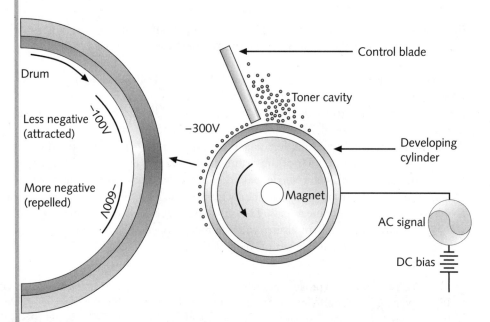

Figure 21-5   In the developing step, charged toner is deposited onto the drum surface

The negatively charged toner is more negative than the −100 V on the drum surface but less negative than the −600 V surface. This means that the toner is attracted to the −100 V area of the drum surface (the −100 V area is positive relative to the toner). The toner is repelled from the −600 V part of the drum surface, which is negative relative to the toner.

A+CORE
  5.1 The result is that toner sticks to the drum where the laser beam has hit and is repelled from the area where the laser beam has not hit.

You can adjust printer density manually at the printer or through software controlling the printer. With laser printers, when you adjust print density, you are adjusting the DC bias charge on the developing cylinder, which controls the amount of toner attracted to the cylinder, which, in turn, results in a change in print density.

Step 5: Transferring. In the transferring step, the transfer charging roller, or transfer corona (shown in Figure 21-2), produces a positive charge on the paper that pulls the toner from the drum onto the paper when the paper passes between the transfer charging roller and the drum. The static charge eliminator (refer again to Figure 21-2) weakens the positive charge on the paper and the negative charge on the drum so that the paper does not adhere to the drum, which it would otherwise do because of the difference in charge between the two. The stiffness of the paper and the small radius of the drum also help the paper move away from the drum and toward the fusing assembly. Very thin paper can wrap around the drum, which is why printer manuals usually instruct you to use only paper designated for laser printers.

Step 6: Fusing. The fusing step causes the toner to bond with the paper. Up to this point, the toner is merely sitting on the paper. The fusing rollers apply both pressure and heat to the paper. The toner melts and the rollers press the toner into the paper. The temperature of the rollers is monitored by the printer. If the temperature exceeds an allowed maximum value (410 degrees F for some printers), the printer shuts down.

The previous steps describe how a black-and-white printer works. Color laser printers work in a similar way, but the writing process repeats four times, one for each toner color of cyan, magenta, yellow, and black. Then the paper passes to the fusing stage, where the fuser bonds all toner to the paper and aids in blending the four tones to form specific colors.

Ink-Jet Printers

A+CORE
  5.1 Ink-jet printers don't normally provide the high-quality resolution of laser printers but are popular because they are small and can print color inexpensively. Most ink-jet printers today give photo-quality results, especially when used with photo-quality paper. Until this new technology was developed, increasing the quality of an ink-jet printer meant increasing the dpi (dots per inch). Earlier ink-jet printers used 300 $\times$ 300 dpi, but ink-jet printers today can use as many as 4800 $\times$ 1200 dpi. Increasing the dpi has drawbacks. Doing so increases the amount of data sent to the printer for a single page, and all those dots of ink on the page can produce a wet page. An improved technology that gives photo-quality results mixes different colors of ink to produce a new color that then makes a single dot. Hewlett-Packard calls this PhotoREt II color technology. HP mixes as many as 16 drops of ink to produce a single dot of color on the page.

21

Ink-jet printers tend to smudge on inexpensive paper, and they are slower than laser printers. The quality of the paper used with ink-jet printers significantly affects the quality of printed output. Only use paper designed for an ink-jet printer, and to get the best results, use a high-grade paper. Figure 21-6 shows one example of an ink-jet printer.

A+CORE
5.1

Figure 21-6   An example of an ink-jet printer

How an Ink-Jet Printer Works

An ink-jet printer resembles a dot-matrix printer in several ways. Both printers use a print head that moves across the paper, creating one line of text with each pass. Also, both types of printer put ink on the paper using a matrix of small dots, although ink-jet printers use much smaller dots than dot-matrix printers do. (You will learn more about dot-matrix printers later in the chapter.)

Different types of ink-jet printers form their droplets of ink in different ways. Printer manufacturers use several technologies, but the most popular is the bubble-jet. Bubble-jet printers use tubes of ink that have tiny resistors near the end of each tube. These resistors heat up and cause the ink to boil. Then, a tiny air bubble of ionized ink (ink with an electrical charge) is ejected onto the paper. A typical bubble-jet print head has 64 or 128 tiny nozzles, all of which can fire a droplet simultaneously. Plates carrying a magnetic charge direct the path of ink onto the paper to form shapes.

Ink-jet printers include one or more ink cartridges. When purchasing an ink-jet printer, look for the kind that uses two separate cartridges, one for black ink and one for three-color printing. If an ink-jet printer does not have a black ink cartridge, then it produces black by combining all colors of ink to produce a dull black. Having a separate cartridge for black ink means that it prints true black and, more important, does not use the more expensive colored ink. You can replace the black cartridge without also replacing the colored ink cartridge.

Figure 21-7 shows two ink cartridges. The cartridge on the left contains red, blue, and yellow ink (officially named magenta, cyan, and yellow), and the cartridge on the right contains black ink. The print head assemblage in the figure is in the center position

A+*CORE*
   5.1

because the top cover has been lifted. Normally when the printer is not in use, the head assemblage sits to the far right of the printing area. This is called the home position and helps protect the ink in the cartridges from drying out.

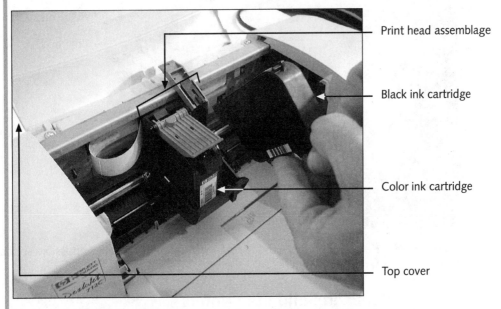

— Print head assemblage

— Black ink cartridge

— Color ink cartridge

— Top cover

Figure 21-7   The ink cartridges of an ink-jet printer

Dot-Matrix Printers

A+*CORE*
   5.1

Dot-matrix printers are less expensive than other types of printers, but they don't give nearly the print quality. Many desktop PC users have replaced them with ink-jet or laser printers. The one reason you still see so many around is that they are impact printers and can print multicopy documents, which some businesses still find useful. A dot-matrix printer has a print head that moves across the width of the paper, using pins to print a matrix of dots on the page. The pins shoot against a cloth ribbon, which hits the paper, depositing the ink. The ribbon provides both the ink for printing and the lubrication for the pinheads.

Occasionally, you should replace the ribbon of a dot matrix printer. Although the print head can wear out, replacing it is probably not cost-effective because it costs almost as much as the printer itself. If the print head fails, buy a new printer. Overheating can damage a print head (see Figure 21-8). Keep the print head as cool as possible so that it will last longer. Keep the printer in a cool, well-ventilated area, and don't use it to print more than 50 to 75 pages without allowing the head to cool down.

21

$A^{+}_{}$CORE
5.1

Print head

Figure 21-8   Keep the print head of a dot-matrix printer as cool as possible so that it will last longer

Thermal Printers and Solid Ink Printers

$A^{+}_{}$CORE
5.1

Two relatively new printer technologies that are similar to each other are thermal printers and solid ink printers. Both are non-impact printers that use heat to produce printed output. Thermal printers use wax-based ink that is heated by heat pins that melt the ink onto paper. The printer's print head containing these heat pins is as wide as the paper. The internal logic of the printer determines which pins get heated in order to produce the printed image. Thermal printers are popular in retail applications for printing bar codes and price tags. A thermal printer can burn dots onto special paper as done by older fax machines (called direct thermal printing) or the printer can use a ribbon that contains the wax-based ink (called thermal wax transfer printing). One variation of thermal printing uses thermal dye sublimation technology to print identification cards and access cards.

Solid ink printers such as the Xerox Phaser 8200 store ink in solid blocks, which Xerox calls ColourStixs. The sticks or blocks are easy to handle and several can be inserted in the printer to be used as needed, avoiding the problem of running out of ink in the middle of a large print job. The solid ink is melted into the print head which spans the width of the paper. The head jets the liquid ink onto the paper as it passes by on a drum. The design is simple, print quality is excellent, and solid ink printers are easy to set up and maintain. The greatest disadvantage to solid ink printing is the time it takes for the print head to heat up to begin a print job, which is about 15 minutes. For this reason, some solid ink printers anticipate a print job might be coming based on previous use of the printer and automatically heat up.

Table 21-1 lists some printer manufacturers. We now turn our attention to how Windows handles print jobs, then to installing a printer on a computer and sharing it with others on the network.

Table 21-1   Printer manufacturers

Printer Manufacturer	Web Site
Brother	www.brother.com
Canon	usa.canon.com
Hewlett-Packard	www.hp.com
IBM	www.ibm.com
Lexmark	www.lexmark.com
Okidata	www.okidata.com
SATO	www.satoamerica.com
Seiko Epson	www.epson.com
Tally	www.tally.com
Xerox	www.xerox.com

How Windows Handles Print Jobs

When supporting printers using Windows, it is helpful to understand how Windows manages print jobs using one of these methods:

- For Windows 9x or Windows NT/2000/XP using a PostScript printer, the print job data is converted to the PostScript language. PostScript is a language used to communicate how a page is to print and was developed by Adobe Systems. PostScript is popular with desktop publishing and the typesetting industry and heavily used with the MAC OS.

- For Windows 9x applications using a non-PostScript printer, the print job data is converted to Enhanced Metafile Format (EMF). This format embeds print commands in the data to help speed printing.

- For Windows 2000/XP, a printer language that competes with PostScript is PCL (Printer Control Language). PCL was developed by Hewlett-Packard but is considered a de facto standard in the printing industry. Many printer manufacturers use PCL.

- Text data that contains no embedded control characters is sent to the printer as is. When DOS applications use this type of printing, the data is called raw data and the print job is sent directly to the printer, bypassing the printer queue.

Normally, when Windows receives a print job from an application, it places the job in a queue and prints from the queue, so that the application is released from the printing process as soon as possible. Several print jobs can accumulate in the queue, which you can view in the Printer window. This process of queue printing jobs is called **spooling**. (The word spool is an acronym for simultaneous peripheral operations on line.) Most printing from Windows uses spooling.

If the printer port, printer cable, and printer all support bidirectional communication, the printer can communicate with Windows. For example, Windows 2000 can ask the printer how much printer memory is available and what fonts are installed. The printer can send messages to the OS, such as an out-of-paper or paper-jam message.

21

INSTALLING AND SHARING A PRINTER

A printer can be connected to a port on a computer, and then the computer can share the printer with others on the network. There are also network printers that have Ethernet ports that can be used to connect the printer directly to the network. Each computer on the network that uses the printer must have printer drivers installed so the OS on each computer can communicate with the printer and provide the interface between applications it supports and the printer. This section covers how to install a local printer, how to share that printer with others on the network, and how a remote computer on the network can use a shared printer. A printer connected to a computer by way of a port on the computer is called a **local printer**, and a printer accessed by way of a network is called a **network printer**. A computer can have several printers installed. Windows designates one printer to be the **default printer**, which is the printer Windows prints to unless another is selected.

Install a Local Printer

$A+\genfrac{}{}{0pt}{}{CORE}{\genfrac{}{}{0pt}{}{1.8}{5.1}}$ Follow these steps to install a local printer:

1. Physically attach the printer to the computer by way of a parallel port, serial port, 1394 port, USB port, SCSI port, IEEE 1394 port, PC Card connection, infrared connection, or wireless access point. Recall from Chapter 10 that, for a parallel port connection, use an IEEE 1284-compliant printer cable. For wireless printers, verify the software for the wireless port on your PC is installed and the port is enabled. For infrared wireless printers, place the printer in line of sight of the infrared port on the PC. (Most wireless printers have a status light that stays lit when a wireless connection is active.)

2. Install the printer drivers. There are two approaches to do this. You can have Windows install the driver, or you can use the printer manufacturer's installation program. In most cases, it is best to use the printer manufacturer's method. The exception to this is if you have several similar printers installed. Windows does a better job of preventing files used by one printer installation from being overwritten by files from another installation.

   a. To use the manufacturer's installation process, insert the printer driver CD that comes bundled with the printer in the CD-ROM drive, and follow directions on-screen to install the printer.

   b. Alternately, you can use the Windows Printer window to install the printer drivers. For Windows 98 and Windows 2000, click Start, Settings, and Printers to open the Printers window. For Windows XP, to open the Printers and Faxes window, click Start, Control Panel, Printers and Faxes (in Classic view) or Printers and Other Hardware (in Category view). Click Add a Printer and follow the Add Printer wizard to install the printer drivers.

3. After you install the printer drivers, test the printer. To do this, open the Printers or Printers and Faxes window and right-click the printer. Select Properties from the shortcut menu. Click the General tab and then click the Print Test Page button.

From the Printers window (Printers and Faxes window for Windows XP) you can also delete printers, change the Windows default printer, purge print jobs in order to troubleshoot

A+*CORE*
1.8
5.1

failed printing, and perform other printer maintenance tasks. If a printer is giving problems or you want to upgrade the printer drivers in order to add new functionality, search the printer manufacturer's Web site for the latest drivers for your printer and operating system. Download the drivers to a folder on the hard drive such as C:\Downloads\Printer, and then double-click the driver file to extract files and launch the installation program to update the printer drivers.

Share a Printer with Others in a Workgroup

A+*CORE*
5.1

Using Windows, to share a local printer, File and Printer Sharing must be installed, and to use a shared printer on a remote PC, Client for Microsoft Networks must be installed. In most cases, it is easiest to simply install both components on all computers on the network. How to install the components under Windows 98 and Windows 2000/XP was covered in Chapter 18. To share a local printer with others in the workgroup connected to a Windows 98 computer, do the following:

1. Open the Printers window (click **Start**, **Settings**, **Printers**).

2. Right-click the printer you want to share. From the shortcut menu, select **Sharing**. (This Sharing option is grayed out if File and Printer Sharing is not installed.)

3. The Properties dialog box opens with the Sharing tab selected (see Figure 21-9).

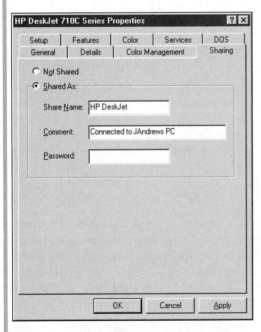

Figure 21-9   When using Windows 98, use the printer Properties window to share a connected printer with other computers on the network

4. Select **Shared As** and give the printer a **Share Name**. Click **OK** to exit.

5. The printer is listed in Network Neighborhood or My Network Places.

21

$A{+}CORE$
5.1

To share a local printer connected to a Windows 2000/XP workstation, do the following:

1. Open the Printers or Printers and Faxes window. Right-click the printer you want to share, and select **Sharing** from the shortcut menu. The printer's Properties dialog box opens, as seen in Figure 21-10 for Windows XP, but Windows 2000 is similar. Select **Share this printer** and enter a name for the printer.

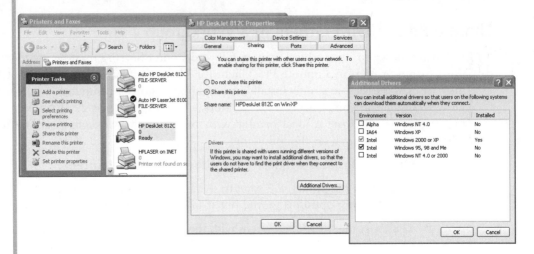

Figure 21-10   Sharing a printer on a Windows XP PC

2. If you want to make drivers for the printer available to remote users who are using an operating system other than the OS being used, then click **Additional Drivers**.

3. The Additional Drivers window appears, as also shown in Figure 21-10. Select the OS. In Figure 21-10, Windows 2000, XP, 95, 98, and Me are selected so that those using these OSs will have the printer drivers they need. Click **OK** twice to close both windows. You might be asked for the Windows installation CD or other access to the installation files. A shared printer shows a hand icon under it in the Printers window.

Using a Shared Printer

Recall that for a remote PC to use a shared network printer, the drivers for that printer must be installed on the remote PC. There are two approaches to installing shared network printer drivers on a remote PC. You can perform the installation using the drivers on CD (either the Windows CD or printer manufacturer's CD), or you can perform the installation using the printer drivers on the host PC. The installations work about the same way for Windows 98 and Windows 2000/XP. The Windows 98 installation is shown here.

To use a printer on the network that is shared, using the manufacturer's printer drivers on CD, do the following using Windows 98:

1. Open the Printers window and double-click **Add Printer**. The Add Printer Wizard window opens. Click **Next**.

2. In response to the question, "How is this printer attached to your computer?", select **Network printer**. Click **Next**. The wizard window in Figure 21-11 opens.

A+CORE
5.1

3. Enter the host computer name and printer name. Begin with two backslashes and separate the computer name from the printer name with a backslash. Or you can click Browse and search the list of shared printers on the network, selecting the printer to install. (If your network is using static IP addressing and you know the IP address of the host PC, you can enter the IP address instead of the host name in this step.) In response to the question, "Do you print from MS-DOS-based programs?", answer Yes if you have any intention of ever doing that, otherwise leave No selected and then click **Next**.

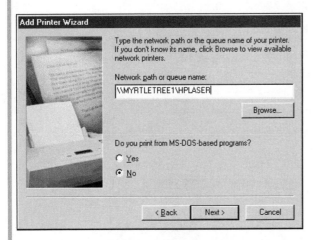

Figure 21-11   To use a network printer under Windows 98, enter the host computer name followed by the printer name

4. Click **Have Disk** to use the manufacturer's drivers, or, to use Windows drivers, select the printer manufacturer and then the printer model from the list of supported printers. Click **Next** when you finish.

5. Enter a name for the printer. You might include the location of the printer, such as 3rd Floor Laser or John's Laser.

6. Sometimes a DOS-based program has problems printing to a network printer. You can choose to associate the network printer with a printer port such as LPT1 to satisfy the DOS application. To do that, click **Capture Printer Port**. The Capture Printer Port dialog box appears (see Figure 21-12). Select the port from the drop-down menu, and then click **OK**.

7. Click **Next** to continue.

8. Choose to print a test page, and then click **Finish**. The network printer is now available for use.

A quicker way to install a shared printer is to use the printer drivers already installed on the host PC. To do that using Windows 98 or Windows 2000/XP, do the following:

1. On the host PC, share the \Windows or \Winnt folder so that printer drivers in this folder are available to others on the network.

21

2. On the remote PC, for Windows 9x, open **Network Neighborhood** and find the printer. Right-click the printer and select **Install** from the shortcut menu. See Figure 21-12. (For Windows 2000/XP, open **My Network Places** and find the printer. Right-click the printer and select **Connect**.)

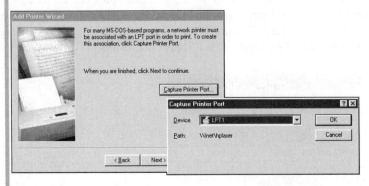

Figure 21-12 Associate a network printer with a printer port to help DOS applications in Windows 98

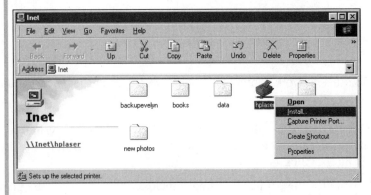

Figure 21-13 Install a shared printer in Windows 98 using drivers on the host computer

3. If the host computer is using the same OS as you are, or, in the case of a Windows NT/2000/XP host computer, if the additional drivers for your OS have been installed, you can use those drivers for the installation. If Windows cannot find the right drivers, it sends you an error message and gives you the opportunity to install the drivers from your Windows CD or the printer manufacturer's CD.

4. Enter a name for the printer, decide how to handle printing from DOS applications, and print a test page to complete the installation.

> **TIP**
> If you must install the shared printer on several PCs in the workgroup, it's easier and faster to use the last method because each PC does not need to read from a CD, and you don't need to carry the CD from PC to PC. After the installations are complete, be sure to remove the shared permission on the host computer's \Windows or \Winnt folder so that this important folder is more secure.

A+CORE 5.1 Other Methods of Sharing Printers over a Network

You have just seen how a printer can be installed as a local printer on one PC and then shared with others in a workgroup. The three ways to make a printer available on a network are summarized here:

- A regular printer can be attached to a PC using a port on the PC, and then that PC can share the printer with the network. (This method was described in the previous section.)

- A network printer with embedded logic to manage network communication can be connected directly to a network with its own NIC.

- A dedicated device or computer called a print server can control several printers connected to a network. For example, HP has software called HP JetDirect, designed to support HP printers in this manner. For more information, see the HP Web site, *www.hp.com*.

If printers are available on the network using one of the last two methods, follow the printer manufacturer's directions to install the printer on each PC. If you don't have these directions, do the following: Download the printer drivers from the printer manufacturer's Web site and, if necessary, decompress the downloaded file. Open the Printers window and start the wizard to add a new printer. Select the option to install a local printer but do not ask Windows to automatically detect the printer. When given the opportunity, choose to create a new port rather than use an existing port (such as LPT1: or LPT2:). Choose to create a standard TCP/IP port. To create the port, you will need the IP address of the printer or the name of the printer on the network. When given the opportunity, click Have Disk so that you can point to and use the downloaded driver files that will then be used to complete the printer installation.

One shortcut you might take to speed up the process of installing a printer connected directly to the network is to install the printer on one PC and then share it on the network. Then, you can install the printer on the other PCs by using Network Neighborhood for Windows 98 or My Network Places for Windows 2000/XP, following directions given earlier. Find the printer, right-click it, and then select Install (for Windows 9x) or Connect (for Windows 2000/XP) from the shortcut menu. The disadvantage of using this method is that the computer sharing the printer must be turned on when other computers on the network want to use the printer.

TROUBLESHOOTING GUIDELINES FOR PRINTERS

A+CORE 5.2 This section first discusses general printer troubleshooting and then explains how to troubleshoot problems specific to each of the three major types of printers. The first steps to prevent problems with printers are to follow manufacturer's directions when using the printer and to perform routine printer maintenance.

21

Printer Maintenance

A+CORE
5.2

Routine printer maintenance procedures vary widely from manufacturer to manufacturer and printer to printer. First, make sure consumables for the printer are on hand such as paper, ink ribbons, colour stixs, toner cartridges, and ink cartridges. For each printer you support, research the printer documentation or the manufacturer's Web site for specific maintenance procedures and how often you should do them. For example, the HP Color LaserJet 4600 printer's maintenance plan says to replace the transfer roller assembly after printing 120,000 pages and replace the fusing assembly after 150,000 pages. The plan also says the black ink cartridge should last for about 9,000 pages and the color ink cartridge for about 8,000 pages. HP sells the image transfer kit, the image fuser kit, and the ink cartridges designed for this printer. The kits, called **printer maintenance kits**, include specific printer components, step-by-step instructions for performing maintenance, and any special tools or equipment you need to do maintenance. The Web site and printer documentation include instructions to command the printer to report how many pages have printed since each maintenance task was performed.

When you perform routine maintenance on a printer, clean inside and outside the printer. Clean the outside of the printer with a damp cloth. Don't use ammonia-based cleaners. Clean the inside of the printer with a dry cloth and remove dust, bits of paper, and stray toner. Don't use an anti-static vacuum cleaner. For a laser printer, wipe the rollers from side to side with a dry cloth to remove loose dirt. Don't touch the soft black roller (the transfer roller) as doing so can cause poor print quality.

 TIP If you get toner on your clothes, dust it off and clean your clothes with cold water. Hot water will set the toner.

Search the printer manufacturer's Web site for lists of common problems and what to do about them. Some Web sites also offer a newsgroup service where you can communicate with others responsible for supporting a particular printer. Following is a guide for general and specific printer troubleshooting. If you have exhausted this list and still have a problem, turn to the manufacturer's Web site for additional information and support.

General Printer Troubleshooting

A+CORE
5.2

Printing problems can be caused by the printer, the PC hardware or OS, the application using the printer, the printer cable, or, in the case of a printer installed on a network, the network. Follow the steps in Figure 21-14 to isolate the problem to one of the following areas:

- The application attempting to use the printer
- The OS and printer drivers
- Connectivity between the PC and the printer
- The printer

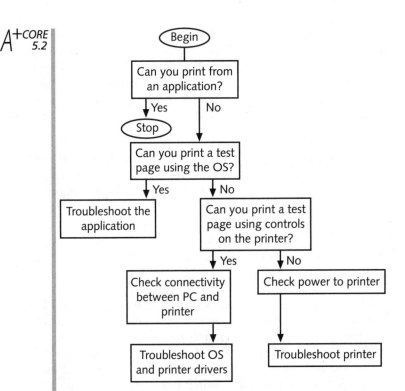

Figure 21-14   How to isolate a printer problem

The sections that follow address printer problems caused by all of these categories, starting with hardware.

Verify a Printer Self-Test Page Can Print

To eliminate the printer as the problem, first check that the printer is powered on, then print a test page on the printer. For directions to print a self-test page, see the printer's user guide. For example, you might need to hold down a button or buttons on the printer's front panel. If this test page prints correctly, it confirms that the printer works correctly. A printer test page generally prints some text, some graphics, and some information about the printer, such as the printer resolution and how much memory is installed. Verify that the information on the test page is correct. For example, if you know that the printer should have 2 MB of on-board printer memory, but it only reports 1 MB, then there is a problem with memory. Also, some printers allow you to flash BIOS on the printer.

21

A+CORE
5.1
5.2

If the self-test page does not print or prints incorrectly (for example, it has missing dots or smudged streaks through the page), then troubleshoot the printer until it prints correctly. Does the printer have paper? Is the paper installed correctly? Is there a paper jam? Try resetting the printer. For a laser printer, check that a toner cartridge is installed. For an ink-jet printer, check that ink cartridges are installed. Check that power is getting to the printer. Check the user guide for the printer and the printer Web site for trouble-shooting suggestions.

If none of these steps works, you may need to take the printer to a certified repair shop. Before you do, though, try contacting the manufacturer. The printer documentation can be very helpful and most often contains a phone number to technical support for the printer manufacturer.

A+CORE
5.2

Problem with the Printer Cable   If the printer self-test worked, but the OS printer test did not work, the problem might be with the printer cable.

- Check that the cable is firmly connected at both ends.

- A business might use an older switch box (sometimes called a T-switch) to share one printer between two computers. A printer cable connects to the printer port of each computer. The two cables connect to the switch box. A third cable connects from the switch box to the printer. A switch on the front of the box controls which computer has access to the printer. Switch boxes were built with older dot-matrix printers in mind. Some switch boxes are not recommended for ink-jet or laser printers that use a bidirectional parallel cable and can even damage a printer. For these printers, remove the switch box.

- Try a different cable. Use a shorter cable. (Cables longer than 10 feet can sometimes cause problems.) Verify that the cable is IEEE 1284 compliant.

- Try printing using the same printer and printer cable but a different PC.

- Enter CMOS setup of the PC, and check how the parallel port is configured. Is it disabled? Set to ECP or bidirectional? Recall that an ECP parallel port requires the use of a DMA channel. Try setting the port to bidirectional.

Problems with Laser Printers

This section covers some problems that can occur with laser printers. For more specific guidelines for your printer model, refer to the printer documentation or the manufacturer's Web site.

Poor print quality due to low toner   Poor print quality, including faded, smeared, wavy, speckled, or streaked printouts, often indicates that the toner is low. All major mechanical printer components that normally create problems are conveniently contained within the replaceable toner cartridge. In most cases, the solution to poor quality printing is to replace this cartridge. Follow these general guidelines:

- If you suspect the printer is overheated, unplug the printer and allow it to cool.

- Remove the toner cartridge and gently rock it from side to side to redistribute the toner. Replace the cartridge. If this solves the problem, plan to replace the toner cartridge soon. To avoid flying toner, don't shake the cartridge too hard.

- If this doesn't solve the problem, try replacing the toner cartridge immediately.

- EconoMode (a mode that uses less toner) may be on; turn it off.

- On some laser printers, you can clean the mirror. Check the user guide for directions.

- A single sheet of paper may be defective. Try new paper.

- The paper quality may not be high enough. Try a different brand of paper. Only use paper recommended for use in a laser printer.

- Clean the inside of the printer with a dry, lint-free cloth. Don't touch the transfer roller.

- If the transfer roller is dirty, the problem will probably correct itself after printing several sheets. If not, then take the printer to an authorized service center.

> **TIP** Extreme humidity may cause the toner to clump in the cartridge and give a low toner message. If this is a consistent problem in your location, you might want to invest in a dehumidifier for the room where your printer is located.

Printer stays in warm-up mode   The warming up message on the front panel of the printer should go off as soon as the printer establishes communication with the PC. If this doesn't happen, try the following:

- Turn off the printer and disconnect the cable to the computer.

- Turn on the printer. If it now displays a Ready message, the problem is communication.

- Verify that the cable is connected to the correct printer port, not to a serial port.

- Verify that data to the installed printer is being sent to the parallel port. For example, open the Properties dialog box of the installed printer, as described above. Verify that the print job is being sent to LPT1, as shown in Figure 21-15.

- Check that the parallel port is enabled in CMOS setup and set to the correct mode.

- Replace the cable.

21

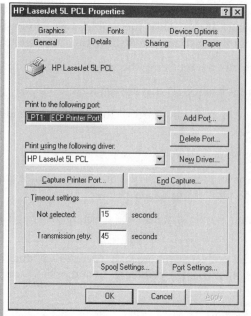

A⁺*CORE*
5.2

Figure 21-15 Verify that print data is being sent to the correct parallel port

A paper jam or paper out message appears

- If paper is jammed inside the printer, follow the directions in the printer documentation to remove the paper. Don't jerk the paper from the printer mechanism, but pull evenly on the paper, with care.

- If there is no jammed paper, then remove the tray and check the metal plate at the bottom of the tray. Can it move up and down freely? If not, replace the tray.

- When you insert the tray in the printer, does the printer lift the plate as the tray is inserted? If not, the lift mechanism might need repair.

- Damp paper can cause paper jams. Be sure to only use dry paper in a printer.

Printed images are distorted If print images are distorted and there is no paper jam, foreign material inside the printer might be interfering with the mechanical components. Check for debris that might be interfering with the printer operation.

Printing is slow Laser printers are rated by two speed properties: the time it takes to print the first page (measured in seconds) and the print speed (measured in pages per minute). Try the following if the printer is slow:

- Space is needed on the hard drive to manage print jobs. Clean up the drive. Install a larger drive if necessary.

- Add more memory to the printer. See the printer manual for directions.

- Lower the printer resolution and the print quality (which lowers the REt settings).

- Verify that the hard drive has enough space.

- Upgrade the computer's memory or the CPU.

A+CORE
5.1
5.2

A portion of the page does not print   For some laser printers, if the printer does not have enough memory to hold the entire page, an error occurs. For others, only a part of the page prints. Some may signal this problem by flashing a light or displaying an error message on their display panels. (Some HP LaserJet printers have a control panel and send an error message for low memory, "20 Mem Overflow.") The solution is to install more memory or to print only simple pages with few graphics. Print a self-test page to verify how much memory is installed. Check the printer guide to determine how much memory the printer can support and what kind of memory to buy.

A+CORE
5.2

Problems with Ink-Jet Printers

This section covers some problems that can occur with ink-jet printers. For more specific guidelines for your printer, refer to the printer documentation or the manufacturer's Web site.

Print quality is poor

- Is the correct paper for ink-jet printers being used? The quality of paper determines the final print quality, especially with ink-jet printers. In general, the better the quality of the paper used with an ink-jet printer, the better the print quality. Do not use less than 20-lb paper in any type of printer, unless the printer documentation specifically says that a lower weight is satisfactory.

- Is the ink supply low, or is there a partially clogged nozzle?

- Remove and reinstall the cartridge.

- Follow the printer's documentation to clean each nozzle.

- In the Printer Setup dialog box, click the Media/Quality tab, then change the Print Quality selection. Try different settings with sample prints.

- Is the print head too close to or too far from the paper?

- If you are printing transparencies, try changing the fill pattern in your application.

Printing is intermittent or absent

- Is the ink supply low?

- Are nozzles clogged?

- Replace the ink cartridges or replenish the ink supply.

Lines or dots are missing from the printed page   The ink nozzles on an ink-jet cartridge occasionally dry out, especially when the printer sits unused for a long time. Symptoms of this are missing lines or dots on the printed page. You had to clean the ink-jet nozzles of older ink-jet printers manually, but now newer printers often let you clean the nozzles automatically, using software or buttons on the front panel of the printer. This section uses the HP 710C series of printers and Windows 98 to describe how to use supporting software to clean the nozzles.

21

A+CORE 5.2

When the printer software is installed, it places a printer toolbox icon on the desktop and adds several tabs to the printer Properties dialog box. Use a tab on the printer Properties dialog box to clean the ink-jet nozzles. Here is what you do for Windows 98:

1. Click **Start**, point to **Settings**, and click **Printers**. The Printers window opens. Right-click the ink-jet printer icon, and select **Properties** from the shortcut menu.

2. Click the **Services** tab. Figure 21-16 shows the list of services available for this printer.

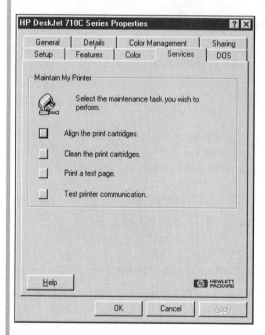

Figure 21-16   Use the Services tab under the printer Properties box to auto-clean the ink-jet nozzles

3. Click **Clean the print cartridges** to clean the ink-jet nozzles automatically.

4. A test page prints. If the page prints sharply with no missing dots or lines, then you are finished. If the page does not print correctly, perform the auto-clean again.

5. You might need to perform the auto-clean procedure six or seven times to clean the nozzles completely. If the problem persists, don't attempt to clean the nozzles manually; contact the manufacturer or vendor for service.

Ink streaks appear on the printed page   Sometimes dust or dirt gets down into the print head assemblage, causing streaks or lines on the printed page. Follow the manufacturer's directions to clean the print cartridge assemblage. Use clean distilled water and cotton swabs to clean the cartridge cradle and the face and edges of the print cartridge, being careful not to touch the nozzle plate. To prevent the ink-jet nozzles from drying out, don't leave the print cartridges out of their cradle for longer than 30 minutes.

$A^{+CORE}_{\quad 5.2}$ | ## Problems with Dot-Matrix Printers

This section covers some problems that can occur with dot-matrix printers. Again, for more specific guidelines for your printer, see the printer documentation or the manufacturer's Web site.

Print quality is poor

- Begin with the ribbon. Does it advance normally while the carriage moves back and forth? If not, replace the ribbon.

- If the new ribbon still does not advance properly, check the printer's advance mechanism.

- Adjust the print head spacing. Look for a lever adjustment you can use to change the distance between the print head and plate.

- Check the print head for dirt. Make sure it's not hot before you touch it. If debris has built up, wipe each wire with a cotton swab dipped in alcohol or contact cleaner.

Print head moves back and forth but nothing prints

- Check the ribbon. Is it installed correctly between the plate and print head?

- Does the ribbon advance properly? Is it jammed? If the ribbon is dried out, it needs to be replaced.

Problems Printing from Windows

$A^{+}_{\ }$ OS 3.3 | If a self-test page works, but you still cannot print to a local computer from Windows, try these things:

- First try to print a test page using the Printers window. Right-click the printer you want to test, and choose Properties from the shortcut menu. Click the Print Test Page button to send a test page to the printer. Verify the correct default printer is selected.

- The print spool might be stalled. Try deleting all print jobs in the printer's queue. Double-click the printer icon in the Printers window. Select Printer, Purge Print Documents. (It may take a moment for the print jobs to disappear.)

- If you still cannot print, reboot the PC. Verify that the printer cable or cable connections are solid.

- Try removing and reinstalling the printer driver. To uninstall the printer driver, right-click the printer icon in the Printers window, select Delete to remove the printer, and then reinstall the printer.

- In CMOS setup, check the configuration of the USB, serial, or parallel port that the printer is using.

21

A+ OS
3.3

- Try another printer driver. It may not print graphics correctly, but if another driver does work at all, then you can conclude that you have a faulty driver. For example, if you have an HP LaserJet 970Cxi, try using the HP LaserJet 970Cse driver. Download and install the correct driver from the printer manufacturer's Web site.

- In the printer's Properties dialog box, click Disable bidirectional support for this printer. The PC and printer might have a problem with bidirectional communication.

- Check the resources assigned to the printer port. Open Device Manager, select LPT1, and click Properties. Verify that the resources are assigned correctly for LPT1 (I/O addresses are 0378 to 037B) and that Device Manager reports "No conflicts."

- In the printer Properties dialog box, try disabling "Check Port State Before Printing."

- Verify printer properties. Try lowering the resolution.

- If you can print from DOS, but not from Windows, try disabling printer spooling. Go to the printer Properties dialog box, and select Print Directly to the Printer. Spooling holds print jobs in a queue for printing, so if spooling is disabled, printing from an application can be slower.

- For Windows 9x, if you have trouble printing from an application, the application may be incompatible with Windows. One way to try to solve this problem is to click Start, Run, and type mkcompat.exe. This utility enables you to troubleshoot and solve problems that may make an application incompatible with a certain version of Windows.

- If you have trouble printing from an application, you can also bypass spooling by selecting Print from the File menu in the application, selecting the option to print to a file, and then dragging that file to the icon representing your printer.

- Try the printer on another PC. Try another power cable and another printer cable.

Troubleshooting Networked Printers

A+ OS
3.3

When troubleshooting problems with connectivity between a PC on the network and a network printer, try these things:

- First check that you can print from the computer that has the printer attached to it locally by printing a test page using the Printer window. Right-click the printer you want to test, and choose Properties from the shortcut menu. Click the Print Test Page button to send a test page to the printer. Verify that the correct default printer is selected.

- If you cannot print from the local printer, solve the problem there before attempting to print over the network.

$A^+_{3.3}$ OS

- Return to the remote computer, and verify that you can access the computer to which the printer is attached. Go to Network Neighborhood or My Network Places, and attempt to open shared folders on the printer's computer. Perhaps you have not entered a correct user ID and password to access this computer; that will prevent you from being able to use that computer's resources.

- Using the Printers window, delete the printer, and then, using Windows 9x Network Neighborhood or Windows 2000/XP My Network Places, reconnect the printer.

CHAPTER SUMMARY

- The three most popular types of printers are laser, ink-jet, and dot-matrix. Laser printers produce the highest quality, followed by ink-jet printers. Dot-matrix printers have the advantage of being able to print multicopy documents.

- The six steps that a laser printer performs to print are cleaning, conditioning, writing, developing, transferring, and fusing. The first four steps take place inside the removable toner cartridge.

- Ink-jet printers print by shooting ionized ink at a sheet of paper.

- The nozzles of an ink-jet printer tend to clog, especially when the printer remains unused. The nozzles can be cleaned automatically by means of printer software or buttons on the front panel of the printer.

- Dot-matrix printers print by projecting pins from the print head against an inked ribbon that deposits ink on the paper.

- Before users on a network can view or access resources on a PC, Client for Microsoft Networks and File and Printer Sharing for Microsoft Networks must be installed, and these resources must be shared.

- When troubleshooting printers, first isolate the problem. Narrow the source to the printer, cable, PC hardware, operating system including the device driver, application software, or network.

KEY TERMS

beam detect mirror	network printer	scanning mirror
control blade	printer maintenance kit	spooling
default printer	REt (Resolution	
local printer	Enhancement	
	technology)	

21

REVIEW QUESTIONS

1. Which of the following ports is *not* considered to be typical of those used to interface with local printers?

   a. IEEE 1394

   b. Network

   c. USB

   d. Infrared

   e. None of the above

2. Of the stages required to get a printout from a laser printer, which is responsible for placing a high electrical charge on the main drum?

   a. Cleaning

   b. Conditioning

   c. Writing

   d. Developing

   e. Fusing

3. Of the stages required to get a printout from a laser printer, which is responsible for the placement of toner on the drum where the electrical charge has been reduced?

   a. Cleaning

   b. Conditioning

   c. Writing

   d. Developing

   e. Fusing

4. Of the stages required to get a printout from a laser printer, which is responsible for ensuring that no residual toner or electrical charge are on the main drum?

   a. Cleaning

   b. Conditioning

   c. Writing

   d. Developing

   e. Fusing

5. Of the stages required to get a printout from a laser printer, which is responsible for ensuring that the toner does not come off onto the user's hand once the paper exits the printer?

   a. Cleaning

   b. Conditioning

   c. Writing

d. Developing

e. Fusing

6. The primary charging roller ensures that a uniform charge of _____ volts is placed onto the drum.

   a. −600

   b. 600

   c. −100

   d. 100

   e. None of the above

7. The ink-jet printer is similar in design to the _____ printer in that it uses a matrix of small dots to create its image.

   a. Laser

   b. Dot matrix

   c. Thermal

   d. Solid ink

   e. None of the above

8. The official names of the colors used in the color ink cartridge for ink-jet printers is:

   a. Black/white/color

   b. Red/blue/yellow

   c. Red/green/blue

   d. Magenta/cyan/yellow

   e. None of the above

9. Of the following printer designs, which made use of an ink ribbon to provide for the transfer of ink onto a sheet of paper?

   a. Laser

   b. Dot matrix

   c. Thermal

   d. Solid ink

   e. None of the above

10. Of the following printer designs, which makes use of the similar technology to that of a photocopy machine to produce output?

   a. Laser

   b. Dot matrix

   c. Thermal

   d. Solid ink

   e. None of the above

21

11. The term associated with the process of accumulating print jobs to be printed by a specific printer is _____.

    a. Queuing

    b. Spooling

    c. Printing

    d. Communicating

    e. Sharing

12. Assuming that a printer installed on a local system was to be configured to be used by many individuals within the same department, how would this particular printer be set up when adding a printer by the operating system?

    a. Local

    b. Network

    c. Both a and b

    d. Neither a nor b

13. The feature that allows for a printer to report to the operating system that the printer is out of paper is an example of:

    a. One-direction communication

    b. Handshaking

    c. Processing

    d. Input/output

    e. Storage

22

ALL ABOUT SCSI

In this chapter, you will learn:

- ♦ About basics of SCSI technology and components
- ♦ How SCSI hard drives compare to IDE drives
- ♦ How to install a SCSI device
- ♦ Setting device IDs during installation
- ♦ Troubleshooting tips for SCSI

In Chapter 8, you learned about IDE hard drives. This chapter covers another technology, SCSI, which provides better performance and greater expansion capabilities for many internal and external devices, including hard drives, CD-ROM drives, DVD drives, and scanners. SCSI devices tend to be faster, more expensive, and more difficult to install than similar IDE devices. This chapter discusses how SCSI technology works, as well as advantages and disadvantages of SCSI.

SCSI BASICS

SCSI (pronounced "scuzzy") stands for **Small Computer System Interface** and is a standard for communication between a subsystem of peripheral devices and the system bus. The SCSI bus can contain, and be used by, up to seven or fifteen devices, depending on the SCSI standard. The SCSI bus controller can be an expansion card called a host adapter or can be embedded on the motherboard. In this section, you will learn how a SCSI subsystem is structured, how it works, and what variations of SCSI there are.

The SCSI Subsystem

A+CORE
1.7

If a motherboard does not have an embedded SCSI controller, the gateway from the SCSI bus to the system bus is the host adapter, a card inserted into an expansion slot on the motherboard. The adapter card, called the **host adapter**, is responsible for managing all devices on the SCSI bus. A host adapter can support both internal and external SCSI devices, using one connector on the card for a ribbon cable to connect to internal devices, and an external port that supports external devices (see Figure 22-1). All the devices and the host adapter form a single daisy chain. In Figure 22-1 this daisy chain has two internal devices and two external devices, with the SCSI host adapter in the middle of the chain.

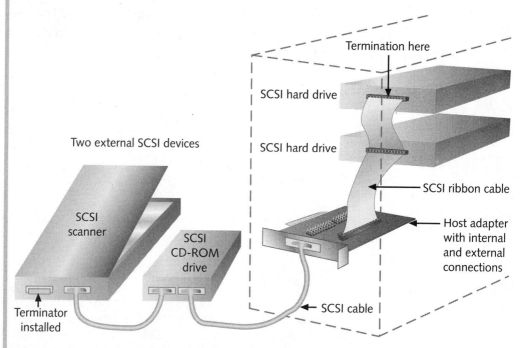

Figure 22-1   Using a SCSI bus, a SCSI host adapter can support internal and external SCSI devices

When a device on the SCSI bus must communicate with the system bus, the data passes through the host adapter. The host adapter keeps up with the interchange between the devices on the SCSI bus and the system bus. SCSI technology has the added advantage of letting two devices on the SCSI bus pass data between them without going through the CPU. This method of data transmission provides a convenient way to back up a SCSI hard drive to a tape drive on the same SCSI subsystem, without involving the CPU.

Figure 22-2 compares IDE and SCSI bus communication. With an IDE drive (on the left in Figure 22-2), the CPU communicates with the hard drive controller, which is contained in the hard drive case, through the system bus. Recall from Chapter 8 that the hard drive controller communicates directly with the system bus. With a SCSI hard drive (on the right in the figure), the CPU communicates over the system bus to the SCSI host adapter, which communicates over the SCSI bus to the SCSI interface controller in the hard drive case. This SCSI interface controller communicates with the hard drive controller, which, in turn, communicates with the hard drive.

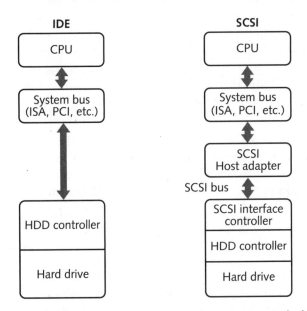

Figure 22-2   SCSI hard drives communicate with the CPU through the SCSI host adapter, but IDE drives communicate directly on the system bus

Many SCSI standards have evolved over several years. The maximum number of devices the SCSI bus can support depends on the type of SCSI being used. Some SCSI buses can link up to seven devices, others up to fifteen. Each device on the bus is assigned a number from 0 to 15 called the **SCSI ID**, by means of DIP switches, dials on the device, or software settings. The host adapter is generally assigned a number larger than all other devices, either 7 or 15; some come factory-set to the highest SCSI ID. Cables connect the devices physically in a daisy chain, sometimes called a straight chain. The devices can

22

be either internal or external, and the host adapter can be at either end of the chain or somewhere in the middle. The SCSI ID identifies the physical device, which can have several logical devices embedded in it. For example, a CD-ROM jukebox—a CD-ROM changer with trays for multiple CDs—might have seven trays. Each tray is considered a logical device and is assigned a **Logical Unit Number (LUN)** to identify it, such as 1 through 7 or 0 through 6. The ID and LUN are written as two numbers separated by a colon. For instance, if the SCSI ID is 5, the fourth tray in the jukebox is device 5:4.

The technology of a SCSI device can be the same as the technology of a similar device that is not SCSI, with the added ability to use the SCSI bus and communicate with the host adapter. A device is a SCSI device not because of its technology, but because of the bus it uses.

Just like an IDE drive, a SCSI drive has its controller mounted inside the drive housing and can have a variable number of sectors per track. Low-level formatting a SCSI drive is sometimes possible, and even recommended by the manufacturer, because the SCSI controller is likely to contain the firmware to do the job. (See the drive's documentation.) In theory, a SCSI drive can simply be an IDE drive with one more chip on the controller card in the drive housing and a different kind of data connection designed to fit the SCSI standard. In practice, however, SCSI drives are of higher quality, having higher rotational speeds and lower seek times than IDE drives. The SCSI chip within the drive housing that controls data transfer over the SCSI bus is called the **SBAC (SCSI bus adapter chip)**.

To reduce the amount of electrical "noise," or interference, on a SCSI cable, each end of the SCSI chain has a **terminating resistor**. The terminating resistor can be a hardware device plugged into the last device on each end of the chain, or the chain can have software-controlled termination resistance, which makes installation simpler.

Now that you've learned the basic structure and function of a SCSI subsystem, let's look closely at two of its important components: host adapters and device drivers.

Host Adapters

An important issue when you install a SCSI bus system for the first time is the sophistication of the host adapter. More expensive host adapters are often easier to install because the installation software does more of the work for the installer and offers more help than does less expensive adapter software. This section discusses issues to consider when selecting a host adapter.

BIOS

A SCSI host adapter controller has BIOS that uses memory addresses on the PC and controls the operation of the SCSI bus. This SCSI controller uses a DMA channel, IRQ, and I/O addresses. You must install a SCSI device carefully to avoid resource conflicts with devices that are not on the SCSI subsystem. When you are looking for a host adapter, look for one that is Plug and Play compatible and has a configuration utility built into its ROM, to make the setup process easier. Check also for software that configures termination and assigns system resources. Working with this software is easier than setting jumpers or DIP switches on the card, because it allows you to make a change without opening the case. Also, look for a host adapter whose BIOS can configure SCSI devices using the bus controlled by the adapter. Finally, see how many devices the BIOS supports; for today's systems and SCSI devices, using a host adapter that supports up to 15 peripherals is best.

Expansion Slot

The host adapter must fit the expansion slot you plan to use. For a Pentium motherboard, you probably can choose either a 16-bit ISA host adapter or a PCI host adapter. Choose the 32-bit PCI bus for faster data transfer rate, instead of the 16-bit ISA bus.

Bus Mastering

Choose a host adapter that uses bus mastering, discussed in Chapter 10, if your system bus supports it. Remember that a bus master attached to the PCI bus can access memory and other devices without accessing the CPU. For PCI buses that do support bus mastering, you have the added advantage that, when bus mastering is used, the SCSI host adapter does not require a DMA channel.

SCAM-Compliant

SCAM (SCSI Configuration AutoMatically or SCSI Configuration AutoMagically, depending on the literature you're reading) is a method by which SCSI devices and the host adapter can be Plug and Play compliant. SCAM-compliant host adapters and devices can assign SCSI IDs dynamically at startup. Many SCSI devices currently in use are not SCAM-compliant, and you will need to set the unique ID on the device, using jumpers, rotary dials, or other methods. Newer SCSI host adapters use software that comes with the card to configure the SCSI BIOS. With the software, you can set the SCSI IDs, SCSI parity checking, termination, and system resources used by the card.

There are two levels of SCAM. Level 1 requires that the devices, but not the host adapter, be assigned an ID at startup by software. Level 2 requires that the host adapter, as well as the devices, be assigned an ID at startup by software. SCSI devices must be SCAM-compliant to carry the logo "Designed for Windows." Some older host adapters that are not SCAM-compliant are configured by jumpers.

Table 22-1 lists vendors for SCSI host adapters.

22

Table 22-1   Vendors for SCSI host adapters

Vendor	Web Site
Adaptec (now owned by DPT)	*www.adaptec.com* or *www.dpt.com*
SONICBlue Inc.	*www.sonicblue.com*
Promise Technology	*www.promise.com*

SCSI Device Drivers

SCSI device drivers are needed to enable an operating system to communicate with a host adapter. Many computers have some SCSI interface software in their system BIOS—enough, in fact, to allow a SCSI hard drive to be the boot device of the system. The system BIOS can access the SCSI drive, execute the load program in the drive's Master Boot Record, and load the SCSI device drivers stored on the hard drive into memory. If a system has two hard drives, one IDE and one SCSI, the IDE drive must be the boot device, unless system BIOS can support booting from a SCSI drive even when an IDE drive is present. This is because the motherboard BIOS takes precedence over the BIOS on the SCSI host adapter, which generally includes driver support for hard drives.

For most SCSI devices, support is not built into the host adapter BIOS or the system BIOS, and separate drivers are required. Although many drivers are available, using the drivers recommended or provided by the device vendor is best. Two popular driver types are **Advanced SCSI Programming Interface (ASPI)** and **Common Access Method (CAM)**. Both these device driver standards describe the way the host adapter communicates with the SCSI device driver. ASPI, the more popular of the two, was originally developed by Adaptec and then licensed to other makers of SCSI devices. With CAM, a single driver can control several host adapters.

The manufacturer of the host adapter usually provides the SCSI driver on floppy disk or CD-ROM. Windows 9x, Windows NT, Windows 2000, and Windows XP all have built-in support for many SCSI devices. These OSs also provide SCSI drivers for a SCSI CD-ROM drive on their rescue disks, such as the Windows 9x startup disk, so that you can have access to the SCSI CD-ROM drive when troubleshooting a failed boot.

Variations in SCSI

A+CORE
1.7
4.3

Just as with IDE/ATA standards, SCSI standards have improved over the years and use different names. SCSI standards are developed by the SCSI T10 Technical Committee (*www.t10.org*) and sent to ANSI, which publishes and maintains the official versions of the standards. The SCSI Trade Association, which promotes SCSI devices and standards, can also be accessed at *www.t10.org*. In addition to varying standards, SCSI also uses different types of cabling and different bus widths. This section covers variations within SCSI technology.

Bus Width

The two general categories of all SCSI standards used on PCs have to do with the width in bits of the SCSI data bus, either 8 bits **(narrow SCSI)** or 16 bits **(wide SCSI)**. In almost every case, if the SCSI standard is 16 bits, then the word *wide* is in the name for the standard. In most cases, the word *narrow* is not mentioned in names for 8-bit standards. Narrow SCSI uses a cable with a 50-pin connector (also called an A cable), and wide SCSI uses a cable with a 68-pin connector (also called a P cable).

 TIP The wide SCSI specification allows for a data path of 32 bits, although this is not broadly implemented in PCs. When you see a SCSI device referred to as wide, you can generally assume 16 bits.

Signaling Methods Used on SCSI Cables

A SCSI cable can be built in two different ways, depending on the method by which the electrical signal is placed on the cable: single-ended and differential. Both types of cables send a signal on a pair of twisted wires. In **single-ended (SE) cables**, one of the wires carries voltage and the other is a ground; in **differential cables**, both wires carry voltage and the signal is calculated to be the difference between the two voltages (see Figure 22-3). A single-ended cable is less expensive than a differential cable, but the maximum cable length cannot be as long because data integrity is not as great. With differential cabling, signal accuracy is better; noise on the line and electromagnetic interference are less likely to affect signaling because the reading is the difference between the two signals rather than the amplitude of one signal. Differential signaling also sends an extra verifying signal for each bit, providing greater reliability and reducing the chance of data errors.

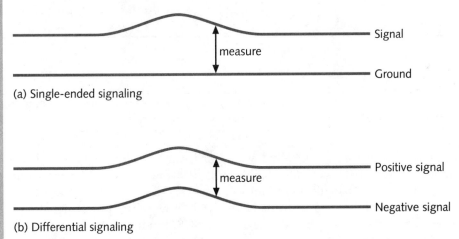

Figure 22-3 A SCSI pair of wires can carry a signal using (a) ground and a signal, or (b) a positive and negative signal, but differential signaling is less likely to be affected by noise on the line

22

A+CORE
  1.7

When differential signaling was first introduced, the difference in voltage between the two wires was high (called **High Voltage Differential**, or **HVD**). This required a large amount of power and circuitry and made it impossible to mix differential and single-ended devices on a system without burning out the hardware. HVD became obsolete with the introduction of the SCSI-3 standard. The introduction of **Low Voltage Differential (LVD)** signaling and termination made it possible to develop less expensive, low-voltage interfaces on the device, host adapter, cables, and terminators. As its name implies, LVD signaling uses lower voltages on the two-wire pair. It provides for cable lengths up to 12 meters (about 39.4 feet) and is required with Ultra SCSI standards. There is a type of LVD signaling called LVD/SE multimode that can work with SE devices and cables. If an LVD/SE device is used on a bus with SE devices, it uses the SE signaling method, which is slower and cannot accommodate longer cable lengths. Table 22-2 lists and describes the four types of cables.

Table 22-2   SCSI cables

SCSI Cable	Maximum Length (meters and feet)	Maximum Speed	Transfer Rate	Description
Single-ended (SE)	3 M (10 ft) for wide or 6 M (20 ft) for narrow SCSI	20 MHz	40 Mbps	One wire in the pair is ground.
High voltage differential (HVD)	25 M (82 ft)	20 or 40 MHz	40 Mbps	Both wires in the pair have high voltage.
Low voltage differential (LVD)	12 M (40 ft) for 15 devices or 25 M (80 ft) for 7 devices	320 MHz	80 Mbps	Both wires in the pair have low voltage.
LVD/SE multimode				If one SE device is on the bus, the smaller length and speed apply.

CAUTION

Never use an HVD device on a bus with SE or LVD devices, because the high voltage put on the cable by the HVD device can destroy the low-voltage devices.

Cables for both narrow SCSI and wide SCSI can be either single-ended or differential. Single-ended, HVD, and LVD cables look the same, so you must make sure that you use the correct cable. It's important to know that you cannot look at a cable, the cable connector, or the connector on a device and know what type of signaling it uses. It is possible that connecting an HVD device to a SCSI bus using SE or LVD devices will burn them up with the high voltage from the HVD device. Look at the device documentation to learn what type of signaling a device uses, or look for a symbol on the device that indicates the signaling method. Figure 22-4 shows the different symbols used on devices and cables to show what kind of signaling they use.

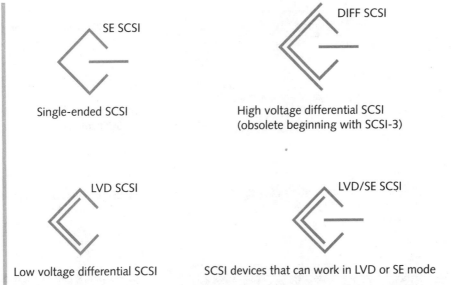

Figure 22-4   These symbols tell what type of signaling a device or cable uses

Adapters are available for mixing single-ended and differential devices and cables, but using them is not recommended. Mixing single-ended and differential signaling types is not a good idea because of the different ways they transmit data. Even with adapters, incompatible connections between single-ended and differential signals can damage both the host adapter and the devices connected to it. An exception to this principle is LVD/SE devices designed to work with either LVD or SE and revert to SE mode whenever the two are connected. Even then, however, know that the device is running at a slower speed than it could run if connected to an all-LVD signaling system, and that all cables in the system must meet the shorter SE standard lengths.

Connectors Used with SCSI Cables

The connector type or the number of pins on a SCSI cable connector is not affected by the signaling method used. Within each signaling method, the number of pins can vary. Figure 22-5 shows just a few of the many types of SCSI connectors. Although there are two main types of SCSI connectors, 50-pin (A cable) and 68-pin (P cable), there are other, less common types as well, such as the 80-pin SCA (Single Connector Attachment) connector used with some hot-swapping drives. Only 80-pin connectors supply power to the device in the connector; other devices require separate power connections. A SCSI bus can support more than one type of connector, and you can use connector adapters in order to plug a cable with one type of connector into a port using another type of connector.

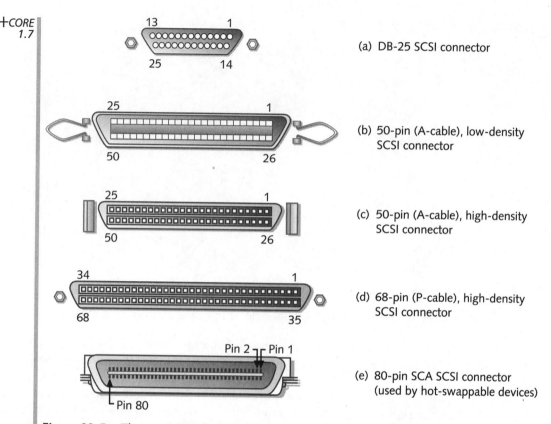

(a) DB-25 SCSI connector

(b) 50-pin (A-cable), low-density SCSI connector

(c) 50-pin (A-cable), high-density SCSI connector

(d) 68-pin (P-cable), high-density SCSI connector

(e) 80-pin SCA SCSI connector (used by hot-swappable devices)

Figure 22-5   The most popular SCSI connectors are 50-pin, A cable connectors for narrow SCSI and 68-pin, P cable connectors for wide SCSI

> **TIP** If you select a host adapter that supports both 50-pin connections and 68-pin connections, you can add a variety of devices to your system without purchasing a second host adapter.

For each type of connector, there can be variations in shape and pin density. Different companies and device manufacturers can make different connector types. For example, in an attempt to trim the size of the connector, a 25-pin SCSI connector was designed for narrow SCSI. The problem was that this connector looked like a parallel port connector. Never plug a SCSI connector into a parallel port or vice versa; you can damage equipment, because the signals work completely differently.

The good news in all this variety is that adapters are generally available to connect one type of connector to another, meaning that you can mix wide and narrow SCSI devices that use different connector variations. If you have any wide devices on your system at all, the cable from the host adapter must have a 68-pin connector, and you will need to use converters to attach 50-pin narrow devices.

TIP When constructing an external SCSI chain, attach wide devices first (closest to the host adapter), and finish the chain with your narrow devices.

Most recent SCSI devices and buses use D-shaped 50-pin or 68-pin connectors that cannot be plugged in wrong. Older 50-pin connectors did not have this shape and could be oriented incorrectly. To line up a 50-pin connector to an internal SCSI device, look for a red or blue stripe on one side of the cable; this stripe lines up with pin 1 on the connector. Look also for a tab on one edge of the connector and a corresponding notch where you are to insert it.

The SCSI bus inside a computer is a ribbon cable, and the device connectors for internal devices are plugs at different positions on the cable. Having multiple connectors on the SCSI bus (see Figure 22-6) enables you to connect multiple internal devices easily. One end of the bus attaches to the host adapter, and for best results, you should always plug a device into the last connector on the cable.

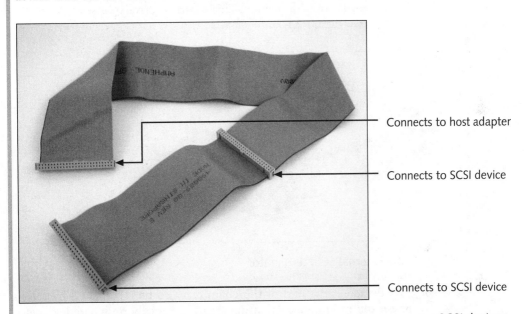

Connects to host adapter

Connects to SCSI device

Connects to SCSI device

Figure 22-6   This 50-pin SCSI ribbon cable can accommodate two narrow SCSI devices

For external SCSI chains, there are two connectors on each device; both can send or receive information. That means it doesn't matter which connector on one device is linked to which connector on the next. A cable goes from the host adapter to a connector on the first device, then another cable goes from the second connector on the first device to a connector on the second device, and so on. The last connector on the last device must be filled with a terminator, unless that device provides software termination. External SCSI

22

chains work like some Christmas lights: if one goes out, they all go out. Therefore, when connecting devices in an external SCSI chain, you should make sure to snap in the retaining clips or wires to complete the connection.

A+CORE 1.7 ## Termination

Termination prevents an echo effect from electrical noise and reflected data at the end of the SCSI daisy chain, which can cause interference with data transmission. Each end of a SCSI chain must be terminated, and there are several ways to do that:

- The host adapter can have a switch setting that activates or deactivates a terminating resistor on the card, depending on whether or not the adapter is at one end of the chain.

- A device can have either a single SCSI connection requiring that the device be placed at the end of the chain, or the device can have two connections. When a device has two connections, the second connection can be used to connect another device or to terminate the chain by placing an external terminator on the connection. This external terminator serves as the terminating resistor (see Figure 22-7).

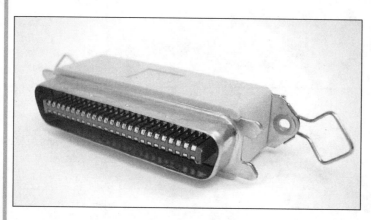

Figure 22-7   External SCSI terminator

- The device at the end of the chain can also be terminated by a resistor physically mounted on that device in a specially designated socket.

- Some devices have built-in terminators (internal terminators) that you can turn on or off with a jumper setting on the device.

- Termination can be controlled by software.

Figure 22-1 shows the terminators needed at the end of both internal and external SCSI chains. In the figure, there is no terminator on the host adapter, which has both internal and external devices attached to it. Only when you have both types of devices attached to a host adapter do you remove termination from the host adapter.

A+CORE
1.7

There are several types of terminators:

- **Passive terminators**, the least reliable type, are used with SCSI-1 devices that operate at low speed and at short distances. They use simple resistors only and are rarely used today, as they are not sufficient for today's faster SCSI devices and longer cabling distances. Passive termination should only be used with narrow SCSI.

- **Active terminators** include voltage regulators in addition to the simple resistors used with passive termination. Most of today's single-ended SCSI cables use active termination, which was recommended with SCSI-2. Active termination is used with wide SCSI and required with fast SCSI. It also works better over longer distances than passive termination.

- **Forced perfect terminators (FPTs)** are a more advanced version of active terminators and include a mechanism to force signal termination to the correct voltage, eliminating most signal echoes and interference. FPTs are more expensive and more reliable than passive and active terminators.

Passive terminators, active terminators, and FPTs are all used with single-ended SCSI cables. Differential cables use either HVD or LVD terminators.

A+CORE
1.7
4.3

SCSI-1, SCSI-2, and SCSI-3

The three major versions of SCSI are SCSI-1, SCSI-2, and SCSI-3, commonly known as Regular SCSI, Fast SCSI, and Ultra SCSI. SCSI-1 was the original version of the SCSI standard. It covered the design of wiring on the SCSI bus but did not include a common command set. Therefore, there were still a lot of incompatibilities between SCSI-1 devices. With SCSI-1, only an 8-bit data bus was used, and there could be only seven devices besides the host adapter.

SCSI-2 improved the standard by developing a common command set so that devices could communicate with each other more easily. It also introduced wide SCSI, which expanded the width of the data bus to 16 bits and the number of possible devices to 15. SCSI-2 also made parity checking of the data bus mandatory.

SCSI-3, which has grown to be a set of standards rather than a single standard, supports both parallel and serial data transmission, supports FireWire connections, and increases the possible rate of data transfer to 320 MB/sec and higher. The **SPI (SCSI Parallel Interface)** standard is part of SCSI-3 and specifies how SCSI devices are connected. There have been three versions of SPI; the latest is Ultra 320 SCSI. Beginning with Ultra SCSI (SCSI-3), the SCSI standard supports SCAM, which you learned about earlier in the chapter. SCSI-3 uses an 8-, 16-, or 32-bit data bus and supports up to 32 devices on a system.

22

$A+{}^{CORE}_{\substack{1.7 \\ 4.3}}$

 TIP Because SCSI can be so difficult to configure, a growing trend in the industry is to replace SCSI with FireWire (IEEE 1394), especially since some newer high-end motherboards provide FireWire support. Another contender to replace SCSI is FCAL (Fiber Channel Arbitrated Loop), which uses fiber optic cabling. Both FireWire and FCAL use serial data transmission. FCAL is used on higher-end systems than FireWire.

Because there are several variations of SCSI standards, when you buy a new SCSI device, you must be sure that it is compatible with the SCSI bus you already have, taking into consideration that some SCSI standards are backward-compatible. If the new SCSI device is not compatible, you cannot use the same SCSI bus, and you must buy a new host adapter to build a second SCSI bus system, increasing the overall cost of adding the new device.

Table 22-3 summarizes characteristics of the different SCSI standards. Other names used in the industry for these standards are also listed in the table. Note that both Fast SCSI (SCSI-2) and Ultra SCSI (SCSI-3) have narrow and wide versions.

Table 22-3   Summary of SCSI standards

Standard Name	Standard Number	Bus Width (Narrow = 8 bits, Wide = 16 bits)	Transfer Rate (MB/sec)	Maximum Number of Devices
Regular SCSI	SCSI-1	Narrow	5	8
Fast SCSI or Fast Narrow	SCSI-2	Narrow	10	8
Fast Wide SCSI or Wide SCSI	SCSI-2	Wide	20	16
Ultra SCSI, Ultra Narrow, or Fast-20 SCSI	SCSI-3	Narrow	20	8
Wide Ultra SCSI or Fast Wide 20	SCSI-3	Wide	40	16
Ultra2 SCSI or SPI-2	SCSI-3	Narrow	40	8
Wide Ultra2 SCSI	SCSI-3	Wide	80	16
Ultra3 SCSI or SPI-3	SCSI-3	Narrow	80	8
Wide Ultra3 SCSI or Ultra 160 SCSI	SCSI-3	Wide	160	16
Ultra 320 SCSI (Ultra4 SCSI or SPI-4)	SCSI-3	Wide	320*	16

*SPI-4 is expected to soon be rated at 640 MBps and then 1,280 MBps.

Table 22-4 summarizes cable specifications for the SCSI standards listed in Table 22-3.

Table 22-4   SCSI standard cable specifications

SCSI Standard Name	Maximum Length of Single-Ended Cable (Meters)	Maximum Length of Differential Cable (Meters)	Cable Type
Regular SCSI	6	25	50-pin
Fast SCSI or Fast Narrow	3	25	50-pin
Fast Wide SCSI or Wide SCSI	3	25	68-pin
Ultra SCSI, Ultra Narrow, or Fast-20 SCSI	1.5	25	50-pin
Wide Ultra SCSI or Fast Wide 20	1.5	25	68-pin
Ultra2 SCSI or SPI-2		12 LVD	50-pin
Wide Ultra2 SCSI			68-pin
Ultra3 SCSI or SPI-3		12 LVD	50-pin
Wide Ultra3 SCSI or Ultra 160 SCSI		12 LVD	68-pin
Ultra 320 SCSI (Ultra4 SCSI or SPI-4)		12 LVD	68-pin

COMPARING IDE AND SCSI

Before we move on to how to install SCSI devices, let's compare SCSI to IDE technology. When selecting hard drives and other devices, you need to know which technology they use and the advantages and disadvantages of each. When you use a single disk drive with an operating system such as Windows 98 or Windows Me, you may actually find that an IDE drive provides better performance than a comparable SCSI drive. Features of SCSI drives that are improvements over IDE increase performance mainly where a heavy load is placed on a system and on its components—for example, when multiple hard drives are installed on a high-end server. Also, some operating systems, such as Windows 2000 and XP, include increased support for SCSI features and can take better advantage of them.

Consider the following issues when choosing between an IDE hard drive and a SCSI hard drive:

- IDE supports only four internal devices; SCSI supports both internal and external devices and allows you to add more devices to a system. If you don't have enough expansion drive bays with IDE, this can solve the problem.

- SCSI devices are generally higher quality than IDE devices and more expensive.

- IDE devices require a separate IRQ for each device; SCSI requires only one for the entire chain.

22

- Both IDE and SCSI are generally backward-compatible, in that most faster hardware can work with slower devices.

- A SCSI hard drive with its supporting host adapter and cable costs more than an IDE hard drive.

- A SCSI subsystem provides faster data transfer than an IDE drive, although the SCSI bus is the source of the performance rather than the hard drive technology.

- SCSI generally provides better performance than IDE and is often used on high-demand servers.

- A good SCSI host adapter allows you to connect other SCSI devices to it, such as a printer, scanner, or tape drive.

- Without SCSI technology, if you have two IDE drives on the same IDE channel, only one of them can be busy at any one time. For instance, without SCSI, if one of your IDE devices is a CD-ROM, the hard drive must wait for the CD-ROM to complete a task before it can work again. With SCSI, two or more devices can operate simultaneously. If you plan to transfer a lot of data from CD-ROM to hard drive, this is a good reason to choose SCSI.

In summary, SCSI is more expensive than IDE but gives you better performance.

 TIP It is possible, but not recommended, to mix SCSI and IDE devices on a system. Both types of devices will try to monopolize the PCI bus, and you may experience resource conflicts as a result.

INSTALLING SCSI DEVICES

As you learned, there are many different types of SCSI and many variations within the components of a SCSI subsystem. Although the installation of a SCSI system may sound complicated and requires many decisions about what components to buy, the installation instructions for SCSI devices and host adapters are usually very thorough and well written. If you carefully follow all instructions, SCSI installations can be smooth and problem free. This section covers how to install SCSI devices, beginning with a host adapter and then moving on to a scanner and a hard drive as examples. First, let's look at some basic steps for SCSI installation:

1. Set any jumpers or switches on the host adapter, install it in the correct expansion slot on your motherboard, and install the host adapter drivers.

2. For each device that has them, use jumpers or switches to assign the SCSI ID.

3. Attach cabling to the host adapter and then to each device.

4. Verify that both ends of the SCSI chain are terminated.

5. Power up one device. After you verify that it works, power up the next device. Continue until you verify that all devices work.

6. Install drivers and software required to interface between the SCSI subsystem and the operating system.

Installing a Host Adapter Card

A+CORE 1.2   For a Plug and Play system using Windows 9x or Windows 2000/XP, follow these general steps to install a host adapter:

1. Install the card in an expansion slot.

2. In most cases, default settings for the host adapter are correct, but you can change or verify these settings using the setup program. For example, to use a setup program that comes on a floppy disk bundled with the adapter, boot the PC from the floppy disk. The disk boots the system (using DOS) and automatically executes the SCSI setup program. In this example of one setup program, the two options on the opening menu are SCSI Disk Utilities (for installing a SCSI hard drive) and Configure the Host Adapter. Select **Configure the Host Adapter.** You see the host adapter configuration screen (see Figure 22-8).

Figure 22-8   Setup software included with a SCSI host adapter is used to change SCSI BIOS settings on the card

3. Verify the settings. Under the Advanced Configuration Options in Figure 22-8, you see two settings: enable or disable Plug and Play, and enable or disable SCAM support. Both are normally set to enable. Note in Figure 22-8 that the SCSI ID for the host adapter is 7 and that parity checking is enabled. After verifying settings, exit the setup program, remove the floppy disk, and reboot.

4. When Windows loads, it senses a new hardware device and automatically launches the Add New Hardware Wizard. Because Windows supports the host adapter, it loads the device drivers automatically and installs the host adapter.

22

A+CORE
1.2
1.7

5. To verify that the host adapter is correctly installed, open **Device Manager**. Double-click **SCSI controllers**. The Adaptec host adapter should appear, as shown in Figure 22-9 for Windows 98. Select the host adapter and click **Properties** to display the host adapter Properties dialog box, also shown in Figure 22-9. Click the **Resources** tab to note the resources assigned to the card by Plug and Play. (For Windows 2000/XP Device Manager, to view a device's properties, right-click the device and select **Properties** from the shortcut menu.)

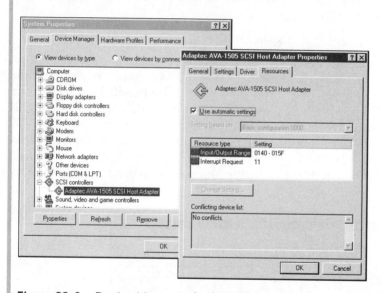

Figure 22-9   Device Manager displays the newly installed host adapter

 TIP   Notice the broken diamond symbol in Figure 22-9, which you saw earlier in Figure 22-4. The symbol for single-ended SCSI devices is sometimes used to symbolize SCSI in general.

After you install the host adapter, you are ready to install the external SCSI device. For example, if the device is a SCSI scanner, follow these directions:

1. Install the software to run the scanner, which includes the scanner driver.

2. Plug the SCSI cable into the host adapter port.

3. Plug the other end of the cable into the scanner.

4. Set the SCSI ID on the scanner.

5. Connect the scanner's power cord to a wall outlet, and turn on the scanner.

6. Restart your PC and test the scanner.

SETTING DEVICE IDs DURING INSTALLATION

A+CORE
1.2
1.7

If your SCSI subsystem is SCAM–compliant, SCSI IDs are assigned automatically. However, SCAM does not work unless your OS, devices, and host adapter all support the SCAM standard. Without SCAM compliance, you must set device SCSI IDs manually. Remember that each ID must be unique; no two devices on the same SCSI channel can have the same ID number. (If you have more than one SCSI adapter on a system, you can reuse IDs.) For narrow SCSI, the IDs are 0–7, and for wide SCSI, the IDs are 0–15. Generally, you can assign almost any ID number to any device. However, the host adapter usually has the ID 7 or 15, and some devices may come from the manufacturer with their IDs already set. Many SCSI hard drives, for example, are automatically set to SCSI ID 6.

To set IDs for external devices, you use either a push-button selector or rotary selector, as shown in Figure 22-10. The push-button selector has buttons to increase and decrease the number, and the rotary selector works like a radio dial that you turn to the number you want. Some ID selectors for external devices are designed to be adjusted with a screwdriver, so that you cannot accidentally change the ID by bumping the device.

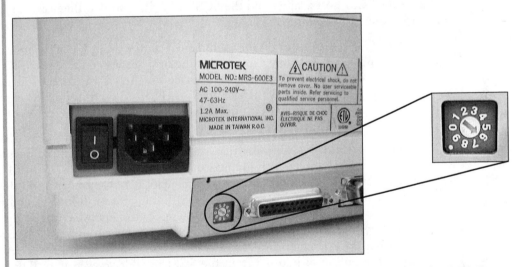

Figure 22-10   This rotary dial on the rear of a SCSI scanner is used to set the SCSI ID, which is now set to 6

To set IDs for internal devices, you use a set of jumpers on the device. Most newer devices use a binary code to set IDs, with three pin pairs for narrow SCSI and four pin pairs for wide SCSI. Figure 22-11 shows the jumper settings for wide SCSI IDs.

22

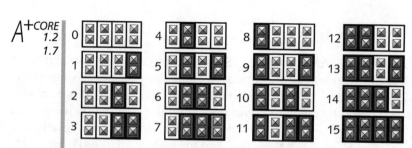

Figure 22-11 Wide SCSI ID binary jumper settings for internal devices

Installing a SCSI Hard Drive

A+CORE
1.2
1.7

When you install a SCSI hard drive, make sure that your host adapter and the cables you use are compatible with the SCSI drive. The vendor can help you here. Read the documentation for both the SCSI host adapter and the hard drive before beginning; most SCSI documentation is well written and thorough. In addition to the procedure already discussed in Chapter 8 for IDE hard drives, a SCSI installation requires that you configure the SCSI host adapter and the SCSI hard drive so that they can communicate with each other. This is done as follows:

1. *Set SCSI IDs.* Set the ID for each device on the SCSI bus. The host adapter documentation probably explains that the host adapter must be set to ID 7 or 15. If the hard drive is to be the boot device for the system, its ID is likely to be 0. The second hard drive ID is usually 1. These ID settings might be set by jumpers or DIP switches on the drive.

2. *Disable or enable disk drive and hard drive controllers.* If the host adapter has a built-in disk drive controller that you are not using, it might be necessary to disable the controller with jumpers or DIP switches, or from the SCSI software setup program. The host adapter documentation explains how to do this. Incidentally, if you are not using a SCSI hard drive or disk drive controller on your motherboard, you must disable these controllers by setting jumpers or DIP switches on the motherboard or by changing settings in CMOS setup. See the documentation for your motherboard. Sometimes CMOS setup gives you the option of booting from the SCSI hard drive even if an IDE hard drive is installed.

3. *Check terminating resistors.* Devices on both ends of the bus must have terminating resistors. Check the documentation for the two devices on each end of the SCSI chain to see how the termination is done.

4. *Run CMOS setup for a SCSI system.* After you physically install the SCSI host and drive, tell setup that the SCSI system is present. Remember that for SCSI devices, the computer does not communicate with the hard drive directly but interfaces with the SCSI host adapter. To use a SCSI hard drive, some computers require that you tell setup that no hard drive is present. The SCSI host provides that information to the computer during startup. Sometimes, the computer

A+CORE
1.7

setup lets you choose a SCSI hard drive type. That's all it needs to know; the SCSI host adapter takes over from there. To recognize a SCSI drive, some computers require that the drive type be set to 1 in CMOS setup.

5. *Load SCSI device drivers.* Windows operating systems offer their own SCSI drivers, although if the host adapter documentation recommends that you use the adapter's driver instead, then do so. After you physically install the drive and change CMOS setup, the next step in any hard drive installation is to boot from a floppy disk. The hard drive package will include a bootable disk or CD that loads the device driver to access the SCSI system.

TROUBLESHOOTING SCSI DEVICES

A+CORE
1.7
2.1

When you use a variety of SCSI devices, installation and configuration can get complicated. To make this process as easy as possible, keep these general tips in mind:

- As always, keep detailed notes on device installation and configuration for use in troubleshooting and backtracking, and always read all documentation for devices you are trying to add to and use with your system. Record all switch and jumper settings for your SCSI devices. Record all system resources and addresses used by the host adapter.

- If you are adding several SCSI devices to your system, add them one at a time rather than all at once. First install the host adapter and, if you are using one, the SCSI hard drive, and make sure they work before you try to install additional peripherals.

- Use components of good quality. Do not sacrifice quality just to pay a little less. For example, higher-quality cables usually experience less degradation of data and less interference, and higher-quality active terminators generally do a better job than cheaper passive ones, even if you have some devices that are not Fast SCSI.

- Limiting cable length whenever possible helps to improve performance and reduces the chance that data will become corrupted.

Here are some things to check if you have problems with installing SCSI devices:

- SCSI drivers will look for their devices when the computer boots, so make sure to turn on all external SCSI devices before you turn on the computer.

- Check the connections of all SCSI cables, power connections, and adapters. Sometimes moving and reattaching them can clear up connection problems.

- Many problems with SCSI devices are caused by incorrect termination. Remember that both ends of a SCSI chain must be terminated and that termination should be disabled at all other points in the chain. If the host adapter is at one end of the chain, it must have termination enabled; if it is in the middle of the chain, it must have termination disabled.

22

A+CORE
1.7
2.1

- Check with your motherboard's manufacturer to make sure you have the most updated BIOS, so that PCI slots operate correctly. Also check to make sure you have up-to-date drivers for your SCSI devices.

- Install a PCI host adapter in a PCI bus that supports bus mastering—not all PCI slots on older motherboards do. Try removing the host adapter and reseating it in another PCI slot.

After you install SCSI devices, if you also have IDE devices, your system attempts to boot from the IDE drive first. To cause it to boot from a SCSI drive, you must either change the boot order or remove the non-SCSI drives to cause it to boot from a SCSI drive. If your system has only SCSI drives installed and still will not boot, check these things:

- The BIOS setup drive configuration for your computer should be set to "No Drives Installed." Most BIOSs only support IDE drives. If you tell the system that no drives are installed, it attempts to boot from another device, such as a SCSI drive.

- Verify that the SCSI drive that you want to boot from is partitioned, that it has a primary partition, and that the boot partition is set as active.

- If nothing else works, back up the SCSI hard drive and then do a low-level format on it. A Format utility is included with the host adapter for this purpose.

CHAPTER SUMMARY

- The SCSI bus requires a controller embedded on the motherboard or on a host adapter inserted into an expansion slot. If the motherboard has a SCSI controller, a SCSI port or connector will be somewhere on the board. The host adapter is the more common way of supporting SCSI.

- The term *SCSI hard drive* refers more to the bus used by the drive than to the technology of the drive. Internally, SCSI and IDE drives work in basically the same way.

- There are several variations of SCSI buses and devices, including SCSI-1, SCSI-2, SCSI-3, Wide SCSI, Ultra SCSI, and Ultra Wide SCSI.

- Every SCSI bus subsystem requires a SCSI controller and unique SCSI IDs assigned to each device, including the host adapter.

- The SCSI host adapter should generally be set to ID 7 or 15, since these IDs have the highest priority.

- The narrow SCSI bus has an 8-bit data path, and the wide SCSI bus has a 16-bit data path.

- Each end of the SCSI bus must have a terminating resistor, which can be controlled by hardware or software.

- Narrow SCSI uses a 25-pin or 50-pin connector (also called an A cable), and wide SCSI uses a 68-pin connector (also called a P cable).

- The two types of SCSI cabling are single-ended and differential.

- There are three types of termination for single-ended cabling: passive, active, and forced perfect.

- There are two types of termination for differential SCSI cabling: HVD and LVD. HVD became obsolete with the introduction of SCSI-3. HVD uses a higher voltage than LVD signaling does.

- When selecting a SCSI host adapter, consider the SCSI standards the adapter supports, the bus slot the adapter will use, the device driver standard used by the host adapter, the issue of single-ended versus differential SCSI, SCAM compliance, and whether or not the host offers bus mastering.

- Each device on a SCSI bus is assigned a number from 0 to 15, called the SCSI ID. Logical devices within a physical device, such as trays within a CD changer, are assigned a separate number called a LUN.

- The two main types of SCSI device drivers are ASPI and CAM. When selecting a host adapter, you should pick one that supports either ASPI or CAM.

- You can limit the chance of data becoming corrupted by buying high-quality cables, limiting cable length, and using high-end terminators.

- If you have an IDE hard drive and a SCSI hard drive installed on the same system, the system attempts to boot from the IDE hard drive first. If you want to boot from a SCSI drive, you must change the boot order in Setup or remove the non-SCSI drives.

- One of the most common causes for problems with the SCSI subsystem is incorrect termination.

KEY TERMS

active terminator
Advanced SCSI Programming Interface (ASPI)
Common Access Method (CAM)
differential cable
forced perfect termi- nator (FPT)
High Voltage Differential (HVD)
host adapter

Logical Unit Number (LUN)
Low Voltage Differential (LVD)
narrow SCSI
passive terminator
SBAC (SCSI bus adapter chip)
SCAM (SCSI Configuration AutoMatically)

SCSI (Small Computer System Interface)
SCSI ID
single-ended (SE) cable
SPI (SCSI Parallel Interface)
terminating resistor
termination
wide SCSI

22

REVIEW QUESTIONS

1. When making use of devices that utilize the SCSI interface, the card that is inserted into the motherboard to control these devices and coordinate the transfer of data is referred to as a:

   a. Controller card

   b. Host adapter

   c. DE controller

   d. EIDE controller

   e. None of the above

2. Which interface technology allows devices like hard drives to communicate directly with the CPU through the system bus?

   a. IDE

   b. SCSI

   c. PCMCIA

   d. All of the above

   e. None of the above

3. Which of the following values represents the number of devices that can be connected to the SCSI bus?

   a. 15

   b. 16

   c. 32

   d. 64

   e. 128

4. The SCSI ID identifies logical devices and the Logical Unit Number identifies the physical device.

   a. True

   b. False

5. A service technician installs an additional hard drive unit on the same SCSI bus where the only hard drive unit is functioning. Upon system boot-up, the system does not boot; rather, the system "hangs." What is the most likely cause of the problem?

   a. The second hard drive is not a SCSI drive.

   b. The first drive is set up as a "master/single drive."

   c. The first drive is set up as a "slave."

   d. The technician failed to install the terminating resistor in the second drive.

   e. None of the above

6. Upon system boot-up, the on-board system BIOS is used to configure the mother-board for data transfer between itself and the installed SCSI hard drive unit.

   a. True

   b. False

7. Two general categories exist for the SCSI interface: narrow SCSI and wide SCSI. Wide SCSI is expected to offer a SCSI data bus width of _____ bits.

   a. 8

   b. 16

   c. 32

   d. 64

   e. 128

8. A service technician is called upon to replace a defective hard drive unit from a system. Upon careful inspection, the technician finds that the hard drive unit is using a 50-pin connector as the interface connection. The technician orders a new _____ hard drive to replace the defective unit.

   a. IDE

   b. EIDE

   c. Narrow SCSI

   d. Wide SCSI

   e. None of the above

9. Using _____ SCSI cables, one of the wires carries voltage and the other carries ground.

   a. Single-ended

   b. Differential

   c. Twisted

   d. Straight

   e. None of the above

10. The symbol ⟨⟩ indicates what type of signaling a device or cable uses.

   a. Single-ended SCSI

   b. Differential SCSI

   c. Twisted cable

   d. Straight cable

   e. None of the above

11. The SCSI connector that is classified as "P cable connector" uses how many pins?

    a. 34

    b. 40

    c. 50

    d. 68

    e. 80

12. The SCSI connector that was developed to allow for hot-swappable devices is the _____ pin connector.

    a. 34

    b. 40

    c. 50

    d. 68

    e. 80

13. The type of terminator that is recommended for SCSI-2 devices is the:

    a. Passive terminator

    b. Active terminator

    c. Forced perfect terminator (FPT)

    d. Any of the above

    e. None of the above

14. Of the three major versions of SCSI, which made parity checking of the data bus mandatory?

    a. SCSI-1

    b. SCSI-2

    c. SCSI-3

    d. SCSI

    e. None of the above

15. Assuming a SCSI interface, the SCSI ID of the host adapter is always set to:

    a. The first SCSI ID setting on the chain (ID 0)

    b. The highest SCSI ID number on the chain

    c. The setting of the ID number doesn't matter for the host adapter.

23

PURCHASING A PC OR BUILDING YOUR OWN

In this chapter, you will learn:
- Some guidelines to use when purchasing a PC
- How to prepare for assembling a PC yourself
- How to assemble a PC from separately purchased parts

This chapter presents guidelines for purchasing a new PC and detailed, step-by-step procedures for building a PC from parts. If you need a computer for your own personal use, consider assembling it yourself, not necessarily to save money but to benefit in other ways. If you don't want to build a PC, you must choose between purchasing a brand-name PC or a clone.

After-sales service and support are probably the most important criteria to consider when purchasing a PC. In general, a brand-name PC (such as Dell or Gateway) might cost more but generally you will get better service and support than you will for a PC built with parts manufactured by companies whose names you don't recognize. Important reasons for choosing to build your own PC are the knowledge gained and complete control over every part purchased, which allows you to make your own customized integrated system.

SELECTING A PERSONAL COMPUTER TO MEET YOUR NEEDS

So far, this book has been full of information concerning which computers, peripheral devices, operating systems, and software to buy and how to manage and maintain them once they are yours. However, hardware and software change daily, and it's important to stay informed if you make buying decisions or give purchasing advice on an ongoing basis.

$A^{+CORE}_{1.9}$ Sometimes it is appropriate to upgrade an existing PC rather than purchase a new one. Consider adding more memory, upgrading the CPU or adding a second CPU, adding a second hard drive, upgrading the video card, upgrading the motherboard, and adding additional fans for cooling. Generally, if the cost of the upgrade does not exceed half the value of the current system, an upgrade is appropriate if the resulting system does not contain legacy components that prevent the upgraded system from performing well. Don't upgrade a computer system that is older than five years as the cost of upgrade will probably exceed the value of the current system. In this case, a new PC is your best option.

You can choose one of three alternatives when selecting a PC: buy a brand-name PC, buy a clone, or buy parts and assemble a PC yourself—which, in effect, results in your own personally designed clone.

A brand-name PC, sometimes called an **IBM-compatible PC**, is a PC manufactured by a company with a widely recognized name such as Hewlett-Packard, Packard Bell, Dell, Gateway, or IBM. A **clone** is generally understood to mean a PC assembled by a local company with parts manufactured by several companies. There are advantages and disadvantages to purchasing both brand-name and clone PCs, in the areas of warranties, service contracts, and ease of obtaining replacement and additional parts. For instance, while it may seem advantageous that brand-name PCs and most clones come with some software already installed, the software is not necessarily standard, brand-name software. The preinstalled software can be any variety of shareware, unknown software, and so forth, and the documentation and original installation disks for the software may not be included in the total package.

When selecting a computer system that will include both hardware and software, begin by taking an overall view of the decisions you must make. Start by answering these questions:

- How will the computer be used now and in the future?
- What functionality do you want the computer to have (within its intended use)?
- What hardware and software do you need to meet this functionality?
- What is your budget?
- If you determine that a clone meets your needs, do you want to assemble it yourself?

In order to make the best possible decision, consider the first question to be the most important, the second question the next most important, and so on. For example, if you intend to use the computer for multimedia presentations and accessing the Internet, the functionality required is considerably different from that of a computer used for software development.

After you identify the intended purpose of the computer, list the functionality required to meet the needs of the intended purpose. For example, if the computer is to be used for playing games, some required functionality might be:

- Ability of the hardware to support game software

- Excellent video and sound

- Sophisticated input methods, such as a joystick or controller

If the computer is to be used for software development, required functionality might include:

- The ability to support the standard hardware and software environment that most customers using the developed software might have

- The ability to run software development tools and hardware to support the software

- A high-quality monitor and a comfortable keyboard and mouse for long work hours

- A removable, high-capacity storage device for easy transfer and storage of developed software

- Reliable warranty and service to guarantee minimal downtime

After the required functionality is defined, the next step, defining what hardware and software are needed, is much easier. For example, if a comfortable keyboard designed for long work hours is required, begin by researching the different types of keyboards available, and try out a few in stores if necessary. It would be a mistake to purchase the cheapest keyboard in the store for this intended purpose. However, for game playing, an expensive, comfortable keyboard is probably not needed because most games use other input devices. Spending your resources on a sophisticated joystick probably makes more sense.

As noted above, the least possible amount of downtime is a required functionality for software development. This is also true for many business-use computers, and it is the most important reason businesses choose brand-name computers over clones.

Purchasing a Brand-Name PC vs. a Clone

As you have most likely noticed, brand-name PCs generally cost more than clone PCs with similar features. One reason is that you pay extra money for after-sales service. For example, some PCs come with a three-year warranty, a 24-hour-service help line with a toll-free number, and delivery of parts to your place of business. A clone manufacturer might also give good service, but this may be due to the personalities of a few employees rather than to company policies. Most likely, clone company policies are not as liberal and all-encompassing as those of a brand-name manufacturer. Most brand-name manufacturers provide additional support generally not provided by clone manufacturers, such as functional Web sites, updated drivers and utilities, and online troubleshooting or user manuals.

23

On the other hand, many brand-name manufacturers use nonstandard parts with their hardware and nonstandard approaches to setting up their systems, making their computers more proprietary than clones. One of the most common ways for a brand-name manufacturer to make its computer more proprietary is to put components, such as support for video, directly on the motherboard rather than use more generic expansion cards.

Additionally, rather than being updated by a setup program in BIOS, the CMOS setup program might be stored on the hard drive. The shape and size of the computer case might be such that a standard motherboard does not fit; only the brand-name board will do. These practices can make upgrading and repairing brand-name PCs more difficult, because you are forced to use the brand-name parts and brand-name service. Also, in some areas of the country, it may be difficult to find authorized dealers and service centers for brand-name PCs.

Selecting Software

Your decisions about software selection are driven by the functionality requirements for the PC, as identified in the previous sections. Choose the operating system first. For Windows, more than likely you will want to select the latest OS supported by your system. Currently, that is Windows XP Professional or Windows XP Home Edition. For the corporate market where security and remote access are important, choose Windows XP Professional. When choosing application software, consider these questions:

- What do you want the software to do? (This will be defined by your answers to the functionality questions listed earlier.)

- Is compatibility with other software or data required? Consider compatibility with your existing system as well as with office systems if you telecommute.

- Is training available, if you do not already have the skills needed to use the software?

- How good is the software's documentation?

- What are the company's upgrade policies?

- How well known or popular is the software? (The more popular, the more likely you'll find good training materials, trained people, technical support, and other compatible software and hardware.)

Caution is in order if you are buying a brand-name or clone computer with preinstalled software that you are not familiar with. The software may not provide the functionality you need and may not have good documentation, reliable upgrades, or support. Unless you feel that you have the skill to manage this software, you're probably better off staying with mainstream-market software. One way to identify which brand of software is the most prevalent in the industry is to browse the computer books section of a local bookstore, looking for the software that has the most "how to" books written about it. Also see trade magazines, the Internet, and your local retailer.

Selecting Hardware

The two most important criteria to consider when selecting hardware are compatibility and functionality. Begin by considering the motherboard. (See Chapter 5 for more information about how to select one.) Here are other topics you should consider:

- Use only 100 percent Plug and Play components, and be certain the BIOS is ACPI compliant.

- If you intend to use the PC for multimedia applications, including games, you want a high-speed CPU, a high-quality video card, and plenty of memory.

- If you plan to use the PC for heavy network use, buy a PC with plenty of processing power.

- If you connect to the Internet using a modem, buy a high-quality one.

- When selecting a computer case, keep in mind that tower cases generally offer more room than desktop units and are easier to work with when adding new devices. Make sure the case has a reset button and, if security is an issue, a key lock in order to limit access to the inside of the case. Some cases even have a lock on the floppy drive to prevent unauthorized booting from a floppy disk.

- Select a power supply that will supply enough power for your components. (Refer to Chapter 4 for help on calculating the total power needs of your system.)

- In addition to the power supply fan and CPU fan, consider buying an auxiliary fan for additional cooling. Fans are not expensive and can help keep a lower temperature inside the case.

- The documentation for a component should be easy to read and comprehensive, and the manufacturer's Web site should offer easy-to-find technical support and the latest drivers.

- A device should have a warranty and be compatible with all hardware and software in your system.

Internal devices are usually less expensive than external devices, because external devices have the additional expenses of their own power supply and case. Internal devices also offer the advantage of not taking up desk space, and their cables and cords are neatly tucked away. An advantage of external devices is that they can be moved easily from one computer to another.

If you've ever shopped for a peripheral device, such as a printer or a sound card, you know what a large variety of features and prices are in today's market. Research pays. In

23

general, when selecting a device for an existing system or when building a new system, you should know the following about your computer system:

- Which CPU, system bus, and local bus you have

- How much memory you have

- What size hard drive your system has

- Which OS you are using and what version it is (for example, Windows 2000 Professional or Windows XP Home Edition)

- How much space is available on your hard drive

- For internal devices, how many drives, bays, or expansion slots and what kinds of slots are free in your computer

 TIP When buying a device and other components that the device will use, such as an expansion card or cable, they are more likely to be compatible if you buy everything from the same source.

Selecting a Total Package

When selecting a complete computer package, including hardware and software, consider these points:

- What hardware and software are included? Are the hardware and software compatible with those found on the general market? (For example, if you want to upgrade your video card or word processor, how difficult would that be?)

- What is the warranty and return or exchange policy?

- What onsite or local service is available? Do you know anyone who has used this service, and was it satisfactory?

- Is the system ACPI and Energy Star compliant? (For information about ACPI and Energy Star, see Chapter 4.)

- What software comes preinstalled?

- What documentation or manuals come with the system?

- Does the manufacturer maintain a Web site with useful support features, utilities, and updates?

- Does the motherboard allow for expansion of RAM?

- What expansion slots are not being used? (Always allow some room to grow.)

- Can features such as video on the motherboard be disabled if necessary? (Refer to Chapter 5 for other guidelines on selecting motherboards.)

- How much does the system cost?

When considering price, keep in mind that high-priced to middle-range-priced PCs are most likely to be network compatible and easily expandable; they offer a broader range of support and have had extensive testing of vendor products for reliability and compatibility. Low-priced PCs may not have been tested for network compatibility; they offer a limited range of support; and the quality of components may not be as high.

> Beware of pirated software installed on preassembled PCs. Vendors sometimes sell counterfeit software by installing unauthorized software on computers. This practice is called **hard-disk loading**. Vendors have even been known to counterfeit disk labels and Certificates of Authenticity. Look for these warning signs that software purchased from vendors is pirated: it has no end-user license, mail-in product registration card, documentation, or original CDs; documentation is photocopied; or disks have handwritten labels. Accept nothing less than the original installation CDs for all installed software.

When considering preinstalled software, remember that sometimes unneeded software is more of a hindrance than a help, needlessly taking up space. For example, it is not uncommon for a brand-name computer to come with three or four applications for Internet access (for example, America Online, CompuServe, and Microsoft Network) because of licensing agreements distributors have with online providers. Typically, only one is needed. Sometimes having more than one on your computer causes problems.

PREPARING TO BUILD YOUR OWN PC

Assembling your own PC takes time, skill, and research, but it can be a great learning experience. You might even want to consider it your "rite of passage" toward being a PC technician. All the skills needed to be a PC technician are tested: research, knowledge of user needs and the computer market, planning, organization, patience, confidence, problem solving, and extensive knowledge of both hardware and software. If you intend to become a corporate-level technician, you most certainly should put together at least one whole PC before starting your first job.

However, don't build your PC to save money, because you probably won't. The total price of all parts usually about equals the price of a comparable clone PC that is prebuilt. Here are a few good reasons to assemble your own PC:

- The whole process can be quite fun.

- Knowledge is power. The knowledge and experience gained in researching the parts to buy, studying the documentation, and finally assembling the PC cannot be overemphasized.

- When you buy all the parts and software for a PC individually, you also get the documentation for each hardware component. This is most likely not the case when you buy a preassembled PC. If you plan to upgrade your PC later, having this documentation can be very valuable.

23

- Many prebuilt PCs come with software preloaded. You may not receive the original CDs or disks or the documentation for these programs That can be a problem when you try to maintain your system and most likely indicates that the software is distributed illegally. (Don't accept preinstalled software unless it also includes the installation disks and documentation.) When you buy each software package individually, you are assured that the distribution is legal, and you have the installation disks, CDs, and documentation.

- When you purchase each computer part individually, you are more likely to understand exactly what you are buying, and you can be more particular about the selection of each component. You have control over the brand and features of each component in the PC.

Here are a few reasons why you might not want to build your own PC:

- If you are in a rush to get a PC up and running, assembling your own is probably not a good idea, especially if you are a first-time builder. The process takes time and requires patience, and the first time you do it, you most likely will make a few mistakes that will need to be resolved.

- Individual parts may be warrantied, but if you build your own PC, there is no overall warranty on the PC. If a warranty or a service agreement is important, then look for a ready-built PC with these services included.

- Clone PCs have been tested to ensure that individual components are compatible. When building your own PC, it is possible you might select incompatible components. For this reason, buy high-quality mainstream components to best ensure compatibility.

- Don't plan to assemble a PC for the first time unless you have access to an experienced technician or a technical service center you can consult if you encounter a problem you cannot resolve. For example, you might buy all the parts from a store that has a service center. The store might offer to assemble the PC for you for a charge ($50 to $75 is about right). If you find you cannot resolve a problem, you can always go back to the store for this service.

- Remember, you probably won't save money assembling the PC.

Getting Ready for Assembly: Selecting Parts

If you have decided to buy parts and assemble a PC, expect the process to take some time. The motherboard and expansion cards are full of connections, ports, and perhaps jumpers, and you must read the documentation carefully to determine just how to configure the motherboard and all components to work together. Technicians in service centers can assemble a PC in less than an hour, but they have already assembled the same group of parts many times!

Planning the assembly of a PC is like packing for a camping trip to a remote location. You must plan for everything you need before you begin. As you select and purchase each part, two things are important: functionality and compatibility with other parts.

Almost every computer needs these essentials: motherboard, CPU, RAM, hard drive, CD-ROM drive (or you can substitute a DVD drive or CD-RW drive for added functionality), floppy drive, case, power supply, video card, monitor, keyboard, and mouse. And, most likely, you also want a sound card and modem. Make careful and informed decisions about every part you buy. Selecting each component requires reviewing your functionality, compatibility, and budget needs and determining what parts meet your criteria. Select the motherboard first, and then select the other parts around this one most important component.

When selecting parts, including the motherboard, carefully examine the documentation. Look for good documentation that you can understand without struggling. When buying parts for your first assembly, you should probably not use mail order. Buy from a reputable local dealer who allows you to examine a part and look at its documentation, and who is willing and able to answer any technical questions you may have. Know the store's return policy and the manufacturer's warranty for each part.

If you can buy the motherboard, CPU, and memory from the same dealer who can help you determine that all three are compatible, do so to avoid problems later with compatibility. The documentation for the motherboard is quite valuable. Make sure it's readable and complete. If it's not, look on the manufacturer's Web site for additional documentation before making the purchase. Does the motherboard support USB, FireWire, or SCSI? The CPU needs at least one fan or cooler. Does the entire system need additional fans? Ask the dealer for recommendations, and read the documentation for the CPU. A dealer often sells a motherboard with the CPU and fan already installed and jumpers on the motherboard set correctly.

After you select the motherboard, CPU, and RAM, select the case and accompanying power supply. Remember the two rules: the case must meet your predetermined functionality, and it must be compatible with other parts (especially the motherboard). Check the motherboard documentation for extra power cords the CPU might require, and make sure the power supply provides these. Next, select the hard drive and other drives.

If the video logic is not included on the motherboard (for clone motherboards it probably is not), select the video card next, and make sure that you have an AGP slot to accommodate it. There are several types of AGP slots. Match your AGP video card to the type your motherboard provides. Last, select other peripherals, including a mouse, keyboard, and monitor.

Getting Ready for Assembly: Final Preparations

When all parts are purchased, prepare well for the assembly. Prepare a work area that is well lit and uncluttered. Before you start, read all documentation and plan the assembly through, from beginning to end. If you have questions or are unsure how to proceed, find answers to your concerns before you begin. For example, if you're not sure how to set the jumpers on the motherboard, even after you read the documentation, take the documentation to your technical support (a dealer, a service center, a knowledgeable friend), and ask for help in interpreting the settings in the documentation before you start the work. Often you can find a detailed diagram of the motherboard on the manufacturer's Web site, complete with proper settings for specific CPUs.

 TIP While working, don't get careless about protecting yourself and your equipment against static electricity. (Review the safety precautions in Chapter 4.) Always use the ground strap on your wrist.

Building a Personal Computer, Step by Step

This section is a step-by-step, detailed description of building a simple Pentium 4 PC that includes a hard drive, a floppy drive, and a CD-ROM drive. Depending on what you decide you want your computer for and what functionality and budget you are operating with, you may choose to build a different PC, with a different CPU and different parts. Documentation and manufacturer Web sites are, as always, good resources for installation procedures and general information on specific parts. While we do not have the space to provide instructions on the assembly of many different PCs, the examples we give will provide you with background and guidance and demonstrate how to approach the task at hand.

The text describes some problems actually encountered during an assembly. I wish I could invite you to work beside me, reading the documentation for that jumper setting, deciding just which card should go in which slot for the best overall fit, and enjoying the pleasure of turning on the PC and seeing it boot up for the first time. However, the best I can do is introduce you to the experience through this book. My hope is that you will one day have the opportunity to experience it yourself.

Overview of the Assembly Process

After the research is done and the parts purchased, organize everything you need to assemble the PC. Have the parts with their accompanying documentation and software available, together with your PC tools. You'll need a safe place to work, with a ground mat and ground strap. Be careful to follow all safety rules and precautions discussed in this and previous chapters. Work methodically and keep things organized. If you find yourself getting frustrated, take a break. Remember, you want the entire experience to be fun!

The general process for putting together a computer is as follows:

1. Verify that you have all parts that you plan to install.

2. Prepare the computer case by installing the case fans and I/O shield, removing the plates that cover the drive bays, and installing the spacers.

3. Install the drives.

4. Determine proper configuration settings for the motherboard, and set any jumpers or switches on the motherboard.

5. Install the CPU and CPU fan.

6. Install RAM in the appropriate slots on the motherboard.

7. Install the motherboard and attach cabling.

8. Install the video card.

9. Plug the computer into a power source, and attach the monitor, keyboard, and mouse.

10. Boot the computer, check the CMOS settings, and make sure that everything is configured and working properly before replacing the computer case. At this point you are ready to install the OS and any other software you want on your system.

Step 1: Verify You Have All the Parts

For the PC we are building in this chapter, the parts purchased before beginning the assembly are listed. The parts to be installed inside the case and some tools are shown in Figure 23-1.

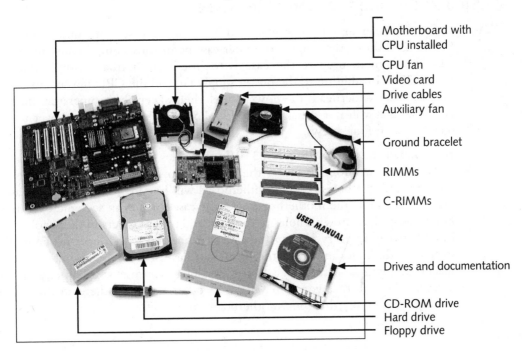

Figure 23-1   Components needed to assemble a PC

23

- ATX case with power supply (ATX12V-compliant power supply required for this motherboard, because the Pentium 4 requires a supplemental power connector)

- Motherboard (Intel Desktop Board D850MV)

- Pentium 4 CPU that runs at 1.5 GHz

- Two 128-bit RIMMs

- AGP video card

- Hard drive (20 GB 5400 RPM ATA100)

- Floppy drive

- CD-ROM drive

- Monitor, mouse, and keyboard

- Cables, cords, drivers, and documentation

Before you begin installation, make sure you have everything you need to complete it, including tools, documentation, and all components. As we discussed in earlier chapters, it is a good idea to have a notebook for all product documentation, lists of the components and settings for your PC, and detailed installation and troubleshooting notes.

Step 2: Prepare the Computer Case

Before you can install components in a computer case, you must prepare the case. Figure 23-2 shows the empty computer case before any components are installed in it. The first step to prepare the case is to install an auxiliary case fan, as shown in Figure 23-3. In addition to the power supply fan and the CPU fan, an auxiliary case fan over the vent underneath the power supply helps keep the temperature inside the case at a level that will not damage the CPU. Position the fan in place over the vent, and secure it with four screws.

Next, install the spacers (Figure 23-4) in the holes on the bottom of the case, to keep the motherboard from touching the case and possibly shorting. When you install the motherboard, the holes on the motherboard will line up with the spacers, as shown in Figure 23-4. Hold the motherboard over the case so you can see where the holes in the motherboard line up with holes in the case, and install spacers in these holes in the case. Install a spacer in every hole in the case that lines up with a hole in the motherboard, so that all the holes in the motherboard can have screws. You should use at least four spacers and will probably use six. However many you use, you will end up with some holes in the case that you don't use. The other holes are there so that the case can accommodate more than one motherboard form factor.

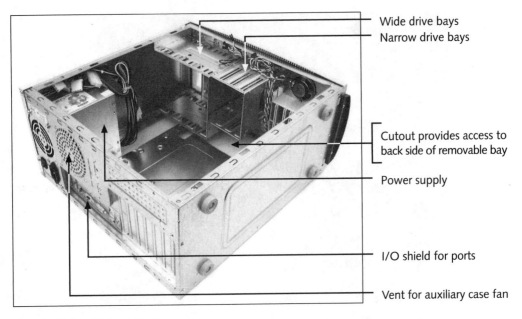

Wide drive bays

Narrow drive bays

Cutout provides access to back side of removable bay

Power supply

I/O shield for ports

Vent for auxiliary case fan

Figure 23-2   The empty computer case

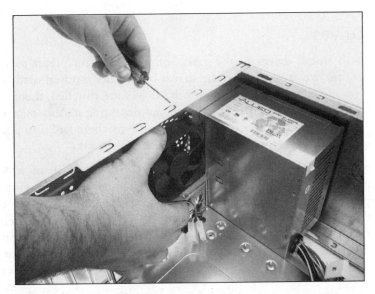

Figure 23-3   Install at least one case fan to provide additional cooling

The next step to prepare the case is to install an I/O shield. Recall that in Chapter 5 you learned how to install an I/O shield in a computer case to help protect ports coming off the motherboard. If the case comes with several shields, as it probably will, select the one that correctly fits the ports on your motherboard.

23

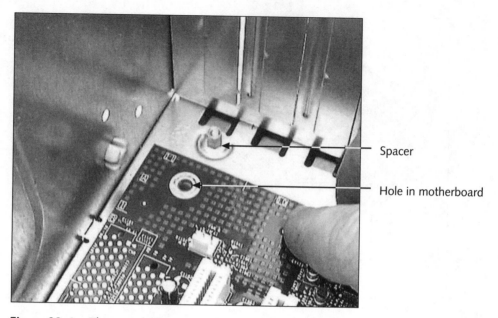

Figure 23-4   The spacers line up with the holes on the motherboard and keep it from touching the case

Step 3: Install Drives

A+CORE 1.2   The next step is to install drives in the case. Some technicians prefer to install the motherboard first, but we are installing the drives before the motherboard because, if the motherboard is already in the case before the drives are installed, there is the risk of dropping one of the drives on the motherboard and damaging it. Also, once the drives are installed, we will not attach power cords until after the motherboard is in place so that the cords will not be in the way when we install the motherboard.

Looking back at Figure 23-2, you can see that this case has a group of wide bays in which we will install the CD-ROM drive and a narrow removable bay in which we will install the floppy drive and hard drive. In Chapter 8 you saw how you can remove a narrow removable bay and install the drives in the bay outside the case, then put the bay with the drives installed back in the case. This case is better designed than the one in Chapter 8 and has a cutout on the back side of the removable bay so that you can install screws on both sides of the drives without removing the bay. The cutout is labeled in Figure 23-2.

When installing drives, be sure to use short screws that will not protrude too deeply into the drive and damage it. The next four sections describe how to install the drives.

$A^{+CORE}_{1.2}$ **Set Jumpers on Each IDE Drive in the System**

Before we get into the details of installing the drives, let's quickly review IDE installations, previously covered in Chapter 8. Recall that there can be up to two IDE controllers on a motherboard, the primary and secondary IDE controllers. Each controller can support up to two drives, a master and a slave, for a total of up to four IDE drives in a system. When possible, leave the hard drive as the single drive on one controller so that performance is not affected. Recall that each IDE drive must be configured as single, master, slave, or cable select. Configuration is normally done by setting jumpers on the drive housing, and the explanation of the jumper settings is most often printed somewhere on the housing. You learned how to set jumpers on an IDE drive in Chapter 8. In our installation, we set the IDE hard drive as the single drive on the primary controller and the IDE CD-ROM drive as a single drive on the secondary controller. Following the settings label on each drive, set the jumpers on each drive to master.

Install the CD-ROM Drive

We decided to install the CD-ROM drive in the top wide bay to keep it up out of the way. Follow these steps and be sure you are wearing your ground bracelet as you work:

- Remove the faceplates from the front of the upper bay.

- Install the CD-ROM drive in the bay, aligning it with the front of the case and securing it with screws, as shown in Figure 23-5. (After the motherboard is installed, we'll also install the CD-ROM data cable, power cord, and audio cord.)

Figure 23-5   Align the CD-ROM drive with the front of the case, and secure it with screws

23

A+CORE
1.2

Install the Hard Drive

This case has only a single bay (the lowest bay) that does not have an opening to the front of the case. Install the hard drive in this last position. Position the hard drive flush with the front of the bay so that it butts up against the computer case. Secure the hard drive with four screws, two on each side of the drive. Note that this computer case has a cutout on the back side of the removable bay, so you do not have to remove the bay to install the drive.

Install the Floppy Drive

Follow these steps to install the floppy drive:

- Place the floppy drive in the bay, noting where the screw holes in the drive align with the side of the bay. On this case, the floppy drive is recessed in the case, and it will fit snugly against the front of the drive bay. On many cases, however, you have to align the floppy drive with the bay and the front of the case so the drive fits flush with the front of the case. How this front cover alignment is done depends on the case design.

- Secure the floppy drive to the bay with four screws, two on each side of the bay (see Figure 23-6).

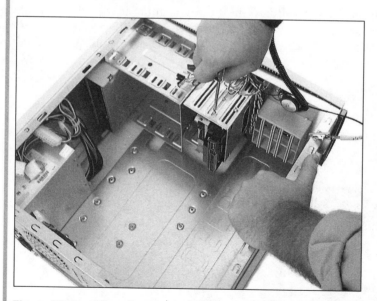

Figure 23-6   After aligning the drives, secure them with screws

Step 4: Set Jumpers or Switches on the Motherboard

A+CORE
1.2
We are installing the Intel Desktop Board D850MV motherboard shown in Figure 23-7 with the processor, fan, and memory modules installed. The diagram in Figure 23-8 will help you identify components on the motherboard. When working with the motherboard or other circuit boards, be particularly concerned about the possibility of ESD damage. Make sure you are properly grounded at all times. Also, try not to touch edge connectors or other sensitive portions of components.

Figure 23-7   The Intel D850MV motherboard

23

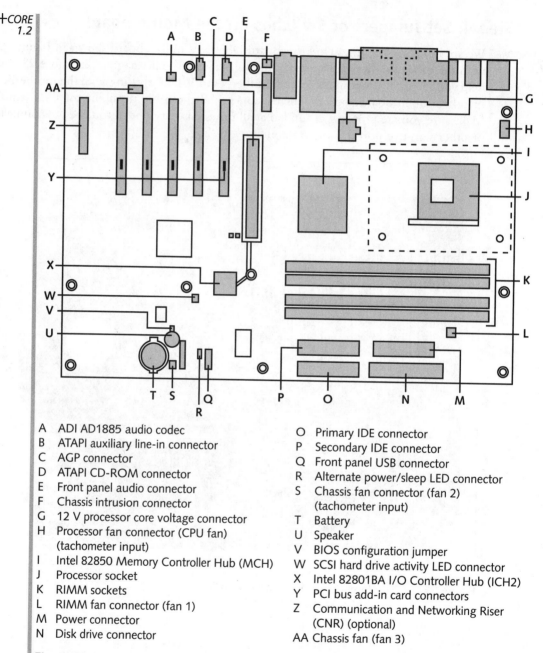

A+CORE 1.2

Figure 23-8   Diagram of the Intel D850MV motherboard

A	ADI AD1885 audio codec	O	Primary IDE connector
B	ATAPI auxiliary line-in connector	P	Secondary IDE connector
C	AGP connector	Q	Front panel USB connector
D	ATAPI CD-ROM connector	R	Alternate power/sleep LED connector
E	Front panel audio connector	S	Chassis fan connector (fan 2)
F	Chassis intrusion connector		(tachometer input)
G	12 V processor core voltage connector	T	Battery
H	Processor fan connector (CPU fan)	U	Speaker
	(tachometer input)	V	BIOS configuration jumper
I	Intel 82850 Memory Controller Hub (MCH)	W	SCSI hard drive activity LED connector
J	Processor socket	X	Intel 82801BA I/O Controller Hub (ICH2)
K	RIMM sockets	Y	PCI bus add-in card connectors
L	RIMM fan connector (fan 1)	Z	Communication and Networking Riser
M	Power connector		(CNR) (optional)
N	Disk drive connector	AA	Chassis fan (fan 3)

Figure 23-9 shows the ports on the back of this motherboard. There are ports for the mouse and the keyboard, four USB ports, a 25-pin parallel port, two 9-pin serial ports, audio and network ports. Note that this motherboard has embedded support for sound and Ethernet, eliminating the need for separate expansion cards to add these features.

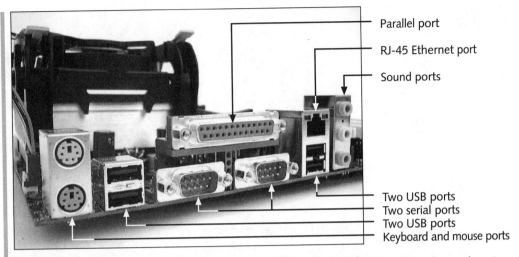

Parallel port

RJ-45 Ethernet port

Sound ports

Two USB ports
Two serial ports
Two USB ports
Keyboard and mouse ports

Figure 23-9 The ports on the D850MV motherboard include network and sound ports

The first thing to do when preparing a motherboard to go into the case is to study the motherboard's documentation and determine what jumpers or DIP switches are on the board and how to set them. Many motherboards support more than one processor or system bus speed, and jumper or DIP switch settings depend on which processor you are installing at what speed. The motherboard we are using in this chapter supports only the Pentium 4 processor running at 1.4, 1.5, 1.6, 1.7, or 1.8 GHz, although more recent Pentium 4 processors can run at higher speeds. The system bus runs at 400 MHz. There are no jumpers or DIP switches to set to configure the processor or bus speed. There is one set of three jumpers that is used to configure the BIOS. The position of this group is shown in Figure 23-8, and the options for the jumpers are shown in Figure 23-10. Set the jumper group to the normal setting so that BIOS uses the current configuration for booting. Once set, the jumpers should be changed only if you are trying to recover when the power-up password is lost or flashing BIOS has failed. Figure 23-11 shows the jumper cap in the normal position.

23

A+CORE
1.2

Jumper Position	Mode	Description
1 ... 3	Normal (default)	The current BIOS configuration is used for booting.
1 ... 3	Configure	After POST, the BIOS displays a menu in CMOS setup that can be used to clear the user and supervisor power-on passwords.
1 ... 3	Recovery	Used to recover from a failed BIOS update. Details can be found on the motherboard CD.

Figure 23-10   BIOS configuration jumper settings

Jumpers set for normal boot

Figure 23-11   BIOS setup configuration jumpers

Step 5: Install the CPU and CPU Fan

A+CORE
1.2

Next, we will install the CPU and the CPU fan on the motherboard. If you look back at Figure 5-7 in Chapter 5, you can see this Pentium 4 installed on the motherboard. Notice in that figure the frame or retention mechanism used to hold the cooler in place. This frame might come separately from the board or be preinstalled. If necessary, follow the directions that come with the motherboard to install the frame.

The next step is to install the CPU. (Again, don't forget to wear your ground strap as you work.) Lift the ZIF socket lever as shown in Figure 23-12. Place the processor on the socket so that the corner marked with a triangle is aligned with the connection of the lever to the socket. After the processor is in place, lower the lever to insert the processor firmly into the socket. As you work, be very careful not to force the processor in at an offset or disoriented position.

Before installing the CPU fan over the CPU, place a small amount of thermal compound on top of the processor. This grease-like substance helps transfer heat from the processor to the heat sink. Do not use too much; if you do, it may squish out the sides and interfere with other components.

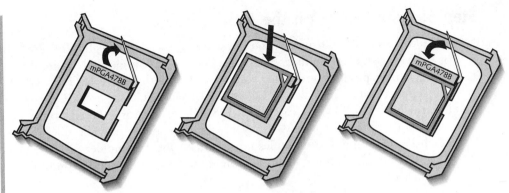

Figure 23-12   Install the processor in the mPGA478B socket

The fan and heat sink are surrounded by a clip assembly; these components together are sometimes called the CPU cooling assembly. Line the clip assembly up with the retention mechanism already installed on the motherboard, and press lightly on all four corners to attach it. Once the fan is in place, push down the two clip levers on top of the CPU fan (Figure 23-13). Different coolers use different types of clipping mechanisms, so follow the directions that come with the cooler. This one was a little difficult to clip onto the processor, and the plastic levers and housing seemed a little flimsy, so proceed with caution.

Figure 23-13   The clip levers attach the cooling assembly to the retention mechanism around the processor

23

Step 6: Install RAM on the Motherboard

A+CORE
1.2

From discussions in Chapter 6, you know how to select the right kind and right amount of RAM for your motherboard, and you know that you should be careful to match size, manufacturer, production batch, and mode. Our motherboard has four RIMM slots that can support from 128 MB to 2 GB of RAM with ECC or non-ECC support. We will be installing two RIMMs, each with 128 MB of memory. Recall from Chapter 6 that when you are installing RIMMs, every memory socket must be filled; sockets that do not have actual memory modules must contain the placeholder C-RIMMs (continuity RIMMs), which do not contain any memory chips but provide continuity throughout the sockets.

The four memory sockets on this motherboard are divided into two banks, bank 0 and bank 1. Install the pair of RIMMs in bank 0, the one closest to the processor as shown in Figure 23-14. These two RIMMs must be the same size and type, 128 MB RDRAM in this case. If you were installing memory in bank 1 as well, that pair of RIMMs would only have to match each other, not the RIMMs in bank 0.

RIMM supporting arms
in outward position

Figure 23-14   Install RIMMs in bank 0

Before inserting each module in its socket, pull the supporting arms on the sides of the socket outward. Notches on the edge of each module will help you orient it correctly in the socket. Insert the module straight down in the socket; when it is fully inserted, the supporting arms should pop back into place.

Step 7: Install the Motherboard and Attach Cabling

$A\!\!+\!^{CORE}_{1.2}$ Let's review what we've done so far. We've prepared the case by installing the auxiliary fan and the spacers, installed drives, and attached the processor, cooling assembly, and memory modules to the motherboard. The next steps are to install the motherboard itself into the case and attach the cabling and power connections.

- Place the motherboard into the case so that the holes on the motherboard align with the holes on the spacers. Attach the motherboard to the case, using the spacers to receive the screws (see Figure 23-15). Be careful not to use excessive force when moving the motherboard into place and attaching it to the case; that could warp the board and damage the circuits on it.

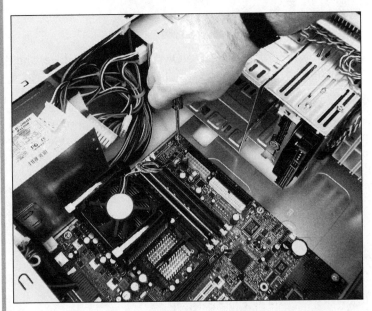

Figure 23-15   Use screws to attach the motherboard to the case via the spacers

- Connect a power cord from the power supply to the case fan. (We did not do this earlier so that the connection between this fan and the power supply would not be in the way when we installed the motherboard.)
- Connect the power cords to the drives, as shown in Figure 23-16. You will connect one to each of the three drives.

23

A+CORE
1.2

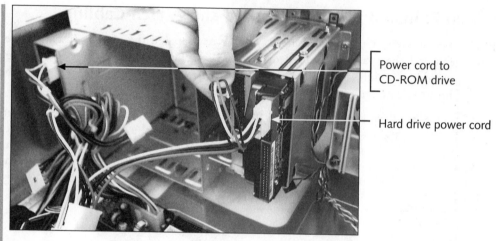

Power cord to
CD-ROM drive

Hard drive power cord

Figure 23-16   Attach power cords to the CD-ROM drive, the hard drive, and the
floppy drive

■ Connect the 4-pin auxiliary power cord, as shown in Figure 23-17. This
cord supplies the supplemental power required for a Pentium 4 processor.
Most processors get all their power from the motherboard and do not
require a separate connection to the power supply, so this is an exception to
the rule. You are likely to have exceptions in your installation as well, which
is why it's so important to read your documentation thoroughly, preferably
before you begin installation.

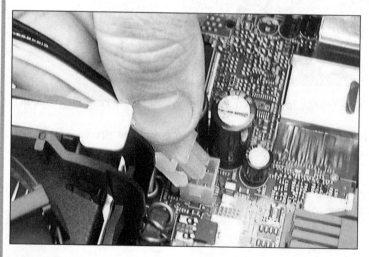

Figure 23-17   The auxiliary 4-pin power cord provides power to the Pentium 4 processor

■ Connect the 20-pin ATX P1 power cord from the power supply to the
motherboard, as shown in Figure 23-18.

Figure 23-18   The 20-pin connector supplies power to the motherboard

- After the power cords are connected, locate and connect the front leads to the switches, speaker, and lights on the front of the case (see Figure 23-19). Note that each front lead is labeled. Sometimes there will be corresponding screen–printed labels on the board to tell you which lead goes on which pins. If the pins are not labeled on the board, as with this motherboard, check your documentation. The motherboard might come with a sticker that goes inside the case and shows a diagram of the motherboard with labels for the front leads. If the motherboard documentation is not clear, you can also check the motherboard manufacturer's Web site for additional documentation. Figure 23-20 shows this motherboard's documentation, which describes the connectors for each of the leads. The power switch lead is already connected to the bank of connectors. Note that there is no connector for a speaker, since the motherboard has its own speaker, and that the ground and +5V connectors are not used.

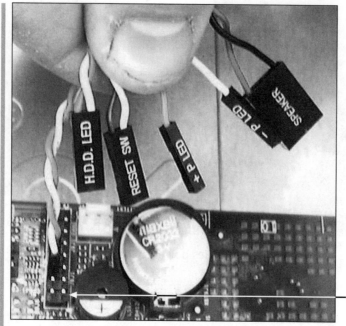

Bank of pins for front leads

Figure 23-19   The front leads provide power to the switches, lights, and speaker on the front of the case

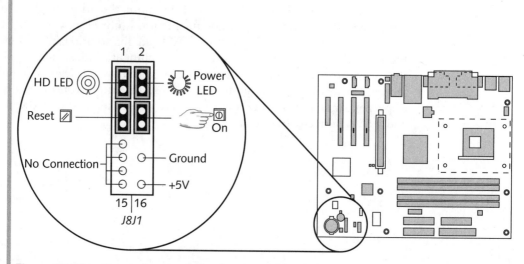

Figure 23-20   Connector group for front panel leads

- Next, install the data cables to each drive (Figure 23-21). Install the floppy drive cable with the twist between the motherboard and the drive, making this drive A in the final configuration. Connect one IDE cable to the hard drive and the primary IDE connector on the motherboard, and connect a

A+CORE
1.2

second IDE cable to the CD-ROM drive and the secondary IDE connector on the motherboard. To orient the cable connectors, look on each drive for a small 1 that indicates pin 1, and align that with the colored edge of the data cable for that drive. Look for pin 1 labeled on the motherboard. (In most cases, pin 1 is next to the power connection on a floppy drive.)

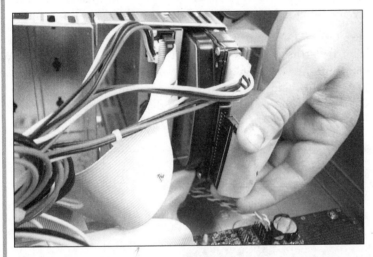

Figure 23-21   Attach data cables from the motherboard to all three drives

■ Normally the CD audio cord connects from the CD-ROM drive to the sound card, in order to play music CDs. Since sound support is embedded on the motherboard, look at the motherboard documentation to determine where to connect the CD audio cord to the board. Connect the CD audio cord to the CD-ROM drive and the other end to the connector on the motherboard, as shown in Figure 23-22.

Figure 23-22   The CD audio cord connects near the sound ports

23

Step 8: Install the Video Card

A+CORE
1.2

The next step is to install the video card, the only expansion card we are including in this installation, since the sound card and network logic are built into this motherboard. In general, when installing an expansion card, first read the documentation for the card and set any jumper switches or DIP switches on the card. Like most cards today, the video card we are installing is Plug and Play compatible and has no jumpers.

Next, select the expansion slot you plan to use on the motherboard, remove the faceplate for the selected slot from the computer case, and insert the card in the slot. We will be inserting this video card into the single AGP slot on this motherboard. There are several different types of AGP slots. The video card we are installing, shown in Figure 23-23, fits into an AGP 4X slot and includes a registration tab that allows the card to fit into an AGP Pro slot.

Registration tab

Figure 23-23   The video card, with a tab that allows it to be used in an AGP Pro slot

Before you install the video card in the AGP slot, install the AGP retention mechanism over the AGP slot. This piece, shown in Figure 23-24, helps stabilize the card. Your motherboard might or might not include this extender.

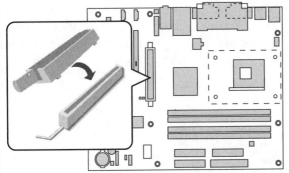

Figure 23-24 The AGP extender helps to stabilize the video card

When inserting a card in an expansion slot, press the card straight down into the slot. As you insert the card, don't allow it to wobble in the slot, because that could widen the slot and prevent a tight fit. Make sure the card is inserted solidly in the slot, and then, using the same screw that held the faceplate in position, screw the card to the computer case (see Figure 23-25).

Figure 23-25 Secure the video card using the same screw that held the faceplate in place

Step 9: Plug In the Computer and Attach External Devices

The installation of devices inside the case is now complete. Before you plug in the computer, make sure that no cords are obstructing the fans. Figure 23-26 shows the case with all internal components installed. Notice that some cables are coiled and tied

23

with plastic ties. (You can also use rubber bands.) This way, they will not be in the way of other components, and the inside of the case will be less cluttered, making it easier to work inside the case when making changes to components. You do not do this, however, until after you test the system to make sure everything works.

Figure 23-26   The case with all the internal components installed

Attach the monitor, keyboard, and mouse, and plug in the computer. You can attach the mouse at this point, or you can leave it off and attach it after you test the system. It is unlikely that the mouse will cause problems during the initial startup process, but you won't really need it, and it is a good idea not to start with anything that you don't absolutely need, especially when first constructing a system.

Step 10: Boot the Computer, Check Settings, and Verify Operation

A+CORE 2.1   It is a good idea to test the system before replacing the case cover, to make changes easier if something goes wrong. However, since some systems require the cover to be on to achieve proper airflow, do not run the system for any length of time without the cover on. Also, some server cases have cover switch latches that do not allow you to power up the system unless the case cover is in place. The boot process and CMOS settings were

A+CORE 2.1

covered in Chapter 3 and reviewed in the general installation process in Chapter 5, which we followed in this chapter. Boot the system and enter CMOS setup by pressing F2. The method to enter setup is different for some motherboards; check the documentation for the motherboard you are using. Refer back to Chapter 5 for the list of CMOS settings you need to check. If you are booting from a floppy disk, insert a bootable setup disk that contains the files that allow you to format the hard drive. (See Chapter 3 for a list of those files.)

When you exit CMOS, the computer will reboot. Observe POST and verify that no errors occur. If there are no errors, congratulations! You have put your system together correctly. (If there are errors, see your motherboard documentation or Appendix A in this book for explanations.) Turn off the computer and slide the case cover back in place, as shown in Figure 23-27. Now you are ready to prepare the hard drive for the OS (Chapter 8) and install the operating system and any other software you need on your system. Figure 23-28 shows the complete system.

Figure 23-27   Slide the case cover back on once you know the system is working

23

Figure 23-28   The complete system

CHAPTER SUMMARY

❑ The most important reason to buy a brand-name PC rather than a clone is after-sales service.

❑ Many brand-name PCs use proprietary designs that force you to use only that particular brand-name's parts and service when upgrading or maintaining the PC.

❑ Middle-range PCs offer more network capability, more expandability, more support, and more prior testing than do low-end PCs.

❑ Some reasons to build your own PC are the knowledge you will gain, the control you will have over the choice of individual parts, the availability of documentation and original software disks, and the satisfaction of having built the PC yourself.

❑ When choosing to build your own PC, be aware that the process will take time, that you will likely encounter problems along the way, that there will be no warranty on the assembled product, and that you probably will not save money.

❑ Plan the project of assembling a PC well. Get answers to any questions you may have on the details before you begin. Keep things organized as you work. Expect the project to be fun.

❑ When assembling a PC, follow this general plan: (1) Verify that you have all parts you plan to install, (2) Prepare the computer case, (3) Install drives, (4) Determine and set jumpers and DIP switches for the motherboard, (5) Install the CPU, CPU fan, and RAM on the motherboard, and then install the motherboard in the case, (6) Attach all cables and power cords, (7) Install the video card and any other expansion cards, (8) Connect the peripherals (mouse, keyboard, and monitor), (9) Plug in the computer, verify that settings are correct and that no errors occur, and replace the computer case, and (10) Install the OS and any other software you need on your system.

KEY TERMS

clone   **hard-disk loading**   **IBM-compatible PC**

REVIEW QUESTIONS

1. Another name given to represent those microcomputers that adhere to the standards set forth by IBM for their systems is _____.

   a. Macintosh

   b. Apple

   c. IBM-compatible

   d. All of the above

   e. None of the above

2. A term associated with a PC that has been assembled by a local company with parts manufactured by several companies is _____.

   a. Macintosh

   b. Apple

   c. IBM-compatible

   d. All of the above

   e. None of the above

3. If it has been decided that a particular piece of software needs to be purchased, which of the following considerations is *not* typically necessary when choosing the proper application software?

   a. What will the software do?

   b. Is the new software compatible with existing software?

   c. How good is the software's documentation?

   d. How much does the software cost?

   e. What are the company's upgrade policies?

4. When considering the purchase of new hardware to be installed into a computer, in considering the BIOS of the hardware under consideration, be certain that it is not only Plug-and-Play (PnP) compliant, but _____ compliant, as well.

   a. PnP-3

   b. ACPI

   c. Hardware

   d. Software

   e. None of the above

23

5. If cost is an issue when purchasing new hardware, which should be purchased?

    a. Internal devices

    b. External devices

    c. There is no cost differential between internal and external devices.

    d. None of the above

6. If a particular piece of hardware being purchased required "local bus access," which areas of the motherboard would need to be verified for capability?

    a. System RAM

    b. System bus

    c. PCI bus

    d. Parallel bus

    e. None of the above

7. When considering the upgrade for system memory, which of the following hardware is being discussed?

    a. RAM

    b. ROM

    c. Floppy drives

    d. Hard drives

    e. Motherboard

8. A service technician determines that a particular user needs to interface twenty devices to a system that he is building for this user. What bus capability should the motherboard possess to handle the interface to the twenty devices?

    a. IDE

    b. EIDE

    c. ESDI

    d. SCSI

    e. USB

9. If a user requested an upgrade of their video subsystem to a video card that was intended for use with complex gaming software, which bus would need to be incorporated onto the motherboard to address this need?

    a. IDE

    b. EIDE

    c. USB

    d. PCI

    e. AGP

10. Assuming the installation of an IDE-based CD-ROM drive as the only device on a chain, how would the drive need to be configured and where would the interface cable need to connect to on the motherboard?

    a. Master, connected to the primary IDE controller

    b. Slave, connected to the primary IDE controller

    c. Master, connected to the secondary IDE controller

    d. Slave, connected to the secondary IDE controller

    e. None of the above; IDE-based devices can be installed onto any controller as they are assigned ID numbers by the controller.

11. Assuming that the motherboard has four slots to accept memory intended as "System Memory," in which slot should the service technician install the first module, assuming that the slots are numbered Bank 0–Bank 3?

    a. Bank 0

    b. Bank 1

    c. Bank 2

    d. Bank 3

    e. None of the above

12. Power cables can be inserted into system devices in any way; the device will handle the coordinating polarity.

    a. True

    b. False

13. The type of power supply connector that can be expected from an ATX-type power supply is:

    a. Single multi-wire connector

    b. Dual multi-wire connector

    c. Single one-wire connector

    d. Dual one-wire connector

    e. None of the above

23

24

TROUBLESHOOTING AND MAINTENANCE FUNDAMENTALS

In this chapter, you will learn:

♦ About your role as a PC technician in troubleshooting and maintenance, and tools available to help you in those roles

♦ How to approach a troubleshooting problem

♦ How to develop a preventive maintenance plan and what to
include in it

This chapter gives you some common-sense guidelines to solving computer problems. In trying to solve a computer problem, you want to
avoid making the situation worse by damaging the equipment, software, or
data, or by placing undue stress on the user. When approaching a computer
problem, follow the important safety precautions that you have learned in
other chapters as well as the ones you will learn in this chapter.

TROUBLESHOOTING PERSPECTIVES AND TOOLS

As a PC troubleshooter, you might have to solve a problem on your own PC or for someone else. As a PC technician, you might fulfill four different job functions:

- *PC support technician.* A PC support technician works on-site, closely interacting with users, and is responsible for ongoing PC maintenance. Of the four technicians listed here, a PC support technician is the only one responsible for the PC before trouble occurs and, therefore, is able to prepare for a problem by keeping good records and maintaining backups (or teaching users how to do so).

- *PC service technician.* A PC service technician goes to a customer site in response to a service call and, if possible, repairs a PC on-site. PC service technicians are usually not responsible for ongoing PC maintenance but do usually interact with users.

- *Bench technician.* A bench technician works in a lab environment, might not interact with users of the PCs being repaired, and is not permanently responsible for them. Bench technicians probably don't work at the site where the PC is kept. They may be able to interview the user to get information about the problem, or they may simply receive a PC to repair without being able to talk to the user.

- *Help-desk technician.* A help-desk technician provides telephone or online support. Help-desk technicians, who do not have physical access to the PC, are at the greatest disadvantage of the four types of technicians. They can only interact with users over the phone and must obviously use different tools and approaches than technicians at the PC.

This chapter emphasizes the job of the on-site PC support technician. However, the special needs and perspectives of the service technician, bench technician, and help-desk technician are also addressed.

Troubleshooting Tools

Several hardware and software tools can help you diagnose and repair computer problems. The tools you choose depend on the amount of money you can spend and the level of PC support you provide.

Essential tools for PC troubleshooting are listed here. All but the bootable rescue disk can easily be purchased in one handy PC toolkit:

- Bootable rescue disk for any OS you might work on (You may need several different ones.)

- Ground bracelet and/or ground mat

- Flat-head screwdriver

- Phillips-head or cross-head screwdriver

- Torx screwdriver set, particularly size T15

- Tweezers, preferably insulated ones, for picking pieces of paper out of printers or dropped screws out of tight places

- Chip extractor to remove chips (to pry up the chip; a simple screwdriver is usually more effective, however)

- Extractor, a spring-loaded device that looks like a hypodermic needle (When you push down on the top, three wire prongs come out that can be used to pick up a screw that has fallen into a place where hands and fingers can't reach.)

The following tools might not be essential, but they are very convenient:

- Multimeter to check the power supply output (This is discussed in Chapter 4.)

- Needle-nose pliers for holding objects in place while you screw them in (especially those pesky nuts on cable connectors)

- Flashlight to see inside the PC case

- AC outlet ground tester

- Small cups or bags to help keep screws organized as you work

- Antistatic bags to store unused parts

- Pen and paper for taking notes

- Diagnostic cards and diagnostic software

- Utility software

- Virus detection software on disks

Keep your tools in a toolbox designated for PC troubleshooting. If you put disks and hardware tools in the same box, don't include a magnetized screwdriver, and be sure to keep the disks inside a plastic case. Make sure the diagnostic and utility software you use is recommended for the hardware and software you are troubleshooting.

Bootable Rescue Disk

Recall from Chapter 3 that an essential tool for PC troubleshooting is a bootable rescue disk. Not only can it boot the PC even when the hard drive fails, but you are ensured of the cleanest boot possible. By *clean boot* we mean that the boot does not load any extraneous software, drivers, or other memory-resident programs (TSRs) that might be loaded from startup routines on the hard drive.

Diagnostic Cards and Software

Although not essential, many hardware and software tools can help you diagnose a PC problem. Before purchasing these tools, read the documentation about what they can and cannot do, and, if possible, read some product reviews. The Internet is a good source

24

of information. One hardware diagnostic tool, a diagnostic card, is discussed next. Then we will look at several diagnostic software applications.

POST Diagnostic Cards   **Diagnostic cards** are designed to discover and report computer errors and conflicts at POST. If you have a problem that prevents the PC from booting, you can install the diagnostic card in an expansion slot on the motherboard and then attempt to boot. The card monitors the boot process and reports errors, usually as coded numbers on a small LED panel on the card. You then look up the number in the documentation that accompanies the card to get more information about the error and its source.

Examples of these cards are:

- Amber Debug Card by Phoenix Technologies (*www.phoenix.com*)
- PCI Error Testing/Debug Card by Trigen Industries (*www.computex.com.tw*)
- POSTcard V3 by Unicore Software, Inc. (*www.unicore.com*)
- Post Code Master by MSD, Inc. (*www.msd.com*)
- POSTmortem Diagnostics Card by System Optimization, Inc. (*www.sysopt.com*)

Diagnostic Software   **Diagnostic software** is generally used to identify hardware problems. Although many diagnostic software programs are available, here we look at only a few. If the software rates itself as being at the professional level, it generally assumes greater technical expertise and also provides more features than end-user or novice-level software. The most effective diagnostic software does not run from the OS, because the OS might sometimes mask a hardware problem. Here are a few examples of diagnostic software.

- *PC-Technician by Windsor Technologies, Inc.* This professional-level PC diagnostic software loads and operates without using the PC's installed operating system, because it has its own proprietary OS built in. Results are thus unaltered by any errors in the PC's OS. PC-Technician can relocate itself during testing and successfully test all of main memory. The ability to relocate is important, since software that tests memory cannot test the portion where it is currently loaded. PC-Technician bypasses standard ROM BIOS when translation mode is used by the system, so that the diagnostic software communicates directly with the hard drive controller. PC-Technician comes with test plugs (called loop-back plugs) that test parallel and serial ports by looping data out of and back to the port. These loop-back tests (also called wrap tests) determine that hardware ports are working. There is a downloadable version of this software called TuffTEST-Pro. For more information, see the company's Web site, *www.windsortech.com*.

- *PC-Diagnosys by Windsor Technologies, Inc.* This software is designed for less experienced PC technicians and end users; it is smaller, easier to use, and less expensive than PC-Technician. See *www.windsortech.com*.

General-Purpose Utility Software

Utility software can be designed to diagnose problems, repair and maintain the software on a PC, recover corrupted or deleted data on the hard drive or floppy disks, provide security, monitor system performance, and download software updates from the Internet. The utility software might use the installed operating system or might provide its own. Four useful utilities for solving hardware and software problems are outlined in Table 24-1.

Table 24-1   Utility software used to solve PC problems

Software	Manufacturer's Web Site	Description
Norton Utilities by Symantec	*www.symantec.com*	Norton Utilities by Symantec is general-purpose, user-friendly, utility software that provides a variety of functions, including the ability to recover lost or damaged data from a hard drive.
CheckIt Suite by Smith Micro Software	*www.checkit.com*	CheckIt by Smith Micro is a general-purpose software and hardware utility product that includes hard drive testing, performance testing, port testing (loop-back plugs included), and setup for resource conflicts.
PartitionMagic by PowerQuest	*www.powerquest.com/ partitionmagic*	PartitionMagic lets you create, resize, and merge partitions on a hard drive without losing data. You can use the software to easily run multiple operating systems, convert file system types, and fix partition table errors.
SANDRA Pro by 3B Software	*www.3bsoftware.com*	SANDRA Pro is benchmarking, diagnostic, and tune-up software that can be used to solve hardware and software problems.

> **TIP** In addition to general-purpose utility software, you should have antivirus software available to scan for viruses when you are diagnosing a PC problem and also use the software regularly to prevent viruses from attacking your system. See Chapter 9 for a list of antivirus software.

YOUR APPROACH TO TROUBLESHOOTING

 A+CORE 2.2 | When a computer doesn't work and you're responsible for fixing it, you should generally approach the problem first as an investigator and discoverer, always being careful not to compound the problem through your own actions. If the problem seems difficult, see it

24

$A^{+CORE}_{2.2}$ as an opportunity to learn something new. Ask questions until you understand the source of the problem. Once you understand it, you're almost done, because most likely the solution will be evident. Take the attitude that you can understand the problem and solve it, no matter how deeply you have to dig, and you probably will. In this section we look at how to approach a troubleshooting problem, including how to interact with the user and how to handle an emergency.

Fundamental Rules

$A^{+CORE}_{2.2}$ Here are a few fundamental rules for PC troubleshooting that I've found work for me.

Make backups before making changes Whether you are working on hardware or software, always back up essential programs and data before working on a computer.

Approach the problem systematically Start at the beginning and walk through the situation in a thorough, careful way. This one rule is invaluable. Remember it and apply it every time. If you don't find the explanation to the problem after one systematic walk-through, then repeat the entire process. Check and double-check to find the step you overlooked the first time. Most problems with computers are simple, such as a loose cable or circuit board. Computers are logical through and through. Whatever the problem, it's also very logical.

Divide and conquer This rule is the most powerful. Isolate the problem. In the overall system, remove one hardware or software component after another, until the problem is isolated to a small part of the whole system. Here are a few examples of applying this rule:

- Remove any memory-resident programs (TSRs) to eliminate them as the problem.

- Boot from a disk to eliminate the OS and startup files on the hard drive as the problem.

- Remove any unnecessary hardware devices, such as a scanner card, internal modem, and even the hard drive.

Once down to the essentials, start exchanging components you know are good for those you suspect are bad, until the problem goes away.

Don't overlook the obvious Ask simple questions. Is the computer plugged in? Is it turned on? Is the monitor plugged in? Most problems are so simple that we overlook them because we expect the problem to be difficult. Don't let the complexity of computers fool you. Most problems are easy to fix. Really, they are!

Check simple things first   It is more effective to first check the components that are easiest to replace. For example, if the video does not work, the problem may be with the monitor or the video card. When faced with the decision of which one to exchange first, choose the easy route: exchange the monitor before the video card.

Make no assumptions   This rule is the hardest to follow, because there is a tendency to trust anything in writing and assume that people are telling you exactly what happened. But documentation is sometimes wrong, and people don't always describe events as they occurred, so do your own investigating. For example, if the user tells you that the system boots up with no error messages, but that the software still doesn't work, boot for yourself. You never know what the user might have overlooked.

Become a researcher   Following this rule is the most fun. When a computer problem arises that you can't easily solve, be as tenacious as a bulldog. Read, make phone calls, ask questions, then read more, make more calls, and ask more questions. Take advantage of every available resource, including online help, the Internet, documentation, technical support, and books such as this one. What you learn will be yours to take to the next problem. This is the real joy of computer troubleshooting. If you're good at it, you're always learning something new.

Write things down   Keep good notes as you're working. They'll help you think more clearly. Draw diagrams. Make lists. Clearly and precisely write down what you're learning. Later, when the entire problem gets "cold," these notes will be invaluable.

Reboot and start over   This is an important rule. Fresh starts are good for us and uncover events or steps that we might have overlooked. Take a break; get away from the problem. Begin again.

Establish your priorities   This rule can help make for a satisfied customer. Decide what your first priority is. For example, it might be to recover lost data, or to get the PC back up and running as soon as possible. Consult the user or customer for advice when practical.

Keep your cool and don't rush   In an emergency, protect the data and software by carefully considering your options before acting and by taking practical precautions to protect software and OS files. When a computer stops working, if unsaved data is still in memory or if data or software on the hard drive has not been backed up, look and think carefully before you leap! A wrong move can be costly. The best advice is not to hurry. Carefully plan your moves. Read the documentation if you're not sure what to do, and don't hesitate to ask for help. Don't simply try something, hoping it will work, unless you've run out of more intelligent alternatives!

Don't assume the worst   When it's an emergency and your only copy of data is on a hard drive that is not working, don't assume that the data is lost. Much can be done

A+CORE
2.2

to recover data. Recall that if you want to recover lost data on a hard drive, don't write anything to the drive; you might write on top of lost data, eliminating all chances of recovery.

Know your starting point Before trying to solve a computer problem, know for certain that the problem is what the user says it is. If the computer does not boot, carefully note where in the boot process it fails. If the computer does boot to an OS, before changing anything or taking anything apart, verify what does and what doesn't work, preferably in the presence of the user.

Gathering Information

A+CORE
2.2

When you are trying to solve a computer problem, the rules just explained will prepare you to apply a successful course of action. Before you take corrective action, however, you need to gather as much information about the situation as possible. This section covers ways to gather information on a computer problem you are troubleshooting.

Interacting with the User

Ask the user to explain exactly what happened when the computer stopped working. What procedure was taking place at the time? What had just happened? What recent changes did the user make? When did the computer last work? What has happened in the meantime? What error messages did the user see? Re-create the circumstances that existed when the computer stopped in as much detail as you can. Make no assumptions. All users make simple mistakes and then overlook them. If you realize that the problem was caused by the user's mistake, take the time to explain the proper procedures, so that the user understands what went wrong and what to do next time.

Use diplomacy and good manners when you work with a user to solve a problem. For example, if you suspect that the user dropped the PC, don't ask, "Did you drop the PC?" Put the question in a less accusatory manner: "Could the PC have been dropped?" If the user is sitting in front of the PC, don't assume you can take over the keyboard or mouse without permission. Also, if the user is present, ask permission before you make a software or hardware change, even if the user has just given you permission to interact with the PC.

When working at the user's desk, consider yourself a guest and follow these general guidelines:

- Don't talk down to or patronize the user.
- Don't take over the mouse or keyboard from the user without permission.
- Don't use the phone without permission.
- Don't pile your belongings and tools on top of the user's papers, books, etc.

A+CORE
2.2

■ Accept personal inconvenience to accommodate the user's urgent business needs. For example, if the user gets an important call while you are working, delay your work until the call is over.

Whether or not you are at the user's desk, you should follow these guidelines when working with the user:

■ Don't take drastic action such as formatting the hard drive before you ask the user about important data that may not be backed up.

■ Provide users with alternatives where appropriate before making decisions for them.

■ Protect the confidentiality of data on the PC, such as business financial information.

■ Don't disparage the user's choice of computer hardware or software.

■ If you make a mistake or must pass the problem on to someone with more expertise, be honest.

In some PC support situations, it is appropriate to consider yourself as a support to the user as well as to the PC. Your goals may include educating the user as well as repairing the computer. If you want users to learn something from a problem they caused, explain how to fix the problem, and walk them through the process if necessary. Don't fix the problem yourself unless they ask you to. It takes a little longer to train the user, but it is more productive in the end because the user learns more and is less likely to repeat the mistake.

Ask the user questions to learn as much as you can about the problem. Refer to Chapter 4 for several sample questions, the most important being, "Can you show me how to reproduce the problem?"

Investigating the Problem on the Computer

After you interview the user, the next step in troubleshooting is to gather as much information as you can about the problem by examining the computer. Find out these things:

■ What operating system is installed?

■ What physical components are installed? What processor, expansion cards, drives, and peripheral devices are installed? Is the PC connected to a network?

■ What is the nature of the problem? Does the problem occur before or after the boot? Does an error message appear? Does the system hang at certain times? Start from a cold boot, and do whatever you must do to cause the problem to occur. What specific steps did you take to duplicate the problem?

■ Can you duplicate the problem? Does the problem occur every time you do the above steps, or is the problem intermittent? Intermittent problems are generally more difficult to solve than problems that occur consistently.

24

$A^{+CORE}_{2.2}$ **Isolating the Problem**

The next step in problem solving is to isolate the source of the problem by doing the following.

Consider the possibilities Given what you've learned by interviewing the user, examining the computer, and duplicating the problem, consider what might be the source of the problem, which might or might not be obvious at this point. For example, if a user complains that his Word documents are getting corrupted, possible sources of the problem might be that the user does not know how to save documents properly, the software or the OS might be corrupted, the PC might have a virus, or the hard drive might be intermittently failing.

Eliminate simple things first In our example of the problem with corrupted Word documents, the most obvious or simplest source of the problem is that the user is not saving documents properly. Eliminate that possibility as the source of the problem before you look at the software or the hard drive. Another example is a CD-ROM drive that does not work. The problem might be that the CD is scratched or bent. Check that first.

Eliminate the unnecessary This rule can be applied in many ways—for example, when the PC does not boot successfully. In this case, it is often unclear if the problem is with the hardware or software. When using Windows 9x or Windows 2000/XP, you can boot into safe mode and eliminate much of the OS customized configuration. But if you still have problems, you may be able to boot from your bootable rescue disk(s).

Boot from a disk that you know is good and that has a minimal OS configuration (i.e., no Config.sys or Autoexec.bat files). By doing so, you eliminate all the application software loaded at startup on the PC and much of the OS. If the problem goes away, you can deduce that the problem is with (1) the software on the PC or (2) the hard drive and/or its subsystem that is used as the boot device.

If you suspect the problem is caused by faulty hardware, eliminate any unnecessary hardware devices. If the PC still boots with errors, disconnect the network card, the CD-ROM drive, the mouse, and maybe even the hard drive. You don't need to remove the CD-ROM or hard drive from the bays inside the case. Simply disconnect the data cable and the power cable. Remove the network card from its expansion slot. Remember to place it on an antistatic bag or ground mat, not on top of the power supply or case. If the problem goes away, you know that one or more of these devices is causing the problem. Replace them one at a time until the problem returns. Remember that the problem might be a resource conflict. If the network card worked well until the CD-ROM drive was reconnected and now neither works, try the CD-ROM drive without the network card. If the CD-ROM drive works, you most likely have a resource conflict.

A+CORE
2.2

Trade good for suspected bad When diagnosing hardware problems, this method works well if you can draw from a group of parts that you know work correctly. Suppose the monitor does not work; it appears dead. The parts of the video subsystem are the video card, the power cord to the monitor, the cord from the monitor to the PC case, and the monitor itself. Also, don't forget that the video card is inserted into an expansion slot on the motherboard, and the monitor depends on electrical power. Suspect each of these five components to be bad; try them one at a time. Trade the monitor for one that you know works. Trade the power cord, trade the cord to the PC video port, move the video card to a new slot, and trade the video card. When you're trading a good component for a suspected bad one, work methodically by eliminating one component at a time. Don't trade the video card and the monitor and then turn on the PC to determine if they work. It's possible that both the card and the monitor are bad, but assume that only one component is bad before you consider whether multiple components need trading.

In this situation, suppose you keep trading components in the video subsystem until you have no more variations. Next, take the entire subsystem—video card, cords, and monitor—to a PC that you know works, and plug each of them in. If they work, you have isolated the problem to the PC, not the video. Now turn your attention back to the PC: the motherboard, the software settings within the OS, the video driver, etc. Knowing that the video subsystem works on the good PC gives you a valuable tool. Compare the video driver on the good PC to the one on the bad PC. Make certain the CMOS settings, software settings, etc., are the same.

Trade suspected bad for good An alternate approach works well in certain situations. If you have a working PC that is configured similarly to the one you are troubleshooting (a common situation in many corporate or educational environments), rather than trading good for suspected bad, you can trade suspected bad for good. Take each component that you suspect is bad and install it in the working PC. If the component works on the good PC, then you have eliminated it as a suspect. If the working PC breaks down, then you have probably identified the bad component.

Intermittent Problems

Intermittent problems can make troubleshooting challenging. The trick in diagnosing problems that come and go is to look for patterns or clues as to when the problems occur. If you or the user can't reproduce the problem at will, ask the user to keep a log of when the problems occur and exactly what messages appear. Show the user how to get a printed screen of the error messages when they appear. Here's the method:

- For simple DOS systems, the Print Screen key directs the displayed screen to the printer.

- In Windows, the Print Screen key copies the displayed screen to the Clipboard.

24

A+CORE
2.2

- Launch the Paint software accessory program and paste the contents of the Clipboard into the document. You might need to use the Zoom Out command on the document first. You can then print the document with the displayed screen, using Paint. You can also paste the contents of the Clipboard into a document created by a word-processing application such as Word.

PREVENTIVE MAINTENANCE

So far we have mainly discussed how to troubleshoot problems that have already occurred. In this section, we will discuss some steps you can take to prevent certain computer problems from occurring in the first place. The more preventive maintenance work you do to begin with, the fewer problems you are likely to have later, and the less troubleshooting and repair you will have to do.

If you are responsible for the PCs in an organization, make and implement a preventive maintenance plan to help prevent failures and reduce repair costs and downtime. In addition, you need a disaster recovery plan to manage failures when they occur. PC failures are caused by many different environmental and human factors, including heat, dust, magnetism, power supply problems, static electricity, human error (such as spilled liquids or an accidental change of setup and software configurations), and viruses. The goals of preventive maintenance are to reduce the likelihood that the events that cause PC failures will occur and to lessen the damage if they do occur.

When designing a preventive maintenance plan, consider what you can do to help prevent each cause of PC failure, and write into the plan the preventive actions you can take. Think through the situation caused by each problem. What would happen to the PC, the software, the data, the user's productivity, and so on, if a failure occurred? What would you do and what materials would you like to have in that situation? What can you do ahead of time to help make the situation less disastrous? Your answers to those questions will lead you to create effective preventive maintenance and disaster recovery plans. This section focuses on the preventive maintenance plan.

For example, consider the problem caused by a user accidentally changing the CMOS setup. What can you do to prevent that from occurring? If it does occur, how can you solve the problem? What can you do now to prepare for that event? By answering these three questions, you might arrive at these preventive maintenance and recovery procedures: (1) make a backup copy of setup on floppy disk, (2) label the disk and keep it in a safe place, (3) educate the user about the importance of not changing setup, and (4) keep a maintenance record of this PC, including the last time setup was backed up.

When a PC Is Your Permanent Responsibility

When you are the person responsible for a PC, either as the user or as the ongoing support person for the PC and the user, prepare for future troubleshooting situations. This section describes tasks and procedures for doing this.

Organize the Hard Drive Root Directory

In the root directory, keep only startup files for your system and necessary initialization files for the software. Software applications or files containing data don't belong in the root directory, although these applications sometimes put initialization files in the root directory to be used when they first load. Keep application software files and their data in separate directories.

Filenames and extensions can help identify files that application software puts in the root directory to initialize itself. For example, Prodigy.bat is a DOS batch file that the Prodigy software uses to execute. Other software packages often use .bat files for this same purpose. Other file extensions to look for as initialization files are .ini, .bin, and .dat. If you are not sure of the purpose of one of these files, leave it in the root directory. Some software packages might not work if their file isn't in the root directory.

Create Rescue Disks

After you clean up the root directory, make a set of rescue disks for the OS, and test your disks to make sure that they work; label them with the computer model, date, and OS version; and keep them available at the PC. If you have problems with the hard drive, you can use these disks to boot the PC.

Document All Setup Changes, Problems, and Solutions

When you first set up a new computer, start a record book about this computer, using either a file on disk or a notebook dedicated to this machine. In this notebook or file, record any changes in setup data as well as any problems you experience or maintenance that you do on this computer. Be diligent in keeping this notebook up to date, because it will be invaluable in diagnosing problems and upgrading equipment. Keep a printed or handwritten record of all setup data for this machine, and store the record with the hardware and software documentation.

 TIP You can also keep a record of all troubleshooting you do on a computer in a word-processing document that lists all the problems you have encountered and the solutions you used. This will help you save time in troubleshooting problems you have encountered before. Store the document file on a floppy disk that you keep with the computer's documentation.

If you are not the primary user of the computer, you might want to keep the hardware documentation separate from the computer itself. Label the documentation so that you can easily identify that it belongs to this computer. Some support people tape a large envelope inside the computer case, containing important documentation and records specific to that computer. Keep the software reference manuals in a location that is convenient for users.

24

Record Setup Data

Keep a record of CMOS, showing hard drive type, drive configuration, and so on. Use a CMOS save program, or use Norton Utilities or similar third-party utility software to save the setup data on a floppy disk. This information should be stored on a floppy disk along with the software necessary to use it. Label the disk with the PC type, date, and any information needed to use the disk. Put the disk in a safe place.

If you don't have access to software to save setup data, use the Print Screen key to print the setup screens. If the Print Screen key does not work while you view setup on the PC, carefully copy down on paper all settings that you changed from the default settings. CMOS can lose these settings, and you will want to be able to reconstruct them when necessary. To do that, you would restore default settings and then use your written record to change the ones that you set manually. Also keep a record of DIP switch settings and jumper settings on the motherboard. You can record these settings the first time you remove the cover of the machine. At the very least, record the settings before you change them! Keep all this information in your notebook.

When installing an expansion card, write information about the card in your notebook, and keep the documentation that came with it in your notebook. If you must change jumper settings or DIP switches on the card, be certain to write down the original settings before you change anything. When the card is configured correctly, write down the correct settings in your notebook or on the documentation for the card. It is unlikely that a user will accidentally change these settings and then ask you to fix them, but you never know!

Take Practical Precautions to Protect Software and Data

If software files become corrupted, the most thorough approach is to restore the software from backups or to reinstall the software. To simplify both of these time-consuming tasks, here are a few suggestions:

- Before you install a new software package, back up the Windows 2000/XP system state.

- For Windows 9x, because many software packages overwrite files in the \Windows\System directory during installation, if you have the hard drive space, back up this entire directory before you begin an installation.

- Don't compress your hard drive, because compressed drives are more likely to become corrupted than those that are not compressed.

- Don't store data files in the same directory as the software, so that there will be less chance of accidentally deleting or overwriting a software file.

Back up original software   According to copyright laws, you have the right to make a backup of the installation CD or floppy disks in case the CD or disks fail. The copyright most likely does not allow you to distribute these backup copies to friends, but you can keep your copy in a safe place in the event that something happens to the original.

Back up data on the hard drive   Don't expect the worst but prepare for it! If important data is kept on the hard drive, back up that data on a regular basis on tape (using utility software designed for that purpose), on removable hard drives, on floppy disks, or on a company file server. Don't keep important data on only one medium.

A Preventive Maintenance Plan

In addition to the guidelines given in the previous sections, it is important to develop an overall preventive maintenance plan. If your company has established written guidelines for PC preventive maintenance, read them and follow the procedures necessary to make them work. If your company has no established plan, make your own. A preventive maintenance plan tends to evolve from a history or pattern of malfunctions within an organization. For example, dusty environments can mean more maintenance, whereas a clean environment can mean less maintenance. Table 24-2 lists some guidelines for developing a preventive maintenance plan that may work for you.

> **TIP** Dust is not good for a PC because it insulates PC parts like a blanket, which can cause them to overheat; therefore, ridding the PC of dust is an important part of preventive maintenance. Some PC technicians don't like to use a vacuum inside a PC because they're concerned that the vacuum might produce ESD. Use compressed air to blow the dust out of the chassis, power supply, and fan, or use a special antistatic vacuum designed to be used around sensitive equipment.

Table 24-2   Guidelines for developing a PC preventive maintenance plan

Component	Maintenance	How Often
Inside the case	• Make sure air vents are clear. • Use compressed air to blow the dust out of the case, or use a vacuum to clean vents, power supply, and fan. • Ensure that chips and expansion cards are firmly seated.	Yearly
CMOS setup	• Keep a backup record of setup (for example, using Norton Utilities or CMOS Save).	Whenever changes are made
Floppy drive	• Only clean the floppy drive when the drive does not work.	When the drive fails
Hard drive	• Perform regular backups. • Automatically execute a virus scan program at startup. • Defragment the drive and recover lost clusters regularly. • Don't allow smoking around the PC. • Place the PC where it will not be jarred, kicked, or bumped.	At least weekly At least daily Monthly Always Always

24

A+CORE 3.1 **Table 24-2**   Guidelines for developing a PC preventive maintenance plan (continued)

Component	Maintenance	How Often
Keyboard	• Keep the keyboard clean. • Keep the keyboard away from liquids.	Monthly Always
Mouse	• Clean the mouse rollers and ball.	Monthly
Monitor	• Clean the screen with a soft cloth. • Make sure air vents are clear.	At least monthly Always
Printers	• Clean out the dust and bits of paper, using compressed air and a vacuum. Small pieces of paper can be removed with tweezers, preferably insulated ones. • Clean the paper and ribbon paths with a soft, lint-free cloth. • Don't re-ink ribbons or use recharged toner cartridges. • If the printer uses an ozone filter, replace it as recommended by the manufacturer. • Replace other components as recommended by the manufacturer.	At least monthly or as recommended by the manufacturer
UPS/ Suppressors	• Run weak battery test. • Run diagnostic test.	As recommended by manufacturer
Software	• If directed by your employer, check that only authorized software is present. • Regularly delete files from the Recycle Bin and \Temp directories.	At least monthly
Written record	• Keep a record of all software, including version numbers and the OS installed on the PC. • Keep a record of all hardware components installed, including hardware settings. • Record when and what preventive maintenance is performed. • Record any repairs done to the PC.	Whenever changes are made

The general idea of preventive maintenance is to do what you can to make a PC last longer and give as little trouble as possible. You may also be responsible for ensuring that data is secure and backed up, that software copyrights are not violated, and that users are supported. As with any plan, when designing your preventive maintenance plan, first define your overall goals, and then design the plan accordingly. The guidelines listed in Table 24-2 primarily address the problems that prevent a PC from lasting long and from performing well.

Moving Equipment

A+CORE
3.2

When shipping a PC, remember that rough handling can cause damage, as can exposure to water, heat, and cold. The PC can also be misplaced, lost, or stolen. When you are preparing a PC for shipping, take extra precautions to protect it and its data. Follow these general guidelines when preparing to ship a PC:

- Back up the hard drive onto a tape cartridge or other backup medium separate from your computer. If you don't have access to a medium that can back up the entire drive, back up important system and configuration files to a floppy disk or other media. Whatever you do, don't ship a PC that has the only copy of important data on the hard drive, or data that should be secured from unauthorized access.

- Remove any removable disks, tape cartridges, or CDs from the drives. Make sure that the tapes or disks holding the backup data are secured and protected during transit. Consider shipping them separately.

- Turn off power to the PC and all other devices.

- Disconnect power cords from the electrical outlet and the devices. Disconnect all external devices from the computer.

- If you think someone might have trouble later identifying which cord or cable belongs to which device or connection, label the cable connections with white tape or white labels.

- Coil all cords and secure them with plastic ties or rubber bands.

- Pack the computer, monitor, and all devices in their original shipping cartons or similar boxes with enough packing material to protect them.

- Purchase insurance on the shipment. Postal insurance is not expensive and can save you a lot of money if materials are damaged in transit.

Disposing of Used Equipment

A+CORE
3.3

As a PC technician, it will often be your responsibility to dispose of used equipment and consumables, including batteries, printer toner cartridges, and monitors. Table 24-3 lists such items and how to dispose of them. Manufacturer documentation and local environmental regulators can also provide disposal instructions or guidance. Monitors and power supplies can contain a charge even after the devices are unplugged. To discharge the capacitors in either type of device, place a screwdriver across a hot prong and the ground prong of the electrical connections, as shown in Figure 24-1. To discharge the actual CRT in a monitor, the monitor must be opened. Ask a technician trained to fix monitors to do this for you.

A+CORE
3.3
5.2

Figure 24-1   Discharge the capacitors in a monitor before disposal

A **material safety data sheet (MSDS)** explains how to properly handle substances such as chemical solvents. An MSDS includes information such as physical data, toxicity, health effects, first aid, storage, disposal, and spill procedures. It comes packaged with the chemical, or you can order one from the manufacturer, or find one on the Internet (see *www.ilpi.com/msds*).

Table 24-3   Computer parts and how to dispose of them

Part	How to Dispose
Alkaline batteries including AAA, AA, A, C, D, and 9 volt	Dispose of these batteries in the regular trash. First check to see if there are recycling facilities in your area.
Button batteries used in digital cameras, Flash Path, and other small equipment Battery packs used in notebooks	These batteries can contain silver oxide, mercury, lithium, or cadmium and are considered hazardous waste. Dispose of them by returning them to the original dealer or by taking them to a recycling center. To recycle, pack them separately from other items. If you don't have a recycling center nearby, contact your county for local regulations for disposal.
Laser printer toner cartridges	Return these to the manufacturer or dealer to be recycled.
Ink-jet printer cartridges Computers Monitors Chemical solvents and cans	Check with local county or environmental officials for laws and regulations in your area for proper disposal of these items. The county might have a recycling center that will receive them. Discharge a monitor before disposing of it.

Fire Extinguishers

No discussion of preventive maintenance would be complete without mentioning the importance of having a fire extinguisher handy that is rated to handle fires ignited by electricity. The National Fire Protection Association (NFPA), an organization that creates standards for fire safety, says a fire has one of three ratings:

- *Class A.* A fire that is fueled by ordinary combustible materials such as wood, trash, or clothes

- *Class B.* A fire that is fueled by flammable liquids such as oil, gasoline, kerosene, propane gas, and some plastics

- *Class C.* A fire that is ignited and heated by electricity

It's the Class C fire that we are concerned about in this discussion. For a fire to be rated as a Class C fire, regardless of what is burning, the fire must have been ignited by electricity and must keep burning because electrical energy is providing heat. If you take away the electrical current, then the fire becomes a Class A or Class B fire. Mount a fire extinguisher rated for Class C fires near your workbench but not directly over your work area. If equipment were to catch on fire, you wouldn't want to have to reach over it to get to the fire extinguisher. Know how to use the extinguisher.

CHAPTER SUMMARY

- ❏ Tools for solving computer problems include a repair kit, bootable disk, and diagnostic hardware and software.

- ❏ Two important rules when troubleshooting are to eliminate unnecessary hardware and software and to trade components you know are good for those you suspect may be bad.

- ❏ Learn to ask the user good questions (using good manners and diplomacy) that help you understand the history behind the problem.

- ❏ One good method of solving intermittent problems is to keep a log of when they occur.

- ❏ Problems with computers can be divided into two general groups: those that prevent the computer from booting successfully and those that occur after the computer boots.

- ❏ Diagnostic cards give error codes based on POST errors.

- ❏ Diagnostic software performs many tests on a PC. Some of these software programs use their own proprietary operating systems.

- ❏ Utility software can update and repair device drivers and applications. Some utility software downloads these updates from the Internet.

- ❏ Keep a bootable disk containing the root directory files of your system.

24

- Keep backups of hard drive data and software.

- Keep a written record of the CMOS setup, or save it on disk.

- PC failures are caused by many environmental and human factors, including heat, dust, magnetism, power supply problems, static electricity, spilled liquids, viruses, and human error.

- The goals of preventive maintenance are to make PCs last longer and work better, protect data and software, and reduce repair costs.

- A PC preventive maintenance plan includes blowing dust from the inside of the computer case, keeping a record of setup data, backing up the hard drive, and cleaning the mouse, monitor, and keyboard.

- Protecting software and hardware documentation is an important preventive maintenance chore.

- Never ship a PC when the only copy of important data is on its hard drive.

- A Class C fire extinguisher is rated to put out a fire ignited and kept burning by electricity.

KEY TERMS

diagnostic cards   diagnostic software   material safety data sheet (MSDS)

REVIEW QUESTIONS

1. The type of technician that would work on-site and interact closely with users is a:

   a. PC support technician

   b. PC service technician

   c. Bench technician

   d. Help-desk technician

   e. None of the above

2. One of the "tools" that is recommended for any individual troubleshooting the PC is what is referred to as a bootable rescue disk. Modern-day operating systems have allowed for one bootable rescue disk to be used for any operating system installed on a PC.

   a. True

   b. False

3. A service technician would like to upgrade the system memory and CD-ROM drive in a particular system. What is the first thing that the technician should do before starting the system upgrade?

   a. Unplug the system from power

   b. Backup the system hard drive

   c. Ensure that the system is properly grounded

   d. Ensure that the new hardware documentation is available for reference

4. If it is suspected that some aspect of the operating system is corrupt, the system should be booted to what level?

   a. The graphical user interface (GUI) without network support

   b. The graphical user interface (GUI) with network support

   c. The graphical user interface (GUI) with TSRs installed

   d. The command line

   e. None of the above

5. A service technician receives a call stating that the system locks up whenever a particular application is executed, and it is suspected that the system hard drive is defective. One of the first activities a good system troubleshooter will do *prior* to replacing suspected defective hardware is _____.

   a. Reconfigure the suspect application

   b. Reinstall the suspect application

   c. Increase the amount of system memory in the system

   d. Reboot the system and try the suspect application again

   e. None of the above

6. A user reports that documents were no longer coming out of the printer after sending them to a locally installed printer via a word processing program. The first course of action the service technician should do is:

   a. Reinstall printer drivers

   b. Replace the printer

   c. Check that power is applied to the printer

   d. Check that the appropriate printer was selected by the word processing program when the user printed

   e. None of the above

24

7. A user reports to a service technician "I can't print…" The technician asks the user what that means, and the response is "I'm pressing the 'Print Screen' button and nothing is coming out of the printer…" What follow-up question would be best for the technician to ask next?

   a. "How much memory is installed on that system?"

   b. "What operating system is installed on that system?"

   c. "Which CPU is installed on that system?"

   d. "How much hard drive space is left on that system?"

   e. "How much did you pay for that system?"

8. What is the recommended maintenance schedule for the defragmentation of a typical system hard drive?

   a. Daily

   b. Weekly

   c. Monthly

   d. Yearly

   e. When the device fails

9. What is the recommended maintenance schedule for cleaning floppy drives?

   a. Daily

   b. Weekly

   c. Monthly

   d. Yearly

   e. When the device fails

10. Prior to physically moving a PC from one location to another, it is very important to first:

    a. Remove power from the system

    b. Reboot the system into safe mode

    c. Adequately cushion the system

    d. Back up the secondary storage onto tape or other backup media

    e. Contact a moving company

11. The class rating for a fire extinguisher appropriate for extinguishing a PC-related fire that is running is:

    a. Class A

    b. Class B

    c. Class C

    d. Any of the above

    e. None of the above

ERROR MESSAGES AND THEIR MEANINGS

The following table of error messages and their meanings can help you when you are diagnosing computer problems. For other error messages, consult your motherboard or computer documentation.

A+ OS
3.1
CORE
2.1

Error Message	Meaning of the Error Message and What to Do
Bad sector writing or reading to drive	Sector markings on the disk may be fading. Try ScanDisk or reformat the disk.
Bad command or file not found	The OS command just executed cannot be interpreted, or the OS cannot find the program file specified in the command line. Check the spelling of the filename and, for DOS or when working from a Windows startup disk, check that the path to the program file has been given to the OS.
Beeps during POST	Before the video is checked, during POST, the ROM BIOS communicates error messages with a series of beeps. Each BIOS manufacturer has its own beep codes, but the following are examples of some BIOS codes. For specific beep codes for your motherboard, see the Web site of the motherboard or BIOS manufacturer.
One single beep followed by three, four, or five beeps	Motherboard problems, possibly with DMA, the CMOS setup chip, timer, or the system bus.
Two beeps	The POST numeric code is displayed on the monitor.
Two beeps followed by three, four, or five beeps	First 64K of RAM has errors.
Three beeps followed by three, four, or five beeps	Keyboard controller has failed or video controller has failed.
Four beeps followed by two, three, or four beeps	Problem with serial or parallel ports, system timer, or time of day.
Continuous beeps	Problem with power supply.
Configuration/CMOS error	Setup information does not agree with the actual hardware the computer found during the boot. May be caused by a bad or weak battery or by changing hardware without changing setup. Check setup for errors.
Insufficient memory	This error happens under Windows when too many applications are open. Close some applications. A reboot may help.

A+ OS
3.1
CORE
2.1

Error Message	Meaning of the Error Message and What to Do
Hard drive not found	The OS cannot locate the hard drive, or the controller card is not responding.
Fixed disk error	The PC cannot find the hard drive that setup told it to expect. Check the cables, connections, power supply, and setup information.
Incorrect DOS version	When you execute a DOS external command, the OS looks for a program file with the same name as the command. It finds that this file belongs to a different version of the OS than the one that is now running. Use the Setver command in Autoexec.bat.
Invalid drive specification	The PC is unable to find a hard drive or a floppy drive that setup tells it to expect. Look for errors in setup, or for a corrupted partition table on the hard drive.
Invalid or missing Command.com	This may be caused by a nonbooting disk in drive A. Remove the disk and boot from drive C. Command.com on drive C may have been erased, or the path could not be found.
No boot device available	The hard drive is not formatted, or the format is corrupted, and there is no disk in drive A. Boot from a floppy and examine your hard drive for corruption.
Non-system disk or disk error	Command.com or one of two OS hidden files is missing from the disk in drive A or the hard drive. Remove the disk in drive A and boot from the hard drive. Use the SYS command to restore system files.
Not ready reading drive A: Abort, Retry, Fail?	The disk in drive A is missing, is not formatted, or is corrupted. Try another disk.
Numeric codes during POST	Sometimes numeric codes are used to communicate errors at POST. Some examples for IBM XT/AT error codes include:
Code in the 100 range	Motherboard errors or errors in CMOS setup
Code in the 200 range	RAM errors
Code in the 300 range	Keyboard errors
Code in the 500 range	Video controller errors
Code in the 600 range	Floppy drive errors
Code in the 700 range	Coprocessor errors
Code in the 900 range	Parallel port errors
Code in the 1100–1200 range	Async (communications adapter) errors
Code in the 1300 range	Game controller or joystick errors
Code in the 1700 range	Hard drive errors
Code in the 6000 range	SCSI device or network card errors
Code in the 7300 range	Floppy drive errors

A+ OS
3.1
CORE
2.1

Error Message	Meaning of the Error Message and What to Do
Track 0 bad, disk not usable	This usually occurs when you attempt to format a floppy disk using the wrong format type. Check the disk type and compare it to the type specified in the format command.
Write-protect error writing drive A:	Let the computer write to the disk by setting the switch on a 3½-inch disk or removing the tape from a 5¼-inch disk.
Missing operating system, error loading operating system	The MBR is unable to locate or read the OS boot sector on the active partition or there is a translation problem on large drives. Boot from a floppy and examine the hard drive file system for corruption.
Unknown error at POST	See the Web site of the system BIOS manufacturer: • AMI BIOS: *www.ami.com* • Award BIOS and Phoenix BIOS: *www.phoenix.com* • Compaq: *www.hp.com* • Dell: *www.dell.com* • IBM: *www.ibm.com*
Error in Config.sys line *xx*	There is a problem loading a device driver or with the syntax of a command line. Check the command line for errors. Verify the driver files are in the right directory. Reinstall the driver files.
Himem.sys not loaded, missing or corrupt Himem.sys	Himem.sys is corrupted, not in the right directory, or not the right version for the currently loading OS. Verify Himem.sys.
Device not found	Errors in System.ini, Win.ini or the registry. Look for references to devices or attempts to load device drivers. Use Device Manager to delete a device or edit System.ini or Win.ini.

B

ASCII CHARACTER SET AND ANSI.SYS

ASCII (American Standard Code for Information Interchange) is a coding system used by personal computers to store character data, such as letters of the alphabet, numerals, some symbols, and certain control characters. There are 128 characters defined by the standard ASCII character set. Each ASCII character is assigned an 8-bit code that converts to a decimal number from 0 to 127, although in the standard set, the first bit is always 0. The first 31 values, which are nonprintable codes, are for control characters used to send commands to printers or other peripheral devices. Files that store data as ASCII characters are sometimes called ASCII files, ASCII text files, or simply text files. ASCII can be read by most text editors and word processors and is considered the universal file format for personal computers. Autoexec.bat is one example of an ASCII file.

In addition to the standard ASCII character set, some manufacturers use an extended ASCII character set that is specific to their equipment and is not necessarily compatible with other computers. The extended ASCII character sets use the codes 128 through 255.

The American National Standards Institute (ANSI), an organization responsible for many computer standards, developed an extended character set using codes 128 through 255 that includes special characters such as letters in an international alphabet and accents, currency symbols, and fractions. ANSI has also defined a series of control codes that can be used to control monitors. For example, a sequence of control codes can clear a monitor, cause characters to be displayed upside down, or put color on a DOS screen. Ansi.sys is a device driver that, when loaded in a DOS environment, provides these monitor and keyboard functions. Ansi.sys is loaded from the Config.sys file with this command:

```
Device=C:\DOS\Ansi.sys
```

Some DOS programs need Ansi.sys loaded in order to interpret the extended character set entered from the keyboard, display these characters on the screen, and control the monitor in other ways.

Table B-1 lists the standard ASCII character set. Note that items 2 through 32, the control characters, and the extended ASCII character set are not included.

Table B-1 Standard ASCII character set

Item Number	Symbol	Meaning	ASCII in Decimal Representation	ASCII in Binary Representation	ASCII in Hex Representation
1	.	Null	0	0000 0000	0
33	b/	Space	32	0010 0000	20
34	!	Exclamation point	33	0010 0001	21
35	"	Quotation mark	34	0010 0010	22
36	#	Number sign	35	0010 0011	23
37	$	Dollar sign	36	0010 0100	24
38	%	Percent sign	37	0010 0101	25
39	&	Ampersand	38	0010 0110	26
40	'	Apostrophe, prime sign	39	0010 0111	27
41	(	Opening parenthesis	40	0010 1000	28
42	)	Closing parenthesis	41	0010 1001	29
43	*	Asterisk	42	0010 1010	2A
44	+	Plus sign	43	0010 1011	2B
45	,	Comma	44	0010 1100	2C
46	-	Hyphen, minus sign	45	0010 1101	2D
47	.	Period, decimal point	46	0010 1110	2E
48	/	Slant	47	0010 1111	2F
49	0		48	0011 0000	30
50	1		49	0011 0001	31
51	2		50	0011 0010	32
52	3		51	0011 0011	33
53	4		52	0011 0100	34
54	5		53	0011 0101	35
55	6		54	0011 0110	36
56	7		55	0011 0111	37
57	8		56	0011 1000	38
58	9		57	0011 1001	39
59	:	Colon	58	0011 1010	3A
60	;	Semicolon	59	0011 1011	3B

Table B-1   Standard ASCII character set (continued)

Item Number	Symbol	Meaning	ASCII in Decimal Representation	ASCII in Binary Representation	ASCII in Hex Representation
61	<	Less than sign	60	0011 1100	3C
62	=	Equals sign	61	0011 1101	3D
63	>	Greater than sign	62	0011 1110	3E
64	?	Question mark	63	0011 1111	3F
65	@	Commercial at sign	64	0100 0000	40
66	A		65	0100 0001	41
67	B		66	0100 0010	42
68	C		67	0100 0011	43
69	D		68	0100 0100	44
70	E		69	0100 0101	45
71	F		70	0100 0110	46
72	G		71	0100 0111	47
73	H		72	0100 1000	48
74	I		73	0100 1001	49
75	J		74	0100 1010	4A
76	K		75	0100 1011	4B
77	L		76	0100 1100	4C
78	M		77	0100 1101	4D
79	N		78	0100 1110	4E
80	O		79	0100 1111	4F
81	P		80	0101 0000	50
82	Q		81	0101 0001	51
83	R		82	0101 0010	52
84	S		83	0101 0011	53
85	T		84	0101 0100	54
86	U		85	0101 0101	55
87	V		86	0101 0110	56
88	W		87	0101 0111	57
89	X		88	0101 1000	58
90	Y		89	0101 1001	59
91	Z		90	0101 1010	5A
92	[	Opening bracket	91	0101 1011	5B
93	\	Reverse slant	92	0101 1100	5C
94	]	Closing bracket	93	0101 1101	5D

Table B-1   Standard ASCII character set (continued)

Item Number	Symbol	Meaning	ASCII in Decimal Representation	ASCII in Binary Representation	ASCII in Hex Representation
95	^	Caret	94	0101 1110	5E
96	_	Underscore	95	0101 1111	5F
97	`	Acute accent	96	0110 0000	60
98	a		97	0110 0001	61
99	b		98	0110 0010	62
100	c		99	0110 0011	63
101	d		100	0110 0100	64
102	e		101	0110 0101	65
103	f		102	0110 0110	66
104	g		103	0110 0111	67
105	h		104	0110 1000	68
106	i		105	0110 1001	69
107	j		106	0110 1010	6A
108	k		107	0110 1011	6B
109	l		108	0110 1100	6C
110	m		109	0110 1101	6D
111	n		110	0110 1110	6E
112	o		111	0110 1111	6F
113	p		112	0111 0000	70
114	q		113	0111 0001	71
115	r		114	0111 0010	72
116	s		115	0111 0011	73
117	t		116	0111 0100	74
118	u		117	0111 0101	75
119	v		118	0111 0110	76
120	w		119	0111 0111	77
121	x		120	0111 1000	78
122	y		121	0111 1001	79
123	z		122	0111 1010	7A
124	{	Opening brace	123	0111 1011	7B
125	l	Split vertical bar	124	0111 1100	7C
126	}	Closing brace	125	0111 1101	7D
127	~	Tilde	126	0111 1110	7E
128	Δ	Small triangle	127	0111 1111	7F

C

THE HEXADECIMAL NUMBER SYSTEM AND MEMORY ADDRESSING

Understanding the number system and the coding system that computers use to store data and communicate with each other is fundamental to understanding how computers work. Early attempts to invent an electronic computing device met with disappointing results as long as inventors tried to use the decimal number system, with the digits 0–9. Then John Atanasoff proposed using a coding system that expressed everything in terms of different sequences of only two numerals: one represented by the presence of a charge and one represented by the absence of a charge. The numbering system that can be supported by the expression of only two numerals is the base 2, sometimes called binary, numbering system, invented by Ada Lovelace many years before, using the numerals 0 and 1. Under Atanasoff's design, all numbers and other characters would be converted to this binary number system, and all storage, comparisons, and arithmetic would be done using it. Even today, this is one of the basic principles of computers. Every character or number entered into a computer is first converted into a series of 0s and 1s. Many coding schemes and techniques have been invented to manipulate these 0s and 1s, called **bits** for **bi**nary dig**its**.

The most widespread binary coding scheme for microcomputers, which is recognized as the microcomputer standard, is called the ASCII (American Standard Code for Information Interchange) coding system. (Appendix B lists the binary code for the basic 127-character set.) In ASCII, each character is assigned an 8-bit code called a **byte**. Table C-1 lists the terms used in the discussion of how numbers are stored in computers. The byte has become the universal single unit of storage for data in computers everywhere.

Table C-1   Computer terminology

Term	Definition
Bit	A numeral in the binary number system: a 0 or a 1
Byte	8 bits
Kilobyte	1,024 bytes, which is 2^{10}, often rounded to 1,000 bytes
Megabyte	Either 1,024 kilobytes or 1,000 kilobytes, depending on what has come to be standard practice in different situations. For example, when calculating floppy disk capacities, 1 megabyte = 1,000 kilobytes; when calculating hard drive capacity, traditionally, 1 megabyte = 1,024 bytes
Gigabyte	1,000 megabytes or 1,024 megabytes, depending on what has come to be standard practice in different situations
ASCII	American Standard Code for Information Interchange coding scheme used for microcomputers, which assigns a 7- or 8-bit code to all characters and symbols. See Appendix B for more information
Hex	Short for hexadecimal. A number system based on 16 values (called base 16), which is explained in detail below. Uses the sixteen numerals 0, 1, 2, 3, 4, 5, 6, 7, 8, 9, A, B, C, D, E, and F. Hex numbers are often followed by a lowercase h to indicate they are in hex (example: 78h).

Computers convert binary data into the hexadecimal (hex) number system because it is much less complex for computers to convert binary numbers into hex numbers than into decimal numbers, and it is much easier for human beings to read hex numbers than to read binary numbers. This way, even though the actual processing and inner workings of computers use the binary system, they often display information using the hex system.

Learning to "Think Hex"

One skill a knowledgeable computer support person must have is the ability to read hex numbers and convert hex to decimal and decimal to hex. Once you understand one numbering system (decimal), you can understand any numbering system (including binary and hexadecimal), because they all operate on the same basic principle: place value. So we begin there.

Place Value

A key to understanding place value is to think of a number system as a method of grouping multiple small units together until there are enough of them to be packed into a single larger group, then grouping multiple larger groups together until there are enough of them to form an even larger group, and so on. In our (decimal) number system, once there are 10 units of any group, that group becomes a single unit of the next larger group. So, groups of 10 units are packed into groups of tens; groups of 10 tens are packed into groups of hundreds; groups of 10 hundreds are packed into groups of thousands, and so forth.

An easy way to understand number systems is to think of the numbers as being packaged for shipping, into boxes, cartons, crates, truckloads, and so on. For the decimal numbering system, consider packing widgets (units) into boxes (tens) which are packed into cartons (100s) which are packed into crates (1000s), and so forth. The same analogy works for binary, decimal, and all other number systems.

Our friend Joe, in Figure C-1, is a widget packer in the shipping department of the ACE Widget Co. Joe can ship single widgets, or he can pack them in boxes, cartons, crates, and truckloads. He can fit three, and only three, widgets to a box; three, and only three, boxes into one carton ($3 \times 3 = 9$ widgets); three, and only three, cartons into one crate ($3 \times 9 = 27$ widgets); and three, and only three, crates into one truck ($3 \times 27 = 81$ widgets). He is not allowed to pack more widgets into boxes, cartons, crates, or truckloads than those specified. Neither is he allowed to send out a box, carton, crate, or truckload that is not completely filled.

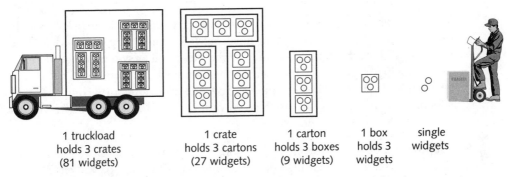

| 1 truckload holds 3 crates (81 widgets) | 1 crate holds 3 cartons (27 widgets) | 1 carton holds 3 boxes (9 widgets) | 1 box holds 3 widgets | single widgets |

Figure C-1   Joe in the shipping department groups widgets in singles, boxes, cartons, crates, and truckloads—all in groups of three

Joe receives an order to ship out 197 widgets. How does he ship them? The answer is shown in Figure C-2. Joe sends out 197 widgets grouped into 2 truckloads ($2 \times 81 = 162$ widgets), 1 crate (27 widgets), no cartons, 2 boxes ($2 \times 3 = 6$ widgets), and 2 single widgets. We can write this grouping of widgets as 21022, where the "place values" from left to right are truckloads, crates, cartons, boxes, and units, which in this case are (in decimal) 81 widgets, 27 widgets, 9 widgets, 3 widgets, and single widgets. Notice that each "place value" in our widget-packing system is a multiple of 3, because the widgets are grouped into three before they are packed into boxes; the boxes are grouped into three before they are packed into cartons, and so on. By grouping the widgets into groups of 3s in this manner, we converted the decimal number (base 10) 197 into the ternary number (base 3) 21022. Joe's widget-packing method is a base three, or ternary, system. The numerals in the ternary number system are 0, 1, and 2. When you get to the next value after 2, instead of counting on up to 3, you move one place value to the left and begin again with 1 in that position, which represents 3. So, counting in base 3 goes like this: 0, 1, 2, 10, 11, 12, 20, 21, 22, 100, 101 and so on. This is the same as Joe's never shipping out 3 of any one group unless they are packed together into one larger group. For example, Joe wouldn't ship 3 individual boxes, he would ship one carton.

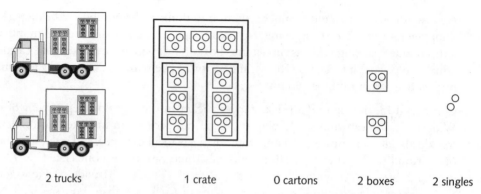

2 trucks   1 crate   0 cartons   2 boxes   2 singles

Figure C-2   Joe's shipment of 197 widgets: 2 truckloads, 1 crate, 0 cartons, 2 boxes, and a group of 2 singles

You can easily apply the widget-packing analogy to another base. If Joe used 10 instead of three, he would be using base ten (decimal) rules. So, numbering systems differ by the different numbers of units they group together. In the hex number system, we group by 16. So, if Joe were shipping in groups of 16, as in Figure C–3, single widgets could be shipped out up to 15, but 16 widgets would make one box. Sixteen boxes would make one carton, which would contain 16×16, or 256, widgets. Sixteen cartons would make one crate, which would contain 16×256, or 4,096, widgets.

Suppose Joe receives an order for 197 widgets to be packed in groups of 16. He will not be able to fill a carton (256 widgets), so he ships out 12 boxes (16 widgets each) and 5 single widgets:

$12 \times 16 = 192$, and $192 + 5 = 197$

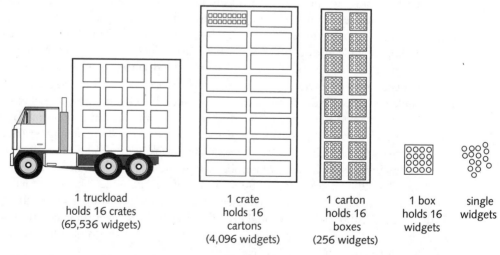

1 truckload
holds 16 crates
(65,536 widgets)   1 crate
holds 16
cartons
(4,096 widgets)   1 carton
holds 16
boxes
(256 widgets)   1 box
holds 16
widgets   single
widgets

Figure C-3   Widgets displayed in truckloads, crates, cartons, boxes, and singles grouped in 16s

You approach an obstacle if you attempt to write the number in hex. How are you going to express 12 boxes and 5 singles? In hex, you need single numerals in hex to represent the numbers 10, 11, 12, 13, 14, and 15 in decimal. Hex uses letters for these numerals. The letters A through F are used for the numbers 10 through 15. Table C-2 shows values expressed in the decimal, hex, and binary numbering systems. In the second column in Table C-2, you are counting in the hex number system. For example, 12 is represented with a C. So you say that Joe packs C boxes and 5 singles. The hex number for decimal 197 is C5 (see Figure C-4).

Table C-2   Decimal, hex, and binary values

Decimal	Hex	Binary	Decimal	Hex	Binary	Decimal	Hex	Binary
0	0	0	14	E	1110	28	1C	11100
1	1	1	15	F	1111	29	1D	11101
2	2	10	16	10	10000	30	1E	11110
3	3	11	17	11	10001	31	1F	11111
4	4	100	18	12	10010	32	20	100000
5	5	101	19	13	10011	33	21	100001
6	6	110	20	14	10100	34	22	100010
7	7	111	21	15	10101	35	23	100011
8	8	1000	22	16	10110	36	24	100100
9	9	1001	23	17	10111	37	25	100101
10	A	1010	24	18	11000	38	26	100110
11	B	1011	25	19	11001	39	27	100111
12	C	1100	26	1A	11010	40	28	101000
13	D	1101	27	1B	11011			

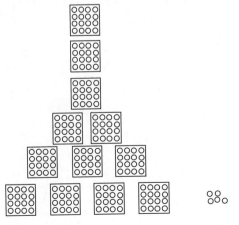

Figure C-4   Hex C5 represented as C boxes and 5 singles = 197 decimal

For a little practice, calculate the hex values of the decimal values 14, 259, 75, and 1,024 and the decimal values of FFh and A11h.

How Exponents Are Used to Express Place Value

If you are comfortable with using exponents, you know that writing numbers raised to a power is the same thing as multiplying that number times itself the power number of times. For example, $3^4 = 3 \times 3 \times 3 \times 3 = 81$. Using exponents in expressing numbers can also help us easily see place value, because the place value for each place is really the base number multiplied by itself a number of times, based on the place value position. For instance, look back at Figure C-1. A truckload is really $3 \times 3 \times 3 \times 3$, or 81, units, which can be written as 3^4. A crate is really $3 \times 3 \times 3$, or 27, units. The numbers in Figure C-1 can therefore be written like this:

Truckload = 3^4 Crate = 3^3 Carton = 3^2 Box = 3^1 Single = 3^0

(Any number raised to the 0 power equals 1.) Therefore, we can express the numbers in Figure C-2 as multiples of truckloads, crates, cartons, boxes, and singles like this:

	Truckloads	Crates	Cartons	Boxes	Singles
21022 (base 3)	2×3^4	1×3^3	0×3^2	2×3^1	2×3^0
Decimal equivalent	162	27	0	6	2

When we sum up the numbers in the last row above, we get 197. We just converted a base 3 number (21022) to a base 10 number (197).

Binary Number System

It was stated earlier that it is easier for computers to convert from binary to hex or from hex to binary than to convert between binary and decimal. Let's see just how easy. Recall that the binary number system only has two numerals, or bits: 0 and 1. If our friend Joe in shipping operated a "binary" shipping system, he would pack like this: 2 widgets in a box, 2 boxes in one carton (4 widgets), two cartons in one crate (8 widgets), and two crates in one truckload (16 widgets). In Figure C-5, Joe is asked to pack 13 widgets. He packs 1 crate (8 widgets), 1 carton (4 widgets), no boxes, and 1 single. The number 13 in binary is 1101:

$$(1 \times 2^3)+(1 \times 2^2)+(0 \times 2^1)+(1 \times 2^0)= 8 + 4 + 0 + 1 = 13$$

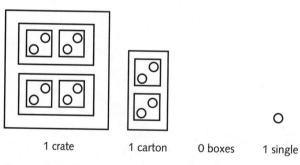

  1 crate   1 carton   0 boxes   1 single

Figure C-5 Binary 1101 = 13 displayed as crates, cartons, boxes, and singles

C

Now let's see how to convert binary to hex and back again. The largest 4-bit number in binary is 1111. This number in decimal and hex is:

```
binary 1111 = 1 group of 8 = 8
              1 group of 4 = 4
              1 group of 2 = 2
                  1 single = 1

                    TOTAL = 15 (decimal)
 Therefore, 1111 (binary) = 15 (decimal) = F (hex)
```

This last calculation is very important when working with computers: F is the largest numeral in the hex number system and it only takes 4 bits to write this largest hex numeral: F (hex) = 1111 (binary). So, every hex numeral (0, 1, 2, 3, 4, 5, 6, 7, 8, 9, A, B, C, D, E, and F) can be converted into a 4-bit binary number. Look back at the first 16 entries in Table C-2 for these binary values. Add leading zeroes to the binary numbers as necessary.

When converting from hex to binary, take each hex numeral and convert it to a 4-bit binary number and string all the 4-bit groups together. Fortunately, when working with computers, you will almost never be working with more than 2 hex numerals at a time. Here are some examples:

1. To convert hex F8 to binary, do the following: F = 1111, and 8 = 1000. Therefore, F8 = 11111000 (usually written 1111 1000).

2. To convert hex 9A to binary, do the following: 9 = 1001, and A = 1010. Therefore, 9A = 1001 1010.

Now try converting from binary to hex:

1. To convert binary 101110 to hex, first group the bits in groups of 4, starting at the right and moving left, adding leading zeros as necessary: 0010 1110.

2. Then convert each group of 4 bits in binary to a single hex numeral: 0010 = 2, and 1110 = E. The hex number is 2E.

Writing Conventions

Sometimes when you are dealing with hex, binary, and decimal numbers, it is not always clear which number system is being used. If you see a letter in the number, you know the number is a hex number. Binary numbers are usually written in groups of four bits. This book follows the convention of placing a lowercase h after a hex number, like this: 2Eh.

Memory Addressing

Computers often display memory addresses in the hex number system. You must either "think in hex" or convert to decimal. It's really easier, with a little practice, to think in hex. Here's the way it works:

Memory addresses are displayed as two hex numbers. An example is C800:5

The part to the left of the colon (C800) is called the *segment address*, and the part to the right of the colon (5) is called the *offset*. The offset value can have as many as four hex digits. The actual memory address is calculated by adding a zero to the right of the segment address and adding the offset value, like this: `C800:5 = C8000 + 5 = C8005`

The first 640K of memory is called conventional memory. Look at how that memory is addressed, first in decimal and then in hex (assuming 1 kilobyte = 1,024 bytes):

`640K = 640 × 1,024 = 655,360`

There are 655,360 memory addresses in conventional memory, where each memory address can hold 1 byte, or 8 bits, of either data or program instructions. The decimal value 655,360 converted to hex is A0000 (10×16^4). So, conventional memory addresses begin with 00000h and end with A0000h minus 1h or 9FFFFh. Written in segment-and-offset form, conventional memory addresses range from 0000:0 to 9FFF:F.

Recall that upper memory is defined as the memory addresses from 640K to 1,024K. The next address after 9FFF:F is the first address of upper memory, which is A0000, and the last address is FFFFF. Written in segment-and-offset terms, upper memory addresses range from A000:0 to FFFF:F.

Here is one way to organize the conversion of a large hex value such as FFFFF to decimal (remember F in hex equals 15 in decimal).

FFFFF converted to decimal:

```
15 × 16⁰ = 15 × 1 =                 15
15 × 16¹ = 15 × 16 =               240
15 × 16² = 15 × 256 =            3,840
15 × 16³ = 15 × 4096 =         61,440
15 × 16⁴ = 15 × 65,536 =      983,040

          TOTAL =          1,048,575
```

Remember that FFFFF is the last memory address in upper memory. The very next memory address is the first address of extended memory, which is defined as memory above 1 MB. If you add 1 to the number above, you get 1,048,576, which is equal to 1024 × 1024, which is the definition of 1 megabyte.

Displaying Memory with DOS DEBUG

In Figure C-6 you see the results of the beginning of upper memory displayed. The DOS DEBUG command displays the contents of memory. Memory addresses are displayed in hex segment-and-offset values. To enter DEBUG, type the following command at the C prompt and press Enter:

`C:\> DEBUG`

Type the following dump command to display the beginning of upper memory (the hyphen in the command is the DEBUG command prompt) and press Enter:

`-d A000:0`

Memory is displayed showing 16 bytes on each line. The A area of memory (the beginning of upper memory) is not used unless the computer is using a monochrome monitor or this area is being used as an upper memory block. In Figure C-6, the area contains nothing but continuous 1s in binary or Fs in hex. The ASCII interpretation is on the right side. To view the next group of memory addresses, you can type *d* at the hyphen and press Enter. DEBUG displays the next 128 addresses.

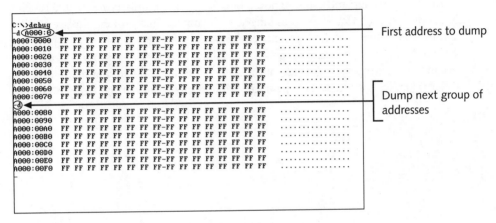

Figure C-6   Memory dump: -d A000:0

The A and B ranges of upper memory addresses (upper memory addresses that begin with A or B when written in hex) are used for monochrome monitors. The C range contains the video BIOS for a color monitor. Figure C-7 shows the dump of the beginning of the C range.

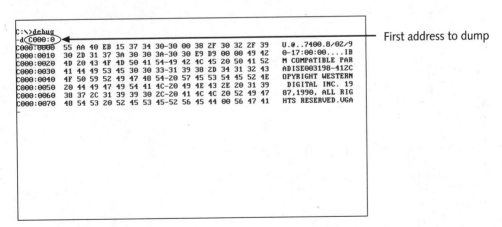

Figure C-7   Memory dump: –d C000:0

There is more than one way—in fact there are many ways—to identify the same segment-and-offset value. Try these commands to display the same upper memory addresses:

```
-d C000:0
-d BFF1:00F0
-d BFFF:0010
-d BEEE:1120
```

In summary, reading and understanding binary and hex numbers are essential skills for managing computers. All data is stored in binary in a computer and is often displayed in hex. Memory addresses are often displayed in hex segment-and-offset terms. An address in memory can be written in a variety of segment-and-offset values. The actual memory address is calculated by placing one zero to the right side of the segment address and adding the resulting value to the offset value. To exit DEBUG, type *q* for quit and press Enter at the hyphen prompt.

D

THE PROFESSIONAL PC TECHNICIAN

As a professional PC technician, you can manage your career by staying abreast of new technology and striving for top professional certifications. In addition, you should maintain excellent customer relationships, behave with professionalism, and seek opportunities for joining professional organizations. As you know, PC technicians provide service to customers over the phone or online, in person on-site, and sometimes in a shop where they have little customer contact. While each setting poses specific challenges, almost all of the recommendations made in this appendix apply across the board.

WHAT CUSTOMERS WANT: BEYOND TECHNICAL KNOW-HOW

Probably the most significant indication that a PC technician is doing a good job is that his or her customers are consistently satisfied. You should provide excellent service and treat customers as you would want to be treated in a similar situation. One of the most important ways to achieve customer satisfaction is to do your best by being prepared, both technically and nontechnically. Being prepared includes knowing what customers want, what they don't like, and what they expect from a PC technician.

Your customers can be "internal" (you both work for the same company) or "external" (your customers come to you or your company for service). Customers can be highly technical or technically naive, represent a large company or simply own a home PC, be prompt or slow at paying their bills, want only the best (and be willing to pay for it) or be searching for bargain service, be friendly and easy to work with or demanding and condescending. In each situation, the key to success is always the same: don't allow circumstances or personalities to affect your personal commitment to excellence.

Listed below are some traits that distinguish one competent technician from another in the eyes of the customer.

- *Have a positive and helpful attitude.* A positive and helpful attitude helps to establish good customer relationships.

- *Be dependable.* Customers appreciate those who do as they say. If you promise to be back at 10:00 the next morning, be back at 10:00 the next morning. If you cannot keep your appointment, never ignore your promise. Call, apologize, let the customer know what happened, and reschedule your appointment.

- *Be customer-focused.* When you're working with or talking to a customer, focus on him or her. Make it your job to satisfy this person, not just your organization, your boss, your bank account, or the customer's boss.

- *Be credible.* Convey confidence to your customers. Being credible means being technically competent and knowing how to do your job well, but a credible technician also knows when the job is beyond his or her level of expertise and when to ask for help.

- *Maintain integrity and honesty.* Don't try to hide your mistakes, not with your customer or with your boss. Everyone makes mistakes, but don't compound them by a lack of integrity. Accept responsibility and do what you can to correct the error.

- *Know the law with respect to your work.* For instance, observe the laws concerning the use of software. Don't use or install pirated software.

- *Act professionally.* Customers want a technician to look and behave professionally. Dress appropriately for the environment. Consider yourself a guest at the customer's site.

- *Perform your work in a professional manner.* If a customer is angry, allow the customer to vent, keeping your own professional distance. (You do, however, have the right to expect a customer not to talk to you in an abusive way.)

SUPPORT CALLS: PROVIDING GOOD SERVICE

Customers want good service. Even though each customer is different and might expect different results, the following characteristics consistently constitute good service in the eyes of most customers.

- The technician responds and completes the work within a reasonable time.

- For on-site visits, the technician is prepared for the service call.

- The work is done right the first time.

- The price for the work is reasonable and competitive.

- The technician exhibits good interpersonal skills.

- If the work extends beyond a brief on-site visit or phone call, the technician keeps the customer informed about the progress of the work.

Planning for Good Service

Whether you support PCs on the phone or online, on-site, or in a shop, you need a plan to follow when you approach a service call. This section surveys the entire service situation, from the first contact with the customer to closing the call. Follow these general guidelines when supporting computers and their users:

- Almost every support project starts with a phone call. Follow company policies to obtain the specific information you should take when answering an initial call.

- Don't assume that an on-site visit is necessary until you have asked questions to identify the problem and asked the caller to check and try some simple things while on the phone with you. For example, the customer can check cable connections, power, and monitor settings, and can look for POST error messages.

- Be familiar with your company's customer service policies. You might need to refer questions about warranties, licenses, documentation, or procedures to other support personnel or customer relations personnel. Your organization might not want you to answer some questions, such as questions about upcoming releases of software or new products, or questions about your personal or company experience with supporting particular hardware or software.

- After reviewing your company's service policies, begin troubleshooting. Take notes, and then interview the customer about the problem so you understand it thoroughly. Have the customer reproduce the problem, and carefully note each step taken and its results. This process gives you clues about the problem and about the technical proficiency of the customer, which helps you know how to communicate with the customer.

- Search for answers. If the answers to specific questions or problems are not evident, become a researcher. Learn to use online documentation, expert systems, and other resources that your company provides.

- Use your troubleshooting skills. Isolate the problem. Check for user errors. What works and what doesn't work? What has changed since the system last worked? Reduce the system to its essentials. Check the simple things first. Use the troubleshooting guidelines throughout this book to help you think of approaches to test and try.

- If you have given the problem your best, but still haven't solved it, ask for help. You learn when to ask for help from experience. Once you have made a reasonable effort to help, and it seems clear that you are unlikely to be successful, don't waste a customer's time.

- After a call, create a written record to build your own knowledge base. Record the initial symptoms of the problem, the source of the problem you actually discovered, how you made that discovery, and how the problem was finally solved. File your documentation according to symptoms or according to solutions.

Making an On-Site Service Call

When a technician makes an on-site service call, customers expect him or her to have both technical and interpersonal skills. Prepare for a service call by reviewing information given you by whoever took the call. Know the problem you are going to address; what computer, software, and hardware need servicing, and the urgency of the situation. Arrive with a complete set of equipment appropriate to the visit, which might include a tool kit, flashlight, multimeter, grounding strap and mat, and bootable disks that have been scanned for viruses.

Set a realistic time for the appointment (one that you can expect to keep) and arrive on time. When you arrive at the customer's site, greet the customer in a friendly manner. Use

Mr. or Ms. and last names rather than first names when addressing the customer, unless you are certain that the customer expects you to use first names. The first thing you should do is listen; save the paperwork for later.

As you work, be as unobtrusive as possible. Don't make a big mess. Keep your tools and papers out of the customer's way. Don't use the phone or sit in the customer's desk chair without permission. If the customer needs to attend to his or her own work while you are present, do whatever is necessary to accommodate that.

Keep the customer informed. Once you have collected enough information, explain to the customer what the problem is and what you must do to fix it, giving as many details as the customer wants. When a customer must make a choice, state the customer's options in a way that does not unfairly favor the solution that makes the most money for you as the technician or for your company.

After you have solved the problem:

- Allow the customer time to be fully satisfied that all is working before you close the call. Does the printer work? Print a test page. Does the network connection work? Can the customer log on to the network and access data on it?

- If you changed anything on the PC after you booted it, reboot one more time to make sure that you have not caused a problem with the boot.

- Review the service call with the customer. Summarize the instructions and explanations you have given during the call. This is an appropriate time to fill out your paperwork and explain to the customer what you have written.

- Explain preventive maintenance to the customer (such as deleting temporary files from the hard drive or cleaning the mouse). Most customers don't have preventive maintenance contracts for their PCs and appreciate the time you take to show them how they can take better care of their computers.

Phone Support

When someone calls asking for support, you must control the call, especially at the beginning. Follow these steps at the beginning of a service call:

- Identify yourself and your organization. (Follow the guidelines of your employer as to what to say.)

- Ask for and write down the name and phone number of the caller. Ask for spelling if necessary. If your helpdesk supports businesses, get the name of the business that the caller represents.

- Your company might require that you obtain a licensing or warranty number to determine if the customer is entitled to receive your support free of charge, or that you obtain a credit card number, if the customer is paying by the call. Get whatever information you need at this point to determine that you should be the one to provide service, before you start to address the problem.

- Open up the conversation for the caller to describe his or her problem.

Providing phone support requires more interaction with customers than any other type of PC support. To give clear instructions, you must be able to visualize what the customer is seeing at his or her PC. Patience is required if the customer must be told each key to press or command button to click. Help-desk support requires excellent communication skills, good phone manners, and lots of patience. As your help-desk skills improve, you will learn to think through the process as though you were sitting in front of the PC yourself. Drawing diagrams and taking notes as you talk can be very helpful.

If you spend many hours on the phone at a help desk, use a headset instead of a regular phone to reduce strain on your ears and neck. If you are accidentally disconnected, call back immediately. Don't eat or drink while on the phone. If you must put callers on hold, tell them how long it will be before you get back to them. Don't complain about your job, your company, or other companies or products to your customers. A little small talk is okay and is sometimes beneficial in easing a tense situation, but keep it upbeat and positive. As with on-site service calls, let the user make sure that all is working before you close the phone call. If you end the call too soon and the problem is not completely resolved, the customer can be frustrated, especially if it is difficult to contact you again.

When the Customer Is Not Knowledgeable

A help-desk call is the most difficult situation to handle when a customer is not knowledgeable about how to use a computer. When on-site, you can put a PC in good repair without depending on a customer to help you, but when you are trying to solve a problem over the phone, with a customer as your only eyes, ears, and hands, a computer-illiterate user can present a very challenging situation. Here are some tips for handling this situation:

- Don't use computer jargon while talking. For example, instead of saying, "Open Windows Explorer," say, "Using your mouse, right-click on the Start button and select Explore from the menu."

- Don't ask the customer to do something that might destroy settings or files without first having him or her back them up carefully. If you think the customer can't handle what you need done, then ask for some on-site help.

- Frequently ask the customer what he or she sees on the screen to help you track the keystrokes and action.

- Follow along at your own PC. It's easier to direct the customer, keystroke by keystroke, if you are doing the same things.

- Give the customer plenty of opportunity to ask questions.

- Compliment the customer whenever you can, to help the customer gain confidence.

- If you determine that the customer cannot help you solve the problem without a lot of coaching, you may need to tactfully request that the caller have someone with more experience call you.

When solving computer problems in an organization other than your own, check with technical support instead of working only with the PC user. The user may not be aware of policies that have been set on the PC to prevent changes to the OS, hardware, or application software.

When the Customer Is Overly Confident

Sometimes a customer is proud of what he or she knows about computers. This type of customer may want to give advice, take charge of a call, withhold information that he or she thinks you don't need to know, or execute commands at the computer without letting you know, so that you don't have enough information to follow along. A situation like this must be handled with tact and respect for the customer. Here are a few tips:

- When you can, compliment the customer concerning his or her knowledge, experience, or insight.

- Ask the customer's advice. Say something like, "What do you think the problem is?" (However, don't ask this question of customers who are not confident because they most likely don't have the answer and might lose confidence in you.)

- Slow the conversation down. You can say, "Please slow down. You're moving too fast for me to follow. Help me understand."

- Don't back off from using problem-solving skills. You must still have the customer check the simple things, but direct the conversation with tact. For example, you can say, "I know you've probably already gone over these simple things, but could we just do them again together?"

- Be careful not to accuse the customer of making a mistake.

- Use technical language in a way that conveys that you expect the customer to understand you.

When the Customer Complains

When you are on-site or on the phone, a customer might complain to you about your organization, products, or service, or the service and product of another company. Consider the complaint to be helpful feedback that can lead to a better product or service and better customer relationships. Here are a few suggestions on how to handle complaints and customer anger:

- Be an active listener, and let the customer know that he or she is not being ignored. Look for the underlying problem. Don't take the complaint or the anger personally.

- Give the customer a little time to vent, and apologize when you can. Then start the conversation from the beginning, asking questions, taking notes, and solving problems. If this helps, don't spend a lot of time finding out exactly whom the customer dealt with and what exactly happened to upset him or her.

- Don't be defensive. It's better to leave the customer with the impression that you and your company are listening and willing to admit mistakes.

- If the customer is complaining about a product or service that is not from your company, don't start off by saying, "That's not our problem." Instead, listen to the customer complain. Don't appear as though you don't care.

- If the complaint is against you or your product, identify the underlying problem if you can. Ask questions and take notes. Then pass these notes on to whoever in your organization needs to know.

- Sometimes simply making progress or reducing the problem to a manageable state for the customer reduces his or her anxiety. As you are talking to a customer, summarize what you have both agreed on or observed so far in the conversation.

- Point out ways that you think communication could be improved. For example, you might say, "I'm sorry, but I'm having trouble understanding what you want. Could you please slow down, and let's take this one step at a time."

When the Customer Does Not Want to End a Phone Call

Some customers like to talk and don't want to end a phone call. In this situation, when you have finished the work and are ready to hang up, you can ease the caller into the end of the call. Ask if there is anything that needs more explanation. Briefly summarize the main points of the call, and then say something like, "That about does it. Call if you need more help." Be silent about new issues. Answer only with "yes" or "no." Don't take the bait by engaging in a new topic. Don't get frustrated. As a last resort, you can say, "I'm sorry, but I must go now."

When You Can't Solve the Problem

You are not going to solve every computer problem you encounter. Knowing how to escalate a problem to those higher in the support chain is one of the first things you should learn on a new job. When escalation involves the customer, generally follow these guidelines:

- Before you escalate, first ask knowledgeable coworkers for suggestions for solving the problem, which might save you and your customer the time and effort it takes to escalate it.

- Know your company's policy as to how to escalate. What documents do you fill out? Who gets them? Do you remain the responsible "support" party, or does the person now addressing the problem become the new contact? Are you expected to still keep in touch with the customer and the problem, or are you totally out of the picture?

- Document the escalation. It's very important to include the detailed steps necessary to reproduce the problem, which can save the next support person lots of time.

- Pass the problem on according to the proper channels of your organization. This might mean a phone call, an online entry in a database, or an e-mail message.

- Tell the customer that you are passing the problem on to someone who is more experienced and has access to more extensive resources. In most cases, the person who receives the escalation will immediately contact the customer and assume responsibility for the problem. However, you should follow through, at least to the point where you know that the new person and the customer have made contact.

- If you check back with the customer only to find out that the other support person has not called or followed through to the customer's satisfaction, don't lay blame or point fingers. Just do whatever you can to help within your company guidelines. Your call to the customer will go a long way toward helping in the situation.

RECORDKEEPING AND INFORMATION TOOLS

If you work for a service organization, it will probably have most of the tools you will need to do your job, including forms, online recordkeeping, procedures, and manuals. In some cases, help-desk support personnel may have software to help them do their jobs, such as programs that support the remote control of customers' PCs (one example is pcAnywhere), an online help utility, or a problem-solving tool developed specifically for their help desk.

There are several types of resources, records, and information tools that can help you with your work supporting PCs, such as the following:

- Specific software or hardware that you support must be available to you to test, observe, and study, and to use to re-create a customer's problem whenever possible.

- You should have a copy of—and be familiar with—the same documentation that the user sees.

- Hardware and software products generally have more technical documentation than just a user manual. This technical documentation should be made available to you by a company when you support its product.

- Online help targeted specifically to field technicians and help-desk technicians is often available for a product. This online help will probably include a search engine that works by topics, words, error messages, and the like.

- Expert systems software is designed and written to help solve problems. It uses databases of known facts and rules to simulate human experts' reasoning and decision-making processes. Expert systems for PC technicians work by posing questions about a problem, to be answered either by the technician or by the customer. The response to each question will trigger another question from the software, until the expert system arrives at a possible solution or solutions. Many expert systems are "intelligent," meaning that the system will record your input and use it in subsequent sessions to select more questions to ask and approaches to try.

- Call tracking can be done online or on paper. Most organizations will have a call-tracking system that tracks (1) the date, time, and length of help-desk or on-site calls, (2) causes of and solutions to problems already addressed, (3) who did what, and when, and (4) how each call was officially resolved. Call-tracking software or documents can also be vehicles used to escalate calls when necessary and to track the escalation.

PROFESSIONAL ORGANIZATIONS AND CERTIFICATIONS

The work done by PC technicians has been viewed as a profession only within the past few years. The one most significant certifying organization for PC technicians is the Computing Technology Industry Association (CompTIA, pronounced "comp-TEE-a"). CompTIA sponsors the A+ Certification Program, and manages the A+ Service Technician Certification Examination, which measures the knowledge of job tasks and behavior expected of entry-level technicians. To become certified, you must pass two test modules: the A+ Core Hardware exam and the A+ Operating System Technologies exam. A+ Certification has industry recognition, so it should be your first choice for certification as a PC technician. As evidence of this industry recognition, these companies now include A+ Certification in their requirements for employment:

- ENTEX Information Services requires that all service employees have A+ Certification.

- GE Capital Services requires that all service employees have A+ Certification one year after hire.

- Okidata requires that all field service technicians have A+ Certification.

- Packard Bell requires all employees to be A+ certified within 90 days of hire.

Some other organizations where A+ Certification is mandatory are Aetna U.S. Healthcare; BancTec, Inc.; Computer Data, Inc.; Computer Sciences Corp.; Delta Airlines; Dow Jones & Company; the FBI, the U.S. Department of Justice; Gateway; Tandy Corporation; TSS IBM; US Airways; and Wang.

CompTIA has over 13,000 members from which include every major company that manufactures, distributes, or publishes computer-related products and services. For more information about CompTIA and A+ Certification, see the CompTIA Web site at *www.comptia.org*.

Other certifications are more vendor-specific. For example, Microsoft, Novell, and Cisco offer certifications to use and support their products. These are excellent choices for additional certifications when your career plan is to focus on these products.

Why Certification?

Many people work as PC technicians without any formal classroom training or certification. However, by having certification or an advanced technical degree, you prove to yourself, your customers, and your employers that you are prepared to do the work and are committed to being educated in your chosen profession. Certification and advanced degrees serve as recognized proof of competence and achievement, improve your job opportunities, create a higher level of customer confidence, and often qualify you for other training and/or degrees.

In addition to becoming certified and seeking advanced degrees, the professional PC technician should also stay abreast of new technology. Helpful resources include on-the-job training, books, magazines, the Internet, trade shows, interaction with colleagues, seminars, and workshops. Probably the best-known trade show is COMDEX and Windows World, where you can view the latest technology, hear industry leaders speak, and network with vast numbers of organizations and people. For more information about COMDEX and Windows World, see the Web site *www.comdex.com*.

PROTECTING SOFTWARE COPYRIGHTS

As a computer support technician, you will be faced with the legal issues and practices surrounding the distribution of software. When someone purchases software from a software vendor, that person has only purchased a license for the software, which is the right to use the software, and does not legally *own* the software; he or she therefore does not have the right to distribute the software. The right to copy the work, called a copyright, belongs to the creator of the work or others to whom he or she has transferred this right.

As a PC technician you will be called upon to install, upgrade, and customize software. You need to know where your responsibility lies in upholding the law, especially as it applies to software copyrights. Copyrights are intended to legally protect the intellectual property rights of organizations or individuals to creative works, whether they be books, images, or, in the case of this discussion, software. While the originator of a creative work is the original owner of a copyright, the copyright can be transferred from one entity to another.

The Federal Copyright Act of 1976 was designed in part to protect software copyrights by requiring that only legally obtained copies of software be used; the law also allows for one backup copy of software to be made. Making unauthorized copies of original software violates the Federal Copyright Act of 1976, and is called software piracy, or, more officially, software copyright infringement. Making a copy of software and then selling it or giving it away is a violation of the law. Because it is so easy to do this, and because so many people do it, many people don't realize that it's illegal. Normally, only the person who violated the copyright law is liable for infringement; however, in some cases, an employer or supervisor is also held responsible, even when the copies were made without the employer's knowledge. The Business Software Alliance (a membership organization of software manufacturers and vendors) has estimated that 26 percent of the business software in the United States is obtained illegally.

Site licensing, whereby a company can purchase the right to use multiple copies of software, is a popular way for companies to provide software to employees. With this type of license, companies can distribute software to PCs from network servers or execute software directly off the server. Read the licensing agreement of any software to determine the terms of distribution.

One of two associations committed to the prevention of software piracy is the Software Information Industry Association, a nonprofit organization that educates the public and enforces copyright laws. Their Web address is *www.siia.net*, and their antipiracy hotline is 1-800-388-7478. Another organization is the Business Software Alliance, which manages the BSA Anti-Piracy Hotline at 1-888-NOPIRACY. The BSA can also be reached at their e-mail address: software@bsa.org. Their Web site is *www.bsa.org*. These associations are made up of hundreds of software manufacturers and publishers in North and Latin America, Europe, and Asia. They promote software raids on large and small companies, and, in the United States, they receive the cooperation of the U.S. government to prosecute offenders.

What Does the Law Say?

The Federal Copyright Act of 1976 protects the exclusive rights of copyright holders. It gives legal users of software the right to make one backup copy. Other rights are based on what the copyright holder allows. In 1990, the United States Congress passed the Software Rental Amendment Act, which prevents the renting, leasing, lending, or sharing of software without the expressed written permission of the copyright holder. In 1992, Congress instituted criminal penalties for software copyright infringement, which include imprisonment for up to five years and/or fines of up to $250,000 for the unlawful reproduction or distribution of 10 or more copies of software.

What Are Your Responsibilities Under the Law?

Your first responsibility as an individual user is to use only software that has been purchased or licensed for your use. As an employee of a company that has a site license to use multiple copies of the software, your responsibility is to comply with the license agreement. It is also your responsibility to purchase only legitimate software. Purchasers of counterfeit or copied software face the risk of corrupted files, virus-infected disks, inadequate documentation, and lack of technical support and upgrades, as well as the legal penalties for using pirated software.

E

INTRODUCING LINUX

Unix is a popular OS used to control networks and to support applications used on the Internet. A variation of Unix is Linux (pronounced "Lih-nucks"), an OS originally created by Linus Torvalds when he was a student at the University of Helsinki in Finland. Basic versions of this OS are available for free, and all the underlying programming instructions (called source code) are also freely distributed. Like Unix, Linux is distributed by several different companies, whose versions of Linux are sometimes called distributions. Popular distributions of Linux are shown in Table E-1. Linux can be used both as a server platform and a desktop platform, but its greatest popularity has come in the server market. Hardware requirements for Linux vary widely, depending on the distribution and version installed.

Table E-1 Popular Linux distributions

Name	Comments	Web site
Red Hat Linux	The most widely used distribution in the world, from Red Hat Software	www.redhat.com
OpenLinux	Produced by The SCO Group (formerly Caldera International). Aimed at business users	www.sco.com
UnitedLinux	A Linux distribution created by multiple Linux vendors as a common base product on which numerous Linux applications can be designed to run	www.unitedlinux.com
TurboLinux	Focused on providing high-end, specialized server software to businesses	www.turbolinux.com
Mandrake	Built on Red Hat Linux with many additional packages. Popular at retail outlets	www.mandrakelinux.com
Stampede	A distribution optimized for speed	www.stampede.org
Debian	A noncommercial Linux distribution targeted specifically to free software enthusiasts. Debian does not have a company behind it. It is created and maintained by developers of free software.	www.debian.org
SuSE	The leading German distribution. Increasingly popular in the United States	www.SuSE.com
Yellow Dog Linux	A version of Linux for Macintosh computers, written for the PowerPC processor	www.yellowdoglinux.com

For more information on Linux, see *www.linux.org* as well as the Web sites of the different distributors of Linux.

Some of the advantages and disadvantages of Linux are:

- Linux rarely crashes.

- Basic versions can be downloaded and installed free of charge.

- Linux distributions that include technical support and software packages are available at a lower cost than other operating systems.

- Linux has strong features for handling network connections.

- Source code is available to users, enabling customization of the development environment.

- Linux on an inexpensive PC is an excellent training tool for learning Unix.

- Linux can be difficult to install, particularly for users who are not familiar with Unix commands.

- Most distributions of Linux run from a command line, which can be difficult for casual users to operate.

- Documentation can be spotty.

- Optimizing a Linux system can take a significant investment of time and research.

- Not as many desktop applications are available for Linux as for Windows, though a Windows-like office suite (Star Office) can be installed.

Network services such as a Web server or e-mail server often are provided by a computer running the Linux operating system. Linux is well suited to support various types of servers. Because Linux is very reliable and does not require a lot of computing power, it is sometimes used as a desktop OS, although it is not as popular for this purpose because it is not easy to use.

As a PC support technician, you should know a little about Linux, including a few basic commands, which are covered in this appendix. You will learn about root and user accounts, file structure, some common commands, and how to use the vi editor. The material in this section is meant as a general introduction to the OS. The organization of files and folders, the desktop's appearance, and the way each command works might be slightly different with the distribution and version of Linux you are using.

Root Account and User Accounts

Recall that an operating system is composed of a kernel, which interacts with the hardware and other software, and a shell, which interacts with the user and the kernel. Linux is a Unix-like operating system, and, just as with other versions of Unix, can use more than one shell. The default shell for Linux is the Bash shell. The name stands for "Bourne Again Shell" and takes the best features from two previous shells, the Bourne and the Korn shells.

For a Linux or Unix server, the system administrator is the person who installs updates to the OS (called patches), manages backup processes, supports the installation of software and hardware, sets up user accounts, resets passwords, and generally supports users. The system administrator has root privileges, which means that he or she can access all the functions of the OS and the principal user account is called the root account. The administrator protects the password to the root account because this password gives full access to the system. When the administrator is logged on, he or she is logged on as the user root. You can use the *who* command to show a list of all users currently logged on to the system. In the example shown below, typing *who* shows that three users are currently logged on: the root user, james, and susan.

```
who
root      tty1   Oct  12  07:56
james     tty1   Oct  12  08:35
susan     tty1   Oct  12  10:05
```

The Linux command prompt for the root user is different from the command prompt for ordinary users. The root command prompt is #, and other users have the $ command prompt.

Directory and File Layout

The main directory in Unix and Linux is the root directory and is indicated with a forward slash. (In Unix and Linux, directories in a path are separated with forward slashes, in contrast to the backward slashes used by DOS and Windows.) Use the *ls* command, which is similar to the DOS Dir command, to list the contents of the root directory. The command (*ls -l /*) and its results are shown in Figure E-1. Notice that the *-l* parameter is added to the command, which displays the results using the long format, and that there are spaces included before and after the parameters of the command. Also notice in the figure the format used to display the directory contents. The *d* at the beginning of each entry indicates that the entry is a directory, not a file. The other letters in this first column have to do with the read and write privileges assigned to the directory and the right to execute programs in the directory. The name of the directory is in the last column. The rights assigned the directory can apply to the owner of the directory, to other users, or to an entire group of users.

Table E-2 lists directories that are created in the root directory during a typical Linux installation. The actual list of directories for a Linux computer that you work with may be a little different, because the directories created in the root directory depend on what programs have been installed.

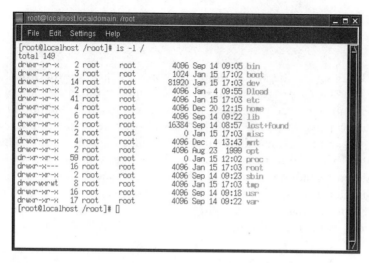

Figure E-1   A directory listing using the ls command

Table E-2   Directories in a typical Linux root directory

Directory	Description
/bin	Contains programs and commands necessary to boot the system and perform other system tasks not reserved for the administrator, such as shutdown and reboot
/boot	Consists of components needed for the boot process, such as boot loaders
/dev	Holds device names, which consist of the type of device and a number identifying the device. Actual device drivers are located in the /lib/modules /[kernel version]/ directory.
/etc	Contains system configuration data, including configuration files and settings and their subdirectories. These files are used for tasks such as configuring a user account, changing system settings, and configuring a domain name resolution service.
/home	Contains user data. Every user on the system has a directory in the /home directory, such as /home/jean or /home/scott, and when a user logs on, that directory becomes the current working directory.
/lib	Stores common libraries used by applications so that more than one application can use the same library at one time. An example is the library of C programming code, without which only the kernel of the Linux system could run.
/lost+found	Stores data that is lost when files are truncated or when an attempt to fix system errors is unsuccessful
/opt	Contains installations of third-party applications such as Web browsers that do not come with the Linux OS distribution
/root	The home directory for the root user; contains only files specific to the root user. Do not confuse this directory with the root directory, which contains all the directories listed in this table.

Table E-2   Directories in a typical Linux root directory (continued)

Directory	Description
/sbin	Stores commands required for system administration.
/tmp	Stores temporary files, such as the ones that applications use during installation and operation.
/usr	Constitutes the major section of the Linux file system and contains read-only data.
/var	Holds variable data such as e-mail, news, print spools, and administrative files.

E

Linux Commands

This section describes some basic Linux and Unix commands, together with simple examples of how some are used. As you read along, be aware that all commands entered in Linux or Unix are case sensitive, meaning that uppercase and lowercase matter. Table E-3 shows some common commands for Linux and Unix. This is not meant to be a comprehensive list of commands but simply to list some that might be useful to you in working with files, directories, network connections, and system configuration. In the rest of the section, you will learn how to use a few common commands. For all of these procedures, assume that you are in your home directory (which would be /home/<*yourname*>/).

Table E-3   Some common Linux and Unix commands

Command	Description
cat	Lets you view the contents of a file. Many Linux commands can use the redirection symbol > to redirect the output of the command. For example, use the redirection symbol with the cat command to copy a file: `cat /etc/shells > newfile` The contents of the shells file are written to newfile.
cd	Change directory. For example, `cd /etc` changes the directory to /etc.
chmod	This command changes the attributes assigned to a file and is similar to the DOS Attrib command. For example, to grant read permission to the file myfile: `chmod +r myfile`
clear	Clears the screen. This command is useful when the screen has become cluttered with commands and data that you no longer need to view.
cp	Used to copy a file: `cp <source> <destination>`
date	Entered alone, this command displays the current system date setting. Entered in the format `date <mmddhhmmyy>`, this command sets the system date. For example, to set the date to Dec 25, 2003 at 11:59 in the evening: `Date 1225235903`
echo	Displays information on the screen. For example, to display which shell is currently being used, enter this command: `echo $SHELL`
fdisk	Creates or makes changes to a hard drive partition table: `fdisk <hard drive>`

Table E-3   Some common Linux and Unix commands (continued)

Command	Description
grep	Searches for a specific pattern in a file or in multiple files: `grep <pattern> <file>`
hostname	Displays a server's FQDN: `hostname`
ifconfig	Used to troubleshoot problems with network connections under TCP/IP. This command can disable and enable network cards and release and renew the IP addresses assigned to these cards. For example, to show all configuration information: `ifconfig -a` To release the given IP address for a TCP/IP connection named eth0 (the first Ethernet connection of the system): `ifconfig eth0 -168.92.1.1`
kill	Kills a process instead of waiting for the process to terminate: `kill <process ID>`
ls	The ls command is similar to the DOS Dir command, which displays a list of directories and files. For example, to list all files in the /etc directory, using the long parameter for a complete listing: `ls -l /etc`
man	Displays the online help manual called man pages. For example, to get information about the echo command: `man echo` The manual program displays information about the command. To exit the manual program, type q.
mkdir	This command makes a new directory: `mkdir <directory>`
|more	Appended to a command to display the results of the command on the screen one page at a time. For example, to page the ls command: `ls |more`
mv	Moves a file or renames it, if the source and destination are the same directory: `mv <source> <destination>`
netstat	Shows statistics and status information for network connections and routing tables: `netstat`
nslookup	Queries domain name servers to look up domain names: `nslookup`
ping	Used to test network connections by sending a request packet to a host. If a connection is successful, the host will return a response packet. `ping <host>`
ps	Displays the process table so that you can identify process IDs for currently running processes (once you know the process ID, you can use the `kill` command to terminate a process): `ps`
pwd	Shows the name of the present working directory: `pwd`
reboot	Reboots the system: `reboot`
rm	Removes the file or files that are specified: `rm <file>`
rmdir	This command removes a directory: `rmdir <directory>`
route	Entered alone, this command shows the current configuration of the IP routing table. Entered in the format `route [options]`, it configures the IP routing table.
traceroute	Shows the route of IP packets; used for debugging connections on a network: `traceroute <host>`
useradd	Adds a user to a system: `useradd [option] <user>`

Table E-3   Some common Linux and Unix commands (continued)

Command	Description
userdel	Removes a user from a system: `userdel <user>`
vi	Launches a full-screen editor that can be used to enter text and commands: `vi <file>`
whatis	Displays a brief overview of a command. For example, to get quick information about the `echo` command: `whatis echo`
who	Displays a list of users currently logged in: `who`

Editing Commands

When you add options and file or directory names to a command, it can get quite long, and if you make a mistake while typing the command, you will want to edit it. Also, once the command has been entered, you can retrieve it, edit it, and press Enter to reissue the command. Some shells allow you to use the arrow, Backspace, Insert, and Delete keys to edit command lines, and other shells do not allow you to use these keys. Instead, use the following keystrokes to edit a command line:

- Alt+D   Delete a word
- Ctrl+K   Delete from the current position to the end of the line
- Ctrl+A   Move the cursor to the beginning of the command line
- Alt+B   Move the cursor left one word
- Alt+F   Move the cursor right one word

For example, follow these steps to edit a command line:

1. Type **who is this** but DO NOT press Enter.
2. To move one word to the left, press **Alt+B** so that your cursor is positioned on the word "is."
3. To delete the word "is," press **Alt+D**.
4. To delete the portion of the command line that follows the current cursor position, press **Ctrl+K**.
5. To move the cursor to the beginning of the command line, press **Ctrl+A**.

Viewing the Shells File

The shells file in the /etc directory contains a list of available shells to use on a Linux system. Each shell incorporates slightly different support for programming and scripting languages. Additionally, different Linux shells may use keystrokes other than the ones you just learned in supporting command line editing; the keystrokes in the procedure in the last section work in Bash, the default Linux shell. To determine whether you are using the Bash shell, type `echo $shell` and press Enter. If you see the output /bin/bash, you are using the Bash shell. If you are not using the Bash shell, type `bash` and press Enter to change to the Bash shell.

To view a list of available shells:

1. Type **cat /etc/shells**, and then press **Enter**.

2. A list of available shells appears. This list may include the entries /bin/bash, /bin/bsh, /bin/csh, /bin/sh, /bin/tcsh, and /bin/zsh. Notice that all these shells are stored in the /bin directory. Type **clear**, and then press **Enter** to clear the screen.

3. Type **cat –n /etc/shells**, and then press **Enter**. Notice that this time, the same list of shells is displayed with a number before each line because you used the –n option. (See Figure E-2.) Notice in the figure that the current user is root.

Redirecting Output

Recall the list of available shells that you created using the **cat** command. When you entered the command **cat /etc/shells**, the list, which is the output of that command, was sent to the screen. What if you wanted to save that list? You would use the **redirection symbol**, which is the greater-than (>) sign, to direct the output to a file, perhaps with the name available_shells. Use these steps:

1. Go to the root directory by typing **cd /** and pressing **Enter**.

2. Type **cat /etc/shells > available_shells**, and then press **Enter**.

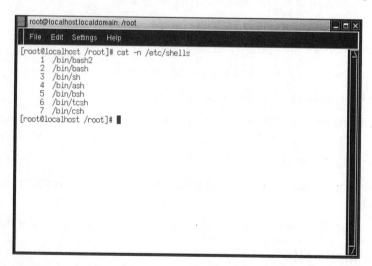

Figure E-2   Use the cat command to display a list of shells

3. Notice that no command output appears on the screen, because the output has been saved to the new file available_shells (the file is created when the command is entered). To view the contents of the file, type **cat available_shells**, and then press **Enter**.

The file was created in the current directory which is the root directory.

Creating a Directory

It is not a good idea to store data files in the root directory, so let's create a new directory to which to move the new file available_shells:

1. Type **mkdir myfiles**, and then press **Enter**. This creates a new directory named myfiles under the current directory, which is root.

2. Type **cd myfiles** to change from the current directory to the new directory.

3. Type **mv /available_shells .** and then press **Enter** (don't overlook the period at the end of the command line; type it, too). This copies the file from the root directory to the current directory, which is /myfiles. The source directory is the root and the destination directory is /myfiles. The period in a command line means the current directory.

4. Type **ls** to see the contents of the myfiles directory. The available_shells file is listed. (See Figure E-3.)

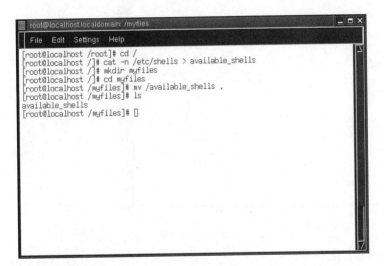

Figure E-3   Creating and moving files to a directory

Using the vi Editor

You were introduced to the vi command in Table E-3 earlier in the appendix. This command launches the vi editor, which got its name because it is a visual editor that was, at one time, the most popular Unix text editor. It is still used with shells that don't allow the use of the arrow, Delete, or Backspace keys. The editor can be used in insert mode, in which you can enter text, or command mode, which allows you to enter commands to perform editing tasks to move through the file. In this section, you will learn how to create and use commands on a text file in the vi editor. All of these commands are case sensitive.

Let's create and work with a file called mymemo.

1. To open the vi editor and create a file at the same time, type the command followed by the filename, as follows: **vi mymemo**

2. The vi editor screen is shown in Figure E-4. Notice that the filename is shown at the bottom of the screen and that the cursor is at the top of the screen.

3. At this point, when you first open the vi editor, you are in command mode, which means that anything you type will be interpreted as a command by the vi editor. Type **i** to switch to insert mode. You will not see the command on the screen, and you do not need to press Enter to execute it. The command automatically switches you to insert mode. When you are in insert mode, the word INSERT will be shown at the bottom of the screen.

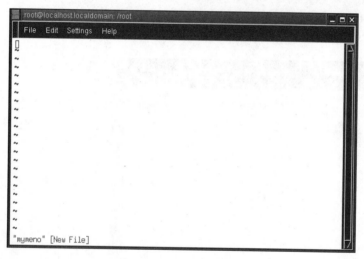

Figure E-4   The vi text editor

4. Type the first two sentences of Step 3 as the text for your memo. If your shell supports it, practice using the arrow keys to move the cursor through the text, up, down, left, and right, one character at a time. You will see the keystrokes used to perform the same movements in Table E-4; they can be used if the arrow keys are not supported.

5. To switch back to command mode, press the **Esc** key. Now you are ready to enter commands to manipulate your text. Type **H** to move the cursor to the upper-left corner of the screen. You must use an uppercase H, because all these commands are case sensitive.

6. Type **w** repeatedly until you reach the beginning of the word "first."

7. Type **dw** to delete the word "first." To delete one character at a time, you would use x; to delete an entire line, you would use dd.

8. To save the file and exit the vi editor, type **:x** and press **Enter**. This will save the file and close the editor.

Table E-4 lists the vi editor commands to move the cursor. There are many more commands to manipulate text, set options, cancel, or temporarily leave a vi editor session. For a more complete list of vi editor commands, see a reference dedicated to Linux.

Window Managers

Because many users prefer a Windows-style desktop, several applications have been written to provide a GUI for Unix and Linux. These GUIs are called window managers. One popular desktop environment software is GNU Network Object Model Environment (GNOME). GNOME (pronounced "guh-nome") provides a desktop that looks and feels like Windows 98, but is free software designed to use a Linux kernel. The major components of a GNOME window are shown in Figure E-5. For more information about GNOME, see the organization's Web site at *www.gnome.org*. Another popular Linux window manager is the KDE Desktop (*www.kde.org*).

Table E-4   vi editor commands

Command	Alternate	Description
Ctrl+B	Pg up	Back one screen
Ctrl+F	Pg down	Forward one screen
Ctrl+U	--	Up half a screen
Ctrl+D	--	Down half a screen
k	Up arrow	Up one line
j	Down arrow	Down one line
h	Left arrow	Left one character
l	Right arrow	Right one character
W	--	Forward one word
B	--	Back one word
0 (zero)	--	Beginning of the current line
$	--	End of current line
NG	--	Line specified by number *n*
H	--	Upper-left corner of screen
L	--	Last line on the screen

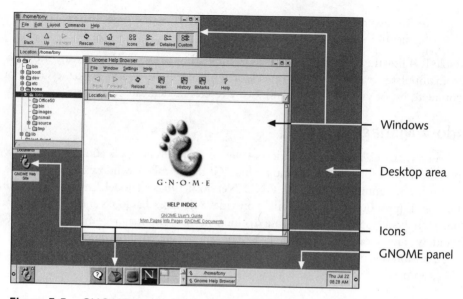

Figure E-5 GNOME is popular desktop environment software used on Linux systems

F

ANSWERS TO CHAPTER REVIEW QUESTIONS

CHAPTER 1

1. Input, Process, Storage, Output
2. c
3. b
4. d
5. c
6. d
7. b
8. c
9. c
10. b
11. d
12. c
13. a
14. b
15. a
16. e
17. c
18. d
19. c
20. d
21. e
22. d

23. a

24. b

25. c

26. c

27. d

28. a

CHAPTER 2

1. b

2. b

3. a

4. c

5. c

6. a

7. d

8. b

9. Device Drivers, System BIOS

10. b

11. a

12. c

13. e

14. e

15. d

16. c

17. b

18. d

19. a

20. b

21. d

22. b

23. b

24. d

25. a

26. b

27. b

28. c

29. b

30. b

31. a

32. b

33. a

34. a. Shortcut on the desktop

   b. Click Start-Programs-*select program*

   c. Use the Run command

   d. Launch the application file by double-clicking the file name in Windows Explorer or the My Computer window.

Chapter 3

1. c

2. b

3. b

4. d

5. d

6. d

7. b

8. b

9. directory table, root directory

10. a

11. b

12. b

13. b

F

14. b

15. b

16. a

17. d

18. c

19. b

20. a

21. d

22. c

23. d

24. c

25. e

26. b

27. Click "Start," then "Settings," then "Control Panel." Once in the "Control Panel," double-click the "Add/Remove Programs" icon. Click the "Startup Disk" tab and then the "Create Disk" button. The Windows CD might need to be available.

28. a

29. b

30. c

CHAPTER 4

1. AT- and ATX-class power supplies

   The AT-class power supply uses two connectors: P8 and P9.

   The ATX-class power supply uses one connector: P1.

2. Yellow: +12VDC

   Blue: −12VDC

   Red: +5VDC

   White: −5VDC

   Black: Ground

3. Molex connectors are the larger, more commonly used connector, and are typically used for devices such as 5 ¼-inch floppy disk drives, hard disk drives, CD/DVD-ROM drives, and tape drives. The mini-connector is significantly smaller than the Molex connector, and is typically used for devices such as 3 ½-inch floppy disk drives.

4. Each Molex connector provides two voltages to peripheral devices, whether both voltages are utilized or not. The red and black wire pair bring +5V to the peripheral device, which is connected to the Molex connector and typically powers the devices' digital logic by way of the circuit board. The yellow and black wire pair bring +12V to the peripheral device, which is connected to the Molex connector and typically powers motors used in disk drives and can also power cooling fans.

5. A spike is typically characterized by a sudden or abrupt change in voltage, where the voltage on a wire is one level at one point in time, suddenly changes to some higher level almost instantaneously, then returns back to the original voltage prior to the voltage spike. A surge is characterized by a change in voltage, typically higher than normal, for a more sustained length of time before returning to proper voltage levels. A sag refers to a condition where the voltage on a wire drops below acceptable tolerances for any length of time.

   Devices such as power conditioners and uninterruptible power supplies (UPSs) are used to treat the power *prior* to entering a device. (Oftentimes, UPSs contain some form of power conditioner so the purchase of an additional power conditioner is not necessary.)

6. Time. The UPS not only needs to be sized to ensure proper power ratings, but it also needs to be sized according to time requirements. It is important to understand that the UPS be allowed to remain on providing power for some length of time, determined by the technician specifying the UPS. So the two factors for UPS sizing are supplied power and the length of time to be able to supply that power.

7. a. The AT-class power supply provides four voltages to peripheral devices: +5V, −5V, +12V, and −12V. It is the ATX-class power supply that also includes a +3.3V supply in addition to those offered by the AT-class power supply.

8. 810 watts

9. b

10. c

11. d

12. c

13. c

14. b

15. a

16. b

17. a

18. c

19. a

20. b

CHAPTER 5

1. a

2. a

3. c

4. c

5. wait state

6. c

7. a

8. d

9. c

10. b

11. Word size is referred to as the internal data path size, i.e., the largest number of bits the CPU can process in once operation.

12. c

13. a

14. c

15. d

16. a

17. c

18. c

19. a

20. b

21. d

22. b

23. b

24. b

25. c

26. a

27. b

28. a

F

CHAPTER 6

1. d

2. a

3. b

4. a

5. b

6. e

7. b

8. a

9. a

10. a

11. a

12. a

13. b

14. c

15. d

16. c

17. a

18. b

CHAPTER 7

1. c

2. a

3. a

4. b

5. a

6. b

7. a

8. b

9. b

10. b

Chapter 8

1. d

2. b

3. b

4. e

5. a

6. e

7. b

8. a

9. c

10. b

11. b

12. d

13. c

14. b

15. a

16. b

17. b

18. d

19. b

20. a

21. d

22. a

23. c

24. c

25. a

CHAPTER 9

1. d

2. a

3. b

4. b

5. c

6. c

7. b

8. a

9. b

10. d

11. a

12. e

13. b

14. c

15. e

16. c

17. a

18. e

19. b

20. d

CHAPTER 10

1. a. Installing the device

   b. Installing the device drive specific to the device

   c. Installing the application software

2. b

3. d

4. a. Backup your hard drive.

   b. Protect the PC from ESD by using an antistatic bracelet or ground mat.

5. e

6. d

7. Default Port Assignments:

Port	IRQ	I/O Address	Port Type
COM1	4	03F8-03FF	Serial
COM3	4	03E8-03EF	Serial
LPT1	7	0378-037F	Parallel

8. b

9. c

10. a

11. a. Standard Parallel Port (SPP)

    b. Enhanced Parallel Port (EPP)

    c. Extended Capabilities Port (ECP)

12. a. Enhanced Parallel Port (EPP)

    b. Extended Capabilities Port (ECP)

13. Extended Capabilities Port (ECP)

14. d

15. d

16. c

17. d

18. d

19. b

20. b

21. Active Matrix

CHAPTER 11

1. b
2. b
3. b
4. d
5. e (the answer is 256 samples or 2^8)
6. b
7. a. CompactFlash

   b. SmartMedia

   c. ScanDisk

   d. Sony Memory Sticks
8. d
9. e
10. e
11. e
12. d
13. c
14. c
15. d
16. b
17. c

CHAPTER 12

1. e
2. b
3. a
4. d
5. b
6. c
7. a

F

8. d

9. e

10. d

11. a

12. c

13. ATTRIB –r –h –s

14. b

15. d

16. a. The System BIOS must be PnP-compliant.

   b. All hardware devices and expansion cards must be PnP-compliant.

   c. The operating system must be PnP-compliant.

   d. 32-bit device drivers must be available either from the manufacturer or the operating system.

17. a. The System Registry

   b. Config.sys

   c. Autoexec.bat

   d. Win.ini

   e. System.ini

18. b

19. b

20. b

21. e

22. a

23. e (the answer is Swap File)

24. c

25. a. BIOS POST and Bootstrap

   b. Loading of the operating system

   c. Loading of the Virtual Device Drivers (VxDs)

   d. Protected Mode Switchover and PnP Configuration

   e. Loading of the remaining operating system components

CHAPTER 13

1. a. Windows 2000 Professional

   b. Windows 2000 Server

   c. Windows 2000 Advanced Server

   d. Windows 2000 Datacenter Server

2. user, kernel

3. user

4. kernel

5. a

6. a

7. d

8. a

9. c

10. d

11. the Hardware Abstraction Layer (HAL); Executive Services

12. Executive Services

13. c

14. d

15. b

16. d

17. a

18. b

19. d

20. a

21. b

22. a

23. b

24. a

25. c

F

CHAPTER 14

1. a

2. a

3. d

4. d

5. c

6. e

7. d

8. d

9. b

10. b

11. a. Information events

b. Warning events

c. Error events

12. d

13. d

CHAPTER 15

1. a

2. c

3. c

4. e

5. b

6. a

7. a

8. a

9. c

10. d

11. e

CHAPTER 16

1. a
2. b
3. b
4. d
5. c
6. c
7. b
8. d
9. c
10. e
11. b

CHAPTER 17

1. b
2. a
3. b
4. d
5. c
6. b
7. a
8. d
9. d
10. b
11. e
12. c
13. c
14. c
15. a

F

16. c

17. b

18. c

19. d

CHAPTER 18

1. b

2. a

3. c

4. e

5. c

6. a

7. d

8. a

9. c

10. b

11. d

12. a

13. c

14. d

15. b

16. e

17. b

18. c

19. d

20. a

21. c

22. c

23. c

24. a

F

25. c

26. a

27. b

28. b

29. b

30. b

31. a

32. b

33. c

34. a

35. b

36. d

37. b

CHAPTER 19

1. b

2. b

3. c

4. e

5. d

6. b

7. c

8. b

9. c

10. e

11. b

12. b

13. d

14. c

15. a

16. d

17. b

18. e

19. a

20. d

CHAPTER 20

1. b

2. b

3. d

4. e

5. b

6. d

7. c

8. c

9. b

10. c

CHAPTER 21

1. b

2. b

3. d

4. a

5. e

6. a

7. b

8. d

9. b

10. a

11. b

12. b

13. b

CHAPTER 22

1. b

2. a

3. a

4. b

5. d

6. b

7. b

8. c

9. a

10. a

11. d

12. e

13. b

14. b

15. b

CHAPTER 23

1. c

2. e

3. d

4. b

5. a

6. c

7. a

8. e

9. e

10. c

11. a

12. b

13. a

CHAPTER 24

1. a

2. a

3. b

4. d

5. d

6. c

7. b

8. c

9. e

10. d

11. c

G

WHAT'S ON THE CD

CertBlaster® software combines knowledge assessment with personalized study recommendations and challenging adaptive testing to help prepare you for the CompTia A+ Certification exam. CertBlaster self-test software helps prepare you for certification through its exclusive Assessment, Recommendation, and Testing™ technology.

Features:

- Personalized recommendation technology builds custom study plans for you.

- Special Focus Drills of missed questions isolate the topics you still need to learn.

- Flexible study modes let you practice with or without hints, references, and notes.

- Realistic certification mode with countdown and randomly composed exams are fresh and challenging every time.

HOW TO USE THE CD

The CD has an Auto-run feature that will work with most computers. Place the CD in your optical drive tray, and the Auto-run should open to the Premier License agreement. If you do not have the capability to Auto-run, select your optical drive in the My Computer directory. Click on Start_Here.exe to start the application.

If you agree to the Terms and Conditions, the installation screen will open. You must select the button in the center of the screen to install the application mentioned above.

GLOSSARY

100BaseT — An Ethernet standard that operates at 100 Mbps and uses STP cabling. Also called Fast Ethernet. Variations of 100BaseT are 100BaseTX and 100BaseFX.

10Base2 — An Ethernet standard that operates at 10 Mbps and uses small coaxial cable up to 200 meters long. Also called ThinNet.

10Base5 — An Ethernet standard that operates at 10 Mbps and uses thick coaxial cable up to 500 meters long. Also called ThickNet.

32-bit flat memory mode — A protected processing mode used by Windows NT/2000/XP to process programs written in 32-bit code early in the boot process.

3-D RAM — Special video RAM designed to improve 3-D graphics simulation.

80 conductor IDE cable — An IDE cable that has 40 pins but uses 80 wires, 40 of which are ground wires designed to reduce crosstalk on the cable. The cable is used by ATA/66, ATA/100, and ATA/133 IDE drives.

802.11b — *See* IEEE 802.11b.

access point (AP) — A device connected to a LAN that provides wireless communication so that computers, printers, and other wireless devices can communicate with devices on the LAN.

ACPI (Advanced Configuration and Power Interface) — Specification developed by Intel, Compaq, Phoenix, Microsoft, and Toshiba to control power on notebooks and other devices. Windows 98 and Windows 2000/XP support ACPI.

active backplane — A type of backplane system in which there is some circuitry, including bus connectors, buffers, and driver circuits, on the backplane.

Active Directory — A Windows 2000 and Windows .NET directory database service that allows for a single point of administration for all shared resources on a network, including files, peripheral devices, databases, Web sites, users, and services.

active matrix — A type of video display that amplifies the signal at every intersection in the grid of electrodes, which enhances the pixel quality over that of a dual-scan passive matrix display.

active partition — The primary partition on the hard drive that boots the OS. Windows NT/2000/XP calls the active partition the system partition.

active terminator — A type of terminator for single-ended SCSI cables that includes voltage regulators in addition to the simple resistors used with passive termination.

adapter address — *See* MAC address.

adapter card — A small circuit board inserted in an expansion slot and used to communicate between the system bus and a peripheral device. Also called an interface card.

administrator account — In Windows NT/2000/XP, an account that grants to the administrator(s) rights and permissions to all hardware and software resources, such as the right to add, delete, and change accounts and to change hardware configurations.

Advanced Options menu — A Windows 2000/XP menu that appears when you press F8 when Windows starts. The menu can be used to troubleshoot problems when loading Windows 2000/XP.

Advanced SCSI Programming Interface (ASPI) — A popular device driver that enables operating systems to communicate with a SCSI host adapter. (The "A" originally stood for Adaptec.)

Advanced Transfer Cache (ATC) — A type of L2 cache contained within the Pentium processor housing that is embedded on the same core processor die as the CPU itself.

AirPort — The term Apple computers use to describe the IEEE 802.11b standard.

alternating current (AC) — Current that cycles back and forth rather than traveling in only one direction. In the United States, the AC voltage from a standard wall outlet is normally between 110 and 115 V. In Europe, the standard AC voltage from a wall outlet is 220 V.

ammeter — A meter that measures electrical current in amps.

ampere or **amp (A)** — A unit of measurement for electrical current. One volt across a resistance of one ohm will produce a flow of one amp.

amplifier repeater — A repeater that does not distinguish between noise and signal; it amplifies both.

ANSI (American National Standards Institute) — A nonprofit organization dedicated to creating trade and communications standards.

answer file — A text file that contains information that Windows NT/2000/XP requires in order to do an unattended installation.

antivirus (AV) software — Utility programs that prevent infection or scan a system to detect and remove viruses. McAfee Associates' VirusScan and Norton AntiVirus are two popular AV packages.

application program interface (API) call — A request from software to the OS to access hardware or other software using a previously defined procedure that both the software and the OS understand.

ARP (Address Resolution Protocol) — A protocol that TCP/IP uses to translate IP addresses into physical network addresses (MAC addresses).

ASCII (American Standard Code for Information Interchange) — A popular standard for writing letters and other characters in binary code. Originally, ASCII characters were seven bits, so there were 127 possible values. ASCII has been expanded to an 8-bit version, allowing 128 additional values.

asynchronous SRAM — Static RAM that does not work in step with the CPU clock and is, therefore, slower than synchronous SRAM.

AT — A form factor, generally no longer produced, in which the motherboard requires a full-size case. Because of their dimensions and configuration, AT systems are difficult to install, service, and upgrade. Also called full AT.

AT command set — A set of commands that a PC uses to control a modem and that a user can enter to troubleshoot the modem.

ATAPI (Advanced Technology Attachment Packet Interface) — An interface standard, part of the IDE/ATA standards, that allows tape drives, CD-ROM drives, and other drives to be treated like an IDE hard drive by the system.

attenuation — Signal degeneration over distance. Attenuation is solved on a network by adding repeaters to the network.

ATX — The most common form factor for PC systems presently in use, originally introduced by Intel in 1995. ATX motherboards and cases make better use of space and resources than did the AT form factor.

audio/modem riser (AMR) — A specification for a small slot on a motherboard to accommodate an audio or modem riser card. A controller on the motherboard contains some of the logic for the audio or modem functionality.

autodetection — A feature on newer system BIOS and hard drives that automatically identifies and configures a new drive in the CMOS setup.

Autoexec.bat — A startup text file once used by DOS and used by Windows to provide backward-compatibility. It executes commands automatically during the boot process and is used to create a 16-bit environment.

Automated System Recovery (ASR) — The Windows XP process that allows you to restore an entire hard drive volume or logical drive to its state at the time the backup of the volume was made.

autorange meter — A multimeter that senses the quantity of input and sets the range accordingly.

Baby AT — An improved and more flexible version of the AT form factor. Baby AT was the industry standard from approximately 1993 to 1997 and can fit into some ATX cases.

back side bus — The bus between the CPU and the L2 cache inside the CPU housing.

backplane system — A form factor in which there is no true motherboard. Instead, motherboard components are included on an adapter card plugged into a slot on a board called the backplane.

backup — An extra copy of a file, used in the event that the original becomes damaged or destroyed.

backup domain controller (BDC) — In Windows NT, a computer on a network that holds a read-only copy of the SAM (security accounts manager) database.

Backup Operator — A Windows 2000/XP user account that can back up and restore any files on the system regardless of its having access to these files.

bandwidth — In relation to analog communication, the range of frequencies that a communications channel or cable can carry. In general use, the term refers to the volume of data that can travel on a bus or over a cable stated in bits per second (bps), kilobits per second (Kbps), or megabits per second (Mbps). Also called data throughput or line speed.

bank — An area on the motherboard that contains slots for memory modules (typically labeled bank 0, 1, 2, and 3).

baseline — The level of performance expected from a system, which can be compared to current measurements to determine what needs upgrading or tuning.

basic disk — A way to partition a hard drive, used by DOS and all versions of Windows, that stores information about the drive in a partition table at the beginning of the drive. Compare to dynamic disk.

batch file — A text file containing a series of OS commands. Autoexec.bat is a batch file.

baud rate — A measure of line speed between two devices such as a computer and a printer or a modem. This speed is measured in the number of times a signal changes in one second. *See also* bits per second (bps).

beam detect mirror — Detects the initial presence of a laser printer's laser beam by reflecting the beam to an optical fiber.

best-effort protocol — *See* connectionless protocol.

binary number system — The number system used by computers; it has only two numbers, 0 and 1, called binary digits, or bits.

binding — The process by which a protocol is associated with a network card or a modem card.

BIOS (basic input/output system) — Firmware that can control much of a computer's input/output functions, such as communication with the floppy drive and the monitor. Also called ROM BIOS.

bit (binary dig**it)** — A 0 or 1 used by the binary number system.

bits per second (bps) — A measure of data transmission speed. For example, a common modem speed is 56,000 bps, or 56 Kbps.

block mode — A method of data transfer between hard drive and memory that allows multiple data transfers on a single software interrupt.

blue screen — A Windows NT/2000/XP error that displays against a blue screen and causes the system to halt. Also called a stop error.

Bluetooth — A standard for wireless communication and data synchronization between devices, developed by a group of electronics manufacturers and overseen by the Bluetooth Special Interest Group. Bluetooth uses the same frequency range as 802.11b, but does not have as wide a range.

BNC connector — A connector used with thin coaxial cable. Some BNC connectors are T-shaped and called T-connectors. One end of the T connects to the NIC, and the two other ends can connect to cables or end a bus formation with a terminator.

boot loader menu — A startup menu that gives the user the choice of which operating system to load such as Windows 98 or Windows 2000 which are both installed on the same system, creating a dual boot.

boot partition — The hard drive partition where the Windows NT/2000/XP OS is stored. The system partition and the boot partition may be different partitions.

boot record — The first sector of a floppy disk or logical drive in a partition; it contains information about the disk or logical drive. On a hard drive, if the boot record is in the active partition, then it is used to boot the OS. Also called boot sector.

boot sector — *See* boot record.

boot sector virus — An infectious program that can replace the boot program with a modified, infected version of the boot command utilities, often causing boot and data retrieval problems.

Boot.ini — A Windows NT/2000/XP hidden text file that contains information needed to build the boot loader menu.

bootable disk — For DOS and Windows, a floppy disk that can upload the OS files necessary for computer startup. For DOS or Windows 9x, it must contain the files Io.sys, Msdos.sys, and Command.com.

bootstrap loader — A small program at the end of the boot record that can be used to boot an OS from the disk or logical drive.

bridge — A device used to connect two or more network segments. It can make decisions about allowing a packet to pass based on the packet's destination MAC address.

bridging protocol — *See* line protocol.

Briefcase — A system folder in Windows 9x that is used to synchronize files between two computers.

broadband — A transmission technique that carries more than one type of transmission on the same medium, such as cable modem or DSL.

broadcast — Process by which a message is sent from a single host to all hosts on the network, without regard to the kind of data being sent or the destination of the data.

brouter — A device that functions as both a bridge and a router. A brouter acts as a router when handling packets using routable protocols such as TCP/IP and IPX/SPX. It acts as a bridge when handling packets using nonroutable protocols such as NetBEUI.

brownouts — Temporary reductions in voltage, which can sometimes cause data loss.

buffer — A temporary memory area where data is kept before being written to a hard drive or sent to a printer, thus reducing the number of writes to the devices.

built-in user account — An administrator account and a guest account that are set up when Windows NT/2000/XP is first installed.

burst EDO (BEDO) — A refined version of EDO memory that significantly improved access time over EDO. BEDO was not widely used because Intel chose not to support it. BEDO memory is stored on 168-pin DIMM modules.

burst SRAM — Memory that is more expensive and slightly faster than pipelined burst SRAM. Data is sent in a two-step process; the data address is sent, and then the data itself is sent without interruption.

bus — The paths, or lines, on the motherboard on which data, instructions, and electrical power move from component to component.

bus mouse — A mouse that plugs into a bus adapter card and has a round, 9-pin mini-DIN connector.

bus riser — *See* riser card.

bus speed — The speed, or frequency, at which the data on the motherboard is moving.

bus topology — A LAN architecture in which all the devices are connected to a bus, or one communication line. Bus topology does not have a central connection point.

byte — A collection of eight bits that is equivalent to a single character. When referring to system memory, an additional error-checking bit might be added, making the total nine bits.

cabinet file — A file with a .cab extension that contains one or more compressed files and is often used to distribute software on disk. The Extract command is used to extract files from the cabinet file.

cable modem — A technology that uses cable TV lines for data transmission requiring a modem at each end. From the modem, a network cable connects to a NIC in the user's PC.

CAM (Common Access Method) — A standard adapter driver used by SCSI.

capacitor — An electronic device that can maintain an electrical charge for a period of time and is used to smooth out the flow of electrical current. Capacitors are often found in computer power supplies.

CardBus — The latest PCMCIA specification. It improves I/O speed, increases the bus width to 32 bits, and supports lower-voltage PC Cards, while maintaining backward compatibility with earlier standards.

cards — Adapter boards or interface cards placed into expansion slots to expand the functions of a computer, allowing it to communicate with external devices such as monitors or speakers.

carrier — A signal used to activate a phone line to confirm a continuous frequency; used to indicate that two computers are ready to receive or transmit data via modems.

CAS Latency (CL) — A feature of memory that reflects the number of clock cycles that pass while data is written to memory.

CAU (Controlled-Access Unit) — *See* MAU.

CCITT (Comité Consultatif International Télégraphique et Téléphonique) — An international organization that was responsible for developing standards for international communications. This organization has been incorporated into the ITU. *See also* ITU.

CD (change directory) command — A command given at the command prompt that changes the default directory, for example CD \Windows.

CDFS (Compact Disc File System) — The 32-bit file system for CD discs and some CD-R and CD-RW discs that replaced the older 16-bit mscdex file system used by DOS. *Also see* Universal Disk Format (UDF).

CD-R (CD-recordable) — A CD drive that can record or write data to a CD. The drive may or may not be multisession, but the data cannot be erased once it is written.

CD-RW (CD-rewritable) — A CD drive that can record or write data to a CD. The data can be erased and overwritten. The drive may or may not be multisession.

central processing unit (CPU) — Also called a microprocessor or processor. The heart and brain of the computer, which receives data input, processes information, and executes instructions.

chain — A group of clusters used to hold a single file.

checksum — A method of error checking transmitted data, whereby the digits are added and their sum compared to an expected sum.

child directory — *See* subdirectory.

child, parent, grandparent backup method — A plan for backing up and reusing tapes or removable disks by rotating them each day (child), week (parent), and month (grandparent).

chip creep — A condition in which chips loosen because of thermal changes.

chip set — A group of chips on the motherboard that controls the timing and flow of data and instructions to and from the CPU.

CHS (cylinder, head, sector) mode — The traditional method by which BIOS reads from and writes to hard drives by addressing the correct cylinder, head, and sector. Also called normal mode.

circuit board — A computer component, such as the main motherboard or an adapter board, that has electronic circuits and chips.

CISC (complex instruction set computing) — Earlier CPU type of instruction set.

clamping voltage — The maximum voltage allowed through a surge suppressor, such as 175 or 330 volts.

clean install — Installing an OS on a new hard drive or on a hard drive that has a previous OS installed, but without carrying forward any settings kept by the old OS, including information about hardware, software, or user preferences. A fresh installation.

client/server — A computer concept whereby one computer (the client) requests information from another computer (the server).

client/server application — An application that has two components. The client software requests data from the server software on the same or another computer.

clock speed — The speed, or frequency, expressed in MHz, that controls activity on the motherboard and is generated by a crystal or oscillator located somewhere on the motherboard.

clone — A computer that is a no-name Intel- and Microsoft-compatible PC.

cluster — One or more sectors that constitute the smallest unit of space on a disk for storing data (also referred to as a file allocation unit). Files are written to a disk as groups of whole clusters.

CMOS (complementary metal-oxide semiconductor) — One of two types of technologies used to manufacture microchips (the other type is TTL, or transistor-transistor logic chips). CMOS chips require less electricity, hold data longer after the electricity is turned off, are slower, and produce less heat than TTL chips. The configuration, or setup, chip is a CMOS chip.

CMOS configuration chip — A chip on the motherboard that contains a very small amount of memory, or RAM—enough to hold configuration, or setup, information about the computer. Also called CMOS setup chip or CMOS RAM chip.

CMOS setup — (1) The chip on the motherboard that holds configuration information about the system, such as date and time, and which CPU, hard drives, or floppy drives are installed. Also called CMOS or CMOS RAM. The chip is powered by a battery when the PC is turned off. (2) The program in system BIOS that can change the values in CMOS RAM.

CMOS setup chip — *See* CMOS configuration chip.

COAST (cache on a stick) — Memory modules that hold memory used as a memory cache. *See* memory cache.

coaxial cable — Networking cable used with 10-Mbps Ethernet ThinNet or ThickNet.

cold boot — *See* hard boot.

combo card — An Ethernet card that contains more than one transceiver, each with a different port on the back of the card, in order to accommodate different cabling media.

Command.com — Along with Msdos.sys and Io.sys, one of the three files that are the core components of the real-mode portion of Windows 9x. Command.com provides a command prompt and interprets commands.

comment — A line or part of a line in a program that is intended as a remark or comment and is ignored when the program runs. A semicolon or an REM is often used to mark a line as a comment.

communication and networking riser (CNR) — A specification for a small expansion slot on a motherboard that accommodates a small audio, modem, or network riser card.

compact case — A type of case used in low-end desktop systems. Compact cases, also called low-profile or slimline cases, follow either the NLX, LPX, or Mini LPX form factor. They are likely to have fewer drive bays, but they generally still provide for some expansion.

Compatibility Mode utility — A Windows XP utility that provides an application with the older

Microsoft OS environment it was designed to operate in.

compressed drive — A drive whose format has been reorganized in order to store more data. A compressed drive is really not a drive at all; it's actually a type of file, typically with a host drive called H.

computer name — Character-based host name or NetBIOS name assigned to a computer.

Config.sys — A text file used by DOS and supported by Windows 9x that lists device drivers to be loaded at startup. It can also set system variables to be used by DOS and Windows.

Configuration Manager — A component of Windows Plug and Play that controls the configuration process of all devices and communicates these configurations to the devices.

connectionless protocol — A protocol such as UDP that does not require a connection before sending a packet and does not guarantee delivery. An example of a UDP transmission is streaming video over the Web. Also called a best-effort protocol.

connection-oriented protocol — In networking, a protocol that confirms that a good connection has been made before transmitting data to the other end. An example of a connection-oriented protocol is TCP.

console — A centralized location from which to execute commonly used tools.

constant angular velocity (CAV) — A technology used by hard drives and newer CD-ROM drives whereby the disk rotates at a constant speed.

constant linear velocity (CLV) — A CD-ROM format in which the spacing of data is consistent on the CD, but the speed of the disc varies depending on whether the data being read near the center or the edge of the disc.

continuity — A continuous, unbroken path for the flow of electricity. A continuity test can determine whether or not internal wiring is still intact, or whether a fuse is good or bad.

control blade — A laser printer component that prevents too much toner from sticking to the cylinder surface.

conventional memory — Memory addresses between 0 and 640K. Also called base memory.

CRC (cyclical redundancy check) — A process in which calculations are performed on bytes of data before and after they are transmitted to check for corruption during transmission.

credit card memory — A type of memory used on older notebooks that could upgrade existing memory by way of a specialized memory slot.

C-RIMM (Continuity RIMM) — A placeholder RIMM module that provides continuity so that every RIMM slot is filled.

cross-linked clusters — Errors caused when more than one file points to a cluster, and the files appear to share the same disk space, according to the file allocation table.

crossover cable — A cable used to connect two PCs into the simplest network possible. Also used to connect two hubs.

CVF (compressed volume file) — The file on the host drive of a compressed drive that holds all compressed data.

data bus — The lines on the system bus that the CPU uses to send and receive data.

data cartridge — A type of tape medium typically used for backups. Full-sized data cartridges are 4 × 6 × ⅝ inches in size. A minicartridge is only 3¼ × 2½ × ⅝ inches in size.

data line protector — A surge protector designed to work with the telephone line to a modem.

data path size — The number of lines on a bus that can hold data, for example, 8, 16, 32, and 64 lines, which can accommodate 8, 16, 32, and 64 bits at a time.

data throughput — *See* bandwidth.

datagram — *See* packet.

DC controller — A card inside a notebook that converts voltage to CPU voltage. Some notebook manufacturers consider the card to be an FRU.

DCE (Data Communications Equipment) — The hardware, usually a dial-up modem, that provides the connection between a data terminal and a communications line. *See also* DTE.

default gateway — The gateway a computer on a network will use to access another network unless it knows to specifically use another gateway for quicker access to that network.

default printer — The printer Windows prints to unless another printer is selected.

defragment — To "optimize" or rewrite a file to a disk in one contiguous chain of clusters, thus speeding up data retrieval.

demodulation — The process by which digital data that has been converted to analog data is converted back to digital data. *See* modulation.

desktop — The initial screen that is displayed when an OS has a GUI interface loaded.

device driver — A program stored on the hard drive that tells the computer how to communicate with an input/output device such as a printer or modem.

DHCP (Dynamic Host Configuration Protocol) server — A service that assigns dynamic IP addresses to computers on a network when they first access the network.

diagnostic cards — Adapter cards designed to discover and report computer errors and conflicts at POST time (before the computer boots up), often by displaying a number on the card.

diagnostic software — Utility programs that help troubleshoot computer systems. Some DOS diagnostic utilities are CHKDSK and SCANDISK. PC-Technician is an example of a third-party diagnostic program.

dial-up networking — A Windows 9x and Windows NT/2000/XP utility that uses a modem and telephone line to connect to a network.

differential backup — Backup method that backs up only files that have changed or have been created since the last full backup. When recovering data, only two backups are needed: the full backup and the last differential backup.

differential cable — A SCSI cable in which a signal is carried on two wires, each carrying voltage, and the signal is the difference between the two. Differential signaling provides for error checking and greater data integrity. Compare to single-ended cable.

digital signature — Digital codes used to identify and authenticate the source of a file or document.

DIMM (dual inline memory module) — A miniature circuit board used in newer computers to hold memory. DIMMs can hold up to 2 GB of RAM on a single module.

diode — An electronic device that allows electricity to flow in only one direction. Used in a rectifier circuit.

DIP (dual inline package) switch — A switch on a circuit board or other device that can be set on or off to hold configuration or setup information.

direct current (DC) — Current that travels in only one direction (the type of electricity provided by batteries). Computer power supplies transform AC to low DC.

Direct Rambus DRAM — A memory technology by Rambus and Intel that uses a narrow, very fast network-type system bus. Memory is stored on a RIMM module. Also called RDRAM or Direct RDRAM.

Direct RDRAM — *See* Direct Rambus DRAM.

directory table — An OS table that contains file information such as the name, size, time and date of last modification, and cluster number of the file's beginning location.

discrete L2 cache — A type of L2 cache contained within the Pentium processor housing, but on a different die, with a cache bus between the processor and the cache.

disk cache — A method whereby recently retrieved data and adjacent data are read into memory in advance, anticipating the next CPU request.

disk cloning — Making an exact image of a hard drive, including partition information, boot sectors, operating system installation, and application software to replicate the hard drive on another system or recover from a hard drive crash. Also called disk imaging.

disk compression — Compressing data on a hard drive to allow more data to be written to the drive.

disk imaging — *See* disk cloning.

Disk Management — A Windows 2000/XP utility used to display and create and format partitions on basic disks and volumes on dynamic disks.

disk quota — A limit placed on the amount of disk space that is available to users. Requires a Windows 2000/XP NTFS volume.

disk thrashing — A condition that results when the hard drive is excessively used for virtual memory because RAM is full. It dramatically slows down processing and can cause premature hard drive failure.

Display Power Management Signaling (DPMS) — Energy Star standard specifications that allow for the video card and monitor to go into sleep mode simultaneously. *See also* Energy Star.

DMA (direct memory access) channel — A number identifying a channel whereby the device can pass data to memory without involving the CPU. Think of a DMA channel as a shortcut for data moving to/from the device and memory.

DNS (domain name service or **domain name system)** — A distributed pool of information (called the name space) that keeps track of assigned domain names and their corresponding IP addresses, and the system that allows a host to locate information in the pool. Compare to WINS.

DNS server — A computer that can find an IP address for another computer when only the domain name is known.

docking station — A device that receives a notebook computer and provides additional secondary storage and easy connection to peripheral devices.

domain — In Windows NT/2000/XP, a logical group of networked computers, such as those on a college campus, that share a centralized directory database of user account information and security for the entire domain.

domain controller — A Windows NT/2000 computer which holds and controls a database of (1) user accounts, (2) group accounts, and (3) computer accounts used to manage access to the network.

domain name — A unique, text-based name that identifies a network.

DOS box — A command window.

Dosstart.bat — A type of Autoexec.bat file that is executed by Windows 9x in two situations: when you select Restart the computer in MS-DOS mode from the shutdown menu or you run a program in MS-DOS mode.

dot pitch — The distance between the dots that the electronic beam hits on a monitor screen.

Double Data Rate SDRAM (DDR SDRAM) — A type of memory technology used on DIMMs that runs at twice the speed of the system clock.

doze time — The time before an Energy Star or "Green" system will reduce 80 percent of its activity.

Dr. Watson — A Windows utility that can record detailed information about the system, errors that occur, and the programs that caused them in a log file. Windows 9x names the log file \Windows\ Drwatson\WatsonXX.wlg, where XX is an incrementing number. Windows 2000 names the file \Documents and Settings\user\Documents\ DrWatson\Drwtsn32.log. Windows XP calls the file Drwatson.log.

DriveSpace — A Windows 9x utility that compresses files so that they take up less space on a disk drive, creating a single large file on the disk to hold all the compressed files.

drop height — The height from which a manufacturer states that its drive can be dropped without making the drive unusable.

DSL (Digital Subscriber Line) — A telephone line that carries digital data from end to end, and can be leased from the telephone company for individual use. DSL lines are rated at 5 Mbps, about 50 times faster than regular telephone lines.

DTE (Data Terminal Equipment) — Both the computer and a remote terminal or other computer to which it is attached. *See also* DCE.

dual boot — The ability to boot using either of two different OSs, such as Windows 98 and Windows 2000.

dual-scan passive matrix — A type of video display that is less expensive than an active-matrix display and does not provide as high-quality an image. With dual-scan display, two columns of electrodes are activated at the same time.

dual-voltage CPU — A CPU that requires two different voltages, one for internal processing and the other for I/O processing.

dump file — A file that contains information captured from memory at the time a stop error occurred.

DVD (digital video disc or digital versatile disk) — A faster, larger CD-ROM format that can read older CDs, store over 8 GB of data, and hold full-length motion picture videos.

dynamic disk — A way to partition one or more hard drives, introduced with Windows 2000, in which information about the drive is stored in a database at the end of the drive. Compare to basic disk.

dynamic IP address — An assigned IP address that is used for the current session only. When the session is terminated, the IP address is returned to the list of available addresses.

dynamic RAM (DRAM) — The most common type of system memory, it requires refreshing every few milliseconds.

dynamic volume — A volume type used with dynamic disks for which you can change the size of the volume after you have created it.

dynamic VxD — A VxD that is loaded and unloaded from memory as needed.

ECC (error-correcting code) — A chip set feature on a system board that checks the integrity of data stored on DIMMs or RIMMs and can correct single-bit errors in a byte. More advanced ECC schemas can detect, but not correct, double-bit errors in a byte.

ECHS (extended CHS) mode — *See* large mode.

ECP (Extended Capabilities Port) — A bidirectional parallel port mode that uses a DMA channel to speed up data flow.

EDO (extended data out) — A type of RAM that may be 10–20 percent faster than conventional RAM because it eliminates the delay before it issues the next memory address.

EEPROM (electrically erasable programmable ROM) — A type of chip in which higher voltage may be applied to one of the pins to erase its previous memory before a new instruction set is electronically written.

EIDE (Enhanced IDE) — A standard for managing the interface between secondary storage devices and a computer system. A system can support up to four IDE devices such as hard drives, CD-ROM drives, and Zip drives.

electromagnetic interference (EMI) — A magnetic field produced as a side effect from the flow of electricity. EMI can cause corrupted data in data lines that are not properly shielded.

electrostatic discharge (ESD) — Another name for static electricity, which can damage chips and destroy motherboards, even though it might not be felt or seen with the naked eye.

Emergency Repair Disk (ERD) — A Windows NT record of critical information about your system that can be used to fix a problem with the OS. The ERD enables restoration of the Windows NT registry on your hard drive.

Emergency Repair Process — A Windows 2000 process that restores the OS to its state at the completion of a successful installation.

emergency startup disk (ESD) — *See* rescue disk.

Emm386.exe — A DOS and Windows 9x utility that provides access to upper memory for 16-bit device drivers and other software.

Encrypted File System (EFS) — A way to use a key to encode a file or folder to protect sensitive data. Because it is an integrated system service, EFS is transparent to users and applications and is difficult to attack.

encrypting virus — A type of virus that transforms itself into a nonreplicating program in order to avoid detection. It transforms itself back into a replicating program in order to spread.

encryption — The process of putting readable data into an encoded form that can only be decoded (or decrypted) through use of a key.

Energy Star — "Green" systems that satisfy the EPA requirements to decrease the overall consumption of electricity. *See also* Green Standards.

enhanced BIOS — A system BIOS that has been written to accommodate large-capacity drives (over 504 MB, usually in the gigabyte range).

EPIC (explicitly parallel instruction computing) — The CPU architecture used by the Intel Itanium chip that bundles programming instructions with instructions on how to use multiprocessing abilities to do two instructions in parallel.

EPP (Enhanced Parallel Port) — A parallel port that allows data to flow in both directions (bidirectional port) and is faster than original parallel ports on PCs that allowed communication only in one direction.

EPROM (erasable programmable ROM) — A type of chip with a special window that allows the current memory contents to be erased with special ultraviolet light so that the chip can be reprogrammed. Many BIOS chips are EPROMs.

error correction — The ability of a modem to identify transmission errors and then automatically request another transmission.

Ethernet — A LAN architecture that uses a bus or star topology, uses CSMA/CD when two computers are trying to gain access to the network at the same time, and is the most popular network architecture in use today.

Execution Trace Cache — A type of Level 1 cache used by some CPUs to hold decoded operations waiting to be executed.

executive services — In Windows NT/2000/XP, a group of components running in kernel mode that interfaces between the subsystems in user mode and the HAL.

expansion bus — A bus that does not run in sync with the system clock.

expansion card — A circuit board inserted into a slot on the motherboard to enhance the capability of the computer.

expansion slot — A narrow slot on the motherboard where an expansion card can be inserted. Expansion slots connect to a bus on the motherboard.

extended memory — Memory above 1024K used in a DOS or Windows 9x system.

extended partition — The only partition on a hard drive that can contain more than one logical drive.

external cache — Static cache memory, stored on the motherboard or inside the CPU housing, that is not part of the CPU (also called L2 or L3 cache).

external command — Commands that have their own program files.

faceplate — A metal plate that comes with the motherboard and fits over the ports to create a well-fitted enclosure around them.

Fast Ethernet — *See* 100BaseT.

FAT (file allocation table) — A table on a hard drive or floppy disk that tracks the clusters used to contain a file.

FAT12 — The 12-bit wide, one-column file allocation table for a floppy disk, containing information about how each cluster or file allocation unit on the disk is currently used.

fault tolerance — The degree to which a system can tolerate failures. Adding redundant components, such as disk mirroring or disk duplexing, is a way to build in fault tolerance.

Fiber Distributed Data Interface (FDDI) — A ring-based network that does not require a centralized hub and can transfer data at a rate of 100 Mbps.

field replaceable unit (FRU) — A component in a computer or device that can be replaced with a new component without sending the computer or device back to the manufacturer. Examples: power supply, DIMM, motherboard, floppy disk drive.

file allocation unit — *See* cluster.

file extension — A three-character portion of the name of a file that is used to identify the file type. In command lines, the file extension follows the filename and is separated from it by a period. For example, Msd.exe, where exe is the file extension.

file system — The overall structure that an OS uses to name, store, and organize files on a disk. Examples of file systems are FAT32 and NTFS.

file virus — A virus that inserts virus code into an executable program and can spread wherever that program is accessed.

filename — The first part of the name assigned to a file. In DOS, the filename can be no more than eight characters long and is followed by the file extension. In Windows, a filename can be up to 255 characters.

firewall — Hardware or software that protects a computer or network from unauthorized access.

FireWire — *See* IEEE 1394.

firmware — Software that is permanently stored in a chip. The BIOS on a motherboard is an example of firmware.

flash ROM — ROM that can be reprogrammed or changed without replacing chips.

flat panel monitor — A desktop monitor that uses an LCD panel.

FlexATX — A version of the ATX form factor that allows for maximum flexibility in the size and shape of cases and motherboards. FlexATX is ideal for custom systems.

flow control — When using modems, a method of controlling the flow of data to adjust for

problems with data transmission. Xon/Xoff is an example of a flow control protocol.

folder — *See* subdirectory.

folder redirection — A Windows XP feature that allows a user to point to a folder that can be on the local PC or somewhere on the network, and its location can be transparent to the user.

forced perfect terminator (FPT) — A type of SCSI active terminator that includes a mechanism to force signal termination to the correct voltage, eliminating most signal echoes and interference.

forgotten password floppy disk — A Windows XP disk created to be used in the event the user forgets the user account password to the system.

form factor — A set of specifications on the size, shape, and configuration of a computer hardware component such as a case, power supply, or motherboard.

formatting — Preparing a new floppy disk for use by placing tracks and sectors on its surface to store information (for example, FORMAT A:). Old disks can be reformatted, but all data on them will be lost.

FPM (fast page mode) — A memory mode used before the introduction of EDO memory. FPM improved on earlier memory types by sending the row address just once for many accesses to memory near that row.

fragmentation — The distribution of data files on a hard drive or floppy disk such that they are stored in noncontiguous clusters.

fragmented file — A file that has been written to different portions of the disk so that it is not in contiguous clusters.

frame — The header and trailer information added to data to form a data packet to be sent over a network.

front-side bus — *See* system bus.

FTP (File Transfer Protocol) — The protocol used to transfer files over a TCP/IP network such that the file does not need to be converted to ASCII format before transferring it.

full AT — *See* AT.

full backup — A complete backup, whereby all of the files on the hard drive are backed up each time the backup procedure is performed. It is the safest backup method, but it takes the most time.

full-duplex — Communication that happens in two directions at the same time.

fully qualified domain name (FQDN) — A host name and a domain name such as *jsmith.amazon.com*. Sometimes loosely referred to as a domain name.

gateway — A computer or other device that connects networks.

GDI (Graphics Device Interface) — A Windows 9x component that controls screens, graphics, and printing.

General Protection Fault (GPF) — A Windows error that occurs when a program attempts to access a memory address that is not available or is no longer assigned to it.

Gigabit Ethernet — The newest version of Ethernet. Gigabit Ethernet supports rates of data transfer up to 1 gigabit per second but is not yet widely used.

gigahertz (GHz) — One thousand MHz, or one billion cycles per second.

global user account — Sometimes called a domain user account, the account is used at the domain level, created by an administrator, and stored in the SAM (security accounts manager) database on a Windows 2000 or Windows .NET domain controller.

graphics accelerator — A type of video card that has an on-board processor that can substantially increase speed and boost graphical and video performance.

Green Standards — A computer or device that conforms to these standards can go into sleep or doze mode when not in use, thus saving energy and helping the environment. Devices that carry the Green Star or Energy Star comply with these standards.

ground bracelet — A strap you wear around your wrist that is attached to the computer case, ground mat, or another ground so that ESD is discharged from your body before you touch sensitive components inside a computer. Also called static strap, ground strap, ESD bracelet.

group profile — A group of user profiles. All profiles in the group can be changed by changing the group profile.

guard tone — A tone that an answering modem sends when it first answers the phone, to tell the calling modem that a modem is on the other end of the line.

Guest user — A user who has limited permissions on a system and cannot make changes to it. Guest user accounts are intended for one-time or infrequent users of a workstation.

HAL (hardware abstraction layer) — The low-level part of Windows NT/2000/XP, written specifically for each CPU technology, so that only the HAL must change when platform components change.

half life — The time it takes for a medium storing data to weaken to half of its strength. Magnetic media, including traditional hard drives and floppy disks, have a half-life of five to seven years.

half-duplex — Communication between two devices whereby transmission takes place in only one direction at a time.

handshaking — When two modems begin to communicate, the initial agreement made as to how to send and receive data.

hard boot — Restart the computer by turning off the power or by pressing the Reset button. Also called a cold boot.

hard copy — Output from a printer to paper.

hard drive — The main secondary storage device of a PC, a small case that contains magnetic coated platters that rotate at high speed.

hard drive controller — The firmware that controls access to a hard drive contained on a circuit board mounted on or inside the hard drive housing. Older hard drives used firmware on a controller card that connected to the drive by way of two cables, one for data and one for control.

hard drive standby time — The amount of time before a hard drive will shut down to conserve energy.

hard-disk loading — The illegal practice of installing unauthorized software on computers for sale. Hard-disk loading can typically be identified by the absence of original software disks in the original system's shipment.

hardware — The physical components that constitute the computer system, such as the monitor, the keyboard, the motherboard, and the printer.

hardware address — *See* MAC address.

hardware cache — A disk cache that is contained in RAM chips built right on the disk controller.

hardware interrupt — An event caused by a hardware device signaling the CPU that it requires service.

hardware profile — A set of hardware configuration information that Windows keeps in the registry. Windows can maintain more than one hardware profile for the same PC.

HCL (hardware compatibility list) — The list of all computers and peripheral devices that have been tested and are officially supported by Windows NT/2000/XP (see *www.microsoft.com/hcl*).

head — The top or bottom surface of one platter on a hard drive. Each platter has two heads.

heat sink — A piece of metal, with cooling fins, that can be attached to or mounted on an integrated chip (such as the CPU) to dissipate heat.

hertz (Hz) — Unit of measurement for frequency, calculated in terms of vibrations, or cycles per second. For example, for 16-bit stereo sound, a frequency of 44,000 Hz is used. *See also* megahertz.

hexadecimal notation (hex) — A numbering system that uses 16 digits, the numerals 0–9, and the letters A–F. Hexadecimal notation is often used to display memory addresses.

hidden file — A file that is not displayed in a directory list. Whether to hide or display a file is one of the file's attributes kept by the OS.

high memory area (HMA) — The first 64K of extended memory.

High Voltage Differential (HVD) — A type of SCSI differential signaling requiring more expensive hardware to handle the higher voltage. HVD became obsolete with the introduction of SCSI-3.

high-level formatting — Formatting performed by means of the DOS or Windows Format program (for example, FORMAT C:/S creates the boot record, FAT, and root directory on drive C and makes the drive bootable). Also called OS formatting.

Himem.sys — The DOS and Windows 9x memory manager extension that allowed access to memory addresses above 1 MB.

hive — Physical segment of the Windows NT/2000/XP registry that is stored in a file.

hop count — *See* time to live (TTL).

host — Any computer or other device on a network that has been assigned an IP address.

host adapter — The circuit board that controls a SCSI bus supporting as many as seven or fifteen separate devices. The host adapter controls communication between the SCSI bus and the PC.

host bus — *See* memory bus or system bus.

host drive — Typically drive H on a compressed drive. *See* compressed drive.

host name — A name that identifies a computer, printer, or other device on a network.

hot-pluggable — *See* hot-swappable.

hot-swappable — A device that can be plugged into a computer while it is turned on and the computer will sense the device and configure it without rebooting, or the device can be removed without an OS error. Also called hot-pluggable.

HTML (HyperText Markup Language) — A markup language used for hypertext documents on the World Wide Web. This language uses tags to format the document, create hyperlinks, and mark locations for graphics.

HTTP (HyperText Transfer Protocol) — The protocol used by the World Wide Web.

HTTPS (HTTP secure) — A version of the HTTP protocol that includes data encryption for security.

hub — A network device or box that provides a central location to connect cables.

hypertext — Text that contains links to remote points in the document or to other files, documents, or graphics. Hypertext is created using HTML and is commonly distributed from Web sites.

i.Link — *See* IEEE 1394.

I/O addresses — Numbers that are used by devices and the CPU to manage communication between them. Also called ports or port addresses.

I/O controller card — An older card that can contain serial, parallel, and game ports and floppy drive and IDE connectors.

IBM-compatible PC — A computer that uses an Intel (or compatible) processor and can run DOS and Windows.

ICMP (Internet Control Message Protocol) — Part of the IP layer that is used to transmit error messages and other control messages to hosts and routers.

IDE (Integrated Drive Electronics) — A standard governing hard drive technology and how secondary storage devices, such as hard drives, CD-ROM drives, and Zip drives, related to a system.

IEEE 1284 — A standard for parallel ports and cables developed by the Institute for Electrical and Electronics Engineers and supported by many hardware manufacturers.

IEEE 1394 — Standards for an expansion bus that can also be configured to work as a local bus. It is expected to replace the SCSI bus, providing an easy method to install and configure fast I/O devices. Also called FireWire and i.Link.

IEEE 1394.3 — A standard, developed by the 1394 Trade Association, that is designed for peer-to-peer data transmission and allows imaging devices to send images and photos directly to printers without involving a computer.

IEEE 802.11b — An IEEE specification for wireless communication and data synchronization that competes with Bluetooth. Also known as Wi-Fi. Apple Computer's version of 802.11b is called AirPort.

IMAP4 (Internet Message Access Protocol version 4) — Version 4 of the IMAP protocol, which is an e-mail protocol that has more functionality than its predecessor, POP. IMAP can archive messages in folders on the e-mail server and can allow the user to choose not to download attachments to messages.

incremental backup — A time-saving backup method that only backs up files changed or newly created since the last full or incremental backup. Multiple incremental backups might be required when recovering lost data.

infestation — Any unwanted program that is transmitted to a computer without the user's knowledge and that is designed to do varying degrees of damage to data and software. There are a number of different types of infestations, including viruses, Trojan horses, worms, and logic bombs.

information (.inf) file — Text file with an .inf file extension, such as Msbatch.inf, that contains information about a hardware or software installation.

initialization files — Configuration information files for Windows. System.ini is one of the most important Windows 9x initialization files.

Installable File System (IFS) — A Windows 9x Plug and Play component that is responsible for all disk access.

Institute of Electrical and Electronics Engineers (IEEE) — A nonprofit organization that develops standards for the computer and electronics industries.

instruction set — The set of instructions, on the CPU chip, that the computer can perform directly (such as ADD and MOVE).

Integrated Device Electronics or **Integrated Drive Electronics (IDE)** — A hard drive whose disk controller is integrated into the drive, eliminating the need for a controller cable and thus increasing speed, as well as reducing price.

intelligent UPS — A UPS connected to a computer by way of a serial cable so that software on the computer can monitor and control the UPS.

interlaced — A type of display in which the electronic beam of a monitor draws every other line with each pass, which lessens the overall effect of a lower refresh rate.

internal bus — The bus inside the CPU that is used for communication between the CPU's internal components.

internal cache — Memory cache that is faster than external cache, and is contained inside 80486 and Pentium chips (also referred to as primary, Level 1, or L1 cache).

internal command — Commands that are embedded in the Command.com file.

Internet Connection Firewall (ICF) — Windows XP software designed to protect a PC from unauthorized access from the Internet.

Internet Connection Sharing (ICS) — A Windows 98 and Windows XP utility that uses NAT and acts as a proxy server to manage two or more computers connected to the Internet.

Internet service provider (ISP) — A commercial group that provides Internet access for a monthly fee. AOL, Earthlink, and CompuServe are large ISPs.

intranet — A private network that uses the TCP/IP protocols.

Io.sys — Along with Msdos.sys and Command.com, one of the three files that are the core components of the real mode portion of Windows 9x. It is the first program file of the OS.

IP (Internet Protocol) — The rules of communication in the TCP/IP stack that control segmenting data into packets, routing those packets across networks, and then reassembling the packets once they reach their destination.

IP address — A 32-bit address consisting of four numbers separated by periods, used to uniquely identify a device on a network that uses TCP/IP protocols. The first numbers identify the network; the last numbers identify a host. An example of an IP address is 206.96.103.114.

IPX/SPX (Internetwork Packet Exchange/ Sequenced Packet Exchange) — A networking protocol suite first used by Novell NetWare, and which corresponds to the TCP/IP protocols.

IRQ (interrupt request) line — A line on a bus that is assigned to a device and is used to signal the CPU for servicing. These lines are assigned a reference number (for example, the normal IRQ for a printer is IRQ 7).

ISA (Industry Standard Architecture) slot — An older slot on the motherboard used for slower I/O devices, which can support an 8-bit or a 16-bit data path. ISA slots are mostly replaced by PCI slots.

ISDN (Integrated Services Digital Network) — A digital telephone line that can carry data at about five times the speed of regular telephone lines. Two channels (telephone numbers) share a single pair of wires.

isochronous data transfer — A method used by IEEE 1394 to transfer data continuously without breaks.

ITU (International Telecommunications Union) — The international organization responsible for developing international standards of communication. Formerly CCITT.

JPEG (Joint Photographic Experts Group) — A graphical compression scheme that allows the user to control the amount of data that is averaged and sacrificed as file size is reduced. It is a common Internet file format. Most JPEG files have a .jpg extension.

jumper — Two wires that stick up side by side on the motherboard and are used to hold configuration information. The jumper is considered closed if a cover is over the wires, and open if the cover is missing.

kernel — The portion of an OS that is responsible for interacting with the hardware.

kernel mode — A Windows NT/2000/XP "privileged" processing mode that has access to hardware components.

key — (1) In encryption, a secret number or code used to encode and decode data. (2) In Windows, a section name of the Windows registry.

keyboard — A common input device through which data and instructions may be typed into computer memory.

LAN (local area network) — A computer network that covers only a small area, usually within one building.

lands — Microscopic flat areas on the surface of a CD or DVD that separate pits. Lands and pits are used to represent data on the disk.

laptop computer — *See* notebook.

large-capacity drive — A hard drive larger than 504 MB.

large mode — A mode of addressing information on hard drives that range from 504 MB to 8.4 GB, addressing information on a hard drive by translating cylinder, head, and sector information in order to break the 528-MB hard drive barrier. Another name for large mode. Also called ECHS mode.

Last Known Good configuration — In Windows NT/2000/XP, registry settings and device drivers that were in effect when the computer last booted successfully. These settings can be restored during the startup process to recover from errors during the last boot.

LBA (logical block addressing) mode — A mode of addressing information on hard drives in which the BIOS and operating system view the drive as one long linear list of LBAs or addressable sectors, permitting drives to be larger than 8.4 GB (LBA 0 is cylinder 0, head 0, and sector 1).

Level 1 (L1) cache — *See* internal cache.

Level 2 (L2) cache — *See* external cache.

Level 3 (L3) cache — *See* external cache.

Limited user — Windows XP user accounts known as Users in Windows NT/2000, which have read-write access only on their own folders, read-only access to most system folders, and no access to other users' data.

line conditioner — A device that regulates, or conditions, power, providing continuous voltage during brownouts and spikes.

line protocol — A protocol used to send data packets destined for a network over telephone lines. PPP and SLIP are examples of line protocols.

line speed — *See* bandwidth.

line-interactive UPS — A variation of a standby UPS that shortens switching time by always keeping the inverter that converts AC to DC working, so that there is no charge-up time for the inverter.

LMHosts — A text file located in the Windows folder that contains NetBIOS names and their associated IP addresses. This file is used for name resolution for a NetBEUI network.

local bus — A bus that operates at a speed synchronized with the CPU frequency. The system bus is a local bus.

local I/O bus — A local bus that provides I/O devices with fast access to the CPU.

local printer — A printer connected to a computer by way of a port on the computer. Compare to network printer.

local profile — User profile that is stored on a local computer and cannot be accessed from another computer on the network.

local user account — A user account that applies only to a local computer and cannot be used to access resources from other computers on the network.

logic bomb — Dormant code added to software that is triggered by a predetermined time or event.

logical drive — A portion or all of a hard drive partition that is treated by the operating system as though it were a physical drive. Each logical drive is assigned a drive letter, such as drive C, and contains a file system. Also called a volume.

logical geometry — The number of heads, tracks, and sectors that the BIOS on the hard drive controller presents to the system BIOS and the OS. The logical geometry does not consist of the same values as the physical geometry, although calculations of drive capacity yield the same results.

Logical Unit Number (LUN) — A number assigned to a logical device (such as a tray in a CD changer) that is part of a physical SCSI device, which is assigned a SCSI ID.

lost allocation units — *See* lost clusters.

lost clusters — File fragments that, according to the file allocation table, contain data that does not belong to any file. The command CHKDSK/F can free these fragments. Also called lost allocation units.

low insertion force (LIF) socket — A socket that requires the installer to manually apply an even force over the microchip when inserting the chip into the socket.

low-level formatting — A process (usually performed at the factory) that electronically creates the hard drive tracks and sectors and tests for bad spots on the disk surface.

low-profile case — *See* compact case.

Low Voltage Differential (LVD) — A type of differential signaling that uses lower voltage than does HVD, is less expensive, and can be compatible with single-ended signaling on the same SCSI bus.

LPX — A form factor in which expansion cards are mounted on a riser card that plugs into a motherboard. The expansion cards in LPX systems are mounted parallel to the motherboard, rather than perpendicular to it as in AT and ATX systems.

MAC (Media Access Control) address — A 6-byte hexadecimal hardware address unique to each NIC card and assigned by the manufacturer. The address is often printed on the adapter. An example is 00 00 0C 08 2F 35. Also called a physical address, an adapter address, or a hardware address.

macro — A small sequence of commands, contained within a document, that can be automatically executed when the document is loaded, or executed later by using a predetermined keystroke.

macro virus — A virus that can hide in the macros of a document file. Typically, viruses do not reside in data or document files.

main board — *See* motherboard.

mandatory user profile — A roaming user profile that applies to all users in a user group, and individual users cannot change that profile.

Master Boot Record (MBR) — The first sector on a hard drive, which contains the partition table and a program the BIOS uses to boot an OS from the drive.

master file table (MFT) — The database used by the NTFS file system to track the contents of a logical drive.

material safety data sheet (MSDS) — A document that explains how to properly handle substances such as chemical solvents; it includes information such as physical data, toxicity, health effects, first aid, storage, disposal, and spill procedures.

megahertz (MHz) — One million Hz, or one million cycles per second. *See* hertz (Hz).

memory — Physical microchips that can hold data and programming, located on the motherboard or expansion cards.

memory address — A number assigned to each byte in memory. The CPU can use memory addresses to track where information is stored in RAM. Memory addresses are usually displayed as hexadecimal numbers in segment/offset form.

memory bus — *See* system bus.

memory cache — A small amount of faster RAM that stores recently retrieved data, in anticipation of what the CPU will request next, thus speeding up access. *See also* system bus.

memory dump — The contents of memory saved to a file at the time an event halted the system. Support technicians can analyze the dump file to help understand the source of the problem.

memory extender — For DOS and Windows 9x, a device driver named Himem.sys that manages RAM, giving access to memory addresses above 1 MB.

memory paging — In Windows, swapping blocks of RAM memory to an area of the hard drive to serve as virtual memory when RAM is low.

memory-resident virus — A virus that can stay lurking in memory even after its host program is terminated.

microATX — A recent version of the ATX form factor. MicroATX addresses some new technologies that have been developed since the original introduction of ATX.

microprocessor — *See* central processing unit (CPU).

Microsoft Management Console (MMC) — A utility to build customized consoles. These consoles can be saved to a file with an .msc file extension.

Mini-ATX — A smaller ATX board that can be used with regular ATX cases and power supplies.

minicartridge — A tape drive cartridge that is only 3¼ × 2½ × ⅗ inches. It is small enough to allow two drives to fit into a standard 5½-inch drive bay of a PC case.

minifile system — In Windows NT/2000/XP, a simplified file system that is started so that Ntldr (NT Loader) can read files from any file system the OS supports.

Mini-LPX — A smaller version of the LPX motherboard.

mixed mode — A Windows 2000 mode for domain controllers used when there is at least one Windows NT domain controller on the network.

MMX (Multimedia Extensions) — Multimedia instructions built into Intel processors to add functionality such as better processing of multimedia, SIMD support, and increased cache.

modem — From MOdulate/DEModulate. A device that modulates digital data from a computer to an analog format that can be sent over telephone lines, then demodulates it back into digital form.

modem eliminator — *See* null modem cable.

modem riser card — A small modem card that uses an AMR or CNR slot. Part of the modem logic is contained in a controller on the motherboard.

modem speed — The speed at which a modem can transmit data along a phone line, measured in bits per second (bps). Also called line speed.

modulation — Converting binary or digital data into an analog signal that can be sent over standard telephone lines.

monitor — The most commonly used output device for displaying text and graphics on a computer.

motherboard — The main board in the computer, also called the system board. The CPU, ROM chips, SIMMs, DIMMs, RIMMs, and interface cards are plugged into the motherboard.

motherboard bus — *See* system bus.

motherboard mouse — *See* PS/2-compatible mouse.

mouse — A pointing and input device that allows the user to move a cursor around a screen and select programs with the click of a button.

MP3 — A method to compress audio files that uses MPEG level 3. It can reduce sound files as low as a 1:24 ratio without losing much sound quality.

MPEG (Moving Pictures Experts Group) — A processing-intensive standard for data compression for motion pictures that tracks movement from one frame to the next and only stores the data that has changed.

Msdos.sys — In Windows 9x, a text file that contains settings used by Io.sys during booting. In DOS, the Msdos.sys file was a program file that contained part of the DOS core.

multicasting — A process in which a message is sent by one host to multiple hosts, such as when a video conference is broadcast to several hosts on the Internet.

multimeter — A device used to measure the various components of an electrical circuit. The most common measurements are voltage, current, and resistance.

multipartite virus — A combination of a boot sector virus and a file virus. It can hide in either type of program.

multiplier — The factor by which the bus speed or frequency is multiplied to get the CPU clock speed.

multiscan monitor — A monitor that can work within a range of frequencies and thus can work with different standards and video cards. It offers a variety of refresh rates.

multisession — A feature that allows data to be read from or written to a CD during more than one session. This is important if the disk was only partially filled during the first write.

Multistation Access Unit (MSAU or MAU) — A centralized hub used in token ring networks to connect stations. Also called CAU.

multitasking — Doing more than one thing at a time. A true multitasking system requires two or more CPUs, each processing a different thread at the same time. Compare to cooperative multitasking and preemptive multitasking.

multithreading — The ability to pass more than one function (thread) to the OS kernel at the same time, such as when one thread is performing a print job while another reads a file.

name resolution — The process of associating a NetBIOS name or host name to an IP address.

narrow SCSI — One of the two main SCSI specifications. Narrow SCSI has an 8-bit data bus. The word "narrow" is not usually included in the names of narrow SCSI devices.

NAT (Network Address Translation) — A process that converts private IP addresses on a LAN to the proxy server's IP address before a data packet is sent over the Internet.

native mode — A Windows 2000 mode used by domain controllers when there are no Windows NT domain controllers present on the network.

NetBEUI (NetBIOS Extended User Interface) — A fast, proprietary Microsoft networking protocol used only by Windows-based systems, and limited to LANs because it does not support routing.

NetBIOS (Network Basic Input/Output System) — An API protocol used by some applications to communicate over a NetBEUI network. NetBIOS has largely been replaced by Windows Sockets over a TCP/IP network.

network adapter — *See* network interface card.

network drive map — Mounting a drive to a computer, such as drive E, that is actually hard drive space on another host computer on the network.

network interface card (NIC) — An expansion card that plugs into a computer's motherboard and provides a port on the back of the card to connect a PC to a network. Also called a network adapter.

network operating system (NOS) — An operating system that resides on the controlling computer in the network. The NOS controls what software, data, and devices a user on the network can access. Examples of an NOS are Novell Netware and Windows 2000 Server.

network printer — A printer that any user on the network can access, through its own network card and connection to the network, through a connection to a standalone print server, or through a connection to a computer as a local printer, which is shared on the network.

NLX — A low-end form factor that is similar to LPX but provides greater support for current and emerging processor technologies. NLX was designed for flexibility and efficiency of space.

NNTP (Network News Transfer Protocol) — The protocol used by newsgroup server and client software.

node — Any computer, workstation, or device on a network.

noise — An extraneous, unwanted signal, often over an analog phone line, that can cause communication interference or transmission errors. Possible sources are fluorescent lighting, radios, TVs, lightning, or bad wiring.

noninterlaced — A type of display in which the electronic beam of a monitor draws every line on the screen with each pass.

non-memory-resident virus — A virus that is terminated when the host program is closed. Compare to memory-resident virus.

nonparity memory — Eight-bit memory without error checking. A SIMM part number with a 32 in it (4 × 8 bits) is nonparity.

nonvolatile — Refers to a kind of RAM that is stable and can hold data as long as electricity is powering the memory.

normal mode — See CHS mode.

North Bridge — That portion of the chip set hub that connects faster I/O buses (for example, AGP bus) to the system bus. Compare to South Bridge.

notebook — A portable computer that is designed for travel and mobility. Notebooks use the same technology as desktop PCs, with modifications for conserving voltage, taking up less space, and operating while on the move. Also called a laptop computer.

NTFS (NT file system) — The file system for the Windows NT/2000/XP operating systems. NTFS cannot be accessed by other operating systems such as DOS. It provides increased reliability and security in comparison to other methods of organizing and accessing files. There are several versions of NTFS that might or might not be compatible.

Ntldr (NT Loader) — In Windows NT/2000/XP, the OS loader used on Intel systems.

NTVDM (NT virtual DOS machine) — An emulated environment in which a 16-bit DOS application resides within Windows NT/2000/XP with its own memory space or WOW (Win16 on Win32).

null modem cable — A cable that allows two data terminal equipment (DTE) devices to communicate in which the transmit and receive wires are cross-connected and no modems are necessary.

octet — Term for each of the four 8-bit numbers that make up an IP address. For example, the IP address 206.96.103.114 has four octets.

ohm (Ω) — The standard unit of measurement for electrical resistance. Resistors are rated in ohms.

on-board ports — Ports that are directly on the motherboard, such as a built-in keyboard port or on-board serial port.

operating system (OS) — Software that controls a computer. An OS controls how system resources are used and provides a user interface, a way of managing hardware and software, and ways to work with files.

operating system formatting — See high-level formatting.

P1 connector — Power connection on an ATX motherboard.

P8 connector — One of two power connectors on an AT motherboard.

P9 connector — One of two power connectors on an AT motherboard.

packet — Segment of network data that also includes header, destination address, and trailer information that is sent as a unit. Also called data packet or datagram.

page fault — An OS interrupt that occurs when the OS is forced to access the hard drive to satisfy the demands for virtual memory.

page file — *See* swap file.

Pagefile.sys — The Windows NT/2000/XP swap file.

page-in — The process in which the memory manager goes to the hard drive to return the data from a swap file to RAM.

page-out — The process in which, when RAM is full, the memory manager takes a page and moves it to the swap file.

pages — 4K segments in which Windows NT/2000/XP allocates memory.

parallel port — A female 25-pin port on a computer that can transmit data in parallel, 8 bits at a time, and is usually used with a printer. The names for parallel ports are LPT1 and LPT2.

parity — An error-checking scheme in which a ninth, or "parity," bit is added. The value of the parity bit is set to either 0 or 1 to provide an even number of ones for even parity and an odd number of ones for odd parity.

parity error — An error that occurs when the number of 1s in the byte is not in agreement with the expected number.

parity memory — Nine-bit memory in which the ninth bit is used for error checking. A SIMM part number with a 36 in it (4 × 9 bits) is parity. Older PCs almost always use parity chips.

partition — A division of a hard drive that can be used to hold logical drives.

partition table — A table at the beginning of the hard drive that contains information about each partition on the drive. The partition table is contained in the Master Boot Record.

passive backplane — A type of backplane system in which the backplane contains no circuitry at all. Passive backplanes locate all circuitry on a mothercard plugged into a backplane.

passive terminator — A type of terminator for single-ended SCSI cables. Simple resistors are used to provide termination of a signal. Passive termination is not reliable over long distances and should only be used with narrow SCSI.

patch — An update to software that corrects an error, adds a feature, or addresses security issues. Also called an update or service pack.

patch cable — A network cable that is used to connect a PC to a hub.

path — (1) A drive and list of directories pointing to a file such as C:\Windows\command. (2) The OS command to provide a list of paths to the system for finding program files to execute.

PC Card — A credit-card-sized adapter card that can be slid into a slot in the side of many notebook computers and is used for connecting to modems, networks, and CD-ROM drives. Also called PCMCIA Card.

PC Card slot — An expansion slot on a notebook computer, into which a PC Card is inserted. Also called a PCMCIA Card slot.

PCI (Peripheral Component Interconnect) bus — A bus common on Pentium computers that runs at speeds of up to 33 MHz or 66 MHz, with a 32-bit-wide or 64-bit-wide data path. PCI-X, released in September 1999, enables PCI to run at 133 MHz. For some chip sets, it serves as the middle layer between the memory bus and expansion buses.

PCMCIA (Personal Computer Memory Card International Association) Card — *See* PC Card.

PCMCIA Card slot — *See* PC Card slot.

PDA (Personal Digital Assistant) — A small, handheld computer that has its own operating system and applications.

peer-to-peer network — A network of computers that are all equals, or peers. Each computer has the same amount of authority, and each can act as a server to the other computers.

peripheral devices — Devices that communicate with the CPU but are not located directly on the motherboard, such as the monitor, floppy drive, printer, and mouse.

physical address — *See* MAC address.

physical geometry — The actual layout of heads, tracks, and sectors on a hard drive. Refer also to logical geometry.

PIF (program information file) — A file used by Windows to describe the environment for a DOS program to use.

pin grid array (PGA) — A feature of a CPU socket whereby the pins are aligned in uniform rows around the socket.

Ping (Packet Internet Groper) — A Windows and Unix command used to troubleshoot network connections. It verifies that the host can communicate with another host on the network.

pinout — A description of how each pin on a bus, connection, plug, slot, or socket is used.

pipelined burst SRAM — A less expensive SRAM that uses more clock cycles per transfer than non-pipelined burst but does not significantly slow down the process.

pits — Recessed areas on the surface of a CD or DVD, separating lands, or flat areas. Lands and pits are used to represent data on a disc.

pixel — A small spot on a fine horizontal scan line. Pixels are illuminated to create an image on the monitor.

Plug and Play (PnP) — A standard designed to make the installation of new hardware devices easier by automatically configuring devices to eliminate system resource conflicts (such as IRQ or I/O address conflicts). PnP is supported by Windows 9x, Windows 2000, and Windows XP.

polling — A process by which the CPU checks the status of connected devices to determine if they are ready to send or receive data.

polymorphic virus — A type of virus that changes its distinguishing characteristics as it replicates itself. Mutating in this way makes it more difficult for AV software to recognize the presence of the virus.

POP (Post Office Protocol) — The protocol that an e-mail server and client use when the client requests the downloading of e-mail messages. The most recent version is POP3. POP is slowly being replaced by IMAP.

port — (1) As applied to services running on a computer, a number assigned to a process on a computer so that the process can be found by TCP/IP.

Also called a port address or port number. (2) Another name for an I/O address. *See also* I/O address. (3) A physical connector, usually at the back of a computer, that allows a cable from a peripheral device, such as a printer, mouse, or modem, to be attached.

port address — *See* I/O address.

port number — *See* port.

port replicator — A device designed to connect to a notebook computer in order to make it easy to connect the notebook to peripheral devices.

port settings — The configuration parameters of communications devices such as COM1, COM2, or COM3, including IRQ settings.

port speed — The communication speed between a DTE (computer) and a DCE (modem). As a general rule, the port speed should be at least four times as fast as the modem speed.

POST (power-on self test) — A self-diagnostic program used to perform a simple test of the CPU, RAM, and various I/O devices. The POST is performed by startup BIOS when the computer is first turned on, and is stored in ROM-BIOS.

power conditioner — A line conditioner that regulates, or conditions, power, providing continuous voltage during brownouts.

power-on password — A password that a computer uses to control access during the boot process.

power scheme — A feature of Windows XP support for notebooks that allows the user to create groups of power settings for specific sets of conditions.

power supply — A box inside the computer case that supplies power to the motherboard and other installed devices. Power supplies provide 3.3, 5, and 12 volts DC.

PPP (Point-to-Point Protocol) — A protocol that governs the methods for communicating via modems and dial-up telephone lines. The Windows Dial-up Networking utility uses PPP.

PPPoE (Point-to-Point Protocol over Ethernet) — The protocol that describes how a PC is to interact with a broadband converter box, such as cable modem, when the two are connected by an Ethernet cable, connected to a NIC in a PC.

preemptive multitasking — A type of pseudo-multitasking whereby the CPU allows an application a specified period of time and then preempts the processing to give time to another application.

primary cache — *See* internal cache.

primary domain controller (PDC) — In a Windows NT network, the computer that controls the directory database of user accounts, group accounts, and computer accounts on a domain. *Also see* backup domain controller.

primary partition — A hard disk partition that can contain only one logical drive.

primary storage — Temporary storage on the motherboard used by the CPU to process data and instructions. Memory is considered primary storage.

printer — A peripheral output device that produces printed output to paper. Different types include dot matrix, ink-jet, and laser printers.

printer maintenance kit — A kit purchased from a printer manufacturer that contains the parts, tools, and instructions needed to perform routine printer maintenance.

private IP address — An IP address that is used on a private TCP/IP network that is isolated from the Internet.

process — An executing instance of a program together with the program resources. There can be more than one process running for a program at the same time. One process for a program happens each time the program is loaded into memory or executed.

processor — *See* central processing unit (CPU).

processor speed — The speed, or frequency, at which the CPU operates. Usually expressed in GHz.

product activation — The process that Microsoft uses to prevent software piracy. For example, once Windows XP is activated for a particular computer, it cannot be installed on another computer.

program — A set of step-by-step instructions to a computer. Some are burned directly into chips, while others are stored as program files. Programs are written in languages such as BASIC and C++.

program file — A file that contains instructions designed to be executed by the CPU.

protected mode — An operating mode that supports preemptive multitasking, the OS manages memory and other hardware devices, and programs can use a 32-bit data path. Also called 32-bit mode.

protocol — A set of rules and standards that two entities use for communication.

Protocol.ini — A Windows initialization file that contains network configuration information.

proxy server — A server that acts as an intermediary between another computer and the Internet. The proxy server substitutes its own IP address for the IP address of the computer on the network making a request, so that all traffic over the Internet appears to be coming from only the IP address of the proxy server.

PS/2-compatible mouse — A mouse that plugs into a round mouse PS/2 port on the motherboard. Sometimes called a motherboard mouse.

public IP address — An IP address available to the Internet.

QIC (Quarter-Inch Committee or **quarter-inch cartridge)** — A name of a standardized method used to write data to tape. These backup files have a .qic extension.

RAID (redundant array of inexpensive disks or **redundant array of independent disks)** — Several methods of configuring multiple hard drives to store data to increase logical volume size and improve performance, and to ensure that if one hard drive fails, the data is still available from another hard drive.

RAM (random access memory) — Memory modules on the motherboard containing microchips used to temporarily hold data and programs while the CPU processes both. Information in RAM is lost when the PC is turned off.

RAM drive — An area of memory that is treated as though it were a hard drive, but works much faster than a hard drive. The Windows 9x startup disk uses a RAM drive. Compare to virtual memory.

RARP (Reverse Address Resolution Protocol) — A protocol used to translate the unique hardware NIC addresses (MAC addresses) into IP addresses (the reverse of ARP).

RDRAM — *See* Direct Rambus DRAM.

read/write head — A sealed, magnetic coil device that moves across the surface of a disk either reading data from or writing data to the disk.

real mode — A single-tasking operating mode whereby a program has 1024K of memory addresses, has direct access to RAM, and uses a 16-bit data path. Using a memory extender (Himem.sys) a program in real mode can access memory above 1024K. Also called 16-bit mode.

Recovery Console — A Windows 2000/XP command interface utility and OS that can be used to solve problems when Windows cannot load from the hard drive.

rectifier — An electrical device that converts AC to DC. A PC power supply contains a rectifier.

refresh — The process of periodically rewriting data, such as on dynamic RAM.

refresh rate — As applied to monitors, the number of times in one second an electronic beam can fill the screen with lines from top to bottom. Also called vertical scan rate.

registry — A database that Windows uses to store hardware and software configuration information, user preferences, and setup information.

re-marked chips — Chips that have been used and returned to the factory, marked again, and resold. The surface of the chips may be dull or scratched.

Remote Assistance — A Windows XP feature that allows a support technician at a remote location to have full access to the Windows XP desktop.

repeater — A device that amplifies signals on a network so they can be transmitted further down the line.

rescue disk — A floppy disk that can be used to start up a computer when the hard drive fails to boot. Also called emergency startup disk (ESD) or startup disk.

resistance — The degree to which a device opposes or resists the flow of electricity. As the electrical resistance increases, the current decreases. *See* ohm and resistor.

resistor — An electronic device that resists or opposes the flow of electricity. A resistor can be used to reduce the amount of electricity being supplied to an electronic component.

resolution — The number of pixels on a monitor screen that are addressable by software (example: 1024 × 768 pixels).

restore point — A snapshot of the Windows Me/XP system state, usually made before installation of new hardware or applications.

REt (Resolution Enhancement technology) — The term used by Hewlett-Packard to describe the way a laser printer varies the size of the dots used to create an image. This technology partly accounts for the sharp, clear image created by a laser printer.

RIMM — A type of memory module used on newer motherboards, produced by Rambus, Inc.

ring topology — A network topology in which the nodes in a network form a ring. Each node is connected only to two other nodes, and a centralized hub is not required.

RISC (Reduced Instruction Set Computing) chips — Chips that incorporate only the most frequently used instructions, so that the computer operates faster (for example, the PowerPC uses RISC chips).

riser card — A card that plugs into a motherboard and allows for expansion cards to be mounted parallel to the motherboard. Expansion cards are plugged into slots on the riser card.

RJ-11 — A phone line connection found on modems, telephones, and house phone outlets.

RJ-45 connector — A connector used with twisted-pair cable that connects the cable to the NIC.

roaming user profile — A user profile for a roaming user. Roaming user profiles are stored on a server so that the user can access the profile from anywhere on the network.

ROM (read-only memory) — Chips that contain programming code and cannot be erased.

ROM BIOS — *See* BIOS.

root directory — The main directory created when a hard drive or disk is first formatted. In Linux, it's indicated by a forward slash. In DOS and Windows, it's indicated by a backward slash.

routable protocol — A protocol that can be routed to interconnected networks on the basis of a network address. TCP/IP is a routable protocol, but NetBEUI is not.

router — A device that connects networks and makes decisions as to the best routes to use when forwarding packets.

sampling rate — The rate of samples taken of an analog signal over a period of time, usually expressed as samples per second, or hertz.

SBAC (SCSI bus adapter chip) — The SCSI chip within a device housing that controls data transfer over the SCSI bus.

SCAM (SCSI Configuration AutoMatically) — A method of configuring SCSI device settings that follows the Plug and Play standard. SCAM makes installation of SCSI devices much easier, provided that the devices are SCAM-compliant.

scanning mirror — A component of a laser printer consisting of an octagonal mirror that can be directed in a sweeping motion to cover the entire length of a laser printer drum.

SCSI (Small Computer System Interface) — A fast interface between a host adapter and the CPU that can daisy chain as many as 7 or 15 devices on a single bus.

SCSI ID — A number from 0 to 15 assigned to each SCSI device attached to the daisy chain.

SDRAM II — See Double Data Rate SDRAM (DDR SDRAM).

secondary storage — Storage that is remote to the CPU and permanently holds data, even when the PC is turned off, such as a hard drive.

sector — On a disk surface one segment of a track, which almost always contains 512 bytes of data.

security accounts manager (SAM) — A portion of the Windows NT/2000/XP registry that manages the account database that contains accounts, policies, and other pertinent information about local accounts.

sequential access — A method of data access used by tape drives, whereby data is written or read sequentially from the beginning to the end of the tape or until the desired data is found.

serial mouse — A mouse that uses a serial port and has a female 9-pin DB-9 connector.

serial port — A male 9-pin or 25-pin port on a computer system used by slower I/O devices such as a mouse or modem. Data travels serially, one bit at a time, through the port. Serial ports are sometimes configured as COM1, COM2, COM3, or COM4.

service pack — See patch.

session — An established communication link between two software programs. On the Internet, a session is created by TCP.

SFC (System File Checker) — A Windows tool that checks to make sure Windows is using the correct versions of system files.

SGRAM (synchronous graphics RAM) — Memory designed especially for video card processing that can synchronize itself with the CPU bus clock.

shadow RAM or **shadowing ROM** — ROM programming code copied into RAM to speed up the system operation, because of the faster access speed of RAM.

shell — The portion of an OS that relates to the user and to applications.

shielded twisted-pair (STP) cable — A cable that is made of one or more twisted pairs of wires and is surrounded by a metal shield.

shortcut — An icon on the desktop that points to a program that can be executed or to a file or folder.

signal-regenerating repeater — A repeater that is able to distinguish between noise and signal. It reads the signal and retransmits it without the accompanying noise.

Sigverif.exe — A Windows 2000/XP utility that allows you to search for digital signatures.

SIMD (single instruction, multiple data) — A process that allows the CPU to execute a single instruction simultaneously on multiple pieces of data, rather than by repetitive looping.

SIMM (single inline memory module) — A miniature circuit board used in older computers to hold RAM. SIMMs hold 8, 16, 32, or 64 MB on a single module.

simple volume — A type of dynamic volume used on a single hard drive that corresponds to a primary partition on a basic disk.

single-ended (SE) cable — A type of SCSI cable in which two wires are used to carry a signal, one of which carries the signal itself; the other is a ground for the signal.

single-voltage CPU — A CPU that requires one voltage for both internal and I/O operations.

slack — Wasted space on a hard drive caused by not using all available space at the end of clusters.

sleep mode — A mode used in many "Green" systems that allows them to be configured through CMOS to suspend the monitor or even the drive, if the keyboard and/or CPU have been inactive for a set number of minutes. *See also* Green Standards.

slimline case — *See* compact case.

SLIP (Serial Line Internet Protocol) — A line protocol used by regular telephone lines that has largely been replaced by PPP.

Smart Multistation Access Unit (SMAU) — *See* MAU.

SMARTDrive — A hard drive cache program that came with Windows 3.x and DOS and can be executed as a TSR from the Autoexec.bat file (for example, Device=Smartdrv.sys 2048).

SMTP (Simple Mail Transfer Protocol) — The protocol used by e-mail clients and servers to send e-mail messages over the Internet. *See* POP and IMAP.

snap-ins — Components added to a console using the Microsoft Management Console.

SNMP (Simple Network Management Protocol) — A protocol used to monitor and manage network traffic on a workstation. SNMP works with TCP/IP and IPX/SPX networks.

socket — *See* session.

SO-DIMM (small outline DIMM) — A type of memory module used in notebook computers that uses DIMM technology and can have either 72 pins or 144 pins.

soft boot — To restart a PC without turning off the power, for example, by pressing three keys at the same time (Ctrl, Alt, and Del). Also called warm boot.

soft power — *See* soft switch.

soft switch — A feature on an ATX system that allows an OS to power down the system and allows for activity such as a keystroke or network activity to power up the system. Also called soft power.

software — Computer programs, or instructions to perform a specific task. Software may be BIOS, OSs, or applications software such as a word-processing or spreadsheet program.

software cache — Cache controlled by software whereby the cache is stored in RAM.

SO-RIMM (small outline RIMM) — A 160-pin memory module used in notebooks that uses Rambus technology.

South Bridge — That portion of the chip set hub that connects slower I/O buses (for example, an ISA bus) to the system bus. Compare to North Bridge.

spacers — *See* standoffs.

spanned volume — A type of dynamic volume used on two or more hard drives that fills up the space allotted on one physical disk before moving to the next.

SPI (SCSI Parallel Interface) — The part of the SCSI-3 standard that specifies how SCSI devices are connected.

spikes — Temporary surges in voltage, which can damage electrical components.

spooling — Placing print jobs in a print queue so that an application can be released from the printing process before printing is completed. Spooling is an acronym for simultaneous peripheral operations online.

SSE (Streaming SIMD Extension) — A technology used by the Intel Pentium III and later CPUs and designed to improve performance of multimedia software.

staggered pin grid array (SPGA) — A feature of a CPU socket whereby the pins are staggered over the socket in order to squeeze more pins into a small space.

standby time — The time before a "Green" system will reduce 92 percent of its activity. *See also* Green Standards.

standoffs — Round plastic or metal pegs that separate the motherboard from the case, so that components on the back of the motherboard do not touch the case.

star bus topology — A LAN that uses a logical bus design, but with all devices connected to a central hub, making a physical star.

star ring topology — A topology that is physically arranged in a star formation but is logically a ring because of the way information travels on it. Token ring is the primary example.

star topology — A LAN in which all the devices are connected to a central hub.

start bits — Bits that are used to signal the approach of data.

startup BIOS — Part of system BIOS that is responsible for controlling the PC when it is first turned on. Startup BIOS gives control over to the OS once it is loaded.

startup disk — *See* rescue disk.

startup password — *See* power-on password.

stateless — Term for a device or process that manages data or some activity without regard to all the details of the data or activity.

static electricity — *See* ESD.

static IP address — An IP address permanently assigned to a workstation.

static RAM (SRAM) — RAM chips that retain information without the need for refreshing, as long as the computer's power is on. They are more expensive than traditional DRAM.

static VxD — A VxD that is loaded into memory at startup and remains there for the entire OS session.

stealth virus — A virus that actively conceals itself by temporarily removing itself from an infected file that is about to be examined, and then hiding a copy of itself elsewhere on the drive.

stop error — An error severe enough to cause the operating system to stop all processes.

streaming audio — Downloading audio data from the Internet in a continuous stream of data without first downloading an entire audio file.

striped volume — A type of dynamic volume used for two or more hard drives that writes to the disks evenly rather than filling up allotted space on one and then moving on to the next. Compare to spanned volume.

subdirectory — A directory or folder contained in another directory or folder. Also called a child directory or folder.

subnet mask — A subnet mask is a group of four numbers (dotted decimal numbers) that tell TCP/IP if a remote computer is on the same or a different network.

subsystems — The different modules into which the Windows NT/2000/XP user mode is divided.

surge suppressor or **surge protector** — A device or power strip designed to protect electronic equipment from power surges and spikes.

suspend time — The time before a "Green" system will reduce 99 percent of its activity. After this time, the system needs a warm-up time so that the CPU, monitor, and hard drive can reach full activity.

swap file — A file on the hard drive that is used by the OS for virtual memory. Also called a page file.

switch — A device used to segment a network. It can decide which network segment is to receive a packet, on the basis of the packet's destination MAC address.

synchronization — The process by which files and programs are transferred between PDAs and PCs.

synchronous DRAM (SDRAM) — A type of memory stored on DIMMs that runs in sync with the system clock, running at the same speed as the motherboard.

synchronous SRAM — SRAM that is faster and more expensive than asynchronous SRAM. It requires a clock signal to validate its control signals, enabling the cache to run in step with the CPU.

SyncLink DRAM (SLDRAM) — A type of DRAM developed by a consortium of 12 DRAM manufacturers. It improved on regular SDRAM but is now obsolete.

Sysedit — The Windows System Configuration Editor, a text editor generally used to edit system files.

system BIOS — BIOS located on the motherboard.

system board — *See* motherboard.

system bus — The bus between the CPU and memory on the motherboard. The bus frequency in documentation is called the system speed, such as 200 MHz. Also called the memory bus, front-side bus, local bus, or host bus.

system clock — A line on a bus that is dedicated to timing the activities of components connected to it. The system clock provides a continuous pulse that other devices use to time themselves.

system disk — Windows terminology for a bootable disk.

System.ini — A text configuration file used by Windows 3.x and supported by Windows 9x for backward-compatibility.

system partition — The active partition of the hard drive containing the boot record and the specific files required to load Windows NT/2000/XP.

system resource — A channel, line, or address on the motherboard that can be used by the CPU or a device for communication. The four system resources are IRQ, I/O address, DMA channel, and memory address.

System Restore — A Windows Me/XP utility, similar to the ScanReg tool in earlier versions of Windows, that is used to restore the system to a restore point. Unlike ScanReg, System Restore cannot be executed from a command prompt.

system state data — In Windows 2000/XP, files that are necessary for a successful load of the operating system.

System Tray — An area to the right of the taskbar that holds the icons of small applets launched at startup.

TAPI (Telephony Application Programming Interface) — A standard developed by Intel and Microsoft that can be used by 32-bit Windows 9x communications programs for communicating over phone lines.

TCP (Transmission Control Protocol) — Part of the TCP/IP protocol suite. TCP guarantees delivery of data for application protocols and establishes a session before it begins transmitting data.

TCP/IP (Transmission Control Protocol/ Internet Protocol) — The suite of protocols that supports communication on the Internet. TCP is responsible for error checking, and IP is responsible for routing.

telephony — A term describing the technology of converting sound to signals that can travel over telephone lines.

terminating resistor — The resistor added at the end of a SCSI chain to dampen the voltage at the end of the chain.

termination — A process necessary to prevent an echo effect of power at the end of a SCSI chain, resulting in interference with the data transmission.

ThickNet — *See* 10Base5 Ethernet.

ThinNet — *See* 10Base2 Ethernet.

thread — Each process that the CPU is aware of; a single task that is part of a longer task or program.

time to live (TTL) — Number of routers a network packet can pass through on its way to its destination before it is dropped. Also called hop count.

token ring — An older LAN technology developed by IBM that transmits data at 4 Mbps or 16 Mbps.

top-level domain — The highest level of domain names, indicated by a suffix that tells something about the host. For example, .com is for commercial use and .edu is for educational institutions.

tower case — The largest type of personal computer case. Tower cases stand vertically and can be as high as two feet tall. They have more drive bays and are a good choice for computer users who anticipate making significant upgrades.

trace — A wire on a circuit board that connects two components or devices.

track — One of many concentric circles on the surface of a hard drive or floppy disk.

training — *See* handshaking.

transceiver — The component on a NIC that is responsible for signal conversion. Combines the words transmitter and receiver.

transformer — A device that changes the ratio of current to voltage. A computer power supply is basically a transformer and a rectifier.

transistor — An electronic device that can regulate electricity and act as a logical gate or switch for an electrical signal.

translation — A technique used by system BIOS and hard drive controller BIOS to break the 504-MB hard drive barrier, whereby a different set of drive parameters are communicated to the OS and other software than that used by the hard drive controller BIOS.

Travan standards — A popular and improved group of standards for tape drives based on the QIC standards and developed by 3M.

Trojan horse — A type of infestation that hides or disguises itself as a useful program, yet is designed to cause damage at a later time.

TSR (terminate-and-stay-resident) — A program that is loaded into memory and remains dormant until called on, such as a screen saver or a memory-resident antivirus program.

UART (universal asynchronous receiver-transmitter) chip — A chip that controls serial ports. It sets protocol and converts parallel data bits received from the system bus into serial bits.

UDP (User Datagram Protocol) — A connectionless protocol that does not require a connection to send a packet and does not guarantee that the packet arrives at its destination. UDP is faster than TCP because TCP takes the time to make a connection and guarantee delivery.

unattended installation — A Windows NT/2000/XP installation that is done by storing the answers to installation questions in a text file or script that Windows NT/2000/XP calls an answer file so that the answers do not have to be typed in during the installation.

Universal Disk Format (UDF) file system — A file system for optical media used by all DVD discs and some CD-R and CD-RW discs.

unshielded twisted-pair (UTP) cable — A cable that is made of one or more twisted pairs of wires and is not surrounded by a metal shield.

upgrade install — The installation of an OS on a hard drive that already has an OS installed in such a way that settings kept by the old OS are carried forward into the upgrade, including information about hardware, software, and user preferences.

upper memory — In DOS and Windows 9x, the memory addresses from 640K up to 1024K, originally reserved for BIOS, device drivers, and TSRs.

upper memory block (UMB) — In DOS and Windows 9x, a group of consecutive memory addresses in RAM from 640K to 1MB that can be used by 16-bit device drivers and TSRs.

UPS (uninterruptible power supply) — A device designed to provide a backup power supply during a power failure. Basically, a UPS is a battery backup system with an ultrafast sensing device.

URL (Uniform Resource Locator) — An address for a resource on the Internet. A URL can contain the protocol used by the resource, the name of the computer and its network, and the path and name of a file on the computer.

USB host controller — Manages the USB bus. For the 400 series Intel chip set, the USB host controller is included in the PCI controller chip. The USB uses only a single set of resources for all devices on the bus.

USB (universal serial bus) port — A type of port designed to make installation and configuration of I/O devices easy, providing room for as many as 127 devices daisy-chained together.

user account — The information, stored in the SAM database, that defines a Windows NT/2000/XP user, including username, password, memberships, and rights.

user component — A Windows 9x component that controls the mouse, keyboard, ports, and desktop.

user mode — In Windows NT/2000/XP, a mode that provides an interface between an application and the OS, and only has access to hardware resources through the code running in kernel mode.

user profile — A personal profile about a user that enables the user's desktop settings and other operating parameters to be retained from one session to another.

User State Migration Tool (USMT) — A Windows XP utility that helps you migrate user files and preferences from one computer to another in order to help a user makes a smooth transition from one computer to another.

V.92 — The latest standard for data transmission over phone lines that can attain a speed of 56 Kbps.

value data — In Windows, the name and value of a setting in the registry.

VCACHE — A built-in Windows 9x 32-bit software cache that doesn't take up conventional memory space or upper memory space as SMARTDrive did.

VESA (Video Electronics Standards Association) VL bus — An outdated local bus used on 80486 computers for connecting 32-bit adapters directly to the local processor bus.

VFAT (virtual file allocation table) — A variation of the original DOS 16-bit FAT that allows for long filenames and 32-bit disk access.

video card — An interface card installed in the computer to control visual output on a monitor. Also called display adapter.

virtual device driver (VxD or VDD) — A Windows device driver that may or may not have direct access to a device. It might depend on a Windows component to communicate with the device itself.

virtual machine — One or more logical machines created within one physical machine by Windows, allowing applications to make serious errors within one logical machine without disturbing other programs and parts of the system.

virtual memory — A method whereby the OS uses the hard drive as though it were RAM. Compare to RAM drive.

virtual real mode — An operating mode that works similarly to real mode provided by a 32-bit OS for a 16-bit program to work.

virus — A program that often has an incubation period, is infectious, and is intended to cause damage. A virus program might destroy data and programs or damage a disk drive's boot sector.

virus signature — A set of distinguishing characteristics of a virus used by antivirus software to identify the virus.

VMM (Virtual Machine Manager) — A Windows 9x program that controls virtual machines and the resources they use including memory. The VMM manages the page table used to access memory.

volatile — Refers to a kind of RAM that is temporary, cannot hold data very long, and must be frequently refreshed.

volt (V) — A measure of potential difference in an electrical circuit. A computer ATX power supply usually provides five separate voltages: +12V, –12V, +5V, –5V, and +3.3V.

voltage — Electrical differential that causes current to flow, measured in volts. *See* volt.

voltmeter — A device for measuring electrical AC or DC voltage.

volume — *See* logical drive.

VRAM (video RAM) — RAM on video cards that holds the data that is being passed from the computer to the monitor and can be accessed by two devices simultaneously. Higher resolutions often require more video memory.

VxD — *See* virtual device driver.

wait state — A clock tick in which nothing happens, used to ensure that the microprocessor isn't getting ahead of slower components. A 0-wait state is preferable to a 1-wait state. Too many wait states can slow down a system.

WAN (wide area network) — A network or group of networks that span a large geographical area.

warm boot — *See* soft boot.

watt (W) — The unit used to measure power. A typical computer may use a power supply that provides 200W.

wattage — Electrical power measured in watts.

WDM (Win32 Driver Model) — The only Windows 9x Plug and Play component that is found in Windows 98 but not Windows 95. WDM is the component responsible for managing device drivers that work under a driver model new to Windows 98.

WFP (Windows File Protection) — A Windows 2000/XP tool that protects system files from modification.

wide SCSI — One of the two main SCSI specifications. Wide SCSI has a 16-bit data bus.

Wi-Fi — *See* IEEE 802.11b.

wildcard — A * or ? character used in a command line that represents a character or group of characters in a filename or extension.

Win16 on Win32 (WOW) — A group of programs provided by Windows NT/2000/XP to create a virtual DOS environment that emulates a 16-bit Windows environment, protecting the rest of the OS from 16-bit applications.

Win386.swp — The name of the Windows 9x swap file. Its default location is C:\Windows.

Win.ini — The Windows initialization file that contains program configuration information needed for running the Windows operating environment. Its functions were replaced by the registry beginning with Windows 9x, which still supports it for backward compatibility with Windows 3.x.

WINS (Windows Internet Naming Service) — A Microsoft resolution service with a distributed database that tracks relationships between NetBIOS names and IP addresses. Compare to DNS.

WinSock (Windows Sockets) — A part of the TCP/IP utility software that manages API calls from applications to other computers on a TCP/IP network.

wireless LAN (WLAN) — A type of LAN that does not use wires or cables to create connections, but instead transmits data over radio or infrared waves.

workgroup — In Windows, a logical group of computers and users in which administration, resources, and security are distributed throughout the network, without centralized management or security.

worm — An infestation designed to copy itself repeatedly to memory, on drive space or on a network, until little memory or disk space remains.

WRAM (window RAM) — Dual-ported video RAM that is faster and less expensive than VRAM. It has its own internal bus on the chip, with a data path that is 256 bits wide.

zero insertion force (ZIF) socket — A socket that uses a small lever to apply even force when you install the microchip into the socket.

zone bit recording — A method of storing data on a hard drive whereby the drive can have more sectors per track near the outside of the platter.

INDEX